HANDBOOK OF LATIN AMERICAN STUDIES: No. 74

A Selective and Annotated Guide to Recent Publications in Art, History, Literature, Music, and Philosophy

VOLUME 75 WILL BE DEVOTED TO THE SOCIAL SCIENCES: ANTHROPOLOGY, GEOGRAPHY, GOVERNMENT AND POLITICS, INTERNATIONAL RELATIONS, POLITICAL ECONOMY, AND SOCIOLOGY

EDITORIAL NOTE: Comments concerning the *Handbook of Latin American Studies* should be sent directly to the Humanities or Social Sciences Editor, *Handbook of Latin American Studies*, Hispanic Division, Library of Congress, Washington, D.C. 20540-4851 or emailed to hlas@loc.gov.

ADVISORY BOARD

Roberto González Echevarría, *Yale University*
Eric Hershberg, *American University*
Scott Hutson, *University of Kentucky*
Peter T. Johnson, *Princeton University*
Franklin Knight, *Johns Hopkins University*
David Scott Palmer, *Boston University*
Susan Ramírez, *Texas Christian University*
Ben Vinson, III, *The George Washington University*

ADMINISTRATIVE OFFICERS
OF THE LIBRARY OF CONGRESS

Carla Hayden, *The Librarian of Congress*
Robin L. Dale, *Associate Librarian for Library Services*
Eugene Flanagan, *Director, General and International Collections Directorate*
Suzanne Schadl, *Chief, Hispanic Division*

REPRESENTATIVE, UNIVERSITY OF TEXAS PRESS

Kerry Webb, *Senior Acquisitions Editor*

HANDBOOK EDITORIAL STAFF

Wendy Acosta, *Editorial Assistant*
Lauren Gattos, *Editorial Assistant*
Patricia Penon, *Library Technician*

HANDBOOK OF LATIN AMERICAN STUDIES: NO. 74
HUMANITIES

*Prepared by a Number of Scholars
for the Hispanic Division of The Library of Congress*

KATHERINE D. McCANN, *Humanities Editor*
TRACY NORTH, *Social Sciences Editor*

2020

UNIVERSITY OF TEXAS PRESS ⟷ *Austin*

International Standard Book Number: 978-1-4773-2098-3
International Standard Serial Number: 0072-9833
Library of Congress Catalog Card Number: 36-32633
Copyright © 2020 by the University of Texas Press.
All rights reserved.
Printed in the United States of America.

Requests for permission to reproduce material from this work should be sent to:
  Permissions, University of Texas Press,
  Box 7819, Austin, Texas 78713-7819

First Edition, 2020

The paper used in the publication meets the minimum requirements of American National Standard for Information Sciences—Permanence of Paper for Printed Library Materials, ANSI Z39.48-1984. ♾

CONTRIBUTING EDITORS

HUMANITIES

Angélica J. Afanador-Pujol, *Arizona State University*, ART
Diana Álvarez Amell, *Seton Hall University*, LITERATURE
Félix Ángel, *Inter-American Development Bank*, ART
Yvette Aparicio, *Grinnell College*, LITERATURE
José R. Ballesteros, *St. Mary's College of Maryland*, LITERATURE
Bradley Benton, *North Dakota State University*, HISTORY
Dário Borim Jr., *University of Massachusetts, Dartmouth*, LITERATURE
Amber Brian, *The University of Iowa*, LITERATURE
John Britton, *Francis Marion University*, HISTORY
Adriana Brodsky, *St. Mary's College of Maryland*, HISTORY
Rogério Budasz, *University of California, Riverside*, MUSIC
José Cardona-López, *Texas A&M International University*, LITERATURE
Bridget María Chesterton, *Buffalo State, The State University of New York*, HISTORY
Matt D. Childs, *University of South Carolina*, HISTORY
Matthew Crawford, *Kent State University*, HISTORY
Tiffany D. Creegan Miller, *Clemson University*, LITERATURE
Paula De Vos, *San Diego State University*, HISTORY
G. Antonio Espinoza, *Virginia Commonwealth University*, HISTORY
César Ferreira, *University of Wisconsin-Milwaukee*, LITERATURE
Erin Finzer, *University of Arkansas at Little Rock*, LITERATURE
María Luisa Fischer, *Hunter College*, LITERATURE
Raphael E. Folsom, *The University of Oklahoma*, HISTORY
Elizabeth Gackstetter Nichols, *Drury University*, LITERATURE
Myrna García-Calderón, *Syracuse University*, LITERATURE
Luis A. González, *Indiana University, Bloomington*, HISTORY
Isadora Grevan de Carvalho, *Rutgers University*, LITERATURE
Mark Grover, *Brigham Young University*, HISTORY
María Constanza Guzmán, *Glendon College, York University*, TRANSLATIONS
Paola Hernández, *University of Wisconsin-Madison*, LITERATURE
Regina Igel, *University of Maryland, College Park*, LITERATURE
Frances Jaeger, *Northern Illinois University*, LITERATURE
John Koegel, *California State University, Fullerton*, MUSIC
Erick D. Langer, *Georgetown University*, HISTORY
Alfred E. Lemmon, *Historic New Orleans Collection*, MUSIC
Peter S. Linder, *New Mexico Highlands University*, HISTORY
Daniel Livesay, *Claremont McKenna College*, HISTORY
Ryan Long, *University of Maryland*, LITERATURE
M. Angélica Guimarães Lopes, *Professor Emerita, University of South Carolina*, LITERATURE

Laura R. Loustau, *Chapman University*, LITERATURE
Mary Ann Mahony, *Central Connecticut State University*, HISTORY
Elizabeth Manley, *Xavier University of Louisiana*, HISTORY
Claire Emilie Martin, *California State University, Long Beach*, LITERATURE
Frank D. McCann, *Professor Emeritus, University of New Hampshire*, HISTORY
Elaine M. Miller, *Christopher Newport University*, LITERATURE
José M. Neistein, *Independent Scholar, Washington, DC*, ART
Mollie Lewis Nouwen, *Pacific Northwest College of Art*, HISTORY
Susana Nuccetelli, *St. Cloud State University*, PHILOSOPHY
Michael O'Brien, *College of Charleston*, MUSIC
Élide Valarini Oliver, *University of California, Santa Barbara*, LITERATURE
Rita M. Palacios, *Conestoga College*, LITERATURE
Suzanne B. Pasztor, *Humboldt State University*, HISTORY
Charles A. Perrone, *University of Florida*, LITERATURE
Jeannine M. Pitas, *University of Dubuque*, LITERATURE
Fabricio Prado, *College of William & Mary*, HISTORY
Susan E. Ramírez, *Texas Christian University*, HISTORY
José Ramón Ruisánchez Serra, *University of Houston*, LITERATURE
Jane M. Rausch, *Professor Emerita, University of Massachusetts-Amherst*, HISTORY
Jonathan Ritter, *University of California, Riverside*, MUSIC
Humberto Rodríguez-Camilloni, *Virginia Polytechnic Institute*, ART
Terry Rugeley, *Historian, Arkadelphia, AK*, HISTORY
William F. Sater, *Professor Emeritus, California State University, Long Beach*, HISTORY
Francisco Solares-Larrave, *Northern Illinois University*, LITERATURE
Peter Szok, *Texas Christian University*, HISTORY
Barbara A. Tenenbaum, *Historian, Washington, DC*, HISTORY
Giovanna Urdangarain, *Pacific Lutheran University*, LITERATURE
Peter Villella, *University of North Carolina at Greensboro*, HISTORY
Stephen Webre, *Louisiana Tech University*, HISTORY
Thomas Whigham, *Professor Emeritus, University of Georgia*, HISTORY
Steven F. White, *St. Lawrence University*, TRANSLATIONS
Jesse Zarley, *St. Joseph's College, Long Island*, HISTORY
Chrystian Zegarra, *Colgate University*, LITERATURE

SOCIAL SCIENCES

Ronald Ahnen, *Saint Mary's College of California*, GOVERNMENT AND POLITICS
Astrid Arrarás, *Florida International University*, GOVERNMENT AND POLITICS
Sherrie Baver, *The City University of New York (CUNY)*, GOVERNMENT AND POLITICS
Melissa H. Birch, *University of Kansas*, POLITICAL ECONOMY
Silvia Borzutzky, *Carnegie Mellon University*, POLITICAL ECONOMY
Federico Bossert, *Universidad de Buenos Aires, Argentina*, ANTHROPOLOGY
Christian Brannstrom, *Texas A&M University*, GEOGRAPHY
Jacqueline Anne Braveboy-Wagner, *The City University of New York (CUNY)*, INTERNATIONAL RELATIONS

Charles D. Brockett, *Sewanee: The University of the South*, GOVERNMENT AND POLITICS
Kathleen Bruhn, *University of California Santa Barbara*, GOVERNMENT AND POLITICS
William L. Canak, *Middle Tennessee State University*, SOCIOLOGY
Jorge Capetillo-Ponce, *University of Massachusetts Boston*, SOCIOLOGY
Ernesto Castañeda-Tinoco, *American University*, SOCIOLOGY
Miguel Centellas, *University of Mississippi*, GOVERNMENT AND POLITICS
David M. Cochran, Jr., *University of Southern Mississippi*, GEOGRAPHY
Jennifer N. Collins, *University of Wisconsin-Stevens Point*, GOVERNMENT AND POLITICS
Christina Conlee, *Texas State University*, ANTHROPOLOGY
Duncan Earle, *Marymount California University*, ANTHROPOLOGY
Scott M. Fitzpatrick, *University of Oregon*, ANTHROPOLOGY
Mario A. González-Corzo, *Lehman College, The City University of New York (CUNY)*, POLITICAL ECONOMY
Clifford E. Griffin, *North Carolina State University*, GOVERNMENT AND POLITICS
Daniel Hellinger, *Webster University*, POLITICAL ECONOMY
John Henderson, *Cornell University*, ANTHROPOLOGY
Peter H. Herlihy, *University of Kansas*, GEOGRAPHY
Silvia María Hirsch, *Universidad Nacional de San Martín, Argentina*, ANTHROPOLOGY
Jonathan Hiskey, *Vanderbilt University*, POLITICAL ECONOMY
Richard Hunter, *State University of New York at Cortland*, GEOGRAPHY
Keith Jamtgaard, *University of Missouri*, SOCIOLOGY
Arthur A. Joyce, *University of Colorado Boulder*, ANTHROPOLOGY
Gregory W. Knapp, *The University of Texas at Austin*, GEOGRAPHY
Félix E. Martín, *Florida International University*, INTERNATIONAL RELATIONS
Daniel Masís-Iverson, *Inter-American Defense College*, POLITICAL ECONOMY
Kent Mathewson, *Louisiana State University*, GEOGRAPHY
Shannan L. Mattiace, *Allegheny College*, GOVERNMENT AND POLITICS
Cecilia Menjívar, *University of California, Los Angeles*, SOCIOLOGY
Mary K. Meyer McAleese, *Eckerd College*, INTERNATIONAL RELATIONS
Erika Moreno, *Creighton University*, GOVERNMENT AND POLITICS
Suzanne Oakdale, *University of New Mexico*, ANTHROPOLOGY
Julio Ortiz-Luquis, *Borough of Manhattan Community College and Brooklyn College, CUNY*, INTERNATIONAL RELATIONS
Carlos Parodi, *Illinois State University*, POLITICAL ECONOMY
Tony Payan, *Rice University*, INTERNATIONAL RELATIONS
Yovanna Pineda, *University of Central Florida, Orlando*, POLITICAL ECONOMY
María Sol Prieto, *Universidad de Buenos Aires, Argentina*, SOCIOLOGY
Enrique S. Pumar, *Santa Clara University*, SOCIOLOGY
David J. Robinson, *Syracuse University*, GEOGRAPHY
René Salgado, *Independent Consultant*, GOVERNMENT AND POLITICS
Clare Sammells, *Bucknell University*, SOCIOLOGY
Isabel Scarborough, *Parkland College*, ANTHROPOLOGY
Joseph Leonard Scarpaci, Jr., *Center for the Study of Cuban Culture & Economy*, GEOGRAPHY
Jörn Seemann, *Ball State University*, GEOGRAPHY
David A. Shirk, *University of San Diego*, POLITICAL ECONOMY

Peter M. Siavelis, *Wake Forest University*, GOVERNMENT AND POLITICS
Russell E. Smith, *Washburn University*, POLITICAL ECONOMY
Scott Tollefson, *National Defense University*, INTERNATIONAL RELATIONS
Brian Turner, *Randolph-Macon College*, GOVERNMENT AND POLITICS
Erica Lorraine Williams, *Spelman College*, SOCIOLOGY

Foreign Corresponding Editors

Franz Obermeier, *Universitätsbibliothek Kiel*, GERMAN PUBLICATIONS
Mao Xianglin, *Chinese Academy of Social Sciences*, CHINESE PUBLICATIONS

Special Contributing Editors

Lucia A. Wolf, *Library of Congress*, ITALIAN LANGUAGE

CONTENTS

	PAGE
EDITOR'S NOTE	xv

ART

SPANISH AMERICA   1

   Precolumbian and Colonial   *Angélica J. Afanador-Pujol and*   1
                                           Humberto Rodríguez-Camilloni
   Precolumbian
     General p. 5
     Mesoamerica p. 6
     South America p. 7
   Colonial
     General p. 9
     Mexico and Central America p. 11
     Caribbean p. 16
     Uruguay p. 16
     Colombia p. 17
     Bolivia and Peru p. 17

   19th-21st Centuries   *Félix Ángel*   21
     General p. 24
     Mexico p. 26
     Central America p. 31
     The Caribbean p. 31
     South America
       Argentina p. 33
       Bolivia p. 34
       Chile p. 34
       Colombia p. 35
       Paraguay p. 37
       Peru p. 37
       Uruguay p. 38
       Venezuela p. 38

   BRAZIL   *José M. Neistein*   39
     Reference and Theoretical
     Works p. 40   *Colonial Period* p. 41

19th Century p. 42   20th-21st Centuries p. 43
Folk Art p. 48   Photography p. 48
City Planning, Architecture, and
Landscape Architecture p. 49
Afro-Brazilian and Indian Traditions p. 52
Miscellaneous p. 53

HISTORY

ETHNOHISTORY		55
Mesoamerica	Bradley Benton and Peter Villella	55
South America	Susan E. Ramírez	70
GENERAL HISTORY	John Britton	83

General p. 84   Colonial p. 93
Independence and 19th Century p. 98
20th Century p. 101

MEXICO		
General	Suzanne B. Pasztor	106
Colonial Period	Paula De Vos and Raphael E. Folsom	114
Independence, Revolution, and Post-Revolution	Suzanne B. Pasztor, Terry Rugeley and Barbara Tenenbaum	129

Independence To Revolution p. 133
Revolution and Post-Revolution p. 147

CENTRAL AMERICA	Peter Szok and Stephen Webre	161

General p. 162   Colonial p. 164   National p. 167

THE CARIBBEAN	Matt D. Childs, Luis A. González, Daniel Livesay and Elizabeth Manley	172

General p. 183   Early Colonial p. 189
Late Colonial and French
Revolutionary Period p. 192
19th Century p. 196   20th Century p. 202

SPANISH SOUTH AMERICA		
Colonial Period	Matthew Crawford, Fabricio Prado and Jesse Zarley	216

Venezuela p. 225   Nueva Granada p. 226
Quito p. 228   Peru p. 229
Bolivia/Charcas p. 234   Chile p. 235
Rio de la Plata p. 238

19th and 20th Centuries		
Venezuela	Peter Linder	245
Colombia and Ecuador	Jane M. Rausch	257

Colombia p. 259   Ecuador p. 271

Peru	G. Antonio Espinoza	274
Bolivia	Erick D. Langer	280
Chile	William F. Sater	288
Argentina, Paraguay, and Uruguay	Adriana Brodsky, Bridget María Chesterton, Mollie Lewis Nouwen and Thomas Whigham	299

    Argentina p. 307
    Paraguay p. 344
    Uruguay p. 347

BRAZIL	Mark Grover, Mary Ann Mahony and Frank D. McCann	351

    General p. 358
    Colonial p. 367
    Empire and National p. 378

LITERATURE

SPANISH AMERICA

Colonial Period	Amber Brian	393

    Individual Studies p. 395
    Texts, Editions, Anthologies p. 399

21st Century Prose Fiction

Mexico	Ryan Long	402

    Prose Fiction p. 403
    Literary Criticism and History p. 414

Central America	Yvette Aparicio, Erin Finzer, with the assistance of Tiffany D. Creegan Miller, Frances Jaeger and Francisco Solares-Larrave	414

    Prose Fiction p. 421
    Literary Criticism and History p. 436

Hispanic Caribbean	Diana Álvarez Amell and Myrna García-Calderón	438

    Prose Fiction p. 446
    Literary Criticism and History p. 458

Andean Countries	José Cardona-López and César Ferreira	464

    Literary Criticism and History
      Bolivia p. 467
      Peru p. 467
    Prose Fiction
      Bolivia p. 468
      Colombia p. 470
      Ecuador p. 474

Peru p. 477
Venezuela p. 484

River Plate Countries   Claire Emilie Martin, Laura R. Loustau
                        and Giovanna Urdangarain   487
  Prose Fiction
    Argentina p. 493
    Paraguay p. 501
    Uruguay p. 502
  Literary Criticism and History
    Argentina p. 505
    Paraguay p. 506
    Uruguay p. 506

Poetry   José R. Ballesteros, María Luisa Fischer,
            Elizabeth Gackstetter Nichols, Rita M. Palacios,
            Jeannine M. Pitas, José Ramón Ruisánchez Serra
                        and Chrystian Zegarra   507
  Anthologies p. 521
  Books of Verse p. 531
  General Studies p. 556
  Special Studies p. 556
  Miscellaneous p. 558

Drama   Paola Hernández and Elaine M. Miller   559
  Plays p. 562
  Theater Criticism and History p. 570

BRAZIL
  Novels   Regina Igel   571
  Short Stories   M. Angélica Guimarães Lopes   579
  Crônicas   Dário Borim Jr   589
  Poetry   Charles A. Perrone   603
  Drama   Isadora Grevan de Carvalho   619
    Original Plays p. 621
    Theater Criticism and History p. 623

TRANSLATIONS INTO ENGLISH FROM THE SPANISH
AND THE PORTUGUESE   María Constanza Guzmán,
            Élide Valarini Oliver and Steven F. White   626
  Anthologies p. 631
  Translations From the Spanish
    Poetry p. 634
    Brief Fiction and Plays p. 642
    Novels p. 644
    Essays, Interviews, and Reportage p. 654
  Translations From the Portuguese
    Brief Fiction and Theater p. 655
    Novels p. 656
    Essays, Interviews, and Reportage p. 657

MUSIC

GENERAL 659

MEXICO *John Koegel* 661

CENTRAL AMERICA AND THE CARIBBEAN
Alfred E. Lemmon 676
The Caribbean (except Cuba) p. 677
Central America p. 681
Cuba p. 681

ANDEAN COUNTRIES *Jonathan Ritter* 684
Bolivia p. 687   Colombia p. 688
Ecuador p. 689   Peru p. 689
Venezuela p. 695

SOUTHERN CONE *Michael O'Brien* 695
Argentina p. 697   Chile p. 700
Paraguay p. 703   Uruguay p. 703

BRAZIL *Rogério Budasz* 703

PHILOSOPHY: LATIN AMERICAN THOUGHT
Susana Nuccetelli 729
General p. 731   Mexico p. 736
Central America p. 737   The Caribbean p. 738
Venezuela p. 738   Colombia p. 738
Ecuador p. 739   Peru p. 740
Bolivia p. 741   Chile p. 742
Brazil p. 743   Uruguay p. 743
Argentina p. 744

INDEX

ABBREVIATIONS AND ACRONYMS 747

TITLE LIST OF JOURNALS INDEXED 757

ABBREVIATION LIST OF JOURNALS INDEXED 763

SUBJECT INDEX 771

AUTHOR INDEX 815

EDITOR'S NOTE

GENERAL AND REGIONAL TRENDS

The apocalyptic drumroll—refugee crises, environmental degradation, rising populism, ossifying political divisions—which is the beat of our times, to be sure, rumbles in Latin America as well. Few countries, leave alone those in Latin America, have been able to sit out the social, political, economic, and environmental maelstrom. Central America, Puerto Rico, Cuba, Venezuela, and Brazil face particularly tumultuous times. The *HLAS* 72 Editor's Note, written shortly before Hurricane María ravaged Puerto Rico and other islands of the Caribbean, commented on the island's rich cultural scene, its lively bookstores, and the promotion of "cooltura" (Volume 72, p. xvi). Two years later, a comprehensive picture of María's destructiveness and the fallout of the callously politicized response continue to emerge with ongoing repercussions for the island's stability. Thousands died during and after the hurricane, some as a direct result of the inadequate rescue efforts, and thousands more left the island, temporarily or permanently, as clean up and restoration of basic services limped along for months. In the introduction to the Puerto Rican fiction section, Myrna García Calderón notes that the infrastructure, economy, and educational system of the island suffered. Among writers, the disaster has led to a "profound reflection on the role of literature and the arts in a society 'venido abajo'" (p. 442). The collection of essays in *Intemperie* (item **1931**), for example, is a "fina reflexión sobre el artista, el arte y los diversos espacios posibles para la creación." While lamenting the impact of the crisis on cultural centers, libraries, bookstores, and publishers, García Calderón finds reason for optimism in the island's resolute cultural response, affirming that "sí, la producción literaria y cultural sigue pujante, contra viento y marea" (p. 446).

The role of laissez-faire capitalism—the most irresponsible version of which invariably found its way to the colonies—and its consequences, many of which are being suffered today, are much on the minds of historians of Latin America. In new approaches to studies of commodities and natural phenomena, historians are drawing connections to global events. Their work shows how political bungling and opportunism inevitably extracted grave humanitarian and environmental costs. The late esteemed Puerto Rican historian, Fernando Picó, made a "significant contribution to environmental studies" with his work on El Niño and the drought of 1847 (item **873**), tethering the island to Atlantic Studies by drawing connections to similar droughts worldwide. He also described how official complacency led to higher death rates, increased internal migration, and greater agricultural disruption. The work of the late Sidney Mintz, another venerable scholar of the Antilles, continues to influence historians and anthropologists. In an article (item **922**) and a monograph (item **921**), April Merleaux shows how sugar production in Puerto Rico influenced US political decisions regarding annexation and transformed people's diets through a dramatic increase in sugar consumption. Her work "reassesses

Sidney Mintz's landmark *Sweetness and Power: The Place of Sugar in Modern History* (1985)." A special edition of *Op Cit: Revista del Centro de Investigaciones Históricas* (available online at *https://revistas.upr.edu/index.php/opcit/*) (item **799**), honors Mintz and his wide-ranging work with a series of essays and a Spanish translation of his "seminal" article. Commodity production and its socioeconomic impacts likewise provide the frameworks for studies of Dominican rum and Peruvian guano. The former, a follow up to a 1988 volume, "intertwines the development of one of the country's now most notable exports with the larger historical narrative of national growth and change" (item **891**). The latter, "an ambitious and complex study," examines the human and environmental costs of guano extraction, as well as the "rise and influence of the technocratic ideal, and the impact of El Niño-Southern Oscillation on historical events" (item **1169**). Historians of Mexico looked at energy and water resources and considered how frequently political and economic policies shape "tastes," often with calamitous consequences for the environment. "To Save the Forests" shows how the Cárdenas government pushed for a shift from the use of charcoal for household energy to petroleum (from state-owned enterprises) as a "patriotic" remedy for the destruction of forests (item **701**), while *Watering the Revolution* describes how short-term political interests ran roughshod over the better judgement of engineers to create a series of dams in the Laguna region with "significant ecological and social consequences" (item **703**).

In this, the United Nations International Year of Indigenous Languages (2019), it is appropriate to note that "Central America has seen an increase in the participation of new literary voices, particularly those of Indigenous and Afro-descendent poets [and] it is no surprise that Indigenous languages see their most realized expression in poetry" (p. 508). "This new poetry is daring, confronting issues of discrimination, racism, class, ethnicity, as well as gender and sexuality" (p. 509). A "monumental" anthology, *Poesía quechua en Bolivia* (item **2164**), which collects the work of more than 70 poets, is "without doubt" the most important work of Bolivian poetry in recent years (p. 512). In Ecuador, a concerted effort by publishers to provide a venue for the best work from previously marginalized voices has resulted in publications like the anthology *Hatun taki: poemas de la madre tierra y los abuelos* (item **2152** and p. 513). Most of the poems in this volume appear in Quechua with Spanish translations. In Peru, university presses are making available works that cannot find an outlet in commercial presses. One example is the bilingual Quechua-Spanish work *Maskhaypa harawin = Harawi de la búsqueda* that tries to capture the inherent musicality of Peruvian voices (p. 517). Counterintuitively, the poetry, and most literary works, from the bilingual nation of Paraguay ignore the daily presence of Guaraní in the country, especially in Asunción. However, two works of poetry selected for *HLAS 74* draw inspiration from Guaraní culture, songs, and wisdom (p. 521): *Ne'e paje* (item **2250**) and *De este río he de beber* (item **2244**).

Several studies focus on the blending of Indigenous song and oral traditions with musical genres as varied as classical symphonies and hip-hop. In these studies, older and more contemporary and more ethnically diverse musical traditions fuse to forge a more inclusive ethnic and national identity. *Filosofía y sabiduría ancestral*, a "hefty work," looks, in part, at ancestral songs within a broader study examining the intersection of Western and non-Western knowledge in Colombia (item **272**). In *Etno-rock* (item **2724**), essays explore "Indigenous rock music, youth, and identity" in southern Mexico. Another study finds Indigenous communities in northwest Mexico blending their oral traditions with cumbia, rock, rap, ranchera, música tropical, and other genres in attempts to find new forms of expression without diluting their Indigenous identity (item **2750**). In similar fashion, the Kaqchikel-Maya, near Lake Atitlán, Guatemala, use hip-hop to "educate youth about their cultural history and identity," connecting the songs to the literary/poetic traditions of the *Chilam Balam* and *Popul Vuh* (item **2785**). Another set of essays (item **2751**) on the Indigenous musical traditions of Chiapas brings together previously published works by prominent scholars, such as Henrietta Yurchenco. (Many of Yurchenco's collected field recordings from the 1940s–70s are available in the American Folklife Center at the Library of Congress.) A new study on the work of Brazilian composer Heitor Villa-Lobos, who combined elements of classical, Indigenous, and folk music in an effort to create a uniquely Brazilian classical sound, includes two studies that question his appropriation of Indigenous melodies and influences (item **2956**).

Today, the ease of digital photography and the allure of social media platforms have triggered the creation of a massive and ever-growing virtual storehouse of images. Every year, billions of images are captured, uploaded, and stored, leading one to question how much visual—and aural—information we unconsciously absorb. Are we forming our own tastes and beliefs or are they shaped for us through a daily barrage of sights, sounds, and visual information? In spite of this abundance and inevitable duplication, a single image retains the power to grab our attention and even haunt us for the rest of our lives. As events drift into history, scholars pore over faded photographs seeking intimate encounters with episodes past. Reproductions of the early 20th-century photos and writings of Henry Bowman, an English immigrant to Chubut, provide an "excellent resource" on early settlement and immigrant life in Patagonia (item **1315**). A number of newly issued books commemorate the 150th anniversary of the arrival of Welsh immigrants to Patagonia. Among them are two coffee-table books that provide visual histories and contextual essays on the Welsh community in Chubut (items **1300** and **1339**). (For those interested in a general history of the Welsh in Patagonia, see item **1337**).

Works of photography can also underscore who is pictured and who is left out. A study (item **96**) of photographic practices in Jamaica and the Bahamas is "mindful of the conditions of race and class and place that facilitate the disappearance of black subjects from the photographic archive." A study on José Christiano de Freitas Henriques Junior (1832–1902), a Portuguese-born photographer who immigrated to Brazil and later moved to Argentina, discusses the significance of his photos and their uses within a social structure heavily influenced by race. His studio portraits, sold at the time as souvenirs, are "the largest set of photographs of the black population in Rio during Emperor Dom Pedro II's era" (item **159**). Labor historians, meanwhile, find that few mediums rival the photograph when it comes to illuminating the realities of workers' lives. Robert Gerstmann's photos of Bolivian miners offer a "wonderful resource for understanding mining and mine labor in the first third of the 20th century" (item **656**). Images by Honduran photographer Rafeal Platero Paz—discussed in an "innovative study" of the 1954 United Fruit Company general strike—provided a counterpoint to the accepted "imagery of colonialism" and helped workers to assert their rights (item **746**). A third work looks at the relationship between artist and subject, viewer and viewed, against the backdrop of the Mexican Revolution and post-Revolution period, analyzing the depiction of workers in murals, prints, and photographs (item **656**).

Photographs also serve as emblems of resistance. Families denied the mortal remains of their loved ones found in photographs their symbolic remains, and used the images to defy the erasure of relatives and friends, while seeking redress for human rights violations. *Fotografía y memoria en la dictadura argentina, 1976–1983* (item **1328**) describes the work of photographers who worked with anti-military organizations like Madres de la Plaza de Mayo. An exhibition at the Memorial da Resistência de São Paulo used photographs and maps to preserve the memory of 119 Chilean leftist militants disappeared by the Pinochet government (item **105**). Another work on collective memory, this one from Argentina, points out that photography "has served to justify both the military dictatorship as well as those groups who fought for the return to democracy" (item **1327**).

A few studies explore the power of images to subtly (or not) inform, influence, shape, and sway perceptions, assumptions, and even state policies. Crespo Armáiz (item **851**) describes how early stereoscopic photographs of Puerto Rico in North American teaching manuals helped reinforce the idea of the island as colony and its inhabitants as *other*. For more than 100 years, the *National Geographic Magazine*, with its familiar bright yellow cover, glossy paper, and sharp photography, has offered a transportive vision of peoples and places near and far. Its images and stories lodged themselves in the collective memory. Three studies (items **892**, **926**, and **927**) explore the magazine's impact on US policies and statecraft in the Caribbean, particularly Cuba and Puerto Rico.

In addition to photographs, scholars consulted a variety of documentary sources, including newspapers, magazines, personal letters, oral testimonies, maps, and censuses to enrich their studies. The ability of the media to influence and reinforce social structures drew the attention of historians. "Innovative and intensive content analysis" of issues of the Colombian magazine *Cromos* from 1930–46 demonstrates how social classes tighten their grip on privileges when threatened or challenged by new ideas and forces (item **1125**); a set of essays on the representations of subaltern peoples shows how constructed cultural perceptions will "define the place of certain people in society" (item **338**), and a study of the Ecuadorian newspapers *Vistazo* and *El Comercio* during the Fifth Centennial (1992) found that their representations of Indians "created a discourse of white-mestizo to counter the 'political demands of the Indigenous movement'" (item **1151**). For nearly 20 years, the director of Brazil's Museu Histórico Nacional, Gustavo Barroso, wrote a column on "little-known events and personalities" of Brazilian history in the magazine *O Cruzeiro*. A study of his essays, which were accompanied by maps, documents, and photos of objects from the museum's collections, concludes that it was "a project aimed at constructing a national identity" and inspiring national pride (item **1536**).[1]

Contributing to the body of work on gender studies, an analysis of the magazine *Damas y Damitas*, aimed at middle- and lower-class women outside of major metropolitan areas, helped teach women to cook—and, not coincidentally, drew them into the consumer class (item **1320**). A "fascinating study" uses radio broadcasts to show the significant role of women in Uruguayan broadcasts in the 1930s–40s (item **1359**). The correspondence between Getúlio and Alzira Vargas—a reminder of the revelatory capacity of intimate letters—"tell[s] us much about the

---

1. The Museu Histórico Nacional was destroyed by a fire on 2 September 2018. Read more about the museum and its collections in the blog post, "National Museum of Brazil: Remembering its Past": blogs.loc.gov/international-collections/2018/11/national-museum-of-brazil-remembering-its-past/.

attitudes of the Vargas family and how they saw Brazil and its leadership" (p. 357), as well as revealing the affection between father and daughter (item **1569**). Another volume, *Getúlio Vargas, meu pai* (item **1546**)—"a gem for historians"—carries on the Vargas legacy in a work started by Alzira and finished by her daughter, Celina, on the build-up to Brazil's entry into World War II and continuing the story into the post-war era.

Among the works using a wide variety of documentary evidence to retell political history is a staggering 1,000-page memoir by a member of the anti-Trujillo revolutionary movement. The volume includes an appendix that "contains a plethora of documents, including official declarations of governance, several exile letters, a previously hidden (and fascinating) cache of documents from the Trujillo resistance movement, correspondence... photographs, and a brief biography of the author" (item **897**). Two volumes of Argentine political manifestos are a "great resource for teaching," given their inclusion of proclamations, public speeches, photographs, poems, letters, and testimonies, some related to lesser-known historical events (item **1414**). Punk music in Peru during and after the Shining Path conflict offered its own cultural manifesto for a generation of musicians. A "provocative, profane, and subversively brilliant study is richly illustrated with photos, song lyrics, reproductions of zines, flyers, and other underground publications" (item **2812**). The relationship between Alberto Lleras Carmago, Colombia's most important 20th-century statesman, and John F. Kennedy is explored through essays, documents, photographs, and a CD with recordings of speeches made during JFK's 1961 visit to Bogotá (item **1090**).[2] The wryly titled *Meia culpa: O Globo e a ditadura militar* studies the role of the influential Rio de Janeiro daily newspaper during the military regime. The paper repeatedly "manipulated facts and subverted society's values," linking the communist danger to the Goulart administration and justifying many of the military's abuses (item **1651**). As the Contributing Editor for Brazilian history asks in a question for the ages, "What would have happened if the newspaper had held to honest standards of journalism?" (p. 357).

Efforts by research libraries worldwide to digitize and provide open access to books, photographs, and manuscripts have presented scholars and autodidacts with an abundant electronic archive to explore. Interestingly, the publication of transcriptions of documents continues unabated. Ethnohistorians, in particular, along with colonial historians, have reaped the rewards of these efforts. In her introduction to the South American ethnohistory section, Susan Ramírez lists no fewer than eight publications that offer transcriptions of primary sources as supplemental materials. The practice is, as she writes, laudable, as the documents substantiate the conclusions of the current studies and access to them may inspire future interpretations (p. 70). Featured among the many transcriptions issued as stand-alone publications are a dossier documenting a 1751 Indigenous uprising against royal taxes (item **975**), a manuscript volume—long thought lost—of 16th-century minutes from the Cabildo de Santiago de Guatemala (item **714**), the first scholarly treatment of the 1566–68 *Códice Guillermo Tovar de Huejotzingo*,

---

2. The Library's Prints and Photographs Division recently acquired images of President Kennedy's Latin American tour by Colombian photographer Leo Matiz. A blog post describing the acquisition is available on the Library's website: blogs.loc.gov/loc/2018/02/new-acquisition-leo-matiz-history-and-fiction-through-photography.

with transcription of the archival *expedientes* (item **201**), and a collection of slave petitions for manumission and sale from 18th-century Chile (item **1004**). It is not entirely surprising that transcriptions continue to be published in hard copy. As the *New York Times* reported, bookstores continue to survive, and in some cases, thrive. Sales at independent bookstores have risen over the past five years and "another challenger to traditional publishing, e-books, has started to fizzle. Sales of digital books fell 3.6 percent [in a third year of decline]," while hardback and paperback sales increased.[3]

Social media has vastly changed how—and how often—we share information. The quirky nature of the information that we choose to share, however, might not have changed as much as we might think. If Insta-influencers think their popularizing of doggie weddings is especially innovative—they'd be wrong. Frank Proctor delved into Inquisition records to find descriptions of small dog marriages and baptisms for his "brilliant, hilarious, and wonderfully lucid article" " *Amores perritos*" (item **510**). His work contributes to the history of animal studies, human emotions, and carnival—and shows that familiar records still yield surprises. It's fortunate that authorities in vice-regal New Spain could allay fears about inoculation and thus save hundreds of lives throughout the 18th and 19th centuries without having to contend with the relentless and reckless spread of vaccination myths that today routinely surge across the internet and ripple through news feeds (item **511**). In Brazil, social media helped rally thousands in support of former president Lula. In a prototypical example of the self-nourishing nature of social media and the internet, the anthology *Lulalivre*Lulalivro* (item **2506**) uses a popular Instagram hashtag within its creative title; includes contributions from the concrete poet Augusto de Campos, who also offered the poems via his Instagram page, poetamenos; and the book itself, which is available online for free download, was distributed at the same social protests it was compiled to support.

The ubiquity of social media and increasing availability of materials online notwithstanding, there remains ample room for traditional archival exploration and fine editorial work. Painstaking research, herculean organizational efforts, and the adroit refashioning of disparate elements into a seamless new whole have yielded several magisterial studies this biennium. From William Taylor, "another masterpiece"—this one on shrines and miracles, and rich with insights, "is at once intricately adorned yet elegant in structure, an awesome achievement and a source of esthetic pleasure" (item **522**). A study of enslaved peoples in Puebla, Mexico (item **520**), based on three years of "impressive and exhaustive research" and resulting in a database of thousands of bills of sale, is "a significant contribution to the history of Afro-Mexicans and of Atlantic world slavery." The work shows how enslaved peoples formed complex social networks and integrated themselves into society until "Poblano slavery gradually faded from existence in the 18th century." In Mexican poetry, the "book of the year" is the collected works of Francisco Hernández, *En grado de tentativa: poesía reunida* (item **2229**). With a humble title that belies the extraordinary breadth of the work, the two-volume, more than 1100-page set avoids the pitfalls of many collected works to provide an instructive guide to the development of a master poet and his oeuvre. New collections of two essential Chilean poets, Gabriela Mistral and Raúl Zurita, reorganize the published

---

3. "Small Bookstores Thrive by Expanding Beyond Books," by Andria Cheng, *New York Times*, 24 June 2019, p. B6.

Editor's Note / xxi

volumes of these prodigious writers to allow fresh readings of their works (items 2295 and 2160).[4] The "long-awaited and important" *Latin American Music Reader: Views from the South* (item 2679) translates a series of "well-known essays and little-known gems" into English, creating connections between non-Spanish/Portuguese speakers and Latin American ethnomusicologists: essential for the novice and specialist alike, and a fine way to introduce students and colleagues to "the rich variety of music scholarship from Latin America." Lastly, Colombian writer Nahum Montt conjures up his own exceptional encounter, bringing together Shakespeare and Cervantes for an imagined conversation and shared cup of rum during a staging of Hamlet in Vallodolid: "'Siempre supe que tenía un hermano de tinta. Lo que nunca imaginé es que fuera español,' le dice Shakespeare a Cervantes" (item 1980).

The encounter of the Indigenous of the Americas and the Caribbean with Europeans has been the purview of ethnohistorians since the inception of the subfield. The "third generation" of Mesoamerican ethnohistorians is "delving beyond social and political history to explore deeper cultural issues such as gender relations, local commerce, and popular religion" (item 244). To achieve a deeper understanding of the Indigenous perspective and its influence during conquest and into the colonial era, scholars from a variety of disciplines—history, art history, literature, and archeology—are drawing on each other's methods and collaborating using documentary and physical evidence. Such interdisciplinary work can radically alter a point of view: "Whereas textual evidence tends to privilege elite perspectives, archeological evidence allows for the study of a broader range of social actors" (item 514). Historians are complicating the longstanding view of "unilateral 'conquest'" with a more nuanced understanding of a "complex 'Aztec-Spanish War'" (item 231). They ask not only what the conquest meant, but how *both* Indigenous and Spaniard saw this new (to them) *other*: how did they comprehend and react to the *other's* religions, histories, and separate stories of the conquest? And how did the Indigenous sense of identity change once confronted with new social structures and ideas? Scholars question when the Indigenous began to see themselves as part of the greater urban life (item 214); posit that churches may have been "symbols of sovereignty," rather than symbols of repression (item 206); and look at documentary evidence like native wills to explore debts, relationships, and priorities (item 226).

In recording their own histories, Indigenous peoples sought to realign the power structures and cling to social standing within a changing landscape. Careful translations and interpretations of the relatively small body of surviving Indigenous histories, contexualized within the history of the era and the lives of the authors, are helping tease out more subtle understandings of religion, culture, and lineage (items 223, 199, 241, and 194, among others). As one ethnohistorian cautions, use of sources can be complicated without an understanding of who wrote them and why. The *Popul Vuh* is a Maya creation myth, but one set down by Franciscan friar Francisco Ximenez. "When considered contextually, then, the *Popul Vuh* in its presently known form is not simply a Maya sacred book, but an indoctrinator's account of the religious errors he intended to extirpate" (item 230). Even as Mesoamerican and South American ethnohistorians show that Indigenous peoples learned to navigate colonial institutions advantageously, the Indigenous were as

---

4. Recordings of the poets reading from their works may be streamed online from the Hispanic Division's archive of recorded writers: www.loc.gov/rr/hispanic/archive.

likely to be victimized. The cases of Indigenous witchcraft before the Real Audiencia de Santiago de Chile "reveal that the language of Christianity, witchcraft, and sorcery served to police the boundaries of social and cultural inclusion and exclusion in central Chile" (item **1007**)—rarely to the benefit of the Mapuche peoples. Other studies remind us that then, as now, family ties and resources, rather than individual will, often meant and mean the difference between success and failure. As Jane Mangan shows in her work on Inca elite during the early years of colonization, "Spanish fathers recognized mestizo children test[ing] boundaries of colonial laws through their last wills and testaments" (item **980**).

Similar works traced the fortunes of the mixed raced children of elite white Jamaican landowners who sought to use their family connections and lineage to gain or maintain social standing and attain prized careers (items **836** and **816**). These are two of the many richly textured works on the British Caribbean, where, from 2013–3017, "historical interest has exploded" (p. 172). Caribbean Studies—in a response to this increased attention—have moved past linguistic and colonizing boundaries. In a special edition of *Small Axe: A Caribbean Journal of Criticism*, the editorial board announced its intention to include more Hispanophone scholarship and encourage the "inclusion of these sometimes doubly marginalized countries and areas into the larger fold of Caribbean Studies," pointing out that the "subregion has long been ignored or silenced through its 'intense' (and arguably ambivalent) 'Americanization and Latin Americanization' since the decline of the Spanish Empire (item **809**). Historians stretched the borders of the Greater Caribbean to encircle the islands as well as the coastlines of South Carolina and Georgia, noting that the entire region "shared similarly sized plantations, comparable economic regimes, somewhat equal demographic divisions, and parallel scourges of disease and environmental disasters" (item **794**, also see item **822**). These studies reveal a more nuanced view of slavery (see p. 137–140). In Barbados, enslaved Africans and imprisoned Central and South American Indigenous peoples were subjected to a brutal "experiment in social control" as the British instituted a "testing ground for a radically new way of extracting profit from human bodies" (items **817** and **813**). The Spanish similarly sent Indigenous prisoners to "toil as bonded laborers in Cuba" (item **812**). The Caribbean region also played a role in the development of North and South American slavery as slave traders stopped off on the islands before continuing to the mainland Americas and, for those on board, to lives in bondage (item **798**). This reckoning with the harsh realities of the past finds its natural denouement in the debate over reparations. Two separate works by historians Hilary Beckles and Verene Shepherd document the long-lasting impact of slavery on the region, making the case for British reparations for crimes against humanity, genocide, and the extraction of profit from human bodies (items **808** and **814**).

To close, we are yet again reminded of the need for clarity of language. The case, here, is of post-independence Argentina where "statesmen needed to define not only what they were fighting for, but what they were fighting against." The insults hurled at 19th-century monarchists were problematic because "words like *impío* or *salvaje* could change their meaning over time in ways that were hardly predictable. And they might signify different things in different parts of the country or depending on the social class of the person using them" (both, item **1325**). The study serves as a cautionary tale about the power of words to inform, but also to mislead. Perhaps today more than ever before, we should reflect on the impact of our words.

CLOSING DATE

With some exceptions, the closing date for works annotated in this volume was 2017. Publications received and cataloged at the Library of Congress after that date will be annotated in the next humanities volume, *HLAS 76*.

ELECTRONIC ACCESS TO THE *HANDBOOK*

HLAS records are searchable through two open-access web sites hosted at the Library of Congress. *HLAS Web*, relaunched with a visual refresh in Fall 2017, is the newer mobile-friendly, ADA-compliant web site (hlasopac.loc.gov). The site offers robust search features; permalinks to individual records; links to many open-access journal articles; and easy options for printing, saving, and exporting lists of records. The site is also compatible with Zotero. *HLAS* records that did not appear in a print volume will not be annotated, and newer records are in a preliminary editorial stage. Currently Volumes 39–74, along with preliminary records for the forthcoming Volumes 75–76, are available. In other words, reviews of publications from the 1970s to the present are searchable via *HLAS Web*. An ongoing conversion project will eventually make the remaining volumes (1–38) available through *HLAS Web*. (See *HLAS 70*, Editor's Note, p. xxiii for more information about the conversion project.) In the meantime, reviews of publications from the mid-1930s onward are accessible via *HLAS Online*.

HLAS Online (www.loc.gov/hlas/), a searchable web-based database, offers electronic access to all volumes of the *Handbook*. website also includes tables of contents and linked introductory essays for Volumes 50–65 (www.loc.gov/hlas/contents.html). The introductory essays for Volumes 1–49 are searchable within the database by using the phrase "general statement." *HLAS Online* offers a trilingual interface (English, Spanish, and Portuguese) and the data is updated weekly. *HLAS Online* is also an OpenURL source, allowing seamless linking from *HLAS* entries to related electronic resources.

CHANGES FROM THE PREVIOUS HUMANITIES VOLUME

Art
Angélica J. Afanador-Pujol appraised works on precolumbian and colonial art of Mesoamerica and New Spain.

History
Bradley Benton and Peter Villella shared responsibility for reviewing works of Mesoamerican ethnohistory. Daniel Livesay provided assessments of works on the British Caribbean. Jesse Zarley examined studies on colonial Chile, Quito, and Nueva Granada. G. Antonio Espinoza commented on works of Peruvian history.

Literature
Amber Brian provided assessments of works on colonial literature. Tiffany D. Creegan-Miller, Frances Jaeger, and Francisco Solares-Larrave collaborated with returning Contributing Editors Yvette Aparico and Erin Finzer to comment on the prose fiction of Central America. Rita Palacios and Jeannine Pitas joined the poetry cohort to review works from Central America and the Southern Cone respectively. Elaine Miller commented on dramatic works from Mexico, Central America, and the Spanish Caribbean. Élide Valarini Oliver evaluated translations from the Portuguese.

Philosophy

Susana Nuccetelli described works of Spanish American philosophy and intellectual history.

ACKNOWLEDGMENTS

This volume marks a significant turning point for the *Handbook*, but one which perhaps will not be noticed by *Handbook* readers. For more than 20 years, Marla Banks has been the programmer behind the print production of *HLAS*, and in more recent years, for the HLAS Conversion Project as well. This year, after 33 years of service, Marla is retiring from the Library. All of us on the *HLAS* staff will miss her ability to track down broken bits of data, spot invalid xml, patiently rerun files to make room for last minute additions and corrections, and generally keep our print production process—and many other technical aspects—humming efficiently behind the scenes. We wish her the best and we are grateful that Library Services has found an equally skilled successor to work with us on future volumes of *HLAS*.

Katherine D. McCann, *Humanities Editor*

ART

SPANISH AMERICA
Precolumbian and Colonial

ANGÉLICA J. AFANADOR-PUJOL, *Associate Professor of Art History and Program Director of the LACMA-ASU Master's Fellowship in Art History, Herberger Institute for Design and the Arts, Arizona State University*
HUMBERTO RODRÍGUEZ-CAMILLONI, *Professor of Architecture and Director, Henry H. Wiss Center for Theory and History of Art and Architecture, Virginia Polytechnic Institute and State University*

MEXICO, CENTRAL AMERICA, CARIBBEAN

THE WORKS REVIEWED FOR *HLAS 74* cover a wide range of topics that provide a greater understanding of art, architecture, and urban and landscape planning both at the local level and in the greater early modern world. Several studies address artistic trade networks in the Americas and the impact of imported goods and artists from Europe to Mexico and the Caribbean. Significantly, some works illuminate the importance of the movement of ideas, materials, and art from the Americas to Spain and throughout Europe. Greater collaboration among authors based in Latin America, Europe, and the US has produced fruitful results with volumes showing diverse expertise and a broader variety of approaches.

Recent studies have provided insight into how Mexico, Latin America, and the Caribbean entered the European imaginary. The noteworthy essays collected in *Altera Roma* (item **26**), as well as *Imágenes de caníbales y salvajes del nuevo mundo* by Yobenj Chicangana-Bayona (item **17**) and *Pictorial Theories by Missionaries in Sixteenth-Century New Spain* by Margit Kern and Richard George Elliott (item **34**), have shown how classical Roman, medieval, and Renaissance precedents, as well as Egyptian hieroglyphs, helped shaped the ways in which Europeans understood and represented the inhabitants of the New World and their artistic production. Alessandra Russo's essay, "An Artistic Journey" (item **23**), connects the discussion of the artistic merits of the work of indigenous peoples to larger debates about the classification of liberal arts in the 16th century. Daniela Bleichmar's *Visual Voyages* (item **16**) addresses the role of images in the creation of scientific knowledge and the conceptualization and transformation of Latin America and Europe.

Studies on materials and techniques have led scholars to explore trade routes, material exchanges, and the added meaning these materials conveyed and continue to convey to precolumbian and viceregal works. The sumptuously illustrated exhibit catalog *Golden Kingdoms: Luxury Arts in the Ancient Americas* (item **1**) highlights the work of scholars whose dedicated study over the past few decades has provided valuable insights about the spread of goldwork techniques and other luxury materials such as jade, shell, and feathers, thus revealing the interconnectedness of South America, Central America, and Mexico. Carmella Padilla and Barbara Anderson's catalog, *A Red like no Other: How Cochineal Colored the World* (item **22**), cleverly unveils the production, use, and meaning of cochineal, a tiny bug originally cultivated in Mexico and Central America and used for artistic pigment and dye, and later gifted and traded, transforming the use of color in textiles and paintings throughout the Americas, Europe, Africa, and Asia. Diana Magaloni Kerpel's *The Colors of the New World* and the studies highlighted in Gabriela Siracusano and Agustina Rodríguez Romero's essay "Materiality Between Art, Science, and Culture in the Viceroyalties (16th-17th Centuries)" also contribute to the discussion of how artists working in the colonial period used specific materials to convey and add meaning to paintings and sculptures (items **35** and **25**, respectively).

Studies on mural, easel, and screen-fold painting have also received renewed attention both for their local contributions and as an expression of regional and inter-regional connections. For the precolumbian period, Mary Ellen Miller and Claudia Brittenham's *The Spectacle of the Late Maya Court* (item **6**) on the Bonampak Maya murals provides a new interpretation of their contents and highlights their connection to the art of other Maya city-states. Similarly, Brittenham's *The Murals of Cacaxtla: The Power of Painting in Ancient Central Mexico* reveals the artists' knowledge of other Mesoamerican regions (see *HLAS 72:196*). Both of these volumes contain extensive high-quality illustrations that make them indispensable for those interested in studying these sites.

Scholars of the viceregal period have looked at artistic contributions both within the context of local traditions and in dialogue with transatlantic art trends. The exhibit catalog, *Painted in Mexico, 1700–1790*, edited by Ilona Katzew provides a comprehensive reassessment of 18th-century Mexican painting and its iconographic and stylistic contributions (item **40**). Sofía Sanabrais' essay, "From Byōbu to Biombo," explores the political and socioeconomic connections between Mexico and Japan that made possible the introduction of folding screens (*byōbu/biombo*) and enabled their production (item **45**).

Recent scholarship on landscape and urban planning of ancient Mesoamerican cities has contributed to a greater understanding of how these spaces are connected to ideology. The collection of essays by distinguished scholars gathered in *La conceptualización del paisaje en la ciudad mesoamericana* offers good examples of different conceptions of the landscape and its connection to the design of cities (item **8**). The catalog *Teotihuacan: City of Water, City of Fire* presents a focused study of this ancient cosmopolitan city, recent archeological findings, and the role of art and architecture, coupled with high-quality images (item **9**).

For the viceregal period, studies on the built environment demonstrate that indigenous ways of connecting to space endured and were adapted to meet the demands of the new government. Barbara Mundy's ambitious book, *The Death of Aztec Tenochtitlan, the Life of Mexico City* provides a theoretically savvy and exemplary visual analysis of the transformation of the Aztec capital Tenochtitlan into the viceregal capital of New Spain (Mexico) (item **38**). By analyzing the construction and representation of the city and its use of space, Mundy demonstrates the role that Aztec governors under the colonial administration played in shaping the city. In addition, recent studies such as those published in the proceedings of the Mayer Center's Symposium *Festivals and Daily Life in the Arts of Colonial Latin America, 1492–1850* and Ana Amigo Requejo's essay in *Iberoamérica en* *perspectiva artística* provide new contributions to our understanding of viceregal spaces in New Spain and the urban experience in La Habana, and the function of ephemeral arts (item **20** and Ana Amigo Requejo in item **24**).

The past few years have seen a robust growth of the scholarship about Catholic art and architecture with researchers exploring new venues. Raquel Pineda Mendoza's *Conjuntos devocionales domésticos de Santa María del Pino, Tepetitlán, Hidalgo* provides a rare glimpse of the transformation of domestic altars and the structures connected to them from precolumbian to viceregal times, particularly within the Otomi community of Santa María del Pino (item **42**). In *Las capillas del Vía Crucis de la ciudad de México*, Alena Robin tackles the challenging work of discussing now extinct chapels of the Stations of the Cross of Mexico City by examining their patronage, function, and, ultimately, destruction (item **44**).

Recent interdisciplinary studies have challenged the vision of convent complexes as static structures, designed according to a pre-existing plan. Instead, they are revealed to be dynamic spaces that grew over several centuries in response to socioeconomic, political, and religious interests, as in the case of the convent complex of Tlaxcala (item **46**). Also in this tenor, the publications by Alessia Frassani highlight the role of Mixtec patrons and practices over several centuries in shaping the art, architecture, and festivities of the church and convent of Santo Domingo and the palace of the indigenous governor at Yanhuitlán, Mexico (items **32** and **31**). The publication of lavishly illustrated catalogs documenting the restoration projects of the Church of Jesus of Nazareth in Atotonilco and the Church of Santa Prisca in Taxco create invaluable records of architectural plans, restoration processes, and rarely published artistic and architectural details (items **30** and **43**).

Several studies are worth mentioning for their investigation of the representation of nuns and the adaptation of European models in the context of New Spain, such as James Córdova's *The Art of Professing in Bourbon Mexico* and Cristina Cruz González's essay, "Beyond the Bride of Christ" (items **28** and **33**). Also in the realm of female representation within the Catholic Church is Jeanette Peterson's exemplary work, *Visualizing Guadalupe* (item **21**). In it, Peterson addresses the subjectivities of viewing and the multilayered meaning of the original Spanish sculpture of the Virgin of Guadalupe, the devotional images created in South America to spread her cult, and the Mexican images of her, as well as the spread of the latter's cult back to Spain.

Recent thematic studies such as Elizabeth Morán's survey on food, art, and culture among the Aztecs (item **7**); María Luisa Vázquez de Ágredos Pascual and Cristina Vidal Lorenzo's examination of fragrances and body paint among the Maya (chapter 9 in item **5**); and David Bindman's study (item **47**) on the representation of race in the Caribbean offer enticing findings and paths of inquiry into areas requiring further investigation. Other areas that have recieved only limited attention and are worthy of future research include precolumbian and colonial works outside the Maya region and central Mexico and colonial furniture and decorative arts. [AAP]

SOUTH AMERICA

Publications reviewed for this biennium reflect significant advances during the past few decades in the history of art and architecture of the precolumbian and Spanish colonial periods. Many studies are models of scholarly rigor and focus on new perspectives on ancient American art and Spanish colonial art. Some of the most noteworthy studies appear in the proceedings of national and international conferences collected in handsome volumes fully documented with notes, comprehensive bibliographies, and fine-quality color illustrations. Excellent examples are *Entre cielos e infiernos: memoria del V Encuentro Internacional sobre Barroco* (item **55**) from the 2009 International Congress on Baroque Art held in La Paz; *Making Value, Making Meaning: Techné in the Pre-Columbian World* (item **10**), from the symposium under the same title held at the Dumbarton Oaks Research Library and Collection, Washington, D.C.; and Ismael Pérez Calderón, ed., *Arte rupestre: actas y ponencias* (item **15**), from the IV "Federico Kauffmann Doig" national symposium on Paleolithic art held in Ayachucho, Peru, between 27 October and 2 November 2010.

Architecture, painting, sculpture, and the decorative arts are evenly represented in both anthologies and single-author monographs. Ramón Mujica Pinilla's *La imagen transgredida: ensayos de iconografía peruana y sus políticas de representación simbólica* (item **60**) is an outstanding contribution to the historiography of Peruvian art primarily from the Spanish colonial period. The volume makes available to a wide audience an anthology of essays originally published in books, catalogs, and journals now out of print. *Visual Culture of the Ancient Americas: Contemporary Perspectives* (item **2**) is an excellent multi-authored volume that pays tribute to international expert in the art of central Mexico Esther Pasztory upon her retirement from the Department of Art History and Archaeology at Columbia University in 2013. Closely reflecting Pasztory's special expertise in Mesoamerican precolumbian art, the collected articles enhance our understanding of specific facets of ancient American art as well as our appreciation of the evolving analytical tendencies related to the broader field of study as it developed and matured.

Rare contributions dedicated to the study of metalwork and glazed ceramics are Anel Pancorvo Salicetti, ed., *Forjando el tiempo: historia del metal en el Perú* (item **12**), and Julio Antonio Gutiérrez Samanez's *Rescate de la cerámica vidriada colonial cusqueña* (item **58**). Both of these publications contain a large number of fine-quality color illustrations incorporated with the texts that permit an appreciation of a cultural heritage from the colonial period that has previously not received the attention it deserves. At the same time, in each case, a valuable visual corpus is provided as a source for future studies.

Two other important publications make accessible the holdings of a public and private museum: *Guía MALI* (item **57**) is a handsome guide to the Museo de Arte de Lima (MALI), Peru. Not only does it provide an indispensable guide to the museum collections—the most complete in the nation—but it also serves as a comprehensive *catalogue raisonné* with fine-quality illustrations and full descriptions of the art works. In turn, Carlos Armando Rodríguez's *Colombia-Ecuador, 3000 años de arte prehispánico: la colección Ziablof* (item **13**) features the private collection of Paul Ziablof consisting of some 1,000 precolumbian pieces from the little-known cultures of Ylama, Tumaco-Tolita, Quimbaya, Sonso, Quebarda Seca, Capulí, Piartal, and Tuza, which developed in southwest Colombia and northwest Ecuador between 700 BC and AD 1550.

Several titles that use iconographic analysis and interpretation explore the relationship between form and meaning. These include *Iconografía intelectual en el Virreinato de la Nueva Granada siglo XVIII: estudio iconográfico, iconológico e histórico de la escuela franciscana, las "defendere", "disputatios" y ofrecimientos* (item **49**); *Pintura colonial cusqueña* (item **51**); and *De Amberes al Cusco: el grabado europeo como fuente del arte virreinal* (item **54**).

It is also worthwhile to mention two international events that included the participation of distinguished scholars in the field. The first of these was the 56th International Congress of Americanists held in Salamanca, Spain, between 15–20 July 2018, that featured three sessions chaired by this author on the topic "The Architecture of the Mendicant Orders in the New World." Papers dealing with Andean colonial themes include "Convento y Templo de Santo Domingo en Tunja, Colombia," by Giovanni Guarnizo Valenzuela, and "La producción arquitectónica de las órdenes religiosas en la región del Altiplano del Lago Titicaca durante el Virreinato del Perú," by Roberto Samanez Argumedo. The second was the Mayer Center Symposium XVIII at the Denver Art Museum on the topic "Materiality: Making Spanish America" held on 1–2 November 2018. Papers presented include "Sculpture at Home in Baroque Lima," by Rafael Ramos Sosa; "Collect, Create and Send: The Objects in the Index of Archbishop of Trujillo, Martínez Castellón," by Olaya Sanfuentes; and "Materiality between Mind and Hands: Some Approaches to Native Creativity in Colonial South America," by Gabriela Siracusano. One hopes the publication of these proceedings will follow in the near future.

Finally, it is my special privilege and honor to dedicate this section to the memory of renowned Bolivian architect, art historian, and friend Teresa Gisbert Carbonell de Mesa, who died on 19 February 2018 at age 91. Universally recognized as the "Grand Dame of the History of Art of the Andean World," Gisbert was the author or coauthor with her late husband, José de Mesa, of numerous books and academic essays considered classics and indispensable reading for studies in the field. Over the decades, her best-known works reviewed in *HLAS* have included *Historia de la pintura cuzqueña* (1962; see *HLAS 25:1177*), *Holguín y la pintura virreinal en Bolivia* (1977; see *HLAS 42:263*), and *Iconografía y mitos indígenas en el arte* (1980; see *HLAS 44:1604*). Featured in this *HLAS* volume is her essay "Los grabados, el 'Juicio Final' y la idolatía indígena en el mundo andino" (item 55). During her life, Gisbert served as director of the Museo Nacional de Arte in La Paz between 1970 and 1976, and as president of the Sociedad Boliviana de Historia in 1983–84. In addition, she was director of the Instituto Boliviano de Cultura between 1985 and 1989, and president of ICOMOS in Bolivia between 1986 and 1992. Without a doubt, her departure has left a big void in the field, and she will be dearly missed with profound gratitude and affection by family, colleagues, and friends. [HRC]

PRECOLUMBIAN

General

1 **Golden kingdoms: luxury arts in the ancient Americas.** Edited by Joanne Pillsbury, Timothy Potts, and Kim N. Richter. Los Angeles, Calif.: The J. Paul Getty Museum and The Getty Research Institute, 2017. 311 p.: bibl., ill., maps.

This comprehensive catalog of the exhibit co-organized by the Getty Museum, the Getty Research Institute, and the Metropolitan Museum of Art explores the development of luxury items, trade, and techniques from precolumbian times until the arrival of Europeans. The exhibit follows the spread of gold techniques from the Andes in South America to Mexico, while emphasizing other materials such as jade, shell, and feathers. Essays by international scholars highlight the kinds of materials used and their meaning, techniques employed, roles of artists, trade networks, and cultural shifts after the arrival of Europeans. Brief insets provide information about archeological sites related to some of the objects and techniques discussed in the essays. The work includes catalog entries of 200 objects and high-quality images. [AAP]

2   Visual culture of the ancient Americas: contemporary perspectives. Edited by Andrew Finegold and Ellen Hoobler. Afterword by Esther Pasztory. Norman: University of Oklahoma Press, 2017. 295 p.: bibl., ill., index, maps, photos.

This elegant multi-authored volume pays tribute to international expert in the art of central Mexico Esther Pasztory upon her retirement from the Department of Art History and Archaeology at Columbia University in 2013. During a period of five decades, Pasztory made a lasting contribution to the study of indigenous and precolumbian art, in terms of both our understanding of specific facets of ancient American art as well as our appreciation of the evolving analytical tendencies related to the broader field of study as it developed and matured. Even though most of the articles collected here reflect Pasztory's specific expertise on Mesoamerican precolumbian art, three important leading studies address the Andean world: "Aesthetics of a Line, Entangled in a Network," by Gary Urton (p. 17–30); "Humboldt and the Inca Ruin of Cañas," by Georgia de Havenon (p. 31–42); and "From a Republic of Letters to an Empire of Images," by Joanne Pillsbury (p. 43–57). Appropriately enough, in one way or another, these studies follow a line of thinking and methodological approach laid down by Pasztory in her own research. The comprehensive list of references (p. 241–278) applies to all of the studies in the publication. [HRC]

Mesoamerica

3   Barnes, William L. The Teocalli of Sacred Warfare and late imperial calendrical rhetoric in the court of Moteuczoma II. (Res/Cambridge, 67/68, 2017, p. 235–255, bibl.)

This essay proposes that the artists who carved the glyphs and images on the Aztec sculpture known as the Teocalli (temple) of the Sacred Warfare (c. 1506–07) organized them into groups that resemble couplets and paired couplets employed by the Aztec noble and priestly class in their discourse. These couplets often use metaphor and metonym to convey meaning, and likewise, the author argues, the calendrical glyphs depicted in the monument are connected to significant dates that link the Aztec rise to power, and the Aztec ruler Moteuczoma II's in particular, to sacred narratives of the earth's creation, the sun, and the realm of the gods. [AAP]

4   Boone, Elizabeth Hill. Who they are and what they wear: Aztec costumes for European eyes. (Res/Cambridge, 67/68, 2017, p. 316–334, bibl.)

Boone analyzes the representation of military, regional, and elite dress in four manuscripts as a response to the European fascination with the costumes of peoples from around the world in the 16th century. She compares Christoph Weiditz's *Trachtenbuch* (Costume Book) produced in Europe with three ethnographic manuscripts produced in Mexico: the *Codex Tudela*, the *Codex Ríos*, and Part Two of the *Codex Ixtlilxochitl*. The author proposes that while all the manuscripts were intended for European consumption, the three manuscripts reproduced in Mexico were accurate cultural representations of costume, but Weiditz's images were based on ideas and amalgamations of images of Amerindians popular in Europe at the time. [AAP]

5   Constructing power and place in Mesoamerica: pre-Hispanic paintings from three regions. Edited by Merideth Paxton and Leticia Staines Cicero. Albuquerque: University of New Mexico Press, 2017. 246 p.: bibl., index.

International scholars bring diverse perspectives to the study of painting and space. For central Mexico, four essays analyze colonial-era Aztec manuscripts and Teotihuacan's murals as a way to understand the use of space and the city's economic interests and political organization. For Oaxaca, one essay explores the representation of family lineages in funerary murals at Monte Albán and another challenges previous identifications of toponyms in Mixtec codices. In the Maya region, five essays identify animals represented in ceramics; the composition of body paints and fragrances among the Maya elite; the centrality of food in murals at Calakmul; iconographic and stylistic changes in Mayapan's murals; and the perseverance of Maya understanding of space in the 17th century. [AAP]

6   Miller, Mary Ellen and Claudia Brittenham. The spectacle of the late Maya court: reflections on the murals of Bonampak. With new reconstruction paintings

by Heather Hurst and Leonard Ashby for the Bonampak Documentation Project. Austin: University of Texas Press, 2013. 261 p.: bibl., ill. (some color), index, maps (some color), 3 plates in pocket. (The William and Bettye Nowlin series in art, history, and culture of the Western Hemisphere)

This work provides an analysis of the courtly murals of Structure 1 in Bonampak (AD 791), Mexico. The authors discuss the history of the mural's discovery and context; their facture in relationship to other Maya courtly art, their surroundings, and the complexity of their program and execution; the connection and tension between text and images and the stories they represent; as well as their function as records of and guides to performances; and the relationship to the politics of the region at their time of creation. Each chapter is richly illustrated with high-quality photographs of the murals and related works. The book also includes a catalog of images and full reconstructions of the murals. For archeologist's comment, see *HLAS 71:98*. [AAP]

7   **Morán, Elizabeth.** Sacred consumption: food and ritual in Aztec art and culture. Austin: University of Texas Press, 2016. 142 p.: bibl., ill., index. (Latin American and Caribbean arts and culture publication initiative (Andrew W. Mellon foundation))

Based on primary and secondary sources from the precolumbian and early viceregal period, this survey points to the centrality of food in Aztec life, art, and culture. The author divides the information in four chapters covering ceremonial consumption in domestic and everyday life, public rituals, cosmovision and religious believes, and the continuation of Aztec food uses in ritual life after the Spanish conquest. The author examines the use of food as a metaphor for cosmic and political transformation and the expression of these beliefs in ritual performances. For ethnohistorian's comment, see *HLAS 72:305*. [AAP]

8   **Paisaje y Diseño Urbano: Interdependencias Conceptuales en la Ciudad Mesoamericana, Precolonial y Colonial** (conference), *México, 2009*. La conceptualización del paisaje en la ciudad mesoamericana. Coordinación de Ángel Julián García Zambrano y María Elena Bernal García. Cuernavaca, Mexico: Universidad Autónoma del Estado de Morelos; México: Juan Pablos Editor, 2015. 220 p.: bibl., ill., maps. (Colección Ediciones Mínimas. Historia; 3)

Conference proceedings of the panel "Paisaje y diseño urbano: interdependencias conceptuales en la ciudad mesoamericana, precolonial y colonial" of the 53rd Congreso Internacional de Americanistas (2009). Essays discuss the conceptualization of the landscape and its connection to identity, memory, and social and temporal order. They address recent findings of man-made caves in Teotihuacan; the symbols of genitals, insemination, and gestation as part of the fertility of Mesoamerican cities; the importance of geographical features for the founding of precolumbian settlements; and the significance of waterways in Tenochtitlan that marked indigenous sacred spaces and routes even after the arrival of Europeans; among other themes. [AAP]

9   **Teotihuacan: city of water, city of fire.** Edited by Matthew Robb. Contributions from Rubén Cabrera Castro *et al.* San Francisco, Calif.: Fine Arts Museums of San Francisco-De Young and University of California Press, 2017. 444 p.: ill.

This work presents a catalog of an exhibit organized by the Fine Arts Museum of San Francisco and the Los Angeles County Museum of Art. Essays by well-known international scholars highlight the recent archeological findings at Teotihuacan's ceremonial pyramids, the city's history and urban planning, its domestic compounds, murals, and other artworks. Contributions explore the diversity of the urban population and art and architecture as ways to unify the city's inhabitants. Objects in the catalog are organized thematically and by the location where they were found. The publication includes high-quality images and maps pointing to the location of objects excavated. [AAP]

South America

10   **Costin, Cathy Lynne.** Making value, making meaning: techné in the pre-Columbian world. Washington, D.C.: Dumbarton Oaks Research Library and Collection, 2016. 489 p.: bibl., ill., index. (Dumbarton Oaks pre-Columbian symposia and colloquia)

This handsome volume in the tradition of fine quality publications by Dumbarton Oaks collects the papers that were presented at the symposium under the same title held in Washington, D.C., on 11–12 October 2013. An excellent introduction by Cathy Lynne Costin (p. 1–30) defines the term "techné" as applied to the themes developed in the symposium and provides a summary of the contents of the papers presented by different scholars. Studies specifically related to the Andean world include: "Telluric Techné and the Lithic Production in Tiwanaku," by John W. Janusek and Patrick Ryan Williams (p. 95–128); "Encoded Process, Embodied Meaning in Paracas Post-Fired Ceramics," by Lisa DeLeonardis (p. 129–166); "Valuing the Local Inka Metal Production in the Tarapacá Valley of Northern Chile," by Colleen Zori (p. 167–192); "New World Metallurgy: A Comparative Study of Copper Production in the South Central Andes and West Mexico," by Blanca Maldonado (p. 193–220); "Spondylus and the Inka Empire on the Far North Coast of Peru: Recent Excavations at Taller Conchales, Cabeza de Vaca, Tumbes," by Jerry D. Moore and Carolina María Vílchez (p. 221–251); "The Artistry of Moche Mural Painting and the Ephemerality of Monuments," by Lisa Trever (p. 253–279); "Crafting Identities Deep and Broad: Hybrid Ceramics on the Late Prehispanic North Coast of Peru," by Cathy Lynne Costin (p. 319–359); and "Shaping Local and Regional Identities: Techné in the Moche Presence at Cerro Castillo, Nepaña Valley, Peru," by Carlos Rengifo (p. 361–390). All texts are well complemented by color photographs, maps, and diagrams, and are fully documented with footnotes and extensive bibliographies. [HRC]

11 Desrosiers, Sophie. El textil como matriz para el desarrollo de las artes plásticas en los Andes. (*Rev. Esp. Antropol. Am.*, 43:2, 2013, p. 477–514, bibl., ill., photos, tables)

This study focuses on the direct links between geometric designs on artwork of various media from several precolumbian cultures of the Peruvian coast and those found on textiles. As a way to identify the actual sources for an extensive design program, the author shows how the understanding of some present weaving practices from the Andean highlands can help in deciphering this relationship, as in particular in the reconstruction of the warp-faced techniques underlying their creation. As a matrix for the development of visual arts in the Andes, the author further argues that warp-faced textiles have played an important role in the history of Andean art and that today they should take their rightful place in being recognized for their contribution to the development of Andean culture and history. Small illustrations integrated with the text help support the author's arguments and additional documentation is presented in the footnotes and bibliography. [HRC]

12 Forjando el tiempo: historia del metal en el Perú. Edición y dirección general por Anel Pancorvo Salicetti. Textos de Luis Repetto *et al.* y fotografía por Daniel Giannoni y Joaquín Rubio. Lima: Apus Graph Ediciones, 2014. 217 p.: bibl., ill. (Intéligo)

This multi-authored deluxe edition provides a comprehensive history of the art of metalwork in Peru from precolumbian times to the 20th century. A brief prologue by Luis Repetto Málaga serves as introduction to the main text, which is divided into three chapters: "La metalurgia en el antiguo Peru: arte y simbolismo," by Régulo G. Franco Jordán (p. 16–99); "Oro y plata en el Virreinato del Perú: minería y economía virreinal," by Jaime Mariazza F. (p. 100–131); and "Entre la conmemoración, las búsquedas expresivas y el refinamiento utilitario," by Gabriela Germaná (p. 132–186). Beautiful color plates alternate with the texts, followed by a comprehensive bibliography and notes arranged by chapters (p. 187–207). In addition, a useful illustrated index to all the plates with captions is provided (p. 209–217). This publication is an indispensable source for further studies with a visual corpus of works from public and private collections not always available to scholars or the general public. [HRC]

Guía MALI. See item 57.

13 Rodríguez, Carlos Armando. Colombia—Ecuador, 3000 años de arte prehispánico: la colección Ziablof. Cali, Colombia: Universidad del Valle, 2013. 200 p.: bibl., ill. Colección Artes y humanidades

This elegant catalog describes a private collection of precolumbian ceramics from Ecuador and Colombia donated in 2011 to the Museo Arqueológico Julio César Cubillos of the Universidad del Valle in Cali, Colombia. Represented in the collection consisting of nearly 1,000 ceramic pieces are the little-known cultures of Ylama, Tumaco-Tolita, Quimbaya, Sonso, Quebrada Seca, Capulí, Piartal, and Tuza, which developed in southwest Colombia and northwest Ecuador between 700 BC and AD 1550. Brief texts introduce each of the cultures, followed by an album of color plates of representative examples pertaining to each. This visual corpus makes available to students and scholars alike a valuable source for future studies. [HRC]

14 **Samaniego Román, Lorenzo A.** Arte mural de Punkurí, Nepeña, Ancash. (*Investig. Soc./San Marcos*, 16:28, junio 2012, p. 15–33, appendices, bibl., ill., maps, photos)

This brief study looks at the pictorial and sculptural decoration of the pre-Inca buildings of Punkurí in the Nepeña Valley on the northern Peruvian coast. The construction with hand-rolled adobe bricks of various shapes is examined as the base for painted figures in low and high relief representing deities and mythical religious scenes depicting humans, fauna, flora, and natural phenomena. Color is mentioned as an important feature of these representations, but unfortunately it cannot be appreciated in the few black-and-white illustrations that accompany the text. The author argues that the mural art of these buildings was linked to the religious worldview of the Andean people as part of the visual language of the artists from the Archaic and formative periods (4000–1000 BC). A close relationship to the development of the artistic style of Sechín, another important contemporary archeological site, is also considered. [HRC]

15 **Simposio Nacional de Arte Rupestre, 4th, Ayacucho, Peru, 2010.** Arte rupestre: actas y ponencias. Edición de Ismael Pérez Calderón. Ayacucho, Peru: Universidad Nacional de San Cristóbal de Huamanga, 2012. 342 p.: bibl., ill.

Popular edition of the proceedings from the IV National Symposium on Paleolithic art held in Ayacucho, Peru between 27 October-2 November 2010. This important academic event which paid tribute to distinguished Peruvian archeologist Federico Kauffmann Doig coordinated the presentation of 19 papers by different scholars highlighting recent discoveries in the field. Petroglyphs from little-known sites in the Andean region are analyzed with concerns for their preservation. Unfortunately, poor quality b/w photographs that accompany the texts do not permit an adequate appreciation of the examples discussed. [HRC]

COLONIAL

General

16 **Bleichmar, Daniela.** Visual voyages: images of Latin American nature from Columbus to Darwin. New Haven: Yale University Press in association with The Huntington Library, Art Collections, and Botanical Gardens, 2017. 226 p.: bibl., color ill., index, maps.

This richly illustrated catalog was published for the exhibition of the same name. Through the analysis of maps, manuscripts, and paintings of Latin America's natural world by indigenous and European artists, the author evaluates the political, economic, and scientific implications of these images and their role in the transformation of Latin America and Europe. Bleichmar studies the histories and dissemination of some of these works; the different value system attached to Latin American commodities; and the process through which fauna, flora, and landscape were classified and understood. [AAP]

17 **Chicangana-Bayona, Yobenj Aucardo.** Imágenes de caníbales y salvajes del nuevo mundo: de lo maravilloso medieval a lo exótico colonial, siglos XV–XVII. Bogotá: Editorial Universidad del Rosario, Universidad Colegio Mayor de Nuestra Señora del Rosario, Escuela de Ciencias Humanas, 2013. 260 p.: bibl., ill. (some color.). (Colección Textos de ciencias humanas)

This detailed iconographic study discusses the European production of images depicting the indigenous inhabitants of the Americas. The author focuses mostly on indigenous representations as good savages and feared cannibals and the precedents for these types in earlier chronicles, illuminated manuscripts, biblical and classical sources, medieval and Renaissance models of the monstrous races of the world and of the Orient, and even in quotidian scenes. The work traces the literary and pictorial genealogy of anonymous works and influential artists such as Johann Froschauer, Hans Holbein, Sébastien Münster, Lorenz Fries, and Theodore de Bry. Includes an extensive bibliography with works in Spanish, Portuguese, French, and some English. [AAP]

18   Diaz, Josef and Suzanne Stratton-Pruitt. Painting the divine: images of Mary in the new world. Albuquerque, N.M.: S.F. Design, llc, 2014. 143 p.: bibl., ill., maps, photos.

Large format, bilingual catalog of an exhibit at the New Mexico History Museum. The artworks depict the Virgin Mary's life and her apparitions in the Viceroyalties of Perú and New Spain from the 17th to the 18th centuries. Exemplary catalog entries include iconographic analysis, high-quality photographs of the 33 paintings, and one sculpture with up-close details, as well as prints and paintings that may have served as inspiration to those images. Accompanying essays explore the history of the collection at the New Mexico History Museum; the artworks housed in New Mexican churches as the expression of local and viceregal patronage, interests, and piety; and the connection between colonial works and those of contemporary artists. [AAP]

19   Londoño Vélez, Santiago. Pintura en América hispana. Tomo I, Siglos XVI al XVIII. Bogotá: Luna Libros: Editorial Universidad del Rosario, 2012. 1 v. (331 p.): bibl., indexes. (América; 2)

This first volume in a trilogy by the same author is a general survey of the art of painting in Spanish America from the 16th through the 18th centuries. The text is developed thematically rather than chronologically, and is divided into four chapters under the titles "Pintura para la evangelización" (p. 1–78); "La estética de la Iglesia triunfante" (p. 79–126); "Adaptaciones y transformaciones del Barroco" (p. 137–264); and "Nuevas imágenes para la razón y la devoción" (p. 265–304). The total lack of illustrations is a major drawback, however, particularly since lengthy descriptions are devoted to the iconography of religious paintings. Nevertheless, the extensive bibliography (p. 305–324) provides a useful guide for further reading. [HRC]

20   Mayer Center Symposium, *12th*, *Denver Art Museum, 2012*. Festivals & daily life in the arts of colonial Latin America, 1492–1850: papers from the 2012 Mayer Center Symposium at the Denver Art Museum. Edited by Donna Pierce. Denver, Colo.: Mayer Center for Pre-Columbian & Spanish Colonial Art at the Denver Art Museum, 2014. 170 p.: bibl., ill., maps, photos.

Enticing publication of the proceedings of the 2012 Mayer Center Symposium. International scholars address the role of festivals by studying the art and architecture and the role of mourning and succession ceremonies for Spanish kings; festivals of the Academy of San Carlos in Mexico City; religious celebrations in Puebla; and indigenous dances in civic festivals in New Spain (today Mexico). Authors study quotidian life by examining objects of daily use such as chairs of Caribbean design and manufacture, women's dress in Argentina, and the changing role of *costumbrista* paintings in Ecuador. High-quality images and extensive bibliographies accompany the essays. [AAP]

21   Peterson, Jeanette Favrot. Visualizing Guadalupe: from Black Madonna to Queen of the Americas. Austin: University of Texas Press, 2014. 332 p.: bibl., index. (Joe R. and Teresa Lozano Long Series in Latin American and Latino Art and Culture)

This eloquently written book addresses the subjectivities involved in viewing and the multivalent meanings of representations of the Virgin of Guadalupe from the 13th to the 18th centuries. It begins in Spain with the sculpture of the Virgin of Guadalupe and continues with the dissemination of its cult in South America and its worship in Mexico as a miraculous painted apparition on cloth. It ends with the analysis of the pious, social, and political networks that enabled the dissemination of the cult of the Mexican Virgin of Guadalupe back to Spain. The author organizes chapters around specific images that mark historical moments and contribute to the discussion of visuality as it connects to theological, cultural, and political issues. [AAP]

22   **A red like no other: how cochineal colored the world: an epic story of art, culture, science, and trade.** Edited by Carmella Padilla and Barbara C. Anderson. Principal photography by Blair Clark. New York: Skira/Rizzoli; Santa Fe, N.M.: Museum of International Folk Art, 2015. 319 p.: bibl., ill. (chiefly color), map, portraits.

Catalog of the exhibit "The Red that Colored the World" by the Museum of International Folk Art, New Mexico. Innovative essays address the artistic uses and trade networks of cochineal, a small bug that grows on the prickly pear cactus and is harvested for its use as a red dye and pigment. Essays by international scholars explore its uses in precolumbian and viceregal works, in European textiles and well-known paintings, in garments in the US Southwest, and in modern-day objects, as well as its trade routes and connection to the slave trade. All items featuring cochineal in the essays were scientifically tested, many of them for the first time. [AAP]

23   **Russo, Alessandra.** An artistic humanity: new positions on art and freedom in the context of Iberian expansion, 1500–1600. (*Res/Cambridge*, 65/66, 2015, p. 352–363, bibl., photos)

Russo proposes that the writing by Catholic missionaries about art and the skills and inventiveness of native artists in Spanish and Portuguese colonies in the 16th century argued for their human and rational nature and therefore the possibility to convert them to Christianity. What is more, in the process of describing the plurality of techniques employed by these native artists and their skills and creations, these Catholic writers participated in larger debates about art and helped redefine "mechanical arts" (painting, sculpture, and architecture) as liberal arts. [AAP]

24   **Simposio Internacional de Jóvenes Investigadores del Barroco Iberamericano, 2nd, *Castellón de la Plana, Spain*, 2015.** Iberoamérica en perspectiva artística: transferencias culturales y devocionales. Edición de Inmaculada Rodríguez Moya, María de los Ángeles Fernández Valle y Carme López Calderón. Castelló de la Plana, Spain: Universitat Jaume I, 2016. 452 p.: bibl., ill. (Col·lecció Amèrica; 35)

Publication of selected papers from the *II Simposio de Jóvenes Investigadores: Arte y patrimonio: Tráficos transoceánicos*, organized by the Centro de Estudios del Barroco Iberoamericano (Spain, 2015). Essays in Spanish, Italian, and Portuguese explore issues of urban planning and architecture; ephemeral artworks, scenic spaces, and literature produced around fiestas and theater; patronage and devotional painting; and the role of noble women as patrons of the arts, collectors, and artistic subjects in the Iberian Peninsula, Latin America, the US Southwest, Florida, and the Caribbean. [AAP]

25   **Siracusano, Gabriela** and **Agustina Rodríguez Romero.** Materiality between art, science, and culture in the viceroyalties (16th-17th centuries): an interdisciplinary vision toward the writing of a new colonial art history. (*Art Trans.*, 9:1, 2017, p. 69–91, bibl., ill.)

The authors summarize four case studies that were part of a three-year international research project developed by the Universidad Nacional de San Martín (Argentina) with the support of the Getty Foundation. The essay contributes to scholarship on the material dimension of artworks and its implication for colonial art in particular. The first two cases analyze indigenous materials and techniques employed in the production of *q'eros* (Inca style vessels) and in Catholic devotional images such as Our Lady of Copacabana by Tito Yupanqui and the *cristos de caña* (Christ figures made from cornstalk paste). The third study focuses on the incorporation of European materials to painting, and the fourth addresses the challenges of restoring a heavily damaged image. [AAP]

Mexico and Central America

26   **Altera Roma: art and empire from Mérida to México.** Edited by John M.D. Pohl and Claire L. Lyons. Los Angeles, Calif.: Cotsen Institute of Archaeology

Press, 2016. 359 p.: bibl., ill., maps. (UCLA Cotsen Institute of Archaeology Press monographs; 83)

Proceedings from the Altera Roma symposium held at the Getty Villa in Los Angeles (2010). Essays from a wide range of experts explore the parallels that Europeans in the 16th century perceived between the Roman Classical and the Aztec worlds. Different chapters address the political organization of the Roman and Aztec world, the role of Aztec architecture and sculpture in establishing the relationships between capital and conquered provinces; and the ways in which Classical and Renaissance and Aztec religious and political concepts and images were conjured and mobilized to promote Spanish imperial interest in New Spain. [AAP]

27 Battcock, Clementina and Alejandra Dávila Montoya. Las láminas de las guerras Tenochcas en Tovar y Durán: variantes y equívocos. (*Rev. Indias*, 77:271, 2017, p. 691–725, bibl., ill.)

This essay examines the relationship between textual accounts and images of the defeat of the city of Azcapotzalco by the Aztecs as recorded in the 16th century in Fr. Diego Durán's *Historia de las Indias de la Nueva España e Islas de la Tierra Firme* and the works attributed to Juan de Tovar known as *Manuscrito Tovar* and *Códice Ramírez*. Through a detailed iconographic analysis the authors propose that plate 11 in Durán's *Historia* represents the defeat of Azcapotzalco and was misidentified by Juan de Tovar as representing the defeat of Coyoacan by Aztec warriors. The authors conclude that Tovar and his team based their images of the defeat of Azcapotzalco on Duran's representation of the defeat of Tlatelolco and Xochimilco. [AAP]

28 Córdova, James M. The art of professing in Bourbon Mexico: crowned-nun portraits and reform in the convent. Austin: University of Texas Press, 2013. 252 p.: bibl., ill., index, photos

Córdova considers the production and iconography of portraits depicting nuns as brides of Christ, attired in a crown of flowers and with a flowering staff of palm in New Spain (Mexico). Through detailed research, he contextualizes the portraits of crowned nuns within convent life, and describes the paintings' connections to early modern portraiture in Spain and New Spain, the indigenous influences on the iconography used, and their production in response to the Bourbon reforms of the late 18th century and the process of identity formation in Mexico. The author shows how the portraits articulated local values and patron-client relationships that wove together sacred and secular concerns. [AAP]

29 Diel, Lori Boornazian. The *Codex Mexicanus* genealogy: binding the Mexica past and the colonial present. (*Colon. Lat. Am. Rev.*, 24:2, 2015, p. 120–146)

Through a careful iconographic analysis, the author proposes that the genealogy of the Mexica (Aztec) ruling family included in the *Codex Mexicanus* emphasizes the family's antiquity, purity, and even divine descent, thus creating a parallel with the Spanish ruling house and its emphasis on *limpieza de sangre* or purity of blood. By presenting the Mexica colonial heirs in this way, the makers of the manuscript emphasized their right to rulership at a time when they had been excluded from the governor's post in the late 1570s and early 1580s. [AAP]

Earle, Rebecca. The pleasures of taxonomy: casta paintings, classification, and colonialism. See item **483**.

30 Espinoza Chávez, Agustín. Restauración del Santuario de Atotonilco: patrimonio mundial = Restoration at the Sanctuary of Atotonilco: World Heritage Site. Guanajuato, Mexico: Ediciones La Rana: Instituto Estatal de la Cultura de Guanajuato, 2015. 302 p.: bibl., color ill., plans.

This bilingual, large-format book describes the history and restoration of the 18th-century sanctuary dedicated to Jesus of Nazareth in Atotonilco, Mexico. Chapters deal with the history, significance, and restoration of the church. The author provides a detailed description of the criteria applied, methods, and materials used for the cleaning, conservation, and restoration processes of the murals, easel paintings, painting frames, sculptures, and exterior of the church. Before and after pictures of the areas and works restored provide an extensive visual record of the changes made during the restoration. The study ends with a brief description of the areas of the church still in need of restoration. [AAP]

31   Frassani, Alessia. Building Yanhuitlan: art, politics, and religion in the Mixteca Alta since 1500. Norman: University of Oklahoma Press, 2017. 195 p.: bibl., ill., index.

This book looks at the history of the building and use of the Santo Domingo convento complex of Yanhuitlán, the devotional images associated with it, the residence of the local rulers, and the village. The book alternates chapters dedicated to the sociopolitical history of the town with those dedicated to its artistic production. It investigates the relationship between indigenous rulers with colonial civic authorities and the Dominican order. The author traces indigenous patronage of the construction, decoration, and festivities of the church. Through the careful analysis of court documents, inventories, and wills, the author proposes the adaptation of Mesoamerican practices throughout the colonial period and modern times. [AAP]

32   Frassani, Alessia. El centro monumental de Yanhuitlán y su arquitectura: un proceso histórico y ritual. (*Desacatos*, 42, mayo/agosto 2013, p. 145–160, bibl.)

Through the analysis of archival documents, this essay examines the historical process of the construction and the ritual and civic uses of the church and convent of Santo Domingo and the palace of the indigenous governor in Yanhuitlán, Mexico. The author posits that these structures and the rituals connected to them were the result of local strategies of adaptation. The layout of the city and its architecture borrowed freely from precolumbian and European precedents and expressed the indigenous appropriation of the new political and religious order. See also item **31**. [AAP]

33   González, Cristina Cruz. Beyond the bride of Christ: the crucified abbess in Mexico and Spain. (*Art Bull.*, 99:4, Oct. 2017, p. 102–132, bibl., ill., photos)

The author traces the art historical lineage of a 1792 Mexican print of a crucified Capuchin abbess and the accompanying sermon, which were banned by the Office of the Holy Inquisition. She argues that the Spanish portraits of crucified nuns that preceded this image were produced in support of monastic reforms that urged members of congregations to live a communal life centered in the imitation of Christ and free of worldly concerns. The Mexican image and sermon, likewise, were also a response to Bourbon reforms with similar aims, but in this case they were banned because the Inquisition perceived them as presenting the abbess as Christ-like to an extreme and the nuns in roles generally reserved for male members of the Church. [AAP]

34   Kern, Margit and Richard George Elliott. Pictorial theories by missionaries in sixteenth-century New Spain: the capacities of hieroglyphs as media in transcultural negotiation. (*Art Trans.*, 8:3, 2016, p. 283–313, bibl., ill.)

This essay compares Catholic friars' perceptions of hieroglyphic writing among Egyptians and among Mexican civilizations. In the case of Egyptian hieroglyphs, friars perceived them as containing philosophical knowledge and as "natural signs of divine revelation" which were part of an original unity of religions before they were purportedly corrupted (except for Christianity). The author proposes that Franciscan friars in the late 16th century and Jesuits in the 18th century believed Mexican hieroglyphic writing, like Egyptian hieroglyphs, contained universal knowledge and resemantisized the symbols in Christian art as signs of divine revelation. [AAP]

35   Magaloni Kerpel, Diana. The colors of the New World: artists, materials, and the creation of the Florentine Codex. Los Angeles, Calif.: Getty Research Institute, 2014. 67 p.: bibl., ill.

This two-part book analyzes the images of the 16th-century illuminated manuscript known as the *Florentine Codex* produced in Mexico by Spanish friar Fr. Bernadino de Sahagún and indigenous artists, informants, and scribes. It provides a context for the production of the manuscript, the artists' training, and their knowledge of classical, Renaissance, and indigenous traditions. In particular, the author investigates the artists' use of pigments to convey meaning and create images that embody indigenous concepts. Her approach combines analysis of the chemical composition of the pigments, the iconography of the images, the Nahuatl text accompanying the images, and ethnographic analogies. [AAP]

36 **Mendoza, Rubén G.** and **Jennifer A. Lucido.** Of earth, fire, and faith: architectural practice in the Fernandino missions of Alta California, 1769–1821. (*CLAHR*, 2:2, Spring 2014, p. 191–237, ill., map, photos)

The authors propose that the friars of Alta California most commonly followed the architectural styles of their home regions in Spain and Mexico rather than the guidelines taught and disseminated by the Colegio de Propaganda Fide de San Fernando in Mexico City, the body in charge of training friars who went on to establish these missions. Many missions show the predominant influence of Vitrubio's *Ten Books of Architecture*, Moorish architecture and sacred geometry, Gothic architecture, and Mexican Baroque, among others. The essay includes several case studies, such as the Presidio of San Carlos de Monterey (including its church), and the missions of Nuestra Señora de la Soledad and San Miguel Arcángel. [AAP]

37 **Mendoza Muñoz, Jesús.** Construcción del convento de monjas capuchinas de Querétaro. Edición conmemorativa del XVII aniversario del Museo de la Ciudad de Santiago de Querétaro (1997–2014). Cadereyta, Mexico: Fondo Histórico y Cultural de Cadereyta, A.C., 2014. 64 p.: bibl., ill. (Serie Divulgación; III)

This study contextualizes the construction of the convent as part of the rise of the secular clergy in Mexico during the 18th century. Through archival research, the author explains the economic circumstances that made possible the founding and construction of the convent in only three and a half years. In particular, he explores the financial contribution and patronage of the influential José de Torres y Vergara, lawyer of the Royal Audiencia, emeritus professor of the Royal University, and Advisor of the Holy Office of the Inquisition. The work provides information about the provenance of some of his wealth, his contribution, and his contract with artists who produced the conventual church's retablo (altar piece), as well as the founding celebrations of the convent. [AAP]

38 **Mundy, Barbara E.** The death of Aztec Tenochtitlan, the life of Mexico City. Austin: University of Texas Press, 2015. 246 p.: bibl., ill., index, maps. (Joe R. and Teresa Lozano Long series in Latin American and Latino art and culture)

This book offers an exemplary analysis of the transformation of the Aztec capital Tenochtitlan into the viceregal capital of New Spain (Mexico) after its conquest by Spaniards. Chapters address representations of the city, its physical spaces, and quotidian practices in order to articulate indigenous adaptation and endurance of spatial uses into the colonial period. The author analyzes major architectural projects, such as waterworks, markets, and administrative centers, and their relationship to Aztec governors of the colonial period. The book combines rich visual analysis of maps, featherworks, codices, feasts, and dances with historical information and archival research. Winner of the 2016 American Association for Latin American Art's Arvey Book Award and the Book Prize in Latin American Studies, Colonial Section of the Latin American Studies Association. For comment by ethnohistorians, see *HLAS* 72:307. For comment by colonial historian, see *HLAS* 72:723. [AAP]

39 **Oles, James.** Art and architecture in Mexico. New York: Thames & Hudson Inc., 2013. 432 p.: bibl., ill., index.

Comprehensive survey of 500 years of Mexican art and architectural history, starting with the viceregal period in the early 16th century and ending with contemporary art. The author organizes the book chronologically with the first four chapters dedicated to colonial art and its transition to independent Mexico, followed by seven chapters dedicated to art produced after independence and into contemporary art. The author pays special attention to the role of visual arts in the construction of identity, the role of institutional patronage, and the representation of indigenous subjects. Color illustrations accompany visual analysis and contextualization of well-known and rarely published works. [AAP]

40 **Painted in Mexico, 1700–1790: Pinxit Mexici.** Edited by Ilona Katzew. Essays and entries by exhibition co-curators Ilona Katzew, Jaime Cuadriello, Paula Mues

Orts, and Luisa Elena Alcalá. Additional entries by Ronda Kasl. Los Angeles, Calif.: Los Angeles County Museum of Art; Mexico City: Fomento Cultural Banamex, A.C.; Munich; New York: DelMonico Books/Prestel Publishing, 2017. 511 p.: bibl., ill., index.

This publication stems from the exhibit by the same name organized by the Los Angeles County Museum of Art and Fomento Cultural Banamex. Accompanying essays by international scholars discuss the work of artists in relation to painting production in Mexico City and in regional centers, iconographic and stylistic traditions and innovations tied to local histories and corporate identities, and the multifaceted work of artists and their participation in ornamental works. These studies emphasize innovations in New Spanish painting as part of a local development, while also studying their connection to international art trends. Extensive catalog entries of over 120 works are divided by thematic groups. Many of the paintings included were restored for the exhibit and had not been previously published. [AAP]

41   Pérez Alacántara, Ivonne Andrea. Reconstrucción de una historia: arqueología de la arquitectura de la iglesia de San Mateo Chalcatzingo, Morelos. México: Instituto Nacional de Antropología e Historia, 2014. 267 p.: bibl., ill. (Colección Arqueología. Serie Logos)

This archeological study examines the architecture of the church, visit chapel, and atrium of San Mateo Chalcatzingo, Mexico. Pérez Alcántara conducts stratigraphic analysis of the walls to determine their construction sequence and the techniques and materials used in the 16th through the 18th centuries. She compares these findings with primary and secondary sources to establish their chronological correlation with social and historical changes in Chalcatzingo and vicereal Mexico. The book includes images of microscopic analysis of the materials, color photographs, plans, and sketches detailing the different construction phases. [AAP]

42   Pineda Mendoza, Raquel. Conjuntos devocionales domésticos de Santa María del Pino, Tepetitlán, Hidalgo. México UNAM, Instituto de Investigaciones Estéticas, 2014. 238 p.: bibl., ill., maps, plans.

This study focuses on rarely documented and analyzed domestic devotional architecture in colonial Mexico, including oratories, niches, and rooms built to welcome pilgrims and visitors within the home. Pineda Mendoza traces their precedents in Spain and precolumbian Mexico and conducts archival research about Nahua structures in central Mexico and surveys surviving structures in the Otomí town of Santa María del Pino, Hidalgo, and other surrounding communities. She addresses the design, contents, and uses of devotional spaces in the homes of Spaniards, their descendants, and indigenous communities, as well as the church regulations of these spaces. The author proposes differences of design based on cultural and devotional variation among these groups. The work includes transcriptions of archival documents, photographs, and architectural plans. [AAP]

43   Restauración de la obra maestra barroca de Taxco de Alarcón: legado y futuro de la iglesia de Santa Prisca = Restoring the Baroque masterpiece of Taxco de Alarcón: the legacy and future of Santa Prisca Church. Coordinación de Norma Barbacci y Norma María Laguna y Ortuña. New York: World Monuments Fund, 2017. 239 p.: bibl., color ill., plans.

This bilingual publication is the result of the restoration efforts of the Santa Prisca Church in Taxco, Guerrero. Essays by different authors discuss the church in relation to urban planning of the colonial town, the history of the church as it was built between 1751 and 1759, its construction structures and techniques, the history of its ongoing architectural restoration efforts from 1997 to 2016, and the various restoration stages. The book includes detailed plans, high-quality images of details, and before and after photos. [AAP]

44   Robin, Alena. Las capillas del Vía Crucis de la ciudad de México: arte, patrocinio y sacralización del espacio. México: UNAM, Instituto de Investigaciones Estéticas, 2014. 307 p.: bibl., ill., index.

The author traces the role of the Third Order of St. Francis, patrons, and artists in the construction, ornamentation, and maintenance of the now lost chapels of the Stations of the Cross built in Mexico City in the late 17th century. Special emphasis is given to questions of patronage by merchants and the role of these chapels in highlighting the Franciscan Order's role as custodians of holy places in Jerusalem and their evangelical mission in the world. The last part of the book addresses the motives behind the destruction of the chapels in the 19th century. The book ends with an appendix of transcribed primary documents. [AAP]

45   Sanabrais, Sofía. From *byōbu* to *biombo*: the transformation of the Japanese folding screen in colonial Mexico. (*Art Hist.*, 38:4, Sept. 2015, p. 779–791, bibl., photos)

This essay discusses the introduction of Japanese folding screens to Mexico in the 17th century, their dissemination among local patrons, and their adaptation to local tastes. Sanabrais clearly traces how these folding screens (known as *byōbu* in Japan and *biombo* in Mexico) were first brought to Mexico as gifts from ambassadors and the Japanese emperor to the viceroyalty's dignitaries and promptly became coveted by other elite members of society. Artists began to produce the *biombos* in Mexico, and like their Japanese counterparts, they depicted mythological scenes, local landscapes, festivals, and references to literary resources. They became part of a robust trade network between Mexico and East Asia. [AAP]

46   Tlaxcala: la invención de un convento. Coordinación de Alejandra González Leyva. Investigación de Jorge Alberto Manrique Castañeda et al. Fotografía de Eumelia Hernández Vázquez. Mapas y planos de Claudia Ivette López Ochoa, Claudia Sabag Moreno y Chac Alejandro Valadés Oliva. México: Facultad de Filosofía y Letras, Dirección General de Asuntos del Personal Académico, UNAM, 2014. 243 p.: bibl., ill. (some color), maps, plans.

This publication is the last of a three-part research project analyzing convent complexes at Tlaxcala, Yanhuitlán, and Yuriria, Mexico. Chapters contributed by interdisciplinary authors address the construction history of the convent complex of Tlaxcala as the result of social, economic, and political processes in the region. The book presents the convent, its church, and art not as static works built in accord with pre-established models, but as unique and changing projects that responded to the needs of the community, as well as to religious, secular, and political interests. This comprehensive study presents a more encompassing way of approaching colonial convents in relation to their documentary history, materials, construction and restoration phases, and its retablo (altar piece) and other artworks. [AAP]

Caribbean

47   Bindman, David. Representing race in the eighteenth-century Caribbean: Brunias in Dominica and St. Vincent. (*Eighteenth-Century Stud.*, 51:1, Fall 2017, p. 1–21, bibl., ill.)

This essay traces the context and artistic production of the Italian artist Agostino Brunias on the island of Dominica and to a lesser extent Saint Vincent and French and British colonies in the 18th century. The author proposes that Brunias' images of women of both African and white settler descent (known as mulatas or mulâtresses) and of Caribs represent a racial fluidity that cannot be seen exclusively as colonial propaganda and anthropological representations. Instead, he proposes that Brunias' images must be seen in the light of several factors such as the varying attitudes among colonial settlers towards sexual relations between settlers and slaves and their offspring, and the different kinds of slavery that predominated throughout the Caribbean islands, among others. For comment by colonial historian, see item **826**. [AAP]

Muñoz Paz, María del Carmen. El obrador de Blas de Abila: maestro platero del siglo XVIII en Santiago de Guatemala. See item **728**.

Uruguay

48   Odriozola Odriozola, Miguel Ángel. De Colonia del Sacramento a Colonia: apuntes del Arq. Miguel Ángel Odriozola Odriozola. Selección de fotografías, planes y croquis, recopilación y verificación de información faltante de Miguel Ángel Odriozola Guillot. Montevideo: Sociedad de Arquitec-

tos del Uruguay, 2012. 239 p.: bibl., ill. (some col.).

Published posthumously, this book contains descriptive notes by the architect Miguel Ángel Odriozola Odriozola on the restoration of historic buildings inside and outside the Barrio Histórico (historic neighborhood) in Colonia del Sacramento, Uruguay. The notes highlight the legacy left by Portuguese, Spanish, and Italian patrons, architects, and builders between the 17th and 19th centuries. The catalog of buildings includes their phases of construction, different restoration interventions, modern-day and older photos, maps of their locations, and plans. The second part of the book includes Odriozola Odriozola's proposals for the adaptation of historic buildings for new purposes, a plan for tourism development at the Port of Yates, his design and construction of new homes, and his partial and proposed restoration of 20th-century buildings. [AAP]

Colombia

49   Del Castillo, Lina; María del Rosario Leal; and Grace McCormick. Iconografía intelectual en el Virreinato de la Nueva Granada siglo XVIII: estudio iconográfico, iconológico e histórico de la escuela franciscana, las "defendere", "disputatios" y ofrecimientos. Bogotá: Universidad Externado de Colombia, Facultad de Estudios del Patrimonio Cultural, Programa de Conservación y Restauración de Bienes Muebles, 2013. 300 p.: bibl., ill.

This comprehensive study by three distinguished scholars examines the development of religious iconography during the Spanish colonial period in the Viceroyalty of Nueva Granada (present-day Colombia). The topics treated in four chapters include "La educación superior en el Virreinato de la Nueva Granada," by Lina del Castillo and Grace McCormick (p. 17–44); "La escuela franciscana a través de treinta y un óleos," by María del Rosario Leal (p. 47–139); "Los retratos de defensa de tesis. Estudio iconográfico e iconológico," by Lina del Castillo (p. 143–217); and "La escolástica en la Nueva Granada a través de dos imágenes pertenecientes a la Catedral Primada de Bogotá. Disputa universitaria entre omasistas y javerianos y agustino doctorándose," by Grace McCormick (p. 219–300). Useful references to primary and secondary sources as well as electronic archives are provided in separate bibliographies. [HRC]

Bolivia and Peru

50   Castañeda Murga, Juan; María del Carmen Espinoza Córdova; and Eduardo Pimentel Carranza. Templos virreinales de los valles de Lambayeque. Lima: Fondo Editorial USMP: Facultad de Ciencias de la Comunicación, Turismo y Psicología, 2015. 231 p.: bibl., ill. (chiefly color), index, maps, portraits.

Divided in four chapters, this book focuses on the religious history and architecture of the northern coast of Peru from the 16th through the early 19th centuries. The first chapter studies the evangelization of this region, its process, and actors. The second chapter focuses on the role of the cofradías (pious organizations formed by lay members of the church). Chapters three and four describe the construction and restoration history of convent complexes, town churches, parish chapels, and their retablos, as well as the devotional chapels of haciendas. The authors combine extensive archival research with field research to provide a view of these buildings, many of which have been destroyed by natural and man-made disasters. [AAP]

51   Cohen Suarez, Ananda. Paintings of colonial Cusco: artistic splendor in the Andes. Photography by Raúl Montero Quispe, with the collaboration of Macarena Deij Prado et al. Translation by Miguel Arisa. Cusco, Peru: Haynanka Ediciones, 2015. 197 p.: bibl., ill.

This work presents an important addition to the study of Cuzco School paintings in colonial Peru by a distinguished scholar with the collaboration of other authors. Two well-documented texts, "Introduction to the Colonial Arts of the Cusco Region" and "European Prints as Sources for Colonial Paintings" (p. 7–21), provide the essential background to the texts that follow, organized by iconographic themes complemented with 158 full-page fine color reproductions of paintings from religious institutions and museums. As indicated in the back cover of the book, the final pages establish thematic continuities among different colonial Andean paintings, such as the indigenous presence in religious art; genealogical trees and lineages; landscapes and the natural world; and representation of the human figure in colonial painting. Captions of the plates give a full description of the scenes represented together with dates, location, and measurements of the works. The selected bibliography provides useful suggestions for further reading. [HRC]

52   Corcuera, Ruth. Gasas prehispánicas. Con la colaboración de Isabel Iriarte. Buenos Aires: CIAFIC Ediciones, 2015. 105 p.: bibl., ill.

This brief text examines the art of gauze textiles from the holdings of the renowned Amano Textile Museum in Lima, Peru. Well represented in the collection are examples from the pre-Inca cultures of Chancay and Paracas that developed along the Peruvian coast. Special attention is given to materials and techniques and the analysis of different designs. The few drawings incorporated with the text show the variety of knots and stitches used by the ancient weavers, but the black-and-white photographs of uneven quality (plates 1–29) do not permit a good appreciation of the important color differentiation. [HRC]

53   Cruz, Pablo. Imágenes en pugna: reflexiones en torno a las producciones visuales indígenas en el ámbito de la minería colonial. (*Bol. Mus. Chil. Arte Precolomb.*, 21:1, 2016, p. 63–78, bibl., ill.)

Through original research, the author provides a synthesis of a series of studies conducted since 1995 at different colonial mining and metallurgical sites in Potosí and in the regions of Chuquisaca, Oruro, and Pacajes, Bolivia. The essay focuses on a series of visual productions linked to contingents of native laborers who were sent to work in major mining centers in the southern Andes during the 16th century and later during the Spanish colonial period. These images are characterized by a high level of abstraction in sharp contrast to the figurative representations and styles of Andean colonial art, thus reflecting both the coercion and the control of images that the Spanish regime and the Catholic Church exercised upon the indigenous population, as well as the latter's recognition and adoption of Christianity and its symbols. In a subtle way, however, by means of these abstract representations, some native traditions and beliefs were preserved. Documentary notes and a list of selected references complement the main text. [HRC]

54   De Amberes al Cusco: el grabado europeo como fuente del arte virreinal. Edición de Cécile Michaud y José Torres Della Pina. Lima: Impulso Empresa de Servicios SAC, 2009. 94 p.: bibl., ill.

This anthology of essays by different authors discusses the importance of European prints as sources for Spanish colonial paintings in Cuzco. The city of Ambers, Belgium, is identified as one of the major centers of production of such prints, which were imported to the American colonies and provide examples of religious iconography that served as visual instruments for the evangelization of the illiterate indigenous population in the Catholic faith. Convincing parallels between print representations and colonial paintings show the significant borrowing of European images and their translation into depictions that added original motifs for a local audience. In particular, the use of striking colors in the paintings (and absent in the prints) reveals the talent of artists that included mestizo and indigenous painters. Fine-quality reproductions of prints and paintings in full color permit a good appreciation of the works. An extensive bibliography (p. 84–91) includes titles of the most recent research on the subject. [HRC]

55   Encuentro Internacional sobre Barroco, 5th, La Paz, 2009. Entre cielos e infiernos: memoria del V Encuentro Internacional sobre Barroco. Organización y edición de Norma Campos Vera. Co-organización por GRISO de Universidad de Navarra. La Paz: Fundación Visual Cultural, 2010. 368 p.: bibl., ill.

This handsome volume collects the proceedings of the 2009 International Congress on Baroque art with contributions of distinguished European and Latin American scholars from 15 countries. The central theme is the dialectic relationship between life and death, angels and demons, sin and sainthood, heaven and hell from the perspective of history, anthropology, art, architecture, literature, music, and theater within an American context. Works specifically related to the Andean world include "Los grabados, el 'Juicio Final' y la idolatría en el mundo andino," by Teresa Gisbert C. and Andrés de Mesa G. (p. 17–42); "¿No escuchas? ¿No ves? Interacciones entre la palabra y la imagen en la iconografía de las postrimerías," by Gabriela Siracusano (p. 75–84); "El apóstol soy yo: José de Arellano y el programa iconográfico de la Cruz de Carabuco," by Diego F. Guerra and Gustavo Tudisco (p. 97–106); "Sensaciones ante el Averno: la prédica sobre las postrimerías y el Infierno de Carabuco," by Leontina Etchelecu and Agustina Rodríguez Romero (p. 107–113); "El Juicio Final de Parinacota," by Paola Cortí Badía, Fernando Guzmán Schiappacasse, and Magdalena Pereira Campos (p. 115–124); "La pintura mural de la iglesia de Santiago de Curahuara de Carangas como patrón iconográfico de la iglesia de la Natividad de Parinacota," by Paola Corti Badía, Fernando Guzmán Schiappacasse, and Magdalena Pereira Campos (p. 125–132); "Diversidad de imágenes en el siglo XVII: el caso de Cohoni," by María Isabel Alvarez Plata P. (p. 203–212); "El cielo y el infierno en las Misiones de Chiquitos: los sermones," by Alcides Parejas Moreno (p. 213–217); "Las casas de Dios y puertas del cielo: las iglesias misionales de Chiquitos y el Templo de Jerusalén," by Eckart Kühne (p. 219–227); "El arcángel San Miguel en la cosmovisión de los chiquitanos," by Sieglinde Falkinger (p. 229–236); "Entre el infierno y el paraíso: el Chaco y sus habitantes en las 'escrituras jesuíticas' del siglo XVIII," by Mara Penhos (p. 237–242); "Cielo/infierno/tentación: la muerte en Caquiaviri," by Lucía Querejazu Escobari (p. 271–278); and "Lo infernal, lo terrenal y lo celestial en la Misión de Moxos," by Víctor Hugo Limpias Ortiz (p. 289–303). All the studies are well documented with copious notes, bibliographies, and many fine-quality color illustrations. [HRC]

56 Escobar Medrano, Jorge Enrique. Historia del arte cusqueño siglos XVI al XIX: la plástica, orígenes y simbiosis. Cusco, Peru: Regresa, 2013. 134 p.: bibl., ill.

This handsome edition treats the development of art and architecture in Cuzco from the 16th to the 19th centuries from an historic perspective. Stylistic developments in Europe during this time period are considered in relation to practices in Cuzco that included work by European and indigenous artists. Selected examples of paintings, sculptures, and architecture represented in fine-quality color plates are used to show the syncretism of European and indigenous themes in what the author calls "la simbiosis en la estilística cusqueña" (p. 79). Questioning the inadequate stylistic term "arte mestizo," the author emphasizes the originality of Andean colonial art as reflected in the Cuzco School of painting. Another important topic discussed in the book is the historic and economic background of Cuzco during the Spanish colonial period and continuity of tradition to the present day (p. 89–132). [HRC]

Forjando el tiempo: historia del metal en el Perú. See item 12.

57 Guía MALI. Edición de Cecilia Pardo. Textos de Ricardo Kusunoki, Sharon Lerner, Natalia Majluf y Cecilia Pardo. Lima: Asociación Museo de Arte de Lima, 2015. 349 p.: bibl., ill.

This handsome guide to the Museo de Arte de Lima (MALI) with texts by Ricardo Kusunoki, Sharon Lerner, Natalia Majluf, and Cecilia Pardo represents another important contribution to the record of fine publications by MALI. Not only does it provide an indispensable guide to the museum collections—the most complete in the nation—but it serves as a comprehensive catalogue raisonné with fine-quality color illustrations and full descriptions of the art works. Precolumbian and colonial art are arranged chronologically and thematically. Major holdings of colonial art include outstanding examples of paintings, sculptures, and decorative arts. The publication includes a useful history of the museum (p. 6–11), followed by chapters that correspond to the various sections of the museum displays: Arte Precolombino (p. 12–141), Arte Colonial (p. 142–191), Arte Republicano (p. 192–235), Arte Moderno (p. 236–271), and Arte Contemporáneo (p. 272–335). The comprehensive bibliography reflects the most recent research corresponding to the different periods. [HRC]

58 Gutiérrez Samanez, Julio Antonio. Rescate de la cerámica vidriada colonial cusqueña. Cusco, Peru: Ministerio de Cultura, Dirección Desconcentrada de Cultura de Cusco, 2016. 278 p.: bibl., ill., maps. (Colección Qillqa Mayu)

This monumental study of the art of glazed ceramics follows 30 years of painstaking research aimed at rescuing the history of its production in Cuzco between the 16th and 19th centuries. The text traces its beginnings as an art imported from Spain and its impact on the Spanish American colony with the creation of a number of shops that produced works of great variety and exceptional beauty. Valuable information is provided regarding the technology and methods of production, distribution, and contemporary efforts to revive the tradition of a vanishing art. A large number of fine-quality color illustrations incorporated with the text permit the appreciation of the richness of this cultural heritage from the colonial period that has previously not received the attention it deserves. In addition, two concluding sections make this publication an invaluable contribution to the study of colonial decorative art: "Anexo 1," consisting of a photographic album of outstanding examples of glazed ceramics (p. 189–201); and "Anexo 2," consisting of fine line drawings that serve as a guide to the iconography of glazed ceramics from Cusco (p. 205–273). Highly recommended for all levels as a reference for future studies. [HRC]

59 Harvey Valencia, Armando and Katherine Harvey Recharte. Trilogía divina: la Basílica Catedral del Cuzco, la Iglesia de la Sagrada Familia y el Triunfo: antología. Cuzco, Peru: Editorial Universitaria, Universidad Nacional de San Antonio Abad del Cusco, 2014. 272 p.: bibl., ill.

This well-documented monograph discusses the Cathedral of Cuzco and its flanking churches of the Sagrada Familia and El Triunfo, considered among the masterpieces of Spanish colonial architecture in Peru. Dating from the 16th and 17th centuries, these buildings offer a harmonious integration of medieval, Renaissance, and Baroque elements. The comprehensive text offers a detailed description and analysis of the architecture of the three buildings and the art works contained therein, complemented with a wealth of graphic documentation including plans, diagrams, and color photographs. References to primary and secondary sources are included in the footnotes and in the general bibliography. A few archival documents are also transcribed in a section of appendices titled "Bula, Ordenanzas y Provisiones" (p. 209–216). [HRC]

60 Mujica Pinilla, Ramón. La imagen transgredida: ensayos de iconografía peruana y sus políticas de representación simbólica. Lima: Fondo Editorial del Congreso del Perú, 2016. 721 p.: bibl., ill.

Outstanding contribution to the historiography of Peruvian art primarily from the Spanish colonial period by distinguished art historian. It makes available to a wide audience an anthology of scholarly essays originally published in books, catalogs, and journals now out of print. The introduction titled "De centros y periferias, originales y copias en el arte peruano" (p. 19–35) provides an overview of the themes treated in the 13 chapters that follow, all models of scholarly research. Beautifully illustrated with color reproductions of paintings and other historical illustrations, the studies focus on iconography and the politics of symbolic representation. Exhaustive visual and written documentation effectively support the arguments presented in the texts. Bibliographic and archival references are provided in footnotes and illustrations are accompanied by full descriptive captions. Major contributions to the study of Spanish colonial painting include Chapter I: "El Niño Jesús Inca y los jesuitas en el Cusco virreinal" (p. 61–85); Chapter III: "Angeles y demonios en la conquista del Perú" (p. 86–124); Chapter IV: "El sermon a las aves o el culto a los ángeles en el Virreinato peruano" (p. 125–173); Chapter VI: "Arte e identidad: las raíces culturales del Barroco peruano" (p. 198–263); Chapter VIII: "Identidades alegóricas: lecturas iconográficas del Barroco al Neoclásico" (p. 374–469); Chapter IX: "Semiótica de la imagen sagrada: la teúrgia del signo en clave americana" (p. 472–505); and Chapter X: "Sobre imagineros e imaginarios andinos: algunas cuestiones metodológicas e históricas" (p. 506–539). [HRC]

61 Webster, Susan Verdi. **Lettered artists and the languages of empire: painters and the profession in early colonial Quito.** Austin: University of Texas Press, 2017. 333 p.: bibl., index.

Through original research based largely on unpublished archival documentation, the author identifies and traces the lives of more than 50 painters who practiced their trade between 1500–1650 in early colonial Quito, Ecuador, revealing their mastery of languages and literacies and the circumstances in which they worked. Contrary to traditional assumptions regarding the work of early Quito artists, who were predominantly Andean, the author establishes that these artists functioned as visual intermediaries and multifaceted cultural translators who harnessed a wealth of specialized knowledge to shape graphic, pictorial worlds for colonial audiences. With abundant visual and written documentation, the author shows that Quiteño artists enjoyed fluency in several areas, including alphabetic literacy and sophisticated scribal conventions in specialized knowledge of pictorial languages: the materials, technologies, and chemistry of painting, in addition to perspective, proportion, and iconography. The book includes a middle section of stunning color plates that complement the black-and-white reproductions of historic prints. Copious notes for each of the chapters are gathered at the end, followed by a comprehensive bibliography. All in all, this work represents an important contribution to the study of Spanish colonial art in Quito. [HRC]

19th–21st Centuries

FÉLIX ÁNGEL, *Former Curator, Cultural Center, Inter-American Development Bank*

THE PRESENT BIENNIUM brings a stimulating publication portfolio to the *HLAS 74* Spanish American art (19th–21st centuries) section. Mexico leads the charge on practically every front, including quantity, followed by Argentina, Colombia, and Chile. Excellent books and articles come from all geographic areas of the Americas: Central America, the Caribbean, South America, and the US, a positive indication of the mostly academic interest in Latin American art outside and beyond the Rio Grande. Dissidence, disobedience, subversion, and intervention are not new words in the lexicon of the arts, least of all in Latin America. The use of these words in the titles of a number of recent analyses appears to deepen their meaning, suggesting the existence of specific manifestations that depend on "attitude" rather than the "object" to give visibility to artwork. At the center of such an attitude is the relationship between expression and genre. Journalist and novelist Laura Restrepo asserts that the only successful revolution of the 20th century was women's denunciation of violence and their roles in leading society (*Hoyesarte.com*, interview by Javier López Iglesias, 31/06/2018). The diverse feminist studies in *HLAS* support Restrepo's claim.

Memory and identity are key components of studies of political and human rights abuses. Misguided, populist beliefs, sometimes intertwined with legitimately elected governments, curtail freedom and democracy in Latin America, with no justification whatsoever except the questionable and unstable realignment of ideological differences which, coupled with outdated rhetoric, violence, and corruption, deter development and quality of life, and benefit small groups whose sole intention is to hold on to power indefinitely.

Constant revision is part of the nature of art history. Conscientious research of neglected materials enables scholars to evaluate, adjust, and correct existing interpretations from a fresh perspective. New narratives on familiar subjects enrich a discipline whose cultivation remains unevenly appreciated in Latin America, although, thankfully, many academic institutions, along with both mature scholars and a younger generation, are filling the gaps. Several strong, well-researched studies on subjects that at first glance appear marginal to the arts are included here, demonstrating how artistic expression has been reformulated, adapted, transformed, or reinvented to bring attention creatively to social issues.

The studies reviewed for *HLAS 74* are varied in topic and theme. *Desobediencias: cuerpos disidentes y espacio subvertidos en el arte en America Latina y Espana 1960–2010*, by Juan Vicente Allaga and Jose Miguel G. Cortes (item **62**), takes note of the increased interaction between Spain and Latin America, exploring the role of feminism and sexual dissidence in both geographic territories. *The Rhetoric of Disobedience: Art and Power in Latin America*, by Eve Kalyva (item **65**), examines art's social function and its ability to act as transformative social praxis, focusing on three collective experiences in Argentina and Chile (1968, 1979, 2000–06) that intersected with the public sphere. *Grupo Proceso Pentagono: politicas de la intervencion 1969–1976–2015*, with texts by Pilar García and Julio García Murillo (item **76**), describes the activity of the art collective (32 projects) and its antagonism toward the Mexican state. *Usina posporno: disidencia sexual, arte y autogestion en la pospornografia*, by Laura Milano (item **101**), proposes a political appropriation of postpornography, anchored in the geographic and symbolic dimensions of Latin America and the fringes of contemporary society, implying the existence of new forms of socialization and collective work. *Octaedro, Los Otros y Axioma: relecturas del arte conceptual en el Uruguay durante la dictadura (1973–1985)*, by May Puchet (item **117**), focuses on the conceptual work of three art collectives active during the dictatorship which were characterized by resistance, experimentation, and the communal process, as opposed to traditional art practices.

Mujeres, feminismo y arte popular, coordinated by Eli Bartra and María Guadalupe Huacuz Elías (item **80**), gathers 18 essays that approach popular art as a process, creating a theoretical relationship among expression, genre, ethnicity, and poverty. The essays also look at the paradox of pop art when the utilitarian factor becomes irrelevant. *Mónica Mayer: si tiene dudas . . . pregunte—una exposición retrocolectiva*, with texts by Karen Cordero Reiman and eight others (item **78**), brings together work developed by the well-known feminist artist, critic, and teacher, individually and in collaboration with other artists, since the early 1970s. *Trazos invisibles: mujeres artistas en Buenos Aires (1890–1923)*, by Georgina G. Gluzman (item **100**), wonders about the meager representation of women artists in public collections and advocates for new narratives that recognize their contribution to the arts of Argentina (the point is valid for the entire region). *Entre lo sagrado y lo profano se tejen rebeldías: arte femnista nuestroamericano*, by Julia Antivilo Peña (item **63**), questions the traditional artistic representation of women, implying that those visions tend to legitimize violence against them. Feminist artists and their history, Antivilo Peña proclaims, have been lifted out of the trenches to form a new field of study.

Performance en México: 28 testimonios 1995–2000, by Dulce María de Alvarado Chaparro (item **70**), refers to the cultural transition initiated by the earthquake of 1985 and other factors that, in the words of Cuauhtémoc Cárdenas, "hopefully encourages others to solve their relations with artistic memory."

Cuerpos sin duelo: iconografías y teatralidades del dolor, by Ileana Diéguez Caballero (item **73**), studies the use of imagery and performing resources in the context of violence and their symbolic connection to "disappeared" people, an abhorrent practice among illegal groups that in some countries is spiraling behind the control of the authorities. *Hotel Mexico: Dwelling on the '68 Movement,* by George F. Flaherty (item **74**), is a metaphor for the contradictions between Mexico's hospitality during the 1968 Olympic Games and the tragic outcome of the Tlatelolco student protest of the same year. The 12 essays in *Mexico . . . nunca más: expresiones artísticas y contextos socioculturales en una era postnacional,* by Héctor Rosales (item **79**), explore identity, technology and postmodernity, urban design, and creativity of the neo-Zapatista movement, among other topics. *Shine: The Visual Economy of Light in African Diasporic Aesthetic Practice,* by Krista Thompson (item **96**), centers on contemporary popular photographic practices mostly in Jamaica and the Bahamas, and their diasporic communities. In his article, Pablo Alonso González (item **93**) examines the implementation of an esthetic imposed in Cuba in line with the official ideology and Soviet social realism. *Neoliberal Bonds: Undoing Memory in Chilean Art and Literature,* by Fernando Blanco (item **104**), is a provocative study. The author looks at the role of the Concertatión (after dictator Augusto Pinochet stepped down), which was responsible for reconfiguring the social fabric, establishing what Blanco calls a new narrative of official memory. Art and literature provide alternative responses and outlooks. *Política del arte: cuatro casos de arte contemporáneo en Colombia,* by Rubén Darío Yepes Muñoz (item **112**), is a case of dissidence within the "established" dissent. Four case studies explain the difference between artists making "institutionalized" art, despite their apparently subversive discourse, and those who are helping to define critical and innovative options. *Spectacular Modernity: Dictatorship, Space, and Visuality in Venezuela, 1948–1958,* by Lisa Blackmore (item **118**), questions the connections between modernity, progress, and stability provided by dictatorial rule in 1950s Venezuela at the expense of democracy.

Jacqueline Barnitz's *Twentieth-century Art of Latin America* (item **64**)—a revised and expanded edition of Patrick Frank's work—is nearly a complete overview of the entire region, though much of Central America and some other countries in the region are not included. Nevertheless, almost 20 years after the publication of the first edition, it remains among the most complete, rigorously researched, and meticulously compiled works of its kind. *Manifestos and Polemics in Latin American Modern Art* (item **66**), edited and translated by Patrick Frank, compiles 65 documents dating from 1900 onward, including some translated into English for the first time. These documents show the concerns of many artists throughout the 20th century, including the need for artistic change and personal views from the symbolic to the political. *Catálogo comentado del acervo del Museo Nacional de Arte: pintura, siglo XX,* Volume I, by Dafne Cruz Porchini and 15 others (item **81**), is a superb publication concentrating on early 20th-century Mexican artists and nationalist and postrevolutionary trends. Concerns with the definition of "Mexican" are implicit. *Dialogos transdisciplinarios V: dialogos con escritores y pintores del siglo XX,* by Julio César Schara (item **85**), gathers 60 interviews conducted between 1972 and 1990 on *Controversias,* a radio program broadcast by UNAM, with a range of prominent Latin American artists, from Siqueiros and Tamayo to Cruz-Diez and Julio Le Parc. The interviews seek to identify the protagonists of the esthetic and literary history of Mexico and Latin America. *Arte, propaganda y diplomacia cultural a finales del cardenismo 1937–1940,* by

Dafne Cruz Porchini (item **72**), focuses on the last three years of the Lázaro Cárdenas government when the social and political agenda went hand-in-hand with a cultural policy aided by modern, technically sophisticated visual propaganda. *El cartel cubano llama dos veces*, by Sara Vega Miche (item **97**), is an absorbing testament to the vitality, originality, and expressiveness of the Cuban postrevolutionary poster. *Espacios críticos habaneros del arte cubano: la década de 1950* (two volumes), by Luz Merino Acosta (item **90**), revisits the art scene in Cuba during the "hinge" decade, gathering articles by about 30 writers. The prologue by Merino Acosta defines the raison d'être of the "critical spaces" where artistic activities occurred.

Two books that share a similar subject matter are worthy of mention. The first, *Artesanos, artistas, artífices: la Escuela de Artes Aplicadas de la Universidad de Chile, 1928–1968*, by various contributors (item **103**), is an attempt to determine the relevance of the School of Applied Arts, despite the difficulty in collecting data and information. The study looks at the School's impact on the evolution of design and how its approach differed from traditional art education. The other study, *Escuelas de artes y oficios en Colombia 1860–1960*, by Alberto Mayor Mora et al. (item **107**), looks back at the impact of an earlier period, presenting a revisionist perspective on the country's insertion into the capitalist world, and studying the organization and pedagogical approaches of art schools. The authors suggest that the leap from workshop to industrial-scale production occurred without a gradual transition.

Scholars, teachers, and aficionados alike will find the works reviewed in the *HLAS 74* 19th–21st century Spanish American art section instructive, illuminating, captivating, intriguing, defiant, and, in some instances, disconcerting. Such a range of possible reactions reflects the precipitous and confusing changes in the economic, political, technological, and ideological landscape. The arts, in spite of being an unfailing source of intellectual stimulation and pleasure, may not offer precise answers to our concerns about the consequences of these changes. The arts, and the exercise of the imagination, however, provide us with the ability to escape the narrow confines of reality, the depressing alleyways of fact, to contemplate reality with a greater and more hopeful understanding of our imperfect world. No matter how difficult and overwhelming the situation, locally and globally, may seem, art reminds us that our existence is a privilege, the acceptance of which places on us the obligation of bearing witness to the human condition and, as is the objective of many artists, of improving it.

GENERAL

62 **Aliaga, Juan Vicente** and **José Miguel G. Cortés.** Desobediencias: cuerpos disidentes y espacios subvertidos en el arte en América Latina y España, 1960–2010. Barcelona; Madrid: Egales Editorial, 2014. 192 p.: bibl., ill. (Colección G)

The use of the body for artistic expression in contemporary art evolved from performance art during the 1960s, one consequence of the cultural revolution that characterized the decade. Performance art eliminated the distinction between art as creation and the artist as creator. It questioned the role of the spectator as a passive observer and became a vehicle for artists to convey their political views. Taking note of the increased interaction between Spain and Latin America, Aliaga and Cortés explore the role that feminism and sexual dissidence have played in both territories recently, showing a change of artistic direction from Anglo-Saxon predecessors. They caution that this survey is not comprehensive. In the first part of the book, Aliaga examines experiences of feminists and others that imply a criticism to heterosexism. The second part, by Cortés, centers on the use of the body in urban spaces (Caracas, Madrid, Santiago de Chile), highlighting how space conditions, and at the same time is conditioned by, the bodies that inhabit cities, and how cities affect the connection between private and public scenarios. The study's goal is to identify some of the locations in Latin America and Spain that have hosted artistic action using the body.

63   **Antivilo Peña, Julia.** Entre lo sagrado y lo profano se tejen rebeldías: arte feminista nuestroamericano. Bogotá: Ediciones Desde Abajo, 2015. 239 p.: bibl., ill. (Feminismos nuestroamericanos)

Antivilo Peña looks at "women's answers to violence through self-representation and mockery of visions about what a woman should be," says Francesca Gargallo Celentani in the prologue of the book. She further declares that those visions internalize (and tend to "legitimize") violence against women. Feminist artists subvert the visions of submission, housewife, obsessive consumer, and sexual object. The study's aim is to learn, understand, and analyze the political praxis of Latin American feminist visual artists that for more than four decades have developed an extensive political and esthetic production. Draws on interviews and information from artists' archives. Useful appendix offers a glossary (*catastro*) of more than 100 feminist artists—half of whom are Mexican—their techniques or vehicles for expression, and website addresses.

64   **Barnitz, Jacqueline.** Twentieth-century art of Latin America: revised and expanded edition. Revised by Patrick Frank. Austin: University of Texas Press, 2015. 435 p.: bibl., index. (The William and Bettye Nowlin series in art, history, and culture of the Western Hemisphere)

Second edition of the 2001 overview of the art and architecture of Latin America. The first edition covered the 20th century up to 1980. The current expanded edition completes the entire century, with the consequential work of a younger generation.

Patrick Frank, coauthor and editor, summarizes his own contribution four ways: 1) updated information and bibliography; 2) improved picture quality; 3) focus on recent scholarship; 4) expanded list of subjects to include topics of recent interest. As with the first edition, some territories and countries are not included in the study (a map of the Americas illustrates the absences): Central America, Paraguay, Puerto Rico, and the Dominican Republic. Perhaps those absences may merit consideration in a third edition. The book as it is, however, is solid and stands the test of time thanks to the dedicated work of Barnitz and her efforts for the arts of Latin America to be recognized. She championed the region's art and artists for more than 50 years, from 1960 until her death in 2017 at age 93.

65   **Kalyva, Eve.** The rhetoric of disobedience: art and power in Latin America. (*LARR*, 51:2, 2016, p. 46–66, bibl., photos)

This article "examines art's social function and its understanding as transformative social praxis." To prove her point, Kalyva relies on three collective experiences that used interdisciplinary methodologies to intersect with the public sphere: *Tucuman Arde* (Argentina, 1968), *Para no morir de hambre en el arte* (Chile, 1979), and *Proyecto Venus* (Argentina 2000–2006). The author describes the relevance of the art projects to social life and evaluates how they help to create a more inclusive and democratic society. As different as the three projects are, they all incorporate social criticism, share a sociological approach to art, and demonstrate a sincere believe in transforming the world.

66   **Manifestos and polemics in Latin American modern art.** Edited and translated by Patrick Frank. Albuquerque: University of New Mexico Press, 2017. 304 p.: bibl., index.

This book compiles 65 documents dating from 1900 onwards. "In Latin America"—Frank states in the preface, "documents are still difficult to access, buried in personal archives and libraries or sometimes—in obscure periodicals, books or manuscripts. This anthology attempts to mitigate that obscurity." Selected topics (from manifestos to interviews) refer to the need and reasons for change in the art world, to personal view of the arts as symbolic and political, and to other related topics. Some of the documents have been translated into English for the first time. Documents are organized across 12 themes, and each theme is organized chronologically. Essays are revealing, though occasionally, the conclusions are debatable.

67 **Peña, Alfonso.** Conversas. San José: Fundación Camaleonart, 2014. 213 p.

This work presents a selection of conversations between the Costa Rican writer and magazine editor and 11 writers, poets, musicians, and artists from Argentina, Brazil, Nicaragua, and Panama (Carlos Barbarito, Floriano Martins, Carlos Calero, and Dima Lidio), and seven from Costa Rica (Sila Chanto, Manuel Monestel, Fabio Herrera, Adriano Corrales, Macarena Barahona, Otto Apuy, and Gerardo González). Peña asks each of them to describe what they do, how they do it, and why. Each interview is preceded by a commentary by Peña. As Colombian writer Omar Castillo points out, "they tell us about forms and manners to apprehend reality, and the 'otherness' that impacts their creative moments."

68 **Superposiciones: arte latinoamericano en colecciones mexicanas.** Curaduría y edición por James Oles. México: CONACULTA, INBA: Fundación Olga y Rufino Tamayo, 2015. 201 p.: bibl., ill.

The work explores the origins of the collection assembled and donated by artist Rufino Tamayo to the eponymous modern art museum in Mexico City. Oles examines selected works from the museum's collections by 12 outstanding Latin American artists, complemented with works by the same artists from three other collections: Mexico's Museo de Arte Moderno, the FEMSA Collection, and the Pérez Simón Collection. Oles' approach is three-pronged: he contextualizes the Tamayo Collection within the history of art collecting in Mexico, while lamenting the lack of public exhibitions dedicated to non-Mexican art. With fragmentary information from the museum's archives, he analyzes the process of assembling the collection, its objective, and the content, and proposes some methodological notes about the exhibition and the works in it. An introduction by Jorge Alberto Manrique concerning the complexity of Latin American art opens the volume, followed by individual essays about each of the artists included in the exhibition. Color reproductions (of middling quality) confirm the excellence of the works exhibited and the consistency of the exhibition overall.

MEXICO

69 **Abstracciones: Nueva York, París, Cuenca, México.** Edición y diseño por Luis Miguel Leon. Textos de Juan Manuel Bonet y Sylvia Navarrete. México: Museo de Arte Moderno, 2015. 228 p.: bibl., ill.

Color and b/w illustrated catalog of 52 artworks by 47 North American, French, Spanish, and Mexican artists, from the collection of Claudia Peralta de Domenech, representing several abstract art movements since the mid-1940s, which were made available to the public for the first time at the Museo de Arte Moderno in Mexico City. Most of the names are immediately recognizable (Motherwell, Rothko, Soulages, Canogar, among them). Essays by Bonet and Navarrete offer reflections on the pieces. All of the discussed works are reproduced and annotated. The catalog includes a checklist and illustrated chronology dating back to 1929. Photographs of the artists, individually and in groups, enable the reader to gain an appreciation for the "pulse"—according to Navarrete—that prevailed when action painting, abstract expressionism, tachism, informalism, and other trends represented in the exhibition were in style.

70 **Alvarado Chaparro, Dulce María de.** Performance en México: 28 testimonios, 1995–2000. México: Editorial 17, 2015. 491 p.: bibl., ill., index. (Colección Diecisiete: teoría crítica, psicoanálisis, acontecimiento; 4)

Performance in Mexico, as defined by Cuauhtémoc Medina in his introduction to Alvarado's study, is "a logical companion for a body and a world of ideas in crisis . . . where social and institutional boundaries have no meaning." He refers to the drastic cultural transition and historical crisis set off by the earthquake of 1985, the Zapatista rebellion, and the escalation of social and political violence. The work is based on Alvarado's enthusiastically received MA thesis in visual arts. Some of the artists included in the study have now passed away, making their testimonies invaluable. Medina states that Alvarado's research is not an "object" of the academy, but rather an affectionate and thought-provoking study, one that may encourage others to consider their relationship with artistic memory as a grand intellectual and corporeal adventure.

71   **Barbosa Sánchez, Alma.** La estampa y el grabado mexicanos: tradición e identidad cultural. México: Universidad Autónoma Metropolitana, Unidad Iztapalapa, Consejo Editorial de la División de Ciencias Sociales y Humanidades, 2015. 306 p.: bibl., ill.

This work offers a sociological, analytical perspective on Mexican printmaking within a long tradition illustrating societal influences and discussing relevant figures. The first part provides an historical assessment, from the 18th century to the present, considering, among other topics, the role of traveling artists, José Guadalupe Posada, Estridentismo, political and social printmaking of the late 1960s, and Oaxaca's Instituto de Artes Gráficas. The second part looks at artistic production, including the techniques employed, the production of editions and commercialization, color, the sustainability of printmaking, and thematic appropriation and invention. Lastly, special attention is given to head printers and editions, market contradictions, and signatures. The study is didactic and although the first part specifically addresses Mexico, the remainder of the book examines printmaking in the broader sense, making the work useful for those interested in the technique, either for commercial use or artistic practice.

72   **Cruz Porchini, Dafne.** Arte, propaganda y diplomacia cultural a finales del cardenismo, 1937–1940. México: Secretaría de Relaciones Exteriores, Dirección General del Acervo Histórico Diplomatico, 2016. 355 p.: bibl., ill., index.

This publication is based on Cruz Porchini's art history PhD thesis which won the 2014 Genaro Estrada award from Mexico's Secretaría de Relaciones Exteriores. The study focuses on the last three years of the Lázaro Cárdenas government, characterized by pragmatism rather than radical innovation, land redistribution, nationalization of railroads and the oil industry, and special interest in the perception of Mexico abroad. The economic, social, and political agenda went hand-in-hand with cultural policy, including technical education, the arts, journalism, and radio, which Cruz Porchini says, shows the consistent tendency in Mexico's postrevolutionary government to modernize rural society. Filmmaking played an important role in the implementation of the government agenda from the moment Cárdenas took office. Although visual propaganda was crucial to the Cárdenas administration, it has been understudied. The author posits that architecture, magazines, posters, and visual arts, all coordinated by the Departamento Autónoma de Prensa y Publicidad (DAPP), attempted to unify and homogenize public opinion. The book's three chapters focus on DAPP, Mexico at the World's Fair in Paris (1937), and cultural and artistic projects in New York (1939–40).

73   **Diéguez Caballero, Ileana.** Cuerpos sin duelo: iconografías y teatralidades del dolor. Nuevo León, Mexico: Universidad Autónoma de Nuevo León, 2016. 437 p.: bibl., ill.

This book was originally published in Argentina after the massacres of Tlatlaya, Ayotzinapa, Apatzingan, Tanhuato-Ecuandureo, and Narvarte. This revised edition was issued in Mexico. The author believes the disappearances, assassinations, and massacres have fundamentally changed Mexico as a country. While many have remained silent in the face of violence, for others, rage has displaced pain. Based on research in Mexico, Peru, Brazil, Argentina, and Colombia, Diéguez Caballero studies the use of imagery and performance in the context of violence, particularly as related to the body and disappearance. As the book demonstrates, performance is one means of creating hope and claiming justice for the many victims of violence.

74   **Flaherty, George F.** Hotel Mexico: dwelling on the '68 Movement. Oakland: University of California Press, 2016. 316 p.: bibl., index.

The book "focuses on the street- and media-savvy prodemocracy movement known as the '68 Movement." The title is a metaphor for the contradiction between the apparent hospitality of Mexico during the Olympics and the considerable social strife among the country's citizens. Ten days before the 1968 Olympic Games began in Mexico City, nearly 300 students were killed by the military in a plaza of a new urban development. The tragedy was one of the outcomes of a turbulent year in which thousands of university and high school students had repeatedly taken to the streets to express their demands for true democracy. They denounced the state's portrait of Mexico as an example of modernization (and of a liberal, free society) and the obfuscation of the violence and other social ills that had plagued the country since the early 1940s. Flaherty argues that while the movement did not represent a real threat, it presented a challenge to the government's claim of legitimacy. The official archives related to the Tlatelolco Massacre and the '68 Movement were classified until 2001, and in 2015 were again closed to public access. Literature, poetry, visual art, and collective memory projects have helped to shed light on the events of that fall. The massacre, Flaherty suggests, "invalidated the state's claim of enlightened technocratic sovereignty and the so-called Mexican Miracle."

75 González Serrano, Manuel. La naturaleza herida: Manuel González Serrano (1917–1960). Textos de María Helena González de Noval et al. México: CONACULTA: INBA, 2014. 159 p.: bibl., ill.

Color-illustrated catalog of an exhibition at the Museo Mural Diego Rivera, with essay contributions exploring the psychological, historical, and botanical aspects implicit in González Serrano's work. He was a self-taught artist who was unsuccessfully treated for paranoid schizophrenia before he died of a heart attack. González Serrano's pictorial production is not exactly surreal; the expression is highly charged. The subject matter is exclusively elements from the plant kingdom: trees, fruits, and flowers convey a metaphor of repressed and subliminal desires, mirroring a dark and elusive personality. Rafael Tovar y de Teresa, president of CONACULTA, introduces the work, stating that the artist is part of the countercurrent to the Mexican School, one of the most interesting chapters of Mexican modernity.

76 Grupo Proceso Pentágono: políticas de la intervención, 1969–1976–2015. Textos de Pilar García y Julio García Murillo. Traducción por Elisa Schmelkes. México: MUAC, Museo Universitario Arte Contemporáneo, UNAM: Editorial RM, 2015. 199 p.: bibl., ill. (Folio MUAC; 037)

Bilingual (Spanish/English) catalog of the first comprehensive exhibition of the archives and artistic output of the art collective whose work is characterized by its antagonism to the politics of the Mexican state. Grupo Proceso Pentágono is an avant garde, political group whose importance and influence for upcoming generations of Mexican artists, particularly conceptual artists, is unquestionable. The exhibit documented the 32 projects that the group developed between 1969 and 2015. The archives are now the property of the Arkheia Center of Documentation and the Museo Universitario Arte Contemporáneo (MUAC). The exhibition also included additional material from private and institutional collections showing diverging viewpoints of group members. The catalog is illustrated in b/w and includes a chronology and bibliography.

77 Kahlo, Frida. Frida Kahlo: retrospective. Exhibition concept by Helga Prignitz-Poda. Essays by Peter Becker et al. Edited by Martin-Gropius-Bau and Bank Austria Kunstforum. New York: Prestel, 2010. 255 p.: bibl., ill.

Color-illustrated, English-language catalog of the first Kahlo exhibition in Austria and the most complete to date in Germany, combining 60 paintings and 80 drawings. Ten different essays approach various facets of the artist's work and life to "grasp the process of maturation in the artist's production" and demonstrate "the fusion of the naked yet complex expression of her own self with the imagery, language, colors, and symbols of Mexican popular culture," in the words of Consuelo Sáizar Guerrero, president of CONACULTA. Top research, printing, and editorial quality will satisfy the most demanding Kahlo follower. Annotations describing the paintings and a chronology are succinct and precise. A collection of photographic portraits of the artist, some of them staged with a calculated intimacy, leave no doubt of Kahlo's celebrity stature in life and the icon she became after her death. She represented and continues to represent a freedom from convention.

Lear, John. Picturing the proletariat: artists and labor in revolutionary Mexico, 1908/1940. See item **656**.

78 **Mayer, Mónica.** Mónica Mayer: sí tiene dudas . . . pregunte—una exposición retrocolectiva. Textos de Karen Cordero Reiman *et al.* México: MUAC, Museo Universitario Arte Contemporáneo, UNAM; Barcelona: RM Verlag, 2016. 271 p.: bibl., ill. (Folio MUAC; 040)

Bilingual, illustrated publication that accompanied the first retrospective exhibition ("retro-collective" is a term suggested by Argentine historian Maria Laura Rosa) of the premier Mexican feminist artist, critic, teacher, and activist. Working since the early 1970s, she is "a multidisciplinary phenomenon in a constant movement between individual and collective work," in the words of Cordero Reiman. The exhibition combines a variety of work made both individually and in collaboration with other artists, including two-dimensional, three-dimensional, and conceptual works and multimedia installations. The exhibition was organized around themes, for instance, Feminism and Training. The catalog and its texts reflect the exhibit's organization, though as Andrea Giunta reminds us in his essay, "It is extremely difficult in a single exhibition to account for the critical force of the associative, performative, and process-based work of Mónica Mayer."

79 **México . . . nunca más: expresiones artísticas y contextos socioculturales en una era postnacional.** Coordinación de Héctor Rosales. Cuernavaca, Mexico: UNAM, 2015. 339 p.: bibl.

This book is the outcome of the project *La identidad nacional mexicana en una era postnacional. Estudios de caso de expresiones artísticas y contextos socioculturales*, developed in 2008–2010 in anticipation of the Mexican Bicentennial. The title refers to the need to eliminate an outdated vision of Mexican identity and to avoid repeating past mistakes. Twelve essays explore identity, technology and postmodernity, popular art and design, urban space, art festivals, creativity of the neo-Zapatista movement, among other topics. Héctor Rosales introduces and closes the book, hoping it may provide answers to questions about Mexico's current identity and future direction.

80 **Mujeres, feminismo y arte popular.** Coordinación de Eli Bartra y María Guadalupe Huacuz Elías. México: Universidad Autónoma Metropolitana, Unidad Xochimilco, División de Ciencias Sociales y Humanidades: Obra Abierta Ediciones, 2015. 191 p.: bibl., ill.

Eighteen essays organized in four chapters approach popular art as a process and not as isolated projects, attempting to create a theoretical relationship between expression and genre, as well as ethnicity. The authors discuss poverty, the unequal conditions in which popular artists manufacture their work, and the challenges for distribution and consumption. All of the essays intentionally include feminism and gender perspectives in their analyses of creation, highlighting how women endow popular art with meaning. Taken together the essays present a case study on popular art in Mexico and the role women play in its development. Essays are in Spanish and Portuguese.

81 **Museo Nacional de Arte (Mexico).** Catálogo comentado del acervo del Museo Nacional de Arte: pintura, siglo XX. Textos de Dafne Cruz Porchini *et al.* Coordinación académica por Dafne Cruz Porchini. México: Museo Nacional de Arte, 2013. 1 v.: bibl., ill.

This work is the first to assess the 20th-century artworks in the collection of the Museo Nacional de Arte (MUNAL) which, for obvious reasons, concentrates on nationalist, postrevolution trends. The authors explore the meaning of "Mexican" identity and ideology and the "vision that Mexicans have of themselves and others" according to contributor Agustín Arteaga Domínguez. Rather than a thematic narrative, the artists are listed alphabetically, from A-G in the present volume. Biographical information on the artists is followed by an analysis of their works. The book also explores the policies adopted by the Mexican government regarding acquisition of artistic goods, philanthropy, patronage, and the merging of other institutional collections, such as the San Carlos Art Academy, with MUNAL. This comprehensive publication goes beyond merely cataloging the MUNAL's collection to situate the works within their artistic, cultural, and social contexts.

82 **Nandayapa, Mario.** Dos movimientos sociales en la gráfica chiapaneca: Guerra de Castas chiapaneca, litografías del siglo XIX, José Pedro Martínez: Mapaches 1914–1920, grabados del siglo XX, Franco Lázaro Gómez. Tuxtla Gutiérrez, Mexico: Consejo Estatal para las Culturas y las Artes de Chiapas, 2014. 78 p.: bibl., ill., index. (Nueva Curaduría. Biblioteca Chiapas)

This work makes available two graphic series from the collection of the Observatorio de la Salvaguarda del Patrimonio Material e Inmaterial de Chiapas. The first is *Guerra de Castas chiapaneca*, eight lithographs commissioned in 1872 from José Pedro Martínez, a disciple of Manuel Manilla (1830–95), depicting an 1869 indigenous uprising in the Tzajaljeme region. The second is *Mapaches 1914–1920* by Franco Lázaro Gómez, recounting the landowners' revolt against Venustiano Carranza. Gómez was one of the first pupils of the Chiapas School of Plastic Arts created in 1945. (He died four years later at age 27.) Both conflicts are attributed to economic and social neglect by the government, and both are deeply important to the history of Chiapas. Demonstrates the connection between the graphic arts and historical events.

83 **Orozco, Gabriel.** Materia escrita: cuadernos de trabajo, 1992–2012. México: Ediciones Era, 2014. 383 p.: bibl., ill., index.

Collection of impressions, ideas, thoughts, drawings, and photographs committed to diary-like *cuadernos* (notebooks), written and edited by the artist himself. The notebooks document two decades of constant traveling and exhibitions in Kortrijk, Frankfurt, Venice, Milan, Mexico City, and New York, among other places. In the content of the *cuadernos* one sees a relationship to the artist's conceptual works. For those not familiar with Orozco's work, the writing may appear disjointed and cryptic, but at the same time will generate curiosity for further investigation.

84 **Rememorar los derroteros: la impronta de la formación artística en la UNAM.** Coordinación de María Esther Aguirre Lora. México: UNAM, Instituto de Investigaciones sobre la Universidad y la Educación: Bonilla Artigas Editores, 2015. 240 p.: bibl., ill. (Historia de la educación / IISUE)

A cultural and intellectual history of the development of art education at UNAM, including the visual arts, music, theater, dancing, and cinematography. The work seeks to answer two questions: How were the formative processes in the artistic field established? And, what conditions existed in each case? The answers are provided in six essays presenting various paths taken by Mexican artists since the time of José Vasconcelos and establishing a means of connecting the past with the unpredictable future.

85 **Schara, Julio César.** Diálogos transdisciplinarios V: diálogos con escritores y pintores del siglo XX. México: Editorial Fontamara; Santiago de Querétaro, Mexico: Instituto de Investigaciones Multidisciplinarias, Universidad Autónoma de Querétaro, Facultad de Ingeniería, 2015. 411 p.: bibl. (Colección Argumentos; 268)

This anthology brings together 60 interviews conducted with important figures of Latin American arts and letters between 1972 and 1990 on *Controversias*, a radio program broadcast by UNAM. The work discusses the protagonists of the esthetic and literary history of Mexico and Latin America in the 20th century. Among the interviewees are David Alfaro Siqueiros, Rufino Tamayo, Carlos Pellicer, Luis Cardoza y Aragón, Raquel Tibol, and Manuel Rodriguez Lozano, along with Carlos Mérida, Carlos Cruz-Diez, Julio Le Parc, and Luis Molinari. Profiles of the interviewees written by Schara precede each conversation.

86 **Terrazas, Eduardo.** Eduardo Terrazas: segunda naturaleza = second nature. México: Editorial RM, 2015. 104 p.: ill.

Color-illustrated, bilingual catalog (Spanish/English) of Terrazas' exhibition at the Museo Carillo Gil covering nearly 50 years of work. Terrazas explores geometric abstraction, the possibilities that a structure may represent development and transformation, and the organic nature of the earth, as Vania Rojas Solís, the museum director, explains. Edward Sullivan's essay places the work of the architect, graphic designer, and installation artist in context generally and within the framework of geometric abstraction. Terrazas has experienced a resurgence of interest among scholars and artists in the past 20 years.

CENTRAL AMERICA

87 **Margarita Quesada Schmidt: no a la realidad.** Coordinación de María José Monge Picado. San José: Fundación Museos Banco Central de Costa Rica, 2015. 78 p.: bibl., ill.

Color-illustrated, bilingual (Spanish/English) catalog of an exhibition highlighting the work of the Cartago schoolteacher (1915–2001) on the 100th anniversary of her birth. Margarita Quesada Schmidt took up painting after retirement and employed watercolor as no one in the country had done before. She rendered landscapes, town scenes, and home interiors in a strong, expressionistic style.

88 **Montero, Carlos Guillermo.** Arte costarricense, 1897–1971. San José: Editorial UCR, 2015. 123 p.: bibl., ill.

In the introduction to his book, Montero explains that it is the result of a long research process that began in 1978 after the Museo de Arte Costarricense was created (1977). It is conceived as a guide to crucial moments in the development of visual arts in Costa Rica. Includes discussion of graphic arts and their connection to modernity, the national fine arts exhibitions of the late 1920s-mid-30s, artists at the forefront of major movements, such as Max Jiménez, Francisco Amighetti, Manuel de la Cruz González, and Group 8. The last chapter is dedicated to the Costa Rican artists who exhibited at the 1st Central American Biennial. The book is generously illustrated in color and b/w.

THE CARIBBEAN

89 **Desquirón, Antonio** and **José Veigas Zamora.** Protagonistas de las artes visuales en Santiago de Cuba. Santiago, Cuba: Fundación Caguayo: Editorial Oriente, 2011. 2 v.: bibl., ill.

A chronological selection of critical writings about artistic activity in Santiago de Cuba aimed at demonstrating the city's importance vis-à-vis art criticism. While not an exhaustive compilation, the portfolio touches on a wide variety of topics and includes research studies, criticism, interviews, exhibition presentations, and essays. Given their promotional character, reviews have been intentionally excluded.

90 **Espacios críticos habaneros del arte cubano: la década de 1950.** Selección y prólogo de Luz Merino Acosta. Habana: UH Editorial: Ediciones Unión, 2015. 2 v. (566 p.): bibl., ill., indexes.

Merino Acosta has selected articles by 30 authors from 15 newspapers, magazines, and exhibition catalogs to recreate the Cuban art scene during the "hinge" decade of the 1950s. The articles, which present an impressive parade of critics and artists, are organized chronologically: Volume I covers 1950–54 and Volume II covers 1955–59. As interesting and revealing as the articles are, they derive greater meaning from a reading of Merino Acosta's prologue defining the raison d'être for the "critical spaces" where art activities took place. Merino Acosta describes the complexity of a new economic model supported by newer information technologies, efficient means of transportation, and the proliferation of spaces for recreation and leisure to provide a context for the cultural life and artistic production on the island. The work draws the reader into the world of art galleries, exhibitions, salons, groups and associations, manifestos, and international biennials. This accessible study is about a paradoxical time for the arts (and everything else) in Cuba that is well documented, but is only beginning to be analyzed.

91 **Fernandez, Segundo J.** Cuban art in the 20th century: cultural identity and the international avant garde. Tallahassee: Florida State University (FSU), 2016. 112 p.

Color-illustrated, English-language catalog of an exhibition curated by Segundo J. Fernandez aimed at "addressing intersections of law, cultural patrimony, international trade, and collecting" in the words of Peter Weishar, dean of the College of Fine Arts of FSU. The catalog includes illustrated sections about the colonial and republican periods and the three modern generations, and ends with examples from some artists belonging to the late modern and contemporary periods, suggesting the scheme under which the exhibition is organized. Also includes essays by Fernandez, Florida International University (FIU) professor Juan A. Martínez, and Paul Niell.

92   **Flores, Tatiana** and **Michelle Stephens.** Contemporary art of the Hispanophone Caribbean islands in an archipelagic framework. (*Small Axe*, 20:3, No. 51, Nov. 2016, p. 80–99, photos)

Recognizing the diversity of the Caribbean as a whole, and of Caribbean Hispanophone culture, the article argues that the "visual arts are uniquely equipped to bridge the region's language and cultural divides." The archipelagic vision, Flores and Stephens state, can support an integrated perspective that includes connectivity and shared histories. For a review of the full journal issue, see item **809**.

93   **González, Pablo Alonso.** Monumental art and hidden transcripts of resistance in revolutionary Cuba, 1970–1990. (*J. Lat. Am. Cult. Stud.*, 25:2, June 2016, p. 271–296, bibl., photos)

Che Guevara believed that the creation of a New Socialist Man required monuments, a concrete rendering of history to help spread the official ideology, much like Soviet socialist realism. This article examines the implementation of such an esthetic. The consciousness that Castro intended for the people included the development of cultural and artistic institutions to unify national and revolutionary projects. Many artists resisted, and, in open opposition to the government, promoted abstract art instead. González has his own explanation to the question of why the revolutionaries adopted social realism as their preferred expression.

94   **González Quesada, Alfons.** Mi tío no se llama Sam: Estados Unidos en la gráfica cubana. Barcelona: RM Verlag: Fundació Casa Amèrica Catalunya, 2016. 119 p.: ill.

Color-illustrated catalog of the exhibition organized at the request of the Fundació Casa Amèrica Catalunya, gathering "visual messages" (posters, billboards, and the like) aimed at the US by the government of Cuba, reflecting the "highest degree of tension" between the two countries on occasion of the reestablishment of diplomatic relations during the administration of President Barack Obama (17 December 2014). The selection reveals a lingering belligerent rhetoric charged with symbolism, in the words of Antoni Traveria, director general of Casa Amèrica Catalunya, Spain. The essay by González Quesada contextualizes the Cuba-US relationship. The highly effective and excellent graphic design reflects the tradition of the Cuban revolutionary poster movement. The catalog includes the text in Catalonian and, in a separate booklet, in English.

95   **Goodman, Walter.** La perla de las Antillas: un artista en Cuba. Prólogo de Olga Portuondo Zúñiga. Edición anotada y corregida. Santiago, Cuba: Editorial Oriente, 2015. 332 p.: bibl., ill., index.

This book is not strictly a diary, but more of a colloquial chronicle about the British painter's experiences while living and working in Santiago de Cuba between May 1864 and November 1868. Goodman moved to Santiago with the artist Joaquín Cuadras Sagarra, a native of the city, after the two met in Italy in the early 1860s. Notes have been arranged, organized, and expanded since Goodman did not always follow a strict chronological order. The years Godman spent in Cuba coincide with a tumultuous social and political time in the Caribbean and Spain: the attempt to reconquer Saint Domingue, the slave revolt in Jamaica, Puerto Rico's "Grito de Lares," Cuba's "Ten Years War," and Spain's war of succession that forced Queen Isabella II to abdicate. The period also saw the rising popularity of photography which, for many artists, meant a diminished ability to make a living painting portraits. Goodman found work in other professions, as a correspondent for *The New York Herald*, for instance. Eventually his sympathy toward abolitionism and Caribbean unity made government authorities suspicious of Goodman, so he left Cuba, taking his notebook with him.

96   **Thompson, Krista A.** Shine: the visual economy of light in African diasporic aesthetic practice. Durham, N.C.: Duke University Press, 2015. 349 p.: bibl., ill., index.

When the author began exploring the photography studios on the streets of Atlanta and New Orleans looking for old photographs of Jamaica and the Bahamas, she was frustrated by the lack of information about black photographers and the communities they pictured. Her study centers on contemporary popular photographic practices, mostly in Jamaica and the Bahamas, and their diasporic communities. Her study is "mindful of the conditions of race and class and place that facilitate the disappearance of black subjects from the photographic archive." The book is profusely illustrated, and the 46 pages of excellent notes demonstrate her commitment to rigorous research.

97   Vega Miche, Sara. El cartel cubano llama dos veces. Edición de Gilberto Padilla Cárdenas. Madrid: Ediciones La Palma; AECID, 2016. 243 p.: bibl., ill. (Colección Cuba; 2)

As Luciano Castillo, director of the Cuban Cinematheque, states, this book recounts the history of Cuban filmmaking through movie posters. In a succinct fashion, Castillo explains how in 1959, after the Cuban Revolution and the creation of ICAIC (Instituto Cubano del Arte e Industrias Cinematográficos), the need to decolonize the screens and cultivate a viewing public contributed to the development of visually dynamic posters. Although prerevolution posters are scarce, the book includes samples as late as 1957. Postrevolution posters, aside from Eduardo Muñoz Bachs (1960), which is a transitional poster, are dated from 1964–2016, and proportionally favor foreign films due to the limited though significant national film production. Vega Miche explains that many of the posters were not considered worth preserving. They were designed to advertise related activities such as film festivals abroad, foreign film week, retrospectives, etc. She has managed, however, to assemble a fascinating collection that is a testament to the vitality, originality, and expressiveness of the Cuban poster.

SOUTH AMERICA

Argentina

98   Bell, Vikki. The art of post-dictatorship: ethics and aesthetics in transitional Argentina. New York: Routledge, Taylor & Francis Group, 2014. 170 p.: bibl., ill., index. (Transitional justice)

The title of this book does not refer exclusively to visual arts. Rather, it is aligned with Foucault's principle of "aesthetics of existence." The attempt to live mindfully in the gap between the past and future "is itself an art . . . a critical and collective engagement with the political arrangements of life." Bell goes through a few case studies (Leon Ferrari, the ESMA trial, Parque de la Memoria, photography in Córdoba, Diana Dowek and Lucila Quieto), organized in chapters discussing "the entwinning of ethics and aesthetics as modes of critique." The force that the past exerts on the future, she states in the introduction, is contingent, and implicitly and explicitly questioned.

99   Frank, Patrick. Painting in a state of exception: new figuration in Argentina, 1960–1965. Gainesville: University Press of Florida, 2016. 206 p.: bibl., ill., index.

This book examines the work of Ernesto Deira, Rómulo Macció, Luis Felipe Noe, and Jorge de la Vega, the four members of the Otra Figuración (or Nueva Figuración) that came about in 1961 in Buenos Aires. The four artists always enjoyed recognition in Latin America; however, as Frank notes, "they are below the horizon of visibility to most observers of modern art" in Europe and North America, despite having exhibited there on multiple occasions. As Frank notes in his analysis, the artists and their work provided a bold response to a tumultuous period in Argentine history. The conclusion examines the years after the group dispersed and the reasons for its diminished prominence and encourages a reevaluation of its relevance. The text is supported by excellent illustrations (in color and b/w), an index, and abundant notes and sources.

100   Gluzman, Georgina G. Trazos invisibles: mujeres artistas en Buenos Aires (1890–1923). Buenos Aires: Editorial Biblos, 2016. 286 p.: bibl., ill., index. (Artes y medios)

Noting the meager representation of female artists in the collection of the Buenos Aires Museo Nacional de Bellas Artes, Gluzman has tangible justification for their study. Long represented solely by Lola Mora, the book centers attention on other women and their contemporary working modes. She explains some of the factors that hampered the ability of women artists to gain prominence up to the late 1920s in Argentina: lack of art education, lack of press attention, lack of support from men and even from other women artists. Acknowledging that the existing literature on women artists is deficient, Gluzman demonstrates that women artists operated in a society that was condescending at best, and, in her closing, advocates not for a parallel canon for women, but for the creation of new narratives that recognize their contribution beyond what she calls "genial exception."

101 **Milano, Laura.** Usina posporno: disidencia sexual, arte y autogestión en la pospornografía. Buenos Aires: Titulo, 2014. 152 p.: bibl., ill.

Milano uses the terms *posporno* and *pospornografía* interchangeably, an artistic and political appropriation of the expression postpornography, anchored in the geographic and symbolic dimensions of Latin America. *Posporno* was born in the fringes of contemporary society out of the queer movement, the revindication of sex work in the 80s, and post-feminism as a critical answer to commercial pornography, "aspiring to portray freedom of genre and plasticity of the body from a dissident view." Acknowledging that *posporno* should propose new forms of socialization and collective work, the author argues that the apparent equity, integration, and tolerance of sexual minorities is an attempt to update the sexual-political heterosexual dominance. The hybrid text combines cultural analysis, feminist critique, interviews, and the like. The study is complemented with a glossary, a list of artists and collectives' practitioners of *posporno*, and a bibliography that includes a list of the videos mentioned in the text.

Bolivia

Medinaceli, Ximena. La Guerra del Pacífico y los ayllus: una lectura de la pintura mural del baptisterio de Sabaya. See item **1215**.

102 **Querejazu, Pedro.** Arte contemporáneo en Bolivia, 1970–2013: crítica, ensayos, estudios. La Paz: Pedro Querejazu Leyton, 2013. 532 p.: bibl., ill., indexes. (Libros de arte; 4)

Compilation of selected critical, didactic, and informative texts about Bolivian art covering 43 years of activity as an art critic, curator, art manager, and educator in Bolivia. The author divides the book in four parts. The first part collects articles written in the 70s and 80s for now-defunct newspapers in La Paz and Santa Cruz. The second part combine texts written for catalogs and the BHN and esART foundations. The third part includes essays about contemporary Bolivian art published in catalogs of international exhibitions, biennials, salons, and specialized art magazines. The fourth part collects commissions for different media. The texts aim to provide the reader with the tools to understand and analyze the works of art, whether a painting, sculpture, or building. Querejazu is by no means the only art critic or cultural journalist in Bolivia; however, he has held nearly every institutional position in La Paz and was an art critic before the profession gained a firm foothold in the country. His writing should not be taken lightly. The present volume chronicles many events in Bolivian art, mostly in La Paz, that otherwise would have been difficult to read about in one place.

Chile

103 **Artesanos, artistas, artífices: la Escuela de Artes Aplicadas de la Universidad de Chile, 1928–1968.** Edición de Eduardo Castillo Espinoza. Textos por Mariana Muñoz Hauer, Pedro Álvarez Caselli, Hugo Rivera-Scott, y Mauricio Vico Sánchez. Santiago: Ocho Libros: Pie de Texto, 2010. 441 p.: bibl., ill., index. Colección Referencias/visuales

A dependency of the Facultad de Artes of the Universidad de Chile, the Escuela de Artes Aplicadas was created in 1928 with the mission to direct artistic education for practical purposes. Considered a reaction to the economic crisis of the late 1920s, the school was created to aid in the formation of a "national identity," a concern shared by most of the subsequent governments until 1973. The school faced administrative and institutional challenges through the years, including suffering the loss of archival documentation. Therefore, the authors acknowledge that it is difficult to assess the impact of the school in its early years, particularly its influence on the evolution of design before 1963 when design was formally integrated into the curriculum of the Universidad de Chile. They conclude, however, that no other institution has provided a similar esthetic program in Chile. The first chapter is dedicated to the history of the school. Chapters 2, 3, and 4 analyze the school's impact on national industry, social transformation and popular art, and art and modernity.

104 Blanco, Fernando A. Neoliberal bonds: undoing memory in Chilean art and literature. Columbus: The Ohio State University Press, 2015. 190 p.: bibl., ill., index. (Transoceanic studies)

The author argues that after the restoration of democracy in Chile, the Concertación de Partidos por la Democracia was responsible for a process of dissolution and reconfiguration of the social fabric of the country at the private and public levels, establishing among other things a new "official narrative of memory," a "change in individual and collective subjectivity," and a "new domestication of impulses." A criticism of Chile's transition governments, Blanco's book looks at the alternative interpretations and perspectives of democratization provided by the arts and literature. The premise of the study is unusual and Blanco offers a provocative analysis of postdictatorial rule in Chile. He also opens a window into the democratization of a country that, however imperfect, many take for granted.

105 Kirby, Cristian. 119: exposição, exposición. Cordenação museológica e editorial por Kátia Felipini Neves. Tradução dos textos por Miriam Osuna. São Paulo: Memorial da Resistência de São Paulo, 2014. 150 p.: bibl., ill.

Bilingual (Portuguese-Spanish) catalog of the exhibition at the Memorial da Resistência in São Paulo (between October 2014 and March 2015), the outcome of a photography project related to the disappearance of 119 Chilean militants of the left during one operation (out of many) carried out during the military dictatorship of Augusto Pinochet in Chile. Portraits of the victims taken from photographs used by their relatives to search for them are placed on newspaper clippings, listing streets or reproducing maps of Santiago neighborhoods, indicating where each person disappeared. Mesquita explains that the exhibit aims at understanding the locations as places of resistance and repression and says that violence should not become commonplace during periods of democracy.

Colombia

Arias Vásquez, Andrés. Politica y vanguardia: la juventud colombiana en las artes plásticas de los años sesenta y setenta. See item **1092**.

106 Gómez Campuzano, Ricardo. Ricardo Gómez Campuzano: visiones de nacionalismo en el arte colombiano. Investigación y textos por Claudia Cristancho Camacho. Fotografías por Victor Robledo. Bogotá: Banco de la Republica, 2014. 125 p.: bibl., ill.

A permanent exhibit of 400 paintings by Ricardo Gómez Campuzano is housed in the late artist's home and studio, which is now part of the Red Cultural del Banco de la República in Colombia. This work is a companion publication for the exhibit. The study emphasizes Gómez Campuzano's successful career. His late 19th-century Spanish Academic style was welcomed by 20th-century Bogotá's traditional society. As modern, newer artistic styles gained a footing in the country, Gómez Campuzano maintained a degree of popularity among members of the conservative, wealthier circles. As the text notes, the artist followed his own path throughout his life and left it to the critics to make their own judgements.

107 Mayor Mora, Alberto. Las escuelas de artes y oficios en Colombia 1860–1960. Vol. 1, El poder regenerador de la cruz. Coinvestigación de Ana Cielo Quiñones Aguilar e Gloria Stella Barrera Jurado. Con la asistencia de joven investigadora Juliana Trejos Celis. Bogotá: Editorial Pontificia Universidad Javeriana, 2014. 1 v.: bibl., ill.

Fascinating and needed study about the impact of the Arts and Crafts Schools in Colombia's economic development from 1860–1960. The study forces a revision about when and how the country inserted itself in the capitalist world, which was generally accepted to be between the second and third decades of the 20th century, and examines the premise that in Colombia productivity went from the workshop to industrial scale without a proper transition. Craftsmen were prevented from, or not encouraged to, acquire technological and scientific advancements, for example; they were also sheltered from ideological training and instructed instead with strict religious behavior and work obligations. Bipartisan violence hampered many efforts to keep the schools up to date. The prologue to the study ponders what could have happened in Colombia if a more dynamic acquisition of knowledge and values had led to the growth of the middle class and the popular sectors. The reader may arrive at his/her own answer after finishing this well-documented study.

108   **Pensamiento visual contemporáneo.** Edición de Margarita María Monsalve Pino. Bogotá: Universidad Nacional de Colombia-Sede Bogotá, Vicerrectoría Académica, Dirección Académica, 2015. 459 p.: bibl., ill.

This book compiles the 2010 Cátedra "Martha Traba" lectures from the Universidad Nacional de Colombia. The chair was created to honor the late Colombian-Argentine art critic and historian. The lectures broadly cover the visual arts and the contemporary implications of the image from artistic, sociological, philosophical, and neurological standpoints.

109   **Ramírez González, Imelda.** Debates críticos en los umbrales del arte contemporáneo: el arte de los años setenta y la fundación del Museo de Arte Moderno de Medellín. Medellín, Colombia: Fondo Editorial Universidad EAFIT, 2012. 265 p.: bibl., ill. (Colección Arena)

This work examines the process and circumstances that resulted in the creation of the Museo de Arte Moderno de Medellín (MAMM) at the end of the 1970s, as an outcome of the Medellín (Coltejer) Biennial (1968, 1970, and 1972). Ramírez asks: Why call an art museum "modern" (instead of contemporary) if the museum is expected to break with the modern tradition? The incompatibility between name and objectives drives the study, buttressed with a generous bibliography and sources, including interviews with people who supported or opposed the creation of the institution. Originally a private institution, it was only in 2017 that the museum was able to build a permanent, physical facility. The museum, despite multiple well-intentioned efforts (as well as erratic and counterproductive ones), has been unable to fulfill its vision and mission, or to acquire a personality that reflects the arts of the city it claims to represent.

110   **Seminario Nacional de Teoría e Historia del Arte, 9th, Medellín, Colombia, 2012.** El arte y la fragilidad de la memoria. Edición de Javier Domínguez Hernández, Carlos Arturo Fernández Uribe, Daniel Jerónimo Tobón Giraldo, y Carlos Mario Vanegas Zubiría. Medellín, Colombia: Universidad de Antioquia, Facultad de Artes: Instituto de Filosofía: Sílaba, 2014. 380 p.: bibl., ill.

This volume compiles presentations from the IX Seminar of Theory and Art History organized by the Instituto de Filosofía of the Universidad de Antioquia with the objective of critically analyzing the relationship between art and memory, specifically how artists come to terms with traumatic events. The essays cover philosophy, museology, art criticism, history, and architectural restoration. Essays focus on colonial and independence eras, Spain's efforts to restore architectural patrimony, and the cycles of violence in the 19th and 20th centuries and the lasting impact of that violence today.

111   **Sinning Téllez, Luz Guillermina and Ruth Nohemí Acuña Prieto.** Miradas a la plástica colombiana de 1900 a 1950: un debate histórico y estético. Bogotá: Universidad Externado de Colombia, 2011. 224 p.: bibl., ill.

A study of national cultural values through an examination of the work of Colombian artists from 1900 to 1950. The artists highlighted in the work were selected by the Consejo Nacional de Patrimonio del Ministerio de Cultura. The authors review Colombia's artistic past, placing it within a social context. Roberto Lleras situates the study, claiming that "no matter what posture one may have, the artistic production of those five decades cannot be ignored. The old and new in the book impress for the beauty of their perspectives and rigorous analysis." Chapters cover landscape, costumbrismo, and sculpture from 1900–30;

academic art and rupture, Bauhaus, Nationalism, artists from Antioquia, and Santiago Martinez Delgado from 1930–50; and a revision of art criticism. According to the authors, 1900–50 was a critical period for the arts in Colombia because "modernity" required accommodations. Citing A. Riga, they suggest that the artistic value of the art production of those years is impossible to separate from historical circumstances.

112   Yepes Muñoz, Rubén Darío. La política del arte: cuatro casos de arte contemporáneo en Colombia. Bogotá: Pontificia Universidad Javeriana, 2012. 161 p.: bibl., ill. (Intervenciones en estudios culturales)

Yepes Muñoz believes that institutionalized art is an elitist field of practices and discourses that excludes many voices. Institutionalized art (represented by critics, historians, museum directors, gallery owners, even "successful" artists, etc.) has become inflexible. Supported by the writings of philosophers Guy Debord and Jacques Rencière, and, to a lesser degree Ernesto Laclau and Chantal Mouffe, Muñoz analyzes the production of four artists, dividing them in two groups. In the first group is Doris Salcedo, a political artist, whose work Muñoz characterizes as unfortunate examples of the depoliticization of politics; and Fernando Pertuz, a self-declared a "resistance" artist, whose work Muñoz sees as trendy and insufficient as a model for political art. In the second group are the art collective *ekolectivo* and the *Práctica artística en la grieta* project by Ludmila Ferrari, representing the potential for politics to be a constructive and transformative force in the life of individuals and communities. Yepes Muñoz closes his stimulating study calling for older, individualistic models to be replaced by collective creation, public versus private art, the implementation of a radical pedagogy, and empowerment instead of exclusion. He believes this artistic repositioning is needed because one artist alone cannot change the world.

Paraguay

113   Bienal Internacional de Asunción, 1st, *Asunción, 2015*. BIA: Primera Bienal Internacional de Asunción, 2015. Asunción: Editorial Servilibro, 2015. 477 p.: ill.

Color-illustrated catalog of the 1st International Art Biennale organized in Paraguay sponsored by the government of Paraguay and the private sector, a joint effort led by the Centro Cultural de la República. The slogan for the event was Grito de Libertad, or "a cry for freedom," a broad framework that allowed the inclusion of nearly every artistic trend currently practiced in the Americas. According to Carmen Zambrini, executive director, the purpose of the Biennale was to provide opportunities for young individuals pursuing a career in the arts and related fields in response to a diminishing interest in art education and a lack of information in Paraguay about the contemporary arts worldwide. An important component of the event was the *Plataforma Educativa* implemented with docents. Descriptions of the exhibited works add value to the publication. A comprehensive table of contents, artist index, and biographical information about the participants would have been useful for the reader.

Peru

114   Imaginación visual y cultura en el Perú. Edición de Gisela Cánepa. Lima: Fondo Editorial, Pontificia Universidad Católica del Perú, 2011. 464 p.: bibl., ill.

This work compiles papers presented in 2008 at a seminar organized by the Facultad de Ciencias Sociales de la PUCP (Pontificia Universidad Católica del Perú) to promote visual anthropology and the creation of a MA degree focused on visual expression as a social phenomenon. Nineteen articles by Peruvian and foreign scholars look at visual culture from prehispanic times to the present. The papers are arranged thematically under theoretical and methodological approach, image and representation, and image and action. As the papers demonstrate, contemporary studies of visual culture necessarily look at issue of representation, truth, and power. Among the papers, a study by Nelson E. Pereyra Chávez on photographic images stands out.

115   Rivera Cachique, Ronald. Arte con ayahuasca: entrevistas sobre el proceso creativo. Lima: La Nave, 2015. 241 p.: bibl., ill. (Serie luz azul; 1)

The Quechua word ayahuasca means "rope of the death" (*soga de los muertos*) and identifies a plant native to the Amazon ecosystem. The inhabitants of the region have used it for hundreds—possibly thousands of years—for various purposes. The word has different meanings depending on the community. The word also identifies a medicinal concoction mixed with *chacruna*, another plant, for ritualistic purposes associated with wellness and contact with a spiritual dimension. Those who drink the beverage experience physical and psychological effects. Use of ayahuasca usually induces energy, magnifies sensibility, and enhances perception and creativity. Rivera interviewed 27 artists who practice or have practiced the ritual of drinking ayahuasca as part of their artistic process (not only in the visual arts, but also in poetry, craftmaking, and storytelling). Rivera refers to the "ayahuasca aesthetic" that searches for answers to the universal, existential questions: Who are we, where do we come from, and where are we going?

Uruguay

116   Caraballo, Jorge. Jorge Caraballo: una exposición antológica. Curación por Manuel Neves. Textos de Enrique Aguerre y Manuel Neves. Traducción al inglés por Adriana Butureira. Montevideo: Museo Nacional de Artes Visuales, 2015. 139 p.: bibl., ill., index.

Illustrated catalog of an exhibition at Montevideo's Museo Nacional de Artes Visuales highlighting the work, career, and life of Caraballo (Montevideo, 1941–2014). Caraballo began practicing Op and Kinetic art as a result of his private studies in Paris with Victor Vasarely. He also studied art theory with Frank Popper, later developing visual poetry and mail art, then returning to geometry in the last two decades of his life. After he and Clemente Padín published *Señales* in Caracas in 1977, they were arrested in Montevideo by the police of the civic-military Uruguayan dictatorship and sent to prison. After his release and the reestablishment of democracy in the country, he resumed his artistic activities. He was a founding member of the Uruguayan Association of Mail Artists (1983), a politically active organization, and wrote other books, among them *En Uruguay la palabra "justicia" significa* (1987) and *Solidaridad*, again with Padín (1991).

117   Puchet, May. Octaedro, Los Otros y Axioma: relecturas del arte conceptual en el Uruguay durante la dictadura (1973–1985). Prólogo de Enrique Aguerre. Montevideo: Yaugurú, 2014. 213 p.: bibl., ill. (Colección Bordes & desbordes; 6)

This study focuses on the conceptual work of three art collectives active during the dictatorship. Their work is characterized by resistance, an emphasis on experimentation, and a communal process. Puchet takes a biographical narrative to provide multiple perspectives. After a brief explanation about the origins and character of Latin American conceptual art and a discussion of the strategies used by conceptual Uruguayan artists to escape the stagnation and censorship of the dictatorship years, she describes each of the groups and interviews their members. The memory-building exercise is fascinating. Puchet provides a record of the experiences of a group of artists whose activity was insufficiently documented, despite the transformative nature of their work in a society traditionally supportive of cultural matters.

Venezuela

118   Blackmore, Lisa. Spectacular modernity: dictatorship, space, and visuality in Venezuela, 1948–1958. Pittsburgh, Pa.: University of Pittsburgh Press, 2017. 268 p.: bibl., ill., index. (Illuminations: cultural formations of the Americas series)

This study examines the paradigm of modernity, progress, and stability in Venezuela provided by dictatorial rule at the expense of democracy throughout the 1950s. Blackmore sets out to demonstrate that social order, visual regimes, and political power cast the Venezuelan population as observers, and not agents, of modernity. The clever analysis comes at a convenient time to examine the intended and unintended consequences of abandoning democracy as a means to an end, whatever that end may be.

119   Manifiesto País. Curación por Lisbeth Salas. Caracas: Sala Mendoza, 2014. 89 p.: ill.

Color-illustrated catalog of an exhibition of 66 posters organized by the Fundación Sala Mendoza (a dependency of the Universidad Metropolitana, Caracas) that aimed at opening dialogue. Sixty-six poets, writers, journalists, and historians were invited to provide a brief text describing the current situation in Venezuela. Salas and the graphic designers Pedro Quintero and César Jara visually interpreted the texts to create the posters, which have a unifying, stylistic similarity.

120 Petit, Edgar. Las artes plásticas en Maracaibo 1860–1920. Maracaibo, Venezuela: SAIEZ, Servicio Autónomo Imprenta del Estado Zulia, 2014. 262 p.: bibl., ill. Colección Cuenca de la luz

A description of artistic activity (mainly painting, drawing, photography, sculpture, and printmaking) around Lake Maracaibo basin between 1860 and 1920. At the time, the port city and capital of Zulia state was an economic hub and a bastion of opposition to the centralist policies of President Guzmán Blanco. Artists demonstrated their opposition through artistic and cultural activities that attracted other artists from the Dominican Republic, Colombia, and elsewhere. The first chapter provides background information about the beginnings of artistic activity in Maracaibo. The second chapter is dedicated to the Drawing School, the first of such institutions created in the state of Zulia, and the role of several artists at its helm. The third and final chapter is dedicated to the influence of Italian painting in the city. Francisco Arias Cárdenas, governor of Zulia, introduces the book, noting that it is not an art history book, but rather a kaleidoscopic view of a complex region determinedly engaged in the national life of Venezuela.

BRAZIL

JOSÉ M. NEISTEIN, *Independent Scholar, Washington, DC*

AS IN RECENT YEARS, the number of scholarly visual arts studies published by university presses has been increasing in several Brazilian states. University presses produced more than half of the books annotated for the Brazilian art section of *HLAS 74*. The majority of these are modified versions of MA and PhD theses; some may become standard reference works in their areas. A collection of primary source materials on Mário Pedrosa, a seminal personality among Brazil's intellectuals and art critics in the second half of the 20th century, seems destined to be a standard reference source (item **123**). *Fronteiras: arte, imagem, história* (item **121**) is also notable for its exploration of the friction between artists and art institutions. The collection of essays on the Baroque in Minas Gerais (item **127**) has quickly become a standard book. Walter Luiz Pereira (item **133**) sheds new lights on 19th-century monumental historical paintings and the political consolidation of the Brazilian Empire under Dom Pedro II.

The subsections of the 20th and 21st Centuries and City Planning and Architecture include the largest numbers of publications. The reassessment of the São Paulo International Bienal on the occasion of its 30th anniversary is of great critical and historical interest (item **155**). The reedition of Aracy Amaral's *Projeto construtivo brasileiro na arte* (item **152**) is very welcome as it has been long out of print. Of historical and critical relevance is Artur Freitas' book on *Arte de guerrilha* (item **142**), an in-depth analysis of avant-garde movements in Brazil under the military dictatorship, particularly in the period from 1969 to 1973. A considerable number of monographs on individual artists appear in the section on modern and contemporary art, most of them vital and creative. Taken together, they contribute their share to the current art scene in the country. Architecture and urbanism have been experiencing a rich wave of scholarly publications. Rodrigo Bastos (item **164**) proposes new ways of looking at colonial settlements in Minas Gerais; Flávio de Lemos Carsalde (item **166**) speculates philosophically on restoration and preservation; Manoela Rossinetti Rufinoni (item **172**) studies urban restoration and preservation; a set of conference proceedings (item **175**) studies architecture as the work of a team, rather than as a solitary accomplishment; Elcio Gomes da Silva (item **174**) studies the palaces of Brasília; and Mara Sánchez Llorens (item **173**) presents the rich artistic personality of Lina Bo Bardi.

Photography offers monographs on three distinguished photographers: Marcel Gautherot (item **161**), Fernando Chiriboga (item **160**) and Christiano Junior (item **159**), and a historical presentation of photography in Recife, Pernambuco (item **162**). The section on Folk Art offers two items: utilitarian pottery-making in a small community in Minas Gerais (item **158**) and the catalog for an exhibition of spontaneous, anonymous artistic expression of ordinary Brazilians (item **157**). Indigenous traditions are represented by an iconographical analysis of the Xingu area (item **177**). Studies of Afro-Brazilian influences focus on architecture (items **168** and **176**), cartography (item **181**), and photography (item **159**). Several items of interest are annotated under the Miscellaneous heading: iconography of Brazil's fauna and flora (item **188**), media and resistance during the military dictatorship from 1964 to 1985 (item **189**), botanic art in the state of Paraná (item **178**), visual documentation of the Portuguese colonies including scientific and art samples (item **181**), a general catalog of the holdings of the Museu de Arte do Rio Grande do Sul Ado Malagoli (item **186**), the Odorico Tavares collection of Brazilian art (item **184**), a study on artists' books (item **190**); and a study on the rarefied world of the small presses in Brazil (item **180**).

REFERENCE AND THEORETICAL WORKS

Barroco: teoria e análise. See item **127**.

121 Fronteiras: arte, imagem, história. Organização por Sheila Cabo Geraldo. Rio de Janeiro: Beco do Azougue Editorial, 2014. 312 p.: bibl., ill.

Fronteiras is a collection of 18 papers presented at the 21st Encontro Nacional de Pesquisadores em Artes Plasticas, do Estado do Rio de Janeiro. Of special interest is the fraught relationship between art and institutions inasmuch as their policies restrict freedom of expression. This friction between artistic institutions and artists raises questions about the legitimacy of experimentation in art. To what extent are artists free and to what extent is artistic development being inhibited by the parameters set by museums and other organizations? The author questions whether artistic expression is autonomous in both universal and Brazilian terms, particularly as art constantly travels between absolute heteronomy and total autonomy, and as sociopolitical conditions impose dialectical controversies. The book offers some valuable theoretical contributions.

Kruchin, Samuel. Kruchin, uma poética da história: obra de restauro. See item **169**.

122 Memória e cultura: itinerários biográficos, trajetórias e relações geracionais. Organização de Milene de Cássia Silveira Gusmão e Raquel Costa Santos. Vitória da Conquista, Brazil: Edições UESB, 2014. 218 p.: bibl., ill.

A collection of 10 essays by 10 authors anchored in social sciences research related to the transmission of knowledge—theoretical and practical—in families from Bahia who have been active in intellectual, cultural, and artistic pursuits for several generations. Writers, essayists, visual artists, photographers, and moviemakers are studied in their local contexts. Some individuals attained national and international stature, like Glauber Rocha, for example.

123 Pedrosa, Mário. Mário Pedrosa: primary documents. Edited by Glória Ferreira and Paulo Herkenhoff. Translated by Stephen Berg. New York: Museum of Modern Art, 2015. 464 p.: bibl., ill., index.

A founder of professional art criticism in Brazil, Mário Pedrosa (1900–81) was an art thinker and charismatic political and intellectual personality who became, and still is, a major icon in Brazilian cultural life. An authority on national and international art, his impact on artists and creative minds was decisive in placing modern Brazilian art on the world map. This publication, part of a series of primary documents related to seminal personalities within the worlds of modern and contemporary art, focuses on a set of carefully selected texts by and about Mário Pedrosa that bear witness to his impact on the national and international avant-garde scenes. Illustrations, chronology, and references provided.

124 Pequeno, Fernanda. Lygia Pape e Hélio Oiticica: conversações e fricções poéticas. Rio de Janeiro: Apicuri, 2013. 126 p., 8 pages of plates: bibl., ill. (Coleção Pensamento em arte)

Originally presented as the author's MA thesis at the Universidade do Estado do Rio de Janeiro, 2007, this comparative study focuses on two major avant-garde artists of Rio de Janeiro, examining their esthetic similarities and divergences. Their common denominator was the reality of political conflict during the military dictatorship in Brazil; the hardest years were from the mid-1960s to the early 80s. Government interference forced the artists to develop new paths. Pequeno handles the contradictions and ambiguities in their work with creative intellectual insights.

125 Vivas, Rodrigo. Por uma história da arte em Belo Horizonte: artistas, exposições e salões de arte. Belo Horizonte, Brazil: Editora C/Arte, 2012. 246 p.: bibl., ill., portraits. (História & arte)

Established in 1897 as the first planned city in Brazil, Belo Horizonte became an active cultural artistic and intellectual center in Brazil. Vivas' PhD thesis analyzes its art scene during three periods: academic art (1918–36); modern art (1936–63); and contemporary art (1964–70). More than a wealth of factual information, the book offers critics' discussions, artists' statements, and cultural producers' texts. A welcome synthesis of the history of modern art in Minas Gerais, and a good starting point for further research.

COLONIAL PERIOD

126 Almada, Márcia. Das artes da pena e do pincel: caligrafia e pintura em manuscritos no século XVIII. Belo Horizonte, Brazil: Fino Traço, 2012. 306 p.: bibl., ill. (Coleção História)

Presented originally as a PhD dissertation, this study of illuminated books and manuscripts and documents in Brazil and, to a lesser extent, in Portugal, is the result of many years of research in both countries and in Spain. Almada's research in public, private, and ecclesiastical libraries, archives, and museums has resulted in a useful contribution to the field of decorative arts during the colonial period. This interdisciplinary analysis covers cultural history, art history, and social history, and provides information on the technical aspects of paper conservation and restoration. Among the many related issues addressed are the importance of the *Livros de compromisso de irmandades* as a main source of ecclesiastical documentation and the role of visual ornamentation in a society that includes the interaction of literate and illiterate cultures. The excellent selection of facsimiles illustrates the points discussed in the text.

127 Barroco: teoria e análise. Organização e apresentação de Affonso Ávila. São Paulo: Perspectiva; Belo Horizonte, Brazil: CBMM, Companhia Brasileira de Metalurgia e Mineração, 2013. 556 p.: bibl., ill., index. (Coleção Stylus; 10)

This work collects articles published in the journal *Barroco*, many translated from other languages, with a special emphasis on Baroque in Minas Gerais. General sections are Do Barroco: temas teóricos; Do Barroco na Europa; Do Barroco na América Latina; Do Barroco no Brasil; and seven essays on city planning, architecture, sculpture, visual arts, literature, poetry, and music. The section on Baroque in Minas Gerais gathers eight essays on the same topics covered in the previous section, on Brazil at large. The international and national scholars who contributed to this publication are among the finest in this field today. Unfortunately the printing of most illustrations, except period documents on paper, are blurred. Color illustrations would have been welcome.

Bastos, Rodrigo. A arte do urbanismo conveniente: o decoro na implantação de novas povoações em Minas Gerais na primeira metade do século XVIII. See item **164**.

128   **Bretas, Rodrigo José Ferreira.** Traços biográficos relativos ao finado Antônio Francisco Lisboa, distinto escultor mineiro, mais conhecido pelo apelido de Aleijadinho. Prefácio de Silviano Santiago. Fotografias de Jomar Bragança. Belo Horizonte, Brazil: Editora UFMG, 2013. 132 p.: ill.

Originally published in an Ouro Preto newspaper in 1858, this text was the first biographical sketch of the Baroque Brazilian master architect and sculptor Aleijadinho (1734–1814), who so intrigued modernist poets Mario de Andrade, Manuel Bandeira, and Carlos Drummond de Andrade in the late 1920s, when they discovered and started reassessing his genius and his role in shaping Brazilian identity. Silviano Santiago provides an introduction and photographer Jomar Bragança presents images of the sculpture and architecture discussed in the text. Among the points addressed is the revival of the neocolonial architecture style in Brazil during and after the modernist movement.

129   **Campos, Adalgisa Arantes.** As Irmandades de São Miguel e as Almas do Purgatório: culto e iconografia no setecentos mineiro. Belo Horizonte, Brazil: Editora C/ Arte, 2013. 247 p.: bibl., ill. (Coleção História e arte)

Colonization of Minas Gerais began ca. 1700 by Portuguese lesser aristocrats, but also criminals, outsiders, and enslaved Africans. Each group brought its own culture, but the spiritual values of the Baroque model prevailed and survived up to the 1850s and beyond. This model absorbs the values of local pagan and African culture, but also dilutes their significance. This book focuses on the cult of the dead as practiced by the lay brotherhood of Saint Michaels, based on Dante's ideas of Purgatory, in order to better understand the meaning of life. Eschatology and the absolvation of the holy souls are studied mainly through the symbolic values of the visual arts artifacts that survived the age, particularly those tied to the ethical values of the Archangel warrior. Based on significant archival research. Blurred reproductions prevent proper evaluation.

Carsalade, Flávio de Lemos. A pedra e o tempo: arquitetura como patrimônio cultural = Stone and time: architecture as cultural heritage. See item **166**.

Chiriboga, Fernando. Relíquias: patrimônio arquitetônico do Nordeste do Brasil. See item **160**.

130   **Derenji, Jussara da Silveira.** Desenhos setecentistas na Sé de Belém. (*An. Mus. Paul.*, 19:2, julho/dez. 2011, p. 107–127, ill.)

This volume is based on an assessment of restoration work done on the cathedral of Belém, a church built from 1748 to 1782, that concluded in 2009. The author offers an analysis of a niche and drawings of its surroundings. More is known about the region's famed architect Antonio Landi (1713–91), than the many anonymous workers—indigenous, mestizo, and black engravers, painters, and sculptors. Nonetheless a study of the cathedral reveals the technical and social changes that occurred during its construction.

131   **Miranda, Marcos Paulo de Souza.** O Aleijadinho revelado: estudos históricos sobre Antônio Francisco Lisboa. Belo Horizonte, Brazil: Fino Traço Editora, 2014. 111 p.: bibl., ill. (Coleção Patrimônio)

Miranda's contribution to the literature on Aleijadinho offers a clearer biographical picture of the noted colonial sculptor and architect. The study is based on many years of archival research.

19TH CENTURY

Beltramim, Fabiana. Sujeitos iluminados: a reconstituição das experiências vividas no estúdio de Christiano Jr. See item **159**.

132 Dias, Elaine. Os retratos de Maria Isabel e Maria Francisca de Bragança, de Nicolas-Antoine Taunay. (*An. Mus. Paul.*, 19:2, julho/dez. 2011, p. 11–43, ill.)

Nicolas-Antoine Taunay, a noted French landscape painter, produced several portraits during his stay at the Rio de Janeiro Court. In 1816, he painted Queen Carlota Joaquina and all of her daughters. In this group, two portraits are special: the paintings which are cataloged as Princess Maria Francisca and Princess Maria Teresa, but are more likely Maria Isabel and Maria Francisca de Assis—both of whom left Brazil that year to marry the Spanish King Fernando VII and his brother Carlos Maria Isidro de Bourbon. In this article, beyond describing the portraits (and analyzing the identities of the portrayed princesses), the article explores court society during the period.

133 Pereira, Walter Luiz. Óleo sobre tela, olhos para a história: memória e pintura histórica nas Exposições Gerais de Belas Artes do Brasil Império (1872 e 1879). Rio de Janeiro: 7Letras, 2013. 177 p.: bibl., ill.

The old Imperial Academy of Fine Arts in Rio organized visual culture by using the monumental historical paintings strongly supported by Emperor Dom Pedro II to symbolically affirm the power of the empire, while also affirming a national identity and consolidating inner unity. The canvasses created by Victor Meirelles and Pedro Américo, representing the past, were intended to stimulate national sentiment. Originally the author's MA thesis, the text underscores the relationship between art and politics, and art as a tool for civil education. Those paintings were widely seen in the salons of 1872 and 1879 under the auspices and the supervision of the Emperor himself. The book is the result of extensive research. The paintings, unfortunately, are poorly reproduced.

20TH–21ST CENTURIES

134 Aguilar, José Roberto. Aguilar. Vol. 1, 1960–1989. Vol. 2, 1990–2010. Texto introdutório por Nelson Aguilar. Textos por Solange Lisboa. Tradução por Melanie Wyffels e Thomaz William Mendoza-Harrell. São Paulo: GPA Projetos Culturais, 2013. 2 v. (519 p.): bibl., ill.

A 50-year retrospective of José Roberto Aguilar (S. Paulo, 1941), painter, video maker, performer, writer, and composer, who often combines all these talents to create outdoor public presentations. Attracted by mythology and the grand literary traditions, he uses quotations in his usually large canvasses reminiscent of Jackson Pollock's drip paintings, but in a very personal, bold manner. The author of five works of fiction, he pioneered video art in Brazil, and triggered some of the finest intellectual minds in the country to write reflexive texts on his output and on innovative art at large. Critics view him as a rebel with a cause for good reasons. He applies colors directly from paint tubes and through sprays and nozzles. No brushes, no spatulas, just action, intense action.

135 Barrão. Coordenação editorial por Luiza Mello e Marisa Mello. Versão en inglês por Rebecca Atkinson e Marise Chinetti de Barros. Rio de Janeiro: Automática Edições Ltda, 2015. 192 p.: bibl., ill. (Arte Bra)

Barrão (Rio de Janeiro, 1959) is basically a self-taught artist. Guided by the logic of bricolage, his work is about making new use of daily objects like domestic appliances, toys, and pottery pieces, forming sculptures of modified objects joined together. He uses similar procedures in his work with music. As Felipe Scovino notes in his text, "Barrão . . . constructs a fictional world inhabited by differences which make use of irreverence, humor and visual poetry, so that from the (supposed) fiction we can reinterpret the world in which we live."

136 Barreto, Adriana. Agora sim. Com curadoria de Alberto Saraiva e Zalinda Cartaxo. Tradução por Regina Alfarano. 2a edição. Rio de Janeiro: Apicuri, 2012. 173 p.: ill.

Adriana Barreto (1949–), painter, sculptor, performer, dancer, choreographer, video artist, photographer, and more, aims at balancing all her creative skills. Her own body is the central point of her creativity, as the dancer on her toes establishes a special path in a sequence that ends in exhaustion. Everything she does intersects with other talents, looking for a point of balance, without limiting the particular areas and mediums she works with. The body is envisaged as a thinking and feeling material that is the center of a complex constellation. Her statements are recorded in an articulate and eloquent interview, and are illustrated by equally eloquent photographs in this publication.

137   **100 anos de artes plásticas no Instituto de Artes da UFRGS: três ensaios.** Organização de Blanca Brites, Icleia Borsa Cattani, Maria Amélia Bulhões e Paulo César Ribeiro Gomes. Porto Alegre, Brazil: UFRGS Editora, 2012. 263 p.: bibl., ill.

Despite their importance on the continent, the Jesuit missions did not establish a tradition in Rio Grande do Sul, where Portuguese colonization later occurred. Consistent art activities hence started with German, Italian, and other immigrants toward the end of the 19th century. The art institute was established in 1910, and eventually became part of the federal university. The institute became a center of teaching and creativity and a focal point for experimentation and the avant-garde. Its centennial is celebrated with this landmark publication that deals with the history and vicissitudes of the institute and offsprings. Texts are in Portuguese and English.

138   **Conduru, Roberto.** Paulo Pasta. Rio de Janeiro: Barléu Edições Ltda., 2013. 215 p.: bibl., ill.

In his dialogue between art and reality, Paulo Pasta's (1959) painting reveals a particularly interesting morphology of geometrical nature. In this conversation, Pasta reveals refinement in the chromatic ambiguity, while working with simple signs and singular colors of great subtlety. As in Mark Rothko's paintings, the morphology of composition is subjected to the reality of color. To achieve the colors that he wants, Pasta works with patience and precision. His pictorial space is generally rectangular and horizontal. A critical text describes his work process.

139   **Dias & Riedweg.** Até que a rua nos separe. Exposição por Dias & Riedweg. Textos por Emilio Kalil *et al.* Rio de Janeiro: Imago Escritório de Arte: NAU Editora, 2012. 219 p.: bibl., ill.

Catalog of an exhibition held at Centro das Artes Hélio Oiticica, Rio de Janeiro, 16 August–30 September 2012, a collaboration between Maurício de Mello Dias (Rio de Janeiro, 1964) and Walter Riedweg (Switzerland, 1955). The exhibition included nine video installations and five sets of photography taken in Rio de Janeiro between 1995 and 2012. "The streets of Rio, from the outskirts to the center, from the so-called asphalt to the favela, are the setting and theme of this show, which reveals the importance of the city to the formulation of the artists' works and everyday lives. . . . In fact the exhibitions are an ode to Rio and to one of its most besotted chroniclers, João do Rio, who in the first years of the 20th century wrote *A alma encantadora das ruas (The Enchanting Soul of the Streets)*."

140   **Entrecopas: arte brasileira 1950–2014.** Organização editorial e curadoria de Wagner Barja. Tradução inglesa por Oto Dias Becker Reifschneider. Brasília: Thesaurus Editora, 2014. 239 p.: color ill.

Catalog of an exhibition held in Brasília to celebrate soccer as a major component of national culture, focusing on the transformations in Brazilian art between the World Cup championships of 1950 and 2014. The wide and representative selection was drawn mainly from the holdings of the Museu de Arte de Brasília and local private collections, and encompasses the major art trends produced in Brazil in a variety of technical media. A thematic thread tying the book together is the idea of urban Brazil claiming its own identity. Excellent color reproductions.

141   **Felix, Nelson.** Nelson Felix: 00c0. Curadoria por Rodrigo Naves. Edição de Júlia Ayerbe e Taisa Palhares. São Paulo: Pinacoteca do Estado, Governo do Estado São Paulo, Secretaria de Cultura, 2015. 1 portfolio: bibl., ill.

Nelson Felix (Rio de Janeiro, 1954–) is an avant-garde artist who works around the world, and whose projects include all sorts of raw materials. He intervenes in conventional spaces and in nature, challenging the environment, but also seeking harmony. In many ways, his output is a melding of all of his projects into each other. His drawings, works in their own right, are also drafts of his monumental projects. This book includes his own conceptual statements as well as essays on and interviews with Tadeu Chiarelli, Rodrigo Naves, Francesco Ferrota Bosch, and others. Photographic essays of the displayed works bear witness to how the artist pushes the limits of every medium he works with.

142   Freitas, Artur. Arte de guerrilha: vanguarda e conceitualismo no Brasil. São Paulo: Edusp, 2013. 358 p.: bibl., ill., index.

Combining esthetic analysis and art criticism, the author discusses the countercultural production of avant-garde artists in Brazil from 1969 to 1973, some of the worst years of the military dictatorship. His purpose is to pinpoint the strategies of guerrilla art or, as Freitas says, the "conceptualist project"—a reaction against censorship, loss of civil rights, and political repression. The complexity of the relationship between art and politics is handled with subtlety and conveyed through clear prose. Art and guerrilla were two faces of the same resistance reality. Freitas, however, rejects both direct sociopolitical analysis and the merely formalistic analysis of the Greenberg tradition.

143   Grassmann, Marcelo. Marcello Grassmann. Pesquisa e seleção dos artigos de Mayra Laudanna. Fotografia das obras de Chris von Ameln. São Paulo: SESI-SP Editora, 2013. 263 p.: bibl., ill.

A world-class craftsman, Grassmann (1925–2013) was one of the finest printmakers and draftsmen in Brazil. Basically self taught, he enjoyed short periods of apprenticeship in Rio de Janeiro and Vienna, where he was influenced by Kokoshka, Pechstein and "Die Brücke"; and classified and acclaimed by critics as expressionist, surrealist, hyperrealist, and more. Grassmann was an artist in the fantastic vein. Ethically and esthetically rigorous and disciplined, he studied medieval and Renaissance printing techniques and was fascinated by the pictorial world of Hieronymus Bosch. He incorporated images of warriors, gentlemen, ladies, and animals unknown by zoology into his work, thus creating a universe of his own characterized by metamorphoses of the monstrous into the lyrical and vice versa. Texts and illustrations cover his wood blockprints, etchings, lithographs, drawings, and interviews, including his many critical remarks.

144   Herkenhoff, Paulo. Tomie Ohtake construtiva. Planejamento e projeto de Max Perlingeiro. Coordenação editorial de Camila Perlingeiro. Versão de Julio Silveira. Rio de Janeiro: Edições Pinakotheke: BTGPactual, 2013. 233 p.: bibl., ill.

Arguably the finest representative of informal abstractionism in Brazil, Tomie Ohtake (Kyoto, 1913-São Paulo, 2015) also had close ties to Brazilian constructivism. However, she avoided being labeled as part of any group or movement, instead seeking a creative spontaneity, thus her connection to geometric abstraction has, prior to this work, not been given much attention. In this work, published to celebrate the centennial of her birth, Herkenhoff reflects on Tomie Ohtake's vast oeuvre, offering new perspectives on her work. Herkenhoff delves deeply into the relationship between the work of Tomie Ohtake and Brazil's "vocation to the constructive reason" as Hélio Oiticica puts it in his writings, emphasizing that Ohtake had her own vital, subtle, spiritual esthetic. Excellent graphic project and color reproductions.

145   Instituto Cultural Itaú. 1911–2011: arte brasileira e depois, na Coleção Itaú = 1911–2011: Brazilian art and after, the Itaú Collection. Com curadoria de Teixeira Coelho. Tradução de Ana Goldberger. São Paulo: Itaú Cultural, 2012. 336 p.: bibl., ill., index.

Catalog of the exhibitions held at the Palácio das Artes, Belo Horizonte (July 2011), Paço Imperial do Rio de Janeiro (November 2011), and the Museu Oscar Niemeyer, Curitiba (2012) with almost 4000 works. The Itaú is one of the most representative sets of Brazilian art; of those, almost 200 by 139 artists were selected to be part of the exhibition meant to be a showcase of Brazilian art production from 1911 to 2011, including paintings, sculptures, prints, drawings, watercolors, mixed media, and installations. Rather than organizing the show chronologically, the curator preferred to arrange the works by themes, styles, and ways of thinking, and grouped by topics, all of which are discussed in individual texts.

146 Jobim, Elizabeth. Elizabeth Jobim. Ensaio por Paulo Venancio Filho. Entrevista por Taisa Palhares. São Paulo: Cosac Naify, 2015. 199 p.: bibl., ill.

Before, during, and after her studies in Rio de Janeiro and New York, Elizabeth Jobim (1957–) established a silent dialogue with a number of artists, both traditional and modern. From the ensuing affinities, and from her observations of the very nature of the art materials she worked with, she gradually developed her own esthetic language, first in drawings, then in paintings on paper and canvas and sculptural objects, from small and intimate to gigantic sizes. Fascinated by the plasticity of line and volume acting in space and color, she explores them with great freedom and vitality. Her work demonstrates rigorous geometry and gestural, vigorous, expressive strokes. In her blocks and installations interacting with space, she poses challenging questions to which she finds intuitive, unexpected, and elegant solutions. Excellent graphic project and color reproductions.

147 Madeira, Angélica. Itinerância dos artistas: a construção do campo das artes visuais em Brasília, 1958–2008. Brasília: Editora UnB, 2013. 283 p.: bibl., ill., index.

A critical approach to 50 years of artistic creativity in a planned city with no traditions whatsoever. This saga is seen through historical, sociopolitical, and esthetic lenses. Madeira's multidisciplinary interpretation combines philosophy, history, and postcolonial studies, and she views the new city as a complex artifact.

148 Marcondes, Ana Maria Barbosa de Faria. Travessia periférica: a trajetória do pintor Waldemar Belisário. São Paulo: Imprensa Oficial, Governo do Estado de São Paulo, 2013. 235 p.: bibl., ill.

While the majority of avant-garde artists in São Paulo came from well-to-do families, other artists, many of them Italian immigrants and their descendents, were working in more conservative directions, and were snubbed by most critics for those reasons. Waldemar Belisário (1895–1983) belonged in the latter group, whose legitimacy was rescued by the more open-minded Mário de Andrade. In and out of the art circuits time and again, Belisário attained recognition towards the end of his life. This well-researched book rescues his work from oblivion. Unfortunately, the color reproductions are poorly printed.

149 Mário de Andrade e seus dois pintores: Lasar Segall e Cândido Portinari. Curadoria de Anna Paola Baptista. Textos de Anna Paola Baptista e Guilherme Bueno. Rio de Janeiro: Museus Castro Maya, 2015. 113 p.: bibl., ill.

Lasar Segall and Cândido Portinari were two of the major modernist painters of Brazil, and the focus of the prolific texts by critic Mário de Andrade from the 1920s to the 1940s. His assessments and reassessments of his favorite painters, the complicated relationships he had with each artist, and their personal and esthetic rivalries defined much of the Brazilian art scene of the time. This publication accompanied exhibits at the Castro Maya Museum in Rio de Janeiro and the Lasar Segall Museum in São Paulo (2015) and commemorated the 70th anniversary of Andrade's death.

150 Meireles, Cildo. Cildo Meireles. Edição de João Fernandes. Texto crítico por Guilherme Wisnik e Sérgio B. Martins. Tradução por Izabel Burbridge e Rui Cascais-Parada. São Paulo: Cosac Naify; Porto, Portugal: Serralves, 2013. 251 p.: bibl., ill.

Avant-garde artist Cildo Meireles (1948–), in his 50 years of production, has been encouraging observers and spectators to actively participate in life. His installations in large dimensions, created from 1967 to 2013, predominate in this catalog of a large exhibition that took place in Serralves, Portugal. Also included are extensive critical essays and color illustrations of his works that combine conceptual and sensorial dimensions, as well as linguistic semantic games and constructive rules that exemplify the artist's favorite themes: territory, values scale, exchange processes, and relations of power. Text and statements by the artist are also presented. Excellent graphic production.

151 As novas regras do jogo: o sistema da arte no Brasil. Organização por Maria Amélia Bulhões. Textos por Nei Vargas da Rosa, Bettina Rupp, e Bruna Fetter. Porto

Alegre, Brazil: Zouk editora, 2014. 141 p.: bibl.

Very interesting study in pocket-book format about the visual arts in Brazil. Offers a historical perspective on the traditional and not-so-traditional relationships among the various participants in the production, exhibition, and circulation of the arts, starting in 1960. Also critically examines how the art world adapts to social, economic, and political conditions and to the cycles of consumer demand. Each contributor draws on personal experience to explore a particular aspect of Brazilian art: artistic practices, entrepreneurship, exhibition to curatorship, and the contemporary Brazilian art market. [F. Angel]

152   **Projeto construtivo brasileiro na arte.** Supervisão, coordenação geral e pesquisa de Aracy A. Amaral. Edição facsimilar. São Paulo: Pinacoteca do Estado, Governo do Estado São Paulo, Secretaria da Cultura, 2015. 357 p.: bibl., ill. (some color).

Arguably one of the most original Brazilian contributions to the international constructivist projects, this publication accompanied the now historic exhibition of São Paulo concretism and its offspring, the neoconcretism movement of Rio de Janeiro. The publication is currently the most important and most encompassing source of research for this area of study. Contains documents, manifestos, texts of the period, visual and literary participant artists, texts from the 1970s, international historical context, and an extensive essential bibliography. For comment on the original 1977 publication, see *HLAS 42:490*.

153   **Ramos, Nuno.** Houyhnhnm. São Paulo: Estação Pinacoteca, 2015. 3 v.: bibl., ill.

Known for the complexity of his art, made of art materials combined with debris of many sorts, Nuno Ramos (São Paulo, 1960-) creates large, expressive, bold, unconventional works and installations exhibited in museums, art galleries, and many other spaces in- and outdoors. This particular show consisted of "Vaselinas" and "Dádivas," created in drawings and reliefs, produced mostly in the very space of the exhibit, and inspired by both the artist's previous works and the Greek myths of Proteus and Menelaus, as well as by Van Gogh and American neoexpressionists. Included in the book are critical essays by curator Lorenzo Mammi, a minute-detailed chronology by Marcelo Vieira, a literary essay by Noemi Jaffe, and photos by several photographers.

154   **Rubens Gerchman: o rei do mau gosto.** Organização por Clara Gerchman. Tradução por Vítor Cortes. São Paulo: J.J. Carol Editora, 2013. 192 p.: bibl., ill.

Rubens Gerchman was a prominent avant-garde artist in Rio de Janeiro. He studied at the Escola Nacional de Belas Artes. With a Guggenheim scholarship, he traveled in Central America and then lived two years in New York, where he experienced the impact of Pop Art. Back in Brazil, he got engaged in protest art and innovative esthetic movements by integrating elements of daily events and the painted word. Later, he converted words into objects with paint and industrial materials. His four children inherited many of his paintings, prints, drawings, objects, correspondence, working materials, and memorabilia that are now part of the archive of the Rubens Gerchman Institute. This book contains a sampling of those items, including statements by and letters from the most representative poets, writers, critics, and artists of his generation, along with his close friends.

155   **30 x bienal: transformações na arte brasileira da 1a à 30a edição.** Curadoria de Paulo Venancio Filho. Textos selecionados por Alberto Tassinari *et al*. Tradução por Matthew Rinaldi e Cid Knipel. São Paulo: Bienal São Paulo, 2013. 305 p.: bibl., ill.

The catalog covers the transformations of Brazilian art as recorded in 30 editions of the São Paulo Bienal, from 1951 to 2012, through a selection of art works of all past editions and a selection of texts published in daily newspapers and specialized magazines. The catalog seeks to recreate the atmosphere of each year, laying out the debates, polemics, and controversies. Despite any controversies, the São Paulo Bienal is arguably one of the world's best international art shows. The event has been responsible for stimulating and shaping modern and contemporary Brazilian art traditions, and helping Brazilian artists gain worldwide recognition, while providing them with opportunities to connect with international artists and other members of the art world.

156   **Verdade, fraternidade, arte: secessão de Dresden, Grupo 1919 e contemporâneos.** Com curadoria de Vera d'Horta. São Paulo: Museu Lasar Segall, 2011. 156 p.: ill.

An offspring of the Wiener Sezession, the Dresdner Sezession brought together a number of young artists whose works exerted a strong impact on the history of modern art at large and on expressionism in particular. Their avant-garde works broke with scholasticism and decorative values, and also with naturalism, cubism, and futurism. Their aim was to criticize societal injustices. Among the artists were Otto Dix, George Grosz, Käthe Kollwitz, and Lasar Segall, who eventually settled down in São Paulo. The catalog of the exhibition shows the 50 works in various media selected from the museum's holdings and from several public and private collections in Brazil to commemorate and honor the artists of that generation and their contemporaries who shared their ideas and esthetic orientation. The introductory text sets the stage for the exhibition. Excellent reproductions, chronology, and documentation included. Texts are in Portuguese and English.

FOLK ART

157   **O Brasil na visualidade popular.** Concepção e curadoria de José Alberto Nemer. Rio de Janeiro: Caixa Cultural, 2007. 134 p.: ill.

Catalog of an exhibition designed to display spontaneous visual, mostly anonymous expressions of ordinary Brazilian people from all over the country, as a statement of their creativity, passionate love for Brazil, and pride in being Brazilians. Rather than scholarly or even analytical, the text is written in an enthusiastically nationalistic tone, focusing strongly on the colors of Brazil's flag, namely green, yellow, and blue. The images themselves, all related to the flag, and featuring saints, politicians, popular icons, fauna, flora, and so forth, are imaginative, cheerful, and engaging, even when linked to propaganda.

158   **Lima, Ricardo Gomes.** O povo do Candeal: caminhos da louça de barro. Rio de Janeiro: Aeroplano Editora, 2012. 458 p.: bibl., ill., maps. (Coleção Circuitos da cultura popular; 5)

Originally presented as the author's PhD thesis (2006, Universidade Federal do Rio de Janeiro), this massive study focuses on utilitarian pottery-making in Cardeal, a community at the São Francisco River basin in northwest Minas Gerais, Central do Brasil. Their production of plain, but very beautiful, painted ceramics is vitally important for the subsistence of the community. This study examines the physical space, generational knowledge, gender and social dynamics, as well as native symbolism, esthetic valves, and state policies for the protection of folklore and craftsmanship. This publication is a model of multidisciplinary research on the field of folk art.

PHOTOGRAPHY

159   **Beltramim, Fabiana.** Sujeitos iluminados: a reconstituição das experiências vividas no estúdio de Christiano Jr. São Paulo: Alameda, 2013. 379 p.: bibl.; ill.

A study of Christiano Junior's photographic work in Rio de Janeiro from 1864 to 1866, which was originally presented as the author's MA thesis at Pontifícia Universidade Católica de São Paulo, 2009. José Christiano de Freitas Henriques Junior (1832–1902) was a Portuguese-born photographer who emigrated to Brazil and later moved to Argentina. The photos studied in this work are mostly studio portraits which were then sold as souvenirs in Brazil. His images are the largest set of photographs of the black population in Rio during Emperor Dom Pedro II's era. This work compares Christiano Junior's photos to the production of other photographers during the same period. The book discusses the various ways in which these photos were used in a society with a social structure heavily influenced by race.

160   **Chiriboga, Fernando.** Relíquias: patrimônio arquitetônico do Nordeste do Brasil. Tradução por Jennifer Sarah Cooper. Natal, Brazil: Intì, 2014. 252 p.: bibl., ill.

Ecuadorian painter, designer, and photographer (the latter is his primary occupation) Fernando Chiriboga has been living in

Natal, Brazil since 1985. In love with Brazilian traditions, he photographed Northeastern Brazil's wealth of religious, secular, and military architecture, monuments, paintings, sculpture, and decorative arts, which date from the 16th to the 20th century in nine states and 15 cities. A representative selection is presented in this publication, along with some basic information on the items. Landscapes, cityscapes, and seascapes are included. While this work does not offer a scholarly analysis or a robust bibliography, it nonetheless provides an excellent visual introduction to the topic.

161 Gautherot, Marcel. Marcel Gautherot: photographies. Sous la direction de Samuel Titan Jr. et Sergio Burgi. Paris: Éditions Hervé Chopin, 2016. 251 p.: ill.

Catalog of an exhibition held at the Maison Européenne de la Photographie, Paris, 15 June–28 August 2016. When Marcel Gautherot (Paris, 1910–Rio de Janeiro, 1996) settled for good in Brazil in 1940 after studies in Paris and travels in Greece, Mexico, and Morocco, he was already an accomplished photographer. Chiefly interested in architecture and people, Gautherot is linked to the history of modern photography in Brazil, where he explored a number of themes through his photography in several areas of the country. Thanks to his close association with architects Oscar Niemeyer and Lúcio Costa he reached the peak of his career as a photographer of Brazil. Noted for his formal discipline and refinement, and his extraordinary esthetic quality, he created a body of work consisting of ca. 25,000 images in b/w and in color. His archives are housed at the Instituto Moreira Salles.

162 Silva, Fabiana Bruce da. Caminhando numa cidade de luz e sombras: a fotografia moderna no Recife na década de 1950. Recife, Brazil: Fundação Joaquim Nabuco, Editora Massangana, 2013. 355 p.: bibl., ill.

Originally presented as the author's PhD thesis at Universidade Federal Rural de Pernambuco (2005), this contribution to the history of photography in Brazil contains the following topics: Perceber e compreender o ato fotográfico; Na história da fotografia, o lugar do Recife; Uma imagem moderna no Recife na década de 1950; Reflexões sobre a fotografia no Recife; Entre história e fotografia, a arte fotográfica do FCCR; Considerações finais: entre fotografias e textos, algumas histórias.

CITY PLANNING, ARCHITECTURE, AND LANDSCAPE ARCHITECTURE

163 Al Assal, Marianna Boghosian. Arquitetura e identidade nacional no Estado Novo: as Escolas Práticas de Agricultura do Estado de São Paulo. São Paulo: FAPESP; Annablume, 2013. 281 p.: bibl., ill.

Based on the author's MA thesis (USP, 2010), this study examines the relationship between nationalism and architecture, and political projects and architecture, during President Getúlio Vargas' dictatorship. The author focuses particularly on the state's intervention in the affairs of São Paulo in the early 1940s when agricultural colleges were established in various areas of the state. The preferred neocolonial style was already anachronistic but very much tied to nationalism. The persistence of that style has not, until now, been assessed in a sociopolitical or historical context.

164 Bastos, Rodrigo. A arte do urbanismo conveniente: o decoro na implantação de novas povoações em Minas Gerais na primeira metade do século XVIII. Florianópolis, Brazil: Editora UFSC, 2014. 245 p.: bibl., ill. Coleção Urbanismo e arquitetura da cidade

Tradition has it that settlements in Minas Gerais were "spontaneous," irregular, with no order whatsoever. This extensively researched book, originally a MA thesis (2003), proposes that those settlements were instead orderly and regular, particularly in the 18th century. To strengthen his argument, Bastos analyzes city planning in Ouro Preto and Mariana, whose architectural traditions can be traced to Portuguese influences during the 16th and 17th centuries. Extensive bibliography and appropriate (albeit poorly printed) illustrations make this work a welcome contribution to the field.

165 Bem, Sueli de. Conversa de patrimônio em Jundiaí. São Paulo: EDUSP, 2014. 374 p.: bibl., ill.

Based on author's PhD thesis, the text deals with the right to information about the historic past of urban dwellings as key to understanding what should be restored or preserved. Architect Sueli de Bem worked in several preservation-related institutions and chose Jundiaí in São Paulo state as a case study for her research and reflections on historic preservation in the 21st century. Jundiaí has a colonial past, a railway tradition that brought industry to the town, and its own contemporary issues and contradictions. Documental sources and bibliography are provided.

166 **Carsalade, Flávio de Lemos.** A pedra e o tempo: arquitetura como patrimônio cultural = Stone and time: architecture as cultural heritage. Tradução para o inglês por Marcel de Lima Santos. Belo Horizonte, Brazil: Editora UFMG, 2014. 639 p.: bibl., ill.

A philosophical inquiry on preservation and restoration of architectural structures and urban spaces seen from hermeneutical and phenomenological perspectives in order to understand architecture as historical patrimony. The author studies the relationship between architecture and the other arts as well as the contradictions of architectural intervention to preserve a "patrimony object." This is a relevant contribution to the speculative aspects of a major problem. Rich illustrations and extensive bibliography.

167 **Costa, Sabrina Studart Fontenele.**
Edifícios modernos e o traçado urbano no centro de São Paulo (1938–1960). São Paulo: Annablume, 2015. 251 p.: bibl., ill., maps.

This book examines urban transformations and the skyscrapers built in the new city center around the Praça da República in São Paulo, from the 1940s to the 1960s. The interplay between the public and the private sectors and the new economic context demanded new legislation, which in turn, stimulated a new approach to the rentability of spaces changing the connections between private and commercial spaces. As buildings changed, urban life itself changed and new forms of commerce, entertainment, shopping styles, and public and private life developed.

168 **Do Valongo à favela: imaginário e periferia.** Organização de Clarissa Diniz e Rafael Cardoso. Textos por Carlos Gradim *et al.* Versão em inglês por Anthony Doyle. Rio de Janeiro: Odeon Instituto: Museu de Arte do Rio, 2015. 223 p.: bibl., ill.

In the 19th century Cais do Valongo, in the Rio de Janeiro port area, was the largest slave trade market in the world. The catalog of this exhibition points to the tragedy of slavery and the African diaspora, and to the development of favelas in Rio as the most conspicuous feature of the new exclusion of freed slaves in the postcolonial period. Texts discuss the contribution of Afro-Brazilians to the development of Rio de Janeiro's cityscape, as well as to Brazil at large. The authors reflect on the origins, imagery, and representations of Rio's port over time. Well illustrated with historical iconography, modern art, and photography.

169 **Kruchin, Samuel.** Kruchin, uma poética da história: obra de restauro. Tradução por Elizabeth Rayes. São Paulo: C4, 2012. 356 p.: bibl., ill.

Architect Samuel Kruchin is known for his restorations of major public, residential, and industrial buildings originally built from the 1860s to the 1940s. He has shown concern for their relevance as they relate to the history of the city of São Paulo and other cities in São Paulo state. This book covers several of his projects, and has as a "central theme the analysis of the concepts of interventions and the specific methodological procedures that those works involve. . . . This publication also presents theoretical texts, with the purpose of altering the discussion about the architectural heritage while being historically visible."

170 **Lemos, Carlos Alberto Cerqueira.** Da taipa ao concreto: crônicas e ensaios sobre a memória da arquitetura e do urbanismo. Organização por José Tavares Correia de Lira. São Paulo: Três Estrelas, 2013. 303 p.: bibl., ill., index.

The work collects articles by Carlos Alberto Cerqueira Lemos (1925), most of them previously published in the Brazilian newspaper *Folha de São Paulo*. Lemos is one of the chief historians of Brazilian architecture and a professor at FAU-USP. He has been a champion for the defense and preservation of the architectural and urban patrimony of the country. With over 50 essays, this book bears witness to his struggles to convey the value of urban architecture to fellow Brazilians. The essays are analytical and polemic, and show the value of preserving collective patrimony of São Paulo and other cities.

171   Mello, Joana. O arquiteto e a produção da cidade: a experiência de Jacques Pilon, 1930–1960. São Paulo: Annablume, 2012. 257 p.: bibl., ill.

Based on her PhD thesis (Universidade de São Paulo, 2010), Mello uses the life and career of French architect Jacques Pilon (1905–62) as an example of foreign architects who contributed to the development of modern architecture in São Paulo and the creation of the megalopolis and its urban features. This thoughtful study shows how urban architecture develops out of and helps inform the social and economic circumstances of cities.

172   Rufinoni, Manoela Rossinetti. Preservação e restauro urbano: intervenções em sítios históricos industriais. São Paulo: Editora FAP-UNIFESP, 2013. 358 p.: bibl., ill.

Rufinoni looks at problems related to the preservation and interpretation of urban patrimony, including how to assess architecture and city planning today and how to achieve harmony between built patrimony and the material and immaterial dimensions that make up cities and life in them. It is also important to consider the legacy left for future generations. As the author states, "we must look for new forms of understanding and respecting the preexisting features of cities, and how to coexist with them and their transformations." Extensive national and international bibliography and photographic materials.

173   Sánchez Llorens, Mara. Lina Bo Bardi: objetos y acciones colectivas. Buenos Aires: Diseño Editorial, 2015. 313 p.: bibl., ill. (Textos de arquitectura y diseño)

Before immigrating to Brazil in 1946, Lina Bo Bardi (Rome, 1914-São Paulo, 1992) studied and practiced architecture in her native Italy. Her work was influenced by European avant-garde and Bauhaus styles (the latter absorbed during a stay in Chicago). She fell in love with Brazil, where she also practiced architecture. Bo Bardi strove to include local elements in her work. Her innovative design ideas included the use of thousands of industrial and craft objects. This study explores her extraordinary imagination and creativity from the intricate structures to the minute details.

174   Silva, Elcio Gomes da. Os palácios originais de Brasília. Brasília: Câmara dos Deputados, Centro de Documentação e Informação: Edições Câmara, 2014. 403 p.: bibl., ill. (Série Arte e cultura; 11)

Based on meticulous analyses of the original documentation and plans for the construction of public buildings in Brasília from 1956 to 1961, Silva studies the contributions of engineer Joaquim Cardozo to the esthetic ideas of architect Oscar Niemeyer. Joaquim Cardozo's analytical geometry equations were crucial to building Niemeyer's designs, including the now iconic columns of the Palácio do Planalto and the Palácio Alvorada, and the domes of the Congresso Nacional. Silva meticulously studies each of the palaces, always bearing in mind the indissoluble relationship between artistic creation and engineering support. This visually rich volume is a welcome scholarly contribution to the history of architecture in Brazil.

175   Simpósio "Memória, Trabalho e Arquitetura," *São Paulo, 2010.* Memória, trabalho e arquitetura. Organização de João Marcos Lopes e José Lira. São Paulo: CPC, Centro de Preservação Cultural, USP: EDUSP, 2013. 367 p.: bibl., ill. (Estudos CPC; 3)

Collection of 20 papers originally presented at the Simpósio "Memória, Trabalho e Arquitetura," held 6–7 December 2010 at the Universidade de São Paulo, reassessing the conventional idea of architecture as a solitary intellectual accomplishment. The papers describe architecture as a process of giving materiality to history, which includes technical elements and decorative work and is reliant on industrial progress.

176   Weimer, Günter. Inter-relações afro-brasileiras na arquitetura. Curitiba, Brazil: PUCPRess; Porto Alegre, Brazil: ediPUCRS, 2014. 325 p.: bibl., ill.

This interdisciplinary study combines architecture, history, and anthropology. Subdivided into three parts, the text presents varieties of African architecture and city and village planning, the development of African architecture in the

Brazilian diaspora, and finally the presence of Brazil in African architecture—the latter introduced by freed slaves who returned to their countries of origin. This publication is already considered a fundamental reference in the field. Includes many images and a glossary of African and other terms.

AFRO-BRAZILIAN AND INDIAN TRADITIONS

Beltramim, Fabiana. Sujeitos iluminados: a reconstituição das experiências vividas no estúdio de Christiano Jr. See item **159**.

Da cartografia do poder aos itinerários do saber. See item **181**.

Do Valongo à favela: imaginário e periferia. See item **168**.

177   Pacheco, Ana Paula Soares. A arte através do tempo: uma análise iconográfica dos desenhos xinguanos. Cruz das Almas, Brazil: Editora UFRB, 2015. 164 p.: bibl., ill.

This study provides an iconographical analysis of the human and geographical nature of the Xingu area in Brazil, considered sacred by the native Amerindian culture of that region. Explanations of the graphic representations of humans, animals, supernatural beings, and fetishes are based on research from the 19th century by Prince Adalbert of Prussia to the present. These images are studied from iconographic, anthropological, and artistic perspectives, indicating the symbolic and mythological elements present in the drawings. The iconography described here is still produced today in the majority of those cultures.

Weimer, Günter. Inter-relações afro-brasileiras na arquitetura. See item **176**.

MISCELLANEOUS

178   Arte botânica no Paraná. Coordenação de Projetos de Raul Böing. Produção executiva de Simone Ribeiro. Versão para o inglês de Silvia M.K. Breiby e Danusa P. Corradine Knuth. Curitiba, Brazil: Centro de Ilustração Botânica do Paraná-CIBP, 2014. 280 p., 128 pages of plates: bibl., ill., indexes.

Although European naturalists and botanical artists have been recording Brazilian flora in drawing, watercolors, oil painting, lithographs, and etchings since the 16th century, it was not until recent decades that Brazilian artists started producing similar work. After Margaret Mead's botanical watercolors resulting from her Brazilian expeditions were met with international critical acclaim, several centers of scientific art illustration have been flourishing in the country. The Centro de Ilustração Botânica do Paraná (CIBP) was established in the late 1990s, and has been very productive since. This publication, focusing on the flora of the state of Paraná, gathered almost 200 species illustrated by 15 local artists. A caption accompanies each work. Includes extensive scholarly texts.

179   Basbaum, Ricardo. Manual do artista-etc. Rio de Janeiro: Azougue Editorial, 2013. 264 p.: bibl.

This collection of 24 essays by art critic Ricardo Basbaum is mainly based on his concept of the flux between art and discourse, looking at the new systems as a "necessity of seeking for new patterns of relationship between texts and art works that lead us to believe that writing can play a marvelous role in the expansion of the senses if the works are linked to the art works in a special and interesting way."

180   Creni, Gisela. Editores artesanais brasileiros. Belo Horizonte, Brazil: Autêntica; Rio de Janeiro: Fundação Biblioteca Nacional, 2013. 159 p.: ill.

This carefully planned and printed book leads the reader through the rarefied world of the small presses in Brazil. The editors concentrate on very limited editions, usually hand-printed books of (more often than not) Brazilian and foreign poets, aimed at bibliophiles. Those editions combine high-quality texts illustrated by fine artists and laid out with graphic refinement. In some cases, the books, artworks in their own right, are made by the poet. This book includes some of the best examples of these Brazilian limited editions.

181   Da cartografia do poder aos itinerários do saber. Com curadoria de Catarina Pires, Paulo Bernaschina, e Emanoel Araujo. São Paulo: Museu Afro Brasil, Governo do Estado São Paulo, Secretaria da Cultura, 2014. 239 p.: bibl., ill., index, maps.

Catalog of an exhibition held in Portugal in 2012, then in 2014 in an enlarged version, at Oca Ibirapuera, São Paulo, to celebrate 10 years of the Museu Afro Brasil and the centennial of the Faculdade de Ciências, Universidade da Coimbra. Texts by various scholars, past and present, point to the advancement of scientific research in Portugal in a variety of fields, including anthropology, natural sciences, medicine, astronomy, mathematics, philosophy, botany, and mineralogy. In order to better understand and dominate its colonies in Africa, Asia, and the Americas, Portugal attempted to gather scientific information about those lands and therefore gathered representative samples of naturally occurring and human-made objects, including artwork. The exhibit included objects and artwork from several countries.

182 As descobertas do Brasil: o olhar estrangeiro na construção da imagem do Brasil. Organização de Ana Cecilia Impellizieri Martins e Monique Sochaczewski. Textos de Jean Marcel Carvalho França, Teresa Cribelli, e Maurício Parada. Rio de Janeiro: Casa da Palavra, 2014. 239 p.: bibl., ill.

This book tells the story of how foreigners saw Brazil since the colonial era and discusses the many immigrants who helped create the richness and complexity of the country. History chronicles, documents, diaries, and biographical information are illustrated with engravings, drawing, maps, and photos. Useful for the classroom, the book provides an introduction to Brazil.

183 História e cultura estudantil: revistas na USP. Organização por José Tavares Correia de Lira. São Paulo: Centro de Preservação Cultural da USP: EDUSP, 2012. 339 p.: bibl., ill.

A survey of the student magazines from the early 1900s to the present produced in various departments of the Universidade de São Paulo. Of special interest are the artwork and design of the covers of the publications.

184 Modernidade: coleção de arte brasileira Odorico Tavares. Curadoria e organização por Emanoel Araujo. São Paulo: Museu Afro Brasil, 2013. 215 p.: bibl., ill., index

Catalog of an exhibition held at the Museu Afro Brasil between 25 April and 4 August 2013. Poet, writer, journalist, world traveler, and art collector Odorico Tavares (1912–80), was an enthusiast of Brazilian art and of art at large. He befriended and supported many of his contemporary artists, promoted their major solo-shows, helped found several art museums in Brazil, and acquired works of Brazilian modernism, as well as colonial sculptures, folk art, Afro-Brazilian art, and works by European artists he befriended such as Miró, Picasso, Rouault, De Pisis, and others. Some of his poems and texts on his own collection—one of reverential quality—are included in this catalog. An attractive graphic project with excellent color reproductions.

185 Mulheres de outrora, bordados de agora. Organização de Jaci Ferreira e Olinda Evangelista. Prefácio de Tânia Aiello Vaisberg. Maringá, Brazil: EDUEM, 2013. 80 p.: bibl., ill.

Biographies and letters of 50 Brazilian women of stature in the arts, illustrated with embroidery by 15 women and one man, inspired by the personalities and accomplishments of their models, all of them national icons.

186 Museu de Arte do Rio Grande do Sul Ado Malagoli. MARGS: catálogo geral. Coordenação geral de Raul Holtz. Tradução de Camila Pasquetti. Porto Alegre, Brazil: Museu de Arte do Rio Grande do Sul Ado Malagoli, 2013. 468 p.: ill., index.

Established in the mid-19th century, this museum has about 3,600 holdings (as of 2012), including paintings, sculpture, works on paper, mixed media, and installation. All of them are reproduced in this catalog in small photos, presented in alphabetical order by the artists' first names. Eight essays by different scholars precede the illustrations. Their topics are: Programa de apoio ao patrimonio cultural brasileiro, Apresentação de um patrimonio artistico, A memória das coisas, Programa e estratégia museológica, a excelencia de um acervo, and O projeto de digitalização do acervo do MARGS. Good source for research.

187 Pedrosa, Mário. Mario Pedrosa. Organização de César Oiticica Filho. Rio de Janeiro: Beco do Azougue Editorial, 2014. 189 p.: bibl., index. (Encontros)

In addition to being one of the most active Brazilian intellectuals of the 20th century, Mario Pedrosa (1900–81) was also instrumental in some of the major transformations in art and politics in Brazil from 1945 to 1981 and beyond, and arguably vital for the development of concretism in Brazil. His sharp intellect and vision as an art critic are evident in his interviews with noted artists and intellectuals over a period of more than 30 years. He was also influential in the international art scene.

188   **Representações da fauna no Brasil: séculos XVI–XX.** Organização de Lorelai Kury. Contribuções de Felipe F. Vander Velden, Bruno Martins Boto Leite, Lorelai Kury, Magali Romero Sá, e José Luiz de Andrade Franco. Versão para o inglês de Chris Hieatt. Rio de Janeiro: Andrea Jakobsson Estúdio, 2014. 280 p.: bibl., ill.

Seven scholarly essays provide a broad account of five centuries of representation of fauna in Brazil—both native plants and those brought by Europeans during and after colonization. Most of the illustrated species are done artistically, in color, sepia, and black and white. The authors describe the changing historical view of Brazil's environment from the colonial-era perspective of environment as a marvel of God's creation to contemporary scientific and ecological approaches. The contributions include Catholic missionaries' views and naturalists' studies, among others. As Lorelai Kury puts it, the book discusses the "profound and gradual changes in the attitudes of humans . . . from Providentialism to the belief that man was just one more among God's creatures." Excellent graphic layout and printing.

189   **Resistir é preciso. . . .** Organização de Fabio Magalhães. Textos de Miriam Leitão, Fabio Magalhães e José Luiz Del Roio. São Paulo: Editora Instituto Vladimir Herzog, 2013. 194 p.: bibl., ill.

Brazil was governed by a military dictatorship from 1964 to 1985. This exhibition aimed to shed light on the role of the media and artists in acts of resistance; an underground media of resistance expanded across the country during that time. The exhibit gathered an impressive collection of works of art that shows the vigor with which artists clamored for democracy and denounced the abuses and crimes of the dictatorship. During the years of military rule, thousands of people were arrested and tortured, hundreds were killed, and many are still missing. Facsimiles, snapshots, and posters show the realities of those days.

190   **Sousa, Márcia Regina Pereira de.**
O livro de artista como lugar tátil. Florianópolis, Brazil: UDESC, Universidade do Estado de Santa Catarina, 2011. 230 p.: bibl., ill., index.

This study deals with the definitions of artists' books, handcrafted objects produced as unique works of art or in very limited editions. Based on traditional bookmaking, artists' books expand the notion of a book as an object, experimenting with their physical, tactile, and esthetic aspects. The text examines theoretical and technical issues of bookmaking and artists' books, focusing on Brazilian production. The author views artists' books as a sculpture of sorts within the context of the fine arts.

HISTORY

ETHNOHISTORY
Mesoamerica

BRADLEY BENTON, *Professor of History, North Dakota State University*
PETER VILLELLA, *Associate Professor of History, University of North Carolina at Greensboro*

AS DEMONSTRATED BY the articles and books reviewed in this bibliography, the ethnohistory of Mesoamerica remains a fertile and productive area of professional scholarship. Due to the antiquity and diversity of its human traditions and the sheer quantity of its material sources, countless avenues remain to be explored. Meanwhile, given ever-evolving analytical techniques and concerns, there is much to learn by revisiting and reinterpreting more familiar and synthetic sources.

Both of these approaches are evident among the most recently published ethnohistorical scholarship on Mesoamerica. Some works apply proven methods to unstudied communities, while others return to well-traveled paths with fresh questions and interpretive lenses. The overall trend is toward the ongoing diversification of the field, as traditional ethnohistorical concerns and methods provide a springboard for exploring new and innovative inquiries. The result is a field in which practitioners continue to seek out new materials and approaches, while also cultivating ever more sophisticated renderings of established findings.

Scholars continue to produce traditional ethnohistorical examinations of specific indigenous communities or social groups, following well-defined and broadly understood divisions. As usual, due to the availability of rich and copious ethnohistorical sources from the early colonial period, the peoples of central and southern Mexico continue to receive the lion's share of scholarly attention, with the Maya *cah* and the Nahua *altepetl*, or ethnic polity, continuing as a primary focal point. Exemplifying studies of this sort are *Vida indígena en la colonia*, edited by María Teresa Jarquín Ortega (item **244**), and Pilar Gonzalbo's research into the process by which Mexico-Tlatelolco (item **214**) became socially and ethnically integrated into the burgeoning urban milieu of 18th-century Mexico City. The Acolhua region of the Nahua world, centered around prehispanic Tetzcoco in today's Estado de México, has attracted a flurry of scholarship lately, as evidenced by recent books by Bradley Benton (item **474**), Patrick Lesbre (item **223**), and Benjamin D. Johnson (item **220**). Lisa Sousa unites proven methods of philology and gender history to shed light on the diverse experiences of colonial Mesoamerican women (item **237**), while Edward Anthony Polanco's essay on Nahua *tiçiyotl*, or healing arts, reveals that close philological and analytical readings of colonial texts still have much to reveal about prehispanic culture and society (item **229**).

Scholars continue to extend ethnohistorical methods pioneered in central and southern Mexico into other parts of Mesoamerica. Multiple new works address the peoples of Michoacán, the Bajío, and Central America. Sarah Albiez's study of the Tarascan state of Michoacán (item **191**) is of particular ethnohistorical importance, as are Juan Ricardo Jiménez Goméz's transcriptions and extended analyses of archival documentation pertaining to the Otomí population of colonial Querétaro (items **216**, **217**, and **218**). In their article, Prudence M. Rice and Don S. Rice hint at a promising model of interdisciplinary scholarship: by placing archeological evidence and colonial-ethnohistorical sources from the central Petén region in dialogue, the authors perceive deep continuities in leadership structures and spatial organization among the lowland Maya from the classic period to the era of Spanish contact (item **232**). Going further, Mesoamerica is invariably well-represented in hemispheric studies of indigenous peoples, such as the recent collection of essays on the native experience in Spanish America edited by Mónica Díaz (item **989**), or Mark Christensen and Jonathan Truitt's exposition of indigenous wills from across the colonial Americas and their ethnohistorical significance (item **226**).

As they have for centuries, Mesoamerican religious systems remain a central academic preoccupation, especially precolonial practices and their colonial-era reverberations. Given the nature of the primary source materials available for such analyses—and the fact that the first Spanish clergy confiscated and destroyed many Mesoamerican religious texts—art historians remain at the forefront of these efforts, along with anthropologists and archeologists. Building on generations of research, their works often pursue emic, endogenous explanations of the spiritual significance of religious practices or cultural phenomena. Patrick Johansson K.'s examination of central Mexican funerary rites exemplifies these efforts (item **219**), as does a new volume, published by Dumbarton Oaks and edited by Vera Tiesler and Andrew K. Scherer (item **235**), that explores ritual uses of fire and body-burning across multiple Mesoamerican societies. A second, perennially prominent area in the study of Mesoamerican religion, addresses colonial-era syncretism, how native beliefs and practices influenced Spanish-American Catholicism and vice versa. The increasing sophistication of this approach, which goes beyond overt beliefs and actions, is modeled by Amara Solari's examination of the "spatial ideologies" of the Maya colonial Yucatan (item **236**). Scholars are also increasingly interested in "indigenous Christianities"—that is, the ways that the religious systems imported from Europe became naturalized and transformed once transplanted to American spiritual soil. A new collection of essays, edited by David Tavárez (item **246**) addresses precisely this idea; while Elizabeth Hill Boone, Louise M. Burkhart, and David Tavárez (item **197**) highlight a pictorial catechism from colonial Atzaqualco to derive insights about Nahua Catholicism and community memory.

Given their complexity, esotericism, and sheer diversity, much scholarship pertaining to Mesoamerican ethnohistory directly addresses the field's sources. Multiple new works highlight a particular document or material source—or a collection of sources—and seek to explain its historical and cultural significance. Maya epigraphy remains a major area of study, as evidenced by Catherine Burdick's article on depictions of prisoners in late classic Maya sculpture (item **202**). Mesoamerican maps and pictorial documents, whether precolonial or colonial, also continue to draw attention, with Baltazar Brito Guadarrama's study (item **201**) of a colonial codex and Néstor I. Quiroga's reinterpretation of the *Popul Vuh* exemplifying this kind of research (item **230**).

Colonial alphabetic documents by native authors or about indigenous culture and history also continue to receive attention. Some new English-language translations of colonial works of ethnohistorical relevance have appeared, such as Stafford Poole's translation of Lorenzo Boturini Benaducci's 18th-century call for a reinterpretation of Mesoamerican history by way of native-authored sources (item **198**). There is also a host of new research into the life and works of the 16th-century Spanish Franciscan friar Bernardino de Sahagún—sometimes considered the first ethnographer of the Americas—much of which derives from a series of investigations at the Instituto de Investigaciones Históricas of the Universidad Nacional Autónoma de México. Pilar Máynez and José Rubén Romero Galván have edited a wide-ranging collection of essays by UNAM's Sahagún scholars (item **243**). Senior collaborator Miguel León-Portilla brought his considerable experience to a generously illustrated edition that essentially replicates the Sahaguntine project for a modern audience (item **222**).

For various reasons, there has been a resurgence of interest in the 17th-century collector and historian Fernando de Alva Ixtlilxóchitl. Descended from Spanish settlers and Nahua nobility, Ixtlilxóchitl is a source for both precontact history and for the colonial world in which he lived. Amber Brian, Bradley Benton, and Pablo García Loaeza recently translated Alva Ixtlilxóchitl's chronicle of the Spanish conquest told from the perspective of a native leader who allied with Hernando Cortés (item **192**). In a separate work, Brian interprets the compilation and posthumous fate of Alva Ixtlilxóchitl's "archive" of ethnohistorical materials, an epistemologically powerful source of knowledge about Nahua history that continues to substantially influence the trajectory of Mesoamerican studies (item **199**). Complementing these works, a special issue of *Colonial Latin America Review*, edited by Camilla Townsend and dedicated to Alva Ixtlilxóchitl, assesses his life and works from multiple angles (items **195**, **200**, **241**, and **245**).

Another group of works reassesses colonial history in the light of Mesoamerican ethnohistorical sources more generally. Most prominently, on the strength of his knowledge of recently rediscovered and reinterpreted colonial indigenous accounts of the Spanish invasion of 1519–21, Matthew Restall (item **231**) questions the very notion of a "conquest"—a five-centuries-old idea—finding it to be a largely self-justifying and triumphalist Spanish invention of later generations rather than an objective description of the historical event itself. Such reinterpretations of familiar materials are certain to continue paying scholarly dividends in coming years.

The field of Mesoamerican ethnohistory clearly remains strong and growing along several trajectories—conceptually, regionally, and methodologically. As more sources are uncovered in archives and collections throughout the region and abroad, and as innovative academic frameworks are applied to previously analyzed artifacts and writings, new discoveries and lines of inquiry continue to emerge. Scholars are also extending established methodologies into heretofore under-researched regions—a process that frequently lends itself to comparative analysis, and therefore challenges the seemingly settled assumptions about more studied communities. Due to the nature of its sources, Mesoamerican ethnohistory invites participation from multiple academic disciplines, including history, art history, archeology, literary studies, and anthropology. Greater scholarly collaboration and interdisciplinarity are sure to yield ever more innovative conclusions. It is also clear from new research that Mesoamericanist scholars are helping to situate the region's place within universal global history and anthropology as an autonomous cradle of human civilization—an effort exemplified by the recent work of Miguel López-Portilla (item **222**). All four trends suggest that the field remains vibrant and productive, with many routes yet to traverse.

191 **Albiez, Sarah.** Contactos exteriores del Estado Tarasco: influencias desde dentro y fuera de Mesoamérica. Zamora, Mexico: El Colegio de Michoacán; México: Fideicomiso "Felipe Teixidor y Monserrat Alfau de Teixor," 2013. 720 p.: bibl., indexes. (Colección Investigaciones)

This work challenges a persistent notion that the Tarascans—and western Mexico more generally—were unique in postclassic Mesoamerica in their isolation and marginality. In fact, the author argues that the Tarascans of Michoacan, especially the members of elite political and social circles within the Tarascan state, maintained contacts not only with the other Mesoamerican groups like the Nahuas, the Maya, and those from Oaxaca, but also with groups much further afield. This latter group includes native peoples in Central and South America as well as those living to the north in the arid regions of present-day Mexico and the US Southwest. The author also documents the multi-ethnic nature of the population of the Tarascan state, composed as it was of Tarascans, Nahuas, Otopames, Chichimecas, and others.

192 **Alva Ixtlilxóchitl, Fernando de.** The native conquistador: Alva Ixtlilxochitl's account of the conquest of New Spain. Edited and translated by Amber Brian, Bradley Benton, and Pablo García Loaeza. University Park: The Pennsylvania State University Press, 2015. 135 p.: bibl. (Latin American originals; 10)

Of part Nahua heritage, don Fernando de Alva Ixtlilxóchitl wrote his "Thirteenth Relation" circa 1608 to demand recognition for the critical services that his great-great-grandfather, a nobleman of Nahua Tetzcoco, had rendered to Cortés in the conquest of Tenochtitlan. In subsequent centuries it became one of the most well-known and oft-cited accounts of the conquest from an indigenous perspective. This slim, readable, and effectively illustrated volume, which includes a substantial introductory essay, is the first English translation of this important text in 50 years. With its action-packed narrative providing a revealing counterpoint to both Spanish and Tenochca accounts of the conquest, *The Native Conquistador* is perfect for undergraduate courses on Mexican and colonial Latin American history.

193 **Ametrano, Lucía.** Crónicas americanas. Montevideo: Ediciones de la Plaza, 2013. 285 p.: bibl.

This heavily illustrated volume, by a graphic designer and art gallery operator, "curates" and exhibits many of the most iconic images of historic Native America. Its Mesoamerican chapters reproduce famous images and descriptive passages derived from important colonial-era European and indigenous-sourced texts about native societies and cultures, such as those by Hernán Cortés, Bernal Díaz del Castillo, Diego Durán, and the *Florentine Codex*. Other chapters showcase images and artifacts from the Andes (for example, Guaman Poma), the La Plata region (de Bry), Brazil (Staden), and British and French North America (Chateaubriand and 19th-century Western artists in the US). The work can be considered a visual introductory guide to the diversity of indigenous American civilizations.

194 **Benton, Bradley.** The lords of Tetzcoco: the transformation of indigenous rule in postconquest central Mexico. New York: Cambridge University Press, 2017. 212 p. (Cambridge Latin American studies)

This political history of Nahua Tetzcoco delves into diverse archival records from Mexico and Spain to trace the vicissitudes of its indigenous dynasty in the generations immediately following the Spanish conquest. In doing so, the author presents a compelling vision of political continuity as well as rupture, challenging many misperceptions regarding the fate of Nahua rulers under colonial rule. While the lords of Tetzcoco maintained a significant degree of local prominence and autonomy into the 1560s, they also faced challenges both external and internal. Ultimately, Benton demonstrates that it was not the conquest that finally undermined traditional native governance in Tetzcoco, but rather in-fighting, exogamy, and a host of economic and social developments that only occurred decades later. For additional comment, see **474**.

195 Benton, Bradley. The outsider: Alva Ixtlilxochitl's tenuous ties to the city of Tetzcoco. (*Colon. Lat. Am. Rev.*, 23:1, 2014, p. 37–52, bibl.)

Bradley Benton references archival sources to challenge the oft-repeated and widely assumed notion that the important chronicler, don Fernando de Alva Ixtlilxóchitl, was a native of the Nahua Tetzcoco that he so patriotically addresses in his writings. Indeed, Benton demonstrates that not only was Alva Ixtlilxóchitl largely raised in Mexico City, he was culturally and politically estranged from the leadership of Tetzcoco itself. Thus, when the viceroy appointed Alva Ixtlilxóchitl governor of Tetzcoco in 1613—an act that historians have interpreted as proof of the chronicler's prominence there—local residents received him as an outsider and reacted so negatively that his term ended early. This article forces us to rethink our understanding of Alva Ixtlilxóchitl's famous chronicles.

196 Bialuschewski, Arne. Slaves of the buccaneers: Mayas in captivity in the second half of the seventeenth century. (*Ethnohistory/Columbus*, 64:1, Jan. 2017, p. 41–63)

The historiography of slavery in the early modern Atlantic world has long emphasized the Middle Passage from Africa, while scholarship on the age of piracy has focused on rivalries between the various European empires. In this article, the author identifies a different kind of suffering at the nexus of slavery and piracy, wherein marauders raided the coasts of Tabasco and Yucatán, taking Maya slaves for themselves or to sell on the black market. Well-documented and researched, the article suggests that, in some places, native peoples suffered not only from the impositions of the colonial regime, but also from the lawlessness that resulted from that regime's inability to control the extent of its claimed territory.

197 Boone, Elizabeth Hill; Louise M. Burkhart; and David Tavárez. Painted words: Nahua Catholicism, politics, and memory in the Atzaqualco pictorial catechism. Washington, D.C.: Dumbarton Oaks Research Library and Collection, 2017. 386 p.: bibl., index. (Studies in pre-Columbian art and archaeology; 39)

This important study is the first work to fully "translate" a pictorial catechism, also known also as a Testerian manuscript. The authors explicitly reject the label "Testerian," however, as giving too much agency to New Spain's early missionary friars and too little to the native painters who were involved in producing these intriguing documents. The specific pictorial catechism analyzed in this volume, known by its catalog data at the Biblioteque Nacional de France as Fonds mexicain 399, is here dubbed the Atzaqualco Pictorial Catechism. The authors have determined that the manuscript encodes a Nahuatl version of Catholic doctrine, even though it is not glossed in any language. This interdisciplinary collaboration by three leading scholars of Mesoamerican art history, history, and anthropology deciphers the Nahuatl-based pictorial text sign-by-sign, providing the complete Nahuatl text and an English translation. For colonial historian's comment, see item **476**.

198 Boturini Benaducci, Lorenzo. Idea of a new general history of North America: an account of colonial native Mexico. Edited and translated by Stafford Poole. Foreword by Susan Schroeder. Norman: University of Oklahoma Press, 2015. 288 p.: bibl., ill., index.

The publication of Stafford Poole's translation of Lorenzo Boturini's 1746 original reflects the current trajectory of Mesoamerican studies. Boturini proposed to rewrite the precolumbian history of Mesoamerica by way of the artifacts and texts of its native peoples, thereby contesting the accounts of outsiders who, he argued, were ignorant and dismissive of indigenous historical knowledge. He also sought to substantiate the apparition story of the Virgin of Guadalupe. Poole's translation acknowledges that today's academic historians and literary experts share many of Boturini's beliefs regarding the extensive historical value of native artifacts and texts. In conjunction with Susan Schroeder's foreword, the volume is useful for English-speaking scholars of ancient Mesoamerica, colonial New Spain, and the history of Mexican creolism and *guadalupanismo*. For comment by colonial literature specialist, see item **1721**.

199   **Brian, Amber.** Alva Ixtlilxochitl's native archive and the circulation of knowledge in colonial Mexico. Nashville: Vanderbilt University Press, 2016. 196 p.: bibl.

This work examines the collection of pictorial and alphabetic texts amassed and preserved by don Fernando de Alva Ixtlilxóchitl, a turn-of-the-17th-century historian of mixed heritage, which was later gifted by don Fernando's son to don Carlos de Sigüenza y Góngora, a white Creole intellectual. The passing of the collection from a bicultural family with strong ties to native communities to a white Creole family, Brian argues, complicates our understanding of the intellectual circles of colonial New Spain, forcing us to acknowledge a closer connection between native and white Creole authors and historiography and giving native and mestizo thinkers a greater role in the intellectual environment of colonial Mexico.

200   **Brian, Amber.** The original Alva Ixtlilxochitl manuscripts at Cambridge University. (*Colon. Lat. Am. Rev.*, 23:1, 2014 p. 84–101, bibl., photos)

In this article, Amber Brian traces the strange fortunes of the original, signed manuscripts of don Fernando de Alva Ixtlilxóchitl (d. 1650), whose invaluable chronicles of prehispanic central Mexico and Acolhuacan had been lost to scholars for almost two centuries before being rediscovered in the 1980s. The content and circuitous path of these texts, from Alva Ixtlilxóchitl's own collection, through the hands of 18th-century Mexican antiquarians, to the Cambridge University Library, illustrate the collaborative historiographical realm in which Alva Ixtlilxóchitl worked and in which they later circulated, as well as the fate of Mexico's historical patrimony more generally during the chaotic 19th century.

201   **Brito Guadarrama, Baltazar.** Códice Guillermo Tovar de Huejotzingo. Libro 1, Estudio introductorio. Libro 2, Códice. Puebla, Mexico: Gobierno del Estado de Puebla, Secretaría de Cultura, 2011. 133 p.: bibl.

This two-volume work is the first scholarly treatment of what the author has named the *Códice Guillermo Tovar de Huejotzingo*, a 1566–68 document housed in Mexico's Biblioteca Nacional de Antropología e Historia. Volume 1 provides a glyphic analysis of the pictorial elements, as well as a paleographic transcription and Spanish translation of the Nahuatl alphabetic glosses. Brito proposes a "Huejotzingo school" of manuscript painting on the model of Donald Robertson's 1959 "schools" of Tenochtitlan, Texcoco, and Tlatelolco. The final chapter of volume 1 includes a transcription (and translation from the Nahuatl when necessary) of the archival *expedientes* that accompany the codex. Volume 2 is a high-quality facsimile of the archival documents, 15 folios in all, including the pictorial codex itself (fol. 1r-2v) and the accompanying Nahuatl and Spanish alphabetic texts.

202   **Burdick, Catherine.** Held captive by script: interpreting "tagged" prisoners in late classic Maya sculpture. (*Anc. Mesoam.*, 27:1, Spring 2016, p. 31–48, bibl., ill., photos, tables)

This article examines Maya representations of captives in southern late classic stone relief sculptures, principally from the southern Petén and Chiapas. Many of these captives were "tagged" with hieroglyphic text, usually on their thighs. Burdick argues that these texts were added to depictions of captives as a way to visually subjugate these prisoners and mark them as a possession, in the same way that the Maya labeled inanimate objects to demonstrate ownership. Visually labeling prisoners served to enhance the power and prestige of their captors.

203   **Castañeda de la Paz, María.** Verdades y mentiras en torno a don Diego de Mendoza Austria Moctezuma. México: UNAM, Instituto de Investigaciones An-

tropológicas; Tenango de Doria, Mexico: Universidad Intercultural del Estado de Hidalgo; Zinacantepec, Mexico: El Colegio Mexiquense, 2017. 426 p.: bibl., ill., indexes, maps.

This book takes up the fascinating story of don Diego de Mendoza, a 16th-century *cacique* and *gobernador* of Tlatelolco. After his death, and over the course of the colonial period, don Diego's fame and importance grew; he came to be associated with the Moctezumas (descendants of the Aztec ruler at the time of contact) and with the Hapsburgs of Austria. And families from as far away as the present-day state of Hidalgo claimed him as their ancestor. Castañeda painstakingly analyzes the glut of documents pertaining to don Diego to sort fact from fiction. She concludes that much of the documentation surrounding the *cacique* was produced in the 17th and 18th centuries and constitutes a repurposing, even outright falsification of the original 16th-century texts.

204 De Catemahco a Tezcoco: origen y desarrollo de una ciudad indígena. Edición de Javier Eduardo Ramírez López. Texcoco, Mexico: Diócesis de Texcoco A. R., 2017. 291 p.: bibl.

This edited anthology includes essays by Mexican, European, and US scholars on the town of Tetzcoco, located in the eastern basin of Mexico, which was one of the most powerful polities of central Mexico at the time of Spanish contact. The essays range in chronological coverage from the prehispanic period to the end of the 18th century and, taken as a whole, attempt to provide a fairly broad and linear account of Tetzcoco's indigenous history. Two chapters veer slightly from this trajectory in order to devote more space to discussions of the Church in early colonial Tetzcoco. Moreover, two 19th-century texts of local interest have been transcribed with introductory essays and appended to the volume.

205 Cortés Máximo, Juan Carlos. De repúblicas de indios a ayuntamientos constitucionales: pueblos sujetos y cabeceras de Michoacán, 1740–1831. México: Instituto de Investigaciones Históricas, Universidad Michoacana de San Nicolás de Hidalgo, 2012. 317 p.: bibl. (Colección Bicentenario de la independencia; 16)

This work explores the relationships and tensions between *cabecera* and *sujeto* towns in Michoacán in the late colonial and early independence periods. The author provides a fine-grained analysis of local government across Michoacán in this period, basing his conclusions on records of local elections and legal suits. He also explores the issues that the independence movements and violence created for local native governance, noting that the instability provided opportunities for native leaders to reclaim control over certain aspects of local rule and for *sujetos* to transform themselves into *cabeceras* in many cases. He concludes with an examination of the challenges faced by local native leaders under the dictates of the new republican government of the state of Michoacán.

206 Crewe, Ryan. Building in the shadow of death: monastery construction and the politics of community reconstitution in sixteenth-century Mexico. (*Americas/Washington*, 75:3, July 2018, p. 489–523, bibl., photos)

Crewe's article seeks to understand how the great mendicant *doctrina* churches and convents of central Mexico could have been built by native communities that, only years earlier, had suffered near-collapse as a result of waves of epidemic disease. How could communities crippled by mass death have mobilized labor and resources to construct these massive buildings? The author is particularly interested in the political and social forces that drove these building projects and argues that they were only possible because they served real needs within the native communities in which they were built. Namely, Crewe asserts that they stood as powerful symbols of local native sovereignty, filling the same roles played by the prehispanic *teocalli*, or temples, a role that was particularly important following the existential crises provoked by demographic collapse.

207 Dehouve, Danièle. A play on dimensions: miniaturization and fractals in Mesoamerican ritual. (*J. Anthropol. Res.*, 72:4, Winter 2016, p. 504–529, bibl., ill.)

This article examines the practice of using miniaturized objects during ritual practices among native peoples in Mesoamerica. The author is particularly interested in developing a typology of miniaturization, drawing on 15th- and 16th-century Aztec archeological evidence as well as modern-day ethnography among the Tlapanecs (or *me'phaa*) from the state of Guerrero, Mexico. Dehouve characterizes miniaturization as having landscape, cosmic, or divine referents; it also sometimes refers metaphorically to childhood or children. She concludes her typology with a discussion of fractal miniaturization.

208   **Las diversidades indígenas en Michoacán.** Coordinación de Juan Carlos Cortés Máximo. Michoacán, Mexico: Instituto de Investigaciones Históricas, Universidad Michoacana de San Nicolás de Hidalgo, 2015. 235 p.: bibl. (Encuentros; 20)

Michoacán is strongly associated with the Purepecha. But, as this edited collection of essays makes apparent, the region has been, and is, inhabited by a variety of native groups, including Nahuas, Matlazincas, Mazahuas, and Otomís. The essays in this volume examine various aspects of the history and present concerns of these groups, ranging in topic from the 16th-century Augustinian evangelization efforts to 18th-century agrarian reform projects to 20th-century conflicts over *ejido* landholding. This is one of the first scholarly works to focus explicitly on non-Purepecha native communities in Michoacan.

209   **Dutt, Rajeshwari.** Business as usual: Maya and the merchants on Yucatán-Belize border at the onset of the Caste War. (*Americas/Washington*, 74:2, April 2017, p. 201–226)

This article explores the Yucatán-Belize border during the Caste War, a place that the author views as both frontier—with contact between the Maya and British—and borderland—where the territorial ambitions of Spain/Mexico, Britain, and the US confronted one another. This relatively uncommon condition allowed for, the author argues, crossracial alliances—with Belizean merchants fighting alongside Maya rebels against the Mexican state—and an unusual degree of freedom of movement for both merchants and Maya. For additional comment, see item **547**.

210   **Dutt, Rajeshwari.** Maya caciques in early national Yucatán. Norman: University of Oklahoma Press, 2017. 183 p.: bibl., index, maps.

This book neatly weaves together the life stories of individual *caciques*, or indigenous nobles, from the Yucatan in the decades following Mexican independence, with an emphasis on a single, well-documented man who exemplifies the caciques' overall experience. Delving into municipal and state archives, Dutt links national developments and local changes, and reveals that Maya caciques struggled to maintain power in what was an increasingly liberal political and economic milieu, thus adopting client relationships with local governmental officials as a survival strategy. The book reminds us that the modern nation-state did not sweep away older structures to begin anew; it developed through ongoing local and regional negotiations, thereby ensuring that the old order would influence its trajectory.

211   **Duverger, Christian.** Crónica de la eternidad: ¿quién escribió la *Historia verdadera de la conquista de la Nueva España*? México: Taurus, 2012. 335 p.: bibl., ill., index. (Historia)

This is a revisionist take on 16th-century Hispanic letters—specifically, on the question of authorship of the famous *True History of the Conquest of New Spain*, commonly attributed to the conquistador and foot soldier Bernal Díaz del Castillo. Primarily by way of a comparative linguistic analysis of this and other 16th-century texts, Duverger concludes that it was originally written by Hernando Cortés himself, late in life, and that it was only attributed to Díaz much later. If nothing else, the book is a reminder that "authorship" in the early modern period was not nearly as concrete and individualized as we expect it to be today, and that this affects the information we have about indigenous peoples and their histories.

212   **Favila Vázquez, Mariana.** Veredas de mar y río: navegación y prehispánica y colonial en Los Tuxtlas, Veracruz. México: UNAM, Coordinación de Estudios de Posgrado, 2016. 286 p.: bibl., ill., maps. (Colección Posgrado; 66)

This work examines the prehispanic and colonial history of navigation in the area of Los Tuxtlas, Veracruz. Drawing upon field excursions and satellite imagery, as well as colonial-era sources—particularly maps—the author proposes a system of prehispanic waterways that challenges scholarly perceptions of the mountains of Los Tuxtlas as being isolated and cut off from the surrounding ecosystems. Instead, the author suggests that the waterways of Los Tuxtlas facilitated intensive and extensive connections with other parts of southeastern Mexico. Such watery connections also allowed native peoples in the region to develop food-production systems that took advantage of and integrated the linked ecosystems at the various altitudes of the *sierra*.

213 Garone Gravier, Marina. Historia de la tipografía colonial para lenguas indígenas. México: CIESAS: Universidad Veracruzana, Dirección Editorial, 2014. 372 p.: bibl.

This work explores the history of indigenous-language typography in New Spain, particularly the adaptations made in novohispanic printmaking to accommodate the previously unwritten native languages Nahuatl and Otomí. Garone Gravier surveys the major genres of native-language printed material, including doctrinal texts, catechisms, collections of sermons, and confessional and sacramental manuals; explores the process whereby native languages came to be written using the letters of the Roman alphabet and the limitations of the Castilian graphic and phonetic system; and provides a census of Nahuatl- and Otomí-language texts published from the16th to the 19th centuries, with an emphasis on the major publishing houses of the region.

214 Gonzalbo, Pilar. Del barrio a la capital: Tlatelolco y la Ciudad de México en el siglo XVIII. México: Centro de Estudios Históricos, El Colegio de México, 2017. 212 p.: bibl.

This work tackles an important perennial issue in Mesoamerican historical studies: how and when did peoples with such powerful and highly localized "micropatriotic" ethnic and political identities cease to refer to themselves as members of a particular barrio (district) with a preconquest heritage, and instead identify as members of broader urban castes and classes? Gonzalbo Aizpurú's contribution focuses on the parish of Santa Catarina Mártir in the Mexico City barrio—and historically discrete Mexica city-state—of Tlatelolco in the late 18th century. Ultimately, the book argues for a more fluid and complex model of the caste system of colonial Mexico, one that incorporates such factors as property ownership, civic role, and education alongside genealogy and appearance.

215 Ibarra Rojas, Eugenia. Entre el dominio y la resistencia: los pueblos indígenas del Pacífico de Nicaragua y Nicoya en el siglo XVI. Ciudad Universitaria Rodrigo Facio, Costa Rica: Editorial UCR, 2014. 146 p.: bibl., indexes.

This work carefully synthesizes early colonial records, explorers' accounts, and chronicles from Mesoamerica with recent archeological scholarship regarding the native population of the Nicaraguan Pacific Coast in the decades following the implementation of Spanish rule. Due to the scarcity of archival materials from the area, the author fills in the gaps with well-defined anthropological theory about the development of discrete sociopolitical "regions" and cultures. She presents an impressionistic, yet very useful introduction to the human history of the region in clear and empirical terms, replete with maps and tables that illustrate both the changes wrought by European intrusion as well as the underlying continuities.

216 Jiménez Gómez, Juan Ricardo. Autos civiles de indios ante el alcalde mayor del pueblo de Querétaro a finales del siglo XVI. Querétaro, Mexico: Instituto de Estudios Constitucionales/Miguel Angel Porrúa, 2014. 448 p: bibl., index.

These three volumes (see items **217** and **218**) present transcriptions of complex archival sources bearing on the colonial development of the modern state of Querétaro and its municipalities. Each consists of a full and unedited transcription of archival material, preceded by an extended introductory essay establishing the historical context necessary for understanding the documents. In each volume, Jiménez Gómez adeptly identifies and explains the relevant colonial-era political, legal, and economic systems shaping the transcribed primary sources. His approach allows the reader to determine which issues were unique to Querétaro and which are illustrative of colonial Mexico more generally. In addition to the history of Querétaro, these volumes will be helpful as guides for graduate students preparing to do archival research.

217 **Jiménez Gómez, Juan Ricardo.** Fundación y evangelización del pueblo de indios de Querétaro y sus sujetos, 1531–1585: testimonios del cacique don Hernando de Tapia y otros indios españoles en el Pleito Grande, entre el Arzobispado de México y el Obispado de Michoacán. Querétaro, Mexico: Universidad Autónoma de Querétaro, 2014. 327 p.: bibl., index, maps. (Serie El derecho)

For annotation, see item **216**.

218 **Jiménez Gómez, Juan Ricardo.** Los pleitos por las tierras entre españoles e indios de la Congregación de Bernal a finales del siglo XVIII y principios del XIX. Querétaro, Mexico: Universidad Autónoma de Querétaro; México: MAPorrúa, 2014. 348 p.: bibl., index. (Serie La historia)

For annotation, see item **217**.

219 **Johansson K., Patrick.** Miccacuicatl: las exequias de los señores mexicas. México: Libros de Godot, 2016. 456 p.: bibl., ill. (Primer Círculo. Etnohistoria)

This is a sweeping examination of representations of death and mortality across multiple 16th-century Nahuatl-language and Nahua-influenced sources by an editor of *Estudios de cultura nahuatl*, one of the most iconic journals of Nahua history and culture. Johansson explores essentially every major text—alphabetic, pictorial, and mixed—by 16th-century Nahuas and Nahuatl-speaking friars and interprets them according to anthropological theories regarding the meaning and purpose of funeral rites. Based on this analysis, the author argues that the Nahuas (and their Toltec predecessors) did not share the clear Western distinction between life and death; rather, they believed life and death to be fully integrated and inseparable, with mortality being a defining feature of life itself.

220 **Johnson, Benjamin D.** Pueblos within pueblos: tlaxilacalli communities in Acolhuacan, Mexico, ca. 1272–1692. Boulder: University Press of Colorado, 2017. 268 p.: bibl., index.

This book follows the history of what the author calls *tlaxilacalli*, or the commoner-dominated constituent parts of Nahua *altepetl*, in the region of Acolhuacan in the eastern basin of Mexico around Tetzcoco. With an imaginative readings of colonial-era sources, Johnson examines the Acolhua *tlaxilacalli* beginning as far back as the 13th century, continuing through the formation of the Aztec and Spanish empires in Acolhuacan, and concluding in the 17th century. Along the way, he offers a case study of the *tlaxilacalli* of Cuauhtepoztlan in the *altepetl* of Tepetlaoztoc. This study is one of the first in decades to focus specifically on sub-*altepetl* Nahua political organization.

221 **Lamadrid, Enrique R.** Tlaxcalans in New Mexico: fading traces, contested legacies. (*N.M. Hist. Rev.*, 91:2, Spring 2016, p. 147–162, bibl., photos)

This article, by a longtime scholar of New Mexican literature, culture, and identity, is an overview of modern research into the changing way that New Mexicans have imagined their state's Indo-Hispanic heritage. The author summarizes the direct and scholarly evidence for the widespread belief that there was a strong Nahua presence in early New Mexico, and argues that there is little evidence that such a population survived the Pueblo Revolt of 1680 intact. LaMadrid then identifies how 18th-century Creoles first, and 20th-century New Mexican poets, activists, and promotors later, amplified and referenced this Nahua heritage to construct New Mexico's unique self-image as a place of deeply rooted multi-culturalism with historical ties to the high civilization of central Mexico.

222 **León Portilla, Miguel.** El México antiguo en la historia universal. Toluca de Lerdo, Mexico: FOEM, Fondo Editorial Estado de México; Chalco, Mexico: Impresora y Editora Xalco, 2016. 219 p.: bibl., ill.

With large, glossy images on every page, this is a beautiful introduction to precolumbian Mesoamerica by one of its most dedicated and respected scholars. Combining archeology, anthropology, and León-Portilla's unmatched knowledge of the 16th-century codices and manuscripts, the book situates ancient Mexico within a comparative timeline of the rise and fall of other large-scale civilizations around the globe, including in India, Mesopotamia, and the Andes. While written for a popular readership, the book's analysis is nonetheless sophisticated and broad—a sort of 21st-century translation of the ethnography of Sahagún. It also reflects upon the history of Mesoamerican studies, with an emphasis on the development of modern empirical scholarship in 20th-century Mexico.

223 Lesbre, Patrick. La construcción del pasado indígena de Tezcoco: de Nezahualcóyotl a Alva Ixtlilxóchitl. Traducción de Mario Zamudio Vega. México: Secretaría de Cultura, Instituto Nacional de Antropología e Historia; Zamora, Mexico: El Colegio de Michoacán; México: CEMCA, Centro de Estudios Mexicanos y Centroamericanos, 2016. 537 p.: bibl., ill. (Colección Investigaciones)

This book, the product of more than 20 years of work, is a close analysis of the alphabetic sources for the history of early colonial Acolhuacan, the region around Tezcoco (Texcoco) in the eastern basin of Mexico. The work is divided into three parts. The first is an examination of early writings from Acolhuacan and the information on prehispanic society that can be gleaned from them. The second part reconstructs a now-lost conquest-era manuscript known as the *Noticias*. The final section examines the works of the two most well-known Acolhuacan writers, Juan Bautista Pomar and don Fernando de Alva Ixtlilxóchitl, whose turn-of-the-17th-century accounts remain among the most oft-cited sources for prehispanic and colonial Tetzcoco and its environs.

224 Melton-Villanueva, Miriam. Cacicas, *escribanos*, and landholders: indigenous women's late colonial Mexican texts, 1702–1832. (*Ethnohistory/Columbus*, 65:2, 2018, p. 297–322, bibl.)

This article deploys multiple forms of analysis, including philology, to Nahuatl-language wills, bills-of-sale, and other notarial records to document the presence of propertied indigenous women at all levels of local society in the Toluca Valley during the 18th and early 19th centuries. It showcases the activities of these *cacicas* in community leadership and independent land management throughout the period, whether single, widowed, or married, thereby challenging notions of female passivity. In focusing on the Nahuatl-language records produced by and for provincial communities, Melton-Villanueva also highlights the complementary role of local Nahuatl scribes in creating and maintaining the semi-autonomous civic societies in which such *cacicas* lived and worked.

225 Los mitos y sus tiempos: creencias y narraciones de Mesoamérica y los Andes. Edición de Alfredo López Austin y Luis Millones. México: Ediciones Era, 2015. 399 p.: bibl., glossary. (Biblioteca Era)

The fourth in a series of collaborations between the authors, this work seeks to provide comparative analysis of the two zones of postclassic cultural achievement: Mesoamerica and the Andes. Written for a broad audience, this volume focuses on the mythology of the two regions. The treatment of Mesoamerican myth, authored by López Austin, constitutes nearly two-thirds of the book. He covers the major Nahua and Maya stories and includes translations of primary-source material for each narrative. There are occasional stories from other indigenous traditions, including Otomí and Zapotec. For each text, López Austin provides a succinct introduction.

226 Native wills from the colonial Americas: dead giveaways in a New World. Edited by Mark Christensen and Jonathan Truitt. Salt Lake City: University of Utah Press, 2016. 276 p.: bibl., ill., index, maps, tables.

This volume effectively argues for, and showcases, the value of wills and testaments as sources for social, economic, and cultural historians of indigenous communities. While addressing indigenous peoples throughout the hemisphere, multiple chapters center on colonial Mesoamerica. In each chapter, a scholar extrapolates information from a single will—the deceased's debts, relationships, and priorities, for example—in order to infer broader lessons about his or her community and era, and then reproduces the entire will in translation. The volume is both a work of scholarship and an innovative and demonstrative how-to guide for researchers intending to delve into testamentary documents.

227 **Nuevas miradas sobre los antiguos michoacanos (México): un diálogo interdisciplinario (symposium), *Vienna, Austria, 2012*.** Nuevas contribuciones al estudio del antiguo Michoacán. Edición de Sarah Albiez-Wieck y Hans Roskamp. Zamora, Mexico: El Colegio de Michoacán, 2016. 283 p.: bibl., ill., index, maps. (Colección Investigaciones)

This edited volume presents recent multidisciplinary work on Michoacán by leading scholars in Mexico, Europe, and the US. The essays proceed chronologically. The first, precontact section of the book opens with archeological research on the site of Malpaís de Zacupa, a settlement that predates the Tarascan state by several centuries. Other contributors to Michoacán's precontact history examine the rise of the Tarascan state and Tarascan social organization as demonstrated in Purepecha-language documentation from the colonial period. The second and third parts of the book deal with contact with Europeans and the integration of the Tarascan state into the Spanish Empire, respectively.

228 **Olivier, Guilhem.** Cacería, sacrificio y poder en Mesoamérica: tras las huellas de Mixcóatl, "serpiente de nube." México: Fondo de Cultura Económica: UNAM: Fideicomiso Felipe Teixidor y Montserrat Alfau de Teixidor: Centro de Estudios Mexicanos y Centroamericanos, 2015. 744 p.: bibl., index. (Sección de obras de antropología)

This text examines the ways in which power and sacrifice in Mesoamerica were bound up within an ideology of hunting. Olivier explores four main themes—hunting implements, deer, the collective hunting ritual associated with the *veintena* festival of Quecholli, and rituals of access to power—to show that hunting, sacrifice, and power were intimately connected. He also gives particular attention to the Nahua god Mixcoatl, patron of the Tlaxcalteca and the hunt.

229 **Polanco, Edward Anthony.** 'I am just a *tiçitl*': decolonizing central Mexican Nahua female healers, 1535–1635. (*Ethnohistory/Columbus*, 65:3, 2018, p. 441–463, bibl.)

This insightful article examines 16th- and early 17th-century Spanish and Nahuatl texts, including Inquisition records, religious codices, and early colonial dictionaries, to revise scholarly portrayals of traditional Nahua healers and healing practices, or *titiçih* and *tiçiyotl*. A close philological reading of such texts combined with anthropological analyses reveal the tendency for non-native colonial writers to misrepresent and misunderstand the activities of both male and female Nahua healers. In this way, Polanco argues that we have inherited a substantially constrained notion of both the breadth and nature of the role of women in Nahua healing practices, one that imposes European categories and definitions where they do not apply.

230 **Quiroga, Néstor I.** Friar Francisco Ximénez and the *Popul Vuh*: from religious treatise to a digital sacred book. (*Ethnohistory/Columbus*, 64:2, 2017, p. 241–270, bibl.)

This article argues for the importance of context in reading the *Popul Vuh*. As we know it today, the famous text is a creation narrative of the K'iché Maya set down in Spanish in the early 18th century by the Franciscan friar Francisco Ximénez, based on an earlier record of precontact oral histories. Quiroga cautions against understanding the *Popul Vuh* in isolation, insisting that it must be regarded as an integral component within fray Francisco's broader work, a manual for evangelizing among the Maya. When considered contextually, then, the *Popul Vuh* in its presently known form is not simply a Maya sacred book, but an indoctrinator's account of the religious errors he intended to extirpate.

231 **Restall, Matthew.** When Montezuma met Cortés: the true story of the meeting that changed history. New York, N.Y.: Ecco, an imprint of Harper Collins Publishers, 2018. 526 p.: bibl., ill., index, maps, tables.

This heavily researched and timely work communicates and extends the most consequential insights from the past 30 years of Mesoamerican studies. Decades of extensive and interdisciplinary research into Mexican ethnohistorical materials has led many, Restall prominent among them, to challenge received notions about why and how the conquistadors successfully defeated the Mexica of Tenochtitlan. Here, Restall reframes the fall of Tenochtitlan in light of contemporary Mesoamerican and Spanish politics and culture, which reveals it to be less of a unilateral "conquest" than a complex "Aztec-Spanish War." He then traces the subsequent historiographical construction of the idea of a conquest and its reproduction in both erudite and popular discourses over the past five centuries.

232 Rice, Prudence M. and Don S. Rice.
Classic-to-contact-period continuities in Maya governance in central Petén, Guatemala. (*Ethnohistory/Columbus*, 65:3, 2018, p. 441–463, bibl.)

The authors of this article place archeological evidence and ethnohistorical sources into direct dialogue in an effort to transcend the methodological and interpretive barriers that typically hinder communication between the two disciplines. They examine lowland Guatemalan Maya epigraphy, the physical layout of excavated classic-era *popol nah* meeting houses, and other structures, and interpret them in light of cultural concepts evident in colonial-era written sources.They suggest the survival of certain "deep" organizational principles, even across the postclassic and contact eras, such as a tradition of dual rulership. The article self-consciously models how Mesoamericanist scholars from disciplines that typically remain aloof from one another might productively communicate and collaborate.

233 Ríos Castaño, Victoria. The herbal of the *Florentine Codex*: description and contextualization of paragraph V in Book XI. (*Americas/Washington*, 75:3, July 2018, p. 463–488, bibl., ill.)

This article examines paragraph V of Book XI of fray Bernardino de Sahagún's 16th-century encyclopedia of Nahua history and culture known as the *Florentine Codex*. Alfredo López Austin has argued that paragraph V—one of three herbals considered indispensable sources for the study of prehispanic medicine—is an independent text that stands on its own apart from the larger codex. Here, Ríos Castaño confirms López Austin's claims, but she also argues that the herbal was nonetheless produced under Sahagún's supervision within the Colegio de Santa Cruz. She asserts, moreover, that it was written with the goal of helping to treat physical illness among the Nahuas. This would have been particularly timely, for *cocoliztli* epidemics were ravaging the native population of central Mexico at precisely this time.

234 Rojas, José Luis de. Imperio Azteca: historia de una idea. Madrid: Rosa María Porrúa Ediciones, 2016. 317 p.: bibl.

This is a succinct review of how ethnographers and scholars over the centuries have conceptualized and represented the so-called "Aztec Empire." The book highlights colonial sources that first conceived of the Aztec world as an "empire." But its primary focus is the modern tradition of research launched by Robert Barlow in the 1940s, who applied anthropological and sociological theories of empire to the Aztec world. The author traces the development of this line of research through the rest of the century, emphasizing the innovations and contributions of numerous scholars and controversies in which they participated. The book is a useful academic review for students preparing to research the social, economic, or political dynamics of the Aztec Empire qua empire.

235 Smoke, flames, and the human body in Mesoamerican ritual practice. Edited by Vera Tiesler and Andrew K. Scherer. Washington, DC: Dumbarton Oaks Research Library and Collection, 2018. 471 p.: bibl., ill., index, maps. (Dumbarton Oaks Pre-Columbian symposia and colloquia)

This volume pushes beyond disciplinary boundaries in search of commonalities, resonances, and linkages connected to the ritual use of fire on human body parts across Mesoamerica and its history, from the 3rd century to today. Among other sources, the contributors consider and juxtapose archeological remains, precolumbian art and epigraphy, colonial-era ethnohistorical texts, and modern oral traditions pertaining to fire and burning bodies across the centuries from Guatemala and Chiapas to Yucatán, southern, central, and western Mexico. The result is a thematic approach to Mesoamerican civilization that goes well beyond the abilities of an individual author or discipline, and which invites ethnographic and anthropological comparisons to fire-related practices from other world traditions.

236   Solari, Amara. Maya ideologies of the sacred: the transfiguration of space in colonial Yucatan. Austin: University of Texas Press, 2013. 212 p.: bibl., ill., index, maps.

Solari approaches the historical question of cultural change among the colonial Yucatecan Maya by way of people's relationship to space. The author examines colonial-era Spanish and Maya texts, images, and architecture, including the Franciscan mission complex of Itzmal, to reveal continuities in the "spatial ideologies" of the pre- and postconquest Maya, how local people understood the spiritual and practical relevance of particular places. Importantly, the friars were often unaware of these continuities, and of their own inadvertent role in sustaining them—for example, by building churches atop indigenous sacred places. Extensively illustrated, the volume ultimately showcases ways that the Maya actively contributed to the religious syncretism of colonial Yucatan.

237   Sousa, Lisa. The woman who turned into a jaguar, and other narratives of native women in archives of colonial Mexico. Stanford, Calif.: Stanford University Press, 2017. 404 p.: bibl., ill., index, maps, tables.

This book derives from the fertile intersection of decades of colonial Mesoamerican ethnohistory and modern innovations in women's history. The result is a vivid exposition of cross-cultural patterns in gender relations among colonial-era Nahuas, Mixtecs, Zapotecs, and Mixes. Sousa addresses a broad range of colonial native women's experiences from birth to death, including girlhood, gender performativity and dress, betrothal and marriage, domestic relations and violence, and sex, as well as gendered public roles in labor, commerce, and political activity. Attention is also given to the influences of class and Spanish institutions and ideologies on gender relations in native communities. Deeply and carefully researched, the book will stand as a reference on the topic for some time.

238   El tiempo de los dioses-tiempo: concepciones de Mesoamérica. Coordinación de Mercedes de la Garza Camino. México: UNAM, 2015. 258 p.: bibl.

This edited anthology explores conceptions of time among native peoples of Mesoamerica, with a strong emphasis on the Maya. The essays cover a range of topics related to the classic, postclassic, and colonial Maya, including the 260-day count, a cycle of 819 days, time in the Maya underworld, the relationship between cosmogonic myth and cyclical ritual practice, colonial-era rebellions and cyclical understandings of time, and coming-of-age rituals. The volume concludes with a wide-ranging examination of the various contexts in which the Maya recorded the passage of time. It suggests that Maya time reckoning was, and is, complex and multifaceted—even at times contradictory—and adds great richness and depth to Maya life.

239   To be indio in colonial Spanish America. Edited by Mónica Díaz. Albuquerque: University of New Mexico Press, 2017. 283 p.: bibl., ill., index.

This edited volume explores the concept of *indio* in the Spanish Empire, with particular attention to the process of identity formation that resulted from the increasing use of this term in legal and social contexts in the colonial period. Both Mesoamerica and the Andes are well represented in this collection. The contributors whose work focuses on Mesoamerica examine such topics as the identities of so-called *indios chinos* and Chichimecs, the limits of native Catholic identity, and native intellectuals' role in formulating identity. In all the essays, the authors highlight the choices that native peoples made in the process of identity formation. For additional comment, see item **989**.

240   Tokovinine, Alexandre. "It is his image with pulque": drinks, gifts, and political networking in classic Maya texts and images. (*Anc. Mesoam.*, 27:1, Spring 2016, p. 13–29, bibl., ill., maps)

This article explores the practice of feasting among the ruling families of classic-period Maya polities. Drawing on Maya hieroglyphic texts and pictorial scenes—on pottery and stone monuments, and in murals—as well as archeological evidence of royal eating and drinking utensils, the author argues that evidence for classic Maya feasting is relatively limited. The depictions seem to commemorate feasting by a small, exclusive group, which usually included high-ranking individuals from other polities. These feasts, the author suggests, are perhaps indicative of a kind of political strategy to cultivate positive relationships with potential rivals.

241   Townsend, Camilla. Introduction: the evolution of Alva Ixtlilxochitl's scholarly life. (*Colon. Lat. Am. Rev.*, 23:1, April 2014, p. 1–17)

In this introduction to a special issue of the *CLAR* devoted to Mexican chronicler don Fernando de Alva Ixtlilxóchitl (ca. 1578–1650), Townsend examines his life and scholarly trajectory. After narrating the known details of his education and early life, she discusses his intellectual connection with the well-known Franciscan fray Juan de Torquemada and the highlights of don Fernando's career in the viceregal bureaucracy of New Spain. Townsend then describes the various accounts that don Fernando wrote concerning the Nahua god Quetzalcoatl. By tracing the evolution of these accounts, she highlights the ways in which don Fernando developed as an author and thinker. For additional comment, see *HLAS* 72:749.

242   Unidad y variación cultural en Michoacán. Edición de Roberto Martínez, Claudia Espejel y Frida Villavicencio. Zamora, Mexico: El Colegio de Michoacán; México: UNAM-Instituto de Investigaciones Históricas, 2016. 281 p.: bibl., ill., index, maps. (Colección Debates)

This edited collection of essays examines a perceived tension in studies of the native cultures of Michoacan, namely, that while there is great ethno-linguistic diversity and substantial change over time in the region, there is also much that unifies it and contributes to a sense of persistence. The first essays explore this tension in the prehispanic period; the second section details the ways in which ideas, language, and ways of life were affected by contact with Spaniards; and the third set of essays examines the rich variety of native speech and tradition across the region today. The contributors approach their topics from a variety of disciplinary traditions: archeology, history, linguistics, and ethnography.

243   El universo de Sahagún: pasado y presente, 2011. Coordinación de Pilar Máynez y José Rubén Romero Galván. México: UNAM, Instituto de Investigaciones Históricas, 2014. 236 p.: bibl., ill. (Serie Cultura náhuatl. Monografías; 35)

This collection is a result of a decade of sustained collaborations among some of the most experienced scholars of Bernardino de Sahagún, the 16th-century Franciscan friar and ethnographer of Nahua culture and society. Since 2005, the authors have been working, under rigid paleographical guidelines, to translate the Nahuatl portions of all 12 volumes of Sahagún's *Florentine Codex*. Half of these essays examine the materiality of the codex for what it reveals about Sahagún and his indigenous collaborators, while the other half advance new insights into Nahua culture that have resulted from the ongoing translation work. Ultimately, the collection is a useful primer for any scholars who intend to use Sahagún's texts to study Nahua culture and history.

244   Vida indígena en la colonia: perspectivas etnohistóricas. Coordinación de María Teresa Jarquín Ortega. México: El Colegio Mexiquense, 2016. 205 p.: bibl.

This collection of essays focusing on indigenous responses and adaptations to colonial rule, exemplifies the current trajectory of colonial Mesoamerican ethnohistory, a well-established historical subfield that emphasizes sources that foreground indigenous thoughts, sentiments, and actions in the retelling of history. The volume explicitly builds upon the ethnohistorical insight that precolumbian indigenous societies and cultures influenced historical development in the centuries following European colonization. Each essay targets a Mesoamerican region, primarily but not exclusively in the Nahua-dominated areas of central Mexico. As befitting a collection in what might be considered the third generation of Mesoamerican ethnohistorical studies, several of the essays delve beyond social and political history to explore deeper cultural issues such as gender relations, local commerce, and popular religion.

245 Villella, Peter B. The last Acolhua: Alva Ixtlilxochitl and elite native historiography in early New Spain. (*Colon. Lat. Am. Rev.*, 23:1, 2014, p. 18–36, bibl., ill.)

This article situates the work of 17th-century Mexican chronicler don Fernando de Alva Ixtlilxóchitl in its appropriate early colonial intellectual milieu. Specifically, the author argues that Alva Ixtlilxóchitl's work should be seen as heir to the rhetorical strategies employed by the native ruling lineage of Tetzcoco in the early colonial period in the face of royal or colonial authority. Both the native rulers and Alva Ixtlilxóchitl conceived of themselves as intrinsically tied to the prehispanic indigenous high nobility of Tetzcoco, but also as quick allies of the Spaniards and eager converts to Christianity. These insights bring nuance to our understanding of Alva Ixtlilxóchitl the man and the author and allow us to better appreciate the ways in which his self-identity shaped his body of written work.

246 Words & worlds turned around: indigenous Christianities in colonial Latin America. Edited by David Tavárez. Boulder: University Press of Colorado, 2017. 329 p.: bibl., index.

This valuable collection of essays showcases an important current trajectory of Spanish-American religious history. While chapters address the Amazon, the Andes, and the Maya, the book deals primarily with central Mexico. Drawing on a range of sources, including native-language texts, images, songs, and performances, the essays explore the indigenization of Christianity in the Americas. Specifically, scholars reveal that Spanish Catholicism necessarily underwent transformations, intentional and unintentional, when imposed upon native peoples. Collectively, the result is less an account of pure "acculturation" or "indoctrination," but rather of subtle, ongoing negotiations and dialogues, explicit and implicit, often strategic, and sometimes subversive, between Spanish clergy and native neophytes, intermediaries, waverers, and believers.

South America

SUSAN E. RAMÍREZ, *Professor of History and Neville G. Penrose Chair of History and Latin American Studies, Texas Christian University*

OVER THE PAST SEVERAL DECADES, ethnohistorians have succeeded in better understanding their subjects by using sources more creatively and crossing disciplinary lines to provide additional perspectives on current and past cultures and peoples. Unceasing inventiveness marks the new additions to a growing literature, reviewed here.

Scholars continue to publish primary sources, usually in appendices, a practice that I have lauded in previous essays as a means of supporting their arguments, while also offering the documents to others for additional interpretations (see items **254**, **255**, **264**, **266**, **274**, **279**, **287**, and **297**). Among the publications reviewed for *HLAS 74* are some standout offerings that expand our discussions and debates, using the analyses of artifacts, such as decorated *qeros* (items **283** and **284**), *topacus* (item **291**), rock forms (item **253**), pottery, stools, drums, textiles, baskets, body painting (item **302**), and ruins. Other authors add rock art (petroglyphs) (item **270**), murals (item **252**), and ceremonies (item **276**).

Ethnographies, often paired with history, geography, and linguistics, add depth to topics that can explain observations and queries from other fields. In this biennial, the oral histories and traditions are paired with professional observations on the Mapuche-Tehuelches of Chile (item **292**); the Wapixana of Brazil (item **281**); the Campa, Ashaninka, Nonatsiguenga, and Cuzqueños of Peru (items **260** and **298**); the Misak of Colombia (item **288**); and the Soraga (item **284**) and people of the Chaco (item **265**) of Bolivia.

To the standard written sources of chronicles, legal documents, administrative texts, testimonies in court cases, petitions and memorials, and travelers accounts (items **256** and **300**), scholars are now analyzing maps (item **261**), myths (items **276** and **304**), songs (item **272**), symbols, names, words, and toponyms (items **248**, **249**, **264**, and **282**), and period illustrations (item **300**). These texts and the comparative uses (items **259** and **279**) that emerge as a consequence provide multidimensional views of both present and past.

I finish by highlighting some exemplary items that should be read by serious practitioners for their methodological contributions. Among them is an article by Guilherme Galhegos Felippe (item **271**) that discusses native inconsistencies and back-tracking observed by settlers in the 17th and 18th centuries. By reading between the lines, Galhegos is able to show convincingly that such behaviors proved to be useful methods for maintaining native group cohesion and integrity. Another study looks at how the Conibo (especially chiefs, other high-ranking natives, captives, and a female informant) contributed their geographical knowledge to the construction of maps in the Alto Ucayali (item **261**). The excellent article by Cecilia Martínez is a methodological model. She looks at the name of a group of Guarani and its transformation into a word that sequentially referred to a linguistic group, a territory, and a type of worker. Even as used today, the word hides a multitude of identities of related peoples who founded new communities (item **282**). The splendid article by José Luis Martínez Cereceda, Carla Díaz, and Constanza Tocornal analyzes the figures and decorations of *qeros*, showing relations between Incas and Antis (jungle inhabitants). The authors conclude that the representations appropriate prehispanic symbols for an indigenous audience and repurpose them to associate the Incas with the prehispanic past as well as with a new, possibly mythic future (item **283**). Finally, a collection of original papers on the southern Andes deals with a series of somewhat familiar topics (e.g., systems of irrigation, verticality, hacienda history, idolatry, native lands and tribute, and Hispanization of the natives), but examines a different, understudied locale. Such regional analyses prove to be a decentering reprieve, given the otherwise strong emphases on studies of the Lima and Cuzco areas (item **275**).

247 Acuña D., **Ángel**. El cuerpo en la memoria cultural Kawésqar. (*Magallania/Punta Arenas*, 44:1, 2016, p. 103–129, bibl.)

An ethnographic study of the Kawésqar people based on 11 months of residence among them. Modern practices are described and contrasted with historical reports of the same cultural folkways. The author covers childbirth and education, gender roles, diet, health, and body decoration and how they changed over time. Significantly, the Kawésqar of today are less healthy than previous generations given changes in their lifestyle, activities, diet, and clothing.

248 Almeida, Carina Santos de and **Ana Lúcia Vulfe Nötzold**. A luta pela terra em território Kaingang: os conflitos na Terra Indígena Xapecó (SC/Brasil) ao longo do século XX. (*Anos 90*, 18:34, dez. 2011, p. 279–303, bibl., map)

This work traces the land struggles of the native Kaingang peoples in the 20th century. From approximately 50,000 hectares in the south of Brazil, their domain has been reduced to 15,000 hectares due to usurpation, fraud, and bureaucratic difficulties. As this occurred, they lost their autonomy and access to natural resources. The author notes that terminology changed as some natives began to live in villages and lead sedentary agricultural lives. These peoples began to be labeled as peasants. This story contrasts with the native Páez of Colombia who successfully expanded their land holdings during colonial times (see items **290** and **296**).

249 Alvarez Lobo, Ricardo. Ensayos amazónicos. Vol. 2, Ensayos de etnohistoria. Lima: Centro Cultural José Pío Aza, Misioneros Dominicos, 2016. 1 v.: bibl.

A volume of essays by a missionary, anthropologist, educator, and public servant. The essays are on the history, economy, culture and language of the Yine. The author writes about the history of the Bajo Urubamba and the Alto Ucayali area and the Piro-Yine and to a lesser extent on the Matsiguengas and Nahuas (or Sharas). His historical topics include crime and vengeance; land tenure; demography, reducciones and parishes of the Alto Ucayali; and the colonization of the Bajo Urubamba. Of the author's four essays on the economy, the essay on the formation of the capitalist market in the Amazon is considered the most complete. In the cultural section are essays on legends and symbols, values, conversion, wisdom, and naming as ways of understanding the native way of thinking. Finally, the author, a near fluent speaker of the Yine language, writes on the structure of the language that gave him insights to the Piro ability to change and adopt.

250 Amayo, Enrique. Mar y olas, rito y deporte: del tup o caballito de totora a la moderna tabla o *surf*—su origen en la Costa Norte del Antiguo Perú (1500 a.C.-1532). Lima: Universidad Nacional Agraria La Molina, 2015. 174 p.: bibl., ill. (some color).

A unique ethnography and history that traces the origins of surfing back thousands of years to the *caballitos de totora* or *tup* that fishermen in Huanchaco (Peru) still use today. Using mostly secondary sources, the author begins with the Caral civilization on the central Coast, mentioning also KonTiki and long-distance maritime navigation across the Pacific in a panoramic review of history. He then writes in more detail about the impact of the conquest on the coastal populations and the survival of the *tup*. In a last section, he deals with the surfboard, balsas Andinas, and Polynesian canoes.

251 Arana Bustamante, Luis. Hacia una perspectiva diacrónica y etnohistórica sobre parentesco andino, linealidad y ayllu. (*Investig. Soc./San Marcos*, 18:32, junio 2014, p. 177–184, bibl.)

A short theoretical article, akin to a historiography, that reflects on the various uses of terms relating to Andean kinship. Among these are matrilineal and patrilineal lineages, *ayllu* (lineage), and house. The work of Lewis Henry Morgan, Denise Arnold, Susan Gillespie, John Victor Murra, A. L. Kroeber, C. Leví-Strauss, and William Isabell, among others are mentioned.

252 Arenas, Marco and **María Carolina Odone.** Despliegues visuales en instalaciones religiosas de los Andes del sur: una reflexión desde el arte rupestre colonial y la etnohistoria. (*Bol. Mus. Chil. Arte Precolomb.*, 21:1, 2016, p. 63–78, bibl., ill.)

An interesting article discussing the continuities in colors, form, themes, and techniques between rock art (*arte rupestre*) and colonial and republican art forms on the interior and exterior walls of church buildings in the Andes. The paintings of the churches of Huayllaripa, Chuquinga, Yaure, Tolapampa, Lagunas, and Markachavi are described. Together, the author argues that they form an indigenous way of communicating that is evident even in the later mural art in similar venues.

253 Barham Ode, Walid. Tambotoco: la trilogía de Guaman. Cusco, Peru: Editorial Pumaruna, 2015. 148 p.: bibl., ill. (some color).

A fascinating exposition on the location of the original Waka Wanakauri (based on a shadow of the Inca and a puma) that the author attests is in the Montaña Pitusiray in the Province of Calca, Valle Sagrado de los Inca. In the first part he discusses the accepted knowledge on the *waka* (shrine, sacred place or object) with its legendary Ventanas de Tambotoco that he states were frequented by all the Incas, given that it was a sacred spot and an oracle. In the second part he supports the thesis that the original location was a secret, using photos, textual citations and maps.

254 **Bauer, Brian S.; Madeleine Halac-Higashimori; and Gabriel E. Cantarutti.** Voices from Vilcabamba: accounts chronicling the fall of the Inca Empire (1572). Boulder: University Press of Colorado, 2016. 235 p.: bibl., index.

A welcome volume containing translations into English of seven documents from the Vilcabamba era, 1536–72, detailing the final decades of Inca rule. The selected documents include the description of Vilcabamba by Baltasar de Ocampo Conejeros, sections of Martín de Murua's chronicle, Augustinian reports, and battlefield and other eye-witness accounts. A critical general introduction and commentaries on each document help provide the historical context of the sources.

255 **Bustamante Paulino, Nicéforo.** La Nación Yacha: territorio, historia, cultura e identidad en Huánuco. Huánuco, Peru: Letra Muerta, 2015. 431 p.: bibl., ill. (color), maps (some color).

A history of the Yacha (Huanuco) by a native son, educator, and academic. Chapters on prehispanic times include a historiography, a discussion of sources, an analysis of social groups, a detailed introduction to the geography, flora and fauna; and information on prehispanic Yacha and the Incas. The colonial era is explored with chapters on the encomienda (including valuable tables with the lists of encomienda grants given out by Francisco Pizarro in 1534 and 1541; one table with the list of encomiendas bestowed by Vaca de Castro in 1543, and another given out by Licenciado Pedro de la Gasca); and the tribute exacted on orders of La Gasca and the Viceroy Marques de Cañete of 1559. The author also covers the visita of 1562; obrajes; haciendas; and reducciones, and resistance to colonization and independence. A long section deals with the economy, technology, and production of the population; as well as festivals, beliefs, music and dance. This represents a massive effort that provides pages and pages of hard-to-find local information.

256 **Caballero Arias, Hortensia.** Desencuentros y encuentros en el Alto Orinoco: incursiones en Territorio Yanomami, siglos XVIII–XIX. Caracas: Ediciones IVIC, 2014. 199 p.: bibl., color ill., maps. (Serie Histórica)

A noteworthy review of the historical sources on the Yamomami Indians in Venezuela from 1750 to the end of the 19th century that recounts how their image became one of a war-like, inaccessible, and uncontrollable people. Accounts that cover the Alto Orinoco and Guayana by Prussian polymath, geographer, and naturalistic scientist Alexander von Humboldt, German botanist and writer Richard H. Schomburgk, English botanist Richard Spruce, explorer Francisco Michelena y Rojas and French traveler Jean Chaffanjon are cited. Particularly important are the colored maps interspersed in the text.

257 **Cabral, Salvador.** Los guaraníes: historia y cultura. Buenos Aires: Corregidor, 2015. 316 p.: bibl., ill.

A synthetic treatment of the cultures and history of the Guaraní peoples, based on chronicles and other primary and secondary sources. Topics covered include the contact between Spaniards and the natives and the transformation of their culture wrought by the encounter. The Jesuit missions figure prominently.

258 **Cañedo-Argüelles Fabrega, Teresa.** El Paraguay colonial: sueño y vigilia de un pueblo itinerante. Buenos Aires: Sociedad Argentina de Antropología, 2014. 103 p.: bibl. (Publicaciones de la Sociedad Argentina de Antropología)

A short volume on colonial Paraguay with discussions on the environment and culture; mestizaje and prejudice; relations between Guaranies and Chaqueños; colonization and conflict; the Jesuit missions; the Franciscan *reducción* (resettlement); the Spanish-Portuguese frontier and the *gaucho* (cowboy).

259 **Carcelén Reluz, Carlos Guillermo.** La mita y el comercio de la nieve en Lima colonial: una aproximación a la historia del medio ambiente. (*Investig. Soc./San Marcos*, 29, dic. 2012, p. 55–64, bibl., ill., tables)

A well-written and organized essay on the ice trade in Lima, especially in the

18th century. The routes and labor involved are documented. The prices are shown to be associated with climate change. A table with the years of El Niño events is especially helpful. A few brief references to the ice trade in Mexico and Guatemala are included.

260   **Carmona Cruz, Aurelio.** La cosmovisión dual de los inkas. Cusco, Peru: Ministerio de Cultura, Dirección Regional de Cultura Cusco, 2013. 149 p.: bibl., ill. (some color).

A book on the worldview of the Incas, written by a Cuzqueño. Among the topics covered are religion, the city of Qosqo, the solar and lunar calendars, duality and complementarity, and traditional medicine. On the last topic, the illness or conditions described include *mal del susto* (loss of the soul), *hallpahap'isqa* (land's punishment when sacrifices are not forthcoming), *qhayqasqa* (failure to respect the ancestor cult), *mal viento* (an illness associated with ancient tombs and mummies in which the body is covered with blemishes), *el supay* (the devil), *amaychura* (a child's illness caused by the body's possession by a dead person's spirit), *mal de ojo* (evil eye), *la enfermedad del acero* (in women, caused by a non-poisonous snake), and *traumatismos* (fractures and the like).

261   **Chauca Tapia, Roberto.** Contribución indígena a la cartografía del Alto Ucayali a fines del siglo XVII. (*Bull. Inst. fr. étud. andin.*, 44:1, 2015, p. 117–138, bibl., maps)

A refreshingly original paper on a relatively new topic—how and when did the native Conibo contribute their geographical knowledge to the construction of maps and sovereignty in the alto Ucayali. The author cites reports with specific indigenous actors and Franciscan missionaries who took part. Native caciques and principales figure prominently, as do, to a lesser extent, captives and a female informant.

262   **Chávez, Samuel Antonio.** Pedagogía de la salvación: un estudio histórico sobre el aporte de la educación adventista en la vida del indígena aymara de Rosario, 1920–1930. Cochabamba: Editorial Nuevo Tiempo de Bolivia, 2012. 278 p.: bibl., ill.

A history of the Adventist Church schools in Rosario (province of Pacajes) from 1920 to 1930. The thesis is that these educational efforts succeeded in teaching indigenous peoples when the prejudices from colonial times undermined the government's efforts to do the same in public schools. Despite some intermittent resistance from the state, politicians, police, military, and the religious establishment, the Adventists succeeded in establishing schools for both male and female students. Eventually, the government realized the need and relented. In one decade, the Adventists established 63 schools with circa 3,000 students. The result is that peasants were transformed into citizens.

263   **Choque Canqui, Roberto.** El indigenismo y los movimientos indígenas en Bolivia. La Paz: Convenio Adrés Bello, Instituto Internacional de Integración: Universidad Nacional Siglo XX, Bolivia, 2014. 381 p.: bibl., ill. (Serie Rebeliones indígenas; 2)

This book by an author who has published extensively on similar themes covers 181 years of Bolivian republican life. Throughout, natives and peasants fight for land, territory, and natural resources. He writes about such conflicts in the highlands against *hacendados* or *terratenientes* from 1874–1953 and in the lowlands from 1990–2006. In the process, he discusses "the Indian," the indigenismo movement, the expansionist hacienda, the Chaco War, the Federación Agrária de La Paz of 1947, the agrarian reform of 1953, political parties, and native mobilizations.

264   **Combès, Isabelle.** De la una y otra banda del río Paraguay: historia y etnografía de los Itatines, siglos XVI–XVIII. Cochabamba, Bolivia: Instituto Latinoamericano de Misionología: Itinerarios Editorial, 2015. 231 p.: bibl., ill. (some color). (Colección Scripta autochtona; 15)

An ethnohistory by an accomplished scholar on the Itatines who live along the River Paraguay. In telling their story, the author relates a tale of a cultural area between Bolivia, Brazil, and Paraguay that is the scene of migrations, exchanges, native alliances, and colonization. Itatin is the name that the Guarayo of Bolivia; the

Kaiowás of Brazil, and the Pai-Tavytera of Paraguay were known by into the colonial era. The eastern groups, living in Brazil and Paraguay, were contacted by and settled by the Jesuits. From primary documents written by early European explorers and missionaries, the author summarizes the demography, political organization, religion and culture of the natives. A second part is a listing of the different ethnic groups, native individuals, and toponyms that appear in the sources from the 16th to the mid-18th century. Part 3 is made up of transcribed documents, including information on the services of Hernando de Salazar (1563); information on the trip of Don Francisco Ortiz de Vergara from Asunción to Santa Cruz in 1565; a list of the Itatines baptized in 1578; information on the mission in the province of Santa Cruz in 1589; the Jesuit annual letter of 1594; letters from missionaries, dated 1600 and 1614; a description of the Itatí in 1633; and an account of the rebellion of Ñanduabuçu of 1643.

265   Combès, Isabelle. Notas de etnohistoria (Chaco y Chiquitania). Santa Cruz de la Sierra, Bolivia: Biblioteca del Museo de Historia, Universidad Autónoma Gabriel René Moreno, 2015. 202 p.: bibl., maps. (Biblioteca del Museo de Historia. Etnohistoria; 5)

An ethnohistory in the form of a compilation of 11 articles on the people of the Chaco and Chiquitania (eastern Bolivia). The chapters are divided into three parts. The first deals with ethnic relations, including writings on how natives view and relate to "the other": the Chanés and Chiriguanos or the Moros of the Chaco. She explores how ethnic names and the ways they changed became markers of the formation and reconfiguration of ethnic groups. Part 2 studies the political organization of the Chanés and Chiriguanos during the colonial era and the 19th century. Part 3 looks at methodology: what work still needs to be done and how to do it.

266   Cornejo Bouroncle, Jorge. Tupac Amaru: la revolución precursora de la emancipación continental. Facsimile edition. Cusco, Peru: Universidad Nacional de San Antonio Abad del Cusco, Facultad de Ciencias Sociales, 2013. 651 p.: bibl., ill. (some color).

This brick-of-a-book is a facsimile and third edition of Cornejo Bouroncle's work, first published in 1949. The author ties the revolutionary movement with the independence that followed. It is based solidly on primary documents, some of which are extensively quoted in the text. It has served several generations already by helping to fortify national identity and culture. The hypothesis of the author is that Tupac Amaru fought for local liberty, justice, and dignity; but his movement, as modern scholars know, has had a global presence and influence.

267   Corominas, Alicia. Desandando La Rioja. La Rioja, Argentina: Nexo Grupo Editor, 2013. 525 p.: bibl., ill.

A massive local history centered on La Rioja that traces the longue durée occupation of the area. The text covers the first Spaniards in the area: Diego de Almagro, Diego de Rojas, Juan Nuñez de Prado, Francisco de Villagra, Francisco de Aguirre, and Juan Pérez de Zurita; the native Diaguita and Calchaqui cultures and their ceremonial centers, economy, and religion; the arrival of the Incas and their worldview; the foundation of La Rioja; colonial labor systems (encomienda, *yanaconazgo* (personal service to an employer, usually in rural areas), and the mita); missionaries; Spanish laws concerning the natives (Leyes de Burgos, Requerimiento, Leyes Nuevas); the war against the Calchaquies; and native resistance.

268   di Salvia, Daniela. La Pachamama en la época incaica y post-incaica: una visión andina a partir de las crónicas peruanas coloniales, siglos XVI y XVII. (*Rev. Esp. Antropol. Am.*, 43:1, 2013, p. 89–110, bibl., ill., tables)

A good review of the 16th- and 17th-century chroniclers' descriptions of the Pachamama, mother earth. The author categorizes the chronicles and shows who borrowed the prose of whom.

269   Dias, Antônio Gonçalves. Brasil e Oceania. Organização por Raymundo Netto. Apresentação e glossário biográfico por Ana Miranda. Fortaleza, Brazil: Armazém da Cultura, 2013. 396 p.: bibl. (Coleção Nordestes; 4)

A comparative report written in the 18th century, on the natives of Brazil and the peoples of Oceania compiled at the request of Emperor don Pedro II by Gonçalves Dias, a member of the Instituto Histórico e Geográfico do Rio de Janeiro. In the first part, the author describes the native Brazilians in the 16th century, based on chronicles, memoirs, and rare books. Chapters focus on the customs and arts of the natives of both the coast and hinterland. He describes the Tupis and their religion, celebrations, dances, government, family life, and their interactions with the French and Portuguese explorers. The second part includes information on the Polynesians, Melanesians, Afurás, Endaménios, and Austrálios. The comparisons comprise a two-page general summary. Overall, the volume is a period-piece reflecting the knowledge and biases of the time it was written.

270   Domínguez Condezo, Víctor. Heroica resistencia de la cultura andina: deslindes sobre la educación y la cultura. Segunda edición. Huánuco, Peru: UDH Universidad de Huánuco; Lima: Editorial San Marcos, 2013. 247 p.: bibl., ill.

A treatise on resistance to formal education that submerges popular culture and fosters discrimination and poverty. The author explores popular culture through oral literature, story-telling, and singing. He associates Hispanization with the loss of native identity. For Huánuco, he discusses legends, petroglyphs, dances and songs, and traditional technology. He describes the Rayguana, a dance of prosperity; postulates that the Quechua Yaru-Huanuco is an example of resistance; and writes on the administration of water. He advocates, finally, for a technical education, that also respects the Andean environment and values.

271   Felippe, Guilherme Galhegos. Estar, e não ser, aliado: a sociabilidade dos índios do Chaco durante o avanço colonial no século XVIII. (*Anos 90*, 22:41, julho 2015, p. 267–298, bibl.)

A noteworthy article describing contacts between the native peoples of the Chaco and settlers trying to establish routes between Buenos Aires and Andean mines, as well as inter-ethnic conflicts in the 17th and 18th centuries. What seemed to Europeans as native inconsistencies and backtracking actually was, from the native's point of view, a traditionally useful method to maintain the cohesion and integrity of the group. Missionaries, reducciones and wars are highlighted.

272   Filosofía y sabiduría ancestral. Edición y compilación por Rafael Gonzalo Angarita Cáceres. Bucaramanga, Colombia: Vicerrectoría Académica, Facultad de Ciencias Humanas, Escuela de Filosofía, Universidad Industrial de Santander, 2015. 531 p.: bibl., ill., maps. (Cátedra Low Maus)

A hefty book on Colombia that highlights the construction of space where Western and non-Western knowledge intersect. Topics include the native concept of time and history, ritual and ceremony, shamanism and native religion, Christianization (of the Muiscas), ancestral songs, roles of native leaders, myths, and intercultural communication.

273   Gómez Gómez, Mauricio Alejandro. Del chontal al ladino: hispanización de los indios de Antioquia según la visita de Francisco de Herrera Campuzano, 1614–1616. Medellín, Colombia: Universidad de Antioquia, Facultad de Ciencias Sociales y Humanas/Historia, Fondo Editorial, 2015. 190 p.: bibl., index. (FCSH investigación)

This book analyzes the Hispanization of the native culture of Antioquia (Colombia) in the 17th century, using such primary sources as the *visita a la tierra* (inspection records). It points out aspects that survived and were even adopted by the Spanish. Some facets of Spanish culture were imposed forcibly by the encomenderos; some were voluntarily adopted by the natives. The book ends with three vignettes of acculturated "ladino-ized" Indians.

274   González Carré, Enrique and Fermín del Pino-Díaz. Aprender e instruir en los Andes: siglos XV–XVI. Lima: Derrama Magisterial, 2013. 207 p.: bibl., ill. (Colección Pensamiento educativo peruano; 1)

An interesting book with two essays on the theme of education. The first by González Carré deals with learning under the Incas. Various life-cycle rituals are described as are the *Yachaywasi*, or "house of knowledge," for boys. For girls, the *acllawasi*, or house of the chosen females, is described. Quotations on the above topics from the chronicles of Garcilaso de la Vega, Martín de Murúa, Felipe Guaman Poma de Ayala, Santa Cruz Pachacuti, Fernando de Montesinos, and others follow. The second essay by Pino-Díaz focuses on the writings of Father Joseph de Acosta. The author discusses European humanism and the Jesuits; Acosta's arrival in Peru; and Mexican and Peruvian schools. A short section of quotes from Acosta's writings follows.

Los grupos subalternos en el nordeste del Virreinato del Río de la Plata. See item **1024**.

275 Historia andina en Chile. Vol. 2, Políticas imperiales, dinámicas regionales y sociedades indígenas. Edición de Jorge Hidalgo Lehuedé. Santiago: Editorial Universitaria, 2014. 1 v.: bibl., ill. (Imagen de Chile)

A valuable collection of original papers on the southern Andes, edited by a recognized authority. Papers based on primary sources cover the Tawantinsuyu; systems of irrigation; verticality; hacienda history, Alacrán Island and the defense of Arica; idolatry in Arica and Atacama; festivals and rituals; caciques; native lands and tribute; mining; enlightened corregidores; and the Hispanization of the natives of the Audienca of Charcas. This is a "must-read" book that balances Lima- and Cuzco-centered research.

276 Historia y cultura en el mundo andino: homenaje a Henrique Urbano. Edición de Johan Leuridan Huys *et al*. Lima: USMP Universidad de San Martín de Porres, Fondo Editorial, Facultad de Ciencias de la Comunicación, Turismo y Psicología, 2016. 210 p.: bibl., ill. (some color).

The publication of nine papers in honor of Henrique Urbano (1938–2014), a prolific student of the history of the Andes. Most of the works deal with themes that Urbano had studied. In addition to the pages dedicated specifically to Urbano and his contributions are works on Andean myths; Pablo José de Arriaga's extirpation of idolatry campaign; Aymara ceremonies; parish churches in Oyon and Huaura; and Archbishop Geronimo de Loayza's view of evangelization. The last chapter deals with the industries that currently disseminate knowledge on Peruvian culture, like movies, television, and radio.

277 Jornadas en Homenaje a Germán Canuhé, 1st, Universidad Nacional de La Pampa, 2014. Investigaciones acerca de y con el pueblo ranquel: pasado, presente y perspectivas: actas. Edición de Claudia Salomón Tarquini y Ignacio Roca. Santa Rosa, Argentina: Subsecretaría de Cultura, Ministerio de Cultura y Educación, Gobierno de La Pampa: EdUNLPam, 2015. 303 p.: bibl., ill.

A volume of selected papers from the meetings on the Ranquel peoples in 2014. A large number of archeologists, linguists, and bilingual educators provide wide-ranging investigations on native identity, exchange, Rosas' campaign of exterminación, frontier diplomacy in the 1840s, Ranquel and peace treaties, native poetry, the Ranquel and the labor market, and native laws and rights.

278 Loayza Portocarrero, José Antonio. Eran tres, dos Túpac y dos Catari: proyecto revolucionario indígena de Tomás Catari, Túpac Amaru y Túpac Catari para la aniquilación de la estructura colonial de opresión, 1780–1781. Cochabamba, Bolivia: Historia Crítica, 2014. 339 p.: bibl., ill. (Historia crítica)

A text on the revolutionary project of Tomás Catari, Túpac Amaru, and Túpac Catari to annihilate the Spanish colonial power structure in the 1780s. In clear, well-organized chapters, the author covers the colonial context and three major revolts. The first is the rebellion of Chayanta led by Tomás Catari. The rebellion of Peru under the leadership of Túpac Amaru and Micaela, his wife, and their fate is the second. The rebellion of La Paz of Túpac Catari is the third major section of the book. A chapter on native ideology follows.

279 López von Vriessen, Carlos. Pillmatun y Linao: dos juegos de pelota de manos originarios de la cultura mapuche. Valparíso, Chile: Ediciones Universitarias de Valparaíso, Pontificia Universidad Católica de Valparaíso, 2013. 307 p.: bibl., ill. (some color), maps.

An interdisciplinary study of two games played by the Mapuche, placed in the historical context of Chile and Mesoamerica. The author uses ethnography, photography, oral traditions, myths, and ethnohistorical accounts to describe the games. Some historical accounts are transcribed as annexes to the main text.

280   Maggiori, Ernesto. Consideraciones y reflexiones acerca de la historia de los pueblos mapuche y tehuelche: ensayo histórico. Trelew Provincia de Chubut, Argentina: Remitente Patagonia, 2015. 607 p.: bibl.

A long essay on the Mapuche and Tehuelche, starting with the Araucanas before the Spanish arrived. It moves on to treat settlement and resistance during the colonial era; independence; German colonization and missions; native revolts and peace treaties; Rosas' Campaña al Desierto; the establishment of native reserves; mega-mining; and native communities in Patagonia.

281   Maia, Delta Maria de Souza. Os Wapixanas da Serra da Moça: entre o uso e desuso das práticas cotidianas (1930–1990). Boa Vista, Brazil: Editora UFRR, EDUFRR, 2014. 136 p.: bibl., ill.

A history of the Wapixana and their interethnic relations with non-Indians and how such interactions changed their social and cultural universe from 1930 to 1990. Education figures prominently in this story. Over time, contact with priests, settlers, and *hacendados* (*fazendeiros*) and others encouraged the Wapixana to replace the use of their language with Portuguese. The history is based on the memories and oral traditions of the Wapixana and ethnographic participant-observations. The author considers changes in the material culture associated with hunting, gathering, and fishing.

282   Martínez, Cecilia. *Tapuy miri, chiquitos, chiquitanos*: historia de un nombre en perspectiva interétnica. (*Bull. Inst. fr. étud. andin.*, 44:2, 2015, p. 237–258, bibl.)

An excellent article, based on primary and secondary sources, on the transformation of the name of a group of natives from a Guarani-given name, referring to small houses or their slave status and translated and simplified by the Spanish to "chiquitos," to a word referring to a linguistic group, to a word for a territory, to a word for a type of worker. Yet, the author states that the words Chiquitos and Chiquitaria hide a multitude of identities that survive to the present and came to be evident in the 20th century as related people began to found new, self-sufficient communities.

283   Martínez Cereceda, José Luis; Carla Díaz; and Constanza Tocornal. Inkas y Antis: variaciones coloniales de un relato andino visual. (*Bol. Mus. Chil. Arte Precolomb.*, 21:1, 2016, p. 9–25, notes, bibl., ill.)

An excellent, even elegant, article on the figures and scenes that appear on colonial *qeros* (drinking beakers). An analysis focuses on the 12.3 percent of the 440 qeros analyzed that show the Incas and the *Antis* (jungle inhabitants). The authors identify the figures and the symbols and the possible narratives they suggest, engaging with interpretations by Tom Cummins and R. Martin. The authors conclude that the qero represent prehispanic symbols which were repurposed into new myths and stories during the colonial period.

284   Mora, Gerardo and Andrea Goytia. Los kerus vivos en Capital Ayllu Soraga y su participación en la fiesta de la Virgen del Rosario. (*Bol. Mus. Chil. Arte Precolomb.*, 21:1, 2016, p. 49–62, bibl., ill.)

An ethnographic description of three pairs of keros (drinking beakers) used in ritual contexts in the Ayllu Soraga (Bolivia). It is interesting that the beakers themselves are described in human terms and are subject to repairs or operations to cure their deterioration. The work covers Inca, colonial, and present times.

285   Morong Reyes, Germán. Saberes hegemónicos y dominio colonial: los indios en el Gobierno del Perú de Juan de Matienzo (1567). Rosario, Argentina: Prohistoria Ediciones, 2016. 323 p.: bibl., ill. (Colección Historia moderna; 7)

The author analyzes the 1567 book on the government of Peru written by Juan de Matienzo, an *oidor* (judge) on the *Audiencia* (Supreme Court) of Charcas. The legal treatise deals with the construction of a colonial government. Much space is dedicated to the discussion of the native's place and role in society. Stereotypes of the native as timid, irrational, drunk, lazy, pagan, and melancholy appear. The issue of native slavery, hotly debated at the time, is discussed with references to Aristotle and Plato.

286 Morrone, Ariel J. Tras los pasos del mitayo: la sacralización del espacio en los corregimientos de Pacajes y Omasuyos, 1570–1650. (*Bull. Inst. fr. étud. andin.*, 44:1, 2015, p. 91–116, bibl., maps, table)

A highly speculative, but provocative work that hypothesizes ritual pathways between *reducciones*, central staging areas for *mitayo* (forced rotating laborers) workers, and the mines of Potosí. The cacique and/or *capitán de mita* organized the travelers and oversaw the rituals along the way, thus (re)establishing memories and reinforcing his legitimacy as a mediator between commoners and the state as well as between the traditional worship of the ancestors and the Catholic Church. The author acknowledges that some data do not fit the model he proposes and suggests that further work is needed to validate his hypothesis.

287 Nicolas, Vincent. Los ayllus de Tinguipaya: ensayos de historia a varias voces. La Paz: Plural Editores, 2015. 491 p.: bibl., ill. (some color), maps (some color).

An impressive panoramic history covering Tinguipaya (Postosí, Bolivia) from the mid-16th century to the early 21st century, based on colonial manuscript documents in archives of Bolivia, Spain, and Argentina; secondary sources; interviews; and dialogues with community members. A critical analysis of the sources permits the author to approximate more closely the relationship of the community to the lands they occupy and use, and to appreciate their strategies of resistance to colonial and republican authorities over time. The author covers the *reducción* of the 16th century, the *cabildo* or town council, tribute, 19th-century struggles to protect their lands, oral histories, the Chaco war, and the Belgrano warriors. The text includes extensive quotes from contemporary documents, including those in native languages (with translations), color photos, and maps. Appendices include transcriptions of the *visita* (inspection) of Fray Luis López of 1593, the ordinances of Diego de Sanabria of 1575, titles from 1726, a land dispute from 1735, and others.

288 Obando Villota, Lorena. Pensando y educando desde el corazón de la montaña: la historia de un intelectual indígena Misak: Avelino Dagua Hurtado. Popayán, Colombia: Editorial Universidad del Cauca, 2016. 150 p.: bibl., ill. (some color), index, maps (some color). (Colección Territorios del saber)

An ethnography on the life of the Misak. The author begins with his encounters with Estanislao Chicunque, *"a cargador de hombres"* (a carrier (literally) or administrator or person responsible for men), who told tales of evangelization and his participation in the war against Peru. He also worked as a porter and merchant, but his narrative fused the historical with ritual, the thunder and lightning, the wind, the songs of birds and the sounds of river and rain that went back as far as the *"tiempo sin tiempo"* (the time without time). Among his stories is the origin of his people and a cacique (Carlos Tamabioy) who had supernatural origins. The author then interviews the *"taita"* Avelino Dagua Hurtado. It is through his apprenticeship with Hurtado that Obando Villota gained entrance to the collective memory, traditions, and histories of the community and came to understand his vision of the world.

289 Oliveira, Susane Rodrigues de. Representações das sociedades indígenas nas fontes históricas coloniais: propostas para o ensino de história. (*Anos 90*, 18:34, dez. 2011, p. 187–212, bibl.)

Theoretical reflections and suggestions for incorporating 16th- and 17th-century historical documents written by Europeans, natives, and mestizos about Indians into the basic history curriculum in Brazil to teach critical thinking. One goal is to reshape public imaginings to overcome the prejudices and negative constructs of some of the sources. Themes, analyses of sample documents, and lesson plans are included.

290 Paredes Cisneros, Santiago. La política del resguardo entre los indios páez del pueblo de Tobooyma (gobernación de Popayán), 1650–1750. (*Hist. Crít./Bogotá*, 58, oct./dic. 2015, p. 33–55, bibl., maps, table)

A good article on the ability of the Páez to appropriate lands, when elsewhere in Northern South America, natives were losing land to Spaniards and castas. Among the factors explaining this success, were the abilities of the caciques to negotiate with Spanish authorities and the absence of many Spaniards and *castas* in the area.

291   **Paz Esquerre, Eduardo.** Sistemas de escritura mochica e inca: la escritura en el mundo. Trujillo, Peru: Fondo Editorial de la Universidad Privada Antenor Orrego, 2015. 142 p.: bibl., ill. (some color).

A book on systems of writing and in particular the system used by the Mochica and Inca peoples of the Andes. The author foreshadows the focus of the book by discussing the ideographs of cuneiform, hieroglyphics, and Chinese characters. He reviews symbols based on phonetics before discussing Hebrew, Greek, and Latin alphabets. Finally, he surveys the evidence that the Mochica used painted lima-bean shaped symbols as a means of communicating. For the Inca, he writes on the *topacus*, square designs woven into tunics of well-placed authorities.

292   **Pérez, Liliana Elizabeth.** Keu-Kenk: política indígena en la Patagonia: 1865–1965. Trelew, Argentina: Remitente Patagonia, 2015. 231 p.: bibl., ill.

An analysis of the politics of the Mapuche-Tehuelches of Patagonia. The author focuses on the people and culture who escaped the "Conquest of the Desert" to reconstitute themselves in community and survive. Pacts, negotiations, diplomacy, dialogue, confrontation and other forms of negotiation and resistance are documented. Oral histories of the GanGan, Yalalaubat, LefiNiyeu, Epulef, and Chalia complement the written record.

293   **Pifarré, Francisco.** Historia de un pueblo: los guaraní-chiriguano. 2a edición corregida y aumentada. La Paz: Fundación Xavier Albó: CIPCA Centro de Investigación y Promoción del Campesinado, 2015. 493 p.: bibl., ill. (some folded), index.

A new, second edition of a long book on the Guaraní-Chiriguanos. It is a basic text that could lead interested readers to additional material on important points. The text starts in the 16th century with discussion of population numbers and the economy. Another chapter discusses Chiriguano relations with other ethnic groups, including the Moxo, the Chiquitano, the Guarayo-Itatin, the Yurakaré, the Tamacoci-Grigotá, the Chore, the Chicha, Paspaya, Churumata and Tomata, the Pocona-Pojo and the Chui of Mizque, the Toba, the Chané, and the Spanish. The colonial era is discussed by century and includes mention of conflicts, missions, and wars. Pages on independence and republican life cover the hacienda, missions, and wars through the second half of the 20th century. Various appendices provide material on Spanish views of the Chiriguanos; demography; the 16th-century Chané, Spanish settlements in the 16th century; missions; and Toba resistance.

294   **Prehistoria en Chile: desde sus primeros habitantes hasta los Incas.** Edición de Fernanda Falabella *et al.* Santiago: Editorial Universitaria: Sociedad Chilena de Arqueología, 2016. 737 p.: bibl., ill.

A huge, serious synthesis and text on the archeology of the prehispanic population up to the rise of the Inca Empire in what is today Chile. Chapters describe the environment and geography of different zones; hunters, gatherers, and fishermen on the coast; the population and activities in the northern valleys; communities of potters (*alfareras*); the populations of Rapa Nui (from circa 800 to 1888 d.C.), and the Incas. This book takes the form of a textbook, uniting state-of-the-art detailed investigative summaries that will long stand as a reference for students and professionals alike. Unfortunately, the title includes the word "prehistory," which robs the subjects of the book of their history. The word "prehispanic" would have conveyed the same idea.

295   **Querejazu Lewis, Roy.** Presencia incaica en el límite andino amazónico, Cochabamba-Santa Cruz. Cochabamba, Bolivia: UMSS, Instituto de Investigaciones Arquitectura y Ciencias del Hábitat: Grupo Editorial Kipus, 2015. 120 p.: bibl., ill. (some color).

A short volume on Inca installations at the frontier between the highlands and the Amazonian zone by a recognized Bolivian historian. The author provides context with chapters on the origins of the Inca Empire and the Inca conquest of the Collasuyus. Then, he documents Inca contacts with the peoples of the Amazonian east and the road system in the region of Pocona. Two chapters review the site of Incallajta and a third describes the fortress (El Fuerte) of Samaipata. The work is based on chronicler accounts and newspaper stories, journal articles and secondary sources, and includes colored pictures of the site.

296   Quiroga Zuluaga, Marcela. Las políticas coloniales y la acción indígena: la configuración de los pueblos de indios de la provincia de Páez, siglos XVII y XVIII. (*Anu. Colomb. Hist. Soc. Cult.*, 42:1, enero/junio 2015, p. 23–50, bibl., table)

A serious article, based on rich primary sources, on the agency of Páez native inhabitants in successfully claiming lands before colonial authorities. This case study contradicts what happened in other parts of Latin America where native peoples continuously lost land to Spanish and *casta* (mixed-blood peoples) usurpation over the centuries (see also **248**). Significantly, too, the author mentions "positional inheritance" as a mechanism for cacique succession.

297   Quispe-Agnoli, Rocío. Nobles de papel: identidades oscilantes y genealogías borrosas en los descendientes de la realeza Inca. Madrid: Iberoamericana; Frankfurt am Main: Vervuert, 2016. 264 p.: bibl., ill., index, map. (Tiempo emulado; 42)

A critical reading of the sources on the genealogies of the descendants of the Inca nobility in a context of social and economic change while living in Mexico. The author focuses on the titles of nobility of the UchuTúpucYupanqui family and the efforts of doña María Joaquina Inca to use the Spanish legal apparatus to re-establish their family's argument. The title refers to the paper trail of *reales cedulas* (royal decrees) and coat of arms used to bolster the family's position. The appendix contains a letter from María Joaquina to Carlos IV (1793); letters between her and the viceroy of Mexico (1789–92); the testimony of a witness on the legitimacy of Juan Uchu and Casilda de la Rosa Ucho (also Uchu) (1696); an encomienda grant (1701); a Real Cedula of Carlos I with a coat of arms (1545); and a description of the coat of arms from 1636. Three genealogies are also reproduced.

298   Rojas Zolezzi, Enrique. Cuando los guerreros hablan: los indígenas campa ashanika y nomatsiguenga y la guerra contra Sendero Luminoso y el movimiento revolucionario Túpac Amaru en la selva central peruana. Lima: Editorial Horizonte, 2016. 329 p.: bibl., maps. (Antropología y etnología; 14)

This volume documents the war among the Campa, Ashaninka, and Nonatsiguenga; adherents of Sendero Luminoso and the Tupac Amaru Revolutionary Movements and the forces of the central government in the jungles of central Peru, a zone propitious to the cultivation of coca and the production of cocaine. The work tells a broader story of the efforts of these native peoples to establish relations with and accommodate the more urban sectors of Peruvian society. The author focuses on the communities and the process of settling down in the 1970s; the production of coca, sugarcane, salt, and iron; early relationships with missionaries; the guerrillas of 1965; and the establishment of native federations and the consequences of the same in building local leadership, regional organizations, and ties to the national government. The story of the struggles between native peoples, settlers, and would-be revolutionaries in the 1980s and early 1990s is juxtaposed against this background. Eventually, the native peoples contributed *ronderos*, groups of armed self-defense forces, to aid government efforts. The effects of this pact on Ashaninka society is told in one of the last segments of the book. The study is based on ethnographic research, newspaper accounts, NGOs and government agency accounts, and secondary sources.

299   Rostworowski de Diez Canseco, María. Los Incas. Lima: Ministerio de Cultura: IEP, Instituto de Estudios Peruanos, 2014. 190 p.: bibl., ill. (Obras completas de María Rostworowski; IX)(Serie Historia andina, 42)

A convenient compilation of the well-loved and respected ethnohistorian María Rostworowski, part of the series of volumes of her complete works. United here are articles published from 1955 to 2000 on the Inca. Contents include the conflict between the Incas and the Chancas, a war that profoundly affected the former and launched their imperial designs; land tenure; the conflict over coca bushes between the Collique and the Quivi; duality; succession; record keeping and the categorization of the population; and the Spondylus trade. The volume includes a CD which accesses maps, videos, and an interview with the author.

300 Sallas, Ana Luisa Fayet. Ciência do homem e sentimento da natureza: viajantes alemães no Brasil do século XIX. Curitiba, Brasil: Editora UFPR, 2013. 334 p.: bibl., ill. (some color), maps, portraits. (Série Pesquisa; 222)

Using the travel accounts and scientific writings of German travelers Prince Maximilian Alexander Philip de Wied-Neuwied (1815–19), Carl Friedrich Phillip von Marthius (1817–20), and Johann Moritz Regendas (1822–25), the author constructs their imaginings of native society and habitat, notably tinged with a sense of Germanic romanticism. The book focuses on the construction of ethnographic images of the people engaged in hunting, warfare, and celebrations. Reproductions of illustrations pepper the text.

301 Sepúlvela Díaz, Jairo et al. El Pucará del Cerro La Muralla: Mapuches, Incas y Españoles en el Valle del Cachapoal. Santiago: Mutante Editores, 2014. 250 p.: bibl., ill. (some color). (Colección Memoria)

A basic history of Mapuches, Incas, and Spaniards since prehispanic times in the Cachapoal Valley of Central Chile, focusing on ruins of a large construction on Cerro La Muralla. Based on chroniclers and travelers accounts and secondary sources, the text surveys the history, mentioning resistance of the *promaucaes* (*puruma* or savage + *awca* or enemy) to Inca incursions; Valdivia's arrival in 1541; and the native war against Spanish settlement.

302 Severi, Carlo et al. Quimeras em diálogo: grafismo e figuração nas artes indígenas. Organização por Carlo Severi y Els Lagrou. Rio de Janeiro: 7Letras, 2013. 334 p.: bibl., ill. (Coleção Sociologia & antropologia)

A book on signs, designs, symbols, and figures on pottery, stools, drums, bones, textiles, baskets, and bodies. Individual chapters treat shamanic rites; narrative and graphic art; Wajana (Wayana) paintings; body painting and decoration; music and song; and trance and ritual. Papers document Ashaninka, Shipibo, Kayapó, Kaxinawa (a Pano-speaking group who live on the boundary between Brazil and Peru), Siona (a Tukono-speaking people of the Colombian jungle boundary with Ecuador), and Wauja (an Arawak-speaking group of the Alto Xingu).

Valcárcel, Luis Eduardo. Luis E. Valcárcel: del indigenismo cusqueño a la antropología peruana. See *HLAS 73:249*.

303 Valenzuela Noguera, Ezequiel. Educación y cultura en los Comentarios reales. Lima: Universidad Inca Garcilaso de la Vega, Fondo Editorial, 2015. 263 p.: bibl., color ill. (Obras escogidas/Historia)

A panoramic view and synthesis on topics of Inca culture and religion included in the work of the Inca Garcilaso de la Vega. Chapters cover the origin of the Incas and el Cuzco, Inca teachings, the Pachacamac cult, imperial laws, scientific accomplishments, music, poetry, the sun cult, schools in Cuzco, land tenure, communal living, the quipu (knotted string counting device), Pachacutec and the formation of the state, exchange, language, and the road system. The volume is based on a close-reading of Garcilaso's work and secondary sources.

304 Vilcapoma Ignacio, José Carlos. Mito y religión en Parinacochas: gentiles, Incas y cristos: documentos del siglo XVII. Lima: Argos Editorial 2015. 91 p.: bibl., ill.

A compilation of oral tradition from 28 pueblos that populate the province of Paucar del Sara Sara (Parinacochas) in southern Ayacucho (Peru). The myths reveal the religious imaginings of the population. Natives, Incas, and Christs travel magic and sacred routes and submit to extraordinary tests. Some of the myths are dramatized in dances in honor of saints and virgins. An appendix contains demographic information from as early as the 17th century.

305 Yaya, Isabel. The two faces of Inca history: dualism in the narratives and cosmology of ancient Cuzco. Boston, Mass.: Brill, 2012. 296 p.: bibl., ill., index, maps. (The early Americas: history and culture; 3)

A detailed and scholarly analysis of the Inca dynasty that attempts to resolve some discrepancies in the sources from the era. The author categorizes early sources into two groups that reflect Cuzco moiety divisions. This leads to a reconsideration of duality, especially in the cosmology and ritual calendar of the ruling elite. The result is an ethnohistorical exploration of how natives construct history.

GENERAL HISTORY

JOHN BRITTON, *Professor Emeritus of History, Francis Marion University*

GOVERNMENTAL INSTITUTIONS and the politics that surround them were central themes in the historical writing on Latin America in the early and middle decades of the 20th century, but social and economic topics gained prominence by the 1960s as historians took on broader research interests and used a "bottom-up" perspective instead of the traditional "top-down" approach. The trend towards more publications on government and politics in the current biennium could be seen as a reversion to older methods and attitudes, but the studies included in this essay and the related annotations are generally based on analyses that place government and politics in their full historical contexts, resulting in a new and often innovative body of work.

Rodríguez O. (item **346**) completed a sweeping examination of the lasting importance of Spanish political culture in the Americas. Publications on the colonial era offer several additional examples. Serrera Contreras (item **382**) produced a survey of Spanish colonial administration under the Hapsburgs. The book edited by Sánchez Santiró (item **366**) contains articles on colonial fiscal practices. Ponce Leiva and Andújar Castillo (item **371**), and Rosenmüller (item **360**) edited two volumes of essays on corruption and administration in Spain and its American empire. The Inquisition is the subject of the scholarly articles collected by Vassallo, Lourenço, and Bastos Mateus (item **370**). Ruan (item **380**) discusses the problems of writing imperial history in 16th century Spain. Tavarez (item **384**) probes the ideas of a Peruvian precursor of the independence movement.

The independence movements were watersheds in Latin American political history. Moreno Luzón and Gutiérrez Viñuales (item **335**) edited a book of essays on the centennial celebrations of independence in Spain, Mexico, and Argentina. Pinto Vallejos, Palma Alvarado, Donoso Fritz, and Pizarro Larrea (item **395**) present a volume on the early national period in Chile and Argentina. Sarracino (item **402**) analyzes the ideas of José Martí on geopolitics and imperialism.

The struggles, conflicts, and violence innate to 20th-century politics are evident in three edited publications: Allier and Crenzel (item **435**) confront political violence, Fernández Rosado and Elías-Caro (item **407**) deal with revolutions, and Aronne de Abreu and Motta (item **408**) discuss authoritarianism. Further work in this area includes Azcona Pastor's monograph (item **409**) on political terrorism, Green's study (item **416**) of political murder, and Bauer's analysis (item **410**) of dictatorship, disappearances, and right-wing extremism in Brazil and Argentina. Pipitone (item **343**) provides an extensive history of the left in Latin America, and the edited volume by Salmerón and Noriega Elío (item **341**) offers essays on an array of political institutions in the Americas and Europe.

Constitutions and the quest for political order are important themes. Eastman and Sobrevilla Perea's edited volume (item **400**) covers the impact of the Spanish Constitution of 1812 in the Americas. Sabato's monograph (item **401**) and Garavaglia and Pro Ruiz's collected essays (item **330**) discuss the process of nation-building throughout Latin America. Gargarella (item **321**) synthesizes a history of the various constitutions adopted by Latin American nations over the two centuries of independence with an emphasis on the Mexican Constitution of 1917.

The historical role of Native Americans continues to receive attention in general publications. Adams (item **306**) provides a broad survey on this large theme from the colonial period to the present. Neira Samanez (item **374**) explores Native American perspectives on events in Mesoamerica and the Andean region. Álvarez-Uría (item **354**) examines the struggles of the Spanish to understand Native American culture in the early colonial period. The selected writings of Native Americans edited by Cortés Navarro and Zamora (item **373**) present a valuable perspective on the colonial period. Carbajal López's (item **363**) assemblage of articles examines mestizaje at the provincial level. Kazanjian (item **392**) looks at the mid-19th century uprising of the Maya in Yucatan in comparative perspective. Reina's volume of essays (item **398**) probes relations between Native Americans and the newly independent national governments in the early 1800s. Zapata's monograph (item **353**) examines the interplay of education and indigenous intellectuals. García Jordán's edited work (item **338**) emphasizes the images of Native Americans in print and visual media.

The enormous influence of the internet has spawned an interest in the importance of communications through print and other media in the past as reflected in the current crop of publications. The colonial period provided some examples: Wolff (item **388**) probed Dutch cartographic interest in the Caribbean, Vilches (item **387**) documents the value of printed manuals and guides for commerce, and Griffin (item **367**) looks into the colonial book trade. Botero Montoya (item **389**) studies the role of public opinion in New Grenada's independence movement, and Pastor Bodmer (item **396**) outlines the transfer of ideas across oceans and political boundaries in the same period. The spread of Charles Darwin's ideas is examined in the edited work by Puig Samper *et al.* (item **315**). Melgar Bao (item **426**) documents the publications of international Communism in Latin America in the 1920s and 1930s. Herrera (item **417**) highlights the movement of artists and art in the time of the Good Neighbor Policy and World War II. Two books concentrate on international communications and propaganda during the Cold War: Iber (item **418**) emphasizes the controversy and fragmentation in this period, while Rupprecht (item **432**) concentrates on the Soviet Union's use of cultural appeals to gain converts. The group of essays edited by Amado Gonzáles, Forniés Casals, and Numhauser (item **316**) recounts the efforts to suppress free speech and communications in the Cold War.

Two unique publications in this biennium deserve special mention. García Ferrari (item **320**) produced a specialized study on the origins and development of fingerprinting in Argentina in the 1890s that also covers the adoption of this process for identification of individuals in other countries in the early 20th century. Putnam's article (item **345**) recognizes the growing availability of web-based digitized archives and other primary sources, such as newspapers but warns that excessive dependence on the still-small universe of digital materials will produce narrow research and a limited intellectual experience.

GENERAL

306 Adams, William Yewdale. Indian policies in the Americas: from Columbus to Collier and beyond. Santa Fe, New Mexico: School for Advanced Research Press, 2014. 332 p.: bibl., index, maps.

A survey of the relations between Native Americans and Europeans from the conquest into the 21st century. Although the word "policy" is in the title, the author places the actions of governments in a cultural framework. The section on the colonial era includes the Spanish, Portuguese,

French, and Dutch, but the emphasis in the postindependence era is on the US with only one chapter on Latin America. Based on published works in English.

307   América: cruce de miradas. Vol. 2. Coordinación de Teresa Cañedo-Argüelles Fábrega. Alcalá de Henares, Spain: Universidad de Alcalá, Servicio de Publicaciones, 2015. 1 v.: bibl. (Obras colectivas humanidades; 49)

An edited volume with a wide range of contributions that delve into several themes. Most of the 33 essays deal with the colonial period and focus on topics such as early explorers, the Casa de Contratación, education, and issues in local government. Articles on the 20th century concern the history of film and art education in Mexico and include an interpretive essay on the political style of Manuel Estrada Cabrera in Guatemala.

308   El auxilio en las ciudades: instituciones, actores y modelos de protección social: Argentina y México: siglos XIX y XX. Coordinación de Juan Manuel Cerdá et al. Zinacantepec, Mexico: El Colegio Mexiquense, A.C; Córdoba, Argentina: Centro de Estudios Históricos, "Prof. Carlos S.A. Segreti", 2015. 503 p.: bibl., ill.

Charitable aid for the poor has taken many forms with varying degrees of impact. This set of 18 articles includes religious organizations, philanthropic societies, political parties, and both local and national governments. Extensive use of primary sources is a strength of these studies. Although there are some statistics, there is much concentration on narrative and descriptive histories. The coupling of Mexico and Argentina invites more comparative analyses.

309   Bulmer-Thomas, V. Empire in retreat: the past, present, and future of the United States. New Haven, Conn.: Yale University Press, 2018. 459 p.: bibl., ill., index, maps.

Although the US is the only nation mentioned in the title, about half of this book concerns Latin America and the impact of US diplomatic, political, business, and military policies therein. Much of the first third of the book deals with 19th-century US expansion and its interventions in Latin America when the Monroe Doctrine became a convenient rationalization for empire. Bulmer-Thomas argues persuasively that the US proclivity for aggressive interventionism elsewhere had its roots in the period that stretched from the 1890s to the 1940s, a half century in which the US encountered anti-imperialism. He also places Latin American-US relations in the Cold War context and in the global environment of recent decades when the US empire began its retreat. A well-known economic historian of Latin America, the author reveals a command of the literature of political and strategic studies.

310   Cacao: producción, consumo y comercio: del período prehispánico a la actualidad en América Latina. Coordinación de Laura Caso Barrera. Madrid: Iberoamericana; Frankfurt am Main: Vervuert, 2016. 408 p.: bibl., ill., maps. (Tiempo emulado: historia de América y España; 48)

These nine scholarly articles offer case studies in the evolution of cacao production, distribution, and consumption from the preconquest Maya through the colonial era. Contributions include archeology, anthropology, and geography as well as history. Caso Barrera's introduction and conclusion give insights into the larger historical context.

311   El carrusel atlántico: memorias y sensibilidades 1500–1950. Dirección de Oscar Álvarez Gila, Alberto Angulo Morales y Alejandro Cardozo Uzcátegui. Caracas: Editorial Nuevos Aires, 2014. 503 p.: bibl., ill. (Serie Historia)

These articles offer a broad sampling of specialized topics within the general framework of circum-Atlantic history. These include immigration, shipping, and political ideas. The port cities of Buenos Aires, Rio de Janeiro, and Cartagena receive particular attention.

312   Cibotti, Ema, América Latina en la clase de historia. Con la colaboración de Agustina Rayes. Nueva edición corregida y aumentada. Buenos Aires: Fondo de Cultura Económica, 2016. 187 p.: bibl., index. (Sección de obras de educación y pedagogía)

Useful guide for the teaching of Latin American history in secondary school and at the college level. Explores general historical issues such as unity and diversity, periodization, and the role of women. Gives much attention to pedagogy, including the use of primary documents as a teaching device.

313   Ciudades sudamericanas como arenas culturales: artes y medios, barrios de élite y villas miseria, intelectuales y urbanistas: cómo ciudad y cultura se activan mutuamente: Bogotá, Brasilia, Buenos Aires, Caracas, Córdoba, La Plata, Lima, Montevideo, Quito, Recife, Río de Janeiro, Salvador, San Pablo, Santiago de Chile. Compilación de Adrián Gorelik y Fernanda Arêas Peixoto. Contribuciones de Ana Clarisa Agüero et al. Traducción de los textos sobre ciudades brasileñas de Ada Solari. Buenos Aires: Siglo Veintiuno Editores, 2016. 466 p.: bibl., ill.

The expanse and variety of urban culture receive ample treatment is this collection of 23 articles. Three contributions are based in the 19th century, and the remaining 20 deal with the 20th and the edge of the 21st century. Buenos Aires and Rio de Janeiro are featured in three articles each, while São Paulo is the subject of four studies. Topics covered are too numerous to mention, but here is a sampling: *lunfardo* in Buenos Aires, accelerated modernization in Caracas, cosmopolitanism in the Copacabana section of Rio, the *bogotazo* in Bogotá.

314   Coloquio Internacional Delitos, Policías y Justicia en América Latina, *Santiago, Chile, 2013*. Delincuentes, policías y justicias: América Latina, siglos XIX y XX. Edición de Daniel Palma Alvarado. Contribuciones de Carlos Aguirre et al. Santiago: Ediciones Universidad Alberto Hurtado, 2015. 515 p.: bibl., ill. (Colección de historia)

The product of an international colloquium on crime, law enforcement, and judiciary in Latin America held in Santiago de Chile in 2013, this group of scholarly articles provides a cross-section of cases in all three dimensions. Five of the 16 deal with Chile. Garcia Ferrari and Galeano concentrate on Argentina in their examination of fingerprinting, while Ricardo Salvatore and Lila Caimari contribute perceptive essays that synthesize research in these understudied fields. For a related work on fingerprinting in Argentina, see item 320.

315   Coloquio sobre Darwinismo en Europa y América *5th, Valdivia, Chile, 2013*. "Yammerschuner": Darwin y la darwinización en Europa y América Latina. Edición de Miguel Ángel Puig-Samper et al. Madrid: Doce Calles, 2014. 351 p.: ill., maps. (Actas)

This collection of 17 scholarly articles covers several topics from material on Darwin's *Beagle* expedition to the impact of his research and the concept of evolution on science, culture, and politics in nine countries including Mexico, Brazil, Cuba, Argentina, and Spain. The word "yammerschuner" is an English approximation of the term used by natives of Tierra del Fuego in their efforts to elicit generosity from the Darwin expedition.

316   Congreso Internacional de Escrituras Silenciadas, *4th, Cusco, Peru, 2014*. Escrituras silenciadas: poder y violencia en la península Ibérica y América. Edición de Donato Amado Gonzales, José F. Forniés Casals y Paulina Numhauser. Alcalá de Henares, Spain: Universidad de Alcalá, Servicio de Publicaciones: 2015. 425 p.: bibl., ill., maps. (Obras colectivas (Universidad de Alcalá))(Obras colectivas humanidades; 46)

A variety of approaches appear in these documented studies, critiques, and opinion pieces. As a group, the 27 contributions offer a multi-faceted portrait of more than five centuries of the suppression of the free expression of political ideas and limitations on the circulation of basic information. This volume is not intended to be a synthesis on this large theme, but it does contain the seeds for general reflection on and analysis of an unfortunately persistent phenomenon.

317   Del espacio cantábrico al mundo americano: perspectivas sobre migración, etnicidad y retorno. Direccion de Óscar Álvarez Gila y Juan Bosco Amores Carredano. Bilbao, Spain: Universidad del País Vasco, 2015. 356 p.: bibl., ill. (Serie de historia medieval y moderna)

These 14 articles provide a diversified picture in a narrowly focused frame on immigration from the Iberian peninsula to several locations in the Americas. The chronological span extends from the 1500s to the early 20th century. Topics include the Sonoran frontier of the 1700s, matrimonial strategies, and family photography.

318 Familias, movilidad y migración: América Latina y España. Coordinación y edición de Gabriela Dalla-Corte Caballero. Rosario, Argentina: Prohistoria Ediciones, 2015. 307 p.: bibl., ill.

The contents of this nicely edited volume are consistent with the title. Migration and its impact on families emerge as main themes in the 20 scholarly articles. Mexico is the subject in five contributions along with four that center on Brazil and three each on Argentina and Colombia.

319 From the ashes of history: loss and recovery of archives and libraries in modern Latin America. Edited by Carlos Aguirre and Javier Villa-Flores. Raleigh, NC: A Contracorriente, 2015. 342 p.: bibl., ill. (History and social sciences series)

Archives can be caught up in political and cultural controversy and accidental tragedy. These nine in-depth studies give a dynamism to the history of history at the very foundation points of the discipline. These case studies include archives that housed or house documents on the Inquisition, slavery, human rights violations in Argentina and Guatemala, and the modern Mexican film industry.

320 García Ferrari, Mercedes. Marcas de identidad: Juan Vucetich y el surgimiento transnacional de la dactiloscopia (1888–1913). Rosario, Argentina: Prohistoria Ediciones, 2015. 312 p.: bibl., ill., index. (Colección Historia de la ciencia; 9)

An excellent study of an important, but previously neglected topic. Argentina's Juan Vucetich was a world class pioneer in the science and practical application of fingerprinting. García Ferrari's work is based on exhaustive research in archives in Argentina and Europe as well as a thorough examination of published documents and monographs. She concentrates on the early work in Argentina, the subsequent experience in Uruguay, and then the international acceptance of fingerprinting. A prime candidate for English translation. For a related work on crime and law enforcement, see item **314**.

321 Gargarella, Roberto. Latin American constitutionalism, 1810–2010: the engine room of the constitution. New York, N.Y.: Oxford University Press, 2013. 283 p.: bibl., index.

An ambitious and well-executed study of a theme in Latin American political history that is too often dismissed to the margins. Gargarella successfully integrates the penchant for the adoption of new constitutions, not as a political device, but as an indication of more fundamental social, political, and economic issues. Mexico's Constitution of 1917 and especially the powers granted to the national government under Article 27 have a prominent place in this book. While the author gives special attention to the role of the "social question" in the 20th century and the rise of human rights protections in the wake of Cold War dictatorships, he concludes that the general absence of broad access to the "engine room" of governmental authority remains the crucial impediment to essential reform.

322 Guerra Vilaboy, Sérgio. Nueva historia mínima de América Latina: biografia de un continente. Santo Domingo: Archivo General de la Nacion, 2015. 740 p.: bibl., index. (Archivo General de la Nación; 228)

A university textbook that covers Latin America from the preconquest to 21st century globalization, in which the author emphasizes the period since independence with stress on the themes of US informal imperialism and Latin American responses to this assertion of power. The author views the fragmentation of Latin America into small and mid-sized nation-states as providing opportunities for the continued expansion of the US after the defeat and dismemberment of Mexico. Guerra Vilaboy terms this process the "recolonización imperialista" that extends into the 20th century, and he connects it to the rise of Fidel Castro.

323 Harvey, Simon. Smuggling: seven centuries of contraband. London: Reaktion Books, 2016. 352 p.

Spans more than six centuries in a worthwhile effort to pull together a wide-ranging narrative history. Latin America appears in Harvey's discussion of the British, Dutch, and French intrusions into the

Spanish Empire of the 16th-century Caribbean and plays a large role in the global context that includes the cocaine trade of the contemporary era. The author's style is fast-paced and should appeal to a general readership.

324 **Hertzman, Marc A.** Fatal differences: suicide, race, and forced labor in the Americas. (*Am. Hist. Rev.*, 122:2, April 2017, p. 317–345)

Hertzman reconsiders the motivations and meaning of suicide among indigenous and African peoples in a thorough and thought-provoking study that stresses the flawed 19th- and 20th-century historiographies on that topic. The article breaks from the European perspectives on suicide with an appreciation of the cultural and religious diversity among those caught in forced labor and slavery.

325 **Historia comparada de las migraciones en las Américas.** Coodinación de Patricia Galeana. Contribuciones de Teodoro Aguilar *et al.* México: UNAM, Instituto de Investigaciones Jurídicas: Instituto Panamericano de Geografía e Historia, 2014. 589 p.: bibl., ill. (Serie Historia del derecho)(Historia comparada en las Américas; 4)

A substantial collection of scholarly articles on a large topic. Migration has played a vital role in the history of the Americas with increasing importance from the late 19th century. These contributions reflect that historiographical trajectory with five articles on the colonial period, four on the 19th century, and the remaining 25 on the 20th and 21st centuries. This volume is a timely reminder that migration has been and continues to be an integral part of human existence. The basic research and diverse methodologies in this collection form a foundation for a major synthesis that would encompass a comparative focus on the policies of the many national governments involved over the centuries and especially on the Mexican-US border since the 1970s.

326 **História da imigração: possibilidades e escrita.** Organização de Elda Evangelina González Martínez *et al.* São Leopoldo, Brazil: Oikos Editora, 2013. 396 p.: bibl., ill. (Coleção Estudos Históricos Latino-Americanos—EHILA; 7)

The potential for research on immigration are quite broad as this selection of 25 essays makes clear. This book is divided into six parts that concentrate on particular themes: one is national (Argentina); others include environmental topics, urbanization, patriotic immigrants (Spanish and German), and subjects in literature and language.

327 **Historia mínima de la expansión ferroviaria en América Latina.** Coordinación de Sandra Kuntz Ficker. México: El Colegio de México, 2015. 361 p.: bibl., ill. (Colección Historias mínimas)

Kuntz Ficker has assembled an excellent set of eight scholarly articles that cover seven major nations in the region and deal with the Antilles in a single chapter. The authors concentrate on railroad construction projects, their business operations, and their impacts on their respective national economies. The appendix has a decade-by-decade and nation-by-nation statistical summary from 1870 to 1970 that includes track mileage, numbers of passengers, amount of cargo, and equipment. The editor's introduction is an impressive synthesis. A prime candidate for English translation.

328 **Imigração na América Latina: histórias de fracassos.** Organização de Cláudio Pereira Elmir y Marcos Antônio Witt. São Leopoldo, Brazil: Oikos Editora: Editora Unisinos, 2014. 246 p., 4 unnumbered pages of plates: bibl., ill. (Coleção Estudos Históricos Latino-Americanos—EHILA; 15)

Historians often undervalue human endeavors that end in failure, but this well-organized volume examines six case studies of immigration projects that were ultimately unsuccessful. The emphasis is on Brazil, but Argentina and Chile are included. An interesting analytical conclusion.

329 **Jornadas de Historia sobre el Descubrimiento de América.** Actas. Vol. 3. Coordinación de la edición por Eduardo García Cruzado. Sevilla, Spain: Universidad Internacional de Andalucía; Palos de la Frontera, Spain: Excmo. Ayuntamiento, 2015. 1 v.: bibl., ill.

This third volume contains 15 new articles on the background, points of origin, and continued interest in the "voyages of discovery." Includes research based on underwater archeology, biographical material on Vicente Yáñez Pinzón, and the Franciscan religious art at La Rábida. Also includes a perceptive study of Wilhelm Sundheim, the mining magnate and promoter of the fourth centennial of the epic voyage.

330 **Latin American bureaucracy and the state building process (1780–1860).** Edited by Juan Carlos Garavaglia and Juan Pro Ruiz. Newcastle upon Tyne, England: Cambridge Scholars Publishing, 2013. 434 p.: bibl., ill., maps.

A reflection of well-structured editorial coordination, these 14 contributions utilize primary sources from national, provincial, and local archives in Latin America to explore the formative process of state-building in the era of transition involving the end of the colonial era and the rise of nation-states. These investigations reveal that, in general, while bureaucratic growth along the lines of North Atlantic models was modest, there were examples of the establishment of government financial agencies and procedures that set budgetary foundations for later expansion of state apparatuses.

331 **Lovera, José Rafael.** Yantares latinoamericanos: ensayos de historia cultural. Caracas: Academia Nacional de la Historia: CEGA Centro de Estudios Gastronómicos, 2014. 221 p. (Biblioteca de la Academia Nacional de la Historia. Estudios, monografías y ensayos; 195)

Intriguing study in culinary history that emphasizes the transatlantic nature of food preparation bringing together the practices and preferences of Latin America with those of Spain. Chronological parameters begin with the early 1800s and extend to the present. Includes country-by-country surveys.

332 **El mar: percepciones, lecturas y contextos: una mirada cultural a los entornos marítimos.** Coordinación de Guadalupe Pinzón Ríos y Flor Trejo Rivera. México: UNAM; México: Instituto Nacional de Antropología e Historia, 2015. 408 p., 16 unnumbered pages of plates: bibl., ill. (some color), maps. (Serie historia general/Instituto de Investigaciones Históricas; 31)

These 14 articles use a variety of academic disciplines to examine the role of oceans in human history over the centuries. Topics include preconquest perceptions of the sea; cartographic history featuring images of sea monsters on early colonial maps; commerce and imperial defense, including Florida and Peru; and various forms of transoceanic communications, including postcards of Veracruz from the early 20th century.

333 **Martin, James W.** Banana cowboys: the United Fruit Company and the culture of corporate colonialism. Albuquerque: University of New Mexico Press, 2018. 252 p.: bibl, index.

A thorough examination of corporate archives and publications gives this book considerable depth in its portrait of the activities of the United Fruit Company in the circum-Caribbean from the late 19th century to 1930. The swagger of the "banana cowboys" on the tropical frontier evolved into a quest for efficiency, profitability, and security that contributed to the transformation of this form of economic colonialism. This study is especially strong on management's relationship with employees from the US as well as local workers. The author also gives attention to the uses of science in dealing with the tropical environment.

334 **Matrimonio: intereses, afectos, conflictos: una aproximación desde la antropología, la historia y la demografía (siglos XVIII al XXI).** Edición de Margarita Estrada Iguíniz y América Molina del Villar. México: Centro de Investigaciones y Estudios Superiores en Antropología Social, 2015. 363 p.: bibl., ill., map. (Publicaciones de la Casa Chata)

Either research in primary documents, or statistical analyses, or a combination of both form the foundations for the 13 contributions to this collection. Topics include familial and financial strategies, Native American and African marriages, endogamy and exogamy. Argentina, Mexico, and Brazil are the focal points for this volume which also includes three articles on transnational matrimony.

335 **Memorias de la independencia: España, Argentina y México en el primer centenario (1908–1910–1912).** Edición de Javier Moreno Luzón y Rodrigo Gutiérrez Viñuales. Madrid: AC/E, Acción Cultural Española, 2012. 270 p.: bibl., colored ill.

Eight general essays combine with illustrations (photographs and drawings) to make for an informative, colorful, and entertaining book that explores how three countries commemorated the independence movements of the early 19th century. The three contributions on art history are complemented by the illustrations.

336 **Mercados en común: estudios sobre conexiones transnacionales, negocios y diplomacia en las Américas (siglos XIX y XX).** Coordinacíon y edición de Maria-Aparecida Lopes y María Cecilia Zuleta. México: El Colegio de México, 2016. 698 p.: bibl., ill., indexes.

The promotion of international commerce through the reduction of tariff barriers and the negotiation of business deals did not emerge sui generis in the post-Cold War globalization. The editors of this volume present 14 scholarly articles that provide case studies dating back to the late 19th century with the expansion of exports from Argentina, Chile, Peru, and Mexico to the nations of the north Atlantic. Other topics include monetary policy, the diplomacy of Sears in Latin America, and petroleum/energy policies. Also includes a perceptive examination of the effects of the Mexican oil expropriation of 1938 in Chile and Uruguay. Well-researched articles with close attention to recent historiography.

337 **Miradas regionales: las regiones y la idea de nación en América Latina, siglos XIX y XX.** Edición de Arturo Taracena Arriola. Compilación de Carolina Depetris y Adam T. Sellen. Mérida, Mexico: UNAM, 2013. 312 p.: bibl., ill., maps. (Ensayos/Centro Peninsular en Humanidades y Ciencias Sociales; 9)

Yucatan is one of the most studied regions in Latin America and its history is the basis for this collection of articles that proposes the development of a comparative framework for regional studies throughout the hemisphere. Rio Grande do Sul of Brazil, La Montaña region of Guatemala, and the Rio Negro region of Argentina are examined alongside eight contributions on various aspects of Yucatecan history.

338 **El mundo latinoamericano como representación, siglos XIX–XX.** Edición de Pilar García Jordán. Barcelona, Spain: Universitat de Barcelona, Publicacions i Edicions; Lima: IFEA, Instituto Francés de Estudios Andinos; Barcelona: TEIAA, Taller de Estudios e Investigaciones Andino-Amazónicos, 2015. 234 p.: bibl., ill.

Constructed mediated cultural perceptions help to define the place of certain groups in society. These nine essays examine in depth the representations of subaltern peoples in a variety of political and economic circumstances. The authors use several types of sources: photographs, written descriptions, censuses, and maps.

339 **Muñoz Serrulla, María Teresa.** La moneda castellana en los reinos de Indias durante la Edad Moderna. Madrid: Universidad Nacional de Educación a Distancia, 2015. 350 p.: bibl., ill. (Arte y humanidades)

Examines the history of Spanish gold and silver money from the 1500s to the 1800s with attention to monetary legislation and policy, techniques of minting, and the circulation of these coins as an international medium of exchange. The written descriptions and the fine color illustrations should be of interest to historians as well as collectors.

Oxford research encyclopedia of Latin American history. See item 800.

340 **Pasiones anticlericales: un recorrido iberoamericano.** Compilación de Roberto Di Stefano y José Zanca. Bernal, Argentina: Universidad Nacional de Quilmes Editorial, 2013. 329 p. (Colección Intersecciones)

Editors de Stefano and Zanca show that anti-clericalism generally involved the assertion of governmental authority at the expense of the Catholic Church in ways that aroused emotional responses from both sides. The politics that surrounded this issue also touched off social and economic considerations that stimulated deeply held beliefs. Uses a country-by-country approach beginning with Spain and Portugal with lengthy chapters on Mexico, Colombia, and Brazil as well as substantial coverage of Peru, Uruguay, and Argentina. Sources include published scholarly works and documentation from contemporary newspapers, pamphlets, and other primary sources.

341 Pensar la modernidad política: propuestas desde la nueva historia política: antología. Edición de Alicia Salmerón y Cecilia Noriega Elío. México: Instituto de Investigaciones Dr. José María Luis Mora, 2016. 476 p.: bibl. (Universitarios)

Assembles some useful essays that argue persuasively that the roles of political institutions, ideas, and movements should be investigated and evaluated in terms of their own vitality and influence and not viewed as dependent on economic forces. These essays include a range of topics: the revolution in British North America, the French Revolution, and the rise of the Nazi Party in Germany. There is also significant Latin American content. Marcello Carmagnani's contribution deals with Latin American elites and Hilda Sabato discusses political citizenship in 19th-century Latin America.

342 Piedra Valdez, José. La misión andina: la historia de la Palabra encarnada en los Andes. Lima: Universidad del Pacífico, 2013. 231 p.: bibl., index.

The role of theology in the evangelization of Andean America figures strongly here, but Piedra Valdez also gives considerable attention to cultural factors. The chronological expanse covers the colonial and national periods. An interesting summary study by a thoughtful scholar of religious history.

343 Pipitone, Ugo. La esperanza y el delirio: una historia de la izquierda en América Latina. México: Taurus: Centro de Investigación y Docencia Económicas, A.C., 2015. 551 p.: bibl., index. (Pensamiento)

A commendable synthesis of the history of the left and left-wing movements in Latin America from the 19th through the early 21st centuries. Pipitone is an economic historian who turned his attention to ideology and political institutions. He includes anarchism, the early versions of communism, "guerrilla communism," populism in various forms including manifestations under Lázaro Cárdenas and Juan Perón, and reformist social democracy.

344 Por la mano del hombre: prácticas y creencias sobre chamanismo y curandería en México y el Perú. Prólogo de Orlando Velásquez Benites. Edición de Silvia Limón Olvera y Luis Millones. Contribuciones de Claudia Rosas Lauro et al. Lima: Fondo Editorial de la Asamblea Nacional de Rectores, 2014. 476 p.: ill. (chiefly color). (Colección Artes y humanidades)

Traditional folk medicine has often been shrouded in mystery and myth but with some medical practices seen as valuable by modern medicine. These articles delve into precolonial and colonial era traditions evaluated within their own cultural ambiences, but also subject to rigorous standards of modern medical science and anthropological and historical methodology. Sharon and Bussman provide a perceptive comparative essay on traditional and modern medicine in Mexico and Peru.

345 Putnam, Lara. The transnational and the text-searchable: digitized sources and the shadows they cast. (*Am. Hist. Rev.*, 121:2, April 2016, p. 377–402)

Perceptive warning about the acceleration of transnational history based on the use of recently digitized sources that entice historians into narrow thematic studies cutting across national borders. Some of these studies are built on a limited understanding of the various national and cultural contexts involved. Putnam's cautionary observation is apt in terms of the overreliance on quick and relatively easy research done without benefit of travel: "We make rookie mistakes."

346 Rodríguez O., Jaime E. Political culture in Spanish America, 1500–1830. Lincoln: University of Nebraska Press, 2018. 279 p.: bibl.

This study of political institutions and ideas includes Spain and the unique environment of Spanish history as essential to understanding the independence era in New Spain and the rest of Spanish America. Rodríguez O calls for a broad re-examination of the continuities from the medieval and early modern eras that influenced the colonies and their subsequent histories as independent nations. The last chapter is a fascinating critique of the relevant historical scholarship from the 1960s to the present.

347 Los rostros de la tierra encantada: religión, evangelización y sincretismo en el Nuevo Mundo: homenaje a Manuel Marzal, S.J. Edición de José Sánchez Paredes y Marco Curatola Petrocchi. Lima: IFEA, Instituto Francés de Estudios Andinos: Fondo Editorial Pontificia Universidad Católica del Perú, 2013. 748 p.: bibl, ill.

The interactions of religion and popular culture in Mexico and Peru form a unifying theme in this collection of 27 essays. The central section on syncretic religion and evangelization provides insights to the colonial era and includes 12 of the contributions. Sánchez Paredes' biographical study of Marzal is a valuable contribution to anthropological scholarship and presents the trajectory of his career as a field anthropologist, a university teacher, and an administrator.

348 Trentmann, Frank and Ana María Otero-Cleves. Paths, detours, and connections: consumption and its contribution to Latin American history. (*Hist. Crít./Bogotá*, 65, julio/sept. 2017, p. 13–28, bibl.)

A review of recently published studies on the history of consumption in the context of the emergence of the field of consumer history, especially in Europe and the US. Authors point out the opportunities for research in Latin America through this relatively new approach.

349 Viajeras entre dos mundos. Edición y compilación de Sara Beatriz Guardia. Presentación de Losandro Antonio Tedeschi. Dourados, Brazil: Editora UFGD, 2012. 943 p.: bibl.

This edited tome contains 46 contributions about women travelers whose perspectives reflect not only their skills as observers, but also their roles as marginal but perceptive players in a patriarchal world that was gradually opening to change. This diverse collection devotes much attention to descriptive writing, but also political and cultural commentary as well as fiction. Tends to concentrate on the 19th and 20th centuries.

350 Visiones de la conquista y la colonización de las Américas. Edición de Francisco Castilla Urbano. Alcalá de Henares, Spain: Universidad de Alcalá, Servicio de Publicaciones 2015. 248 p.: bibl. (Obras colectivas humanidades; 48)

This edited volume contains 10 commentaries on the writings and opinions of a cross-section of historical figures such as Las Casas, Montesquieu, and Martí and national cohorts from Spain and Russia, including the founding fathers of the US. Intended for college students.

351 Wright, Thomas C. Latin America since independence: two centuries of continuity and change. Lanham, Md.: Rowman & Littlefield, 2017. 362 p.: bibl., index. (Latin American silhouettes: studies in history and culture)

This university-level textbook offers a unique structural and thematic cohesiveness that is especially useful at the introductory level. Wright explains five persistent colonial legacies: authoritarian governance, the Catholic Church, rigid social hierarchy, large landed estates, and economic dependency, and then explores their influence since independence. The text also emphasizes the impacts of the Mexican and Cuban Revolutions and their historical contexts.

352 Xu shi cheng ji = Volume of Xu Shicheng. Beijing: Zhong guo she hui ke xue chu ban she, 2013. (Zhong guo she hui ke xue yuan xue zhe wen xuan.)

Professor Xu Shicheng is an honorary member in CASS, former deputy director of the Institute of Latin American Studies. This corpus collects more than 30 articles and research reports published from the 1980s to the first 10 years of 21st century. It is divided into four parts: Politics, Economy, International Relations and Social Culture. Representative works are as follows: *The Change and Development in Latin America since the 1900s*; *The Recent Development and Prospects of the Left in Latin America*; *The Experience and Lessons of Development Strategy in Latin American Countries*; *The Features, History Links and Interrelationship of Culture between China and Latin America*; and *Globalization and Latin American Civilization*. Some of the works are related to all of Latin America and the Caribbean, while others focus on one Latin American country. Among them, there are many works which analyze and comment on the political, economic or social situation with a certain limitation of the times; however they are genuine history records. [Liu Weiguang]

353 **Zapata, Claudia.** Intelectuales indígenas en Ecuador, Bolivia y Chile: diferencia, colonialismo y anticolonialismo. La Habana: CASA, 2015. 610 p., 53 unnumbered p.: bibl.

The content of this book is broader than the title indicates. Zapata provides a general, but clearly delineated discussion of the roles of the three nation-states, the diversity within Native American society, and the activities of educational institutions. The last half of the book is a thematic analysis of colonialism and anticolonialism. Sources include personal interviews and correspondence as well as published material.

COLONIAL

354 **Álvarez-Uría, Fernando.** El reconocimiento de la humanida: España, Portugal y América Latina en la génesis de la modernidad. Madrid: Ediciones Morata, 2015. 367 p.: bibl.

Sociology, history, and philosophy intersect in Álverez-Uría's conceptualization of the Spanish effort to place Native American culture in the framework of the European value system with consequences for political power and economic activity. The author views this intellectual process in secular terms, thereby explaining his use of the concept of modernity. Students of this large theme in Latin American history explored two generations ago by Lewis Hanke will recognize the names Las Casas and Sepúlveda and will revisit the repercussions of their debate.

355 **América y el Tratado de Utrecht de 1713, *México, 2013*.** Resonancias imperiales: América y el Tratado de Utrecht de 1713. Coordinación de Iván Escamilla González, Matilde Souto Mantecón y Guadalupe Pinzón Ríos. México: Instituto de Investigaciones Dr. José María Luis Mora, Consejo Nacional de Ciencia y Tecnología: Instituto de Investigaciones Históricas, UNAM, 2015. 333 p.: bibl., maps. (Historia económica)

These 12 articles add breadth and depth to the understanding of economic and political developments in the Americas in the wake of the Treaty of Utrecht. The editors review the historiography of this era in their introduction that opens the way for detailed examinations of a variety of changes rooted on the American side of the Atlantic. Seven of the contributions deal with patterns of commerce within the Spanish Empire. Three examine the increasing influence of the British in the Americas. A pronounced shift away from the Eurocentric view of the consequences of Utrecht.

356 **Arroyo Abad, Leticia** and **Jan Luiten van Zanden.** Growth under extractive institutions?: Latin American per capita GDP in colonial times. (*J. Econ. Hist.*, 76:4, Dec. 2016, p. 1182–1215, bibl., graphs, map, tables)

Quantitative analysis of per capita income levels in this study indicates that economic dynamism in Peru and especially New Spain from the 1500s to the 1700s pulled these two colonial entities close to the economic performance level of Spain. This conclusion creates an apparent countervailing argument against the establishment of an entrenched dependency status in these large parts of the Spanish Empire in the colonial era.

357 **Baskes, Jeremy.** Staying afloat: risk and uncertainty in Spanish Atlantic world trade, 1760–1820. Stanford, Calif.: Stanford University Press, 2013. 393 p.: bibl., ill., index. (Social science history)

This well-researched and nicely written economic history focuses on risk and commercial enterprises in the late 18th-century Spanish Atlantic. The author examines the development of insurance in relation to commercial practices, the effects of the 1778 promulgation of *comercio libre*, bankruptcies, and the effects of privateering on long-distance trade. The author draws on sources deposited in archives in the Americas and in Europe. [F. Prado]

358 **Beerman, Eric.** El marino cántabro Juan Antonio de Riaño (1757–1810): conferencia pronunciada con motivo del bicentenario de su muerte en el Museo de las Reales Fábricas de Artillería de la Cavada el 25-8-2010. Liérganes, Spain: Asociación Cultural Liérganes XXI, 2012. 51 p.: bibl., ill.

This brief volume commemorates the life of the Spanish colonial official and military officer who served in several campaigns and various assignment in Louisiana, the Gulf Coast, and New Spain from the 1780s until his death in 1810 in the unsuccessful revolt led by Miguel Hidalgo y Costilla.

359 **Borucki, Alex.** Across imperial boundaries: black social networks across the Iberian South Atlantic, 1760–1810. (*Atlan. Stud. Global Curr.*, 14:1, 2017, p. 11–36, bibl.)

This groundbreaking article reveals the establishment and resilience of social networks among African slaves in Buenos Aires and Montevideo that transcended imperial boundaries and laid the basis for a transgenerational culture.

360 **Corruption in the Iberian empires: greed, custom, and colonial networks.** Edited by Christoph Rosenmüller. Albuquerque: University of New Mexico Press, 2017. 228 p.: bibl., index.

Corruption is often mentioned, but it is often difficult to find documentation for in-depth studies. The contributors to this excellent collection surmounted that difficulty as they investigated archival collections in Spain, Portugal, Mexico, Bolivia, and Brazil to provide depth and accuracy to several case studies, including Upper Peru, central Mexico, and the Rio de la Plata region. The articles are thoroughly footnoted and place their findings in the context of current scholarly interpretations.

361 **Crawford, Matthew James.** The Andean wonder drug: cinchona bark and imperial science in the Spanish Atlantic, 1630–1800. Pittsburgh, Pa.: University of Pittsburgh Press, 2016. 284 p.: bibl., ill., index.

This well-written and well-researched monograph examines the incorporation of quina (cinchona) bark into European botanical and medical knowledge. The book looks at the role of quina beyond its historical significance as quinine's predecessor, examining the local and imperial the networks of knowledge (including indigenous peoples) and commerce, and as an imperial commodity. Through extensive archival research, the author presents a study that brings together debates on the history of science, empire, environmental history, and the history of the Atlantic World. [F. Prado]

362 **Donoso, Sebastián I.** Los últimos piratas del Pacífico. Quito: Editorial Planeta del Ecuador, 2014. 303 p.: bibl., index.

Archival research and extensive reading in secondary sources set the foundation for this fast-moving narrative study of a crucial stage in the history of piracy on the Pacific coast of the Spanish American Empire from 1686 to 1695. Combines biographical sketches with colonial institutions. Detailed index is useful for researchers.

363 **Familias pluriétnicas y mestizaje en la Nueva España y el Río de la Plata.** Coordinación de David Carbajal López. Guadalajara, Mexico: Universidad de Guadalajara, 2014. 372 p.: bibl., ill.

A dozen detailed examinations of ethnicity and mestizaje in the late colonial period and the 19th century present the serious scholar with opportunities for comparative analysis. Ten essays concentrate on New Spain/Mexico and two on Argentina. The authors have plumbed the depths of local archives and other unique sources to produce impressive contributions in social history.

364 **Flint, Richard.** Asian mirror of the Americas in the 1500s: a review essay on *The First Circumnavigators* and *A History of Early Modern Southeast Asia*. (*N.M. Hist. Rev.*, 91:4, Fall 2016, p. 467–474)

This review essay on two books dealing with European explorers in the Age of Exploration rises above the usual review function to offer a comparative portrait of this period in East Asian history and Latin American history through the activities of the Portuguese and the Spanish.

365 **La frontera en el mundo hispánico.** Coordinación de Porfirio Sanz Camañes y David Rex Galindo. Quito: Abya Yala, 2014. 535 p.: bibl., ill., maps.

Extensive research by 14 historians establishes the foundation for this set of articles on multiple aspects of frontiers in Spain's American Empire. Heavily based on primary research, these contributions cover themes such as the role of the military, the impact of frontiers on Native Americans, smuggling, missionary work, ad religious ideas. Several of the articles are focused on northern New Spain.

366 **El gasto público en los imperios ibéricos, siglo XVIII.** Coordinación de Ernest Sánchez Santiró. México: Instituto de Investigaciones Dr. José María Luis Mora: Consejo Nacional de Ciencia y Tecnología, 2015. 302 p.: bibl., ill., maps. (Historia económica)

A collaborative volume that delves into the expenditures of the Spanish and Portuguese governments. Editor Sánchez Santiró coordinated the articles to present a portrait of imperial policy as revealed through budgetary priorities that indicated a growing geopolitical concern with defense of the empire and the promotion of internal security. A good balance of statistical information with analytical prose.

367 **Griffin, Clive.** Los Cromberger y los impresos enviados a las colonias españoles en America durante la primera mitad del siglo XVI, con una coda filipina. (*Titivillus*, 1, 2015, p. 251–272)

The transoceanic book trade is an important but seldom studied part of colonial history. Griffin uses archival documents and books published in the 1500s to explore this field that encompasses both business and intellectual history with a concentration on the Cromberger family.

368 **Helg, Aline.** Slave but not citizen: free people of color and blood purity in colonial Spanish American legislation. (*Millars*, 42:1, 2017, p. 75–99)

The legal status of free people of color remains a topic of scholarly concern and, to some extent, dispute. Helg emphasizes the legal barriers faced by Africans released from slavery in contrast to the findings of Ann Twinam. Helg also cites the seminal study by Frank Tannenbaum, *Slave and citizen: the negro in the Americas* (see *HLAS 12:89*), as an historiographical reference point.

369 **Imagining histories of colonial Latin America: synoptic methods and practices.** Edited by Karen Melvin and Sylvia Sellers-García. Foreword by Davíd Carrasco. Albuquerque: University of New Mexico Press, 2017. 283 p.: index. (Religions of the Americas series)

Stimulating essays that concentrate on a single topic, event, or person and then shift adroitly to a more general level to explore various methods of synthesis. The authors are comfortable with their chosen themes, and also evince talent for explaining context and elaborating on the long view of history. Valuable for professional scholars, this volume also has an approach suitable for the college classroom.

370 **Inquisiciones: dimensiones comparadas (siglos XVI–XIX).** Coordinación de Jaqueline Vassallo, Miguel Rodrigues Lourenço y Susana Bastos Mateus. Córdoba, Argentina: Editorial Brujas, 2017. 292 p.: bibl. (El mundo de ayer)

A dozen scholarly articles that relied on published monographs and primary sources to describe the institutional functions of the Inquisition in Spain, Portugal, and their American colonies. Several of the contributors present comparative perspectives on the Spanish and Portuguese versions of this institution.

371 **Mérito, venalidad y corrupción en España y América, siglos XVII y XVIII.** Edición de Pilar Ponce Leiva y Francisco Andújar Castillo. Valencia, Spain: Albatros, 2016. 362 p.: bibl., index. (Colección Historia de España y su proyección internacional; 10)

Archival research underlies these scholarly articles. Generalizations about corrupt practices in the Spanish government and its colonial administration are tested in depth here. The introductory essay provides the first steps for incorporating these findings into a general overview of the Spanish Empire. The comprehensive analytical index will be of value for researchers.

372 **Mira Caballos, Esteban.** Vinos y élites en la América de la conquista. (*Iberoamericana/Madrid*, 15:57, marzo 2015, p. 7–23, bibl., table)

This article uses red and white grape wines and their relatively high costs in the Americas in the 1500s to discuss the dietary transition of the Spanish conquerors and later arrivals. The article notes the increasing importance of indigenous foods in Spanish diets.

373 **Narradores indígenas y mestizos de la época colonial (siglos XVI–XVII): zonas andina y mesoamerica.** Edición de Rocío Cortés Navarro y Margarita Zamora. Lima: Centro de Estudios Literarios Antonio

Cornejo Polar: Latinoamericana Editores, 2016. 383 p.: bibl., facsimiles.

A fruitful approach to the explication of the writings of Native Americans and mestizos. Fifteen selections are reproduced and accompanied by an introduction to explain the historical, cultural, and biographical contexts. Suitable for advanced undergraduates and graduate students.

374 **Neira Samanez, Hugo.** El mundo mesoamericano y el mundo andino. Lima: Universidad Ricardo Palma, Editorial Universitaria, 2016. 478 p.: bibl., ill.

This book is a major work of synthesis that offers a valuable and much-needed perspective drawn from recent research on the conquest and the colonial era. Neira utilizes Native American narratives bolstered by contemporary ethnohistorical methods to emphasize that the Spanish arrival in the Americas was more than a military conquest in that it disrupted and, in many cases, dismembered, but did not destroy, historical patterns in the Middle American and Andean regions. A well-organized piece of scholarship that should have an English translation.

375 **Obermeier, Franz.** Jesuit colonial medicine in South America: a multidisciplinary and comparative approach [Medicina jesuítica en la América del Sur colonial: una aproximación multidisciplinar]. Kiel, Germany: China Center; Universitätsbibliothek, Christian-Albrechts-Universität zu Kiel, 2018 198 p.

The Jesuit reductions of Paraguay and adjacent territories such as the Chiquitania in today's Paraguay, Brazil, Bolivia, and Argentina (1608–1767) are a particularly well-documented area of encounter between Jesuit missionaries and indigenous populations, mainly Guaraní. There are medical texts, mostly in Spanish, from this area, and also a pharmaceutical manuscript in Guaraní, ascribed to the Lay Brother Marcos Villodas (1695–1741) and dated 1725. When the most important Spanish text on the topic by the physician Pedro de Montenegro (1663–1728) was rediscovered in the 19th century, it was called "Materia Medica misionera" in its first edition. Different manuscript versions, some with illustrations, exist. Also available is the recently rediscovered anonymous Spanish "Tratado de . . . cirugia," dated 1725, related to the missions, which represents a major source on the history of medicine in the region. The articles in these conference proceedings focus on various topics: medical terminology adopted by Jesuit manuscripts and dictionaries in Guaraní and Chiquitano, Guaraní anthropological concepts about healing among the Jesuits, newly discovered manuscripts of medical history (a version of a pharmaceutical manuscript ascribed to Villodas in Guaraní from the 18th century, the aforementioned Spanish "Tratado de cirugia," dated 1725) and a history of research about the topic in 19th-century Argentina by Pedro de Arata (1849–1922). A short bibliography of contemporary manuscript sources and South American pharmaceutical inventories is also included. [F. Obermeier]

376 **Quesada, Sarah.** An inclusive "black Atlantic": revisiting historical creole formations. (*Lat. Am. Caribb. Ethn. Stud.*, 10:2, July 2015, p. 226–246, bibl.)

A review article on studies of the process of creolization of African slaves not only in America, but also in Africa in the earliest stages of enslavement. Quesada recognizes the diversity within creolization and the resilience of African culture throughout the process.

377 **Reséndez, Andrés.** An early abolitionist crusade. (*Ethnohistory/Columbus*, 64:1, Jan. 2017, p. 19–40, maps.)

Using information made available by the digitization of some of Spain's colonial archives, this article examines the Spanish Crown's campaign to liberate enslaved indigenous people at scattered points throughout the Empire: northern New Spain, the island of Trinidad, Chile, and the Philippines from the 1660s to the 1680s. Although the campaign freed only a few thousand, it raised many questions surrounding enslavement of Native Americans.

378 **Rex Galindo, David.** *To sin no more*: Franciscans and conversion in the Hispanic world, 1683–1830. Mission San Luis Rey, Calif.: The Academy of American Franciscan History, 2017. 330 p.: bibl.

With a research base that is both extensive and intensive, this book delves deeply into the history of the Franciscans in the Americas. Rex Galindo's concentration on the 29 Franciscan colleges distributed through New Spain, South America, and Spain itself includes examinations of theology, pedagogy, daily life, and recruitment of the young men who became missionaries. Two lengthy chapters cover the work of these missionaries in the field encompassing their efforts to reach the diverse general population of criollo and mestizo peoples as well as the indigenous communities. For Mexican colonial historian's comment, see item **512**.

379 Rowe, Erin Kathleen. After death, her face turned white: blackness, whiteness, and sanctity in the early modern Hispanic world. (*Am. Hist. Rev.*, 121:3, June 2016, p. 727–754)

Sophisticated analysis of Catholic theology's understanding of the differences between skin pigmentation and the moral implications and visualizations of "lightness" or "whiteness" as related to sainthood. Rowe concludes that the Church saw African saints as encouragements for the conversion of African people of the Spanish colonies.

380 Ruan, Felipe E. Prudent deferment: cosmographer-chronicler Juan López de Velasco and the historiography of the Indies. (*Americas/Washington*, 74:1, Jan. 2017, p. 27–55)

Context can be a determining historical influence as this excellent article makes clear. López de Velasco received a royal appointment to write a formal history of the Indies but did not do so before he left official standing in 1591. Ruan's archival research indicates that the "environment of secrecy and censorship" prevalent in the Spanish court led López de Velasco to postpone and eventually avoid that task even though he did complete other important writing assignments.

381 Saldarriaga, Gregorio. Comer y ser: la alimentación como política de la diferenciación en la América española, siglos XVI y XVII. (*Varia Hist.*, 32:58, jan./abril 2016, p. 53–77, bibl.)

This article uses diet as an expression of class status and wealth in colonial Spanish America. Based on some archival research and also classic accounts published in the era under study.

382 Serrera Contreras, Ramón María. La América de los Habsburgo (1517–1700). Sevilla, Spain: Universidad de Sevilla: Fundación Real Maestranza de Caballería de Sevilla, 2011. 467 p.: bibl., index. (Serie Historia y geografía (Universidad de Sevilla); 179)

The title may imply for some readers that this volume is tightly focused on administrative history, but the text presents a sweeping, balanced survey that gives much attention to cultural, economic, and social themes. Prominent among them are the various roles of Native Americans, botanical and dietary history, and the exploitation of silver, gold, and other resources. The author is especially interested in the social structure of the American colonies, the tensions that arose in the Native American communities, and the emergence of a criollo sense of identity. The color illustrations and maps are of exceptionally high quality and serve the content of the book very nicely.

383 Surdich, Francesco. Verso i mari del Sud: l'esplorazione del Pacifico centrale e meridionale da Magellano a Malaspina. Ariccia, Italy: Aracne editrice int.le S.r.l., 2015. 366 p.: bibl., ill. (A11)

The volume reconstructs the long history of the explorations of the Pacific Ocean that started with Vasco Núñez de Balboa in 1513. The author provides a comprehensive treatment of the period of the European expeditions across the Pacific Ocean between the 16th and 17th centuries. While the general approach conventionally uses the periodization defined by the explorers and nations leading the expeditions, the most relevant contribution of this work to the discussion are the extensive references to the vast literature on the voyages, mostly based on primary sources written by the protagonists of the imaginary or factual oceanic explorations and their contemporary critics, as well as a substantial apparatus of critically acclaimed secondary sources. The author is a very well-established expert of the history of the geographic explorations, due to his long-standing teaching career at the Università di Genoa (1970–2014), his more than 200 articles published in the most authoritative scientific journals and conference proceedings, as well as his various monographs. [L.A. Wolf]

384 Tavarez, Fidel J. Viscardo's global political economy and the first cry for Spanish American independence, 1767–1798. (*J. Lat. Am. Stud.*, 48:3, Aug. 2016, p. 537–564)

Peruvian precursor of independence argued from an embryonic nationalist agenda that stressed the economic advantages of a complete break with Spain. The prescient Juan Pablo Viscardo called for Spain's American colonies to establish independence in order to participate in global—especially British—commerce. Tavaras makes good use of primary sources.

385 Valenzuela A., Eduardo. Kerigma: preguntas teóricas en torno a la primera evangelización de América (Antillas, 1510-Nueva España, 1524). (*Hist. Crít./Bogotá*, 58, oct./dic. 2015, p. 13–32, bibl.)

A complex examination of the adjustments by the first wave of missionaries in the evangelization efforts among Native Americans. Valenzuela A. emphasizes the combination of and evolution of theology and pedagogy as these early missionaries dealt with the challenges of mass conversions.

386 Vila Vilar, Enriqueta. El Consulado de Sevilla de mercaderes a Indias: un órgano de poder. Sevilla, Spain: Ayuntamiento de Sevilla, Instituto de la Cultura y las Artes de Sevilla (ICAS) SAHP, Departmento de Publicaciones, 2016. 250 p.: color ill. (Colección Temas libres; 68)

This comprehensive synthesis based on archival research provides an institutional history of the powerful consulado placed in its imperial, economic, and social contexts. Nicely illustrated with mostly color photographs, the work contains detailed footnotes and a list of 1628 individuals involved in 17th-century commerce.

387 Vilches, Elvira. Trade, silver, and print culture in the colonial Americas. (*J. Lat. Am. Cult. Stud.*, 24:3, Sept. 2015, p. 315–334, bibl.)

A valuable scholarly article that concentrates on the use of published commercial manuals by merchants, clerks, and a variety of consumers in the processing and sale of silver in the 1500s and 1600s. Includes insights on the social interactions related to these transactions.

388 Wolff, Jennifer. *Venisti tandem*: Johannes de Laet y la articulación del imaginario geográfico holandés sobre el Caribe, 1625–1641. (*Caribb. Stud.*, 43:2, July/Dec. 2015, p. 3–32, bibl., ill.)

A much-needed and well-researched examination of the Dutch perception of the Caribbean as a means of understanding their piratic, commercial, and colonial interventions in the region. Wolff focuses on the writings of geographer Johannes de Laet and maps produced in the era under study.

INDEPENDENCE AND 19TH CENTURY

389 Botero Montoya, Luis Horacio. La opinión pública en la formación de la ideología de la independencia en la Nueva Granada. Medellín, Colombia: Universidad de Medellín, Sello Editorial, 2014. 290 p.: bibl., ill.

Historical research and communications/social science concepts come together in this study of New Grenada's independence movement. The author used nine newspapers from the 1791–1815 era to analyze the ideological dimensions of the independence movement. An elite group of editorialists and commentators were the opinion leaders with their influence extending beyond the printed page to reach a key segment of the population.

390 Congreso Internacional Las Mujeres en los Procesos de Independencia de América Latina, *1st, Lima, 2013.* Primer Congreso Internacional Las Mujeres en los Procesos de Independencia de América Latina. Edición y compilación de Sara Beatriz Guardia. Lima: Centro de Estudios La Mujer en la Historia de América Latina, CEMHAL, 2014. 495 p.: bibl., ill.

This collection of 43 scholarly articles and interpretive essays covers several themes with helpful discussions of the historiography of women participants in revolutionary movements. Other large topics included are theater, art, the press, literature, and the education of women. There are also several case studies of individual participants. Among the individuals studied in detail are María Parado de Bellido,

Mariquita Sánchez de Thompson, and Juana Manuela Gorriti. A valuable publication because of the breadth of geographical representation: contributors come from Europe, the US, and Australia, as well as several Latin American nations. This volume constitutes a large accomplishment in this area and is an invitation for further research and synthesis.

391 Dulci, Tereza Maria Spyer. As Conferências Pan-Americanas (1889 a 1928): identidades, união aduaneira e arbitragem. São Paulo: Alameda, 2013. 236 p.: bibl. (Coleção Teses / USP, História Social)

This work examines the political and cultural projects surrounding the transnational conferences hosted in different capitals of the Americas between 1889 and 1928. The book pays special attention to questions of pan-Americanism, national identity, US influence in Latin America, and diplomacy. The study draws on sources deposited in Brazilian archives pertaining to the Pan-American conferences of Washington, D.C., Rio de Janeiro, Buenos Aires, Santiago, and Havana. [F. Prado]

392 Kazanjian, David. The brink of freedom: improvising life in the nineteenth-century Atlantic world. Durham, NC: Duke University Press, 2016. 329 p.: ill., index.

The relatively new field of Atlantic history receives an infusion of creative energy in this publication. This seemingly unorthodox, provocative study juxtaposes the experience of the rebellious Maya in Yucatán with the former slave settlers in Liberia in 1847–48. Both attempted to establish freedom (but not a formal nation-state) and both failed, but this nuanced examination of their struggles reveal social and cultural parallels that established the larger context of transatlantic communities and the activism of subject peoples.

393 Massot, Vicente Gonzalo. Los dilemas de la independencia. Buenos Aires: Grupo Unión, 2016. 156 p.: bibl.

Brief thought piece on the course of the independence movements mainly in the Río de la Plata area. Delves into the details of these movements with some comparative references to the revolution against the British in North America, but lacks full scholarly apparatus.

McCarthy, Matthew. Privateering, piracy and British policy in Spanish America, 1810–1830. See item **866**.

394 Ni vencedores ni vencidos: la Guerra del Pacífico en perspectiva histórica. Edición de José Chaupis Torres, Juan Ortiz Benites y Eduardo Cavieres Figueroa. Lima: La Casa del Libro Viejo, 2016. 437 p.: bibl., 2 ill., portraits.

This grouping of Peruvian and Chilean contributors strikes a balance in the overall historiographical impact of the 18 articles in this volume. The authors study in depth the origins of the war, the course of the fighting, and its short-term and long-term consequences. Among the articles are explorations of the influence of Great Britain and the US, the pervasive importance of nitrates, as well as discussions of particular naval and military actions.

395 El orden y el bajo pueblo: los regímenes de Portales y Rosas frente al mundo popular, 1829–1852. Edición de Julio Pinto Vallejos *et al*. Santiago: LOM Ediciones, 2015. 200 p.: bibl. (Historia)

An adroitly focused quartet of historical studies on Argentina and Chile. The authors combine some primary research with published studies to present a rigorous account of the interplay between nation-building, political instability, and populism. Sold groundwork for comparative history.

396 Pastor Bodmer, Beatriz. Cartografías utópicas de la emancipación. Madrid: Iberoamericana; Frankfurt am Main: Vervuert, 2015. 247 p.: bibl., index. (Tiempo emulado: historia de América y España; 43)

A general study of the ideas and idealism associated with the independence movements in Latin America as espoused by intellectual and political leaders in Europe and the US as well as Latin America. Explores the transnational nature of ideas. Among these independence advocates are Rousseau, Locke, Paine, Franklin, and Jefferson as well as Miranda, Gual, Bolívar, and Mier.

397 The politics of the second slavery. Edited by Dale W. Tomich. Albany: State University of New York Press, 2016. 267 p.: bibl., index. (Fernand Braudel Center studies in historical social science)

Slavery was a controversial issue that cut across national boundaries in the Western Hemisphere. These nine articles form a volume that places this deeply divisive issue in particular contexts from Spanish Cuba to the British Caribbean, Brazil, and the US. A significant contribution to Atlantic history and also the efforts to explore commonalities and contrasts in the history of the Americas.

398   **Pueblos indigenas en Latinoamérica: incorporación, conflicto, ciudadanía y representación siglo XIX.** Coordinación de Leticia Reina. México: Instituto Nacional de Antropología e Historia, 2015. 340 p.: bibl., ill. (Colección Historia. Serie Logos)

The troubled interaction of the newly independent nation-states and Native American communities is a main theme in this collection of 10 articles. The authors deal with political, military, and economic developments and the responses of indigenous peoples to these expanding national institutions. Five contributions deal with Mexico, two with Bolivia, and one each concern Argentina, Brazil, and Guatemala.

399   **Las revoluciones en el largo siglo XIX latinoamericano.** Edición de Rogelio Altez y Manuel Chust. Madrid: Iberoamericana; Frankfurt am Main: Vervuert, 2015. 265 p.: bibl. (Estudios AHILA de historia latinoamericana; 12)

This wide-ranging collection covers the varied forms of revolution from 1810 to 1910 prefaced by interesting introductory essays in the first two contributions. The revolutions for independence are the focal points of six of the essays. Cuba's lack of an independence movement is an instructive counterpoint for this volume. Reforma Mexico and the Mexican Revolution of 1910 are the main themes in the last three contributions.

400   **The rise of constitutional government in the Iberian Atlantic world: the impact of the Cádiz Constitution of 1812.** Edited by Scott Eastman and Natalia Sobrevilla Perea. Tuscaloosa, Alabama: The University of Alabama Press, 2015. 304 p.: bibl., ill., index. (Atlantic crossings)

This tightly focused group of articles begins with the origins and advent of Spain's Constitution of 1812 and then follows a variety of historical pathways to illuminate a formative era in Spanish American history. These pathways range from medieval Spain to the independence era in Central America New Granada, Peru, Rio del la Plata, Cuba, and Florida. The contributors combine a detailed knowledge of their specializations with an understanding of larger transnational influences.

401   **Sábato, Hilda.** Republics of the new world: the revolutionary political experiment in nineteenth-century Latin America. Princeton, N.J.: Princeton University Press, 2018. 220 p.

The simplistic notion that views 19th-century Latin American politics as a story of frustration and wasted energy receives a telling body-blow in this thoughtful and well-researched book. Sabato sees these efforts in nation-state building as components of a vast experiment in the Americas. Among the first colonials to break away from the Eurocentric imperial power structure, the Latin American nations have the misfortune of being compared to the US with quick jumps to negative judgements. Instead Sabato documents worthwhile struggles from Argentina to Mexico. Her approach is topical: constitutions, elections, military involvements, political parties, and a most impressive chapter on public opinion.

402   **Sarracino, Rodolfo.** José Martí, nuestra América y el equilibrio internacional. La Habana: Centro de Estudios Martianos, 2015. 197 p.: bibl. (Ala y raíz)

Perceptive analysis of Martí's ideas on anti-imperialism in relation to the prospective independence of Cuba. Includes biographical context for the development of Martí's anti-imperialism with emphasis on the influence of Argentina in his thinking. Gives much attention to his hopes for pan-Hispanic unity as a counter balance against the emerging power of the US. Based on Martí's published works as spelled out in the extensive footnotes.

403   **Secreto, María Verónica.** Fronteiras em movimento: história comparada, Argentina e Brasil no século XIX. Niterói, Brazil: Editora da UFF, 2012. 270 p.: bibl., ill., maps. (Biblioteca/Editora da UFF)

Comparative history requires a carefully structured text based on a broad reading of several relevant authors. Secreto does an outstanding job through the incorporation of the works of Frederick Jackson Turrner, Caio Prado Júnior, Roberto Cortés Conde, Marc Bloch and others with her own research in primary documents and contemporary publications in both countries. The analysis is nuanced and the conclusions reflect the persistent pattern of concentrated land holdings.

404   Tutino, John. New countries: capitalism, revolutions, and nations in the Americas, 1750–1870. Durham, NC: Duke University Press, 2016. 397 p.: ill., index, maps, photos.

A stimulating collection of scholarly articles that brings together the presumably contradictory themes of transnational and transoceanic history and the divergent experiences of nations such as Brazil, Haiti, Mexico, Guatemala, Peru, and Bolivia. The authors include global economic trends alongside the continuations of slavery and indigenous labor regimes. The collection benefits from preliminary conversations of the contributors which gives these studies a special coherence. The editor deserves special commendations.

405   Zeuske, Michael. Out of the Americas: slave traders and the hidden Atlantic in the nineteenth century. (*Atlan. Stud. Global Curr.*, 15:1, 2018, p. 103–135, bibl.)

Originally published in German in 2009, this article has been slightly revised to reflect more recent findings. The "hidden Atlantic" consists of slave trade vessels outfitted in Brazil and Cuba beyond the normal surveillance of the British navy. This article assesses the extent of this phase of the slave trade and points out future research avenues.

20TH CENTURY

406   Arocena, Felipe and Kirk Bowman. Lessons from Latin America: innovations in politics, culture, and development. Toronto, Canada: University of Toronto Press, 2014. 204 p.: ill.

The authors take on the challenge of countering stereotypes of Latin America that have prevailed for over a century in the popular media of the US. The widespread perceptions of backwardness, immaturity, and obsolescence find persuasive rejoinders in thoughtful discussions of women in politics, demilitarization, immigration to the US, the recent history of soccer, and social policies, especially retirement systems. The text concentrates on the last quarter century and benefits from a topical organization.

407   Asociación de Historiadores Latinoamericanos y del Caribe. Congreso. 10th, Santo Domingo, 2011. Las revoluciones del siglo XX en la historia de América Latina y el Caribe: memorias. Compilación de Ángela Altagracia Fernández Rosado y Jorge Enrique Elías-Caro. Ciudad Universitaria, Dominican Republic: Universidad Autónoma de Santo Domingo, 2014. 504 p.: bibl., ill.

The revolutions spawned in Mexico in 1910 and Cuba in 1959 are prominent in this collection of 34 articles and thought pieces. Taken as a whole, these contributions invite the reader to find patterns based on both similarities and differences. Another prominent theme centers on transnational influences as exemplified by movements in countries such as Costa Rica, the Dominican Republic, Uruguay, and Argentina.

408   Autoritarismo e cultura política. Organização de Luciano Aronne de Abreu e Rodrigo Patto Sá Motta. Rio de Janeiro: FGV Editora; Porto Alegre: EdiPUCRS, 2013. 348 p.: bibl.

Various institutional and ideological permutations and combinations that are manifested in authoritarian systems form the central themes in these 12 essays. Brazil is the main focus, but there is also coverage of Chile, Argentina, and Uruguay. Three of the essays deal with issues surrounding economic development. Taken as a whole, this volume is an interesting commentary on Cold War South America.

409   Azcona Pastor, José Manuel and Matteo Re. Guerrilleros, terroristas y revolución (1959–1988): identidad marxista y violencia política en ETA, Brigadas Rojas, Tupamaros y Montoneros. Cizur Menor,

Spain: Thomson Reuters Aranzadi, 2015. 280 p.: bibl., ill. (Humanidades)

This study pulls together the historical roots of radical terrorist groups that emerged in the 1960s and carries them through the 1980s. The authors begin with the Basque-inspired ETA. The bulk of the content concentrates on Uruguay, Argentina, Brazil, and Chile and also includes the influence of these movements in Europe. The authors rely on published documents and interviews. The breadth of this study allows for comparative perspectives on these movements.

410 Bauer, Caroline Silveira. Brasil e Argentina: ditaduras, desaparecimentos e políticas de memória. 2a edição. Porto Alegre, Brazil: Medianiz; ANPUHRS, 2014. 336 p.: bibl.

The dark phases in the histories of these two countries are fully explored in this exemplary comparative study. Bauer uses extensive quotations from documents and measured prose to impart a restrained sense of outrage. The author consulted official archives, legislative and judicial records, and political files to construct a summary view of the dictatorships and their abuse of state power. The struggles for justice in both nations in the aftermath of these events are also covered in depth. This work constitutes an important synthesis for the two nations affected by right-wing extremist culture and policy.

411 Congreso Internacional Ciencias, Tecnologías y Culturas: Diálogo entre las Disciplinas del Conocimiento, Mirando al Futuro de América Latina y el Caribe, *3rd, Santiago, Chile, 2013.* Integração na América Latina: a história, a economia e o direito. Vol. 2. Organización de Eduardo Scheidt, Elian Araúj e Luis Gutierrez San Juan. Jundiaí, Brazil: Paco Editorial, 2014. 470 p.: ill.

The term integration is used in its broadest sense here. Most of the 20 articles deal with one of the various forms of integration, including not only trade and investment, but also politics, law, multiculturalism, and the transfer and validation of postgraduate degrees. Three contributions involve Venezuela and one concerns the portrayal of military dictatorship in Argentina.

412 Dehne, Phillip. How important was Latin America to the First World War? *(Iberoamericana/Madrid,* 14:53, marzo 2014, p. 151–164, bibl.)

A convenient overview of an often-neglected subject. Dehne relies on published works to point out what scholars have done and what needs more attention. For comparison, see Frederick Luebke's work on WWI *(HLAS 52:3056).*

413 Elementos identitarios de la imagen de España, América Latina y de su historia en Albania: análisis estructural y estudio de caso. Edición de José Manuel Azcona y Anastasi Prodani. Madrid: Editorial Dykinson, 2013. 338 p.: bibl., ill.

This edited volume contains a diverse group of essays on popular images across national boundaries. Most pertinent to Latin Americanists is Azcona's historical and statistical study of the image of Spain in Latin America with special reference to economics and business affairs.

414 Encuentro Latinoamericano de Historia Oral, *5th, San Salvador, 2013.* Voces e imágenes de la historia reciente de América Latina. Coordinación de Eugenia López, Jilma Romero Arrechavala, y Alberto del Castillo Troncoso. Managua: UNAN-Managua, 2015. 286 p.: bibl., ill.

This selection of documents in oral history presents a sampling from the left side of the political spectrum on events from the 1920s to the present with emphasis on the last half century. Each section has a brief introduction for context and a bibliography for further reading. Intended for the college classroom.

415 Extendiendo los límites: nuevas agendas en historia reciente. Coordinación de Guillermo Mira y Fernando Pedrosa. Buenos Aires: Eudeba, 2016. 557 p.: bibl., ill.

Sixteen scholarly articles explore the turbulent political history of the 1970s and 1980s with a focus on Argentina, while also touching on events in Chile, El Salvador, Guatemala, Colombia, and Venezuela. A persistent theme in several contributions concerns the determined opposition to authoritarian regimes. As a group, these articles offer a look at transnational factors in the anti-authoritarian movements.

416   Green, W. John. A history of political murder in Latin America: killing the messengers of change. Albany, NY: SUNY Press, 2015. 360 p.: bibl., index, maps. (SUNY series in global modernity)

A competent study of a controversial and often emotional topic. The author states his approach clearly: an examination of right-wing elites who target popular leftist movements. Includes the dirty wars of the Cold War era. Green also discusses the shifting policies of the US. Nations that receive considerable attention are Argentina, Colombia, El Salvador, Guatemala, and Mexico. Little or no coverage on pre-Cold War murders, such as those of Augusto Sandino and Julio Antonio Mella.

417   Herrera, Olga U. American interventions and modern art in South America. Gainesville: University Press of Florida, 2017. 319 p.: bibl., ill., photos.

This excellent study establishes the extensive artistic and cultural interactions that left indelible influences throughout the Western Hemisphere during the WWII period. Franklin D. Roosevelt's administration established exchange programs with the goal of promoting hemispheric unity in the face of Nazi propaganda and the potential Axis threat. These programs moved artists both northward to the US and southward into Latin America. Nelson Rockefeller and Lincoln Kirsten emerge as central figures in the process of creating a transnational market for art in the Americas. Congratulations to the University of Florida Press for the beautifully reproduced color illustrations.

418   Iber, Patrick. Neither peace nor freedom: the cultural Cold War in Latin America. Cambridge, Mass.: Harvard University Press, 2015. 327 p.: bibl., ill., index.

The Cold War's conflicts were fought on many levels and involved more than the stereotypical left versus right battles between the US and the Soviet Union. Iber's book examines the cultural-ideological struggles among leftists engineered by the Soviet Union's World Peace Congress and the Central Intelligence Agency's Congress for Cultural Freedom in Latin America. Even this apparently two-sided contest was, in Iber's astute analysis, broken into fragments as intellectuals, artists, and political activists sought victory for their particular cause and survival for themselves in this highly charged atmosphere. Much concentration on Mexico City and Havana. The author relies on published sources as well as archival material.

419   Islam and the Americas. Edited by Aisha Khan. Gainesville: University Press of Florida, 2015. 348 p.: bibl., ill., index, photos. (New world diasporas)

Pioneering effort that assembles studies of the Muslim presence in 20th- and 21st-century Latin America. The focus is on the circum-Caribbean with four of the 13 articles on Trinidad and Tobago, but the editor also includes contributions on Mexico and Brazil. These articles rely on scholarly documentation.

420   Keller, Renata. The Latin American missile crisis. (*Dipl. Hist.*, 39:2, April 2015, p. 195–222, map, photo)

Provides analytical summaries of the varied responses of Latin American governments to the Cuban missile crisis. These responses included a mix of tolerance for anti-US protests and support for the U.S. blockade of Cuba in Mexico City, right-wing anti-communist responses in Somoza's Nicaragua, and support for US policy in maneuvers for political advantage within the Argentine military. A useful, well-written synopsis.

421   Local Church, global Church: Catholic activism in Latin America from *Rerum Novarum* to Vatican II. Edited by Stephen Joseph Carl Andes and Julia G. Young. Washington, D.C.: Catholic University of America Press, 2016. 353 p: bibl.

This collection studies the many ways in which the Catholic Church was a dynamic force in Latin American politics and society throughout the 20th century. Two of the articles concern Brazil and one each deal with Colombia and Guatemala. Four examine the Mexican Revolution from the 1910s to 1940. Matthew Butler's contribution emphasizes the masculinization of Catholic activism in Mexico, and Robert Curley provide a close examination of the controversial Oklahoma Bishop Francis Kelly and his portrayal of the plight of the

Mexican clergy for readers in the US. Other articles look at grassroots activism such as the Antigonish movement and Catholic sponsorship of Maya cooperatives from 1943 to 1966.

422 **López-Durán, Fabiola.** Eugenics in the garden: transatlantic architecture and the crafting of modernity. Austin: University of Texas Press, 2018. 296 p.: bibl., ill., index. (Lateral exchanges: architecture, urban development, and transnational practices)

This groundbreaking book brings together the study of eugenics, architecture, city planning, and cultural/intellectual history in its discussion of the intermingling of ideas and work of French, Argentine, and Brazilian physicians, architects, and social theorists. Included in the mixture are Jean Baptiste Lamarck, Le Corbusier, and Alexis Carrel from France, José María Ramos Mejía and Emilio Coni of Argentina; and Donat-Alfred Agache and Lucio Costa of Brazil. Racial and racist concepts were integral parts of this transnational movement for social engineering. Anchored by research in the archives of architects and urban planners.

423 **Lutas sociais, intelectuais e poder: problemas de história social.** Organização de Eurelino Coelho e Larissa Penelu. Contribuções de Benito Bisso Schmidt et al. Feira de Santana, Brazil: UEFS Editora, 2012. 272 p.

These essays explore problems related to class and racial conflict, the use of political power, the flaws of capitalism, and the ambiguous position of intellectuals. The last essay examines the roles of Rollie Poppino, his associates, and "Project Columbia" in the early Cold War.

424 **Martínez Lillo, Pedro Antonio** and **Pablo Rubio Apiolaza.** América Latina actual: del populismo al giro de izquierdas. Madrid: Catarata, 2017. 143 p.: bibl. (Colección Investigación y debate; 183)

Succinct discussion of the politics and ideology in the Cold War era that begins with populism in the 1940s and 1950s and then focuses on Castro's revolution and the right-wing "security states" of the 1970s and 1980s. The concluding section examines the rise of neoliberalism and the ideological diversity of the 21st century.

425 **Masera, Gustavo** and **Duilio Lorenzo Calcagno.** El largo camino de la utopía: integración regional en América Latina (1949–1999). Mendoza, Argentina: Editorial de la Universidad del Aconcagua, 2013. 160 p.: bibl.

A small book that presents a substantial and often penetrating analysis of the inherent tensions between globalization and regional economic organizations and arrangements over a crucial half-century. Commentary on the Central American Common Market, the Groupo Andino, and Mercosur. The author uses the broad perspective of political economy rather than a narrow econometric approach.

426 **Melgar Bao, Ricardo.** La prensa militante en América Latina y la Internacional Comunista. México: Instituto Nacional de Antropología e Historia, 2015. 315 p.: bibl., ill., index. (Colección Historia. Serie Logos)

A combination of exhaustive research and perceptive analysis gives this book much value for historians of communism in Latin America. Melgar Bao includes lists of pamphlets and editorials produced by various branches of the Communist Party from 1919 to 1938. *El Machete, El Libertador, Labor,* and *La Correspondencia Sudamericana* are featured publications. The author also discusses the archives that house these publications.

427 **El otro rostro de la inversión extranjera: redes migratorias, empresa y crecimiento económico en México y América Latina.** Coordinación de María Eugenia Romero Ibarra y Javier Moreno Lázaro. México: UNAM, Facultad de Economía, 2014. 1 vol.: bibl., ill.

These nine essays deal with the role of immigrants as entrepreneurs with an emphasis on Mexico. Not only do these case studies expand our knowledge of the connections between immigration and international business, but they also provide valuable portraits of small- to mid-sized firms involved in the process of globalization.

428 **Pérez, Inés.** Consumo y género: una revisión de la producción historiográfica reciente sobre América Latina en el siglo XX. (*Hist. Crít./Bogotá*, 65, julio/sept. 2017, p. 29–48, bibl.)

Helpful review of 66 published works that reflects growing interest in the role of women in the consumer economy with attention to social class, domestic work, and nation-by-nation trends.

429   **Piczenik, José Luis.** Comunidades judías en América Latina. Buenos Aires: Editorial Milá, 2013 214 p.: bibl., ill. (Colección Investigaciones)

A collection of brief, country-by-country surveys of several Jewish communities. The time frame is mainly the early 21st century. The author relies on press reports and also examines the themes of anti-Semitism, Islamic influences, and Israeli tourism.

430   **Rinke, Stefan H.** Latin America and the First World War. Cambridge, England: Cambridge University Press, 2017. 302 p.: bibl., ill., index. (Global and international history)

Latin American history during WWI is frequently neglected by both specialists and generalists, but Rinke show how the impact of the diplomacy, politics, sociocultural change, and commercial relations of the Great War had a lasting impact on the region and its place in world history. This excellent synthesis is based on both published monographs and research in primary documents. Rinke makes good use of words and illustrations from the Buenos Aires publication, *Caras y Caretas,* and *Zig-Zag* of Santiago, Chile as well as other news magazines, newspapers, and archives. His coverage of the external and internal stresses on domestic politics and social institutions is matched by his assessment of the shift in the hemispheric power balance to the US.

431   **Riofrio, John D.** Continental shifts: migration, representation, and the struggle for justice in Latin(o) America. Austin: University of Texas Press, 2015. 198 p.: bibl., index.

The recent intensification of globalization has produced cultural conflicts in the US in which defenders of traditional values have mounted campaigns against the arrival of immigrants, languages, and cultures from other parts of the world—especially Latin America. Riofrio outlines the multiple dimensions of this conflict through the examination of novels, films, and political/ ideological commentary. Prominent figures include Ariel Dorfman, Tommy Lee Jones, and Dylan Rodríguez.

432   **Rupprecht, Tobias.** Soviet internationalism after Stalin: interaction and exchange between the USSR and Latin America during the Cold War. Cambridge, England: Cambridge University Press, 2015. 334 p.: bibl., index.

Much-needed study of a previously neglected aspect of the Cold War: the expansion of the Soviet Union's interest in Latin America in the fields of popular culture, high culture, and academe. Rupprecht builds on his extensive research in Russian language sources to provide new information on the institutional developments that resulted in the growth of knowledge about Latin American history, society, and music. Traces the parallel between the expansion of Latin American studies in the US and the Soviet Union. One chapter is devoted to Latin American students in the Soviet Union. A valuable scholarly study of the "soft side" of Cold War history.

433   **Sánchez Román, José Antonio.** El multilateralismo como intervencionismo: Estados Unidos y la Sociedad de Naciones en América Latina, 1930–1946. (*Rev. Complut. Hist. Am.,* 41, 2015, p. 47–69, bibl.)

Highlights the expansion of US policy influences through the League of Nations and its Fiscal Committee based on the shift from European to US capital investment in Latin America during the 1920s. Considerable commentary on the Good Neighbor Policy viewed from a financial perspective.

434   **Santos, Norma Breda dos.** Latin American countries and the establishment of the multilateral trading system: the Havana Conference (1947–1948). (*Rev. Econ. Polít.,* 36:2, abril/junho 2016, p. 309–329, bibl., graph, tables)

Santos underscores the relative weakness of the Latin American countries and the disadvantages faced by their representatives at the conference that was crucial in the development of the post-WWII world economic environment. The General Agreement on Tariffs and Trade (GATT) emerged in the Havana conference with disadvantages for the developing economies.

435 **The struggle for memory in Latin America: recent history and political violence.** Edited by Eugenia Allier and Emilio Crenzel. New York, N.Y.: Palgrave Macmillan, 2015. 260 p.: bibl., index. (Memory politics and transitional justice)

The violent political conflicts of the last half of the 20th century in Latin America constitute some of the major battlegrounds in the Cold War. This expertly edited volume concentrates on the efforts—often conflicted—that define and analyze the historical understanding of these painful episodes. There are specialized studies of Argentina, Brazil, Chile, and Mexico (in 1968) and six other Latin American countries in this period. One study deals with the declassification of government archives in the US. An important contribution to the historiography of this era.

436 **Transformations of populism in Europe and the Americas: history and recent tendencies.** Edited by John Abromeit et al. London: Bloomsbury Academic, an imprint of Bloomsbury Publishing Plc, 2016. 354 p.: bibl., index.

This edited work places Latin American populism in a large geopolitical framework that includes Europe and the US. Five of the 18 articles deal with Latin America—mainly Argentina, Brazil, Paraguay, and the circum-Caribbean. Latin Americanists will also benefit from the comparative perspective on the "producerist" populism in Germany of the 1920s that cast workers as producers of the nation's wealth and their political rivals as parasites. These essays stress the flexibility of populist ideologies that avoided dogmatic traps that the left often set for itself. The Latin American movements often thrived on the interplay between leaders such as the Peróns and their followers.

437 **Vera, Héctor.** Medición y vida económica: medidas panamericanas y la lucha por un "lenguaje universal para el comercio." (*Estud. Sociol./México*, 32:95, mayo/agosto 2014, p. 231–260, bibl.)

Informative discussion of the necessity for statistical measurements of international trade and the problematic negotiations for the establishment of hemispheric-wide standards in the early 20th century. Historical analysis of a crucial period in the development of quantification methods across national boundaries.

438 **Wright, Thomas C.** Latin America in the era of the Cuban Revolution and beyond. Third edition. Santa Barbara, Calif.: Praeger, 2018. 286 p.: bibl., index, maps.

Revised edition of a widely used textbook. For international relations specialist's comment on the first edition (1991), see *HLAS 55:3881*. For historian's comment on the revised edition (2001), see *HLAS 60:1144*.

MEXICO
General

SUZANNE B. PASZTOR, *Professor of History, Humboldt State University*

THE PERIOD UNDER REVIEW witnessed the appearance of several works that illuminate Mexico's long history of social activism, perhaps reflecting the increasing visibility of protest groups (including #YoSoy132) in the Mexico of the new millennium. Illades provides a brief overview of radical protest from the 19th century to the present (item **451**), Vázquez Toriz and Rappo Míguez make impressive use of sources from the National Agrarian Archive to detail the long history of agrarian activism in one section of Puebla (item **472**), and Sánchez Reséndiz explores the long struggle for autonomy and access to water among villages in eastern Morelos (item **468**). An edited volume by Acevedo Tarazona, Sánchez Parra, and Samacá Alonso (item **439**) focuses on student activism in the 20th and 21st centuries, and Espinosa provides an important addition to the historiography with a study of Catholic student groups during the 20th century (item **449**).

Social and cultural historians continue to produce interesting work, exploring a variety of topics, applying approaches from other disciplines, and discovering novel sources. Gonzalbo Aizpuru and Mayer Celis provide essays on the history of social relations (item **446**), Ruiz Medrano, Roque Puente, and Coronado Guel present a volume built around the exploration of human impacts on landscapes (item **461**), and Gonzalbo offers a collection based on the idea of subjective spaces (item **448**). The social and cultural implications of urban development are at the heart of the collection by Dávalos López and Iracheta Cenecorta (item **442**), Arias examines social life in a rural town (item **441**), and a collection edited by Day utilizes art to examine several themes related to modern Mexico (item **457**). A few authors during the last biennium turned their attention to economic themes. Aboites examines the impact of cotton agriculture in northern Mexico (item **440**), Lavín Higuera offers a detailed look at economic development in Tamaulipas (item **453**), and Flores Torres has assembled a collection on a variety of economic topics (item **463**). Most notably, Beatty provides a compelling exploration of technology in modern Mexico (item **443**). Two important additions to Mexican historiography explore foreign populations in Mexico: Chang analyzes anti-Chinese racism (item **445**), and Dormady and Tamez have assembled essays on the Mormon presence (item **452**). Among other notable works not included in the above categories is a history of relations between Spain and Mexico by Sánchez Andrés and Pérez Herrero (item **467**), an important volume by Pérez Toledo, Miño Grijalva, and Amaio Peñaflores on the history of artisans (item **458**), a survey of narcotrafficking by Valdés Castellanos (item **471**), and a collection of essays on the modern Mexican press assembled by Valles Ruiz, González Victoria, and Vega Jiménez (item **464**).

GENERAL

439 ¡A estudiar, a luchar! movimientos estudiantiles en Colombia y México, siglos XX y XXI. Compilación de Álvaro Acevedo Tarazona, Sergio Arturo Sánchez Parra y Gabriel David Samacá Alonso. Culiacán, Mexico: Universidad Autónoma de Sinaloa, 2014. 251 p.

Most of the selections in this volume came out of an intellectual history conference held in Colombia. Four of the 10 brief studies deal directly with Mexico, including a survey of the movement for autonomy at the national university. Two essays examine student radicalization during the 1970s (touched off by the naming of a new rector) at the Universidad Autónoma de Sinaloa, and one selection details the organization and structure of Mexico's #YoSoy132 movement.

440 Aboites, Luis. El norte entre algodones: población, trabajo agrícola y optimismo en México, 1930–1970. México: El Colegio de México, Centro de Estudios Históricos, 2013. 461 p.: bibl., ill.

This is an extensively researched history of cotton agriculture in Mexico's northern states, including the regions of La Laguna and Mexicali. The author details the demographic shifts and urban development that were linked to cotton, explores the technical aspects of cotton cultivation, and surveys the ways in which this commodity linked Mexico to the US. He also examines the realities of cotton workers' lives, and the crucial role played by the Mexican government in fostering a cotton economy. A major argument is that cotton helped integrate the Mexican north with the rest of the country.

441 **Arias, Patricia.** Retrato escrito: los grupos domésticos y el espacio en Totatiche, Jalsico, 1905–1920. Zapopan, Mexico: El Colegio de Jalisco, 2014. 282 p.: bibl., ill., maps. (Investigación)

This intriguing study combines social demography, history, and ethnography to trace patterns in the social life of a rural town in northern Jalisco. The author utilizes parish census records, ex-votos, and interviews, and she focuses especially on change and continuity at the household level. Totatiche residents developed unique patterns of social reproduction in the context of isolation and a lack of in-migration.

442 **Barrios y periferia: espacios socioculturales, siglos XVI–XXI.** Coordinación de Marcela Dávalos López y Pilar Iracheta Cenecorta. Zinacantepec, México: El Colegio Mexiquense, 2015. 285 p.: bibl., ill., maps.

This intriguing collection of essays by historians and social scientists explores the historical dynamics and implications of urban development. Several authors engage with the issue of how precolonial indigenous communities were transformed by the growth of cities and the political and administrative policies that supported such growth. Most selections deal with Mexico City, with additional studies on communities, populations, and neighborhoods in Michoacán, Oaxaca, Guadalajara, and Aguascalientes.

443 **Beatty, Edward N.** Technology and the search for progress in modern Mexico. Oakland: University of California Press, 2015. 360 p.: bibl., index.

This extensively researched and readable monograph examines technology transfer and technological assimilation from approximately 1870 to 1920. The author uses case studies of sewing machines, glass bottle blowing technology, and the processing of silver and gold with cyanide. Mexico readily adopted new technologies, but local adaptations to such technologies were often problematic. Meanwhile, technical learning lagged behind, hampering Mexico's ability to develop the means to reproduce and maintain new technologies. An important addition to the historiography.

444 **Beezley, William H.** and **Colin M. MacLachlan.** Mexico: the essentials. New York: Oxford University Press, 2016. 227 p.: bibl., ill., index, maps.

This brief volume is intended as a popular introduction to Mexico. Nine chapters survey Mexico's physical, cultural, political, economic, and social landscapes. The authors also highlight the importance of religion, the centrality of Mexico City, the evolution of popular art, and the role of drugs, crime, and immigration in Mexico's history.

445 **Chang, Jason Oliver.** Chino: anti-Chinese racism in Mexico, 1880–1940. Urbana, Ill.: University of Illinois Press, 2017. 257 p.: bibl., ill., index, maps, tables. (The Asian American experience)

This impressive and well-researched study pushes the historiography of postrevolutionary state building in an important new direction. The author traces the history of Chinese settlement in Mexico in the context of Porfirian colonization efforts, explores patterns of anti-Chinese violence during the Revolution, and analyzes the Nationalist Campaign of the 1930s during which thousands of Chinese were expelled from Mexico. He details how anti-Asian discourse helped create a postrevolutionary state based on mestizo nationalism and concludes with an exploration of government policies under President Abelardo Rodríguez that solidified the idea of racialized citizenship. An important contribution.

446 **Conflicto, resistencia y negociación en la historia.** Edición de Pilar Gonzalbo y Leticia Mayer Celis. México: El Colegio de México, 2016. 443 p.: bibl., ill.

The 11 essays in this collection (all but one about Mexico, and most focused on Mexico City) represent a variety of interesting approaches to the history of social relations. The social symbolism of a colonial funerary procession, dynamics among in-laws in 18th-century families, the evolution of attitudes toward orphans, marital conflict among foreign residents of Mexico City, and anti-Chinese discrimination in the early 20th century are among the topics. Additional authors explore the efforts of female domestic workers in Oaxaca to assert their rights, the negotiation of femininity in the 1920s, indigenous strategies of adjustment to the wheat economy in 19th-century Chiapas, the integration of Spaniards into Mexico's postindependence literary community, and the challenges arising from the establishment of federal schools along the northern border in the aftermath of the Mexican Revolution.

447 Desde la otra orilla: miradas extranjeras sobre Querétaro. Compilación de José N. Iturriaga de la Fuente. Santiago de Querétaro, Mexico: Fondo Editorial de Querétaro, 2013. 319 p.: bibl.

This is a collection of 85 brief excerpts that touch upon a variety of aspects of Querétaro. Authors include both well-known and more obscure figures with missionaries, colonial officials, scientists, journalists, and diplomats among them. The majority of the selections belong to the 19th century, though the volume begins with the colonial era and ends with the 21st century.

448 Espacios en la historia: invención y transformación de los espacios sociales. Edición de Pilar Gonzalbo. México: El Colegio de México, 2014. 426 p.: bibl., ill.

This is a collection of social histories (most rather brief and all but two about Mexico) built around the idea of subjective spaces created by symbols, beliefs, traditions, and perspectives. Topics in the first two sections include the experience of the sacred through death rituals in a colonial monastery and through the daily rhythm created by convent bells in colonial Puebla, and 19th-century cultural spaces, including those carved out by female musicians and privileged theatergoers. The remaining two sections of the volume cover a bewildering variety of themes, including the colonial mining complex, female work culture, colonial places of indigenous power, and the segregation of prostitutes in Mexico City's Hospital Morelos.

449 Espinosa, David. Jesuit student groups, the Universidad Iberoamericana, and political resistance in Mexico, 1913–1979. Albuquerque: University of New Mexico Press, 2014. 196 p.: bibl., index.

The author emphasizes the role of the Mexican Catholic Youth Association (ACJM), the National Catholic Student Union (UNEC), and the Jesuit Universidad Iberoamericana in this important addition to the historiography of the Church and of the student movement. He traces the evolution of Church-state relations in the context of the Mexican Revolution, explores the development of the ACJM and UNEC, and their links to conservative causes, including the Cristero Rebellion and the founding of the PAN party. The author demonstrates that in the post-Vatican II era, the Iberoamericana, which had initially trained a generation of business leaders, embraced a more activist orientation, thereby contributing to Mexico's student movement.

450 Ideas, ideólogos e idearios en la construcción de la imagen peninsula. Coordinación de Mario Humberto Ruz y Adam T. Sellen. Izamal, Mexico: Secretaría de Educación del Gobierno del Estado de Yucatán, 2015. 236 p.: bibl., ill., maps (some color).

Seven essays explore the evolution of a regional identity in the Yucatan, with a focus on intellectuals writing about the area, particularly during the 19th century. The volume includes explorations of early English writings on indigenous peoples, Justo Sierra O'Reilly's rendition of a 17th-century Franciscan text on the Yucatan, the work of philologist Juan Pío Pérez in preserving Maya texts and language, and a survey arising from scientific efforts during the French intervention. The last three essays focus on the work of Crescencio Carrillo y Ancona, a 19th-century priest who collected Yucatecan artifacts, founded a museum, and corresponded widely with others about the Yucatan.

451 Illades, Carlos. Conflicto, dominación y violencia: capítulos de historia social. México: Universidad Autónoma Metropolitana, 2015. 251 p.: bibl., ill. (Serie CLA-DE-MA. Historia.)

This brief volume explores the broad sweep of social activism in Mexico from the 19th century to the present era. The author examines the earlier evolution of organizing among skilled workers, agrarian socialism in Queretaro and Guanajuato, and anti-Spanish activity during the Mexican Revolution. Additional chapters analyze Guerrero's long history of unrest, contextualize Mexico's "Black Block" protests during the present century, and trace outstanding examples of contemporary radicalism including the #YoSoy132 movement, and protests surrounding the disappearance of 43 students in Ayotzinapa.

452   **Just south of Zion: the Mormons in Mexico and its borderlands.** Edited by Jason H. Dormady and Jared M. Tamez. Albuquerque: University of New Mexico Press, 2015. 220 p.: bibl., ill., index, map.

In this volume, scholars of Mexico, the American West, the Borderlands, and Mormon history explore various aspects of the Mormon presence in Mexico from the mid-19th to the mid-20th centuries. Selections examine the beginnings of a Mormon presence in Mexico, Mormon missionary efforts, the creation of a transnational identity among Mormons, cross-border relations among the Mormon community, the role of women and Mexican Mormons in shaping the local experience of Mormonism, and the Third Convention movement by which Mexico's Mormons attempted to carve out their own church leadership vis-à-vis Salt Lake. Useful introductory and concluding chapters, provide broader historical context and reflection on the place of Mormonism in the history of Mexico and the Borderlands.

453   **Lavín Higuera, Valentín.** Historia económica de Tamaulipas. Huixquilucan, Mexico: Oak Editorial, 2015. 502 p.: bibl., map.

This is an extensively researched, detailed history from the colonial era to the early 21st century. The author begins with a survey of the colonization of Nuevo Santander, and delves more deeply into 19th-century developments, including the emergence of the port of Tampico, cross-border trade, the development of infrastructure, and the beginning of the oil industry. The exploration of the 20th century underscores the continuing importance of oil, as well as the development of agriculture, cattle ranching, manufacturing, and a maquiladora industry. Appendices provide population data, as well as information on the state's maquilas.

454   **Liu, Wenlong.** Moxige tong shi = The history of Mexico. Shanghai, China: Shanghai she hui ke xue yuan chu ban she [Shanghai Academy of Social Sciences Press (China)], 2014. 419 p.: bibl., graphs, tables. (Shi jie li shi wen hua cong shu [World history and culture series])

This book consists of 11 chapters. It covers the formation and development of early indigenous civilizations, Spain's conquest and colonization of Mexico, colonial society and culture, the independence movement and the difficulties both at home and abroad during the postindependence period, the Reform War and France's interference. It also provides a detailed evaluation of the regime under José de la Cruz Porfirio Díaz and the Mexican Revolution and significant historical events of the mid-20th century to the early 21st century. A clear and logical presentation of Mexican history that benefits from the author's original commentary. [Liu Weiguang]

455   **Lizárraga Sánchez, Salvador** and **Cristina López Uribe.** Living CU 60 years: Ciudad Universitaria UNAM 1954–2014. México: UNAM, 2014. 349 p.: bibl., ill. (some color), maps, plans.

This is an English translation of a volume that emphasizes the architectural evolution and heritage of the national university campus. Authors examine the landscape of El Pedregal, which became the backdrop for the university campus, and detail the process by which architectural designs and concepts were developed and implemented. Additional chapters explore the image of the campus through film, newspapers, and architectural magazines, as well as the relationship of the campus project to the Mexican state. The volume's last section places the campus in a more contemporary context, and includes considerations of the area as a World Heritage site, as well as criticisms of the ways in which urban growth has encroached upon and challenged the architectural integrity of the campus.

456   **Meyer, Jean A.** De una revolución a la otra: México en la historia. México: El Colegio de México, Centro de Estudios Históricos, 2013. 579 p.: bibl.

This is an anthology of 23 previously published writings by the distinguished scholar of the Cristero Rebellion. Three distinct sections bring together studies on Mexico's independence, the Mexican Revolution, and the church-state conflict, including Meyer's analyses of regional differences during the *Cristiada*. Selections span Meyer's career from the 1960s to the present.

457 Modern Mexican culture: critical foundations. Edited by Stuart Alexander Day. Tucson: The University of Arizona Press, 2017. 330 p.: bibl., index.

In this intriguing collection of essays, cultural studies scholars examine a variety of themes relevant to modern Mexico through the lens of art, broadly defined. More historical topics include political messages in the work of graphic artists and mural representations of teachers in the context of the Mexican Revolution, and cultural expressions of the Tlatelolco massacre. Of more contemporary relevance are works that explore representations of young Mexican immigrants (DREAMers), and the use of documentary films to underscore the consequences of corporate agriculture, probe the dynamics between mainstream and grassroots media, and analyze depictions of Mexico's democratic transition and of feminicide in Ciudad Juarez. Additional essays interrogate images of the charro, challenge the notion of Mexican "solitude," examine classism among Mexicans, explore depictions of the Mexican north, and survey the deployment of art in the "post-internet" era. Each chapter contains a list of available primary sources, making this volume a particularly useful source for teachers.

458 El mundo del trabajo urbano: trabajadores, cultura y prácticas laborales. Coordinación de Sonia Pérez Toledo, Manuel Miño Grijalval, y René Amaro Peñaflores. México: El Colegio de México, 2012. 322 p.: bibl., index.

With a primary focus on transformations in the cities of Mexico, Guadalajara, and Zacatecas from the late colonial era into the 19th century, the authors of this collection move beyond traditional approaches to labor history. What emerges is a more complex view of labor systems in colonial cities, as well as a more active role for Indians, mestizos, and Afro Mexicans as artisans in these growing urban areas. Authors also highlight the transformation from an oral culture of guild-based artisan training, to a more formal vocational training linked to literacy, and emphasize the emergence of workers' organizations and activism.

459 El norte de México y la historia regional: homenaje a Ignacio del Río. Coordinación de Marco Antonio Landavazo Arias *et al.* Morelia, Mexico: Universidad Michoacana de San Nicolás de Hidalgo, 2014. 397 p.: bibl., ill. (Encuentros; 18)

This series of essays commemorates the work of a regional historian and emphasizes the northwest. A first section explores the theory and practice of regional history, while a second provides two personal accounts of the life and work of del Río. Remaining essays examine regional histories of the colonial era and of the 19th century. Authors examine sources for ethnohistory of northern peoples, northern colonial institutions as a reflection of negative views of northern peoples, and colonial missionary work in the northwest. Nineteenth-century themes include the integration of Baja California into a newly independent Mexico, elite colonization efforts and the importance of the Catholic Church in Sonora, the politics of public health in Baja California, and demographic changes linked to the development of La Paz.

460 Olveda, Jaime. Autonomía, soberanía y federalismo: Nueva Galicia y Jalisco. Zapopan, Mexico: El Colegio de Jalisco, 2014. 294 p.: bibl., ill. (Investigación)

A study of the relationship between this western region and Mexico's political center, from the colonial era to the centralizing Constitution of 1857. The author examines the effect of the intendancy system, independence, and the federalist constitution of 1824 on local autonomy. The last two chapters trace the effects of a renewed centralism on Jalisco, culminating in the agreement of regional elites to support a strong central authority.

461 Paisajes culturales y patrimonio en el centro-norte de México, siglos XVII al XX. Coordinación de Carlos Rubén Ruiz Medrano, Carlos Alberto Roque Puente, y Luis Edgardo Coronado Guel. San Luis Potosí, Mexico: El Colegio de San Luis,

2014. 418 p.: bibl., ill., maps. (Colección Investigaciones)

This volume of essays takes its cue from geographer Carl Sauer's emphasis on the "cultural history" of human impacts on landscapes. The first section includes studies of colonial Nueva Galicia and the Real de Catorce mining zone, agricultural development in 19th-century San Luis Potosí, salt mining in San Luis Potosí and Zacatecas, the social effects of historical preservation in the city of Zacatecas, and the effects of the revival of mescal in San Luis Potosí in the contemporary era. Essays in the second section attempt to broaden the view of cultural patrimony to include customs, traditions, and identities. Authors examine the Alameda of San Luis Potosí, the "social memory" of railroads and aviation in Mexico, the effects of state-sanctioned ideas of cultural patrimony on Mexico's diverse religious expressions, and effect of transnational migration on musical expression, language, food, and popular traditions.

462 **Pani, Erika.** Soft science: the humanities in Mexico. (*Am. Hist. Rev.*, 120:4, Oct. 2015, p. 1327–1342, bibl.)

The author briefly surveys the debate over the humanities from independence to the contemporary era. She emphasizes both official rhetoric about the humanities and efforts to include history, literature, philosophy, and other fields in academia, particularly in secondary and higher education. After the positivist turn of the late 19th century, humanistic studies regained some credence in the context of revolutionary projects. The humanities themselves, however, lacked popularity at the university level, and have been increasingly eclipsed by scientific and technical fields.

463 **Pereza, revolución y desarrollo empresarial en México: siglos XIX y XX.** Edición de Oscar Flores Torres. San Pedro Garza García, México: Universidad de Monterrey, Centro de Estudios Históricos UDEM, 2011. 199 p.: bibl., ill., index, ports.

In this collection of seven essays, historians, economists, and one archeologist examine a variety of economic themes. Essays on the 19th century examine official attempts to address vagrancy, and German businessmen in 19th-century Monterrey. Twentieth century themes include the economic effect of the Mexican Revolution in Sonora, the evolution of José Cuervo's tequila fortune, politician and businessman Alberto J. Pani, the history of Monterrey's iron foundry, and the politics of oil during the 1970s.

464 **La prensa: un actor sempiterno: de la Primera Guerra Mundial a la posmodernidad.** Coordinación de Rosa María Valles Ruiz, Rosa María González Victoria, y Patricia Vega Jiménez. Pachuca, Mexico: Universidad Autónoma del Estado de Hidalgo, 2014. 438 p.: bibl., ill.

This collection of conference papers, most of which pertain to Mexico, explore the media's role in several contexts, with a primary focus on print journalism. Authors examine the efforts of Lázaro Cárdenas and Manuel Ávila Camacho to shape public opinion through the press, detail coverage of the 1954 Guatemalan coup in Mexican newspapers, and analyze how a PAN publication covered the Cuban Revolution and missile crisis. Three articles examine the print media and student movements during the 1960s and 1970s. Selections on more contemporary themes probe the evolution of journalism in the context of an increasingly dangerous society, and the role of the media in 2009 mid-term elections.

465 **Rosas Salas, Sergio Francisco.** La Iglesia mexicana en tiempos de la impiedad: Francisco Pablo Vázquez, 1769–1847. México: Ediciones EyC, 2015. 379 p.: bibl. (Colección H)

This volume examines the life of the bishop of Puebla in the context of the efforts of the Catholic Church to carve out a role for itself in the transition to an independent Mexico. A seminarian during the era of the Bourbon reforms, parish priest and participant in local politics during the independence era, and Mexico's first envoy to the Vatican, Vázquez was a central figure in the formation of the Mexican nation, supporting an independent, republican Mexico while also asserting and defending the independence and importance of the Church. The author's research is extensive, and is based in part on Vázquez' personal archive.

466 Ruano Ruano, Leticia. La identidad del laico apostólico: Acción Católica Mexicana. Guadalajara, Mexico: Universidad de Guadalajara, 2013. 300 p.: bibl., ill. (Colección Miradas múltiples)

In this study of Acción Católica Mexicana, a social anthropologist focuses on how the members of the organization constructed an identity. The author traces the growth, development, and decline of the ACM, underscores the process of socialization among its members, and makes extensive use of the stories of two Jalisco women who participated in the ACM at its height to demonstrate how activists internalized an ACM ethos.

467 Sánchez Andrés, Agustín and **Pedro Pérez Herrero.** Historia de las relaciones entre España y México, 1821–2014. Alcalá de Henares, Spain: Instituto Universitario de Investigación en Estudios Latinoamericanos, Universidad de Alcalá, 2015 367 p.: bibl., ill. (Colección Instituto Universitario de Investigación en Estudios Latinoamericanos)

The authors of this volume provide a comprehensive look at the diplomatic, economic, and cultural relations between the two countries, as well as an analysis of the changing fate of Mexico's Spanish community. The last three chapters focus especially on the economic aspects of links between Spain and Mexico since the Franco dictatorship, including a consideration of Mexico's interactions with the EU. Includes a useful bibliography.

468 Sánchez Reséndiz, Victor Hugo.
Agua y autonomía en los pueblos originarios del oriente de Morelos. Morelos, México: Libertad bajo Palabra, 2015. 205 p.: bibl., ill., map.

The author, a sociologist with a focus on rural development, is interested in the ways in which three villages in eastern Morelos have sought historically to defend their access to natural resources, while asserting a communal autonomy from central authority. The waters of the Amatzinac River have been central to these efforts, generating activism in the context of Mexico's revolution, and in the later contexts of commercial agriculture and contemporary infrastructure projects, including the Plan Puebla-Panama. Based in part on interviews with local residents, and on research in the Archivo Histórico del Agua.

469 60 años: catálogo de publicaciones INEHRM (1953–2013). Coordinación de Instituto Nacional de Estudios Históricos de la Revolución Mexicana. México: Instituto Nacional de Estudios Históricos de la Revolución Mexicana, 2013. 352 p.: bibl., indexes.

This useful reference work includes an annotated listing of all of the institute's publications (including monographs, facsimiles, periodicals, and digital resources). Although the majority of items pertain to the Mexican Revolution, works on Independence and the 19th and 20th centuries, chronologies, children's books, and commemorative volumes are also indexed.

Tabasco serrano: miradas plurales: geografía, arqueología, historia, lingüística y turismo. See *HLAS 73:40*.

470 Los trabajadores de la ciudad de México, 1860–1950: textos en homenaje a Clara E. Lida. Coordinación de Carlos Illades y Mario Barbosa. México: El Colegio de México, Universidad Autónoma Metropolitana, Unidad Cuajimalpa, 2013. 259 p.: bibl., ill.

This series of eight essays represents preliminary explorations of various aspects of working-class history. Authors explore the relationship between the city's workers and urban modernization, activism among artisans in the Reform era, images of the city's newspaper boys, and the emergence of civil service workers in the early 20th century. Additional essays examine policewomen, lottery workers, Spanish laborers in the context of the Depression, and filmic depictions of child workers.

471 Valdés Castellanos, Guillermo.
Historia del narcotráfico en México. México: Aguilar, 2013. 483 p.: bibl., ill.

This is a useful, general survey by a former director of Mexico's national security organization, who served under President Felipe Calderón. The author combines the research of academics with his own reflections to examine the evolution of the drug trade since the 1920s, US drug policy, and the crime, violence, and political corruption inherent in the drug wars. A key theme is the historical debility of the Mexican state and its security apparatus.

472 **Vázquez Toriz, Rosalía** and **Susana Edith Rappo Míguez.** Campesinos en Puebla: momentos de la historia agraria en ocho comunidades del altiplano mexicano. México: Ediciones de Educación y Cultura, 2011. 121 p.: bibl., ill.

This brief but detailed volume is the result of a university workshop designed to capture the long history and legacy of agrarian activism in east-central Puebla, an area that more recently resisted *Programa Millenium*, a government effort to transform this region into a more industrial corridor. The authors trace the earlier efforts of indigenous peoples and campesinos in eight communities to protect their lands and livelihood from the colonial era through the Mexican Revolution. Well-researched, including extensive documentation from the National Agrarian Archive.

Colonial Period

PAULA DE VOS, *Associate Professor of History and Graduate Advisor, San Diego State University*
RAPHAEL E. FOLSOM, *Assistant Professor of History, University of Oklahoma*

SIMILAR TO *HLAS* 72, publications on colonial Mexican history are divided between revisionist works that provide new lenses for viewing important traditional themes within the field and those that point to new directions in research topics and methodologies. Revisionist works are largely focused around topics of religiosity and the institution of the Catholic Church; issues of race, caste, and class; the role of indigenous elites in the colonial regime and the impact of conquest on their status; Bourbon reforms and independence; economic considerations and networks; and the foundations and development of Creole patriotism. New directions include works on the history of medicine and pharmacy—still a fledgling field, and, most notably, works utilizing new methodologies that involve interdisciplinary collaborations between historians and other researchers across a range of fields, from linguistics to archeology to historical anthropology. These kinds of collaborations allow what Enrique Rodríguez-Alegría has called "mixed epistemologies" (item **514**): by employing a variety of data, including physical artifacts as well as texts, researchers bring together sources and methods from multiple fields to address and understand daily life and material culture among a wider cross section of the colonial population. Another effective, though less novel, methodology employed in several recent publications involves the use of microhistory, assembled from criminal investigations, slave bills of sale, and Inquisition cases, to investigate colonial life. The Diálogos series of University of New Mexico Press has issued a number of important works, and Cambridge University Press deserves special recognition for a series of unique and innovative monographs published in the last two years. The new philology movement also continues with a number of important publications by graduates of UCLA who worked under the direction of Kevin Terraciano.

Marcy Norton's major essay on the subaltern in the early modern Atlantic world arguably established the framework for the direction of revisionism so prominent in the field (item **507**). In her substantial article, Norton examines some of the central tenets that have guided the study of the Spanish Atlantic world through a number of the classics in the field, particularly the work of John Elliott. She argues that, despite the importance of these works, there is still a fundamental neglect of subaltern populations and lack of acknowledgement that Spaniards lived and worked alongside indigenous peoples and those of African descent. Whether responding directly to her calls for such acknowledgement or not, historians have produced a series of works in the last two years that address the complexities of caste and class and call into question any easy acceptance of such categorizations. Jorge Victoria Ojeda and Aurelio Sánchez, for example, recognize an inclusive sort of *convivencia* in colonial Mérida (item **525**); Pablo Miguel Sierra Silva examines how enslaved families formed complex and integrated networks among both slave and free populations of Puebla (item **520**); and Melchor Campos García argues that social class in colonial Mexico was more important than race—that people of African descent occupied many social roles that ran the gamut from high status to low status (item **478**).

In this way, these and other authors have sought to understand better the workings of the caste system and *casta* categories, following in the tradition of R. Douglas Cope and María Elena Martínez. Robert C. Schwaller, for example, expands on their arguments as to the largely fictitious nature of genealogical categorizations of ethnicity and caste and the ineffectuality of laws meant to separate New Spain's populations (item **519**). Ben Vinson, author of a previous monograph on the free colored militia in Bourbon Mexico (see *HLAS 60:1344*), has written a major work on what he calls the "extreme castes," those categories that involved more complicated genealogical backgrounds and that historians have traditionally believed were only theoretical, legalistic categories thought to have little practical significance in day-to-day life (item **526**). Vinson's work contributes to the important and long-neglected history of Afro-Mexican identity, which continues to receive treatment in other important new contributions as well: Pablo Miguel Sierra Silva on the nature of urban slavery in Puebla (item **520**) and Mark Lentz's linguistic study of the rise of Yucatec Maya as a lingua franca in 18th-century Yucatán among Creoles and Afro-Mestizos (item **494**).

Research on *casta* paintings, another subgenre of works on race, class, and caste that has proved very popular of late, continues to build upon and challenge previous works on the subject by Ilona Katzew, Magali Carrera, Susan Deans-Smith, and Sarah Cline (and discussed in Martínez's *Genealogical Fictions* (see *HLAS 66:743*) and Daniela Bleichmar's *Visible Empire* (see *HLAS 72:4*). Schwaller uses interest in the paintings to frame his study, and Rebecca Earle, author of *The Body of the Conquistador* (see *HLAS 70:515*), frames her new study of *casta* paintings around similar arguments about the mutability of the body and malleability of identity in Galenic humoralism to argue against the idea of a firm or fixed *casta* taxonomy (item **483**).

Another subgenre of works on race and caste includes studies of indigenous and Creole elites. Bradley Benton and Peter Villella, for example, both address the postconquest fortunes of indigenous elites (items **194** and *HLAS 72:370* and 755). Benton points out the middling status of Tetzcocan elites who maintained honorific status as a leisure class but, unlike those of Tenochtitlán, did not possess enough power to threaten Spanish rule and gain major concessions and who, unlike Maya caciques, were still too close to the Spanish seat of power to be left largely alone. In his study, Villella traces the status of Nahua elites over the course of the entire colonial period, showing how they sought to maintain favored status within the system by representing their culture and heritage in the context of a priomordial past—a past that Creole elites later sought to appropriate and manipulate for their own patriotic purposes. Stuart McManus also revisits understandings of Creole patriotism in his argument that Creole identity had little to do with American versus Peninsular birth, but rather depended more on Spanish versus non-Spanish identity (item **500**). In this way, both scholars offer major correctives to Brading's classic work on the nature and origins of Creole patriotism. Hillel Eyal's article on networks further underscores the destabilization of accepted understandings of Creole and peninsular networks, arguing that "human capital"—an individual's education and skill level—was a much stronger determinant of economic success in Mexico City than regional, ethnic, or familial networks (item **484**).

Colonial religiosity and institutional Church history persist as staple topics for colonial historians, who continue to deepen our understanding of the complexities of Hispano-Catholicism in New Spain. William Taylor's most recent contribution to the field is a masterful work that explores the history of miraculous images and shrines over the course of the colonial period (item **522**). Related contributions include Jessica Delgado's research on laywomen's participation within the colonial Church (item **481**), Robert Jackson's study of evangelization in Sierra Gorda showing that nonsedentary populations tended to fare worse in mission systems than did sedentary ones (item **490**), and David Rex Galindo's examination of the practice of forced conversion which he argues was much more widespread than the Lascasian narrative implies (item **488**). Galindo also writes about evangelical efforts in Franciscan colleges, important institutions that were established in Spain and the Americas, but have been largely neglected in the historiography. In this way, he builds on Karen Melvin's expansive work on mendicant orders in urban areas of New Spain.

Finally, a series of works focused on Bourbon reforms and the independence era seek to deepen our knowledge of political and economic development in the late colony. Francisco Altables has made a massive contribution to current understanding of the Bourbon government's expansion and control over frontier regions, demonstrating the effectiveness of those actions (item **473**). Eva María Mehl further examines the forced transport of men from mainland New Spain to the Philippines during the later 18th century largely to strengthen the Spanish military presence there as a result of the British occupation of Manila in the Seven Years' War (item **501**). Works focusing on economic themes include Eyal's aforementioned work exploring the reasons for economic success of Peninsular immigrants to New Spain; a distinguished collection of essays edited by María del Pilar Martínez López-Cano *et al.* on fiscal laws, regulations, and budgets in the later 18th century; and John Tutino's examination of "silver capitalism" in New Spain, in which silver production both funded resistance to the Napoleonic invasion of Spain and constituted a prime motive for that invasion (item **485**).

In addition to the valuable revisionist works that serve to deepen our understanding of topics that have long been of interest to colonial historians are several recent publications that introduce innovative topics and methodologies. Still a developing field, the history of medicine in colonial Mexico has received attention in Paul Ramírez's masterfully written work on epidemic disease and public health practices in the late colony, and Paula De Vos discusses the challenges of using colonial documentation to assemble a comprehensive listing and understanding of Nahua materia medica (item **511**). Rodrigo Vega y Ortega also focuses on the importance of indigenous materia medica and the testing of its therapeutic value in the 19th century (item **524**). In addition, historians have adopted a series of new methodologies (or repurposed older ones) to produce a series of innovative works that may be a sign of future directions for the field. These include methodologies resulting from interdisciplinary collaborations as well as a series of enlightening "microhistories" that make creative use of archival documentation.

The first area of interdisciplinary collaboration involves the intertwining of methods and sources used by historians, anthropologists, and archeologists to explore themes related to material culture and daily life within the colony. Authors in this genre argue that the combination of textual sources and artifacts allows researchers to gain a greater understanding of a larger cross section of the colonial population. Enrique Rodríguez-Alegría, for example, "mixes epistemologies" to gauge the impact of Spanish conquest on daily life in the Valley of Mexico (item **514**), while a team of researchers collaborated to produce *Colonial and Postcolonial Change in Mesoamerica*, edited by Rani Alexander and Susan Kepecs (item **480**), a work that purports to implement the ambitious "total history" approach of the Annales school, emphasizing long-term continuities, structures, and conjunctures over individual events. Along similar lines but on a more modest scale, Lourdes Márquez Morfín and Patricia Hernández use skeletal remains from the Valley of Mexico to show the challenges to daily life in colonial Mexico through evidence of violence and hunger that, in addition to well-documented diseases, led to high infant mortality and low life expectancy (item **497**).

In addition to the methods above, other teams of scholars have combined linguistic evidence and methods of art history with archival and printed sources to better understand themes as wide ranging as social and cultural integration to colonial codices and catechisms. In addition to Lentz's previously discussed work on Yucatec Maya, Julia Madajczak and Magnus Pharao Hansen have analyzed Nahua sermons in an effort to explore social hierarchy among Nahua migrants to Guatemala (item **496**). In a particularly impressive effort, Louise M. Burkhart, David Tavárez, and Elizabeth Hill Boone have combined expertise from their respective fields to create a masterful monograph-size study on a pictorial catechism that provides a model for future scholars who seek to reveal the promise and complexities of pre- and postconquest codices (item **476**).

Finally, with regard to innovative works in the field, a number of recent studies have turned to the genre of microhistory pioneered by Carlo Ginzburg, Emmanuel LeRoy Ladurie, and Natalie Davis, among others, to provide unique insights into colonial Mexican society. Pablo Miguel Sierra Silva's groundbreaking work on slavery in Puebla, for instance, consists of a series of "micro-narratives" gained from three years' work in Puebla's notarial archives compiling bills of slave sales (item **520**). Mark Lentz makes good use of criminal court proceedings concerning a mysterious murder of a colonial official in Mérida in order to highlight the complex effects of Bourbon reforms among the colonial population (item **494**). Frances Levine utilizes Inquisition documents to trace the life of Doña Teresa, whose distinctive personality, flamboyance, and wealth attracted suspicion and hatred (item **495**). Two other works use microhistorical approaches to inject humor into our understanding of Novohispanic society. These include Frank T. Proctor's examination of Inquisition cases that focuses on the baptism and marriage of dogs (item **510**) and Martin Austin Nesvig's deeply insightful research into the incompetence of Novohispanic governance that was dominated by desperados, psychopaths, and clowns (item **506**). Such approaches provide unique, entertaining, and revealing new lenses that promote greater understanding of society and culture in colonial Mexico.

COLONIAL

473 Altable, Francisco. Vientos nuevos: idea, aplicación y resultados del proyecto borbónico para la organización del gobierno y el desarrollo de la población y economía de las Californias, 1767–1825. La Paz, Mexico: Universidad Autónoma de Baja California Sur, 2013. 587 p.: bibl., ill. (Cuadernos universitarios)

This study offers a massive contribution to our understanding of one of the Bourbon government's most consequential projects: expanding and gaining control over frontier regions by means of vigorous enlightened government. Those whose research focuses on the ineffectuality of Bourbon reform will find a stumbling block in works such as this one, which details the profound changes that the new policies brought to frontier regions like California. [RF]

474 Benton, Bradley. The lords of Tetzcoco: the transformation of indigenous rule in postconquest central Mexico. New York: Cambridge University Press, 2017. 212 p. (Cambridge Latin American studies)

This substantive examination of Tetzcoco, one of the neighboring city-states of Tenochtitlan and part of the Triple Alliance, brings to light its great significance in the precontact era and traces its fate following Spanish conquest of the Aztec capital. Using mainly textual sources, the author traces the fate of Tetzcocan elites in the early postconquest era. The author argues that the status of Tetzcocan elites remained somewhere between that of Nahua tlatoque (ruling nobles, plural for tlatoani)—who continued to pose a major potential threat to the Spanish and thus were granted major concessions, nobility rights, and encomiendas—and that of caciques in more peripheral regions like Yucatán, who were largely left alone and maintained political control of their cacicazgos. That middling status led to the maintenance of a Tetzcocan elite without political power, a leisure class that largely lost political power, but was not granted extensive holdings. In this way, the Tetzcoco elites lost status, but did not disappear into the peasantry, as evidenced from a 19th-century Tetzcocan lawsuit arguing for status and privilege. For additional comment, see **194**. [PDV]

475 Bock, Ulrike. Entre "españoles" y "ciudadanos": las milicias de *pardos* y la transformación de las fronteras culturales en Yucatán, 1790–1821. (*Secuencia/México*, 87, sept./dic. 2013, p. 9–27, bibl.)

Explores the changing ideologies of pardo militias in the independence era, as evolving laws and ideologies "encountered stubborn facts on the ground." [RF]

476 Boone, Elizabeth Hill; Louise M. Burkhart; and **David Tavárez.** Painted words: Nahua Catholicism, politics, and memory in the Atzaqualco pictorial catechism. Washington, D.C.: Dumbarton Oaks Research Library and Collection, 2017. 386 p.: bibl., index. (Studies in pre-Columbian art and archaeology; 39)

In a series of essays, these three authors combine their extensive and varied expertise regarding the language, culture, and religion of the Nahuas as represented in the images, glyphs, and alphabetical writings of a particular pictorial catechism from the colonial period. The authors study various aspects of the Azaqualco pictorial catechism, whose manuscript currently resides in the National Library of France. The authors trace in detail the history and context of such pictorial catechisms, arguing that early examples represent a transition from precontact to colonial society, and that later catechisms often used the same elements to denote an antiquated and ancient style. They find that this explanation is in line with the catechism in question, which they date roughly to the 17th century. For ethnohistorian's comment, see item **197**. [PDV]

477 Burciaga Campos, José Arturo. Viator intra terram: legados del Camino Real de Tierra Adentro en Zacatecas. Zacatecas, Mexico: Secretaría de Economía del Estado de Zacatecas: Taberna Libraria Editores, 2013. 247 p.: bibl., color ill., index, color maps.

This beautifully produced study of the Camino Real features dozens of full-color photographs and maps, the latter detailing political, geographical, and economic aspects of the lands through which the road ran. Documents from Sevilla and

Madrid in Spain, and Mexico City, Zacatecas, and Fresnillo in Mexico enrich the narrative. [RF]

478 **Campos García, Melchor.** Esclavitud y servidumbre negra en la ciudad de Mérida, Yucatán: 1563–1610. (*Iberoamericana/Madrid*, 15:58, junio 2015, p. 21–44, bibl., tables)

Social class was more important than race in 16th-century Yucatán and people of African descent occupied many social roles, some of them high-status. [RF]

479 **Cázares Puente, Eduardo.** Laberintos de muerte: la Batalla de Monterrey de 1846. Monterrey, Mexico: Universidad Autónoma de Nuevo León, 2013. 172 p. (Ancla de tiempo)

This new account of a critical battle of the US-Mexican War draws on extensive research in local archives. [RF]

480 **Colonial and postcolonial change in Mesoamerica: archaeology as historical anthropology.** Edited by Rani T. Alexander and Susan Kepecs. Albuquerque: University of New Mexico Press, 2018. 448 p.: bibl., ill., index, maps, tables.

This is a major contribution to the literature on world-systems, dependency theory, and the total history approach of the Annales School. The consequence of a series of meetings among ethnohistorians, historical archeologists, and anthropologists, this volume brings together a series of essays on the material culture of Mesoamerica from the precontact period to the present. The authors aim to document historical development in Mesoamerica in the manner of Fernand Braudel's work on Mediterranean civilization and capitalism, highlighting the importance of the longue durée in understanding the long-term structures and continuities of social and economic development. The authors use written sources but mainly focus upon material archeology to bring new insights to the history of development in Mesoamerica in a way that does not privilege elites and, through the continuity of archeological sources over time, fills a number of gaps in the historiography. The authors consciously use historical archeology to conduct their study, which they see as a combination of historical, archeological, and anthropological work. [PDV]

481 **Delgado, Jessica L.** Laywomen and the making of colonial Catholicism in New Spain, 1630–1790. New York, N.Y.: Cambridge University Press, 2018. 278 p. (Cambridge Latin American studies; 110)

In this work, Delgado focuses on laywomen in colonial Mexico and the ways that they participated in the Mexican Catholic Church. In doing so, she challenges the notion of devout and cloistered Mexican women subservient to Church doctrine. Instead, she argues that laywomen and the institutional Church recognized in each other a supporting partnership that would further each other's goals. In this way, then, laywomen shaped the meanings of Catholic worship and ritual and were able to carve out spaces for themselves within colonial society. [PDV]

482 **Díaz Hernández, Magdalena** and **Octavio García.** Esclavos/as y cimarrones, monarquía, poder local y negociación en Nueva Espana. (*Mex. Stud.*, 33:2, Summer 2017, p. 296–319, bibl.)

This article examines a community of escaped slaves who founded the town of Santa Maria de Amapa in 1769. In examining archival documents hitherto ignored, the authors explain a series of confrontations that took place among community members and colonial authorities, during which the community turned in some of their own members in order to receive viceregal authority to establish their town. See also *HLAS 56:1119*. [PDV]

483 **Earle, Rebecca.** The pleasures of taxonomy: casta paintings, classification, and colonialism. (*William Mary Q.*, 73:3, July 2016, p. 427–466, ill.)

This article examines the classification systems employed in designating *casta* categories depicted in the *casta* paintings of 18th-century Mexico. The author draws connections between 18th-century taxonomy of natural flora and fauna and casta categories. She argues that despite the host of excellent literature on *casta* paintings, race, and class in colonial Spanish America, one aspect of casta paintings requires further discussion: the mutability of caste through European ideas of Galenic humoralism in which bodies could change based upon food, diet, regimen, exercise, etc. Thus, despite the genealogical faces forecast, she argues that these categories were not firm or fixed, but changeable and related to issues of pleasure and desire. This stimulating piece could use more input from literature on Linnaean taxonomy and from R. Douglas Cope's arguments about the importance of patronage networks and marriage and naming patterns, which were also factors in the mutability of caste (see *HLAS 56:1137*). María Elena Martínez also argued that the genealogical arguments were inherently fictions, which also would serve to explain the mutability of caste (see *HLAS 66:743*). See also item **519**. [PDV]

484 Eyal, Hillel. Beyond networks: transatlantic immigration and wealth in late colonial Mexico City. (*J. Lat. Am. Stud.*, 47:2, May 2015, p. 317–348, bibl., graphs, tables)

This article examines the various levels of economic success gained by Peninsular Spaniards who migrated to Mexico City in the late colonial period. Earlier studies have examined Spanish immigration to Spanish American colonies and concluded that networks and social capital are largely what determined success in the Americas. The author, however, pushes these conclusions further and concludes that human capital, rather than social capital, was the true determinant of economic success. He finds that, overall, economic success in Mexico City was largely determined by the regions from which the Spaniards came. In the 18th century, Spaniards from northern Spain, particularly the Basque country, tended to be more successful entrepreneurs than their counterparts from southern regions. By examining the archival record thoroughly rather than anecdotally, the author finds that levels of education and acquired skills, i.e., human capital, determined success moreso than social networks. These networks, to be sure, played a very important role in explaining how immigrants were successful—but not why. Literacy rates and greater skill levels, which were associated with northern Spain, were greater determinants of success. This argument questions the emphasis and reliance on networks in Atlantic world historiography. [PDV]

485 La fiscalidad novohispana en el imperio español: conceptualizaciones, proyectos y contradicciones. Coordinación de María del Pilar Martínez López-Cano, Ernest Sánchez Santiró y Matilde Souto Mantecón. México: Instituto de Investigaciones Dr. José María Luis Mora: Instituto de Investigaciones Históricas, UNAM, 2015. 363 p.: bibl., tables. (Historia económica)

A distinguished collection of articles on the laws, regulations, and procedures of the government budget on fees, taxes, and contributions that fund the state. Highlights include an article by Carlos Marichal arguing that, by promoting indebtedness in America in the late 18th century, the Spanish government extracted large amounts of the private capital stock from New Spain which might otherwise have been invested productively. Enriqueta Quiroz offers a provocative critique of John Coatsworth's work on the origins of Mexican underdevelopment, arguing that a sales tax imposed in the late 18th century did not hinder, but rather stimulated, the colonial economy by making funds available to local governments to address local problems. [RF]

486 Flint, Richard. Ditch-irrigated agriculture noted by Spaniards at Santo Domingo Pueblo in 1591: evidence from dating anomalies in the *Memoria de Castaño de Sosa*. (*N.M. Hist. Rev.*, 92:2, Spring 2017, p. 157–180, ill., map)

This detailed study of a tangled colonial document reveals extensive use of ditch irrigation in six Keres pueblos in what is now New Mexico (US). [RF]

487 Folsom, Bradley. Arredondo: last Spanish ruler of Texas and northeastern New Spain. Norman: University of Oklahoma Press, 2017. 324 p.: bibl., index, maps.

This is a well-researched and well-written study of Mexico's independence era as experienced by one of its most prominent losers. Arredondo was a conservative official who opposed independence, but who had a surprisingly extensive influence on the history of northern Mexico. He invited Stephen F. Austin to colonize Texas. And he took as his protégé Antonio López de Santa Ana, future anti-hero of 19th-century Mexico. A distinguished addition to the canon of Spanish Borderlands historiography. [RF]

488 Galindo, David Rex. "Primero hombres, luego cristianos": un análisis sobre la conversión forzosa en la frontera de Texas. (*CLAHR*, 2:3, Summer 2014, p. 405–432)

An elegant and erudite argument that forcible conversion, both in mainstream theology and in practical fact, was a more widely accepted practice than the Lascasian narrative (i.e., peaceful evangelization) would have us believe. Priests were not only protectors of Indians; at times they also cheered Christian violence against them. [RF]

489 García Ruiz, Luis J. Demandas sociales y propiedad imperfecta en Veracruz: el impulso a la enfiteusis, 1760–1811. (*Secuencia/México*, 93, sept./dic. 2015, p. 28–49, bibl.)

Concerned about unproductive lands held in entailed estates, Veracruzanos promoted a nonrevolutionary reform in which peasants received land to live on, the land would be improved, the rich retained their privileges, and the poor avoided the temptation to revolt: long-term leases. [RF]

490 Jackson, Robert H. Frontiers of evangelization: Indians in the Sierra Gorda and Chiquitos missions. Norman: University of Oklahoma Press, 2017. 198 p.: bibl., index.

This is a worthy capstone to a long career of research on native peoples, missions, and historical demography. In this book, Jackson offers a comparative study of sedentary populations in Bolivia and nonsedentary ones in Mexico. His findings indicate that nonsedentary populations generally fared worse in the missions than sedentary ones. Low birth rates and high death rates spelled doom for previously nonsedentary peoples trapped on missions. But: "The Jesuits in the missions in lowland South America cogoverned with native clan chiefs and created an economic system that retained considerable autonomy for native families" (p. 140). Guaraní mission Indians were able to recover from demographic disasters and had relatively robust birth rates. [RF]

491 Jáuregui, Carlos A. Going native, going home: ethnographic empathy and the artifice of return in Cabeza de Vaca's *Relación*. (*Colon. Lat. Am. Rev.*, 25:2, 2016, p. 175–199, bibl.)

This article offers a revisionist interpretation of Cabeza de Vaca's extraordinary journey after being shipwrecked in Florida, living among native peoples, and eventually being "rescued" by Spanish compatriots in northern New Spain. Whereas previous authors have argued that his experiences offer a counternarrative of conquest in which Cabeza de Vaca is viewed as a sympathetic conquistador who displayed empathy toward native peoples and worked as a cultural mediator and critic of the excesses of Spanish cruelty and slave hunting, Jáuregui argues that, in fact, Cabeza de Vaca's story is all about a return to Spanish "civilization" and, as such, offers no apology for Spanish conquest, but rather depicts his journey as inevitably returning to the Spanish fold. [PDV]

492 Jiménez Gómez, Juan Ricardo. Los pleitos por la tierra entre los indios y los hacendados del partido de Tolimán: Querétaro, 1793–1808. Querétaro, Mexico: Tribunal Superior de Justicia del Estado de Querétaro: Universidad Autónoma de Querétaro; México: MÁ Porrúa, 2013. 310 p.: bibl., index, map. (Serie La historia)

This book brings together a detailed and useful collection of documents from late 18th and early 19th century Sierra Gorda. Preceded by a 74-page introductory study, the documents chronicle a land dispute among various communities, focusing on the efforts of the provincial government to resolve those disputes through an iron-fisted repression of the native communities it held responsible, and a restoration of disputed lands to various hacendados. The dispossessed native peoples did not give up the legal fight over their lands, however, and later brought accusations to the authorities in Mexico City. In the process, they left rich and abundant testimonies about the practices, customs, and political realities of the region. A gold mine for historians interested in the enduring legacy of the Chichimeca War. [RF]

493 Lentz, Mark W. Castas, creoles, and the rise of a Maya lingua franca in eighteenth-century Yucatan. (*HAHR*, 97:1, Feb. 2017, p. 29–61)

This fascinating and distinguished article challenges standard narratives of native linguistic decline. In 18th-century Yucatán, knowledge of Maya languages actually expanded as Creoles and Afro-Mestizos adopted Yucatec Maya as a lingua franca for use in courts, local governments, and everyday life. [RF]

494 Lentz, Mark W. Murder in Mérida, 1792: violence, factions, and the law. Albuqerque: University of New Mexico Press, 2018. 328 p.: bibl., index. (Dialogos series)

This book recounts the murder of the provincial governor of Yucatán, Lucas de Gálvez, in 1792. Arriving home one night in his carriage, Gálvez was accosted by an unidentified man dressed as a cowboy who attacked him using a makeshift spear fashioned from a knife tied to a stick. The assailant successfully lodged the spear into the victim's torso, severing his pulmonary artery and piercing his lung, which resulted in his death soon after. Although an investigation was launched immediately, the murderer was not discovered for eight years. Employing the court records of this major criminal investigation, Lentz exploits the detailed information included in the proceedings to document the widespread frustration with Gálvez's reforms as part of the larger Bourbon reform program, thus placing the murderer squarely within local resistance to colonial authority. In doing so, Lentz also traces various networks within colonial society and the complex relations and interactions they entailed. [PDV]

495 Levine, Frances. Doña Teresa confronts the Spanish Inquisition: a seventeenth-century New Mexican drama. Norman: University of Oklahoma Press, 2016. 296 p.: bibl., index.

This study works in a historical genre made popular by Emmanuel Le Roy Ladurie's *Montaillou* (1975) and Carlo Ginzburg's *The Cheese and the Worms* (1976) and then imitated many times over: it takes an Inquisition case as a lens through which to observe the inner workings of a remote historical world. This is an exceptionally successful specimen of the genre. Doña Teresa was a highly educated, willful, irreverent woman whose distinctive personality, flamboyance, and wealth made her attract suspicion and hatred. She also had traveled widely. Born in Italy, she had lived in Cartagena de Indias before arriving in New Mexico. As Stuart Schwartz shows in *All Can Be Saved* (see *HLAS* 66:513), this kind of worldliness often landed people in the Inquisition's prisons. Levine does a spectacular job describing Teresa and her world. The text includes lengthy quotations from trial testimony and, as appendices, 65 pages of translated documents. [RF]

López-Chávez, Celia. Epics of empire and frontier: Alonso de Ercilla and Gaspar Pérez de Villagrá as Spanish colonial chroniclers. See item **1005**.

496 Madajczak, Julia and Magnus Pharao Hansen. Teotamachilizti: an analysis of the language in a Nahua sermon from colonial Guatemala. (*Colon. Lat. Am. Rev.*, 25:2, 2016, p. 220–244, bibl.)

This article examines the particular language used in a Nahua sermon from colonial Guatemala in order to understand social relationships and dynamics in the area. The authors point out that colonial Guatemala was inhabited by a small contingent of Spanish friars and two main groups of Nahua speakers, one group that had fled to the area following the fall of Tula, and the other consisting of allies of the Spanish in the conquest of the area. The authors analyze the language used in this specific sermon from a sociolinguistic perspective to highlight how different dialects of Nahua speakers reflected social hierarchy, in particular differences between local dialects and the prestige dialect of central Mexican Nahuatl. Such a study also sheds light on language training of local missionaries and how they dealt with local vernacular dialects and meanings. [PDV]

497 Márquez Morfín, Lourdes and Patricia Hernández. La esperanza de vida en la ciudad de México (siglos XVI al XIX). (*Secuencia/México*, 96, sept./dic. 2016, p. 6–44, bibl., graphs, tables)

Skeletal remains from the Valley of Mexico provide powerful but unsurprising evidence that life in colonial Mexico was brutal, nasty, and short. High infant mortality, low life expectancy, and much hunger and violence prevailed. [RF]

498 Martínez, Patricia. El tejido familiar de los Sánchez Navarro 1805–1840. Traducción de Pilar Valles. Saltillo, Mexico: R. Ayuntamiento de Saltillo: Archivo Municipal de Saltillo: Archivo para la Memoria de la Universidad Iberoamericana, 2014. 135 p.: bibl., map.

A short study of the family dynamics of the celebrated Sánchez Navarro family of Coahuila, based on the author's UT-Austin MA thesis (1996). Much is known about the political and economic importance of large landed estates. Little is known about the personal lives of the families that ruled them. This book seeks to fill that gap. Letters from the Sánchez Navarro collection at the Benson Library in Austin help provide a more rounded portrait of this powerful family, particularly the women. [RF]

499 McCracken, Ellen. Fray Angélico Chávez and the colonial Southwest: historiography and rematerialization. (*Americas/Washington*, 72:4, Oct. 2015, p. 529–547, photos)

A biographical study of a 20th-century Franciscan of Hispano origins and his massive efforts to document, analyze, and restore New Mexico's colonial history. [RF]

500 McManus, Stuart M. The *Bibliotheca Mexicana* controversy and Creole patriotism in early modern Mexico. (*HAHR*, 98:1, Feb. 2018, p. 1–41, bibl., ill., map)

This major article presents a substantial argument that, in line with a series of scholars such as María Elena Martínez (see *HLAS 66:743*), seeks to offer a revision of traditional ideas of Creole patriotism. In the historiography, which is dominated by the culminating and justifiably well-recognized work of D.A. Brading in *The First America* (see *HLAS 54:941*), Creole patriots have been represented as an elite group apart from peninsular Spaniards who formed a separate identity taking pride in their American heritage. This author, however, challenges the narrative by looking into a particular publication, the *Bibliotheca Mexicana*, which has been identified as one of the key moments in the formation of Creole consciousness. In challenging this notion, the author corroborates the findings of others who have also sought to destabilize the narrative of a separate Creole patriotism that developed during the 18th century. Rather, McManus argues that Creole and Peninsular identity were not viewed as separate, but rather, Spanish heritage was contrasted to that of non-Spaniards. Additionally, Mexican Creoles articulated an identity tied to localized place, most prominently Mexico City, rather than with the whole of New Spain. At the same time, this identity, which had much more to do with long-term residence in the Americas than birthplace, was also compatible with a Pan-American identity and Catholicism. [PDV]

501 Mehl, Eva María. Forced migration in the Spanish Pacific world: from Mexico to the Philippines, 1765–1811. Cambridge, England: Cambridge University Press, 2016. 310 p.: bibl., ill., index, maps.

This book examines the forced transport of men from mainland New Spain to Manila in the late 18th and early 19th centuries to serve as recruits for military service. From 1765 to 1811, 4,000 recruits were rounded up in New Spain and sent to the Philippines. This action was taken to strengthen the Spanish military presence in the Philippines as a consequence of the British occupation of Manila toward the end of the Seven Years' War—from 1762 to 1763. The author examines the ways in which these recruits were chosen and co-opted, often forcibly sent to the Philippines. These men were supposed to help defend Manila but instead caused many more problems with their presence, often requiring hospitalization or imprisonment for illness, drunkenness, absence, and other excesses. This result was largely because, though some migrants were composed of Mexican and Spanish troops, many others had been rounded up during vagrancy campaigns or were convicted criminals, and a number of them had been turned in by family members as well. Mehl studies individual cases of these recruits, examining changing vagrancy laws as well as the relationship between the Empire of New Spain and the Philippines within the viceroyalty, and of the viceroyalty's relationship to Spain. Her study provides a new and unique way to examine imperial relationships and social relations with in the empire as well, particularly in the outpost of Manila about which there is a general paucity of historical writing. [PDV]

502 **Mendoza, Jesús Leticia.** El mito historiográfico de Maximiliano de Habsburgo, segundo emperador de México. Colima, Mexico: Archivo de Letras, Artes, Ciencias y Tecnologias: Archivo Histórico del Municipio de Colima, 2013. 153 p.: bibl.

A study of secondary sources dealing with Maximilian of Habsburg (1832–67). [RF]

503 **Mendoza Muñoz, Jesús.** El Palmar un pueblo en las faldas de la Sierra Gorda. Libro I. Cadereyta, Mexico: Fomento Histórico y Cultural de Cadereyta, 2014. 175 p.: bibl., ill. (Fomento Histórico y Cultural de Cadereyta, Serie de historia; 16)

This short study reviews the documents establishing the community of El Palmar, a town in what is now the state of Hidalgo, in the early 17th century. [RF]

Miño Grijalva, Manuel. El cacao Guayaquil en Nueva España, 1774–1812: (política imperial, mercado y consumo). See item **972**.

504 **Montoya Gómez, María Victoria.** Orden y desorden: una mirada a las representaciones de lo masculino y lo femenino a través de algunos procesos criminales; la Ciudad de México y sus alrededores, 1777–1805. (*Estud. Sociol./México*, 30:88, enero/abril 2012, p. 171–197, bibl.)

The author takes nine criminal cases from late 18th-century Mexico to examine class, gender, marriage, adultery, and Bourbon attempts to regulate all of the above. [RF]

505 **Nemser, Daniel.** Primitive accumulation, geometric space, and the construction of the "Indian." (*J. Lat. Am. Cult. Stud.*, 24:3, Sept. 2015, p. 335–352, bibl., maps)

This article discusses the indigenous policy in which Spanish conquerors used the reorganization of communities into grid patterns to further imperial ends. [RF]

506 **Nesvig, Martin Austin.** Promiscuous power: an unorthodox history of New Spain. Austin: University of Texas Press, 2018. 252 p.: bibl., ill., index, maps.

This book is a hilarious and deeply insightful tour-de-force of research and analysis. Not all will agree with the thesis—the Spanish Empire in 16th-century Mexico was exceedingly weak, incompetently run, and dominated by desperados, psychopaths, and clowns—but all will enjoy and learn from the author's tremendous research and scintillating argumentation. Perhaps the most salient contribution here is that Nesvig has resolved once and for all the vexed question of how to translate the colonial insult, *puto*: "punk-ass bitch." Joking aside, Nesvig has unearthed rich documentation that allows him to offer a series of cogent, detailed microhistorical narratives that all support a provocative overarching argument. This book is comparable in quality to various classics in the genre: *All Can Be Saved: Religious Tolerance and Salvation in the Iberian Atlantic World* by Stuart Schwartz (see *HLAS 66:513*), *The Devil and the Land of the Holy Cross: Witchcraft, Slavery, and Popular Religion in Colonial Brazil* by Laura de Melo e Souza (see *HLAS 52:2963* and *HLAS 62:2165*), and *Voices of Morebath: Reformation and Rebellion in an English Village* by Eamon Duffy (2001). [RF]

507 **Norton, Marcy.** Subaltern technologies and early modernity in the Atlantic world. (*Colon. Lat. Am. Rev.*, 26:1, 2017, p. 18–38)

This significant essay challenges Atlantic world historiography to be more inclusive of subaltern groups, including the myriad cultures of Africa and the African diaspora as well as Native America. Norton provides extensive analysis and critique of some of the central tenets that have guided the study of the Spanish Atlantic world and comparative empires within that world, particularly through the work of John Elliott. She points out that in his works, as well as in other major writings on the impact of the New World on the Old, there is a fundamental division assumed between elite Spaniards and the Native Americans and people of African heritage with whom they would have interacted on a daily basis. Norton suggests that a focus on subaltern technologies, such as the production and flavoring of chocolate, can reveal these interactions and show their great significance for the formation of the Atlantic world. [PDV]

508   Los otros rebeldes novohispanos: imaginarios, discursos y cultura política de la subversión y la resistencia. Coordinación de Carlos Rubén Ruiz Medrano. San Luis Potosí, Mexico: El Colegio de San Luis, 2015. 230 p.: bibl., ill. (Colección Investigaciones)

A distinguished collection of articles on the evergreen topics of resistance and rebellion in New Spain. Caroline Cunhill looks at hybrid consciousness in a Yucatec rebellion in the late 16th century. José Alfredo Rangel Silva analyzes Pame resistance in 18th-century San Luis Potosí. María Concepción Gavira Márquez explores resistance in Michoacán mines. Fernando Olvera Charles scrutinizes borderland dynamics of resistance in 18th-century Nuevo Santander. Natalia Silva Prada considers monarchist rebels over the colony's longue durée. The editor Ruiz Medrano examines the image of the Marian King in the popular imagination. Each essay is marked by detailed research and sophisticated engagement with a polyglot theoretical literature. [RF]

509   Pacheco Rojas, José de la Cruz. El proceso de formación del obispado de Nuevo México. (*N.M. Hist. Rev.*, 91:1, Winter 2016, p. 57–78, table)

Two hundred years of Franciscan efforts culminated in the creation of a bishopric in New Mexico under US rule in 1853. [RF]

Poder y privilegio: cabildos eclesiásticos en Nueva España, siglos XVI a XIX. See item **2756**.

510   Proctor, Frank T. *Amores perritos*: puppies, laughter and popular Catholicism in Bourbon Mexico City. (*J. Lat. Am. Stud.*, 46:1, Feb. 2014, p. 1–28, bibl.)

This brilliant, hilarious, and wonderfully lucid article uses Inquisition cases focusing on the baptism and marriage of small dogs to make a substantial contribution to various fields: Inquisition studies; the history of laughter, carnival, and revolt; the history of human relations with the natural world; and Bourbon reforms. [RF]

511   Ramírez, Paul Francis. Enlightened immunity: Mexico's experiments with disease prevention in the Age of Reason. Stanford, Calif.: Stanford University Press, 2018. 358 p.: bibl., ill., index.

This study focuses on public health practices in viceregal Mexico City in the late 18th and early 19th centuries with a particular focus on epidemic disease and the ways that the population understood disease and contagion, as well as the ways that authorities sought to deal with it. In the first part of the book, the author examines ideas related to the intersection between health, disease, and religion. The second part turns to specific epidemics that ravaged Mexico and the reforms that attempted to deal with these epidemics, including inoculation campaigns throughout the viceroyalty. This study seeks to build on earlier studies of epidemics and inoculation campaigns, delving into Enlightenment ideologies as well as exploring the reasons why parents would allow children to be inoculated in what was an experimental technique that often met significant resistance and questioning. Despite this setting, however, Mexico did undergo a major inoculation campaign in the early 19th century. [PDV]

512   Rex Galindo, David. *To sin no more*: Franciscans and conversion in the Hispanic world, 1683–1830. Mission San Luis Rey, Calif.: The Academy of American Franciscan History, 2017. 330 p.: bibl.

This work focuses on a series of Franciscan colleges that were established in Spain and the Americas beginning in the late 17th century, with the first opened in Querétaro in 1683. The author argues that, despite the attention that Franciscans and their evangelical efforts have received from colonial historians, these colleges have been neglected in the historiography. They were established at a time in which there was a growing sentiment against the regular clergy among secular authorities, but they played a major role in reinvigorating the missionary efforts both in the peripheries of Spanish America as well as in traditional centers of power and influence, including Spain itself. For historian's comment, see item **378**. [PDV]

513   Rincón Frías, Gabriel *et al.* Juan Caballero y Ocio: la generosidad y el poder: los anhelos barrocos del benefactor queretano. Coordinación de Gabriel Rincón Frías. Textos de Rodolfo Anaya Larios, José Ignacio Urquiola Permisán, e Alejandra Medina Medina. Santiago de Querétaro, Mexico: Municipio de Querétaro, 2013. 532 p.: bibl. (Librarius historia)

This rich collection of documents is intended to celebrate the life of Juan Caballero y Ocio, a Queretano priest from a prominent family who made numerous consequential philanthropic gifts. With a stupendous inheritance from his father, Caballero funded construction of various churches and colleges and the repair of various others. He also provided dowries for hundreds of orphan girls. This book includes fascinating material for the transition of the economy of northern Mexico after the fading of the Chichimeca Wars, the intersection of economic and religious life, and the philanthropic uses to which some residents of New Spain put the accumulated spoils of empire. [RF]

514   Rodríguez-Alegría, Enrique. The archaeology and history of colonial Mexico: mixing epistemologies. New York, N.Y.: Cambridge University Press, 2016. 241 p.: bibl., index.

This work examines the early postconquest history of two different sites in the Valley of Mexico: the Aztec capital of Tenochtitlan and the town of Xaltocan in the northern part of the valley. The author uses a combination of historical, anthropological, and archeological methods to examine changes in material life in households of these two different locations to gauge the impact of the Spanish conquest on daily life in the region. Thus, the study provides a social history of the immediate postconquest years, examining the impact of conquest on a cross-section of society that includes elites and commoners. The evidence used includes a combination of historical texts and archeological remains of material culture. Whereas textual evidence tends to privilege elite perspectives, archeological evidence allows for the study of a broader range of social actors. In this way, the author argues, he is mixing epistemologies, using a variety of interdisciplinary methods and approaches. In particular, he examines the use of narrative in the ways that researchers work to draw conclusions from evidence. By critically examining the construction of narrative forms, drawing largely from the arguments of Hayden White, the author analyzes his own ways of inferring conclusions from the variety of evidence he uses. This groundbreaking work will allow more communication and coordination between the disciplines of history and archeology, though including the perspectives of biogeography, agronomy, and horticulture would also complement these approaches. For archeologist's comment, see *HLAS 73:31*. [PDV]

515   Rodríguez Jáuregui, Luis. Nochistlán, de los orígenes a la conquista: invasión, rebelión y pacificación de la Nueva Galicia. Lagos de Moreno, Mexico: H. Ayuntamiento de Lagos de Moreno: Casa de la Cultura de Lagos de Moreno, 2015. 193 p.: bibl., ill., maps.

This short microhistory addressing one of the key communities of Mexico's "near north" is written not by a historian but by a surgeon who is passionate about history. Based entirely on printed sources, but enriched by many maps, illustrations, and photos. For a related work, see *HLAS 70:271*. [RF]

516   Salinero, Gregorio. Rebeliones coloniales y gobierno de las Indias en la segunda mitad del siglo XVI. (*Hist. Mex./ México*, 64:3, enero/marzo 2015, p. 895–936, bibl.)

Multiple challenges to imperial rule in the Americas were met by a creative and flexible Spanish government that deployed judges and courts to win military, financial, and cultural struggles with rebels. [RF]

517   Saucedo González, José Isidro. Poder político y jurídico en Yucatán en el siglo XVI. Prólogo de José Luis Vargas Aguilar. México: UNAM; Mérida, Mexico: Universidad Autónoma de Yucatán, 2014. 157 p.: bibl., ill., maps. (Serie Doctrina jurídica/ Instituto de Investigaciones Jurídicas; 257)

This slim volume presents a short, lucid, and detailed study of the political structures—indigenous, Spanish, and mixed—that came into being in 16th-century Yucatán. [RF]

518   Schwaller, John Frederick. Fr. Agustín de Vetancurt: the "Via crucis en mexicano." (*Americas/Washington*, 74:2, April 2017, p. 119–137, ill.)

This article traces the history of this well-known author (1620–1700) by delving into one of his little-known writings in Nahuatl, a work on the Stations of the Cross that was published in 1680, but of which there is no known extant copy. The author found a manuscript copy of it in the

Academy of American Franciscan History (Washington, DC) and describes its content and unique illustrations. [PDV]

519 Schwaller, Robert C. Géneros de gente in early colonial Mexico: defining racial difference. Norman: University of Oklahoma Press, 2016. 286 p.: bibl., index.

This is a learned, substantial, and provocative contribution to our understanding of race, identity, and ethnicity in colonial New Spain. To see the *"casta* paintings" of the 18th century is to be curious about the society that produced them. This book provides one of the most lucid and insightful accounts of that society available. Spanish colonial law wove together data from petitions from the New World and ancient Mediterranean ideas and prejudices about human difference. The laws governing the Indies reflected royal attempts to respond to the needs and grievances of colonial actors. Yet, "for a number of reasons, colonial subjects in early New Spain did not abide by the spirit or letter of the laws that their own petitions and complaints helped produce" (p. 224). Many new caste groups were the product of the failure of colonial subjects to conform to the law. Schwaller's revelatory finding that more than half of colonial mulatos were a mix of African and indigenous ancestors is proof of the ineffectuality of laws meant to separate blacks and Indians. He also shows that mestizos and mulatos married outside their group more often than *españoles, negros,* and *indios.* Thus, mixing begat more mixing, and groups that considered themselves "pure" were dwindling islands in a rising sea of racial mixture. Schwaller provides rich quantitative and qualitative research on the occupations of mixed-race people, and shows how their roles and opportunities gradually changed over time. This book joins *The Limits of Racial Domination* by R. Douglas Cope (see *HLAS* 56:1137), *Genealogical Fictions* by María Elena Martínez (see *HLAS* 66:743), and *Casta Painting* by Ilona Katzew (see *HLAS* 64:31) on the list of classics in the historiography of race—or, better, *género*— in New Spain. See also item **483**. [RF]

520 Sierra Silva, Pablo Miguel. Urban slavery in colonial Mexico: Puebla de los Ángeles, 1531–1706. Cambridge, England; New York, N.Y.: Cambridge University Press, 2018. 226 p.: bibl., ill., index, maps. (Cambridge Latin American studies; 109)

This work focuses on slavery and the slave trade in colonial Puebla. The author has conducted impressive and exhaustive research, spending three years in notarial and municipal archives in Puebla, compiling a database of thousands of bills of sale of slaves that is supplemented by a wide array of other documentation. In this way, Sierra Silva was able to do both quantitative and qualitative analysis of slave culture in Puebla, a city not typically associated with the slave trade. In compiling this data, the author has reconstructed and uncovered the myriad experiences of and relationships among enslaved families in their daily lives, however incomplete and fragmentary the historical record. The author argues that the slave trade was, indeed, a significant element of the Poblano economy and culture throughout the 17th century, but as slaves became increasingly integrated into Poblano society and made contacts and created networks with the free population, Poblano slavery gradually faded from existence in the 18th century. This work makes a significant contribution to the history of Afro-Mexicans and of Atlantic world slavery. Sierra Silva also argues that the regional urban centers throughout New Spain were important venues for the slave trade, and points out the necessity to study these centers in greater depth, given that much of the historiography focuses on Mexico City, which was not necessarily representative of the whole of New Spain. [PDV]

521 Somohano Martínez, Lourdes.
¿Tiene una historia la Sierra Gorda queretana antes de la llegada del capitán Escandón y fray Junípero Serra a mediados del siglo XVIII?: La Sierra Gorda queretana, 1521–1743. Querétaro, Mexico: Universidad Autónoma de Querétaro Facultad de Filosofía, 2013. 223 p.: bibl. (Colección Academia. Serie Nodos)

This excellent and revealing study addresses the Sierra Gorda before the celebrated evangelizing efforts of Junípero Serra and others. The answer Somohano offers to the question posed in the title is "yes." For the 16th century, she relies mainly on well-known printed sources, both primary and secondary, with a few excursions into archival documents. The documentation for the 17th-century mushrooms, and Somohano makes extensive and fascinating use of it. Documents from Mexico City and Madrid are woven together with data from local archives in Querétaro, San Pedro Escanela, and the municipality of Jalpan. Rich chapters cover the conquest of the region, division of lands, the establishment of mining towns and ranches, the evangelizing efforts of various orders, the office of "protector of Indians," and the development of the slave trade. Among many other findings, it is clear that the Chichimeca War never really ended in this zone, Borderland dynamics continued in abundance, and the years before the advent of Serra and his henchmen were rich with violence, drama, compromise, and achievement. A key point of reference for all future studies of the Borderlands. See also *HLAS 60:1193*. [RF]

522 **Taylor, William B.** Theater of a thousand wonders: a history of miraculous images and shrines in New Spain. New York, N.Y.: Cambridge University Press, 2016. 654 p.: bibl., ill., index. (Cambridge Latin American studies; 103)

The late-career renaissance of William Taylor has yielded yet another masterpiece, this one even more enormous than the others. This study features Taylor's customary oceanic breadth and depth of reading, with footnotes citing the letters of Emily Dickinson, scholarship by art historian Michael Baxandall, philosopher Alexander Nehamas, anthropologists Michael Taussig and Greg Dening, and many more from across disciplines—in addition to the specialized literature on his topic and documents from archives dotting central Mexico. The work is panoramic and mosaic-like, assembling a detailed and massive image with thousands of bright shards of evidence. Taylor emphasizes peculiarity and specificity, but at times steps away and identifies larger patterns: evidence from the early colonial period betrays little interest in miraculous images and shrines. The later 17th century and early 18th, a time of intense distress over idolatry, was also a time of increasingly widespread fascination with, and official sanction for, miraculous shrines and images. A further intriguing observation is that accounts of miracles in Mexico usually lacked the martial edge found in those from Spain: "In general Mexican miracles were less fraught with political and social danger . . . miracles usually protected the righteous. Other than the devil lurking in the wings, enemies of the faith were rarely in sight" (p. 341). More space would be needed to do justice to the richness of the research and abundance of insights found in this book. Like the dome of St. Peter's Basilica, this book is at once intricately adorned yet elegant in structure, an awesome achievement and a source of esthetic pleasure. [RF]

523 **Tutino, John.** Mexico City, 1808: power, sovereignty and silver in an age of war and revolution. Albuquerque: University of New Mexico Press, 2018. 296 p.: bibl., index. (Diálogos series)

In this work, the author traces the history of Mexico City from the mid-18th century to the eve of the independence revolts in 1808. He characterizes Mexico City as the urban core of the Viceroyalty of New Spain that was the engine of what he terms silver capitalism, or the economy in New Spain that was dominated by the production of silver and the agricultural and industrial economies and practices that supported it. He argues that the production of Mexican silver funded resistance to the Napoleonic invasion and that control over silver receipts was a prime factor of Napoleon's rule in Spain. In contrast to most works focusing on independence movements, Tutino argues that historians have neglected the significance of the events of 1808, particularly the municipal response to the removal of the Spanish royal family and debates over who or what bodies now would have legitimate control over New Spain. Such an argument provides a significant corrective to historiography of independence, which tends to focus on events subsequent to the Grito de Dolores and the popular movements associated with Hidalgo and Morelos. [PDV]

524 **Vega y Ortega, Rodrigo.** Los estudios farmacéuticos en el Segundo Imperio a través de la *Gaceta Médica de México*. (*Hist. Ciênc. Saúde Manguinhos*, 23:2, abril/junho 2016, p. 249–265, bibl.)

This article examines 12 essays of pharmaceutical importance that were published in the *Gaceta Médica de México* during the Second Empire, a period that, however brief, witnessed significant investment in and gains for the study of medicine and science. During this time, there was greater emphasis among medical professionals and especially pharmacists upon the professionalisation of their fields, with pharmacists attempting to separate and distance themselves from apothecaries. Part of their effort was devoted to the study of medicinal plants indigenous to Mexico, examining and testing their therapeutic properties in an effort that stemmed from the colonial period to substitute indigenous medicinal plants for imported drugs. [PDV]

Venegas Delgado, Hernán and **Carlos M. Valdés Dávila.** La ruta del horror: prisioneros indios del noroeste novohispano llevados como esclavos a La Habana, Cuba. See item **812**.

525   Victoria Ojeda, Jorge and Aurelio Sánchez. Interetnicidad y espacios de convivencia: españoles, indígenas y africanos en la Mérida novohispana, 1542–1620. (*Secuencia/México*, 92, mayo/agosto 2015, p. 7–36, bibl., ill., maps)

This article examines the demography of early colonial America. The authors examine ecclesiastical documents, particularly marriage registers, to reexamine traditionally held notions of the city's ethnic makeup in contrast to Spanish stipulations that city centers to be inhabited only by Spaniards. They find that Mérida was inhabited by a variety of peoples—a mix of Spaniards, Maya, and people of African descent who interacted to such a degree that the authors label it *convivencia*. They also find that a local community traditionally thought to be inhabited by the Maya was actually an African neighborhood. They argue overall that historians must take into account colonial urban policy of the secular state as well as that of the Church. [PDV]

526   Vinson, Ben. Before mestizaje: the frontiers of race and caste in colonial Mexico. New York: Cambridge University Press, 2018. 284 p., 8 unnumbered pages of plates: bibl., ill. (some color), index, maps (some color). (Cambridge Latin American studies; 105)

In this work, Vinson builds upon his earlier work on the free colored militia in Bourbon Mexico by delving deeper into the meanings of race, ethnicity, and caste in colonial Mexico. Vinson focuses in particular on what he terms the "extreme castes," those *casta* categories that involved more complicated genealogical backgrounds and that many historians have dismissed as relatively minor and unimportant legal categories that had little in the way of any real significance for day-to-day living. By contrast, Vinson uncovers these identities and their meanings, tracing them through marriage patterns and records of slave sales, examining their legacies in the modern period, emphasizing the fluidity of racial categorization, and discussing the problems with received notions of hybridity and mestizaje. This is a major revisionist work in the literature on *castas*, miscegenation, and *limpieza de sangre*. For philosophy specialist's comment, see item **2994**. [PDV]

Independence, Revolution, and Post-Revolution

SUZANNE B. PASZTOR, *Professor of History, Humboldt State University*
TERRY RUGELEY, *Historian, Arkadelphia, AK*
BARBARA TENENBAUM, *Historian, Washington, DC*

INDEPENDENCE TO REVOLUTION
DURING THIS BIENNIUM, historians continue to observe anniversaries and many volumes look at independence and revolution. Political history continues to dominate the works under review, and San Luis Potosí seems to attract the most attention at the state level. The period produced several magisterial works: Guardino on the Mexican-American War (item **564**), Arrioja Díaz Viruell on statistics

and their use (item **597**), Becerril Hernández on tax collections during the French Empire (item **530**), Buve and Falcón on the period after the Mexican-American War (item **579**), Durán-Merk on German immigration (item **546**), Medina García on the use of concepts articulated in the US to explain the Mexican phenomenon (item **577**), Reina on indigenous participation in politics (item **598**), and Ruiz de Gordejuela Urquijo on Spaniards' repatriation of funds after independence (item **604**).

Despite the overwhelming emphasis on political subjects (42 percent), historians have examined other subjects as well. Fewer works cover geography, women, and homosexuality, while several contributions address Mexico's intellectual history including Achim (item **527**), Bueno (item **533**), Depetris (item **543**), Valiant on archeology and its uses (item **615**), and an edited volume on Darwin in Mexico (item **542**). Curiously, many scholars analyze public health issues including Jiménez Marce (item **571**), López on the Porfirian attempt to get Mexicans to use the new crematorium (item **574**), and Quezada Torres (item **594**).

The political focus notwithstanding, economic subjects continue to develop. Historians report on statistics (Arrioja Díaz Viruell in item **597**), tax and tithe collections—Becerril Hernández on taxes (item **530**) and Ortega González on tithes (item **587**), and economic activity on the western part of the border with the US (items **534**, **539**, and **570**). Ruiz de Gordejuela Urquijo sheds new light on why the 1820s and 1830s were so fiscally challenging (item **604**).

Other works worthy of note are Borsò and Gerling *et al.* on Mexican history with insights from Europeans (item **538**), Casas García on Church-state relations (item **591**), and Dutt on the interplay between Yucatán and Belize, which challenges both frontier and Borderlands paradigms (item **547**). Several works examine labor unrest (items **558** and **609**).

Once again, scholars rarely used internet sources in *HLAS* 74. Regrettably, the difficulties inherent in using the internet extend to the possible disappearance of links to archives and shuttering of websites. However, the HathiTrust digital repository is committed to providing permanent online access to many books and documents that support serious investigation (www.hathitrust.org). In addition, the trend of Spanish-speaking historians not consulting English-language sources continues unabated. Such research practices run counter to productive scholarship. [BT]

REVOLUTION AND POST-REVOLUTION

Mexico's 20th century, alternately tempestuous and triumphant, continues to inspire a wealth of historical studies. The most important event of the century began almost as soon as the 19th century ended: the Revolution raged from 1910 to 1920, and Mexicans spent the next 80 years coming to terms with it. The overriding question remains one of discontinuity versus continuity. Did the Revolution bring fundamental change to the society, or was it an event that stirred tempers, spilled blood, and then passed on like a summer storm? Ávila Espinosa and Salmerón Sanginés (item **632**) take on the skeptics by arguing that the Revolution did indeed alter Mexican society. Elsewhere, we may not be witnessing any major paradigm shift in our understanding of the Mexican Revolution, but we do see an expansion of the actors and places under study. The list here is long. In terms of place, Rodríguez Pérez (item **668**) gathers essays exploring Francisco Villa's defeat of federal forces at Zacatecas, a defeat that broke the government of usurper Victoriano Huerta. This same critical battle appears in Sarmiento Pacheco's collection of primary documents (item **681**). Military aspects also dominate Salmerón Sanginés' comprehensive history of the year 1915 (item **683**), when leaders of the ill-fated revolutionary coalition spend their time fighting each other. Carvallo Torres *et al.*'s edited collection of essays reconstructs another pivotal moment of that decade, namely, the 1914 US invasion of Veracruz (item **688**).

Among lesser-known individuals stepping into the foreground we find Juan M. Banderas, the Sinaloan caudillo who changed loyalties with startling facility, and who, not surprisingly, survived the fighting unharmed (item **627**). Similarly, Máximo Castillo fought with three of the major leaders, only to go into a permanent exile in 1914 (item **664**). Fewer people were more anonymous than the Yaquis transported to Yucatán during the Porfirian era; but in Padilla Ramos' recent work (item **672**) their role in the emerging revolutionary conflict becomes clear. Conversely, no one could paint Venustiano Carranza, the self-styled "first chief" of the Revolution, as an unknown, but Plana (item **674**) provides a useful retrospective on his career and achievements. Certainly the most exhaustive and penetrating (and long overdue) study of a key figure is Lomnitz-Adler's history of Ricardo Flores Magón, die-hard anarchist, which details his work with fellow radicals (item **660**).

Studies of science and technology are also finding their way into the history of this critical period. Castro (item **635**) shifts the focus of analysis away from political and military themes by exploring the role that wireless radio played in the revolutionary years, as well as the decades before and after. Olea Franco's edited work on the 1913 overthrow of Francisco Madero explores the photographic and cinematic treatment of those Ten Tragic Days (item **646**). Submarines provided part of the arsenal of devices that Europeans used in their various Mexican interventions, as documented by Mills (item **669**).

A question that has always dogged revolutionary-era political debates: did they matter? Earlier historians have tended to second Mao Zedung's claim that "power grows out of the barrel of a gun," but at least some recent works challenge that dire assertion. Abdo Francis (item **623**) finds that the much-maligned Convention of Aguascalientes, normally taken as Francisco Villa's civilian front, did indeed allow for a valuable airing of perspectives and grievances. Sánchez Tagle reconstructs the political debates of the state of Zacatecas in the decade following 1910 (item **685**). The collected newspaper articles of revolutionary ideologue Luis Cabrera (item **633**) document the emergence of key issues and agendas, with Cabrera himself having been one of the key intellectual spokesmen urging some sort of agrarian reform.

One of the more notable trends for the cycle under review was the appearance of several outstanding volumes related to immigration. Alanís Enciso provides another important look at the repatriation of Mexicans from the US during the 1930s (item **626**), while his earlier volume on the same theme is now available to an English-speaking audience (item **625**). Loza adds significantly to the history of braceros with a work that emphasizes migrants who did not fit the family-oriented, heteronormative ideal (item **661**), while Kang underscores the extent to which the INS and the Border Patrol have had a central role in shaping US immigration policy (item **653**). Not surprisingly, historians also continue to produce works on Spanish immigrants in the context of the Spanish Civil War and the Mexican Revolution. Dávila Munguía (item **642**), Serra Puche *et al.*(item **675**), and Pavón Romero *et al.* (item **641**) have collected essays commemorating 70 years of Spanish exile in Mexico. Leyva Martínez *et al.* document the effect of Spanish man of letters Adolfo Sánchez Vázquez on the National University in the 1950s and 1960s (item **678**). Lisbona examines the presence of the Chinese in Chiapas (item **659**), and Izquierdo focuses on the incorporation of Soviet scientists into

Mexico's universities (item **651**). Finally, immigration of a somewhat different nature appears in Young's study of militant Catholics who fled Mexico for the US during the Cristero War of the 1920s (item **704**).

Women's history also continues to attract scholars. A handful took up the issue of voting rights in a nod to the 70th anniversary of women's suffrage in Mexico (achieved at the national level in 1953). Galeana has assembled a commemorative volume of essays (item **599**), Castillo Ramírez examines the issue through press coverage (item **634**), Mitchell explores a woman's electoral campaign in the context of the 1930s (item **670**), and Augustine-Adams adds the interesting factor of anti-Chinese racism to her analysis of a local suffrage movement (item **630**). Other notable works in the subfield of women's history include Arce's cultural history of *soldaderas* and Afro-Mexican women (item **629**), and Fernández Aceves' compilation focusing on the lives of five women active in the Mexican Revolution and in other causes (item **643**).

Economic history continues to be well represented in the literature. Luna Sánchez underscores the importance of "human intellectual capital" in her study of entrepreneurs (item **662**), while Trujillo Bolio offers a valuable look at the historiography of Mexico's textile industry (item **694**). Solís Hernández *et al.* focuses on industrial growth in several Mexican regions (item **639**), Villavicencio Rojas explores industry and business people in Puebla (item **700**), and the Instituto Mora has published a wide-ranging collection on development in western Mexico (item **676**). Also notable is Covert's study of San Miguel de Allende, which emphasizes the tourism economy as a development model tied to Mexico's neoliberal turn in the latter 20th century (item **637**).

During this biennium, labor historians pushed the subfield in interesting new directions. Lear provides a wonderful study of the link between artists and organized labor in a revolutionary context (item **656**) and Lenti examines the effect of the Tlatelolco massacre of 1968 on government efforts to draw closer to workers under the regime of Luis Echeverría (item **657**). Zamorano-Villarreal investigates the fate of a government project for an ideal working class community in Mexico City (item **705**), and Mendiola García makes a fine case for including street vendors in the history of labor activism in contemporary Mexico (item **666**). Ventura Rodríguez also provides a useful look at the process by which Puebla's local unions became integrated into the national labor movement (item **699**).

A handful of historians turned their attention to the history of education in the context of Mexico's revolution, and to the student movement. (The year 2018 marked the 60th anniversary of the height of that movement, and of the Tlatelolco massacre.) Socialist education during the Cárdenas years is the focus of Trujillo Holguín, who explores local efforts in Chihuahua (item **695**), and of Montes de Oca Navas, who uses textbooks to analyze the nature of elementary education (item **671**). Sosenski examines a little-known initiative by the secretary of education to facilitate "moral" education through a program encouraging saving money and using banks (item **691**). Soler Durán has assembled reflections and commentaries on the events of 1968 (item **665**), Tirado Villegas details the split within the University of Puebla's student movement (item **693**), speeches that reveal the University of Guadalajara's official opposition to the student movement are collected by Díaz Ordaz (item **638**), and Pensado explores the changing face of the Catholic student movement (item **673**).

While cultural and environmental history attracted fewer scholars for the period under review, some notable works in these areas appeared. Pulido Esteva provides an interesting analysis of drinking culture and masculine sociability (item **677**), Smith delves into the relationship between artists and Mexico's postrevolutionary state (item **689**), and Sheppard brings together the issues of representation, authenticity, and the Chicano cultural movement in his analysis of the Mexican Pavilion at Disney's EPCOT Center (item **687**). A particularly outstanding contribution by Wolfe advances our knowledge of Mexico's agrarian reform by examining official efforts to facilitate the distribution of water, while at the same time underscoring the environmental consequences of such efforts (item **703**). Also of interest is Vitz's study linking a transition in the source of cooking fuel to an official narrative that, ironically, praised the environmental benefits of petroleum use (item **701**).

Other valuable contributions appearing during the biennium include diplomatic studies by Sánchez Andrés, who demonstrates Mexico's leading role in supporting the Spanish Republic and denouncing international aggression in the League of Nations (item **684**), and by Hernández Galindo, who provides an intriguing look at surveillance of Japanese immigrants in Mexico during World War II (item **648**). Additionally, Iber examines an American-funded writing center that produced many important Mexican writers during the Cold War (item **649**). On the theme of postrevolutionary state formation, Alexander (item **628**) reconstructs, and significantly revises our understanding of the presidency, while Sola Ayape examines the controversial figure of José López Portillo (1978–82) with a focus on the president's visit to his family's ancestral home in Spain (item **690**). A leading scholar on Chiapas explores the National Indigenous Institute's first coordinating center, which was located in that state (item **658**), and Rangel Lozano and Sánchez Serrano bring together essays exploring a number of the more important of these revolutionary movements of the 1960s and 1970s, together with the state repression that they inspired (item **667**). [SP and TR]

INDEPENDENCE TO REVOLUTION

527 Achim, Miruna. From idols to antiquity: forging the National Museum of Mexico. Lincoln: University of Nebraska Press, 2017. 327 p.: bibl., ill., index. (The Mexican experience)

This work examines the evolution and development of the National Museum of Mexico from its founding in 1825 to 1867. The author shows that because of its turbulent history, little happened for the first decades of its existence despite foreign interest and that José Fernando Ramírez was able to regularize the keeping of antiquities and retain them in Mexico.

528 Bárcenas García, Felipe. Imprenta, economía y cultura en el noreste de México: la empresa editorial de Desiderio Lagrange, 1874–1887. Monterrey, Mexico: Consejo para la Cultura y las Artes de Nuevo León, 2017. 174 p.: bibl., ill., maps, tables. (Memoria del futuro. Concursos)

This important survey covers a little-known subject—the press in Nuevo León and specifically Monterrey. The author concentrates on the work of Desiderio Lagrange, a Frenchman who came to the area around 1860. The study shows how the arrival of talented individuals could implement the decree for a free and vibrant press where there had been none. Recommended.

529 Barrera-Enderle, Alberto. Contrabandear en la frontera: relaciones comerciales clandestinas en la frontera noreste de la Nueva España, 1808–1821. (*Front. Hist.*, 20:1, enero/junio 2015, p. 44–69, bibl., maps)

This study shows how the Provincias Internas de Oriente, the future states of Coahuila, Nuevo León, Tamaulipas, and Texas, developed secret trade relations with areas in the US and were helped decisively by indigenous peoples. This clandestine trade relationship was fostered due to population scarcity and high prices available from Mexico, as the lack of population kept the area from revolting.

530   **Becerril Hernández, Carlos de Jesús.** Hacienda pública y administración fiscal: la legislación tributaria del Segundo Imperio Mexicano, antecedentes y desarrollo. México: Instituto de Investigaciónes Dr. José María Luis Mora: Consejo Nacional de Ciencia y Technología, 2015. 372 p.: bibl., ill., indexes. (Historia económica)

This study analyzes Treasury collections during the French Empire as part of the history of these activities throughout the 19th century. Fills in a very important gap in the literature and helps us understand the empire better. Recommended.

531   **Bloch, Avital H.** and **Margarita Rodríguez.** Colima, la ciudad, en el siglo XIX: espacios, población y mujeres. Colima, Mexico: Colima, Gobierno de Estado, Secretaría de Cultura: Sociedad Colimense de Estudios Históricos A.C.: Puertaberta Editores, S.A. de C.V., 2013. 170 p.: bibl., ill.

Colima is rarely analyzed, but this slender volume looks at the 1841 census for both population demographics and economic participation, together with a discussion of the closing of a religious community there. Offers an interesting contrast to other parts of the republic.

532   **Breve noticia del recibimiento y permanencia de SS. MM. II. en la ciudad de Puebla: Puebla, tipografía de T.F. Neve, 1864.** Puebla, Mexico: Benemérita Universidad Autónoma de Puebla, Dirección de Fomento Editorial, 2013. 110 p.: ill. (Colección Conmemorativa del 150 aniversario del sitio de Puebla de 1863)

This publication contains the official announcement of the 1864 arrival of the royal couple, Emperor Maximilian I and Empress Carlota, along with poetry written for the occasion. Lists of civilian and military personnel and that of women who directed festivities are also included.

533   **Bueno, Christina.** The pursuit of ruins: archaeology, history, and the making of modern Mexico. Albuquerque: University of New Mexico Press, 2016. 267 p.: bibl., index. (Diálogos series)

This book concentrates on how the Mexican state used its ruins as an advertisement for the country abroad, while carefully making the distinction between the glorious Indian of the past and their second-class heirs of the modern state. The author also looks at the life and work of Leopoldo Batres, but differently from Valiant (item **615**). For ethnohistorian's comment, see *HLAS 72:198*.

534   **Busto Ibarra, Karina.** Comercio marítimo en los puertos de La Paz y Santa Rosalía, Distrito Sur de la Baja California, 1880–1910. La Paz, Mexico: Gobierno del Estado de Baja California Sur, Instituto Sudcaliforniano de Cultura: Archivo Histórico "Pablo L. Martínez", 2013. 242 p.: bibl., ill., maps.

This book offers a welcome look at maritime commercial links for a peninsula usually studied in relation to its railroad. The author looks at the port city of La Paz, Baja California Sur, mainly in terms of its foreign links, but notes that the port town of Santa Rosalía was indispensable for the development of the interior.

535   **Cañedo Gamboa, Sergio Alejandro.** Comercio, alcabalas y negocios de familia en San Luis Potosí, México: crecimiento económico y poder político, 1820–1846. San Luis Potosí, Mexico: Colegio de San Luis; México: Instituto Mora, 2015. 282 p.: bibl. (Colección Investigaciones)

This in-depth study focuses on the economic growth of San Luis Potosí during the years before the war with the US. The book contains valuable economic information that helps explain why US arms went through there.

536   **Carrigan, William D.** Forgotten dead: mob violence against Mexicans in the United States, 1848–1928. Oxford, England: Oxford University Press, 2013. 304 p.: appendixes, bibl., index, photos, tables.

This study shows that antipathy toward immigrants from Mexico is hardly a new phenomenon, and that they too were lynched. The authors also note how prejudice against Mexican-Americans seeped into popular culture.

537   **Chaires Zaragoza, Jorge.** Las bases del estado constitucional y democrático de México (1808–1812). Guadalajara, Mexico: Universidad de Guadalajara, 2014. 357 p.: bibl.

This study examines the key years in Mexico during the time of the Napoleonic invasion of Spain. The author argues that this event prompted the development of a constitutional monarchy and then republicanism in Mexico. The work focuses on Bayonne and its role in subsequent developments.

538　**Colonia-independencia-revolución: genealogías, latencias y transformaciones en la escritura y las artes de México.** Edición de Vittoria Borsò y Vera Elisabeth Gerling. Madrid: Iberoamericana; Frankfurt am Main: Vervuert, 2017. 346 p.: bibl., color ill. (MEDIAmericana; 7)

This compilation of 16 essays written by European scholars and edited by a professor of literature at the Universität Düsseldorf (Germany) examines aspects of Mexico from 1500 to the revolution. The contributions indicate different sensibilities using ideas of Foucault and Certeau, and range from analyses of women in the independence movement and images of women during the French intervention. Other essays review the revolution in terms of its history, architecture, literature, film, and photography.

539　**Colonización, economía agrícola y empresarios en el noroeste de México: siglos XIX y XX.** Coordinación de R. Arturo Román Alarcón y Eduardo Frías Sarmiento. México: Universidad Autónoma de Sinaloa, 2014. 209 p.: bibl., ill., maps.

These eight essays address Mexico's northwest spanning from 1741 to 2019, and focus on Sonora, Sinaloa, and Baja California. The studies analyze mainly population and economic trends.

540　**Coloquio Internacional "1910: México entre Dos Épocas," Paris, 2010. 1910: México entre dos épocas.** Edición de Paul-Henri Giraud, Eduardo Ramos-Izquierdo, y Miguel Rodríguez. México: El Colegio de México, 2014. 499 p.: bibl., ill.

This collection of 27 conference papers looks at 1910 as a turning point in Mexican history. The volume is divided into seven sections studying *centenarios* historically, geographically, architecturally inside Mexico, literally, and in comparison with France (Jean Meyer).

541　**Cuando las armas hablan, los impresos luchan, la exclusion agrede . . . : violencia electoral en México, 1812–1912.** Coordinación de Fausta Gantús y Alicia Salmerón. San Juan Mixcoac, Mexico: Instituto Mora, 2016. 429 p.: bibl., ill. (Historia política)

This collection of 12 essays focuses on how electoral violence was as Mexican as tequila, how cartoons and newspapers encouraged it, and how it became an indispensable part of the Mexican electoral tradition. The volume includes two fine pieces on the election of 1828. Recommended. See also item **549**.

542　**Darwin en (y desde) México.** Coordinación de Rosaura Ruiz Gutiérrez, Ricardo Noguera Solano, y Juan Manuel Rodríguez Caso. Textos de Jonathan Hodge et al. México: UNAM: Siglo Veintiuno Editores, 2015. 147 p.: bibl. (Ciencia y técnica)

This volume discusses the impact of the theory of evolution by natural selection in Mexico as early as 1870. Justo Sierra and Gabino Barreda analyzed and used the theory and found it "methodologically deficient." These very insightful works address Darwin and the history of ideas. Recommended.

543　**Depetris, Carolina. El héroe involuntario: Frédéric de Waldeck y su viaje por Yucatán.** Mérida, Mexico: UNAM, 2014. 186 p.: bibl., ill. (some color). (Viajeros. Colección sextante; 4)

This work presents a study of one of the first European travelers to the Maya precolumbian ruins of Mexico and Central America. The author looks at the context in which Waldeck's study of Palenque fits into European discussions of the origins of civilization.

544　**La desamortización civil desde perspectivas plurales.** Coordinación de Antonio Escobar Ohmstede, Romana Falcón y Martín Sánchez Rodríguez. México: CIESAS: El Colegio de México; Zamora, Mexico: El Colegio de Michoacán, 2017. 551 p.: bibl., ill., maps.

This work compiles a series of 13 essays concerning one of the most significant economic and social processes attempted in 19th-century Mexico: the expropriation of land (one essay looks at the same topic in

Guatemala). None of the contributions goes farther north than the state of Hidalgo or Lake Chapala, but they do analyze the fact and effect of turning clerical property into individual holdings from 1856 to beyond the Constitution of 1917. The studies also examine previous views of this question. Recommended.

545 **Documentos y testimonios históricos del sitio a Puebla de 1863.** Compilación de Alberto Enríquez Perea. Puebla, Mexico: Benemérita Universidad Autónoma de Puebla, Dirección de Fomento Editorial, 2013. 265 p.: bibl. (Colección Conmemorativa del 150 aniversario del sitio de Puebla de 1863)

This collection presents 26 documents relating to the siege of Puebla, supplemented by some contemporaneous essays and analyses. The volume is indispensable for understanding how Mexico coped with yet another foreign invasion.

546 **Durán-Merk, Alma.** "In our sphere of life": German-speaking immigrants in Yucatán and their descendants, 1876–1914. Madrid: Iberoamericana; Frankfurt am Main, Germany: Vervuert, 2015. 652 p.: bibl., ill. (Tiempo emulado; 37)

This work offers a significant addition to our understanding of the immigrant phenomenon in Mexico by adding Germans to the mix. The book includes excellent appendices naming the immigrants who came and settled. Extraordinary use of sources. Recommended.

547 **Dutt, Rajeshwari.** Business as usual: Maya and the merchants on Yucatán-Belize border at the onset of the Caste War. (*Americas/Washington*, 74:2, April 2017, p. 201–226)

This study puts the boundary between Yucatán and Belize squarely in the literature of both frontiers and borderlands with Bacalar linking the two. The author shows that territory created polity of its own, one where appeals of racial solidarity with the Yucatecan elite fell on deaf ears. For additional comment, see item **209**.

548 **Los efectos del liberalismo en México, siglo XIX.** Coordinación de Antonio Escobar Ohmstede, José Marcos Medina Bustos y Zulema Trejo Contreras. Hermosillo, Mexico: El Colegio de Sonora; México: Centro de Investigaciones y Estudios Superiores en Antropología Social, 2015. 353 p.: bibl., ill., maps.

This compilation brings together 10 essays concentrating on how the liberal policy of individual land holding affected indigenous peoples. Many essays see the implementation of liberalism as a damaging ideology for rural dwellers. As with many essay collections, this one could have benefitted from a substantial conclusion.

549 **Elecciones en el México del siglo XIX: las fuentes.** Coordinación de Fausta Gantús. México: Instituto Mora: CONACYT, 2015. 501 p.: bibl., facsims., maps. (Historia política)

This collection of 18 essays, only two of which cover the capital, addresses the 19th-century history of elections with an emphasis on sources stemming from a project on the history of electoral practices in Mexico. See especially Andrews on Tamaulipas, Noriega Elío and Salmerón on Veracruz, and Tapia's very welcome look at Mexico City during the occupation in 1847. See also item **541**.

550 **Enchílame otras: comida mexicana en el siglo XIX.** Introducción, selección y notas de Jorge García-Robles. México: Uva Tinta, 2013. 175 p.: bibl., ill. (Colección Microhistorias mexicanas)

This work presents a compilation of quotations from 19th-century Mexicans and non-Mexicans concerning Mexican food and cooking. The excerpts include both praise and pans such as Princess Salm-Salm, who noted that "Mexicans have coffee, but don't know how to prepare it."

551 **Enciso Contreras, José.** El Pobre Diablo: Jesús González Ortega y los orígenes del periodismo en Tlaltenango, Zacatecas. Zacatecas, Mexico: Instituto Zacatecano de Cultura, 2014. 103 p., 180 pages of facsimiles: bibl., ill. (Biblioteca del bicentenario)

The author presents the 55 issues of the weekly newspaper founded by General Jesús González Ortega that ran from 23 December 1853 to 27 June 1857 in Tlaltenango. The study links the end of the newspaper to the promulgation of the new constitution, the forced obedience to it, and the clerical reaction. See also item **555**.

552 **Estrella González, Alejandro.** Libertad, progreso y autenticidad: ideas sobre México a través de las generaciones filosóficas (1865–1925). México: Jus, 2014. 132 p.

This brief study reviews the process of how Mexicans tried to construct an image of their country from the French Empire to the presidency of Calles. Strangely written as if the Revolution had never occurred.

553 **Fierros Hernández, Arturo.** Historia de la salud pública: en el Distrito Norte de la Baja California 1888–1923. Tijuana, Mexico: Consejo Nacional para la Cultura y las Artes, Centro Cultural Tijuana, 2014. 131 p.: bibl., maps. (Divulgación cultural)

This slim volume represents one of the first studies to actually credit Porfirio Díaz as the founder of something good "without buts." The author shows how diseases in the US territory filtered down to Mexico and Mexico's subsequent struggle to maintain public health.

554 **Flores Clair, Eduardo.** Otro escenario de guerra: la diplomacia insurgente: la misión de José Manuel de Herrera (1815–1817). México: Instituto Nacional de Antropología e Historia, 2015. 223 p.: bibl., index. (Coleccion Historia. Serie Sumaria)

This study focuses on documents involving José Manuel de Herrera's mission to New Orleans, letters written by him and José Alvarez de Toledo, and the correspondence of viceregal authorities. The footnotes are a mine of information for nonspecialists. Recommended.

555 **Flores Zavala, Marco Antonio.** Jesús González Ortega: notas biográficas. Zacatecas, Mexico: Instituto Zacatecano de Cultura "Ramon López Velarde", 2013. 267 p.: bibl.

This work places an important general and writer in his time period. The study includes a wealth of his prose and poetry and should be read together with item **551**.

556 **Fontano Patán, Francisco.** La Colonia Manuel González: un éxito dentro de un proyecto fallido. Emiliano Zapata, Mexico: Editora del Gobierno del Estado de Veracruz, 2016. 210 p.: bibl., ill., maps. (Colección Investigaciones)

This work discusses the trajectory of 423 Italian colonists from Liverno who came to Mexico in 1881 to found an agricultural colony in Veracruz called Manuel González after the then-president. The research is supported by a cache of new documents found in the Ministerio de Fomento. The author finds that, by September 1882, less than one year later, a substantial number of colonists had left, which caused the experiment to fail.

557 **Formación y gestión del estado en Chiapas: algunas aproximaciones históricas.** Coordinación de María Eugenia Claps Arenas y Sergio Nicolás Gutiérrez Cruz. Tuxtla Gutiérrez, Mexico: Universidad de Ciencias y Artes de Chiapas; San Cristóbal de Las Casas, Mexico: CESMECA, 2013. 170 p.: bibl., ill.

Six essays and a documental index tell the story of the southernmost Mexican state acquired at independence. Mario Heriberto Arce Moguel looks at the effect of the revolution under Carranza and its rule from 1914 to 1920, which the Chiapan elite in San Cristóbal deeply resented. This collection introduces us to a world not often studied.

558 **Gámez, Moisés.** Cohesión, movilizaciones y tenacidad: trabajadores y empresas en la minería y la metalurgia potosinas, 1880–1926. San Luis Potosí, Mexico: El Colegio de San Luis, 2014. 259 p.: bibl., ill. (Colección Investigaciones)

This study chronicles workers' resistance to capitalist organization, especially in terms of its relation to first the Partido Liberal Mexicano and then to the Confederación Regional Obrera Mexicana (CROM) and its relation to the Revolution. The author outlines the differences in treatment of workers by owners in San Luis Potosí and outlines forms of resistance.

559 **La gloriosa batalla del 21 de octubre de 1863.** Compilación de Rigoberto Nuricumbo Aguilar. Tuxtla Gutiérrez, Mexico: Consejo Estatal para las Culturas y las Artes de Chiapas, 2013. 129 p.: bibl., ill. (some color, some folded). (Presencias)

This study provides a thorough discussion of the little-known battle for control of southern Mexico led by area strongman General Ángel Albino Corzo. Although told by Manuel B. Trens years earlier, this panorama offers important vistas into the life of Chiapas.

560   **Gonzales, Felipe.** Política: Nuevomexicanos and American Political Incorporation, 1821–1910. Lincoln: University of Nebraska Press, 2016. 1053 p.: bibl., ill., index, maps, photos, tables.

This study chronicles the encroachment of the US into New Mexico beginning with the Santa Fe trail, through the official change of sovereignty, almost to statehood in 1912. The author shows how much the nuevomexicanos worked to keep their ways and their lands. The book offers a solid look at the costs to Mexicans of losing political power. Recommended.

561   **González Milea, Alejandro.** El silencio de las aldeas: urbanismo militar y civil del noreste mexicano, siglo XIX. Monterrey, Mexico: Consejo para la Cultura y las Artes de Nuevo León, 2014. 252 p.: bibl., ill., maps, plans. (Memoria del futuro/Concursos)

This work offers a stimulating look at the foundation of urban centers in the north of Coahuila. The study is part of a trend of urban archeology fostered in areas of industrialization. The author connects this urbanism with other trends in areas such as military colonies, war with the US, and other problems of the long frontier.

562   **Grandes financieros mexicanos.** Dirección de Leonor Ludlow. Presentación de Enrique Cárdenas Sánchez. México: LID, 2015. 438 p.: bibl., ill. (Colección Acción empresarial de LID Editorial Mexicana)

This important compendium, written by specialists, lists Mexican financiers and industrialists from 1780 to the present. A must for anyone working on present-day Mexico. Recommended.

563   **Grewe, David.** Ethnizität, Staatsbürgerschaft und Zugehörigkeit im Zeitalter der Revolution: Afroamerikaner und Indigene in Mexiko um 1800 [Ethnicity, citizenship and affiliation in the time of revolution: Afro-Americans and indigenous in Mexico around 1800]. Köln, Germany: Böhlau Köln, 2016. 304 p. (Lateinamerikanische Forschungen; 47)

This study focuses on indigenous and Afro-Mexican groups in Mexico between 1810 and 1846 and their interactions with the state on the basis of their racial and ethnic backgrounds. Indigenous groups ("naturales") were an accepted ethnic category in the colonial era and had their own communities, but the Afro-Mexicans, who were often soldiers in the militia, had to define their status through this profession in order to be accepted. The Afro-Mexicans were listed as Spaniards in the Spanish constitution ratified by the Cortes, considered the first National Assembly in Spain, in 1810–12. Indigenous peoples and their descendants were not recognized as citizens with full political rights. Nation-building efforts during and following the wars of independence implied abolishing social boundaries between indigenous, Spanish, and mestizo groups—all now considered citizens of the new state. Mexican independence therefore granted full citizenship to Afro-Mexicans, but also triggered conflicts, particularly in indigenous communities regarding their representation in the cabildos. [F. Obermeier]

564   **Guardino, Peter F.** The dead march: a history of the Mexican-American War. Cambridge, Mass.: Harvard University Press, 2017. 502 p.: bibl., ill., index, maps.

This is the first major work to look at the Mexican-American War (1846–48) genuinely from both sides. The author conclusively shows how previous accounts of the war citing a lack of Mexican unity as the cause for the US taking over the southwest territory pale in comparison to the more apt explanation: a tremendous economic disparity between the two nations. Winner of the 2018 Bolton-Johnson Prize for best book in English on Latin American history. Highly recommended.

565   **Guzmán, Ricardo** and **Aída Gándara.** The Dos Bocas oil well: science, ideology, memory and discourse. (*Universum/Talca*, 31:2, 2016, p. 75–97, bibl.)

In 1908, the Dos Bocas oil well in Veracruz blew, causing a fire that lasted for two months until it burned out. In this article, the authors examine both official and popular tellings of the story in order to discuss how they fit in either in the discourse of scientific modernization or that of its end.

566   **Hernández Fuentes, Miguel.** La experiencia moderna del tiempo en la prensa mexicana, 1821–1850. México: Universidad Autónoma Metropolitana, Unidad Azcapotzalco, 2013. 118 p.: bibl. (Cuadernos de debate; 8)

This book looks at how Mexicans developed judgments on such issues as progress, march of humanity, the spirit of the century, etc., through studying the press. The author notes that there were many agreements among liberals and conservatives, but also understands that they diverged on how to look at the future.

567   **Hidalgo Pego, Mónica.** Vientos de cambio en la tercera enseñanza: el caso del Colegio de San Ildefonso de México, 1834–1852. (*Secuencia/México*, 91, enero/abril 2015, p. 105–126, bibl.)

This article looks at the Colegio de San Ildefonso and the attempts to reform it. The study begins with a history of educational institutions in Mexico starting in 1809. The author discusses all of the reorganizations during the period with regard to clerical subjects.

568   **Historia de la educación superior en Yucatán: las instituciones (universidad, colegio e instituto), siglos XIX y XX.** Coordinación de Jorge I. Castillo Canché, Roger A. Domínguez Saldívar y José E. Serrano Catzim. Mérida, Mexico: Facultad de Ciencias Antropológicas, Universidad Autónoma de Yucatán, 2017. 270 p.: bibl.

This work brings together eight essays on the history of higher education in Yucatán—from the colonial period to 1922. The essays have very little on the Caste War or the separatist movements of the state. The book is useful for scholars interested in how policies from the center were implemented in this one state.

569   **Independencia, revolución y derecho: catorce miradas sobre las revoluciones de México.** Coordinación de Óscar Cuevas Murillo y José Enciso Contreras. Zacatecas, Mexico: Universidad Autónoma de Zacatecas: Tribunal Superior de Justicia del Estado de Zacatecas, 2012. 391 p.: bibl., port.

This potpourri of 14 essays covers a wide range of issues surrounding revolution in Mexico including the colonial army and a study of agrarian law, 1910–2010. Worth a look.

570   **Intereses extranjeros y nacionalismo en el noroeste de México, 1840–1920.** Coordinación de Ignacio del Río y Juan Domingo Vidargas del Moral. México: UNAM, Instituto de Investigaciones Históricas, 2014. 262 p.: bibl., maps.

This group of five essays addresses foreign economic activity in Mexico from 1848 to 1920. The studies provide a good contrast to the work done on the eastern side of the country.

571   **Jiménez Marce, Rogelio.** Problemática sanitaria y conflictos políticos en una ciudad del centro de Veracruz: la epidemia de cólera morbus de 1833 en Xalapa. (*Secuencia/México*, 91, enero/abril 2015, p. 69–101, bibl.)

This study details how the ayuntamiento of Xalapa prepared for the cholera epidemic of 1833 including street cleaning and the draining of standing water. The paper begins with citations of other works on the subject for both 1833 and 1850.

572   **Lemoine Villicaña, Ernesto.** La revolución de Independencia y el liderazgo de Morelos. Investigación, edición y estudio introductorio de Héctor Cuauhtémoc Hernández Silva. México: Instituto Nacional de Estudios Históricos de las Revoluciones de México, 2015. 233 p.: bibl., ill. (some color), maps (some color).

This volume brings together a richly illustrated selection of articles written by famed historian Ernesto Lemoine on José María Morelos (1765–1815). The work, commemorating the 200th anniversary of Morelos' death, attempts to reinvigorate the legacy of the second major leader of Mexican independence. Morelos is deserving of further study as the head of a genuinely popular movement in the south.

573   **León-Real Méndez, Nora Marisa** and **Blanca López de Mariscal.** Exploratrices europeas: relatos de viaje a México en el siglo XIX. México: Bonilla Artigas, 2016. 214 p.: bibl., ill. (Memoria literatura y discurso; 7)

This fascinating study focuses on five female European travelers who went to Mexico in the 19th century and left behind detailed information on life a la mexicana. Good source for imagining Mexican society during the period.

574 **López, Amanda M.** "An urgent need for hygiene": cremation, class, and public health in Mexico City, 1879–1920. (*Mex. Stud.*, 31:1, Winter 2015, p. 88–124)

This study discusses the Mexican reaction to a Porfirian desire to install a crematorium as a more modern way of dealing with tradition. The vast majority disagreed and ultimately only the very poor had their remains cremated. The author shows how the values of Mexican culture (e.g., the Day of the Dead) defeated the urge for thoroughgoing modernization.

575 **Martínez Rodríguez, Marcela.** Colonizzazione al Messico!: las colonias agrícolas de italianos en México, 1881–1910. San Luis Potosí, Mexico: El Colegio de San Luis; Zamora, Mexico: El Colegio de Michoacán, A.C., 2013. 364 p.: bibl., ill. (Colección Investigaciones)

This is the most thorough study to date on Italian immigration to Mexico. The author sees the development of small colonies as a way of hiding the true nature of the Mexican countryside, with its large-scale properties. The book notes that colonists had difficulties producing more than basic subsistence. Much more detailed and complex than previous studies.

576 **McNamara, Patrick J.** Rewriting Zapata: generational conflict on the eve of the Mexican Revolution. (*Mex. Stud.*, 30:1, Winter 2014, p. 122–149, table)

This study challenges Womack's thesis (see *HLAS 60:1607*) that Zapata's revolt stemmed from an unwillingness to move from the village of Anenecuilco. New documents show, in fact, that the villagers agreed to move, but President Díaz refused to support their relocation. Their frustration boiled over and led to the zapatista movement.

577 **Medina García, Miguel Ángel.** Cambios sociales y rearticulación espacial: el ferrocarril en Jalisco durante el porfiriato. Zapopan, Mexico: El Colegio de Jalisco, 2014. 239 p.: bibl., ill. (Investigación)

This work shows how the Mexican case fits in with scholarly concepts developed in the US, including "social savings," and hypotheses that are counterfactuals. The author seeks to add to the existing literature on railroads by Coatsworth, Kuntz Ficker, and Riguzzi by looking at railroads in Jalisco from 1880 to 1914. The study shows how the confluence of internal and external influences affected both local and international conditions. Recommended.

578 **Mendoza Soriano, Reidezel.** Bandoleros y rebeldes. Vol. 1, Correrías de Heraclio Bernal, Ignacio Parra, José Beltrán Olivas, Tomás Urbina y Francisco Villa. Vol. 2, Correrías de Doroteo Arango, Sabás Baca y Abelardo Prieto. Chihuahua, Mexico: Ediciones del Azar, 2013. 2 v.: bibl., ill.

This two-volume work looks at the phenomenon of banditry and its relation to rebellion and the Maderista part of the Mexican Revolution. The volumes contain many photo reproductions of items taken from both US and Mexican archives. The author emphasizes the strong relationship between banditry, social justice, and the Mexican Revolution.

579 **El México profundo en la gran década de desesperanza (1846–1856).** Coordinación de Raymond Buve y Romana Falcón. Textos de Will Martin Fowler *et al.* México: Ediciones EyC; Puebla, Mexico: Benemérita Universidad Autónoma de Puebla, 2016. 205 p.: bibl., ill., maps.

Not since *Mexican Liberalism in the Age of Mora, 1821–1853* by Charles Hale (see *HLAS 36:2026*) has there been a collection of seven essays concerning the desperate period encompassed in the decade from 1846–56. The compilation hammers home again the lack of unifying geographical features, describing the territories as a series of nations within one. Despite the convenience of such an explanation, new analyses are contesting this vision, although not necessarily its prevalence at the time.

580 **Meyer, Jean A.** Manuel Lozada: el Tigre de Álica: general, revolucionario, rebelde. México: Tusquets Editores, 2015. 350 p.: bibl. (Tiempo de memoria)

This book represents an attempt to write a biography of Lozada in relation to certain topics: Catholicism, agriculture, indigenous peoples, wars, politics, and governing. The work serves as a guide for future biographers and scholars and those who will read their works.

581 **Mier Noriega y Guerra, José Servando Teresa de.** La revolución y la fe: una antología general. Selección y estudio preliminar de Begoña Pulido Herráez. Ensayos críticos de Cristina Gómez Álvarez, Mariana Ozuna Castañeda, y José Javier Villarreal. Cronología de Héctor Fernando Vizcarra y Begoña Pulido Herráez. México: Fondo de Cultura Económica, 2013. 545 p.: bibl., index. (Biblioteca americana. Serie Viajes al siglo XIX)

This work offers a thorough discussion of the life and thought of one of the most important theoreticians of Mexican independence, with an emphasis on politics. Although Mier launched the idea that there was a link between preconquest peoples and Christianity, its significance is not emphasized in this study. Nevertheless the book is essential for understanding the ideology of independence.

582 **Moguel Pasquel, María Carolina.** Un empresario agrícola porfirista en Morelos: el caso de Luis García Pimentel. (*Secuencia/México*, 97, enero/abril 2017, p. 170–199, bibl.)

This paper provides an in-depth look at Luis García Pimentel, who owned two haciendas producing sugar and other products before the Revolution. The study divides his life into first apprenticeship (1874–94) and when he comes into his own. The author shows that in 1919, when he returned to Mexico, he found that both of his haciendas had substantially deteriorated. Ultimately his land was given to neighboring villages.

583 **Moncada González, Gisela.** La gestión municipal: ¿cómo administrar las plazas y los mercados de la ciudad de México? 1824–1840. (*Secuencia/México*, 95, mayo/agosto 2016, p. 39–62, graphs)

This paper concentrates on the inability of Mexico City to regulate city services due to the scarcity of funds and to overlapping jurisdictional issues between the city and the central government. Believing that contracting out such services would solve the problem, the ayuntamiento only managed to create a new class of interest groups. See also item **584**.

584 **Moncada González, Gisela.** La libertad comercial: el sistema de abasto de alimentos en la ciudad de México, 1810–1835. México: Instituto Mora, 2013. 231 p.: bibl., ill., index. (Historia económica)

This study concentrates on the transition between viceregal and republican rule with regard to the food supply in Mexico City. The author looks at the ayuntamiento and the slow shift from protectionism to free trade. She also analyzes the adjustment of markets to new conditions, among other themes. Recommended.

585 **Neufeld, Stephen.** The blood contingent: the military and the making of modern Mexico, 1876–1911. Albuquerque: University of New Mexico Press, 2017. 383 p.: bibl., ill., index.

This long-awaited study focuses more on soldiers than on their commanders. The author explains both army life as the troops experienced it as well as soldiers per se as a manifestation of the nation.

586 **Nichols, James David.** The limits of liberty: mobility and the making of the Eastern U.S.-Mexico border. Lincoln: University of Nebraska Press, 2018. 287 p.: bibl., index. (Borderlands and transcultural studies)

This study shows how after 1836, runaway slaves, indigenous peoples, fugitives, immigrants, and folks on the move entered Mexico before even the northeastern border of Mexico had been drawn. An important contribution to studies of migration, particularly in that Mexico was hardly the haven they sought.

587 **Ortega González, Carlos Alberto.** El ocaso de un impuesto: el diezmo en el Arzobispado de México, 1810–1833. México: Instituto de Investigaciones Dr. José María Luis Mora: Consejo Nacional de Ciencia y Tecnología, 2015. 298 p.: bibl., ill. (Historia económica)

This important study looks at tithes in the archbishopric of Mexico from 1810–33. The collections suffered mightily during the wars of independence, partly from confusion, partly from indifferent harvests. Further complications occurred when parishes remained vacant for years. Ultimately in 1833 the tithe became voluntary, but still continued to produce revenue.

588 **Otras miradas de las revoluciones mexicanas (1810–1910).** Edición de Hilda Iparraguirre Locicero, Massimo De Giuseppe y Ana María González Luna. México: Instituto Nacional de Antropología e Historia, 2015. 426 p.: bibl., ill. (some color).

This collection includes 16 historical and literary essays addressing Mexico in 1810 and 1910, the latter mostly from a European perspective. Particularly of note are papers on the evolution of Mexico's self-perception to *historia patria* (Mestas) and Mexico and the Vatican from the Porfiriato to the revolution (Cannelli).

589 **Pablo Hammeken, Luis de.** Ópera y política en el México decimonónico: el caso de Amilcare Roncari. (*Secuencia/México*, 97, enero/abril 2017, p. 140–169, bibl.)

This fascinating study highlights the connection between the government and the arts. The imprisonment of Italian musical empresario Amilcare Roncari led to a rupture of relations between US Minister to Mexico John Forsyth and the Zuloaga government. The author notes that the government did provide substantial sums to maintain the arts, even in very troubled times. For music specialist's comment, see item **2753**.

590 **Peniche Moreno, Paola.** El cólera morbus en Yucatán: medicina y salud pública, 1833–1853. México: CIESAS Sureste: MAPorrúa, Librero-Editor, 2016. 191 p.: bibl., ill. (Colección peninsular)

This study looks at the ravages of cholera in Yucatán in 1833 and 1853, somewhat later than in the center of the country. The author puts epidemics in a political context, either between federalists and centralists or during the Caste War. She also links poverty to illness, examines the confluence between science and religion, and details the first steps toward public hygiene while urging more comparative studies. This volume belongs to a recent trend looking at the development of public health and scientific approaches following independence.

591 **Por una Iglesia libre en un mundo liberal: la obra y los tiempos de Clemente de Jesús Munguía, primer arzobispo de Michoacán (1810–1868).** Coordinación de Juan Carlos Casas García y Pablo Mijangos y González. Textos de Jorge Carlos Adame Goddard *et al.* México: Universidad Pontificia de México; Zamora, Mexico: El Colegio de Michoacán, 2014. 497 p.: bibl.

This compilation contains 17 essays divided into five parts that discuss Church-state relations in Mexico. The authors cover many distinct issues such as the rights of the clergy during Church reform, which emphasizes the difficulties of creating a laic state given Mexico's heritage. While Connaughton delves into Catholic liberalism, Pani wonders about how the conservative party morphed into a clerical one. Recommended.

592 **La prensa en el porfiriato: procesos políticos en Michoacán, diplomacia y actores sociales en México.** Coordinación de María del Rosario Rodríguez Díaz y Claudia González Gómez. Morelia, Mexico: Instituto de Investigaciones Históricas, Universidad Michoacana de San Nicolás Hidalgo, 2016. 198 p.: bibl., ill. (Encuentros; 26)

This compilation brings together eight essays covering the press during the Díaz regime. Many of the papers look at *El Imparcial*, which functioned as a prominent political organ. The authors also examine the role of *El diario del hogar*, which became a vehicle for the opposition, as well as other newspapers. See also item **603**.

593 **Prieto, Guillermo.** Los San Lunes de Fidel y El cuchicheo semanario: Guillermo Prieto en la Colonia española (enero-mayo de 1879). Edición crítica, estudio preliminar, notas e índexes de Lilia Vieyra Sánchez. Con la colaboración técnica de Carlos Alberto López Villegas y Arturo David Ríos Alejo. Presentación de Guadalupe Curiel Defosse. México: UNAM, Coordinación de Humanidades, Programa Editorial, 2015. 643 p.: bibl., index. (Al siglo XIX, ida y regreso)

Few 19th-century writers could boast of the quantity and quality of their readers as could Guillermo Prieto, often cited as the preeminent costumbrista writer in Mexico. The purpose of his writing was to reveal customs and practices that he hoped to modify or eliminate entirely. To that end, this study offers an important window into Mexican society during that time period.

594 **Quezada Torres, María Teresa.** La higienización de la ciudad de San Luis Potosí durante el siglo XIX. San Luis Potosí, Mexico: Secretaría de Cultura, Gobierno del Estado de San Luis Potosí, 2015. 199 p.: bibl., ill.

This thought-provoking study focuses on the development of urban public health in San Luis Potosí. The author looks at clean water, electric light, epidemics, burial grounds, and markets. She also looks at how changes in the capital filtered down to other states.

595 **Ramos Lara, María de la Paz.** Vicisitudes de la ingenieria en México (siglo XIX). México: UNAM, 2013. 218 p.: bibl., ill. (Ciencia y tecnología en la historia de México)

This work studies the transformation of the school of mines into the Escuela Nacional de Ingenieros, which would collapse at the end of the 19th century. The author indicates that part of the problem was the preference for foreign-trained engineers, which was hardly the case.

596 **Rangel Silva, José Alfredo.** "Para reprimir a este difamador": discursos públicos, valores y orden social en Guadalajara, México, 1885. (*HAHR*, 97:3, Aug. 2017, p. 457–484, bibl.)

This paper studies the beating of opposition journalist Wistano Luis Orozco and how the incident became known nationally as an attack on press freedom as well as on elite values. The situation pitted a society where family and connections held sway against one where personal honesty, intelligence, and hard work were more noble. The author suggests that the incident was also seen as an attack on the state.

597 **Registrar e imaginar la nación: la estadística durante la primera mitad del siglo XIX.** Vol. 1, Jalisco, Estado de México, Nuevo México, Oaxaca, Sinaloa, Sonora y Veracruz. Edición de Luis Alberto Arrioja Díaz Viruell. Zamora, Mexico: El Colegio de Michoacán; Xalapa, Mexico: Universidad Veracruzana, Dirección Editorial; Hermosillo, Mexico: El Colegio de Sonora, 2016. 1 v.: bibl., ill., indexes, maps. (Colección Investigaciones)

This work provides a powerful introduction to the importance and use of statistics in the construction of states and nation-states in the first half of the 19th century in Mexico. These six essays are essential reading for scholars seeking to understand the period. Recommended.

598 **Reina, Leticia.** Cultura política y formas de representación indígena en México, siglo XIX. México: Instituto Nacional de Antropología e Historia, 2015. 291 p.: bibl., ill., maps. (Colección Historia. Serie Logos)

This magisterial study examines indigenous peoples and political participation in 19th-century Mexico. The author stresses that the Pax Porfiriana hardly reached the rebellious countryside. Beautifully argued and important discovery. Recommended.

599 **La República errante.** Textos de Patricia Galeana *et al.* México: Secretaría de Cultura: INEHRM, Instituto Nacional de Estudios Históricos de las Revoluciones de México, 2016. 222 p.: bibl., ill., map. (Historia)

Although this portion of Mexican history (1863–67) was covered by the Discovery television channel, the period has received little scholarly attention. Here the journey receives its due despite a lamentable lack of primary sources. Among the important topics covered are Zubirán Escoto on the Republican army and Jiménez Marce on the literature of the period.

600 **Revolucionarias fueron todas.** Textos de Evelyne Sanchez *et al.* Puebla, Mexico: Benemerita Universidad Autónoma de Puebla, 2013. 214 p.: bibl., ill.

This work contributes to the study of women in the Mexican Revolution. Some topics are familiar, such as the Primer Congreso Feminista, but others, such as Gomez García's look at the effect of the Revolution on the daily lives of women, are refreshingly new.

601 **Rhi Sausi Garavito, María José** and **María del Ángel Molina A.** El mal necesario: gobierno y contribuyentes ante el dilema de las alcabalas, siglos XIX y XX. México: Universidad Autónoma Metropolitana, 2014. 208 p.: bibl., ill. (Biblioteca de ciencias sociales y humanidades. Colección Economía. Serie Estudios)

This work outlines the history of *alcabalas* from colonial times to the 20th century. Long thought of as a vestige of preindependence times, the *alcabalas* stayed in place until José Limantour, Mexico's secretary of the treasury during the Porfiriato, abolished them in 1896. The Porfirians correctly saw this move as unifying Mexico while abolition curtailed state funds.

602   **Rodríguez, María Guadalupe.** Historia social de los bancos en Durango, 1890–1907. Durango, Mexico: Instituto de Investigaciones Históricas, 2015. 203 p.: bibl., ill., maps.

This work discusses how a successful banking enterprise flourished in Durango. The study has much more of an economic focus than a social one as promised in the title.

603   **Rodríguez Díaz, María del Rosario.**
Estados Unidos y América Latina a inicios del siglo XX: una mirada desde México: El diario del hogar. Morelia, Mexico: Universidad Michoacana de San Nicolás de Hidalgo, Instituto de Investigaciones Históricas, 2016. 132 p.: bibl., ill. (Fábrica de historias; 7)

This study examines US foreign policy through the lens of a popular opposition daily, *El diario del hogar*. The author's knowledge of the US is questioned by her insistence on referring to President William Howard Taft as Howard Taft. The book would have benefited greatly from more time at the Library of Congress and including more on Taft through the end of his presidency when he met Díaz. See also item **592**.

604   **Ruiz de Gordejuela Urquijo, Jesús.**
Remesas de caudales españoles durante los primeros años del México independiente, 1821–1827. (*Rev. Complut. Hist. Am.*, 42, 2016, p. 293–317, bibl., tables)

This article offers long-awaited answers to many questions concerning the Mexican economy during the early years of independence—namely where and how much in Mexican pesos the exiled Spaniards shipped outside Mexico from 1821–23 and 1824–28. Precious metals ascended to more than 70 percent of the wealth paid by exporting cochineal. Quite a bit of Mexican silver went to Cuba, England, and Burgundy on French ships. Recommended.

605   **Saffell, Cameron L.** A reexamination of the "bloodless conquest" of Santa Fe. (*N.M. Hist. Rev.*, 91:3, Summer 2016, p. 277–308)

This study re-examines the mythology surrounding the surrender of Santa Fe to General Kearny. The author shows that New Mexico Governor Manuel Armijo probably was not bribed and that he legitimately feared the onslaught of the US army, being considerably outmanned.

606   **Salinas Sandoval, María del Carmen.**
El primer federalismo en el Estado de México, 1824–1835. Zinacantepec, Mexico: El Colegio Mexiquense, A.C., 2014. 235 p.: bibl., maps. (Publicaciones)

Taking her cues from the pioneering work of Nettie Lee Benson (but not Jaime E. Rodríguez O., who is regrettably omitted from the bibliography), the author studies the effect of the Cortes of Cádiz on Mexican federalism and how it impacted the development of the crucial state of México. She discusses the differing approaches of Melchor Múzquiz and Lorenzo de Zavala, who she sees as proposing analytical liberalism.

607   **Sánchez de la O, María de Guadalupe.**
Andamiaje del castigo: el nacimiento de la penitenciaría en Coahuila (1881–1910). Saltillo, Mexico: Quintanilla Ediciones, 2015. 290 p.: bibl., ill.

This study looks at the issue of prisons from colonial times to the beginning of the 20th century. The author concentrates on the framework of crime and punishment in Coahuila, the land of the Madero family. She discovers that rules for the penitentiary were not always followed, despite good intentions. Lamentably, a lack of English-language sources shows that the study neglects so much of the excellent work done in that language.

608   **Sánchez Hidalgo Hernández, Dora.**
La legitimidad de la reforma fiscal: autoridades tributarias y contribuyentes en el mercado de la ciudad de Veracruz, 1875–1889. (*Secuencia/México*, 96, sept./dic. 2016, p. 73–106, bibl., table)

This study delves into how a sales tax regime evolved into a system of indirect taxes in Veracruz at the end of the 19th century. Somehow the head of the ayuntamiento was able to get owners of small shops used to paying the tax and the government to collecting the taxes, a system that he implemented across the board.

Sarazúa, Juan Carlos. Política y etnicidad y servicio militar: dos experiencias paralelas en Mesoamérica: Chiapas y Guatemala, 1808–1871. See item **773**.

609 Sedano Ortega, Mauricio. Los trabajadores del Ferrocarril de Tehuantepec y la huelga "olvidada" de Rincón Antonio (1903). (*Secuencia/México*, 96, sept./dic. 2016, p. 142–166, bibl., tables)

This article discusses the railroad workers' strike in 1903 in a small town in Oaxaca. Workers resorted to strikes to demand better labor conditions, but that did not always lead to changes in the way they related to employers.

610 Soberón Sagredo, Agustín. Diario de don Agustín Soberón Sagredo (1819–1873). Introducción y edición María Isabel Monroy Castillo. Transcripción paleográfica de María Graham Soberón de Armida. San Luis Potosí, Mexico: El Colegio de San Luis: Universidad Autónoma de San Luis Potosí, 2013. 862 p.: bibl., indexes.

This work focuses on the period between 1858–73 in Matehuala, San Luis Potosí, where the author settled permanently in 1842. Excellent source for work on day-to-day issues such as water, telegraph, etc.

611 Terán Fuentes, Mariana. Bosquejo de un inmenso cuadro: liberalismo constitucional y formas de gobierno en Zacatecas, 1823–1846. Con la colaboración de Adolfo Trejo Luna. Zacatecas, Mexico: Universidad Autónoma de Zacatecas: Taberna Libraria Editores, 2015. 543 p.: bibl.

This major study, covering the period from independence to the war with the US, focuses on how centralism worked in one of the most federalist enclaves in Mexico. The book contains lists of state representatives in Zacatecas as well as timelines of political developments in the 19th century.

612 Torget, Andrew J. The Saltillo slavery debates: Mexicans, Anglo-Americans, and slavery's future in nineteenth-century North America. (*in* Linking the histories of slavery: North America and its borderlands. Edited by Bonnie Martin and James F. Brooks. Santa Fe, N.M.: School for Advanced Research Press, 2015, p. 171–196, bibl.)

This chapter provides an excellent summary of the problem of the northern Borderlands for the Mexican nation. The divisive role of slavery appeared early as Texan lobbying helped to keep slavery in Mexico. The author examines debates in the Tejas-Coahuila constitution and finds that, as a last ditch effort, the American colonists sought to use the language of debt peonage to apply to slavery.

613 Tovar y de Teresa, Rafael. De la paz al olvido: Porfirio Díaz y el final de un mundo. México: Taurus, 2016. 342 p., 32 unnumbered pages of plates: bibl., ill., portraits. (Taurus Historia)

Mexico has always struggled with the memory of historical figures whose declines have occurred in the public sphere. Add to that the virtual disappearance of the Porfiriato in Mexico City and the nostalgia was guaranteed to follow. The author demonstrates rare sympathy for a leader who outlived his time.

614 Uribe Soto, María de Lourdes. Prostitutas, rateras y pulqueras: resistencias, poder y control social durante el porfiriato en la ciudad de San Luis Potosí. Aguascalientes, Mexico: Centro de Estudios Jurídicos y Sociales Mispat; San Luis Potosí, Mexico: Maestría en Derechos Humanos de la Universidad Autónoma de San Luis Potosí, 2016. 268 p.: bibl., ill., maps, ports.

This study, based on the author's PhD dissertation, details resistance strategies employed by women of lower status in San Luis Potosí. The author brings insights from James Scott and William Sewell to bear on how the powerless resist. She also makes use of extensive source material from state archives. An ideal next step would be a comparison of San Luis Potosí to other parts of the country.

615 Valiant, Seonaid. Ornamental nationalism: archaeology and antiquities in Mexico, 1876–1911. Leiden, Netherlands: Brill, 2018. 291 p.: bibl., ill., map. (Brill's studies on art, art history, and intellectual history; 20)

This work provides an important look at how Leopoldo Batres, Mexico's first Inspector of Monuments, safeguarded Mexican treasures, although he was manifestly unequipped for the job. He was retained in his post until the end of the Porfiriato because he managed to complete the shoddy excavations of Teotihuacán in time for the independence celebrations of 1910. See also item 533.

616 **Van Young, Eric.** De una memoria truncada a una historia majestuosa: el caso de Lucas Alamán. (*Desacatos*, 50, enero/abril 2016, p. 12–27, bibl., photos)

The author uses insights found in Lucas Alamán's fixation on his family's loss of social status and wealth in an unpublished memoir written in the 1830s. He indicates that Alamán's distress with his own life led him to see Mexican history from independence to his death in 1853 as a monumental failure.

617 **Vázquez, Lourdes Celina.** Que besa su mano . . . : cartas de mujeres a religiosos franciscanos en el siglo XIX. Guadalajara, Mexico: Editorial Universitaria, Universidad de Guadalajara, 2016. 195 p.: bibl., facsims., ill., ports.

This work reviews a collection of documents kept together by Fray Leonardo Sánchez Zamarripa from a Franciscan archive in the province of Jalisco from the 18th and 19th centuries. The collection contains letters from women to friars and priests. The study provides a very important look at a segment of Mexican women.

618 **Vázquez Valenzuela, David.** Mirando atrás: los trabajadores de origen mexicano de Los Ángeles y el Partido Liberal Mexicano, 1905–1911. San Juan Mixcoac, Mexico: Instituto Mora, 2016. 289 p.: bibl., ill., index, maps. (Historia política)

Looking at how the politics in Los Angeles both repeated Mexican sensibility and differed from it, this excellent study analyzes Mexican-American support for the Partido Liberal Mexicano, the Flores Magonista party, during the Revolution. The work should spark a trend that fits Mexican-American lives together with those of families back in Mexico.

619 **Vicente Guerrero (1782–1831): primero tuve patria . . .: recopilación documental.** Presentación y compilación de David Cienfuegos Salgado. México: Instituto de Estudios Parlamentarios "Eduardo Neri," Centro Guerrerense de Estudios Interculturales, El Colegio de Guerrero, 2014. 397 p.: bibl., ill.

This study offers an intriguing look at independence and its aftermath from the perspective of the south and its people. The collection of documents included in the book concerns the assassination of President Guerrero. Hopefully the publication leads to more studies about this important leader.

620 **Vida en Puebla durante el segundo imperio mexicano: nuevas miradas.** Coordinación de Lilián Illades Aguiar. Textos de Miguel Ángel Cuenya Mateos *et al.* Puebla, Mexico: Benemérita Universidad Autónoma de Puebla, Instituto de Ciencias Sociales y Humanidades "Alfonso Vélez Pliego," Dirección de Fomento Editorial, 2017. 323 p.: bibl., ill., maps.

This collection of five essays looks at Puebla during the French Empire. Several thoughtful examinations utilize new documentation to investigate topics such as why the empire took hold (Jacinto), demography under stress (Grajales Porras), the development of manufacturing (Cuenya Mateos), and life in the countryside (Huerta Jaramillo). Recommended.

621 **Visiones históricas de la frontera: cruce de caminos: revoluciones y cambios culturales en México.** Coordinación de Jorge Chávez y Franco Savarino. Ciudad Juárez, Mexico: El Colegio de Chihuahua, 2013. 428 p.: bibl., ill. (Colección Visiones históricas de la frontera)

This collection of 15 essays about the border region addresses widely differing topics from the role of the Apache in the independence of Nuevo Vizcaya and how the Zapatistas were presented in the press in Sinaloa to the idea of revolution in the work of Felix Fulgencio Palavicini, the chronicler of the Constitutional Congress of 1916–17. See also *HLAS 68:719*.

622 **Weiner, Richard.** Antecedents to Daniel Cosío Villegas's post-revolutionary ideology: Justo Sierra's critique of Mexico's legendary wealth and Trinidad Sánchez Santos's assault on Porfirian progress. (*Mex. Stud.*, 30:1, Winter 2014, p. 71–103)

This paper analyzes two schools of thought on the economy prior to the Revolution—that of the *científicos* who debunked the notion of Mexico's natural wealth and lauded Porfirian progress and that of both liberal and conservative opponents of Díaz who questioned his development of the economy and its blatant inequality. Both threads lead to a discussion of their ultimate appearance in the work of Cosío Villegas.

REVOLUTION AND POST-REVOLUTION

623 Abdo Francis, Jorge. De las armas a los argumentos: la Soberana Convención Revolucionaria cien años después. Villahermosa, Mexico: Universidad Juárez Autónoma de Tabasco, 2014. 126 p.: bibl. (Colección Félix Fulgenio Palavicini, política y sociedad)

The Convention of Aguascalientes (October-November 1914) is most commonly known for inaugurating a political front for the ultimately unsuccessful alliance between Francisco Villa and Emiliano Zapata. The author argues that the Convention-born government achieved greater success than is commonly recognized, particularly in airing ideas and political platforms that later governments adopted. This brief but informative study will certainly interest revolutionary scholars.

624 Agua la boca: restaurantes de la Ciudad de México en el siglo XX. Introducción, selección y comentarios por Arturo Reyes Fragoso. México: Uva Tinta Ediciones, 2013. 175 p.: ill. (Colección Microhistorias mexicanas)

The author, a journalist, has assemble a variety of sources, including restaurant reviews, profiles of chefs, menus, and works of fiction, to provide a series of anecdotes about Mexico's history from the end of the Porfirian regime to the 1990s. The evolution and variety of Mexico's gastronomy is evident, as is the prevalence of restaurants in several key political events, including the assassination of Alvaro Obregón.

625 Alanís Enciso, Fernando Saúl. They should stay there: the story of Mexican migration and repatriation during the Great Depression. Translated by Russ Davidson. Chapel Hill, N.C.: The University of North Carolina Press, 2017. 246 p.: bibl., index. (Latin America in translation/en traducción/em tradução)

English edition of an important work by a leading scholar on migration history. See *HLAS 67:1574*.

626 Alanís Enciso, Fernando Saúl. Voces de la repatriación: la sociedad mexicana y la repatriación de mexicanos de Estados Unidos 1930–1933. San Luis Potosí, Mexico: El Colegio de San Luis; Tijuana, Mexico: El Colegio de la Frontera Norte; Zamora, Mexico: El Colegio de Michoacán, 2015. 387 p.: bibl., ill., index. (Colección Investigaciones)

This important volume is based on extensive research in local, state, and federal archives, including archives along the Mexican border, as well as newspapers and interviews. The author surveys the context in which the US expelled over 300,000 Mexicans during the Great Depression, and details the response in Mexico, which included attacks on immigrant communities in that country. He examines the efforts of Mexicans to assist the return migrants, explores the ambivalent attitudes that Mexicans, Mexican politicians, and the Mexican media had toward them, and outlines official efforts to provide land and assistance to the returnees.

627 Alarcón Amézquita, Saúl Armando. En la línea de fuego: Juan M. Banderas en la Revolución. Culiacán, Mexico: H. Ayuntamiento de Culiacán; Sinaloa, México: Servicios Editoriales Once Ríos, 2013. 508 p.: bibl., ill.

The Mexican Revolution rode on the backs of hundreds of leaders, some thoroughly researched and others almost completely unknown. Somewhere in the middle we find Juan M. Banderas, military and political strongman of Sinaloa. He rose with the original revolt of Francisco Madero, shifted his loyalties to Emiliano Zapata, and eventually ended up a high-ranking officer in the Constitutional army. While today his home state has acquired a reputation as a narcotics mecca, this book reminds us of its critical role in the revolutionary process. Revolutionary specialists and students of western Mexico will want to read this volume.

628 **Alexander, Ryan M.** Sons of the Mexican Revolution: Miguel Alemán and his generation. Albuquerque: University of New Mexico Press, 2016. 245 p.: bibl., index. (Diálogos series)

Historians often point to the years 1946–52 as a turning point in modern national history, a time when President Miguel Alemán moved the country to the right toward industry and private initiative. This work poses a more moderate reading of Alemán and his political associates, arguing that they did in fact attempt to follow most of the Revolution's inherited ideals, but were constrained by both international pressures and the limits of state power. This study will stir debates and reinterpretations among those interested in the formation of the post-WWII state.

629 **Arce, B. Christine.** México's nobodies: the cultural legacy of the soldadera and Afro-Mexican women. Albany: State University of New York Press, 2017. 331 p.: bibl., ill., index. (Suny series, Genders in the global South)

The author analyzes cultural forms, including music, films, poetry, and prose, in this exploration of the ubiquitous figures of the *soldadera* and the *mulata*, and of black musical styles. The first section of the book examines the trope of the *soldadera*, including explorations of the figures of Adelitas and Cucarachas. The second section engages with the African presence in Mexico's cultural imaginary, from the colonial figure of La Mulata de Córdoba to Mexican Son music and the performances of Toña la Negra.

630 **Augustine-Adams, Kif.** Women's suffrage, the anti-Chinese campaign, and gendered ideals in Sonora, Mexico, 1917–1925. (*HAHR*, 97:2, May 2017, p. 223–258)

The author examines local women's activism in the context of racism and of gender ideals that circumscribed their behavior and their political rights. She focuses on two women whose support for suffrage was eclipsed by their virulent racism, and explores the rhetoric of a Sonora newspaper that echoed their anti-Chinese sentiment, while also supporting a beauty contest that endorsed a racist and classist notion of the ideal woman.

631 **Aurrecoechea, Juan Manuel.** Imperio, revolución y caricaturas: El México bárbaro de John T. McCutcheon. México: Editorial Itaca: Secretaría de Cultura, 2016. 331 p.: bibl., ill.

McCutcheon, a political cartoonist for the *Chicago Tribune*, was a war correspondent during the US intervention of Veracruz, and interviewed Venustiano Carranza and Pancho Villa. The author of this study places McCutcheon's work firmly in the context of Manifest Destiny and American imperialism. The first section of the book provides biographical and historical context for McCutcheon's work while examining American press coverage of Mexico's revolution. The second section reproduces and analyzes the cartoons.

632 **Ávila Espinosa, Felipe Arturo** and **Pedro Salmerón Sanginés.** Historia breve de la Revolución Mexicana. México: Instituto Nacional de Estudios Históricos de las Revoluciones de México, Secretaría de Educación Pública: Siglo Veintiuno Editores, 2015. 318 p.: bibl. (Revoluciones)(Serie Clásicos)(Historia)

The authors provide their own overview of the events of 1910–20. In so doing, they pose an upward revision to challenge the previous downward revision. Put simply, the authors argue that the Revolution really did bring significant change to Mexican society, including a mobilized population, a radically overhauled state, and a sweeping agrarian reform. Grand-scale revolutionary thinkers will want to consider this brief, if compactly written, synthesis.

633 **Cabrera, Luis.** Obras políticas del Lic. Blas Urrea. México: INEHRM: Siglo Veintiuno Editores, 2015. 449 p.: bibl. (Historia)(Clásicos)

Reshuffle the letters in "Lic. Blas Urrea," and you discover Luis Cabrera, one of the key ideological architects of the Mexican Revolution. This volume brings together newspaper articles by Cabrera dating from the late Porfirian era to the final weeks of Francisco Madero's presidency, covering everything from late Porfirian political parties to Nicaraguan poet Rubén Darío. *Obras políticas* will find its most passionate readership among political scientists and intellectual historians.

634 **Castillo Ramírez, Guillermo.** El debate sobre el sufragio femenino en la prensa tapatía (1946–1955). Guadalajara, Mexico: Universidad de Guadalajara, 2013. 203 p.: bibl. (Colección del Centro de Estudios de Género; 4)

Analyzes the coverage of two main Guadalajara newspapers of the suffrage movement on the national and local levels. Including editorial coverage, as well as opinions of journalists, political parties, Church, lay groups and suffragettes who published in these papers. The author is concerned with the main arguments on both sides of the debate, as well as notions of men, women, and citizenship revealed in that debate. The author emphasizes two main Guadalajara newspapers in this study of the coverage of the suffrage movement on the local and national levels. He examines editorials, as well as the opinions of journalists, political parties, the Catholic Church, lay groups, and suffragettes, which appeared in these papers. Main arguments in the debate, as well as notions of men, women, and citizenship are analyzed.

635 **Castro, J. Justin.** Radio in revolution: wireless technology and state power in Mexico, 1897–1938. Lincoln: University of Nebraska Press, 2016. 268 p.: bibl., index. (The Mexican experience)

Those hoping to create a new society have to spread the word somehow, and in early 20th-century Mexico, radio became one of the mediums of choice. This book traces the arrival of wireless technology, its gradual penetration into military and public affairs, and its key role in the emerging one-party developmentalist state. Radio naturally speaks to anyone with an interest in the revolutionary era, but also adds to the growing literature on the history of technology in Latin America.

636 **Una concepción atlántica del americanismo: en los pasos de François Chevalier.** Edición de Véronique Hébrard. Paris: Éditions des archives contemporaines, 2013. 139 p.: bibl.

Few individuals approach the late François Chevalier's impact on the bewildering topic of landholding in New Spain. This book brings together essays exploring the diverse influence of his works. Chevalier's "men rich and powerful" may not read it, but colonialists certainly will.

637 **Covert, Lisa Pinley.** San Miguel de Allende: Mexicans, foreigners, and the making of a World Heritage Site. Lincoln: University of Nebraska Press, 2017. 289 p.: bibl., index, maps, photos. (The Mexican experience)

This well-researched study examines the evolution of a tourism economy and an influential expatriate community in San Miguel. The author examines conflict over this development model, as well as ways in which San Miguel's transformation affected ideas of local and national identity. When Mexico's national government finally embraced the town as a historic monument, it reflected a neoliberal model for Mexico's future.

638 **Díaz Ordaz, Gustavo.** El movimiento estudiantil de 1968 y la UdeG: discursos en el Consejo General Universitario de la Universidad de Guadalajara el 30 de junio de 1966 y el día 5 de septiembre de 1968. Guadalajara, Mexico: Taller Editorial, La Casa del Mago, 2011. 141 p.: bibl., ill.

This brief volume assembles the speeches given by university personnel in support of President Gustavo Díaz Ordaz and in opposition to Mexico's student movement.

639 **Empresa, empresarios e industrialización en las regiones de México, siglos XIX y XX.** Coordinación de Oliva Solís Hernández, José Óscar Ávila Juárez y Alfonso Serna Jiménez. Querétaro, Mexico: Universidad Autónoma de Querétaro, Editorial Universitaria, 2015. 303 p.: bibl. (Colección academia. Serie nodos)

This collection of eight essays focuses on industrial growth from the Porfiriato to the 1960s. A first section includes essays on Monterrey's industrial and urban growth, Guadalajara's textile industry, Baja California's tourist industry, the failed partnership between Fiat and Deisel Nacional auto companies, as well as a comparison of industrialization in Mexico and Japan. The second section offers three studies of industrial growth in Querétaro, touching upon the role of the railroad, regional differences in growth, and the efforts of a local newspaper to encourage industrial activity.

640 Estrada Saavedra, Marco. La comunidad armada rebelde y el EZLN: un estudio histórico y sociológico sobre las bases de apoyo zapatistas en las cañadas tojolabales de la Selva Lacandona (1930–2005). Segunda edición corregida y aumentada. México: El Colegio de México, 2016. 614 p.: bibl., ill., maps.

This is a revised and updated edition of the author's earlier study of the municipality of Las Margaritas (see *HLAS 66:931*). The study details the process by which the Tojolabal community was transformed by the pastoral activism of Liberation Theology and by a more explicitly political activism by leftist groups. The emergence of the EZLN guerrilla movement created conflict within the community over these two models of change. Includes a brief postscript reflecting on 20 years of the EZLN struggle.

641 Estudios y testimonios sobre el exilio español en México: una visión sobre su presencia en las humanidades. Edición de Armando Pavón Romero, Clara Inés Ramírez González y Ambrosio Velasco Gómez. México: Bonilla Artigas Editores: CONACYT, Consejo Nacional de Ciencia y Tecnología, 2016. 497 p.: bibl. (Pública memoria; 4)

This volume brings together selections from a conference commemorating 70 years of Spanish exile in Mexico. The emphasis is on exiles in the fields of the humanities and social sciences. An initial section provides historiographical commentary on the topic, as well as general commentary on the influence of Spanish exiles. The second and lengthiest section features explorations of several exiles who contributed to Mexico's intellectual life. A very brief third section, features two personal testimonies of the exile experience, a Mexican account of the last moments of José Gaos, and an account of the Ateneo Español de México, which came to house one of the largest libraries on the exile experience and the Spanish Civil War.

642 Exiliados de la guerra civil española, en México: sociedad, política y ciencia. Edición de Carmen Alicia Dávila Munguía. Morelia, Mexico: Universidad Michoacana de San Nicolás de Hidalgo, Instituto de Investigaciones Históricas, 2015. 200 p.: bibl., ill. (Encuentros; 19)

Historians from Mexico, Spain, and Cuba contributed to this volume of essays commemorating the Spanish exile. Topics include expatriate youth in Morelia, the exile of a Spanish military leader, and the story of a socialist historian displaced first from Spain and then from the Dominican Republic. Several additional selections underscore the importance of Spaniards who contributed to Mexico's intellectual life, including Spanish scholars who came to work at the Universidad Michoacana, legal experts who were incorporated into Mexico's national law school, and Spanish scientists.

643 Fernández Aceves, María Teresa. Mujeres en el cambio social en el siglo XX mexicano. México: CIESAS: Siglo Veintiuno Editores, 2014. 348 p.: bibl., ill. (Sociología y política)

The authors intend a "postrevisionist" cultural history that details the lives and activities of five women in the context of the Mexican Revolution, postrevolutionary state-building, and its aftermath. The women (four from Jalisco and one from Spain) were active in different factions of the revolution, in the anticlerical movement, and in the labor and campesino movements. Their lives underscore the gendered nature of revolutionary social change, and illustrate the role of women in the construction of new notions of citizenship and power.

García, Jerry. Looking like the enemy: Japanese Mexicans, the Mexican state, and US hegemony, 1897–1945. See *HLAS 73:1490*.

644 González y González, Luis. Luis González y González: independencia y revolución. Selección y prólogo de Álvaro Ochoa Serrano. México: El Colegio de México, 2013. 473 p.: bibl. (Antologías)

Even more than the title suggests, *Independencia y revolución* is really two different books stitched together: two studies by the late Luis González y González. Each work is informed by an extensive knowledge of Mexican history and accented by the author's deep ties to his home state of Michoacán. The breadth of the work makes it read like a synthesis of national history with a century missing somewhere in the middle.

645 **Gutiérrez Quintanilla, Lya.** Zapata: voces y testimonios. Cuernavaca, Mexico: Secretaría de Información y Comunicación, Gobierno del Estado de Morelos, 2014. 314 p.: ill.

The agrarian revolution of Emiliano Zapata remains the biggest thing that ever happened in the state of Morelos, and shows no sign of lessening its grip on the country's historical imagination. Zapata presents an anthology of memories and commentaries drawn from (quite old) former Zapatista combatants, their grandchildren, historians, and contemporary Morelos political figures. Their statements provide interesting, if necessarily heterogeneous, perspectives on a revolution that lost the battle but nevertheless won the war for restored agrarian rights. The Zapatista hard-core will flock to this volume, but scholars of the broader sweep of revolutionary history will enjoy it as well.

646 **Los hados de febrero: visiones artísticas de la Decena Trágica.** Edición de Rafael Olea Franco. México: El Colegio de México, 2015. 436 p.: ill. (Serie Literature mexicana; XVI)

The 10-day overthrow of President Francisco Madero in February 1913 will likely haunt Mexico for many years to come, and continues to generate intensive scholarship. *Los hados* brings together a surprising collection of essays regarding the literary, photographic, and cinematic treatment of the Ten Tragic Days. Mexican revolutionary scholars and cultural historians will appreciate the depth that these essays add to our understanding of that terrible moment.

647 **Heatherton, Christina.** University of radicalism: Ricardo Flores Magón and Leavenworth Penitentiary. (*Am. Q.*, 66:3, Sept. 2014, p. 557–581, bibl., ill., photos)

This study examines the Kansas jail as a meeting and education space for radicals who were held under the Espionage Act. As one of the prison's international inmates, Flores Magón contributed to the prison newspaper, taught in the prison's night school, and earned the trust of his fellow radicals before his suspicious death. The author also emphasizes the role of José Martínez, an immigrant from Chihuahua who served in the US military during WWI.

648 **Hernández Galindo, Sergio.** La guerra contra los japoneses en México durante la Segunda Guerra Mundial: Kiso Tsuro y Masao Imuro, migrantes vigilados. México: Itaca, 2011. 158 p.: bibl., ill.

This fascinating study examines the efforts of the US and Japan to monitor and control Japanese immigrants in Mexico as part of the war effort. The author focuses on two first-generation immigrants: one a naturalized Mexican with significant wealth and important connections that enabled him to evade detention; the other more recently arrived and of a more modest background, who spent much of the war in detention. Based on research in declassified documents from all three countries, as well as interviews with Mexico's Japanese community, including Masao Imuro and the children of Kiso Tsuro.

649 **Iber, Patrick.** The Cold War politics of literature and the Centro Mexicano de Escritores. (*J. Lat. Am. Stud.*, 48:2, May 2016, p. 247–272)

This article examines a writing center, established in 1951, and funded by the Rockefeller Foundation and the CIA. Although the Center trained a host of important postwar Mexican writers, including Juan Rulfo, Carlos Fuentes, Elena Poniatowska, and Rosario Castellanos, it did not succeed in advancing the political goals of the US.

650 **Inclán Fuentes, Carlos.** Perote y los nazis: las políticas de control y vigilancia del estado mexicano a los ciudadanos alemanes durante la Segunda Guerra Mundial (1939–1946). México: UNAM; Xalapa, Mexico: Gobierno del Estado de Veracruz, 2013. 249 p.: bibl., ill. (Colección La pluralidad cultural en México; 34)

Anyone who has made an historical pilgrimage into the interior of the state of Veracruz knows the solitary fortress of Perote, constructed by Spain as an armory in the waning days of its Empire. Since that time, Perote has held a wide number of criminals and political dissidents. Here we read of how the Mexican government used the place to incarcerate Nazi spies and sympathizers, along with a number of political troublemakers that it wanted to silence. Here they did hard time indeed, although the author rightly reminds us that Mexico's internment numbers pale beside those of the wartime US. The book offers a valuable addition to the growing body of work on Mexico's experiences in WWII.

651 **Izquierdo, Isabel.** Los científicos de la ex URSS inmigrantes en México: ¿quién soy yo, después de todo? México: Bonilla Artigas Editores, 2015. 181 p.: bibl. (Pùblica memoria; 3)

The author is interested in the subjective identity of scientists who came to Mexico in the 1990s as part of a program that placed them in two public universities. She emphasizes the socialization of two generations of Soviet scientists, how they experienced immigration, and how they came to understand their role as scientists in Mexico. This study incorporates interviews with the scientists themselves, as well as their Mexican counterparts

652 **Jiménez Marce, Rogelio.** "Atender las necesidades del vecindario": las políticas de la Junta de Administración Civil de Jalapa para evitar la carestía y la especulación de alimentos, 1914–1917. (*Secuencia/ México*, 89, mayo/agosto 2014, p. 85–117, bibl.)

This study examines the effect of the Mexican Revolution on the civilian population by exploring the steps taken by local officials in Jalapa, Veracruz, to prevent food shortages. Acting in concert with state officials and with merchants to lessen increases in the price of foodstuffs, the Jalapa council moderated the impact of wartime shortages.

653 **Kang, S. Deborah.** The INS on the line: making immigration law on the US-Mexico border, 1917–1954. Oxford, UK: Oxford University Press, 2017. 282 p.: bibl., index.

This extensively researched study demonstrates the extent to which the INS and the Border Patrol have been instrumental in creating immigration regulations and shaping national immigration policy. The author traces this dynamic from the agricultural labor program of the WWI era through the Bracero Program and Operation Wetback. Mid-level INS officials on the border, as well as members of the Border Patrol, held complex and often contradictory views of the border, working to secure the line while at the same time facilitating a transnational economy and society. An important history with implications for current thinking about immigration and the border.

654 **Kiddle, Amelia M.** Mexico's relations with Latin America during the Cárdenas era. Albuquerque: University of New Mexico Press, 2016. 307 p.: bibl., index.

The years of President Lázaro Cárdenas (1934–40) saw Mexico at the high tide of revolutionary changes, including advances in land reform, labor rights, and national sovereignty. Amelia Kiddle demonstrates that while a handful of conservative Latin American quarters found these changes deeply unsettling, most other Spanish- and Portuguese-speaking nations saw Mexico as the "lighthouse of America." This book explores multiple dimensions of Mexico's role as regional leader in the Depression years, and will find a place on the desks of those seeking to understand the still-controversial Cárdenas presidency.

655 **Kosack, Edward** and **Zachary Ward.** Who crossed the border?: self-selection of Mexican migrants in the early twentieth century. (*J. Econ. Hist.*, 74:4, Dec. 2014, p. 1015–1044, bibl., graphs, map, tables)

The authors examine border crossing manifests and US and Mexican census records to glean information about the quality of migrants and the effect of their migration on Mexico and the US. They focus on the recorded height of migrants during the 1920s, showing that taller laborers tended to leave for work in the US, and speculating on the implications of this.

656 **Lear, John.** Picturing the proletariat: artists and labor in revolutionary Mexico, 1908/1940. Austin: University of Texas Press, 2017. 366 p.: bibl., ill. (Joe R. and Teresa Lozano long series in Latin American and Latino art and culture)

This intriguing study examines the close relationship between artists and organized labor from the eve of the Mexican Revolution to the shift away from the radicalism of the 1930s. The author analyzes the ways in which workers were represented in murals, prints, and photographs, and he includes a consideration of lesser-known artists. He also emphasizes the role of gender in artistic depictions of workers.

657 **Lenti, Joseph U.** Redeeming the revolution: the state and organized labor in post-Tlatelolco Mexico. Lincoln: University of Nebraska Press, 2017. 355 p.: bibl., index, photos. (The Mexican experience)

This study explores the link between the Tlatelolco massacre and renewed government efforts to ally with organized labor, thus redeeming its revolutionary credentials. The author describes union opposition to the student movement and Luis Echeverría's efforts through specific economic policies to reassert the government-worker relationship. These efforts culminated in the New Federal Labor Law of 1970. Despite organized labor's tendency to embrace collaboration with the government, however, female unionists and electrical workers revealed a gap between the regime's rhetoric of worker democracy and the reality of a tightly controlled labor movement.

658 **Lewis, Stephen E.** Rethinking Mexican indigenismo: the INI's Coordinating Center in highland Chiapas and the fate of a utopian project. Albuquerque: University of New Mexico Press, 2018. 343 p.: bibl., index.

This excellent study explores the work of the Instituto Nacional Indigenista (INI)'s first center, created in 1951. The author emphasizes the innovative nature of the center's efforts, which sought to transform indigenous lives, and he analyzes the difficulties faced by reformers. Architects of indigenismo faced significant problems on the ground, and by the 1970s, their initiatives were criticized by many, including the indigenous peoples themselves.

659 **Lisbona, Miguel.** Allí donde lleguen las olas del mar . . . : pasado y presente de los chinos en Chiapas. Chiapas, Mexico: CONACULTA, 2014. 284 p.: bibl., ill.

The author focuses on the Chinese in the province of Soconusco, with an emphasis on the first half of the 20th century. The first part of the study examines the contemporary presence of the Chinese, the complexities of their self-identification, and the contributions of Chinese food and the dragon dance to local culture. A second section is more historical, tracing the origins of the Chinese presence, challenges to that presence, and examples of Chinese associations, including a local branch of the Kuomintang.

660 **Lomnitz-Adler, Claudio.** The return of comrade Ricardo Flores Magón. Brooklyn, N.Y.: Zone Books, 2014. 594 p.: bibl., index.

The author's encyclopedic narrative reconstructs not only the life and career of life-long revolutionary Ricardo Flores Magón, but also reconstructs the network of US sympathizers who helped him and his fellow anarchists to wage their struggles: initially against the dictatorship of Porfirio Díaz, and later against the emerging revolutionary state. Readers learn how Flores Magón's Liberal Party rose to prominence, but also witness its painful defeat and decline, a fate symbolized above all by its intransigent leader's death in Leavenworth Prison. This book joins the prestigious list of monumental biographies of the Mexican revolutionary period.

661 **Loza, Mireya.** Defiant braceros: how migrant workers fought for racial, sexual, and political freedom. Chapel Hill: The University of North Carolina Press, 2016. 237 p.: bibl., index. (The David J. Weber series in the new borderlands history)

The author has played a key role in capturing oral histories from both sides of the border. She utilizes these histories to reveal the complexities of the bracero experience, with a particular emphasis on indigenous migrants, braceros who did not fit the family-oriented, heteronormative ideal, and workers who challenged their condition through political organizing. The study includes examinations of the activism of the National Alliance of Mexican Braceros, and Bracero Justice Movement.

662 **Luna Sánchez, Patricia.** Gestión empresarial de las haciendas del Altiplano potosino 1899–1941: capital intelectual estructural. San Luis Potosí, Mexico: El Colegio de San Luis: Archivo Histórico del Estado de San Luis Potosí; Santiago de Querétaro, Mexico: Universidad Autónoma de Querétaro, 2015. 508 p.: bibl., ill., maps. (Colección investigaciones)

This is an excellent study of how entrepreneurs in western San Luis Potosí successfully responded to changing situations in Mexico, particularly the Mexican Revolution and subsequent agrarian reforms. The author has done extensive research in local and national archives, in private and commercial correspondence, and through interviews with descendants of entrepreneurs. She focuses on four businessmen, demonstrating the importance of their knowledge and experience ("human intellectual capital") in adapting to changing circumstances.

663 **Márquez Morfín, Lourdes.** La sífilis y su carácter endémico en la ciudad de México. (*Hist. Mex./México*, 64:3, enero/marzo 2015, p. 1099–1161, bibl., tables)

Utilizing an interesting array of sources including studies of skeletons from different social groups, the author explores the prevalence of syphilis in the capital city during the 19th century. She provides the social and demographic context for the historical emergence of syphilis in Mexico, discusses treatments and public health efforts to combat the disease in the 19th century, and emphasizes soldiers and prostitutes as particularly identified with the spread of syphilis. Evidence reveals that syphilis touched all social and ethnic groups.

664 **Máximo Castillo and the Mexican Revolution.** Edited by Jesús Vargas Valdés. Translated by Ana-Isabel Aliaga-Buchenau. Baton Rouge: Louisiana State University Press, 2016. 202 p.: index, map, photos.

Máximo Castillo fought under the revolutionary banners of new fewer than three major leaders—Francisco Madero, Pascual Orozco, and finally as an independent loosely allied with Emiliano Zapata—but his career ended in 1914 when he was captured and sent into what turned out to be a permanent exile. This long-forgotten personal memoir takes us into the confidence of a man who saw those momentous early years first-hand, and who lived tell his own version of events. A historical piece, to be certain, but also one of surprising literary merit.

665 **Memoria histórica del 68 en México: antología.** Edición de Alcira Soler Durán. Cuernavaca, Mexico: Universidad Autónoma del Estado de Morelos, 2014. 304 p.: bibl., ill.

This volume brings together nine previously published commentaries in commemoration of the 50th anniversary of the student movement. Authors reflect on the precursors, global context, evolution, and significance of the movement. Includes the words of some who participated directly in the events of 1968.

666 **Mendiola García, Sandra C.** Street democracy: vendors, violence, and public space in late twentieth-century Mexico. Lincoln: University of Nebraska Press, 2017. 271 p.: bibl., index, photos. (The Mexican experience)

The author focuses on the vendors of Puebla, and on the independent Union of Street Vendors. From the 1970s through the 1990s, vendors and local university students united in resisting an increasingly neoliberal state that was determined to suppress union activity, and supportive of "urban renewal" efforts that removed vendors from public spaces. The study details vendor tactics for asserting their rights, and state violence against such activism.

667 **México en los setenta: ¿guerra sucia o terrorismo de estado?: hacia una política de la memoria.** Edición de Claudia E.G. Rangel Lozano y Evangelina Sánchez Serrano. Chilpancingo, Mexico: Universidad Autónoma de Guerrero; México: Editorial Itaca, 2015. 297 p.: bibl., charts.

The 1960s and 1970s witnessed a series of rural guerrilla insurgencies; while in no way resembling the revolutions imagined by Karl Marx, they fired the popular imagination and brought on a state repression of frightful proportions. These days the wars have ended, but the interpretations have not. The essays of this book explore various aspects of the Genaro Vázquez and Lucio Cabañas movements, both of which ended in death and failure. The works included here be of value for those interested in recent Latin American history, or in gauging the limits of state tolerance for dissent.

668 **1914: definiendo el rumbo de una nación.** Edición de María Cristina Rodríguez Pérez. México: Centenar100 Toma de Zacatecas, 1914–2014: Asociación de Historiadores A.C. Elías Amador: CONACULTA: IZC, Instituto Zacatecas de Cultura, 2014. 171 p.: bibl.

Francisco Villa's defeat of the federal army at Zacatecas in June 1914 marked a watershed moment in Mexican history, the last stand of the old Porfirian security forces and the beginning of a bloody duel between rival revolutionary armies. The seven essays of this brief volume explore such diverse perspectives as the battle's military aspects, its effect on the Zacatecas urban population, and its role as inspiration for later film and literature. A multidisciplinary work on a moment that changed the nation forever.

669 Mills, Bill. Treacherous passage: Germany's secret plot against the United States in Mexico during World War I. Lincoln: Potomac Books, an imprint of the University of Nebraska Press, 2016. 226 p.: bibl., index, photos.

As if military carnage and frequent changes of government were not enough, Mexicans of the 1910s had to contend with the international espionage spun out of WWI. This books recounts German schemes to disrupt American shipping and supply U-boats off Mexico's west coast. Most of these plans came to naught, but they give some idea of the unpredictable nature of the times, and of the dogged resourcefulness of both German and US intelligence. *Treacherous Passages* will principally appeal to scholars interested in the Mexican Revolution's international dimensions, but its rollicking narrative of agents and double-agents recommend it to the general reader as well.

670 Mitchell, Stephanie Evaline. Revolutionary feminism, revolutionary politics: suffrage under Cardenismo. (*Americas/Washington*, 72:3, July 2015, p. 439–468, tables)

This study explores the 1937 electoral campaign of María del Rufigio García, co-founder of Mexico's Communist Party and secretary general of Frente Único Pro-Derechos de la Mujer. The unsuccessful campaign revealed both the Frente's determination to confront President Lázaro Cárdenas on the issue of women's citizenship, and the ongoing political struggles that led Cárdenas to retreat from his support of suffrage.

671 Montes de Oca Navas, Elvia. La educación socialista en México, 1934–1940: discursos y textos escolares. Toluca, Mexico: Instituto Mexiquense de Cultura, 2014. 139 p.: bibl. (Colección Documentos y testimonios)

This brief volume utilizes history and reading textbooks issued by the Secretary of Public Education to examine the nature of elementary education during the presidency of Lázaro Cárdenas. The author surveys the context in which socialist education developed, and discusses the form that it took. Subsequent chapters provide a general look at the content of the official textbooks with reference to earlier texts and to the new precepts of socialist education.

672 Padilla Ramos, Raquel. Los irredentos parias: los yaquis, Madero y Pino Suárez en las elecciones de Yucatán, 1911. México: Instituto Nacional de Antropología e Historia, 2011. 211 p.: bibl., ill., maps. (Colección Historia. Serie Logos)

The relocation of rebellious Yaqui Indians from their Sonoran homeland to the gulag of the Yucatecan henequen haciendas formed a key irritant in the toxic atmosphere of late Porfirian Mexico. This brief but illuminating volume takes us through their lives as unwilling workers on the peninsula's haciendas, as combatants in early revolutionary uprisings, and above all as fodder for the political controversies of the day. *Irredentos parias* will find a place among scholars of the southeast, but also speaks to the larger question of how a seemingly ironclad dictatorship degenerated into sheer mayhem.

673 Pensado, Jaime M. El Movimiento Estudiantil Profesional (MEP): una mirada a la radicalización de la juventud católica mexicana durante la Guerra Fría. (*Mex. Stud.*, 31:1, Winter 2015, p. 156–192)

The author is concerned with the evolution of a Catholic student movement, established in the 1940s with a decidedly anticommunist bent. In the context of postwar developments, including the struggle for university autonomy, labor struggles, Cold War interventionism, decolonization, Vatican II, and the counterculture, the MEP became more progressive, even radical, in its outlook.

674 Plana, Manuel. Venustiano Carranza (1914–1916): el proceso revolucionario en México ante la disolución de las instituciones. México: El Colegio de México; Saltillo, Mexico: Centro Cultural Vito Alessio Robles, 2016. 421 p.: bibl., index. (Jornadas; 170)

Venustiano Carranza was the kind of man that other men dislike: obstinate, calculating, and too successful for his own good. But he nevertheless managed to usher Mexico out of the chaos of 1914 and toward the beginnings of its current political order. This book reviews his major challenges and triumphs, and will attract the attention of those trying to understand how states recover from their own ashes. For comment on *Venustiano Carranza, 1911–1914*, see *HLAS 68:990*.

675 **Política y sociedad en el exilio republicano español.** Edición de Mari Carmen Serra Puche, José Francisco Mejía Flores, y Carlos Sola Ayape. México: UNAM, Centro de Investigaciones sobre América Latina y el Caribe, 2015. 293 p.: bibl. (Colección exilio iberoamericano; 2)

The selections in this volume focus primarily on the political and diplomatic responses to the Spanish Civil War and to the issue of Spanish exiles in the Americas. Most selections have Mexico as the main point of reference. Topics include Mexico's policy toward the Second Republic and toward the republican government in exile, Mexico-Cuban diplomatic relations in the context of the Spanish Civil War, communist refugees in 1940s Mexico, and the impact of Spanish jurists in Mexico. Several essays go beyond Mexico to examine the experiences of individual exiles, as well as groups of exiled Spaniards (including Basques and Galicians) in Latin America and the Caribbean. Concluding chapters analyze aspects related to the return of exiles to Spain.

676 **Problemas del desarrollo económico en el occidente de México: los recursos y sus usos en una perspectiva de largo plazo, siglos XIX y XX.** Coordinación de José Alfredo Pureco Ornelas. México: Instituto de Investigaciones Dr. José María Luis Mora: Consejo Nacional de Ciencia y Tecnología, 2015. 276 p.: bibl., ill., index, maps. (Historia económica)

In this collection, historians, rural studies specialists, and social anthropologists emphasize the natural, human, and financial resources that have shaped economic development in three states. Essays on Jalisco examine rural social stability during the Porfiriato, a 19th-century project to drain Magdalena Lake, the migration of sugar workers during the Bracero era, and the emergence of an informal tequila sector in the context of contemporary globalization. Studies on Michoacán examine land use among *hacendados* during the 19th century, the evolution of public financing in the aftermath of the revolution, and the development of irrigation works from the 1920s to 2001. A single selection on Sinaloa explores the commercial development of Culiacán and Mazatlán.

677 **Pulido Esteva, Diego.** ¡A su salud!: sociabilidades, libaciones y prácticas populares en la ciudad de México a principios del siglo XX. México: El Colegio de México, 2014. 226 p.: bibl.

This interesting study examines drinking culture and state attempts to regulate it from the late Porfirian era through the 1920s. The author provides an overview of the city's drinking establishments and their customers, analyzes the relationship between city authorities and such establishments, and examines elite discourse on drinking and alcoholism. He also emphasizes the persistence of a popular culture that embraced the sociability of drinking, particularly among men. This masculine sociability resisted attempts at state regulation and reform.

678 **Raíces en otra tierra: el legado de Adolfo Sánchez Vázquez.** Compilación de Gustavo Leyva Martínez *et al*. México: Universidad Autónoma Metropolitana, Unidad Iztapalapa: Ediciones Era, 2013. 203 p.: bibl.

In 1939, man of letters Adolfo Sánchez Vázquez came to Mexico fleeing the dictatorship of Francisco Franco. The essays of this book explore Sánchez's impact on generations of humanities students via his essays and his teaching at UNAM. *Raíces* provides important perspectives on the cultural and educational climate of Mexico during the boom years of the 1950s and 1960s, and reminds us of the immense contribution made by exiles from the fallen Spanish Republic.

679 Ramos Aguirre, Francisco. Revolucionarios a la carta. Ciudad Victoria, Mexico: Glera Editorial, 2012. 95 p.

The author has assembled anecdotes, testimonies, and recipes in this brief attempt to recount the eating habits of elites and the popular classes alike in the context of the Mexican Revolution.

680 La revolución de las mujeres en México. México: SEP, Secretaría de Educación Pública: INEHRM, Instituto Nacional de Estudios Históricos de las Revoluciones de México, 2014. 182 p.: bibl., ill.

This brief volume brings together seven essays to commemorate the achievement of women's suffrage in Mexico. The authors include historians, and specialists in law, political science, sociology, and literature. Selections survey the national and international context of the suffrage movement, highlight the work of key figures such as Hermila Galindo, trace the steps taken toward suffrage, and analyze the political rights of Mexican women in a contemporary context.

681 La Revolución en Zacatecas y la Batalla de 1914: a través de documentos inéditos del Archivo Histórico del Estado de Zacatecas (agosto de 1910-octubre de 1915). Edición de Oliverio Sarmiento Pacheco. Zacatecas, Mexico: CONACULTA: IZC, Instituto Zacatecano de Cultura, 2014. 390 p.: bibl.

This volume offers researchers an impressive collection of transcribed original documents dealing with the 1914 battle of Zacatecas, in which Pancho Villa decisively destroyed the federal army, and with it, any hopes of restoring the Porfirian order. Because most of these documents are federal army papers, they tend to present the loser's side of the contest, but discerning historians can read beyond the face value of the words. Sarmiento's collection will appeal to anyone studying the military history of the Mexican Revolution.

682 Rivera Mir, Sebastián. "Latin American news agency should be formed . . .": las agencias de noticias internacionales en el México posrevolucionario, 1920-1934. (Secuencia/México, 92, mayo-agosto 2015, p. 167-192, bibl.)

The author is interested in the strategies deployed by the Mexican government to control news and information coming out of Mexico, and to counter negative propaganda about the Mexican Revolution. Central to these efforts was state support of specific foreign news agencies.

683 Salmerón Sanginés, Pedro. 1915: México en guerra. México: Editorial Planeta Mexicana, 2015. 350 p.: bibl., ill., maps.

As the title suggests, 1915 presents a comprehensive reexamination of what may well have been the critical year of the Mexican Revolution, the moment that sorted victors from vanquished and policy directions from the ideological roads not taken. The book leans more toward the military side of events, but its implications are broad. Salmerón argues that foreign intervention ultimately played a minor role in the actual outcome of events; that Francisco Villa had little option except to throw himself into the catastrophic battle of Celeya; and that the defeated popular forces advanced a far more coherent and comprehensive national vision than is often supposed. This is a major work in terms of studies of the critical (and bloody) decade of 1910-20.

684 Sánchez Andrés, Agustín and Fabián Herrera León. Contra todo y contra todos: la diplomacia mexicana y la cuestión española en la Sociedad de Naciones, 1936-1939. Santa Cruz de Tenerife, Spain: Idea, 2011. 420 p.: bibl., index.

What emerges from this important study is a picture of a Mexico that was, from the start, a leading voice against outside aggression in Spain and elsewhere. After surveying the process by which Mexico was finally accepted into the League of Nations, the authors analyze the expression of Mexican diplomacy within the League, quoting extensively from Mexican diplomats, including Narciso Bassols and Isidro Fabela. Mexico played a major role not only in supporting the Spanish Republic, but also in calling attention to the League's inability to support the policy of nonintervention.

685 Sánchez Tagle, Héctor. El liberalismo en su laberinto: la revolución mexicana en Zacatecas, 1910-1917. Zacatecas, Mexico: Instituto Zacatecano de Cultura "Ramón López Velarde", 2015. 479 p.: bibl.

Drawing largely on newspapers and the Secretary of Defense archives, Sánchez Tagle reconstructs the political and military currents that swept over the state between the uprising of Francisco Madero and the coming triumph of the Constitutionalist order. Throughout, the author argues that the nation's self-proclaimed revolutionaries were really nothing more than updated 19th-century liberals. *El laberinto* presents a history that is at once national and intensely regional.

686 **Sesenta años de lucha por el sufragio femenino en México, 1953–2013.** Edición de María del Rocío García Olmedo. Puebla, Mexico: Benemérita Universidad Autónoma de Puebla, Dirección de Fomento Editorial, 2014. 412 p.: bibl.

This commemorative volume brings together essays on the antecedents of suffrage, and on the actual campaign to achieve it. Authors in the first section examine the role of Hermila Galindo, survey initiatives in the Yucatán, highlight the work of female journalists, and detail regional activism in Sinaloa, Puebla, and Tabasco, all in the context of the Mexican Revolution. The second section explores process of obtaining the vote and the right to run for office on the national level, and includes essays on regional experiences in Puebla, Coahuila, Guanajuato, Tlaxcala, and Hidalgo.

687 **Sheppard, Randal.** Mexico goes to Disney World: recognizing and representing Mexico at EPCOT Center's Mexico pavilion. (*LARR*, 51:3, 2016, p. 64–84, bibl.)

The author examines the process by which the Mexican pavilion, opened in 1982 as a permanent exhibit, was created. The pavilion combined touristic images promoted by Mexico's own postrevolutionary regime. At the same time, Disney looked to Mexican-American artists from East Los Angeles to give authenticity to the display. These artists, tied to the Goez Art Gallery and Studio, were part of a burgeoning Chicano cultural movement, and themselves looked to images promoted by the Mexican state in their search for identity.

688 **Simposio Bienal de Historia Naval en México, 1st, Veracruz, Mexico; Distrito Federal, Mexico, 2014.** La invasión a Veracruz de 1914: enfoques multidisciplinarios. Compilación de Guillermo Alejandro Carvallo Torres, Leticia Rivera Cabrieles y Marisol Fernández Pavón. México: Secretaría de Marina-Armada de México, 2015. 645 p.: bibl., ill., maps.

The US occupation of the port of Veracruz in 1914 remains one of the most well known and consequential foreign military interventions in modern Latin American history. The 21 essays of this volume shed considerable light on the event, its background, and its consequences. *Invasión de Veracruz* has much to offer to anyone seeking to understand one of the most critical events of Mexico's watershed year of 1914.

689 **Smith, Stephanie J.** The power and politics of art in postrevolutionary Mexico. Chapel Hill: University of North Carolina Press, 2017. 275 p.: bibl., index.

This is an extensively researched account of the relationship between artists (including muralists and printmakers) and Mexico's Communist Party, and between artists and the Mexican state from the 1920s to the 1940s. The author also emphasizes the influence of female artists, including Tina Modotti, Aurora Reyes, and the importance of transnational influences in shaping Mexico's cultural and political response to international fascism.

690 **Sola Ayape, Carlos.** El tlatoani de Caparroso: José López-Portillo, México y España. México: Editorial Fontamara, 2015. 301 p.: bibl., ill., map. (Argumentos; 266)

Mexicans will come to an understanding on controversial President José López Portillo about the time that people in the US reach agreement on Richard Nixon. This volume explores how the often grandiose "Jolopo" made a pilgrimage to his ancestral home in Caparroso, Spain, and in the process reestablished diplomatic ties with Spain, acrimoniously severed since the days of the Civil War. *El tlatoani* combines modern presidential and diplomatic history.

691 **Sosenski, Susana.** Educación económica para la infancia: el ahorro escolar en México (1925–1945). (*Hist. Mex./México*, 64:2, oct./dic. 2014, p. 645–711)

The author examines a program created by the Secretary of Education to encourage the habit of saving money and using banks among schoolchildren and their families. She explores both the development and functioning of the program, and the response of children, parents, teachers, and school officials to this initiative. In the end, this government program of financial and "moral" education was circumscribed by the needs and demands of those affected by it.

692   **Tiempos de zozobra: miradas, rostros y latitudes de la revolución en Zacatecas.** Edición de Xochitl del Carmen Marentes Esquivel y Limonar Soto Salazar. Zacatecas, Mexico: Instituto Zacatecano de Cultura "Ramón López Velarde", 2015. 232 p.: bibl.

This collection of 10 essays explores a broad gamut of themes, all relating to the experiences of Zacatecas—both city and state—during the 10 years of the Mexican Revolution. In addition to the more familiar political and economic perspectives, *Tiempos de zozobra* includes cultural explorations, including an expected reconstruction of how two leading musicians experienced the conflicts. Regional, but rewarding at a larger level as well.

693   **Tirado Villegas, Gloria.** El movimiento estudiantil de 1961: en la memoria histórica de la Universidad Autónoma de Puebla. Puebla, Mexico: Benemérita Universidad Autónoma de Puebla, Dirección de Fomento Editorial, 2012. 187 p.: bibl., ill.

The author provides a detailed account of the student movement that pitted liberal students inspired by the Cuban Revolution against more conservative elements in the university, Catholic Church, and local government. In the end, a more secular and self-governing version of the university prevailed.

694   **Trujillo Bolio, Mario A.** La manufactura de hilados y tejidos en la historiografía mexicana, siglos XVIII y XIX: obrajes, protoindustrias, empresariado y fábricas textiles. (*Secuencia/México*, 97, enero/abril 2017, p. 30–60, bibl.)

This useful survey of scholarship highlights both seminal works on Mexico's textile industry, as well as trends in the study of this topic from the latter 20th century to the present. The author's analysis is built around four themes: the debate over whether colonial *obrajes* were a form of proto-industrialization, the process by which mechanization transformed textile manufacturing during the 19th century, regional studies of the textile industry, and textile entrepreneurs.

695   **Trujillo Holguín, Jesús Adolfo.** La educación socialista en Chihuahua 1934–1940: una mirada desde la Escuela Normal del Estado. Chihuahua, Mexico: Universidad Autónoma de Chihuahua, 2015. 212 p.: bibl., ill. (Textos universitarios; 112)

This well-researched study examines the development and deployment of socialist education through the state's Escuela Normal. The author explains the process by which socialist education was adopted, and details the role of student groups, cultural brigades, and cultural programs in diffusing it. He profiles the main figures involved in spreading the national educational project, and concludes with a consideration of the decline of socialist education after 1936.

696   **Trujillo Muñoz, Gabriel.** Años de lucha, años de guerra: la identidad bajacaliforniana en tiempos de cambio, 1933–1953. Tijuana, Mexico: Consejo Nacional para la Cultura y las Artes, 2015. 191 p.: bibl. (Divulgación cultural)

Baja California's unique position—far away from Mexico City and directly adjacent to the dynamism of California state—have made it somewhat atypical relative to older and more densely populated parts of the republic. This book explores Baja's transition from territory to state, together with the closely linked process of incorporation into national lines of authority. *Años de lucha* fills an important space in our understanding of Mexico's northern border region.

697   **Urías Horcasitas, Beatriz.** Un mundo en ruínas: los intelectuales hispanófilos ante la revolución mexicana, 1920–1945. (*Iberoamericana/Madrid*, 50, June 2013, p. 147–160, bibl.)

This is a brief examination of the conservative critique of the Revolution by a group of conservative intellectuals. The author focuses on lay (as opposed to Catholic) conservatives. These intellectuals, including Miguel Alessio Robles and José Vasconcelos, warned of the danger of the democratizing tendency of the Revolution, and embraced a concept of *mestizaje* with Creole culture at its center.

698   Valles Salas, Beatriz Elena and Beatriz Corral Raigosa. La presencia femenina en el Instituto Juárez, 1872–1957. Durango, Mexico: Universidad Juárez del Estado de Durango, Instituto de Investigaciones Históricas, 2014. 229 p.: bibl., ill., index.

This is a general survey, based on archives of Durango's state university, of the development of post-secondary education in the state. The author emphasizes the gradual inclusion of women, first in teacher training and, with time, in a variety of professional fields of study.

Véjar Pérez-Rubio, Carlos. Las danzas del huracán: Veracruz y La Habana en los años treinta. See *HLAS 73:1507*.

699   Ventura Rodríguez, María Teresa. El sindicalismo oficial en Puebla, 1938–1952. Puebla, Mexico: Benemérita Universidad Autónoma de Puebla, Dirección de Fomento Editorial, 2014. 311 p.: bibl. (Colección Historia)

The author uses local and national archives, as well as interviews and union newspapers, to trace the process by which the state's unions became more integrated with the national labor movement. She examines the activism of Puebla's labor organizations surrounding the presidential election of 1940 and in the context of WWII, the postwar clash between local labor groups, and the final achievement of a more peaceful solidarity linked to national political power. Includes biographical profiles of two important labor leaders, as well as transcriptions of interviews with a prominent Confederación Regional de Obreros Mexicanos (CROM) figure and with the founder of Puebla's communist party.

700   Villavicencio Rojas, Josué Mario. Industria y empresarios en Puebla, 1940–1970: una aproximación a la historia económica regional. Puebla, Mexico: Instituto de Ciencias Sociales y Humanidades "Alfonso Vélez Pliego," Benemérita Universidad Autónoma de Puebla, 2013. 278 p.: bibl., graphs, ill., maps, tables.

The author has conducted extensive research in Puebla's business and property registry. Part one traces changes in the location and scope of industrial companies, demonstrating the persistence of the textile industry amid a gradual diversification. Part two profiles the industrial class, from the Spanish textile magnates to Mexican and Syrio-Lebanese entrepreneurs. Most of this era was dominated by light industry and family-owned businesses.

701   Vitz, Matthew. "To save the forests": power, narrative, and environment in Mexico City's cooking fuel transition. (*Mex. Stud.*, 31:1, Winter 2015, p. 125–155)

This study examines the shift from charcoal to petroleum as the chief source of household energy. Beginning with Lázaro Cárdenas and continuing into the 1940s, this shift was facilitated by a narrative that linked charcoal use to the environmental destruction of forests, and supported the state-owned oil company as a patriotic answer to conservation.

702   Weis, Robert. The revolution on trial: assassination, Christianity, and the rule of law in 1920s Mexico. (*HAHR*, 96:2, May 2016, p. 319–353, bibl.)

The author provides a detailed analysis of the arguments used by the government in the 1928 trial of José de León Toral, Álvaro Obregón's assassin. Despite President Plutarco Elías Calles' public insistence that the trial underscored Mexico's emergence as a nation of laws, undergirded by a new "revolutionary spirituality," the event revealed a divided Mexico in which political expediency remained the norm.

703   Wolfe, Mikael. Watering the revolution: an environmental and technological history of agrarian reform in Mexico. Durham, N.C.: Duke University Press, 2017. 317 p.: bibl., ill., index, maps, tables.

This important study focuses on the Laguna region of Durango and Coahuila from the late 19th to the late 20th centuries. The author examines the efforts of politicians and federal engineers (*técnicos*) to transform this area with dams, canals, and groundwater pumps, in the context of the Mexican Revolution's commitment to redistributing and conserving water. While *técnicos* understood the environmental consequences of such technology, short-term interests prevailed over conservationism, resulting in significant ecological and social consequences.

704 Young, Julia Grace Darling. Mexican exodus: emigrants, exiles, and refugees of the Cristero War. Oxford, England: Oxford University Press, 2015. 271 p.: bibl., index.

Once a forbidden topic, Mexico's Cristero War of 1926–29 now enjoys a growing literature. This most recent study documents the activities of Cristeros in their US exile. The religiously motivated insurgents picked up some sympathetic hearings in places like El Paso, San Antonio, and Los Angeles, but predictably fell flat in their efforts to organize a Cristero army abroad. The book will appeal not only to students of this armed conflict, but also to anyone trying to untangle the perpetually knotty relationship between the US and Mexico.

705 Zamorano-Villarreal, Claudia Carolina. Vivienda Mínima Obrera en el México posrevolucionario: apropiaciones de una utopía urbana (1932–2004). México: CIESAS: CONACYT, Consejo Nacional de Ciencia y Tecnología, 2013. 266 p.: bibl., ill. (Publicaciones de la Casa Chata)

This intriguing study explores a short-lived project to create an ideal working class community in Mexico City. The author is concerned with tensions inherent in the project, which drew in "radical" architects, politicians, and the inhabitants themselves. Each group appropriated the space on their own terms, and to their own ends. Incorporates architectural illustrations and interviews with some of colonia Michoacana's original families.

CENTRAL AMERICA

PETER SZOK, *Professor of History, Texas Christian University*
STEPHEN WEBRE, *Professor Emeritus of History, Louisiana Tech University*

HISTORICAL PRODUCTION ON Central America increases in maturity as both regional and foreign scholars explore unfamiliar topics, or explore familiar topics in unfamiliar ways. Recent important archival discoveries have enriched colonial historiography. Long believed lost, the reappearance of the *Libro segundo del cabildo* (item **714**) sheds new light on Guatemala in the early 16th century, while new documentary evidence brought to the surface by Kramer (item **725**) offers important findings on the background and early career of Juan Rodríguez Cabrillo. The relationship of the Roman Catholic Church to colonial society and economy is the subject of innovative new studies by Leavitt-Alcántara (item **708**) and Fernández Sagastume (item **719**). Colonial cultural life finds welcome attention in new studies of silversmiths by Muñoz Paz (item **728**), reports of ceremonies and celebrations by Sánchez Mora (items **732** and **733**), and indigenous influence on colonial music by Singer (item **734**). The vogue for studies of African influence in colonial history may be passing. Nonetheless, important new works by Thornton (item **736**) and Madrigal Muñoz (item **727**) augment existing scholarship. Finally, Solórzano Fonseca (item **735**) makes a new contribution to an old debate in his essay on the contact-era population of Costa Rica.

Encouraged by ongoing attention to the bicentennial of Central American independence, expected to peak in 2021 with a planned international symposium to take place in Chiapas, works distinguished by quality research and original analysis continue to appear. Major examples are the study of political elites by Madrigal Muñoz (item **709**) and the collection assembled by Boza and colleagues (item **713**), both of which focus on Costa Rica and stress continuity over discontinuity. The impact of the early 19th-century political crises on indigenous communities finds effective treatment in studies by Pollack (item **731**) and Hawkins (item **722**).

Works on Costa Rica continue to figure heavily among recent publications on the national period, although thematic emphasis has shifted in response to the recent commemoration of the 200th anniversary of the birth of president and national hero Juan Rafael Mora Porras (1814–59), who is viewed in different ways by Acuña Ortega (item **738**), Díaz Arias (item **749**), Fallas Santana (item **753**), Molina Jiménez (item **765**), and Rodríguez Sáenz (item **771**). Texts by and about Mora are collected by Aguilar Piedra and Vargas Araya (items **767** and **770**). Meanwhile, Costa Rica's 1948 Civil War continues to receive attention, most recently by Díaz Arias (item **748**) and in the collection of sources from the losing side edited by Barahona Riera (item **766**).

In neighboring Nicaragua, studies on Augusto C. Sandino and the movement he inspired still dominate the scholarship. A substantial new biography of Sandino himself was penned by Bendaña (item **742**), while the Frente Sandinista is dealt with at length by Midence (item **764**). Recent military histories of the Sandinista Revolution and the later Contra War include works by Bonilla López (item **744**) and Duque Estrada Sacasa (item **750**). Rueda Estrada (item **772**) examines Nicaraguan reality since 1990. Studies of the Somoza era by Gómez (item **757**), López Maltez (item **761**), and Traversari (item **777**) complement attention to later events.

El Salvador's Civil War of 1979–92 and the peace process that ultimately brought an end of sorts to the carnage are covered by Ayalá (item **741**), Chávez (item **745**), and the collected testimony of Mayorga and others (item **751**). The role of women in the struggle is revealed by the personal experiences gathered by Drago and Ramos (item **776**), while the Jesuit commitment to social justice is addressed by Gould (item **759**) and Hernández Pico (item **760**). The much-studied indigenous uprising of 1932 and the brutal repression that followed are reassessed by Mejía Burgos (item **763**).

Notable for Guatemala are the article by Gibbings (item **756**) on the 19th-century debate on forced labor and the new book by Taracena Arriola (item **774**) on the reception of Spanish Republican exiles. For its part, Honduras is represented by a new journal (item **710**) and by an innovative study by Coleman (item **746**) on photography as an instrument of struggle against banana empire hegemony. Certain familiar topics remain durable. In addition to the aforementioned works by Gibbings and Coleman, innovative studies on capitalist export agriculture include those by Bohme on pesticides (item **743**) and Peters Solórzano (item **768**) on German investment and coffee expansion in Costa Rica. Finally, two studies from Panama mark the 50th anniversary of the Canal Zone riots of 1964 (items **739** and **780**).

GENERAL

706 **Cunin, Elisabeth** and **Odile Hoffmann.** From colonial domination to the making of the nation: ethno-racial categories in censuses and reports and their political uses in Belize, 19th–20th centuries. (*Caribb. Stud.*, 41:2, July/Dec. 2013, p. 31–60, bibl., tables)

This article describes the racial categories in Belizean censuses and explains that they have changed over time, reflecting the country's complex trajectory from colony to independence to neoliberal society. For a review of the Spanish-language version of this article, see *HLAS* 70:767.

707 **La historiografía costarricense en la primera década del siglo XXI: tendencias, avances e innovaciones.** Edición de David Díaz Arias, Iván Molina Jiménez, y Ronny Viales Hurtado. San José: Editorial UCR, 2014. 324 p.: bibl., ill. (some color).

This work brings together conference papers that provide insights on recent developments in colonial and modern historiography of Costa Rica, including scholarship on women, masculinity, economics, the environment, and social history.

708   Leavitt-Alcántara, Brianna. Alone at the altar: single women and devotion in Guatemala, 1670–1870. Stanford, California: Stanford University Press, 2017. 297 p.: bibl., index.

Based on extensive research in wills and other archival materials, the author reveals how widows, spinsters, and other unattached women provided material support for the Church, worship, and affiliated institutions and activities.

709   Madrigal Muñoz, Eduardo. Poder económico y lazos sociales de una elite local en los últimos años del régimen colonial y en la independencia: Costa Rica, 1821–1824. (in Caravelle/Toulouse, 101, 2013, p. 87–108, bibl.)

In this article, the author demonstrates the continuity of elites in early 19th-century Costa Rica by employing prosopographic and social network analyses of membership of independence-era *juntas de gobierno*.

710   *Memorias: Revista de la Maestría en Historia Social y Cultural de la UNAH*. Vol. 1, julio/dic. 2017. Tegucigalpa: Universidad Nacional Autónoma de Honduras.

This is the first issue of new journal that is distinguished by a focus on Honduran history as well as by bold graphics and eccentric typography. The contents include articles, essays, documents, and book and film reviews. Among notable items in this issue are articles on Church life in early Tegucigalpa by Mirian Fernández Sagastume (see item **719**) and Julio Sevilla and on the history of education by Oscar Zelaya and Moisés Mayorquín. The issue also features essays on cultural historiography by Rolando Sierra Fonseca and on representations of the devil by Jorge Alberto Amaya. One curious addition is the text of a *licenciatura* thesis defended in 1898 by future dictator Tiburcio Carías Andino (1932–49) on the question of whether or not mechanization of industry has improved conditions for the poor.

711   Preston, Douglas J. The lost city of the Monkey God: a true story. New York: Grand Central Publishing, 2017. 326 p., 16 unnumbered pages of plates: bibl., ill. (some color), index, maps.

This journalistic account of high adventure in the Honduran rainforest features history and archeology against the backdrop of deadly serpents, gruesome tropical diseases, and political intrigue following the 2009 coup d'état.

712   Sibaja Chacón, Luis Fernando and Chester Zelaya. Nicoya: su pasado colonial y su anexión o agregación a Costa Rica. San José: EUNED, 2015. 365 p.

Originally published under a different title in 1974 (see *HLAS 41:8694*). The authors explain that this updated 2015 book is a completely different work, integrating advances in scholarship during the intervening 40 years. The book addresses the border between Costa Rica and Nicaragua on the Nicoya Peninsula.

713   Simposio De colonia a república: economía, política e iglesia en Costa Rica (1709–1892), *Museos del Banco Central de Costa Rica, 2017.* De colonia a república: economía, política e iglesia en Costa Rica, siglos XVII–XIX. San José: Fundación Museos Banco Central de Costa Rica, 2017. 316 p.: bibl., ill. (some color), maps.

These conference proceedings bring together original essays by recognized specialists who treat different aspects of the transition from the old regime to a nation state in Costa Rica. The contributors include Alejandra Boza Villarreal on frontier indigenous groups, Patricia Clare Rhoades on environmental change, Verónica Jerez Brenes on the dissolution of *cofradía* assets, Esteban Corella Ovares on the legacy of Bourbon military reforms, Elizet Payne Iglesias on the impact of Cádiz reforms on native communities, Manuel Benito Chacón Hidalgo on the political symbology of coinage, Carmela Velázquez Bonilla on the role of the Roman Catholic clergy in independence, and David Díaz Arias on the significance of commemorative dates.

COLONIAL

714 Antigua (Guatemala). Ayuntamiento. Libro segundo del Cabildo de la çibdad de Santiago de la provinçia de Guatemala començado a XXVII de mayo de MDXXX años. Coordinación de la edición de Wendy Kramer. Edición de Jorge Luján Muñoz y Wendy Kramer. Transcripción paleográfica de Wendy Kramer con Edgar F. Chután Alvarado. Wellfleet, Mass.: Plumsock Mesoamerican Studies (PMS); La Antigua, Guatemala: Centro de Investigaciones Regionales de Mesoamérica (CIRMA); Ciudad de Guatemala: Academia de Geografía e Historia de Guatemala (AGHG); Universidad del Valle de Guatemala (UVG); New York, N.Y.: Hispanic Society of America (HSA), 2018. 394 p.: bibl., facsims., ill., map. (Biblioteca "Goathemala" / Academia de Geografía e Historia de Guatemala; XXXV)

This work presents a faithful scholarly transcription of a manuscript volume containing city council minutes from 1530–41 for Santiago de Guatemala. The document was presumed to be lost until 2010, when it turned up in the library of the Hispanic Society of America in New York. Informative introductions by Wendy Kramer and Christopher H. Lutz summarize the volume's significance for early postconquest historiography as well as what is known of its chain of possession during its prolonged absence from public view.

715 Cano Borrego, Pedro Damián. La moneda en el Reino de Guatemala durante el siglo XVIII. (*Anu. Estud. Centroam.*, 42, 2016, p. 161–180, bibl.)

This article presents a technically inclined account of the 1731 establishment of the Guatemala mint and the coinage it produced. Contrary to official expectations, local coining of silver did not relieve the colony's chronic shortage of metal money.

716 Capítulos provinciales de la Orden de la Merced en el Reino de Guatemala (1650–1754). Transcripción, estudio preliminar, notas e índices de Fr. José Zaporta Pallarés. Revisión por Gerardo Ramírez Samayoa. Guatemala: Academia de Geografía e Historia de Guatemala, 2014. 694 p.: bibl., color ill., index, maps. (Biblioteca Goathemala; XXXIV)

Due to the survival of archival records, the activities of Mercedarian friars in colonial Central America may be better documented than those of either of their more numerous rival orders, Dominicans or Franciscans. This elegant edition of provincial chapter minutes is accompanied by a sound scholarly introduction by the order's most distinguished living historian.

717 Caso Barrera, Laura. Tratamiento del cuerpo y control social entre los mayas itzaes, siglo XVII–XVIII. (*Anu. Estud. Am.*, 72:2, julio/dic. 2015, p. 631–660, bibl., photos, tables)

Based largely on documentary evidence associated with the Maya Itza', this study explores the centrality of the human body in the Maya worldview in terms of nahualism and a fear of witchcraft; body modification, including tatooing, scarification, and penile mutilation; torture, human sacrifice, and cannibalism; and other related beliefs and practices. Despite Church opposition, many of these practices continued after conquest. See also *HLAS 62:208*.

718 Conover Blancas, Carlos. De los frentes de batalla a los linderos tangibles en el sureste novohispano: la demarcación de los límites de los territorios ampliados a los establecimientos británicos del Walix por la convención de Londres de 1786. (*Rev. Hist. Am./México*, 152, 2016, p. 91–133, bibl., maps)

This article provides a historical background of the current border between Mexico and Belize.

719 Fernández Sagastume, Mirian Leavel. Capellanías del Convento San Diego: auge minero y élites en el Real de Minas de Tegucigalpa durante el siglo XVIII. (*Memorias/Tegucigalpa*, 1, julio/dic. 2017, p. 33–56, bibl., ill., tables)

An expansion of mining and stock raising financed investment in *capellanías*, which contributed to the material development of the Church in the Tegucigalpa region. A preference for mortgaging slaves and livestock suggests the land held little value without them.

720 Fernández Sagastume, Mirian Leavel. Métodos misionales de los franciscanos en la Taguzgalpa, Honduras (1574–1810). (*in* De Mérida a Taguzgalpa: Seráficos y predicadores en tierras mayas, chiapanecas y xicaques. Coordinación de José Manuel A. Chávez Gómez. México: Secretaría de Cultura, Instituto Nacional de Antropología e Historia, 2018, p. 71–92)

This book chapter offers a useful narrative introduction to the topic with citations to appropriate primary materials.

721   Gámez Casado, Manuel. Buscando el enemigo inglés: expediciones de guardacostas españolas al golfo del Darién, 1767–1768. (*Anu. Estud. Am.*, 75:1, 2018, p. 211–234, bibl.)

This overview of the Spanish-British rivalry for control of the Darien isthmus emphasizes defensive measures undertaken in the 18th century and especially on coastal reconnaissance expeditions dispatched to locate, identify, and quantify both British and indigenous settlements.

722   Hawkins, Timothy. Fighting Napoleon in Totonicapán. (*Lat. Am./Orlando*, 61:4, Dec. 2017, p. 490–510, bibl.)

In the wake of the 1808 French invasion of Spain, fear of sabotage, subversion, and invasion gripped Spain's American possessions. Local colonial officials such as those in the remote northwestern Guatemalan highlands became important elements in an organized response orchestrated by Spanish agents in Washington, DC.

723   Ibarra Rojas, Eugenia. Los indígenas de la cuenca del río San Juan (o Desaguadero) en el siglo XVI ante el descubrimiento español del río. (*Anu. Estud. Centroam.*, 40, 2014, p. 115–137, bibl.)

This study of the early exploration of the San Juan River is set in the context of native peoples' existing use of the river and Spanish dependence upon their geographical knowledge and willingness to collaborate. The detailed narrative is based largely on familiar printed sources.

724   Jones, Owen H. Language politics and indigenous language documents: evidence in colonial K'ichee' litigation in seventeenth-century highland Guatemala. (*Americas/Washington*, 73:3, July 2016, p. 349–370)

The record of a lawsuit about a land dispute reveals the activity of indigenous-language notaries. The range of practice and clientele were much broader and more complex than commonly assumed. For ethnohistorian's comment, see *HLAS* 72:272.

725   Kramer, Wendy. El español que exploró California: Juan Rodríguez Cabrillo (c. 1497–1543): de Palma del Río a Guatemala. Córdoba, Spain: Diputación de Córdoba, 2018. 237 p.

This new biography of Juan Rodríguez Cabrillo is based on previously unexamined archival materials. Among other things, the author locates Cabrillo's birthplace in Spain, rather than in Portugal as traditionally thought. She also suggests he had a New Christian background; she describes his important role in early colonial society; and she questions the authorship of a frequently cited description of the 1541 destruction of Santiago de Guatemala (see *HLAS 14:1836*).

726   Lovell, W. George; Christopher H. Lutz; and Wendy Kramer. Atemorizar la tierra: Pedro de Alvarado y la conquista de Guatemala, 1520–1541. Guatemala: F&G Editores, 2016. 224 p.: bibl., ill. (some color), map.

This work provides an accessible translation of relevant parts of *HLAS* 70:798, addressing the early postconquest years of Guatemalan history.

727   Madrigal Muñoz, Eduardo. Solidaridades afromestizas: compadrazgo y padrinazgo entre la población de sangre africana en el primer libro de bautizos de Cartago (1594–1680). (*Caravelle/Toulouse*, 106, 2016, p. 121–146, bibl.)

Patterns of *compadrazgo* (ritual co-parenthood) reflected in sacramental records reveal extensive interaction among different ethnic and socioeconomic groups, as well as maintenance of appropriate social distance.

728   Muñoz Paz, María del Carmen. El obrador de Blas de Abila: maestro platero del siglo XVIII en Santiago de Guatemala. Guatemala: Universidad de San Carlos de Guatemala, Dirección General de Investigación y Centro de Estudios Urbanos y Regionales, 2017. 107 p.: bibl., ill.

This richly illustrated study sees the Avila workshop as a family enterprise, focusing not only on the esthetic aspects of gold and silversmithing, but also on the social organization of production and the position in social hierarchy of master craftsmen.

729 Obregón, Clotilde María and **Patricia Sibaja Amador.** Diccionario biográfico costarricense: siglos XVI y XVII. San José: EUNED, Editorial Universidad Estatal a Distancia, 2015. 183 p.

This volume presents biographical sketches of colonial-era Costa Ricans, mostly Spanish elites, but also including some indigenous Americans. Entries vary in quality; some are long on fact, others are long on editorial comment. The introduction to colonial institutions and local geography is a useful starting point for scholars who are new to the field.

730 Pinzón Ríos, Guadalupe. De zona olvidada a plataforma de expansión: Centroamérica en las representaciones cartográficas y proyectos navales ingleses (1680–1742). (*Anu. Estud. Am.*, 75:1, 2018, p. 185–210, bibl., maps)

The author reports on British expansionist interest in an interoceanic passage as reflected in maps and other strategic documents related to Central America.

731 Pollack, Aaron. Protesta en Patzicía: los pueblos de indios y la *vacatio regis* en el reino de Guatemala. (*Rev. Indias*, 78:272, 2018, p. 147–173, bibl.)

This study contributes to our understanding of pre-independence mobilization in highland Guatemala. The author examines local protest and official and elite responses in the context of a power vacuum in Spain, Cádiz reforms, outbreaks of violence in other colonies, and divisions within indigenous society. Not all mobilizations of the era were aimed at independence or even autonomy.

732 Sánchez Mora, Alexánder. Guatemala por Fernando sétimo: crisis dinástica, juegos de lealtad y afirmación del poder local en una relación de fiestas. (*Rev. Hist./Heredia*, 75, enero/junio 2017, p. 155–182)

The author examines colonial *relaciones de fiestas* as both historical documents and literary productions. He argues that the documents are not meant simply to preserve the record of festivities marking major public events, but also to evoke emotional responses of group loyalty and cohesion, which is particularly important in the case of the accession of Ferdinand VII due to the circumstances in which it occurred.

733 Sánchez Mora, Alexánder. Las relaciones de fiestas impresas del reino de Guatemala, siglos XVII a XIX. (*An. Acad. Geogr. Hist. Guatem.*, 91, 2016, p. 115–146, ill.)

Based on a sample of 44 texts, the author proposes a scheme for classifying and describing one specific genre of colonial literary imprints. Reports of public celebrations marked important deaths, loyalty to the monarch of the time, and religious observances. See also item **732**.

734 Singer, Deborah. Música colonial: otredad y conflicto en la Catedral de Santiago de Guatemala. (*Temas Am.*, 37, dic. 2016, p. 88–104)

The author sees musical performances in religious ceremonies as a means of ratifying indigenous place in the colonial world, while at the same time reinforcing the native's status as "other." The message is contained in the lyrics of *villancicos de indios*, but also in the incorporation of indigenous instruments, dance traditions, and vocal style.

735 Solórzano Fonseca, Juan Carlos. La población indígena de Costa Rica en el siglo XVI al momento del contacto con los europeos. (*Anu. Estud. Centroam.*, 43, 2017, p. 313–345, bibl.)

This study challenges the widely accepted figure of a population of 400,000 indigenous peoples in Costa Rica in the 16th century in favor of a much lower late-19th-century estimate by Bishop Bernardo Augusto Thiel. Noting conflicting evidence from archeological and ethnographic sources, the author suggests a significant depopulation before the arrival of the Spanish, possibly reflecting the impact of the interruption of long-distance trade occasioned by the classic Maya collapse.

736 Thornton, John K. The Zambos and the transformation of Miskitu Kingdom, 1636–1740. (*HAHR*, 97:1, Feb. 2017, p. 1–27)

This study documents the African roots of the Zambos' rise to dominate the

Miskitu kingdom, with an emphasis on military experience acquired during tribal warfare in Africa.

737 Webre, Stephen. Más allá de la Verapaz: fray Francisco Morán, O.P. (1590–1664). (*in* De Mérida a Taguzgalpa: Seráficos y predicadores en tierras mayas, chiapanecas y xicaques. Coordinación de José Manuel A. Chávez Gómez. México: Secretaría de Cultura, Instituto Nacional de Antropología e Historia, 2018, p. 141–151)

In a departure from the order's Las Casas legacy, a Dominican friar advocated for Spanish settlement and armed force to reduce the notoriously resistant inhabitants of Guatemala's northern frontier.

NATIONAL

738 Acuña Ortega, Víctor Hugo. Costa Rica: la fabricación de Juan Rafael Mora (siglos XIX–XXI). (*Caravelle/Toulouse*, 104, 2015, p. 31–46)

This study outlines Mora's rise to mythic status as a hero of resistance to William Walker. The author sees the process as originating with Mora himself, then evolving with different stages of the nation's history.

739 Araúz, Celestino Andrés. Jorge E. Illueca y la gesta patriótica de enero de 1964. Panamá: Bufete Illueca, 2014. 445 p.: bibl.

This narrative account of the 1964 riots highlights future president Illueca's role in public debates. Illueca served as head of the National Association of Lawyers and helped galvanize support for renegotiating the canal agreement. He subsequently served as special ambassador to the US. The book was conceptualized as a counterpoint to the existing historiography focused on student contributions. Includes extensive writings by Illueca.

740 Arias Castro, Tomás Federico. 150 años de historia de la masonería en Costa Rica 1865–2015: biografía histórica del presbítero Dr. Francisco C. Calvo. San José: Editorial Costa Rica, 2015. 356 p.: bibl., ill. (Colección nueva biblioteca patria; 8)

This sympathetic biography describes the life of Dr. Francisco Calvo, a priest and key figure in the development of Costa Rican Freemasonry. The author emphasizes the intellectual and personal formation that allowed Calvo to embrace both his faith and his masonic association.

741 Ayalá, Berne. En el silencio de la batalla. El Salvador: Editorial Expedición Americana, 2014. 597 p.

This testimonial account of the Salvadoran Civil War is by a prolific writer and former member of the FAL—Fuerzas Armadas de Liberación (Armed Forces of Liberation).

742 Bendaña, Alejandro. Sandino: patria y libertad. Managua: Anamá Ediciones, 2016. 472 p., 96 unnumbered pages: bibl., ill., index, maps.

This weighty exploration of Sandino's political development focuses on his early life, his experiences in Mexico, and his work for US companies. The author depicts his thinking as assuredly flexible. While exposed to an array of intellectual influences, Sandino confidently fashioned his own positions, combining nationalism with anti-imperialism and class-based perspectives. See also *HLAS 66:1080*.

743 Bohme, Susanna Rankin. Toxic injustice: a transnational history of exposure and struggle. Oakland: University of California Press, 2015. 343 p.: bibl., ill., index.

This well-researched study of globalization is presented from the perspective of polemics surrounding the DBCP pesticide (dibromochloropropane). The author examines the multinational use of DBCP pesticide on banana plantations in Central America and the efforts of workers in Nicaragua and Costa Rica to seek justice in national and foreign contexts, including in the US court system.

744 Bonilla López, Douglas. La reserva de Sandino. Managua: Douglas José Bonilla López, 2013. 296 p.: bibl., ill.

This first-person account describes the reserve battalions' role in combating the US-backed contras in Nicaragua in the 1980s. The author is a retired lieutenant colonel in the Nicaraguan army.

Cascante Segura, Carlos Humberto. La política exterior de Costa Rica (1850–2010). See *HLAS 73:1509*.

745   Chávez, Joaquín Mauricio. How did the civil war in El Salvador end? (*Am. Hist. Rev.*, 120:5, Dec. 2015, p. 1784–1797, bibl., photos)

This article presents an overview of the Salvadoran peace process, emphasizing the FMLN's ideological flexibility and its willingness to relinquish Marxist-Leninist ideology in favor of a social democratic orientation. In exchange for government security reforms, the FMLN agreed to participate in electoral politics, facilitating the ARENA-led neoliberal restructuring of the country.

746   Coleman, Kevin P. A camera in the garden of Eden: the self-forging of a Banana Republic. Austin: University of Texas Press, 2016. 312 p.: bibl., ill., index, maps, photos.

This innovative study of United Fruit operations in El Progreso, Honduras, combines labor and social history with an analysis of competing imaginings of progress. The author focuses on the 1954 strike and the work of local photographer Rafael Platero Paz. Platero Paz played a key role in what Coleman describes as a visual challenge to the imagery of colonialism.

747   Correspondencia de los diplomáticos franceses en Costa Rica (1889–1917). Ciudad Universitaria Rodrigo Facio, Costa Rica: Editorial UCR, 2015. 173 p.: bibl., ill.

This volume brings together a collection of French consular correspondence discussing a variety of topics, including political figures, elections, and party politics, as well as relations with Germany and the US, and the influence of businessmen such as Minor Cooper Keith. Orlando Salazar Mora provides an introductory essay.

748   Díaz Arias, David. Crisis social y memorias en lucha: guerra civil en Costa Rica, 1940–1948. Ciudad Universitaria Rodrigo Facio, Costa Rica: Editorial UCR, 2015. 381 p.: bibl. (Colección Historia de Costa Rica)

This work offers an important synthetic account of the Costa Rican Civil War, its political origins and its memories. The author situates Rafael Ángel Calderón Guardia in the broader context of Latin American populism. He argues that exaggerated partisanship surrounding the caudillo provoked an equally fervent opposition and gave rise to violent conflict.

749   Díaz Arias, David. La era de la centralización: estado, sociedad e institucionalidad en Costa Rica, 1848–1870. Ciudad Universitaria Rodrigo Facio, Costa Rica: Editorial UCR, 2015. 73 p.: bibl. (Cuadernos de historia de las instituciones de Costa Rica; 29)

This overview of mid-19th century Costa Rica underlines President Juan Rafael Mora's consolidation of executive power and the socioeconomic and cultural changes associated with the advance of coffee exports.

750   Duque Estrada Sacasa, Esteban. Nicaragua: ¡insurrección! 1977–1979. Managua: Esteban Duque Estrada Sacasa, 2014. 426 p.: bibl., ill., maps.

This work offers an encyclopedic account of the Sandinista insurrection with a focus squarely on military operations. The author provides biographical information on dozens of protagonists in the Guardia Nacional and the FSLN.

751   El Salvador, de la guerra civil a la paz negociada. Textos de Román Mayorga *et al.* San Salvador: Secretaria de Cultura de la Presidencia El Salvador, Dirección de Publicaciones e Impresos, 2014. 177 p.: bibl.

This volume provides a compilation of reflections on the Salvadoran civil war, the subsequent peace process, and legacies from prominent figures involved in the conflict.

752   Escolán Romero, Gabriel. Ritmos de crecimiento, reestructuraciones sociales y enfrentamiento político: el paisajismo rural salvadoreño en las vísperas de las reformas liberales, 1860–1880 (II). (*ECA/San Salvador*, 69:737/738, abril/sept. 2014, p. 257–277, tables)

This study examines Salvadoran rural society on the eve of liberal reforms, emphasizing the paucity of capitalist accumulation, subsistence agriculture, and weak state institutions.

753   Fallas Santana, Carmen Maria. Costa Rica frente al filibusterismo: la guerra de 1856 y 1857 contra William Walker: defensa y fortalecimiento de las instituciones del estado. Ciudad Universitaria Rodrigo Facio, Costa Rica: Editorial Universidad de

Costa Rica, 2015. 123 p.: bibl. (Cuadernos de historia de las instituciones de Costa Rica; 26)

This study reviews the familiar history of the National Campaign in Costa Rica framed within the context of state development. The author argues that the efforts of President Juan Rafael Mora Porras to strengthen finances and governmental authority were critical to Walker's defeat.

754 **Fernández Hellmund, Paula D.** Nicaragua debe sobrevivir: la solidaridad de la militancia comunista argentina con la Revolución Sandinista (1979–1990). Argentina: Imago Mundi, 2015. 295 p.: bibl., ill. (Colección Indeal)

This oral history describes the Argentine Communist Party's support of the Sandinista Revolution, which took place amidst declining Soviet influence and the party's embrace of more revolutionary positions. Despite the leftward turn, participants in Brigada General San Martín tended to leave the party following their return to Argentina.

755 **Fuentes orales, emigración española y desarrollo socioeconómico en Centroamérica.** Edición de José Manuel Azcona. Textos de Nuria González Alonso et al. Cizur Menor, Spain: Thomson Reuters Aranzadi, 2015. 711 p.: bibl., ill. (chiefly colored). (Humanidades)

This eclectic collection of 13 essays addresses Spanish immigration to Central America from the 16th to the 21st centuries, with topics as varied as the conquest, literature, investments, military missions, film, and art. Nicaragua and El Salvador receive particular attention.

756 **Gibbings, Julie.** "Shadow of slavery": historical time, labor, and citizenship in nineteenth-century Alta Verapaz, Guatemala. (*HAHR*, 96:1, Feb. 2016, p. 73–107, bibl.)

This study examines *mandamiento* (forced labor) and historical discourse in Alta Verapaz. While state officials argued that forced labor was necessary to move Guatemala toward modernity, K'eqchi' patriarchs and sympathetic ladinos drew on similar teleological narratives to associate the institution with feudalism and other precapitalist structures.

757 **Gómez, Juan Pablo.** Autoridad, cuerpo, nación: batallas culturales en Nicaragua (1930–1943). Managua: Instituto de Historia de Nicaragua y Centroamérica de la Universidad Centroamericana, IHNCA-UCA, 2015. 239 p.: bibl., ill.

This book presents a cultural reinterpretation of the Somoza dynasty. The author emphasizes the role of intellectuals, especially Pablo Antonio Cuadra, the Church, and military officials in fashioning a Catholic and authoritarian identity which supported the rise of dictatorship and survived the Sandinista Revolution. For comment by literary specialist, see item **1866**.

758 **González, Luis Felipe.** Textos históricos, educativos y biográficos. Compilación de Elías Zeledón Cartín. Heredia, Costa Rica: EUNA, 2015. 2 v.: bibl.

This multivolume work presents a compilation of historical and educational writings by this prominent 20th-century intellectual.

759 **Gould, Jeffrey L.** Ignacio Ellacuría and the Salvadorean revolution. (*J. Lat. Am. Stud.*, 47:2, May 2015, p. 285–315)

This article presents a detailed examination of the political thinking of martyred UCA rector and Jesuit priest Ignacio Ellacuría. Disagreements between Ellacuría and the revolutionary left regarding the Junta Revolucionaria del Gobierno reflect a common disjuncture (*desencuentro*) between potential collaborators, shaped by class, ethnic, and gender differences.

760 **Hernández Pico, Juan.** Luchar por la justicia al viento del espíritu: autobiografía y esbozo de historia de mi generación. San Salvador: UCA Editores, 2014. 447 p.: portraits.

This autobiography of the influential Jesuit describes his commitment to social justice and his generation's engagement with critical episodes of the Cold War in Central America.

761 **López Maltez, Nicolás.** Historia de la Guardia Nacional de Nicaragua. Tomo I. Managua: N.A. López Maltez, 2014. 1 v.: bibl., ill.

This is the first of a projected two-volume history of the Nicaraguan National Guard. The author traces the rise of this military institution from its precursors in the late 19th century to Somoza's consolidation of power in 1937. The study digs deeply into US occupation, political intrigues, and the campaign against Sandino. Includes dozens of photos from the period.

762   Matamoros Hüeck, Bosco. El encanto del poder. Managua: Hispamer, 2015. 225 p.: ill., index.

This volume presents short reflections on key Nicaraguan figures of the 20th and early 21st centuries by a political analyst, former diplomat, and FDN spokesperson.

763   Mejía Burgos, Otto. 1932, un mito fundacional. Prólogo de Rafael Lara-Martínez. San Salvador: Editorial Universidad Don Bosco, 2016. 198 p.: bibl., ill.

This primary source investigation purports to challenge binary interpretations of El Salvador's 1932 conflict as more than a Communist-inspired insurrection or a state-sponsored attempt at ethnocide. The author underlines various historical, structural, and circumstantial factors that prompted the revolt and its suppression.

764   Midence, Carlos. Sandinismo y revolución: resistencia, liberación, justicia y cambio en las luchas de nuestros pueblos. Managua: Editorial Universitaria Tutecotzimí, 2016. 711 p.: bibl.

This voluminous study focuses on the FSLN, tying its formation and trajectory to Sandino and to the movement for national liberation, stretching into the 21st century.

765   Molina Jiménez, Iván. La cicatriz gloriosa: estudios y debates sobre la Campaña Nacional: Costa Rica (1856–1857). San José: Editorial Costa Rica: Imprenta Nacional: Ministerio de Cultura y Juventud, SINABI, 2014. 179 p.: bibl., index. (Colección nueva biblioteca patria; 2)

This study reviews the historiographical and literary debates surrounding the National Campaign, Juan Santamaría, and Juan Rafael Mora. The author emphasizes the political function of narratives which he associates with moments of national commemoration.

766   Nuevos documentos de 1948: los proscriptos. Prólogo, investigación, selección y notas de Macarena Barahona Riera. San José: Editorial Costa Rica, 2015. 402 p.: bibl., ill. (Colección Nueva biblioteca patria; 7)

This study presents documents intended to illuminate the perspective of defeated parties in the 1948 Civil War in Costa Rica. Writings include essays by José Albertazzi Avendaño, Rosendo Argüello Rodríguez, Manuel Mora Valverde, José Meléndez Ibarra, and Carlos Luis Fallas Sibaja.

767   Palabra viva del Libertador: legado ideológico y patriótico del Presidente Juan Rafael Mora para la Costa Rica en devenir. Edición de Raúl Aguilar Piedra y Armando Vargas Araya. San José: Eduvisión, 2014. 459 p.: bibl., ill.

This volume compiles the speeches and writings of Costa Rican president Juan Rafael Mora Porras from before, during, and after the National Campaign. Includes an extensive chronology of Mora's life and a sympathetic essay by the volume's editors.

768   Peters Solórzano, Gertrud. El negocio del café en Costa Rica, el capital alemán y la geopolítica, 1907–1936. Heredia, Costa Rica: EUNA, Editorial Universidad Nacional (EUNA), 2016. 527 p.: bibl., Ill.

This exhaustive treatment of German involvement in coffee production in Costa Rica is framed within the context of international economics and geopolitical tensions during the period.

769   Pico de Coaña de Valicourt, Yago. Treinta y cuatro años después: el asalto a la Embajada de España en Guatemala. Burgos, Spain: Editorial Dossoles, 2014. 162 p.: ill., map. (Colección La valija diplomática; 44)

This book reproduces the memoir of a Spanish diplomatic representative who was sent to Guatemala to investigate the 1980 assault on the Spanish embassy. Includes the author's 1982 report on the massacre, as well as other valuable documents from the period.

770   Polifonía del Padre de la Patria: ciento treinta atisbos, narraciones y testimonios sobre el capitán general Don Juan Rafael Mora, presidente de la República de 1849 a 1859. Edición de Armando Vargas Araya. San José: Eduvisión, 2014. 469 p.: bibl., ill.

This collection of writings about Costa Rican president Juan Rafael Mora Porras includes texts from national and foreign authors, stretching from Mora's time to the 200th anniversary of his birth. See also item 767.

771 **Rodríguez Sáenz, Eugenia.** Campaña Nacional, crisis económica y capitalismo: Costa Rica en la época de Juan Rafael Mora (1850–1860). San José: Editorial Costa Rica, 2014. 147 p.: bibl., ill., index. (Colección nueva biblioteca patria; 4)

In this economic history of the Central Valley during the National Campaign, the author suggests that the conflict coincided with a global economic downturn, drying up credit for small coffee farmers and accelerating their expropriation by larger producers.

772 **Rueda Estrada, Verónica.** Recompas, recontras, revueltos y rearmados: posguerra y conflictos por la tierra en Nicaragua, 1990–2008. México: Instituto de Investigaciones Dr. José María Luis Mora: Consejo Nacional de Ciencia y Tecnología: Centro de Investigaciones sobre América Latina y el Caribe, UNAM, 2015. 518 p.: bibl., index, map. (Historia internacional)

This chronicle of military demobilization, heavily reliant on oral histories, suggests that excombatants rearmed following the government failure to reintegrate them into the rural sector. Rearmament in postwar Nicaragua formed part of the longer-term peasant struggle for land.

773 **Sarazúa, Juan Carlos.** Política y etnicidad y servicio militar: dos experiencias paralelas en Mesoamérica: Chiapas y Guatemala, 1808–1871. (*Rev. Hist. Am./México*, 152, 2016, p. 135–162, ill.)

This article reviews the impact of military service on ethnic identities during the period of transition from colonial to republican rule and examines how the process in Guatemala differed from that in neighboring parts of Mexico.

774 **Taracena Arriola, Arturo.** Guatemala, la República Española y el Gobierno Vasco en el exilio (1944–1954). Mérida, Mexico: UNAM, Centro Peninsular en Humanidades y Ciencias Sociales; Zamora, Mexico: El Colegio de Michoacán, A.C., 2017. 543 p.: bibl., ill., index. (Ensayos; 17)

Based largely on a trove of manuscript records discovered in the basement of the Guatemalan embassy in Paris, this study provides a detailed account of the reception of Spanish Republican exiles by the Arévalo and Arbenz administrations in Guatemala.

775 **Textos vivos: los pueblos indígenas de Guatemala en los escritos del Ejército Guerrillero de los Pobres—EGP.** Guatemala: Centro Rolando Moran, 2015. 176 p.: bibl., ill.

This valuable collection of EGP texts, testimonials, and interviews covers the revolutionary group's relationship to indigenous people and their role in the civil war.

776 **Tomamos la palabra: mujeres en la guerra civil de El Salvador: (1980–1992).** Edición de Margarita Drago y Juana Ramos. San Salvador: UCA Editores, 2016. 295 p.: ill., maps. (Colección Testigos de la Historia; 15)

This work compiles the testimonials of 20 women who participated in the armed uprising against the Salvadoran state. The subjects represent varied socioeconomic, political, and geographic backgrounds, suggesting a diversity of female experiences.

777 **Traversari, Gabriel.** La hija del dictador: conversaciones con Lillian Somoza Debayle. Prólogo de Julio Valle Castillo. Managua: Editorial La Prensa, 2014. 266 p., 34 pages of plates: ill. (some color), portraits.

This book publishes interviews with Lillian Somoza Debayle shortly before her death in 2003. Somoza Debayle was the daughter of Anastasio Somoza García and the wife of Guillermo Sevilla Sacasa, Nicaragua's longtime ambassador to the US. The conversations cover childhood, adolescence, and adulthood, treating a broad array of topics.

778 **Vargas Arias, Claudio Antonio.** Hacia la consolidación del Estado liberal en Costa Rica (1870–1890). Ciudad Universitaria Rodrigo Facio, Costa Rica: Editorial UCR, 2015. 75 p.: bibl. (Cuadernos de historia de las instituciones de Costa Rica; 27)

This thin volume examines the institutional, social, and ideological foundations of the liberal state in Costa Rica; its transition toward democratic, electoral practices; and its association with the country's agro-export economy.

779 **Vásquez Monzón, Olga.** Mujeres en público: el debate sobre la educación femenina entre 1871 y 1889. Prólogo de Juan José Tamayo. San Salvador: UCA Editores, 2014. 198 p.: bibl., facsims., ill., portraits. (Colección estructuras y procesos. Serie mayor; 34)

This study discusses the growth of female education in the late 19th century, which is seen as a product of the liberal reformers, who in opposition to the Catholic Church were determined to pursue secularization and to use schools as a means of socialization.

780 **Zúñiga C., Juan Cristóbal.** La gesta heroica del nacionalismo panameño: causas y consequencias inmediatas del 9 de enero de 1964: análisis documental histórico-jurídico. Panamá: Cultural Portobelo, 2015. 262 p.: bibl. (Biblioteca de autores panameños; 255)

This revision of a 1977 thesis for a BA degree in law at the Universidad de Panamá suggests that both the 1967 and 1977 canal treaties constituted betrayals of the 1964 uprising and the historic fight to eliminate the US colonial presence in Panama.

THE CARIBBEAN

MATT D. CHILDS, Associate Professor of History, University of South Carolina
LUIS A. GONZÁLEZ, Librarian for Latin American Studies, Spanish and Portuguese, Chicano-Riqueño Studies, Latino Studies, and European Studies, Indiana University, Bloomington
DANIEL LIVESAY, Associate Professor of History, Claremont McKenna College
ELIZABETH MANLEY, Associate Professor of History, Xavier University of Louisiana

BRITISH CARIBBEAN

AS A REGION, the Caribbean has experienced some of the most extreme versions of the historical forces shaping the Americas. Imperialism, native genocide, and slavery were in certain ways more intensely practiced in the West Indies than on the mainland. Likewise, resistance, uprisings, and anticolonial intellectualism were arguably developed more powerfully there too. Scholars of the 20th-century British Caribbean have long produced insightful examinations of the postcolonial progress and challenges facing the region. In more recent decades, as "Atlantic History" has prospered, scholars of the early-modern period have also revealed the critical importance of the Anglophone Caribbean to world events. As historians of this earlier era have sketched out more of the outlines of slavery, oppression, and economic underdevelopment that came out of the colonial period, greater continuities have emerged to clarify the struggles of the present. This assessment of publications on the British Caribbean covers the years 2013 to 2017, a period during which historical interest in the field has exploded.

With the near eradication of native populations in the British Caribbean, scholars have struggled to tell indigenous histories. In recent years, however, that has begun to change. Archeological evidence, coupled with deep archival investigations, have produced clearer images of aboriginal life immediately before and after Europeans arrived. But much is still obscured, due in large part to successive waves of European imperialism that devastated indigenous populations while simultaneously complicating their social statuses. Melanie Newton argues that the attempted annihilation of Antillean peoples in the 17th century transformed into a legal genocide to strip Amerindians of their indigenous designation (item **818**). This effort worked alongside a slave trade in native peoples within the Greater Caribbean that blurred the distinction between indigenous and African servants. Additional work is still needed in this area, but these scholarly forays signal highly encouraging trends.

Much of the literature on the British Caribbean continues to focus on plantation slavery. With roughly two million kidnapped Africans arriving to the region over the course of the transatlantic slave trade, this period is critical to understanding the economic, political, and demographic history of the West Indies. The online publication of the Trans-Atlantic Slave Trade Database (slavevoyages.org) more than a decade ago launched many investigations into the quantitative character of human trafficking. In recent years, though, scholars have redirected their attention toward the human and political elements of the barbaric trade. Sowande' Mustakeem documents, in vivid detail, the sufferings of captured Africans at sea by delineating the variety of experiences based on age, health, and gender (item **796**). Gregory O'Malley demonstrates the crucial position of the British Caribbean as an enslaved clearinghouse in the Americas, while Nicholas Radburn carefully reconstructs the ways that a Jamaican trader carried out the business (items **798** and **839**). Both William Pettigrew and Abigail Swingen further underscore the importance of the Caribbean slave trade: in these cases as a battleground of British politics (items **825** and **837**).

Despite a consensus on the scale and centrality of the transatlantic slave trade in the Caribbean, its initial effects continue to roil debate. The forcible transportation of Irish servants complicates early definitions of West Indian bondage. Simon Newman contends that New World plantations were testing grounds for novel labor regimes that subjugated both European and African workers. During Barbados' early colonial years, he argues, white servants experienced effectively the same type of abuse as black counterparts—until indentures turned too expensive and African labor became much cheaper (item **817**). Jerome Handler counters this position by asserting that the legal and customary precedents against Africans made them distinctive in their oppression on the plantation from the beginning (item **815**). Irish servants were originally mistreated for various reasons that were eventually mollified by the arrival of Africans, but there is substantial evidence that Barbados' legal codes were quite early in distinguishing between African and European laborers.

The solidification of plantation slavery, worked exclusively by African labor at the end of the 17th century, produced enormous profits and inhumane conditions that scholars continue to investigate exhaustively. Many studies chart, in close detail, the economics of plantation agriculture, and their brutal effects on those forced to toil. This scholarship has also paid close attention to the ways in which Caribbean outposts were tightly linked—economically, politically, and geographically—with one another, and with the broader Americas. Two substantial monographs deploy a comparative approach not only to provide a refined sense of British Caribbean slavery, but also to demonstrate the ways that it was part of modern economic development (items **829** and **831**). Notably, there has been a renewed interest in the enslaved family experience on plantations as well, especially around the effects of slavery on children.

How enslaved people responded to their treatment is still a challenging question for scholars in this field. Most studies have walked away from interpretations that put enslaved agency solely into the polarized categories of resistance and accommodation. Survival, instead, appears to have been a more salient goal for most enslaved people. Religious practices, particularly that of obeah, have often been interpreted as a form of rebellion. But recent work charts obeah's multifaceted and polysemous character. Planters themselves, disconnected from the actual maneuvers of enslaved people, often cooked up conspiracies of rebellion. Marisa Fuentes thoughtfully considers much of the challenge in recovering the enslaved perspective; she methodically details the archival silences and obstacles that often deliberately misrepresented those unable to record their own viewpoints (item **832**).

For individuals who made their way out of slavery, life could nevertheless still present significant trials. Analyses of free people of color have emerged, in part, because the group made a stronger archival impression than their enslaved peers. Businesswomen of color, along with white women, were critical agents in the economies of Britain's West Indian territories. Likewise, Jamaica's most elite inhabitants of color were closely connected to white relatives, demonstrating the importance of family connection to racial status (item **836**). Yet their biographies reveal areas of opportunity that existed only within highly circumscribed spaces in a region dominated by racial oppression. These stories have nonetheless helped to diversify the narratives of social life in the British West Indies.

The dominance of slavery in the colonial Caribbean has dictated much of the scholarship on the region, but recent work has also sought to uncover the small, but distinct civil society that existed for free people. Carla Pestana provides a thorough overview of England's conquest of Jamaica and the early struggles for colonial dominance (item **819**). Her work questions the role of piracy in Jamaica's initial years, though Mark Hanna insists that privateering was critical to the colony's development (item **790**). Additional scholarship chronicles the social life of free whites through their financial activities, cosmopolitan engagement with the Enlightenment, and architectural investment that allowed planters to remove themselves from the ugly realities of their business. Indeed, white colonists worked aggressively to portray themselves as sophisticated people at the service of an equally refined state. Although focused on free society, each of these publications helps to add greater complexity to the historical changes that enslaved people experienced in the British Caribbean.

The illumination of colonial rulers during slavery has helped scholars of the post-emancipation period make stronger assessments of life after bondage. Religious reforms imposed a great deal of colonial control over freed people after the emancipation act of 1834. Multiple authors use that religious context to explain a series of governmental crackdowns on Afro-Caribbean people in the mid-19th century. Each of these was a moral panic argument about the supposed depredations of black people, which whites used to justify imperial oppression and "civilizing" processes. Those strictures, combined with a devastated regional economy, inspired multiple uprisings and revolts, which historians have recently documented with stunning detail. Once again, comparisons are helpful. Matthew Smith charts the parallel stories of Jamaica and Haiti in the 19th and 20th centuries to show the role that direct and indirect imperialism played in the Caribbean (item **878**). Each of these cases reveals the ways that colonial regimes continued to oppress people of color long after slavery's shackles fell off.

The discontent felt across Britain's West Indian territories shaped some of the 20th century's most important and brilliant intellectuals. The British Caribbean produced a number of key figures in the Pan-African and black consciousness movement. Their biographies continue to inspire scholars of the 20th century. Eric

Williams has been subject to several notable works in recent years that chart not only the politician's global influence, but also his historical and cultural reach. Much of the current attention to Caribbean intellectualism has led to an exploration of its influence across the Americas and the globe. In some cases, those studies have maintained a principal examination of great figures, but in many others, the focus has shifted to the less famous adherents of radical black ideologies. Two important works on Rastafarianism explore both the founders of the religion as well as what typical congregants thought about it and how they expressed the practice in their own lives and global travels (items **889** and **931**). The movement of West Indians across the English- speaking world created a cauldron of black political thought that ultimately inspired everyday people to demand justice against colonial rule. Lara Putnam (item **934**) and Birte Timm (item **948**) demonstrate how mistreatment at home, migration abroad, and global networking produced a truly international activist movement rooted in the Caribbean experience. Nevertheless, the political particularities of each island produced their own experiences of decolonization in the mid-20th century, as well as continued imperial influence from the US.

Scholars of the British Caribbean have constructed a long historical timeline with recurring patterns of abuse, racial injustice, and colonial oppression that endures today. These are not merely intellectual concerns, but ones with pressing importance for a region still struggling with its history. Although it has been subject to fits and starts, the reparations movement has gained strong support from Caribbean academics. Both Hilary Beckles and Verene Shepherd have made impassioned pleas for reparations, based on careful calculations about the profit extracted from West Indians by the British government, British companies, and British families (items **808** and **814**). Beckles and Shepherd concede that the request has not been an easy political argument, but that the history of expropriation and abuse is entirely clear.

Taken together, a compelling and—in some ways—coherent portrait of the British Caribbean emerges through these various pieces of scholarship. The legacy of empire, slavery, genocide, and racism informs each of the periods in question. There is still more to do, however. Although scholars have effectively demonstrated the global dimension of the British Caribbean, there remains a woeful lack of publications on the connections between European empires in the region. Likewise, significant gaps exist in the institutional history of the British Caribbean. Many courts, businesses, legislatures, religious denominations, fraternal orders, newspapers, hobby organizations, and cultural clubs have not yet had their own analyses, leaving much of the vibrancy and complexity of Caribbean life undocumented. Scholars living outside the West Indies must be more persistent in doing research in Caribbean archives to help uncover these stories. At the same time, however, Caribbean scholars have successfully revealed how crucial the region is to Latin America and the wider world. [DL]

PUERTO RICO

If one accepts that the preoccupations of the present generally inform or give shape to the retrospective gaze of historians, one can perhaps begin to understand the overriding interest of scholars of Puerto Rico in interrogating the Caribbean nation's modern history from diverse theoretical and methodological perspectives. The centennial of the enactment of the Jones Act of 1917 prompted conferences and publications that examined historical, social, political, and juridical aspects of the landmark, yet controversial legislation granting US citizenship to the people of Puerto Rico. *CENTRO Journal* and *Op. Cit.*—leading academic journals in the field of Puerto Rican Studies—dedicated special issues to the timely topic (items **890** and **930**, respectively).

A growing body of literature deals with the contributions of prominent political leaders and intellectuals to the formation of modern Puerto Rico. On the one hand, these works are heavily concentrated on *autonomismo* and *estadismo*, two of the main political currents in 20th-century Puerto Rican politics. On the other, this scholarship explores key aspects of the history of the Estado Libre Asociado (or Commonwealth of Puerto Rico), established in 1952. A reprint of selected writings of Luis Muñoz Rivera, the influential *autonomista* leader, appears in *Campañas políticas (1890–1916)* (item **795**). The Centro Interamericano para el Estudio de las Dinámicas Políticas (CIEDP) at the Universidad Interamericana maintains a vigorous research agenda on political elites. Recent volumes focus on Antonio Fernós Isern, the intellectual architect of the Estado Libre Asociado (item **899**), and Rafael Martínez Nadal, a leading advocate of the Puerto Rican statehood movement during the 1920–40 period (item **935**). As is customary in these publications, the volumes contain extensive appendices of ancillary materials, including select speeches and personal correspondence. The creation of the Estado Libre Asociado continues to generate scholarly interest. Carlos Zapata Oliveras addresses the intense constitutional debates and contested political negotiations between Puerto Rican leaders (particularly Luis Muñoz Marín and Fernós Isern), the US executive office, and the US Congress over the creation of the political system that granted a degree of self-rule to the people of Puerto Rico (item **953**). Fernando Bayrón Toro provides a comprehensive history of elections and political parties in Puerto Rico dating back to the early 19th century (item **782**).

The lens of culture has fostered insightful analyses of understudied aspects of modern Puerto Rican society and politics. This line of inquiry has also elucidated the contributions of intellectuals to the formulation of government policies. In a study of sugar industry reforms introduced by the Partido Popular Democrático during the 1940s, Rubén Nazario Velasco examines the critical role of leading intellectuals in the development of an agrarian discourse that challenged the domination of sugar interests on the island (item **928**). Martín Cruz Santos highlights the figure of Águedo Mojica Marrero, an organic intellectual who gave shape to cultural nationalism in Puerto Rico (item **893**). The intersection of sports, culture, and politics has been fertile ground for historical inquiry. Antonio Sotomayor shows how the athletic development project introduced by the Partido Popular Democrático dovetailed with the ruling party's political and economic program (item **944**). The sports program generated broad-based support from the citizenry for the government, ultimately reinforcing colonial bonds between Puerto Rico and the US. As a US territory, the Cold War had far-reaching political, economic, and social repercussions in Puerto Rico. A stimulating volume edited by Manuel Rodríguez Vázquez and Silvia Álvarez Curbelo takes us beyond the conventional accounts of the Cold War as a predominantly binary struggle between world powers (item **947**). In their everyday life, people in Puerto Rico experienced the Cold War in complex and contradictory ways, suggesting that high-stakes conflicts for global power had a manifestly local cultural dimension.

Critical engagement of photographic discourse has advanced the knowledge of relations between Puerto Rico and the US since the era of the Spanish-Cuban-American War of 1898. In her landmark book-length study of the representations of the Caribbean region (particularly Cuba and Puerto Rico) in the photographs and captions of *National Geographic*, Laura Muñoz Mata argues that photographs are complex, polysemic records that do not simply reflect, but at times serve to shape and influence US relations toward the countries of the Caribbean (item **927**). In a 2017 journal article, she continues this research agenda, focusing on the Caribbean sugar industry (item **926**). The visual discourse of sugar estates in the photographs in *National Geographic* suggests both modernization led by North American capital investments in technology and infrastructure, and shifts in US political interests toward the Caribbean over time. Jorge Luis Crespo Armáiz's article complements the work of Muñoz Mata (item **892**). For historian Crespo Armáiz, the textual and visual representations of Puerto Rico in the pages of *National Geographic* challenge the magazine's manifest editorial line of scientific objectivity, suggesting that these representations mirror the shifts in US economic, political, and military interests in Puerto Rico. Another work by Crespo Armáiz, *Estereoscopía y sujeto colonial*, makes a significant contribution to colonial photography studies (item **851**). Drawing on largely untapped sources—collections of stereoscopic photographs—he examines the construction of a colonial visual imaginary of Puerto Rico since 1898. The scholar also shows how this imaginary was extensively consumed in North American schools, universities, and libraries in the form of teacher's manuals during the first decades of the 20th century.

Using an array of oral and archival sources, scholars have documented the personal experiences of ordinary people in Puerto Rican society. The late anthropologist Sidney W. Mintz provided an insightful reflection on the use of oral history and life history as appropriate methodologies for the study of modern agrarian societies (item **923**). His now classic *Worker in the Cane* (1960; see *HLAS* 23:650), translated into Spanish as *Taso, trabajador de la caña* (1988; see *HLAS* 52:1943), pioneered the use of life history methodology in anthropological research on rural workers. Carmelo Rosario Natal unearths the story of Juana Agripina, a Creole enslaved woman from Ponce, based on the extant case file she lodged to claim her freedom in 1865 (item **876**). This remarkable legal document sheds new light on the agency of enslaved people in 19th-century Puerto Rico. Similarly, Raquel Rosario Rivera has published the first scholarly biography of Mariana Bracety, a woman leader of the Grito de Lares rebellion against Spain in 1868 (item **877**). Rosario Rivera recovered important information on Bracety's life from the previously untapped resource of a recorded interview with Bracety's long-time female household companion.

Migration to and from Puerto Rico has also been the subject of stimulating research. Ivette Pérez Vega provides a prosopographical study of the foreign-born merchant class of Ponce during the early decades of the 1800s (item **871**). Merchants were key actors in the transformation of the southern municipality into a booming sugar-producing economy based on slave labor. José Lee-Borges traces the history of the first Chinese migrants to Puerto Rico (item **864**). Arriving during the 1860s from the Dominican Republic and Cuba, the Chinese were brought in as prisoners by the Spanish colonial authorities to work on road construction and public works projects. This work fills a gap in the historiography of Caribbean immigration. Drawing on records of the Puerto Rican Department of Labor, Edgardo Meléndez shows the government's active role in the development and implementation of a well-planned migrant workforce program from the island to the US mainland during the 1940s and 1950s (item **918**).

Recent scholarship in social, economic, and diplomatic history has deepened our understanding of Puerto Rico's past and present. Kathryn Renée Dungy explores the experience of free people of color in early 19th-century Puerto Rico (item **854**). She argues that the Puerto Rican case introduces nuances into the understanding of race and race relations in colonial societies in the Black Atlantic. Focusing on the Ministerio de Ultramar, established in 1863 to oversee Spain's overseas territories, Adel Ben Othman analyzes the foreign relations of Spain with Cuba and Puerto Rico, the last colonial possessions of the former European power in the Americas (item **846**). Edwin Borrero González studies the history of the coastal railway network, documenting its development and eventual decline in the 1950s (item **847**). Research on the once-dominant sugarcane industry continues to command scholarly interest. Heriberto Medina Vera examines the social composition and political discourse of the forces opposing the sugar reforms introduced by the New Deal program during the 1930s (item **917**). Not only native capital, the scholar argues, but also cane growers and workers mobilized against these reforms. Javier Alemán Iglesias writes on the historiography of the *colonato*, the class of growers who supplied sugarcane to the modern central mills (*centrales*) in 20th-century Puerto Rico (item **883**). In a microhistory of Guayama, a southern sugarcane-growing region, Alexis Oscar Tirado Rivera analyzes local struggles against both the expansion of North American absentee investments in the sugar industry and transportation as well as US government policies promoting the use of English in schools (item **949**). Jorge Duany provides an accessible, yet authoritative introduction to Puerto Rico's modern history, covering topics such as national identity and Americanization, the Puerto Rican diaspora in the US, the current debt crisis, and other relevant issues in US-Puerto Rican relations (item **789**).

Examination of resistance continues to attract scholarly attention. Focusing on the slave conspiracy of 1812 in Puerto Rico, Antonio Pinto traces connections between this historical event, the Aponte rebellion in Cuba, and the slave plot in Santo Domingo during the same year (item **874**). A unifying feature of these slave plots was the collaboration between slaves and free people of color. Jorell Meléndez-Badillo combines social and cultural history approaches to explore the largely autonomous, grassroots mobilization of agricultural workers during the historic 1905 strike in the sugarcane fields of southern Puerto Rico (item **919**). Both studies highlight agency on the part of enslaved peoples and workers in these struggles.

Also of note is research in the burgeoning fields of environmental studies and food studies focusing on Puerto Rico. Fernando Picó delves into a largely forgotten chapter in 19th-century Puerto Rican history, the severe drought of 1847, investigating the social impact of a so-called natural disaster (item **873**). He places the local case in the global perspective of a drought, propelled by the El Niño weather phenomenon. A significant contribution to environmental studies, this work was the preeminent historian's last book-length publication before his untimely passing in 2017. April Merleaux investigates the shifts in patterns of sugar consumption in the US market and the attendant transformation of the diet of people in Puerto Rico as the outcome of policies established by the US government during the New Deal era and World War II (items **921** and **922**).

Welcome reflections on historiographical and anthropological writing about Puerto Rico appear in Gervasio Luis García's book (item **856**) and in a special issue of *Op. Cit.* dedicated to the late Sidney W. Mintz (item **799**). Among other subjects, García analyzes the discursive strategies that 19th-century intellectuals used to circumvent the censorship of Spanish authorities. The journal special issue includes the Spanish-language translation of Mintz's seminal article "The Caribbean as a Socio-cultural Area" (1966), a biography, and two additional essays: one reviewing the intellectual context at the time his essay was written, and the other assessing Mintz's scholarly contributions to the field of Caribbean Studies. [LG]

DOMINICAN REPUBLIC
In the historiography of the Dominican Republic in the 20th century, several major periods and approaches continue to hold sway in the imaginations—and agendas—of scholars. The US occupation (1916–24), the era of the Trujillo dictatorship (1930–61), and the postdictatorship and second US intervention (1961–65) remain entrenched as the most covered periods in modern Dominican history and they are generally covered from a political or personal (memoir) perspective. While a number of temporal and thematic holes remain gaping—to wit, Amaury Rodríguez and Nelson Santana's recent series of lists of potential research topics in their online journal *Esendom* ("Ten Research Ideas about Dominicans You Should Pursue, Part 1"; https://esendom.com/cultura/2018/2/8/ten-thesis-ideas-about- dominicans-that-you-should-pursue-part-1)—the trend toward a more inclusive historiography continues slowly but surely, staking claims in previously neglected periods and addressing well-trodden ground with rigorous and innovative analytical approaches.

Following a trend established with the publication of *The Dominican Republic Reader* edited by Lauren Derby, Eric Paul Roorda, and Raymundo González and part of the Duke University Press series of readers (see *HLAS 71:1124*), modern Dominican history is becoming more visible in encyclopedic reference texts. An example is Eric Paul Roorda's *Historical Dictionary of the Dominican Republic*, which offers a thorough overview of people, places, events, and concepts in Dominican history (item **806**). In addition, a number of contributions to the new *Oxford Research Encyclopedia of Latin American History* (Krohn-Hansen, Manley, Moulton, Wooding, Yoder, and Roorda (forthcoming)), all solicited by Lauren Derby, demonstrate an expanding breadth of coverage in Dominican historical studies, as well as its broader relevance to Latin American studies as a whole (item **800**).

Continuing trends that are more standard in Dominican historiography, a number of selections in this volume return to the first US occupation of the Dominican Republic (1916–24). This is not to say that this historic ground has been completely trampled, although several of the selections on the period offer little in the way of new primary source-based analysis (items **900** and **929**). Of the three works included here written to commemorate the 100th anniversary of the Marine arrival in 1916, only one, written (posthumously) by a member of the Academia Dominicana de la Historia and a highly esteemed scholar of the discipline, offers substantially new material (item **884**). While all three do indeed serve as an important reminder of the eight-year derogation of sovereignty in the hands of US occupiers, as well as the valiant resistance of Dominican men and women through political, civil, and military avenues, new directions in research on the period should continue to mine the vast historical sources available in both the Dominican Republic and the US, as well as expand into cultural, literary, and social fields in order to better chart both the occupation and its aftermath. The publications by Micah Wright and Isabel Delores de Leon are examples of research in progress by early-career scholars that indicate important new directions in creative uses of sources and expansion into new lines of inquiry (items **896** and **952**).

Much like the occupation, texts continue to be produced about the Trujillo period—including its resistance activities—that reify existing knowledge, sometimes in ways that do a disservice to efforts to nuance this long period of dictatorship. Several texts here focus in on the Trujillato and/or authoritarianism, contributing to the ongoing conversation of the hows and whys of the three-decade regime (item **907**), although there has been a shift in perspective in that nearly all of these works have begun to move beyond an insular focus and nod to the questions of how the particularities of the Dominican case shed light on authoritarian and militaristic regimes across Latin America and the Caribbean (item **950**). As testament to the expanding and more comparative approach to Dominican scholarship, one study on the attempted assassination of Rómulo Betancourt by the Trujillo regime offers research completed entirely in Venezuela (item **924**). Similarly, an assessment of the US film coverage of Trujillo in 1936 demonstrates how crucial a role film history and media studies may play in our understanding of US-Dominican relations during the regime (item **905**). Shedding light on the lesser-known (and shocking/not shocking) activities of the regime and the documents produced during that period is also evidenced in a number of new, if not terribly innovative, studies of the movement of resistance against Trujillo (items **888** and **897**). Finally, several studies that extend beyond the period of dictatorship seek to integrate Dominican history into larger regional narratives of interstate relations (items **805** and **880**).

Continuing in its practice of unearthing and publishing troves of primary documents and its deep and abiding reverence for the resistance movement, the Archivo General de la Nación (AGN) facilitated a collaboration with the Academia Dominicana de la Historia (ADH) helmed by historian Bernardo Vega that made accessible a collection of correspondence between Angel Morales and Sumner Welles (1930–50) and treats the efforts of long-exiled Morales to unseat the three-decade dictator (item **951**). The close relationship between the AGN and the ADH—evidenced by several texts selected included in this section—is a crucial connection that links the personnel and resources of the nation's archival treasures with its most celebrated historians. Facilitated by AGN director Roberto Cassá's membership in the elite group of historians, a significant number of texts were produced when Bernardo Vega took the helm of the ADH in 2016 (items **884** and **951**).

Moreover, in an effort to construct a "complete history" of the Dominican Republic, the ADH also began publishing a series of six texts in 2013, covering "from the indigenous peoples, through the conquest, the configuration of Creole society, the emergence of the nation between 1790 and 1880, the advent of modernization, the dictatorial regime of Trujillo, and the last decades of the 20th century" (item **910**, p. 15). In the presentation of the series, Bernardo Vega, then president of the Academy, argues that not only would the collected volumes offer a "new historiography, using new sources and revising old paradigms", but also that each of the 16 essays in this fifth volume on the Trujillo regime (p. 15–16) presented "very novel" approaches to the characterization of the dictatorship, Trujillo's claim of the presidency, economic conditions and Trujillo's business "empire," political and military struggles, the Haitian massacre, World War II, international relations, crimes and repression, resistance, daily life, literature, and architecture. Contributions from Roberto Cassá, Bernardo Vega, Edwin Croes Hernández, Alejandro Paulino Ramos, Eliades Acosta Matos, Rafael Darío Herrera, Nelson Moreno Ceballos, Luis Gómez Pérez,

Odalía G. Pérez, and Omar Rancier anchor the text (item **910**). Regardless of its claim to a new historiography and new analytical lenses, gender, sexuality, and, most importantly, women are glaringly absent from the national narrative. No women are on the advisory board for the series (despite the current president of the ADH being a woman); no female scholars contributed to the volume; and there is precious little mention of women in the text (the Mirabal sisters not even meriting a subheading).

However, concurrent with the publication of the primary-document anthology *Cien años de feminismos dominicanos* (see *HLAS 72:1023*), there has been an increased public and academic interest in the role of women in Dominican history since 2017. In addition to a surprising number of journalistic pieces in the nation's daily newspapers and magazines, there has been a growth in the publication of books addressing women in the political realm (item **906**). Attention to gender and sexuality as crucial links in the structure and function of domestic and international politics continues to expand in interest—both scholarly and popular—in modern Dominican historiography (item **811**). Building on the work of the past half-decade (at least), each of the essays in a special issue of the journal *Small Axe*, curated and edited by Maja Horn and David Scott, speaks to this trend, but also challenges other scholars to continue to widen their historical analyses of women, gender, and sexuality (item **810**).

Still, biographies and primary document collections addressing "important men" in Dominican history continue to dominate the field, including volumes on Carlos Morales Languasco, Ulises Heureaux, and Juan Pablo Duarte (items **898**, **858**, and **862**, respectively). Several important points should be noted, however, as the compilation of documents gathered by Cyrus Vesser on former dictator Ulises Heureaux demonstrates the continued commitment of the AGN to making their collections more available to the public, the period covered by the documents in the collection on Morales Languasco represents a relatively understudied era, and the bibliographic treatment of Dominican founding father Juan Pablo Duarte by Orlando Inoa provides a useful resource and thorough display of commitment to the study of the famous figure. In addition, an homage to historian Emilio Cordero Michel demonstrates the breadth and depth of his scholarly reach, expanding beyond such "great men" history to illustrate a number of crucial interventions into Dominican historical studies (item **786**).

Finally, there is some glimmer of indication that the first Balaguer period (1966–78) is beginning to receive the scholarly attention it demands and that new areas of research in the 20th century are opening up. Included here is work on the African Methodist Episcopal Church in the Dominican Republic (item **895**), as well as scholarship on the *doce años*—from standard treatments of Balaguer to citizen complaints of prostitution and identity politics vis-à-vis television stardom (item **885**).

In a recent edition of the Caribbean journal *Small Axe*, Ada Ferrer kicked off the publication's call to expand their own focus to include the Hispanophone Caribbean in their research and publication agenda (item **809**). Ferrer's contribution grappled with a definition for that new focus, ultimately pushing readers to consider a shift toward the transnational, to at once transcend the primacy of "national perspectives" while also looking locally (to see globally). True to their commitment of expansion in that issue, *Small Axe* has embraced modern Hispaniola in their subsequent editions, including the July 2018 special focus on Dominican gender and sexuality (item **810**).

Ferrer made the call for a transnational lens at the same time that a group of scholars—the Transnational Hispaniola collective—sought to redirect studies of Haiti and the Dominican Republic to look at the island as a whole. In what might be called their mission statement in the *Radical History Review* (115, Winter 2013, p. 26–32), they challenged scholars "to consider the island and its people as a whole." After several conferences and many scholarly exchanges, 13 scholars, including editors April J. Mayes and Kiran C. Jayaram, came together to produce *Transnational Hispaniola: New Directions in Haitian and Dominican Studies* (item **811**). While the collection incorporates a number of disciplines, it will be of interest to historians of the modern Caribbean because several of the essays force readers to consider "new narratives"—of the present and the past—that reject the notion of a divided Hispaniola and offer instead a history that intertwines both sides of the island (see particularly Bragadir, Eller, Manley, and Tavárez).

Sadly, work on Haitian-Dominican relations, mostly coming from journalists and non-Dominicanist scholars, continues to reinforce a mostly solidified and predominantly ahistorical hatred between the two sides of the island (item **791**). Pushing back against this narrative that pits the Dominican Republic as always against Haiti, Dió-genes Abréu offers, in *Sin haitianidad no hay dominicanidad (cartografía de una identidad que se bifurca)*, a more nuanced historical analysis of the inextricable relationship between the two countries (item **781**). As he argues, the Haitian heritage in Dominican identity is undeniable; the irony of course is that, given the legacies of the Trujillato, scholars and activists must make the effort to point out that such linkages are, in fact, undeniable. Suggesting "cognitive alternatives" to the racist and shameful commentaries that have appeared recently across Dominican media about Haitians and Haitian-Dominicans, Abréu argues that the syncretic relationship between the two nations has been denied in Dominican historiography only through a "trampa ideológical." Crucial to creating these "cognitive alternatives" is a need to critically assess the moments in Dominican history and historiography in which animosities and stereotypes have hardened into perceived truths. Much like work conducted previously by Richard Turits, Lauren Derby, and Edward Paulino (see *HLAS 62:1250–1251*, *HLAS 67:1189*, and *HLAS 72:1103*, respectively), among others, new work also chips away at some of the most hardened spots of the Trujillato, as Amelia Hintzen does with her article in the *New West Indian Guide (NWIG)* (item **908**). Similarly, two other very distinct offerings challenge existing understandings of race, nation, and the relations between the two sides of the island (items **800** and **880**).

Other significant trends in the study of 20th-century Dominican Republic include an emphasis on combining cultural analysis—literature, music, and foodways—with historical perspectives for a more comprehensive understanding of Dominican identity and contemporary realities. Undertaking a review, for example, of foreign press coverage between the fall of Trujillo and the overthrow of President Juan Bosch (item **941**), presenting a comprehensive 20th-century history of the rum industry (item **891**), or compiling interviews of nearly 30 modern bachata performers (item **943**) represent essential moves toward a more comprehensive historical picture. Moreover, as indicated in the last edition of *HLAS*, literary studies of the Dominican Republic and Hispaniola more broadly continue to carefully meld meticulous textual readings—as products of a particular time and space—with historical analysis and speak to questions of collective memory, race, gender, and identity across the island (item **936**).

In sum, recent scholarship challenges the linguistic, historical, racial, and other barriers that make Hispaniola both part of and marginalized from Latin American and Caribbean scholarship. Demanding that scholars and popular audiences consider the island as central to the corpus of work on the region or, in Dixa Ramírez's words, as the "navel" of the postcolonial Americas, this new work aims to put Hispaniola back at the "crossroads" of studies of the hemisphere. [EM]

GENERAL

781 Abréu, Dió-genes. Sin haitianidad no hay dominicanidad: cartografía de una identidad que se bifurca. Santo Domingo: Editora Nacional, 2014. 263 p.: bibl., ill. (Colección Ultramar)

This work offers a nuanced analysis of the inextricable relationship between the two sides of the island of Hispaniola. The author argues that the Haitian heritage in Dominican identity is undeniable and seeks to offer "cognitive alternatives" to the racist and shameful commentaries that have appeared recently across Dominican media about Haitians and Haitian-Dominicans. The text looks at traditionally defined historiographical periods from the colonial period to the 2010 earthquake, offering sometimes surprising examples to support its thesis of Haitian-Dominican syncretism and skillfully employing oral histories throughout. Winner of the Premio Letras de Ultramar de Ensayo 2013. [EM]

782 Bayrón Toro, Fernando. Historia de las elecciones y los partidos políticos de Puerto Rico, 1809–2012. 8a edición ampliada. Río Piedras, Puerto Rico: Ediciones Gaviota, 2016. 650 p.: bibl., ill., maps, portraits.

This work presents a revised and enlarged edition of a comprehensive history of elections, political parties, and general background information on Puerto Rican politics dating back to the early 1800s. Includes a catalog of governors and lawmakers. For a review of the 7th edition, see *HLAS 65:1573*. [LG]

783 Beckles, Hilary. The first black slave society: Britain's "barbarity time" in Barbados, 1636–1876. Kingston: The University of the West Indies Press, 2016. 296 p.: bibl., index.

As the first American colony to be structured wholly around slavery, Barbados was a radical experiment in human exploitation. Beckles follows the social, political, economic, and legal structures put into place that made the island a slave society (rather than simply a society with enslaved people). Likewise, he traces the ways that Barbados became a model for plantation systems in the Greater Caribbean. This monograph acts as a focused history of Barbados as well, culminating in an analysis of the War of General Green in 1876, in which workers pushed back against economic exploitation nearly a half century after emancipation. [DL]

784 Los caminos del Moncada. Textos de Servando Valdés Sánchez et al. Habana: EH, Editora Historia, 2013. 246 p.: bibl.

This collection of 11 essays and articles was published on the 60th anniversary of the Moncada assault led by Fidel Castro. Many of the individual chapters, a few of which have been previously published, analyze the political events leading up to the Moncada assault such as political mobilization and the situation of the peasantry. Other chapters specifically examine the reaction to the Moncada assault by different sectors of Cuban society and how the event was covered in the press. A valuable collection of essays for understanding the importance of the failed Moncada attack in the revolutionary process. See also *HLAS 64:1098*. [MDC]

785 Caribbean Irish connections: interdisciplinary perspectives. Edited by Alison Donnell, Maria McGarrity, and Evelyn O'Callaghan. Kingston: The University of the West Indies Press, 2015. 341 p.: bibl., ill., index, maps.

This volume contains 17 separate articles on the interlinkages between Ireland and the Caribbean from the 17th century to the present. The first collection of articles examines the history of Irish migration to the Caribbean, the group's place and influence on colonial plantations, and its religious contribution to the West Indies. The second set of articles explores issues of identity and cultural performance within Irish-Caribbean society. A final group analyzes literary and political connections between Ireland and the Caribbean. Each section evaluates the notion, popularized by Derek Walcott, of "a deep collective bond of cultural subalternity" between the two locations and people (p. 4). [DL]

786 **Cordero Michel, Emilio.** Obras escogidas. Ensayos I. Presentación de Eliades Acosta Matos. Santo Domingo: Archivo General de la Nación, Departamento de Investigación y Divulgación, 2015. 401 p.: bibl., index. (Archivo de la nación; CCLIV)

This work presents an homage to Emilio Cordero Michel through a series of 10 essays written by the distinguished historian and member of the Dominican Academy of History over the course of his career, ranging in topics from the Haitian Revolution to the precolonial economy to the April Revolution and second US intervention. The volume, presented by Eliades Acosta Matos, is the first of a planned series to celebrate the "militant revolutionary, committed journalist, guerrillero, political activist, university professor, and always lucid, coherent, and combative historian." One essay, appearing here in English, was published in 1965 by the US Progressive Labor Party, while the remainder were presented and/or published (in Spanish) originally in the Dominican Republic and other Latin American countries. [EM]

787 **Cuba y España: procesos migratorios e impronta perdurable (siglos XIX y XX).** Edición de José Manuel Azcona y Israel Escalona. Madrid: Editorial Dykinson, 2014. 316 p., 7 unnumbered pages of plates: bibl., ill.

This edited collection of 18 chapters chronicles the experience of Cuban migrants to the island during the 19th and 20th centuries. The first half of the volume takes a regional and institutional approach by chronicling the formation of Spanish cultural associations in cities and regions across Cuba, such as Spanish "casinos" in interior towns. The second half examines the ongoing cultural influence of Spain in Cuba during the 20th century through film, literature, and art. [MC]

788 **Dillman, Jefferson.** Colonizing paradise: landscape and empire in the British West Indies. Tuscaloosa: The University of Alabama Press, 2015. 249 p.: bibl., index. (Atlantic crossings)

The Caribbean landscape was a sight of natural paradise and horrific human abuse. In this study, Dillman assesses the ways that European colonizers approached the West Indian environment. The Spanish held a bifurcated view of Edenic lushness, paired with Satanic savagery. Building off the Iberian model, the English likewise took a split view: one in which the landscape was holy, but the labor within it was hell. Dillman contends that the vices of piracy, alcohol, and slavery fed into stereotypes of Caribbean danger, pushing white West Indians to promote cultivated gardens as evidence of imperial mastery over a wild climate. [DL]

789 **Duany, Jorge.** Puerto Rico: what everyone needs to know. New York, N.Y.: Oxford University Press, 2017. 189 p.: bibl., index, maps.

This work presents an accessible introduction to Puerto Rico's modern history. Duany illuminates key aspects of national identity and Americanization, migration and the Puerto Rican diaspora in the US, and current issues in US-Puerto Rico relations. [LG]

790 **Hanna, Mark G.** Pirate nests and the rise of the British Empire, 1570–1740. Chapel Hill: The University of North Carolina Press, 2015. 448 p.: bibl., ill., index, maps.

This monograph tackles piracy in a global British Empire, but it contains a crucial chapter about privateering in Jamaica. After England took Jamaica from the Spanish in 1655, the island struggled to defend itself against possible reconquest. Moreover, royal treaties in the years after the Restoration appeared to threaten the safety and financial stability of Jamaica, compelling many colonists to support piratical activity in the region before a slave-based economy had fully formed. Hanna works through the history of Jamaica's early decades under

British rule to argue that pirates were critical to the political and economic stability of the young colony. [DL]

791   Lamb, Valerie and Lauren Dundes.
Not Haitian: exploring the roots of Dominican identity. (*Soc. Sci.*, 6:4, 2017, p. 132–143, bibl.)

Exemplary of the ways in which scholars have helped fuel the lie that all Dominicans are anti-black and anti-Haitian, this very sweeping look at race in the Dominican Republic from a purportedly social science perspective merely serves to duplicate the problems that divide the island. The five-paragraph "History of Hispaniola" that presents broad-sweeping claims like "most Dominicans identify as indio" (without evidence and citing scholars who do not work on the DR) and the use of travel guides as sources of Dominican attitudes are demonstrative of the problems with this "literature review supplemented by interview data." Moreover, the reliance on US-focused scholars as a foundation for their work ignores (and negates) the scholarship of many Dominican-centered scholars who have provided much more nuanced and sophisticated analyses of racial identity in the Dominican Republic. When Dominican-based scholars are engaged, their work is in large part misrepresented. [EM]

792   Martin, John Angus. Island Caribs and French settlers in Grenada, 1498–1763. St George's, Grenada: The Grenada National Museum Press, 2013. 438 p.: bibl., ill., index, maps.

This monograph compiles information on nearly every aspect of Grenada's history over the first three centuries of its colonization. The study begins with a consideration of the native Carib population, including reflections on European misperceptions of the people. Martin then charts the warfare and destruction brought by Spanish colonization, early British attempts to capture the island, French success at establishing a permanent outpost in 1649, and finally English conquest in 1763. The Island Caribs remain a primary focus of the book throughout each of these periods, as their role in the colony shifted with every transformation. Martin also charts several of the key episodes of genocide in the island, including the 1650–1651 massacre at Sauteurs. [DL]

793   Méndez Serrano, Manuel Reinaldo.
La isla del día después: un viaje a la Cuba real. Valencia, Spain: Aduana Vieja, 2014. 493 p.

This well-written, contemporary travel account of Cuba offers insights into the contradictions of contemporary Cuba during the last years of Fidel Castro's life. [MC]

794   Mulcahy, Matthew. Hubs of empire: the Southeastern Lowcountry and British Caribbean. Baltimore, Md.: Johns Hopkins University Press, 2014. 244 p.: bibl., index, maps. (Regional perspectives on early America)

This study argues for a redrawing of the historic map. The author proposes that Britain's major Caribbean islands, and the coastal region from South Carolina to Georgia, composed one distinct zone in the colonial period. This "Greater Caribbean" region shared similarly sized plantations, comparable economic regimes, somewhat equal demographic divisions, and parallel scourges of disease and environmental disasters. Mulcahy chronicles the individual histories of these colonies to demonstrate their analogous developments. He also charts direct networks and associations between migrants, as well as the warfare and trade, that tied the Greater Caribbean together. [DL]

795   Muñoz Rivera, Luis. Campañas políticas (1890–1916). Seleccionadas y recopiladas por Luis Muñoz Marín. Prólogo de Julio E. Quirós Alcalá. Edición especial. San Juan: Universidad Interamericana de Puerto Rico, 2015. 590 p.: bibl., ill., ports.

This book reprints selected writings by Luis Muñoz Rivera (1859–1916), an influential leader in Puerto Rican politics from the late 1800s through his premature death in 1916. Originally published as a three-volume set in 1925 by Muñoz Rivera's son, Luis Muñoz Marín (1898–1980), himself a central figure in modern Puerto Rican politics. Mostly consists of columns in *La Democracia*, Muñoz Rivera's newspaper, but also contains letters and speeches. [LG]

796 **Mustakeem, Sowande' M.** Slavery at sea: terror, sex, and sickness in the Middle Passage. Urbana: University of Illinois Press, 2016. 262 p.: bibl., ill., index, map. (The new Black studies series)

Joining a long historiography on the transatlantic slave trade, Mustakeem's book delves into the more challenging topic of the emotional and physical experience of the Middle Passage. Focusing primarily on British slaving from Africa to the Americas, particularly the Caribbean, this study interrogates how captive Africans reported their experiences, as well as how enslavers and observers noted what those experiences might have been like. Mustakeem asks fresh questions about the Middle Passage, especially about the ways that gender, age, and infirmity could have influenced the type of suffering humans faced within transatlantic trafficking. [DL]

797 **Neira Vilas, Xosé.** Galicia en Cuba: lingua, Rosalía, loitas. Santiago de Compostela, Spain: Consello da Cultura Galega, 2013. 463 p.: bibl., ill. (Autores & textos)

Written in Galician, the book chronicles through mini-biographies the presence and role of Galicians in Cuba in the 19th and 20th centuries. In particular, the author emphasizes Galicians who fought on the side of Cuban independence and their role in contributing to the cultural and social life of the new independent nation. Over 100 pages of primary sources documents on Galicians in Cuba are included in the book. [MDC]

798 **O'Malley, Gregory E.** Final passages: the intercolonial slave trade of British America, 1619–1807. Chapel Hill: University of North Carolina Press, Chapel Hill, 2014. 394 p.: bibl., ill., index.

Although principally focused on North America, this study offers a key insight into the importance of the Caribbean to the Atlantic slave trade. The Middle Passage primarily took Africans directly to the West Indies and South America. But this often was not the concluding destination for captives. O'Malley charts the next stage of trafficking for those first landed in the Caribbean, tracing their eventual arrivals in Mexico and British North America. He shows how important this intercolonial trade from the Caribbean was to plantation societies in mainland America. [DL]

799 **Op. Cit.: Revista del Centro de Investigaciones Históricas.** 23, 2014/2015, Historia y antropología: homenaje a Sidney Mintz. Río Piedras: Universidad de Puerto Rico, Facultad de Humanidades, Departamento de Historia.

This special issue of *Op. Cit.* is dedicated to Sidney Mintz (1922–2015), distinguished scholar of the Caribbean. The volume includes the Spanish-language translation of Mintz's seminal article "The Caribbean as a Socio-Cultural Area" (1966; see *HLAS 29:8468* and *HLAS 31:1969*), a biography, plus two additional essays: one reviewing the intellectual context at the time of his essay, and the other assessing Mintz's scholarly contributions to the field of Caribbean Studies. [LG]

800 **Oxford research encyclopedia of Latin American history.** Oxford, England: Oxford University Press, 2018. <http://latinamericanhistory.oxfordre.com>

Begun in 2014 and helmed by Editor-in-Chief William Beezley, this online collection of essays stands out from standard encyclopedias as it aims to present new and innovative work from a wide range of interests across Latin American history. Described as "a comprehensive digital research encyclopedia that describes Latin America's peoples and experiences from precolumbian to contemporary times" that contains "essays mak[ing] the region's compelling past come alive by using the latest analyses, and by taking advantage of opportunities not available to traditional printed encyclopedias." Since it began, essays on the Dominican Republic have been included thanks to the editorial work of Lauren Derby, and now cover topics as diverse as Dominican baseball, US foreign relations and dictators, masculinity, Dominican-Haitian border relations, the murder of the Mirabal sisters (forthcoming), and the disappearance of Jesús Galíndez during the Trujillato. [EM]

801 **Palomares Ferrales, Eugenia.** Bajo el sol de la Sierra. La Habana: Casa Editorial Verde Olivo, 2013. 164 p.: bibl., ill., maps.

This work presents the personal biography of the author's father, Cecilio

Pastor Palomares López, who participated in the 26 de julio armed guerrilla struggle and was killed at the battle of Palma Mocha. The brief biography includes a series of sources documenting his political life. Also of particular interest is the process of commemorating and memorializing his life and his contributions to the Cuban Revolution in the form of monuments and anniversaries that are chronicled in the volume. [MDC]

Pamphile, Léon Dénius. Contrary destinies: a century of America's occupation, deoccupation, and reoccupation of Haiti. See *HLAS* 73:1533.

802 **Paton, Diana.** The cultural politics of Obeah: religion, colonialism and modernity in the Caribbean world. Cambridge, England: Cambridge University Press, 2015. 361 p.: bibl., index. (Critical perspectives on empire)

Obeah, as Paton describes, is an amorphous term that symbolizes Afro-Creole traditions in the Caribbean to some, and criminal acts of rebellion to others. Unlike other West Indian religions, it does not have a set hierarchy, priesthood, or liturgy, making it open to wide varieties of interpretation. This study charts the African traditions brought to the Caribbean that consisted of sets of religious and social customs which were lumped into the title of "obeah." Fear of enslaved uprisings produced an initial prohibition against obeah practice, first in Jamaica, and then across the Caribbean. Increased interest in African religious traditions after emancipation led to further excoriations of obeah in the hopes of distancing individual colonies from comparisons to Haiti and Vodou. Paton follows this persecution through the 20th century, up to a consideration of its reassessment in the present day. [DL]

803 **Perera Díaz, Aisnara** and **María de los Ángeles Meriño Fuentes.** El cabildo carabalí viví de Santiago de Cuba: familia, cultura y sociedad (1797–1909). Santiago de Cuba: Editorial Oriente, 2013. 305 p.: bibl., ill. (Bronce colección)

This work offers an excellent analysis of the fraternal and religious organization formed by Africans to meet their spiritual and social needs. The authors provide one of the few detailed analyses of a single cabildo over a century, stressing how it served to reinforce an African identity. [MC]

804 **Pérez Concepción, Hebert.** Sobre los Estados Unidos y otros temas martianos. Santiago de Cuba: Editorial Oriente, 2015. 236 p.: bibl. (Bronce colección)

This collection of essays and research articles analyzes José Martí's writing on the US, some of which have been previously published. The volume is part of a resurgence of interest in Martí's writing over the last 20 years—with particular attention to his comments on race relations and US imperialism as both topics have been recast in light of contemporary discussion of Cuban racism in the 21st century and changing relations between the US and Cuba. [MDC]

805 **Pérez Memén, Fernando.** Ensayos sobre historia social, política y cultural de la República Dominicana y de México. Santo Domingo: Banco Central de la República Dominicana, 2015. 398 p.: bibl., index. (Colección del Banco Central de la República Dominicana; 213) (Serie ciencias sociales; 36)

This collection of essays highlights a number of the links between the Dominican Republic and Mexico. The volume brings together a rather eclectic gathering of topics, including from the colonial period (the Church, Montesinos in Mexico, Toussaint L'Ouverture), during independence and restoration (Hidalgo and Duarte, sovereignty), along with biographies (Pedro Henríquez Ureña, Eugenio Maria de Hostos, Dede Mirabal, Juan Bosch, Joaquín Balaguer, Carlos Morales Troncoso) and literary analysis. Written by the former ambassador to Mexico, many of the pieces included were originally talks given there or essays treating connections between the two nations. [EM]

806 **Roorda, Eric Paul.** Historical dictionary of the Dominican Republic. Lanham, Md.: Rowman & Littlefield, 2016. 394 p.: bibl. (Historical dictionaries of the Americas)

A thorough and useful guide for new students of Dominican history, this reference book written by diplomatic historian Eric Paul Roorda provides excellent coverage of the major issues, personalities, events, and terms in Dominican history, but also deftly incorporates US-Dominican relations into the collection of entries. The work contains over 500 crosslisted entries that are categorized alphabetically and appendices covering a chronology of Dominican heads-of-state, the nation's provinces, and a reference bibliography; a succinct but thorough chronology opens the text to provide appropriate context. This publication represents the 11th country covered in this series that began in the early 1990s and is edited by Jon Woronoff. [EM]

807 Saunders, Gail. Race and class in the colonial Bahamas, 1880–1960. Gainesville: University of Florida Press, 2016. 371 p.: bibl., index.

This race and class analysis of the Bahamas focuses on the 1880s-1960s, a period during which the entrenched, though extra-legal, segregation prevalent in most spheres of Bahamian society were not necessarily parallel to those across other British West Indian colonies, but instead mirrored the inflexible color line of the US. [C.E. Griffin]

Schwartz, Stuart B. Sea of storms: a history of hurricanes in the greater Caribbean from Columbus to Katrina. See *HLAS 73:541*.

808 Shepherd, Verene. Jamaica and the debate over reparation for slavery: an overview. (*in* Emancipation and the remaking of the British Imperial world. Manchester, England: Manchester University Press, 2014, p. 223–250)

In this book chapter, the author walks through each stage of the transatlantic slave trade, and the experience of plantation slavery, to make a case for British reparations to the Caribbean. She argues that the scope of the slave trade, and of slavery itself, were wholly organized around profits and wealth extraction from African bodies. Moreover, she argues that Atlantic slavery functioned, effectively, as a genocide. The lack of investment in infrastructure during the colonial period produced, in her telling, a continual plantation system through the 20th century. This argument forms her case for reparations, and she concludes with precise calculations on how much is potentially owed to the Caribbean, as well as how West Indian politicians might approach the issue. [DL]

809 *Small Axe: A Caribbean Journal of Criticism.* Vol. 20, No. 3, Issue 51, Nov. 2016. Edited by Vanessa Pérez-Rosario. Durham, N.C.: Duke University Press.

This special edition of *Small Axe* announces the efforts of the editorial board to incorporate more Hispanophone Caribbean scholarship into this peer-reviewed print journal. Managing editor Vanessa Pérez-Rosario provides a provocative introductory essay, "On the Hispanophone Caribbean Question" while Ada Ferrer tackles the place of the historiographies of Puerto Rico, Cuba, and the Dominican Republic (along with the wider Spanish colonial territories) in her "History and the Idea of Hispanic Caribbean Studies." Both essays, along with the other pieces in the edition, provide compelling arguments for a reassessment of the category of the Hispanophone Caribbean as well as the inclusion of these sometimes doubly marginalized countries and areas into the larger fold of Caribbean studies. As Pérez-Rosario notes, it seems obvious to include the Hispanophone islands and territories in "any serious study of the Caribbean" and yet the subregion has long been ignored or silenced through its "intense" (and arguably ambivalent) "Americanization and Latin Americanization" since the decline of the Spanish Empire (p. 22). The fact that there are multiple "Caribbeans" and a "discordant overlap in the histories of the Spanish Caribbean," Ferrer argues, only serves to expand possible analytical frames for scholars in extremely fruitful ways; in other words, such a deframing supports the claim of many scholars that the histories of the region are, in fact, "at the core of the history of the modern world" (p. 63–64). [EM]

810 *Small Axe: A Caribbean Journal of Criticism.* Vol. 22, No. 2, Issue 56 July 2018. Edited by Maja Horn and David Scott. Durham, N.C.: Duke University Press.

Small Axe: A Caribbean Journal of Criticism has been actively incorporating work on the Hispanophone Caribbean since 2016 in their quarterly publication. This issue offers a special section of scholarship on gender and sexuality in the Dominican Republic edited by Maja Horn. In addition to Horn's incisive introductory comments, the selection of essays includes a reflection on Dominican latinidad through literature by

Sharina Maillo-Pozo, an analysis of LGBT activism by Ana-Maurine Lara, a study of Dominican media darling María Montez by Danny Méndez, a transnational approach to Dominican pride and the politics of gay rights by Rachel Afi Quinn, a complication of race, gender, and the imperial gaze by Dixa Ramírez, an analysis of the silences in the historical record surrounding women by Elizabeth Manley, and a reflection on the history of sexuality studies in the Dominican Republic by Carlos Decena and Fátima Portorreal. As Horn notes, the collection speaks not only to the "current vitality and multiplicity of approaches" to Dominican gender and sexuality on and beyond the island, but also to the importance of such work to the larger field of Caribbean studies. [EM]

811   Transnational Hispaniola: new directions in Haitian and Dominican studies. Edited by April J. Mayes and Kiran C. Jayaram. Gainesville: University of Florida Press, 2017. 273 p.: bibl., index.

The product of a long and fruitful collaborative effort to think across the island of Hispaniola, this collection edited by Mayes and Jayaram offers selections in history, literary studies, anthropology, ethnomusicology, and cultural studies. The goals of the book—and its antecedent collective—include fostering and uniting scholarly endeavors across Hispaniola and among its diasporas/*diasporas*/*diaspora*, connecting with social activisms that "resist political exclusion, racism, anti-Haitian xenophobia, gender inequality, and discrimination based on sexuality," and creating "new narratives" that recognize and amplify the long, complicated, and ultimately positive relationships between Haiti and the Dominican Republic, but also between the island and the rest of the Caribbean. Twelve contributing chapters range in disciplinary and temporal focus, and cover topics as diverse as engaged scholarship and pedagogy, sex and tourism, literature, citizenship, and the politics of place and space. [EM]

812   Venegas Delgado, Hernán and Carlos M. Valdés Dávila. La ruta del horror: prisioneros indios del noroeste novohispano llevados como esclavos a La Habana, Cuba. Segunda edición. Coahuila, Mexico: Gobierno del Estado de Coahuila de Zaragoza, 2014. 229 p.: bibl., ill., maps. (Biblioteca Coahuila de derechos humanos)

This fascinating analysis covers the often ignored and overlooked transportation of indigenous prisoners from Mexico to toil as bonded laborers in Cuba. Drawing upon sources from Mexico, Cuba, and Spain, the authors demonstrate that long into the 18th century and up until Mexico's independence, an indigenous prisoner trade route transported rebellious Native Americans from the border region of Coahuila to Cuba. [MDC]

EARLY COLONIAL

Arcangeli, Myriam. Sherds of history: domestic life in colonial Guadeloupe. See *HLAS 73:182*.

813   Arena, Carolyn. Indian slaves from Guiana in seventeenth-century Barbados. (*Ethnohistory/Columbus*, 64:1, Jan. 2017, p. 65–90)

Lacking a settled indigenous population, Barbados became a site of maritime trauma for Central and South American natives brought to the island as enslaved laborers. English theorists advocated the forced transportation of Amerindians from the beginning of Barbados' colonization in the early 17th century, despite the fact that Europeans had started decrying native enslavement. Indians from Guiana joined a nebulous class of servants arriving to the island, but white officials soon began to lump them together with bound Africans into a racialized caste of laborers. Arena notes that Caribbean warfare increased the number of enslaved natives on Barbados, and planters continued to purchase them into the 18th century, even as indigenous enslavement came to be seen as immoral. [DL]

814   Beckles, Hilary. Britain's black debt: reparations for Caribbean slavery and native genocide. Kingston, Jamaica: University Of West Indies Press, 2013. 292 p.: bibl., index.

This monograph makes an historical and political case for Britain to repay the Caribbean for the crime of slavery. Beckles provides a detailed history of Britain's involvement in the Caribbean: beginning with the Amerindian genocide of early colonization, to the horrors of the Middle Passage, to the various abuses and expropriations committed under slavery that extracted profit and also inflicted violence. These historical facts line-up, according to Beckles, with definitions of crimes against humanity, as established by the UN and other organizations. He outlines a path by which the government of the United Kingdom, various British businesses originally connected to slavery, and the Church of England could pay back the Caribbean for those profits. More uncertain, however, are the ways in which grassroots movements in the West Indies can overcome a recent reticence by Caribbean governments to push for reparations. See also *HLAS 70:852*. [DL]

815 **Handler, Jerome S.** Custom and law: the status of enslaved Africans in seventeenth-century Barbados. (*Slavery Abolit.*, 37:2, 2016, p. 233–255)

Handler contributes to the ongoing debate about attitudes toward Africans in the early years of English colonization in the Caribbean. Tacking against a consideration of Barbadian statutes, Handler instead looks at customary notions of Africans on the island in its early colonial decades. He argues that Iberian legal precedents, English traditions of property ownership, and preexisting British beliefs of African inferiority, resulted in enslaved blacks being put immediately into a distinctive category. From the beginning, Handler contends, African servitude was seen as heritable, lifelong, devoid of human rights, and property-based. [DL]

816 **Livesay, Daniel.** West meets east: mixed-race Jamaicans in India, and the avenues of advancement in imperial Britain. (*Atlan. Stud. Global Curr.*, 14:3, 2017, p. 382–398, bibl.)

This article presents the case studies of three mixed-race Jamaican families of elite backgrounds who attained upward social mobility—and acceptance into British society as white people—after migrating to South Asia to work for the East India Company. As racial prejudice hardened in Britain toward the end of the 18th century, elite Jamaicans of color faced more challenges to recast their identities as white. [LG]

817 **Newman, Simon P.** A new world of labor: the development of plantation slavery in the British Atlantic. Philadelphia: University of Pennsylvania Press, 2013. 327 p.: bibl., ill., index, map. (The early modern Americas)

As England's first major Caribbean colony, Barbados was an experiment in social control. In this study, Newman examines the traditions of labor in Britain and Africa to paint a contrasting image of the worker exploitation that developed in Barbados. Newman counters certain historiographical claims that white servitude in the Americas was not initially as abusive as that of African slavery. Instead, he argues that in the opening decades of the island's colonial regime Barbadian planters worked indentured servants as brutally as enslaved Africans. As European labor grew more expensive, and African labor less so, a more racialized form of servitude emerged. But Barbados was nevertheless a testing ground for a radically new way of extracting profit from human bodies. [DL]

818 **Newton, Melanie J.** The race leapt at Sauteurs: genocide, narrative, and indigenous exile from the Caribbean archipelago. (*Caribb. Q./Mona*, 60:2, June 2014, p. 5–28)

This article examines "three incidents as acts of genocide" during the colonial invasions of the Lesser Antilles by the Spanish, French, and British (p. 6). Each event, separated by more than a century, was marked by an attack and attempted annihilation of the indigenous populations of the islands by European colonizers. For the British, this extended into a bureaucratic eradication as well. When they exiled the so-called Black Caribs of St. Vincent, British officials insisted that the group was not aboriginal—which would have made them entitled to certain legal protections—but instead maintained that they were of enslaved African descent with virtually no legal rights. This activity has precipitated an erasure of native populations from the Caribbean generally. [DL]

819 **Pestana, Carla Gardina.** The English conquest of Jamaica: Oliver Cromwell's bid for empire. Cambridge, Mass.: The Belknap Press of Harvard Uni-

versity Press, 2017. 362 p.: bibl., ill., index, maps.

Pestana analyzes in rigorous detail the "Western Design" implemented by England's Lord Protector Oliver Cromwell (1599–1658) to augment England's colonial presence in the early Caribbean. She assesses English conceptions of the West Indies, alongside growing theories about empire and conquest at the time of the plan. England's military failed to take the island of Hispaniola, but effectively established itself in Jamaica. Pestana demonstrates, however, the difficulty that the English had in fully colonizing the island due to challenges in subduing enslaved populations, eliminating an ongoing Spanish presence, and building a successful economy. [DL]

820   Reichert, Rafal B. Sobre las olas de un mar plateado: la política defensiva española y el financiamiento militar novohispano en la región del Gran Caribe, 1598–1700. Mérida, Mexico: UNAM, 2013. 176 p.: bibl., ill.

This work offers a new angle on Spain's military fortification of its Spanish Caribbean colonies. Unlike other studies that focus on the era of the Bourbon Reforms and in particular the expansion in military projects in the wake of the Seven Years' War, the author examines the relationship between the colony of New Spain and its role in financing and supplying the Caribbean colonies of Hispaniola, Puerto Rico, Cuba, and Florida during the 17th century. [MDC]

821   Roberts, Justin. Surrendering Surinam: the Barbadian diaspora and the expansion of the English sugar frontier. (*William Mary Q.*, 73:2, 2016, p. 225–256)

Roberts centers 17th-century Barbados as a key colonial outpost that radiated political, legal, and migratory influence throughout the rest of the Americas. He considers why England relinquished claims to Suriname after the Treaty of Breda, arguing that metropolitan officials used the surrender, in part, as a way of checking the power of an overly ambitious Barbadian planter class driven toward expansionism. This action proved to be a decisive transformation for the Caribbean, as English interests in the region moved away from South America and toward the Greater Antilles. [DL]

822   Rugemer, Edward B. The development of master and race in the comprehensive slave codes of the Greater Caribbean during the seventeenth century. (*William Mary Q.*, 70:3, 2013, p. 429–458)

According to Rugemer, slave societies in the Greater Caribbean developed their slave codes in conversation with one another, rather than simply adopting and adapting most of Barbados' early edicts. This study looks at the initial legal codes of Barbados, Jamaica, and South Carolina to show the ways that each location built off the statutes of the other, and perfected the law to suit their particular colonial regimes. Rugemer highlights Jamaica's 1684 Slave Act as an overlooked legal document in the development of Atlantic slave codes. Moreover, he contends that these edicts show an early differentiation between African and European servants. [DL]

823   Sharples, Jason T. Discovering slave conspiracies: new fears of rebellion and old paradigms of plotting in seventeenth-century Barbados. (*Am. Hist. Rev.*, 120:3, 2015, p. 811–843)

Tracing an alleged conspiracy among enslaved Barbadians in 1692, Sharples analyzes the ways in which enslavers not only interpreted supposed information about potential acts of rebellion, but also how they attempted to anticipate the potential for violence. Sharples argues that planters—who struggled to comprehend African communication—assessed speculative violence by enslaved people by looking at classical examples of rebellion, along with recent Catholic plots in Europe. These comparisons were the chief frame through which Barbadians attempted to make sense of enslaved resistance, though they soon adapted these views to the West Indian context. Sharples cautions scholars from taking enslavers' claims about conspiracies at face value, as those plots were often as much an invention of the masters as they were actual plans of the oppressed. [DL]

824   Shaw, Jenny. Everyday life in the early English Caribbean: Irish, Africans, and the construction of difference. Athens: The University of Georgia Press,

2013. 259 p.: bibl., ill., index, map. (Early American places)

This monograph principally examines the place of Irish migrants, who arrived in both forced and voluntary capacities, to the Caribbean. The author argues that social, religious, and ethnic distinctions were all crucial and complicated markers of difference in the early years of British colonization. When kidnapped Africans were brought to the West Indies, however, those categories slowly started to simplify around basic conceptions of race. Shaw traces the legal and cultural developments in this period, but also includes pieces of speculative nonfiction to understand the experiences of the Caribbean's working and enslaved classes. [DL]

825 **Swingen, Abigail L.** Competing visions of empire: labor, slavery, and the origins of the British Atlantic empire. New Haven, Conn.: Yale University Press, 2015. 271 p.: bibl., index, map.

Swingen's monograph is largely a study of British court politics swirling around the topic of slavery, and more specifically about the Royal African Company. Specifically, her analysis uncovers the ways in which particular British political forces drove the transatlantic slave trade to the Anglophone Caribbean. She argues for the centrality of slavery in British visions about an integrated empire, and the ways that Caribbean governors were steeped in those debates. This analysis puts the West Indies forward as a crucial site and source of influence for the English Civil War and the Glorious Revolution. [DL]

LATE COLONIAL AND FRENCH REVOLUTIONARY PERIOD

826 **Bindman, David.** Representing race in the eighteenth-century Caribbean: Brunias in Dominica and St. Vincent. (*Eighteenth-Century Stud.*, 51:1, Fall 2017, p. 1–21, bibl., ill.)

As one of the most prolific artists of the 18th-century British Caribbean, Agostino Brunias' portraits have long been used by scholars to assess colonial West Indian life. Bindman traces the history of Brunias' visit to the Lesser Antilles, which was prompted by the British official William Young. Countering other scholarly interpretations, Bindman argues that Brunias did not create his portraits either to advertise the colonies or to produce anthropological sketches. Instead, the Italian-born painter sought profit and influence among the Creole white population, who desired idyllic portrayals of their West Indian homes and lives. For comment by art historian, see item 47. [DL]

827 **Bollettino, Maria Alessandra.** "Of equal or of more service": black soldiers and the British Empire in the mid-eighteenth-century Caribbean. (*Slavery Abolit.*, 38:5, 2017, p. 510–533)

In the first half of the 18th century, officials in the British Caribbean relied strongly on enslaved auxiliaries to ward off foreign invasion, as well as to support imperial missions to other West Indian outposts. Bollettino assesses the various reasons why black laborers were valued: including beliefs about African strength, views about Creole immunities to tropical diseases, and knowledge of local landscapes, labor skills, etc. She argues that this enthusiasm for black soldiers came about much earlier than previous scholarship has suggested, and she puts the issue of black military mobilization into a larger, Atlantic context. [DL]

828 **Burnard, Trevor G.** Planters, merchants, and slaves: plantation societies in British America, 1650–1820. Chicago, Ill.: The University of Chicago Press, 2015. 357 p.: bibl., ill., index, maps. (American beginnings, 1500–1900)

In this study, Burnard explores the development of the plantation system in three places: the Chesapeake, the Lowcountry, and the Caribbean. He argues that although the plantation system often remained static for long periods of time, it nevertheless transformed over the long 18th century—shaped by momentous events and broad trends across the Atlantic World. Jamaica is held out as somewhat distinctive compared to the rest of the British Caribbean. But, throughout, Burnard assesses how white society at all levels came to support and drive the plantation system that oppressed so many individuals of African descent. [DL]

829 **Burnard, Trevor G.** and **John Garrigus.** The plantation machine: Atlantic capitalism in French Saint-Domingue and British Jamaica. Philadelphia: University

of Pennsylvania Press, 2016. 350 p.: bibl., ill., index, maps. (The early modern Americas)

This monograph compares Jamaica and Saint Domingue—two incredibly similar slave colonies overseen by two different empires—from 1740 to 1788. The authors argue that Caribbean plantations were industrial (or proto-industrial) machines that refined a particular type of exploitative global economy. As they meticulously describe the plantation systems and experiences of enslaved people in both locations, the authors also assess the transformations that occurred in the Caribbean during three critical periods: the Seven Year's War, the American Revolution, and the lead-up to the French Revolution. Ultimately, they contend that local conditions were most critical in the developments of plantation economics, along with the racial justifications used to support them. [DL]

830   **Candlin, Kit** and **Cassandra Pybus.**
Enterprising women: gender, race, and power in the revolutionary Atlantic. Athens: University of Georgia Press, 2014. 241 p.: bibl., index. (Race in the Atlantic world, 1700-1900)

With a focus on the Southern Caribbean—especially the islands ceded to the British in 1763—Candlin and Pybus document the lives of women of color who gained wealth and influence in brutal colonial regimes. These were critical spaces for racial negotiation, as the ceded islands often encompassed multiple European traditions and legal structures that complicated social and racial statuses. Each chapter presents a major biography of a woman of color making advancements in the bustling 18th-century Atlantic economy, alongside parallel stories of similar women constructed from much smaller, more fragmentary sources. The authors argue that these women were not just participants in that larger economic and political world, but that they were often central figures within it. [DL]

831   **Dunn, Richard S.** A tale of two plantations: slave life and labor in Jamaica and Virginia. Cambridge, Mass.: Harvard University Press, 2014. 540 p.: bibl., index.

As the title indicates, this monograph explores two plantations in great detail: one in Virginia and one in Jamaica. The author focuses on enslaved life in both places, and the ways in which plantation economics influenced unfree households. In Jamaica, Dunn traces nearly a century-long history of the Mesopotamia plantation up to emancipation in 1833. He reveals the personal experiences of enslaved households to show the divergences of their organization, the particular effects of interracial coupling, and the sometimes muted responses among workers to larger political events. The work succeeds brilliantly at uncovering the personal biographies of a number of enslaved households within Mesopotamia's boundaries, and the ways in which their lives moved over time. [DL]

832   **Fuentes, Marisa J.** Dispossessed lives: enslaved women, violence, and the archive. Philadelphia: PENN University of Pennsylvania Press, 2016. 217 p.: bibl., ill., index, maps. (Early American studies)

Fuentes seeks to uncover the lives of enslaved women in colonial Bridgetown, Barbados, but also reflects on the archival silences that keep such stories from being told. She documents several case studies of enslaved runaways, businesspeople, "criminals," and others to demonstrate the ruthlessness of slavery in urban spaces, as well as the added challenges facing women in Caribbean slavery. Comparisons to white women reveal the added persecution that race imposed. Fuentes argues that the recorders of slavery obscured and buried the experiences of enslaved women, and that the promotion of elites of color in colonial narratives ultimately hid the sexual and physical violence that the enslaved endured. [DL]

833   **Gerbner, Katharine.** "They call me Obea": German Moravian missionaries and Afro-Caribbean religion in Jamaica, 1754-1760. (*Atlan. Stud. Global Curr.*, 12:2, 2015, p. 160-178)

This article presents a case study of Zacharias George Caries, the first German Moravian missionary to Jamaica. During his relatively short stint on the island, Caries came to be seen by parishioners as a sort of seer, or individual of spiritual prowess. At one point, Caries noted that the Afro-Jamaicans to whom he had been preaching called him "Obea." Gerbner explores the meaning of this appellation to argue for a wider definition of the concept of obeah than previously believed. She contends that European religious traditions were part of the syncretic organization and practice of obeah on the island. [DL]

834 Greene, Jack P. Settler Jamaica in the 1750s: a social portrait. Charlottesville: University of Virginia Press, 2016. 288 p.: bibl., index. (Early American histories)

Focusing entirely on the middle decade of the 18th century, this study sketches out the social and economic life of England's most profitable Caribbean colony at its exploitative height. Examining inventory, map, and other data, Greene creates a cartography of the island, divided into core, periphery, and near-periphery areas. His research calls into question certain basic assumptions, such as the total dominance of sugar during this period, along with the distribution of enslaved people in urban and rural spaces. He also reveals a tremendous amount about people of color living in the major cities of Spanish Town and Kingston. [DL]

835 Limia Díaz, Ernesto. Cuba entre tres imperios: perla, llave y antemural. Segunda edición corregida. La Habana: Casa Editorial Verde Olivo, 2014. 292 p.: bibl., ill., maps.

Drawing largely from secondary sources, this study provides an analysis of colonial Cuba's foreign relations. The author focuses mainly on how Cuba became enveloped into conflicts between England and Spain during the 18th century and culminating with the Seven Years' War and the Occupation of Havana in 1762. [MC]

836 Livesay, Daniel. Privileging kinship: family and race in eighteenth-century Jamaica. (*Early Amer. Stud.*, 14:4, 2016, p. 688–711)

This article argues that family belonging was a critical part of one's racial status in 18th-century Jamaica. The study examines the petitions of several hundred free individuals of mixed heritage to the island's legislature asking for concessions from certain race-based laws. One of the most critical parts of these petitions was a biographical statement that included family lineages to white fathers and relatives in order to bolster a case for legal privileges. Livesay contends that Jamaica's elites of color operated in a social world in which their family history was nearly as important as their skin coloration. [DL]

837 Pettigrew, William A. Freedom's debt: the Royal African Company and the politics of the Atlantic slave trade, 1672–1752. Chapel Hill: The University of North Carolina Press, 2013. 262 p.: bibl., ill., index.

As a monopoly, the Royal African Company struggled to expand its political reach beyond the Stuart court. Pettigrew explains how private traders used the language of freedom to destroy the company's monopoly, allowing for an explosion of slave trading in the 18th-century Atlantic. The dissolution of the monopoly, Pettigrew argues, created greater political buy-in to slave trading among Britons for a large portion of the 18th century, bringing many hundreds of thousands of Africans to the British Caribbean. He also profiles various West Indian merchants and planters who created a successful lobbying campaign against the Royal African Company, which was critical in bringing down the monopoly. [DL]

838 Portuondo Zúñiga, Olga. Una derrota británica en Cuba. La Habana: Editora Historia, 2015. 249 p.: bibl., ill., maps.

This work is a reprint of the 2000 edition with a new prologue and additions by the author. Portuondo presents an analysis of the War of Jenkins Ear that brought European military fighting between Spain, France, and Britain to the Caribbean. In particular, she focuses on Cuba's role in the war and the military battles in Santiago and Guantánamo and their geopolitical ramifications for New World empires. The book also includes several primary source documents that provide insights into the Caribbean theater of the war and the social and political history of the region during this period. [MDC]

Prado, Fabrício Pereira. Trans-imperial networks in the crisis of the Spanish monarchy: the Rio de Janeiro-Montevideo connection, 1778–1805. See item **1617**.

839 Radburn, Nicholas. Guinea factors, slave sales, and the profits of the transatlantic slave trade in late eighteenth-century Jamaica. (*William Mary Q.*, 72:2, 2015, p. 243–286)

Through a biographical sketch of John Tailyour, a Scottish merchant in Kingston, this article assesses the detailed economics of slave trading at the end of the 18th century. Tailyour became rich after less than a decade's residence in Jamaica, and brought those profits with him back to Scotland. Radburn outlines the process through which Tailyour so quickly built up his career by painstakingly noting the Jamaican and British contacts he cultivated, as well as by cross-referencing newspaper accounts to tally the financial growth of Tailyour's trade. Altogether, the article provides an in-depth and complex look at how slave trading operated on the ground in the British Caribbean. [DL]

840   Reid, Ahmed and David B. Ryden.
Sugar, land markets and the Williams Thesis: evidence from Jamaica's property sales, 1750–1810. (*Slavery Abolit.*, 34:3, 2013, p. 401–424)

The "Williams Thesis" that West Indian slavery was in economic decline in the years leading up to the abolition of the slave trade gets another look in this article. Continuing on Ryden's recent work, he and Reid explore land prices in Jamaica in the decades before England abolished its slave trade. Land transaction sales indicate increasing prices over the course of the 18th century, especially in the areas around Kingston. But planter overextension, coupled with a plummeting of sugar prices, saw a collapse of land value after 1800. Reid and Ryden thus argue against a *longue durée* decline, in favor of a more immediate one in the years before abolition. [DL]

841   Robertson, James Craufurd.
Eighteenth-century Jamaica's ambivalent cosmopolitanism. (*History/London*, 99:37, 2014, p. 607–631)

As a site of brutal plantation slavery, colonial Jamaica was often not considered to be a spot for enlightened thinking. Robertson contends in this article, however, that the Enlightenment did not pass by Jamaica. Instead, colonists undertook grand European tours, built elegant homes, read contemporary literature, hosted internationally known scholars and luminaries, and kept up their own scientific inquiries. Moreover, the island's major cities of Kingston, Spanish Town, and Port Royal, were on par with many of their North American peers in terms of population and cultural institutions. But, as Robertson concludes, this was a cosmopolitanism built upon racial division; one that could not easily survive emancipation. [DL]

842   Vasconcellos, Colleen A. Slavery, childhood, and abolition in Jamaica, 1788–1838. Athens: The University of Georgia Press, 2015. 151 p.: bibl., ill., index. (Early American places)

This monograph analyzes the experience and perception of youth among Afro-Jamaican people during slavery and the apprenticeship period. Vasconcellos reflects closely on the challenges of studying young people under slavery, with so few first-person sources available. Early chapters focus particularly on the debates around youth and slavery in Parliament, as well as in Jamaican society, as reformers hoped to improve childhood health in order to end the slave trade. As emancipation neared, young Jamaicans were considered the prime targets for evangelical efforts to "civilize" the enslaved population. Finally, Vasconcellos concludes by demonstrating how difficult and damaging the apprenticeship period was for young adults. [DL]

843   Walker, Christine. Pursuing her profits: women in Jamaica, Atlantic slavery and a globalising market, 1700–60. (*Gend. Hist.*, 26:3, 2014, p. 478–501)

This article argues for the importance of free women in the Jamaican colonial economy, especially because so much scholarship has assumed—incorrectly—that the island had very few white women in the 18th century. Walker demonstrates that, even though they suffered under a number of legal constraints around property ownership, free women were active agents in trade and the perpetuation of slavery. This was true not just for elite women, who often were crucial creditors in Jamaica, but also for those of more modest means who acted as seamstresses, pen owners, and innkeepers. As enslavers, their attitudes and actions toward the enslaved could often differ significantly from white, male peers. The findings of this study challenge the notion that Jamaica was a wholly patriarchal society in the 18th century. [DL]

19TH CENTURY

844 Abreu Cardet, José Miguel and **Luis Álvarez-López.** Guerras de liberación en el Caribe hispano, 1863–1878. Santo Domingo: Archivo General de la Nación, 2013. 262 p.: bibl., ill. (Archivo General de la Nación; 193)

This pioneering co-authored volume brings together the Dominican War for Restoration 1863–65, The Cuban Ten Years' War 1868–78, and the 1869 Puerto Rican Grito de Lares into a single frame of analysis. Rather than treating these events only in their singular colonial situation as episodes of national history, the authors have shown the interconnections between the events as a Caribbean-wide phenomenon. [MDC]

845 Álvarez Álvarez, Luis and **Olga García Yero.** El pensamiento cultural en el siglo XIX cubano. La Habana: Editorial de Ciencias Sociales, 2013. 231 p.: bibl.

This work presents a concise and selective overview of the major Cuban intellectuals of the 19th century, focusing in particular on José Antonio Saco, Domingo del Monte, Félix Varela, and most notably José Martí. The authors analyze published writings of well-known intellectuals to scrutinize how Cuban culture was being defined in the process of moving from a colony to a nation. [MDC]

Ayala Lafée-Wilbert, Cecilia; Werner Wilbert; and **Ariany Calles.** Juan Pablo Duarte en la Venezuela del siglo XIX: historia y leyenda. See item **1051**.

846 Ben Othman, Adel. Ultramar en la política española: Cuba y Puerto Rico (1863–1898). Prólogo de Jesús Ignacio Fernández Domingo. Madrid: Pigmalión, 2015. 246 p.: bibl. (Colección Magíster de Pigmalión)

This work provides a history of the foreign relations of Spain with both Cuba and Puerto Rico, the last colonial possessions of the former European power in the Americas during the second half of the 19th century. The study focuses on the role of the Ministerio de Ultramar, established in 1863, to oversee the government of these territories. Based on the author's doctoral dissertation. [LG]

847 Borrero González, Edwin. Los ferrocarriles en Puerto Rico (1850–1957): historia económica, política, social, cultural y jurídica. Cayey, Puerto Rico: Mariana Editores; Dominican Republic: Impreso en Serifraf, S.A., 2016. 486 p.: bibl., ill., maps.

This study presents a history of the coastal railway network established in Puerto Rico stretching from the early planning stages in the 1850s through its development and eventual decline in the 1950s. The research is based mainly on records drawn from the Archivo General de Puerto Rico in San Juan. [LG]

848 Browne, Randy M. Surviving slavery in the British Caribbean. Philadelphia: University of Pennsylvania Press, 2017. 279 p.: bibl., index, map. (Early American studies)

When Britain took over Berbice (present-day Guyana) from the Dutch, it kept open the "fiscal," an agency that heard complaints from enslaved people claiming to have been victims of illegal treatment. This book explores the fiscal records to uncover the methods by which enslaved individuals survived in Berbice, and the ways in which they navigated relationships with enslavers. The author advocates for a subtler reading of enslaved agency—one not so strictly polarized between rebellion and accommodation. Instead, as these records show, issues such as family, religious tradition, and labor hierarchies created multiple pathways of negotiation between freedom and bondage. [DL]

849 Cabrera Peña, Miguel. ¿Fue José Martí racista?: perspectiva sobre los negros en Cuba y Estados Unidos: una crítica a la Academia norteamericana. Madrid: Editorial Betania, 2014. 464 p.: bibl. (Colección Ensayo)

This lengthy and extended essay examines from historiographical and political perspectives the various interpretations of José Martí on the question of race. In particular, the author is critical of intellectuals and academics who have drawn attention to certain silences and absences in Martí's political statements and writings on race to make arguments about what Martí meant. Polemical in tone, but well-researched and deserves to be read by scholars of Cuban race relations more broadly and those focusing on José Martí in particular. [MC]

850 **Cento Gómez, Elda.** Nadie puede ser indiferente: miradas a las guerras (1868-1898). Santiago de Cuba: Editorial Oriente, 2013. 333 p.: bibl., ill., maps. (Colección Historia. Bronce)

This study offers a regional perspective on the Wars of Independence in the province of Camagüey rather than in the well-known theaters of political and military action in Havana and Oriente. Drawing upon municipal and regional archives, the author examines how the 30 years of fighting in particular impacted the civilian population, with insights into how slavery became transformed during the struggle against Spanish colonial rule. [MDC]

851 **Crespo Armáiz, Jorge Luis.** Estereoscopía y sujeto colonial: la contribución de la fotografía estereoscópica en la construcción del otro puertorriqueño (1898-1930). Gurabo, Puerto Rico: Universidad del Turabo, Sistema Universitario Ana G. Méndez, 2015. 245 p.: bibl., ill. (some color), index.

This work draws on largely untapped sources—collections of stereoscopic photographs or stereoviews—to examine the construction of a visual colonial imaginary of Puerto Rico since 1898 and the dissemination and consumption of this visualized knowledge in North American schools, universities, and libraries in the form of teacher's manuals during the first decades of the 20th century. Lavishly illustrated. Significant contribution to colonial photography studies. [LG]

852 **Dalby, Jonathan R.** "Such a mass of disgusting and revolting cases": moral panic and the "discovery" of sexual deviance in post-emancipation Jamaica (1835-1855). (*Slavery Abolit.*, 36:1, 2015, p. 136-159)

Through an extensive analysis of the Surrey Assize cases, this study reconstructs a key period of cultural attack against recently freed Jamaicans. Prior to emancipation, only one percent of Assize Court cases dealt with sex offenses. Yet, in the two decades after emancipation, that figure rose to 14 percent. The author examines the language within these cases to argue that judges and colonial observers manufactured a sense of sexual panic as a way to undercut the position of Afro-Jamaicans. He argues that the economic and social turbulence of the post-emancipation period allowed jurists to justify such claims, creating a criminal crackdown that sowed the seeds for the Morant Bay Rebellion in 1865. See also *HLAS 62:1087*. [DL]

853 **Dumont, Henri.** Los orígenes de la antropología en el Caribe. Revisión y anotaciones de Gabino La Rosa y Lourdes S. Domínguez. San Juan: Ediciones Puerto, 2013. 204 p.: bibl., ill.

This work is a reprint with critical annotation of Dumont's 1875 volume titled *Antropología y patología comparadas de los negros esclavos*. Dumont interviewed and studied the enslaved population and reproduced many images of the enslaved people from a racist scientific approach to argue for a connection between race and criminality. [MDC]

854 **Dungy, Kathryn Renée.** The conceptualization of race in colonial Puerto Rico, 1800-1850. New York: Peter Lang, 2014. 132 p.: bibl., ill., index, maps. (Black studies and critical thinking; 47)

The experience of communities of free people of color in early 19th-century Puerto Rico introduces nuances into our understanding of race and race relations in colonial societies in the Black Atlantic. To that end, this study draws on a variety of archival sources, including census and marriage records. [LG]

855 **Fryer, Christienna D.** The moral politics of cholera in postemancipation Jamaica. (*Slavery Abolit.*, 34:4, 2013, p. 598-618)

Roughly eight percent of Jamaica's population died in a two-year cholera epidemic, beginning in 1850, that was part of a global wave of disease. Rulers and commentators on the island were quick to link the disease to a sense of moral failure on the part of Afro-Jamaicans who had only recently been freed. Mostly, medical personnel claimed that cholera spread due to the supposed unhealthiness, laziness, and filthy living of the recently emancipated. Jamaica's economic struggles at the time served to arouse a sense of panic in which future prevention became more important than contemporary treatment. Sanitation programs, the author argues, became a path by which reformers could then attempt to "civilize" those suffering in poverty. [DL]

856 **García, Gervasio Luis.** Historia bajo sospecha. Río Piedras, Puerto Rico: Publicaciones Gaviota, 2015. 280 p.: bibl., ill., index.

This study provides a perceptive critical examination of historiographical writing on Puerto Rico. Important chapters cover the discursive strategies used by 19th-century intellectuals to circumvent the censorship of Spanish authorities, and the ideological negotiations of early 20th-century political leaders vis-à-vis US rule in Puerto Rico. Mostly composed of works previously published in print and online publications. [LG]

857 **Goodridge, Sehon S.** Facing the challenge of emancipation: a study of the ministry of William Hart Coleridge, first bishop of Barbados, 1824–1842. Kingston: Canoe Press; St Michael, Barbados: Barbados Museum and Historical Society, 2014. 131 p.: bibl., ill., index, plates.

This work reprints Goodridge's 1981 study of Coleridge and the role that the Anglican Church played in Barbados' transition from slavery to freedom. Goodridge provides an overall history of the Church in Barbados for its first two centuries of colonization before turning to the efforts of Coleridge to proselytize on the island as its first bishop. Specific topics include assessments of Coleridge's attempts to improve education on the island, as well as a reflection on his attitudes toward conversion and social change in the emancipation and apprenticeship period. [DL]

858 **Heureaux, Ulises.** Antología de cartas de Ulises Heureaux (Lilís). Edición y compilación de Cyrus Veeser. Santo Domingo: Archivo General de la Nación, 2015. 488 p.: bibl., index. (Colección presidentes dominicanos)(Archivo General de la Nación; CCXLIX)

A collection of documents from the pen of former dictator Ulises Heureaux, another primary document collection from the publications department of the AGN and a part of their Dominican Presidents series, this rather massive collection charts the correspondence written by Heureaux to various recipients between 1894 and 1898. Historian Cyrus Veeser, who has published extensively on US foreign policy particularly in the early part of the century, curated the collection and provides a thorough introduction. While the selection of letters covers only part of the presidency of the man more commonly known as Lilís (1882–99), the collection manages to convey the elements that distinguished the man as, Veeser argues, "cosmopolitan, multilingual, financier, and diplomat" (p. 23). To wit, the letters were destined for locations across the Caribbean, the US, and Europe; a number of them highlight the dictator's financial relationship with the Santo Domingo Improvement Company. While the letters may hide the more notoriously dictatorial side of the leader through polite and careful text, they certainly help clarify a number of the fiscal and international tactics that kept him in power for 17 years, as well as the many tentacled legacies of those manuevers. [EM]

859 **Hoffmann, Odile.** British Honduras: the invention of a colonial territory: mapping and spatial knowledge in the 19th century. Belize: Cubola Productions; France: Institute de Recherche pour la Development, 2014. 79 p.: bibl., ill., map.

Using a number of historical and contemporary maps, this study charts the growth of colonization in 19th-century Belize. Officials used maps to navigate territory, but also to delimit the extent of state and economic control. Hoffmann provides a close analysis of the challenges of cartographic investigation, alongside a detailed assessment of how colonization extended over Belize decade by decade. These ongoing developments include the path of conquest over indigenous peoples through British warfare, as well as representations of racial segregation in the years after emancipation. Along the way, Hoffmann examines how maps themselves transformed over the 19th century to reflect different governmental and personal interests. [DL]

860 **Hutton, Clinton A.** Colour for colour, skin for skin: marching with the ancestral spirits into War Oh at Morant Bay. Kingston: Ian Randle Publishers, 2015. 259 p.: bibl., ill., index, photos.

One of the most important moments in postemancipation Jamaican society was the 1865 Morant War—also known as the Morant Bay Rebellion. In this study, Hutton examines the ways in which planters continued to exploit workers, more than a generation after emancipation, to precipitate the war. He follows the ideological and political views expressed by the revolutionaries who took part, the factors which stymied their success, and the fallout of the war, when Britain transformed its governance of Jamaica. Future tensions and uprisings emerged directly as a result of the 1865 uprising. [DL]

861 **Inniss, Tara A.** "This complicated incest": children, sexuality, and sexual abuse during slavery and the apprenticeship period in the British Caribbean, 1790–1838. (*in* Sex, power, and slavery. Edited by Gwyn Campbell and Elizabeth Elbourne. Athens: Ohio University Press, 2014, p. 253–271)

This study delves into the topic of youthful sexuality—including issues of sexual abuse and incest—within the enslaved community of Barbados in the decades leading up to emancipation. Enslaved children, especially girls, were aggressively sexualized by planters and overseers, leading to near constant sexual violence. Inniss proposes a number of different routes for scholars to explore enslaved sexual history, including studies of same-sex relationships and relations among kin. She concludes with several case studies of sexual and physical assault against young children during the period of apprenticeship. [DL]

862 **Inoa, Orlando.** Bibliografía de Juan Pablo Duarte. Santo Domingo: Letragráfica, 2014. 199 p. (Serie Vintage books)

An exhaustive compilation of all the work that has been produced in the past five decades on the much-applauded "founding father" Juan Pablo Duarte, this annotated bibliography provides an invaluable tool to scholars of Duarte, the 19th-century Dominican Republic, and Dominican literature and historiography more broadly. Includes books, scholarly articles, newspaper and magazine articles, and even printed speeches and official state declarations honoring the man. [EM]

863 **Jemmott, Jenny M.** Ties that bind: the black family in post-slavery Jamaica, 1834–1882. Kingston: The University of the West Indies Press, 2015. 263 p.: bibl., ill., index, map.

Assessing life after slavery, Jemmott's work tacks away from structural analyses of family organization and toward considerations of relational experiences. West African traditions of extended family care bolstered the Jamaican nuclear family, particularly during lean economic periods. Men took a much more active role, she claims, than previous studies have suggested. Jemmott also argues that the family became a source of political warfare in the 19th century, when officials and reformers insisted that black Jamaicans did not properly care for their relatives, while those families countered that supportive kinship was an instrumental force in the maintenance of their freedom. Both sides battled for control over education, marriage, and supervision of children during the period. [DL]

864 **Lee-Borges, José.** Los chinos en Puerto Rico. San Juan: Ediciones Callejón, 2015. 436 p.: bibl., ill., index, maps, portraits. (Coleccion en fuga)

This welcome study addresses the origins and trajectories of the first Chinese migrants introduced from the Dominican Republic and Cuba to Puerto Rico as prisoners forced to work in public works projects since the 1860s. The author presents the social imaginary of the Chinese community in Puerto Rico. Fills a gap in the historiography of Caribbean immigration. [LG]

865 **Lightfoot, Natasha.** Troubling freedom: Antigua and the aftermath of British emancipation. Durham, N.C.: Duke University Press, 2015. 320 p.: bibl., index, maps, photos.

Although it nominally freed enslaved people, British emancipation in 1834 created a host of problems for those released from bondage. This study discusses Antigua's particular version of slavery, its 1831 rebellion, the aftermath of emancipation, and the island's 1858 uprising over job scarcity and labor control. Lightfoot examines ordinary people's experiences with, and reactions to, these events. She argues that the post-1834 period produced more aggressive forms of surveillance by the state, religious reformers, and employers, all of which resulted in far less freedom than that promised by emancipation. Moreover, she contends that violence and restrictions on freedom had a stronger impact on Antiguan women. [DL]

866 **McCarthy, Matthew.** Privateering, piracy and British policy in Spanish America, 1810–1830. Woodbridge, England: Boydell Press, 2013. 184 p.: bibl., ill., index.

This study examines the role and impact of piracy and privateering on the maritime activities during the Spanish American wars for independence. Drawing largely from the British National Archives and Parliamentary Papers, the author is able to show how the political and military events related to Latin American independence created new opportunities for privateers to contract out their services, which subsequently fostered a resurgence in piratical activity that most scholarship tends to limit to the 16th to the 18th centuries. [MDC]

867 **Meriño Fuentes, María de los Ángeles** and **Aisnara Perera Díaz.** Del tráfico a la libertad: el caso de los africanos de la fragata Dos Hermanos en Cuba (1795–1837). Santiago de Cuba: Editorial Oriente, 2014. 379 p.: bibl., ill. (Bronce colección)

This book presents one of the most detailed studies to date of the Cuban slave trade in the 19th century. The authors skillfully and insightfully move between a microhistory of the slave ship *Dos Hermanos* to the macrohistory of the transatlantic slave trade, the African diaspora, and the rivalries among empires. Accompanying the book is nearly 100 pages of original documents. [MDC]

868 **Monteith, Kathleen E.A.** Boom and bust in Jamaica's coffee industry, 1790–1835. (*J. Caribb. Hist.*, 47:1, 2013, p. 1–27)

Coffee boomed in Jamaica after 1790 due to the drop of supply from the Haitian Revolution. In this article, Monteith traces the growth, and ultimate decline, of the profitability of coffee on the island in the final decades of slavery. She provides a close examination of the economic returns on coffee, the disruptions in trade caused by the Napoleonic Wars, as well as the political debates over protectionism at the time. Through this study, Monteith offers a complex analysis of the Jamaican economy as it evolved. She argues that assessing the dynamics of slave trading does not adequately address the multiple issues—such as war, trade liberalization, etc.—that factored into whether Jamaica was in economic decline or ascension at the beginning of the 19th century. [DL]

869 **Navarro Carballo, José Ramón.** Vicisitudes sanitarias de la Tercera Guerra de Cuba. Villaviciosa, Spain: Ediciones Camelot, 2015. 306 p.: bibl.

This work offers a history of the conditions and ailments of Spanish soldiers in Cuba's final war for independence and the medical services provided to soldiers who fought there. The book is more a chronicling of sanitary and health services offered than a medical history approach to the war. The text also provides reproductions of important primary source documents. [MDC]

870 **Nuestros reveses y victorias: causas y experiencias (1868–1958).** Edición de María Luisa García Moreno. Tercera edición corregida y actualizada. La Habana: Casa Editorial Verde Olivo, 2014. 245 p.: bibl., ill.

This traditional military history, written from a teleological perspective, explains Cuba's 100-year struggle for independence that culminates in the 1959 Revolution. The 19th-century Wars for Independence, the Cuban Republic, and the 1933 Revolution are written from the perspective of explaining what they did not achieve and the work left to be accomplished by the 1959 Revolution. [MDC]

871 **Pérez Vega, Ivette.** Las sociedades mercantiles de Ponce (1816–1830). San Juan: Academia Puertorriqueña de la Historia: Ediciones Puerto Inc., 2015. 448 p.: bibl., ill., maps. (Biblioteca de la Academia)

This prosopographical study analyzes the foreign-born merchant class of Ponce during the early decades of the 1800s. Through their control of trade and financing, merchants were key actors in the transformation of the southern municipality into a booming sugar-producing economy based on slave labor. [LG]

872 **Petley, Christer.** Plantations and homes: the material culture of the early nineteenth-century Jamaican elite. (*Slavery Abolit.*, 35:3, 2014, p. 437–457)

Petley explores the homes, possessions, and culture of Jamaica's plantocracy in the final years of the island's most profligate and profitable period. He profiles two of the most elite colonial Jamaicans at the time: Simon Taylor and John Cunningham. Through probate inventories, Petley chronicles the extreme wealth that both men possessed, including not only luxurious homes on massive tracts of land, but also large numbers of enslaved people toiling to support them. Yet the two men were also the last of their kind before the island's economy transformed in the lead-up to emancipation. [DL]

873 **Picó, Fernando.** Puerto Rico y la sequía de 1847. San Juan: Ediciones Huracán, 2015. 207 p.: bibl.

This study delves into a largely forgotten chapter in 19th-century Puerto Rican history—the severe drought of 1847. Specifically, the author investigates the social impact of a so-called natural disaster. Picó places the local case in the global perspective of a drought, propelled by the El Niño weather phenomenon that caused major disruptions in societies throughout the Atlantic world. A significant contribution to environmental studies. [LG]

874 **Pinto, Antonio J.** Negro sobre blanco: la conspiración esclava de 1812 en Puerto Rico. (*Caribb. Stud.*, 40:1, Jan./June 2012, p. 121–149, bibl., graphs, ill.)

This article traces connections between the slave conspiracy of 1812 in Puerto Rico, the Aponte rebellion in Cuba, and the slave plot in Santo Domingo during the same year. A unifying feature of these slave plots was the collaboration between slaves and free people of color. The author highlights the peculiarities of the Puerto Rican case: the conspiration spread to areas beyond San Juan; after slaves, poor white people formed the second largest group of conspirators; and the punishment delivered by the Spanish colonial authorities was relatively moderate. [LG]

875 **Rodríguez La O, Raúl.** Limbano Sánchez y la independencia de Cuba. La Habana: Instituto Cubano del Libro, Editorial de Ciencias Sociales, 2015. 207 p.: bibl., facsims., ill.

This work publishes a document collection from Cuban and Spanish archives detailing the role of Limbano Sánchez in Cuba's 19th-century wars for independence. The documents provide details on Sánchez's active role in the Ten Years' War (1868–78), the Guerra Chiquita (1879–80), and other political and insurrectionary activity in the cause of Cuban independence until his death in 1885. [MC]

876 **Rosario Natal, Carmelo.** Soy libre!: el grito de Agripina, la esclava rebelde de Ponce. San Juan: Ediciones Puerto, Inc., 2013. 67 p.: bibl., facsims.

This study unearths the story of Juana Agripina, a Creole enslaved woman from Ponce, based on the extant case file, or *expediente*, she lodged to claim her freedom in 1865. This remarkable legal document sheds new light not only on the workings of the Spanish legal system, but more importantly, on the agency of enslaved people seeking liberation in 19th-century Puerto Rico. [LG]

877 **Rosario Rivera, Raquel.** Mariana Bracety: una patriota que no claudicó. San Juan: Academia Puertorriqueña de la Historia: Asociación Puertorriqueña de Investigación de Historia de las Mujeres, 2014. 259 p.: bibl., ill.

This is the first scholarly biography of Ana María Bracety, better known as Mariana Bracety, an iconic figure of the Grito de Lares rebellion against Spain in 1868. The study draws on previously untapped oral and archival sources in Spain, Puerto Rico, and elsewhere. [LG]

Singleton, Theresa A. Slavery behind the wall: an archaeology of a Cuban coffee plantation. See *HLAS 73:193*.

878 **Smith, Matthew J.** Liberty, fraternity, exile: Haiti and Jamaica after emancipation. Chapel Hill: The University of North Carolina Press, 2014. 409 p.: bibl., ill., index, maps.

This monograph seeks to integrate the histories of Jamaica and Haiti from the period after slavery and apprenticeship to the dawn of the First World War. Smith explores the shared experiences and social structures forged during the era of slavery to reveal divergent—yet similar—paths. Whereas Jamaica came under more intense metropolitan rule during the 19th century, Haiti fell under stronger foreign influence and meddling in its government. Both countries experienced a shared US intervention in the 20th century. Throughout this period, Jamaicans and Haitians moved frequently between the two locations, creating extended families in both nations, as well as building shared ideologies and regional perspectives. [DL]

879   Turner, Sasha. Contested bodies: pregnancy, childrearing, and slavery in Jamaica. Philadelphia: PENN University of Pennsylvania Press, 2017. 316 p.: bibl., ill., index, maps. (Early American studies)

Turner focuses on the politics around enslaved reproduction in Jamaica at the turn of the 19th century, when antislavery activism was at its height. She argues that pregnancy and childbirth became the central point of interaction between enslaved people and free society during this period. Reformers believed that increased reproduction could eliminate the need for the slave trade, as well as civilize enslaved families. Plantation managers contended that increased surveillance would heighten their power over enslaved workers. Enslaved people themselves, however, pushed back and took over as much control of pregnancy and childbirth as they could. Altogether, this monograph reveals that enslaved women were some of the most important actors in Jamaican plantations. [DL]

880   Vásquez Frías, Pastor. Misiones dominicanas en Haití. Tomo 1, Primeras misiones 1866–1876. Tomo 2, El general Luperón, el Partido Azul y los gobiernos haitianos, 1877–1887. Santo Domingo: Somos Artes Gráficas, 2014. 2 v.: appendices, bibl., ill., photos.

A two-volume study covering the 20-year period between 1866 and 1887 and the Dominican diplomatic corps appointed to Haiti during that time, this work is an outgrowth of the author's previous research on the origins of migration from Haiti to the Dominican Republic. Rather than focus on the formal treaties and conventions signed (between the two nations), the author seeks to find out how the relations between the two nations began and functioned in a regular way; to that end, this work represents a careful and well-sourced detailing of those first two decades. Endorsed by revered ambassador and scholar Rubén Silié, who notes the work's strength in highlighting "the strong historical linkages between the two nations," the study also provides a number of useful appendices, including transcribed (and original) presidential statements, treaties, death notices (Tomas Bobadilla), and diplomatic correspondence. [EM]

881   Zeuske, Michael. Amistad: a hidden network of slavers and merchants. Translated from the German by Steven Rendall. American edition. Princeton, N.J.: Markus Wiener Publishers, 2014. 268 p.: bibl., ill., index, maps.

This study provides a fresh interpretation on the well-known *Amistad* slave ship revolt that carried a cargo of human captives bound for Cuba, but subsequently landed in the US once the enslaved Africans rebelled. Drawing upon previously unknown sources, Zeuske is able to map out the connections between illegal transactions, falsified documents, and reputable merchants that linked the clandestine trade together. [MDC]

882   Zhongguo ren yu Guba du li zhan zheng = The Chinese and Cuba's independence wars. Edited by Pang Bing'an zhu bian. Beijing: Xin hua chu ban she, 2013. 182 p.: bibl., ill.

This book tells the story of how the editor collected and stored for decades a valuable historical document written by a famous Cuban patriot and published in Germany in 1892 (later republished in Cuba in 1946), which praised the heroic deeds of the Chinese during Cuba's Wars of Independence. After several decades, the editor returned the document to Cuba, and the Cuban Embassy in China donated it to the Chinese National Museum for the permanent collection. Prior to returning the document, the editor relayed the story to Fidel Castro, who then wrote an inscription on the document in favor of the donation. The book contains the complete Chinese translation of the document and biographical information about several famous Chinese-Cubans. The editor is the former deputy director of Xinhua News Agency (China). [Mao Xianglin]

20TH CENTURY

883   Alemán Iglesias, Javier. El origen del colono en Puerto Rico: un balance historiográfico del agricultor de la industria azucarera en el siglo XX. (*Rev. Indias*, 78:273, 2018, p. 533–560)

This historiographical essay focuses on the development of the *colonato*, the class of growers who supplied sugarcane to the modern central mills (*centrales*) in 20th-century Puerto Rico. The author proposes a research agenda anchored in comparative studies of the sugar industry in the Hispanic Caribbean and the use of archival and oral sources to improve understanding of the social and economic profiles of *colonos* and their political roles. [LG]

884 **Artículos recopilados sobre la ocupación norteamericana de 1916.** Edición de Vetilio Alfau Durán. Santo Domingo: Academia Dominicana de la Historia, 2016. 237 p.: index. (Academia Dominicana de la Historia; CXXXI)

An impressive set of primary documents, meticulously culled from national newspapers at the time of the first US occupation and published posthumously from a collection of the author by the Dominican Academy of History, this work charts the US marine intervention of the Dominican Republic (1916–24) in its very first year. Drawn from *Listín Diario*, *El Radical*, and *La Bandera Libre* primarily, the 95 articles contained in this volume, some of which were first published elsewhere, demonstrate the tenor of debate that surrounded the arrival of US marines, but also the manner in which newspapers sought to keep the public informed of the ongoing struggle to maintain sovereignty. [EM]

885 **Balaguer, Joaquín.** Joaquín Balaguer: cartas, artículos, conferencias, discursos y documentos inéditos. Compilación, introducción, y notas de Cándido Gerón. Santo Domingo: Editora Centenario, 2015. 390 p.: ill., index.

Divided into two parts with the first covering the period between 1930 and 1996 and the second focusing specifically on correspondence between Balaguer and the US Department of State immediately following the *ajusticiamiento* of Trujillo, this collection represents an addition to the available primary sources on long-time president Joaquín Balaguer. While a bit short on analysis (in the form of a brief six-page introduction), the collection provides some interesting correspondence with individuals who would later find themselves in opposition to the Trujillato (Andrés Requena, José Almoina), individuals well-known as regime accomplices (Johnny Abbes García, Rafael Paíno Pichardo), and individuals from the Church and foreign diplomatic corps. Materials also cover Balaguer's roles in the Trujillo regime (including speeches and writings from that period), as well limited publications from the "doce años" (1966–78) and his final term as president (1990–96). While the organization of materials seems to lack a clear logic and original source citations are not always provided, the contained documents offer important glimpses into the man and his style of leadership. [EM]

886 **Barrio Batista, Magrid** and **Ismael Alonso Coma.** Historia del colegio americano en Guantánamo. Guantánamo, Cuba: Editorial El Mar y la Montaña, 2013. 95 p., 6 unnumbered pages of plates: bibl., ill. (Investigación)

This study provides a brief and insightful account of the American religious school established in Guantánamo affiliated with the Episcopal Church of the US. The authors investigate the role of the school as a private institution. Particular attention is paid to the relationship between the school and Cuban students and families in Guantánamo before private schools were nationalized by the 1959 Revolution. [MDC]

887 **Blanco Rodríguez, Juan Andrés** and **Alejandro García Álvarez.** Legado de España en Cuba. Madrid: Sílex, 2015. 287 p.: bibl., ill.

This study examines the continued migration of Spaniards to Cuba in the 20th century after Cuban independence from Spain. The authors pay particular attention to the formation of migrant associations and their mutual-aid activities in building immigrant communities throughout the island. Notably, many of the buildings that housed the immigrants' cultural associations later became *casas de cultura* during the 1959 Revolution. [MDC]

888 **Bofill Pérez, María Antonia.** La olvidada expedición a Santo Domingo en 1959. Santo Domingo: Archivo General de la Nación, 2015. 204 p.: bibl., ill., index. (Archivo General de la Nación; CCXXIX)

Written by the daughter of a member of the Cuban rebel army and participant in a failed expedition against Trujillo in August 1959 (José Antonio Bofill Carbonell), this volume includes a narrative of the attempted attack (nominally supported by the Castro regime), as well as interviews conducted by the author, short biographies of the lost participants, and primary documents connected to the events. Its central focus is on the group of Cuban *guerrilleros* who had followed up on the Dominican attack more widely known as Constanza, Maimón, and Estero Hondo the previous June and who, after being discovered by a Haitian ship, were imprisoned and tortured. Of the group of 30, only five were eventually returned to their native Cuba. [EM]

889 **Bonacci, Giulia.** Exodus!: heirs and pioneers, Rastafari return to Ethiopia. Translated by Antoinette Tidjani Alou. Foreword by Elikia M'Bokolo. Kingston: The University of the West Indies Press, 2015. 482 p.: bibl., ill., index, maps.

Bonacci provides a sweeping history of pan-Africanism, Garveyism, and Rastafarianism through an analysis of Caribbean repatriation to Africa. She gives a wide-ranging account of the "Back-to-Africa" movement, but also looks closely at several hundred West Indian migrants who relocated to Shashemene—the area given by Ethiopia's Emperor Haile Selassie I to all black people wishing to settle. The end of the Italo-Ethiopian war opened up the land to migrants after WWII, offering an opportunity to fulfill a key goal of the black consciousness movement. However, Bonacci demonstrates the challenges that Shashemene faced, as relations with the Ethiopian state and people were often in tension. The book delves into the details of many of the migrants' lives, providing a bottom-up investigation of the movement and its goals. [DL]

890 ***Centro Journal.*** Vol. 29, No. 1, Spring 2017, U.S. citizenship in Puerto Rico: one hundred years after the Jones Act. Edited by Charles R. Venator-Santiago and Edgardo Meléndez. New York, N.Y.: Center for Puerto Rican Studies.

Published on the centennial of the enactment of the Jones Act of 1917, this special issue of the *Centro Journal* provides in-depth analyses by prominent social scientists and legal experts on the history, legal interpretation, and long-lasting political legacy of the landmark legislation that granted US citizenship to the people of Puerto Rico. Contains 12 articles plus a preface. For political scientist's comment, see *HLAS 73:1137*. [LG]

891 **Chez Checo, José.** El ron en la historia dominicana. Tomo 2, Siglos XX y XXI. Santo Domingo: Centenario de Brugal, 2014. 1 v.: bibl., ill.

In this second volume of a history of rum in the Dominican Republic sponsored by the Brugal & Co., noted historian José Chez Checo narrates the development of the industry across the 20th century, from the decade and a half prior to the US occupation in 1916 through the centennial anniversary of Brugal rum in 1988 and their expansion globally into the 21st century. The study follows up on the first volume (covering the precolonial period to the end of the 19th century) published by Chez Checo in 1988 on the corporation's centennial anniversary. Like several other similar works sponsored by the nation's most dominant industries (notably beer and tobacco), this study intertwines the development of one of the country's now most notable exports with the larger historical narrative of national growth and change. [EM]

892 **Crespo Armáiz, Jorge Luis.** De la prosperidad a la resistencia: la representación de Puerto Rico en la revista *National Geographic*, 1898–2003. (*Caribb. Stud.*, 42:1, Jan./June 2014, p. 3–43, bibl., photos)

The textual and visual representations of Puerto Rico in the pages of the *National Geographic* challenge the magazine's manifest editorial line on scientific objectivity, suggesting that these representations are in line with shifts in the preoccupations of the larger economic, political, and military interests of the US in Puerto Rico. This study complements the work of historian Laura Muñoz Mata (see items **926** and **927**). [LG]

893 **Cruz Santos, Martín.** Afirmando la nación . . .: políticas culturales en Puerto Rico (1949–1968). San Juan: Ediciones Callejón, 2014. 281 p.: bibl., ill. (Colección En fuga. Ensayos)

This work explores the role of organic intellectuals in the formulation and implementation of the cultural program of the Partido Popular Democrático (PPD) and its iconic creation, the Instituto de Cultura Puertorriqueña. The author centers on Águedo Mojica Marrero—scholar, cultural agent, and lawmaker—who played a key role in the development of cultural nationalism in Puerto Rico. [LG]

894 Davidson, Christina Cecelia. Black Protestants in a Catholic land: the AME Church in the Dominican Republic 1899–1916. (*NWIG*, 89:3/4, Jan. 2015, p. 258–288, bibl.)

This study of the African Methodist Church in the Dominican Republic is a refreshing reminder of the new work on religion and the Dominican-African diaspora (see, for example, item **895**) but also of the need to continually question accepted "truths," including the stories we tell about American Protestants in the Dominican Republic in the early 20th century. Part of a larger work in progress on the AME, this article clarifies much about the church's work across several regions in the country (Samaná, Santo Domingo, and the southeast), its engagements with immigrant West Indian laborers, and the ways it served as "a space in which leaders and parishioners imagined themselves in relation to other black people in the Dominican Republic and elsewhere" (p. 265). [EM]

895 Davidson, Christina Cecelia. Disruptive silences: the AME Church and Dominican-Haitian relations. (*J. Africana Relig.*, 5:1, 2017, p. 1–25, bibl.)

Another contribution to the work of charting the history of the African Methodist Church (AME) in the Dominican Republic, this article (honorable mention, Haiti-Dominican Republic Section Prize, LASA) also helps explain how and why the church failed to support Haitians and Haitian-Dominicans in their current struggles over citizenship. In looking back to early to mid-20th century records of the AME's involvement in both Haiti and the Dominican Republic, as well as the Dominican branch's marginalization from the larger organization, Davidson posits that the silences created around the church's work on the island are an even bigger issue than neglect for it congregants and present a much larger crick in the links of African diasporic solidarity. See also item **894**. [EM]

896 De León Olivares, Isabel Dolores. Resistencias discursivas de intelectuales de República Dominicana durante la ocupación estadounidense de 1916–1924: nacionalismo, antiimperialismo e hispanismo. (*Tzintzun*, 62, julio/dic. 2015, p. 108–148)

Contributing to a growing field of studies of the US occupation of the Dominican Republic (see, for example, *HLAS 71:1416* and *HLAS 72:1115*), this article focuses on the intellectual discourse used by the elite cadre of leaders of the resistance movement to mobilize the cultural concepts of nationhood for a reclaimed sovereignty. De León makes a compelling claim for an understanding of the use of hispanidad at this moment that runs contrary to how scholars have predominantly focused on its use as a deflection of shared Haitian and African ancestry. Rather, the author argues, the Dominican case illustrates how hispanidad, during the early 20th century, was used across the Caribbean and Latin America as a key element in an anti-imperialist campaign against the US. [EM]

897 Despradel, Fidelio. Fidelio: memorias de un revolucionario. Santo Domingo: Archivo General de la Nación, 2015. 2 v.: appendices, ill., indexes. (Archivo General de la Nación; CCXXXIII–CCXXXIV)

Revolutionary memoir and selection of primary documents by the extremely prolific member of the 14 de Junio Movement Fidelio Despradel, this two-volume set is an over 1000-page homage to the efforts of the revolutionary generation(s) of the 1940s, 50s, and 60s, as well as to the author's own role in the valiant, if challenged, revolutionary movement. Published by the AGN, the two volumes attempt to cover the period from 1865 through 1965, with the first volume addressing the Despradel family history from that initial date through the eve of the April Revolution and the second volume treating the events of the 1965 April Revolution and its aftermath. The appendix in the second volume also contains a plethora of documents, including official declarations of governance, several exile letters, a previously hidden (and fascinating) cache of documents from the Trujillo resistance movement, correspondence between the 1J4 and the incarcerated members of the 1963 insurrection, a large glossy section of photographs, and a brief biography of the author. The sum total of these primary materials supports the supposition that a large portion of such direct evidence of the resistance remains within private/secret archives. [EM]

898 Documentos del gobierno de Carlos F. Morales Languasco 1903–1906. Compilación de Alfredo Rafael Hernández Figueroa. Santo Domingo: Archivo General de la Nación, 2015. 400 p.: bibl., index. (Archivo General de la Nación; CCLIII)(Colección Presidentes dominicanos)

This volume, one of the many anthologies of primary documents being produced by the AGN, covers a relatively understudied yet crucial period in Dominican history. Containing an array of government documents, all culled from the collections of Laws and Decrees, Foreign Relations, and Interior, this contribution to the AGN's series on Dominican presidents offers a view on the provisional presidency of Carlos Felipe Morales Languasco between 1903 and 1906, as well as a series of materials from 1907 establishing a case for espionage against him. A priest and resident of Puerto Plata, Morales Languasco came into his role following the period known as "Lilismo" (Ulises Heureaux); like the collection of documents from Heureaux (see item **858**), this anthology spotlights the fiscal, social, and political turmoil that led up to the first US occupation in 1916. [EM]

899 Dr. Antonio Fernós Isern: de médico a constituyente. Edición de Héctor Luis Acevedo. Con la ayuda de editores asociados José Luis Colón González y Néstor R. Duprey Salgado. San Juan: Universidad Interamericana de Puerto Rico, Recinto Metropolitano, CIEDP, Centro Interamericano para el Estudio de las Dinámicas Políticas, 2014. 843 p.: bibl., ill. (some color), index, portraits. (Colección Raíces de nuestra épica)(Colección Publicaciones compartidas)

This work delves into the life and political career of Antonio Fernós Isern, a trained physician, a statesman (he was Resident Commissioner from 1945–65), and a key figure of the so-called Generation of 1940 in Puerto Rico. As the intellectual architect of the Estado Libre Asociado (Commonwealth), he advocated and proposed legislation supporting a form of self-government for Puerto Rico. Speeches, newspaper columns, bills, correspondence, and other relevant documents appear in an appendix. [LG]

900 Espínola, Ramón Emilio. Remembranzas: crónicas de la ocupación 1916–1924: la era de los Estados Unidos. Santo Domingo: Argos, 2016. 158 p.: bibl., ill.

This short volume, written in light of the 100th anniversary of the landing of the US marines, seeks to serve as a reminder of the Dominican struggle to maintain sovereignty in light of the overwhelming force of the US across the region at this historical moment. Minimal sources are provided to support the facts enumerated in the text, although interesting new elements of guerrilla resistance and labor resistance to the occupation are offered by the author. Espínola argues, again without source citations, that the occupation started a "true emancipatory revolution" for Dominican women; while true that the period saw a revolutionary movement of women, it is an extremely reductive—and problematic— claim to lay its cause at the feet of foreign occupiers. Still, the references to revolutionary (male and female) figures and labor activism could be engaged as fodder for future research. [EM]

901 Fajardo Estrada, Ramón. Yo seré la tentación: María de los Ángeles Santana. La Habana: Letras Cubanas, 2013. 846 p.: bibl., ill., portraits.

This lengthy and insightful biography delves into the life of one of Cuba's most influential female actresses of the 20th century. The study draws upon a diverse range of sources and connects Santana's life to other intellectual and cultural developments in Cuba and abroad. In sum, the biography does more than just chronicle María de los Ángeles Santana's life; it also sheds light into the emergence and evolution of the Cuban entertainment industry during the early and mid-20th century. [MDC]

902 Fornet, Jorge. El 71: anatomía de una crisis. La Habana: Letras Cubanas, 2013. 324 p.: bibl., index.

This work provides a detailed intellectual, political, and cultural interpretation of the year 1971 in Cuba. Moving between constructing a detailed historical timeline of the year and telescoping forward the consequences for the future of Cuban society, the author subtly lays out some of the historical tendencies that will manifest themselves over the next several decades—often written in the form of a lesson for the present. [MDC]

903 Francos Lauredo, Aurelio. Los puentes de la memoria: vascos en Cuba. Vitoria, Spain: Servicio Central de Publicaciones del Gobierno Vasco, 2011. 337 p.

This insightful biographic collection is constructed by oral histories of a dozen Basque migrants who have settled and lived in Cuba over the course of the 20th century. Especially worthwhile is the reproduction of images depicting material cultural objects that are coveted and passed from one generation to another, indicating the importance of the migrants' Basque origins and their adaption to life in Cuba. [MDC]

904 Fraser, Adrian. The 1935 riots in St Vincent: from riots to adult suffrage. Kingston: The University of the West Indies Press, 2016. 240 p.: bibl., index, maps.

The Caribbean saw a spate of riots in the 1930s due to labor organizing and the outgrowths of the global Great Depression. Unlike its West Indian neighbors, which were still largely dependent upon sugar and banana monocultures, St. Vincent's economy was not centered on these products (arrowroot and cotton, instead, dominated). Riots broke out in St. Vincent when island officials began debating customs and taxation changes that potentially would have raised consumer prices and increased unemployment. Fraser follows the events of the riots closely, charting the various reactions to the protests, as well as the trials against those who participated. He concludes with an examination of the island's extension of suffrage in 1951 to show the breadth of experiences in Caribbean political activism of the 20th century. [DL]

905 García-Crespo, Naida. Picturing "the tightest little tyranny in the Caribbean": the march of time and a 1936 United States-Dominican diplomatic crisis. (*Film Hist.*, 29:4, 2017, p. 89–111, bibl., photos)

Using a newsreel-like film production ("An American Dictator") to highlight a minor, if overlooked diplomatic tussle between the US and the Dominican Republic, this article focuses on the boundaries of the Good Neighbor policy as well as the uncertain alliances between the two nations in the early years of the dictatorship; the author demonstrates the importance of looking beyond traditional source materials to understand the complex relations between the two nations. [EM]

906 Gerón, Cándido. Minerva Bernardino: trayectoria en defensa de los derechos de la mujer. Santo Domingo: Editora Centenario, 2015. 231 p.: ill., indexes.

This study, which focuses on the international affairs of the much-abhorred figure, unfortunately falls into the category of a largely uncritical (even laudatory) evaluation of this well-known regime sicaria and provides no references for its biographical claims, making the contained materials largely suspect and not useful. A chapter on Jesús Galíndez, whose disappearance was no doubt facilitated by Bernardino's connections in New York, also sits uncomfortably at the end of the book along with the documents the ambassador used to argue she had nothing to do with the crime. Also included are a series of letters and various materials concerning Bernardino, ranging from a letter she received from Horacio Vásquez in 1927 to certificates of appreciation, to correspondence with members of the Pan American Union, the Inter-American Commission of Women, and various others concerning the "First Dominican Women's Assembly" convened in 1943. The home of these primary sources, the only ones referenced, is not disclosed. [EM]

907 Gerón, Cándido. Trujillo: la cultura del terror. Santo Domingo: Editora Centenario, 2015. 303 p.: bibl., ill., index.

Incorporating a fair number of primary documents, this study on the "psychopathological aspects" of Trujillo and his political career provides essays on the dictator's military career and rise to power in 1930 and an "archeology of behavior" of the notorious leader. The documents, which take up the rest of the text, include over 100 transcribed confidential memorandum from the Servicio de Inteligencia Militar (SIM) and other military officers, foreign diplomats (reporting on exile activities), and press reports. Most are from the final years of the regime, although unfortunately no sourcing information is provided for any of them. Additionally, the author has included a number of reproductions of newspaper pages listing both the members of the Trujillo secret police (*caliés*) and political prisoners (both appearing in the paper *1/4* in early 1962) and an unsourced list of the regime's secret police. [EM]

908   Hintzen, Amelia. "A veil of legality": the contested history of anti-Haitian ideology under the Trujillo dictatorship. (*NWIG*, 90:1/2, Jan. 2015, p. 28–54, bibl.)

A fascinating study of labor policy before and after the 1937 Haitian Massacre, this article sheds light on the Trujillo regime's possible reasons for ordering the genocide. Hintzen argues that "archival evidence suggests that the regime was frustrated with the lack of support in rural communities for anti-Haitian policies" and sought to manifest its power in such a way as to "compel obedience from local officials who had resisted central state involvement" (p. 42). Meticulously sourced through a variety of state department files at the AGN, the study also demonstrates the importance of looking at labor policy following the massacre, that of isolating Haitian and Haitian-Dominican laborers on sugar plantations and policing their cultural practices, as central to a larger understanding of the state-sponsored genocide and development of anti-Haitianism. [EM]

909   **Historia de Cuba.** Textos de José Abreu Cardet *et al*. Santo Domingo: Búho, 2013. 469 p.: bibl., ill., index. (Archivo General de la Nación; CLXXXVI)

This collection of seven individually authored chapters chronicles the history of Cuba from its indigenous past through the 1959 Revolution. The novelty of the volume is that all of the authors are from the interior province of Holguín. Consequently, even though they are writing a synthetic national history of Cuba, the regional elements stand out unlike most histories of Cuba that tend to narrate from a notably Havana-centric perspective. [MDC]

910   **Historia general del pueblo dominicano.** Tomo 5, La dictadura de Trujillo (1930–1961). Coordinación general por Roberto Cassá y Genaro Rodríguez Morel. Santo Domingo: Academia Dominicana de la Historia, 2014. 1 v.: bibl., ill., indexes, maps. (Academia Dominicana de la Historia; CV, CXX)

In an effort to construct a "complete history" of the Dominican Republic, the Dominican Academy of History began publishing a series of six texts in 2013, covering "from the indigenous peoples, through the conquest, the configuration of Creole society, the emergence of the nation between 1790 and 1880, the advent of modernization, the dictatorial regime of Trujillo, and the last decades of the 20th century" (p. 15). In this, the fifth volume (but the second to be published) covering the Trujillato, chapter subjects include the characterization of the dictatorship, Trujillo's claim of the presidency, economic conditions and Trujillo's business "empire," political and military struggles, the Haitian massacre, WWII, international relations, crimes and repression, resistance, daily life, literature, and architecture. Contributions from Roberto Cassá, Bernardo Vega, Edwin Croes Hernández, Alejandro Paulino Ramos, Eliades Acosta Matos, Rafael Darío Herrera, Nelson Moreno Ceballos, Luis Gómez Pérez, Odalís G. Pérez, and Omar Rancier anchor the text. Citations generally provide excellent direction for future study, although most of the material cited is secondary in nature, as would be expected in this type of work. [EM]

911   **Hoefte, Rosemarijn.** Suriname in the long twentieth century: domination, contestation, globalization. New York, N.Y.: Palgrave Macmillan, 2014. 294 p.: bibl., index.

This synthesis approaches Suriname's history through the lenses of cultural, ethnic, gender, and political factors with an emphasis on immigration. The mining and export of bauxite has been a driving force since the 1920s. Hoefte also discusses the urban history of Paramaribo and the disorder and other problems that appeared in the wake of independence in the 1970s. The author maintains a firm grasp on the connections between Suriname's domestic social and political history with its often overwhelming international connections. Extensive footnotes indicate heavy use of Dutch sources. [J. Britton]

912 **Kohan, Néstor.** En la selva: los estudios desconocidos del Che Guevara: a propósito de sus *Cuadernos de lectura de Bolivia*. Buenos Aires: Amauta Insurgente Ediciones; Barcelona: Yulca Editorial; Buenos Aires: Ediciones La Llamarada, 2013. 464 p.: bibl., ill.

This study examines the notes Che Guevara took as he read various books during his Bolivia Campaign of 1966–67. The contribution and insights of the volume are developed from the author moving beyond the quotidian analysis of his diary entries to analyze what philosophical and political works influenced his evolving radical thoughts during his last year of his life. [MDC]

913 **The legacy of Eric Williams: Caribbean scholar and statesman.** Edited by Colin A. Palmer. Kingston: University of the West Indies Press, 2015. 268 p.: bibl., map.

This edited volume explores a number of elements of Eric Williams' life and scholarship that emerged from a 2011 conference at Oxford University to celebrate the centenary of his birth. Entries include both reassessments of the "Williams Thesis" and the influence of the scholar's work on current examinations of capitalism. The work also contains reflections on the role that Williams had on postcolonialism and Caribbean integration, as well as on the man himself. [DL]

914 **The legacy of Eric Williams: into the postcolonial moment.** Edited by Tanya L. Shields. Jackson: University Press of Mississippi, 2015. 221 p.: bibl., ill., index. (Caribbean studies series)

This edited volume emerged out of a 2002 conference on the influence of Eric Williams. The first section of articles considers his biographical origins in Trinidad alongside the development of his academic and public intellectualism. The second set of contributions delves into the particular history of Williams as a political figure, especially in his role as prime minister of Trinidad and Tobago. A final section of articles reflects on Williams's legacy—both positive and negative—within the postcolonial Caribbean and the academy. See also item **913**. [DL]

915 **Leonard Percival Howell and the genesis of Rastafari.** Edited by Clinton A. Hutton *et al.* Kingston: University of the West Indies Press, 2015. 274 p.: bibl., ill., portraits.

As a celebration of the 130th anniversary of Leonard Howell's birth, this edited collection of articles assesses the life and influence of the man traditionally thought to have first publicly declared the divinity of Emperor Haile Selassie of Ethiopia. Powell would go on to serve as an instrumental pioneer and leader in the Rastafari religion that emerged out of this declaration. Each of the articles dissects different elements of Howell's life and legacy in the movement. The contributors include traditional scholars as well as Rastafari practitioners. [DL]

916 **Manley, Elizabeth S.** The paradox of paternalism: women and the politics of authoritarianism in the Dominican Republic. Gainesville: University Press of Florida, 2017. 319 p.: bibl., index, photos.

The author demonstrates the ways in which women activists from across the political spectrum engaged with the state by working within both authoritarian regimes and inter-American networks, founding modern Dominican feminism, and contributing to the rise of 20th-century women's liberation movements in the Global South. [C.E. Griffin]

917 **Medina Vera, Heriberto.** La guerra del azúcar: la batalla contra las reformas a la industria azucarera de Puerto Rico (1934–1940). Río Piedras, Puerto Rico: Publicaciones Gaviota, 2015. 413 p.: bibl., ill.

This work examines the social composition and political discourse of the forces opposing the reforms in Puerto Rico's once-dominant sugar industry introduced by the New Deal program during the 1930s. The author challenges the perceived wisdom that opponents to these reforms supported the interests of absentee North American sugar corporations. Not only native capital, the author argues, but also cane growers and workers mobilized against these reforms. [LG]

918 **Meléndez, Edgardo.** Sponsored migration: the state and Puerto Rican postwar migration to the United States. Columbus: The Ohio State University Press,

2017. 260 p.: bibl., ill., index. (Global Latin/o Americas)

This incisive investigation focuses on the development and implementation of a well-planned policy by the government of Puerto Rico not only to encourage migration from the island to the US mainland but also to promote the incorporation of Puerto Ricans as a migrant workforce in the US during the 1940s and 1950s. The Puerto Rican government's role in the management of migration is gleaned from careful research in local archives, particularly the records of the Department of Labor. See also *HLAS 72:1088*. [LG]

919 **Meléndez-Badillo, Jorell A.** Imagining resistance: organizing the Puerto Rican southern agricultural strike of 1905. (*Caribb. Stud.*, 43:2, July/Dec. 2015, p. 33–81, bibl., tables)

This study combines social and cultural history approaches to explore the largely autonomous, grassroots mobilization of agricultural workers during the historic 1905 strike in the sugarcane fields of southern Puerto Rico. Sugar workers deployed their agency, developing militancy and a discourse of contestation, through their worker-run night schools, public meetings, the labor press, and the actions of their local labor union organization. [LG]

920 **Méndez, Danny.** Charytín Goyco, la rubia de América: a case study of television stardom in the Dominican Republic in the 1970s. (*Stud. Lat. Am. Pop. Cult.*, 33, 2015, p. 27–40)

Engaging Dominican television personality Charytín Goyco to look more deeply at the Dominican Republic of the 1970s, this article provides a nuanced look at race and class tensions under the Balaguer *doce años* (1966–78). In addition to beginning the work of charting a period that is vastly understudied, Méndez's work here (as elsewhere) brings fresh sources and analytical perspectives to modern Dominican history. [EM]

921 **Merleaux, April.** Sugar and civilization: American empire and the cultural politics of sweetness. Chapel Hill: University of North Carolina Press, 2015. 302 p.: bibl., index.

This work examines the US sugar industry from the late 19th century through the New Deal period in the mid-1930s, describing the significant shifts in patterns of sugar consumption within the domestic market and its territories, including Puerto Rico. The author reconsiders Sidney Mintz's landmark *Sweetness and Power: The Place of Sugar in Modern History* (1985). [LG]

922 **Merleaux, April.** Sweetness, power, and forgotten food histories in America's empire. (*Labor/Durham*, 12:1/2, May 2015, p. 87–114, bibl.)

This study attributes the increased consumption of processed sugar in Puerto Rico and the attendant transformation in people's diet to policies established by the US government during the New Deal era and WWII. The author reassesses Sidney Mintz's landmark *Sweetness and Power: The Place of Sugar in Modern History* (1985). See also item **921**. [LG]

923 **Mintz, Sidney Wilfred.** Taso's life: person and community. (*Caribb. Stud.*, 40:1, Jan./June 2012, p. 2–14, bibl., photos)

This article provides an insightful reflection on the use of oral history and life history as appropriate methodologies for anthropological inquiry of modern agrarian societies. The study dwells on the author's classic *Worker in the Cane: A Puerto Rican life history* (1960; see *HLAS 23:650*), translated into Spanish as *Taso, trabajador de la caña* (1988; see *HLAS 52:1943*), featuring the life history of Anastasio (Taso) Zayas, a sugarcane worker from southern Puerto Rico. [LG]

924 **Mondolfi Gudat, Edgardo.** El día del atentado: el frustrado magnicidio contra Rómulo Betancourt. Caracas: Editorial Alfa, 2013. 223 p.: bibl. (Coleccion Hogueras; 65)

Covering a fascinating yet often skimmed over moment in the history of the Trujillato, this book addresses head-on the assassination attempt on Venezuelan president Rómulo Betancourt by the regime of Rafael Trujillo in June 1960. Like many of the horrific acts that occurred toward the end of the regime, people are often shocked to hear about the lengths Trujillo went to in an effort to assert his power globally and locally, and yet countless stories remain unwritten. Thanks to the files in the Fundación Rómulo Betancourt and the work of Mondolfi Gudat, a number of these holes are beginning to be filled. [EM]

925 Morales Tejeda, Aida Liliana; Mariela Rodríguez Joa; and Edelsi Palermo Liñero. Testigos patrimoniales de una gesta histórica. Santiago de Cuba: Ediciones Santiago, 2013. 257 p.: bibl.

Published in commemoration of the 60th anniversary of the 1953 assault on the Moncada Barracks, this volume consists of a collection of essays by different authors documenting and explaining historical buildings, monuments, and locations in Santiago and other nearby towns. The volume provides insights into the process of memorializing and commemorating Cuban history, and supplies documents accounting for how the historical relevance of structures is validated. The book thus serves as both a historical guide to many locations and a manual for how buildings and monuments are elevated and recognized as national patrimony. [MDC]

926 Muñoz Mata, Laura. Esplendor y decadencia del cultivo de caña en el Caribe: la mirada de *National Geographic*. (*Memorias/Barranquilla*, 13:31, enero/abril 2017, p. 39–74, bibl., photos)

This study analyzes a set of 80 photographs from the *National Geographic* depicting the growth and decline of the sugar industry in the Caribbean, including Puerto Rico, from 1898 through the early 1990s. The photographs provide a visual discourse not only of modernization enabled by North American capital investments in sugar technology and infrastructure, but also of transformations in US political interests in the Caribbean over time. See also items **892** and **927**. [LG]

927 Muñoz Mata, Laura. Fotografía imperial, escenarios tropicales: las representaciones del Caribe en la revista *National Geographic*. México: Instituto Mora: El Colegio de Michoacán, 2014. 433 p.: bibl., ill., index, map. (Historia internacional)

This landmark study addresses the representations of the Caribbean region, particularly Cuba and Puerto Rico, in the photographs and captions appearing in the original English-language edition of *National Geographic* from 1898 to the present. The author views photographs as complex, polysemic records that do not simply reflect, but at times shape and influence, US relations toward the countries of the Caribbean. See also items **892** and **926**. [LG]

928 Nazario Velasco, Rubén. El paisaje y el poder: la tierra en el tiempo de Luis Muñoz Marín. San Juan: Ediciones Callejón, 2014. 385 p.: bibl., ill. (Colección en Fuga. Ensayos)

This work elucidates the ideological, cultural, and political foundations as well as the long-lasting impact on the sugar industry of the agrarian reforms introduced by the Partido Popular Democrático during the 1940s in Puerto Rico. The author addresses the critical contributions of leading intellectuals to the development of an agrarian reformist discourse that challenged the domination of sugar interests on the island. [LG]

929 Novas, José C. Los gavilleros: la lucha nacionalista contra la ocupación, 1916–1924. Santo Domingo: Argos, 2016. 143 p.: bibl., ill.

Like several other volumes published in 2016, this work is motivated by the need to remind the Dominican public of the 100th anniversary of the start of US occupation, and it offers a broad but brief overview of the eight-year Marine occupation from a predominantly political/military perspective. Focused on the rebel resistance, a force the author considers greater than any other revolutionary movement that preceded it, the book details (although with minimal source citations) the movements of the rebel force against the occupying US Marines between 1916 and 1922. There is also a nod to the resistance activism of women, as well as the civil responses to foreign rule. [EM]

930 *Op. Cit.: Revista del Centro de Investigaciones Históricas*. 24, 2016/2017, Citizenship/Ciudadanía. Río Piedras: Universidad de Puerto Rico, Facultad de Humanidades, Departamento de Historia.

Dedicated to the centennial of the Jones Act enacted in 1917, this special issue of *Op. Cit.* includes three articles specifically addressing the topics of US citizenship and Puerto Rico's current political status. See also *HLAS* 73:1137. [LG]

931 Palmer, Colin A. Inward yearnings: Jamaica's journey to nationhood. Kingston: The University of the West Indies Press, 2016. 252 p.: bibl., index.

Palmer narrates the key moments and forces behind Jamaica's independence from Britain in the middle of the 20th century. He reflects on the long historical trends of African slavery, Garveyism, colonialism, and Rastafarianism, among others, along with close explorations of Jamaica's 1938 labor riots, the foundations of the country's two prominent political parties, and the origins of its early governmental leaders. Much of the monograph's second half focuses on battles between Alexander Bustamante and Norman Manley, culminating in Jamaica's exit from the West Indies Federation to found its own nation. Throughout, Palmer delves into the ways that racial consciousness did, and did not, influence Jamaican culture and politics. [DL]

932 Pérez Rivero, Roberto and **José Abreu Cardet.** Cierra . . . viene el derrumbe: reflexiones y relatos sobre la guerra de guerrillas en la llanura oriental. Santiago de Cuba: Editorial Oriente, 2013. 230 p.: bibl., ill. (Bronce. Colección Historia)

This insightful study examines the guerrilla fighting and organization in the regions outside of the Sierra Maestra, with a particular focus on the province of Holguín. Utilizing published and archival sources, along with interviews with surviving combatants, the authors provide details on how the 26 de July Movement expanded into urban and lowland zones during the revolutionary struggle. [MDC]

933 Pérez Sánchez, Yusleidy. Jorge Mañach, el ABC y el proceso revolucionario del 30 (1920–1935). Holguín, Cuba: Empresa Poligráfica de Holguín, ARGRAF, 2014. 194 p.: bibl. (Pinos nuevos. Ensayo)

These insightful extended essays in the Pinos Nuevos series examine the political thought of Jorge Mañach from slightly revisionist perspectives. Unlike earlier works that focused on radical intellectuals, student leaders, and labor groups that propelled the 1933 Revolution, the author argues that Mañach's importance and legacy needs to be reconsidered and should not be reduced to just representing bourgeois middle class ideas. [MDC]

Pettinà, Vanni. A preponderance of politics: the Auténtico governments and US-Cuban economic relations, 1945–1951. See *HLAS* 73:1534.

934 Putnam, Lara. Global child-saving, transatlantic maternalism, and the pathologization of Caribbean childhood. (*Atlan. Stud. Global Curr.*, 11:4, 2014, p. 491–514)

This article explores imperial interest in Caribbean childrearing practices. Putnam examines the 1945 report by the West India Royal Commission (WIRC), which attempted to provide a more scientific assessment of Caribbean families than previous analyses, but which nevertheless replicated much of those prior studies' use of racial blame. Although the WIRC carried forward a specific anti-racist approach, Putnam argues that it imposed European norms of middle-class domesticity onto Caribbean families in its critique. This approach fueled future efforts that sought strong reforms in the direction of such European notions of civility. [DL]

935 Rafael Martínez Nadal: una vida, un ideal. Edición de José Luis Colón González. San Juan: Universidad Interamericana de Puerto Rico: Museo Prócer Rafael Martínez Nadal, 2015. 680 p.: bibl., facsims., ill. (some color), index, portraits.

This collection of essays focuses on the life and contributions of Rafael Martínez Nadal (1877–1941), the leading advocate of the Puerto Rican pro-statehood movement during the 1920–1940 period. An extensive appendix section includes speeches, correspondence, and relevant records depicting his political trajectory. [LG]

936 Ramírez, Dixa. Colonial phantoms: belonging and refusal in the Dominican Americas, from the 19th century to the present. New York: New York University Press, 2018. 315 p.: bibl., ill., index. (Nation of nations. Immigrant history as American history)

An impressive look at the ways literary and historical production in the Dominican Republic from 1850 ("a crucial period for the creation of a unified national culture") through the present day have resisted the silencing, or as Ramírez frames it, ghosting, that defines the nation according to imperial dominant racial narratives and geopolitical hierarchies (p. 32, p. 35). While rooted in literary studies, the author deftly engages with historical sources and cultural artifacts to construct a study that is unique and compelling, but also highly in sync with larger efforts to construct new and more inclusive narratives for the island. The range of inquiry is impressive—from the poetry and prose of Salomé Ureña (1850–97) to contemporary female writers, late 20th-century sex work, Dominican-American film, and musical/performance artists—and her work convincingly reminds us of the island's place as the region's "navel," symbolizing its "geographic" and "conceptual" centrality to much larger patterns of conquest, colonization, imperialism, and an ever-present resistance to such dominating discourses. Winner of the Isis Duarte Book Prize. [EM]

937 **Rodríguez, Rolando.** Rebelión en la República: auge y caída de Gerardo Machado. La Habana: Editorial de Ciencias Sociales, 2013. 3 v.: bibl. (Historia)

This multivolume set presents an encyclopedic albeit hagiographic account of the overthrow of the Machado dictatorship in 1933. Drawing from political records, trade union literature, and US government reports, the author explains how a broad coalition of Cuban society came together to topple the dictatorship, but ultimately was undermined through US intervention shortly after the revolution came to power. [MDC]

938 **Rodríguez, Rolando.** La revolución que no se fue a bolina. La Habana: Editorial de Ciencias Sociales, 2013. 732 p.: bibl., index. (Historia)

Drawing upon sources from Cuban and especially US archives detailing consular and ambassadorial activities, the author provides a lengthy and detailed analysis of US-Cuban relations in the first half of the 20th century. In particular, Rodríguez concentrates on the 1930s and the specific machinations of US ambassador Summer Welles during the 1933 Revolution. [MDC]

939 **Rodríguez, Rolando.** Los vientos huracanados de la historia. Selección y notas de Fernando Carr Parúas. La Habana: Editorial de Ciencias Sociales, 2013. 314 p.: bibl., ill., index. (Colección Premio nacional de ciencias sociales; séptimo título)

This collection brings together previously published essays by one of the Cuban Revolution's favored intellectuals and historians. The essays deal with Rodríguez's writing on the independence struggle, José Martí's vision of the nation, and political, social, and race relations during the republic. Particularly noteworthy is the biographical introduction by Elier Ramírez Cañedo that recounts the historian's role as an intellectual in service of the 1959 Cuban Revolution. [MDC]

940 **Rojas, Rafael.** Fighting over Fidel: the New York intellectuals and the Cuban Revolution. Translated by Carl Good. Princeton, N.J.: Princeton University Press, 2016. 300 p.: bibl., ill., index.

This study offers an insightful analysis of the varying reactions by liberal and radical American intellectuals to Fidel Castro and the Cuban Revolution. The author demonstrates how the Cuban Revolution often served as an example and empirical case study to put into action the new social movements of the 1960s, and it was a polemical dividing point separating the Old Left and the New Left. Largely drawn from well-known radical and liberal publications as well as memoirs and personal correspondence of New York intellectuals. [MDC]

941 **Saneaux, Sully** and **Ramona Hernández.** La República Dominicana y la prensa extranjera: Mayo 1961-Septiembre 1963: (desde la desaparición de Trujillo hasta Juan Bosch). Santo Domingo: Biblioteca Nacional Pedro Henríquez Ureña, 2013. 459 p.: bibl., ill., index. (Serie: Historia)

A review of the foreign press from the fall of Trujillo (1 May 1931) through the overthrow of President Juan Bosch (30 September 1963), this volume highlights the extensive (if selective) coverage of Dominican events in US and Latin American newspapers as well as in Russian, French, Chinese, and several global news agencies. Identifying one publication per country (with the exception of the US), the authors reviewed a total of 1,810 articles for the study in an effort not to point out veracity (or lack thereof) in this foreign coverage, but rather to explain why so many Dominicans of the diaspora have an extremely limited understanding of the nation's history. Part of a planned series (with the next to include coverage of the April Revolution), this volume also seeks to contribute to a widening conversation about external visions of the Dominican Republic. [EM]

942 **Scott, David.** Omens of adversity: tragedy, time, memory, justice. Durham, N.C.: Duke University Press, 2014. 219 p.: bibl., index.

This work dissects the issue of temporality and the perception of time as it was experienced during the Grenada Revolution, which lasted from 1979 to 1983. A Marxist-Leninist uprising that captured much of the socialist activism circulating in the Caribbean at the time, the revolution dissolved within four years due to intraparty conflict and US military intervention. Throughout the text, Scott considers the way that the revolution collapsed the scale of political timeframes, especially in the struggle between socialism and global neoliberalism. Yet, he also reflects on the ways that time can heal and reinterpret revolutionary activities. [DL]

943 **Sellers, Julie A.** The modern bachateros: 27 interviews. Jefferson, N.C.: McFarland and Company, Inc., 2017. 232 p.: bibl., ill., index.

A collection of 27 interviews with well-known Dominican performers of modern or "urban" bachata, performers the author refers to as "modern bachateros." Defining it as the musical form that developed in diasporic communities following the end of the Trujillato and one that "reflects the multicultural and multilingual realities of Dominican migrants and the children," the author argues that it is "a blend of bachata, hip-hop, R&B, rap, and other genres" (p. 5). The performers, presented through edited interview transcripts ("organizing each story into an overarching framework, providing context and chronology, and making connections among ideas," p. 19) form a collective that Sellers argues "reflects a transnational, multicultural, and bilingual production of identity" (p. 20). [EM]

944 **Sotomayor, Antonio.** Un parque para cada pueblo: Julio Enrique Monagas and the politics of sport and recreation in Puerto Rico during the 1940s. (*Caribb. Stud.*, 42:2, July/Dec. 2014, p. 3–40, bibl., photos, table)

Sports serve as a window to understand the complexities of Puerto Rican politics during a transitional period in the nation's modern history. This article shows how the athletic development project introduced by the Partido Popular Democrático dovetailed with the ruling party's political and economic program, not only generating broad-based support from the citizenry to these policies, but ultimately reinforcing colonial bonds between Puerto Rico and the US. [LG]

945 **Teel, Leonard Ray.** Reporting the Cuban Revolution: how Castro manipulated American journalists. Foreword by Patrick Washburn. Baton Rouge: Louisiana State University Press, 2015. 242 p.: bibl., index. (Media and public affairs)

This study provides an account of the relationship between Fidel Castro and the American press corps during the guerrilla struggle and the subsequent process of consolidating power. The work draws exclusively from English-language sources by analyzing the well-known published writing and personal papers of journalists such as Herbert Matthews. The book is insightful for its analysis of the role played by American journalists in informing the US public and shaping popular opinions about Cuba, but offers only limited observations of the Cuban perspective. [MDC]

946 **Teelucksingh, Jerome.** Ideology, politics, and radicalism of the Afro-Caribbean. New York: Palgrave Macmillan, 2016. 238 p.: bibl., index.

Following the lives of eight prominent Caribbean thinkers, this monograph explores the social and economic history of the West Indies in the 20th century. Each chapter links the biographies of Marcus Garvey, C.L.R. James, George Padmore, Tubal Uriah Butler, Arthur Lewis, Eric Williams, Walter Rodney, and Kwame Ture to black activism and radical politics of the modern Caribbean. It is a Caribbean story, told within a global context, that puts particular focus on the early political protests of the 1920s and 30s, as well as on the more developed postcolonial movements of the 1960s and 70s. [DL]

947 Tiempos binarios: la Guerra Fría desde Puerto Rico y el Caribe. Edición de Manuel R. Rodríguez Vázquez y Silvia Álvarez Curbelo. San Juan: Ediciones Callejón, 2017. 411 p.: bibl., ill., maps. (Colección En Fuga. Ensayo)

This study seeks to understand the complex and contradictory experience of the Cold War in Puerto Rico and the Caribbean region through everyday cultural, social, and political dynamics at the national and regional levels. The lens of culture calls into question conventional accounts of the Cold War as a predominantly bipolar conflict between world powers vying for geopolitical interests. [LG]

948 Timm, Birte. Nationalists abroad: the Jamaica Progressive League and the foundations of Jamaican independence. Kingston: Ian Randle Publishers, 2016. 459 p.: bibl., index.

With much of modern Jamaican political history filtered through contests between rival parties, the Jamaican Progressive League (JPL) and the People's National Party (PNP), this book explores the influence of the JPL in the island's eventual independence. Formed in New York in 1936 by expatriate Jamaicans, the Progressive League was considerably more radical in its anticolonial stance than many political organizations in the Caribbean. The author contends, through an extensive examination of the League's 30-year history, that Jamaican independence was much more of a global effort than previous studies have claimed. [DL]

949 Tirado Rivera, Alexis Oscar. Historia de una ciudad: Guayama 1898–1930. Caguas, Puerto Rico: Ediciones Bayoán, 2014. 234 p.: bibl., ill. (Arte y cultura)

This work presents a microhistory of Guayama, a southern Puerto Rican town where sugar growing and cattle raising dominated the economy. The author explores local struggles not only against the expansion of North American absentee investments in the sugar industry and transportation, but also against US government policies promoting the use of English in schools. [LG]

950 Uribe Peguero, Eurípides Antonio. Militares y autoritarismo: en 100 años de evolución política (1916–2016). Santo Domingo: Eurípides Antonio Uribe Peguero, 2015. 691 p.: bibl., index.

An incredibly ambitious undertaking, this volume spans 100 years of military history in just under 700 pages and seeks to delineate the *"rol incisivo"* of the armed forces in the political history of the nation. The study begins with the US occupation in 1916 as this intervention both constituted the modern Dominican armed forces and also was the foundation of *"toda la dominación posterior"* (p. 19). Uribe Peguero, former admiral of the Dominican navy, presents the study as both a student of history and a "living witness" to (some) of the events that form the central core of the study, although concurrently seeks to provide a "dispassionate" analysis of the interactions between military and state that buttressed so many years of authoritarianism. While the study would benefit from more extensive citations to allow for further analysis of this important topic, it nonetheless makes a contribution to the efforts of explaining the long hold of authoritarianism in the Dominican Republic. [EM]

951 Vega, Bernardo. Correspondencia entre Ángel Morales y Sumner Welles. Santo Domingo: Archivo General de la Nación, 2013. 684 p.: bibl., ill., index. (Archivo General de la Nación; CCV)(Academia Dominicana de la Historia; CXV)

Another valuable collection of transcribed primary documents from the Archivo General de la Nación, this 600-plus page volume covers an extensive correspondence between resistance leader Ángel Morales and US diplomat Sumner Welles (1930–50) and treats the efforts of long-exiled Morales to unseat the three-decade dictator Rafael Trujillo. A collaboration between the AGN and the Academia Dominicana de la Historia (ADH) helmed by noted historian (and ADH president) Bernardo Vega, the volume is arranged chronologically with introductory notes provided by the author before each year (or several years) of correspondence. Brief biographical sketches at the beginning of the text provide background on the two men. Sources for these primary materials include the personal archives of Welles' son, the private collection of exiled anti-Trujillo activist Ángel Morales, and the FDR Presidential Library in Hyde Park, N.Y. Although the entirety of the collection has now been digitized by the AGN, the selections contained in this volume highlight not only the personal side of diplomacy, but also the Trujillato as seen by the resistance, the regime's careful maneuvering of US interlocutors, and the politics of life-long exile. [EM]

Véjar Pérez-Rubio, Carlos. Las danzas del huracán: Veracruz y La Habana en los años treinta. See *HLAS 73:1507.*

952   **Wright, Micah.** Building an occupation: Puerto Rican laborers in the Dominican Republic, 1916–1924. (*Labor/Durham,* 13:3, 2016, p. 83–103, bibl.)

Filling some crucial silences in the historiography, this article, sourced predominantly from the US occupation records at NARA, grapples with both labor and the immigration of Puerto Rican workers during the US occupation of the Dominican Republic. In illustrating how such imported labor was initially termed "un-Antillean," it also speaks to larger threads of Caribbean solidarity in the face of US intervention, the shifting realities of Puerto Ricans during the period of US neocolonial empire in the Caribbean, and Dominican resistance to the abrogation of sovereignty. [EM]

953   **Zapata Oliveras, Carlos R.** Luis Muñoz Marín, Estados Unidos y el establecimiento del Estado Libre Asociado de Puerto Rico (1946–1952). San Juan: Universidad Interamericana de Puerto Rico, 2015. 591 p.: bibl., ill.

This study chronicles the intense constitutional debates and contested political negotiations between Puerto Rican leaders, the US executive office, and the US Congress over the creation of the Estado Libre Asociado, or Commonwealth of Puerto Rico, in 1952. The author focuses on the actions of Luis Muñoz Marín to attain self-rule for Puerto Rico as a US territory. [LG]

954   **Zequeira Motolongo, Alfonso** and **Alberto Alvariño Atiénzar.** Alfredo Alvarez Mola: un pequeño gigante: diario inédito de Alfredito. Prólogo Fidel Castro Ruz. La Habana: Casa Editora Abril, 2015. 196 p., 26 unnumbered pages: bibl., ill. (some color).

Alfredo Alvarez Mola was an urban worker who organized banking clerks and staff through a labor union to become more active in the protest against the Batista dictatorship. This work provides insights into how some of the professional ranks channeled their political militancy into action and joined the 26th of July Movement. The book also includes a transcription of his diary and other primary sources documenting his participation. [MDC]

SPANISH SOUTH AMERICA
Colonial Period

MATTHEW CRAWFORD, *Professor of History, Kent State University*
FABRICIO PRADO, *Associate Professor of History, College of William & Mary*
JESSE ZARLEY, *Assistant Professor of History, St. Joseph's College*

NUEVA GRANADA
RECENT SCHOLARLY TRENDS in the study of the Kingdom and subsequent Viceroyalty of Nueva Granada (which included portions of modern Panama, Ecuador, Colombia, and Venezuela) have breathed new life into how we understand the 18th century. These works provide innovative directions for the study of slavery and slave resistance and for the examination of the colonial economy.

One of the most stirring topics in the history of slavery and slave resistance is the escaped slave communities known as *palenques*. Alfonso Cassiani Herrera's short study of the most famous Colombian escaped slave community, Palenque Magno, challenges the notion that such communities persisted for decades or even centuries because of their isolation from colonial society and the plantation regime (item **961**). Instead, this case reveals that slave communities, like the El Cobre community in Cuba, at times sought recognition by the Spanish Crown in order to achieve the status of town and receive the protections and privileges which that entailed. Palenque Magno's story, and that of its leaders, creates fascinating opportunities to compare scholarship on the engagement of Afro-descendant and enslaved peoples with colonial legal institutions and the creation of legal identities within and beyond colonial society. The new primary document collection *Voces de esclavitud y libertad* offers such an opportunity by collecting and transcribing Spanish legal documents related to slavery in Colombia (item **968**). Drawn from archives across Colombia, this collection focuses on three primary reasons why slaves and free Afro-descendant people chose to engage with the Spanish legal regime (life and death, freedom and manumission, and military service). These documents allow students and scholars to consider how colonized peoples learned the language and limits of the Spanish system of justice, and how they creatively interpreted and employed these understandings to form their own identities and petition for protections and freedom from the crown against abusive masters and employers. Combined, these works provide helpful comparative points to other slave societies in the Americas, as well as with the rich body of scholarship on indigenous peoples' engagement with colonial legal systems in Colombia and elsewhere.

While classic economic history has fallen by the wayside with North American Latin Americanists or has been reinvigorated by cultural considerations, it has been the most dominant scholarly trend in this region. Nevertheless, recent national studies and approaches represent a diversity of revisions and new directions in the field of economic history. Topics covered include fiscal policy and taxation (item **965**), environmental impacts of conquest (item **962**), the formation of Spanish towns (item **964**), tropical commodity exchange (item **972**), political economic methodology (item **965**), the dispersion of political economic thought (item **960**), and the relationship between Jesuit haciendas and nascent capitalism (item **970**), to name a few. Representative of the breadth of research are Claudia Milena Pico's essay collection on fiscal and tax policy (item **965**) and Jesús Bohórquez's consideration of the circulation and restriction of political economic treatises in the 18th century (item **960**). While the former plumbs the late colonial period to better understand the post-independence Colombian economy bequeathed by the Spanish, Bohórquez examines how political economy became an embraced and reviled mode of governance and reform in Bourbon Spain and Nueva Granada. This growing body of scholarship has much to contribute to understandings of imperial reform, local networks of political power and economic accumulation, and the interplay between environment, production, and consumption. [JZ]

PERU

Finely dressed slaves, pious women, indigenous intellectuals, Portuguese immigrants, and Afro-Peruvian physicians are just a few of the diverse cast of characters that populate the pages of recent scholarship on colonial Peru. By far, the vast majority of new studies on colonial Peru have focused on illuminating the myriad ways in which the different social and ethnic groups shaped colonial societies and manipulated imperial structures as they formed their identities and asserted their agency in the context of Spanish colonial rule in the Andes. Various studies have significantly enriched our understanding of these groups especially in the case of indigenous peoples and peoples of African descent. While remaining sensitive to the discrimination and oppression that indigenous Andeans and Afro-Peruvians faced, these studies also show how members of these groups actively participated in colonial society and played a vital role in the Spanish colonial enterprise, even as other studies show how the traditional frameworks of colonial and imperial history remain inadequate for capturing the complexity of the lived experience. Most importantly, many of these recent studies shed new light on the ways in which the history of colonial Peru is integral not just to our understanding of Latin America, but also to our understanding of the Spanish Empire, the Iberian Atlantic, the early modern world, and even the roots of modernity.

One of the most significant and exciting trends in recent scholarship has been the attempts to locate the roots of modernity or some aspect of modernity in the Spanish Empire or the broader Iberian Atlantic world. Much of this scholarship has effectively shown that, rather than being the antithesis of modernity and its various phases from the Renaissance to the Enlightenment, the Iberian world fully engaged with these various episodes in the development of modernity. To that end, some scholars have begun to refer to the region as early modern Latin America—a designation that displaces colonialism as the most central or fundamental feature of this period. In *The Matter of Empire*, Orlando Bentancor embraces these revisionist tendencies and makes a compelling argument for locating the instrumental metaphysics of scientific modernity in the intellectual and cultural currents of the Spanish colonial project in the 16th and early 17th centuries (item **974**). Peru figures prominently as much of Bentancor's study deals with the ways in which Spanish efforts to exploit the fabulously rich silver mines at Potosí contributed to the formulation of an imperial metaphysics that emphasized the manipulation of both human and natural resources for the good of empire.

While several studies have reframed the history of Peru in terms of empire in order to emphasize the centrality of the Andean world to narratives of modernity and its epistemology, other studies have highlighted the transatlantic ties between Peru and Spain to reframe colonial Peru as part of the Atlantic World. For example, Jane Mangan analyzes the way in which the Spanish Empire was constituted by transatlantic familial networks in the era of conquest by focusing on families in Lima, Arequipa, and Seville (item **980**). In particular, this study shows how the lived experience and complexity of mixed families resulting from the unions between Spaniards and indigenous people undermined Spanish efforts to articulate and enforce rigid structures of class and caste in early colonial societies. José Carlos de la Puente Luna applies a similar transatlantic lens to analyze the formation of indigenous identities and the assertion of indigenous agency during the conquest of Peru and more than a century afterwards (item **984**). De la Puente Luna emphasizes indigenous efforts to manipulate the political discourse and legal structures of Spanish colonialism for their own purposes from the Audiencia in Lima to the Royal Court in Madrid. Like Mangan's book, this study unsettles stereotypes about indigenous Andeans during the early decades of Spanish colonial rule by piecing together the cosmopolitan trajectories of those who shrewdly engaged the new imperial structures to which they were forcibly subjected.

Related lines of inquiry and scholarship have offered additional insight into the identities, experiences, and activities of indigenous Andeans during the colonial period. The collection of essays edited by Monica Días examines the question of what it meant to be an "indio" in Spanish colonial society with particular attention to the ways in which indigenous peoples fashioned their identities collectively and individually (item **989**). Featuring four essays focused on the Andean world, this volume enriches our understanding of the indigenous experience by highlighting not only the diversity of roles and identities espoused by indigenous peoples but also the agency of indigenous peoples in employing colonial institutions and epistemologies to their own ends. By looking at the making of identities, some recent studies focus on the ways in which indigenous peoples navigated the legal and institutional contexts of Spanish colonial rule. Two articles show how indigenous peoples in the Andes asserted their legal and political agency through the continued power and influence of the office of *cacique* (item **977**) and the skillful manipulation of the legal concept of "custom" to secure various rights and privileges (item **983**). Ofelioa Huamanchumo de la Cuba subjects several genres of administrative and legal documents from 16th-century Peru to philological and linguistic analysis in order to show the ways in which the paperwork of governance was a site for the articulation of indigenous identities and agency in the face of the processes of colonization and evangelization (item **978**). As a group, these studies represent the important ways that scholars continue to enrich our understanding of the diversity of the indigenous experience in colonial Peru by employing new methods, sources, and conceptual frameworks.

Coincident with the burgeoning interest in the history of Africans and people of African descent in the broader early modern world, the social and cultural history of Afro-Peruvians has also featured prominently in recent scholarship. While the experience of slavery remains a major topic of research, other studies have called attention to the diversity of experiences and wide variety of roles played by Afro-Peruvians in the colonial period. Among the works produced is the first scholarly biography of Fray Martín de Porres, a *mulato* in late 16th and early 17th-century Lima who became a saint in 1962 (item **976**). While he was in some ways an exceptional case, Porres' biography provides new insight into Catholic religiosity in colonial Peru and the ways in which Afro-Peruvians navigated and challenged the racial hierarchies of colonial society. The case of Porres is unique in that a cult developed around him during his life and gave rise to the movement to have him canonized. Such efforts permit historical analysis of Porres' afterlife—as much as his life—as a way to track how the meaning of Porres in Peruvian society and culture has evolved since the 17th century. Another recent study shows how Afro-Peruvians participated in the intellectual life and medical community of Lima in the late colonial and early Republican periods (item **979**). These studies enrich the history of Afro-Peruvians beyond an exclusive focus on their experiences as enslaved and marginalized peoples. While mulatos like Porres and mixed-race surgeons and physicians still faced discrimination and persecution in their societies, their stories illuminate the limits of possibility for people of Afro-Peruvian descent in colonial Peru. At the same time, Tamara Walker offers new insight into the experience of enslaved Africans in Peru through a cultural history of clothing that examines the ways in which slaves appropriated and used clothing (item **993**). Perhaps the most innovative feature of this strand of scholarship is that these studies offer broader insights into the contours and tensions of colonial Peruvian society even though their focus is restricted to the history of one specific group: Afro-Peruvians.

Additional studies have made important and novel contributions to the historiography of colonial Peru by focusing on other marginalized groups including women, immigrants, and Jews. Nancy Van Deusen focuses on female spirituality through an examination of the experiences of several female saints in 17th-century Lima (item **991**). Moving beyond the inquisitorial sources which tend to cast female spirituality as deviant, Van Deusen's study employs contemporary spiritual biographies and others sources to show how women experienced the sacred while also navigating, and at times challenging, the patriarchy and misogyny that pervaded colonial society in Peru. Another study that moves beyond inquisitorial records in order to shed new light on a key group in colonial Peru is Gleydi Sullón Barreto's book that focuses on the experience of Portuguese immigrants in Lima from the late 16th century to the late 17th century (item **988**). This book challenges the longstanding assumption (dating back to the colonial period) that Portuguese immigrants were crypto-Jews and *conversos* by offering a comprehensive social history of this migrant community that emphasizes the variety of social and economic roles that they played in colonial Lima. While these studies have largely eschewed inquisitorial records, Ana Schaposchnik explicitly focuses on the Inquisition and its archival records in a recent study that reconstructs the experiences of crypto-Jews in 17th-century Lima (item **987**). This study not only recovers the history of colonial Lima's Jewish community, but also explores the ways that the Inquisition shaped colonial Peruvian society through public and symbolic displays of punishment and power. Together, these studies show how well-known inquisitorial records and new archival and print sources can yield a deeper understanding of the tensions of colonial society, the disciplinary power of the colonial state, and the heterogeneous experiences of marginalized groups, especially in the urban spaces of colonial Peru.

One final trend in recent scholarship is a renewed interest in the rebellions, revolutions, and independence movements of the late 18th- and early 19th-century Andean world in conjunction with recent anniversaries of these key episodes in Peruvian history. Pablo Ortemberg has produced a novel study that traces the symbolic dimensions of political power during the transition from colonial to republican rule in Peru (item **982**). Focusing on the period from 1735 to 1828, this study examines how festivals, processions, and other public rituals in Lima exhibited both continuity and change, while articulating social and political tensions as a new republic and national identities emerged in the early decades of the 19th century. If such public rituals played an important role in the constitution of political legitimacy, so too did political discourse. A recent study by Luis Daniel Morán Ramos demonstrates current scholarly interest in the history of political discourse during the period of the independence movements. In his book, Morán Ramos compares royalist and counterrevolutionary discourse that appeared in print in Lima with the revolutionary discourse that appeared in print in Buenos Aires to investigate competing and changing notions of key concepts, such as "revolution" (item **981**). The events of specific rebellions and independence movements continue to attract attention, especially the indigenous uprisings in the Andean highlands during the 1780s. Charles Walker offers the first major study of the Tupac Amaru rebellion to appear in English in several decades (item **992**). This study enriches the history of this rebellion by giving greater attention to the role of women, especially Micaela Bastides, the role of the Catholic Church, and the importance of geography. Walker also emphasizes the significance of violence, as does Pilar Roca in her work on Amaru. Roca focuses on the systematic violence of the Spanish colonial enterprise in Peru as represented by the prosecution and punishment of Amaru and his associates in the wake of their uprising. She also points to the prevalent and persistent violence against women in colonial society (item **986**).

The transcription and publication of archival sources have also made an important contribution to the scholarship on colonial Peru. Such activities are not only acts of scholarship in themselves, but also serve the vital function of facilitating future research by scholars interested in colonial Peru. The works reviewed for *HLAS 74* include three examples of critical and scholarly editions of primary sources that have appeared in recent years. One is the transcription of the dossier from 1751 that resulted from the investigation into the activities of Gregorio Taco, the indigenous leader of a protest against royal taxes in Andagua near Arequipa (item **975**). The case of Gregorio Taco, who was the custodian of a powerful Andean mummy, offers useful insight into the persistence and evolution of Andean religious practice, and sheds light on forms of indigenous resistance in the later colonial period. The second published primary source is a transcription and critical edition of a report to the Crown written by Antonio de Ulloa, a Spanish naval officer, scientific traveler, and colonial administrator, describing his efforts to implement reforms to the mercury mines in Huancavelica in the late 1750s and early 1760s (item **990**). The source provides insight into one of the most important sectors of the colonial economy and vividly demonstrates the challenges of colonial administration during the era of the Bourbon Reforms. Finally, building on recent interest in the life and activities of the reform-minded bishop of Trujillo, Baltasar Jaime Martínez, Susan Ramírez offers a transcription and critical edition of nine manuscripts related to Martínez's efforts to establish primary schools for indigenous children in the 1780s (item **985**). The existing documents from this unique educational initiative offer further insight into the ways in which the members of colonial Peruvian society engaged with the ideals of Enlightenment and reform that pervaded the Americas and the Atlantic world in the late 18th century.

As always, the scholarship reviewed here represents but a small sampling of the excellent publications in Spanish and English that continue to enrich and refine our understanding of colonial Peru and its place in the early modern world. Taken together, these studies offer new and important insights not just using overlooked or underused sources but also by applying new methodologies and new conceptual frameworks to make sense of these sources. Recent scholarship on colonial Peru remains at the cutting edge of historiographical and scholarly trends prevalent in other fields of history. Social and cultural history figure prominently, as do intellectual and political history. One conspicuous omission is that the vast majority of these studies focus on urban life and urban spaces with a number of studies on Lima alone. Consequently, one of the challenges for future scholarship will be to determine whether the findings and insights are relevant for rural areas in colonial Peru. At the very least, the methodological and conceptual insights of several of these studies represent potentially useful tools for doing the history of colonial Peru and the Spanish Empire beyond cities. [MC]

CHILE
With the bicentennials of Spanish American independence looming large, recent scholarship on colonial Chile (primarily by historians) has taken up three key issues: the political culture of Bourbon rule leading up to the outbreak of the inde-

pendence wars, the significant impact of the indigenous Mapuche people on Chile and the Spanish Empire, and the collection and transcription of primary documents relating to slavery and indigenous diplomacy.

Monographs by Jaime Valenzuela Márquez (item **1010**) and Verónica Undurraga Schüler (item **1008**) join classic studies of colonial New Spain by investigating the importance of public ceremonies and honor to Spanish rule in 18th-century Chile. In kindred ways, they contest the notion that the transition from Hapsburg to Bourbon rule in Spain signified a shift away from Church dominance and local, patronage-based rule to peninsular domination and secular reform across the Indies. They both uncover the enduring importance of public interactions for identity, legitimacy, and prestige for men and women of distinct social classes. Valenzuela shows how Bourbon reformers and pro-independence patriots conceded to popular demand for public religious and secular rituals. He examines visual images, like fetishes and paintings, and the ceremonial role of institutions like the military and administrative bureaucracies. Undurraga addresses honor as a status, not a sentiment, in Chile by using judicial documents to explore how non-elite men (scribes, merchants, peons, and artisans) and some women understood and litigated differing conceptions of honor. This honor, she finds, differed in important ways from the "honor of origins" of the Iberian peninsula which was connected to nobility, titles, and *limpieza de sangre* (purity of blood). Both contributions provide new directions for thinking about gender, hierarchy, and political culture in urban colonial Chile.

A second important wave of scholarship turns away from urban centers like Santiago to the countryside and the south. The indigenous Mapuche people of what is today southern Chile and western Argentina successfully defeated the Spanish conquest in the late 16th century and maintained their autonomy until the 1880s. This made them famous across the Spanish Empire and earned their homelands the title *flandes indiano* or the Flanders of the Indies. José Manuel Zavala (item **1006**) and his coeditors provide an invaluable collection of primary sources for comparative study of indigenous peoples and borderlands in the Americas. His focus is on the interethnic treaty negotiations, known as *parlamentos*, which took place between the Mapuche and the Spanish along Chile's southern frontier from 1593 until 1803. The volume collects treaties and descriptions of these negotiations that were scattered across archives in the Atlantic world and glossed over by official histories. The documents offer fascinating insights into Mapuche diplomatic customs, practices of authority, and notions of identity. In a different vein, Celia López-Chávez (item **1005**) provides a literary analysis of Spanish epic poetry (*Historia de Nueva México* and *La Araucana*) written in response to 16th-century rebellions by the Acoma people of Nueva Mexico and the Mapuche as a means to understand Spanish imperialism and indigenous resistance in the aftermath of the conquest. The analysis of other literary works in conversation with the historical context in which they were written offers an exciting avenue for expanding Borderlands and frontier studies in colonial North and South America.

Finally, Zavala and Undurraga Schüler (items **1006** and **1008**) respectively provide readers with access to primary sources in Spanish related to and produced by historically marginalized peoples in Chile: the Mapuche and African slaves. While Zavala's team performed the herculean task of locating and compiling this broad and fragmented corpus of sources related to a common theme in Chilean ethnohistory, Undurraga breaks surprisingly new ground by making accessible primary documents related to slavery and freedom in colonial Chile. Undurraga's document collection, focused on urban central Chile, provides a helpful guide to the transcription process and a fine-grained exposition of how enslaved people actually accessed the legal system, including the types of legal authorities, intermediaries, and the petitions they used. The corpus of documents along with the introductory essay demonstrate that African slavery, alongside the "other slavery" of indigenous peoples, was not a minor footnote in Chile's history. Rather, Chileans developed permanent practices for the institution during the colonial period through which scholars and students can gain comparative insights into gender and freedom, legal identities, discourses, and knowledge of enslaved men, women, and families. [JZ]

RIO DE LA PLATA

In the mid-2010s, the historiography on colonial Rio de la Plata has maintained its traditional interest in social and economic history, as well as on indigenous history and frontier studies. New publications on the significance of Atlantic connections, urban populations, demography, slavery, and early phases of colonization attest to the vitality of the field. Because of the bicentennial celebration of the independence war in the Viceroyalty of Rio de la Plata, works focusing on the revolutionary period continued to appear, with particular focus on plebeian and elite groups and state formation. Historical works centered on the colonial and national state formation in Upper Peru have been a focal point of many political and economic histories. A number of works offer transcribed editions of important colonial sources, which will undoubtedly benefit the next generation of scholars of the region.

Building on the deep-rooted tradition of research on Rio de la Plata's social and economic history, Raúl Fradkin's edited volume offers several case studies of popular political participation in different regions of the viceroyalty (item **1047**). Another edited volume offers an essential contribution to the research on subaltern groups in current day northeastern Argentina and Paraguay, focusing mostly on the different roles of indigenous and African-descended people in the area (item **1024**). Ana Fanchin provides a well-researched analysis of family dynamics and their significance for politics and hierarchy within colonial society (item **1022**). The effect of the Bourbon Reforms on marriage is at the center of the study by Guillermo Quinteros (item **1035**). Social mobility in colonial times is the focus of an edited volume (item **1045**), and Marcelo Gullo's work examines popular resistance to imperialism and anti-British ideologies in Argentina (item **1025**). A publication of conference proceedings examines the social history of institutions and power in Rio de la Plata and Brazil (item **1041**), while Pablo Fucé analyzes the social and political power of institutional rituals in colonial Montevideo (item **1023**). The rituals of power are also at the center of Silvana Smietniansky's study (item **1042**). The social and economic processes of Jujuy are at the center of studies by Enrique Cruz (item **1020**) and Dolores Estruch (item **1021**). Mercedes Avellaneda utilizes the two colonial rebellions in the 18th and 19th centuries as a window into the dynamics between Guarani, Jesuits, and Spanish settlers (item **1015**). An edited volume of conference proceedings brings together scholars from Brazil and Uruguay to examine slavery and freedom in the 19th-century Uruguay-Brazil borderlands (item **1040**). Fernando Suárez Saavedra offers a comprehensive overview of sex life and sexuality in the Andes from precolumbian times to the 18th century (item **999**).

The significance of Atlantic processes in shaping the politics and economic development of Rio de la Plata are brought to the forefront in José Carlos

Chiaramonte's comparative study of federalism in the Americas (item **1018**). Paola Revilla Orías' work examines the influence of Enlightenment ideas in the Audiencia de Charcas (item **998**). Jeremy Baskes examines the consequences of the end of the fleet system and the introduction of *comercio libre* on long-distance trade and finances in the late colonial period (item **357**). The incorporation of quina (cinchona) as a commodity of empire is at the center of Matthew Crawford's well-researched piece (item **361**). Loyalist and monarchist political projects are the object of Aguerre Core's well-argued work about Montevideo during the revolutionary decade of 1810 (item **1012**). Tejerina and Contera's edited volume brings together several essays examining "the other" in Rio de la Plata, including the "other" as the Portuguese, the indigenous peoples, the British, and even "other" ideas (item **1019**). Political and national identity projects surrounding the Pan-American conferences in the 19th and 20th centuries are the object of Tereza Dulci's book (item **391**). Washington Ashwell presents an overview of the economic development of Paraguay from early conquest to the eve of the War of the Triple Alliance (item **1014**). Pacho O'Donnell utilizes the events of 1815 to examine the different political and military projects competing for control over the Banda Oriental (item **1030**). Transatlantic dynamics are also at the center of Alejandro Sambrizzi's examination of Portuguese, Dutch, French, and British intrusions in colonial Rio de la Plata (item **1038**).

Significant contributions on indigenous peoples and frontier regions have been published between 2013 and 2017. Diego Bracco's work examines the military participation of Charrua and Minuane in wars against and in alliance to Spaniards (item **1017**). The military role of the Guarani in the context of the Treaty of Madrid and the conflicts with the Portuguese is at the center of Juan José Arteaga's study (item **1013**). Florencia Roulet's publication provides a compilation of firsthand accounts describing the indigenous groups of Patagonia and the Southern Andes in the colonial period (item **1036**).

A series of recent titles focuses on political and military history, including works examining the trajectories of Rio de la Plata viceroys (item **1032**) and analyzing different facets of the British invasion: Ismael Pozzi Albornoz looks at the battles and disputes over Colonia do Sacramento in 1806 (item **1034**), while Juan Carlos Luzuriaga investigates the reconquest of Buenos Aires (item **1028**). Mariano Moreno and Manuel Belgrano receive new vistas in the works of Felipe Pigna (item **1033**) and an edited volume (item **1031**), with special attention given to both men's intellectual influences and political writings.

In recent years, scholars have published a number of transcriptions of primary sources that will benefit students of the region in the coming decades. The medical treatise written by Jesuit priest José Sanchez Labrador between 1771 and 1776 was published by Elaine Fleck (item **1039**). The 18th-century natural history of Upper Peru by Marcos Jiménez de la Espada was transcribed and a received critical prologue by Juan Francisco Bedregal Villanueva (item **997**). Several first-hand accounts of the Paraguayan War appeared in Lecio Gomes de Souza's multivolume work (item **1043**). Bismark Cuéllar Chávez offers a plethora of primary sources about the colonial past of the region of Santa Cruz de la Sierra (item **996**).

The current historiographical production about colonial Rio de la Plata denotes not only the continued vitality of the field, but also the significance of dialogue with Atlantic World history and the importance of transnational approaches. The number of recent publications of transcribed sources (or inclusion of transcribed sources in more extensive studies) also provides renewed resources for new studies on the region. [FP]

VENEZUELA

955 González, Hermann. Una historia de nuestra frontera oriental: las colonias holandesas en Guayana "cambian de dueño" (1795–1814). Caracas: Academia Nacional de la Historia, 2014. 238 p.: bibl., ill. (Biblioteca de la Academia Nacional de la Historia. Estudios, monografías y ensayos; 196)

This work presents a posthumously published history of the Dutch colonies of Esequibo and Demerara, which pertained to the Captaincy General of Venezuela and subsequently to the Republic of Guyana. The author traces the changing sovereign control of this region beginning with Holland's cessation to Britain in 1796, to support Venezuela's international claims to redraw its eastern border. Despite a presentist political purpose, the study demonstrates extensive research in Spanish and British archives for understanding interimperial competition, piracy, and slave revolt in this portion of the circum-Caribbean during the Age of Revolution and independence. [JZ]

956 Hernández González, Manuel. En el vendaval de la Revolución: la trayectoria vital del ingeniero venezolano José de Pozo y Sucre (1740–1819). Caracas: Fundación Centro Nacional de Historia, 2013. 123 p.: bibl. (Colección monografías)

This short biographical sketch focuses on an underappreciated Spanish-trained engineer from Caracas. Pozo y Sucre participated in the measuring missions to carve out the new Viceroyalty of Río de la Plata, in the war against the French Revolution and the Napoleonic invasion of Spain, and in the first *junta suprema* in Cádiz. With close family ties to Francisco de Miranda and Alexander von Humboldt, Pozo y Sucre offers a fascinating example of the plight and cosmopolitanism of educated, upper-crust Creole *americanos* during the late 18th and early 19th centuries. This work serves as a case study of the fluid and contingent nature of loyalty to the Spanish monarchy or to the pro-independence movements within the broad current of Spanish liberalism during and following the Napoleonic invasion of the Iberian Peninsula. [JZ]

957 Langue, Frédérique. Rumores y sensibilidades en Venezuela colonial: cuando de historia cultural se trata. Caracas: Fundación Buría, 2010. 148 p.: bibl.

This series of essays develops a cultural analysis and *histoire des mentalités* of Creole identity formation in late-colonial Venezuela. The book begins with extensive reviews of the relevance and meaning of cultural history in Europe and Latin America and historiographical trends in colonial Venezuelan history. The author then presents analyses of aristocratic Creole politics in relation to mestizo middling and elite groups by looking at discourses, celebrations, and condemnations of honor, rumor, and sin. Finally, the work considers institutional tensions within and between *criollos* and *peninsulares* and the Catholic Church as they played out in the growing public sphere. [JZ]

958 Leal, Ildefonso. Historia de la Universidad de Caracas 1721–1827. Segunda edición. Caracas: Academia Nacional de la Historia: Banco Central de Venezuela, 2013. 584 p.: bibl., ill. (chiefly color), color map.

This work presents a pedagogical and institutional history of the Universidad de Caracas. The author recounts its transformation from a colonial Catholic institution originating as the Colegio Seminario de Santa Rosa in a 1592 *Real cédula* to its crucial role in late colonial caraqueño society. While including chapters on student life and colonial society, the majority of the study focuses on the internal history of the institution, offering chapters on the development of the core curricula—from philosophy and theology to music. This new edition adds two chapters extending the story through the wars of independence and the foundation of the Universidad Repúblicana. For a review of the first edition published in 1963, see *HLAS 26:837*. [JZ]

959 Rey Fajardo, José del. La República de las Letras en la Babel étnica de la Orinoquia. Caracas: Academia Nacional de la Historia, 2015. 696 p.: bibl. (Académicos actuales; 10)

This wide-ranging religious and cultural history covers the missionary work of the Company of Jesus (Jesuit Order) in the Llanos of the Orinoco River. The study draws on extensive and underutilized archives of the order to look at the many actors (missionaries, Llanos and orinoqueño indigenous peoples) and ideas who encountered one another around these frontier missions. The book goes beyond a strict religious history of the missionaries, though several are profiled, to detail how the literate priests' encounters with indigenous peoples produced extensive textual records of indigenous beliefs, stories, customs, and language. An extremely detailed bibliographic record provides a fruitful point of comparison for other episodes of frontier missionary politics and the spiritual conquest. [JZ]

NUEVA GRANADA

960   **Bohórquez Barrera, Jesús.** Luces para la economía: libros y discursos de economía política en el Atlántico español durante la era de las revoluciones (Nueva Granada, 1780–1811). Bogotá: Instituto Colombiano de Antropología e Historia, 2014. 206 p.: bibl. (Colección Cuadernos coloniales; XVII)

This work presents an intellectual history, inspired by Foucault, of the emergence of political economy as a new project for governance and economic thought in the 18th and early 19th centuries, and its circulation in Nueva Granada. Bohórquez places the fields of commerce and agriculture at the heart of the study, though not in an empirical sense. Rather, the author is interested in how the tools and ideas of reason and rational governance came to be applied to the study and promulgation of policy regarding commercial exchanges. Of particular interest is the study of the writing, circulation, and prohibition of political economy literature across the Atlantic. Complements studies of the Bourbon Reforms, the Age of Revolution, and the transimperial Atlantic world. [JZ]

961   **Cassiani Herrera, Alfonso.** Palenque Magno: resistencias y luchas libertarias del Palenque de la Matuna a San Basilio Magno 1599–1714. Cartagena de Indias, Colombia: Icultur: Ataole, 2014. 190 p.: bibl., ill., maps.

This work presents a short history of an escaped slave (*cimarrón*) community (*palenque*) in the modern Colombian province of Cartagena from its foundation until it earned Spanish recognition as a town in 1714. The author surveys in detail previous studies of the *palenque* before delving into the important leaders of the community, their forms of resistance and representation, and ultimately their strategies of relating to Spanish colonial society. Fascinating comparative case for studies of slave resistance and Maroon communities in the circum-Caribbean as the leaders achieved the status of colonial town over a century after its foundation, rather than choosing to stay in active isolation from the Spanish. [JZ]

962   **La economía colonial de la Nueva Granada.** Edición de Adolfo Meisel Roca y María Teresa Ramírez G. Bogotá: FCE: Banco de la República, 2015. 399 p.: bibl., ill., maps. (Sección de obras de economía)(Colección del Banco de la República)

This book is the product of a seminar organized by the Banco de la República of Colombia to better understand the colonial economy of Colombia. The compilation includes nine essays based on conference presentations. The collection aims to explore the environmental and economic consequences of the Spanish conquest and colonial rule in their own right, and in terms of the legacy they bequeathed to republican Colombia. Contributors approach a wide range of topics of interest to environmental, economic, and social historians of colonial Latin America—land use and ecosystems, demography, gold, agriculture, financial policies, currency, commerce, and colonial economists. Includes a valuable link to an online appendix with all of the maps, figures, and charts from the book. [JZ]

963   **Eissa-Barroso, Francisco A.** The Spanish monarchy and the creation of the Viceroyalty of New Granada (1717–1739): the politics of early Bourbon reform in Spain and Spanish America. Leiden: Brill, 2017. 326 p.: bibl., ill., index, map. (Early American history series: the American colonies, 1500–1830; 6)

This study offers an Atlantic-scale diplomatic history of the circumstances surrounding the creation, suppression, and recreation of the Viceroyalty of New Granada under the reign of Spain's first Bourbon king, Philip V (1701–46). The author privileges debates over how to stabilize and administer the American economy between Spanish and Spanish American reformers represented in the court of Madrid. In examining inter-elite factional battles, the work highlights how Philip's reform agenda marked a transition from a Hapsburg juridical form of rule (based on audiencias and delegation of power) to more administrative royal rule. Extremely useful for the fine-grained discussion of how the mechanisms of reform were debated, contested, and implemented by Creole and peninsular Spanish actors. [JZ]

964   Guerrero Rincón, Amado Antonio; Silvano Pabón Villamizar; and Carmen Adriana Ferreira Esparza. Poblamiento y economía: orígenes de los asentamientos urbanos en el nororiente colombiano durante la colonia. Bucaramanga, Colombia: Dirección Cultural, Universidad Industrial de Santander, 2014. 248 p.: bibl., maps. (Colección Temas y autores regionales)

This work provides a history of the origin and development of towns in northeastern Colombia. The authors examine the constitution of roughly a dozen Spanish and indigenous towns (*pueblos de indios*) to consider how settling and organizing European Spanish, mestizos, and indigenous peoples took place, and how this intertwined religious conversion, secular administration, and authority. They place particular emphasis on the precision of terminology for how the Spanish aimed to settle and occupy the new world. The study considers the city as a political and juridical space with power placed under a sovereign, not simply a dense human settlement defined by structures or architecture. The authors also suggest more contextual treatment of terms like *reducir, poblar, congregar,* and *erigir,* which scholars have used interchangeably or uncritically. [JZ]

965   Pico, Claudia Milena. Historia económica de Colombia: fiscalía y moneda entre los siglos XVI y XIX. Bogotá: Ediciones Unisalle, Universidad La Salle, Facultad de Ciencias Económicas y Sociales, 2016. 64 p.: bibl. (Apuntes de clase; 113)

This work presents a brief introduction to two areas of the economic history of Colombia from the early colonial period through the 19th century. The book begins with a methodological essay for prospective students of economic history and political economy to complement the existing fields of social and political history, and serves as a basis for comparative studies. The final two essays draw on quantitative and qualitative sources found in Colombia to point to continuities in issues of taxation and money across the colonial/national divide. The author touches on policy, the practical and moral dimensions of credit, debt, banking, money supply, and metal backing of currency. [JZ]

966   Pita Pico, Roger. Tahúres, chicherías y celebraciones monárquicas en el Santander colonial. Bucaramanga, Colombia: Editorial, Proyecto Cultural de Sistemas y Computadores, 2014. 191 p.: bibl., ill. (chiefly colored).

This collection of three historical essays and an appendix of historical documents explores social life through vice (gambling and chicha production) and royal ritual in the northeast of Nueva Granada. The author steps away from the overtly political and economic focus on Bourbon Reform policy to consider how gambling, chica production and consumption, and Spanish attempts to regulate them, open new vantage points to consider how mixed-race, lower class colonial subjects asserted cultural attitudes and customs to defend their economic practices. The studies aptly reveal how Spanish concerns with morality and immorality intertwined with economic questions of social peace, mestizo business owners, and royal monopolies (or *estancos*) on aguardiente. Relevant to studies of gender, race, popular culture, and the origins of a public sphere in the colonial Americas. Includes an appendix of transcribed documents relating to royal celebrations. [JZ]

967   Sociedad, política y cultura en Colombia siglos XVIII–XIX: (enfoques, problemas y tendencias). Edición de José Trinidad Polo Acuña y Rafael Enrique Acevedo Puello. Medellín, Colombia: La Carreta Editores E.U.; Cartagena, Colombia: Universidad de Cartagena, 2015. 297 p.: bibl.

This collection of 10 micro studies examines power, writing, and social representation in the provinces of Cartagena, Santa Marta, Mompox, Riohacha, and Maracaibo in the former Captaincy General of Venezuela. The studies are primarily focused on the 19th century, but also include helpful social histories of classic late-18th century topics, such as race and representation in colonial census data, criminality, and the politics of creating new indigenous communal landholdings in exchange for loyalty. Postindependence topics include waning loyalties for Bolívar and Santander, the capacity of educated *pardos* to advance in republican administration through personal and political networks, the limits of citizenship, provincial rivalries, and civil war. Directly engages with North American and Spanish literature on race and popular political culture, Spanish liberalism, and ethnohistory. [JZ]

968 **Voces de esclavitud y libertad: documentos y testimonios, Colombia, 1701–1833.** Transcripción y estudio preliminar de Orián Jiménez Meneses y Edgardo Pérez Morales. Popayán, Colombia: Editorial UC, Editorial Universidad del Cauca, 2013. 305 p.: bibl.

This edited and transcribed collection brings together 36 historical documents related to slavery and freedom in Colombia. The documents are drawn from archives across Colombia (Buga, Cali, Bogotá, Popayán, Medellín) and organized into three categories: life and death (including wills), slavery and freedom, and military service. An introductory essay emphasizes the need for studies of slavery in Colombia to conceptualize freedom as a category inseparable from slavery, and to return to the original documents which include the voices and testimonies of slaves and *libertos* employed as soldiers and tradespeople. The selection of documents displays the complexity of interactions between slaves, officers, masters, patrons, clients, and institutions characterized by violence, abuse, deference, but also love and paternalism. Of interest for comparative legal and cultural histories of slavery, manumission, and emancipation, as well as for the study of the history of race in Bourbon South America. [JZ]

QUITO

969 **Barriga López, Leonardo.** Quito, por la independencia. Quito: CCE Benjamín Carrión: Academia Nacional de Historia, 2015. 574 p.: bibl., ill.

This work offers a Creole- and elite-centered patriotic history of Quito's experiences following the Napoleonic invasion of Spain in 1808 until the reassertion of Spanish rule in the early 1810s. The author examines the pro-independence insurgencies in 1809, Quiteños' responses to the 1812 Spanish liberal constitution, and ideas about more rights for *americanos* within the Empire. While little space is given to the actions and contributions of Afro-Quiteños, women, and indigenous peoples, or politics of loyalty to Spain, the narration and extensive transcription of primary sources related to priests, Creole leaders, and the independence movements make this a useful introduction to Quito's part in the Nueva Granadan independence story. [JZ]

970 **Cushner, Nicholas P.** Hacienda y obraje: los jesuitas y el inicio del capitalismo agrario en Quito Colonial, 1600–1767. Traducción al español, estudio introductorio, y notas de Gonzalo Ortiz Crespo. Quito: Instituto Metropolitano de Patrimonio, 2011. 399 p.: bibl., ill. (some color), index. (Biblioteca básica de Quito; 38)

This is the first Spanish translation of *Farm and Factory: the Jesuits and the Development of Agrarian Capitalism in Colonial Quito, 1600–1767* (see HLAS 42:2675), which coincided with Ecuador's bicentennial independence celebration. The book presents a social history of the formation of capitalist relations in the inter-Andean regions near Quito during the Spanish colonial period. The author utilizes local Jesuit archives to examine the Company of Jesus' hacienda, Chillo Compañia, and suggests that private property ownership, reinvestment in agricultural techniques, a mobile workforce, and money-based economy represented nascent capitalism. This analysis focuses on an understudied case in the growing field of history of capitalism. A helpful introduction from the translator situates the study and the hacienda in the context of the bicentennial of Ecuadorian independence. An appendix includes transcribed documents and a glossary of key terms. [JZ]

971 **Espinosa, Carlos R.** El Inca barroco: política y estética en la Real Audiencia de Quito, 1630–1680. Quito: FLACSO Ecuador, 2015. 309 p.: bibl., color ill. (Atrio)

This work, based on the author's PhD dissertation, offers a political and visual study of the Audiencia of Quito's only instance of neo-inca revival in the postconquest period. Espinosa examines the rituals, language, and displays of Spanish Royal and Inca revivalist politics used by the *corregidor* of Ibarra, the self-proclaimed "Inca King," Alonso Florencia Inca, in the 1660s. The subject is especially curious given that the predominant indigenous inhabitants of Ibarra were *carangue*, who had suffered massacres at the hands of the Inca Huayna Cápac in the 16th century. The book offers fascinating insights into the incorporation of indigenous nobility by the early colonial administrative system, and the conflicts generated by Inca revivalism outside the core regions of the Viceroyalty of Peru. Includes an extensive appendix of transcribed documents from the legal case against Florencia Inca and many beautiful reproductions of paintings from the era. [JZ]

972 **Miño Grijalva, Manuel.** El cacao Guayaquil en Nueva España, 1774–1812: (política imperial, mercado y consumo). México: El Colegio de México, 2013. 323 p.: bibl., maps.

This book provides an account of a relatively unknown facet of the Bourbon reforms in Spanish America: the trade of cacao between Guayaquil, in the Audiencia of Quito, and Veracruz in New Spain. The study reveals how the more bitter but affordable cacao guayaquil (as opposed to the sweeter, upper-class preferred cacao from Tabasco, Caracas, and Soconusco) experienced growing demand in urban New Spain alongside the 18th-century demographic growth. This elucidating case study describes a tropical commodity and its entanglement with Spanish Creole and peninsular debates over free trade or monopoly in Americas, imperial reform, and the politics of consumption and class in the 18th and early 19th centuries. While focusing more on the politics of legality, import, and export, the author provides a thought-provoking comparison to slave society commodity producers in the circum-Caribbean. [JZ]

973 **Núñez Sánchez, Jorge.** Las milicias del corregimiento de Chimbo: siglos XVIII y XIX. Quito: Ministerio de Defensa Nacional, 2014. 169 p.: bibl., ill. (Biblioteca de la defensa. Colección histórica (Quito))

This work provides an official narrative history of the Spanish and Ecuadorian militias from the Chimborazo region, which lay midway between the capitol of the Audiencia (in Quito) and the port of Guayaquil. The author draws on records from the Archivo de Indias to reveal how the formation of militias responded to indigenous uprisings, which characterized the Andes in the late 18th century, and defense of the coastline from pirates and imperial rivals. Of comparative relevance to those interested in the Bourbon Reforms and partisan politics sparked by the outbreak of independence movements across Nueva Granada. Includes appendices with data on militia service. [JZ]

PERU

974 **Bentancor, Orlando.** The matter of empire: metaphysics and mining in colonial Peru. Pittsburgh, Pa.: University of Pittsburgh Press, 2017. 404 p.: bibl., index. (Illuminations: cultural formations of the Americas series)

This book examines the intellectual and cultural history of the Spanish Empire in the 16th and early 17th centuries. The author illuminates the metaphysical instrumentalism central to the Spanish imperial project as reflected in writings on politics, natural history, and mining from 1520 to 1640. Such evidence is used to develop an argument for locating the roots of modernity in scholasticism and imperial metaphysics of the Iberian world. [MC]

China y Perú: en el arte y la cultura. See item **1168**.

975 **Culto a los ancestros, hechiceros y resistencia colonial: el case de Gragorio Taco, Arequipa, 1750.** Edición de Luis A Galdames R. y María Marsilli. Artículos de Luis Millones y Frederic Duchesne. Arica, Chile: Cinosargo Ediciones, 2012. 579 p.

In 1751, Joseph de Arana, the corregidor of Condesuyos, arrested Gregorio Taco, the indigenous leader of an uprising against royal taxes in Andagua, an indigenous community near Arequipa. The subsequent investigation resulted in a massive dossier into the activities of Taco and the indigenous community in Andagua. This book is a transcription of that dossier with a critical introduction. As the subsequent investigation revealed, Taco was not just an economic and political leader in the indigenous community but also a religious leader in his capacity as the custodian of Cuyag Mama, the most powerful mummy among several that were the center of worship in a local, Andean ancestor cult. This dossier provides excellent insight into the persistence of Andean religious beliefs during the colonial period even after the extirpation campaigns of the 17th century. It also sheds light on the forms of indigenous resistance to Spanish colonial rule in the Andean region. [MC]

976 **Cussen, Celia L.** Black Saint of the Americas: the life and afterlife of Martín de Porres. New York: Cambridge University Press, 2014. 292 p.: bibl., ill., index. (Cambridge Latin American studies; 99)

This book is the first scholarly study of the life and cult of Fray Martín de Porres (1579–1639), a mulato from colonial Lima who was canonized in 1962. Porres spent much of his life as a voluntary lay servant and healer at the convent of El Rosario in Lima. The first half of the book focuses on Porres' biography and the experience of Afro-Peruvians and *castas* that challenged the imagined racial and ethnic divisions of colonial social hierarchy. The second half of the book uses the development of the cult of Porres to explore the dynamics of religion and society in colonial Lima and argues that limeños embraced the cult because of Porres' mixed race. [MC]

977 **Graubart, Karen B.** Learning from the Qadi: the jurisdiction of local rule in the early colonial Andes. (*HAHR*, 95:2, May 2015, p. 195–228, bibl.)

This article examines the way in which the legal and political incorporation of Muslim communities into the Christian kingdoms of late medieval Iberia informed the legal and political incorporation of indigenous communities in early colonial Latin America with a focus on the Andean region. The author analyzes the political jurisdiction of caciques (ethnic lords) in colonial Latin America and challenges recent scholarship that has argued that the Spanish colonial project undermined the office of the cacique. Instead, this article argues that the jurisdiction of caciques was real and meaningful to indigenous peoples in Spanish colonial society. [MC]

978 **Huamanchumo de la Cuba, Ofelia.** Encomiendas y cristianización: estudio de documentos jurídicos y administrativos del Perú, siglo XVI. Piura, Peru: Facultad de Humanidades, Universidad de Piura, 2013. 213 p.: bibl. (Estudios y ensayos; 8)

This study offers a philological and linguistic analysis of different genres of legal and administrative documents prevalent in 16th-century Peru. The author focuses on four main genres: *Cartas de petición, Memorias, Instrucciones de visita,* and *Visitas*. Through linguistic analysis, this book provides insight into the ways in which these kinds of texts reflected the influence of the processes of colonization and evangelization in colonial Peru. The various chapters engage with ethnohistory and pay attention to how these texts served as sites of interaction between Spanish colonists and indigenous peoples as well as sites for the articulation of indigenous identity and agency. [MC]

979 **Jouve Martín, José Ramón.** The black doctors of colonial Lima: science, race, and writing in colonial and early republican Peru. Montréal: Kingston: McGill-Queen's University Press, 2014. 209 p.: bibl., ill., index, ports. (McGill-Queen's/Associated Medical Services studies in the history of medicine, health, and society; 41)

José Pastor de Larrinaga (1758–c.1821), José Manuel Dávalos (1758–1821), and José Manuel Valdés (1767–1843) were all Afro-Peruvian medical practitioners in Lima who lived during the transition from colonial to republican Peru. Through a prosopographical study of these three individuals, this book examines the experience of surgeons and doctors of African descent in Peru primarily in the period from 1760 to 1840. The analysis emphasizes the ways in which the biographies of these individuals undermine the common assumption that Afro-Peruvians were excluded from academic and professional spaces of science and medicine because of their race. The study also highlights the divisions and hierarchies within Lima's black community by showing how these three prominent medical practitioners sought to distance themselves from other Afro-Peruvians. In addition to tracing their careers in science and medicine, this book also explores the ways in which Larrinaga, Dávalos, and Valdés engaged with the broader political and social issues of their time such as independence and slavery. [MC]

980 Mangan, Jane E. Transatlantic obligations: creating the bonds of family in conquest-era Peru and Spain. Oxford, England; New York: Oxford University Press, 2016. 247 p.: bibl., ill., index, maps.

This book provides new insight into the impact of Spanish colonialism on the structure and lived experience of families in urban centers of Peru and Spain from the 1530s to 1600. The author focuses on families in the cities of Lima, Arequipa, and Seville, and highlights the role of family networks in Spain's transatlantic Empire. Drawing on legal and notarial documents, chapters explore the ways in which elite Inca families navigated the early years of Spanish colonization, the processes whereby Spanish fathers recognized mestizo children, how Spanish men and women negotiated the Spanish Crown's efforts to regulate marriage in colonial society, the role of family networks in facilitating emigration from Spain to Peru, the patterns of everyday family life in indigenous-headed families and blended families in colonial Andean society, and the ways in which parents—especially fathers—provided for their children and tested the boundaries of colonial laws through their last wills and testaments. The book argues that families in practice undermined the structures of class and caste of colonial society in Peru. [MC]

981 Morán Ramos, Luis Daniel. Batallas por la legitimidad: la prensa de Lima y de Buenos Aires durante las guerras de independencia. Los Olivos, Peru: Universidad de Ciencias y Humanidades Fondo Editorial, 2013. 291 p.: bibl., ill.

Building on renewed interest in the Latin American independence movements associated with recent bicentennial celebrations, this book examines the role of printing and newspapers in Lima and Buenos Aires during the period of the wars for independence. This study is an intellectual and cultural history of public and political discourse focusing on the changing meaning of concepts like "independence" and "revolution." The methodology that relies on comparing political discourse in Lima, a center of royalist and counterrevolutionary sentiment, and Buenos Aires, a center of support for revolution and independence, and is a feature that distinguishes this study relative to existing scholarship on the topic. [MC]

982 Ortemberg, Pablo. Rituales del poder en Lima, 1735–1828: de la monarquía a la república. Lima: Fondo Editorial, Pontificia Universidad Católica del Perú, 2014. 402 p.: bibl., ill. (some color).

Festivals, processions, and other rituals played a vital role in constituting political power and authority in Peru during the transition from Spanish viceroyalty to independent republic. This book tracks the changes and continuities in rituals of power in Lima from 1735 to 1828. While recognizing that those in power often organized such spectacles, this study emphasizes the ways in which these rituals not only reinforced authority and unity but also provided a space for articulating social and political tensions. Individual chapters focus on rituals to celebrate different aspects of colonial and republican rule including the arrivals of viceroys; royal proclamations; celebrations of the births, weddings, and deaths of the royal family; and military victories—as well as rituals to celebrate competing visions of the political community during the rise of independence movements and the ceremonial activities that articulated a vision of Peru as a republic. The book explores several important themes in order to highlight the techniques for maintaining or establishing legitimacy in times of significant change. [MC]

983 Premo, Bianca. Custom today: temporality, cutomary law, and indigenous enlightenment. (*HAHR*, 94:3, Aug. 2014, p. 355–379, bibl.)

This article explores the myriad ways in which indigenous peoples used the notion of "custom" in litigation in late 18th-century Latin America. Focusing on cases from Ferreñafe in northern Peru (1781), Lima (1782), and Oaxaca (1760), the article reviews several episodes that challenge the opposition between the enlightened reforms of the

Bourbons to indigenous custom prevalent in existing scholarship. The evidence shows that "custom" was a malleable concept deployed by indigenous litigants to make arguments for rights and privileges rooted in their achievement and service rather than ancestry and inheritance. [MC]

984 **Puente Luna, José Carlos de la.** Andean cosmopolitans: seeking justice and reward at the Spanish royal court. Austin: University of Texas Press, 2018. 345 p.: bibl., index.

This study examines the legal and political activities of indigenous Andeans in the context of the Spanish Empire. Drawing on fragmentary archival records, the book focuses on the movement of people and information between the Royal Audiencia of Lima to the Spanish Court in Madrid from the 1530s to the 1690s. Individual chapters provide new insight by foregrounding indigenous agency and indigenous perspective on a range of topics from the political power of the pueblo to the ways in which native Andeans used and shaped the discourse of the "Nation of the Indies" to close examinations of indigenous experiences in legal courts and the vice-regal court in Peru as well as legal courts and the royal court in Madrid. Along the way, the book makes an important contribution by showing the ways in which indigenous identities could be situational as well as the ways in which indigenous peoples played a role in the making of the Spanish Atlantic World. [MC]

985 **Ramírez, Susan E.** Al servicio de Dios y de Su Majestad: los orígenes de las escuelas públicas para niños indígenas en el norte del Perú en el S. XVIII. Con la colaboración de José Carlos de la Puente Luna y Fernando Arturo Siles Quezada. Santiago de Surco, Peru: Fondo Editorial de la Asamblea Nacional de Rectores, 2014. 383 p., 2 folded leaves of plates: bibl., ill., map. (Colección Artes y humanidades)

This book provides a transcription and critical edition of 11 manuscripts of Baltasar Jaime Martínez, Bishop of Trujillo, in the "Estado" section of the Archivo General de Indias in Seville. The manuscripts relate to Martínez's efforts to establish primary schools for indigenous boys and girls in the 1780s. These schools were unique in colonial Peru for their focus on educating indigenous children and teaching practical skills, inculcating Christian belief and respect for the Crown, and assimilating indigenous children to Hispanic culture. As such, these documents provide insight not only into this unique colonial enterprise, but also into the impact of the ideals of Enlightenment and reform in late 18th-century Peru. The book includes an introductory essay by Susan Ramírez and a table listing the primary schools established in Trujillo in the late 18th century. [MC]

986 **Roca, Pilar.** Terror en los Andes: la violencia como sistema en el Perú colonial. Lima: Universidad de Ciencias y Humanidades, Fondo Editorial, 2013. 350 p.: bibl.

Violence—in various forms—was an important part of Spanish colonial rule. This book-length essay emphasizes the use of violence by the Spanish colonial state by focusing on the prosecution and punishment of the Inca José Gabriel Túpac Amaru and his family and associates for the crime of *lese majesty* in the early 1780s in the viceroyalties of Peru and Río de la Plata. The first half of the essay argues that violence was a systemic feature of colonial rule and Spanish efforts to oppress indigenous peoples and the culture. Another major theme is the prevalence of violence against women, and the second half of the essay focuses on the state violence directed at indigenous women, such as Micaela Bastidas Puyucahua, Tomasa Tito Condemayta, and Bartolina Sisa, for their role in the Túpac Amaru uprising. The essay is accompanied by 21 appendices that range from transcriptions of key documents to an extensive list of individuals accused of supporting the uprising and the repercussions that they faced. This study provides a vital reminder of the important role of violence in the Spanish colonial enterprise in South America. [MC]

987 **Schaposchnik, Ana Edith.** The Lima Inquisition: the plight of crypto-Jews in seventeenth-century Peru. Madison: The University of Wisconsin Press, 2015. 291 p.: bibl., index.

This book offers new insight into the symbolic importance of the Inquisition in Lima and a profile of the experience of crypto-Jews in colonial Latin America. As a study of the Inquisition, the book attempts to refocus attention on the disciplinary function of the Inquisition and argues that this institution fulfilled this function not through a preponderance of cases but through using individual trials and punishments as potent examples. At the same time, this study seeks to highlight the experience of the crypto-Jewish community and, in particular, those individuals that went on trial. While drawing on studies of the Inquisition's activities in Spain, Mexico, and Peru, the book presents a detailed study of La Complicidad Grande, a period from 1635 to 1639 when the Lima Inquisition handled nearly one hundred trials for crypto-Judaism, and the Auto General de Fe in 1639. The author gives particular attention to the impact of the Inquisition's trials and public punishments not just on crypto-Jews but on the broader colonial society of 17th-century Peru. [MC]

988 Sullón Barreto, Gleydi. Extranjeros integrados: portugueses en la Lima virreinal, 1570–1680. Madrid: Consejo Superior de Investigaciones Científicas, 2016. 303 p.: bibl., ill. (Estudios americanos. Tierra nueva; 2)

This book offers a social history of the community of Portuguese immigrants in Lima in the years before, during, and after the union of the Spanish and Portuguese Crowns. Chapters focus on four different aspects of daily life for the Portuguese in colonial Lima: legal and social lives, integration and assimilation, economic activity, and religiosity and material culture. This study looks beyond the archives of the Inquisition to challenge the prevalent stereotype in the scholarship that Portuguese immigrants to colonial Peru were primarily *conversos* and Jews. Drawing on evidence from notarial records, this book shows that *conversos* and Jews were only one group in a heterogeneous Portuguese community. The author highlights the ways in which members of the Portuguese community interacted and integrated with limeño society. [MC]

989 To be indio in colonial Spanish America. Edited by Mónica Díaz. Albuquerque: University of New Mexico Press, 2017. 283 p.: bibl., ill., index.

This collection of essays examines various processes of individual and collective identity-making by indigenous peoples in the context of the colonial societies of Mexico and Peru. The studies emphasize the agency of indigenous peoples in their ability to understand and manipulate different institutions, languages, and rhetorical strategies. Each essay uses specific artifacts or documents to illuminate native epistemologies as well as the diversity and flexibility of indigenous identities in different contexts. Four of the essays deal specifically with colonial Peru and the Andean World including Rolena Adorno's comparative study of Felipe Guamán Poma de Ayala, Fernando de Alva Ixtilxóchitl, Fray Martín de Murúa and Carlos de Sigüenza y Góngora; Nancy van Duesen on indigenous slaves in Lima; Rachel O'Toole on the mercantile identities of indigenous muleteers in Trujillo; and Rocio Quispe-Agnoli on the negotiation of Andean notions of the sacred. For additional comment, see item **239**. [MC]

990 Ulloa, Antonio de. Relación de gobierno del Real de Minas de Huancavelica (1758–1763). Edición, estudio introductorio y notas de Kendall W. Brown y José J. Hernández Palomo. Lima: Banco Central de Reserva del Perú: IEP, Instituto de Estudios Peruanos, 2016. 328 p.: bibl., facsim., index, map, portrait. (Serie Historia económica; 26)(Fuentes y clásicos de la historia económica del Perú; 2)

In 1757, Antonio de Ulloa (1716–95) was named governor of the province of Huancavelica, home to the most important mercury mines in South America. This book offers a transcription and critical edition of Ulloa's report to the Crown upon the conclusion of his service as governor in 1763. In the report, Ulloa discusses his time managing the Santa Bárbara mine, the mining guild, and the royal treasury, while also providing a description of the local governments in Huancavelica and Angaraes. This primary source provides valuable insight into the challenges that the agents of the Spanish Crown faced when attempting to introduce reforms to the mining sector in colonial Peru. This edition serves a critical function in making this rare and important archival document more accessible to the scholarly community. [MC]

991 Van Deusen, Nancy E. Embodying the sacred: women mystics in seventeenth-century Lima. Durham, N.C.: Duke University Press, 2017. 272 p.: bil., index.

This innovative study of female spirituality in 17th-century Lima offers a prosopography of several female saints in colonial Lima including Rosa de Lima, Ángela de Carranza, María Jacina Montoya, and Josefa Portocarerro Laso de la Vega. By focusing on the ways in which well-known and lesser-known women experienced the sacred, this study offers new insights into female piety in a context of patriarchy and misogyny. The author looks beyond inquisitorial records and examines spiritual biographies and other sources in order to develop new insight into the experience of spirituality shared among women. Such an approach emphasizes that women's spiritual experience transcended their ability to navigate the patriarchy of early modern Catholicism, which has been the main focus in earlier studies. Closer attention to sacred objects, sacred acts, and sacred spaces highlights the ways in which women not only learned about the sacred from each other but also developed a diversity of sacred experiences—a key feature of the book that challenges assumed universality and stability of categories like "female mystic" and "pious woman." [MC]

992 Walker, Charles F. The Tupac Amaru rebellion. Cambridge, Mass.: The Belknap Press of Harvard University Press, 2014. 347 p.: bibl., ill., index, maps.

This book offers the first major account and analysis of the Tupac Amaru Rebellion in English in several decades. It expands the chronology of the rebellion and argues for the importance of events after the execution of Tupac Amaru in 1781. The book also provides an account of Micaela Bastides, Amaru's wife, as a central player and presents new insight into the role of the Catholic Church in the rebellion. The author gives special attention to the theme of violence associated with the intensification of the conflict as well as to the ways in which the geography of Upper Peru shaped the conflict. An essential study for those interested in revolts and rebellions in colonial Peru. The book is available in Spanish translation as *La rebelión de Tupac Amaru* (2015). [MC]

993 Walker, Tamara J. Exquisite slaves race, clothing, and status in colonial Lima. New York, N.Y.: Cambridge University Press, 2017. 240 p.: bibl., index.

This book examines the meaning of clothing in Lima during the 18th century. Focusing on a close reading of criminal and civil cases regarding slaves accused of stealing clothes and other luxury items as well as a wealth of supporting documents, the author provides new insight into the lived experience of African slaves and peoples of African-descent in colonial Peru while also attending to the ways in which limeños of all walks of life understood and navigated the complexities of colonial society, culture, and identity through the acquisition and use of clothing. [MC]

BOLIVIA/CHARCAS

994 Balderrama Román, Rolando A. Yo soy el primer poblador que entró en este valle: Garci Ruiz de Orellana: orígenes de la Villa de Oropesa del Valle de Cochabamba 1548–1593. Cochabamba, Bolivia: Grupo Editorial Kipus, 2016. 786 p.: bibl., facsims.

This detailed and exhaustively referenced study examines the early Spanish settlers in Cochabamba Valley. The life trajectory of Garci Ruiz de Orellana serves as the narrative thread for the author to examine different facets of early colonial Cochabamba, including extensive interactions with indigenous peoples (including the Kjanas), enslavement and trade of indigenous peoples, foundations of Spanish towns, and commercial and religious observations. The book contains an unusually high number of transcribed passages from primary sources embedded in the text. [FP]

995 Bedregal Villanueva, Juan Francisco. Tras el oro de Chuquiabo: en busca de un tiempo olvidado. La Paz: Concejo Municipal de La Paz, 2013. 173 p.: bibl., ill. (some color).

This study presents an overview of the history of the Chuquiabo Valley and the foundation of the city of La Paz. The work is published by the municipality of La

Paz. The author examines the political and economic processes of the Spanish conquest and the foundation of the city. Based on ecclesiastical and administrative records, the book illuminates the early years of colonization and the civil war among Spanish settlers. Contains a plethora of colored maps and images of paintings and artifacts from the period. [FP]

996 **Cuéllar Chávez, Bismark Alberto.** Historia de Santa Cruz. Tomo 1, Período prehistórico y colonial: desde el origen del hombre hasta el año 1825. Santa Cruz, Bolivia: Bismark A.C.Ch. Historia, Turismo & Cultura, 2015. 1 v.: bibl., ill. (some color).

This work offers an overview of the history of the province of Santa Cruz de la Sierra, Bolivia, from precolumbian times to 1825. The study is mostly centered on Spanish colonial agents, the economy, and the society at large. The author presents numerous images of precolumbian art, paintings, maps, flags, and some transcribed primary sources. [FP]

Jackson, Robert H. Frontiers of evangelization: Indians in the Sierra Gorda and Chiquitos missions. See item **490**.

997 **Jiménez de la Espada, Marcos.** Relaciones geográficas indianas collao y charcas. Compilación y prólogo de Juan Francisco Bedregal Villanueva. La Paz: Ediciones Fondo Editorial Municipal Pensamiento Paceño, 2014. 224 p.: bibl., ill.

This book provides a transcription of the 18th-century work of Jiménez de la Espada (1831–98) with a prologue by Juan Francisco Bedregal Villanueva. This critical edition of the natural history of the region includes geographical references and administrative considerations. The original document was produced during the author's travels through Spanish South America (Upper Peru). [FP]

998 **Revilla Orías, Paola.** La autonomía revolucionaria de la Real Audiencia de Charcas hacia 1809: cimientos de un Estado independiente. Sucre, Bolivia: Casa de la Libertad; La Paz: Fundación Cultural, Banco Central de Bolivia, 2009. 375 p.: bibl.

This well-researched and abundantly documented study focuses on the Real Audiencia de Charcas. The book presents a detailed account of the institutional history of the Audiencia, including the political and social relationships of regional and local elites. Additionally, the author analyzes the circulation of books, enlightened ideas, and the intellectual and political ideas that influenced the Audiencia in the eve of the wars of independence. [FP]

999 **Suárez Saavedra, Fernando.** El placer de los placeres. Tomo I, Historia de la sexualidad en Bolivia desde la época prehispánica hasta fines de la colonia. Sucre, Bolivia: Fernando Suárez Saavedra, 2011. 1 v.: bibl., index.

This study examines sexuality and sex life in the Viceroyalty of Peru from the 16th to the 18th centuries. The work provides an overview of sex life and sexuality among Incas, Aymaras, and peoples of eastern Bolivia, among other groups. Marriage, prostitution, polygamy, and incest are topics of individual chapters. The author also examines religious practices and ideas about sex, sodomy, love spells, slavery and sexuality, and chastity. [FP]

1000 **Vhiestrox Herbas, Herland.** Extensión de las provincias de Santa Cruz en la colonia. Santa Cruz de la Sierra, Bolivia: Fondo Editorial del Gobierno Autónomo Municipal de Santa Cruz de la Sierra, 2015. 120 p.: bibl., ill., maps (1 folded).

This study provides a military historical and geographical account of the process of occupation and territorialization of the province of Santa Cruz from the colonial period to the early 19th century. The book contains a plethora of maps on different periods of occupation of the region. [FP]

CHILE

1001 **Albornoz, María Eugenia.** Experiencias de conflicto: subjetividades, cuerpos y sentimientos en Chile siglos XVIII y XIX. Santiago: Acto Editores, 2015. 174 p.: bibl., ill. (Colección Traspasos)

Three presentations originally given by the author in French translated into Spanish that discuss the politics and experiences of gender, race, and sentiment in Santiago, Chile, from 1739 to 1860. Using slander lawsuits and other legal records, the first chapter uncovers the complicated and contradictory ways women of different social classes use racialized terms like "mulata" to insult and affirm differences among themselves. The second uses similar sources to uncover how slander cases offer instances of the rhetoric and expression of love and affection between couples separated by distance. Such reflections on well-worn judicial sources provide a thought-provoking meditation on the unstable and contested meanings of casta categories and gendered relations in urban Chile. [JZ]

1002 Cartes Montory, Armando. Un gobierno de los pueblos . . . : relaciones provinciales en la Independencia de Chile. Valparaíso, Chile: Ediciones Universitarias de Valparaíso, Pontificia Universidad Católica de Valparaíso, 2014. 415 p.: bibl.

Recasts Chile's independence process from the point of view of the provinces of Coquimbo, Concepción, Valdivia, and Chiloé. Joins a growing body of scholarship questioning the celebratory, and largely capital city—and elite-centered, patriotic histories of nationhood. Places the Chilean experiences in hemispheric and Atlantic contexts of Hispanic liberalism and crises of Spanish rule while also challenging the overwhelming focus on Santiago-based patriot leaders. Instead, the author describes the dynamic political traditions of provincial actors, ranging from middling classes to autonomous indigenous Mapuche, in towns, cities, and their cabildos (councils) that shaped the reception of pro-independence and pro-Spanish attitudes. Challenges the idea of Chile's uniquely stable and rapid consolidation of constitutional rule and national identity by showing how they were debated, negotiated, and fought over within and between provinces. [JZ]

1003 Gaune, Rafael. Descifrando el Flandes indiano: adaptación misionera, escritura anticuaria y conversión religiosa en la obra del jesuita Diego de Rosales, en Chile, siglo XVII. (CLAHR, 2:3, Summer 2014, p. 317–351)

Critical reinterpretation of the original characterization of colonial Chile as the "Flanders of the Indies," or flandes indiano. Instead of a simple geographic analogy used to capture the frequent and tenacious Mapuche indigenous resistance to the Spanish conquest, the author suggests Jesuit Diego de Rosales (1605–77) coined the term to express the Company of Jesus' desire to understand and adapt to non-Catholic cultures in order to eventually settle and convert them. Through a close reading of Book I of Rosales' famous Historia general de Chile, Flandes indiano and the public and private catalogs of the Jesuits in Chile, the study uncovers how the Jesuit practices of accomodatio and antiquitates infused Rosales' analogy and his approach to the Mapuche. Resonates with other studies of the Spanish "spiritual conquest," frontiers and missions, and interethnic exchange in Asia, the Americas, Europe, and Africa. [JZ]

1004 González Undurraga, Carolina. Esclavos y esclavas demandando justicia: Chile, 1740–1823: documentación judicial por carta de libertad y papel de venta. Santiago: Editorial Universitaria, 2014. 293 p.: bibl., 2 ill., index. (Imagen de Chile)

Transcribed and edited collection of slave petitions for freedom and sale from 18th-century Chile until abolition in 1823. Includes 50 legal cases found in Chile's National Archive divided into four sections: demands for justice by enslaved men, women, families, and married couples. In addition to presenting an overview of recent scholarship, the introductory essay provides a helpful guide to transcription and a marvelous fine-grained exposition of the mechanics of how slaves accessed the legal system. While primarily focused on urban cases and domestic slaves in Santiago courts (78 percent), these rich documents should be of value to those interested in recent directions in studies of transatlantic slavery in the Americas and the Atlantic World such as gender and freedom, free womb laws, the legal identities, discourses, and knowledge of enslaved men and women, and kinship and families. [JZ]

1005 López-Chávez, Celia. Epics of empire and frontier: Alonso de Ercilla and Gaspar Pérez de Villagrá as Spanish colonial chroniclers. Norman: University of Oklahoma Press, 2016. 308 p.: bibl., ill., index, maps.

Comparative literary-historical analysis of Alonso de Ercilla's La araucana and Gaspár de Villagra's Historia de la Nueva

México, two epic poems written on the northern and southern margins of the Spanish Empire in the aftermath of the conquest of Chile and the suppression of the Acoma Pueblo revolt in Nueva México (1599). Argues that a lack of historical context on the writing of epic poetry has led literary scholars of Spain's Golden Age to focus on chroniclers and dismiss epic poetry as unfaithful descriptions of historical reality. A close reading of both poems (with passages in their original Spanish and in translation) illuminates the violent and textual tensions between observations framed by Iberian legal and literary traditions and global monarchy, and physical and cultural spaces controlled by indigenous peoples resisting Spanish imperialism. [JZ]

1006 Los parlamentos hispano-mapuches, 1593–1803: textos fundamentales. Edición de José Manuel Zavala. Con la colaboración de Cristian Lineros Pérez et al. Temuco, Chile: Ediciones Universidad Católica de Temuco, 2015. 493 p.: bibl., ill., index, maps.

Most complete and extensive transcribed compilation of the *actas* and *relaciones* of *parlamentos*, or diplomatic treaty-making encounters between the Spanish and Mapuche peoples, which took place in southern Chile and western Río de la Plata (Argentina) during the colonial period. Introductory essay outlines the origins and definition of *parlamentos*, ethnohistorical debates over their meaning and interpretation, as well as the semantic and politico-cultural genesis and fusion of indigenous negotiation and Iberian legal traditions. Contributes to growing scholarly interest in Spanish borderlands and frontiers, autonomous indigenous peoples, and the contested meanings of colonial pacts and vassalage by making accessible in a single volume these fascinating traces of interethnic diplomacy. Provides students and scholars a wealth of primary sources to analyze and consider Mapuche people's creative rituals and responses to Spanish colonialism. [JZ]

1007 Plaza Salgado, Camila Belén. Brujos, indios y bestias: imaginarios de lo maléfico y marginalidad en el Reino de Chile, 1693–1793. (*Front. Hist.*, 20:1, enero/junio 2015, p. 124–149, bibl.)

Interprets how Spanish Catholic imagery and language of evil as an explanation for wrongdoing in 18th-century criminal and civil cases in central Chile continued to define Mapuche peoples as others in a time of political and territorial instability. Elucidates how despite Chile never having established a Tribunal of the Inquisition, the Real Audiencia still heard cases which called into question the Catholic faith of the accusers and accused. Instances of Mapuche claiming to be good Catholics and non-Mapuche claiming to have been bewitched by indigenous people reveal that the language of Christianity, witchcraft, and sorcery served to police the boundaries of social and cultural inclusion and exclusion in central Chile. [JZ]

1008 Undurraga Schüler, Verónica. Los rostros del honor: normas culturales y estrategias de promoción social en Chile colonial, siglo XVIII. Santiago: Editorial Universitaria: DIBAM, Dirección de Bibliotecas, Archivos y Museos: Centro de Investigaciones Diego Barros Arana, 2013. 428 p.: bibl., facsims., ill. (Colección Sociedad y cultura; LIII)

Critical legal study of the meaning of honor in 18th-century Santiago. Uncovers a "polyphonic register of honor" with competing definitions and actors, such as artisans, merchants, scribes, and peons, claiming this organizing principle of colonial life as much as their elite counterparts. Also reveals how women could claim honor for themselves and be part of men's honor claims. Provides an important case for those interested in comparative or hemispheric questions of gender, honor, and law in the colonial Americas. Rigorous examination of judicial documents related to *injurias y calumnias*, *riñas, lesiones físicas*, and *homicidio* and *expedientes* regarding marriage, patrimony, and wills found in Chile's National Archive. A table derived from the document appears in an appendix. [JZ]

1009 Urbina Carrasco, María Ximena. La sospecha de ingleses en el extremo sur de Chile, 1669–1683: actitudes imperiales y locales como consecuencia de la expedición de John Narborough. (*Magallania/Punta Arenas*, 44:1, 2016, p. 15–40, bibl., ill.)

This study examines local, continental, and Atlantic repercussions of an English expedition to the southern shores of Chile during the late 17th century. The author provides a fresh perspective on the rivalry between the British and Spanish in the South Pacific instead of the Caribbean or North America. Aptly demonstrates the strategic importance of the Straits of Magellan and the defensive fortifications in Chiloé and Valdivia to Madrid, the Viceroyalty of Peru, and the Captaincy General of Chile, despite southern Chile's geographic isolation and its lack of mineral wealth and indigenous labor. The author's previous work on Osorno allows her to point to the important intersection between naval history and ethnohistory by revealing the Spanish fear of unconquered Mapuche-Huilliche serving as a Fifth Column in aid of their rivals. [JZ]

1010 Valenzuela Márquez, Jaime. Fiesta, rito y política: del Chile borbónico al republicano. Santiago: DIBAM Dirección Bibliotecas, Archivos y Museos, Centro de Investigaciones Diego Barros Arana, 2014. 469 p.: bibl., ill. (Colección Sociedad y cultura; LIX)

The author's previous study of Hapsburg political and religious festivals in Chile extended to how Bourbon reformers and pro-independence patriots sought legitimacy during the last century of Spanish rule in Chile. This work contributes to critical studies of the Bourbon Reforms in Latin America by looking at how Baroque rituals, public ceremonies, and visual culture continued to be central to local rule (military, administrative, and ecclesiastical) despite the enlightened aspirations of the Crown. A close analysis of sources ranging from protocols for public ceremonies, paintings, and institutional correspondence (reproduced in the text and in an extended appendix), shows efforts to sideline the Church and its rituals at the imperial level belied the importance of such cultural practices for the legitimacy and prestige of local actors and subjects. [JZ]

1011 Venegas Espinoza, Fernando. De Tralca-mawida a Santa Juana: despliegue histórico de una localidad en la frontera del BíoBío, 1550–1980. Valparaíso, Chile: Ediciones Universitarias de Valparaíso, Pontificia Universidad Católica de Valparaíso, 2014. 179 p., 5 unnumbered pages: bibl., ill.

A micro-historical analysis of the Spanish fort of Santa Juana, founded in the early 17th century on the southern shores of the Bío-Bío River. Like the site's original Mapuche name (Tralca-mawida, or "thunder mountain"), explores the fort as an important locus for understanding precolumbian culture, interethnic politics, conquest, and colonization along Chile's southern frontier. Since it was produced as part of a Chilean Ministerio de Obras Públicas project to emphasize the patrimonial significance of Santa Juana, the work provides a helpful introduction to Mapuche-Spanish relations, indigenous social organization, and the economic and political development of the region up to the late 20th century. Also includes reproductions of architectural sketches, maps, and photographs of the area. [JZ]

RIO DE LA PLATA

1012 Aguerre Core, Fernando. Los últimos españoles: autonomía y lealtad a la Corona en el Montevideo insurgente (1800–1815). Montevideo: Librería Linardi y Risso, 2012. 235 p.: bibl., ill.

This well-researched study investigates the causes of Montevideo's loyalism towards Spain in the early phase of the war of independence in Rio de la Plata. The author suggests that commercial interests and a large number of bureaucrats and other officers of the Spanish Empire ensured the city's elites' loyalty to Spain. The book examines the trajectory of the Spanish elites in Montevideo under the different political regimes from 1808 to 1825. This volume is a synthesis of previous works on the wars of independence by the same author with the addition of new sections and new insights based on additional sources. The author draws on administrative and privates records published in Uruguay, and on manuscripts from archives in Spain. [FP]

1013 Arteaga, Juan José. Conflicto y jesuitas en las fronteras del imperio: las misiones guaraníes. Segunda edición. Lima: Ediciones El Virrey, 2015. 386 p.: bibl., ill.

This study examines the role of the Jesuits as agents of empire from a transnational perspective. The author focuses on the period around the Treaty of Madrid (1750) until its nullification in 1761 in Rio de la Plata. The book explores the expedition to demarcate limits between Spanish and Portuguese dominions that brought to the region relevant authorities of both Spanish and Portuguese empires (Marques de Valdelirios and Gomes Freire). The monograph examines in detail the use of Guarani troops by the Spanish Empire against Colonia del Sacramento and the personal networks of governor Pedro de Cevallos. [FP]

1014 Ashwell, Washington. Historia económica del Paraguay: de sus orígenes al gobierno de Carlos Antonio López (1536–1862). Asunción: Servilibro, 2015. 248 p.: bibl.

This work offers an overview of Paraguay's economic development from colonial times to the late 19th century. The author examines different periods of Paraguay's political history and contrasts the country's economic situation with different economic ideologies, such as physiocracy, economic liberalism, and economic nationalism. Early Spanish colonization, the independence period, and the decades leading to the War of the Triple Alliance are analyzed in detail. Connections to Argentina and Brazil are highlighted. The book is written for a general audience. [FP]

1015 Avellaneda, Mercedes. Guaraníes, criollos y jesuitas: luchas de poder en las Revoluciones Comuneras del Paraguay: siglos XVII y XVIII. Asunción: Academia Paraguaya de la Historia: Editorial Tiempo de Historia, 2014. 297 p.: bibl., ill.

This social history of the conflicts between Jesuits and the cabildo of Asunción in the 17th and 18th centuries has a particular focus on two colonial insurrections against Jesuits in the province: one in the 17th century (1642–50) and the Comuneros Rebellion (1724–35). This well-researched work provides extensive information on indigenous and Jesuit leadership. The book presents maps, tables with demographic data, and censuses of 1735 Pueblos del Paraná (based on Nusdorffer's information).

1016 Boneo, Martín Francisco and Juan Cruz Jaime. El intendente olvidado de Buenos Aires: biografía de D. Martín Boneo y Villalonga. Buenos Aires: Letemendia Casa Editora, 2013. 264 p.: bibl., color ill.

This biographical study investigates Martín Boneo y Villalonga, a Spanish bureaucrat and naturalist who was involved in urban planning, cartographic expeditions, and colonial administration in Buenos Aires. The authors argue that Boneo's work has similarities to the works of Azara and Humboldt. Includes colored plates, maps, reproductions of colonial paintings, and numerous transcribed primary sources. [FP]

1017 Bracco, Diego. Con las armas en la mano: Charrúas, Guenoa-Minuanos y Guaraníes. Montevideo: Planeta, 2013. 224 p.: bibl., ill., maps.

This work provides an overview of indigenous groups during the colonial period in present-day Uruguay. There is a major emphasis on indigenous military participation in conflicts both in favor of and against Spanish forces. The author argues for the importance of indigenous military failures and successes in shaping the pace of colonization, Spanish military strategies, and the emergence of modern nations. Includes maps, historical images, and transcribed primary sources. [FP]

1018 Chiaramonte, José Carlos. Raíces históricas del federalismo latinoamericano. Buenos Aires: Sudamericana, 2016. 314 p.: bibl.

This work represents a significant contribution to the political history of Latin America through the examination of political ideas and projects centered around federalism. Based on solid documentary evidence and in dialogue with an expansive historiography, the author presents this magisterial work comparing different versions of federalist ideas and constitutions. The study transcends mere comparison between federalism in Argentina and the US by mapping the interconnections, different regional adaptions, and diverse courses of development of federalist ideas circulating in the Atlantic. [FP]

1019 Combatir al otro: el Río de la Plata en épocas de antagonismos: 1776–1830. Coordinación de Marcela V. Tejerina y Carmen S. Cantera. Bahía Blanca, Argentina: EdiUNS, 2016. 263 p.: bibl. (Serie

Extensión. Colección Ciencias Sociales y Humanidades)

This edited volume examines alterity in Río de la Plata, including questions of gender, imperial competition, and conflicting ideologies, during the late colonial period and the wars of independence. The authors focus on the Portuguese presence in the Río de la Plata, the British invasions, the penetration of liberal ideas in the region and the ensuing debates on the press, the role of women during revolutionary times, and the role of religious institutions in times of war. [FP]

1020 Cruz, Enrique Normando. Del fuerte a la hacienda: historia de una frontera colonial (Virreinato del Río de la Plata, siglos XVIII y XIX). San Salvador de Jujuy, Argentina: Purmamarka Ediciones, 2014. 145 p.: bibl., ill.

This work presents a social and economic history of the city of San Salvador de Jujuy in colonial Salta. The book examines the foundation of the colonial settlement by Spaniards and the changes that occurred in the 18th and 19th centuries when colonists pushed the frontier further. Indigenous rebellions, military expansion, and commercial development are at the center of this well-researched monograph that draws on administrative and ecclesiastic records from different archives in Argentina and Spain. [FP]

1021 Estruch, Dolores. El ejercicio del poder en el Jujuy colonial: enlaces y tensiones entre la jurisdicción civil y la eclesiástica: siglo XVI–XVIII. Buenos Aires: La Bicicleta Ediciones, 2017. 305 p.: bibl. (Colección Hipótesis)

This work presents a social history of power in colonial Jujuy. The well-researched monograph explores the building of the jurisdiction of San Salvador de Jujuy and the legal conflicts derived from it. The author analyzes the relationships between secular and religious authorities, local political participation (*vecinos*), and the establishment of colonial military power in the region. The book draws on sources from archives in Spain, Bolivia, and Argentina. [FP]

1022 Fanchin, Ana. El hogar, la familia y las alianzas: San Juan de la Frontera (siglos XVII–XVIII). Rosario, Argentina: Prohistoria Ediciones, 2015. 279 p.: bibl., ill., tables.

This work provides a social history of the border region of San Juan de la Frontera in the eastern Andes in current-day Argentina during the 18th century. Family networks and dynamics, as well as inter-racial dynamics, are at the center of the study. The book includes tables with demographic data for whites, blacks, and indigenous peoples. [FP]

1023 Fucé, Pablo. El poder de lo efímero: historia del ceremonial español en Montevideo (1730–1808). Montevideo: Linardi y Risso, 2014. 445 p.: bibl.

This study examines rituals and ceremony in colonial Rio de la Plata, with an emphasis in Montevideo. The author discusses the history of the ephemeral and nonverbal rituals and symbols in the life of colonial cities. Based on administrative, ecclesiastical, and private records from archives in Spain, Uruguay and Argentina, the book focuses on rituals connected to political ceremonies, especially the monarch, local authorities, and ties of loyalty. The work also includes rituals involving indigenous peoples (Minuanes). [FP]

1024 Los grupos subalternos en el nordeste del Virreinato del Río de la Plata. Compilación de María Laura Salinas y Hugo Beck. Rosario, Argentina: Prohistoria Ediciones, 2015. 271 p.: bibl., ill. (Colección Universidad; 45)

This edited volume includes nine essays that examine subaltern groups in Corrientes, Paraguay, Misiones, and parts of Brazil during the 18th and 19th centuries. The chapters are well written and well researched; the authors focus on indigenous participation in the labor force in cities and rural areas, indigenous participation in the military, African-descended people in Paraguay, and the relationship between spatial transformations and subaltern groups. The volume presents several theoretical articles on the history of subaltern groups in Latin America.

1025 Gullo, Marcelo. La historia oculta: la lucha del pueblo argentino por su independencia del imperio inglés. Buenos Aires: Editorial Biblos, 2013. 221 p.: bibl. (Historia)

This revisionist essay aimed at a general audience examines the economic influence of Great Britain in the history of Argentina. The author traces the origin of British influence to the colonial period and denounces the alliances of regional oligarchies and foreign interests. The book argues that since the 19th century the Argentine people have resisted different forms of British economic and military imperialism. [FP]

1026 **Güttner, Carlos Hermann.** Pedrito Ríos, el tamborcito de Tacuarí. Buenos Aires: Ediciones Fabro, 2014. 239 p.: bibl., ill.

This study focuses on the historical, literary, and official memory of Pedro Ríos, a popular character from Corrientes. Pedro Ríos was identified with both Corrientes regional identity and Argentine national identity. The author examines poems, myths, oral histories, legislative projects to honor Ríos' memory, and existing monuments in honor of Pedro Ríos. [FP]

1027 **The improbable conquest: sixteenth-century letters from the Río de la Plata.** Edited and translated by Pablo García Loaeza and Victoria L. Garrett. University Park: The Pennsylvania State University Press, 2015. 121 p.: bibl., index. (Latin American originals; 9)

The 9th volume of the Latin American Originals series presents letters from Spaniards who attempted to found a colony in the Río de la Plata estuary. The book presents eight documents written between 1537 and 1556 revealing the difficulties, persistent efforts, and failures of colonizers in the region. The volume includes letters written by Pedro de Mendoza, Isabel de Guevara, Domingo de Irala, Francisco Galán, Juan Pavón, Francisco de Andrada, Martín Gonzáles, and Domingo Martínez. [FP]

1028 **Luzuriaga, Juan Carlos.** La reconquista de Buenos Aires: el cenit de Montevideo colonial. Montevideo: Editorial Planeta, S.A., 2017. 278 p., 8 unnumbered pages of plates: bibl., ill. (chiefly color).

This work presents a military history of the British invasions of Buenos Aires and Montevideo (1806–07). The author examines in detail the movement of forces and military strategies in Buenos Aires and Montevideo, political factions, and demographics of military forces involved in the fighting. The appendix provides tables of number of troops, wounded soldiers, and the death toll among Spanish and British forces. [FP]

Massot, Vicente Gonzalo. Los dilemas de la independencia. See item **393**.

1029 **Molina, Raúl A.** La Ciudad de la Santísima Trinidad escondía al diablo en sus entrañas: crónica de los primeros cincuenta años de Buenos Aires. Buenos Aires: Tejuelo Editores: Instituto Argentino de Ciencias Genealógicas, 2015. 359 p.: bibl., ill., index.

This is the first-time publication of a posthumous work by Raúl Alejandro de Molina (1897–1973), portraying the first 50 years of the colonization of Buenos Aires. The author presents chronicles of daily-life events involving historical characters in Buenos Aires during the late 16th and early 17th centuries. Topics range from contraband trade to local politics, to poetry and entertainment. The book contains illustrations by the author. [FP]

Morán Ramos, Luis Daniel. Batallas por la legitimidad: la prensa de Lima y de Buenos Aires durante las guerras de independencia. See item **981**.

1030 **O'Donnell, Pacho.** 1815: la primera declaración de independencia argentina. Buenos Aires: Aguilar, 2015. 264 p.: bibl.

This study of the years surrounding Argentina's declaration of independence has a particular focus on the conflicts in the Banda Oriental and the political relationship between José Gervasio Artigas and the leaders of Buenos Aires. The text, suitable for general audiences, has nationalistic undertones. The author examines the influence of Spain and Brazil in Rio de la Plata, and offers biographical accounts of independence leaders such as Artigas, Rivera, Rondeau, Sarratea, Belgrano, among others. Good introductory reading for a nonspecialist audience. [FP]

1031 **El otro Belgrano: lejos del mito, cerca de una visión: escritos y documentos.** Buenos Aires: Editorial Museo Archivo Raggio, 2015. 285 p.: bibl. (Colección Antorchas)

Five essays from historians and sociologists re-examine the political, intellectual, and social life of Manuel Belgrano. The contributions focus on Belgrano's family life, his late colonial career, his participation in the wars of independence, and his trajectory as a political leader. The book includes several transcribed documents, such as a marriage record, Belgrano's will, and Belgrano's essay "Causas de la destrucción de la conservación y engradecimiento de la naciones" published on 19 May 1810 in the *Correo de Comercio*. [FP]

Los parlamentos hispano-mapuches, 1593–1803: textos fundamentales. See item **1006**.

1032 Pieroni, Agustín. El virreino y los virreyes. Buenos Aires: Editorial Dunken, 2015. 357 p.: bibl.

This work presents a political and social history of the area of the Viceroyalty of Rio de la Plata. The author includes a description of economic activities (mining, shipping, farming), population (including women, enslaved Africans, indigenous peoples), cities, and biographic information on all of the viceroys of Rio de la Plata. The work is based on mostly published primary and secondary sources. [FP]

1033 Pigna, Felipe. La vida por la patria: una biografía de Mariano Moreno. Buenos Aires: Planeta, 2017. 442 p.: bibl.

This work presents a biography of Mariano Moreno, one of the main characters of the early revolutionary period in Buenos Aires. The essay, written for a general audience, is mostly based on published primary and secondary sources. The author aims to dissipate the myths surrounding the character of Moreno by closely examining his familial life, his intellectual influences, and the polemics surrounding his translation of Rousseau's *Social Contract*, his own "Representacion de los Hacendados," and the "Plan de Operaciones." This solid introductory book is useful for both scholars of the period and neophytes to the topic of the wars of independence in Rio de la Plata. [FP]

1034 Pozzi Albornoz, Ismael R. 1807 ataque a Colonia del Sacramento y combate del arroyo San Pedro: bautismo de fuego de las milicias criollas. Buenos Aires: Edivérn, 2014. 170 p.: bibl., ill.

This work presents a military history of the British invasion of Rio de la Plata utilizing the understudied case of the battles surrounding Colonia do Sacramento. Based on British and Spanish sources, the author provides a detailed examination of the military tactics, the movement of people, and the motivation of the main British and Spanish officers in the Banda Oriental. He also examines in detail the trajectories of Spaniard Francisco Xavier de Elio and Brit Theodore Dennis Pack. The book contains 20 additional transcribed primary sources from the Archivo General de la Nación (Buenos Aires) and the Museo Mitre. [FP]

1035 Quinteros, Guillermo O. La política del matrimonio: novios, amantes y familias ante la justicia: Buenos Aires, 1776–1860. Rosario, Argentina: Prohistoria Ediciones, 2015. 235 p.: bibl. (Colección Historia argentina; 27)

This study examines familial conflicts in 18th- and 19th-century Buenos Aires. The author pays special attention to the new policies enacted by the Crown regarding "undesirable" marriages, how the new laws were received by different social groups, and the challenges of authorities in applying the reforms. Specific chapters examine the relationship between state and family, violence within families, marriages, and love and desire. [FP]

1036 Roulet, Florencia. Huincas en tierra de indios: mediaciones e identidades en los relatos de viajeros tardocoloniales. Buenos Aires: Eudeba, 2016. 438 p.: bibl., ill., index. (Temas. Historia)

This work examines travel narratives from the early 19th century in Patagonia and the southern Andes (current-day Argentina and Chile). The book includes information on Pampas, Tehuelches and Huilliches, Pehuenches, and Araucanian indigenous groups. The author provides information on demography, gender, culture, and geographical descriptions. Includes transcriptions of the "Diario del viaje de Justo Molina de Chillán," among other primary sources. [FP]

1037 Salas, Alberto Mario. Crónica y diario de Buenos Aires, 1806–1807. Buenos Aires: Ediciones Biblioteca Nacional, 2013. 2 v.: bibl., ill. (Colección Reediciones y antologias; 25)

This work offers a historical chronicle of colonial Buenos Aires before and after the English invasions (1806–07). Social, economic, and political history are interspersed with daily episodes, colonial entertainment, and religious life. This is a revised and extended edition of the work published as *Diario de Buenos Aires, 1806 y 1807* in 1981 (see *HLAS 44:2778*). This posthumous edition was produced based on the author's unpublished papers. [FP]

1038 **Sambrizzi, Alejandro.** Ojos de plata: invasiones al Río de la Plata antes del ataque inglés de 1806–1807. Buenos Aires: Alejandro Sambrizzi, 2014. 134 p.: bibl.

This work offers an overview of foreign invasions in Rio de la Plata during the period of Spanish colonialism. The author describes early British, French, Dane, and Dutch incursions in the region from the 16th to the early 19th century. Includes material on Francis Drake among other privateers. [FP]

1039 **Sánchez Labrador, José.** As artes de curar em um manuscrito jesuítico inédito do Setecentos: o Paraguay natural ilustrado do padre José Sánchez Labrador (1771–1776). Organização de Eliane Cristina Deckmann Fleck. São Leopoldo, Brazil: Editora Oikos Ltda.: Editora Unisinos, 2015. 590 p.: bibl., ill. (Coleção Estudos Históricos Latino-Americanos—EHILA; 21)

This work provides a transcription of the medical treatise "El Paraguay natural ilustrado" written in Paraguay between 1771 and 1776 by Jesuit priest José Sánchez Labrador with a critical introduction by Eliane Fleck. The book presents descriptions of natural phenomena, landscapes, and animals (quadrupeds, fish, birds, and amphibians). Includes scientific descriptions of plants with consideration about their economic potential. Of interest for historians of science, medicine, and colonialism. [FP]

1040 **Seminário Escravidão, Fronteiras e Relações Internacionais no Império do Brasil, *Universidade do Rio de Janeiro, 2011*.** As fronteiras da escravidão e da liberdade no sul da América. Organização de Keila Grinberg. Textos de Carla Menegat *et al.* Rio de Janeiro: FAPERJ: 7Letras, 2013. 228 p.: bibl., ill., maps.

This edited volume examines the social and political dynamics of slavery and freedom in the 19th-century Brazil-Uruguay borderlands. Authors from Brazil and Uruguay examine legal disputes over slaves who crossed borders in search of freedom, illegal enslavement of free blacks in Uruguay, among other diplomatic and legal disputes between Uruguayan and Brazilian citizens and authorities. Includes several graphs and tables with economic, legal, and demographic data. [FP]

1041 **Seminario Internacional Diálogos entre Brasil y Argentina: Historia e Historiografía, *Mariana, Brazil, 2013*.** Historia, poder e instituciones: diálogos entre Brasil y Argentina. Coordinación de María Elena Barral e Marco Antonio Silveira. Rosario, Argentina: Prohistoria Ediciones: Universidad Nacional de Rosario, 2015. 267 p.: bibl. (Colección Universidad; 44)

The conference papers in this edited volume are centered on the question of power and institutions in Brazil and Rio de la Plata. Authors from Brazil, Uruguay, Argentina present well-researched case studies examining the social and political role of institutions such as the Church, the colonial state, civic organizations, the national state, and welfare systems. The book's coverage spans the 16th to the 20th centuries. Case studies include religious institutions, warfare, political institutions in indigenous settlements, rural militias in Spanish Rio de la Plata, educational policies in 19th-century Brazil, and labor unions in the national period. [FP]

1042 **Smietniansky, Silvina.** Ritual, tiempo y poder: una aproximación antropológica a las instituciones del gobierno colonial (Gobernación del Tucumán, siglos XVII y XVIII). Rosario, Argentina: Prohistoria Ediciones, 2013. 299 p.: bibl. (Historia & cultura; 9)

This well-written and thoroughly researched monograph examines the social construction of institutions of power in 17th- and 18th-century Tucumán. The author deploys an anthropological framework to understand the construction of imperial institutions, religious authority, and social hierarchy. Analysis of rituals surrounding political life, church life, and family life are at the center of this study. The author utilized ecclesiastical records, wills and probate records, and administrative and legal sources. [FP]

1043 Souza, Lécio Gomes de. Bacia do Paraguai: geografia e história. Vol. 2–3. 2a. edição. Campo Grande, Brazil: Instituto Histórico e Geográfico de Mato Grosso do Sul, 2012. 2 v.: bibl., ill. (Série Memória sul-mato-grossense)

These volumes offer a geographic description of areas within the Paraná River basin, including parts of Brazil, Paraguay, and Argentina. The author presents extensive data on rivers, soils, plants, and a history of occupation of the region. Includes many transcriptions of primary sources describing the region (mostly from the period of the War of the Triple Alliance 1864–70). For a review of vol. 1, see item 1627. [FP]

1044 Territorios de lo cotidiano, siglos XVI–XX: del antiguo Virreinato del Perú a la Argentina contemporánea. Coordinación de Mónica Ghirardi. Rosario, Argentina: Prohistoria Ediciones, 2014. 306 p.: bibl., ill. (Colección Actas; 28)

This compilation of articles examines multiple facets of the daily lives of common subjects in colonial Peru and Rio de la Plata. The authors analyze the motivations, passions, suffering, and social aspirations of plebeians in colonial Spanish America. The essays focus on the daily life of subaltern groups in Upper Peru, Buenos Aires, and Paraguay. Studies of family life and loyalty in Buenos Aires and Catamarca, slavery in the Royal Mint of Potosí, daily life in indigenous towns, questions of order and disorder, and identity formation, among other topics, make of this book an essential addition to the social history of colonial Rio de la Plata. [FP]

1045 Vecinos y pasantes: la movilidad en la colonia. Dirección de Susana Frías. Textos de Ana Teresa Fanchín et al. Estudio crítico a cargo de Gladys Massé. Buenos Aires: Academia Nacional de la Historia, 2013. 182 p.: bibl., ill. (Serie Estudios de población; 7)

This edited volume examines physical and social mobility in colonial Rio de la Plata from the 17th century to the early 19th century. Chapters look at patterns of migration and marriage, as well as ecclesiastical, indigenous, and Spanish settlers' networks. Specific studies focus on the regions of Areco, Corrientes, San Juan, Buenos Aires, and Banda Oriental. [FP]

1046 Villagrán San Millán, Martín R. Ejército y milicias de Buenos Aires a Tumusla, 1776–1825. Salta, Argentina: Fondo Editorial, Secretaría de Cultura de la Provincia de Salta, 2015. 2 v.: bibl., ill., maps.

This study examines the different military forces in Rio de la Plata during the viceregal and revolutionary periods. The multivolume work includes demographic data, along with economic and logistical considerations. Using military and administrative sources, the author presents a wealth of primary sources and data regarding military conscription, warfare strategies, and equipment. Includes transcriptions of primary sources, images, and maps. [FP]

1047 ¿Y el pueblo dónde está?: Contribuciones para una historia popular de la revolución de independencia en el Río de la Plata en el siglo XIX rioplatense. Edición de Raúl O. Fradkin. Edición corregida y aumentada. Buenos Aires: Prometeo Libros, 2015. 252 p.: bibl. (Colección Historia argentina)

This compilation of eight articles examines the significance of popular political participation in late colonial and revolutionary Rio de la Plata. The authors present theoretical discussions on the historiography of popular classes. Political participation of plebeians in revolutionary Buenos Aires, slaves' and freed-blacks' politics in Cuyo, popular groups in the Banda Oriental and in Salta, and indigenous diplomacy in the Pampas and Patagonia are the subjects of well-researched case studies. For a review of the 2008 edition, see *HLAS 68:1554*. [FP]

19th and 20th Centuries
Venezuela

PETER LINDER, *Professor of History, New Mexico Highlands University*

VENEZUELA'S ONGOING POLITICAL AND ECONOMIC crises continue to deepen. Amid severe political divisions, the economy faces catastrophic levels of inflation and ongoing scarcities of basic economic needs. Recently published historical works reflect this deplorable situation to a considerable degree. Most of the works reviewed in this section have a political focus, and many draw explicit or implicit connections between Venezuela's historical past and the conflictive present. The historiography of 19th-century Venezuela remains a focus of much of the work reviewed, particularly the era of independence and its immediate aftermath. Some publications explore diverse aspects of the life of Simón Bolívar and the ways in which contending interests have utilized his image since the 19th century. Historians have paid somewhat less attention to other members of the revolutionary generation. Several recent studies attempt to reimagine independence or analyze it from new perspectives and angles, at times while questioning the nature of independence itself. The 20th century remains another primary focus of recent research. Of particular interest has been the exploration of the post-World War II era, especially the transitions from military rule to electoral democracy and the politics of the Cold War in Venezuela. Fewer studies deal with regional or local history than in previous volumes; most works reviewed for this volume focus on national issues. Still, a limited number of intriguing studies of local history, environmental history, and the history of natural catastrophes invite analysis. National political divisions color historical research and writing. Several authors seek to identify the origins of the nation's current polarization, while the professionalization of historical writing noted in previous *HLAS* introductory essays continues apace.

    The era of independence remains a major—perhaps the major—focus of historical writing since the last *HLAS* volume. Many works deal with the process of independence and the end of Spanish colonial rule. In one useful study, Manuel Alberto Donís Ríos analyzes the roles that clerics played in the constituent congresses of the revolutionary decade, exploring their motives and the results of their participation, demonstrating that many ecclesiastics participated fully in the politics of the era (item **1060**). Several works also examine the roles that individual *criollos* played; most of those profiled were civilians, rather than soldiers; this focus represents something of a departure, as military participants have traditionally received more attention. The emphasis on the events and politics of independence informs many recent publications. One valuable work presents a new edition of the memoir of Dr. José Francisco Heredia, an *oidor* of the Audiencia of Caracas, a staunch royalist, and a defender of the prerogatives of the Audiencia against patriots and royalist military commanders alike (item **1064**). A new edition of a classic study profiles peninsular physician and politician Francisco Isnardi (item **1086**). In addition, a collection of biographies of clerics and civilians coordinated by Jean Carlos Brizuela and José Alberto Olivar demonstrates that debates and discussions in civil society and the institutions of colonial administration in Venezuela's capital and elsewhere throughout the region preceded the military rebellion (item **1069**). In a collection of essays edited by Jorge Bracho *et al.*, contributors explore the origins of republicanism in the 19th century, suggesting that the contradictions inherent in republicanism extended far beyond the achievement of Venezuelan independence (item **1077**). Two books by Francisco Alfaro Pareja examine the process of independence and its aftermath; one concentrates on "the hidden history" of negotiation and agreements as opposed to an exclusive focus on the military conflicts of the era (item **1048**), and the other characterizes the struggles for independence as "a process of searching for peace" (item **1049**). Rogelio Altez analyzes the rise and fall of the First Republic (1810–12) and concludes that the outbreak of a movement in favor of Venezuelan independence was a reaction to the declining efficacy of colonial rule and institutions (item **1050**).

Simón Bolívar remains the subject of much work dealing with independence. Many recent studies probe the Liberator's origins and early life, seeking an understanding of his later career. A pair of recent works explore Bolívar's personal and intellectual formation. The first is a collection of essays profiling Simón Rodríguez, the tutor of the Liberator in his youth, focusing on his pedagogical approach and its relevance for both the history of education in Venezuela and contemporary educational issues in the Bolivarian Republic (item **1085**). R.J. Lovera De-Sola likewise examines Bolívar's early life and education and particularly his sojourns in the US and Europe (item **1070**). The study seeks to understand Bolivar's outlook and personality and his later career as a soldier, statesman, and politician. Bolívar's military career has also attracted attention. Manuel Hernández González studies Bolívar's *Campaña Admirable* and the notorious 1813 "Declaration of War to the Death" (item **1065**). He deems the declaration to be both a significant error and a political and military disaster.

Several works examine Bolivarian symbolism. With a preface by Germán Carrera Damas, Maureen Shanahan and Ana Maria Reyes' collection consists of essays that enumerate the evolution of Bolívar's image and persona (item **1084**). Essays within the collection investigate changing political uses of Bolívar's image and how Bolivarian "relics"—swords, icons, and even his remains—have been used by contending political actors and interest groups. In a similar vein, Ecuadorian historian Jorge Núñez advances an explicitly revisionist view of the Liberator (item **1076**). He asserts that Bolívar was dark-skinned and small of stature, with a love of dancing and conversation; in other words, that Bolívar was a man of the people despite his undeniable abilities, and that his image has been hijacked and "whitened" by elites in the 19th and 20th centuries.

Several recent studies concentrate on the city of Caracas as a focal point for the struggles associated with independence. Pedro Cunill contributes a brief study examining population changes in Caracas during the independence era, characterizing it as an "insurgent historiography" of the capital (item **1057**). Guillermo González Durand offers a bicentennial history examining the evolution of Caracas and *caraqueño* society in the 18th century and noting the rapid changes occurring in the first years of the insurgency, transforming the city in the two years leading up to the cataclysmic 1812 earthquake (item **1061**). Another recent work explores the history and culture of the capital city: María Elena D'Alessandro Bello examines Caracas' past and present through a variety of lenses, including literature, popular histories, and dialects (item **1058**).

In comparison to previous volumes, only limited recent work on the post-independence 19th century has emerged. Nonetheless, three standout works merit a mention. Cecilia Ayala Lafée-Wilbert, Werner Wilbert, and Ariany Calles present two essays analyzing the Venezuelan career of Dominican leader General Juan Pablo Duarte (item **1051**). Duarte arrived in Venezuela in 1845 and played a key role in mid-century Venezuelan politics along with members of his family. Yoston Ferrigni examines the economic strategies that liberal leaders pursued between 1810 and the mid-19th century and argues that the models that the elites of Caracas and other regions embraced were derived largely from European and American theories that did not reflect Venezuelan realities (item **1062**). In addition, a collection of essays provides insights into some aspects of fin- de-siècle Venezuelan culture (item **1056**). The collection focuses on the 1895 publication of the *Primer libro venezolano de literatura, ciencias y bellas artes*—derived largely from the Caracas journal *El Cojo ilustrado*—as evidence of an emerging distinctively Venezuelan culture, and a crucial milestone in the intellectual history of the nation and national debates about the nature of modernity. Luis Rincón Rubio provides a potentially useful catalog for the *protócolos de escribanos* from Maracaibo province, corresponding to the period between 1790 and 1836 (item **1079**); it is a companion work to his earlier 2009 catalog (see *HLAS 66:1575*). The work has great potential for exploring the social and cultural history of the Maracaibo region.

Several recent publications focus on the 20th century, in particular on politics. Most of the studies under review explore transitions to democracy in the mid-20th century. Some analyze mid-20th century political parties in the decades after General Juan Vicente Gómez's death in 1935. In a few cases, historians compare the turmoil of Venezuela in the 1940s implicitly or explicitly with the current political turmoil. Marco Tulio Bruni Celli explores the 18 October 1945 civil-military uprising that brought Acción Democrática (AD) to power (item **1053**). Sócrates Ramírez's award-winning study looks at the October 1945 civil-military takeover that resulted in the ouster of General Isías Medina Angarita, which was in truth a revolutionary seizure of power (item **1082**). The later history of AD also receives scholarly attention. Carlos Marín's work examines the fracturing of the party in the wake of the 1958 restoration of civilian rule after a decade of military rule and the emergence of the Movimiento de Izquierda Revolucionaria (MIR) as a separate political organization, leading to the outbreak of armed insurgency in the 1960s (item **1071**). Other political parties also receive scholarly attention. In her study of a regional political party, the Unión Federal Repúblicana (UFR), Nelly J. Hernández Rangel characterizes the conservative party based in Mérida as a response to the rise of Acción Democrática and an expression of regional desire for political autonomy in the face of AD national policies (item **1066**).

The Cold War in Venezuela has roused the interest of several historians. Several works investigate various aspects of Venezuela's involvement in the global competition between the US and the Soviet Union. Mauribel Bravo and Mykel Navas seek to provide an ideologically balanced assessment of the impact of the Cold War on Venezuela's transition from dictatorship to democratic rule between 1958 and 1962 (item **1052**). Another work relies on the speeches and correspondence of AD leader Rómulo Betancourt to argue that AD was an authentically revolutionary political movement in the context of the early Cold War. A new collection of essays edited by Alejandro Cardozo Uzcátegui examines numerous aspects of Venezuela's experience during the Cold War, including Venezuela's internal politics, economic policies, civil-military relations, and international relations from the 1950s until the 1990s (item **1088**). Aragorn Storm Miller analyzes Cold War relations between the US and Venezuela in the decade after the January

1958 overthrow of the military dictatorship, and concludes that the Venezuelan experience represents a success for US foreign policy in Latin America (item **1073**). Another study that focuses on popular political mobilization in the second half of the 20th century is Alejandro Velasco's fascinating book about the 23 de Enero barrio in Caracas (item **1087**). Velasco argues that the inhabitants have for decades used a sophisticated repertoire of tactics to negotiate with the national state, from Marcos Pérez Jiménez's military regime of the 1950s to Hugo Chávez Frías' populist government in the 2000s.

Contemporary political history continues to draw the attention of researchers. A pair of works illuminate various aspects of the political career of Hugo Chávez Frías. Miguel Angel Martínez Meucci provides a pointed critique of the contemporary political crisis in Venezuela, criticizing the international community for "appeasement" in allowing the regimes led by Hugo Chávez Frías and his successor Nicolás Maduro to remain in office without any serious challenge (item **1072**). Another publication worthy of attention is a compilation of Chávez's discourses from *Aló Presidente,* providing first-hand accounts of his early life, military career, and political formation (item **1055**).

In addition to political history, a limited number of economic and social histories of 20th-century Venezuela have been published. Though few, they provide innovative approaches to the nation's recent past. Anthropologist María Victoria Padilla has produced an original examination of the catastrophic drought and resultant famine striking the Paraguaná Peninsula of Falcón in 1912; the author asserts that such catastrophes represent failures of state policy and economic systems (item **1078**). Based on accounts of German travelers and residents in the region, Lorena Puerta Bautista's study explores changes in the Zulian landscape occasioned by the oil boom of the early 20th century (item **1080**). Two additional works explore the history of the oil industry in the 20th century. Another regional study involving the oil industry's history is Sebastián Rafael Navarro Rodríguez's exploration of the development of the industry in eastern Venezuela from 1938–58 (item **1075**). A final study focused on oil is Rafael Quiroz Serrano's nationalist analysis of oil policy before Chávez's ascent to power (item **1081**). The author asserts that before 2001, Venezuela's oil policy was antinationalist and did not benefit Venezuelans significantly.

One recent work explores the roles of the Catholic Church in 20th-century Venezuela. Augustín Moreno Molina provides a narrative account of the interactions between Church leaders and political figures of Venezuela's 20th century (item **1074**). A single work of diplomatic history analyzes Venezuela's diplomatic relations with South Korea. Written by Norbert Molina Medina, the study argues that Venezuela's relations with that Asian nation have become increasingly close and cordial over the last 50 years (item **1067**).

Finally, a handful of general works deserve mention. Two essay collections explore the role of the military in Venezuela over time. A collection edited by Alejandro Cardozo Uzcátegui and Luis Alberto Buttó investigates the interactions between civil and military authorities to argue that praetorianism has been a constant from independence to the present (item **1068**). Another collection edited by Luis Albert Buttó *et al.* explore civil-military relations from the independence era until the 1990s, without making specific connections to the current political situation (item **1059**).

Two works of general history are explicitly pedagogical. One is a collection of brief biographies of prominent politicians and intellectuals; author President

Rafael Caldera intended the collection for use in teaching (item **1054**). Napoleón Franceschi González and Freddy Domínguez present a collection—compiled by two education professors—of primary sources fundamental for the teaching of Venezuelan history (item **1063**).

In conclusion, the last two years have seen a distinct decrease in the publication of historical works on the 19th and 20th centuries. Nonetheless, the excellence of the studies and collections reflects ongoing improvements in the quality of research. Many of the works provide insights into the history of the independence era, while studies exploring the Cold War in Venezuela reflect a lively interest in how Venezuelans understood the conflict and their roles in it.

1048 Alfaro Pareja, Francisco. La historia oculta de la Independencia de Venezuela: de la guerra idealizada a la paz imperfecta. Caracas: Editorial Alfa, 2016. 254 p.: bibl. (Colección Trópicos; 120. Historia)

This book presents a reassessment of the nature of the process of Venezuelan independence. Noting that Venezuela's early 19th-century historiography stresses warfare and the actions of Bolívar and other leading figures, the author seeks to refocus the historical study on what he terms the "hidden history" of independence—the history of negotiation, agreement, and relatively peaceful interactions between those participating in the conflict. The author argues that the struggles for independence evolved, went through three distinct phases, and extended until 1846. He characterizes the independence process as one involving both violence and "pacific regulations." Prologue by Tomás Straka.

1049 Alfaro Pareja, Francisco. El iris de la paz: paz y conflictos en la independencia de Venezuela. Castelló de la Plana, Spain: Universitat Jaume I, 2014. 217 p.: bibl., ill., index. (Cooperació i solidaritat. Estudis; 12)

This work provides new perspectives on Venezuelan independence. The author notes that the prevailing historiographical traditions focus on independence as a military phenomenon. In contrast, he argues that Venezuela's struggle is best understood "as a process of searching for peace." He asserts that historical emphasis on the role of violence in the independence movement reflects the political situation prevailing in Venezuela during the late 20th century. He further characterizes the independence movement as an intricate process that combined fighting, negotiation, truces, and agreements and regulations. See also item **1048**.

1050 Altez, Rogelio. Desastre, independencia y transformación: Venezuela y la primera República en 1812. Castelló de la Plana, Spain: Universitat Jaume I, 2015. 285 p.: bibl. (Col·lecció Amèrica; 31)

This work offers a stimulating analysis of the establishment of the First Republic (1810-12) and its ultimate defeat. The author concludes that despite the nationalist depictions of the wars of independence as inevitable and inherently just, the early movement in favor of Venezuelan independence must be understood as a violent upheaval occurring in the context of colonial society and the Spanish imperial system, a system of declining efficacy.

1051 Ayala Lafée-Wilbert, Cecilia; Werner Wilbert; and Ariany Calles. Juan Pablo Duarte en la Venezuela del siglo XIX: historia y leyenda. Santo Domingo: Banco Central de la República Dominicana, 2014. 203 p.: bibl., ill., maps. (Colección del Banco Central de la República Dominicana; 197)(Serie ciencias sociales; 33)

This work brings together two largely laudatory essays exploring the Venezuelan residence and activities of General Juan Pablo Duarte and his family. Originally from Santo Domingo, General Duarte went to Venezuela in 1845. A key figure in the struggle for independence of the Dominican Republic, Duarte fled with his family to Venezuela in response to political persecution and they became residents of Caracas. The authors utilize documentary collections in both the Dominican Republic and

Venezuela and refute many prevalent accounts about Duarte's stay in Venezuela. The authors argue that despite some depictions, he was not a quixotic dreamer but rather a "pragmatic revolutionary."

1052 Bravo, Mauribel and **Mykel Navas.** Transición de la dictadura a la democracia representativa en Venezuela: 1958–1962. Caracas: s.n., 2014. 169 p.: bibl., ill.

Reacting to a perceived lack of impartiality in existing accounts of the era in which military rule gave way to a civilian regime (1958–62), the author notes the "ideological" permeation of current historiography and seeks to portray this account as a comprehensive one, focusing on all relevant causes. The author argues that the end of the Pérez Jiménez regime and the rise of a representative system was a societal crisis. Based on newspaper accounts, participants' accounts, and political manifestos, the work pays particular attention to the impact of the Cold War on Venezuelan policy and society.

1053 Bruni Celli, Marco Tulio. El 18 de octubre de 1945. Prólogo de Francisco Suaniaga. Edición a cargo de Guillermo Amaro. Caracas: La Hoja del Norte, 2014. 801 p.: bibl. (Ensayo)

Written in response to a perceived return to militarism under Hugo Chávez Frías and Nicolás Maduro, this work presents a detailed analysis of the 18 October 1945 civil/military uprising that toppled the government of Isías Medina Angarita. A confidant of Rómulo Betancourt and many other protagonists in the events of the uprising, the author argues that the revolt that overthrew the Medina government resulted from the regime's political incompetence and authoritarianism.

1054 Caldera, Rafael. Moldes para la fragua: nueva serie. Prólogo de Ramón Guillermo Aveledo. Caracas: Cyngular, 2016. 178 p.: bibl. (Biblioteca Rafael Caldera; VI)

This works brings together a posthumous collection of biographical sketches by former president Rafael Caldera (1916–2009). Produced explicitly for didactic purposes, the collection includes profiles of political, intellectual, and religious figures from Venezuela and other nations. The leaders profiled include Eduardo Frei, Caracciolo Parra León, Pedro Grases, and Juan Carlos Puig.

1055 Chávez Frías, Hugo. Cuentos del arañero. Compilación de Orlando Oramas León y Jorge Legañoa Alonso. Tafalla, Spain: Txalaparta, 2013. 256 p.: ill.

This book presents a thought-provoking compilation of Hugo Chávez Frías' addresses on the long-running weekly television program *Aló Presidente*. The presidential addresses included in the study provide an autobiography of sorts. Vignettes presented explore Chávez's early life, military career, the events that contributed to his radicalization and his emergence as a would-be revolutionary, and his perspective on Venezuela's history and prospects for the future. For a related work, see *HLAS 73:1194*.

1056 Cuatro miradas: a propósito del *Primer Libro Venezolano de Literatura, Ciencias y Bellas Artes de 1895*. Compilación de Janicce Martínez y Alexandra Mulino. Caracas: Fondo Editorial de la Facultad de Humanidades y Educación, Universidad Central de Venezuela, 2014. 154 p.: bibl., ill. (Colección Estudios. Educación)

This provocative compilation of essays focuses on the 1895 publication of the *Primer libro venezolano de literatura, ciencias y bellas artes*. The authors examine this key publication from the perspectives of history, pedagogy, social psychology, and sociology. The authors contend that the *Primer libro* was an important example of the evolution of a distinctively Venezuelan culture and literature. This development involved not only the publication of the book but also that of the periodical *El Cojo ilustrado*, which provided much of the material for the book. The *Primer libro* is thus a key work in the intellectual history of turn-of-the-century Venezuela.

1057 Cunill, Pedro. Geohistoria de la Caracas insurgente, 1810–1812. Caracas: Archivo General de la Nación, Centro Nacional de Historia, 2012. 63 p.: bibl.

A brief study of the history and geography of Caracas from 1810 to 1812. This publication is an excerpt from a longer work, Cunill's three-volume *Geografía del poblamiento venezolano en el siglo XIX* (see *HLAS 51:2968*). The intent of the work is to provide an insurgent historiography of the people, for the people, and with the people.

1058 D'Alessandro Bello, María Elena. Caracas, la ciudad de la memoria: ensayos de cultura urbana. Saarbrücken, Germany: Editorial Academica Espanola, 2014. 93 p.: bibl., index.

This collection of brief essays explores the city of Caracas' origins and past through language and culture. Specific topics explored include popular histories, novels, languages, the changing roles played by women in caraqueño society, and even the smells and tastes unique to the city.

1059 De la hueste indiana al pretorianismo del siglo XX: relaciones civiles y militares en la historia de Venezuela. Con ensayos de Luis Alberto Buttó et al. Coordinación de Raúl Meléndez M., Luis Alberto Buttó, y José Alberto Olivar. Valencia, Venezuela: Asociación de Profesores Universidad de Carabobo, 2012. 216 p.: bibl., 1 ill.

This edited volume explores civilian-military relations in Venezuela from the last years of the colonial period until the end of the 20th century, "from a strictly academic perspective," meaning that the authors do not explicitly attempt to connect the research with the contemporary political situation.

1060 Donís Ríos, Manuel Alberto. Los curas congresistas: la actuación de los sacerdotes como diputados en los congresos republicanos de 1811, 1817, 1819 y 1821. Caracas: Academia Nacional de la Historia, 2012. 483 p.: bibl. (Colección Bicentenario de la independencia)

This comprehensive study examines the participation of clerics in the political ferment of the independence era in Venezuela. The author observes that there has been no detailed research focused on the roles played by the clergy in the struggle for independence and asserts that clerics—particularly those from the province of Mérida—participated fully in the political debates and deliberations of the Congreso Nacional and the congresses of 1817, 1819, and 1821. The clerical participants in the congresses espoused a variety of positions on the issues that Venezuela faced, with some joining the patriot cause as chaplains or even combatants, while others emerged as ardent defenders of the king and the royalist cause. The author insists nonetheless that all were in one way or another "defenders of the rights and privileges of the Catholic Church."

1061 Durand González, Guillermo. Caracas en tiempos revueltos, 1810–1812. Caracas: Instituto Municipal de Publicaciones, Alcaldía de Caracas, 2012. 282 p.: bibl., ill.

This work presents a bicentennial history of Caracas in the first two years of the patriot insurgency. Noting that there has been no systematic study of Caracas between 1810 and the massive earthquake of March 1812, the author examines the urban space and public discourse in the capital city. After exploring the impact of the Enlightenment and the Bourbon Reforms on Caracas, the author argues that between 1750 and 1810 colonial authorities produces a body of ordinances profoundly influenced by the Enlightenment. The second part of the book focuses on the two years between 1810 and the earthquake of 26 March 1812, in which three-quarters of the city was destroyed. The author argues that just as the city had developed a comprehensive set of ordinances for the governance of a mature colonial society, the political changes following 19 April 1810 and the challenges involved in rebuilding after a devastating seismic event rendered the city a very different place.

1062 Ferrigni, Yoston. El laberinto del progreso: problemas y estrategias de la economía en Venezuela, 1810–1858. Caracas: Fundación Bancaribe para la Ciencia y la Cultura, 2014. 398 p.: bibl., ill.

This work examines the economic strategies that Venezuela's liberal leaders embraced in the decades after 1810. The author asserts that Venezuela's political and social elites looked to Great Britain and the US as models and framed Venezuela's economic problems as consequences of Spain's backwardness and the supposedly negative impact of a racially mixed population. The author also explores the political implications of pursuing orthodox liberal economic policies. The study concludes that the colonial administrative apparatus survived long after independence, and questions of how to reconcile economic growth, social equality, and democracy continue to afflict contemporary Venezuelan society.

1063 Franceschi González, Napoleón and **Freddy Domínguez.** Antología documental: fuentes para el estudio de la historia de Venezuela, 1776–2000. Caracas: Universidad Metropolitana, 2012. 468 p.: bibl.

This collection of documents relates to the history of Venezuela from the 1770s until 2000. Compiled by two professors of teacher education, the collection is explicitly pedagogical in its purpose. The professed goal of the publication is to provide an accessible and comprehensive compilation of documents for students and teachers, seeking the "systematic study of Venezuelan history." The collection is organized chronologically and reflects orthodox views of Bolívar, the struggle for independence, and 19th- and 20th-century history.

1064 Heredia, José Francisco. Memorias sobre las revoluciones de Venezuela, 1812–1817. Estudio preliminar a la tercera edición venezolana de Alí Enrique López Bohórquez. Tercera edición venezolana. Caracas: Academia Nacional de la Historia: Banco Central de Venezuela, 2014. 417 p.: bibl. (Colección Bicentenario de la independencia)

Published as part of the bicentennial observances, this work presents a new edition of the independence memoirs of an *oidor decano* and interim regent of the Audiencia of Caracas, Dr. José Francisco Heredia y Mieses. In the introductory essay, Alí Enrique López Bohórquez characterizes Heredia as both a royalist and a tireless advocate for the powers and prerogatives of the Audiencia, both in opposition to the patriot cause and the pretension of the military leaders prosecuting the struggle against them. The work includes a useful documentary appendix.

1065 Hernández González, Manuel. La guerra a muerte: Bolívar y la Campaña Admirable (1813–1814). Santa Cruz de Tenerife, Spain: Ediciones Idea, 2014. 254 p.: bibl. (Desde América; 39)

This detailed analysis of the Venezuelan Second Republic focuses on the violence directed against Spaniards and Canary Islanders by the republican government and military. Given formal sanction by Bolívar's "Declaration of War to the Death," the cruel treatment of *canarios* and peninsular Spaniards resulted in the murder of more than two thousand men. The author argues that the policy grew out of the class and social antagonisms in late colonial Venezuela and characterizes Bolívar's declaration as a serious policy error enacted by the *Mantuano* elite that contributed markedly to the later outrages perpetrated by Boves and Morales. The author rejects traditional depictions of Bolívar as an infallible political genius and portrays the elite of Caracas as a class defined by their economic interests and their prejudices.

1066 Hernández Rangel, Nelly Josefina. Unión Federal Republicana: un partido político merideño, 1946–1948. Mérida, Venezuela: Ediciones El Lápiz, 2013. 165 p.: bibl., ill.

This brief historical study examines the Unión Federal Repúblicana (UFR), a Mérida-based regional political party of the late 1940s. The author traces the origins of the party from conservative anti-Marxist civic leagues in the aftermath of the death of Juan Vicente Gómez in December 1935. The leagues arose in support of the government of Eléazar López Contreras. The UFR became a dominant force in regional politics and eventually was subsumed into COPEI, the Venezuelan Christian democratic political party. She argues that the UFR was an authentic expression of the conservative, Catholic outlook of Mérida's population, and a legitimate effort to revitalize federalism after a long era of despotic and centralized government under the leadership of Castro and Gómez while supporting conservative, anti-Marxist policies. Above all, the author argues that the rise of the UFR was a reaction against the effects of modernity in Venezuela and an intent to impede the expansion of rival organization Acción Democrática into the Andean states. Originally the author's MA thesis, this work represents an effort to encourage more research into local and regional political history.

1067 Historia de las relaciones diplomáticas Venezuela—Corea (1965–2015) = **Han'guk kwa Penesuella kan ŭi 50–yŏn ujŏng.** Compilación de Norbert Molina Medina. Caracas: Embajada de la República de Corea en Venezuela; Mérida, Venezuela: Universidad de Los Andes, Centro de Estudios de África, Asia y Diásporas Latinoamericanas y Caribeñas "José Manuel Briceño Monzillo", 2015. 312 p.: bibl., color ill., 2 color maps.

This work presents a brief history of Venezuela's diplomatic ties with the Republic of South Korea. The study notes that some 50 years have passed since the establishment of formal diplomatic and commercial relations, and argues that the relationship has become significantly closer in recent years. Includes documentary appendices.

1068 **El incesto republicano: relaciones civiles y militares en Venezuela, 1812–2012.** Dirección de Alejandro Cardozo Uzcátegui y Luis Alberto Buttó. Caracas: Editorial Nuevos Aires, 2013. 218 p.: bibl. (Serie Historia)

This compilation of essays explores the role played by militarism in Venezuela's political history from before independence until the present. The authors seek to demonstrate that militarism and praetorianism have been continuous in Venezuela's modern history and remain a constant in the era of the Bolivarian Republic.

1069 **Levitas y sotanas en la edificación republicana: proceso político e ideas en tiempos de emancipación.** Textos de María Soledad Hernández Bencid et al. Coordinación de Jean Carlos Brizuela y José Alberto Olivar. Venezuela: Subdirección de Investigación y Postgrado UPEL-IPR El Mácaro, 2012. 208 p.: bibl.

This collection of brief biographies explores the roles played by clerics and civilians in the independence and early republican period. The general argument is that the military struggles for the independence of Venezuela were preceded by debates and discussions conducted within civil society. The authors collectively seek to trace the origins of Venezuela as a civil republic back to the statesmen of the early 19th century. The authors include many of the best-known Venezuelan historians of national politics. The underlying assumption of the authors is to valorize civilian politics and political debate, while referring explicitly to contemporary political and social divisions.

1070 **Lovera De-Sola, R.J.** Simón Bolívar en el tiempo de crecer: los primeros veinticinco años, 1783–1808. Caracas: Editorial Alfa, 2016. 344 p.: bibl. (Colección Trópicos; 121. Historia)

This work offers an analysis of the early life of Simón Bolívar (1783–1830). Based on primary sources—many previously unknown—the author examines key events of Bolívar's early life and the environment from which he emerged as a young man of 25 in 1808. The author argues that Bolívar's experiences, particularly the extended periods he spent in Europe and the US, were crucial in shaping his outlook, character, and later career. He also characterizes the Venezuela into which the Liberator was born as a mature colonial society, the elite of which—Bolivar's generation—were the architects of the independence movement, while most of the older *criollos* would have been satisfied with the prospect of greater autonomy within the Spanish imperial system.

1071 **Marín, Carlos Alfredo.** Dos islas, un abismo: AD a MIR, 1948–1960. Caracas: Fundación Celarg, 2011. 194 p.: bibl. (Nuestra América; 4)

This work examines the divisions within the Acción Democrática (AD) political party that resulted in the creation of the Movimiento de Izquierda Revolucionaria (MIR), one of the most important of the leftist political movements of the second half of the 20th century, in April 1960. The author traces the evolution of the MIR as a faction within Acción Democrática and attributes the split to the profound pressures created by the military regimes in control of Venezuela from 1948 to 1958. He characterizes the split as in some ways a generational conflict and argues that the founding leaders of AD felt threatened by the militancy and energy of the "hotheads" who would eventually create the MIR. The militant young members of the party felt entitled to seize control based on their role in the armed struggle against the coup regime.

1072 **Martínez Meucci, Miguel Ángel.** Apaciguamiento: el referéndum revocatorio y la consolidación de la Revolución Bolivariana. Caracas: Editorial Alfa, 2012. 512 p.: bibl., ill. (Colección Hogueras; 58)

This work offers a historical analysis of the current political crisis in Venezuela. The author provides a detailed narrative of the decline of the Fourth Republic and the rise, survival, and ultimate triumph of Hugo Chávez Frías. The author characterizes the political process unfolding in Venezuela in the first decade of the 21st century as the progressive dismantling of liberal democracy and accuses the US, the European Union, and individual state actors as having engaged in appeasement in allowing the consolidation of a state he characterizes as authoritarian. He asserts that the rise of Chávez's movement is part of a worldwide phenomenon, the rise to power of "illiberal regimes."

1073 **Miller, Aragorn Storm.** Precarious paths to freedom: the United States, Venezuela, and the Latin American Cold War. Albuquerque: University of New Mexico Press, 2016. 278 p.: bibl., index.

This work provides a detailed historical study of US-Venezuelan relations during the Cold War, particularly those of the decade following 1958. Relying primarily on sources from US and Dominican diplomatic archives and US presidential library collections, the author examines the effects of US policy in Venezuela. He identifies Venezuela as "the critical arena of the hemispheric Cold War because of its tangible and psychological importance to the US, the Dominican Republic, and Cuba and because of the efforts of Venezuelans to reinterpret, alter, exploit, or resist US, Soviet, Chinese, and Cuban policies and ideologies." The author asserts that Venezuela was both an exceptional case and a major foreign policy success for the US in the Cold War because of the preservation of electoral democracy in an era in which most Latin American republics were under military rule.

1074 **Moreno Molina, Agustín.** Hechos y personajes de la historia políticaeclesiástica venezolana del siglo XX. Caracas: Universidad Católica Andrés Bello, 2013. 417 p.: bibl.

This work presents a narrative account of events involving the Catholic Church in Venezuela during the 20th and 21st centuries, written from a generally proclerical perspective. The author provides a description of the actions of the Venezuelan church and its relations with national authorities in power from Cipriano Castro to Hugo Chávez Frías. He then seeks to relate the Catholic experience and actions of practitioners of the faith with the specific circumstances of time and space. The study is critical of contemporary and earlier officials' actions and attitudes toward the Catholic faith and its representatives in Venezuela.

1075 **Navarro Rodríguez, Sebastián Rafael.** Venezuela petrolera: el asentamiento en el oriente, 1938 a 1958. Trafford rev. ed. Bloomington, Ind.: Trafford Pub., 2011. 149 p.: bibl., ill.

Written by a historian with a business background, this study—orthodox in approach—analyzes the oil industry in eastern Venezuela, particularly in the states of Anzoategui, Guárico, and Monagas, from 1938 to 1958. The author notes that the men and women who first came to the eastern oilfields in the 1930s had to contend with a harsh climate, isolation, and endemic disease, and succeeded in creating a thriving and dynamic regional economy. Based primarily on published primary sources and personal archives.

1076 **Núñez, Jorge.** Simón Bolívar, el libertador. Quito: Eskeletra Editorial, 2012. 229 p.: bibl.

This work offers a revisionist assessment of the life and legacy of the Liberator Simón Bolívar. The author asserts that Bolívar was short of stature, dark-complected, and a lover of dancing and conversation. He characterizes conventional portrayals and depictions of Bolívar as reflecting racist stereotypes and post facto whitewashing, seeking to convey an image of a tall, light-complected, heroic Bolívar. He also argues that despite being in some senses a typical Latin American, Bolívar was in many ways an exceptionally accomplished leader and visionary.

1077 La opción republicana en el marco de las independencias: ideas, política e historiografía, 1797–1830. Coordinación de Jorge Bracho, Jean Carlos Brizuela, y José Alberto Olivar. Textos de Mariano Nava Contreras *et al.* Presentación de Edgardo

Mondolfi Gudat. Caracas: Universidad Metropolitana, 2012. 317 p.: bibl., ill.

This useful collection of essays explores the origins of republicanism in the decades of the late 18th and early 19th centuries. The authors assert that the foundation of a republican government was a complex and conflictive process, fraught with contradictions that persisted for centuries after independence. Among the essays are an examination of the intellectual and political evolution of republicanism and the role of the Catholic Church in the region's political and institutional environment, and a study on the evolution of ideas about modernity in the era of independence. Historiographical discussions center on the effort and need for regional and local analyses. A section at the end of the work focuses on historiographical integration and the development of the positivist and nationalist historiographic schools of the era.

1078 Padilla, María Victoria. El año del hambre: la sequía y el desastre de 1912 en Paraguaná. Coro, Venezuela: Gobernación del Estado Falcón, Instituto de Cultura del Estado Falcón INCUDEF: Fundación Literaria León Bienvenido Weffer: Grupo Tiquiba, 2012. 189 p.: bibl., ill.

This work presents an anthropologist's analysis of drought and famine occurring on the Paraguaná Peninsula in Falcón in 1912. The author observes that the study of natural disasters has been neglected, particularly in the context of Venezuelan history, arguing that "disasters do not enter the collective memory unless they represent something in political and institutional history or the nationalist historiography." She argues that the 1912 famine in Paraguaná was the result not only of a natural disaster—the prolonged drought that struck the northern reaches of the peninsula—but also of a lack of institutional support from national and state authorities for the poor. She also blames the distortion of the national and regional economies by market forces and the economic interests of the family of Juan Vicente Gómez.

1079 Protocolos de escribanos en el Registro Principal del Estado Zulia (1790–1836): catálogo integral y extractos documentales. Textos de Luis Rincón Rubio et al. Maracaibo, Venezuela: Academia de Historia del Estado Zulia, 2015. 698 p.: bibl., indexes.

Funded by Harvard University's Program for Latin American Libraries and Archives, this useful catalog lists the *protocólos de escribanos* housed in the Registro Principal del Estado Zulia in Maracaibo. The documents cataloged are the scribes' archives corresponding to the period between 1790 to 1836, which according to the editor consist of more than 10,000 documents, including bills of sale, powers of attorney, wills, manumissions, and bonds. The editor notes that the period from which the documents derive was one in which the Maracaibo region was undergoing "important administrative, cultural, and political changes." See also *HLAS 66:1575*.

1080 Puerta Bautista, Lorena. Los paisajes petroleros del Zulia en la mirada alemana, 1920–1940. Caracas: Archivo General de la Nación: Centro Nacional de Historia, 2010. 120 p.: bibl., ill., 1 map. (Colección Bicentenario; 4)

The author explores changes in the landscapes of Zulia during the oil boom of the early 20th century. The author based the study on the travel writings of Germans living in Venezuela, specifically Julia Bornhorst and Wilhelm Georgi, who spent extended periods in the Maracaibo region during the oil boom. The study argues that oil transformed the Zulian landscape and population, infrastructure, ecology, and economy.

1081 Quiroz Serrano, Rafael. Marchas y contramarchas del petróleo en Venezuela, 1989–2001. Caracas: Editorial Panapo, 2011. 224 p.: bibl., ill.

This work offers a history of the Venezuelan oil industry from its beginnings in 1889 until 2001. The author's purpose is to explore oil policy and its consequences during the decade immediately before the election of Hugo Chávez Frías. He argues that Venezuela's policy before 1999 was antinationalist and so informed by neoliberalism as to be a treasonous attempt to "dismantle the Venezuelan state." He characterizes the official policy of the Carlos Andres Pérez administration as "the internationalization of Venezuelan petroleum."

1082 Ramírez, Sócrates. Decir una revolución: Rómulo Betancourt y la peripecia octubrista. Caracas: Academia Nacional de la Historia: Fundación Bancaribe para la Ciencia y la Cultura, 2014. 284 p.: bibl. (Colección Premio Rafael María Baralt)

This award-winning study reexamines the 1945 revolt that brought Acción Democrática (AD) to power in 1945 while deposing Isías Medina Angarita and ushering in three years of reformist or revolutionary policy. Based largely on documents in the Betancourt archives, the work focuses primarily on the statements made by Rómulo Betancourt and other AD leaders to understand the concept of revolution as used by the participants in the October revolt. The author seeks to push back against recent historiography that calls into question the "revolutionary character" of the revolt and argues that at the time, the movement was truly revolutionary.

1083 Rey Fajardo, José del. Nosotros también somos gente indios y jesuitas en la Orinoquia. Caracas: Academia Nacional de la Historia, 2011. 697 p., 2 folded leaves of plates: bibl., ill., indexes, folded maps. (Biblioteca de la Academia Nacional de la Historia; 270. Fuentes para la historia colonial de Venezuela)

Written by the premier historian of the Jesuit Order in Venezuela, this work presents an exploration of the relations between the Jesuits and the indigenous peoples of the Orinoco basin, particularly those commonly targeted by the Caribes and their European partners for enslavement. The author argues that it is necessary to provide detailed information about the people—perhaps as many as 200,000 or more—enslaved and sold from this region. The author's focus is on the Jesuits' efforts to learn and teach using the languages spoken in the region. The work contains several useful appendices. See also item **959**.

Rey Fajardo, José del. La República de las Letras en la Babel étnica de la Orinoquia. See item **959**.

1084 Shanahan, Maureen G. and Ana María Reyes. Simón Bolívar: travels and transformations of a cultural icon. Gainesville: University Press of Florida, 2016. 273 p.: bibl., index.

Inspired in part by Germán Carrera Damas' 1969 essay on the cult of the Liberator (see *HLAS 32:2418* for the original publication and *HLAS 46:2825* for a follow-up 1983 article), this fascinating collection of essays explores Simón Bolívar's evolving image and the ways in which that image has been put to use in the last two centuries. The editors note in their introduction that Bolívar has "become the quintessential myth mined for authority and legitimacy." Individual contributions examine the interaction between images and ideology in painting, music, opera, and film, and the uses made of Bolívar's portraits, swords, and physical remains. Germán Carrera Damas contributes the preface.

1085 Simón Rodríguez: y las pedagogías emancipadoras en nuestra América. Textos de Carla Wainsztok *et al.* Buenos Aires: Ediciones del CCC, Centro Cultural de la Cooperación Floreal Gorini, 2013. 152 p.: bibl.

This collection of essays investigates the historical role and the pedagogy of Simón Rodríguez, tutor and confidant of the Liberator. The authors argue that educators/teachers have a responsibility for developing a "pedagogy of liberation" for the 21st century and see in Rodríguez's teaching a guide on how to develop such a pedagogy in Venezuela and even beyond.

1086 Vannini de Gerulewicz, Marisa. El misterio de Francisco Isnardi. Venezuela: Fundavag Ediciones, 2014. 224 p.: ill. (Colección Calle real; 10)

With an introductory essay by Edgardo Mondolfi Gudat, this publication is a new edition of the classic work about Francisco Isnardi, a key member of the independence generation, a peninsular Spaniard, Cádiz native, and medical doctor. The work is both a biography of Isnardi—who played a crucial role in the political debates leading to the declaration of Venezuela's First Republic—and also a history of the first years of the independence movement. Isnardi was one of the authors of the declaration of Venezuelan independence of 5 July 1811. Originally published in 2001 (see *HLAS 62:1550*).

1087 Velasco, Alejandro. Barrio rising: urban popular politics and the making of modern Venezuela. Oakland: University of California Press, 2015. 321 p.: bibl., index.

This fascinating study examines popular democracy in Caracas during the Fourth Republic (1958-98). Using the 23 de Enero barrio—containing high-rise apartments built by the military dictatorship in the 1950s—as a case study of the functioning of popular democracy in the capital city, the author argues that the inhabitants of the neighborhood have actively participated in electoral and party politics since 1958 but take to the streets in public protests and demonstrations in response to governmental neglect or deception. The author concludes that the relationship between the inhabitants of 23 de Enero and the government of Hugo Chávez Frías is quite similar to that of previous democratic governments; the inhabitants employ a spectrum of political strategies in their relations with the state, including participation in electoral politics, public protest, and even armed resistance.

1088 Venezuela y la Guerra Fría. Dirección de Alejandro Cardozo Uzcátegui. Caracas: Editorial Nuevos Aires: Universidad Simón Bolívar, Centro Latinoamericano de Estudios de Seguridad: Consorcio GEO, 2014. 293 p.: bibl. (Serie Historia)

Originating as a project of the Centro Latinoamericano de Estudios de Seguridad of the Universidad Simón Bolívar, this collection of essays focuses on the Cold War in Venezuela. The authors include many prominent Venezuelan historians and political scientists, and the studies explore diverse aspects of Venezuela's politics, economy, and culture during the decades after World War II. Most of the authors aver that Venezuela was not merely subservient to the US during the Cold War, and that, rather, Venezuela's civilian and military leadership sought to pursue national goals and priorities and sometimes disagreed with or defied the representatives of the US. For a related work, see item **1073**.

Colombia and Ecuador

JANE M. RAUSCH, *Professor Emerita of History, University of Massachusetts-Amherst*

SINCE *HLAS* 72, the number of investigations into Colombian history has continued to grow. The XVIII Congreso Colombiano de Historia held in Medellín 10–13 October 2017 confirmed this trend with 451 national and international scholars who presented papers in addition to 26 lecturers and two *"conversaciones"* in which six invited guests participated. This impressive output is supported by journals sponsored by major Colombian universities, such as *Historia y Sociedad* (Universidad Nacional sede Medellín), *Historia Crítica* (Universidad de los Andes), *Historia y Memoria* (Universidad Pedagógica y Tecnológica), and the online journal, *HISTORelo*, also based at the Universidad Nacional sede Medellín. These publications have combined with the venerable *Anuario Colombiano de Historia Social y de la Cultura* (begun in 1963 by the Universidad Nacional de Colombia sede Bogotá) and the Biblioteca Luis Angel Arango's lavishly produced *Boletín Cultural y Bibliográfico* to allow more Colombian academics to get their works in print.

International scholars interested in Colombian history have also proliferated. In their introduction to the updated Spanish edition of *Los colombianistas* (item **1099**), editors Peralta and LaRosa note that in the 18 years since the book first appeared in English, the study of Colombian history has undergone a grand transformation when measured by the increasing number of North American and European investigators and the growth of scholarly output. The Biblioteca Luis Angel Arango as well as the Academia Colombiana de Historia are publishing more PhD theses; foreign presses are printing more works on Colombia; non-Colombian scholars are working in new areas such as sociology, anthropology, art, and music, and interchanges between disciplines and colleagues are more numerous and of higher quality. What is still missing, as Peralta and La Rosa point out, is the creation of centers specializing in Colombian Studies at North American universities, such as those that already exist for Brazil, Mexico, and Cuba. At present, PhD and MA candidates who want to do their theses on Colombia are scattered across the US, and for those in residence outside Colombia, achieving a PhD in Colombian history is a difficult task indeed. A university that specializes in Colombian Studies at the graduate level would promote the exchange of information, the pooling of human resources, and the circulation of ideas. Unfortunately, at this time, the establishment of such a center remains an unrealized dream.

Turning now to the independence era, the wave of interest generated by bicentennial celebrations of independence in Colombia led to the publication of three important anthologies. Cortés Guerrero (item **1094**) has assembled essays written by 17 academics, examining the impact of independence on multiple aspects of the new nation's development; Bonilla's book (item **1100**) includes eight essays dealing with the war's effect on the 19th-century economy; while the 10 essays in Almario García's volume (item **1091**) focus on the position of castes and races between 1810–30.

The 16 entries dealing with the 19th century focus on a variety of topics. Five studies concern accommodation of subalterns—Afro-Colombians and/or indigenous peoples (items **1103**, **1126**, **1137**, **1140**, and **1141**). Three essays offer new approaches to the 19th-century economy: (items **1111**, **1114**, and **1124**) and two examine the educational reform of 1870 (items **1116** and **1139**). Perhaps the most groundbreaking offering in this group however is Del Castillo's iconoclastic overview of Colombia's l9th century, which suggests that Colombian leaders invented the notion of "colonial legacies," and created a new science of republicanism (item **1101**).

Among studies dealing with the 20th century there are five biographical studies: Alberto Lleras Camargo (item **1090**), Alfonso López Michelson (item **1115**), Eduardo Santos (item **1120**), Diego Luis Córdoba (item **1121**), and Esmeralda Arboleda (item **1127**). In addition, *La nación sentida* (item **1095**), is a kind of collective biography that offers unique insight into the Colombian worldview after Gaitán's assassination in 1949.

The *Boletín Bibliográfico y Cultural* broke new ground by assembling four essays on the changing situation of Colombian youth (items **1092**, **1112**, **1132**, and **1136**), and three authors provide very different interpretations of the high and low points of Colombia's 20th-century development (items **1109**, **1110**, and **1113**).

Continuing the trend noted in past *HLAS* volumes, publications about Ecuador continue to lag in quantity and quality behind those concerning Colombia. Two exceptions are the volumes written by Ayala Mora, which reconceptualize the periodization of Ecuador's history. The first (item **1147**) is a collection of seven essays ranging from 12,000 a.c. to the present; the second (item **1148**) is a survey of the country's historiography that is intended to better prepare future scholars and teachers of national history.

Nineteenth-century entries include two intriguing works. Espinosa Fernández de Córdoba and Aljovín de Losada (item **1152**) offer a refreshing revisionist view of conservative political language and conclude that Conservatives and Liberals shared many common values, while Barrera-Agarwal (item **1149**) recounts an incident in 1895 when a Chilean ship sailed to Japan under an Ecuadorean flag and contributed to the resignation of President Luis Cordero Crespo. Of the eight works concerning the 20th century, especially notable are Becker's examination of FBI files regarding Ecuador from 1944 to 1984 (item **1150**), and a three-volume journalistic account written by former vice-chancellor Kintto Lucas who outlines his interpretation of events occurring between 1990 and 2015 (item **1157**).

COLOMBIA

1089 Acuña Rodríguez, Olga Yanet. De las urnas a la movilización popular: elecciones presidenciales de 1970 en Colombia. (*Secuencia/México*, 96, sept./dic. 2016, p. 193–225, bibl., photo, table)

Careful, extensive research examines aspects of the blatant electoral fraud in the April 19, 1970 election of Misael Pastrana Borrero and the techniques used by the established political actors to prevent the return to power of Rojas Pinilla and his newly-formed ANAPO party. Shows that the masses regarded this process as a travesty of the democratic system by claiming their role as citizens and demanding their rights, filing complaints with various institutions, and engaging in mobilization and protest leading to the M-19 armed movement.

1090 Alberto Lleras Camargo y John F. Kennedy: amistad y política internacional: recuento de episodios de la Guerra Fría, la Alianza para el Progreso y el problema de Cuba. Compilación de Carlos Caballero Argáez et al. Bogotá: Universidad de Los Andes, Escuela de Gobierno Alberto Lleras Camargo, 2014. 185 p.: ill.

Affirming that Alberto Lleras Camargo was Colombia's most important 20th-century statesman, this volume includes essays, documents, photographs, and text exploring his friendship with John F. Kennedy. It focuses on Kennedy's visit to Bogotá on December 17, 1961 and his discussion with Lleras regarding the "problem of Cuba" as an obstacle to the success of the recently launched Alliance for Progress. Includes an essay describing the origin of the Barrio Kennedy after the president's assassination. Also included is a CD with recordings of the speeches that were presented during the visit. Essential reference for anyone interested in Colombian-US relations in the 1960s.

1091 Almario García, Óscar. Castas y razas en la Independencia neogranadina, 1810–1830: identidad y alteridad en los orígenes de la Nación colombiana. Bogotá: Universidad Nacional de Colombia, Comisión para la Celebración del Bicentenario de la Independencia, 2013. 278 p. (Colección Comisión para la Celebración del Bicentenario de la Independencia)

Prompted by the commemorations of the Bicentenario of Colombian Independence, Almerio García has compiled 10 essays and/or papers previously published during the last three years related to the independence period. The emphasis is on questions of identity and the positions of castes and races during the origin of the Colombian nation. Topics range from whether the Bicentenario should be celebrated at all to the role of blacks in the war of Independence. Helpful for suggesting new lines of inquiry related to the period between 1810 and 1830.

1092 Arias Vásquez, Andrés. Politica y vanguardia: la juventud colombiana en las artes plásticas de los años sesenta y setenta. (*Bol. Cult. Bibliogr.*, 51:93, 2017, p.23–39, bibl., ill.)

Observes that the "baby boom" generation supplied the universities with more students than ever before, including a massive number women. Discusses the various groups of artists and their work, the influence of the Cuban Revolution, US Peace Corps, and the Alliance for Progress. Regards José Gómez Sicre, director of the Salón Esso de Artistas Jóvenes and Marta Traba as two of the most powerful figures. Concludes that it was the tension between the ideas of these two individuals that permitted Colombian art to develop its own techniques of expressionism, abstract, and conceptualism. Other artists were Pedro Alcántara, Norman Mejía, Augusto Rendón, and Leonel Góngora.

1093 Aristizábal García, Diana Marcela.
"Supermercados *made in*": conexiones, consumo y apropiaciones. Estados Unidos y Colombia (siglo XX). (*Hist. Crít./Bogotá*, 65, julio/sept. 2017, p. 139–159, bibl.)

Careful analysis of primary and secondary sources in order to trace the evolution of consumer marketing in Colombia from small bodegas to self-service supermarkets during the 20th century. Deals with the development of local supermarket markets such as Tia, Carulla, and Exito, and foreign concerns such as Sears based in the US. Shows how they expanded in the 1950s and continued, until the end of the century, to adjust and accommodate their establishments to the varying customs of the population. Concludes that Colombian merchants actively participated in developments in consumer marketing drawing on their own local experiences. Helpful contribution to a little studied topic.

1094 El bicentenario de la independencia: legados y realizaciones a doscientos años. Edición de José David Cortés Guerrero. Bogotá: Universidad Nacional de Colombia-Sede Bogotá, Vicerrectoría de Sede, Dirección Académica, 2014. 468 p.: ill., some color.

In 2010, during the bicentennial of Colombia's independence, the Cátedra Manuel Ancízar at the Universidad Nacional held a series of conferences inviting scholars from different disciplines to meditate about the significance of this event. Predictably the participants offered multiple reflections on the process of change over 200 years. This handsomely produced anthology contains essays written by 17 academics arranged in six sections that investigate the impact of independence on Colombian territorial division; ideas; Liberalism and institutionalization; social groups and subaltern sectors; art; religion and daily life; and historiographical symbolism. The collection demonstrates that many questions remain to be answered about the meaning of independence and that these topics should be approached from a variety of view points.

1095 Braun, Herbert. La nación sentida: Colombia, 1949. El país se busca en sus palabras. Bogotá: Penguin Random House Grupo Editorial, S.A.S., 2018. 546 p.: ill.

As a continuation of his now classic *Mataron a Gaitán*, Braun traces developments during the months following the events of April 9, 1948 using telegrams, stories, press articles, and speeches. Focusing on the experiences of six representative individuals, he seeks to present the impressions of public and anonymous people during 1949 when Colombians felt the impact of the assassination and were contemplating the portent of the future. By connecting these varied sources, he has created a unique book which has the ability to capture the sensibility of the country and the historical conditions and circumstances that give form to today's Colombia. The product of over 30 years of contemplation, the volume is a major contribution for understanding what it means to be Colombian.

1096 Cacua Prada, Antonio. Antonio Nariño, el colombiano de todos los tiempos. Bogotá: Panamericana Editorial, 2012. 270 p. (Personajes de la Independencia; v. 4)

Antonio Nariño (1765–1823) was an administrator and journalist, best known as the "Precursor" for his role in the Independence movement. Well-written biography is a condensed version of a more extensive work published in 2008 by a distinguished historian and foremost authority on Nariño. Narrates the most important events in his life including his translation and publication of "The Rights of Man;" his enlistment in the patriot forces in 1810; his publication of 'La Bagatela;' his presidency of Cundinamarca (1812–1813); leadership of the military campaign in the south in 1813; and imprisonment by the Spanish (1813–1819). Informative introduction to career of a key independence figure.

1097 Castrillón Gallego, Catalina. Todo viene y todo sale por las ondas: formación y consolidación de la radiodifusión colombiana, 1929–1954. Medellín, Colombia: Editorial Universidad de Antioquia, 2015. 142 p.: ill. (Clío)

Excellent in-depth study of the processes of the constitution and formation of the radio broadcasting and the radio audience in Colombia during the media's so-called "golden age" 1929–54. Describes the broadcasting stations, the types of radio receptors, the hours and duration of transmission. Discusses the types of programs that included those for entertainment, those directed at children, and radio dramas. Most importantly, the author considers the nature of the audience and the impact of radio listening on the lives of ordinary Colombians. Major contribution to understanding the modernization of Colombian life in the 20th century.

1098 Cerón Rengifo, Carmen Patricia.
Amerindios y europeos en manuales escolares de historia de América: Colombia, 1975–1990. (*Anu. Colomb. Hist. Soc. Cult.*, 42:1, enero/junio 2015, p. 83–113, bibl.)

Analysis of depictions of Amerindians and Europeans in eight representative Latin American history textbooks published in Colombia between 1975 and 1990. Concludes that Amerindians are consistently located in a prior and inferior position relative to Europeans who are positively represented as providers of civilization. Thus, a Eurocentric perspective is imposed, and conquest and colonization are justified as essential processes for civilizing America. Notes that the period before the arrival of Europeans is usually categorized as "prehistory," suggesting that nothing of hisorical importance occurred until after 1492. Concludes that the texts justify the actions of the conquistadors and colonizers as "necessary and inevitable in order to civilize America." No surpises here, but interesting research nevertheless.

1099 Los colombianistas: una completa visión de los investigadores extranjeros que estudian a Colombia. Entrevistas de Victoria Peralta and Michael LaRosa. Edición actualizada. Bogotá: Academia Colombiana de Historia, 2015. 320 p.

The object of this book, originally published in English in 1997, was to gather information about 31 non-Colombian scholars specializing in Colombian history. Each interviewee responded to 10 questions concerning their personal background and their reasons for focusing on Colombia. The resulting data underscored problems foreigners encountered when studying Colombia, exposed underresearched topics, and sought to strengthen contacts between foreign and Colombian academicians. The Academia Colombiana de Historia commissioned this Spanish edition to provide a record of the past and to emphasize transformations that occurred during the past two decades. A brief "Presentación" outlines some of these changes, and the original list of non-Colombian scholars has been updated to include younger writers at work in 2015. An excellent source for anyone interested in the development of Colombian studies.

1100 Consecuencias económicas de la independencia. Edición de Heraclio Bonilla. Bogotá: Universidad Nacional de Colombia, Comisión para la Celebración del Bicentenario de la Independencia, 2012. 231 p.: ill., some color. (Colección Comisión para la Celebración del Bicentenario de la Independencia)

Prompted by the Bicentenario de Independence celebration, eight members of the Grupo de Historia Económica y Social of the History Department of Universidad Nacional sede Bogotá, directed by Professor Heraclio Bonilla, offer essays suggesting fresh approaches dealing with the war's impact on economic and national state development between 1780 and 1839. Muños R. traces quantitative changes of alcabala income; Torres Moreno analyzes mining developments; Bonilla looks at the migration of international capital; Moreno R. reviews foreign trade; Perilla Cárdenas traces the financing of armies during the war; Forerro Polo looks at kidnapping in the context of the war; Pérez considers the Junta de Secuestros during the Reconquista; while López Arévalo examines internal public debt between 1819–39. Bibliography included after each essay. Essential for students of the independence era.

1101 Del Castillo, Lina. Crafting a republic for the world: scientific, geographic, and historiographic inventions of Colombia. Lincoln: University of Nebraska Press, 2018. 382 p.

Iconoclastic interpretation of 19th-Colombian history suggests that after winning independence, there were no "colonial legacies" except those invented by "the vibrant postcolonial public sphere in Colombia." Colombian leaders then went on to tackle these so-called "legacies" to forge a republic in a hostile world of monarchies and empires. The book explores how the struggle at the vanguard of radical republican equality fomented innovative contributions to social science, history, and the calculation of equity through land reform. Deeply researched monograph concludes that the Colombians created a new science of republicanism. Complex and provocative study designed to challenge long accepted ideas of the nature of Colombia's 19th century.

1102 Los desterrados del paraíso: raza, pobreza y cultura en Cartagena de Indias. Edición de Alberto Abello Vives y Francisco Javier Flórez Bolívar. Cartagena de India, Colombia: Maremágnum, 2015. 479 p.: ill., maps.

This massive volume, containing multi-disciplinary essays by 18 authors, seeks to explain how and why Cartagena, a city that in 1810 was a "pearl" in the Spanish Empire, "betrayed itself" and declined over the next 200 years due to racial discrimination and scorn for African culture. In enumerating the conditions that led to this decline, the essayist suggests that deterioration has been minimized by the exertions of individuals belonging to the humble classes and by efforts through politics, labor, education, music, art, and culture to negotiate, question, and conteract the city's decline and reclaim its former glory.

1103 Díaz Casas, María Camila. Salteadores y cuadrillas de malhechores: una aproximación a la acción colectiva de la 'población negra' en el suroccidente de la Nueva Granada, 1840–1851. Popayán, Colombia: Editorial Universidad del Cauca, 2015. 277 p.

Impressive dissertation research seeks to answer the question: "What were the characteristics and influences of the collective action of the black population between 1840 and 1851 in bringing about the definitive abolition of slavery in Colombia?" Focus is on the provinces of Cauca, Buenaventura, and Popayán, and the narrative is divided into four phases: the period during the War of the Supremes; black collective armed action between 1840–43; black legal action between 1844–47, and black involvement in democratic societies. Concludes that contrary to traditional interpretations, blacks using both violent and peaceful strategies were agents in winning their unconditional freedom in 1851.

1104 Duque Muñoz, Lucía et al. Impactos territoriales en la transición de la colonia a la república en la Nueva Granada. Bogotá: Universidad Nacional de Colombia-Sede Bogotá, Facultad de Ciencias Humanas, Departamento de Geografía [y] Departamento de Historia, 2013. 202 p.: ill.

Essays by four geographers at the Universidad Nacional reveal how the tools of cartography can inform our understanding of historical developments. Chapter 1 by Delgado considers the impact of the wars of Independence as historical geographical phenomena. In Chapter 2, Jiménez analyses how the colonial spacial organization generated a reconstruction of regional economies due to British influence after independence. Chapter 3 by Williams Montoya studies the restructuring of the systems of cities that promoted the ascendancy of Bogotá and the decline of Cartagena. In Chapter 4 Duque Muñoz reviews explorations of New Granada by naturalists, geographers, and cartographers. Clear, beautiful maps illustrate key points throughout the volume. Essential source for scholars of early national period.

1105 Earle, Rebecca. España y la independencia de Colombia, 1810–1825. Bogotá: Universidad de los Andes, Facultad de Ciencias Sociales, Departamento de Historia, 2014. 250 p.: maps.

Spanish translation of a book originally published in English in 2000. Basing her examination on documents viewed in Seville, Bogotá, and Popayán archives, Earle suggests that the Spanish rather than the patriots were primarily responsible for the loss of New Granada due to the Crown's political incompetence, incoherent ideology, and internal conflicts, as well as personal animosity between the Spanish officials. Analysis is clearly presented and accessible to a wide range of readers. Highly recommended.

1106 Escobar Guzmán, Brenda. De los conflictos locales a la guerra civil: Tolima a finales del siglo XIX. Bogotá: Academia Colombiana de Historia, 2013. 308 p.: ill. (Biblioteca de historia nacional; CLXIX)

Innovative analysis of the Regeneración Era from the local perspective. Suggests that conflicts before and during the development of the Thousand Days War allowed subaltern sectors of Tolima a larger scope of action than previously acknowledged. Uses archival and published sources to show that the period was one of profound transformation in terms of colonization, adoption of new economic activities, and changes in political divisions. Argues that the war promoted new ideologies challenging the strict identification of Liberals versus Conservatives. Major contribution to regional history and subaltern studies in Colombia.

1107 Estrada Orrego, Victoria; Oscar Gallo; and **Jorge Márquez Valderrama.** Retórica de la cuantificación: tuberculosis, estadística y mundo laboral en Colombia, 1916–1946. (*Hist. Ciênc. Saúde Manguinhos*, 23:2, abril/junho 2016, p. 277–299, bibl., graph, table)

Informative research traces the application of tuberculosis statistics in Colombian medical discourse, the gap between these statistics and official data as well as the relationship between the quantitative dynamics, the anti-tuberculosis campaign and the objectification of tuberculosis in the labor world in Colombia from the beginning of the campaign in 1916 to the inclusion of tuberculosis in the list of professional diseases in 1946. Also analyzes the role labor statistics played in the development of the Colombian social security system and in the definition of professional diseases.

1108 Galán-Guerrero, Luis Gabriel; Juan Carlos Rodríguez-Raga; and **Laura Wills Otero.** Los viajes olvidados de la democracia: circulación y apropiación de la legislación electoral en Colombia, 1855–1886. (*LARR*, 51:4, 2016, p. 139–162, bibl.)

Complex essay reviews the various ways that legislation adopted in Colombia both by states and the central government was circulated via newspapers, bookstores, and shops within Colombia and throughout Europe and the US. Offers an analysis of how various sectors of society adopted aspects of this legislation in different contexts and speculates on the impact that knowledge of these numerous constitutions and electoral laws had on a world still dominated by empires and monarchs.

1109 Gutiérrez Sanín, Francisco. El orangután con sacoleva: cien años de democracia y represión en Colombia (1910–2010). Bogotá: IEPRI, 2014. 527 p.: ill. (Biblioteca IEPRI 25 años)

Intensive analysis of the opposing views suggesting that Colombia is either Latin America's oldest democracy or a terrorist regime—a contradiction colorfully described by Darío Echandía as an "orangutan wearing a jacket." Text is divided into three parts in which the author carefully explores both interpretations. Rejects facile solutions to this anomaly and suggests that investigators should explore more deeply each of these embedded sides of Colombian political development. Includes wide-ranging and extensive bibliography. Key contribution for interpreting Colombian history.

1110 Henderson, James D. Colombia's narcotics nightmare: how the drug trade destroyed peace. Jefferson, N.C.: McFarland & Company, Inc., 2015 230 p.: ill., map.

Authoritative history of Colombia's illegal drug traffic originally published in Spanish in 2012. Six chapters detail the Medellín and Cali cartels' war against the Colombian government, the revolutionary guerrilla war against the government, the paramilitary war against the guerillas, and the way in which the government finally put a stop to the cartel-financed bloodshed. Author's conclusion that the US-sponsored Plan Colombia to eradicate the trade was a positive development is controversial, but he does make a strong case that the program was "necessary and proper." Narrative is accessible to undergraduates as well as professionals. Includes a helpful glossary and extensive bibliography.

1111 Hoz, Joaquín Viloria de la. Negocios en la frontera: agricultura, comercio y actividad extractiva en La Guajira colombiana, 1870–1930. (*Caribb. Stud.*, 42:1, Jan./June 2014, p. 183–224, bibl., map, tables)

Solid archival analysis of commercial activities in Guajira as well as the institutional and natural limits that the merchants endured between 1870 and 1930. Suggests a cross-border economy developed in a frontier region characterized by lack of institutional presence, a large indigenous population, absences of colonization, and active trade with Venezuela, Curaçao, Jamaica, and other islands. Concludes that employers linked to extractive activities such as salt, pearls, and dyewood could not create the necessary institutions or entrepreneurial context to consolidate the Guajira economy as a productive network based on endogenous production with competitive companies and a labor market adjusted to national legislation.

1112 Jiménez Becerra, Absalón. Una mirada al movimiento estudantil colombiana, 1954–1978. (*Bol. Cult. Bibliogr.*, 51:93, 2017, p. 5–21, bibl., ill.)

Colombian sociologist reviews the organization and impact of student groups after 1922, tracing the evolution of their demands to improve conditions in public and private universities and their political actions. During the Gómez dictatorship the students organized the Federación Universitaria Colombiana calling for an autonomous university academically, administratively, and financially. They collaborated in the overthrow of Rojas in 1957 and in the 1960s organized strikes to press their demands on the Frente Nacional governments. The movement became more militant in 1971 after police killed seven students during a protest in Cali. Concludes that university youth activities were viewed both with fear and romanticism as they sought to promote a general transformation of Colombian society.

1113 Karl, Robert A. Forgotten peace: reform, violence, and the making of contemporary Colombia. Oakland: University of California Press, 2017. 321 p.: bibl., ill., index, maps, tables.

Explores how Colombians grappled with violence between 1957 and 1966 during and after the period known as La Violencia, a term that came into being in the mid-1960s. Adopts a variegated methodological approach that combines a biographical focus on individual actors with an analysis of broader trends in public discourse. Also maps spatial patterns of violence and political changes while drawing on archival materials and classic texts. Result is a vivid narrative and sweeping reinterpretation of the mid-20th-century conflicts that provides a new explanation for the emergence of the FARC guerrillas and offers important implications for the peace efforts today.

1114 Lenis Ballesteros, César Augusto. Los *Dorados* de la Revolución de Independencia: proyectos e innovaciones en la minería antioqueña. (*Hist. Soc./Río Piedras*, 29, julio/dic. 2015, p. 229–257, bibl.)

Investigation seeks to show the continuity between Creole efforts at gold mining in Antioquia in the late 18th century and projects begun by elites in the early and late 19th century. Emphasis is placed on technological developments and contributions of foreigners—Swiss, French, English, and German—who, in the years after independence, introduced the miners to new techniques in mineralogy, geology, hydraulics, and metallurgy. As a result, by the second half of the century, mining methods had become more modern and scientific.

1115 López Michelsen, Alfonso. López sin tapujos: antología de los escritos más polémicos de Alfonso López Michelsen. Bogotá: Debate, 2015. 291 p.: bibl.

López Michelsen (1913–2007) was the founder of the Movimiento Revolucionario Liberal (MRL) and the president of Colombia between 1974–78. Juan Leonel Giraldo has brought together a collection of López Michelson's essays on 11 general topics previously published in books and newspaper articles. With the understanding that there are already many biographies of López Michelson, Giraldo has created this selection of essays in order to provide insight into the author's political ideas and his views of various aspects of Colombia's history, politics, and culture. Primarily of interest to students of Colombia's contemporary history.

1116 Malkún Castillejo, Willian. Educación y política en el estado soberano de Bolívar, 1857–1885. Cartagena de Indias, Colombia: Editorial Universitaria, 2013. 265 p.: bibl.

Analysis of the school reform of 1870 in the state of Bolívar with a special emphasis on its efforts to diminish the role of the Catholic Church and to form good citizens. Suggests that unlike their counterparts in Cundinamarca and Boyacá, clergy in Bolívar did not oppose the reform, but the costs of the civil war of 1876 instigated by religious concerns, was a significant blow to Bolívar's educational budget. Political instability, continual economic crises, and objections of parents to the reform likewise took a toll on elementary and university education. Despite these difficulties, author concludes that "the radical project in Bolívar established an education presence in all the provinces of the state."

1117 Mejía de Mesa, Marietta. Entre la mutua dependencia y la mutua independencia: el Hospital San Ignacio y la Facultad de Medicina de la Universidad Javeriana, 1942–1990. Bogotá: Pontificia Universidad Javeriana Bogotá, 2013. 342 p.: bibl., ill. (Taller y oficio de la historia)

Traces the development of hospitals in Bogotá during the course of the 20th century with an emphasis on the establishment of the Faculty of Medicine at the Universidad Javeriana in 1942 along with its plans to create a cooperative relationship with a soon-to-be-built Hospital San Ignacio. Investigates foreign influence in Colombian medicine and problems with the Ley 67 of 1935 concerning the medical profession. Narrates the history of Hospital San Ignacio whose construction, due to economic difficulties and in the context of the European war, was delayed for two decades. An important contribution to the history of Colombian medicine.

1118 Mesa Chica, Darío. Miguel Antonio Caro: el intelectual y el político. Bogotá: Universidad Nacional de Colombia, Sede Bogotá, Facultad de Ciencias Humanas, Departamento de Sociología, 2014. 164 p. (Biblioteca abierta; 428. Colección General. Sociología)

Miguel Antonio Caro, linguist, legislator, and acting president of Colombia 1892–1898 was a distinguished orator and philosopher known for his strong defense of the Hispanic tradition. This volume is a collection of Mesa's lectures and student responses during a graduate seminar at the Departamento de Sociología of the Universidad Nacional that examined Caro's views concerning political economy and the adoption of paper money. Mesa's reflections call attention to Caro's complex personality and set aside his markedly conservative ideology to present him as a thinker whose value in Colombia's natural life should not be reduced to his partisan activities.

1119 Monsalvo Mendoza, Edwin. Presidencialismo vs. provincialismo: el control de los poderes locales en Colombia. (*Caribb. Stud.*, 42:1, Jan./June 2014, p. 135–162, bibl.)

Reviews political developments in Cartagena province during the 1830s to provide new insights into Santander's presidency (1832–37). Through analysis of letters, press, leaflets, and contemporary testimonies, suggests that the 1836 election was a critical turning point because it enabled a moderate faction of liberalism to come to power thanks to efforts of local leaders within the provinces. Concludes that leaders in peripheral territories could and did challenge the power of the central government, and that this tendency eventually led to a two party system in the 1840s.

1120 Morales Benítez, Otto. Eduardo Santos. Tomo 1, Apuntes para una biografía política. Tomo 2, Cartas, discursos, artículos y otros documentos. Bogotá: Intermedio, Universidad del Rosario, 2016. 2 vol.: ill.

Eduardo Santos (1888–1974) was a lawyer, Liberal, longtime editor of *El Tiempo* and president of Colombia from 1938 to 1942. Moralez Benítez, a prolific historian, spent three decades gathering materials related to Santos. These two volumes represent a distillation of his findings. The first volume examines Santos' family antecedents and principal aspects of his presidency. It concludes with a brief section concerning his exile in the early 1950s. The second volume is a compilation of documents, speeches, and letters that Santos composed during his presidency as well as his personal correspondence with Paul Rivet and Gabriela Mistral. This dual publication is not a fully developed biography, but it does contain much previously obscure information that will interest historians of mid-20th century Colombia.

1121 Mosquera, José E. Diego Luis Córdoba: mito y realidad: historia de las luchas de los chocoanos por la creación del departamento del Chocó, 1830–1947. Medellín, Colombia: Editorial L. Vieco, 2015. 247 p.: bibl., ill. (Serie Debates)

Revisionist view of Chocó's stuggle to achieve departmental status in 1947. Based on archival and published materials, the text is divided into two parts: the first analyzes efforts between 1830–1905 to create an Intendencia Nacional. The second deals with 1905–47. Author suggests that during this period, Diego Luis Córdoba promoted the struggle to attain departmental status, but that historians have overemphasized his role. Rather than being the "father of the creation of the Department of Chocó," Córdoba built on the efforts of many other leaders. Essential study challenging the mythology surrounding Córdoba's career.

1122 **Murillo Sandoval, Juan David.** La aparición de las librerías colombianas: conexiones, consumos y giros editoriales en la segunda mitad del siglo XIX. (*Hist. Crít./Bogotá*, 65, julio/sept. 2017, p. 49–69, bibl.)

Study of the development of bookstores in Colombia in the early 19th century. Examines the commerce of book circulation and the bookselling profession and notes the importance of book catalogs and international trade for the consolidation of bookstores. A useful sketch of 19th-century booksellers and their connections to commercial, editorial, and political networks.

1123 **Ospina Ovalle, Carlos.** Los años en que Colombia recuperó la esperanza: cómo la aplicación coordinada de política y estrategia logró la recuperación social, económica y de seguridad de la nación colombiana. Medellín, Colombia: Universidad Pontificia Bolivariana, 2014. 572 p., 1 unnumbered page: bibl., ill. (chiefly color), color maps. (Colección Nuevo pensamiento político contemporáneo; 8)

Excellent and straightforward tactical, strategic, and political analysis of the government's Political, Defense and Democratic Security Plan 2002 and its Patriotic Military Plan that was eventually successful in ending the decades-long battle with the FARC. Author is a retired general and professional historian who was involved in these actions. Far more than just a history of Colombia from 1960 to 2014, the book traces the ups and downs of the long struggle, and shows why the FARC was unable to succeed in overturning the government. Suggests that the government's eventual success offers a model that can be applied in other regions of the world suffering similar conditions.

1124 **Otero-Cleves, Ana María.** Foreign machetes and cheap cotton cloth: popular consumers and imported commodities in nineteenth-century Colombia. (*HAHR*, 97:3, Aug. 2017, p. 423–456, bibl., ill.)

Well-written and researched study examines the consumption of foreign machetes and textiles by peasants, smallholders, and artisans in 19th-century Colombia. Shows that popular sectors of society were the largest consumers of foreign goods and as such were able to change markets conditions and make specific demands regarding the quality of imported products intended for their consumption. Shows that popular classes chose imported goods for their quality rather than price and were active participants as consumers in the developing national economy. Concludes that popular sectors were critical agents in national and international markets and as such were functional citizens in their new nation.

1125 **Peralta, Victoria.** Distinciones y exclusiones: en busca de cambios culturales in Bogotá durante las Repúblicas Liberales: una historia cultural de Bogotá (1930–1946). Bogotá: Academia Colombiana de Historia, 2013. 318 p.: bibl., ill. (Biblioteca de Historia Nacional; CLXX)

Innovative and intensive "content analysis" of issues of the magazine *Cromos* between 1930 and 1946 reveals how Bogotá elites sought to create a facade of modernity in Colombia by emulating developments in Europe and the US. Argues that this trend fortified the ability of the upper class to control the political, economic, and social destiny of Colombia when its hegemony was being challenged by the arrival of new methods of mass communication. Suggests that this process, which was also occuring in other Latin American countries, enabled elites to solidify their superiority over the subordinate classes thus increasing inequalities between groups. An important contribution to 20th-century social and cultural history.

1126 **Pérez Benavides, Amada Carolina.** Nosotros y los otros: las representaciones de la nación y sus habitantes, Colombia, 1880–1910. Bogotá: Editorial Pontificia Universidad Javeriana, 2015. 327 p.: illustrations (some color), maps (chiefly color). (Opera eximia Abstracts.)

Revised dissertation compares the ways white (or "notables"), blacks ("afrodescendientes") and indigenes were represented in the writings and pictures of *Papel Periódico Ilustrado*, the Museo Nacional, and the reports of missionaries at the turn of the 19th century. Volume reproduces 68 illustrations, 11 graphs, and nine maps, suggesting that these representations have influenced political, cultural, and social practices. Artisans and campesinos were rarely portrayed which raises new questions about the nature of the Colombian population in the late 19th century and argues that new approaches should be employed to recover the contributions of these underrepresented groups.

Pico, Claudia Milena. Historia económica de Colombia: fiscalía y moneda entre los siglos XVI y XIX. See item **965**.

1127 Pinzón de Lewin, Patricia. Esmeralda Arboleda: la mujer y la política. Bogotá: Taller de Edición-Rocca, 2014. 457 p.: ill. (Biografía)

Esmeralda Arboleda (1921–97) was a feminist, senator, minister, and diplomat from Valle de Cauca. Authoritative biography recounts her early life, her university studies, her graduation as a lawyer, her participation in the struggle for women's right to vote in Colombia (that was only granted in 1954), and her subsequent political and diplomatic career. Although Arboleda's efforts were praised by Presidents Alberto Lleras Camargo and Carlos Lleras Restrepo, and she remained active in national and international causes, this is the first study of her life, and consequently a major contribution to Colombian feminist studies.

1128 Pita Pico, Roger. El saqueo de los ornamentos y las alhajas sagradas en las Guerras de Independencia de Colombia: entre la represión política y la devoción religiosa. (*Rev. Complut. Hist. Am.*, 43, 2017, 179–202, bibl.)

Analysis of the looting, transformation and destruction of church ornaments during the Wars of Independence. Shows that these sacred pieces were immersed in a context marked by political polarization, religious devotion, and the desire of Republicans and Spaniards to acquire resources for the war efforts. In 1821 the republican government decided to sell gold and silver items not considered sacred and apply the profits to public education. It returned other artifacts to the churches. Provides insight into the Church-state struggle during the early years of independence.

1129 Popayán en el siglo XX: algunas perspectivas sobre su historia urbana. Edición de Natalia Cruz Gómez, Natalia Cobo Paz, y Alexander Díaz Munévar. Popayán, Colombia: Editorial UC, Editorial Universidad del Cauca, 2016. 149 p.: bibl., ill., index.

Collection of three essays that deals with aspects of the 20th-century history of Popayán. Topics include discussion of improvement of hygiene in the city between 1920–35; analysis of the uses of public spaces between 1930–40; and the perceptions of the terrible earthquake of 1983 that transformed the city and initiated a population boom. Taken together, the essays amplify understanding of the modern history of the city by recovering forgotten voices and social sectors and refuting the image of Popayán as simply a well-preserved artifact of Spanish colonial rule. The essay on the impact of the earthquake, now almost forgotten, is especially moving. In short, volume is a useful contribution to urban and regional history.

1130 Porto Cabrales, Raúl. Memoria histórica del béisbol de Bolívar y de Cartagena, 1874–1948. Cartagena de Indias, Colombia: Universidad de Cartagena, 2013. 339 p., 1 unnumbered p.: bibl., ill.

First installment of a proposed three-volume history recording the "genesis, evolution and development of baseball in Cartagena and Bolívar" from 1874 to the present. Porto Cabrales, a respected journalist, notes that this is a subject that has been completely neglected by academics. As a result he has relied on newspapers, personal archives, and oral testimonies to put together a coherent, comprehensive, and well-written outline of the emergence of this sport on Colombia's Caribbean coast. In addition to the text, he includes a helpful chronology of significant events, a glossary of baseball terms, extensive statistics, and multiple photographs of key players. An innovative and promising contribution to Colombia's understudied sport history.

1131 La Quintiada (1912–1925): la rebelión indígena liderada por Manuel Quintín Lame en el Cauca: recopilación de fuentes primarias. Compilación de Julieta Lemaitre Ripoll. Bogotá: Universidad de los Andes, 2013. 339 p.: bibl. (Colección Historia y materiales del derecho)

Manuel Quintín Lame (1880–1967), and advocate of indigenous rights, was a key leader in a native rebellion in Cauca between 1914 and 1925. Volume contains a collection of letters, telegrams, press notices, and official documents related to the movement. Following this section are three introductory essays: Lemaitre Ripoll examines the way Lame used law to promote indigenous rights; Karla Escobar places the rebellion in the context of the modernization that Colombia was experiencing; and Paulo Bacca, drawing on primary and secondary accounts, provides an account of Lame's personal history. A major contribution to the study of native movements and conflict over land in the early 20th century.

1132 Reina Rodríguez, Carlos Arturo. Rock and roll en Colombia: el impacto de una generación en la transformación cultural del país en el siglo XX. (Bol. Cult. Bibliogr., 51:93, 2017, p. 23–39, bibl., ill.)

An examination of the ways that music united and gave vitality to youth in the 1960s and 1970s. Shows how radio and television promoted the new genre of "rock and roll." Despite the disapproval of established authorities who saw it as a new method of North American penetration into Colombian culture, young people adopted the hippie style and discotheques appeared in various parts of Bogatá. Due to the inability to import electric guitars, Colombian bands adapted their own versions. A major event was the Festival de Ancón held in Medellín, June 18–20 1971. Known as the Colombian Woodstock, it attracted between 15,000 and 30,000 young people. In the 1990s, Medellín replaced Bogotá as the most "rock" oriented city in the country.

1133 Reza, Germán A de la. El intento de integración de Santo Domingo a la Gran Colombia, 1821–1822. (Secuencia/México, 93, sept./dic. 2015, p. 65–82, bibl.)

Analyzes the factors that influenced the decision of the "State of Spanish Haiti" to join Gran Colombia during its brief political existence from December 1821 to February 1822. The research findings underscore the complexity of the Dominican strategy. Emphasizes the importance of Bolívar's support for the integration of Santo Domingo to "Gran Colombia," which if completed might have effected important changes in the situation of Spanish control of Cuba and Puerto Rico.

1134 Rincón, Carlos. Íconos y mitos culturales en la invención de la nación en Colombia. Bogotá: Pontificia Universidad Javeriana, 2014. 374 p.: 1 ill. (Colección 2010; 3)

Amid statements that due to persistent violence, Colombia is close to being a "failed state," a distinguished scholar seeks to investigate the Colombian cultural memory that has coalesced around myths that through the centuries have made Colombia a nation. The myths he identifies include Nuestra Señora del Rosario de Chiquinquirá stemming from the colonial era; Simón Bolívar from the Independence era, and in the 19th-century the image of Colombia as the Athens of Latin America which is fortified by the culture of poets. Insightful but dense narrative that draws upon and includes a wide-ranging bibliography.

1135 Rodríguez Cuadros, José Darío. Génesis, actores y dinámicas de la violencia política en el Pacífico nariñense. Bogotá: Odecofi-Cinep, Pontificia Universidad Javeriana, 2015. 155 p.: bibl., ill. (some color), color maps. (Colección Territorio, poder y conflicto)

Investigation seeks to explain why between 1990 and 2012 conflicts in the Pacific department of Nariño have greatly increased. Emphasizes that transformations in the region's economic and social life have led to structural problems. These are exacerbated by the department's complicated geography that provides a strategic corridor to the Pacific for contraband and coca commerce as well as a refuge for illegal armed groups fighting in the interior regions of the country. Draws on interviews and printed sources. Includes an excellent series of maps and graphs.

1136 Ruiz Patiño, Jorge Humberto. Juventud y deporte en Colombia en la primera mitad del siglo XX. (*Bol. Cult. Bibliogr.*, 51:93, 2017, p. 57–71, bibl., ill.)

In a stimulating essay, Colombian sociologist examines the impact of sports on the concept of youth in Colombia during the first half of the 20th century. Nineteenth century diversions consisted of theater plays, bullfighting, cockfighting, and gambling. Show how the introduction of the bicycle, tennis, basketball, soccer, and polo represented modern values of progress, health, and hygiene. Organized sport was restricted to youths of the upper class, including women who gained more freedom to participate. In public schools the government promoted physical education for the popular class. Notes how these new activities created a gulf between younger and the older generation who clung to traditional diversions, and suggests that as professional sports became popular, there was a fear that youth would become passive spectators rather than active participants.

1137 Salgado Hernández, Elizabeth Karina. Estrategias de negociación y resistencia indígena a la colonización del occidente de Antioquia, 1880–1920. (*Hist. Soc./Río Piedras*, 29, julio/dic. 2015, p. 171–201, bibl.)

Investigation into the social, cultural, economic and political actions undertaken by the indigenous communities living in the reservation of San Carlos de Cañasgordas against the colonization process in western Antioquia between 1880 and 1920. During that time, the government was making final distributions of the collective ownership of land in the basins of the Sucio and Murri rivers. Despite persistent pressure from colonizers, the indigenous peoples made use of judicial and administrative procedures as well as their economic relations with neightboring settlers to obtain favorable resolutions from the local authorities affirming their control of their land. An excellent example of Indian agency at the turn of the 20th century.

Sociedad, política y cultura en Colombia siglos XVIII–XIX: (enfoques, problemas y tendencias). See item **967**.

1138 Torres Cendales, Leidy Jazmín. ¿Progreso, disciplina y masculinidad?: un caso de sodomía en la Universidad Nacional de los Estados Unidos de Colombia, 1880. (*Hist. Soc./Río Piedras*, 29, julio/dic. 2015, p. 121–151, bibl.)

Careful investigation of an act of sodomy presumably committed by two philosophy and literature students at the Universidad Nacional in 1880. After an analysis of the disciplinary system of the university, the possible meanings of sexual contact between men in the late 19th century, and the power relations revealed by the documents, the author shows how the case destabilized and at the same time reaffirmed the control system and the physical and behavioral standards within the institution. Presents the actions of the two men as an escape mechanism from the harsh surveillance toward students as well as exposing the regulation and behavioral rule imposed on the students. Fascinating insight into gender relations in the late 19th century.

1139 Tovar Bernal, Leonardo. Enseñanza religiosa y poder clerical: Estados Unidos de Colombia, 1863–1886. (*Anu. Colomb. Hist. Soc. Cult.*, 44:2, julio/dic. 2017, p. 304–330, bibl.)

The 1863 Constitution of Colombia and the 1870 Organic Decree regarding elementary public education included articles that seemed to limit the Catholic Church's control of education. Through an analysis of school textbooks representative of the period, essay shows how despite the aforementioned regulations, religious education was widespread in schools and remained practically untouched by attempts to impose limits on it. In spite of the efforts of government authorities, the textbooks continued to comply with papal teachings set out by Pope Pius IX in *Syllabus Erromun* (1864) and Pope Leo XIII in *Aeterni Patris* (1879).

1140 Valencia Llano, Alonso. Afrodescendientes en el Valle del Cauca: ensayos históricos. Palmira, Colombia: Universidad del Valle, Sede Palmira, 2015. 130 p.

Suggests that since Afrodescendientes formed the largest minority in the population of the Valle del Cauca, their role in the history of the region, previously ignored, deserves further investigation. This compilation of essays, some previously published, discusses their participation and is organized in three sections: "Contributions of Afrodescendientes to the Development of the Valle del Cauca;" "Role of Popular Sectors in the Independence of the Valle del Cauca," and "Slaves during the First Fifty Years of the Republic." Useful starting place for researchers concerned with delving more deeply into the experience of Afrodescendientes in Colombian history.

1141 Valencia Llano, Alonso. Entre la resistencia social y la acción política: de bandidos a políticos. Cali, Colombia: Universidad del Valle, Departamento de Historia, 2014. 144 p.: bibl. (Colección Historia y espacio)

Distinguished professor uses archival, periodical, and secondary sources to show how under Spanish rule marginalized social groups in the Cauca Valley integrated themselves into republican society during the 19th century. Groups studied include slaves, peons working on haciendas or hatos, free campesinos, small rural merchants, rebels and individuals categorized as *bandidos* or *bandoleros*, and urban domestic servants and vagrants. Discusses the tensions caused by the abolition of the colonial region and emphasizes how, during the new republic, poor whites, blacks, mulatos and mestizos, by invoking liberal views of "el pueblo soberano" "Liberty, equality and fraternity," or by owning a piece of land, were able to improve their status and even, in some cases, become political actors in the Liberal Party.

1142 Vargas Álvarez, Sebastián. La investigación sobre las conmemoraciones rituales en Colombia, siglos XIX–XXI: balance historiográfico. (*Anos 90*, 22:42, dez. 2015, p. 207–235, bibl.)

Commemorative rituals—at times called "civil ceremonies" and at others "Patriotic holidays"—since the 19th century have played an important role in nation-state building and legitimization in Colombia during the past two centuries. Three-part essay first defines the problems of ritual commemorations as an object of study that forms parts of a more general concern of history and social sciences about the politics of memory and public uses of history. Next, it presents an inventory and brief analysis of contemporary inquiries on this subject in Colombia. Final section balances the conclusions of the two approaches and suggests possible new theoretical and methodological paths on ritual commemorations research.

1143 Walker, Alexander. Colombia, siendo una relación geográfica, topográfica, agricultural, comercial, política, &c. de aquel pays. Tercera edición. Caracas: Academia Nacional de la Historia, 2014. 2 volumes: ill.

New Venezuelan edition of an extensive description of Ecuador, Colombia and Venezuela originally published in English and Spanish in 1822. Editor Alexander Walker drew heavily on the accounts written by Alexander von Humboldt and François DePons. The original edition was promoted by Francisco Antonio Zea. Volume I includes essays by Pedro Cunill Grau, who analyzes the sources for the work and Juan Carlos Reyes, who explores questions concerning its authorship. It has a map of the territory drawn in 1814 and four chapters describing the geographic and natural characteristics of Gran Colombia, information on the Spanish population and various groups of indigenous peoples. The three chapters in Volume II cover agricultural and animal products, commerce, history, and politics. Useful and basic reference for anyone researching the independence era.

1144 Yie Garzón, Maite. Del patrón-Estado al Estado-patrón: la agencia campesina en las narrativas de la reforma agraria en Nariño. Bogotá: Pontificia Universidad Javeriana, 2015. 309 p.: bibl., ill., indexes. (Colección Academia)

Authoritative explanation of agrarian reform between 1960 and 1970 by privileging the campesinos' memories of their experiences on the Hacienda de Bomboná in Nariño. Suggests that the reform was propelled not by the efforts of the state, but through campesino activism. Describes the patrón-campesino relationship. Emphasizes that campesinos took pride in their role in bringing about change. Author reaches these conclusions through a careful examination of archival and published sources as well as extensive interviews with campesinos conducted in 2007. Volume provides a new approach while offering novel insights into the study of Colombian agrarian reform.

1145 Zapata Giraldo, Juan Gonzalo. Reforma radical en el estado de Santander, 1850–1885. Bogotá: Universidad del Rosario, 2016. 342 p.: bibl., maps. (Colección Textos de ciencias humanas)

This revised PhD thesis is based on an exhaustive review of archival sources and offers an in-depth examination of political, economic, and social developments in the state of Santander during the period of Radical rule, 1850–85. After a review of the general political policies adopted by federal governments in 1864, the author emphasizes the development of reforms in three sectors: finance, railroads, and education. He concludes that the conduct of the regime in Santander during this period stands as one of the Radical Liberals' most successful achievements.

1146 Zarama Rincón, Rosa Isabel. Pasto: cotidianidad en tiempos convulsionados, 1824–1842. Bucaramanga, Colombia: Dirección Cultural, Universidad Industrial de Santander, 2012. 2 vol.: bibl. (Colección Bicentenario; 21)

Revised doctoral thesis reviews local archival sources to present a detailed examination of the social and cultural life of the people of Pasto in the first three decades after independence. While earlier histories have emphasized the resistance of *pastusos* to incorporation into New Granadan armies, this study provides a comprehensive view of the life of women in convents, the pulperías, indios concertados and merchants, priests and bishops, mule drivers and soldiers. Volume I sets the geographic scene and includes chapters on the municipal council, and the political integration of Pasto into Nueva Granada, while Volume II focuses on economic and religious life. Outstanding regional history and essential reference for students of the first half of the 19th century.

ECUADOR

1147 Ayala Mora, Enrique. Historia, tiempo y conocimiento del pasado: estudio sobre periodización general de la historia ecuatoriana: una interpretación interparadigmática. Quito: Universidad Andina Simón Bolívar, Sede Ecuador, Corporación Editora Nacional, 2014. 198 p.: bibl., ill., indexes. (Colección Temas; 23)

Leading Ecuadorian historian proposes and justifies in a series of seven essays a new schema for delineating the periodization of Ecuador's history which will take into account new insights provided by research completed in the last 30 years. The epochs he outlines are as follows: Época Aborigen (12000 a.c to 1529); Época Colonial (1529–1806); Independencia y Étapa Colombiana (1808–30); and Étapa Republicana (1830-present). There are further divisions in each época. For example: he divides the Época Republicana into three subperiods: Primer período: Proyecto nacional criollo (1830–95); Segundo período: Proyecto nacional mestizo (1895–1960); Tercer período: Proyecto nacional de la diversidad (1960 to the present). While sure to provoke criticism, this new organization should be helpful to scholars and students alike.

1148 Ayala Mora, Enrique. Historiografía ecuatoriana: apuntes para una visión general. Quito: Universidad Andina Simón Bolivia, Ecuador, Corporación Editora Nacional, 2015. 196 p.: bibl., indexes. (Biblioteca de historia 45)

Distinguished historian provides a brief general vision of the developments of the historiography of Ecuador from the colonial times to the 21st century. The work is divided by periods, stages, themes, and tendencies, and reviews efforts by individual authors and institutions. Although the narrative is accessible to the uninitiated, the work, addressed to serious historians interested in Latin America and Ecuador, is intended to encourage the formation of future scholars and teachers of history. Extols the professionalization of the discipline since the 1970s, but concludes that much work needs to be done on the subject of Ecuador's independence era and the impact of the development of the nation state on the native populations. Indispensable volume for anyone interested in investigating Ecuadorean history.

1149 Barrera-Agarwal, María Helena. Anatomía de una traición: la venta de la bandera. Tungurahua, Ecuador: Casa de la Cultura Ecuatoriana, Núcleo del Tungurahua, 2015. 176 p.: bibl.

In 1895 Chile sold the warship *Esmeralda* to José María Caamaño on the condition that he would sell it to Japan, then involved in a war with China. According to the arrangement, Caamaño did sell the *Esmeralda* back to Chile, which, not wanting to jeopardize its neutrality in the Sino-Japanese war, allowed it to sail for Yokohama under an Ecuadorean flag. Enemies of Caamaño accused him of betraying Ecuador, and the incident contributed to resignation of Ecuador's president, Luis Cordero Crespo. Using archival documents Barrera-Agarwal challenges this interpretation. She suggests that American businessman Charles Flint was behind the event and cites the incident as example of growing US involvement in South American affairs after the US Civil War. Provocative but solid work.

1150 Becker, Marc. The FBI in Latin America: the Ecuador files. Durham, N.C.: Duke University Press, 2017. 322 p.: bibl., ill., index. (Radical perspectives: a radical history review book series)

During WWII, the FBI used a program called Special Intelligence Service (SIS) to assign 700 agents to combat Nazi influence in Latin America. By 1943, FBI director J. Edgar Hoover shifted their focus from Nazism to communism. This book is an analysis of the trove of surveillance documents produced by FBI agents in Ecuador that provides a new perspective on events in 20th-century Ecuador, the activities of the Latin America left, and broad-based social movements. Among other conclusions, it suggests that the Ecuadorean left did not speak with one voice; that regional and ideological disputes divided Communist leaders, and that some activists collaborated with the US in the war against the Nazis, while others cared more about local activities.

1151 Cabrera Hanna, Santiago. Hispanismo, mestizaje y representaciones indígenas durante el quinto centenario en Ecuador: *Vistazo* y *El Comercio*. (*Anu. Colomb. Hist. Soc. Cult.*, 42:1, enero/junio 2015, p. 213–244, bibl., photos)

Based on newspaper articles published in *Vistazo* and *El Comercio* in 1992 during the Fifth Centennial, the essay examines representation of Indians with special attention to reports about the centennial and opinion articles. Suggests that native images inserted into the public memory at this time served as an underpinning of national white-mestizo discourse in opposition to demands issued by indigenous organizations. Concludes that two motivations inspired these false images: to affirm intermixing with Spanish blood and to serve as an ideological and cultural counter to political demands of the indigenous movement. The result was the reaffirmation of myths regarding the discovery of America.

1152 Espinosa Fernández de Córdoba, Carlos and Cristóbal Aljovín de Losada. Conceptos clave del conservadurismo en Ecuador, 1875–1900. (*Anu. Colomb. Hist. Soc. Cult.*, 42:1, enero/junio 2015, p. 179–212, bibl.)

Refreshing revisionist view of conservative political language in Ecuador during the last third of the 19th century. Suggests positions were an expression of political modernity as well as a discourse involving dialogue with liberal concepts. Explores conservative ideas of "Catholic freedom," "Catholic civilization" and "perfect society" and the reciprocal manner in which these concepts were defined relative to liberal notions. Analyzes polysemantic political categories in a context of struggle and in relation to the rise of modernity. Concludes that despite their differences, Conservatives and Liberals shared common values regarding progress, individual and collective liberty, and religion, but their responses to these values were opposite at times.

1153 Gomezjurado Zevallos, Javier. Quito: historia del cabildo y la ciudad. Quito: Javier Gomezjurado Zevallos, 2015. 611 p.: bibl., ill., maps.

Prominent Ecuadorean historian provides a comprehensive history of the cabildo in the city of Quito. Beginning with the origin of the institution in medieval Spain, he traces its transfer to Quito in the 16th century. Subsequent chapters cover the development of the institution chronologically by centuries. Volume concludes with the list of Quito mayors from 1946 to 2015. Based on review of archival materials stored in the AGI in Geville, the Archivo Metropolitano and the Archivo Nacional de Historia of Quito along with private archives. Extensive footnoting and bibliography but to index. Successfully argues that the history of the cabildo is tantamount to the history of the city. A key recource for scholars.

1154 González Leal, Miguel Ángel. Historiando la crisis de 1859. (*Ecuad. Debate*, 93, diciembre 2014, p. 47–62, bibl.)

The political crisis of 1859, which preceded the regime of García Moreno (1860–75), could easily have led to the break up of Ecuador into regions. This provocative essay is a methodological reflection on the significance of this crisis. Argues that while historians usually trace the cause to the international conflict over borders, they haven't given significant importance to the problem of regionalism and the failure of efforts to create a state combining three large regions: Sierra Norte, Sierra Sur, and Costa. Calls for more careful review of the situation in Guayaquil and lists the types of sources that should be consulted.

1155 Hamerly, Michael T. and Miguel Díaz Cueva. Bibliografía de bibliografías ecuatorianas, 1885–2010. Primera edición en español. Quito: Universidad Andina Simón Bolívar Ecuador: Corporación Editoria Nacional, 2013. 207 p.: bibl., indexes. (Biblioteca de ciencias sociales; 73)

An invaluable guide to 400 bibliographies in English and Spanish produced between 1885 and 2010, including some only available online. The entries are preceeded by an historiographical guide to resources and publications about Ecuador. The bibliographies include works related to the humanities, social sciences, and the natural sciences. A name index, subject indexes in Spanish and English, and a chronological index provide multiple ways of unearthing heretofore hidden gems of information. Published in an easily portable paperback, this volume should be part of every Latin American Studies collection and by the hand of every scholar of Ecuador. [The Editor]

1156 López Baquero, Patricio. Ecos de revuelta: cambio social y violencia política en Quito, 1931–1932. Quito: Abya Yala, Universidad Politécnica Salesiana, 2011. 176 p.: bibl., ill. (Serie Tesis)

Well-written narrative investigates two questions: What were the basic characteristics of increasing social agitation between 1931 and 1932?, and what factors explain social mobilization at the time? Using primary sources, including newspapers, maps, interviews, and extensive secondary accounts, the author suggests that the era marked the entrance of civil society into the institutional political arena. Also indicates that the fall of Dr. Isidro Ayora's government in 1932 marked the end of a civilian, authoritarian, and modernizing era that cumulated in the "four-days war" and led to the accession of Velasco Ibarra.

1157 Lucas, Kintto. Ecuador cara y cruz: del levantamiento del noventa a la Revolución Ciudadana. Tomo I, Una década de luchas sociales, 1990–2001. Tomo II, Entre la esperanza popular y la decepción, 2001–2006. Tomo III, Luces y sombras de la Revolución Ciudadana, 2007–2015. Quito: Ediciones CIESPAL, 2015. 3 vols.: bibl. (Colección Periodística y nuevas culturas informativas; 2–4)

Unusual three-volume journalistic account written by a former vice-chancellor of Ecuador who blends history, interviews, and analysis to provide an account of Ecuadorean history between 1990 and 2015 that is designed to engage the reader. Volume I covers the period between 1990 and 2001 focusing on the Indigenous Movement, the crisis of neoliberalism, and US policy toward Latin America in general. Volume II deals with the five years between 2001 and 2006 whent the population had reason to hope for political, economic, and social change only to find their expectations unfulfilled. Volume III describes the success and failures of the so-called Citizens Revolution (2007–2015) from the election of Rafael Correa. It examines the constituent process, the contradictions of the political project, and the doubts and perspectives for the future. There are no footnotes, but Volume I includes a bibliography.

1158 Pérez Ramírez, Gustavo. La Revolución Juliana y sus jóvenes líderes olvidados. Quito: Academia Nacional de Historia, 2014. 273 p.: bibl., ill.

The Revolution of July 9, 1925 (Revolución Juliana) was the military intrusion into Ecuadorian politics that ousted President Gonzalo S. Córdova and imposed a seven-number ruling junta. Book seeks out to cut through intellectul controversies concerning this event by focusing on the young officers who engineered the coup. Based on sustained and arduous investigation, Pérez Ramirez analyzes the program of the Liga Militar. Emphasizing their patriotism summed up by the motto "Honor and Dignity," he provides detailed biographies of each of the eight youthful leaders and an anthology of their ideas. A serious volume that reaffirms the importance of the event as a turning point in Ecuadorian history.

1159 **Prieto, Mercedes.** Estado y colonialidad: mujeres y familias quichuas de la Sierra del Ecuador, 1925–1975. Quito: FLACSO Ecuador, 2015. 272 p.: bibl., ill. (Serie Atrio)

Well-researched study explores the relations between the state and rural Quichua women living outside principal highland cities between 1925 and 1975. Employs four approaches: First, analysis of the writings by indigenous peoples and intellectuals to reveal varied concepts concerning the family, maternity, and work. Second, exploration of the participation of the native women in the judicial processes. Third, an examination of elitist and indigenous narratives concerning campaigns to integrate the latter into the state. Finally, investigation of community development in the provinces of Imbabura and Chimbozoa. Concludes that the result of these actions was to create colonial subjects partially controlled by the state, and that the experience of rural Quichua women in relation with the state contrasts with the methods used to organize women living in the cities.

1160 **Torre, Carlos de la Espinosa.** De Velasco a Correa: insurrecciones, populismos y elecciones en Ecuador, 1944–2013. Quito: Universidad Andina Simón Bolivar Ecuador, 2015. 243 p.: bibl. (Biblioteca de historia; 44)

Examines four elections in which candidates used populists rhetoric against their establishment opponents to gain power: Velasco Ibarra in 1960; Bucaram in 1996; Correa in 2006 and 2013. Finds that these campaigns were branded as corrupt because people, normally marginalized from political decisions, retook power. Concludes that populism is not a passing phenomenon tied to the first phases of modernization, but rather a distinctive political strategy that gains power by manipulating the struggle between the oligarchy and the people.

1161 **Torres Dávila, Víctor Hugo.** Estado e industrialización en Ecuador: modernización, fricciones y conflictos en los años cincuenta. Quito: Abya Yala, 2012. 167 p.: bibl.

Analysis of the development of industrialization in Ecuador in the second half of the 1950s as a consequence of the new phase of the country's ties to the world capitalistic system and not as a response to the industrial sector that was sheltered by "accidental protectionism" and fuctioned as an appendix to the hacienda, agro-export, and commercial economy. Argues that it was the state and not the industrial social class that promoted the need for industrialization, thus demystifying the virtues attributed to the industry as the creator of wellbeing, modernization and social dynamism. Important contribution to explanation of Ecuador's 20th century economic development.

Peru

G. ANTONIO ESPINOZA, *Associate Professor of History, Virginia Commonwealth University*

1162 **Armas Asín, Fernando.** La invención de la propiedad: Valle del Rímac: siglos XVI–XX. Lima: Universidad de Lima, Fondo Editorial, 2014. 216 p.: bibl., color maps. (Colección Investigaciones)

Based on extensive archival research, the author studies the conceptual and legal changes that land property went through in the Rímac Valley, where the city of Lima is located. Includes discussion of *censos* or annuities, agricultural land and water use, the impact of the railroad, and the effects of increasing urbanization.

1163 Bergel, Martín. De canillitas a militantes: los niños y la circulación de materiales impresos en el proceso de popularización del Partido Aprista Peruano, 1930–1945. (*Iberoamericana/Madrid*, 15:60, dic. 2015, p. 101–115, bibl., photos)

This article examines the role of children in spreading printed political propaganda for the Peruvian Aprista Party (APRA), first as newsboys and later on as clandestine messengers.

1164 Carey, Mark P. Mountaineers and engineers: the politics of international science, recreation, and environmental change in twentieth-century Peru. (*HAHR*, 92:1, Feb. 2012, p. 107–141)

Sophisticated article that advocates integrating environmental history with the history of science, to restore the agency of non-European peoples, and to achieve a better understanding of the complexity of the production and circulation of knowledge. Focusing on the scientific activities of the German Alpine Society in the northern highlands of Peru, describes the diverse responses of local power holders, scientists, entrepreneurs, and lower class residents, and explains their motivations.

1165 Caro Cárdenas, Ricardo. "La comunidad es base, trinchera de la guerra popular": izquierda, campesinismo y lucha armada: Huancavelica, 1974–1982. (*Bull. Inst. fr. étud. andin.*, 43:2, 2014, p. 265–283, bibl.)

This article enriches the scholarship on both the pre-civil war left and Shining Path in Peru, by following the career of peasant activist Justo Gutiérrez Poma. Based on archival primary sources and oral testimonies, Caro Cárdenas analyzes the social networks and political ties of an insurgent cadre who does not fit the profile of the Shining Path leaders studied so far.

1166 Casanova Rojas, Felipe; Alberto Díaz Araya; and Daniel Castillo Ramírez. Tras los pasos de la muerte: mortandad en Tacna durante la Guerra del Pacífico, 1879–1880. (*Historia/Santiago*, 50:2, dic. 2017, p. 399–441, bibl., tables)

The stationing of Peruvian and Bolivian troops in Tacna negatively impacted the state of the province's public health and the local economy. While the newcomers brought disease, they also suffered from local problems. This well-researched study demonstrates the overwhelming influence of the War of the Pacific on this Peruvian province. [W. Sater]

1167 Chile en el Perú: la ocupación a través de sus documentos, 1881–1884. Estudio preliminar y recopilación de Carmen Mc Evoy. Lima: Fondo Editorial del Congreso del Perú, 2016. 855 p.: bibl.

A collection of more than 400 documents related to the Chilean occupation of Peru (1881–84), during the War of the Pacific. The original documents, located in Chilean archives, include military and administrative reports issued by the invading forces, complaints from foreign diplomats living in Peru, letters from Peruvian functionaries to Chilean officers, and press clips, among others. They illustrate topics such as the financial and logistical mechanisms of the occupation, the reliance of the invaders on the mail and the telegraph for communication, the ideological role of the press, and the strategies of resistance and adaptation used by locals. In the preliminary study, Carmen McEvoy introduces the collected documents, reviewing the existing historical literature on the occupation.

1168 China y Perú: en el arte y la cultura. Lima: Universidad Ricardo Palma: Instituto Confucio URP, 2014. 181 p.: bibl., ill. (some color), maps (some color).

A survey of the Chinese presence in Peru. Successive waves of migration arrived, starting in the 16th century when a few Chinese worked on the ships that plied the Philippine-Acapulco route and then traveled south. Another dates from the middle of the 19th century when Chinese agricultural workers arrived on the coast. This volume collects recent studies on the culture and religion of the migrants, the Chinese district of Lima, and Chinese traditional medicine. [S. Ramírez]

1169 Cushman, Gregory T. Guano and the opening of the Pacific world: a global ecological history. Cambridge; New York: Cambridge University Press, 2013. 392 p.:

bibl., ill., index, maps, tables. (Studies in environment and history)

Ambitious and complex study centered on the Pacific Ocean as the stage where the search for fertilizers and other raw materials, and their extraction and near exhaustion, was closely associated with competition among imperial powers, the exploitation of human labor, and rising economic inequalities. Also examines environmental degradation, the rise and influence of the technocratic ideal, and the impact of El Niño-Southern Oscillation on historical events.

1170 **Degregori, Carlos Iván.** How difficult it is to be God: Shining Path's politics of war in Peru, 1980–1999. Edited and with an introduction by Steve J. Stern. Translated by Nancy Appelbaum *et al.* Madison: The University of Wisconsin Press, 2012. 250 p.: bibl., index, maps. (Critical human rights)

English translation of the final work by the late leading expert on Shining Path. Reorganized and abridged to make it more accessible to a non-Peruvian audience and/or those unfamiliar with the history of the Shining Path. Degregori challenged the interpretive value of *lo Andino*, an Andean cultural essence inherent to indigenous peasants that crystallized them into eternal "others" to whites and mestizos who were presumed to be, in contrast, historically dynamic. Instead, Degregori focused on the internal and external politics of the Shining Path's insurgency, including its ideological dimensions, its relationship with other social forces, the social and political consequences of the internal war, and the conditions that favored and threatened the work of the postwar Peruvian Truth and Reconciliation Commission. Degregori's insights have influenced the recent scholarship on the Shining Path, and some of the concepts that he put forward—such as the myth of progress through education in 20th-century Peru—deserve further inquiry and discussion. For comment by political scientist, see *HLAS 73:1257*.

1171 **Delgado Benites, Francisco Javier.** Los guerrilleros de Santiago de Chuco en la guerra con Chile. Lima: Instituto de Investigación en Ciencias y Humanidades: Juan Gutemberg Editores Impresores, 2013. 99 p: ibibl., ill.

The author pays homage to the local irregulars of the Santiago de Chuco province (Northern Peru) who fought against the invading Chilean army in the Battle of Huamachuco (July 10, 1883). Partly fictionalized account and partly historical narrative, the book is based on a limited number of printed documents and some oral testimonies, and includes local anecdotes as well as information about a few guerrilla leaders. Strong condemnation of Chilean invaders.

1172 **En el nudo del imperio: independencia y democracia en el Perú.** Edición de Carmen Mc Evoy, Mauricio Novoa, y Elías Palti. Lima: IFEA Instituto Francés de Estudios Andinos, UMIFRE 17, CNRS/MAE: IEP Instituto de Estudios Peruanos, 2012. 499 p.: bibl. (Serie Estudios sobre el bicentenario; 1)(Actes & mémoires de l'Institut français d'études andines; 31)

Collection of 19 essays on the dynamics of Peruvian independence, investigating the position of Peru within the Spanish Empire in South America, the consequences of independence, and the country's adoption of a republican system.

1173 **Espinoza, G. Antonio.** Education and the state in modern Peru: primary schooling in Lima, 1821-c. 1921. New York, NY: Palgrave Macmillan, 2013. 283 p.: bibl., ill., index, maps. (Historical studies in education)

Wonderful summary of educational policy of primary schools in Peru for the first century after independence. The author elaborates on the complexities of how the elites tried to provide education to children in the capital city of Lima. The fine-grained and well-sourced analysis deals with curriculum, class issues, and the way in which racial theories affected and impeded education for Lima's children. [E. Langer]

1174 **Fitzpatrick-Behrens, Susan.** The Maryknoll Catholic mission in Peru, 1943–1989: transnational faith and transformation. Notre Dame, Ind.: University of Notre Dame Press, 2011. 315 p.: bibl., index. (From the Helen Kellogg Institute for International Studies)

An inquiry into the role that religion played in the modernization of Peru, through the evolving methods and experiences of the Maryknoll missionaries. The Maryknoll began their activities in Latin America in the context of the New Deal and early years of WWII. The Maryknoll originally sought to promote orthodoxy vis-à-vis folk Catholicism, and to counter communism by providing material aid to the poor. Initially focused on the rural areas of the Puno region, Maryknoll gradually expanded their activities to major cities. Influenced by the Second Vatican Council (1962–65) and the Conference of Latin American Bishops meeting in Medellín (1968), Maryknoll was one of the Catholic organizations that became more progressive in the 1960s. While the progressive Church embraced Liberation Theology's preferential option for the poor, male clergy based in Lima remained at the top of the ecclesiastical power hierarchy. Female missionaries sometimes gained closer access to local communities, due to their formally subordinate role. Maryknoll also promoted knowledge about, and respect for, indigenous culture.

1175 Gootenberg, Paul. Fishing for Leviathans? Shifting views on the liberal state and development in Peruvian history. (*J. Lat. Am. Stud.*, 45:1, Feb. 2013, p. 121–141)

A refined analysis of recent historiographical interpretations of state and development in Peru. In the 1970s and 1980s, structuralist-dependency approaches focused on the failure of postcolonial elites to build a strong state, a cohesive national community, and a capitalist economy. In the latter part of this period, the New History expanded and added nuance to this perspective by adopting a bottom-up examination of society. In the 1990s, the historical scholarship took a "political turn," focusing instead on the origins of "citizenship" and "civil society." Gootenberg persuasively advocates reconciling these historiographical waves, by addressing the impact of economics, institutional frameworks, and inequalities, on citizenship and politics.

1176 Heilman, Jaymie Patricia. Yellows against reds: campesino anticommunism in 1960s Ayacucho, Peru. (*LARR*, 50:2, 2015, p. 154–175, bibl.)

Important contribution to the emerging history of the Cold War at the grassroots level. Examines the use of anti-communist rhetoric by indigenous peasantry, and the consequences it had.

1177 La Serna, Miguel. The corner of the living: Ayacucho on the eve of the Shining Path insurgency. Chapel Hill: University of North Carolina Press, 2012. 286 p.: bibl., index, photos. (First peoples: new directions in indigenous studies)

Fascinating study of the civil war in Peru (1980–92) through the experiences of Chuchi and Huaychao, two rural villages in the Ayacucho region. Based on archival primary sources and ethnographic work, La Serna convincingly argues that power relations, intra- and inter-communal conflicts, and cultural understandings of authority, conditioned the responses of peasants to the Shining Path and violence.

1178 La Serna, Miguel. In plain view of the Catholic faithful: Church-peasant conflict in the Peruvian Andes, 1963–1980. (*HAHR*, 95:4, Nov. 2015, p. 631–657, bibl.)

In an effort to understand the decline of the Catholic Church's influence in the rural areas of the central Andes, and the parallel rise of evangelical Protestantism, this article examines the conflict between peasants and clergy in the village of Chuschi. The author concludes that the regional Church's conservatism, within a context of peasant mobilization and national political reform, led to a rupture between both sides. Based on substantial archival research and oral testimonies.

1179 Martin, Guillemette. Vivir el conflicto lejos de los campos de batalla: la comunidad alemana del Perú y la Primera Guerra Mundial. (*Bull. Inst. fr. étud. andin.*, 44:2, 2015, p. 259–281, bibl., photos)

This article examines the representations of Germany's role in the First World War, as presented in two contemporary periodical publications published by the German community living in Peru. Largely overlooked by the scholarship, these publications tried to influence local public opinion, which was predominantly supportive of the Allies.

1180 Maxwell, Keely. Tourism, environment, and development on the Inca trail. (*HAHR*, 92:1, Feb. 2012, p. 143–171, maps, photos, table)

The author focuses on the Inca Trail in the southern Peruvian Andes to present a case study of the environmental impact of tourism in Latin America. From the expedition led by North American archeologist Hiram Bingham in 1911, to the conservation regulations issued by the national government in 2000, to the present, the Inca Trail has been a site of competing modernization projects and narratives of development.

1181 **Memorias del caso peruano de esterilización forzada.** Compilación e investigación de Alejandra Ballón. Lima: Biblioteca Nacional del Perú, Fondo Editorial, 2014. 319 p.: bibl., ill. (Colección Las palabras del mudo)

This is the first scholarly book published in Peru on the program of forced sterilizations carried by the authoritarian regime of Alberto Fujimori. From 1996 to 2000, political authorities in complicity with high-ranking healthcare officers sterilized more than 270,000 women and over 22,000 men without their informed consent. Four essays examine this violation of human rights, one of the many human rights abuses that Fujimori's regime carried, from the perspective of political economy, public health, medical ethics, and the law, respectively. The book includes testimonies from victims and healthcare professionals.

1182 **La modernización de la república: la prensa científica del Perú (1827–1829).** Compilación y estudio introductorio de Alejandro Málaga Núñez-Zeballos. Lima: Fondo Editorial de la Asamblea Nacional de Rectores, 2013. 362 p.: bibl., ill., index. (Colección Artes y Humanidades)

A sample of articles published in *Memorial de Ciencias Naturales y de Industria Nacional y Extranjera*, a periodical edited by Mariano de Rivero y Ustáriz and Nicolás Fernández de Piérola. The sample includes articles on mining, mineralogy, and metallurgy; the periodical also published articles on agriculture, antiquities, geography, chemistry, botany, and medicine.

Monrroy, Gustavo. La Confederación Perú-Boliviana: los inicios de la República y el proyecto de Santa Cruz. See item **1216**.

1183 **Necochea López, Raúl.** A history of family planning in twentieth-century Peru. Chapel Hill: University of North Carolina Press, 2014. 234 p.: bibl., ill., index.

An original historical analysis of family planning, including policy-making as well as the role of national and international actors and organizations. Critiques existing demographic transition theory, demonstrating that biomedical knowledge used to control fertility originated before the 1960s and had diverse origins, not just the US. Also shows that demand for family planning had both financial motivations, as well as those related to interpersonal relations. More broadly, the author illustrates that foreign organizations that promoted birth control had to negotiate their interests with those of preexisting local actors.

Ni vencedores ni vencidos: la Guerra del Pacífico en perspectiva histórica. See item **394**.

1184 **Peralta Ruiz, Víctor.** La guerra civil peruana de 1854: los entresijos de una revolución. (*Anu. Estud. Am.*, 70:1, enero/junio 2013, p. 195–219, bibl.)

The author of this article persuasively argues for more a detailed study of the political contexts in which civil wars happen, and for greater attention to the role of rural populations in these conflicts. Demonstrates the key function of shifting alliances and patronage in the successful war that General Ramón Castilla waged against elected President General José Rufino Echenique.

1185 **Perú.** Vol. 2, 1830–1880, La construcción nacional. Dirigido por Carlos Contreras. Madrid: Taurus: Fundación MAPFRE, 2015. 1 v.: bibl., ill., index. (América Latina en la historia contemporánea)

This is the second volume about Peru within the collection titled América Latina en la Historia Contemporánea. Prominent specialists present synthetic chapters dedicated to Peruvian politics, foreign policy, economics, society, and culture.

1186 **Quichua Chaico, David.** Huamanga: sociedad, haciendas e instituciones (1825–1830). Ayacucho, Peru: Lluvia Editores; CEHRA, Centro de Estudios Históricos Regionales Andinos; AHAYACUCHO, Asociación de Historiadores de Ayacucho, 2015. 126 p.: bibl., ill.

Study on Huamanga province, examines the economy before and after independence, haciendas, local demographics, the secular and ecclesiastical bureaucracy, and the university. Largely based on primary sources.

1187 Rénique C., José Luis. Imaginar la nación: viajes en busca del "verdadero Perú" (1881–1932). Lima: Congreso de la República: IEP Instituto de Estudios Peruanos: Ministerio de Cultura; Wanchaq, Cusco: Ministerio de Cultura, Dirección Desconcentrada de Cultura de Cusco Subdirección de Interculturalidad, 2015. 514 p.: bibl., ill. (Serie Perú problema, 42)

The author proposes an "historical reading," as opposed to an "ideological" one, of the ways in which local authors imagined the Peruvian nation in the late 19th- and early 20th centuries. Includes chapters on Manuel González Prada, Clorinda Matto de Turner, Enrique López Albújar, Ventura García Calderón, José de la Riva-Agüero, Abraham Valdelomar, Luis E. Valcárcel, José Carlos Mariátegui, and Víctor Raúl Haya de la Torre.

1188 Roca-Rey, Christabelle. La propaganda visual durante el gobierno de Juan Velasco Alvarado (1968–1975). Lima: Instituto Frances de Estudios Andinos: Instituto de Estudios Peruanos, 2016. 167 p.: bibl.

An analysis of the visual propaganda of the regime of General Juan Velasco Alvarado, as presented in official posters and publications. The author argues that these images represented a cultural shift, from a negative portrayal of the indigenous population, peasants, and workers, as backward and compliant, to a positive one that associated these social groups with heroism and national identity.

1189 Sala i Vila, Núria. Justicia conciliatoria durante el liberalismo hispano en el Perú: el caso de Huamanga. (*Anu. Estud. Am.*, 69:2, julio/dic. 2012, p. 423–450, bibl., tables)

This article examines the impact that the 1812 Constitution, and the judicial conciliation process it mandated, had in the highland Huamanga region from 1812 to 1814, and from 1820 to 1824. Based primarily on the conciliatory justice record books kept by the mayors who decided the cases, the article also provides some information about these officers.

1190 Salinas Sánchez, Alejandro. Polos opuestos: salarios y costo de vida 1821–1879. Lima: Seminario de Historia Rural Andina, Fondo Editorial, Universidad Nacional Mayor de San Marcos, 2013. 356 p.: bibl.

Based on a large sample of manuscript and printed primary sources, the author examines the evolution of wages and the cost of living in Peru, from independence to right before the War of the Pacific. Includes information on tax rates and tax collection, government salaries, urban and rural wages, the income of individual entrepreneurs and professionals, and household expenditures.

1191 Sánchez, Roberto. From sharecroppers to *lancheros*: Afro-Peruvians in Tambo de Mora, 1876–1932. (*MACLAS Lat. Am. Essays*, 26/27, 2012/2013, p. 56–72, map, tables)

Sánchez examines the migration of Afro-Peruvian day laborers and sharecroppers from the rural areas of Chincha province, and their settlement in the port of Tambo de Mora, where they became boatmen, fishers, and dockworkers. In the process, Sánchez argues, Afro-Peruvians experienced cultural and social mestizaje, within the context of national modernization. Partly based on local manuscript censuses from 1895, 1918, and 1932.

1192 Urrutia, Jaime. Aquí nada ha pasado: Huamanga siglos XVI–XX. Lima: COMISEDH: IFEA: IEP, 2014. 378 p.: bibl., ill., maps. (Número 64 de la serie Estudios Históricos del IEP)(Tomo 318 de la Serie "Travaux de l'Institut français d'études andines)

This book gathers the works published by the author in the decades of 1980 and 1900. It examines the colonial and republican economy, the rural communities and their conflicts, and political radicalism, among other topics of regional history.

1193 Valladares Quijano, Manuel. El paro nacional del 19 de julio de 1977: movimientos sociales en la época del "Gobierno Revolucionario de las Fuerzas Armadas." Lima: Facultad de Ciencias Sociales, Universidad Nacional Mayor de San Marcos: Pakarina, 2013. 146 p.: bibl., ill.

Synthesis of the July 1977 National Strike in Peru, presenting a broad perspective on the main political and social actors involved in this historical event. Based mainly on secondary sources, mentions reference to printed primary documents but does not quote them.

1194 **Vásquez Medina Luis.** La verdad detrás de la Guerra del Pacífico: el Imperio Británico contra el sistema americano de economía en Sudamérica. Lima: Arquitas, 2012. 296 p. (some folded): bibl., ill. (some color).

The author claims that the War of the Pacific between Chile and Peru was part of the struggle between the "British oligarchic imperial system" and the "American system of sovereign republics." The book is clearly partial to the US, as a presumed source of support for Latin American nationalists, and critical of Great Britain, which the author considers a "threat" to humanity. As an annex, includes a text written by far right US political activist Lyndon LaRouche.

1195 **Whipple, Pablo.** La gente decente de Lima y su resistencia al orden republicano: Jerarquías sociales, prensa y sistema judicial durante el siglo XIX. Lima: IEP Instituto de Estudios Peruanos; Santiago: Centro de Investigaciones Diego Barros Arana, 2013. 220 p.: bibl. (Estudios históricos; 62)

While Peruvian colonial society defined *decencia* by social and racial factors, republican discourse construed it as virtuous, individual behavior. In this brilliant book, Whipple uses the tension between both understandings of *decencia* as a lens to study postindependence public opinion, civil justice, and social control in Peru. Largely based on periodical sources, the book demonstrates that, in the first three decades after independence, elites used satire and gossip in newspapers to assert their social status and influence legal proceedings. Over time, elites managed to refocus judgment of private and public behavior on the lower classes as a means of social control.

1196 **Yokota, Ryan Masaaki.** Ganbateando: the Peruvian Nisei Association and Okinawan Peruvians in Los Angeles. (*in* Transnational crossroads: remapping the Americas and the Pacific. Lincoln: University of Nebraska Press, 2012, p. 427–460, bibl.)

Original study on the complex migratory history of Okinawan Peruvians, from the late 19th century to the 1990s, analyzing the process within multiple contexts such as Japanese state formation, Peruvian attitudes toward Asian immigrants, and US diplomatic and immigration policies. Using archival primary sources and interviews, Yokota shows that Okinawans living in the US nowadays have forged a transnational identity.

Bolivia

ERICK LANGER, *Professor, Georgetown University*

THE PRODUCTION OF HISTORICAL WORKS on Bolivia is thriving, despite the great structural problems for historians in the country. In the past three years, a number of young Bolivian and foreign scholars have shown their staying power and have continued to publish on important topics. Many PhD dissertations continue to be written on Bolivian history in many parts of the world. Some have been published as monographs in Bolivia and elsewhere, and articles based on dissertation research have appeared in some of the most prestigious journals of the field. In addition, more seasoned scholars continue to publish and, as usual, many Bolivian writers who are not formally trained in history have produced noteworthy and, at times, challenging works. Although not all of the regions of Bolivia receive equal attention (some continue to be underserved), in general scholarly interest has remained strong, even in regions traditionally not covered as well, such as the Santa Cruz area. Also, over the past few years, interest in the Chaco War has attracted more sophisticated work that goes beyond the military history or soldier biographies.

We are on the cusp of various bicentennial celebrations in the independence wars. The Vice Presidency of Bolivia has begun to republish some of the best works on Bolivian history as part of the "Biblioteca del Bicentenario" series, with new forewords by distinguished historians. While these works generally are not cited in this section, it is nevertheless a shot in the arm of the Bolivian publishing business and the reappearance of many classic works is welcome. The initiative has stimulated the publication of new works as well.

As always, political history remains one of the strongest fields. On the basis of her research in 19th-century Bolivia, Marta Irurozqui develops her ideas about how violence intersects with elections and the creation of the notion of citizenship (item **1211**). A compendium of older articles on the Battle of La Tablada during the independence wars, though mostly military history, also deals with its political implications (item **1198**). Hernando Armaza Pérez del Castillo's book on the resistance to the mostly foreign-born patriot army after independence provides an important corrective to the hagiographies of the "liberators" who remained to lead the country in the first few years (item **1197**). Gustavo Monrroy complements Armaza's perspective from the Peruvian side by examining the Peru-Bolivian Confederation (1836–39), at a time when many of the same actors—foreigners and nationals—were in charge of Peru and Bolivia (item **1216**). To this we can add Heraclio Bonilla's compendium of essays (item **1200**), many of which touch on Bolivia (as well as on Ecuador and Peru). This useful mix of previously published and new essays shows the breadth of his inquiries, from indigenous communities and the War of the Pacific to Andean integration. For more recent political periods, it is worth reading a quasi-political novel, which is essentially a biography of the controversial forerunner of the MNR, President Germán Busch, written by the famous nationalist intellectual and founder of the MNR, Carlos Montenegro (1903–53) (item **1217**). In turn, Andrey Shchelchkov and Pablo Stefanoni offer a (item **1209**) primer on leftist parties in early 20th-century Bolivia, with a good leavening of primary documents copied from the Moscow Comintern archives. For more recent leftist literature, Yolanda Tellez's compilation of previously unpublished transcripts of recordings of one of the most consequential Bolivian leftists, Marcelo Quiroga Santa Cruz, is of interest (item **1218**). Mauricio Belmonte Pijuán's tome addresses Mario Gutiérrez's frustrated attempts to negotiate with Chile over access to the Pacific during the Banzer dictatorship (item **1199**), illuminating the role of the right-wing Falange Party, active in the mid-20th century.

Social history remains important, such as the marvelous book on Radio Illimani, the most important and oldest radio station in Bolivia, by Cristóbal Coronel Quisbert (item **1202**). An encyclopedic effort at covering Japanese immigration to Bolivia, especially important in the lowlands, has been translated from the original Japanese and provides a solid overview of the influence of Japanese in the country (item **1212**).

As usual, most regions of the country are represented in Bolivian social and economic history. The handsome volume of images by German photographer Robert Gerstmann provides a beguiling photographic record of the mining regions in Bolivia in the early 20th century (item **1210**). In addition to a collection of spectacular photos, the volume includes comments by people whose lives are similar to the laborers and peasants pictured. Pilar Mendieta's edited volume on modernity in Oruro during the first third of the 20th century analyzes the city's social history (item **1227**). A companion piece is the book by Virgilio Rodríguez Quispe, also on urban modernity, but in this case on the city of La Paz (item **1221**). Mining in the La Paz region, specfically, the important copper mine of Corocoro, finally gets the scholarly treatment that it deserves in a valuable publication by Teodoro Salluco Sirpa (item **1223**). A magisterial book with a broad scope by Gustavo Rodríguez Ostria incorporates decades of his writing in one volume (item **1220**) and touches on mining over the 19th century, and the regional economies of Cochabamba and Santa Cruz departments. On a smaller scale, Huascar Rodríguez García studies a bandit gang in Punata, Cochabamba, in the last years of the 19th century (item **1219**).

Santa Cruz has recently produced more serious historical works, in part because of the existence of the museum and archive under the direction of Paula Peña Hasbún of the public Universidad Gabriel René Moreno in Santa Cruz city. She supervised the publication of two edited volumes on the independence wars in Santa Cruz, one tome devoted to classic articles on the topic and the second one to new approaches, often by young historians (items **1207** and **1224**, respectively). For a later period, Víctor Hernán Rojas Vásquez examines the role of the Santa Cruz Comité Cívico in regional identity formation from the Chaco War to the Banzer dictatorship (item **1222**). Likewise, Fernando Aníbal García Enríquez shows the central role of sugar cane production in Santa Cruz (item **1205**), complementing Gustavo Rodríguez Ostría's aforementioned work, though from a perspective that asserts the value of Santa Cruz regionalism.

The history of indigenous peoples always looms large in Bolivia. Finally, the Oruro communities are getting the attention they have deserved. In an article based on a section of her PhD dissertation, Hanne Cottyn examines the effects of the 1874 law abolishing indigenous communities on the Oruro ayllus (item **1203**). Ximena Medinaceli illuminates the views of the indigenous communities about modernization based on the spectacular murals in the Sabaya church in Carangas, Oruro (item **1215**). Carmen Soliz, focusing mostly on the La Paz region, shows how the MNR revolutionary government after 1952 had to take into account the indigenous communities in their agrarian reform program, despite their principle goal of reforming the hacienda system (item **1226**). Two efforts by distinguished historians on the Bolivian educational system also largely focus on indigenous peoples. Françoise Martinez's book on the Liberal period (1898–1920) is especially useful for its examination of educational reformer Georges Rouma and the implementation of his vision of "regenerating the Indian race" (item **1214**). Brooke Larson also tackles the same topic in an article, showing how the Bolivian elites went from attempting universal education for all to proposing only manual education for the Indian masses by the early 20th century (item **1213**).

Military history is combined with social history, especially for the Chaco War. Trifonio Delgado Gonzalez's diary of the war shows a working-class man aware of the class and racial differences in the war (item **1204**). Bridget Chesterton's edited book takes on the contextual issues of the war (item **1201**). The majority of contributions are from Bolivianists, though there are a few chapters on Paraguay. Rather than treating the conduct of the war, the book addresses other issues, such as the treatment of Bolivian prisoners of war, the rhetorical creation of a "Great Paraguay," the treatment of Chaco Indians by Bolivia, Paraguay, and Argentina prior to the war, continuities of unionism before and after the war in

Bolivia, among other topics. Lastly, Ricardo Scavone analyzes diplomatic relations between Bolivia and Paraguay after the war (item **1225**).

A vigorous debate is also unfolding about the role of resources and development in Bolivia, stimulated perhaps by the rhetoric of the current leftist-nationalistic government of Evo Morales. Molly Geidel takes the Peace Corps to task for their naïve attempts to Americanize rural Bolivians (item **1206**). Kevin Young focuses on resource nationalism after 1952, attempting to explain the country's history by examining how different political factions wanted to use Bolivia's wealth of natural resources (items **1228** and **1229**). A response to these works is Lawrence Heilman's book on USAID in Bolivia. He claims that, overall, the development agency did a lot of good in Bolivia before its expulsion by President Morales in 2008 (item **1208**).

In conclusion, the historiography of Bolivia continues to expand into different areas. Bolivian scholars, many of whom received their academic training in La Paz or Santa Cruz, collaborate with international historians. Studies of Cochabamba seem to have fallen somewhat by the wayside and, unfortunately, Beni and Pando do not get the attention they merit. However the historical production on Oruro continues to develop. On balance, the history of Bolivia continues to evolve in important and stimulating ways.

1197 **Armaza Pérez del Castillo, Hernando.** Libertarse de sus propios libertadores: de Ayacucho a la Guerra del Pacífico: política y diplomacia, 1824–1884. La Paz: Plural Editores, 2014. 518 p.: bibl., ill.

More of a polemic than a professionally produced historical work (though based on primary documents), this book shows how and why Bolivia had to liberate itself from the Colombian/Venezuelan *libertadores* in the first decades of independence. The author tries to redeem the role of his ancestor Gen. Mariano Armaza (1787–1839) in an attempt to throw out patriot foreigners. The study treats the period mostly to 1841. This is a revised and augmented version of *Gracias al 31 de diciembre: Bolivia entre la presidencia de Bolívar y la muerte de Gamarra*, which was first published in 1992.

1198 **La Batalla de la Tablada: 200 años; 1817–14 y 15 de abril–2017; estudios, testimonios, documentos y bibliografía.** Compilación, introducción y anotación de Juan Ticlla Siles. Tarija, Bolivia: Ideas Positivas, 2017. 326 p.: bibl., facsims., ill.

A compendium of accounts of the battle on April 14–15, 1817, that sealed the victory of the patriot side during the independence wars. The book also includes useful documents on the battle, plus a bibliography. A historiographical tour-de-force.

1199 **Belmonte Pijuán, Mauricio.** A la deriva y sin grumetes: el falangismo enfoca la cuestión marítima nacional: ensayo sobre la gestión diplomática del ex canciller Mario Gutiérrez G., 1971–1973. La Paz: Inventa Publicidad e Impresos, 2013. 120 p.: bibl., ill. (some color).

This study of Bolivian foreign minister Mario Gutiérrez's efforts to negotiate access to the Pacific with Chile (1971–73) shows the difficulties of these efforts even during a time when the dictatorships of Hugo Banzer and Augusto Pinochet agreed on so many other issues. Nevertheless, commercial interactions flourished.

1200 **Bonilla, Heraclio.** La metamorfosis de los Andes: guerra, economía y sociedad. Cochabamba, Bolivia: Grupo Editorial Kipus; La Paz: Centro de Estudios para la América Andina y Amazónica, 2014. 562 p.: bibl. (Nuestra América; 1)

This work presents a compendium of essays by Heraclio Bonilla, one of the most important Andeanist historians. He examines the Andes as a historical concept, the role of indigenous communities in the Andes, the history of indigenous communities, Andean integration, the role of debt in Ecuador, Bolivia, and Peru, and a summary of the War of the Pacific, where he takes to task Florencia Mallon and

Nelson Manrique's ideas that the peasants who resisted the Chilean army were truly nationalist. A mixture of good previously published essays and some new additions.

Casanova Rojas, Felipe; Alberto Díaz Araya; and Daniel Castillo Ramírez. Tras los pasos de la muerte: mortandad en Tacna durante la Guerra del Pacífico, 1879–1880. See item **1166**.

1201 The Chaco War: environment, ethnicity, and nationalism. Edited by Bridget María Chesterton. London; Oxford; New York: Bloomsbury Academic, an imprint of Bloomsbury Publishing Plc, 2016. 219 p.: bibl., ill., index, maps.

A great series of essays, mostly on the context before and after the Chaco War from both the Bolivian and Paraguayan perspectives. Includes essays on Bolivian prisoners in Paraguay, how there is more continuity than previously thought about leftist activity in Bolivia before the war, the attempt to build a canal to the Pilcomayo River before and during the war, the use of a botanical garden to claim a larger Paraguayan *Lebensraum*, the treatment of indigenous peoples by Bolivian, Argentine, and Paraguayan authorities before the war, the topic of energy and oil nationalism as causes for the war, and the uses of the archeology of the war. For Paraguayan historian's comment, see item **1492**.

1202 Coronel Quisbert, Cristóbal. Ondas que provocan: Radio Illimani, los estados y el nacionalismo. Bolivia: Friedrich Ebert Stiftung: Editorial Gente Común: Edición Limitada, 2013. 231 p.: bibl., ill.

An excellent and detailed history of Radio Illimani, the pioneer radio station in Bolivia from its initial broadcast in 1929 to 2013. The study provides political context and describes how the radio changed over time, since Radio Illimani is the official radio of the Bolivian state. In a way, the work offers a political history of Bolivia over the past century.

1203 Cottyn, Hanne. Mantener la exvinculación a raya: reformas liberales y derechos comunitarios en Carangas, 1860–1930. (*Umbrales/La Paz*, 29, 2015, p. 97–132)

This well-documented study examines the efforts of Oruro indigenous communities to preserve their lands and their community structures from usurpation and destruction by the state and other actors, especially after the 1874 law that in theory abolished indigenous communities. The author analyzes the legal maneuvers that the community leaders used, and shows that this approach brought about serious internal conflicts as well. One of the few studies of this type on what continues to be one of the most important indigenous regions in the country.

1204 Delgado Gonzales, Trifonio. Carne de cañón: ¡ahora arde, kollitas!: diario de guerra, 1932–1933. Prólogo de Silvia Rivera Cusicanqui. Introducción, notas y edición de Guillermo Delgado P. La Paz: Plural Editores, 2015. 224 p.: bibl., ill., index.

This work publishes a valuable diary of a soldier of the Chaco War. The author was a worker from Patiño Mines and fought in the first year of conflict. The writings show well the type of warfare in the region, the comradery of the soldiers, and the disdain for the war. The text is written in a very expressive Spanish and presents the view of a regular soldier.

1205 García Enríquez, Fernando Aníbal.
Historia de la industria azucarera cruceña: desde la fundación de la ciudad hasta los ingenios modernos del siglo XXI. Santa Cruz, Bolivia: Fondo Editorial Gobierno Autónomo Municipal de Santa Cruz de la Sierra, 2013. 390 p.: bibl., ill., maps.

A unique effort to write the history of Santa Cruz using the history of sugar production. The study is mostly based on published sources, with some newspapers. The author interprets Santa Cruz history as one of neglect because of the lack of support of the sugar industry by the national government. The analysis of Franciscan missions is not well thought out; it presumes the missions were major manufacturers of sugar and also assumes that Chiriguanos were willing producers of sugar, a doubtful proposition.

1206 Geidel, Molly. The Peace Corps, population control, and cultural nationalist resistance in 1960s Bolivia. (*in* Peace Corps fantasies: how development shaped the global sixties. Minneapolis: University of Minnesota Press, 2015, p. 187–229)

This book chapter provides a devastating critique of the Peace Corps efforts in Bolivia before it was kicked out by the leftist Bolivian government in 1970. The author shows how the Peace Corps volunteers tried to modernize the peasant population by changing their identities and culture. The study addresses gender dynamics and discusses at length the film *Yawar Mallku* that helped bring about the Peace Corps' expulsion because of accusations of sterilizing women against their will. For sociologist's comment, see *HLAS 73:2193*.

1207 La guerra de la independencia en Santa Cruz de la Sierra, según sus historiadores, 1810–1825. Edición de Paula Peña Hasbún. Santa Cruz de la Sierra, Bolivia: Biblioteca del Museo de Historia, Universidad Autónoma Gabriel René Moreno, 2015. 239 p. (Biblioteca del Museo de Historia; 6)

This work presents a useful compendium of previously published essays written by Santa Cruz authors from the late 19th to the early 21st century on the process of independence in the Bolivian lowlands. The book also includes some transcribed documents from 1815. See also item **1224**.

1208 Heilman, Lawrence C. USAID in Bolivia: partner or patrón? Boulder, Colo.: FirstForumPress, 2017. 346 p.: bibl., index.

An important evaluation of the role of USAID by a long-time veteran of the institution. The author's access to primary source materials for the agency is unmatched. The book argues that USAID bureaucrats in Bolivia tried to do the best for the country, at times despite contradictory goals from Washington, DC. The study evaluates all of the USAID administrators in Bolivia, showing that some were more effective than others. Heilman argues that, on balance, USAID aided significantly in the economic development of the country.

1209 Historia de las izquierdas bolivianas: archivos y documentos (1920–1940). Coordinación de Andrey Shchelchkov y Pablo Stefanoni. La Paz: Centro de Investigaciones Sociales; Instituto de Historia Universal de la Academia de Ciencias de Rusia, 2016. 392 p.: bibl.

A great primer for leftist movements in the first third of the 20th century in Bolivia. Seven strong essays address the Bolivian left in the early 20th century. In general, 19th-century antecedents are not considered. Most of the book is dedicated to primary documents, many from Comintern (Communist International) archives in Moscow. The documents in many ways show how poorly leftists understood Bolivian social and political realities and how truly irrelevant the left was until the Chaco War (1932–35). Very few documents on the 1927 Chayanta Rebellion or on the Chaco War are included in the study.

1210 Imágenes de la revolución industrial: Robert Gerstmann en las minas de Bolivia (1925–1936). Edición de Pascale Absi y Jorge Pavez O. Textos de Pascale Absi et al. La Paz: Plural Editores, 2014. 383 p.: ill. (some color), color map.

A wonderful resource for understanding mining and mine labor in the first third of the 20th century. The plentiful photos are accompanied by citations from miners. Nine essays by established scholars explain mining technology, mining companies, and Robert Gerstmann and his professional trajectory as a photographer in Bolivia.

1211 Irurozqui, Marta. Infracción electoral y violencia política en la construcción de la ciudadanía en América Latina: propuesta conceptual a partir del caso boliviano (1825–1952). (*Ecuad. Debate*, 93, dic. 2014, p. 99–121, bibl.)

This study presents a theoretical summary of the concept of citizenship in Latin America before universal suffrage. The author argues that not only the act of voting, but what happened before and after the vote, counts for understanding how people understood this act of citizenship. While many people were excluded from voting, they could still participate in elections in other ways. Repression and violent acts affirmed citizenship, since it showed the value of voting. The concept of civic citizenship, based on the ideas of Iberian *vecindad*, was more important than the rule-based civil citizenship.

1212 Los japoneses en Bolivia: 110 años de historia de la inmigración japonesa en Bolivia. Coordinación de Iyo Kunimoto.

La Paz: Plural Editores; Santa Cruz, Bolivia: Federación Nacional de Asociaciones Boliviano-Japonesas; Yokohama-shi, Japan: Asociación Nippon-Bolivia, 2013. 359 p.: bibl., ill.

This work represents a greatly amplified Spanish edition of a 2000 Japanese-language book that makes an encyclopedic attempt to cover (and celebrate) all of Japanese immigration to Bolivia. The publication is organized by departments (La Paz, Beni, Pando, Santa Cruz) and colonies (Okinawa and San Juan), and focuses on the past few decades. The analysis misses some classic older works in English, such as Tigner (see *HLAS 45:5351*).

1213 Larson, Brooke. La invención del indio iletrado: la pedagogía de la raza en Bolivia. (*Umbrales/La Paz*, 29, 2015, p. 133–172)

This study argues that after the early 20th century, inspired by racialist ideology, the Bolivian elites abandoned the idea of universal education and instead created a pedagogy for Indians that concentrated on menial and mechanical skills appropriate for their racially inferior status.

1214 Martinez, Françoise. "Régénérer la race": politique éducative en Bolivie (1898–1920). Paris: IHEAL éditions, 2010. 455 p.: bibl., ill. (some color), index, maps, portrait. (Collection Travaux et Mémoires; 83)

The book shows that the effort to educate the Bolivian masses during the Liberal era (1899–1920) revolved around "civilizing" the indigenous population in public schools. The author's analysis focuses on the efforts of the Belgian Georges Rouma, who was invited by the Bolivian government to design a program to modernize the country through education.

1215 Medinaceli, Ximena. La Guerra del Pacífico y los ayllus: una lectura de la pintura mural del baptisterio de Sabaya. (*Bol. Mus. Chil. Arte Precolomb.*, 21:1, 2016, p. 79–93, bibl., ill.)

A marvelous short essay describing the late 19th-century paintings inside the Sabaya church, located close to the border with Chile. The author shows that the paintings were done from the indigenous perspective, from the ayllus of Carangas, which demonstrate the notion of progress and nationhood within the indigenous community. The study argues that the indigenous communities, only a decade after the War of the Pacific, were fully aware of their nationality and their role in the commercial and technological progress of the era.

1216 Monrroy, Gustavo. La Confederación Perú-Boliviana: los inicios de la República y el proyecto de Santa Cruz. Lima: Universidad de Ciencias y Humanidades, Fondo Editorial, 2013. 164 p.: bibl., ill.

This collection brings together three essays on the Peru-Bolivian Confederation (1836–39) from the Peruvian perspective, with a documentary collection at the end. The essays deal with the constitution of the confederation project and relations between Peru and Ecuador during this period, and provide a brief summary of how four Peruvian historians of different epochs evaluated the confederation.

1217 Montenegro, Carlos. Germán Busch y otras páginas de historia de Bolivia. Prólogo y notas de Mariano Baptista Gumucio. La Paz: Levylibros Librería y Editorial, 2014. 350 p.: bibl., ill. (some color).

This novelized biography of former Bolivian president Germán Busch (1937–39) serves as a precursor to the 1952 social revolution. The book is a 1938 manuscript from Carlos Montenegro, the nationalist paladin of the Movimiento Nacionalista Revolucionario (MNR) party, published here for the first time. This interesting read helps us understand Montenegro's intellectual development that led him to write his influential 1943 *Nacionalismo y coloniaje* (see *HLAS 9:3293*).

1218 Quiroga Santa Cruz, Marcelo. Un libro para escuchar a Marcelo Quiroga Santa Cruz. Compilación de Yolanda Téllez. La Paz: Muela del Diablo Editores, 2013. 155 p.: bibl., ill.

Téllez has compiled previously unpublished transcripts of speeches and interviews with Marcelo Quiroga Santa made between 1963–80, along with a series of his essays. Quiroga Santa Cruz is one of the most consequential leftists in Bolivia. This selection of his thoughts and words will be indispensable for those seeking to understand Bolivian politics and society.

1219 Rodríguez García, Huascar. Bandidos y policías: la cuadrilla de Punata: una organización político-criminal en Cochabamba, 1890–1898. Santa Cruz de la Sierra, Bolivia: Editorial El Pais: Heterodoxia, 2016. 158 p.: bibl., ill. (Ciencias sociales/historia; 40)

This marvelous little book describes the political banditry of the Crespo brothers in the Valle Alto of Cochabamba. The author, a sociologist, shows how the bandits, tied to the Conservative Party, threatened and killed Liberals in the last decade of the 19th century. The study also demonstrates the ties between authorities and village toughs in the Bolivian countryside.

1220 Rodríguez Ostria, Gustavo. Capitalismo, modernización y resistencia popular, 1825–1952. La Paz: Vicepresidencia del Estado Plurinacional, Centro de Investigaciones Sociales, 2014. 547 p.: bibl., ill.

This compendium brings together essays from one of the most influential historians of modern Bolivia. Taken together, they show how capitalism developed in the country since independence. The first section deals with mine laborers from independence to the Revolution of 1952. The case study of the Guadalupe Mining Company stands out. The second part concentrates on the peasants of Cochabamba from the mid-19th century to 1952 and the third part on the interaction between Cochabamba and Santa Cruz from 1880 to the Chaco War (1932). The essays are based on earlier work published in articles and short books. An important Marxist interpretation of Bolivian history.

1221 Rodríguez Quispe, Virgilio. Impacto de la modernidad en la ciudad de La Paz, 1900–1920. La Paz: Centro de Estudios para la América Andina y Amazónica, CEPAAA: La Pesada Ediciones: Pasanaku Editorial de La Pesada Ediciones, 2015. 260 p.: bibl., ill. (Historia boliviana; 4)

An impressive snapshot of La Paz at the beginning of the 20th century, analyzed under the concept of modernity. The author looks at internal and external "landscapes," showing how modern technology and ideas about urban areas transformed the city of La Paz.

1222 Rojas Vásquez, Víctor Hernán. Región y poder central en Bolivia: Santa Cruz de la Sierra 1938–1971. Santa Cruz de la Sierra, Bolivia: Biblioteca del Museo de Historia: Universidad Autónoma Gabriel René Moreno, 2015. 382 p. (Biblioteca del Museo de Historia, Región y Poder Central en Bolivia Santa Cruz de la Sierra 1938–1971; 8)

This work provides a close political narrative of a crucial period in the history of Santa Cruz. The study highlights the role of the Comité Cívico in the defense of regional interests. The author shows that present-day regional demands originated from Santa Cruz's long experience with fighting for autonomy within the Bolivian political system. He also underplays national policies, especially the development plans of the MNR governments from 1952 to 1964.

1223 Salluco Sirpa, Teodoro. La explotación del cobre en el distrito minero de Corocoro a principios del siglo XX, 1900–1930. La Paz: Universidad Mayor de San Andrés, Facultad de Humanidades y Ciencias de la Educación, Carrera de Historia, 2013. 247 p.: bibl., ill.

A somewhat mechanical description of the copper mining companies in Corocoro during the early 19th century. Most evidence comes from regional governmental institutions. Good coverage on mining companies, supplies, labor, labor conditions, and the role of the state. No non-Spanish language sources are used, leaving out other important studies on these copper mines.

1224 Santa Cruz en la guerra de independencia: nuevas aproximaciones. Edición de Paula Peña Hasbún. Santa Cruz de la Sierra, Bolivia: Biblioteca del Museo de Historia, Universidad Autónoma Gabriel René Moreno, 2017. 306 p.: bibl. (Biblioteca del Museo de Historia; 7)

This useful compendium of essays written by Santa Cruz authors covers the process of independence in the Bolivian lowlands. Essays vary from traditional military history, analysis of a slave revolt, independence in Moxos, a historiographical essay, and an examination of the first two prefects of Santa Cruz, to a review of a selection of documents relating to the 1810 revolution. Other than the Moxos essay, the book includes very little on the role of frontier Indians, who were crucial to the fight. See also item **1207**.

1225 Scavone, Ricardo. Después de la guerra: las relaciones paraguayo-bolivianas desde el Tratado de Paz hasta 1952. Asunción: Servilibro, 2013. 169 p.: bibl.

This valuable short study examines Paraguayan-Bolivian diplomatic relations after the Chaco War (1932–5). The Paraguayan author's even-handed analysis describes how both countries' foreign offices worked together to overcome old resentments and to bring about friendly relations as a means to diminish the influence of other neighboring countries. Despite good diplomatic relations, the countries were unable to overcome mutual ignorance of each other or promote much commercial activity.

1226 Soliz, Carmen. "Land to the original owners": rethinking the indigenous politics of the Bolivian agrarian reform. (*HAHR*, 97:2, May 2017, p. 259–296, table)

This valuable study contributes to our understanding of the 1952 Bolivian Revolution and its agrarian reform policies. The author argues that, despite its preference for giving land to the hacienda peons who worked the estates, the revolutionary government also had to accept the return of hacienda land to indigenous communities. This policy brought about difficult-to-resolve conflicts in the countryside between ex-peons and communities that lasted at least into the 1970s.

1227 Vivir la modernidad en Oruro 1900–1930. Coordinación de Pilar Mendieta. Textos de Weimar Giovanni Iño Daza *et al.* La Paz: IEB, Instituto de Estudios Bolivianos; Stockholm: Asdi, 2010. 336 p.: bibl., ill. (Colección Relaciones interétnicas)

This collection of essays examines Oruro in the late 19th and early 20th centuries. All but one of the contributions deal with the history of the city of Oruro. After an introductory essay on modernity in Oruro by Pilar Mendieta, the book contains chapters on different topics by her students. Themes include the presence of foreigners, *chicheras*, the postal service, mental health and other social problems, the public library, photography, and Indian education. Some essays are more sophisticated than others.

1228 Young, Kevin A. Blood of the earth: resource nationalism, revolution, and empire in Bolivia. Austin: University of Texas Press, 2017. 275 p.: bibl., ill., index.

A useful addition to the literature of nationalism in Latin America. This study focuses on the government that emerged after the 1952 Bolivian Revolution, which used the leftist nationalist discourse that the Bolivian people should own the country's resources, to come to power. The author shows how that discourse changed after the revolution and became more conservative, though resource nationalism remained an important constraint on Bolivian politics and in anti-imperialist rhetoric. Important for understanding current Bolivian politics.

1229 Young, Kevin A. From Open Door to nationalism: oil and development visions in Bolivia, 1952–1969. (*HAHR*, 97:1, Feb. 2017, p. 95–129, ill., map.)

Based in large part on author's book, *Blood of the Earth* (see item **1228**), this article shows that the Bolivian revolutionary regime after 1955 allowed private investment in the hydrocarbon sector despite its avowed resource nationalism. In 1969 the leftist Alfredo Ovando Candia regime nationalized the Gulf Oil Company in Bolivia as a means of thwarting greater radicalization, which would have meant redistribution of oil resources rather than state control.

Chile

WILLIAM SATER, *Professor Emeritus of History, California State University, Long Beach*

THE PUBLICATION OF EDITED VOLUMES, while useful, typically do not inspire great joy: too often the various authors, like modern dancers, move in almost sublime indifference to the efforts of their colleagues. However, two recent works, both in the Historia Política de Chile, 1810–2010 series under the general editorship of Ivan Jaksic, prove the exception. Under the guidance of Juan Luis Ossa Santa Cruz (item **1259**) and Francisca Rengifo (item **1260**), the first two of a proposed four-book series, trace the political development of Chile as well as its various institutions. Comprehensive and extremely well researched, these volumes provide a researcher with a wonderful entry point for those interested in Chilean political history. In a similar vein, Alejandro San Francisco, in conjunction with a team of Chilean scholars, has produced two of four volumes dealing with Chile from 1960 to 2010 (item **1279**). Incorporating a variety of sources, these books, as well as the future works, are essential for anyone wishing to begin their research projects.

Scholars continue to concentrate first on the Allende regime, the 1973 coup, the Pinochet years, and the latter's collapse. Marco Álvarez Vergara studied one of the stalwarts on the left, MIR, its history and its evolution (item **1232**), although Cristián Pérez (item **1270**) questions its skills, as well as that of other leftist armed groups, to confront bourgeois governments. Perhaps because of their history as outliers—as Rolando Álvarez Vallejos (item **1283**) noted—and the ability of the Juventud Comunista to train future militants, the Communists, according to Carmen Hertz, Apolonia Ramírez, and Manuel Salazar (item **1257**) managed both to survive the savage repression of the Pinochet government, and even to prosper in the post-1988 period. Franck Gaudichaud (item **1250**) has written a superb work—based on his PhD dissertation from a French university—explaining the formation and functioning of Santiago's *cordones industriales* as well as giving examples of worker support for the UP government. Contrary to popular belief, Cuba's aid to the anti-Pinochet forces, while useful, did not prove as significant as that of European groups. Not all the resistance to Pinochet was violent. As Horacio Eloy documents (item **1247**), a group of literary journals spearheaded opposition to the Pinochet government. This work provides a comprehensive list of items published throughout Chile at the time, as well as interviews and examples of literary works. Not surprisingly, as Stephen Andes notes (item **1233**), the Church strongly opposed separation from the state, but when that occurred, in 1925, it did not quietly return to the rectory. Instead the Church continued to participate in the nation's political life, working to advance its agenda. As we know, the Church spearheaded opposition to Pinochet. Miguel Mansilla, Juan Sepuúlveda, and Luis Orellana (item **1265**) note that the Evangelicals joined their Catholic brethren to oppose the dictatorship and help the poor.

As Rodrigo Araya Goméz (items **1234** and **1267**) and Azun Candina (item **1240**) note, the labor unions, including those of public employees, constituted the bedrock of resistance to the dictatorship and later became the basis for the emergence of new political forces. Manuel Salazar chronicles the activities of a businessman, Jorge Schindler, who used his chain of pharmacies to provide cover to various Communist and other activists. José Varas (item **1285**) also resisted, although less violently, by broadcasting from Moscow, citing the atrocities of the Pinochet government. One of those he should have mentioned is Ingrid Olderock (item **1253**), a singularly vile woman who used animals as part of her interrogation techniques to extract information from her victims. Curiously, Cuba, for all of its statements in support of Compañero Allende provided only lukewarm support for the anti-Pinochet forces, in part because of infighting in the exile community and Havana's self-interest (item **1256**). The Pinochet regime not only divided the nation, but also splintered the right, which eventually realized that it could not depend on the General. In an earlier period of repression, the *ley maldita* forced some Chileans to flee for exile in Argentina, Mexico, or Guatemala. Those who settled in Mexico fared better than their fellow refugees in Guatemala, although in both cases they supported the governments of Árbenz and Arévalo (item **1274**).

Studying the evolution of the Chilean state is a relatively new topic for research. Thanks to Antonio Dougna and Roberto Gerón, we can follow the growth of Chile's judiciary from independence to the late 19th century. Francisca Rengifo (item **1272**) edited an excellent series of articles on the evolution of the Chilean state, including a study of the development of the nation's social security system. One of the problems that developed was the establishment of a legal distinction between benefits received by those classed as obreros and those called *empleados*. In his epic study, Gabriel Salazar Vergara (item **1277**) looks at the emergence of the Chilean state and its political parties, delving into the formation of the nation and its political entities. This singularly outstanding work is not to be missed. As part of this program of nation-building, according to Sol Serrano, Macarena Ponce de Leó, and Francisca Rengifo (item **1258**), the state used a century of education, not merely to produce a literate populace, but to integrate the rural and urban populations into the nation. Jael Goldsmith Weil has written an interesting study (item **1251**) of the creation of the government's milk program, which evolved from ensuring sanitary milk to providing it to the nation's children. Oscar Mac-Clure Hortal (item **1264**) traces how the Chilean state created institutions to educate and care for the nation's health. But, as Diego Ortúzar points out (item **1269**) the state enjoyed more success in eradicating hookworm from Lota's coal pits than silicosis from the northern copper camps.

Assuring social order proved a more onerous, if not difficult task. As Ivette Lozoya López indicates (item **1263**), unrest roiled the countryside, although the author describes the rural bandits as rebels against the society, rather than common criminals. As Paulo Álvarez Bravo shows in the case of Legua, a suburb of Santiago (item **1231**), the government often resorted to brutal tactics to keep the lower classes in line. Ironically, as the state expanded its power, which it used to protect property, it tolerated private interests carving up Patagonia, much to the detriment the indigenous community and the local working class.

One of the few articles to deal with politics, but not with the Allende period, is Patricio Navia's work (item **1268**) showing that the Cura de Catapilco did not dramatically contribute to the Allende's 1958 defeat at the hands of Jorge Alessandri. Isabel Torres Dujisin (item **1282**) concentrates on the two post-1958 presidential elections, as well as that of Allende, providing a treasure trove of statistical data, as well as a description of the various campaigns. Victor Farías (item **1248**) has provided a biography of Ricardo Lagos who was instrumental in leading the nation after Alwyn's term ended, while Jaime Hales Dib (item **1254**) offers an insider's view of the Allende-Pinochet period.

Women's history continues to prosper. María Huidobro (item **1244**) and Gabriel Salazar et al. (item **1273**) have compiled some excellent essays dealing with women since the colonial period, while Eliana Largo explores the development of feminism (item **1239**). Gloria Angelo Mladinic (item **1261**) describes the importance of women in developing Magallanes. If Ingrid Olderock was Chile's Ilsa Koch, Biddy Forstall Comber (item **1249**) was, if not its Alice Roosevelt Longworth, than an acute observer, providing a superb insight into the life of the Anglo-Chileans who ran the *salitreras*. While historians might find her memoirs of limited value, they nonetheless lift the corner of a gilded age, at least for the English administrators. Juan Salinas Toledo (item **1278**) describes not so much the role of women, as the fashions they adopted.

José Benoga has provided two wonderful volumes (items **1236** and **1237**) on the evolution of Chile's landholding system and its impact on Chile's political and economic life. Extremely well researched and epic in its vision, it is essential for all economic and social historians. But the landholding oligarchy was not as monolithic as believed. Indeed, Manuel Llorca-Jana and others clearly demonstrate through the study of *catastros agrícolas* that the mining elites used their newly found funds to buy their way into the nation's social aristocracy (item **1262**). As Alberto Harambour concludes (item **1255**), the exploitation of the lower classes, so often associated with the *fundos*, also occurred in the newly opened Patagonian region. Ángel Soto (item **1281**) reveals that the 1967 Agrarian Reform law precipitated widely differing views, both on the cause of the land tenure problem and the purpose of its resolution. Leonardo Mazzei da Grazia (item **1266**) does a superb job tracing the economic development of Concepción as well as illuminating the contribution of Italian immigrants to that area.

Diplomatic historians will find it worthwhile to consult Francisco González Errázuriz's excellent work (item **1252**) on French involvement in the War of the Pacific which noted that Paris, unlike Washington, accepted the right of Chile to annex territory from its defeated foes. As if Chilean anger were not enough, Felipe Casanova Rojas and two other scholars (item **1166**), note that the stationing of Allied troops in Tacna adversely impacted its economy and spread disease, perhaps causing more immediate damage than the Chileans.

In sum, these recent works not only amplify our understanding of some already explored issues, but open new areas of study. Reading these publications and assisting scholars, particularly those outside of Chile, to undertake our work of historical inquiry has been a fruitful experience.

1230 Allard, Raúl. Ambientes múltiples: testimonios de cinco décadas en el desarrollo de Valparaíso, Chile y América Latina. Santiago: RIL Editores, 2013. 556 p.: bibl., ill.

A collection of essays and remembrances by a prominent educator who was instrumental in nurturing various academic institutions in Valparaíso, among other places. In addition to working abroad with Chilean and other international leaders, he served as a public servant in Chile.

1231 Álvarez Bravo, Paulo. Legua Emergencia: una historia de dignidad y lucha. Santiago: Ediciones Universidad Diego Portales, 2014. 309 p.: bibl., ill., maps.

Tragic tale of the police's repression in the Legua district of Santiago where the authorities, often citing the high crime rate, brutally maltreated the area's residents and denied them their basic civil rights. Based on more than 120 interviews, shows how neighborhood organizations managed to obtain judicial relief from police brutality and address social issues. Excellent example of the history of the lower class.

1232 Álvarez Vergara, Marco. La constituyente revolucionaria: historia de la fundación del MIR chileno. Santiago: LOM Ediciones, 2015. 169 p.: bibl. (Historia)

Superb study on the evolution of MIR as it moved from a Castro-inspired organization to embrace armed struggle against the bourgeois state. Relying on a variety of sources, particularly interviews, it offers new insights into MIR. Essential to understanding the political life of late 20th century.

1233 Andes, Stephen Joseph Carl. The Vatican and Catholic activism in Mexico and Chile: the politics of transnational Catholicism, 1920–1940. Oxford, UK: Oxford University Press, 2014. 250 p.: bibl., index. (Oxford historical monographs)

The Roman Catholic Church saw the Conservative Party as its vanguard in the fight against the separation of Church and state and the Constitution of 1925. Once both had been implemented, various Catholic intellectuals began to deal with social issues, eventually forming the Christian Democratic Party. Well-researched study of a key party.

1234 Araya Gómez, Rodrigo. Organizaciones sindicales en Chile: de la resistencia a la política de los consensos: 1983–1994. Santiago: Ediciones Universidad Finis Terrae, 2015. 330 p.: bibl. (Colección Historia)

Labor unions were crucial in the resistance to the Pinochet dictatorship. Superb analysis of Chile's labor force and CUT's efforts to reconstitute itself as a viable force in Chilean politics. Provides new information on the post-Pinochet period.

1235 Baradit, Jorger. Historia secreta de Chile. Santiago: Sudamericana, 2015. 169 p.: bibl.

A series of vignettes exploring a diverse set of topics which could have remained secret without negatively altering our knowledge of Chilean history.

1236 Bengoa, José. Historia rural de Chile central. Tomo 1, La construcción del Valle Central de Chile. Santiago: LOM Ediciones, 2015. 1 v.: bibl., ill., indexes (Historia)

Superb comprehensive study of the hacienda system which replaced the encomienda and shaped Chile's political, economic, and social system, inculcating values and cementing the subordinate relationship between *inquilino*, the patron, and Church. Lavishly illustrated, deeply researched, and highly insightful, this work offers a key to understanding how Chile evolved.

1237 Bengoa, José. Historia rural de Chile central. Tomo 2, Crisis y ruptura del poder hacendal. Santiago: LOM Ediciones, 2015. 1 v.: bibl., ill., indexes (Historia)

Due to a primitive landholding system, a lack of investment, and indifference, Chile's hacienda system failed to feed the nation, even as it deprived numerous people of employment. The collapse of the salitreras denied Chile's *fundos* of a market, while challenging the nation's social system.

Challenges from the left and the Church undermined the hacienda system.

1238 Berguño Hurtado, Fernando. Los soldados de Napoleón en la independencia de Chile (1817–1830). Santiago: RIL Editores, 2015. 343 p.: bibl., ill.

Numerous high-ranking French officers, veterans of Napoleon's army, served and trained the pro-independence military that defeated Spanish troops. Inspired by various motives, including self-promotion, some of these men remained in Chile where they married and produced children who also served in the military and the government.

1239 Calles caminadas: anverso y reverso. Estudio y compilación de Eliana Largo. Santiago: Centro de Investigaciones Diego Barros Arana, 2014. 552 p.: bibl., ill., index. (Fuentes para la historia de la república; XXXVII)(Ediciones de la Dirección de Bibliotecas, Archivos y Museos)

Excellent collection of interviews from various feminist leaders tracing events beginning with the original movement for women's suffrage in the early 20th century through the present time. The book addresses issues such as abortion, gay rights, and feminism. An interesting work, although lacking an overarching theme.

1240 Candina, Azun. Clase media, Estado y sacrificio: la Agrupación Nacional de Empleados Fiscales en Chile contemporáneo (1943–1983). Santiago: LOM Ediciones, 2013. 241 p.: bibl., ill.

Study of a public employees' labor union, which demonstrates that, unlike their counterparts, the members saw themselves as dedicated and patriotic public servants, and certainly not as "obreros" in the legal sense. Places union members within the context of Chilean public and economic life as they and their organization worked on behalf of society and anti-Pinochet forces.

1241 Chile-Colombia: diálogos sobre sus trayectorias históricas. Edición académica de Fernando Purcell y Ricardo Arias Trujillo. Santiago: Instituto de Historia, Facultad de Historia, Geografía y Ciencia Política, Pontificia Universidad Católica de

Chile: RIL Editores; Bogotá: Departamento de Historia, Facultad de Ciencias Sociales, Universidad de los Andes Colombia, 2014. 297 p.: bibl., ill.

A series of essays written by Chilean and Colombian scholars trying to accentuate the two nations' similarities as well as differences. Offers useful interpretations of various aspects of the historical development of the countries.

1242 Cohen Ventura, Jacob. Desde Macedonia, Turquía y Europa: judíos en la Araucanía: una historia en imágenes. Santiago: RIL editores, 2016. 514 p.: ill.

Charming and informative study of how Jews, initially from Macedonia, Turkey, and Greece, migrated to Chile in the early 19th century. Profusely illustrated, it demonstrates how these immigrants assimilated into Chilean society, as well as revealing their relations with local society, including the Araucanian Indians. Marvelous source for those interested in regional and ethnic history.

1243 Conflictos y tensiones en el Chile republicano. Edición de Carlos Donoso Rojas y Pablo Rubio Apiolaza. Santiago: RIL Editores, Universidad Nacional Andrés Bello, 2014. 289 p.: bibl.

Excellent series of essays which deal with different aspects of Chilean history from the 19th to late 20th century. Well worth reading for those interested in the various topics covered. Contains an excellent bibliography.

1244 De heroínas, fundadoras y ciudadanas: mujeres en la historia de Chile. Edición de María Gabriela Huidobro. Viña del Mar, Chile: Universidad Andrés Bello; Santiago: RiL Editores, 2015. 200 p.: bibl., ill.

A variety of essays, written by various scholars who describe the roles of women, some of them prominent, during different periods: the colonial period, the Republic, and the more modern epoch. By emphasizing the achievements of women, the work provides access to overshadowed contributions.

1245 Díaz Araujo, Enrique. El allendismo chileno. Buenos Aires: Ediciones Buen Combate, 2013. 194 p.: bibl. (Cuadernos rojos)

An anti-Allende tract blaming him and his followers for the debacle that befell Chile. Based on largely skewed secondary sources, it is too biased for the serious scholar, even the most conservative, to use with confidence.

1246 Dougnac Rodríguez, Antonio and **Roberto Cerón Reyesl.** Una silueta de la jurdicatura chilean en el siglo XIX. (*Bol. Acad. Chil. Hist.*, 82:125, 2016, p. 7–82, bibl.)

While Chile erected its postindependence legal system on the Spanish tradition, it eventually created a new and independent judiciary, based on regional centers and sometimes specific designated tasks, surmounted by a Supreme Court. Using primary sources, this work concentrates on efforts of specific jurists. A somewhat tedious work, but worthwhile.

1247 Eloy, Horacio. Revistas y publicaciones literarias en dictadura (1973–1990). Santiago: Piso Diez Ediciones, 2014. 234 p.: bibl., ill.

A group of literary journals spearheaded opposition to the Pinochet government. This work provides a comprehensive list of items published throughout Chile, as well as interviews and examples of literary works. Essential source of intellectual as well as political historians.

1248 Farías, Víctor. Ricardo Lagos y el Chile nuevo. Santiago: Editorial Maye, 2013. 120 p: bibl., ill.

Beginning his career as a leftist, Lagos opted to operate within the economic parameters instituted by the Pinochet and Concertación governments. Although excoriated by the extreme left, his advocacy of moderation allowed the country to function without falling into the trap of ultrapartisanship.

1249 Forstall Comber, Biddy. Crepúsculo en un balcón frente a los Andes: ingleses y la pampa salitrera. Santiago: Centro de Investigaciones Diego Barros Arana, DIBAM, Dirección Bibliotecas, Archivos y Museos: Editorial Universitaria, 2015. 427 p.: bibl., ill. (Testimonios)

Charming anecdotal description of a pampa-born Anglo Irishwoman who lived in the British-administered salitreras in the mid-20th century. Provides insights into the life of expatriates in the almost incestuous Anglo-Chilean community, as well as the workers they commanded.

1250 Gaudichaud, Franck. Chile 1970–1973: mil dias que estremecieron al mundo: poder popular, cordones industriales y socialismo durante el gobierno de Salvador Allende. Traducción de Claudia Marchant. Santiago: LOM Ediciones, 2016. 467 p.: bibl., ill., indexes, maps. (Historia)

A French doctoral dissertation that describes in great detail the creation and functioning of Santiago's *cordones industriales* as well as other spontaneous worker organizations that developed up during Allende's regime. Extremely well researched and richly illustrated, the study analyzes the role of worker-controlled groups and their tensions with the Moneda. Essential for understanding the UP government.

1251 Goldsmith Weil, Jael. Milk makes state: the extension and implementation of Chile's state milk programs, 1901–1971. (*Historia/Santiago*, 50:1, junio 2017, p. 79–104, bibl., graphs, tables)

Beginning as a private charity dedicated to addressing childhood malnutrition, the milk program evolved into a state enterprise that fostered a domestic dairy industry that produced and monitored the equality of milk. The Christian Democrats accelerated the process, as the government stressed the use of dehydrated milk.

1252 González Errázuriz, Francisco Javier. La diplomacia norteamericana y las negociaciones de paz durante la Guerra del Pacífico: la mirada frances. (*Bol. Acad. Chil. Hist.*, 82:125, 2016, p. 167–192, bibl.)

France, unlike the US, recognized that Chile could annex Peruvian and Bolivian territory as a price for peace and thus supported its draconian demands. Clumsy and under economic pressure, Washington could not prevent European intervention in Latin America.

1253 Guzmán Jasmen, Nancy. Ingrid Olderock: la mujer de los perros. Santiago: CEIBO Ediciones, 2014. 175 p.: bibl., ill. (Colección Investigación)

Olderock, a self-acknowledged Nazi, joined the Carabineros where she trained female officers in interrogation techniques that included using dogs to violate the Pinochet regime's male and female prisoners. A particularly ruthless and unrepentant operative, she became involved in Operation Condor. If true, the book adds a singularly horrible insight into the military government's activities.

1254 Hales Dib, Jaime. La rueda de la historia: testimonio de un protagonista. Santiago: Ediciones Radio UChile, 2014. 498 p.: bibl. (Colección Testimonios)

The son of a prominent politician, Alejandro Hales, and a Christian Democrat lawyer, Hales Dib recounts the events preceding Allende's election and his fall. Highly critical of the Concertación, the military, the US, and the existing socioeconomic system, as well as his Christian Democratic Party, he still hopes to change Chile.

1255 Harambour, Alberto R. Soberanía y corrupción: la construcción del Estado y la propiedad en Patagonia austral (Argentina y Chile, 1840–1920). (*Historia/Santiago*, 50:2, dic. 2017, p. 555–596, bibl., ill., photos)

Once "pacified," Chile's southernmost province became the target of greedy business interests which, in collusion with corrupt politicians, introduced sheepherding in the area. Essentially operating outside the law, these interests created an economic fiefdom for the pastoral interests.

1256 Harmer, Tanya. View from Havana: Chilean exiles in Cuba and early resistance to Chile's dictatorship, 1973–1977. (*HAHR*, 96:1, Feb. 2016, p. 109–146, bibl.)

Cuban assistance to the anti-Pinochet forces, while useful, proved less significant than those elements operating in Europe and elsewhere. Cuban reluctance and internecine struggles limited the resistance's ability to alter the situation. Well-researched article dealing with a crucial period in the post-coup era.

1257 Hertz, Carmen; Ramírez, Apolonia; and Manuel Salazar. Operación Exterminio: la represión contra los comunistas chilenos (1973–1976). Santiago: LOM Ediciones, 2016. 392 p.: bibl., ill., index. (Colección Nuevo periodismo)

Traces the Pinochet government's coup and its program to destroy the Partido Comunista and its adherents. Provides an excellent overview of the development of the party, its various organizations, as well as its resistance to the coup and the ensuing regime. Provides biographies of the party's leadership and their ultimately tragic fate. Excellent study for those interested in post-Allende period.

1258 Historia de la educación en Chile, 1810–2010. Vol. 1, Aprender a leer y escribir, 1810–1880. Vol. 2, Educación nacional, 1880–1930. Edición de Sol Serrano, Macarena Ponce de León y Francisca Rengifo. Santiago: Taurus, 2012. 2 v.: bibl., ill.

Beginning with independence, education proved crucial to integrating Chile's diverse population into the new nation. Initially designed to create a literate population, educational policies eventually incorporated the rural sector. Shows the development of a cadre of teachers, with the creation of normal schools, and the production of school texts. The school emerges as important to improving health and vocational education. Contains a wealth of useful statistics which will advance the study of education.

1259 Historia política de Chile, 1810–2010. Vol. 1, Prácticas políticas. Edición de Iván Jaksic y Juan Luis Ossa Santa Cruz. Santiago: Fondo de Cultura Económica: Universidad Adolfo Ibañez, 2017. 506 p.: bibl. (Sección de obras de historia)

A superb series of essays tracing how Chile slowly integrated various elements—women, the poor, the middle class, the peasantry, the military, and labor—into the political process. While this increasingly intricate mechanism initially functioned, it collapsed into a military dictatorship. The essays and the bibliography that undergirds them make this volume essential.

1260 Historia política de Chile, 1810–2010. Vol. 2, Estado y sociedad. Edición de Iván Jaksic y Francisca Rengifo. Santiago: Fondo de Cultura Económica: Universidad Adolfo Ibañez, 2017. 474 p.: bibl. (Sección de Obras de historia)

Outstanding collection of original essays explaining the creation and evolution of the Chilean state, as well as how it manifested itself in areas such as foreign relations, creation of the judiciary, the social welfare system, the secularization of society, labor relations, and education. Extremely well researched study with an excellent bibliography.

1261 Historias de mujeres inmigrantes de Magallanes: más importante que el oro. Recopilación de Gloria Angelo Mladinic. Santiago: Ediciones Radio Universidad de Chile, 2015. 285 p.: bibl., ill.

Fascinating stories of the various women of different nationalities who settled in the Magallanes region, describing their lives, their tribulations, and their influence on the economy. Also traces the backgrounds of the various women and the influences in their lives.

1262 Llorca-Jaña, Manuel et al. La agricultura y la élite agraria chilena a través de los catastros agrícolas, c.1830–1855. (*Historia/Santiago*, 50:2, dic. 2017, p. 597–639, bibl., tables)

Demonstrates that until the second half of the 19th century, postindependence Chilean agricultural elites managed to preserve their hold on the land. The emerging mining elite, in part to diversify their economic position, used their new wealth to buy into the aristocracy. A superb article based upon extensive use of agricultural records.

1263 Lozoya López, Ivette. Delincuentes, bandoleros y montoneros: violencia social en el espacio rural chileno, 1850–1870. Santiago: LOM Ediciones, 2014. 149 p.: bibl. (Historia)

Sees rural violence as creating a sense of identity, as well as demonstrating the anger of the nation's lower class against the socioeconomics changes produced by the evolving economy. Like Hobsbawn, the author does not see those breaking the law—including numerous women—as criminals, but as those acting against the social order and "traditional" values.

1264 Mac-Clure Hortal, Óscar. En los orígenes de las políticas sociales en Chile, 1850–1879. Santiago: Universidad Alberto Hurtado 2012. 468 p.: bibl., ill., index. (Colección de historia)

The Chilean state devoted substantial sums to providing its citizens with an education, trying to create healthy living conditions, and guaranteeing health care. The impetus for these enlightened social policies originated not only in the government, but in various citizens groups.

1265 Mansilla, Miguel Ángel; Juan Sepúlveda; and Luis Orellana. Cuando el opio se rebela: la Confraternidad Cristiana de Iglesias (evangélicas) en su crítica a la dictadura militar y su proyecto de sociedad (1981–1989). (*Rev. Cienc. Polít./Santiago*, 35:2, 2015, p. 327–345, bibl.)

Because evangelical churches tended to concentrate their activities in Santiago's poorest barrios, they identified with the lower classes. Using documents, the authors show that the Protestant elements espoused causes, such as providing economic support, to help the deprived. Additionally, these organizations advocated for a restoration of political liberties.

1266 Mazzei de Grazia, Leonardo. Historia económica regional de Concepción, 1800–1920. Concepción, Chile: Ediciones del Archivo Histórico de Concepción, 2015. 260 p.: bibl., ill. (Colección Bío-Bío)

A superb collection of essays by an outstanding scholar who has specialized in Concepción. Traces the province's economic development and includes interesting material on Italian immigrants and their contribution to the area. Provides an extensive bibliography demonstratng Mazzei de Grazia's contribution to Chile's historiography.

1267 Movimiento sindical en dictadura: fuentes para una historia del sindicalismo en Chile, 1973–1990. Edición de Rodrigo Araya Gómez. Santiago: Ediciones Universidad Alberto Hurtado, 2015. 219 p.: bibl., ill. (Colección de historia. Serie Chile contemporáneo)

Divided into three phases, this is a collection of primary source materials, documenting how organized labor responded to the Pinochet regime. A work of limited value, although useful for learning how labor refused to accept military rule.

1268 Navia, Patricio, and Ignacio Soto Castro. El efecto de Antonio Zamorano, el Cura de Catapilco, en la derrota de Salvador Allende en la elección presidencial de 1958. (*Historia/Santiago*, 50:1, dic. 2017, p. 121–139, bibl., graphs, tables)

Utilizes the latest statistical methods to show that, contrary to popular belief, Zamorano's candidacy did not siphon votes away from Allende in 1958. The Cura drew support, votes, and financial support not only from the left, but also from right-wing communities and communes.

Ni vencedores ni vencidos: la Guerra del Pacífico en perspectiva histórica. See item 394.

1269 Ortúzar, Diego. La política de las enfermedades profesionales: anquilostomiasis y silicosis en Chile, 1920–1940. (*Estud. Soc./Santa Fe*, 25:49, segundo semestre 2015, p. 183–210)

The Chilean government belatedly recognized that certain diseases—hookworm in the Lota coal pits and silicosis in the northern copper mines—afflicted the work force. Beginning in the post-1925 period, the Moneda confronted these ailments, enjoying more success in eradicating the southern problem, than in the north where the issue was more embedded in work regulations. Interesting study showing interaction between the government and the economy.

1270 Pérez, Cristián. Vidas revolucionarias. Santiago: Editorial Universitaria, 2013. 437 p.: bibl. (Testimonios)

Contrary to some, the MIR and other extreme leftist groups lacked the skills and weapons to challenge either the Allende or the Pinochet governments. An extremely detailed study of the MIR, FPMR, and other organizations. This well-researched work provides a detailed account of the left's activities in Chile, even before Allende's election, as well as in Bolivia. Includes an extensive biographical study of the various participants, their allies, and their foes. Essential work.

1271 La religión en la esfera pública chilena: ¿laicidad o secularización? Edición de Ana María Stuven. Santiago: Ediciones Universidad Diego Portales, 2014. 337 p.: bibl. (Colección Ciencias sociales e historia)

Series of essays that deal with religion, its place in Latin America as well as in Chile. The material on Chile is particularly useful, especially for the late 19th-century and on the issue of separation of Church and state.

1272 Rengifo, Francisca. Desigualdad e inclusión: la ruta del estado de seguridad social chileno, 1920–1970. (*HAHR*, 97:3, Aug. 2017, p. 487–521, bibl., ill.)

The urbanization and industrialization of Chile spawned a series of social and economic problems. In the 1920s, Chile's state created a social security system that developed into a bifurcated system which differentiated between white collar, blue collar, industrial, and agrarian workers as well as those employed by the public and private sectors. The result was an patchwork of benefits.

1273 La revolución permanente: historia social de las mujeres en Chile. Edición de Gabriel Salazar et al. Madrid: Niram Art, 2015. 587 p.: bibl., ill.

An excellent collection of essays, each dealing with a different era: the pre- and postcolonial Mapuche, colonial women, women's economic emancipation in the 19th and early 20th centuries, and their final liberation. Contains some excellent sources and bibliography.

1274 Rivera Mir, Sebastián. El otro exilio chileno en México y Guatemala, 1948–1951: militancia transnacional en los orígenes de la Guerra Fría. (*Historia/Santiago*, 50:1, enero/junio 2017, p. 209–240, bibl.)

The Ley Maldita forced various Chilean communists to seek exile, first in Mendoza, and then in Mexico and Guatemala, where they worked against the González Videla government. Those who settled in Guatemala, where they labored for Juan José Arévalo and Juan Jacobo Árbenz, had an easier time than in Mexico, although the latter government did provide some support.

1275 Rubio Apiolaza, Pablo. Los civiles de Pinochet: la derecha en el régimen militar chileno, 1983–1990. Santiago: DIBAM Dirección de Bibliotecas, Archivos y Museos, Centro de Investigaciones Diego Barros Arana, 2013. 346 p.: bibl., ill. (Colección Sociedad y cultura; LV)

A rare look at Chile's right during the dictatorship's last days, combining a history of that spectrum. Based on extensive research, it shows how a schism developed as the political system evolved, particularly when the right realized that it could not rely on Pinochet.

1276 Salazar Salvo, Manuel. La lista del Schindler chileno: empresario, comunista, clandestino. Santiago: LOM Ediciones, 2014. 203 p.: bibl., ill.2 (Memorias)

No relation to the famous Oscar Schindler, Jorge Schindler organized a chain of emergency pharmacies in Concepción and Santiago which provided a cover, as well as a source of support, for Communists and other leftists, as well as organizing the remnants of the Party to oppose the Pinochet government.

1277 Salazar Vergara, Gabriel. La enervante levedad histórica de la clase política civil: Chile, 1900–1973. Santiago: Debate, 2015. 1139 p.: bibl. (Debate Historia)

An almost encyclopedic study, analyzing the Chilean state. Describes a fusion of the political and economic elites who ruled the nation, perpetuating the political system in which they wielded an enormous economic stake. Sees the political parties as forces to structure the state and the economy without much regard for the people they supposedly served. Brilliant and well researched, the is work is imperative for scholars.

1278 Salinas Toledo, Juan Luis. Linda, regia, estupenda: historia de la mode y la mujer en Chile. Santiago: El Mercurio; Providencia, Chile: Aguilar, 2014. 340 p., 17 unnumbered p.: bibl., ill., index.

Written by a fashion editor, describes the interplay between fashion and women over the past 60 years. Although preoccupied with appearing chic, Chilean women consider motherhoood to be their preeminent role. Also includes some observations on why Chilean designers never seem to capitalize on the numerous models, including a Miss Universe, that the country produced.

1279 San Francisco, Alejandro. Historia de Chile: 1960–2010. Tomo 1, Democracia, esperanzas y frustaciones: Chile a mediados del siglo XX. Tomo 2, El preludio de las revoluciones: El gobierno de Jorge

Alessandri. Santiago: CEUSS, 2016 2 vol.: bibl., index.

Providing a panoramic overview of the period from 1950 to 1973, these volumes meld the study of politics, economics, social, and intellectual history with a superb bibliography and numerous pictures and illustrations. A must for all interested in Chilean history, economic, and culture.

1280 **Santibáñez Rebolledo, Camilo.** Los trabajadores portuarios chilenos y la experiencia de la eventualidad: los conflictos por la redondilla en los muelles salitreros, 1916–1923. (*Historia/Santiago*, 50:2, julio/dic. 2017, p. 699–728, bibl., map)

World War I disrupted the nitrate industry, creating chaos in the labor market and precipitating strikes and boycotts. The workers attempted to stabilize the labor market so that all could work. Eventually the government became involved, creating a labor allocation system in an attempt to eliminate favoritism and corruption.

1281 **Soto, Ángel.** Monólogos para la historia: Discursos parlamentarios en torno al proyecto de ley de reforma agraria. (*Bol. Acad. Chil. Hist.*, 82:125, 2016, p. 192–201, bibl.)

Although Frei's reform of the agrarian sector eventually became law, support was neither unanimous nor uniform: some saw it as a moral issue, others as an economic measure. Interesting article showing how these opinions vary. Drawn from the congressional debates, this article helps historians understand at least some of the motivations of the voters.

1282 **Torres Dujisin, Isabel.** La crisis del sistema democrático: las elecciones presidenciales y los proyectos políticos excluyentes: Chile 1958–1970. Prólogo de Alan Angell. Santiago: Centro de Investigaciones Diego Barros Arana; DIBAM-Dirección de Bibliotecas, Archivos y Museos: Editorial Universitaria, 2014. 421 p.: bibl., ill. (Imagen de Chile)

Excellent study which examines the influence of the elections of 1968, 1964, and 1970 that depicted the candidates as potential saviors, polarizing Chilean society and leading to the 1973 coup. Contains a wealth of statistical information and examples of the various electoral tactics employed by competing factions as they tried to influence the nation. Essential for historians of modern Chile.

1283 **Un trébol de cuatro hojas: las juventudes comunistas de Chile en el siglo XX.** Edición de Rolando Álvarez Vallejos y Manuel Loyola T. Santiago: Ariadna; América en Movimiento, 2014. 311 p.: bibl., ill. (Colección Izquierdas)

Excellent compilation of the activities of the Communist Youth in Chile at various critical times. Although of varying quality, these essays provide insights into the acts of the youth organizations, particularly earlier. Includes interviews of five activists, some of whom left the Party and others who remained faithful to the cause.

1284 **Valdivia Ortiz de Zárate, Veronica.** Los tengo plenamente identificados: seguridad interna y control social en Chile, 1918–1925. (*Historia/Santiago*, 50:1, enero/junio 2017, p. 241–271, bibl.)

The government ignored constitutional guarantees protecting political liberties, initially, to stop presidential abuses, and then, after 1917, to limit worker and radical political ideology. Among the measures adopted was an identification system and the creation of the *carnet* to control the population.

1285 **Varas, José Miguel.** Escucha Chile Radio Moscú. Santiago: LOM Ediciones, 2012. 150 p.: ill. (Colección Crónicas)

A series of programs produced by José Varas, a political exile who broadcast from the Soviet Union where he worked as a correspondent in opposition to the Pinochet regime. Most of his reporting described the countless atrocities committed by the dictatorship. A predictable work, which adds very little to our knowledge.

1286 **Venegas Valdebenito, Hernán** and **Diego Morales Barrientos.** Un caso de paternalismo industrial en Tomé: familia, espacio urbano y sociabilidad de los obreros textiles (1920–1940). (*Historia/Santiago*, 50:1, enero/junio 2017, p. 273–302, bibl., photo)

In hopes of improving productivity and regulating the workforce, the Sociedad Nacional de Paños tried to create a sense of community. By relying on hiring based on family ties and creating a series of social programs, the company fostered paternalism to make their workers good employees.

Argentina, Paraguay, and Uruguay

ADRIANA BRODSKY, *Professor of History, St. Mary's College of Maryland*
BRIDGET MARÍA CHESTERTON, *Professor of History, Buffalo State, The State University of New York*
MOLLIE LEWIS NOUWEN, *Assistant Professor of Liberal Arts and Department Head of Humanities, Pacific Northwest College of Art*
THOMAS WHIGHAM, *Professor Emeritus of History, University of Georgia*

ARGENTINA, PARAGUAY, AND URUGUAY (INDEPENDENCE TO 1880)
THE VARIOUS POLITICAL SHIFTS in the modern Platine states continue to shape historical scholarship in that part of the world. Under the government of President Kirchner in Argentina, for instance, historical work of a left-populist orientation received official sanction together with occasional financial subventions. This gave historians of that persuasion an outsized role in Argentine scholarship and over several years they produced a substantial number of studies, some useful, others little better than polemical tracts. With the electoral victory of Mauricio Macri in December 2015, however, the subventions dried up in Argentina and even the monies regularly provided to young scholars by the nonpartisan CONICET have been harder to come by. In consequence, there has been an overall downturn in the volume of historical publications coupled with a renewed dependence on the non-academic market. "Left-populist" titles have slipped into obscurity, a trend that has been both good and bad. Standards for evidence have generally improved in recent years, but the "bottom-to- top" histories that made up such an important and promising part of the scholarly profile during the first decade of the 21st century are largely on hiatus these days (with the works of Di Meglio—items **1350** and **1351**—standing out as happy exceptions). Perhaps one could argue that politicized works are better than none at all.

That said, there are more than a few titles recently published in Argentina that compel our interest for their insight and solidity. There are new and attractive biographical accounts of key historical figures, such as Sarmiento, Lavalle, Andrade, and Belgrano (items **1323, 1332, 1342, 1369, 1418, 1437,** and especially **1391**). Several innovative studies on political culture have also appeared, including Fradkin and Gelman's investigation of leadership under Rosas (item **1369**); Cantera's book on revolutionary discourse and vocabulary (item **1325**); Eujanian's study of republican discourse and fundamental texts (item **1364**); Tarcus' account of the reception among Argentines of the literature of Romantic Socialism (item **1477**); and Blumenthal's intriguing article on how the bodies of national heroes can become instruments in the development of partisan politics (item **1312**). Provincial studies—always a significant focus in Argentine historiography—have continued to appear in goodly number. In this respect, we might note excellent works on Corrientes (items **1335** and **1454**); Córdoba (items **1345** and **1450**); Santa Fe (item **1421**); Catamarca (item **1435**); and Mendoza (item **1316**). One strikingly interesting work on the history of Argentine natural history museums by Podgorny and Lopes must be pointed (item **1451**). An excellent look at Rosas' relations with the Indians should also be noted in Cutrera's lively study of frontier "diplomacy" (item **1346**). Finally, Martínez deserves congratulations for reintroducing a theme long absent from secular literature—the history of the Argentine Church in the early national period (item **1420**).

Neither Paraguay nor Uruguay could count on the support rendered to certain Argentine scholars by the Kirchner government and, not surprisingly, scholars in those countries produced far fewer historical studies in recent years. That said, there have been a few works deserving of more than passing attention from readers. Chesterton's efforts in throwing light on the history of the Paraguayan Chaco are a case in point and they continue to inspire interest from readers on several continents (items **1492**, **1493**, and **1494**). They clearly promise more to come. Vázquez Franco, for his part, shows that advanced age is no barrier to producing pioneering work, in this case, on the 1828 events leading to Uruguayan independence (item **1519**). Lastly, the intriguing field of Afro-Uruguayan research is here well represented in a compelling study of slaves in the Uruguayan north by Palermo (item **1515**). [TW]

ARGENTINA (LATE 19TH CENTURY TO 20TH CENTURY)

Among the works reviewed for *HLAS 74*, provinces and territories have been a major focus. Bonaudo's edited work looks specifically at Tucumán, Santa Fe, Río Negro, and Neuquén (item **1458**). Mases and Zink have also produced a fine edited volume focusing on the territorial era with a strong focus on labor (item **1360**). Córdoba province is the focus of an array of new scholarship. Pavoni's book on politics and political culture will be of great interest to many (item **1445**). Camaño's article specifically delves into the political arena of the city of Río Cuarto (item **1322**). Vidal and Blanco's edited volume is from a working group on the public sphere and political culture from a comparative perspective, most of the essays focus on the province of Córdoba (item **1363**). For Santa Fe, often with an emphasis on the city of Rosario, Bertero and her coauthors explore the growing association movement, particularly Masonic lodges (item **1308**), while Micheletti takes on historical writing and the ways history is imagined (item **1429**). At the city level, Megías *et al.* focus on the debates about identity within the public sphere of the city of Rosario from the late 19th century onward (item **1303**). Both Horowitz (item **1394**) and Roldán (item **1462**) have new articles that approach the growth and popularity of soccer in the early 20th century, focusing particularly on neighborhoods: Horowitz for Buenos Aires and Roldán for Rosario. Martocci takes on the Province of La Pampa, and the role of the Socialist Party (item **1422**). Vignoli, writing about the Sociedad Sarmiento in Tucumán (prior to the foundation of the University of Tucumán), demonstrates its importance as a site of male sociability and intellectual upward mobility (item **1484**).

The history of business and capitalism in the provinces is another area with some excellent new volumes. Tucumán is the focus of Moyano's work, which tackles the sugar industry through the lens of business history (item **1436**). Richard Jorba continues the fine work that has already been done on the Mendoza wine industry with his exploration of its social and economic implications, particularly regarding class structure (item **1459**). Mayer, also looking at industry, examines the public-private partnership of the railroads in the province of Buenos Aires (item **1426**).

Biographies were a popular genre in the past two years, particularly those focusing on figures of importance in the late 19th and early 20th centuries. New works include Martí's evaluation of Juan Manuel de Rosas and his legacy (item **1419**), Glück's intellectual biography of Juan Álvarez (item **1381**), de Marco's popular study on Leandro N. Alem (item **1417**), Galasso's accessible biography of Yrigoyen (item **1373**), and Losada's re-evaluation of Marcelo T. de Alvear and his legacy (item **1410**). Marchante's popular profile of José Menéndez, a Patagonian businessman, is part biography, part history of environmental destruction (item **1291**). Finally, Olivera has written a biography of Wilhelm Vallentin, a little-known German economist, traveler, and founder of a colony in Chubut (item **1442**). Peronist biographies are their own subcategory with new scholarship on some of the most important Peronist leaders. Works include a pro-Peronist profile of the man himself by Gúzman Suárez (item **1390**), Cloppet's intimate biography of Perón and letters from his assignment in Rome (item **1338**), Mercado's biography of Raúl Apold, entitled *El inventor del peronismo* (item **1427**), and Sorín's work on John William Cooke, chosen by Perón to lead the party following the 1955 coup (item **1472**). Soler's biography of Ricardo Balbín includes plenty of documents: material published in *Adelante*, as well as letters received from citizens regarding the imprisonment or disappearance of family members (item **1471**).

Gender, sexuality, and women's studies continue to be a rich vein of scholarship that shows no sign of abating. An excellent edited volume, this one by Giordano, Ramacciotti, and Valobra, focuses on the little-studied topic of divorce in the mid-20th century, with a particular focus on the period in 1955–56 when it was briefly legal (item **1341**). Ehrick adds a fascinating new perspective on women and their voices with her study of radio in Argentina and Uruguay (item **1359**), while rural women and the changing gender roles from the 1930s to the 1960s are the focus of de Arce's book (item **1294**). Ledesma Prietto adds to the conversation with an examination of the medical discourse in the anarchist movement surrounding sexuality and maternity (item **1404**). Periodicals featuring women were also the subject of new studies, particularly Caldo's examination of *Damas y damitas*, a home economics magazine for women, exploring the written transmission of culinary knowledge and its impact on non-elite women (item **1320**), and Gallo's book on four periodicals devoted to rights for women in the early 20th century—*Unión y Labor, Nuestra Causa, Vida Femenina,* and *Mujeres de América* (item **1375**). This biennium also produced a new edition of short writings by early 20th-century feminist icon Alfonsina Storni (item **1476**).

Leftist political movements and labor in the early 20th century continue to draw scholarly attention. Ceruso's work is an exhaustive examination of labor between 1916 and 1932, including all major industries and the various leftist political movements to which many workers belonged (item **1331**). Iñigo Carrera approaches the 1930s by exploring radical labor mobilization and organization, which has often been ignored in the periods between democratic rule and the Peronist years (item **1397**). Looking to transnational linkages and ideologies, Pittaluga's new study of Argentine responses to the Russian Revolution of 1917 is a fascinating rumination on the nature of leftist politics and the meaning of revolution (item **1448**). In Poy's new article, he calls for a more systematic examination of the Socialist Party in its early years, and presents an example of his method in an analysis of the early Socialist Congresses, from 1896–1908 (item **1453**). Labor and the laws surrounding labor protections and accidents are the focus of two new articles—Maddalena examines the period up to the labor law of 1915 (item **1411**) and Stagnaro looks at the various legal and legislative strategies to deal with labor accidents from 1904–46 (item **1475**). Finally, an English translation of Bayer's classic *Rebellion in Patagonia* will appeal to many English readers interested in the history of the left in Argentina (item **1305**).

The "infamous decade" of the 1930s is receiving more and more scholarly attention from a variety of perspectives. Blacha's new work examines the power relations of the elite in the 1930s, arguing that the 1916–30 period was a brief democratic interlude and that the 1930s were a return to normal for Argentine political culture (item **1311**). Friedmann's article on The Black Front in Argentina, a party that broke with the Nazis and became critical of Hitler and his state, is a good addition to the growing historiography on fascism and antifascism (item **1370**). The nationalist and anti-imperialist group FORJA was another response to the infamous decade. Godoy's new work studies the sociological and theoretical implications of the group (item **1382**).

Immigration continues to be a focus of scholarship this biennium. One of the most noteworthy is Hyland's examination of Arabic-speaking immigrants, primarily in Argentina's northwest during the early 20th century. For linguistic reasons, the topic that has received little prior attention (item **1396**). Cristóforis' text, created for undergraduates at the Universidad de Buenos Aires, is a basic but good introduction to the subject, focusing in particular on the province of Buenos Aires (item **1343**). Cristóforis, this time with Tato, also produced an edited volume exploring the reactions of the Spanish immigrant community to the two World Wars and the Spanish Civil War, as well as their links to the home country (item **1387**). Bravo Herrera approaches Italian literature about emigration to Argentina, particularly the works related to identity (item **1317**). Cruset's work compares Basque and Irish immigrants (item **1344**), while the volume put together at the behest of the Asturian center of Mar del Plata by Da Orden, Ortuño de Martínez, and Derbiz celebrates the history of that migratory flow (item **1347**). Bryce and Sheinin's edited collection includes a few essays on how immigrant communities claimed their place in a new nation (item **1412**). The book, more broadly, explores the changes in the meaning of citizenship throughout Argentina's history. An essay in the collection edited by Philp likewise focuses on citizenship and its link to human rights (the book also discusses other aspects of the history of Córdoba) (item **1479**).

Jewish immigrants in particular continue to be a focus of scholarship. Especially noteworthy is Brodsky's wide-ranging work on the Sephardim in Argentina, vital to our expanding understanding of Jewish life (item **1318**). Avni continues to add to the conversation, this time with an investigation of the "white slave trade" in both Argentina and Israel (item **1296**). Dujovne analyzed Argentine Jewish culture by reconstructing the world of the Jewish book and the actors who participated in their production, distribution, and consumption (item **1357**). In a journalistic style, Huberman attempts to retell the story of the *Weser*, the first boat of Jewish immigrants (item **1395**), while Muchnik explores the history of his own Jewish family and other immigrant families to Argentina (item **1438**).

Welsh immigration received special attention this biennium due to the 150th anniversary of Welsh settlement in Patagonia. Gavirati and Williams' edited volume is the most wide-ranging and academic of the new works (item **1337**). Other works include Barzini's accessible photo book on the town of Dolavon (item **1300**), a translation of Davies' 1892 work relating his own experience as a Welsh immigrant (item **1348**), Lo Presti's oversize photo book of the Welsh in Chubut with reproductions of many little-seen early photographs (item **1339**), and Pérez and Lo Presti's edition of Henry Bowman's writings and early photographs of his Patagonian surroundings (item **1315**).

A few studies of Argentine foreign policy appeared this biennium, though much remains to be done. Semán's study of blue-collar workers appointed by Perón to attaché positions at embassies throughout the world is a fascinating chapter of the Cold War in Latin America that has received little attention (item **1468**). Finally, Pérez Stocco's work (item **1446**) on the peace process during the Chaco War and the diplomacy of Carlos Saavedra Lamas is also notworthy.

Periodicals received a great deal of attention, with some works already mentioned in conjunction with gender studies. One of the strongest is Di Stefano's, a theory-based work examining the "discursive community" around the anarchist publications *La protesta* and *La protesta humana* (item **1353**). Ospital and Mateo's edited volume, focusing on the publication *SERVIR*, explores the presence of economic nationalist thought in the years before Peronism (item **1292**). Rubinzal and Zanca's article takes up the case of *Primeras armas*, a Catholic magazine for boys, published between 1935 and 1955 (item **1466**).

Culture and memory are the subject of a number of strong new studies. Montaldo's wide-ranging and theoretically sophisticated book (item **1431**) on the rise of mass culture in the late 19th and early 20th century looks at elements as disparate as circuses, tango, and population growth. The work will be of use to a range of scholars. Eujanian, Pasolini, and Spinelli's edited volume grapples with Argentine celebrations and commemorations of the past, particularly independence (item **1361**). The book by Quinteros (item **1340**) on the commemoration of the May Revolution of 1810 includes several essays on the narratives crafted by the Perón governments about the origins of the modern nation (other sections discuss representations of the revolution during the 1820s and the 2000s). Varela's book on tango, while not written as a professional history, nonetheless has good information on tango and its attendant culture through the years (item **1482**).

Some of the synthetic work of this biennium would be of particular use at the undergraduate level or as an overview. Gallo's work, spanning the years 1850–1930, is a good introduction to the nation-making period in Argentina for those wanting a concise overview (item **1376**), while Tarruella offers an accessible account of Argentina and the First World War (item **1478**). Lida's examination of the Catholic Church in Argentina from the 1870s to the 1960s is a broad look at an important institution (item **1408**).

A number of works are pointing to new and exciting directions in the scholarship on early 20th-century Argentina. Many of these works engage their subjects from a variety of perspectives and examine the ramifications of the topic under study. Harari's detailed analysis of the automotive industry (1952–76) (item **1392**) includes a discussion of Peronist policies and the role of the working class. Rieznik, writing about the history of observatories in Córdoba and La Plata, shows how the mapping of the southern sky had meaning far beyond the scientific (item **1460**). Part intellectual history, part transnational history of psychiatry and psychoanalysis in the Cold War, Vezzetti's work is an intriguing take on the links between leftist politics and the treatment of mental health in Argentina (item **1483**). Finally, media, children, and immigrants are the focus of Rojkind's article about the Sambrice case and attendant media sensation over the 15-year-old immigrant and would-be assassin of President Julio A. Roca (item **1461**).

Some areas of study saw few new books since the publication of *HLAS* 72. Indigenous groups were the subject of a few new books, only one an academic study. Mases' new book approaches the history of the indigenous from a variety of perspectives while linking it to the social question of the late 19th century (item **1423**). Intended for popular audiences, Sosa's book explores the Patagonian feather trade and its impact on the indigenous population (item **1473**) and Valko's study examines the campaigns of attrition against native peoples (item **1481**). Other works of note this biennium include González Bollo's history of census-taking and its attendant bureaucracy in Argentina (item **1384**) and the edited volume by Sierra, Pro, and Mauro in appreciation of their mentor, Marta Bonaudo, which loosely examines politics and political culture in Argentina and Spain during the first half of the 20th century (item **1349**).

The topic of Peronism, predictably, continues to generate academic interest, and some of the trends identified in our *HLAS* 72 essay have solidified. Among other issues, writers have focused on Peronism in provincial settings, relationships with the military, political culture, youth and political participation, and resistance after 1955 and during the dictatorship. Our understanding of the ways that Peronism worked on a provincial and local level continues to grow. The Province of La Pampa (briefly known as the Province of Eva Perón in the early 1950s) received sustained attention, with three monographs focusing on Peronism there, including Ferrari's work (item **1365**). Liscia focused on Peronism through the lens of La Pampa's women, using interviews with them to ground her work (item **1409**). Some scholars were looking at the ways Peronism was experienced on a very local level, including Klappenbach's edited volume about La Plata (item **1470**), Marcilese's detailed examination of the city of Bahía Blanca (item **1416**), and Camaño Semprini's exploration of Río Cuarto (item **1321**).

Among the new studies are examinations of the 1955 coup. Besse and Rodríguez's edited volume approaches the coup against Perón with scholars from a range of fields examining images, the press, silence, and memory (item **1354**). Furman examines the fascist Alianza Libertadora, the group behind the 1955 coup, interviewing the remaining participants and situating the group within its historical context (item **1372**). Other works of note include Canton and Acosta's volume, which uses quantitative data to refutes Germani's hypothesis about the importance of internal migrants in the rise of Perón (item **1326**). Guy's fascinating new book uses the letters written to Juan and Eva to demonstrate the charismatic bonds engendered by Peronism (item **1389**). Finally, Montes de Oca examines the links between the Peronist government and the Ustasha, the Croatian fascist paramilitary group which was allowed to settle in Argentina after World War II (item **1432**).

Those who opposed Peronism also have received a great deal of attention, from political parties to humanist Catholics. Nállim brings together full spectrum of anti-Peronism forces and their roots in his new book, which will be of interest to a wide range of scholars (item **1439**). Two of the strongest additions are Herrera's book on the Socialist Party's fortunes during and after Peronism (item **1393**) and Lichtmajer's examination of the Radical Party in Tucumán under Peronism (item **1407**).

Peronism in the years following 1955 received a great deal of attention. Adamovsky and Buch discuss the origins and uses of three famous Peronist symbols: the badge, the Peronist song ("Marcha Peronista"), and the drums (*bombo*), adding to an existing literature on Peronist popular culture (item **1415**). A book by Souroujon looks at the use of Peronist symbols by Carlos Saúl Menem (item **1474**). Sepúlveda explores the lives of women as they participated in these tumultuous decades (item **1469**). Others who focused on the post-1955 period include Antúnez (item **1293**) on the rise of revolutionary Peronism (and the conflict it generated for the Peronist orthodoxy) in the provinces of Buenos Aires, Córdoba, Mendoza, Santa Cruz, and Salta; Leoni and Solís Carnicer (item **1405**) with a comparison of the processes of political centralization during the first and second Peronist periods in the provinces of Corrientes and Chaco; Chaves (item **1333**), with oral histories of members of the Peronist Resistance (a period understood by this author as including the dictatorship) in the city of La Plata; and Getselteris (item **1379**) on the revolutionary armed group called La Compañía de Monte, which was active in Tucumán. The book by Bustos *et al.* (item **1440**) focuses on the life, union activism, and assassination of two trade union leaders in Córdoba. Pacheco reconstructs the work of Montoneros in the Greater Buenos Aires (item **1444**), while Merenson focuses on women prisoners in Villa Devoto (item **1428**).

Several memoirs describe the 1970s, and the experiences of youth. Grabois' memoir (item **1386**) recounts his experiences as he moved from the Socialist Youth to the Peronist Party. Garavaglia discusses his experiences as a member of Montoneros (item **1378**), and Muchnik and Pérez narrate their accounts of the times (item **1371**). Mangiantini's book on the conflicts between leftist groups regarding armed struggle includes an excellent historiographical chapter on the topic (item **1413**). Two works focus on relationships between Peronism and the military: Gorza examines the 1960 uprising led by Iñíguez (item **1385**) and Arrosagaray studies the one led by General Juan José Valle (item **1295**).

Binder's book on the Trelew massacre (1972) includes a short summary of the main events, but focuses on the 2012 trial, which exposed the role of intelligence agencies and the development of state terrorism (item **1309**). A few collections of primary sources to note: Baschetti's collection of Peronist ephemera, fliers, and pamphlets covering the 1945–83 period (item **1301**), and Casullo and Caramés two-volume compilation (1890–1956 and 1956–76) containing a wide array of documents—not exclusively Peronist—, including proclamations, public speeches, cultural artifacts, debates, polemic, editorials (item **1414**). Some of these documents are easy to translate for use in the classroom, making the volumes a good choice for those interested in teaching with primary sources.

Several books have focused on the period known as the "Onganiato" (1966–70). Galván and Osuna (item **1452**) begin their study with an excellent historiographical discussion of the period, and focus mostly on social changes and the existing political culture; other essays in the collection discuss the policies adopted by Onganía's government. Ferraris' book describes the period of the "Revolución Argentina" by tracing the connections between Onganía's government and Spain, and explaining Onganía's conservatism in light of that relationship (item **1366**). Figallo's book (item **1367**) also focuses on the relationships between Argentina and Spain, but not exclusively during the Onganía period. She includes a detailed bibliographic essay. An excellent article by Ben and Insausti covers the history and strategy of the Frente de Liberación Homosexual (Homosexual Liberation Front) during the highly repressive period of the Onganiato until the dictatorship (item **1306**). They uncover the connections members sought to make with the New Left even when, ideologically, the two groups were not on the same page.

Besides the books already mentioned in connection with Peronism and "Peronist Resistance" during the dictatorship, Finchelstein's work on the ideological origins of the "Dirty War" is an excellent analysis of the local manifestations of fascism (item **1368**). Two articles by Castillo Troncoso discuss the role of photojournalism both in covering the military dictatorship and antimilitary groups (like the Mothers of Plaza de Mayo) and its effect on collective memory (items **1327** and **1328**).

The 1980s and the return to democracy is the focus of a few books. Masi's work discusses how Raúl Alfonsín built his leadership (item **1424**). González and Basile's study focuses on youth, political culture and the arts, and it includes a chapter on gay resistance during this period (item **1399**).

Erlich's book on Argentina's policy over the Malvinas adds to a growing collection of material on the topic (item **1362**). This book ends with a very useful discussion of the policy changes and continuities regarding the islands. Work on more recent events continues to appear. Moreira's article adds to a growing literature on the relationship between politics and sports (in this case, soccer) (item **1434**). The article discusses the early 2000s and the mutually beneficial relationship between soccer clubs and politicians during elections. Ronchi's excellent study of the Hogar Obrero (a cooperative association founded in 1905 by socialists Juan B. Justo and Nicolás Repetto) discusses its demise in the 1990s, and details the changing objectives of the institution throughout its history (item **1463**). [AB and MN]

PARAGUAY AND URUGUAY (LATE 19TH CENTURY TO 20TH CENTURY)
There are a few promising trends in Paraguayan historiography. Of note is the work of Fuentes Armandas who dissects the term *legionario* in order to better understand post-War of the Triple Alliance historiography. This text is a remarkable sea-change in Paraguayan historiography in that it moves beyond the nationalist perspective of earlier works(item **1497**). Also significant is the work of Duarte (item **1496**), which demonstrates that the Paraguayan diplomatic corps was not isolated, but instead was actively engaged with its counterparts in the region. In the same vein, the edited volume by Chesterton (item **1492**) strives to undermine the more traditional nationalist historiography of the Chaco War in Paraguay by bringing together historians whose work shows an understanding of environmental and transnational histories. Moreover, the works by Brezzo (item **1498**), and Chesterton and Isaenko (item **1494**) demonstrate how outside actors have influenced the understanding of war and nationalism in Paraguay. American historians, including Chesterton (item **1493**) and White (item **1502**), contribute to a greater understanding of gender in Paraguayan history.

Nevertheless, traditional narratives about nationalism and uncritical compilations, including the works of Salum-Flecha (item **1499**) and Olmedo Zorilla (item **1500**), are still being published.

An interest in intellectual history is a clear trend in recent Uruguayan historiography, including the works of Giorgi (item **1509**), Gregory (item **2136**), Magri (item **1511**), and Reis (item **1516**). These texts untangle the complex web of Uruguayan intellectual through studies of the country's most prominent thinkers. Magri's text, for example is a *longue durée* study of Uruguayan political thought. Another clear trend is the publication of institutional histories of Uruguay's most important social, economic, and political bodies. This includes Chagas and Trullen's narrative social history (item **1507**) of the Caja Obrera. Morales' text about *fútbol* in Uruguay also falls into this trend of instructional history, with a focus on politics and the role of sports in shaping concepts of nationalism (item **1513**).

Two other works examine more common themes in Uruguayan historiography: the struggle against the dictatorship and the history of immigration. Sasso's text (item **1518**) narrates the harrowing moments of survival for the Tupamaro's struggle against dictatorship and Martínez (item **1512**) recounts the history of a small group of Russian settlers in rural Uruguay. [BMC]

ARGENTINA

1287 Abmeier, Angela. Kalte Krieger am Rio de la Plata?: die beiden deutschen Staaten und die argentinische Militärdiktatur (1976–1983) [Cold War in the La Plata region? The two German states and the Argentine military dictatorship (1976–1983)]. Düsseldorf, Germany: Droste Verlag, 2017. 562 p.: bibl., ill., index. (Schriften des Bundesarchivs; 76)

The relationship between West Germany (Bundesrepublik Deutschland) and East Germany (Deutsche Demokratische Republik) and the impact of Cold War political tensions on foreign policy is the backdrop for a study of the relations between both German states and Argentina. East Germany followed the foreign policy of the Soviet Union which allowed little leeway for political maneuvering. Both states had a tendency to see the Argentine dictatorship as less dangerous than the Chilean one. Argentine army officials successfully hid their crimes in contrast to the international scandals that Pinochet's torturers caused. West Germany criticized Argentine human rights violations but maintained strong economic ties with the country—even selling weapons to Argentina. At the same time, West Germany intervened diplomatically behind the scenes to try to help Germans—and later Argentines—who were imprisoned in the country. Even during the Falkland/Malvinas War between Great Britain and Argentina in 1982, the two German states did not coordinate foreign policy efforts to exert pressure on the Argentine military junta to democratize. [F. Obermeier]

1288 Abrego, Verónica. Erinnerung und Intersektionalität: Frauen als Opfer der argentinischen Staatsrepression (1975–1983) [Memory and intersectionality: women as victims of Argentine state repression (1975–1983)]. Bielefed, Germany: Verlag, 2016. 558 p. (Mainzer historische Kulturwissenschaften; 25)

This study focuses on gender and the repression of rebellious women during the Argentine dictatorship from 1975 to 1983. "Intersectionality" is used here as a category to show that plural factors created suppression. Class, gender, ethnicity, or body (the latter as part of the competitive capitalist society) were interwoven and interacted. In analyzing memory, the discursive factor of the social inequality that produces subalternity has to be examined. How did women's memories preserve their experiences? Do women's narratives create a specific feminine memory of repression? Based on a reading of four relevant texts (Pilar Calveiros, *Poder y desaparición* (1998), Graciela Fainstein, *Detrás de los ojos* (2006), Manuela Fingueret, *Hija del silencio* (1999) (see *HLAS* 60:3689 and *HLAS* 70:2276) and María Teresa Andruetto, *La mujer en cuestión* (2003)), the study shows that these works are seen as a rewriting and recreation of memory, even those which are fictitious. These texts reproduce a symbolic gender order and note the significance of gender within power relations and within works of individual and collective memory by women. [F. Obermeier]

1289 Acosta, José Virgilio. Huéspedes no convencionales en el vecindario que llaman "de Goya". Corrientes, Argentina: Moglia Ediciones, 2016. 352 p.: bibl.

The little port city of Goya has long provided the southern stretches of the province of Corrientes with a convenient door through which the regional ranching economy has exported its hides, meat, and cheeses to the outside world. The overall exportation of such products from Corrientes has always been modest compared to that of Entre Rios, Santa Fe, and Buenos Aires province, but that does not mean that Goya has played a negligible role in the fluvial economy. In fact, because it has long been recognized as a key entrepot at the edge of a potentially rich ranching frontier, Goya always attracted the attention of some unusual historical figures, including the Scottish merchants J.P. and W.P. Robertson, the French explorer Alcides d'Orbigny, and more recently, the Polish writer Witold Gombrowicz, author of the nearly untranslatable *Ferdydurke* (1937). Each one of these get some biographical treatment in this text (together with information on several Correntino military men). This result is occasionally interesting, though in no way does this study replace the more traditional work of Hernán Félix Gómez. [TW]

1290 **Alonso, Aldo Fabio.** El peronismo en La Pampa: conformación partidaria y construcción estatal, 1945-1955. Rosario, Argentina: Prohistoria Ediciones, 2015. 358 p.: bibl. (Colección Historia política hoy; 02)

Alonso has written a deeply researched book about the specific nature of Peronism in the province of La Pampa, arguing that Peronism helped citizens of the province feel fully integrated into the nation and the political process. This work is a strong addition to the growing historiography on Peronism throughout Argentina, and the way it worked in different localities. La Pampa is a particularly good case study, because it was during this period that it became a province (from a national territory) and was even briefly renamed "Eva Perón" before the end of the first Peronist era, demonstrating its strong ties to Peronism. [MLN]

1291 **Alonso Marchante, José Luis.** Menéndez, rey de la Patagonia. Prólogo de Osvaldo Bayer. Buenos Aires: Losada, 2014. 351 p.: bibl., ill.

A wide-ranging biography of José Menéndez, whose business interests in Patagonia in the late 19th and early 20th centuries contributed to the destruction of the land, its indigenous inhabitants, and the plants and animals that flourished there. Written in a narrative, journalistic style, the book will be of some interest to scholars but seems to be intended more for popular audiences. [MLN]

1292 **Antes de Perón y antes de Frondizi: el nacionalismo económico y la revista** *Servir*: **1936-1943** Compilación de María Silvia Ospital y Graciela Mateo. Buenos Aires: Imago Mundi, 2015. 137 p.: bibl., ill., index. (Colección Bitácora Argentina)

Ospital and Mateo have edited a series of essays focusing on the publication *SERVIR*, published by the Escuela de Estudios Argentinos and promoting an early version of economic nationalism. Topics range from energy to navigable rivers, from the intellectual underpinnings of nationalism to economic development. [MLN]

1293 **Antúnez, Damián Horacio.** Caras extrañas: la tendencia revolucionaria del peronismo en los gobiernos provinciales (Buenos Aires, Córdoba, Mendoza, Santa Cruz y Salta, 1973-1974). Rosario, Argentina: Prohistoria Ediciones, 2015. 361 p.: bibl. (Colección Historia política hoy; 03)

This book focuses on the provincial governments of Oscar Bidegain (Buenos Aires), Ricardo Obregón Cano (Córdoba), Alberto Martínez Baca (Mendoza), Jorge Cepernic (Santa Cruz) and Miguel Ragone (Salta), to understand how the crises evident in these provinces during this time period led to the removal of these men from power. These crisis were embedded in the conflicts between the Peronist orthodoxy and those with revolutionary tendencies (*Tendencia-Ortodoxia*). [AMB]

1294 **Arce, Alejandra de.** Mujeres, familia y trabajo: chacra, caña y algodón en la Argentina (1930-1960). Bernal, Argentina: Universidad Nacional de Quilmes Editorial, 2016. 320 p.: bibl., ill. (Colección Convergencia)

Focusing on the pampean region and north of Argentina, de Arce examines the role of women and gender, often ignored in the rural historiography. In an era of great change—from the political and structural crisis of the 1930s to the shifts in social mores and expansion of possibilities for production in the 1960s—de Arce demonstrates the ways that women made their mark in agriculture. The book is an important addition to the growing historiography on both rural areas and women and gender. [MLN]

1295 **Arrosagaray, Enrique.** La resistencia y el general Valle. Buenos Aires: Punto de Encuentro, 2016. 324 p.: bibl.

The book details the work done by General Juan José Valle in coordinating the Peronist resistance movement in preparation for a military revolt that aimed to free all political and trade union prisoners, call for elections, and make Peronism legal again. The book incorporates interviews collected in 1995-96 with 30 participants in the movement and families of the 32 members killed. [AMB]

1296 **Avni, Haim.** "Clientes," rufianes y prostitutas: comunidades judías de Argentina e Israel frente a la trata de blancas. Traducción del hebreo por Margalit Mendelson. Revisión por Florinda F. Goldberg. Buenos Aires: Leviatán, 2014. 381 p.: bibl., index.

Tracing the "white slave trade" of the late 19th and early 20th century that many Jews participated in as prostitutes, madams, pimps, and clients, Avni shows the ways that Jews protested and participated in the trade. Unlike many other studies of worldwide prostitution networks, Avni includes Israel in his work, creating a book very focused upon the Jewish experience with the "white slave trade." [MLN]

1297 **Azcona Pastor, José Manuel** and **Víctor Guijarro Mora.** La utopía agraria: políticas visionarias de la naturaleza en el Cono Sur, 1810–1880. Madrid: Consejo Superior de Investigaciones Científicas, 2015. 271 p.: bibl., ill. (Estudios sobre la ciencia)

An interesting and suggestive exploration of how 18th-century European utopianism met its greatest challenge in the reality of the 19th-century Argentine countryside. The ideal of nature, it seemed, yielded to practical dangers and hardships before eventually being transformed into a new ideal epitomized in Alberdi's observation *gobernar es poblar.* Technological progress in this environment became the loadstone for the future, the new goal for immigrants and Argentines alike. Thus did technology merge with the new utopianism. [TW]

1298 **Barcos, María Fernanda.** Pueblos y ejidos de la campaña bonaerense: una historia sociojurídica de los derechos de propiedad y la conformación de un partido: Mercedes, 1780–1870. Rosario, Argentina: Prohistoria Ediciones, 2013. 254 p.: bibl., ill. (Colección Historia argentina; 22)

A well-researched look at land usage, politics, and the evolution of property rights in the Bonaerense countryside, specifically in the ejido of the Guardia de Luján (Mercedes), during the 19th century. The study offers few surprises, but is relentless in tracking down details about this one small region. In this, it has the strength of a nicely crafted doctoral thesis, but it does not go much beyond those strengths in offering an argument that is more broadly applicable. [TW]

1299 **Barreto Constantín, Ana María.** Vida de un caudillo: Justo José de Urquiza: reseña biográfica. Buenos Aires: Editorial Dunken, 2014. 94 p.: bibl.

A figure as central to Argentine history as Justo José de Urquiza (1801–70) deserves a thorough, well-researched, and insightful biography. He received it in Beatríz Bosch's 1971 *Urquiza y su tiempo* (See *HLAS 44:3161*). This new "book," by contrast, is a paper-thin summary that adds nothing. [TW]

1300 **Barzini, Jorge.** Dolavon: su historia. Trelew, Argentina: Remitente Patagonia, 2014. 219 p.: ill.

An oversize glossy photo-filled book chronicling the history of Dolavon, a center of Welsh settlement in Chubut. Intended for a popular audience, the book nonetheless has a wealth of photographs that may be of use to scholars. [MLN]

1301 **Baschetti, Roberto.** Lo que el viento (no) se llevó: efémeras, volantes y panfletos peronistas, 1945–1983. Edición ampliada. Buenos Aires: Pueblo Heredero Editorial, 2013. 185 p.: ill.

A collection of Peronist flyers, ephemera, handwritten notes, photos, and posters printed between 1943 and 1983. The material is presented chronologically in eight chapters, focusing on important events in the history of Peronism. The project was published for the 70th anniversary of the creation of Peronism. [AMB]

1302 **La Batalla de Salta: 20 de febrero de 1813.** Compilación de Inés Zadro Wierna. Edición "Bicentenario de la Batalla de Salta" (1813–2013). Salta, Argentina: Fondo Editorial, Secretaría de Cultura de la Provincia de Salta, 2013. 102 p.: bibl., 1 ill. (Colección Memoria cultural)

Six short studies on the 1813 engagement drawn from longer historical works written between 1913 and 1987. Occasionally interesting. [TW]

1303 **Las batallas por la identidad: visiones de Rosario.** Textos por Alicia Megías et al. Rosario, Argentina: Editorial Municipal de Rosario, 2014. 163 p.: bibl., ill.

A collection of essays exploring the battles over identity (of the title) in Rosario that began in the second half of the 19th century and lasted over 100 years. The authors describe the competing visions of the press, Catholic Church, political parties, intellectuals, artists, and businessmen during this century of modernization. The period is one in which Rosario was growing and changing, and the essays address politics, the red-light district, relations with the Church, and the memorialization of the city and its history. [MLN]

1304 **Bauck, Sönke.** Nüchterne Staatsbürger für junge Nationen: Die Temperenzbewegung am Rio de la Plata [Sobriety for young nations: temperance campaigns in the Río de La Plata region]. Stuttgart, Germany: Steiner, 2018. 64 p. (Beiträge zur europäischen Überseegeschichte; 106)

Nation-building among young nations often implied referring to a specific set of republican values, amongst them sobriety which led to abstinence campaigns in Argentina. The study shows how these social movements were embedded in the nation-building process throughout the history of the La Plata-region. [F. Obermeier]

1305 **Bayer, Osvaldo.** Rebellion in Patagonia. Chico, Calif.: AK Press, 2016. 506 p.: index.

Newly translated for English-speaking readers, Bayer's classic of labor unrest and violence is written in his characteristic narrative style. Bayer conducted interviews and research to write the book, but his personal feeling and voice appear throughout the work in this leftist classic. For comment on the original Spanish-language version, see *HLAS 44:3153*. [MLN]

1306 **Ben, Pablo** and **Santiago Joaquin Insausti.** Dictatorial rule and sexual politics in Argentina: the case of the Frente de Liberación homosexual, 1967–1976. (*HAHR*, 97:2, May 2017, p. 297–325)

This important article explores the history of the short-lived Frente de Liberación Homosexual during the highly repressive period of the Onganiato, and until the beginning of the 1976 dictatorship, when it dissolved. It explains the strategies followed by their members, the shared beliefs and divergences with other youth political groups. [AMB]

1307 **Bernasconi, Eduardo Guillermo.** La patria vieja: historia de un destino frustrado. Buenos Aires: Editorial Dunken, 2016. 2 v.: bibl.

This study constitutes a massive opus, over 1,000 pages in two volumes, that in fact says very little. At the beginning, its author asserts with pride that he is not an historian who has "visited archives and repositories of documents in search of materials to feed a knowledge of the past." Instead, he is a Peronist lawyer from Santa Fe who wishes to offer to readers the full product of many years of "meditations" on the history of his country from 1810 through the mid-1860s. It is not very edifying and rarely rises above the hackneyed arguments of José María Rosa, Fermín Chavez, and Arturo Jauretche—and they said it better 40 years ago. [TW]

1308 **Bertero, Eliana; Pini, Valeria;** and **Matías Vicentín.** Logia Armonía: masones y librepensadores en la esfera pública: Santa Fe, 1889–1921. Santa Fe, Argentina: EdicionesUNL, Secretaría de Extensión, Universidad Nacional del Litoral, 2015. 191 p.: bibl.

The authors of this work argue that the rise of Masonic lodges in Argentina was part of the growing association movement of the late 19th century—from mutual aid societies to philanthropic organizations. It is also part of the shift toward a more secular and modern worldview, particularly the participation in the public sphere, which the authors show in its specifics in Santa Fe, particularly Rosario. The book contains a section at the back with primary sources and a membership roll, which may be of interest to scholars. [MLN]

1309 **Binder, Axel et al.** Diario del juicio: la masacre de Trelew, 40 años después. Rawson, Argentina: Provincia del Chubut, Secretaría de Cultura: Fondo Editorial Provincial, 2015. 274 p.: bibl.

More than a book about the massacre, this book provides a daily account of the trial related to the massacre (originally published in blog form). The trial was carried out 40 years after the killing of 16 political prisoners in 1972. The trial exposed the role of intelligence agencies, and the development of state terrorism. The first chapter presents a short summary of the main events of the massacre. [AMB]

1310 **Biondo, Gabriela Anahí.** Montoneros ¿peronistas? Bahía Blanca, Argentina: En un Feca, 2015. 135 p.: bibl., ill.

An undergraduate thesis project, Biondo argues that Montoneros were not Peronists. The book is aimed at a popular audience. [MLN]

1311 **Blacha, Luis Ernesto.** La clase política argentina, 1930–1943: la oposición ausente y la pérdida de poder. Bernal, Argentina: Universidad Nacional de Quilmes Editorial, 2015. 271 p.: bibl. (Colección Convergencia: entre memoria y sociedad)

Using an interdisciplinary focus, but with a particular emphasis on sociology and the theories of Norbert Elias, Blacha explores the political elite during the "infamous decade" of the 1930s and into the 1940s. Arguing that the 1930s were a return to politics as normal after the democratic interlude from 1916–30, Blacha is interested in the power relations within the political elite, both as a group and as individuals. [MLN]

1312 **Blumenthal, Edward.** Lavalle's remains: the political uses of the body in exile and return. (*HAHR*, 97:3, Aug. 2017, p. 387–421, bibl.)

The postmortem perambulations of the cadavers of important statesmen would appear to be a major subtheme in Argentine history. Who can forget the many strange adventures that the embalmed Eva Perón made before finally coming back to her homeland? As Professor Blumenthal demonstrates in this concise article, the pattern goes back a long way, at least to the time of General Juan Lavalle, who died in a military engagement in Jujuy in 1841, but whose ashes only reached Buenos Aires 20 years later. Along the way, his remains took many interesting trips through Chile, Bolivia, and Argentina, thus providing a different take on the power of exile to shape a political role, in this case, after the historical figure has died. Different political factions either demanded the "return" of Lavalle, or adamantly opposed it. These demands often asserted a place in Argentine politics for Lavalle that the man would never have recognized for himself in life. Exile groups even saw themselves as guardians for his ashes. Many have commented on how national symbols have been created and taken on a life of their own over the years. This fascinating piece shows that a man's remains can undergo the same metamorphosis, yielding to the secular age an equivalent of a holy relic. Lenin's corpse is clearly not the only example of such a phenomenon. [TW]

1313 **Bonatti, Andrés** and **Javier Valdez.** Una guerra infame: la verdadera historia de la Conquista del Desierto. Buenos Aires: Edhasa, 2015. 238 p.: bibl., ill.

It almost goes without saying these days that any study that offers a "true history" of any event or epoch is bound to offer more hyperbole and fuzziness than depth. This sparsely referenced work on the Conquest of the Desert is no exception. It repeats the usual accusations against the Argentine army and landed elite, but presents no new information or interpretations. It might be better to stick to John Lynch, Tulio Halperín, and if one wishes to go very far back, to Estanislao Zeballos. [TW]

1314 **Botana, Natalio R.** Repúblicas y monarquías: la encrucijada de la independencia. Buenos Aires: Edhasa, 2016. 279 p. (Ensayo)

For more than 30 years Natalio Botana has been blazing trails in the complex, but always rewarding area of Argentine political history. To my knowledge he has yet to write a study that is not readable, well-researched, and intelligently argued. This latest work, which examines the different political challenges facing the newly consolidated national regime, show that Botana has lost none of his flair or relevance. He points out that none of the factors usually associated with independence—the form of government, the rights of individuals, the relation among provinces—had as yet been decided in Argentina in 1816. He also notes that the atmosphere for honest political debate was so abysmal that the impulse in favor of republican institutions was really no better than an accident. This thesis, which contradicts several generations of perceived wisdom, is sure to provoke—but in a very good way. [TW]

1315 **Bowman, Henry Edward.** La cámara y la pluma en el valle y la meseta: memorias y fotografías de Henry Bowman. Estudio, selección y notas por Liliana E. Pérez y Pablo Lo Presti. Rawson, Argentina: Gobierno del Chubut, 2015. 186 p.: bibl., ill. (Biblioteca del sesquicentenario Tegai Roberts)

Henry Bowman, immigrant to Chubut, left behind a vast trove of early 20th-century photographs and writings that are reproduced in this oversized book. Of interest to anyone tracing the history of photography in Argentina, the book is also an excellent resource for those interested in life in the early years of settlement in Patagonia and immigrant life in rural Argentina. [MLN]

1316 **Bransboin, Hernán.** Mendoza federal: entre la autonomía provincial y el poder de Juan Manuel de Rosas. Buenos Aires: Prometeo Libros, 2014. 251 p.: bibl.

Argentine historiography tends to treat Rosismo as a political force of Bonaerense origin that acted to shape and twist the federalist dynamic in the provinces. Rarely do we see a treatment where provincial federalism influences Rosismo. This quite attractive analysis of federalism in Mendoza between the 1830s and 1852 demonstrates quite clearly that Rosismo had its provincial face in regions very distant from the Pampas. It served to maintain a new stability or to reinforce the old stability associated with the landholding elite. It also affected politics by assuring that meaningful power increasingly rested in the hands of the provincial governor, who in turn checked the centrifugal factors that had always defined Mendocino affairs. The price for this stability was cooperation with Rosas. Bransboin makes an impressive contribution in identifying the various alliances that kept representative government alive in Mendoza despite the compromises with the Restaurador de las Leyes. He recognizes, however, that much more needs to be done. It might be added that similar analyses should be attempted for other provinces, especially Jujuy, La Rioja, San Juan, and Santiago del Estero. [TW]

1317 **Bravo Herrera, Fernanda Elisa.** Huellas y recorridos de una utopía: la emigración italiana a la Argentina. Palabras preliminares de Romano Luperini y Antonio Melis. Buenos Aires: Teseo, 2015. 371 p.: bibl., ill.

Bravo Herrera explores the literature in Italian surrounding Italian immigration to Argentina, a topic that has surprisingly received little attention. The author addresses questions of identity, nationality, and the social and economic contexts of both Argentina and Italy when analyzing the texts. The book will be of interest to scholars of immigration, but all of the many quotes from Italian sources are not translated into Spanish. [MLN]

1318 **Brodsky, Adriana Mariel.** Sephardi, Jewish, Argentine: creating community and national identity, 1880–1960. Bloomington: Indiana University Press, 2016. 280 p.: bibl., ill., index, maps. (Indiana series in Sephardi and Mizrahi Studies)

Brodsky has written a wide-ranging and deeply researched book about the Sephardi Jews of Argentina, a population that has all too often been neglected in the historiography. A diverse group of immigrants and their descendants from around the Mediterranean, Brodsky explores topics from cemeteries to philanthropy, women's lives to education. The book will be of use to scholars interested in Jewish and immigrant life throughout Latin America. [MLN]

1319 **Bustos Argañaráz, Prudencio.** Luces y sombras de Mayo: un análisis descarnado de la Revolución de 1810. Córdoba, Argentina: Ediciones del Boulevard, 2011. 226 p.: bibl.

After stating that the 1810 Revolution continues to be one of the most polemic-ridden themes to emerge from Argentine history, the author sets out to obliterate, or at least to puncture, many of key myths associated with his nation's independence movement. Much of this has been done before, of course, but Bustos Argañaraz, writing as one of Córdoba's premier historians, does offer a provincial optic that is too often absent from the literature. He may spends too much citing revisionist writers from the mid-1900s who should be left to speak for themselves, but it is hard to argue with the thesis that popular legends have twisted the events of 1810 into something unrecognizable. It is probably a good thing to be reminded that things were different from what the myth-makers would have us believe, but also it would have been better had this book included more original research. [TW]

1320 Caldo, Paula. Revistas, consumos, alimentación y saberes femeninos: la propuesta de *Damas y Damitas*, Argentina, 1939–1944. (*Secuencia/México*, 94, enero/abril 2016, p. 210–239, bibl.)

Caldo focuses on the publication *Damas y Damitas*, aimed at middle- and lower-class women in small cities and suburban and rural areas. Led by the knowledge of domestic economist Julia Elena Bordieu, the magazine was a way to transmit culinary information to a wide array of women who acted as cooks and consumers. [MLN]

1321 Camaño Semprini, Rebeca. Peronismo y poder municipal: de los orígenes al gobierno en Río Cuarto (Córdoba, 1943–1955). Rosario, Argentina: Prohistoria Ediciones, 2014. 176 p.: bibl., ill. (Colección Historia política hoy; 01)

Focusing on the city of Río Cuarto in the province of Córdoba, Camaño Semprini looks at Peronism and its manifestations on a micro level. Part of the growing historiography focusing on the ways different communities experienced the first Peronist government, the book is short but will be of use to the many scholars looking at Peronism from a variety of locations outside Buenos Aires. [MLN]

1322 Camaño Semprini, Rebeca. El radicalismo riocuartense: renovación partidaria, sectores conservadores y fascismo en los años treinta. (*Estud. Soc./Santa Fe*, 25:49, segundo semestre 2015, p. 11–30)

Focusing on the 1930s, Camaño shows the ways that the Radical Party changed in the face of new challenges from the right. Led by the Radical Youth, who formed alliances with the parties of the left, these changes ultimately led to a break with the Radical Party for the youth, who created an anti-fascist coalition with the leftist parties. [MLN]

1323 Camogli, Pablo. Andresito: historia de un pueblo en armas. Buenos Aires: Aguilar, 2015. 261 p.: bibl., ill.

This is probably the most complete treatment of Andresito Guacurarí since Jorge Machón pioneered the reconsideration of the Indian caudillo in the 1990s. But that is only saying just so much. The available documentation on Andresito is remarkably thin for a man who was Artigas' adopted son, and unfortunately, Camogli has a habit of dishing out populist rhetoric whenever proof is wanting; he is particularly fond of loaded terms like "genocide" and "revindication." Readers are thus advised to examine this work with care, and if the analysis seems too stridently Kirchnerista, it probably is. [TW]

1324 Canciani, Leonardo. Fuerzas armadas y militarización de los guardias nacionales en la frontera sur de Argentina (provincia de Buenos Aires, 1862–1879). (*Rev. Complut. Hist. Am.*, 43, 2017, 259–283, bibl., graphs, maps, tables)

A useful examination of the militarization of frontier communities in Buenos Aires province from the time of Pavón to 1879. The army was only just becoming an appreciable entity during those years, and Canciani shows how service on the frontier became the key to promotion and institutional cohesion. [TW]

1325 Cantera, Carmen Susana. Déspotas, invasores, usurpadores y anarquistas: representaciones rioplatenses de los 'otros': enemigos y extranjeros durante las primeras décadas del siglo XIX. Bahía Blanca, Argentina: EdiUNS, 2016. 266 p.: bibl. (Serie Extensión. Colección Ciencias sociales y humanidades)

Postindependence Argentina witnessed the elaboration of a whole new political vocabulary to describe circumstances and challenges facing the not-quite cohesive nation-state. In this respect, the country's political figures were not that different from the Frenchmen of 1789, the Haitians of 1800, and the Russians of 1917. In all of these cases, in order to win support, statesmen needed to define not only what they were fighting for, but what they were fighting against. This need provides Professor Cantera with material to describe the "Other," a decidedly 20th-century term that she usefully applies to the revolutionary era more than 100 years earlier. The words used to attack the monarchists and various illiberal elements were often meant to be insulting, but were not necessarily false. As Cantera notes, moreover, words like *impío* or *salvaje* could change their meaning over time in ways that were hardly predictable. And they might mean different things in different parts of the country or depending on the social class of the person using them. Of course, in a political environment that inspired a wide variety of dualisms (Federalism versus Centralism; City versus Countryside; Barbary versus Civilization), it would be curious not to find a certain sensitivity to language in political circles. That said, while this study makes excellent use of newspapers, gazettes, and political tracts (and the always-useful *Biblioteca de Mayo*), it lacks the lexicographical precision provided by, for example, Ezequiel Martínez Estrada. This is less a criticism than a simple observation that much remains to be done. [TW]

1326 Canton, Darío, and **Luis R. Acosta.** Una hipótesis rechazada: el rol de los migrantes internos según Gino Germani en los orígenes del peronismo: una investigación con datos de los archivos de la Cámara Nacional Electoral. Con la colaboración de Jorge R. Jorrat. Buenos Aires: Librería Hernández, 2013. 121 p.: bibl., ill.

Canton and Acosta have published a point-by-point analysis of Gino Germani's famous hypothesis that internal migrants were essential in the 1946 election of Juan Domingo Perón. The authors look closely at the voting data for the Buenos Aires metropolitan area to test the thesis, one of the foundational analyses of Peronism. They find that for the greater Buenos Aires area at least, internal migrants were not the decisive factor Germani posited, but that his larger points about structural changes in the economy and society that began in the 1930s were still valid. The book will be an invaluable resource for anyone working on Peronism and wanting more hard data—the authors include an array of charts and quantitative data. [MLN]

1327 Castillo Troncoso, Alberto del. Algunas reflexiones en torno al fotoperiodismo y la dictadura en la historiografía argentina reciente. (*Secuencia/México*, 96, sept./dic. 2016, p. 226–277, bibl., photos)

This article surveys the changes brought about in the collective memory of Argentina during the last four decades, stressing the role played by photographs in such process, by analyzing scholarly production on this topic. Photography, the author claims, has served to justify both the military dictatorship and those groups who fought for the return to democracy. [AMB]

1328 Castillo Troncoso, Alberto del. Fotografía y memoria en la dictadura argentina, 1976–1983. Entrevista con Eduardo Longoni. (*Secuencia/México*, 95, mayo/agosto 2016, p. 215–258, ill.)

This essay centers on the coverage of the military dictatorship, in particular by photographers who worked alongside anti-military groups, like the Mothers of Plaza de Mayo. The article includes an extensive interview with Eduardo Longoni, who was one such photographer. [AMB]

1329 **Caudillos, política e instituciones en los orígenes de la nación argentina.** Compilación de Roberto Schmit. Los Polvorines, Argentina: Ediciones UNGS, Universidad Nacional de General Sarmiento, 2015. 235 p.: bibl., ill. (Colección Humanidades)

Schmit and three other historians examine different aspects of mid-19th century federalism in Entre Ríos. The latter province, which had boasted the seat of government before the 1861 battle of Pavón, had to adjust to a smaller scale of politics afterwards and yet still had to tolerate or adjust to the authoritarian inclinations of Justo José de Urquiza. This book is a good place to start in analyzing how Entrerriano politicians managed to meet the challenge. [TW]

1330 Caviasca, Guillermo. La revolución de la independencia: Moreno, Artigas y San Martín, proyectos para crear una nación. La Plata, Argentina: De la Campana, 2016. 239 p.: bibl. (Campana de palo)

This study advances the rather dubious claim that the Argentine struggle for independence owed more to precedents established during the Túpac Amaru revolt of the late 1780s than to European intellectual influences during the subsequent period. The author tries to make the case for José Gervasio Artigas and (to a lesser extent) José de San Martín as popular leaders reflecting the clamor of the lower classes for a revolutionary regime instead of the elite-based order that the Unitarios ultimately imposed in Argentina. One can see how attractive this idea might be for readers who came of age during the Kirchner years, but it lacks evidence. A few disjointed citations to authority taken from the *Grundrisse* by Marx and from Perry Anderson's *Lineages of the Absolutist State* will not do the trick. Readers interested in the period should look elsewhere. [TW]

1331 Ceruso, Diego. La izquierda en la fábrica: la militancia obrera industrial en el lugar de trabajo, 1916–1943. Buenos Aires: Imago Mundi, 2015. 277 p.: bibl., index. (Colección Archivos: estudios de historia del movimiento obrero y la izquierda; 4)

Ceruso has written an important addition to the historiography of labor in Argentina, focusing on the organizing of the pre-Peronist years. A deeply researched book that includes the major industries of the era, Ceruso traces the early years of organizing and strikes along with the leftist political movements that many workers joined, from anarchism to communism to syndicalism. Broken into chapters covering only a few years, the book will be useful to all scholars working on the period and those interested in labor and leftist politics. [MLN]

1332 Chaves, Claudio Enrique. El revisionismo histórico liberal: vida y obra de Olegario V. Andrade. Buenos Aires: Editorial Dunken, 2015. 361 p.: bibl.

Many politicians in 19th century Argentina saw themselves primarily as poets. It follows that they saw their efforts to construct the nation mainly in the light of an artistic project. Esteban Echeverría and Carlos Guido y Spano come to mind in this respect, as does, after a fashion, Bartolomé Mitre. A name encountered less frequently is Olegario V. Andrade (1839–82), born in Río Grande do Sul of a mother who hailed from Entre Ríos. It is with the complex politics and the sensuous poetry of the latter province that Andrade's name is usually associated. Given how close he was to the great questions of the day, he clearly deserves an insightful biographical treatment. Unfortunately, this is not it. The author draws principally from older secondary sources, but offers little new information. Nor does he systematically address Andrade's sizable journalistic work. He treats key terms like "revisionism" and "liberalism" with scant regard for precision (though he promises a lot). As written, moreover, Chaves' book needs extensive editing just to make his points clear. Readers who are hoping to find a biography of Andrade that will repeat the success of Tulio Halperín's examination of José Hernandez will be disappointed. [TW]

1333 Chaves, Gonzalo Leónidas. Rebelde acontecer: relatos de la resistencia peronista. Buenos Aires: Ediciones Colihue, 2015. 284 p.: bibl. (Serie Protagonistas)

Chaves has gathered oral histories of the Peronist resistance "from the perspective of the city of La Plata." Defining the period of resistance as 1955 to 1983, Chaves focuses on important events, like the steelworkers strike of 1959, the take-over of the meatpacking company Lisandro de la Torre in 1959, the national strike of 1979, and others. [AMB]

1334 Chiappero, Rubén Osvaldo. Esperanza urbana: aportes a la historia del urbanismo del siglo XIX en el oeste de Santa Fe, Argentina. Santa Fe, Argentina: Universidad Católica de Santa Fe, 2015. 172 p.: bibl., ills. (chiefly color).

Nineteenth century urbanization in the interior and Littoral provinces of Argentina received its most profound impulse as part of the state's ongoing efforts to settle the countryside, which hitherto had been open and unproductive space. This present work, an abbreviated version of the author's doctoral thesis, examines how this process unfolded in the western districts of Santa Fe province. Chiappero maintains that the key moment for urban development in this area came after 1853 when contracts were signed between the provincial government and Aaron Castellanos, a key entrepreneur in the cereals trade. The subsequent establishment of the city of Esperanza represented not an outgrowth of the older colonial model for urban development but instead the consolidation in urban form of modern political, economic and social structures tied to the Atlantic economy. This study works well with other studies of Argentine urbanization, such as those of Jorge Hardoy and James Scobie. [TW]

1335 Chiaramonte, José Carlos. Mercaderes del litoral: economía y sociedad en la provincia de Corrientes, primera mitad del siglo XIX. Corrientes, Argentina: Universidad Nacional del Nordeste, 2016. 526 p.: bibl.

The appearance of the first edition of this study (see HLAS 56:2994) set off a wave of laudatory reactions from scholars in Argentina and elsewhere. They clearly had a classic on their hands. And in the 25 years that have passed since that time, the dazzling reputation of this study has never wavered. It is easy to see why. Chiaramonte provided a superbly detailed analysis of the regional economy, focusing on the province of Corrientes, and showing how merchants managed political actors and sculpted them into a machine that effectively organized regional interests—and precisely during that stage of national consolidation when chaos supposedly reigned. It was a masterly study back in 1991 and still is today. This new edition has been conceived in part as a homage to Chiaramonte, and contains a 200-page addenda that includes reviews and updates, an exhaustive Chiaramonte bibliography, interviews, and several short autobiographical sketches. When I first met Chiaramonte in his Mexican exile during the early 1980s, he was extremely generous to me, though decidedly down on his luck because the army had thrown out his notes and collections of photocopies of documents when they forced him to flee Argentina. This book represents a great victory over that sad moment, and deserves to be read by a whole new generation of students. [TW]

1336 Cicerchia, Ricardo. Raros artefactos: travesías, idearios y desempeños de la sociedad civil en la construcción de la modernidad, Argentina 1850–1930: postdatas de la historia cultural. Rosario, Argentina: Prohistoria Ediciones, 2016. 191 p.: bibl., ill. (Colección Historia argentina; 29)

Cicerchia's book identifies various objects and cultural currents through which to explore the creation of modernity in Argentina. He focuses on a variety of artifacts, from the poetry of José Mármol to the beautification program of Charles Thays, from dinosaur excavations to postcards. Although short, the different focus of each chapter will be of interest to a variety of scholars. [MLN]

1337 150 años de Y Wladfa: ensayos sobre la historia de la colonización galesa en la Patagonia. Compilación por Marcelo Gavirati y Fernando Williams. Rawson, Argentina: Gobierno del Chubut, 2015. 389 p.: bibl., ill. (Biblioteca del sesquicentenario Tegai Roberts)

A collection of essays about the history of the Welsh community in Patagonia, the book is the most academic of the recent contributions marking the 150th anniversary of their arrival. From the mechanisms of their arrival and settlement to the ways that the Welsh language transferred to Patagonia, the volume has an array of works from scholars on both sides of the Atlantic. [MLN]

1338 Cloppet, Ignacio Martín. Perón en Roma: cartas inéditas (1939–1940): amores y política. Buenos Aires: Ediciones Fabro, 2015. 317 p.: bibl., ill., index.

The book is mostly an intimate biography of Perón in the years before Eva Duarte, with a particular emphasis on Perón's relationships with women. The letters of the title are to María Tizón, his sister-in-law during the time he was posted to Europe (1939–41). The work and letters will be of interest to those working on Peronism—the letters are personal, but reveal his impressions of Mussolini and events in Europe as they occurred. [MLN]

1339 La colonia galesa del Chubut en imágenes: de los comienzos al Centenario. Selección y textos por Pablo Alberto Lo Presti. Adaptación al galés por Ana Chiabrando Rees. Traducción al inglés por Pablo Fabián García. Rawson, Argentina: Secretaría de Cultura de la Provincia del Chubut, 2015. 388 p.: ill. (Biblioteca del sesquicentenario Tegai Roberts)

An oversize book of photographs of the early years of the Welsh community in Chubut. In Spanish, English, and Welsh, the work has an enormous array of photographs of the Welsh, the indigenous of the region, and the landscape. The beginning of the book has a series of historical essays that situate the photographs. [MLN]

1340 La conmemoración de la Revolución de Mayo: prensa gráfica, historia y política, siglos XIX–XXI. Compilación de Guillermo O. Quinteros. La Plata, Argentina: Centro de Historia Argentina y Americana (FAHCE, IdICHS, UNLP-CONICET): Laboratorio de Estudios en Comunicación,

Política y Sociedad (Facultad de Periodismo y Comunicación Social), Universidad Nacional de La Plata, 2013. 254 p.: bibl. (Serie Estudios/Investigaciones; 46)

Excellent collection of works detailing the way in which the May Revolution of 1810 was portrayed during various periods in Argentine history and in different newspapers. The chapters focus on the narratives about the origin of Argentina and when those narratives were created. Three essays discuss the representation of the May Revolution during Peronist governments, one during the early years of the *Gaceta Mercantil* (1820s), and two during the 2000s. [AMB]

1341 Contigo ni pan ni cebolla: debates y prácticas sobre el divorcio vincular en Argentina: 1932–1968. Edición de Verónica Giordano, Karina Ramacciotti y Adriana María Valobra. Buenos Aires: Editorial Biblos, 2015. 181 p.: bibl. (Colección Ciudadanía e inclusión)

A fascinating edited volume that deals with divorce in Argentina. After an examination of the political debates surrounding divorce in the early 1930s, the contributors then focus a great deal of attention on the 1955–56 period, when divorce was briefly legal. The book begins to wind down in 1968, with legal reforms that make divorce easier overall. Using cases which have been little-studied, the authors approach divorce from a variety of perspectives—personal, political, and legal. The book will be of use to all scholars working on gender and women's topics, as well as legal and judicial history. [MLN]

1342 Correspondencia epistolar (1855–1881). Selección, edición crítica, estudio preliminar por Lucila Pagliai. San Martín, Argentina: UNSAM Edita, 2015. 183 p.: bibl. (Colección Biblioteca Furt. Serie Archivo Alberdi)

A great many public figures who find themselves in important positions during key periods of their countries' history have private thoughts that are difficult to guess at, much less understand. Juan Bautista Alberdi (1810–84), author of the Argentine Constitution of 1853, was certainly such a man. Hence, it is a good day when a quantity of private correspondence between the great jurist and a longtime friend is placed before the scholarly audience. Francisco Javier Villanueva only knew Alberdi for a short time while the latter was a young exile in Chile, but their friendship endured for many years, and was unaffected by distance, political circumstance, or personal tragedy. Though much still remains hidden in those epistles, both men wrote with considerable candor and the assiduous researcher should find much that is useful in this compilation. Of particular interest are Alberdi's ruminations on European politics, the Paraguayan War, provincial rebellions, and the rise and fall of Bartolomé Mitre. [TW]

1343 Cristóforis, Nadia Andrea de. Inmigrantes y colonos en la provincia de Buenos Aires: una mirada de largo plazo (siglos XIX–XXI). Buenos Aires: Editorial de la Facultad de Filosofía y Letras, Universidad de Buenos Aires, 2016. 133 p.: bibl., ill. (Colección Libros de cátedra)

A concise introduction to the major issues and themes in Argentine immigration history. Created for undergraduates at the University of Buenos Aires, the book is useful for its broad overview of immigration from its beginnings in the 19th century to today. [MLN]

1344 Cruset, María Eugenia. Nacionalismo y diásporas: los casos vasco e irlandés en Argentina (1862–1922). La Plata, Argentina: Universidad Nacional de La Plata, Cátedra Libre de Pensamiento y Cultura Irlandesa: Ediciones Lauburu, 2015. 244 p.: bibl., ill.

A comparative look at the Basque and Irish immigrants to Argentina—both relatively small, well-financed groups with a chain migration pattern in the 19th century. Cruset is particularly interested in the idea of a diaspora, which she explores in some depth. Although the book will be of some interest to scholars, the sources are primarily secondary, not primary. [MLN]

1345 Cucchi, Laura. Antagonismo, legitimidad y poder político en Córdoba, 1877–1880. Bahía Blanca, Argentina: EdiUNS, 2015. 312 p. (Serie Extensión. Colección Estudios sociales y humanidades)

Certain moments in 19th-century Argentine political history have never quite lost their controversial character. One such moment came in 1880 when national leadership shifted decisively to Julio Roca and the Partido Autonomista Nacional. This development, which ushered in conservative rule for the better part of a generation, is usually seen from the perspective of backroom plotting (and front-room grandstanding) in Buenos Aires. Where Cucchi makes an attractive contribution is to analyze the changing picture from the perspective of the city and province of Córdoba. It is a complex and rather juicy story, and every bit as full of pugilistic politics as that in Buenos Aires. It helped launch Miguel Juárez Celman onto the national stage. Cucchi has done a solid job of tracing events, political current, and changing standards of comportment by sifting through myriad documents from the provincial archives, and more importantly, from the surprisingly lively Cordobesa newspapers. A well-crafted study. Recommended. [TW]

1346 Cutrera, María Laura. Subordinarlos, someterlos y sujetarlos al orden: Rosas y los indios amigos de Buenos Aires entre 1829 y 1855. Buenos Aires: Teseo, 2013. 399 p.: bibl., ill.

Despite its unwieldy title (which is drawn from a decree of Juan Manuel de Rosas), this is a sharp and concise analysis of the Restaurador's relations with the Indians of Buenos Aires province. Cutrera is principally interested in the "friendly" Indians with whom Rosas constructed a working relation that brought a measure of security, if not peace, to the southern frontier. It has long been recognized that Rosas spoke Pampa very well, but this work also points out that native leaders knew how to work with him, effectively pushing their own interests at the same time. An excellent study, similar in scope and orientation to those of Jorge Gelman, Juan Carlos Garavaglia, and, with a few reservations, John Lynch. [TW]

1347 Da Orden, María Liliana; Bárbara Ortuño Martínez; and **Walter Derbiz.** Historia(s) de la inmigracion asturiana en Mar del Plata. Mar del Plata, Argentina: EUDEM, 2014. 160 p.: bibl., ill.

Created for the centennial of the Asturian Center of Mar del Plata, the work details the history of the Asturian community in Mar del Plata from its late nineteenth-century migratory flow to the present. Full of excellent photographs of the community, the book shows the ways that Asturians integrated themselves into the seaside resort. [MLN]

1348 Davies, Jonathan Ceredig. Patagonia: el modo de vida en la colonia galesa y una crónica sobre los indios y sus costumbres. Introducción por Liliana E. Pérez y Pablo Lo Presti. Traducción por Pablo F. García. Trelew, Argentina: Remitente Patagonia, 2015. 92 p.: ill.

Davies, a Welsh immigrant who lived in Patagonia for sixteen years during the late 19th century, returned to Wales and gave a series of lectures about his time in Argentina. The lectures, originally published in English in 1891, are reproduced in this small book, useful for those interested in the history of Welsh community, immigration, and early Patagonian settlement. [MLN]

1349 Desde la historia: homenaje a Marta Bonaudo. Edición de María Sierra, Juan Pro y Diego Mauro. Buenos Aires: Imago Mundi, 2014. 361 p.: bibl. (Colección Bitácora argentina)

Covering an array of topics relating to modern Argentine and Spanish history, the volume was created by the students of historian Marta Bonaudo. With 15 articles ranging from an examination of Republican exiles to the correspondence of a teacher in 1930s and 1940s Argentina, the overarching organization is loose and primarily focused on politics and political culture. [MLN]

1350 Di Meglio, Gabriel. 1816: la trama de la independencia. Buenos Aires: Planeta, 2016. 300 p.

A half-hearted attempt to unravel the Gordian knot of Platine politics in the crucial year of 1816. De Magio wants to do well, but he is no Alexander and his sword cuts only just so deep. Instead of focusing on one key dynamic, he tries to cover everything, claiming full mastery over matters military, social, economic, and cultural. He fails to gain much traction in any of his preferred categories, and even his political speculations draw too uncritically from secondary works of left-revisionism and worn-out *dependentismo*. This is not one of his better efforts. [TW]

1351 **Di Meglio, Gabriel.** ¡Viva el bajo pueblo!: la plebe urbana de Buenos Aires y la política entre la Revolución de Mayo y el rosismo. Buenos Aires: Prometeo Libros, 2013. 346 p.: bibl. (Colección Historia argentina)

Di Meglio has spent more than a decade analyzing the role of the urban masses in setting the parameters of politics in Argentina's early national period. The several works that he has produced on this theme have all been sophisticated and extensively documented, just as one might expect from a scholar associated with the Ravignani Institute. This work, which is the second edition of the first one he wrote in 2006 (see *HLAS 66:1869*), demonstrates why the whole series has been successful. As he suggests, the plebe often leads, it does not merely follow. And when we think of the urban poor setting trends in the era of Perón, Menem, and the Kirchners, it is useful to remember that their historical pedigree goes back a long time. [TW]

1352 **Di Pasquale, Mariano.** Entre la experimentación política y la circulación de saberes: la gestión de Bernardino Rivadavia en Buenos Aires. (*Secuencia/México*, 87, sept./dic. 2013, p. 51–65, bibl.)

The author attempts to locate profundities in the political discourse of the Rivadavian era and does not get very far. Once we manage to get past the postmodern perambulations and clichés, it becomes obvious that what is convincing in this short study is not new and what is new is not convincing. [TW]

1353 **Di Stefano, Mariana.** Anarquismo de la Argentina: una comunidad discursiva: géneros, enunciación, estilos y lenguas en *La protesta humana* y *La protesta*. Buenos Aires: Cabiria, 2015. 216 p., 16 unnumbered p.: bibl., ill. (Colección Elementos)

Di Stefano has written a theory-based approach to two anarchist periodicals from the late 19th and early 20th centuries—*La Protesta Humana* and *La Protesta*. She is interested in the "discursive community" created by the two newspapers. She does a thorough job of analyzing the two papers, and ends with a useful discussion of Esperanto. [MLN]

1354 **16 de junio de 1955, bombardeo y masacre: imágenes, memorias, silencios.** Edición de Juan Besse y María Graciela Rodríguez. Buenos Aires: Editorial Biblos, 2016. 184 p.: bibl., ill. (Historia)

This edited volume approaches the overthrow of Juan Peron from a variety of perspectives—images, the press, silence, and memory. Focusing on the day of the coup, scholars from an array of fields grapple with the significance of the coup and its aftermath. The book will appeal to any scholar of Peronism. [MLN]

1355 **Documentos para la historia del general don Manuel Belgrano.** Organización de Instituto Belgraniano Central. Buenos Aires: El Instituto, 2015. 7 v.: bibl., ill. (t. 3, v. 2, t. 4–7: Documentos)

Useful compilation of materials—correspondence, reports, treaties—taken from various provincial and national archives and covering Belgrano's experiences between 1813 and 1814. [TW]

1356 **Domínguez Paredes, Raúl Alejandro.** Entre la fidelidad al rey y a la Revolución de Mayo: el Cabildo de Jujuy en la década revolucionaria (1810–1820). San Salvador de Jujuy, Argentina: Purmamarka Ediciones, 2015. 95 p.: bibl. (Colección Estudios americanistas)

A brief and not very convincing look at the cabildo of Jujuy during the early revolutionary age. Most of what the study has to offer is drawn from the Archivo Capitular de Jujuy, published in 1944. There is much more to be done on this topic but Domínguez Paredes just scratches the surface. [TW]

1357 **Dujovne, Alejandro.** Una historia del libro judío: la cultura judía argentina a través de sus editores, libreros, traductores, imprentas y biliotecas. Buenos Aires: Siglo Veintiuno Editores, 2014. 240 p.: bibl. (Metamorfosis)

This book describes the world of the Jewish book in Buenos Aires, starting with the first editorial projects in 1910 until the late 1960s and early 1970s. It focuses on editors, intellectuals, translators, printers, patrons, cultural associations, as well as on political parties. The book also explores the social conditions that defined the modes of reception and local circulation of the ideas produced in the main centers of Jewish culture. The book focuses mostly on the Ashkenazi community. [AMB]

1358 **Durán, Juan Guillermo.** Un malón sobre la Villa de la Paz: el robo del vestido de la Virgen paceña: Mendoza 1868. Buenos Aires: Agape Libros, 2015. 255 p.: bibl., ill.

Slowly but surely the complicated history of Indian-white relations on the Argentina frontier gets written and all the varied instances of cooperation and aggression, once left encompassed by broad generalities, finally get their proper attention. The case here involves the incursions of Ranquel Indians against the little Mendocino community of La Paz in November 1869 and their desecration of the image of the Virgin held within the local church. There is not much that is particularly profound in this tale, nor any real scholarly analysis, but the author nonetheless deserves praise for having scoured the archives, the libraries, and the relevant contemporary newspapers for anything throwing light on the incident. Scholars of Lucio Mansilla who recall his great memoir of time spent among these same Indians will want to peruse this work. [TW]

1359 **Ehrick, Christine.** Radio and the gendered soundscape: women and broadcasting in Argentina and Uruguay, 1930–1950. New York, N.Y.: Cambridge University Press, 2015. 231 p.: bibl., ill., index.

A fascinating new direction in the study of women and gender in the Río de la Plata, Ehrick's book explores the pivotal role that women played in radio broadcasting during the 1930s and 1940s. An innovative way for women to have a voice—literally— female broadcasters covered a variety of content and formats. Ehrick highlights some of the most interesting—Montevideo's all-women radio station, Niní Marshall's wildly popular comedy broadcasts, and the political broadcasts of Eva Duarte de Perón. Located at the nexus of gender and sound studies, this is a book that will appeal to a wide array of scholars. [MLN]

1360 **En la vastedad del "desierto" patagónico . . . : estado, prácticas y actores sociales (1884–1958).** Edición de Enrique Mases y Mirta Zink. Rosario, Argentina: Prohistoria Ediciones, 2014. 254 p.: bibl., ill. (Colección Estudios y problemas; 4)

This edited volume contains scholarship on the territorial period in Patagonia. The first section deals with the state and political structures, while the second approaches the array of social actors—from children to workers—that populated the Patagonian region. Well-researched by an array of leading scholars, the book is a good addition to the growing scholarship on the growth and development of peripheral areas. [MLN]

1361 **Episodios de la cultura histórica argentina: celebraciones, imágenes y representaciones del pasado, siglos XIX y XX.** Coordinación por Alejandro C. Eujanian, Ricardo Pasolini, y María Estela Spinelli. Buenos Aires: Editorial Biblos, 2015. 209 p.: bibl. (Historia)

This edited volume grapples with the way Argentines and Argentine history have remembered and commemorated the past. More than half of the articles deal with independence celebrations and commemorations, and the rest the ways that the past is perceived through memoir, essays, and the press. The book will be useful to all those exploring celebrations of the past and historiography. [MLN]

1362 **Erlich, Uriel.** Malvinas, soberanía y vida cotidiana: etapas y perspectivas de la política exterior argentina a 50 años de la Resolución 2065 (XX) de Naciones Unidas. La Plata, Argentina: EDULP, Editorial de la Universidad de La Plata; Villa María, Argentina: Eduvim, Editorial Universitaria Villa María, 2015. 274 p.: bibl. (Nuestras Malvinas. Ensayo)

The book presents a history of Argentine foreign policy regarding the Islas Malvinas after the passing of UN Resolution 2065 (XX) in 1965. The resolution was an acknowledgement on the part of the international community that there was a conflict, and it initiated a series of negotiations between the UK and Argentina. The book discusses how those initial negotiations were interrupted by the war in 1982, and how Argentine foreign policy has developed since then. The conclusion includes a useful summary of the differences between the policies followed during different periods, as well as the continuities between them. [AMB]

1363 **Espacio público en Argentina, fines s. XIX-primera mitad s. XX: partidos, catolicismo, sociabilidad.** Edición de Gardenia Vidal y Jessica Blanco. Córdoba, Argentina: Editorial Brujas, 2016. 316 p.: bibl., ill.

An edited volume that grew out of a research group on the public sphere and political culture from a comparative perspective. The works are divided into sections on political parties, associations, sociability, gender, Catholicism and politics. Focusing mostly on Córdoba with a few articles on Buenos Aires, Santa Fe, and Mendoza, the articles show strong scholarly work on topics that need more attention—from the internal politics of political parties in provincial Argentina to the creation of rural clubs and associations. [MLN]

1364 **Eujanian, Alejandro C.** El pasado en el péndulo de la política: Rosas, la provincia y la nación en el debate político de Buenos Aires, 1852-1861. Bernal, Argentina: Universidad Nacional de Quilmes Editorial, 2015. 308 p.: bibl. (Colección La ideología argentina y latinoamericana)

An excellent study of the republican discourse of the mid-19th century that reflects and refines the earlier theses of Jorge Myers. In carefully analyzing key texts and legislative reports, the author challenges the traditional binary structure of Argentine politics with Liberal Centralists ranged against Rosista Federalists, and finds that the ideological parameters of these times were decidedly more fluid and contingent than is usually argued. The broad historiographical debates that helped define the "nation" in Argentina require a more organic approach, he argues, before we can understand what politicians wanted to create in the country. The role of fundamental texts, like *Martín Fierro* and the *Historia de Belgrano* (see *HLAS 8:3375*) will need to be reconsidered along the way. He suggests that we pay closer attention to the legislative debates throughout the entire period if we wish to find useful clues. [TW]

Fernández Hellmund, Paula D. Nicaragua debe sobrevivir: la solidaridad de la militancia comunista argentina con la Revolución Sandinista (1979–1990). See item **754**.

1365 **Ferrari, Jorge Luis.** Historia del peronismo en La Pampa (1945–1956). Buenos Aires: Ediciones Biebel, 2016. 282 p.: bibl. (Biblioteca Inter Pares)

Ferrari's book fits into two growing strands of historiography—the increased analysis of the National Territories and their place in the nation, and the history of Peronism in areas outside of the metropolitan centers. The study is a good start, but scholars will find few footnotes and a lack of source citation that make it less than ideal for academic purposes. [MLN]

1366 **Ferraris, María Carolina.** La influencia del franquismo en la dictadura de Onganía: autoritarismo y desarrollismo durante la Guerra Fría. Rosario, Argentina: Prohistoria Ediciones, 2017. 199 p.: bibl. (Colección Universidad ; 56)

The book traces the connections between the Spain under Franco (during the 1960s) and the government of Onganía in Argentina. It explains why the "Revolución Argentina" imitated the authoritarian and religious conservatism of Spain rather than borrowing from the models followed by France or the US. [AMB]

1367 **Figallo Lascano, Beatriz J.** Argentina y España: entre la pasión y el escepticismo. Buenos Aires: Teseo; Rosario, Argentina: IDEHESI CONICET, Nodo Rosario, 2014. 342 p.: bibl. (Relaciones internacionales)

This book summarizes the history of the relationship between Spain and Argentina, starting with colonial times and ending with Juan Domingo Perón. A shorter second chapter focuses on the last few decades. The book includes an excellent bibliographical chapter on the topic. The book was originally part of a project that would focus on the relationship between Spain and each Latin American country. [AMB]

1368 **Finchelstein, Federico.** The ideological origins of the dirty war: fascism, populism, and dictatorship in twentieth century Argentina. Oxford, England: Oxford University Press, 2014. 214 p.: index.

The book demonstrates how Argentina's Dirty War was rooted in fascist ideology and embodied in the local nationalists. The country's road to fascism started in the 1920s and 1930s, and then was shaped by

Peronism, right-wing organizations in the 1960s and 1970s, and the military dictatorship of the 1970s. The author also stresses that Argentine fascism was different from the German and Italian counterparts: Argentine fascists did not want to conquer the world, nor achieve a permanent state of war; they wanted to eliminate all political opponents, concentrate economic and political capital, and, later, win the war in the South Atlantic. The first part of the book (1900–45) traces the origins and development of fascism and anti-Semitism in Argentina; the second part analyzes the intellectual path of fascism during Peronism, and after. [AMB]

1369 Fradkin, Raúl O. and Jorge Gelman. Juan Manuel de Rosas: la construcción de un liderazgo político. Buenos Aires: Edhasa, 2015. 475 p.: bibl., ill. (Biografías argentinas)

An excellent biographical treatment of the Restorer of the Laws that goes beyond the classic study of Adolfo Saldías (see *HLAS 12:2093*) and the more modern empirical study of John Lynch (see *HLAS 44:3300*) by focusing on the construction of a specifically Argentine form of political leadership. Fradkin and Gelman reject the traditional dualist analyses in addressing this question. They offer instead a more nuanced interpretation of how a caudillo can organize political alliances that cut across classes and respond effectively to changing times. While it is true that Rosas submitted the landholding elites to a sharp discipline, he also allowed them sufficient room to operate successfully in their own spheres. Fradkin and Gelman place a lot of juicy meat on this bone, and in so doing, produce one of the best works on Rosas to appear in years. [TW]

1370 Friedmann, Germán. El Frente Negro en la Argentina durante la década de 1930. (*Iberoamericana/Madrid*, 15:57, marzo 2015, p. 39–57, bibl.)

Originally part of the Nazi Party, the Germany-based National Socialist Black Front broke with Hitler in 1930 because of the fascist nature of the party he had created. Friedmann explores the little-told history of the Black Front in Argentina, part of the larger South American contingent of followers, critical of Hitler and his actions in Germany during the 1930s. The article points the way to a fruitful area of study that needs more scholarship. [MLN]

1371 Furia ideológica y violencia en la Argentina de los 70. Edición de Daniel Muchnik y Daniel Pérez. Buenos Aires: Ariel, 2013. 297 p.: bibl. (Periodismo & actualidad)

Critical first-person accounts of the authors about the years of violence and death in the 1970s. The narratives explore how the Latin American left failed to accept the violence unleashed by the Cuban Revolution, and consider the betrayal of the Revolution's ideals. [AMB]

1372 Furman, Rubén. Puños y pistolas: la extraña historia de la Alianza Libertadora Nacionalista, el grupo de choque de Perón. Buenos Aires: Sudamericana, 2014. 346 p., 16 unnumbered pages of plates: bibl., ill., index.

Focusing on the fascist group the Alianza Libertadora Nacionalista, Furman interviewed the last remaining survivors of the group to get their perspectives on the work of the group during the first Peronist administration. The work will be valuable to all scholars working on the political culture of the Peronist years, as well as those tracing the far-right politics of the 1930s (the group was founded in 1937) and the interplay of different political factions during a time of great change in Argentina. The book also contains many photographs and an appendix containing the platform of the group. [MLN]

1373 Galasso, Norberto. Don Hipólito: vida de Hipólito Yrigoyen. Buenos Aires: Colihue, 2013. 297 p.: bibl., ill. (Grandes biografías)

An accessible biography of President Yrigoyen, leader of the Radical Party in the 1910s and 1920s. Intended more for non-historians, the book nevertheless contains a great deal of information about Yrigoyen. [MLN]

1374 Gallo, Claudio Rodolfo. "Claroscuros" de la historia argentina: 1806–1945. Buenos Aires: Editorial Dunken, 2014. 701 p.: bibl.

Gallo has written a series of anecdotes illustrating various aspects of Argentine history. Written for a popular audience, the work has no notes and is a personal journey of the aspects of history one man finds important—the author himself. [MLN]

1375 Gallo, Edit Rosalía. Periodismo político femenino: ensayo sobres las revistas feministas en la primera mitad siglo XX. Buenos Aires: Instituto de Investigaciones Históricas Cruz del Sur, 2013. 94 p.: bibl., ill.

A short book focusing on four periodicals that focused on the rights of women in the early 20th century—*Unión y Labor, Nuestra Causa, Vida Femenina,* and *Mujeres de América.* Some journals were explicitly political, while others more generally worked for expanding the possibilities for women in Argentina and the Americas. The book is a good introduction to the early feminist press, with information about the reach and focus of each publication. [MLN]

1376 Gallo, Ezequiel. La república en ciernes: surgimiento de la vida política y social pampeana, 1850–1930. Buenos Aires: Siglo Veintiuno Editores, 2013. 238 p.: bibl. (Historia y cultura)

A short overview of the formative years of the Argentine republic, the book primarily engages with political and economic history. Gallo focuses on the two projects of the period: the formation of a new society and the creation of a stable republican system. Succinct and well-researched (Gallo is a leading Argentine historian), the work would be of use to undergraduates or graduate students requiring an overview of this seminal period in the creation of modern Argentina. [MLN]

1377 Garavaglia, Juan Carlos. La disputa por la construcción nacional argentina: Buenos Aires, la Confederación y las provincias, 1850–1865. Buenos Aires: Prometeo Libros, 2015. 235 p.: bibl., ill. (Colección Historia argentina)

Another excellent study in Argentine quantitative history by the late Juan Carlos Garavaglia, who here tackles the thorny question of how state revenues were collected and applied to the broader project of creating a modern nation. Not surprisingly, he finds that much of the monies flowing from the customs house to the exchequer were applied to the creation of a modern military. This inclination was particularly salient, as Garavaglia points out, in understanding the conflict between the Paraná-based Confederation and the very strong, if ephemeral, State of Buenos Aires. [TW]

1378 Garavaglia, Juan Carlos. Una juventud en los años sesenta. Buenos Aires: Prometeo Libros, 2015. 208 p.: bibl., ill.

This book is divided into 10 parts, detailing the life of historian Juan Carlos Garavaglia, in particular his membership in the Montoneros as a youth. It does not aim to be a history book about the 1950s, 1960s, and 1970s, but the narrative is a wonderful first-person account by someone involved in important national events. [AMB]

1379 Getselteris, Gonzalo. Desde el monte: la Compañía de Monte vencerá. Lanús Oeste, Argentina: Nuestra América, 2015. 556 p.: bibl., ill.

The book presents a historical narrative of the events in the province of Tucumán, in particular the work done by the Compañia de Monte "Ramón Rosa Jimenez," made up of activists of the ERP (People's Revolutionary Army) and PRT (Workers' Revolutionary Party). The author has included many first-person accounts as well as material from magazines and newspapers. The author focuses more on their reasons for fighting than on their ultimate failure. The discussion of conditions in Tucumán in the early 1970s is excellent. [AMB]

1380 Gigliotti, Carlos Alberto. Amanecer de un 3 de Febrero: historia del combate de San Lorenzo. Buenos Aires: Ediciones Argentinidad, 2013. 160 p: bibl., ill.

A spotty account of San Martín's debut as military commander during the independence struggle. Occasionally useful for the military historian. [TW]

1381 Glück, Mario. La nación imaginada desde una ciudad: las ideas políticas de Juan Álvarez, 1898–1954. Bernal, Argentina: Universidad Nacional de Quilmes Editorial, 2015. 357 p.: bibl., ill. (Colección Intersecciones)

An intellectual biography of Juan Álvarez, political thinker of the early 20th century. Glück pays special attention to his writings about the nation and positivism, particularly *Las guerras civiles argentinas.* The work will fit into the larger panorama of historians working on intellectual history and the ideas about nationalism of the late 19th and early 20th century. [MLN]

1382 **Godoy, Juan.** La forja del nacionalismo popular: la construcción de una posición nacional en la "Fuerza de Orientación Radical de la Joven Argentina" (FORJA). Buenos Aires: Punto de Encuentro, 2015. 497 p.: bibl.

Godoy explores the history and significance of the nationalist and anti-imperialist group FORJA. Founded in the middle of the 1930s, FORJA was a response to the difficulties of the infamous decade, both political and economic. Godoy, a sociologist, is interested in the theoretical and sociological implications of the movement, particularly its anti-colonialism and strategies for national liberation, which he compares with contemporary situations in Argentina. [MLN]

1383 **Goldman, Noemí.** Mariano Moreno: de reformista a insurgente. Buenos Aires: Edhasa, 2016. 280 p.: bibl. (Biografías argentinas)

A superior biography of Moreno (1778–1811), the lawyer-turned-patriot who might best be understood as the John Adams of Argentina. Goldman has always been one of the most solid scholars working with the Ravignani Institute, and her command of archival documents and periodical literature of the early 1800s demonstrates that she is still on top of her game. Her Moreno is a thoughtful and talented young man forced by circumstances down the road to insurgency, a process that gave his political liberalism a sharp revolutionary edge. It is in examining Moreno's transformation from lawyer to ideologue that Goldman makes her real contribution, forming her study, as it were, into a *bildungsroman*. She is to be congratulated for avoiding the wild speculations that have swirled around Moreno since the 1970s, demonstrating once again that fact-based history is the best. [TW]

1384 **González Bollo, Hernán.** La fábrica de las cifras oficiales del Estado argentino (1869–1947). Bernal, Argentina: Universidad Nacional de Quilmes Editorial, 2014. 284 p.: bibl. (Convergencia)

González Bollo has written an exploration of the history of census-keeping and its bureaucracy, showing the changes and ultimate centralization of the institutions. He explores the economic meanings of record-keeping, and the role of the state in this broad look at the official figures generated throughout the country during its modernization and consolidation. The implications for economic history and the role of the state vs. local governments in record-keeping will be of use to a variety of scholars. [MLN]

1385 **Gorza, Anabella.** Peronistas y militares: una vieja relación en un nuevo contexto. (*Estud. Soc./Santa Fe*, 25:49, segundo semestre 2015, p. 31–62)

This essay utilizes the uprising led by Miguel Ángel Iñíguez on November 30, 1960 to return Peronism to power to analyze the relationship between Peronism and the military, especially during the resistance, and between civilians and the army during the same period. In particular, it asks why some within Peronism sought members of the armed forces to carry out a coup-de-état, and why some members of the forces were eager to participate. [AMB]

1386 **Grabois, Roberto.** Memorias de Roberto "Pajarito" Grabois: de Alfredo Palacios a Juan Perón (1955–1974). Buenos Aires: Corregidor, 2014. 557 p.: bibl., ill.

First person account of Roberto Grabois, leader of the FEN (National Student Front), member of the Socialist Youth, and then part of the Peronist movement. The book covers the years 1955–74. [AMB]

1387 **Las grandes guerras del siglo XX y la comunidad española de Buenos Aires.** Edición de Nadia Andrea de Cristóforis y María Inés Tato. Buenos Aires: EFFL FILO: UBA Facultad de Filosofía y Letras, 2014. 226 p.: bibl. (CS)

Part of the ever-growing historiography on Spanish immigrants and their descendents in Argentina, this edited volume focuses on the links and reactions of people of Spanish origin in Buenos Aires during WWI, the Spanish Civil War, and WWII. The work expands our knowledge of the ways that people continued to have contact with their country of origin, even if they were second or third-generation immigrants. The book will be useful to those working on immigration to Argentina as well as those exploring the reactions within Argentina to the "major wars of the 20th century." [MLN]

1388 Guerras de la historia argentina. Compilación de Federico G. Lorenz. Buenos Aires, Argentina: Ariel, 2015. 352 p.: bibl. (Historia)

A first-class compilation of war-and-society studies from the time of the Guerra Guaranítica in the 1750s to the Malvinas War of 1982. These 15 studies offer summary treatments of the individual conflicts and general analyses of the political and social effects on Argentina. Though the coverage here is broad rather than deep, several of the studies are excellent models of how to address these questions in a nuanced fashion. In this respect, the works of Raúl Fradkin, Alejandro Rubinovich, and Santiago Garaño deserve particular praise. [TW]

1389 Guy, Donna J. Creating charismatic bonds in Argentina: letters to Juan and Eva Perón. Albuquerque: University of New Mexico Press, 2016. 173 p.: bibl., index. (Diálogos series)

Using the thousands of letters sent to Juan and Eva Perón, most of them from the first Five-Year Plan, initiated in 1946, Guy explores the nature of charisma and leadership. With letters from people, many of them poor and working-class, Guy is able to examine the ways that ordinary people responded to the populist team of the Peróns. Guy also brings in children and the elderly, two groups seldom studied in modern Argentine political history. Accessible even to undergraduates, this will be a useful book for an array of scholars. [MLN]

1390 Guzmán Suárez, M. Silvinar. Perón: la revolución del pueblo. Buenos Aires: Editorial Dunken, 2015. 590 p.: bibl., ill.

Gúzman Suárez has written a very pro-Peronist look at the life of Juan Domingo Perón. Using long sections from primary sources, many written by Perón himself, the author explores the revolutionary nature of Peronism and its many successes. Because it is an explicitly political examination of Perón's life, it will primarily be useful to scholars working on Peronist political thought. [MLN]

1391 Halperín Donghi, Tulio. El enigma Belgrano: un héroe para nuestro tiempo. Buenos Aires: Siglo Veintiuno Editores, 2014. 138 p.: bibl., ill. (Historia y cultura)

Tulio Halperín Donghi was widely considered the most insightful historian that Argentina produced during the second half of the 20th century, and this, his final work, demonstrates clearly that, even in his mid-80s, he was still writing innovative history. His topic here is Manuel Belgrano (1770–1820), the iconic hero of the independence struggle, the fair-haired patriot of May who Bartolomé Mitre and José María Paz attempted to turn into the George Washington of the south. Halperín has little patience for such simplifications. His Belgrano is a much more nuanced figure, with one foot in the past and the other in the distant future, who was well out of his depth with his own time. He was a charismatic individual and a hopeless political dreamer. But, as Halperín points out, the positive feelings that he generated gave him a universal appeal—and it never left him even when he failed. This is the enigma of the book title, which like the enigmas of Borges' fiction, can never be fully explained, but tend to tell us more about Belgrano's admirers than about the man himself. This is a marvelous study, providing an analysis that is at once more intimate and more suggestive than any previously written. It is a fitting valedictory for a great historian. [TW]

1392 Harari, Ianina. A media máquina: procesos de trabajo, lucha de clases y competitividad en la industria automotriz argentina (1952–1976). Buenos Aires: Ediciones ryr, 2015. 280 p.: bibl., ill. (Investigaciones CEICS; 13)

The book seeks to understand why Argentina will likely never be able to develop a car industry of global reach. It focuses both on the history of the industry as well as on the history of the working class. It covers the years 1952 through 1976, detailing the changes in the type of work brought about by the arrival of new capital (and therefore new companies): Kaiser, Fiat, and Renault. [AMB]

1393 Herrera, Carlos-Miguel. ¿Adiós al proletariado?: El Partido Socialista bajo el peronismo (1945–1955). Buenos Aires: Imago Mundi, 2016. 260 p.: bibl., index. (Colección

Archivos: estudios de historia del movimiento obrero y la izquierda; 6)

Herrera examines the problems the Socialist Party faced during the first Peronist administration, issues that led to the ultimate decline of the party. The author identifies a few factors that led to the problems, including the death of party leader Juan B. Justo and a new generation taking over in the 1930s, persecution by the military government preceding Perón's presidency and during the early Peronist years, and finally the role socialists played in the overthrow of Perón and ensuing government. For a party that was long the representative of the left in Argentina, Herrera's account of the fall of the socialists is an important contribution to the growing literature on anti-Peronism. [MLN]

1394 Horowitz, Joel. Football clubs and neighbourhoods in Buenos Aires before 1943: the role of political linkages and personal influence. (*J. Lat. Am. Stud.*, 46:3, Aug. 2014, p. 557–585)

Horowitz examines football clubs within the neighborhood and association culture of the early 20th century in Buenos Aires, noting the importance of the club for neighborhood identity. The author also traces the linkages between football and politics—as clubs needed more resources, they turned to politicians and the wealthy for help, and those politicians then turned to the clubs for political support in these pre-Peronist years. [MLN]

1395 Huberman, Silvio. Los pasajeros del *Weser*: la conmovedora travesía de los primeros inmigrantes judíos a la Argentina. Buenos Aires: Sudamericana, 2014. 267 p.: appendix, bibl.

Written in a journalistic style, Huberman attempts to recreate the voyage of the *Weser*, the boat that brought the first Jewish immigrants to rural Argentina. Although the book will be of some interest to scholars, there are no footnotes for the material, only a bibliography. [MLN]

1396 Hyland, Steven. More Argentine than you: Arabic-speaking immigrants in Argentina. Albuquerque: University of New Mexico Press, 2017. 289 p.: bibl., index.

One of the first studies of Arabic-speaking immigrants to Argentina, Hyland's book explores the transnational lives of the often-divided Syrian-Lebanese community in Argentina's Northwest. A group that ultimately achieved great success in Argentina, Hyland shows its origins through an array of documentation that illuminates the class divisions and issues the immigrants faced in the early decades of their settlement. The book will be of great interest to scholars working on immigration throughout Latin America and the Arabic-speaking diaspora. Includes a fascinating chapter on the activities of girls and women. [AMB & MLN]

1397 Iñigo Carrera, Nicolás. La otra estrategia: la voluntad revolucionaria (1930–1935). Buenos Aires: Imago Mundi, 2016. 319 p.: bibl., ill, index. (Colección Confrontaciones PIMSA)

Writing directly in response to the vast historiography on workers during the Peronist years, Carrera posits a different approach to the pre-Peronist 1930s and the ways that workers organized themselves. "The Other Strategy" of the title is the radical current among many workers who wanted to tear down the structures that oppressed them, rather than work within the existing political framework. Many workers were active in protesting their conditions and treatment, despite the often-authoritarian governments of the "infamous decade." The book will be an excellent bridge for scholars working on both the early 20th century (when radical ideologies like anarchism were somewhat common) to those studying Perón and his successful alliances with workers' groups starting in the early 1940s. [MLN]

1398 Jornadas Internacionales de Historia de la Iglesia y las Religiosidades en el NOA, 4th, *Cafayate, Argentina, 2013*. Representaciones sobre historia y religiosidad: deshaciendo fronteras. Rosario, Argentina: Prohistoria Ediciones, 2014. 417 p.: bibl., ill. (Colección Universidad; 39)

A compilation of 23 papers on varying aspects of the history of the Roman Catholic Church in Argentina, originally presented at the 4th Jornadas Internacionales de la História de la Iglesia y las Religiosidades en el Nordoeste Argentino, held at Cafayate (Salta) in September 2013. The principal factor that ties these works together is a consideration of how the Church affected the settlement of the frontier in the 18th and 19th centuries. The northwestern provinces get particular attention, and it is well that they do, for Jujuy, Salta, and Santiago del Estero rarely get the emphasis they deserve. Not surprisingly in a compilation of this size, some of the studies are better than others. The short studies of Fernando Torres Londoño, Miriam Moriconi, and Susana Monreal, all concerning the Jesuit Order, are among the best, but historians of Argentine art will appreciate Ana Cecilia Aguirre's study of the Hungarian sketch artist Lajos Szalay (1909–95), whose work at the University of Tucumán boasted many marvelous religious allusions. [TW]

1399 **Juventudes, políticas culturales y prácticas artísticas: fragmentos históricos sobre la década de 1980.** Coordinación de Alejandra Soledad González y María Verónica Basile. Textos de María Sol Bruno et al. Córdoba, Argentina: Alción Editora, 2014. 158 p.: bibl., ill.

Part of a larger project on the recent cultural history of Argentina, these essays add new understanding to the 1980s, to the history of the city of Córdoba, and to political and cultural youth practices. The contributors focus on popular urban music, gay resistance, university student practices, and theater. [AMB]

1400 **Landaburu, Roberto E.** Crónicas de fronteras. Buenos Aires: Letemendia Casa Editora, 2015. 241 p., 16 unnumbered pages of plates: bibl., ill.

The author of these 26 vignettes concerning frontier life and Indian-white relations in 19th-century Argentina notes at the outset that they bear no relation to each other whatsoever. Nor does he offer any overarching thesis to pull them together. That said, and recognizing the obvious limitations, the vignettes can be very attractive if we judge them from the model suggested by the *Tradiciones peruanas* of Ricardo Palma (see *HLAS 56:3733*) or those essays that graced the various volumes in Beezley and Ewell's series *Human Tradition in Latin America*. That is to say, any reader looking for a good anecdote, properly referenced, will find something here to admire. [TW]

1401 **Lanteri, Ana Laura.** Acerca del aprendizaje y la conformación político-institucional nacional: una relectura de la "Confederación" argentina, 1852–1862. (*Secuencia/México*, 87, sept./dic. 2013, p. 69–95, bibl.)

Lanteri here attempts to reconceptualize the history of the Argentine Confederation (1852–1861), placing relatively more emphasis on congressional politics than is usually the case and relatively less emphasis on individual politicians such as the caudillo Justo José de Urquiza. The study, which treats the Confederal Congress as an arena of "apprenticeship," is certainly interesting but not altogether convincing. [TW]

1402 **Lanteri, Ana Laura.** Se hace camino al andar: dirigencia e instituciones nacionales en la "Confederación" (Argentina, 1852–1862). Rosario, Argentina: Prohistoria Ediciones, 2015. 282 p.: bibl., ill. (Colección Historia política hoy; 06)

A well-crafted examination of the politics of the Confederation (1852–61), focusing on provincial interests and the development of new political classes. Lanteri wants to emphasize the prosopographical side of this question though she actually provides only limited information on the protagonists and their interrelations. Her study works better as an institutional history in that it shows—very perceptibly—how the different branches of the Confederal government managed to construct the checks, but not really the balances associated with modern statecraft. This fact proved especially challenging for politicians confronting the personality of Justo José de Urquiza and what he represented of the *ancien régime*. [TW]

1403 **Larguía, Alejandro.** Félix de Aguirre. Buenos Aires: Corregidor, 2013. 268 p.: bibl., ill.

Not much is known about the history of federalism in Corrientes and the Misiones, and what is known was covered 90 years ago by Hernán Félix Gómez and Manuel Florencio Mantilla, and more recently, by Jorge F. Machón (see *HLAS 60:2927*). This present work, which looks into the career of a key Artiguista commander in the 1810s (and an important Misionero political figure in the next decade) summarizes what is already known but presents no real surprises. [TW]

1404 Ledesma Prietto, Nadia. La revolución sexual de nuestro tiempo: el discurso médico anarquista sobre el control de la natalidad, la maternidad y el placer sexual: Argentina, 1931–1951. Buenos Aires: Editorial Biblos, 2016. 201 p.: bibl. (Colección Ciudadanía e inclusión)

Focused on decoupling women's sexuality from the social pressure to become mothers, Ledesma Prietto analyzes the discourse from a variety of sources within anarchism and the medical establishment. The author argues that the anarchist perspective was one of disruption, particularly against eugenicist models, because it promoted the individual and sexual rights of women and supported those who chose to not become mothers. An important addition to the growing literature on medical and reproduction, in addition to its clear position within gender and sexuality studies. [MLN]

1405 Leoni, María Silvia and María del Mar Solís Carnicer. Peronismo, diseño institucional y centralización política: un análisis a partir de dos espacios subnacionales argentinos: Corrientes y Chaco, 1946–1955. (*Iberoamericana/Madrid*, 15:60, dic. 2015, p. 61–79, bibl.)

The authors present a comparison of the political transformations of two provinces during the Peronist years, with the intention of analyzing the workings of Peronism in two different provincial contexts. Corrientes suffered important changes, the most important of which was the imposition of changes to the electoral system for the 1948 elections. Chaco, on the other hand, became a province during and thanks to Peronism, and the 1951 Constitution guaranteed a strong executive with power held in check by the federal government. [AMB]

1406 Levine, Alex and Adriana Novoa. !Darwinistas!: The construction of evolutionary thought in nineteenth century Argentina. Leiden, Netherlands: Brill, 2012. 279 p.: bibl., index. (History of science and medicine library, 27)(Scientific and learned cultures and their institutions; 5)

This is a solid and readable contribution to the history of ideas in Argentina, specifically, how Argentine intellectuals received and adapted Darwinism to meet their own needs and to help refine notions of national identity. In addition to offering two chapters explaining conflicting interpretations (natural selection versus esthetic selection, etc.), Levine and Novoa also offer 80 pages of selected texts taken from figures who acknowledged being influenced by Darwin. These include Hermann Burmeister, Domingo F. Sarmiento, Florentino Ameghino and José Ingenieros. For a comment on a companion volume, see *HLAS 70:1346*. [TW]

Lichtmajer, Leandro. La articulación de una estrategia política opositora al peronismo: radicales, periodistas y prensa escrita en Tucumán, 1943–1949. See *HLAS 73:1351*.

1407 Lichtmajer, Leandro. Derrota y reconstrucción: el radicalismo tucumano frente al peronismo 1943–1955. Sáenz Peña, Argentina: EDUNTREF Editorial de la Universidad Nacional de Tres de Febrero, 2016. 270 p.: bibl., ill. (Análisis político: teoría e historia)

Lichtmajer provides a new perspective on the Peronist years in Tucumán by focusing on the history of the Radical Party during that time. As his title makes clear, it was a time of rebuilding and reassessment for the party, which had been in control of the province from 1935–43, years that it had little control in most of the rest of Argentina. Tracing the fortunes of the Radicals at the same time the Peronists were in control, Lichtmajer also illuminates the particularity of Tucumán and the sugar plantation society that existed there. [MLN]

1408 Lida, Miranda. Historia del Catolicismo en la Argentina entre el siglo XIX y el XX. México: Siglo Veintiuno Editores, 2015. 269 p., 1 unnumbered p.: bibl., ill. (Historia y cultura)

Focusing on the period between the first Vatican Council in 1870 and the second, which began in 1962, Lida has written a fine history of Catholicism in a period of nation-building and secularization. Focusing on the Church itself and also its place in the society and culture, Lida's book will be a welcome addition to the larger historical perspective on the role of the Church in Argentina. In this modernizing period in

Argentine society, Lida shows the ways that the Church struggled against some changes and embraced others. [MLN]

1409 Liscia, María Herminia Beatriz di.
Mujeres y política: memorias del primer peronismo en La Pampa. La Pampa, Argentina: Instituto Interdisciplinario de Estudios de la Mujer: EdUNLPa; Buenos Aires: Miño y Dávila Editores, 2013. 169 p.: bibl., ill.

Based on a series of interviews with a variety of women from the province of La Pampa, Liscia explores how their gender shaped their experience with Peronism. The women reflected on a variety of topics, from their first experiences voting to their feelings about Eva Perón to motherhood. Unlike many other books about Peronism in areas outside Buenos Aires, Liscia focuses on individual voices (often silent in other works) and allows the protagonists to speak for themselves. [MLN]

1410 Losada, Leandro. Marcelo T. de Alvear. Buenos Aires: Edhasa, 2016. 349 p.: bibl., ill. (Biografías argentinas)

Losada's biography of Radical Party leader and president of Argentina (1922–28) Marcelo T. de Alvear is a reevaluation of his legacy. At times an ally and at others a rival or critic of Hipólito Yrigoyen, the founder and other main leader of the Radical Party, Losada focuses most of the book on the post-1930 years, when the Radicals were out of power. He documents Alvear's support for and and response to the coup that removed Yrigoyen in 1930, and Alvear's subsequent leadership of the Radical Party. His exile from and return to Argentina and politics in the middle of the "infamous decade" of the 1930s is an important part of Losada's new look at his life, that of an elite leader of a primarily middle and lower-class party with a complicated relationship to power. [MLN]

1411 Maddalena, Pablo. El Departamento Nacional del Trabajo y su relación con la Ley de Accidentes Laborales de 1915. (*Estud. Soc./Santa Fe*, 25:49, segundo semestre 2015, p. 95–124)

Maddalena explores the discussions surrounding labor accidents and the role of the state in the early 20th century, arguing that the DNT was not as central to the conversation as has been previously claimed. He believes that a variety of political actors, from across the political spectrum, were the key motivators behind the 1915 law. Squarely situated in the early 20th-century milieu, the article captures the wide-ranging concerns of the early 20th century and the creation of a modern Argentine state. For a related study on the Ley de Accidentes Laborales, see item **1475**. [MLN]

1412 Making citizens in Argentina. Edited by Benjamin Bryce and David Sheinin. Pittsburgh: University of Pittsburgh Press, 2017. 263 p.: bibl., index. (Pitt Latin American series)

This book brings together essays that seek to explore the meaning of citizenship and how that meaning changed over time. The authors examine laws regulating citizenship, as well as studying immigrant associations, science and cultural citizenship, racial ideas, sport and gender, among others, to understand the complex understandings of citizenship by various groups. The last two chapters focus on this notion during and after the military dictatorship. [AMB]

1413 Mangiantini, Martín. El trotskismo y el debate en torno a la lucha armada: Moreno, Santucho y la ruptura del PRT. Buenos Aires: El Topo Blindado, 2014. 215 p.: bibl. (Colección Controversias)

The book covers the crisis and debates that led to the break-up of the PRT (Partido Revolucionario de los Trabajadores or Workers' Revolutionary Party) in 1967–68. Of note is the author's analysis of the discussion within the group led by Nahuel Moreno regarding the role of armed struggle, even before their dispute with Mario Roberto Santucho. Important last chapter on the historiography of this topic. [AMB]

1414 Manifiestos políticos argentinos: antología. Tomo 1, 1890–1956. Tomo 2, 1956–1976. Edición y guión por Mariana Casullo y Diego Caramés en colaboración con Matías Farías y Adriana Petra. Buenos Aires: Cultura Argentina, 2014–2015. 2 v.: bibl., ill.

Volume One brings together manifestos (including proclamations and public speeches), intellectual interventions (as seen in debates, polemics, editorials), and cultural artifacts (including photographs, paintings, poems, letters, memoirs, and testimonies) not attempting to be exhaustive, and not utilizing exclusively well-known historical events and periodization. Each section (a range of years) is contextualized in a few paragraphs before the documents. Volume Two contains similar documents and is divided into two chapters: 1956 to 1966 and 1966 to 1976. Within each chapter, the material is organized topically. Great resource for teaching.The textual material is in Spanish, but photos, and other sources are very useful for all. [AMB]

1415 **La marchita, el escudo y el bombo: una historia cultural de los emblemas del peronismo, de Perón a Cristina Kirchner.** Edición de Ezequiel Adamovsky y Esteban Buch. Buenos Aires: Planeta, 2016. 367 p.: bibl.

The book discusses the origins and uses of three Peronist symbols: the badge, the Peronist song (Marcha Peronista), and the drums (*bombo*). Using these symbols as focus, the book proposes a cultural history of Peronism and of Argentina; it alludes to the history of the uses of other badges, other instruments, and how the Peronist song was created in conversation with images and speeches of Perón. See also items **2829** and **2830**. [AMB]

1416 **Marcilese, José.** El peronismo en Bahía Blanca: de la génesis a la hegemonía. Bahía Blanca, Argentina: EdiUNS, 2015. 234 p.: bibl., ill. (Serie Extensión. Colección Estudios sociales y humanidades)

Another good addition to the growing historiography of the first Peronist administration, this work focused on the city of Bahia Blanca, a small port city in Buenos Aires province. Marcilese examines the relationships between the Peronist party in the city while also taking it to a very local level—looking at neighborhood groups and clubs and the ways they dealt with the new Peronist phenomenon. Even though it was part of the province, Peronism played out very differently in Bahia Blanca than it did in Buenos Aires, making this a valuable contribution to the scholarship. [MLN]

1417 **Marco, Miguel Angel de.** Alem: caudillo popular, profeta de la república. Buenos Aires: Emecé, 2015. 334 p., 16 plates: bibl., ill.

A narrative biography of Leandro N. Alem, an essential figure in late 19th-century Argentine politics. Soldier, senator, leader of the "Revolution of 1890," founder of the Unión Cívica Radical, Alem is key to understanding the political landscape of the decades before 1900. Written for a popular audience, the book contains no footnotes or traditional citations, though each chapter has a bibliography. [MLN]

1418 **Marco, Miguel Angel de.** Sarmiento: maestro de América, constructor de la nación. Buenos Aires: Emecé, 2016. 413 p.: bibl.

The author, former president of the Argentine Academy of History, has specialized in recent years in producing good quality biographies of key Argentine political figures of the 19th century. This latest effort concerns Domingo Faustino Sarmiento, the famous author of *Facundo*, and president of the republic from 1868 to 1874. Because Sarmiento was so fundamentally important in promoting public education and the cultural life of his nation, the fact that he was driven so manifestly by narrow political concerns often gets underemphasized in the literature. De Marco will have none of that. His Sarmiento is a political animal, thinking about power arrangements in Buenos Aires while in exile in Chile, thinking about national elections while ambassador in Washington, and thinking about leaving a permanent political legacy as he was about to step down from office. He was also a prickly character, quick to take offense, and quick to offer insulting repartee when the situation called for prudence. All this De Marco gets right, and thus generally endorses the conventional picture of Sarmiento the politician. That said, De Marco's overall approach is entirely orthodox. He has uncovered no new information and explored no new archives or documentary collections. The fact that he writes so concisely, however, will attract readers to this biography notwithstanding. This is a well-executed rather than profound work and should be read on that basis. [TW]

1419 **Martí, Gerardo Marcelo.** Juan Manuel de Rosas: poder, destierro y regreso: 1845–1989. Villa Martelli, Argentina: Ediciones AqL, 2014. 503 p.: bibl., ill.

Martí's intimate biography of Rosas focuses on the end of his reign and his subsequent exile in England. The author is also interested in Rosas' enduring power as a political symbol, and explores the changing nature of his legacy. The work contains an appendix with some primary sources. The book will be useful to those working on political history, particularly the 19th century. [MLN]

1420 Martínez, Ignacio. Una nación para la Iglesia argentina: construcción del estado y jurisdicciones eclesiásticas en el siglo XIX. Buenos Aires: Academia Nacional de la Historia, 2013. 574 p.: bibl.

Argentine historiography usually reserves an important but somewhat isolated niche for works highlighting the history of the Church. We get some excellent histories of missionary labors in the colonial era (those of Guillermo Furlong Cardiff still standing out after many years) and some useful biographical works on individual churchmen such as Déan Funes. But these studies are directed inwardly for the most part and tend to eschew the more problematic question of how the Church affects and overlaps with secular society in Argentina's broader trajectory as a nation. This excellent study of royal, revolutionary, provincial, and national patronage is thus not only unusual—it is exciting. Martínez traces Church-state relations from the time of the late Bourbon *patronato* to the era of secularization in the 1860s. He notes that there were many different interpretations of the Church's proper role in Argentine society and what seems written in stone today was in no sense guaranteed during the long sunset of colonial thinking and the consolidation of republican institutions. A very solid study. [TW]

1421 Martiren, Juan Luis. La transformación farmer: colonización agrícola y crecimiento económico en la provincia de Santa Fe durante la segunda mitad del siglo XIX. Buenos Aires, Argentina: Prometeo Libros, 2016. 266 p.: bibl. (Prometeo bicentenario)

The Ravignani Institute has long overseen the training of fine economic historians with the late Jorge Gelman, for instance, producing brilliant analyses of the ranching economy in Buenos Aires province and the Banda Oriental. This new study thus follows in the wake of an established line of highly creative work. Martirén focuses on economic change in the southern districts of Santa Fe province in the second half of the 19th century. The transformation that this region underwent from primitive ranching economy to modern cereal exporter was emblematic of what Richard Scobie once termed the "revolution on the Pampas." Martirén supplies an impressive array of data to show how it happened, and how three agricultural colonies systematically worked to foment a broader development in the region, some 1,700,000 hectares sown with high-quality wheat by the end of the century. [TW]

1422 Martocci, Federico. La política cultural del Partido Socialista en el Territorio Nacional de La Pampa: dispositivos y prácticas de intervención de sus dirigentes e intelectuales (1913–1939). Santa Rosa, Argentina: EdUNLPam, 2015. 266 p.: bibl. (Colección Libros académicos de interés regional)

Based on an MA thesis for social science, Martocci's study is an institutional and intellectual look at socialists in the early 20th century. The book explores the ways that socialists organized and imagined themselves away from the political capital, at the margins of national political life. Martocci's work is part of the growing historiography on political life outside of Buenos Aires and the history of the national territories. [MLN]

1423 Masés, Enrique. Estado y cuestión indígena: el destino final de los indios sometidos en el sur del territorio (1878–1930). Buenos Aires, Argentina: Prometeo Libros, 2010. 327 p.: bibl., ill. (Colección de Estudios Patagónicos)(Prometeo Bicentenario)

Linking the treatment of the indigenous to the "social question" of the late 19th century, Mases has written a book that approaches the history of indigenous peoples from a variety of perspectives, using an array of documentation. Locating the debates over indigenous peoples and their treatment to the creation of the modern nation of Argentina, Mases details the ways that the state attempted to integrate into white Euro-Argentine society, from the military and law to forced domestic labor. A must-read for scholars of indigenous life in Argentina and anyone interested in how the "indigenous question" played out in a country interested in presenting and preserving whiteness. [MLN]

1424 **Masi, Andrés Alberto.** Los tiempos de Alfonsín: la construcción de un liderazgo democrático. Buenos Aires: Capital Intelectual, 2014. 509 p.: bibl., index.

Analysis of Raúl Alfonsín's leadership during the years of the transition to democracy. The author argues that works on Alfonsín have focused on the political and socioeconomic problems encountered during his presidency, but the construction and consolidation of his leadership and the influence of the economy on his ability to lead have not been sufficiently studied. [AMB]

1425 **Mata de López, Sara.** Conflicto y violencia en tiempos de crisis: Salta (Argentina) en las primeras décadas del siglo XIX. (*Secuencia/México*, 90, sept./dic. 2014, p. 33–56, bibl.)

This interesting but rather uneven work seeks to define and analyze the interconnective elements that explain the insensate violence of Salteño politics in the 1810s and 1820s. All the usual culprits are referenced—the relations with Buenos Aires, the avarice and power-hunger of the landed elite, the ambitions of petty caudillos, and the unrealized quest for a better life on the part of the masses. What is not addressed is the plain fact that violence breeds violence; no mechanistic explanation can approximate the sheer passion of bloodlust in providing an understanding for why people behave with such brutality, whether the site is 19th-century Salta, early 20th-century Namibia, or today's Syria. [TW]

1426 **Mayer, Mirko Edgardo.** El Ferrocarril Provincial de Buenos Aires, 1912–1930: un abordaje desde la perspectiva de la historia de empresas. Buenos Aires: EC, Ediciones Cooperativas, 2013. 192 p.: bibl., ill. (Colección Tesis y tesinas de historia económica)

Based on a Master's thesis, Mayer's work looks at the public-private partnership that created the provincial railroad in Buenos Aires. The author is interested in the role of the state in infrastructure and business ventures, and the links to private business. The work will be useful to those interested in the modernization of the country and capitalist innovation. [MLN]

1427 **Mercado, Silvia D.** El inventor del peronismo: Raúl Apold, el cerebro oculto que cambió la política argentina. Buenos Aires: Planeta, 2013. 368 p., 8 unnumbered leaves: bibl., ill., index. (Espejo de la Argentina)

Mercado has written a biography of Apold, "the best-kept secret in Peronism," who led the Subsecretary of Information and Press during the first Perón administrations. A shadowy figure who was most comfortable manipulating and pushing the Peronist agenda in the background, Mercado has written a fascinating work that has strong parallels (which she points out) with the Kirchner years and their relations with the press. Dealing with the nature and goals of the political press, freedom of speech and press, and the ways that Peronist governments have manipulated the media to their own ends, the work is important for understanding both the past and future of journalism in Argentina. [MLN]

1428 **Merenson, Silvina.** Y hasta el silencio en tus labios: memorias de las ex presas políticas del Penal de Villa Devoto en el transcurso de la última dictadura militar en la Argentina. Dirección de Rosana Guber. Buenos Aires: IDES, Centro de Antropología Social; La Plata, Argentina: Ediciones Al Margen, 2014. 169 p.: bibl. (Colección La otra ventana)

This book is based on 32 interviews with former female prisoners during the military dictatorship in Argentina. Historian and social anthropologist Merenson analyzes these narratives and reassembles the gender construction of the "resistance," the sense of guilt, and the body. Fascinating discussion. [AMB]

1429 **Micheletti, Maria Gabriela.** Historiadores e historias escritas en entresiglos: sociabilidades y representaciones del pasado santafesino, 1881–1907. Buenos Aires: Lumiere, 2013. 273 p.: bibl.

Micheletti writes about the ways that residents of Santa Fe, primarily Rosarinos, wrote and thought about their past in the late 19th and early 20th centuries. Writing from outside the capital of Buenos Aires and at a time when history was not professionalized, writers in Santa Fe wanted to make sense of their own context and importance in the nation, particularly revered figures like Estanislao "El Gaucho" López. The book is an important look at the trajectory of historical writing in Argentina, particularly because it is not focused on Buenos Aires. [MLN]

1430 Minutolo de Orsi, Cristina V. Manuel Belgrano: 1816: unidad e independencia americana. Buenos Aires: Instituto Nacional Belgraniano, 2016. 359 p.: bibl. (Ensayos)

For better or worse, certain historical figures are oversubscribed in the scholarly literature. In the US, we see Lincoln in that position, and in Great Britain, Churchill. In Argentina, we see Manuel Belgrano. In the case of all three, the supposition in every new study is the same: that if we discover which shoe the protagonist slipped on first thing in the morning, we will have in our hand some essential key to the man's personality such that all his history, which will be conveniently appended, will present itself in a new light. Except that it never does. The present work is a good example of the general trend. We learn all about Belgrano's plans to promote "national unity" in the 1810s, an effort that was invariably frustrated by political dissolution and the rise of *caudillismo*. We learn of his plans to incorporate elements of Incaic administration in the elaboration of a modern Platine state. We also learn that he failed to achieve his goals and that he was a great patriot. These were all things that readers in the 1920s knew from works produced at that time by the Academia Nacional de Historia. Here, Minutolo de Orsi cites Ricardo Rojas but does not get much further. She omits mention of Tulio Halperín Donghi (a serious error on her part) and gives no attention to revisionist analyses (many of which treat Belgrano in an indirect way that nonetheless deserves mention). Above all, Minutolo de Orsi sticks to the conventional, and by thus avoiding debate, she assures that no one will consult her work. [TW]

1431 Montaldo, Graciela R. Museo del consumo: archivos de la cultura de masas en Argentina. Buenos Aires: Fondo de Cultura Económica, 2016. 387 p.: bibl. (Tierra firme)

Montaldo's book is a wide-ranging exploration of the growing mass culture in the late 19th and early 20th centuries, from tango and circuses to population growth. The work uses a great deal of theoretical work to analyze the sources and period, drawing from literature, history, sociology, and cultural studies. [MLN]

1432 Montes de Oca, Ignacio. Ustashas: el ejército nazi de Perón y el Vaticano. Buenos Aires: Sudamericana, 2013. 318 p.: bibl.

Montes de Oca has written a narrative history of the Ustasha, the Croatian fascist paramilitary group. Through help from the Vatican (and Western intelligence agencies who wanted help in the anti-Communist fight), many successfully made it to Argentina. Perón welcomed them because he shared many of their ideologies—anti-Communist, nationalist, and Catholic. Close to Perón during his first presidency, Croats continued to help him throughout his exile and return, as well as the Peronist Menem government, elected in 1989. Written without any footnotes, it would be primarily of interest to a popular audience. [MLN]

1433 Moralidades y comportamientos sexuales: Argentina, 1880–2011. Edición de Dora Barrancos, Donna Guy y Adriana Valobra. Buenos Aires: Editorial Biblos, 2014. 412 p.: bibl., ill. (Colección Ciudadanía e inclusión)

An edited volume that will take the history of gender and sexuality into new directions, the authors have assembled an array of scholars and articles that explore a variety of topics surrounding morality and sexuality in Argentina. From examinations of prostitution and popular ideas about sexuality in the late 19th century to contemporary explorations of law and sexual rights, the book will be of interest to a wide array of scholars working on modern Argentine history, gender studies, and anyone interested in the history of sexuality. [MLN]

1434 Moreira, María Verónica. Juego electoral y relaciones políticas en el fútbol argentino. (*Hist. Quest. Debates*, 29:57, julho/dez. 2012, p. 127–149)

This article studies the relationships that soccer club leaders, fans and mainstream politicians create during (club) elections. In particular, the author focuses on the mid and late 2000s, on a soccer club in the province of Buenos Aires. The findings confirm how politics and soccer work in tandem: the club obtains "favors" and politicians gain supporters. [AMB]

1435 Moreno, Alicia del Carmen. Afromestizos en Catamarca: familias y matrimonios en la primera mitad del siglo XIX. Buenos Aires: Editorial Dunken, 2014. 218 p.: bibl., ill.

For reasons that are both frustrating and obvious, the province of Catamarca has never gained its fair share of attention in the quite ample regional historiography of Argentina. For that reason, we need to celebrate a bit when a good work comes along that successfully places the province in a broader thematic context. That is the case in this unusual study of the Afro-Argentine population of Catamarca in the early 1800s. By examining censal and matrimonial documents from provincial and Church archives, Moreno has succeeded in throwing a concentrated light on a part of the population that was once very important but has for the most part slipped into obscurity. Her work, which is solid and well-researched, bears comparison with that of Alex Borucki (see *HLAS 72:1159*), George Reid Andrews (see *HLAS 66:1901*), and Miguel Angel Rosal (see *HLAS 48:2828*). [TW]

1436 Moyano, Daniel. Desde la empresa: firmas familiares y estructura empresarial en la industria azucarera tucumana (1895–1930). Buenos Aires: Prometeo Libros, 2015. 208 p.: bibl., ill. (Prometeo bicentenario)

One of a number of new studies of the Argentine economy to approach the subject from the perspective of the businesses themselves, Moyano's book tackles the early growth and development of the sugar industry in Tucumán. Moyano has been able to assemble an array of quantitative sources that help to illuminate the business practices of the various producers and their links to banks. This book is an important addition to the fast-growing scholarship on Tucumán's sugar industry. [MLN]

1437 Moyano, Marcelo. Juan Lavalle, una biografía. Buenos Aires: Ediciones Fabro, 2012. 762 p.: bibl., ill.

A 762-page biography of Lavalle (1797–1841), the early Unitarian military leader who rose to prominence at the end of the Cisplatine War, but could not find a role for himself afterwards. He ended his career with a "permanent succession of military and personal setbacks" until death in the form of "friendly fire" finally overtook him in Jujuy. Moyano is a frequent contributor to *Todo Es Historia*, and evidently hopes that this study will supply every known detail about the life of Lavalle, which it comes close to doing. There are extensive materials presented on military campaigns, political alliances, and the various houses that Lavalle occupied during his life. The study lacks an overarching thesis, however, which may not necessarily be a bad thing. Bartolomé Mitre tried unsuccessfully to turn Lavalle into the epitome of liberal patriotism. Moyano, by contrast, appears comfortable in leaving Lavalle to his "permanent contradictions." [TW]

1438 Muchnik, Daniel. Inmigrantes, 1860–1914: la historia de los míos y de los tuyos. Buenos Aires: Sudamericana, 2015. 229 p.: bibl.

Part family history and part history of immigration in Argentina, Muchnik's book is written for a popular audience. Tracing the journey of his Ashkenazi Jewish ancestors to Argentina and the Jewish Colonization Association settlements, Muchnik focuses specifically on the rural immigrants. [MLN]

1439 Nállim, Jorge. Las raíces del antiperonismo: orígenes históricos e ideológicos. Buenos Aires: Capital Intelectual, 2014. 284 p.: bibl.

Nállim explores the diversity of anti-Peronism, from conservatives to communists, while also interrogating the strands that pulled the different groups together (or apart). He also argues that both Peronism and anti-Peronism arose from the particular historical circumstances of the 1930s. For the author, the period 1930–55 is one in which both sides developed their ideas and arguments within three discrete political periods—1930–37, 1938–46, and 1946–55. An excellent scholarly work that will be of use to those working on the political and ideological history of mid-20th century Argentina. [MLN]

1440 El negro Atilio: un trabajador, un líder sindical combativo, un militante político revolucionario: libro homenaje a 40 años de su asesinato. Edición de lda Bustos et al. Córdoba, Argentina: Unión Obrera Gráfica Cordobesa: Confederación General del Trabajo, Regional Córdoba: Editorial Filosofía y Humanidades, UNC, 2014. 235 p., 20 unnumbered plates: bibl., ill.

This book is a compilation of testimonies about Atilio Lopez and Juan Jose Varas, two trade union militants from Córdoba who were murdered in 1974. The testimonies seek to reconstruct their private lives, their union activism, and their political struggles. The book is divided into chapters that cover these topics. [AMB]

1441 Ocampo, Emilio. La independencia argentina: de la fábula a la historia. Buenos Aires: Claridad, 2016. 380 p.: bibl.

The principal thesis of this new study follows fairly closely from that of Juan Bautista Alberdi, who held that the standard foundational myths of Argentina—which place San Martín at the center—are not an adequate way to analyze the independence struggle, that, in fact, the Liberator's advent signaled an unfortunate trend towards *caudillismo* in Argentine politics. This was a perfectly reasonable, if not entirely new, argument even in Alberdi's time. But it is only one of several that Ocampo puts forward. He is particularly interested in giving the English their proper due in fomenting changes of long-lasting impact in the country. Unlike a younger generation of readers, who are used to thinking in dualist terms that pose traditional "Mitrista" against left-revisionist approaches, Ocampo holds that neither of the two interpretations work all that well. [TW]

1442 Olivera, Gastón Alejandro. Del desamparo al imperio: Wilhelm Vallentin y el proyecto de colonización del Chubut bajo el signo del Kaiserreich, 1890–1914. Buenos Aires: Prometeo Libros, 2015. 208 p.: bibl., ill. (Prometeo bicentenario)

Olivera's thesis for his Licenciatura, published as the result of a contest, follows the life of Dr. Wilhelm Vallentin, economist, traveler, and creator of a German colony in the Patagonian region of Chubut. The work is primarily a biography, and weaves in intellectual history as well as the transnational nature of Vallentin's hopes and project. Olivera offers a new perspective on the growing historiography of Patagonia. [MLN]

1443 Olmedo, Ernesto. Los militares y el desarrollo social: frontera sur de Córdoba, 1869–1885. Buenos Aires: Aspha, 2014. 232 p.: bibl.

A somewhat specialized study, well-researched, on how the Argentine army was the chief factor in taming the southern districts of Córdoba, and bringing them under effective occupation in the final third of the 19th century. [TW]

1444 Pacheco, Mariano. Montoneros silvestres: 1976–1983: historias de resistencia a la dictadura en el sur del conurbano. Buenos Aires: Planeta, 2014. 437 p.: bibl. (Espejo de la Argentina)

The book reconstructs the memories and trajectories of Montonero militants in Greater Buenos Aires (*Conurbano bonaerense*) and details their resistance activism during the years of the dictatorship. [AMB]

1445 Pavoni, Norma L. Facciones, partidos y clientelismo político: en la Córdoba de entre siglos, 1890–1912. Córdoba, Argentina: Editorial Universidad Nacional de Córdoba, 2016. 348 p.: bibl.

A deeply researched work that will be of use to scholars working on topics related to politics in Córdoba and Argentina overall in the late 19th and early 20th century. Pavoni focuses on political identity and the clientelism as main themes of the work, and her discussion of clientelism in particular will be of use to anyone attempting to make sense of Argentine political culture in the modern era. The book also contains a very useful appendix with primary sources and lists of important players organized by their role in the political process. [MLN]

1446 Pérez Stocco, Sandra. La paz del Chaco: Carlos Saavedra Lamas y la participación de la Cancillería argentina

(1932–1938). Godoy Cruz, Argentina: Jagüel Editores de Mendoza; Mendoza, Argentina: Universidad Nacional de Cuyo, Facultad de Filosofía y Letras, Instituto de Historia Americana y Argentina, 2014. 364 p.: bibl., ill.

Pérez Stocco has written an examination of the peace process in the Chaco War (between Bolivia and Paraguay) and the role that Argentina, particularly Carlos Saavedra Lamas, played in that peace. She examines the variety of interests in the region, how Argentina navigated those, and the larger picture of the war and Argentine foreign policy during a chaotic time in global affairs—1932–35. The book is a welcome addition to a small historiography on Argentina and its foreign policy. [MLN]

1447 **Pigna, Felipe.** Manuel Belgrano: el hombre del bicentenario. Buenos Aires: Planeta, 2016. 437 p.: bibl.

The rise to political dominance of former president Kirchner witnessed the concomitant rise of a populist interpretation of Argentine history that, because it privileges assertions over facts, is unlikely to improve the state of Platine historiography. Felipe Pigna, a journalist-turned-scholar, has been at the forefront of this trend and invariably reflects its many contradictions. On the one hand, as demonstrated in this new work on Manuel Belgrano, his work is very readable. There are heroes and villains on all sides, and each appears to have an overly prescient grasp of the country's political trajectory; none are confounded by events beyond their control and none are average people just trying to muddle along. In some earlier period, such an interpretation would be discounted for verging on the romantic. Today, it seems more palatable because *la turba* likes it and because the scholarly elite does not, the latter fact being held as proof of its fundamental value. Readers who prefer to see historical analyses bolstered by evidence will want to consult Tulio Halperín. [TW]

1448 **Pittaluga, Roberto.** Soviets en Buenos Aires: la izquierda de la Argentina ante la revolución en Rusia. Buenos Aires: Prometeo Libros, 2015. 399 p.: bibl., index. (Colección Historia argentina)

Pittaluga's study of responses among the Argentine left to the Russian Revolution and its aftermath will be of great interest to those working on early 20th century leftist movments as well as those interested in texts and transnational linkages. Using an array of documents, including a great deal of theoretical background, the author explores the ways that leftist Argentines conceived of revolution and its meanings and their own understandings of the events in Russia. Through his work, Pittaluga demonstrates the differences of opinion on the Argentine left and the ways that those disagreements manifested themselves through the questions brought up by the Bolshevik Revolution. [MLN]

1449 **Plaza Navamuel, Rodolfo Leandro.** San Martín y Güemes: libertad para los pueblos de la Unión. 2o edición. Salta, Argentina: Centro de Investigaciones Genealógicas de Salta, Mundo Editorial, 2015. 134 p.: bibl., ill.

A journalistic treatment of Güemes and San Martín, broadly destitute of analysis and with little in it that is novel. [TW]

1450 **Población y sociedad en tiempos de lucha por la emancipación: Córdoba, Argentina, en 1813.** Edición de Sonia Colantonio. Córdoba, Argentina: CIECS, CONICET-UNC, 2013. 523 p.: bibl.

Slowly but surely, quantitative historians fill in the many lacunae that have thus far bedeviled our understanding of the interior provinces of Argentina during the first years of independence. The process has never been easy. Even now there is terra incognita that needs to be scouted. That said, every once in a while we encounter a truly solid work, and insofar as the province of Córdoba is concerned, this is clearly it. The editor and her associates have produced seven essays that can be considered together or apart. All the essays focus on demographic data derived from the 1813 census (and from other documentation held in the provincial archive). Life expectancy among different groups is examined, as are internal migrations and fertility, the status of children and the elderly, and the overall effects of militarization on a relatively isolated rural society. The research often confirms what we would expect of trends in such a place. For example, marriages were often informal—not because of social tolerance or heterodoxy but because of the lack of clerics or officials to notarize documents. But who would have thought Indians and pardos were more commonly encountered in the provincial capital than in the countryside? Demographers will be particularly impressed with this work; other scholars will use it occasionally, especially when they wish to test propositions derived exclusively from the Bonaerense case. [TW]

1451 **Podgorny, Irina** and **María Margaret Lopes.** El desierto en una vitrina: museos e historia natural en la Argentina, 1810–1890. Rosario, Argentina: Prohistoria Ediciones, 2014. 317 p.: bibl., ill., index. (Colección Historia de la ciencia; 8)

Since well before Charles Darwin visited Juan Manuel de Rosas at his military headquarters in Patagonia, European scientists displayed great interest in the natural history of Argentina—its flora, fauna, and the fossilized examples of its antediluvian creatures. It was only a matter of time before Argentine intellectuals took up an interest in the same things, celebrating the nation's natural wonders and attempting, after a fashion, to understand them, as if gaining a scientific knowledge of the *ombú* and the *vizcacha* were tantamount to a patriotic act. Irina Podgorny and Maria Margaret Lopes' study looks at this process by examining one of its more striking productions—public and private museums. Their work is superb, touching not only on the establishment of institutions in Buenos Aires, but describing in judicious detail the contributions of provincial museums, all of which had something interesting to offer. One particularly fascinating area that the authors describe is the theoretical debate engendered by various paleontologists regarding Argentina's prehistory and the effect that these loud disagreements had in orienting museum collections and interpretations. The authors erred, perhaps, in not consulting Stephen Bell's work on Aimé Bonpland (see *HLAS 68:1556*), but this one lacuna offers nothing more than the tiniest of quibbles. In every other particular, their study is excellent. [TW]

1452 **Política y cultura durante el "Onganiato": nuevas perspectivas para la investigación de la presidencia de Juan Carlos Onganía (1966–1970).** Compilación por Valeria Galván y Florencia Osuna. Rosario, Argentina: Prohistoria Ediciones, 2014. 197 p.: bibl. (Colección Actas; 26)

The book begins with an excellent historiographical discussion of the period known as the "Onganiato," citing the questions that had guided the (very few) works devoted to this period in Argentine history. Moving beyond what has already been covered (violence, and the liberal economic project which consolidated after 1976), the book focuses on new questions: namely the communitarian project (*comunitarismo*), the corporativist ideology, and the trajectories of the Catholic public servants. The book is divided into two sections: the first part focuses on social and political cultural changes; the second part deals with state projects and the public policies adopted by this government. [AMB]

1453 **Poy, Lucas.** Los primeros congresos del Partido Socialista argentino (1896–1908): consideraciones para un análisis social y político. (*Rev. Eur. Estud. Latinoam. Caribe*, 99, Oct. 2015, p. 47–67, tables, graphs)

Poy writes about the need for a more systematic study of the Socialist Party, and the methodological considerations historians should take into account. As an example, the author carefully examines the early congresses of the Party, giving readers a detailed account of the origins of the Socialist Party. Because the article is so narrowly focused, it is useful for its methodological discussions and consideration of the congresses between 1896–1908. [MLN]

1454 **Ramírez Braschi, Dardo.** Política correntina en tiempos de guerra: 1865–1870. Corrientes, Argentina: Moglia Ediciones, 2016. 131 p.: bibl.

The province of Corrientes has always had an anomalous character with its political loyalties oriented towards the Argentine Republic and yet with an underlying identity linked to a Guaraní past more redolent of Paraguay than of Buenos Aires. Normally, this unusual status inspires a reaction of simple curiosity, but in 1865, when the armies of Marshal Francisco Solano López invaded the province, its contradictions became strikingly apparent. As Dardo Ramírez Braschi points out in this slim but concise work, provincial politics split along three lines—a faction devoted to Buenos Aires and the liberal cause of President Mitre; a federal faction associated with Governor Urquiza of Entre Ríos (and the southern ranching elites generally); and a third faction, the smallest of the three, that chose open collaboration with Marshal López and the Paraguayans. After the latter were driven out and the provincial capital retaken by Allied troops, the province went to war with itself. While the great battles of Tuyutí and Curupayty were being fought across the border in Paraguay, in Corrientes, a series of desultory confrontations took place that, even if they ended in Liberal victory, still involved any number of compromises, deals, and broken promises. All this Ramírez Braschi details, using materials garnered from local newspapers and the provincial archive. The whole effect, which in some other context might be of limited interest, is a good deal more interesting, for it illustrates the problem of political consolidation at a particularly perilous moment for the nation. [TW]

1455 Ratto, Silvia. Redes políticas en la frontera bonaerense (1836–1873): crónica de un final anunciado. Bernal, Argentina: Universidad Nacional de Quilmes, 2015. 241 p.: bibl., ill. (Serie Investigación)

An attempt to analyze the social and political relations on the Bonaerense frontier between 1836 and 1873, with particular attention paid to the "diplomacy" practiced by indigenous leaders with their Creole counterparts and vice-versa. Generally speaking, this study promises more than it delivers, but is nonetheless is a useful contribution in a field where questions still outnumber answers. [TW]

1456 Recalde, Héctor. Clericalismo y anticlericalismo en América Latina (1810–1915): el caso de Argentina. Buenos Aires: GEU, Grupo Editor Universitario, 2016. 455 p.: bibl.

An interesting and well-crafted account of Church-state relations in Argentina during the era of secularization in the second half of the 19th century. Though lacking documentation from the Vatican archive, this study has the virtue of clarity in covering the various debates on marriages, cemeteries, and social policy, and does make up for the lack of primary documentation by offering a full analysis of Church policies as defined in the *Revista Eclesiástica del Arzobispado de Buenos Aires*. With some understatement, the author qualifies Church-state confrontations as a "love-hate relation." [TW]

1457 Regime der Anerkennung: Kämpfe um Wahrheit und Recht in der Aufarbeitung der argentinischen Militärdiktatur [Searching for recognition: the fight for law and rights in the historical reappraisal of the Argentine military dictatorship]. Edited by Alexander Hasgall. Bielefeld, Germany: Verlag, 2016. 328 p.: bibl. (Histoire; 95)

The author focuses on the notion of "recognition," i.e. how Argentine society slowly recognized the crimes perpetrated during the military dictatorship in Argentina from 1975 to 1983. He aims to show how the truth about these crimes, including torture and the estimated 30,000 murders, was slowly recognized. During the early days of the dictatorship, groups of parents such as the Madres de la Plaza de Mayo were nearly the only ones to speak openly about the desaparecidos in their demonstrations. Later, human rights NGOs worked on an international level to pressure for hearings in the US Congress. In the transition period to democracy, the first amnesty laws protected the perpetrators, later when they were abolished, the courts of justice were slow to document the killings and to punish those responsible. Likewise, the Army was averse to recognizing its involvement in crimes until 1995, which was a first step towards later trials of the main political figures and army members involved in human rights violations and assassinations. Truth seeking and the moral obligation of the democratic state to react to past violence were important for the "recognition" of these abuses. Thus documenting the fate of the desaparecidos became part of new power relations and gave the victims' families the possibility of acknowledging and coming to terms with their losses and traumas. [F. Obermeier]

1458 Representaciones de la política: provincias, territorios y municipios (1860–1955). Coordinación por Marta

Bonaudo. Buenos Aires: Ediciones Imago Mundi, 2017. 211 p.: bibl. (Colección Bitácora argentina)

This edited volume explores the political norms of the provinces of Tucumán, Santa Fe, Río Negro and Neuquén. The work also addresses the beginning of the modern administrative state and the ways that it took hold at the local level. [MLN]

1459 Richard Jorba, Rodolfo A. Empresarios ricos, trabajadores pobres: vitivinicultura y desarrollo capitalista en Mendoza, 1850–1918. Rosario, Argentina: Prohistoria Ediciones, 2010. 279 p.: bibl., ill., maps. (Colección Historia argentina; 8)

An extremely well-researched volume on Mendoza's wine industry and the society and economy it created. The book is particularly good for its analysis of the class divisions that plagued Mendoza's society and the ways it was manifested in politics and urban growth. Richard-Jorba includes many tables with quantitative data that will be of use to other scholars, and the work itself will be of interest to those working on topics related to the wine industry and economic growth of the provinces in the late 19th and early 20th centuries. [MLN]

1460 Rieznik, Marina. Los cielos del sur: los observatorios astronómicos de Córdoba y de La Plata, 1870–1920. Rosario, Argentina: Prohistoria Ediciones, 2011. 220 p.: bibl., index. (Colección Historia de la ciencia; 4)

A good contribution to the growing history of science in Argentina, focusing on the history of the observatories in Córdoba and La Plata. The author posits the notion of a "southern sky" that these observatories mapped and presented, and it allowed Argentine scientists to enter worldwide conversations and debates. Rieznik looks at the ways that the professionalization of the field, the creation of national institutions, and the consolidation of the nation state were entwined. The book will be of interest to a variety of scholars working on science and the late19th- and early 20th-century period. [MLN]

1461 Rojkind, Inés. El caso Sambrice: niños, prensa y política en Buenos Aires a fines del siglo XIX. (Iberoamericana/ Madrid, 15:60, dic. 2015, p. 87–100, bibl.)

Rojkind takes on the case of Tomás Sambrice, the 15-year-old would-be assassin of President Julio A. Roca. The author addresses political participation, media, and the ways ordinary people involved themselves in political movements. Sambrice was an immigrant and legal minor, as such, the case also brings up questions about immigration, childhood, and the meanings of being Argentine in the 1890s. [MLN]

1462 Roldán, Diego P. Circulación, difusión y masificación: el futbol en Rosario (Argentina), 1900–1940. (Secuencia/ México, 93, sept./dic. 2015, p. 137–161, bibl.)

An exploration of the expansion and massification of football in Rosario, Roldán approaches the topic from the early clubs, local competitions, and conflicts over fairness during play. This article is part of a slowly growing historiography of sport and football in particular in urban settings. [MLN]

1463 Ronchi, Verónica. La cooperación integral: historia del "Hogar Obrero". Buenos Aires: Ediciones Fabro, 2016. 541 p.: bibl.

The book chronicles the foundation, development and ultimate decline and death of the cooperative association "El Hogar Obrero," founded in Buenos Aires in 1905 by Juan B. Justo and Nicolas Repetto. Part of a larger program led by the Socialist Party, the initial objective was to help build homes for those who could not afford to; later, the cooperative added health assistance, bank, supermarkets, libraries, kindergartens, and other recreational spaces. The book moves chronologically until the cooperative's demise in 1991. Excellent work. [AMB]

1464 Roselli, Manuel H. Historia de Reconquista. Santa Fe, Argentina: UNL, Universidad Nacional del Litoral, 2017. 195 p.: bibl.

This is a local history of the sort that denizens of Wichita, Sioux City, and Amarillo are doubtlessly familiar with. In telling the story of colonization and settlement in the northern ranges of Santa Fe province, the author focuses fitfully on questions of land, of rural penury, of Indian raids, and political divisiveness leading up to the establishment of the town of Reconquista in 1872. The documentary bases for this particular study are rather thin, but one does not need to be José Hernández or Frederick Jackson Turner to recognize that the frontier produces more legends than definitive analyses. More work will have to be done in the archives. [TW]

1465 Rubé, Julio Horacio. Tiempos de guerra en América del Sur: Argentina y Chile 1826–1904: diplomacia, armas y estrategia. Buenos Aires: Editorial Eder, 2015. 644 p.: bibl.

It seems very odd in a study of Argentine-Chilean relations to refer in the title to "times of war" since the two countries never actually faced each other in such a conflict. That said, the competition between the two countries was very real, especially in the Patagonian territories during the late 19th century. Surrogates, usually in the form of provincial caudillos, did contest control in the bordering areas, and there was always bad blood expressed in public statements and foreign policy memoranda. Rubé's very thorough examination touches on all this, drawing on a quite vast array of documentary sources and secondary accounts. It is probably not the definitive work on the topic but at 644 pages, it certainly should not be ignored. [TW]

1466 Rubinzal, Mariela, and José Zanca. *Primeras Armas* y sus pequeños lectores en la Argentina católica de entreguerras. (*Iberoamericana/Madrid*, 15:60, dic. 2015, p. 117–132, bibl., photos)

A short article detailing the history of the Catholic children's magazine *Primeras armas* (published between 1935 and 1951). The publication was intended for boys, making them into "little soldiers" of Christ, and allowing them a limited voice as readers and occasional contributors. Catholic children's literature has received little scholarly attention and clearly deserves more. [MLN]

1467 Sarmiento, los Estados Unidos y la educación pública. Coordinación de Luis M. Savino. Buenos Aires: Centro de Estudios Americanos, 2015. 230 p.: bibl. (Serie Bicentenario)

Visitors to Boston who wish to take a walking tour of the city may chance to find among the many monuments to American patriots of the Revolutionary Age an unlikely statue of Domingo Faustino Sarmiento, whose accompanying brass plaque reads "A Friend of the American People." So he was. And if we would like to believe that friendship often manifests itself in imitation, we can fully understand why the Argentine president (1868–72) so wished to copy for his country the system of public education that pundits so regularly criticize in the US today. He had seen with his own eyes how primary and secondary schools had turned a disorderly North American population into a society of law and prosperity. And since he reasoned that his own country suffered from comparable restraints, it followed that the establishment of a similar system of public education could transform it into a modern nation. It did not quite happen that way, of course, but it was not for lack of trying. This compilation of 12 different studies shows how, with the help of US-based educational theorists and a small army of Yankee schoolmarms, Sarmiento tripled the number of students in the country in less than three years and saw Argentina's rate of illiteracy drop substantially. Sarmiento's various inspirations are touched on, as well as the challenges he faced in bringing his program to fruition. All the studies contained herein are good, but Javier F. García Basalos' article on Sarmiento' s objectives as defined in his short-lived journal *Ambas Americas* is particularly noteworthy. It shows that while "Don Yo" admired the North Americans, his support was not without its limits. In fact, what he liked about the North Americans was not necessarily, what they liked about themselves. [TW]

1468 Semán, Ernesto. Ambassadors of the working class: Argentina's international labor activists and Cold War democracy in the Americas. Durham: Duke University Press, 2017. 309 p.: bibl., index.

Focusing on the labor attachés sent around the world as emissaries of Perón's Argentina, Semán adds a fascinating chapter to the already-voluminous historiography around Peronism and labor, yet with a new twist. By sending these blue-collar workers, Perón was issuing a strong message to the US about the importance of economic nationalism and his unwillingness to bow to imperialist demands. A well-researched and documented work that will be of great interest to an array of scholars both on Argentina and international labor. [MLN]

1469 Sepúlveda, Patricia Graciela. Mujeres insurrectas: condición femenina y militancia en los '70. Bernal, Argentina: Universidad Nacional de Quilmes, Publicaciones Ciencias Sociales, 2015. 293 p.: bibl., ill. (Serie Tesis)

The author explores the lives of 15 women political activists during the 1970s in Argentina. Their stories were either given by themselves or members of their families. The author seeks to understand these women's struggles to be recognized and treated equally, within a context in which their positions went against prescribed gender roles. The book also interrogates how memory works. [AMB]

1470 Sobre los orígenes del peronismo: reseña histórica del Partido Justicialista de La Plata, 1945–1955. Dirección por Fernando Klappenbach. Esta edición ha sido auspiciada y declarada de interés cultural por la Secretaría de Cultura de la Nación. Buenos Aires: Editorial Docencia, 2014. 248 p.: bibl., ill. (Biblioteca testimonial del bicentenario)

Klappenbach and the other contributors to the volume explore the roots of Peronism in La Plata. The book contains many membership lists, quotes from Peronist literature of the time, and an appendix of a variety of primary sources. The book will be of most use to scholars of Peronism—it is not a narrative history. [MLN]

1471 Soler, Ricardo, and **Raúl H. Pistorio.** Ricardo Balbín: biografía documentada. Colaboración de Rolando R. Carreras y Humberto J. Vignoli. Prólogo por Juan Manuel Casella. Buenos Aires: Corregidor, 2014. 331 p.: bibl., ill.

This biography of Ricardo Balbín starts in the 1930s, documenting his first years in politics. It details his work for the newspaper *Adelante* (many of the articles he published there are included), and it gathers comments from various important politicians. It also contains a list of letters he received from citizens regarding the imprisonment or disappearance of family members. [AMB]

1472 Sorín, Daniel. John William Cooke: la mano izquierda de Perón. Buenos Aires: Planeta, 2014. 622 p.: bibl. (Espejo de la Argentina)

A biography of John William Cooke, the man named by Juan Domingo Perón to lead the Peronist Party following the coup against him in 1955 and subsequent exile. The work is well-organized and written in an engaging style—it will be useful to those working on Peronism as well as those researching the 1960s and the tangled politics of that era. [MLN]

1473 Sosa, Norma. Cazadores de plumas en la Patagonia: singulares intercambios ente tehuelches y cristianos. Villa Adelina, Argentina: Patagonia Sur Libros, 2015. 207 p.: bibl., ill.

Focusing on the late 19th-century feather trade in Patagonia, Sosa explores the lives of the array of characters involved, from indigenous Tehuelches to marginalized white Argentines to Europeans looking for fortune. Each chapter is told in a narrative style and is geared more toward popular readers than professional historians. [MLN]

1474 Souroujon, Gastón. El peronismo vuelve a enamorar: la articulación de un imaginario político durante el gobierno de Menem. Rosario, Argentina: Homo Sapiens Ediciones, 2014. 273 p.: bibl., ill. (Colección Politeia)

Souroujon seeks to understand the rise of Carlos Saúl Menem in the 1980s, by analyzing the need to maintain alive Peronist symbols (but distancing himself from the trade union leadership) within a liberal democratic language proposed by Raúl Alfonsín. Most importantly, the author stresses that a government's legitimacy and identity can only be achieved by successfully through the leadership's successful articulation of a political imaginary. The book covers topics such as the uses of Perón by Menem, the construction of a charismatic relationship, the political myth of Argentina as a first world country, the ideas about neoliberal forces, among others. [AMB]

1475 Stagnaro, Andrés. La Ley de Accidentes del Trabajo y los debates promovidos para la creación de un fuero laboral (Argentina, 1904–1946). (*Estud. Soc./Santa Fe*, 26:50, enero/junio 2016, p. 111–143)

A history of the debates surrounding labor laws and a court specifically designed for labor, which was eventually legislated in 1944. The article is narrowly focused on the law and legal debates that coursed through the political process and will be of great interest to legal and labor historians. For a related study on the Ley de Accidentes Laborales, see item **1411**. [MLN]

1476 Storni, Alfonsina. Escritos: imágenes de género. Colección dirigida por Carlos Dámaso Martínez. Villa María, Argentina: EDUVIM, 2014. 362 p.: bibl. (Letras y pensamiento en el Bicentenario)

A newly issued collection of the works of early 20th-century writer and feminist icon Alfonsina Storni. The book is of short-form writing, not the poetry for which she is more widely known, much of which was published in *La Nación*. [MLN]

1477 Tarcus, Horacio. El socialismo romántico en el Río de la Plata (1837–1852). Buenos Aires: Fondo de Cultura Económica, 2016. 382 p.: bibl., index. (Sección de obras de historia)

Students today are apt to conflate socialist theory with Marxism, thus missing a major chapter in the historical development of modern ideology. But readers of the mid-19th century were much attracted to the romantic socialism that predated Marx, and saw in the writings of Saint-Simon, Fourier, and Louis Blanc an appealing blueprint for the future. Those few readers in Buenos Aires and Montevideo who had access to such writings, which they saw as frankly revolutionary, looked to the Romantics for some degree of guidance. This new study by Horacio Tarcus examines this process between 1837, when socialist writings first appeared in the porteño press, and 1852, when these same ideas gained a greater hearing with the fall of Rosas. As a history of ideas, this study is first-rate, and particularly shines in its examination of how new concepts were propagated in the Platine urban environment, finding their apogee with Esteban Echeverria's *Dogma Socialista* and the writings of Alberdi. A particular strength of Tarcus's study is the attention he places on Montevideo, where the exile community gave considerable energy to the debate on the future of the Platine states. [TW]

1478 Tarruella, Ramón D. 1914: Argentina y la Primera Guerra Mundial. Buenos Aires: Aguilar, 2014. 220 p.: bibl.

An account written in a narrative, journalistic style of Argentina's relationship to the events of the First World War in Europe. The book contains few notes and will be of limited value to scholars, but would be of interest to a popular audience or lower-level undergraduates. [MLN]

1479 Territorios de la historia, la política y la memoria. Compilación de Marta Philp. Córdoba, Argentina: Alción Editora, 2013. 256 p.: bibl.

The book brings together historians from the province of Córdoba working on historiographical and political issues as well as on memory. The first part focuses on the history of Córdoba; the second discusses two authors (Carlos S. A Segreti and Sergio Bagú) and their historiographical interventions. The third section introduces works on the Communist Party, and on the links among political power, citizenship, and human rights. [AMB]

1480 Una y otra vez, Sarmiento. Coordinación de Mauricio Meglioli y Ricardo de Titto. Buenos Aires: Prometeo Libros, 2016. 283 p.: bibl., index.

The title tells it all: this is a grab-bag of 17 short studies on Domingo Faustino Sarmiento's place in the broad trajectory of Argentine history. It is the result of a plan launched in 2011 by the Biblioteca Franklin in San Juan to sponsor a series of talks on Sarmiento offered by various historians, essayists, and political scientists. All the usual names are here: Natalio Botana, Félix Luna, Tulio Halperín, and Noé Jitrik. And then there are a few figures who, though less well-known, offer quite sharp observations on "Don Yo" and his efforts to define (or redefine) Argentina. As a whole, the published talks seem somewhat iconoclastic, which, depending on cases, can be a strength or a weakness. Thoughtful readers will either smile at this or shake their heads, but doubtlessly they will find things of interest here without too much difficulty. Sarmiento continues to fascinate. [TW]

1481 Valko, Marcelo. Cazadores de poder: apropiadores de indios y tierras. Buenos Aires: Peña Lillo: Ediciones Continente, 2015. 331 p.: bibl., ill. (Biblioteca Artillería del pensamiento)

A narrative history written in a literary style about the campaigns of attrition against the indigenous. Though it will be of interest to some scholars, the book is primarily intended for a popular audience. [MLN]

1482 Varela, Gustavo. Tango y política: sexo, moral burguesa y revolución en Argentina. Buenos Aires: Ariel, 2016. 250 p.: bibl. (Historia)

A history of tango with particular emphasis on the culture and society from which it came, Varela's book covers topics that have been presented in great detail in other works. Although the book is not making new arguments, the mix of primary and secondary sources make it accessible and enjoyable for scholars and popular audiences alike. [MLN]

Vence Conti, Agustina. Deuda externa y gobernabilidad en Argentina: la historia de Roca, Pellegrini y el proyecto de conversión de deuda de 1901. See *HLAS 73:1888*.

1483 Vezzetti, Hugo. Psiquiatría, psicoanálisis y cultura comunista: batallas ideológicas en la guerra fría. Buenos Aires: Siglo Veintiuno Editores, 2016. 290 p. (Sociología y política)

Focusing on the period following the Second World War until the 1960s, Vezzetti explores the era in which psychiatry and psychoanalysis were moving toward a more socially integrated approach and away from a strictly medical understanding of mental health issues. As part of this turn in Argentina, many practitioners were coming to their work from a leftist perspective, often explicitly communist. Part intellectual history, part transnational history of psychiatry and psychoanalysis in the Cold War (Buenos Aires to Paris and back), Vezzetti brings to life a little-explored chapter in Argentina's history. [MLN]

1484 Vignoli, Marcela. Sociabilidad y cultura política: la Sociedad Sarmiento de Tucumán, 1880–1914. Rosario: Prohistoria Ediciones, 2015. 163 p.: bibl., ill. (Colección Historia política hoy; 04)

A narrowly focused dissertation on the intellectual Sociedad Sarmiento, which acted as a site of male sociability and learning in the years before the establishment of the University of Tucumán in 1914. The members of the Sociedad, most of them graduates of the newly formed public school system and many of them teachers in that same system, were part of a new chapter in the history of Tucumán. The upwardly-mobile members of the Sociedad showed the ways that non-elite men were able to use education and sociability to be more fully part of the civic and political life of the province. [MLN]

1485 Vilar, Juan Antonio. La Confederación Argentina: época de Rosas, 1829–1852. Paraná, Argentina: Facultad de Ciencias de la Educación, Universidad Nacional de Entre Ríos, 2016. 154 p.: bibl. (Serie académica)

The term "confederation" has an odd character in Argentine historiography, with some scholars limiting its use to that period in which the country was dominated by Justo José de Urquiza (and its capital was at Paraná and not Buenos Aires) while other scholars use it as a synonym for the entire early national period, that is, from the time of independence in 1810 up to the battle of Pavón 51 years later. Probably the least-encountered definition of "confederation" has the term demarcating the governorship of Juan Manuel de Rosas (1829–52). It is this latter definition that Professor Vilar places front and center in this rather abbreviated account. His thesis holds that the Rosista regime represented an alliance between provincial federalists and Bonaerense landowners who thought of themselves as federalists, but who behaved like the centralists they claimed to oppose. This idea is not very original. Indeed, Adolfo Saldías argued something very similar to it during the late 19th century and Miron Burgin did the same 50 years later. As an Entrerriano, Vilar might be expected to add a provincial dimension to this rather complex story, but he does not get very far from a process of cherry-picking from various classical and a few revisionist texts. He comes nowhere near offering the documents-rich analysis that he promises in the one-page prologue. Indeed, the only detail that his book offers that was new to me was where Vilar observes that today's Correntinos still harbor resentment toward the Entrerrianos over the latter's support for Rosas at Laguna Limpia and Vences. This seems an improbably long time to hold a grudge. As for the rest, there is not really much here. Readers will want to stick to Beatríz Bosch, José Luis Busaniche, Tulio Halperín Donghi, and of course, Saldías. [TW]

¿Y el pueblo dónde está?: Contribuciones para una historia popular de la revolución de independencia en el Río de la Plata en el siglo XIX rioplatense. See item 1047.

1486 Yurman, Pablo. Nación y confederación: Rosas y el Pacto Federal de 1831. Buenos Aires: Imago Mundi, 2014. 139 p.: bibl., index. (Colección Bitácora Argentina)

The Pacto Federal of 1831 has received relatively little attention from modern historians and we have to go back almost to the time of Adolfo Saldías to find treatments that focus on its juridico-institutional character. Both modern scholars and modern readers, it would seem, prefer history driven by the ambitions of men—either heroes or villains—than by the legal machines that they create. It is thus a good day when a scholar tackles the Federal Pact, which set the structural parameters for government in Argentina that were eventually subsumed by the legal structures of the Confederation. Yurma concentrates on the creation and operation of the Representative Commission set up by the Pacto, which supposedly united the interests of Buenos Aires with those of Santa Fe, Entre Ríos, and Corrientes. This is an interpretive work and introduces little in the way of new research, but, historiographically, it is well balanced. Mainly for the specialist in the Rosas era.[TW]

1487 Zubizarreta, Ignacio. Unitarios en Argentina ¿los buenos o los malos de la historia?: la contrucción antagónica de la imagen de una facción política. (*Iberoamericana*/Madrid, 49, March 2013, p. 67–85, bibl.)

One would think that the time had long gone when it would be necessary to point out the limitations of a dualistic, "unitarian versus federal" interpretation of Argentine historiography. This author appears to think otherwise. He wishes to remind us that there was more to Unitarian thinking than the parodies produced by Rosista propagandists and their spiritual heirs in the 20th century. Fair enough, but this was already old news 40 or 50 years ago. [TW]

1488 Zubizarreta, Ignacio. Unitarios: historia de la facción política que diseñó la Argentina moderna. Buenos Aires: Sudamericana, 2014. 219 p.: bibl.

Zubizarreta traces the history of the Unitarian party from its beginnings in 1820, just after independence, to its return in 1852 after the fall of Juan Manuel de Rosas. The author is not just interested in the liberal ideas of the party, which acted as the opposition to Rosas, but in the legacy of Unitarian ideas in Argentina. Exploring the nature of centralism, factionalism, and the importance of interrogating European models, Zubizarreta has written a book that will be of use to scholars of the early 19th century and Argentine political history overall. [MLN]

PARAGUAY

1489 Abreu, Sergior. La vieja trenza: la alianza porteño-lusitana en la Cuenca del Plata (1800–1875). 2a edición. Montevideo: Planeta, 2014. 413 p.: bibl.

An interpretive work that asserts the existence of a long-term alliance between Portuguese/Brazilian and Spanish/Argentine interests in the broader Platine region. The author, who was foreign minister in the Lacalle government, was born in Paraguay, and sees a natural connection between his birth country and Uruguay, both of which were victimized by the "alliance." This argument adopts the general parameters of Luis Alberto de Herrera and other Blanco historians, but is not especially convincing. For every instance of supposed cooperation between Rio de Janeiro and Buenos Aires in the period under consideration, there were two or three instances of sharp rivalry. Even the war of 1864–70, which did inspire an alliance between the two, were largely forced on Brazil and Argentina by the unexpected bellicosity of the Paraguayan president.[TW]

1490 Alonso González, José Luis and **Juan Manuel Peña López.** El año de la sangre: la guerra contra el Paraguay: 1865–

1866. Córdoba, Argentina: Abrazos, 2017. 478 p.: bibl.

A rather spotty account of military action during the first year of the Triple Alliance War, or to be more specific, of the period from October 1865 to October 1866, which the authors offer as a more salient chronology. It is not very obvious why they chose to cover these particular months, and in any case, they fail to add much to the classic accounts of Beverina, Centurión, and Tasso Fragoso. Alonso and Peña appear to be somewhat indifferent to citing sources, which makes this work seem more, not less, derivative of the earlier treatments. [TW]

1491 Baratta, Maria Victoria. ¿Aliados o enemigos?: las representaciones de Brasil en el debate público argentino durante la guerra del Paraguay, 1864–1870. (*Rev. Hist./São Paulo*, 172, jan./junho 2015, p. 43–75, bibl., photo)

A short but suggestive look at how Argentine newspapers promoted the alliance with Brazil at the time of the Paraguayan War, and how this promotion itself shaped the development of a national identity in the 1860s. [TW]

1492 The Chaco War: environment, ethnicity, and nationalism. Edited by Bridget María Chesterton. London; Oxford; New York: Bloomsbury Academic, an imprint of Bloomsbury Publishing Plc, 2016. 219 p.: bibl., ill., index, maps.

This is a strikingly interesting compilation of studies on the 1932–1935 Chaco War between Paraguay and Bolivia. Unlike the standard military analyses usually associated with this topic, this study takes as its focus the overlap between the natural environment of this spectacularly isolated region and the heated politics that the two countries developed as part of their respective notions of nationalism. This overlap owes much of its historiographical innovation to Chesterton's previous work, *Grandchildren of Solano López* (2013), which stressed the linkages between exploration and national identity. Here she spreads her wings even more widely, overseeing eight other scholars in their examinations of such subjects as Bolivian labor unions during the conflict; the role and reactions of indigenous peoples; the much-referred to but little studied factor of foreign oil companies and their supposed manipulation of politics in Asunción and La Paz; and the use of pack animals. The contributors offer much that has never been previously considered. All of these studies are attractive, but Ben Nobbs-Thiessen's piece "Channeling Modernity" offers something more in its happily ironic reminder that modern engineering was once regarded as a magical catalyst for the Chaco. This connects the dreams of the region's past with the not-quite realized promises of the present, and demonstrates that utopian estimations never quite left the Chaco scene. For Bolivian historian's comment, see item **1201**. [TW]

1493 Chesterton, Bridget María. Composing gender and class: Paraguayan letter writers during the Chaco War, 1932–1935. (*J. Women's Hist.*, 26:3, Fall 2014, p. 59–80)

This article considers how Paraguayan gender and class norms were subverted during the Chaco War (1932–35) with Bolivia so that lower-class men in Paraguay could correspond with elite women in the capital. The article uses letters from private Asunción collections to narrate how women contained any perceived romantic advances though the use of the taboo mother-son sexual relationship. And, as the article recounts, although men and women of different classes corresponded during the war in order to maintain morale, after the conflagration, these relationships quickly, and often tersely, burned out. [BMC]

1494 Chesterton, Bridget María and Anatoly V. Isaenko. A white Russian in the green hell: military science, ethnography, and nation building. (*HAHR*, 94:4, Nov. 2014, p. 615–648, bibl., maps)

Except in the most exaggerated writings of certain nationalists, the Chaco Boreal rarely receives attention as a catalytic factor in the consolidation of Paraguayan identity. Scholars and casual observers would not be remiss in thinking the region an afterthought, appropriate to a discussion of Mennonite colonization or the 1932–35 war with Bolivia, but otherwise unworthy of consideration. This innovative article by Chesterton and Isaenko shows how wrong such a generalization can be. While on the surface a conventional account of White Russian General Ivan Belaieff's mapping of the Chaco interior in the 1920s, in fact this study shows how the region captured the imagination of Paraguayans who, against all the historical antecedents, proceeded to make it their own. Belaieff had charted portions of the Caucasus in earlier years and had similarly made them recognizably Russian in the minds of many denizens of Moscow and St. Petersburg. The analogy, which suggests structural similarities between Chechens or Circassians and Makka or Toba, certainly seems attractive. So does the argument that military geographers and ethnographers can play a key role in formulating national identities rather than simply filling in the empty spaces on the map. Chesterton and Isaenko have done a fine job of research in unusual documents, many of them in the Russian language. They have succeeded in turning a topic that on the surface seems arcane into something central to modern thinking in Paraguay. [TW]

1495 Díaz-Duhalde, Sebastián. La última guerra: cultura visual de la guerra contra Paraguay. Barcelona: Sans Soleil Ediciones, 2015. 263 p.: bibl., index. (Pigmalión)

Scholars of visual culture and art theorists may occasionally find things of interest in this quick look at how painters and sketch artists addressed the Paraguayan War (1864–70). Historians will find it sorely incomplete, ignoring as it does the famous woodcut prints of *El Centinela* and *Cabichuí*, and generally leaving aside any consideration of Brazilian images on the war. Readers interested in a fuller exposition should turn to Miguel Angel Cuarterolo, Lucrecia Johansson, Ricardo Salles, and Ticio Escobar. [TW]

1496 Duarte, Luis María. José Irala: política y diplomacia paraguaya a principios del siglo XX. Asunción: Intercontinental Editora, 2014. 361 p.: bibl.

This diplomatic history of Paraguay lucidly argues that the narrative of Paraguayan diplomatic isolation is a myth that must be deconstructed. Written by a former politician, this text adds to Paraguay's notable diplomatic histories of the 20th century, particularly the voluminous work that has been done on the Chaco War. Although the text is ostensibly about José Irala—a Paraguayan diplomat—as noted in the title, this work also outlines the larger struggles and development of the Paraguayan diplomatic coups. The text is bound to be a classic in the history of Paraguayan diplomacy. [BMC]

1497 Fuentes Armadans, Claudio José. La maldición del legionario: cómo se contruyó un estigma político autoritario en el Paraguay. Asunción: Editorial Tiempo de Historia, 2016. 380 p.: bibl., ill.

An exciting contribution to Paraguayan intellectual history by a young Paraguay scholar that recounts how the word *legionario* was used by various Paraguayan political parties from the end of the War of the Triple Alliance (1864–70) up to the present day to demonstrate disloyalty to nation or traitors. *Legionarios* were Paraguayans who joined the allies—Brazil, Argentina, and Uruguay—to fight the Paraguayan troops. The text uses varied sources, including political speeches, newspapers, personal correspondence, to name a few, to demonstrate that all political parties and even international actors use the term *legionaries* when trying to undermine a political enemy. [BMC]

1498 La Guerra del Paraguay en primera persona. Edición de Liliana María Brezzo. Asunción: Editorial Tiempo de Historia, 2015. 347 p.: ill., maps, facsim.

This book is a rich set of documents collected by the Argentine Estanislao Zeballos in the late 19th century in the hopes of putting together a text to be titled *Historia de la Guerra del Paraguay*. His intentions had been to narrate the history of the war through its major actors. His project, however, never came to fruition. The introduction to this work by Liliana Brezzo outlines the life of Zeballos, how the documents were collected, and what Zeballos had planned to write. What survives in this volume is a valuable collection of oral interviews and correspondence between Zeballos and various participants of the war. These sources amount to an oral history of the War of the Triple Alliance before oral history was a formal historical subdiscipline. [BMC]

1499 **Salum-Flecha, Antonio.** Historia diplomática del Paraguay: de 1811 hasta nuestros días. Asunción: Intercontinental Editora, 2012. 596 p.: bibl., ill.

Text is a revised edition of book originally published in 1983 and again in 1990. This classic study of Paraguayan nationalism and law is used in law schools in Paraguay to teach diplomacy. It outlines the various international agreements that Paraguay entered into with its neighbors. In particular the text narrates the "unfair" and "unequal' treatment of the terms of the end of the War of the Triple Alliance in 1870. Describes how the treaty led to various other "unbalanced" treaties, in particular those related to border negotiations with Argentina and Brazil. This is not a diplomatic history of those who negotiated the treaties, but rather a close legal study surrounding the text of various treaties, which accounts for its thematic, not chronological organization. [BMC]

1500 **Testimonios para no olvidar: entrevistas a víctimas de la dictadura, a 26 años del golpe.** Entrevistas de Elvira Olmedo Zorrilla. Asunción: Servilibro, 2015. 218 p.: ill.

Olmedo is a Paraguayan journalist who interviews survivors of the brutal Stroessner region. The text is an oral history of the dictatorship and each subject interviewed was asked about his or her experiences and the result of those experiences. She does not offer any synthesis or analysis of the interviews. There is however a notable section about the repression of the press as various journalists are asked what role the press played in either propping up or opposing the regime. [BMC]

1501 **Uma tragédia americana: a Guerra do Paraguai sob novos olhares.** Organización de Fernando da Silva Rodrigues y Fernando Velôzo Gomes Pedrosa. Curitiba, Brazil: Editora Prismas, 2015. 583 p.: bibl., ill. (some color), map, portraits. (Coleção História militar e estratégia)

Another grab-bag of article-length studies on the 1864–1870 Triple Alliance War, neither better nor worse than the usual run of such compilations. The editors are hoping that the various authors will explore the relation of their narrow topics to the historiographical trend that scholars in today's Brazil call the Nova História Militar. The authors tend to resist that packaging, however, and demand that their work be considered on its own basis. By that measure, of the sixteen studies presented, only four really count as being strictly original: that by Francisco José Corréa-Martins on the participation of children in the conflict; that by Alberto del Pino Menck on the photography occasioned by the struggle; that by Marcelo Santos Rodrigues on the celebrations that were held to note the end of the war; and that by Silva Rodrigues on life-pensions and veterans' claims in the early 1900s left over from Paraguay 30 years earlier. [TW]

1502 **White, John Howard.** Prodigal sons and beardless machos: labor, migration, and masculinity at Itaipú Binacional, Alto Paraná, Paraguay, 1974–1980. (*HAHR*, 94:4, Nov. 2014, p. 649–679, bibl., ill., photos)

This article examines the construction of Paraguayan masculinity in the borderlands region between Paraguay and Brazil during the building of Itaipú dam during the 1970s. The author mines the newspaper of the Paraguayan business Conempa to explain how a nation with an agricultural workforce struggled to meet the demands of a large industrial project. White's work is one of the first studies about the construction of masculinity in Paraguay and thus an important contribution to gender studies for the nation. It is one of the many new projects on Itaipú currently underway by American-based researchers. [BMC]

URUGUAY

1503 **Artigas hoy: testimonios sobre historia Uruguaya.** Edición de Gonzalo Abella *et al.* Montevideo: Ediciones Cruz del Sur, 2016. 196 p.: bibl., ill., map.

Eight different scholars (or aficionados) of José Gervasio Artigas offer snippets of autobiography along with assorted observations on the Protector de los Pueblos Libres. Nothing new here. [TW]

1504 **Azcuy Ameghino, Eduardo.** Historia de Artigas y la independencia argentina. Buenos Aires: Ediciones CICCUS, 2015. 390 p.: bibl.

Because the Uruguayans wish to portray José Gervasio Artigas as their national hero, there is a tendency in the historiography to downplay his role in the broader Platine region, which was extensive but also ambiguous. Azcuy Ameghino certainly recognizes the extent of Artigas' contribution to regional politics but is less forthcoming on the ambiguity. This study, which originally appeared in the early 1990s, portrays Artigas not so much as a rural caudillo, which is the traditional depiction, but as a convinced democrat and social reformer, especially innovative in matters of land redistribution. Such an interpretation has been part of the left-revisionist corpus of Argentine historiography for some time and certainly deserves to be taken seriously. That said, it almost goes without saying that it is a risky position to maintain because it is based so fundamentally on what Artigas said rather than what he did. And he said a great many things, some of which contradict Azcuy Ameghino's thesis. The latter's work does depend on a base of documents drawn fitfully from the Archivo Artigas and the AGN, however. And in an age where historians appear to be long on assertions and short on the use of evidence, that surely is a point in his favor. [TW]

1505 Berro: la obra de un estadista. Edición de Ernesto Berro Hontou. Montevideo: Ediciones de la Plaza, 2015. 382 p., 16 unnumbered leaves of plates: bibl., ill. (Los Blancos; III)

The Berro family has produced several important figures in the political history of the Oriental Republic and in that of the Blanco (or National) Party. In this case, we find a passable biography of Bernardo Berro (1803–1868) by one of his descendants (aided by five other Blanco historians). While the work does veer a bit too often into apologia, it confirms many details taken from Berro's own correspondence and from 19th-century newspapers. Unfortunately, the work throws no new light on the tragic—and somewhat convoluted—events of February 1868, during which don Bernardo was murdered at the same time as his rival, the Colorado caudillo Venancio Flores. [TW]

1506 Borges, Leonardo and **Armando Olveira Ramos.** El enigma de Purificación. Montevideo: Editorial Fin de Siglo, 2015. 198 p.: bibl., ill., maps.

The quest for new pieces in the jigsaw puzzle of Artiguismo can seem very compulsive on occasion. Usually scholars or antiquarians turn up a new letter or two that they hope will throw sufficient light on the figure of José Gervasio Artigas to suggest broader conclusions. But the majority of the new found pieces end up being just that—pieces. The present effort will likely take a similar trajectory. The author is interested in determining the location of Purificación, Artigas's "capital" in the Uruguayan countryside. He writes that many sites have been argued for, from a camp along the Río Negro in the southwest to another spot on the Río Daymán in the northwest. Since the "capital" was temporary and mobile, the location could have been both, or either, or neither. Mr. Borges is inclined to think that Purificación was situated on or near the Heredero Ranch (near the confluence of the Daymán and they Uruguay), but can offer no preponderance of evidence one way or the other. Nor is his assertion that this is an important consideration all that convincing in itself. [TW]

1507 Chagas, Jorge; and **Gustavo Trullen.** Banco La Caja Obrera: una historia, 1905–2001. Montevideo: Perro Andaluz Ediciones, 2009. 439 p.: bibl., ill.

Founded in 1905, severely damaged by the economic crisis in Argentina in 1982, and closed in 2001, the Caja Obrera served, according to the authors, not only a place of financial importance in Uruguay, but also a human one. They note that the bank formed a community that is fundamental to understanding Uruguayan history in the 20th century. The authors credit the bank with developing modern advertising, institutionalizing medical care, and generally helping to modernize the country. The text is full of oral testimonies to validate the authors' premise that the bank was a progressive influence over Uruguayan finance and society until its closure. Most interesting—although not well developed is the chapter on female employees of the bank who first entered in 1950. Text does border on the hagiographic, if such a thing is possible for an institution. [BMC]

1508 Dotta Ostria, Mario and **Rodolfo González Rissotto.** Leandro Gómez: artiguista, masón, defensor heroico de la independencia nacional. Montevideo: Ediciones de la Plaza, 2014. 547 p., 12 pages of plates: bibl., ill. (some color), color map.

Raymond Chandler once wrote that there are "flustered old ladies of both sexes (and no sex) and almost all ages who like their murders scented with magnolia." Such would appear to be the case with Masonic historians who seek to find in the clandestine machinations of their lodges the explanation for every turn of event in their country's past. In this case, two Freemasons (one a repentant communist) address the career of Leandro Gómez, the Blanco hero who died facing Brazilian interventionists during the Flores rebellion of 1864–65. Gómez has always attracted the attention of Blanco apologists, probably because so few figures in Uruguayan political life at that time can be called heroic. But Dotta Ostría and González Rissotto take their praise to a whole new level, qualifying Gómez as an "integral man," noteworthy for his sense of honor and decency that contrasts so vividly in their minds with today's politicians. Not surprisingly, he, too, was a Freemason, a proponent of public education and responsible charity. Dotta and González are both traditional scholars who use standard empirical methodologies, and their study works fairly well as political history. Their celebration of the Freemasons' role in situating Gómez, on the other hand, is a bit farfetched. [TW]

1509 **Giorgi, Alvaro de.** Sanguinetti: la otra historia del pasado reciente. Montevideo: Editorial Fin de Siglo, 2014. 319 p.: bibl.

This intellectual biography of Julio M. Sanguinetti, president of Uruguay after the dictatorships of the 1970s and the 1980s, outlines his major intellectual contributions to Uruguayan politics by studying his speeches and his journalistic contributions, in particular those written immediately following the fall of the dictatorship. He is studied in close comparison to Batlle, although the author does not see him as the intellectual child of Batlle. The text seeks to put Sanguinetti in line with other great Uruguayan political intellectuals. [BMC]

1510 **Maggi, Carlos.** El libro de Artigas. Montevideo: Editorial Fin de Siglo, 2014. 143 p.: facsimiles.

Carlos Maggi was a Colorado politician, a skilled political essayist, and probably one of the greatest promoters of the traditional nationalist depiction of the Protector de los Pueblos Libres. In the 1950s, hardly a book or article was written on Artigas that did not reflect his influence (or authorship). But as his ongoing debate with Guillermo Vásquez Franco at the beginning of the new century has illustrated, Maggi long ago ceased producing new interpretations. The present study promises work that is "fresh, intelligent and audacious," but delivers very little that has not been seen before. [TW]

1511 **Magri, Altair.** De José Batlle y Ordóñez a José Mujica: ideas, debates y políticas de vivienda en Uruguay entre 1900 y 2012. Montevideo: Comisión Sectoral de Investigación Científica (CSIC) de la Universidad de la República, 2015. 191 p.: bibl. (Biblioteca plural)

A social scientist describes the complexities of housing in 20th-century Uruguay and specifically Montevideo in this study. The opening chapters consider the larger theoretical questions concerning housing in Europe and Uruguay's regional neighbors. The later chapters consider the role of public financing and housing legislation. The later chapters are broken down into smaller units of time (a decade or two) with a close statistical analysis of housing and related legislation in each time period. There is little analysis of how these statistics influenced the everyday lives of Uruguayans. [BMC]

1512 **Martínez, Virginia.** Los rusos de San Javier: perseguidos por el zar, perseguidos por la dictadura uruguaya: de Vasili Lubkov a Vladimir Roslik. Segunda edición. Montevideo: Ediciones de la Banda Oriental, 2013. 298 p.: bibl., 32 unnumbered pages of plates, ill.

A study completed on the 100th anniversary of the founding of the Russian settlement of San Javier in Uruguay. This text outlines the original struggles of the community in Uruguay. Already outsiders in Russia because of their religious beliefs, this small community of Russians who separated from the Russian Orthodox Church and immigrated to Uruguay in search of a better life. They struggled economically and were one of the least successful immigrant groups according to Uruguayan politicians, who held the group in contempt both because of their unusual religious practices, lack of economic success, and their founder's Vasili Lubkov's relations with young women. The group was the object of suspicion during the Cold War because of their Russian heritage. The text is well researched and contains transcriptions of the original sources that were used to produce the book. [BMC]

1513 Morales, Andrés. Fútbol, identidad y poder, (1916–1930). Montevideo: Editorial Fin de Siglo, 2013. 214 p.: bibl.

This study of the politics of *fútbol* in Uruguay does not bother with the history of play nor players, but rather considers how politics influenced the creation of teams in Uruguay and later, how ideas of nationalism shaped international participation for the Uruguayan national team. The text is highly influenced by the works of Antonio Gramsci, Benedict Anderson, and Eric Hobsbawm, and as such considers how ideas of hegemony, identity, and power created the Uruguayan *fútbol* culture. Much more than a simply a sport history, it is a political, institutional, and intellectual history of Uruguay. [BMC]

1514 Nocera, Eduardo Luis. Quién es Artigas: viajando tras sus pasos. Tomo 1, Viajando tras sus pasos. Tomo 2, Entre Buenos Aires y Montevideo. Merlo, Argentina: Instituto Superior Dr. Arturo Jauretche, 2015–2016. 2 v: ill. (Colección Patria grande)

A team of minor revisionist historians associated with the Vivian Trías Institute goes on a tour, passing through all the territories where Artigas is said to have operated, from Montevideo and the Uruguayan interior to Paraguay. Along the way, they meet with various scholars and sundry antiquarians and ask some interesting questions, most of which they appear to already know the answers to. For the diligent reader willing to plow through two volumes, both of which are over 600 pages in length, an occasional nugget (or glitter of pyrite) may be gleaned from the creek bed. [TW]

1515 Palermo, Eduardo R. Tierra esclavizada: el norte uruguayo en la primera mitad del siglo XIX. Montevideo: Tierradentro Ediciones, 2013. 303 p.: bibl., ill., maps.

In a little country with a relatively large capital city, it is sometimes easy to forget that under-studied regions have added their own portion of pepper and salt to the *puchero* of national history. The setting here is the Uruguayan north, a land of flat plains that merges without geographical interruption into Brazil's Rio Grande do Sul. The proximity to Brazil presented the region with an unusual status—for it was through those territories that runaway slaves passed on their way south to freedom in the early 19th century. The north, in this sense, bears some resemblance to the free states providing way-stations on the "underground railroad" of the US, but there the similarity ends. As Palermo points out, the region tolerated the "peculiar institution" until 1846, and Afro-Uruguayans suffered much as their Brazilian cousins did until that time. They created a vibrant culture, true enough, but their status as slaves was what defined them. Though Palermo's study of this region and its people should not be counted in the same breath as the excellent work of Alex Boruki, still it is a workman-like effort, studded with archival references, tables, and interesting illustrations. On this basis, it deserves attention. [TW]

1516 Reis, Mateus Fávaro. Americanismo(s) no Uruguai: os olhares entrecruzados dos intelectuais sobre a América Latina e os Estados Unidos (1917–1969). São Paulo: Alameda, 2014. 347 p.: bibl., ill.

Aimed at Brazilian audiences, this work is a close study of three Uruguayan political intellectuals Emilio Frugoni, José Antuña, and Carlos Quijano. The text navigates Uruguayan intellectual history through a study of the men's work, biographies, and their places within Uruguayan historiography. Reis seeks to understand Uruguayan intellectual thought and how intellectuals placed Uruguayan nationalism in the larger context of Pan-Americanism and resistance to US hegemony. The work studies Uruguayan thought in what the author labels the "long twentieth century." The text also contextualizes Uruguayan intellectual history along the with Batllismo and the writing of Rodó and his work, *Ariel*. [BMC]

1517 **Ricca, Javier.** Artigas 1814: secretos de una revolución. Montevideo: Ediciones el Mendrugo, 2015. 299 p.: bibl.

A regional journalist and author of several works on yerba mate and the "secrets" of Platine history here tackles José Gervasio Artigas and the nascent Oriental nationalism associated with his name. Ricca evidently aspires to be a full-fledged left-revisionist, even noting toward the end that "only the hand that erases can write the truth." He seems not to realize that historians deal in likelihoods and possibilities and not "truths," and, in any case, assertions of conspiracies without any real evidence makes for shoddy historical writing. Readers should definitely look elsewhere. [TW]

1518 **Sasso, Rolando W.** Tupamaros: la derrota: de Pando a la caida de Sendic. Montevideo: Fin de Siglo Editorial, 2015. 286 p.: bibl.

This is the fourth title by the same author of a series about the Moviemiento de Liberación Nacional (Tupamaros) that concludes that the failure of the organization was the direct result of military disasters and failures to properly screen new recruits. The text contains many oral testimonies, newspaper articles, and archival material about the Tupamaros and relays exciting details about military operations and a jailbreak by members of the Tupamaros from the Punta Carreta prison. The book moves quickly with exhilarating details. [BMC]

1519 **Vázquez Franco, Guillermo.** Traición a la patria: la Convención Preliminar de Paz. Montevideo: Ediciones Mendrugo, 2014. 471 p.: bibl.

With good reason Guillermo Vázquez Franco is frequently considered the dean of modern Uruguayan historians, and in many ways the most innovative scholar on the Uruguayan scene. With his many historiographical works, he has made a career out of butchering sacred cows in the practiced manner of a gaucho wielding a *facón* on the *pampa húmeda*. Under his active pen, more than a few of the old national myths have yielded their place of dominance to a much more nuanced, ambiguous interpretation of Oriental history. Here he offers readers a thorough and well-written analysis of the 1828 convención that led to Uruguayan independence. The product of 10 years of research, this study traces diplomatic negotiations between Brazil and the Platine states that led up to the Convención. It will likely become the definitive work on the topic. Nonetheless, it might be argued, that its title is ill-chosen; it implies deliberate betrayal of an established nation-state— Argentina—by the diplomat delegated to sign the final agreements that were afterwards held to be favorable to Brazil. But that diplomat, Manuel José García, was looking not to betray but to effect a compromise, as demonstrated in Vázquez Franco's text. In sum, the book is excellent, the title regrettable. [TW]

BRAZIL

MARK GROVER, *Former Area Studies Bibliographer, Brigham Young University*
MARY ANN MAHONY, *Professor of History, Central Connecticut State University*
FRANK D. McCANN, *Professor Emeritus of History, University of New Hampshire*

COLONIAL PERIOD

MANY BRAZILIANS have only a minimal knowledgeable of their colonial past. Because of an inadequate history curriculum in the schools, they are generally aware of celebrated events, heroes and villains, and the institution of slavery. Most have some knowledge about the push into the interior by the Bandeirantes, the role of Jesuit priests in educating the indigenous peoples, and the hero of the beginning of the independence movement, Tiradentes. Students may also be aware of the destruction of the indigenous population by the Portuguese conquest and the negative aspects of slavery, but there still is a strong belief in the myth of racial equality. Though historians continue to publish on these major personalities and events, recent historiography often emphasizes lesser-known aspects of colonial history and looks at less-studied regions of the country. The historiography of the colonial period continues to benefit from the publication of thesis and dissertations from universities all over the country. The introduction of this new research into the school curriculum would be beneficial.

A major event in Brazilian colonial historiography of the past four years was the publication of a three-volume collection of essays by Civilização Brasileira on all aspects of Brazilian colonial history: *O Brasil colonial*, organized by João Fragoso and Maria de Fátima Gouvêa (item **1580**). This set provides a valuable summary of the historiography of the past 25 years, including research approaches and debates. It is an essential text and reference publication for Brazilian history. Also important are regional histories such as a three-volume set on the colonial history of the state of Rio Grande do Sul: *A fronteira* by Tau Golin (item **1596**). This set provides a detailed history and analysis of the evolution of Brazil in the southern region, investigating relationships and contacts with Spanish neighbors. An additional interesting set is a history of newspapers in Brazil that begins by exploring their introduction to the country from the arrival of the Portuguese crown in 1807 to independence in 1822: *História dos jornais no Brasil* by Matias M. Molina (item **1605**).

Two volumes focus on Brazilian personalities of the period. One by Jaime Cortesão, one of Portugal's preeminent historians of Brazilian history is the reprint of the seminal 1954 biography of António Raposo Tavares (item **1584**), Brazil's most well-known bandeirante. (The volume includes a valuable introductory essay by Fernando A. Novais from the Universidade de São Paulo.) Portuguese historian Eugénio dos Santos produced a new biography of Dom Pedro I that offers both Brazilian and Portuguese perspectives on the Emperor (item **1706**).

There were publications of older dissertations, including two important studies of slavery and the Inquisition both written more than 30 years ago: *Da escravidão ao trabalho livre: Brasil, 1550–1900* by Luiz Aranha Corrêa do Lago (item **1531**), and *O momento da Inquisição* by Sonia A. Siqueira (item **1626**). Even though these publications include only limited updating from their early form as dissertations, they continue to be significant for their inclusion of details, facts, and stories not readily available otherwise. They also provide an overview of both Brazilian and international historiography from period in which they were written. While it's a shame that they were not published years ago, one hopes their new accessibility will help them find a wide audience.

The Dutch occupation of northeastern Brazil, 1630–54, continues to be of interest to scholars. Two valuable publications take different approaches to the era. The first, *A guerra do açúcar: as invasões holandesas no Brasil* by Carlos Roberto Carvalho Daróz (item **1587**), addresses a gap among existing works by exploring the military history of the period. The second, *Guerra e pacto colonial: a Bahia contra o Brasil holandês (1624–1654)* by Wolfgang Lenk (item **1600**), views the occupation from the periphery in the state of Bahia. This publication suggests loose and limited control by the Dutch outside Pernambuco.

Slavery and the Church, while more traditional subjects, continue to be of interest to historians. *Networks and Trans-Cultural Exchange: Slave Trading in the South Atlantic, 1590–1867* edited by David Richardson and Filipa Ribeiro da

Silva (item **1608**) sheds light on the movement of slaves and other goods from Africa, particularly Angola. The movement of slaves within Brazil is examined in a series of essays from a 2006 conference held in Rio de Janeiro, Seminário Internacional "Nas Rotas do Império: Eixos Mercantis, Tráfico de Escravos e Relações Sociais no Mundo Português" (item **1622**). A groundbreaking publication (item **1528**) studies runaway slave communities (*quilombos*), not only as hiding places during the colonial period, but as post-emancipation rural peasant communities that provided a place for former slaves, and as present-day migrant settlements.

The online availability of the Inquisition archives in Portugal at the Arquivo Nacional da Torre do Tombo continues to be an important source of information, particularly on material culture and attitudes towards women and children. One valuable study (item **1579**) provides information about home and work by examining the list of sequestered goods seized from converted Jews (Cristãos Novos).

Given the ready availability of documentation on Minas Gerias, the state continues to appear in studies of colonial life. *Fama pública: poder e costume nas Minas setecentistas* by Marco Antonio Silveira (item **1625**), is an interesting study of material culture that examines household goods and products related to work. *A piedade dos outros: o abandono de recém-nascidos em uma vila colonial, século XVIII* by Renato Franco (item **1592**) is a study of the treatment of abandoned children in the city of Ouro Preto. This study suggests that Minas society, particularly religious organizations, had significant concerns for children, while at the same time showing little compassion towards the enslaved population, which was treated with disdain and violence.

For many years, Brazilian historiography has focused on the northern region of the Amazon. A unique volume, *Pedro Teixeira, a Amazônia e o Tratado de Madri* organized by Sérgio Eduardo Moreira Lima and Maria do Carmo Strozzi Coutinho (item **1615**), looks at Pedro Teixeira, an important explorer of the Amazon River basin. In addition to providing a narrative history of his 1673 exploration trip, the work includes 200 valuable pages of transcriptions of documents and contemporary maps. A second study (item **1588**), with essays by Brazilian and Surinamese historians, examines Brazil's northernmost state, Roraima, a region infrequently studied by colonial historians.

Finally, two notable publications take fresh approaches to history. The first is a study of the Brazilian forest, *Na presença da floresta: Mata Atlântica e história colonial*, by Diogo de Carvalho Cabral (item **1581**). Though this is a theme that has drawn attention in the past, this volume examines the forest as a symbol that continues to be important for the history of Brazil. The second publication in an innovative examination of terminology in Brazilian history, tracing the meaning of words and concepts that began in colonial Brazil: *Dar nome ao novo: uma história lexical da Ibero-América entre os séculos XVI e XVIII: (as dinâmicas de mestiçagens e o mundo do trabalho)* by Eduardo França Paiva (item **1613**). This volume connects the country's history to the present by suggesting that words, meanings, and understanding of modern-day Brazil extend back to its colonial past. [MG]

EMPIRE TO REPUBLIC

Scholarship on Brazilian history from the Empire to the Old Republic, especially by Brazilian scholars, continues to grow in quantity and quality, reflecting Brazil's recent investment in higher education. New universities, new MA and PhD programs, new scholarly journals, and new academic presses have all contributed to the growing collection of first-rate monographs, articles, and collections of essays being published in Brazil. This development also reflects the now regular publication in Portuguese of important scholarship on European, US, African, and Caribbean history, and particularly the African Diaspora and labor history, which allows Brazilian scholars to engage in broader historiographical discussions and address questions.

Four important trends noted in *HLAS* 72 continue to characterize the work in this biennium: 1) scholarship about regions beyond the Rio-São Paulo corridor continues to represent a growing contribution to Brazilian history; 2) historians of Brazil are uncovering and conducting research using underutilized or never-before-used documentary sources, in part as a reflection of the previous trend; 3) historians of Brazil are breaking down boundaries between historical periods, especially between the Empire and the Old Republic; and 4) for all of this innovation, with few exceptions, most work in this biennium focuses on the same themes that have been common in the past two decades—slavery and freedom, politics, economics, immigration, journalism, medicine, foreign policy, and labor history. Gender history, environmental history, and the history of capitalism have attracted little attention, at least as evidenced by the materials reviewed here.

For decades, with relatively few exceptions, historians of 19th- and early 20th-century Brazil emphasized the experiences of Rio de Janeiro or São Paulo, while colonial historians tended to focus on Minas Gerais and the Northeast. That research was excellent, but left students and scholars with little knowledge of the history of less economically and politically powerful regions. This biennium includes marvelous research on regions at the center of Brazilian scholarship, as well as new research on the boundary regions of Bahia and Minas Gerais (items **1554** and **1705**), Espirito Santo (item **1703**), Maranhão (item **1681**), Paraná (item **1637**), Pernambuco (item **1582**), Piauí (item **1634**), and Matto Grosso do Sul (item **1668**) during the imperial and early republican periods. This expansion of interest in the history of farther flung areas is a reflection of higher education in those regions, and the increasing emphasis on archival research among Brazilian scholars.

As has been the case for many years, some of the strongest work on Brazilian history during this period examines questions of slavery and freedom, as well as the causes and consequences of abolition, particularly from the perspective of the enslaved or formerly enslaved. Of particular note is Roquinaldo Ferreira's "Biografia como história social", which traces the history of the Ferreira Gomes family in Angola and Brazil (item **1662**). Angela Alonso's *Flores, votos e balas*, a comprehensive study of abolitionism in Brazil, is not to be missed (item **1632**). Three volumes of essays bring together research by established and younger scholars of slavery and freedom and indicate the growing maturity and sophistication of the field. All three contribute to the examination of the key period leading up to and just after emancipation from the perspective of those who experienced liberation, but they also argue cogently for blurring boundaries between historiographies of enslaved and free labor, and the Empire and Old Republic (items **1565**, **1667**, and **1697**). Two prize-winning monographs by new PhDs are particularly notable in this area. Rafael Costa's *Escravizados na liberdade* studies free workers in 19th-century Rio de Janeiro, but always in the context of their presence in a world of enslaved workers, finding that they played important roles in the abolitionist movement (item **1652**). Paulo Cruz Terra's *Cidadania e trabalhadores: cocheiros e carroceiros no Rio de Janeiro (1870–1906)* explores the history of free and enslaved transportation workers and their efforts to be considered full citizens (item **1714**).

Similarly, several collections of essays bring together senior and junior scholars from Brazil and the US to expand our understanding of the contours of the Brazilian state, its strengths and weaknesses (item **1657**), slavery and freedom (items **1565, 1567,** and **1697**) as well as the urban histories of Rio de Janeiro and Minas Gerais from the colonial period through the 20th century (item **1680**). Economic history is represented by several publications, covering topics from colonial history through 20th-century economic development. While many of the themes have been addressed before, the case studies and approaches are new. Exports and industrialization remain important issues, but reexaminations of long-held assumptions (item **1631**) and studies of topics rarely addressed, including cacao, tropeiros—the muleteers who transported goods—and patent laws represent important contributions (items item **1522, 1647,** and **1657**).

Gender history, and specifically the history of masculinity, is the subject of an important new collection of essays organized by Mary del Priori and Marcia Amantino, the former well known for organizing the multivolume studies on the history of private life and women's history in Brazil. The essays in this collection explore the ways in which different groups of Brazilians—enslaved Africans, priests, soldiers, elites—understood their masculine identities (item **1677**). A compendium of essays published over many years, Jocélio Teles dos Santos' *Ensaios sobre raça, gênero e sexualidades no Brasil*, is one of the few texts to consider LGBTQ history (item **1559**).

The history of ideas about political power, magic, and/or religion is an important, but rarely approached topic. Luís Santiago's prize-winning study of the concept of the *"corpo fechado"* and its relationship to rural political power offers a fascinating exploration of a little-examined topic—the notion within northeastern Brazilian popular culture that certain powerful men in rural areas cannot be killed (item **1705**).

Scholars have also expanded our understanding of several other important topics. Publications this biennium include works on indigenous history, a topic which until the year 2000, the quincentenary of the Portuguese conquest of Brazil, still had received very little attention (item **1637**). Scholarship on the history of government administrative structures in Brazil (item **1660**) also emerged. Sports history is represented by a fascinating contribution (item **1527**), as Wilson Gambeta explores the relationship between sports and modernization in Brazil, ostensibly focusing on soccer in São Paulo, but also introducing what may be the first discussion of bicycling in Brazil. Given how popular horse racing, auto racing, cycling, swimming, and volleyball became among Brazilians during the 20th century, the lack of attention to such social and cultural activities is curious. Environmental history yielded an important study with an extensive bibliography (item **1534**).

Happily, this biennium boasts several collections of primary sources that should not be missed. The first is the reproduction of the 1906 Census of Rio de Janeiro. The second is a four-volume collection of primary sources on the independence movement in Brazil (items **1670, 1671, 1672,** and **1673**). Items in these volumes include pamphlets of all sorts, from letters to analyses, speeches, sermons, and poetry. The volumes will allow students and scholars without access to the originals to consult a vast array of materials produced by the intellectuals of the period. All graduate schools with programs in Latin American history, literature, or politics should acquire a set of these volumes, as they will allow graduate students and advanced undergraduates to write theses using original documents from the period that are otherwise unavailable.

Given the recent cuts to education spending and to funding for research and scholarship, this outpouring of high-quality scholarship by Brazilians may not continue at its current pace. Antipoverty programs designed to allow parents to keep their children in school have been slashed. A constitutional amendment in 2016 limited increases in spending on education and health care to the inflation rate for the next 20 years.[1]

Since 2016, funding for research at the CNPq, the National Council for Scientific and Technological Development, has dropped below that of 2001.[2]

Predoctoral and postdoctoral fellowships alike have been cut significantly and fewer scholars are able to conduct research or travel. Given the cuts to US humanities and social science funding, as well as to international education and foreign language training, the future of scholarship on Brazilian history does not seem as bright as it did as recently as two years ago. [MAM]

NATIONAL PERIOD

In the selection of books and articles for this volume some themes appear salient: the 1930s and World War II continue to fascinate, Getúlio Vargas holds a portion of the stage, the coup of 1964 and the military regime draw attention, as does the US relationship. For the Brazilian story with the widest perspective there is Lilia Moritz Schwarcz and Heloisa Murgel Starling's *Brasil: uma biografia* (item **1561**) that manages to take the reader through the whole of the country's history with engaging and constantly attractive prose that elucidates and instructs. Even the most well-read scholars will find this book entertaining and useful.

For the 1930s, the books by João Bertonha on Integralism (item **1642**), Fernando da Silva Rodrigues *et al.* on propaganda (item **1679**), Samantha Viz Quadrat and Denise Rollemberg on 20th-century dictatorships (item **1678**), and Renato Coutinho on the Flamengo football club (item **1653**) capture important aspects of the decade. Marly de Almeida Gomes Vianna organized a group of scholars who plunge into secret police archives to show how foreigners who raised suspicions were investigated during the Estado Novo (item **1698**). Brazil's World War II experience is examined in clear prose by English author Neill Lochery, showing how the war years affected Brazilian development (item **1687**). A fascinating collection of oral histories, organized by Marilia Freidenson (item **1646**), relate the experiences of Jews fleeing Europe to resettle in Brazil. They provide a starting point for researchers grappling with the complexities of such painful emigration. Alexandre Busko Valim's inquiry provides new details about the activities of the wartime Office of the Coordinator of Inter-American Affairs in Brazil (item **1568**). The Office played a key role in preparing the Brazilian people for the country's involvement in the conflict. For an analysis of Brazil's military participation in the Italian campaign, there is Dennison de Oliveira's book (item **1542**). The section treating the decision to demobilize the Expeditionary Force immediately is a notable contribution.

Books by Flávia de Sá Pedreira and Giovana Paiva de Oliveira examine the impact on Natal, Rio Grande do Norte, of having the huge US Parnamirim airbase

---

1. Katarzyna Doniec, Rafael Dall'Alba, Lawrence King. "Brazil's Health Crisis in the Making," *The Lancet*. Vol. 392, 1 September 2018, p. 731. https://www.thelancet.com/pdfs/journals/lancet/PIIS0140-6736(18)30853-5.pdf.

2. G. Wilson Fernandes *et al.* "Dismantling Brazil's Science Threatens Global Biodiversity Heritage." Perspect. Conserv. Ecol. https://www.researchgate.net/figure/Resources-of-the-Brazilian-National-Council-for-Scientific-and-Technological-Development_fig1_319445810.

nearby (items **1541** and **1544**). The city's social life, its economy, and even its slang were profoundly altered. They go beyond simplistic images to create complex portraits of the interactions between the thousands of American military personnel and the local population. Alzira Vargas do Amaral Peixoto provided considerable detail regarding the buildup to Brazil's entry into the war and the war years themselves. This extended volume of her *Memórias,* instigated by her daughter Celina, will likely cause some interpretive revisions (item **1546**). Alzira had been writing short pieces to enlarge the Vargas story to his death in 1954, but never finished it. Celina gathered the essays together, provided explanatory notes, and wrote biographical sketches of most of the important personalities.

Celina also played an energizing role in the publication of the correspondence between Alzira Vargas do Amaral Peixoto and her father Getúlio during his "exile" in São Borja and his reelection to the presidency. *Volta ao poder,* edited by Adelina Novaes e Cruz and Regina da Luz Moreira, is a great contribution to research on the inter-regnum between the two Vargas governments (item **1569**). These letters tell us much about the attitudes of the Vargas family and how they saw Brazil and its leadership. The affection between father and daughter is palpable. She addressed him as "Querido Gé" or "Querido Papai" and he used the nickname "Rapariguinha" (little girl) for her. The letters were hand carried by trusted friends to avoid government spies.

The postwar era and relations with the US are brought into focus by Antônio Tota in his study of Nelson Rockefeller and his development activities in Brazil (item **1566**). The book is a major contribution to the study of Brazilian-American relations after the war.

This selection of books is especially rich in studies of the military intervention of 1964 and the 21-year military regime. Geraldo Cantarino's examination based on English diplomatic archives is particularly significant (item **1645**). The British were a bit removed from the emotions of the events and so might have been more objective than American diplomats. It is helpful that the history runs from 1963 to 1979. Political scientists Clóvis Brigagão and Trajano Ribeiro have written a highly useful biography of Leonel Brizola, who as the volatile governor of Rio Grande do Sul did much to stimulate worry among the military and the Brazilian right (item **1644**). The fact that he was President João Goulart's brother-in-law gave his violent language added weight.

The 1964 coup was a civilian-military affair, a fact too easily forgotten. Edwaldo Costa makes that clear in his book on the role that the Rio de Janeiro newspaper *O Globo* played throughout the military era (item **1651**). Its columns steadily proclaimed the communist danger and linked it to the Goulart government and justified much illicit behavior during the military regime. The editors continually manipulated facts and subverted society's values. What would have happened if the newspaper had held to honest standards of journalism? Paulo Amorim's study of the fourth estate (*O quarto poder*) offers some reason for optimism (item **1636**). Flavio Tavares surveyed Washington archives to uncover American involvement in the coup (item **1563**).

Marcus Napolitano, Rodrigo Czajka, and Rodrigo Motta mustered scholars to probe Brazil's communist movements in an insightful and useful manner (item **1649**). Angela Alonso and Miriam Dolhnikoff organized a multi-authored volume on the coup that asks who was under threat (item **1693**). The testimony of first-hand participants is a special strength of this book. As the regime hardened in the late 1960s, torture of prisoners and murder of suspected subversives became more common. Marcelo Godoy's examination of the Destacamento de Operações de Informação—Centro de Operações de Defesa Interna (DOI-CODI) is a landmark study (item **1666**). It is based on interviews with DOI agents, who perhaps wanted to soothe troubled consciences. The view of the regime's dungeons is deeply disturbing. Milton Pinheiro led another group of scholars who examine the regime's attack on nationalist populism that militarized the Brazilian state (item **1658**).

Daniel Sasaki's investigation of the fate of Panair do Brasil shows that not only did the regime harm individuals, but even storied companies were done in by caprice and jealousy (item **1560**). Panair's quality was never matched by its envious replacements. Grimaldo Zachariadhes coordinated a volume (item **1692**) that probes the meaning of the military years and asked what kind of a country Brazilians want. Certainly they do not want a dictatorship. The story of how the regime ended is in José Ribeiro's biography of Tancredo Neves who led Brazil out of the darkness only to be struck down before he could become president (item **1555**). The search for meaning is clear in Lucas Figueiredo's study of the Comissão Nacional de Verdade and its pursuit of the regime's records, which supposedly had not been destroyed (item **1524**). These books point toward the obvious conclusion that the results of 1964 coup and the subsequent military-controlled governments were too high a price to pay for whatever satisfaction was gained in deposing Goulart. [FDM]

GENERAL

1520 Assumpção, Maurício Torres. A história do Brasil nas ruas de Paris. Rio de Janeiro: Casa de Palavra, 2014. 479 p.: bibl.

Readable narrative history of well-known Brazilians in Paris that includes images and addresses of the places where they lived or socialized. [MAM]

1521 Canale, Dario. O surgimento da Seção Brasileira da Internacional Comunista (1917–1928). São Paulo: Fundação Maurício Grabois: Anita Garibaldi, 2013. 413 p.: bibl., ill.

The text is the Portuguese translation of a previously unpublished 1986 Karl Marx University Phd. thesis on the relationship between the Brazilian Communist Party and Comintern based on important primary sources and an extensive bibliography. [MAM]

1522 Chambouleyron, Rafael. "*Como se hace en Indias de Castilla*": el cacao entre la Amazonía portuguesa y las Indias de Castilla, siglos XVII y XVIII. (*Rev. Complut. Hist. Am.*, 40, 2014, p. 23–43, bibl.)

Well-researched article that argues that the expansion of cacao in Maranhão was a result of, among other factors, the legacy of Spanish control of the Portuguese Empire. [MAM]

1523 Döbrich, Wolfgang. 190 Jahre Kirche gestalten: Gemeinde, Ämter und Dienste in der Evangelischen Kirche Lutherischen Bekenntnisses in Brasilien: Studien zu Mission, Ökumene und aktuellen Partnerschaften der Evangelisch-Lutherischen Kirche in Bayern (ELKB) [190 years of building a church: parishes, duties and services in the Evangelical Lutheran Church in Brazil]. Neuendettelsau, Germany: Erlanger Verlag für Mission und Ökumene, 2015. 548 p.: bibl., maps.

The Evangelical Lutheran Church in Brazil (Igreja Evangélica de Confissão Luterana no Brasil) has approximately 700,000 members today. The church started in Brazil in the 19th century with the arrival of Protestant migrants. The Swiss established Nova Friburgo (Province of Rio de Janeiro) in 1824 and the Germans established São Leopoldo (in Rio Grande do Sul), and Blumenau (in Santa Catarina) in 1854. Lutherans were present in Rio de Janeiro from 1827 on. This study shows the slow building of church structures in the nearly 200 years since. [F. Obermeier]

1524 Figueiredo, Lucas. Lugar nenhum: militares e civis na ocultação dos documentos da ditadura. Coordenação da coleção por Heloisa Maria Murgel Starling. São Paulo: Companhia das Letras, 2015.

237 p.: bibl., ill., index. (Coleção Arquivos da repressão no Brasil)

Between November 2012 and July 2013, the *Comissão Nacional de Verdade* organized and oversaw a small team of historians and journalists to search for the archives of the various repressive units of the armed forces. At the end of the military regime there was a deliberate effort to hide the records of corruption, disappearances, murders, and torture. Without them it would be very difficult to apportion responsibility and the process of returning to democracy would be more problematic. The result was the creation of a collection of *Arquivos da Repressão no Brasil* which is now open to researchers. Anyone taking on a project related to repression will want to have this book in hand. It explains how the documents were handled, organized, and stored. General Leônidas Pires Gonçalves, minister of the army under President Sarney, asserted that nothing was destroyed (p. 207). One hopes that is true and researchers will unearth the full story. [FDM]

1525 Fischer, Brodwyn M. The Red Menace reconsidered: a forgotten history of communist mobilization in Rio de Janeiro's favelas, 1945–1964. (*HAHR*, 94:1, Feb. 2014, p. 1–33, bibl.)

The article appraises the role of the Communist Party in protecting Rio's favelas from forced removal. While rural land reform has been the object of much study and analyses, the world of the urban poor has enjoyed less attention. Oddly, despite their success in obtaining permanence for the favelas, the communists seemingly have been less enthusiastic about their urban accomplishments. This is a finely done study of an overlooked topic. [FDM]

1526 Gallo, Carlos Artur. Do luto à luta: um estudo sobre a Comissão de Familiares de Mortos e Desaparecidos Políticos no Brasil. (*Anos 90*, 19:35, julho 2012, p. 329–361, bibl., graph)

The military decades still weigh heavily on Brazil. The murdered and disappeared cannot demand justice, but their families have been doing so. This article analyzes how the families organized themselves to demand that the Brazilian state accept responsibility for the human rights violations, that the circumstances of the deaths and disappearances be made public, that the guilty be held to account, and that the memory of these events be preserved. Their struggle continues. [FDM]

1527 Gambeta, Wilson. A bola rolou: o Velódromo Paulista e os espetáculos de futebol (1895–1916). São Paulo: SESI-SP Editora, 2015. 430 p.: bibl. (Memória e sociedade)

Prize-winning monograph on the introduction of soccer to São Paulo that connects the process to a broader history of sport and modernization in São Paulo. Interesting material on cycling in Brazil. Based on extensive research in primary sources and a broad bibliography. [MAM]

1528 Gomes, Flávio dos Santos. Mocambos e quilombos: uma história do campesinato negro no Brasil. São Paulo: Claro Enigma, 2015. 235 p.: bibl., ill., index. (Coleção Agenda brasileira)

An important element of the slave experience in Brazil was the formation of runaway slave communities. There were numerous communities throughout Brazil whose history extended far beyond the end of slavery, most to the present time. This book examines the history of quilombos from their foundation as rural peasant communities populated primarily by runaway slaves, to their growth following abolition as former slaves looked for land. The author suggests that quilombos were not just a product of one period, but a fluid rural evolution extending over the entire history of Brazil. An important part of this volume is a chart listing all the known communities. [MG]

1529 Hörner, Erik. Até os limites da política: a "Revolução Liberal" de 1842 em São Paulo e Minas Gerais. São Paulo: Alameda, 2014. 372 p.: bibl.

Extensively researched and detailed discussion of the liberal revolts against the centralizing imperial government. [MAM]

1530 Ipanema, Cybelle de. História da Ilha do Governador. 2a edição revista e ampliada. Rio de Janeiro: Mauad X, 2013. 223 p.: bibl., ill.

A revised and expanded edition of a volume published in 1991 by a prominent historian of the city of Rio de Janeiro (see *HLAS 54:3326*). The Ilha do Governador is an island in the northern part of Guanabara Bay connected to the city of Rio de Janeiro. The island has a rich history separate from the center of the colonial capital city. The focus of this history is on unique elements of the region often not included in traditional histories of Rio de Janeiro. The history covers more than 450 years and concludes with brief descriptions of the different neighborhoods of the city at the end of the 20th century. [MG]

1531 **Lago, Luiz Aranha Corrêa do.** Da escravidão ao trabalho livre: Brasil, 1550–1900. São Paulo: Companhia Das Letras, 2014. 781 p.: bibl., ill. (some color), maps.

The publication of the author's 1978 Harvard University dissertation, revised, updated, and translated into Portuguese. The volume is an important study of slavery in agricultural southern Brazil where the use of slaves was primarily on coffee plantations. The author examines slavery by comparing the coffee plantations of Rio de Janeiro, Espírito Santo, Minas Gerais, and São Paulo with slavery in the three southern Brazilian states. The study evaluates the transition from slavery to abolition. The author also includes a detailed study of different forms of labor in Brazilian agriculture. Though the arguments relate more to ideas about slavery in the Americas in the 1960s, this publication is a long overdue and welcome addition to the study of slavery in Brazil. [MG]

1532 **Lobato, Sidney da Silva.** Família e sobrevivência cotidiana na foz do Amazonas, 1944–1964. (*Anos 90*, 22:42, dez. 2015, p. 353–373, bibl.)

The article examines family survival strategies in Macapá, Amapá. Often when the husband fell ill, or mistreated the wife, she would leave. If there were children she could not support, she might offer one or more for adoption. In 1950 the male population exceeded the female by 1,744. Illiteracy was high. The women who migrated to Macapá tended to work as domestics to help sustain their families. Others washed clothes. A significant number of women ran their own households. The ideal family of a man working outside the home and the woman managing the house and children was more of an elite situation, than a working class one. [FDM]

1533 **Losada, Janaina Zito.** Brazilian historiography and the environment: contributions by Sérgio Buarque de Holanda and the contemporary environmental history debate. (*Hist. Ciênc. Saúde Manguinhos*, 23:3, July/Sept. 2016, p. 653–668, bibl.)

Brazil's preeminent 20th-century historian Sérgio Buarque de Holanda tackled historical problems such as national identity, settlement, and society. His *Raizes do Brasil* (1936) (see *HLAS 14:62a* and *2262*) is still influential as are his other books. Setting his work within Brazil's tropical climate and environment, he was able to show how humans interacted with and affected the world around them. This article is a useful excursion into his worldview and historical mindset that can be read profitably by anyone wishing to understand Brazilian history. [FDM]

1534 **Losada, Janaina Zito** and **José Augusto Drummond.** Espíritos cheios de bichos: a fauna nas viagens de Louis Agassiz e Richard Francis Burton pelo Brasil oitocentista. (*Varia Hist.*, 31:55, jan./abril 2015, p. 253–284, bibl.)

Interesting contribution to environmental history with extensive bibliography. [MAM]

1535 **Machado, José Lucio da Silva.** O sertão e o cativo: escravidão e pastoreio, os Campos de Palmas—Paraná, 1859–1888. Porto Alegre, Brazil: PPGH UPF: FCM Editora, 2015. 193 p.: bibl., ill. (Coleção Malungo ; 23)

Contribution to the study of slavery in cattle ranching and outside of large plantations. [MAM]

1536 **Magalhães, Aline Montenegro** and **Claudia Barroso Roquette-Pinto Bojunga.** Segredos da história do Brasil revelados por Gustavo Barroso na revista *O Cruzeiro*, 1948–1960. (*Estud. Hist./Rio de Janeiro*, 27:54, julho/dez. 2014, p. 345–364, bibl.)

The photo magazine, *O Cruzeiro*, began in 1928–29, and throughout its existence it provided a visual record of Brazil. From

1948 into 1960 Gustavo Barroso, director of the Museu Histórico Nacional and a recognized scholar, edited a section on Brazilian history that was characterized by eulogistic prose and colorful illustrations. His intention was to educate and encourage the public to be proud of their country by calling attention to little-known events and personalities of the past. It was a project aimed at constructing a national identity. Many of the maps, documents, and photos of objects were from the museum's collections, which, of course, turned to ashes in the tragic fire of September 2, 2018. Sadly, it is likely that the most complete collection of Barroso's work disappeared in the fire. [FDM]

1537 **Monteiro, Mário Ypiranga.** Fundação de Manaus. 5a. edição ilustrada e revista. Manaus, Brazil: Cultura Edições Governo do Estado, 2012. 267 p.: bibl.

The fifth edition of a history of the city of Manaus originally published in 1948. Monteiro was a well-known educator and scholar of both the city and the Amazon region, who passed away in 2004 at the age of 95. The volume is a basic descriptive history of the evolution of the city, examining the selection of the land, construction of the original fort, growth, and political activities. This volume includes minor revisions and the addition of a few photographs by the author's son that were not in the previous volumes. [MG]

1538 **Moraes, Julio Lucchesi.** São Paulo: capital artística: a cafeicultura e as artes na belle époque (1906–1922). Rio de Janeiro: Beco do Azougue, 2014. 247 p.: bibl. (Pensamento brasileiro. Série pesquisa & reflexão)

Quantitative and qualitative history of the development of the arts in São Paulo during the highpoint of the coffee economy. [MAM]

1539 **Moratelli, Thiago.** Operários de empreitada: os trabalhadores da construção da Estrada de Ferro Noroeste do Brasil (São Paulo e Mato Grosso, 1905–1914). Campinas, Brazil: Editora Unicamp, 2013. 267 p.: bibl., ill., maps. (Coleção Várias histórias; 38)

Well-researched and well-written labor history of the workers recruited to build the railroad that connected São Paulo to Matto Grosso, produced by a promising young scholar who made extensive use of the Arquivo Leuenroth and documents from Matto Grosso. [MAM]

1540 **Neder, Gizlene.** As reformas políticas dos "homens novos": Brasil Império: 1830–1889. Rio de Janeiro: Editora Revan, 2016. 270 p.: bibl.

Study of the secularization of politics and the law over the course of the nineteenth century. History of ideas. [MAM]

1541 **Oliveira, Giovana Paiva de.** Natal em guerra: as transformações da cidade na Segunda Guerra Mundial. Natal, Brazil: Editora da UFRN, 2014. 201 p.: bibl., ill., maps.

The author has an academic background in architecture and urbanism and set out to examine the changes in Natal's physical plant during the world war. That naturally led her to focus on the roles and visions of the city's social, political, and economic elites. The focus provides the book's strengths and some weaknesses. She makes use of the local newspapers, which were not always accurate. Brazil entered the war in August, not September, 1942 (p. 99). One of the best chapters treats the effects of so many American soldiers on the social life of the city, especially via the USOs. Hopefully more such social history will give a more detailed story. [FDM]

1542 **Oliveria, Dennison de.** Extermine o inimigo: blindados brasileiros na Segunda Guerra Mundial. Curitiba: Juruá Editora, 2015. 217 p.

Brazilian authorities hoped that the experiences of their army in World War II would result in the country's modernization. This book studies two aspects of that process: the first was the action in combat of the 1st Reconnaissance Squadron of the Brazilian Expeditionary Force in the Italian campaign; and the second the creation of the first Armored Division in the Brazilian army. The author reviews the prewar period, the pursuit of arms purchases from Germany and the US, emphasizing that the secrecy kept lower-ranked officers in the dark. Throughout he highlights the thinking of Plínio Pitaluga, who led the Reconnaissance Squadron in Italy. Using individual cases, he provides considerable information regarding the training that Brazilians received in the US, as well as the eventual composition of expeditionary force units. The many lengthy quotations from participants give the text immediacy. The fact that Hitler had ordered the German forces to hold their positions at any cost meant that they did not have a plan for orderly retreat, which ultimately contributed to their defeat. Oliveria's discussion of why the FEB was demobilized and how its personnel were marginalized after the war is an important contribution to the study of Brazil's war role. [FDM]

1543 Palacios, Guillermo. Política externa, tensões agrárias e práxis missionária: os capuchinhos italianos e as relações entre o Brasil e o Vaticano no início do segundo reinado. (*Rev. Hist./São Paulo*, 167, julho/dez 2012, p. 193–222, bibl.)

This article by well-respected Mexican historian of Brazil addresses an unusual but important topic, diplomatic relations between the Brazilian state and the Vatican, and their role in dealing with agrarian unrest. Largely based on Vatican sources. [MAM]

1544 Pedreira, Flávia de Sá. Chiclete eu misturo com banana: carnaval e cotidiano de guerra em Natal, 1920–1945. 2a edição revista e ampliada. Natal, Brazil: Editora da UFRN, 2012. 290 p.: bibl., ill.

The author follows relations between the US and Brazil to create the bases in the northeast and provides considerable detail about relations between American personnel and Brazilians in Natal. The gradual arrival of American soldiers and sailors at Natal in the early 1940s coincided with a drought that caused a migration from the interior into the capital city. The population increase produced a food supply crisis and a rise in prices. The Americans shipped in their own food and had farms producing grains, pigs and chickens, while Natal had rationing. They also bought a lot from local stores which pushed up prices. People in Natal commented on the lack of blacks among the Americans (p. 117). The military was then segregated. For the "Yankees" despite the war "it was a real 'fiesta' in Natal" (p. 119). American soldiers were encouraged to learn Portuguese; the Parnamirim newspaper *Foreign Ferry News* opined that it would improve their chances with local women. Music, samba, and carnival are important subthemes throughout the book. The American presence even affected names given babies. Between 1942 and 1946 there was an increasing number of Davids, Lesters, Richards, Marthas, etc. Some of such babies were likely the result of the night-life at the Wander Bar and other like establishments. This is the best study of the American wartime presence in Natal. [FDM]

1545 Pedrosa, Fernando Velôzo Gomes. Violência e pacificação no Caribe: tropas brasileiras em operações de paz na República Dominicana (1965–1966) e no Haiti (2004–2005): um estudo comparado. Rio de Janeiro: Biblioteca do Exército, 2015. 266 p.: bibl., ill. (Bibilioteca do Exército publicação; 921. Coleção General Benício; 520)

Brazil's role as a UN peacekeeper is important to its international status. This book compares the 1965 experience in the Dominican Republic with the 2004 mission in Haiti. The Dominican event included the rare occasion when American forces were under the command of a Brazilian general. Rather than under UN sponsorship, the Brazilians were part of the Inter-American Peace Force aimed at preventing a feared communist takeover. By contrast the effort in Haiti was aimed at preventing chaos after the government collapsed. Brazil's motivation included obtaining a permanent seat on the UN Security Council. There was also heavy involvement in humanitarian assistance. Together the two experiences provided training in special operations dealing with irregular forces and, importantly, improving logistical capacity in long distance operations abroad. [FDM]

1546 Peixoto, Alzira Vargas do Amaral. Getúlio Vargas, meu pai: memórias de Alzira Vargas do Amaral Peixoto. Notas de Celina Vargas do Amaral Peixoto, Francisco Reynaldo de Barros e Érico Melo. Edição definitiva, incluindo segundo livro inédito. Rio de Janeiro: Objetiva, 2017. 551 p.: ill., index.

This is a gem for historians. Alzira's daughter Celina organized this new edition. Originally published in 1960, this edition has been enriched by notes, including helpful biographical identifications, and, most importantly, by 164 pages of Alzira's unpublished writings carrying the story to 1954. The style is simple and direct and her perspectives so engaging that the book is difficult to put down. This is an important contribution to the historical literature that is likely to ignite more research on the Vargas era. Simply put, do not miss this book. [FDM]

1547 Pena Rodríguez, Alberto. A guerra da propaganda: Portugal, Brasil e a Guerra Civil de Espanha: imprensa, diplomacia e fascismo. Colaboração especial de Maria Luiza Tucci Carneiro, Heloisa Paulo e Esther Gambi Giménez. Porta Alegre, Brazil: EdiPUCRS, 2014. 354 p.: bibl., ill. (Série comunicação; 47)

The idea behind the book was to examine how the propaganda campaign of the Spanish Fascists affected thinking in Portugal and Brazil. Salazar's Portugal fully supported Franco's war on the Second Spanish Republic. The republic sought to capture the loyalty of the large Spanish immigrant population in São Paulo. The nature of propaganda changed during the conflict and influenced how propaganda was carried on during the world war. The civil war was not only a military struggle it also was a war of ideas and ideals. The roles of Brazilian police and diplomats are given good coverage. [FDM]

1548 Peres, Fernando Antonio. João Penteado: o discreto transgressor de limites. São Paulo: Alameda, 2012. 335 p.: bibl., ill.

The text is a history of the role of anarchist João Penteado in the development of São Paulo's Escola Moderna, which, according to the author, was the principal initiative of São Paulo's anarchists. It is based on the author's revised PhD dissertation in education at the University of São Paulo. Sources include newspapers and magazines, as well as Penteado's personal archive. MAM

1549 Pinto, Paulo Roberto Margutti. Historia da filosofia do Brasil: (1500-hoje). Vol. 1, O periodo colonial (1500–1822). São Paulo: Edições Loyola, 2013. 1 v.: bibl.

Volume one of a projected three-volume history of philosophy in Brazil with an emphasis on writers who focus on Brazil and not on outside ideas. The volume shows that Brazil did have a colonial philosophy separate from Europe that influenced the evolution of thought in Brazil to the present. The book does demonstrate the uniqueness of Brazilian philosophy, though the author does overstate the distinctiveness of Brazilian thought. [MG]

1550 Priori, Angelo and Verônica Karina Ipólito. DOPS, a cidade de Rolândia (PR) e a repressão aos imigrantes de origen alemã, 1942–1945. (*Varia Hist.*, 31:56, maio/agôsto 2015, p. 547–580, bibl.)

Brazilian entry into World War II, American fears of possible German immigrant uprising, and the Estado Novo's logic of social control propelled the political police (DOPS) to repress, control, and monitor immigrant communities in the south of Brazil. This article focuses on a town in Paraná state that was the object of repression. Unfortunately all Germans and descendants were considered suspect and treated accordingly. The authors seek to find the impact of this undiscriminately applied persecution had on individual lives of victims. Interestingly some of the immigrants were Jews fleeing the Nazis. Keeping "German" customs excited the suspicion of the police. Despite the contradiction, such Jews were lumped with others from Germany as "Axis subjects" (p. 560). The authors argue that the "German threat" or conspiracy were myths that helped justify the Estado Novo. [FDM]

1551 Queler, Jefferson J. A roupa nova do presidente: a politização da imagem pública de Jânio Quadros (1947–1961). (*An. Mus. Paul.*, 19:2, julho/dez. 2011, p. 45–69, ill.)

Author seeks to refute the widely accepted image of Quadros as a personalist demagogue. He argues that his gestures and clothes deserve more attention and that he projected himself as a Christian Democrat, who was particularly interested in improving the lives of the poor and avoiding class struggle. His Independent Foreign Policy aimed at cultivating trade with Eastern Europe was, the author argues, based on the principle of self-determination of peoples. For sources he leaned heavily on photos and stories in *O Cruzeiro and Manchete*. [FDM]

1552 **Rezzutti, Paulo.** D. Pedro, a história não contada: o homem revelado por cartas e documentos inéditos. São Paulo: Leya, 2015. 429 p.: bibl., ill.

Biography of Dom Pedro I written for a popular audience, but based on important primary sources with color illustrations. [MAM]

1553 **Ribeiro, Daniele Corrêa,** Tramas da loucura na Corte Imperial: ciência, caridade e redes de sociabilidade no Hospício de Pedro II (1883–1889). Curitiba: Editora Prismas, 2015. 207 p.: bibl. (Coleção Patrimônio cultural, museus & turismo)

Well-documented history of the Dom Pedro II Psychiatric Hospital, that includes appendices documenting patients and diagnoses. [MAM]

1554 **Ribeiro, Eduardo Magalhães.** Estradas da vida: terra e trabalho nas fronteiras agrícolas do Jequitinhonha e Mucuri, Minas Gerais. Belo Horizonte: Editora UFMG, 2013. 346 p.: bibl., maps. (Humanitas)

Study of the settlement of the Jequitinhonha and Mucurí River Valleys that emphasizes land acquisition and labor control. This region has only recently begun to be studied. [MAM]

1555 **Ribeiro, José Augustor.** Tancredo Neves: a noite do destino. Rio de Janeiro: Civilização Brasileira, 2015. 866 p.: bibl., ill.

The first biography of the man elected to lead Brazil back to democracy, but who tragically died before assuming the presidency. The author was his press spokesman during the presidential campaign and thus had a close view of the man and the politician. It is worth recalling that Tancredo had been minister of justice in the second Vargas government, prime minister in the parliamentary experiment of 1961, and in 1984 was the collective opposition's choice as candidate for the presidency. He transformed the indirect election into a direct one thanks to great popular support. The author convincingly argues that Tancredo was one of the greatest Brazilians of the 20th century. This is a biography not to be missed. [FDM]

1556 **Rinke, Stefan H.** Alemanha e Brasil, 1870–1945: uma relação entre espaços. (Hist. Ciênc. Saúde Manguinhos, 21:1, Feb. 2014, p. 299–316, bibl.)

This excellent article traces the relationship between Brazil and Germany across decades replete with wars, regime changes, economic and scientific advances, until the destruction of World War II. Germans saw the empty spaces of Brazil as the "last free continent" (p.15) where the Reich could live out its colonial dreams. Allied fears of German areas in Brazil ignored the deep divisions between Catholics and Protestants, newcomers and old settlers, clashing attitudes of migrants from different parts of Germany, and the power of Brazilian nationalism. This article succinctly examines the positive and negative aspects of the bi-national relationship over time and should be read by anyone interested in German migration to Brazil. [FDM]

1557 **Rocha, Simone.** Eugenia no Brasil: análise do discurso "científico" no Boletim de Eugenia, 1929–1933. Curitiba, Brazil: Editora CRV, 2014. 104 p.: bibl.

Examination of the eugenics journal *Boletim de Eugenia* from the perspective of the history of science. [MAM]

1558 **Sant'Anna, Denise Bernuzzi de.** História da beleza no Brasil. São Paulo: Editora Contexto, 2014. 205 p.: bibl., ill.

Brazilians hold beauty to be a good to be striven for and perfected to a high degree. A few decades ago one could tell a person's economic class by the state of their teeth, no more thanks to better dental care. The author studies changes in ideas of beauty and how they were propagated by advertisements, films, the press, and television. For much of the Brazilian past, white skin was prized over dark tones, and the author discusses at length the effect of racial prejudice on notions of beauty. Sadly, she observes that "the preference for 'morena' skin many times indicated an intolerance for black skin" (p.78). The 20th century was the golden age of transformation via creams, exercise, and even plastic surgery. Fashions played their part. This book is an engrossing tale that also instructs. It is a serious topic that deserves this kind of careful study. [FDM]

1559 **Santos, Jocélio Teles dos.** Ensaios sobre raça, gênero e sexualidades no Brasil: séculos XVIII–XX. Salvador, Brazil: Edufba, 2013. 177 p.: bibl.

This collection of essays by a leading anthropologist and historian of Bahia brings together five previously published and two unpublished works covering topics from ideas of race in 18th-century Bahia to transvestism in the 20th century. Well worth reading. [MAM]

1560 **Sasaki, Daniel Leb.** Pouso forçado. Revisão técnica de Jorge Ferreira. 2a edição, ampliada. Rio de Janeiro: Editora Record, 2015. 488 p.: bibl., ill., index.

Panair do Brasil brought the style, efficiency, and glamour of Pan American Airways to Brazil's internal aviation. It began as PAA's subsidiary. Milton Nascimento's song "Nas Asas de Panair" captured the collective popular memory of the airline touted as Brazil's best. From 1930 to 1965 Panair set the standard for quality in Brazilian air travel. For Brazilians "it was the synonym for aviation, the great pride of the nation's aviation" (p.17). The "Panair standard" has not been equaled since its demise. Unfortunately, the company did not die because of its business practices, but rather because of the jealousy of certain members of the Brazilian Air Force that controlled civil aviation, Brigadeiro Eduardo Gomes at their head. The coup of 1964 gave Panair's enemies the power to ground it in a "forced landing." Its competitor Varig was in on the plot and had its planes positioned to take over the many routes Panair had pioneered. It is a tale that shows the damage that jealousy and envy can do. [FDM]

1561 **Schwarcz, Lilia Moritz** and **Heloisa Murgel Starling.** Brasil: uma biografia. São Paulo: Companhia das Letras, 2015. 694 p.: bibl., ill., index.

The authors close the introduction to their fascinating book with the idea that "Brazil certainly was another world" (p.49). It was a mestiço world. And this is certainly a different history. The writing is jargonless, and has the comfortable tone of an extended set of reader-friendly essays. The authors managed to utilize much of recent historical research. The development of citizenship, and frequently its absence, is a thread throughout the book, as is the continual current of violence and inequality. Brazil's past and present have a lot of similarities. [FDM]

1562 **Silva, Juremir Machado da.** Jango: a vida e a morte no exílio: como foram construídos, com ajuda da mídia, o imaginário favorável ao golpe e as narrativas sobre as suspeitas de assassinato do presidente deposto em 1964. Porto Alegre, Brazil: L&PM Editores, 2013. 372 p.

João Goulart was a weak president, when Brazil desperately needed a very strong one. The author's basic question is: who was João Goulart? Was Brazil on the edge of becoming a communist state? Was the US behind the coup? Was the later guerrilla movement merely a reaction to the dictatorship? Who was responsible for Jango's death? Were his medications altered? These questions form the structure of the book, which reads like a police thriller. The odd thing is that in this book so full of direct quotations there is no indication of sources. Which calls up another question: how did this book get published? [FDM]

1563 **Tavares, Flavio.** 1964: o golpe. Porto Alegre, Brazil: L&PM, 2014. 315 p.: bibl., ill.

This account, which is partially an eye-witness explanation of some events, is tied together with research carried on in American archives. He was particularly searching for information on how the US supported and financed the conspirators. He appears captivated by the extensive documentation on Operation Brother Sam, which unfortunately for his tale, never landed on Brazil's shore. [FDM]

1564 **Teixeira, Melissa.** Making a Brazilian new deal: Oliveira Vianna and the transnational sources of Brazil's corporatist experiment. (*J. Lat. Am. Stud.*, 50:3, Aug. 2018, p. 613–641, bibl.)

The term corporatist is often applied to the *Estado Novo* (November 1937 to October 1945). The principal thinker behind that label was Francisco José de Oliveira Vianna, an official in the Ministry of Labor. A major intellectual figure of his time, who this author asserts was on a par with Gilberto Freyre and Sergio Buarque, but being tagged as a retrograde authoritarian, he was written out of the canon. This article makes a strong argument that he should be restored. His embrace of ideas behind the Roosevelt era New Deal inserted corporatism into global debates regarding the state's role in economic recovery and social welfare. Teixeira argues that the *"Estado Novo* needs to be studied in this global context." (p. 615) This is impressive research and analysis. [FDM]

1565 **Tornando-se livre: agentes históricos e lutas sociais no processo de abolição.** Organização por Maria Helena P.T. Machado y Celso Thomas Castilho. São Paulo: EDUSP, 2015. 479 p.: bibl.

Significant collection of articles by junior and senior scholars of enslavement and freedom, that examines complexities of struggles for freedom and abolition by enslaved and freed persons from several different perspectives, but always asserting the agency of those who suffered enslavement. Essential reading for anyone interested in Brazilian abolition. [MAM]

1566 **Tota, Antônio Pedro.** O amigo americano: Nelson Rockefeller e o Brasil. São Paulo: Companha das Letras, 2014. 477 p.: bibl., ill., index.

This is a very interesting and highly useful book by a scholar who has steeped himself in the details and byways of Brazilian-American relations. The book follows the career of Nelson Rockefeller and his fascination with Brazil. Rockefeller believed in Brazil's future and invested money to develop various types of enterprises with Brazilian partners that he thought would contribute to Brazil's development. Often Brazilians suspected his motives. Why would a rich American care what happened in Brazil? Toto does a fine job explaining why he cared and how he sought to help. This is a captivating read that shows that Republicans can have a heart. [FDM]

1567 **O Vale do Paraíba e o Império do Brasil nos quadros da segunda escravidão.** Organização de Mariana Muaze y Ricardo Salles. Rio de Janeiro: FAPERJ: 7Letras, 2015. 573 p.: bibl.

This important collection of esays brings together junior and senior scholars of slavery in Brazil's Paraíba Valley using Dale Tomich's concept of the Second Slavery, a term referring to the expansion of chattel slavery in the Atlantic World after the Haitian Revolution. [MAM]

1568 **Valim, Alexandre Busko.** O triunfo da persuasão: Brasil, Estados Unidos e o cinema da política de boa vizinhança durante a II Guerra Mundial. São Paulo: Alameda, 2017. 335 p.

The book studies the role of film in persuading the Brazilian population to support the allied cause in World War II. This social history of cinema in the intensive propaganda campaign that the Office of the Coordinator of Inter-American Affairs waged in Brazil enlightens and startles. Hollywood films were shown throughout the country from the smallest towns in Amazonia to the major cities. So many American newsreels were shown that in distant rural areas people thought that Franklin Roosevelt was the president of Brazil. This book is a good read that is highly recommended. [FDM]

1569 **Vargas, Getúlio.** Volta ao poder: a correspondência entre Getúlio Vargas e a filha Alzira. Vol. 1, 1946 a 1948. Vol. 2, 1949 a 1950. Organização por Adelina Novaes e Cruz e Regina da Luz Moreira. Rio de Janeiro: FGV Editora: Ouro sobre Azul, 2018. 2 v.: ill.

These two volumes are a major publication event and a significant contribution to the study of the Vargas era. The publication in 1995 of the diaries of Getúlio Vargas reshaped the historiography of the Vargas era. These two volumes fill in the enormous gap between the overthrow of Vargas in 1945 and his reelection in 1950. They consist of the 568 letters and notes, totaling 1,650 pages, exchanged between Alzira Vargas and her father from 1946 to 1950. The letters discuss and inform regarding personalities, issues, political parties, and pros and cons of how to proceed. They show Alzira to have been a major, if not the principal, adviser to her father. The volumes may reshape the historiography. Ilustrated with many photos. Highly recommended. [FDM]

1570 **Vasconcelos, Cláudio Beserra de.** Os militares e a legitimidade do regime ditatorial (1964–1968): a preservação do Legislativo. (*Varia Hist.*, 29:49, jan./abril 2013, p. 333–358)

Overthrowing a government requires that what replaces it be considered legitimate. This article explores the contradiction of an imposed regime based on military force seeking democratic legitimacy by maintaining the Congress. The author rightly concentrates his attention on the period 1964 through 1968. But for the arbitrary regime to maintain the support of the civilian upper and middle class it had to look like something other than it was. At the end of 1968, Deputy Márcio Moreira Alves gave an impassioned speech recommending boycotting the 7th of September parade and suggesting that girls not date military men. The army demanded that his parliamentary immunity be lifted so he could be punished, but the Congress refused to do so. The crisis ended with the issuing of Institutional Act #5, which greatly expanded the General-President's powers, including an ability to close the Congress. The lights of democracy dimmed considerably. [FDM]

1571 **Weimer, Rodrigo de Azevedo.** Felisberta e sua gente: consciência histórica e racialização em uma família negra no pós-emancipação rio-grandense. Rio de Janeiro: FGV Editora, 2015. 272 p.: bibl.

This pathbreaking research provides a multigenerational oral history of the family of the ex-slave Felisberta that emphasizes her descendants' memories about enslavement and how they change over time. [MAM]

COLONIAL

1572 **Albuquerque, Maria Betânia Barbosa.** Beberagens indígenas e educação não escolar no Brasil colonial. Belém, Brazil: Fundação Cultural do Pará Tacredo Neves, 2012. 167 p.: ill. (Selo Ildefonso Guimarães de literatura)

This volume is a study of the manufacture, use, and significance of alcoholic beverages within the Tupinamba indigenous group. This group lived primarily in the region of São Luis in the state of Maranhão in the Brazilian Amazon. The thesis of the book is that the manufacture of these products required a sophistication not acknowledged by scholars. Valuable examination of the plants of the region and the techniques required to produce the desired products. The author emphasizes the role of women in the production of alcoholic beverages. [MG]

1573 **Amado, Janaína** and **Leny Caselli Anzai.** Luís de Albuquerque: viagens e governo na Capitania de Mato Grosso, 1771–1791. São Paulo: Versal Editores, 2014. 394 p.: bibl., ill.

Luís de Albuquerque was the captain general of the captaincy of Mato Grosso from 1771 to 1791. His mandate was to strengthen the Portuguese claim to this western region by doing a variety of projects, including building the Beira Fort in the present state of Rondônia. The authors discovered his diaries in the Newberry College Library in Chicago. This publication provides a history and analysis of the activities and success of Albuquerque. Included are illustrations of the time and photographs of the present. The diaries and accompanying documents are reproduced. A beautiful volume of great value to historians of the 18th-century frontier. [MG]

1574 **Anselm Eckart, S.J. e o Estado do Grão-Pará e Maranhão setecentista (1785).** Organização de Nelson Papavero e Antonio Porro. Belém, Brazil: Museu Paraense Emílio Goeldi, 2013. 404 p.: bibl., ill., maps.

Eckart was a German Jesuit who came to Maranhão, Brazil in 1753 and remained in the region until he arrested and sent to Portugal in 1757 by order of the Marques de Pombal. During his time in Brazil, he was involved in numerous activities, including excursions up the Amazon to study indigenous culture and languages. He was freed from prison in 1777 and returned to Germany where he wrote his memoirs. In 1785, he published a series of notes on various topics related to the region of Brazil where he had lived. This volume is a study of Eckart's time in Brazil, and a publication of his original works with a Portuguese translation. Included are, *Os Aditamentos, Falsidades da relação abreviada*, and *Vocabulário da lingua Brazil*. In the appendix is a list of objects confiscated from him at the time of his arrest. With this publication, valuable documents on the 18th-century Amazon are now available in Portuguese in one collected volume. [MG]

1575 **Bacelar, Jeferson.** A comida dos baianos no sabor amargo de Vilhena. (*Afro-Asia/Salvador*, 48, 2013, p. 273–310)

Luís dos Santos Vilhena was a professor of Greek in Bahia who arrived in Brazil in 1787. His volume *Recopilação de notícias soteropolitanas e brasílicas* (Compilation of News on Salvador and Brazil), popularly known as "The Letters of Vilhena," is an important source of information about the region. This article examines Bahian food and eating habits from information gleaned from the Vilhena descriptions. [MG]

1576 **Barganhas e querelas da escravidão: tráfico, alforria e liberdade (séculos XVIII e XIX).** Organização de Gabriela Dos Reis Sampaio, Lisa Earl Castillo e Wlamyra Albuquerque. Salvador, Brazil: Edufba, Editora da Universidade Federqal da Bahia, 2014. 358 p.: bibl., ill., maps.

Ten essay by historians connected to the Grupo de Pesquisa Escravidão e Invenção da Liberdade (Slavery and the Invention of Freedom) in the graduate history department of the Universidade Federal da Bahia. The purpose of the research group is to study all aspects of slavery and its abolition using primary source materials. Most essays are about slavery in Bahia. The essays vary in subject and quality with the majority focusing on manumission. [MG]

1577 **Bellini, Lígia.** A coisa obscura: mulher, sodomia e inquisição no Brasil colonial. Segunda edição. Salvador, Brazil: EDUFBA, 2014. 113 p.: bibl.

A second edition of the revision of the author's master's thesis from Universidade Federal da Bahia first published in 1989 by Editora Brasiliense under the same title. There are only minimal changes from the original 1989 publication. The study examines accusations in the 1592 Inquisition visit regarding sexual activities of gay women. [MG]

1578 **Berbel, Márcia Regina; Parron, Tâmis;** and **Rafael de Bivar Marquese.** Slavery and politics: Brazil and Cuba, 1790–1850. Translated by Leonardo Marques. Albuquerque: University of New Mexico Press, 2016. 362 p.: bibl., index.

A comparative study of 18th-century slavery in Cuba and Brazil. A translation of a Brazilian publication, *Escravidão e Política: Brasil e Cuba, 1790–1850*, São Paulo: HUCITEC, 2010, this study suggests that even through the two countries have obvious differences, the presence of a similar slave system resulted in comparable historical patterns. The authors believe that the events of the Haitian Revolution, the evolution of Iberian constitutional structures in the early part of the century, and the parliamentary experiences in both countries resulted in slavery being at the center of society. [MG]

1579 **Braga, Isabel M.R. Mendes Drumond.** Bens de hereges: inquisição e cultura material, Portugal e Brasil, séculos XVII–XVIII. Coimbra, Portugal: Imprensa da Universidade de Coimbra, 2012. 426 p.: bibl., maps. (Investigação)

A study of material culture described in investigations done by the Catholic Inquisition in cases related to Jews who had converted to Catholicism (Cristãos Novos). The author examines the confiscated property and then analyzes the items in relation to house, kitchen, clothing, jewelry, work items, and books. This inquiry provides an analysis of home and work life. However, these homes cannot be considered typical since many belonged merchants. Studies such as this demonstrate the value of detailed Inquisition records in providing information on life in Portugal and Brazil. [MG]

1580 **O Brasil colonial.** Vol. 1, 1443–1580. Vol. 2, 1580–1720. Vol. 3, 1720–1821. Organização de João Fragoso e Maria de Fátima Gouvêa. Rio de Janeiro: Civilização Brasileira, 2014. 3 v.: bibl.

This three-volume set is a major event in the study and historiography of colonial Brazil. It brings together important essays on the evolution of Portuguese America from its European discovery to Brazil's independence. The authors, primarily from Brazil, are major scholars of the different periods, issues, and debates. The volumes are divided chronologically according to political events. Each volume provides descriptive and analytical information on population, economics, society, culture, and politics. The essays are written using traditional approaches for the most part, although some use new approaches and methodology. The audience for this set are academics and advanced university students, but will be of interest to sophisticated lay readers of history. Each essay includes an extensive and up-to-date bibliography with references and discussion of historiography for each period and topic. This collection is a summary of Brazilian research approaches, debates, and historiography of colonial Brazil of the past 25 years. It will be an important reference and text of colonial Brazil for many years. [MG]

1581 Cabral, Diogo de Carvalho. Na presença da floresta: Mata Atlântica e história colonial. Rio de Janeiro: Garamond, 2014. 535 p.: bibl., ill. (Garamond universitária)

The importance of the forest in the evolution of Brazilian colonial history is symbolically shown by the country's name which comes from a tree—Pau-Brasil. Its wood became the first and most important trade commodity during the first 50 years of Brazil's history. The author, a geographer, provides an interpretive history of the role of the forest in the evolution of the country. The forest was not just an ecological presence, but also an important social and philosophical influence, extending beyond the initial exploration of Brazil, shaping and influencing most aspects of colonial life. An interesting addition to the historiography that shows the forest as much more than just an economic factor in the history of Brazil. [MG]

1582 Cantarelli, Rodrigo. Contra a conspiração da ignorância com a maldade: a Inspetoria de Monumentos de Pernambuco. Recife, Brazil: Fundação Joaquim Nabuco, Editora Massangana, 2014. 236 p.: bibl.

Study of the establishment of the first agency in Pernambuco to save colonial monuments and the role of Gilberto Freyre and other intellectuals in the process. [MAM]

1583 Caratti, Jônatas Marques. O solo da liberdade: as trajetórias da preta Faustina e do pardo Anacleto pela fronteira rio-grandense em tempos do processo abolicionista uruguaio (1842–1862). São Leopoldo, Brazil: Oikos Editora, 2013. 454 p.: bibl., ill. (Coleção Estudos Históricos Latino-Americanos; 10)

An examination of the impact of the 1842 Uruguayan abolition of slavery in the southern state of Brazil, Rio Grande do Sul, between 1840–60. This is a revision of the author's unusually high quality master's thesis. The study looks at a variety of unique aspects of slavery on the frontier such as slave rebellions, slave escapes into Uruguay, sending Brazilian slaves to work in Uruguay, and the commerce of slaves in general on the border after the signing of the 1851, Tratado de Devolução de Escravos (Treaty for the Return of Slaves), between Uruguay and Brazil. This volume suggests an often-unrecognized complexity of slavery and abolition on the frontier. [MG]

1584 Cortesão, Jaime. Raposo Tavares e a formação territorial do Brasil. Edição Fac-símile. São Paulo: Fundap, 2012. 454 p.: bibl., ill., index. (Coleção Paulista)

This volume, originally published in 1954, is one of the seminal books for an understanding colonial Brazilian history. Cortesão, a Portuguese historian who lived more than 17 years in Brazil, published numerous volumes on Brazil. This volume, a facsimile printing of the original, tells the story of António Raposo Tavares, Brazil's most famous bandeirante (explorer) whose expeditions were the largest in the history of colonial Brazil extending over 6,200 miles to the Rio de la Plata Basin, the slopes of the Andean mountains, and the mouth of the Amazon. His activities provided proofs for Portugal's claim of land far beyond the limits of the Treaty of Tordesillas. The volume includes an excellent introductory essay by Fernando A. Novais of the Universidade de São Paulo. [MG]

1585 Costa, Heraldo Batista da. Tolerância religiosa: criação dos "cemitérios ingleses" no Brasil Colônia: Rio de Janeiro 1808–1811. Rio de Janeiro: Chama Editora, 2014. 128 p.: bibl., ill.

A brief history of a British cemetery in the Gamboa section of Rio de Janeiro. This cemetery provided a place for the burial of Protestants and foreigners in the city. The volume is an interesting case study of change resulting from British influence on Portuguese and Brazilian politics and society. [MG]

1586 Cultura, arte e história: a contribuição dos jesuítas entre os séculos XVI e XIX. Organização de Adriana Romeiro e Magno Moraes Mello. Belo Horizonte, Brazil: Fino Traço Editora, 2014.

277 p.: bibl., ill. (some color). (Coleção História)

A collection of 10 essays on the worldwide influence of Jesuits in the 19th century. The essays were presented at a 2010 conference held at the Universidade Federal de Minas Gerais. The presentations have an international focus looking at Jesuits in Brazil, Portugal, the Philippines, Spain, and Venezuela. All essay are in Portuguese. The collection provides an example of high quality research being done on the Jesuit influence and impact in the Luso-Brazilian and Spanish world. [MG]

1587 Daróz, Carlos Roberto Carvalho. A guerra do açúcar: as invasões holandesas no Brasil. Recife, Brazil: Editora UFPE, 2014. 448 p.: bibl., ill.

A history of the Dutch occupation of northeastern Brazil during the 17th century. The author is a professor of military history and has taught at the military college is Recife. The focus of this history is different from traditional economic and political approaches, analyzing instead the 30-year period as military and war history. Using traditional sources, the volume does not provide significant new information. [MG]

1588 Dos caminhos históricos aos processos culturais entre Brasil e Suriname. Organização de Reginaldo Gomes de Oliveira e Andrea Idelga Jubithana-Fernand. Tradução de Lourival Novais Néto. Boa Vista, Brazil: Editora UFRR, 2014. 183 p.: bibl., ill.

A collection of essays by scholars from the Universidade Federal de Roraima and Suriname's only university, Anton de Kom Universiteit van Suriname. Roraima is the northernmost state of Brazil bordering Venezuela and Guyana. Most of the essays focus on the colonial period examining social interaction between Native Americans, Europeans, and African slaves in this northern region of the Amazon. The essays by scholars from Suriname are translated into Portuguese. This is a unique collection on a region seldom examined in the historical literature of colonial Brazil. [MG]

1589 Educação, sociedade e cultura na América portuguesa: estudos sobre a presença jesuítica. Organização de Fábio Eduardo Cressoni. Curitiba, Brazil: Editora CRV, 2012. 170 p.: bibl.

Five essays written by masters' students from the Universidade Metodista de Piracicaba examining different aspects of Jesuit education in Brazil. The issues discussed are not new and have been the subject of numerous publications. The purpose of this collection is to approach traditional issues with new paradigms related to contemporary ideas of education. The research is interesting though not significantly unique from previous works on the topic. [MG]

1590 Felippe, Guilherme Galhegos. A cosmologia construída de fora: a relação com o outro como forma de produção social entre os grupos chaquenhos no século XVIII. Jundiaí, Brazil: Paco Editorial, 2014. 373 p.: bibl.

An examination of European documents describing 18th-century indigenous groups in the geographic region called the Chaco Plain, the Gran Chaco, or Dry Chaco. This region is the lowland area of the Rio de la Plata basin that includes portions of the Brazilian states of Mato Grosso and Mato Grosso do Sul, The focus of the analysis is on three aspects of Chaco cosmology: war, economics, and food production and consumption. Though most of the documentation is negative, the author's analysis results in an understanding and appreciation of the culture and ideology of this region of indigenous South America. [MG]

1591 Ferreira, Elisangela Oliveira. "Mulheres de fonte e rio": solicitação no confessionário, misoginia e racismo na Bahia setecentista. (Afro-Asia/Salvador, 48, 2013, p. 127–171)

A study of inquisition documents (1702–22) related to accusations made as the result of confessions to priests. The author evaluates the terminology used by men in testimonies and demonstrates not only the presence, but the prevalence, of racism, prejudice, and mistrust of women in society. The author also shows that there was additional racism toward black female slaves in descriptions of sexual behavior. [MG]

1592 Franco, Renato. A piedade dos outros: o abandono de recém-nascidos em uma vila colonial, século XVIII. Rio de Janeiro: FGV Editora, 2014. 254 p.: bibl., ill.

An examination of the practice of 18th-century charity for abandoned children in the city of Ouro Preto, Minas Gerais, principally within religious organizations. This was a period of economic growth, social evolution, and political conflict due to mining and exportation of minerals, primarily gold. A study of the charitable activities of the Church provides a window into the compassion and concern that existed within a society that also included the horrors of slavery. The volume is a publication of a revised masters' thesis from the Universidade Federal Fluminense. [MG]

1593 Françozo, Mariana de Campos. De Olinda a Holanda: o gabinete de curiosidades de Nassau. Campinas, Brazil: Editora Unicamp, 2014. 287 p.: bibl., color ill.

A revision of the author's dissertation in anthropology from the Universidade de Campinas. During the Dutch occupation of Brazil, 1630–54, the governor, João Maurício de Nassau, made a collection of artifacts, paintings, books, plants, and animals that were taken to the Netherlands and put on display. This volume describes how the collection was built, what it included, and how it was displayed in Europe. The author suggests motives and outcomes of the project. Color photographs of some of the items are included. This volume adds some new information about this significant period in the history of the Brazilian colonial northeast. [MG]

1594 Garcia, Elisa Frühauf. Identidades e políticas coloniais: guaranis, índios infiéis, portugueses e espanhóis no Rio da Prata, c. 1750–1800. (*Anos 90*, 18:34, dez. 2011, p. 55–76, bibl.)

An examination of the political and social divisions within the indigenous population of the upper Río de la Plata region between 1750 and 1800. Rejecting the traditional view of indigenous groups strictly divided between the two European powers, the Spanish and Portuguese, the author looks at relationships within and between the different ethnic populations. This analysis suggests that instead of a simple division of the population based on Spanish control of Christianized Indians, the region's actual partition was complicated and based on economic, ethnic, and political relationships between different indigenous groups. [MG]

1595 Gentes das ilhas: trajetórias transatlânticas dos Açores ao Rio Grande de São Pedro entre as décadas de 1740 a 1790. Organização de Ana Silvia Volpi Scott, Gabriel Santos Berute e Paulo Teodoro de Matos. São Leopoldo, Brazil: Oikos Editora, 2014. 220 p.: bibl., ill., maps.

The captaincy of Rio Grande de São Pedro was an administrative region of Brazil centered in the present state of Rio Grande do Sul. The region historically was always populated by a variety of peoples, including blacks and Indigenous. This book of eight essays is a study of immigration to the region by Portuguese from the Azores. By placing Azorean immigration within the context of migration to Brazil in general and migration to the country's southern region in particular, the volume augments our understanding of the peoples who populated South America's largest country. [MG]

1596 Golin, Tau. A fronteira. Vol. 3, 1763–1778—História da brava gente e miseráveis tropas de mar e terra que conquistaram o Brasil meridional. Porto Alegre, Brazil: L&PM Editores; Passo Fundo, Brazil: Méritos Editora 2002. 1 v. (832 p.): ill. (some col.), maps (some col.)

This set is an excellent study of the evolution and expansion of a southern state of Brazil, Rio Grande do Sul. In volume 3, the author examines the final period of conflict between Spain and Portugal for control of southern Brazil and Uruguay. This volume examines in detail, the conflicts, war, and legal battles between the two European powers. It describes events that resulted in the formation of the final boundaries between the two countries. His general thesis is that regardless of political boundaries, the frontier is different because of the connection to the history of the relationship between two countries. [MG]

1597 González Sánchez, Carlos Alberto. La cultura escrita en el mundo Atlántico colonial: Brasil y América del norte. Claves historiográficas, retos y perspectivas. (*Rev. Indias*, 73:259, sept./dic. 2013, p. 633–662, bibl.)

González Sánchez is a professor of early modern history at the University of Seville. His research focuses on the role of written and iconographic communication in the Atlantic world. This article is a summary essay of Brazilian and British North American historiography related to the production of books, the role of libraries, and written communication, primarily during the colonial period. The author demonstrates similarities and consistency in the history that suggests the need for a common history for the Americas, rather than a study focused on Spanish colonies separate from the rest of Brazil. [MG]

1598 Inventário dos lugares de memória do tráfico Atlântico de escravos e da história dos africanos escravizados no Brasil. Organização de Hebe Mattos, Martha Abreu e Milton Guran. Niterói, Brazil: PPGH-UFF, 2014. 111 p.: bibl., ill.

An identification and description of 100 places of importance related to the history of slavery in Brazil. Scholars and experts on the history of slavery were consulted as to the geographic location and significance of the places in history. The listings are organized according to function. The entries are in Portuguese with an English translation, and include the scholars consulted and references in the literature that identify the place. This project is an important first step in documenting the geographic history of slavery in Brazil. [MG]

1599 Kobelinski, Michel. Ufanismo e ressentimento: de Minas Gerais aos sertões de São Paulo (século XVIII). São Paulo: Annablume, 2012. 379 p.: bibl., ill.

Ufanism is the expression of excessive national pride and the exaltation of qualities while minimizing or completely ignoring the negative. In this volume, the author examines conflicting reactions and social manipulation in Minas Gerais during the government of Morgado de Mateus between 1765 and 1774. The author believes the root of the conflict in this period emanates from the Guerra dos Emboadas, 1707–09, between Paulista and non-Paulista claims to gold in Minas Gerais. The author examines the role of arrogance and myth in this conflict with São Paulo in the evolution of the history of colonial Minas Gerais. The volume is a reworking of the authors dissertation and provides a unique view of the history of a conflict in the state of Minas Gerais that continued into the 19th century. [MG]

1600 Lenk, Wolfgang. Guerra e pacto colonial: a Bahia contra o Brasil holandês (1624–1654). São Paulo: Alameda Casa Editorial, 2013. 478 p.: bibl., ill.

Based on the author's 2009 dissertation from UNICAMP (Universidade Estadual de Campinas), this work tells the history of the state of Bahia during the 30-year period of Dutch occupation of the Brazilian Northeast. The thesis of the book is that the Portuguese elite of the state of Bahia were able to maintain a measure of political separation and economic independence from Dutch political control centered in Recife. When the war against the Dutch began, the unified Portuguese front enabled them to regain rapid control of the region. This is an interesting study of the Dutch occupation from the periphery. [MG]

1601 Martins, Alexandre and Luiz Sabeh. Boca Maldita: blasfêmias e sacrilégios em Portugal e no Brasil nos tempos da Inquisição. Organização de Geraldo Pieroni. Jundiaí, Brazil: Paco Editorial, 2012. 153 p.: bibl.

An examination of activities that antagonized, provoked, and upset the Catholic Church during the period of the Inquisition. Sacrilege generally suggests actions, whereas blasphemy connotes speech that is insulting or disrespectful. The authors examine definitions, practices, and outcomes of different types of activities that disrespected the Church. Both Brazil and Portugal are examined. The essays are short and descriptive with limited analysis and add little to our understanding of the Church. [MG]

1602 Menz, Maximiliano Mac. A Companhia de Pernambuco e Paraíba e o funcionamento do tráfico de escravos em Angola, 1759–1775/80. (*Afro-Asia/Salvador*, 48, 2013, p. 45–76, graphs, tables)

The author is professor of history at the Universidade Federal de São Paulo. His research has focused on the economic history of slave trafficking, financing, and transport from Angola between 1730 and1807. This article looks at the public-private partnership of the Pernambuco and Paraíba Company (Companhia Geral de

Comércio de Pernambuco e Paraíba) founded in 1759 by the Pombal government. The company had a monopoly on commerce in the region. The article suggests that the Portuguese government was able to control the slave trade through the dominant role of this company. [MG]

1603 Miranda, Bruno Romero Ferreira.
"Doentes e incapazes para marchar": vida e morte no exército da Companhia Neerlandesa das Índias Ocidentais no nordeste do Brasil, 1630–1654. (*Hist. Ciênc. Saúde Manguinhos*, 22:2, abril/junho 2015, p. 337–353, bibl.)

An examination of the frequency and types of diseases suffered by European soldiers during the Dutch occupation of northern Brazil between 1630 and 1654. Beyond describing the diseases, the author examines the causes and treatments used. The author suggests that disease was more important in the occupation than has been indicated in the literature. [MG]

1604 Miranda Neto, Manoel José de. A utopia possível: Missões Jesuíticas em Guairá, Itatim e Tape, 1609–1767, e seu suporte econômico-ecológico. Brasília: Fundação Alexandre de Gusmão, 2012. 237 p.: bibl., ill. (some color), index, maps.

A history and analysis of Jesuit missions in the frontier region between present-day Brazil, Paraguay, and Uruguay. The author provides a chronological history of the missions from their establishment to the expulsion of the Jesuits from Latin America in 1767. His purpose is to examine the missions focusing on the economy and indigenous abuse. The books fits well in recent historiography that studies the missions in terms of economic development and social consequences, rather than political significance. [MG]

1605 Molina, Matias M. História dos jornais no Brasil. Vol. 1, Da era colonial à Regência (1500–1840). São Paulo: Companhia das Letras, 2015. 1 v.: bibl., ill., index.

Volume one of a projected three-volume history of newspapers in Brazil. The objective of the set is to provide a descriptive history of individual newspapers, personalities, and influences on journalism during the period studied. The restrictions imposed by the Portuguese government on printing and publication resulted in little activity in Brazil until the arrival of the Portuguese Crown in 1808. Consequently, the bulk of the book focuses little on the colonial period before this date. [MG]

1606 Moreno, Alessandra Zorzetto. Vivendo em lares alheios: filhos de criação e adoção em São Paulo colonial e em Portugal, 1765–1822. São Paulo: Annablume, 2013. 374 p.: bibl.

A study of childcare outside the home during the final phase of the colonial period. Using a variety of sources, the author identifies the options that existed for taking care of children. The study examines both positive practices of acceptance of non-relative children and adoption, as well as unfortunate practices of child labor and child slavery. This volume provides a unique look at social life in colonial Brazil. [MG]

1607 Myrup, Erik. Power and corruption in the early modern Portuguese world. Baton Rouge: Louisiana State University Press, 2015. 241 p.: bibl., ill., index.

A readable examination of governance in the early Portuguese Empire. Using as his theme the role and functioning of social networks, the author suggests that Portuguese power was based on informal networks of patronage and influence underlying the formal colonial political structure. The author bases his conclusion primarily on an examination of the institution of colonial government, the Overseas Council. The volume includes only two chapters specifically on Brazil; however, the author used numerous studies of the Brazilian colonial period. Myrup's volume suggests a weaker colonial political structure than has been suggested. [MG]

1608 Networks and trans-cultural exchange: slave trading in the South Atlantic, 1590–1867. Edited by David Richardson and Filipa Ribeiro da Silva. Leiden, Netherlands: Brill, 2015. 278 p.: bibl., index. (Atlantic world: Europe, Africa and the Americas, 1500–1830, 1570–0542 ; volume 30)

Eight essays in English on trade in the Atlantic written by European, Brazilian, and US scholars. The essays establish the prevalence of Angola in trade but also show that other regions of Africa were involved in Portuguese trade. The collection includes a valuable essay on Mozambique. The essays describe the different aspects of the trade beyond slaving activities, focusing on the trade as part of cultural encounter and exchange. The underlying theme of the essays is that the power and influence of Portuguese/Brazilian merchants weakened as competition from other European contenders increased. [MG]

1609 Novinsky, Anita Waingort et al. Os judeus que construíram o Brasil: fontes inéditas para uma nova visão da historia brasileira. São Paulo: Planeta, 2015. 286 p.: bibl., ill.

A summary history of Judaism in colonial Brazil by four professor from the Universidade de São Paulo. The authors suggest that the story of Judaism in Brazil is not widely known and often ignored by Brazilian historians due, in part, to discrimination and racism in Brazil. The work is partly based on manuscripts recently made available in the Portuguese archives of the Inquisition housed in the Arquivo Nacional da Torre do Tombo in Lisbon. The volume illuminates the Jewish side of Brazilian history and suggests that there was significant persecution of Jews and cristãos-novos (New Christians) during the colonial period. [MG]

1610 Obermeier, Franz. Brasilien "für die Jugend und das Volk" Kinder- und Jugendliteratur aus und über Brasilien vom 18. Jahrhundert bis in die Mitte des 20. Jahrhunderts [Brazil for young adult readers and in popular literature: children's and young adult literature about and from Brazil from the 18th century to the mid-20th century]. Kiel, Germany: Universitätsbibliothek, 2016. 319 p.: ill. <http://macau.uni-kiel.de/receive/macau_publ_00001314>

In-depth study of Brazil in children and young adult literature from the mid-18th century to the mid-20th century sheds light on German, French and US views of Brazil. Works from the end of the 19th century include texts in Portuguese texts, mainly written for schools in Brazil. The early 19th-century texts focus on sentimental stories, while those from the later 19th century emphasize adventure-stories. The fictional texts are based on authentic travel literature and natural histories. Texts published in the US, some of them dime novels, focus on the masculinity of the young Americans going to Brazil in search of adventure and personal development. The German texts explore the personal experience of young adults coming from the bourgeoisie often striving to reconquer a lost place in society. Later German colonization in southern Brazil becomes an important motive for writing fictional works about the South American country. For instance, some 19th-century German novels warn about the difficult situations that German settlers faced in Brazil. The Portuguese texts demonstrate the republican project of writing morally suitable fiction and informative reading books for school children to inform them about their country. Despite all the prejudices exhibited in the texts about foreign people, black, mestizo, or indigenous population and the often prevailing idea of Brazil as an uncivilized land (mainly the Amazonian region), all these texts are important for the Brazilian image abroad and among young Brazilians. [F. Obermeier]

1611 Ordem crítica: a América portuguesa nas "fronteiras" do século XVIII. Organização de Guilherme Amaral Luz, Jean Luiz Neves Abreu e Mara Regina do Nascimento. Belo Horizonte, Brazil: Fino Traço editora, 2013. 235 p.: bibl., ill. (Coleção História)

Nine essays on 18th-century Brazil on a variety of topics. The authors have a connection to universities in the state of Minas Gerais, though the research extends beyond this region. The collection provides an assessment of research patterns and the production of Brazilian scholars writing on this period. [MG]

1612 Paiva, Asséde. Brumas da história: ciganos & escravos no Brasil. Volta Redonda, Brazil: Nova Gráfica e Editora, 2012. 188 p.: bibl., ill.

An examination of the role of gypsies in the selling and trading of slaves, primarily in Rio de Janeiro. The author suggests that the perception of a significant involvement of gypsies in the slave trade was actually a myth created by historians who read a few accounts by foreign observers which described gypsy involvement in the selling and trafficking of slaves. These accounts led some historians to conclude an active role of gypsies in the slave trade. Through the examination of the documents recording the sale of slaves, the author found a limited involvement and showed that the majority of slave transactions were conducted by more traditional elite economic figures. The author suggests that gypsies were outcasts in colonial Brazilian history with limited financial resources and that the Brazilian gypsy population in general followed a pattern of life similar to their European counterparts due to tradition and discrimination within Brazilian society. [MG]

1613 **Paiva, Eduardo França.** Dar nome ao novo: uma história lexical da Ibero-América entre os séculos XVI e XVIII: (as dinâmicas de mestiçagens e o mundo do trabalho). Belo Horizonte, Brazil: Autêntica, 2015. 301 p.: bibl., color ill.

An innovative study of the meaning of words and concepts emanating from the colonial period that continue to the present. The author, a historian of slavery, suggests that Ibero-American concepts of race, identity, and self, have their origin in the slave world and the Africanization of work. Social relations including miscegenation and marriage between free and slave were important in the formation of societal definitions. The author believes that abolition and the first years of freedom resulted in alterations of those concepts. He suggests that the institution of slavery has universal influence and he examines both the Brazilian and the Spanish American experiences. [MG]

1614 **Para além das Gerais: dinâmicas dos povos e instituições na América portuguesa Bahia, Goiás e Mato Grosso.** Coordenação de Fernando Lobo Lemes. Organização de Avanete Pereira Sousa, Eduardo José Reinato e Nauk Maria de Jesus. Goiânia, Brazil: Editora da PUC Goiás, 2015. 403 p.: bibl., ill.

Examining the general expansion of Portugal in Africa and South America, the book suggests that the primary reason for the extension of Portuguese settlements in colonial Brazil beyond the coastal regions into the interior was to search for gold and silver. Historians have traditionally focused on the region of Minas Gerais with limited acknowledgement that other regions, namely Goiás, Mato Grosso, and Bahia were part of the expansion. The essays examine issues and subjects connected to these other areas and their economic and social connections with Minas Gerais. The essays suggest that historians need to be more expansive in their research. [MG]

1615 **Pedro Teixeira, a Amazônia e o Tratado de Madri.** Organização de Sérgio Eduardo Moreira Lima e Maria do Carmo Strozzi Coutinho. Brasília: Fundação Alexandre de Gusmão, 2016. 309 p.: bibl., maps. (História diplomática)

Pedro Teixeira was the first European to travel the entire length of the Amazon River. In 1637, Teixeira, a Portuguese explorer, led a large expedition consisting of 47 canoes, 70 soldiers and 1,200 natives, up the Amazon, exploring the Rio Negro, and discovering the Madeira River before finally reaching the Spanish settlement of Rio Quijos. The expedition took eight month to reach Quijos and included significant exploits and adventures. Some of the expedition went further into Spanish territory, primarily by foot, to reach the city of Quito several months later. This volume includes five essays that examine the importance of the expedition and describe the primary sources that document the journey. The volume also includes 200 pages of transcribed documents as well as 10 contemporary maps. The study concludes that Portugal, rather than Spain, was able to lay claim to the territory of Brazil primarily due to Teixeira's expedition. [MG]

1616 **Pérez, José Manuel Santos.** Brazil and the politics of the Spanish Habsburgs in the South Atlantic, 1580–1640. (*in* South Atlantic, past and present. Edited by Luiz Felipe De Alencastro. Dartmouth, Mass.: Tagus Press at UMass Dartmouth, 2014, p. 104–120)

The crowns of Spain and Portugal were united between 1580–1640. This unification had a significant effect on the Portuguese Empire in a variety of areas including culture. The author suggests that Brazil underwent a less significant "Castilianization" than did Portugal. Brazilians were able to maintain independence from the Spanish influence. [MG]

1617 Prado, Fabrício Pereira. Trans-imperial networks in the crisis of the Spanish monarchy: the Rio de Janeiro-Montevideo connection, 1778–1805. (*Americas/Washington*, 73:2, April 2016, p. 211–236.)

Prado is a professor of history at College of William and Mary. His research focuses on the Río de la Plata region during the Bourbon period. In this article, he examines the establishment of the Viceroyalty of Rio de la Plata combined with the expulsion of the Portuguese from Uruguay. By examining social and commercial networks of merchant elites in the Rio de la Plata region, the author suggests that Montevideo merchants used trans-imperial connections specifically with the Portuguese, to communicate and interact with Spain. He shows the emergence of Montevideo as competition with Buenos Aires as a center for Atlantic trade. The article describes how these interactions reinforced, rather than weakened, the Spanish Empire, and at the same time strengthened the economic position of Montevideo in the Spanish empire. [MG]

1618 Raizes medievais do Brasil moderno: ordens religiosas entre Portugal e o Brasil. Coordenação de João Marinho dos Santos e Manuela Mendonça. Lisboa: Academia Portuguesa da História, Centro de História da Sociedade e Cultura, 2012. 363 p.: bibl.

A collection of essays by primarily Portuguese historians examining Portuguese religious orders in Brazil. The overlying theme of the collection is that the modern political and religious environment of the Catholic Church in Brazil has roots in the foundations of these orders in colonial Brazil. Though this volume includes valuable research on the Church, unfortunately, the volume lacks a unifying essay. [MG]

1619 Representações do sertão: poder, cultura e identidades. Organização de Renato da Silva Dias e Jeaneth Xavier de Araújo. São Paulo: Humanitas, 2013. 434 p.: bibl. (Coleção História diversa; 1)

A collection of essays on the hinterland of Brazil in the captaincy Minas do Ouro in the present state of Minas Gerais during the 18th-century period of exploration and the gold rush. The book is divided into two sections. The first includes essays on historical themes characteristic of a frontier society including examinations of revolts, violence, slave rebellions, and criminal activities. The second group of essays studies topics outside of traditional frontier themes. The authors examine the evolution of a society influenced by religious activities and folk celebrations. Included are studies of women and families, road development, and political events. This volume is an interesting collection of essays that provides new insights and interpretations of the evolution of Minas Gerais during a tumultuous time. [MG]

1620 Rodrigues, Jaime. Um perfil de cargos e funções na marinha mercante luso-brasileira, séculos XVIII e XIX. (*Anos 90*, 22:42, dez. 2015, p. 295–324, appendix, bibl., tables)

Using registration records of Portuguese ships from the mid-18th to the mid-19th centuries, the author examines the positions and functions of the crews. Beyond a descriptive analysis, the author discovered that the national and ethnic origins of the crews indicates an unexpected diversity among the men aboard ship. [MG]

1621 Santa Cruz: de legado dos jesuítas à pérola da Coroa. Organização de Carlos Engemann e Marcia Amantino. Rio de Janeiro: EdUERJ, 2013. 352 p.: bibl., ill., maps.

A study of the Jesuit settlement in the present-day Santa Cruz neighborhood in the city of Rio de Janeiro. Eleven essays study the plantation using documentation found in inventories and court cases between 1759 and 1801. The book includes three sections: Jesuit administration, slavery, and the post-Jesuit period when the plantation was under first Portuguese and then Brazilian governmental control. The book is a case study of Jesuit economic and social power in colonial Brazil. [MG]

Seminário Escravidão, Fronteiras e Relações Internacionais no Império do Brasil, *Universidade do Rio de Janeiro, 2011*. As fronteiras da escravidão e da liberdade no sul da América. See item **1040**.

1622 Seminário Internacional "Nas Rotas do Império: Eixos Mercantis, Tráfico de Escravos e Relações Sociais no Mundo

Português", *Universidade Federal do Rio de Janeiro, Programa de Pós-Graduação em História Social, 2006*. Nas rotas do Império: eixos mercantis, tráfico e relações sociais no mundo português. Organização de João Fragoso et al. 2a edição. Vitória, Brazil: EDUFES, 2014. 623 p.: bibl., ill.

A collection of papers on colonial trade routes that examines the movement of goods and slaves in colonial Brazil. Shows how the trade impacted population growth, social evolution, and political development. Originally published in Portugal, this is a reprint with minor changes. [MG]

1623 **Silva, Augusto da.** O governo da ilha de Santa Catarina e sua terra firme: território, administração e sociedade (1738–1807). Rio de Janeiro: Ministério da Justiça, Arquivo Nacional, 2013. 235 p.: bibl. (Prêmio Arquivo Nacional de Pesquisa—2011)

A study of 18th century Portuguese administration on the southern island of Santa Catarina, the city of Florianopolis. A revision of the author's dissertation from the Universidade de São Paulo, the book provides a case study of peripheral Portuguese government outside of the political center in Rio de Janeiro. The author demonstrates that the political and legal aspects of the government were influenced more by local needs and demands than by a strict adherence to the dictates of Lisbon. [MG]

1624 **Silva, Filipa Ribeiro da.** The Dutch and the consolidation of the seventeenth-century south Atlantic complex, c. 1630–1654. (*in* South Atlantic, past and present. Dartmouth, Mass.: Tagus Press at UMass Dartmouth, 2014, p. 83–103)

In this chapter, the evolution and expansion of trading and commerce in the South Atlantic is examined, focusing on the Dutch West India Company and Dutch private merchants based in northeast Brazil during the occupation of the region. The Dutch presence significantly disrupted trade between Brazil and Angola. Trade between the two regions did not recover until the Dutch were expulsed from Brazil. [MG]

1625 **Silveira, Marco Antonio.** Fama pública: poder e costume nas Minas setecentistas. São Paulo: Hucitec Editora, 2015. 356 p.: bibl., color ill. (Estudos históricos; 89)

The publication of a 2000 dissertation from the Universidade de São Paulo. The book studies material culture in the region of Vila Rica in 18th-century Minas Gerais. The book provides a portrait of life among the different classes of society. The result is an examination of the power and social structure that developed in a period of economic boom and expansion. [MG]

1626 **Siqueira, Sonia A.** O momento da Inquisição. João Pessoa, Brazil: Editora Universitária, 2013. 706 p.: bibl., one folded ill. (Coleção Videlicet)

The publication of a doctoral dissertation defended at the Universidade de São Paulo in 1968. The author is a leading expert on the topic and has published other works on the Inquisition since 1968 using this research. The volume provides in one place an extensive history of the establishment of the Inquisition in Brazil, the administration of the office, and evaluation of procedures used. Suggested as a "new classic," the volume makes valuable information available to the public that had been a challenge to find. It does not include new research done over the past 50 years, but is a foundational study that needed to be published. [MG]

1627 **Souza, Lécio Gomes de.** Bacia do Paraguai: geografia e história. Vol. 1. 2a. edição. Campo Grande, Brazil: Instituto Histórico e Geográfico de Mato Grosso do Sul, 2012. 1 v.: bibl., ill. (Série Memória sul-mato-grossense)

A reprinting of Volume 1 of a three-volume set published in a little-known 1978 edition. This version has only limited updating. The region described is the drainage region surrounding the Rio Paraguai in western extremes of the states of Mato Grosso and Mato Grosso do Sul. The author provides geographic descriptions and summaries of the history of the region. The volume is of interest because it provides information on a little-known region of Brazil. For a review of the reprint of vols. 2–3, see item **1043**. [MG]

1628 **Souza e Mello, Marcia Eliane Alves de.** Perspectivas sobre a "nobreza da terra" na Amazônia colonial. (*Rev. Hist./São Paulo*, 168, 2013, p. 26–68)

A look at the formation of local political elites in 18th-century Amazon by examining the election history of the Belém City Council. The study focus on the election of Luís Francisco Barreto in 1741. The author suggests the importance of networks related to family connections, marriage, and economic relationships as important factors in the ascendency of local citizens into positions of power. [MG]

1629 **Souza Junior, José Alves de.** Negros da terra e/ou negros da Guiné: trabalho, resistência e repressão no Grão-Pará no período do Diretório. (*Afro-Asia/ Salvador,* 48, 2013, p. 173–211)

An investigation of the captive labor force in the northern Amazon region of Grão-Pará and Maranhão in the late 18th century. The author shows that epidemics and oppressive treatment resulted in a high mortality rate amongst native slaves justifying an increase in the African slave trade. The author suggests that the exploitation and oppression of African slaves gave rise to the formation of a rebellion identity manifested by strong forms of collective resistance that in turn led to increased repression by the slave owners. [MG]

1630 **Zanon, Dalila.** Bispos de São Paulo: as diretrizes da Igreja no século XVIII. São Paulo: Annablume: FAPESP, 2012. 221 p.: bibl.

This book examines religious organizations and their influence in the functioning of the captaincy of São Paulo during the second half of the 18th century. The book is a revision of a masters' thesis from the University of Campinas, Unicamp. The author's approach is to use the biographies of the first three bishops of the dioceses of São Paulo to demonstrate the influence of the Church on the entire community. The volume provides an interesting look at the day-to-day activities of the bishops as related to ecclesiastical functions within the environment of civil and religious activities. [MG]

EMPIRE AND NATIONAL

1631 **Absell, Christopher David** and **Antonio Tena-Junguito.** Brazilian export growth and divergence in the tropics during the nineteenth century. (*J. Lat. Am. Stud.,* 48:4, Nov. 2016, p. 677–706)

This article offers a reexamination of a long-held assumption about Brazilian economic growth—that it was not very strong in the early imperial period—and offers a convincing argument that it has been undervalued. Ties Brazilian export growth to the abolition of slavery in the British Caribbean. [MAM]

1632 **Alonso, Angela.** Flores, votos e balas: o movimento abolicionista brasileiro (1868–88). São Paulo: Companhia das Letras, 2015. 529 p.: bibl., index.

Important study of abolitionism in 19th-century Brazil, based on extensive research in primary sources in Brazil and the US. Comprehensive list of sources and bibliography. [MAM]

1633 **Alsina Júnior, João Paulo Soares.** Rio-Branco: grande estratégia e o poder naval. Rio de Janeiro: FGV Editora, 2015. 403 p., 12 unnumbered plates: bibl., ill., index.

In designing Brazil's foreign relations at the start of the 20th century the Baron of Rio-Branco emphasized that Brazil's diplomats had to be well prepared intellectually to mobilize their ethical and juridical arguments in defense of national interests. But it is often forgotten that he considered military power essential to achieve hegemony in South America. For that reason he arranged training in Imperial Germany for a group of officers who would later be called the "Young Turks" so that they could reform and modernize the Brazilian army. For the Navy, the Baron had the biggest of the era's warships constructed in Britain. This study of Rio-Branco's thinking and efforts to build Brazil's power is an extremely welcome addition to the diplomatic and military literature. It sets a new standard for such studies. [FDM]

1634 **Alvarenga, Antonia Valtéria Melo.** Nação, país moderno e povo saudável: política de combate à lepra no Piauí. Teresina, Brazil: EDUFPI, 2013. 343 p.: bibl., ill. (some), color map.

Revised PhD dissertation of promising junior scholar of the social history of modernization and public health who explores the history of national efforts at extinguishing leprosy in the context of previously unexplored issues related to the state of Piauí. Based on previously unexplored primary sources. Extensive bibliography. [MAM]

1635 Alves, Jolinda de Moraes. Assistência aos pobres em Londrina, 1940/1980. Londrina, Brazil: EDUEL, 2013. 372 p.: bibl., ill.

The text is based on a doctoral dissertation at the Universidade Estadual Paulista-Assis that provides rich detail about social assistance in Londrina, Paraná. The coffee boom in the north of Paraná produced considerable wealth, but also heart-rending poverty. The deep frosts of 1975 destroyed the coffee groves and plunged the workers into unemployment and a struggle to survive. Without education and skills, the search for employment was often hopeless. Abandoned children, orphans, and juvenile delinquents became commonplace. The author examines how the public authorities worked to change this difficult social reality. The churches set up asylums for the elderly and shelters where beggars and itinerants could pass the night. The state became legally responsible for assistance to abandoned children. The author notes that before the Constitution of 1988 there was no public policy of social assistance. The book analyzes the first state instruments of social assistance via a 1993 program. In the following year Londrina created a Municipal Council of Social Assistance that sought to coordinate public and private efforts. The author argues that these efforts generated a new culture of social assistance. Along the way she provides a good deal of the social history of the north of the state. [FDM]

1636 Amorim, Paulo Henrique. O quarto poder: uma outra história. São Paulo: Hedra, 2015. 553 p.: bibl., ill., index.

The book analyzes the changes in Brazilian media since the 1960s, as the country went from being mostly agricultural to industrial. An international journalist, the author brings a broad perspective to writing about his homeland. This is another intimate way to look at the post-64 era. He tells lots of stories that provide interesting sidelights to major events and certainly major personalities. [FDM]

1637 Amoroso, Marta Rosa. Terra de índio: imagens em aldeamentos do Império. São Paulo: Editora Terceiro Nome, 2014. 243 p.: bibl. (Antropologia hoje)

This study of indigenous people in 19th-century Paraná state is based on the unusually detailed reports to the provincial and federal governments by Capuchin missionary Frei Timotheo de Castelnuovo. [MAM]

1638 Aragão, Isabel. Da caserna ao cárcere: uma identidade militar-rebelde construída nas prisões (1922–1930). Jundiaí, Brazil: Paco Editorial, 2013. 432 p.: bibl., ill.

Extensively researched study of the development of a military ethos in the 1920s and the issues that led to military rebellions and imprisonment. [MAM]

1639 Arraes, Ricardo. Batalhão Suez: história, memória e representações dos soldados brasileiros (1957–1967). Rio de Janeiro: Editora Multifoco, 2013. 374 p.: bibl., ill., maps.

It is almost forgotten that Brazil has sent its soldiers as UN peacekeepers ever since the first such mission in the Sinai in 1957. It was an adventure for those 6,300 young men who stood between the Israelis and the Egyptians. The particular strength of the book results from the interviews that the author conducted with participants. Brazil's role in UN peacekeeping deserves more attention. [FDM]

1640 Avella, Aniello Angelo. Teresa Cristina de Bourbon: uma imperatriz napolitana nos trópicos, 1843–1889. Rio de Janeiro: EDUERJ, 2014. 238 p.: bibl., ill., maps.

A brief biography of the second Empress of Brazil by Italian scholar of literature that aims to place her in the context of broader relationships between Italy and Brazil. [MAM]

1641 Bartholazzi, Rosane Aparecida. Os italianos no noroeste fluminense: estratégias familiares e mobilidade social, 1897–1950. Rio de Janeiro: Garamond, 2013. 342 p.: bibl. (Garamond universitária)

Well-researched study of Italian immigration to Rio de Janeiro from a family history perspective that includes a discussion of the families' conditions prior to immigration to Brazil and concludes with a review of remissions paid to relatives in Italy by Italians in Brazil. [MAM]

1642 Bertonha, João Fábio. Integralismo: problemas, perspectivas e questões historiográficas. Prefácio por Marion Brepohl. Maringa, Brazil: EDUEM, 2014. 225 p.: bibl.

Integralismo's persistence even after its seeming destruction in the Vargas era makes it more than an historical curiosity. Bertonha is a careful student of the movement and here provides an extremely knowledgeable guide that summarizes the existing literature and points the way to deeper research and analysis. He gives us a critique of the historiography and an explanation of the evolution of the movement. Very useful. [FDM]

1643 Brame, Fernando Ribeiro Conçalves. O império sobre os trilhos. Vol. I, Estradas de ferro e desarticulação socioespacial do Rio de Janeiro. Vol. II, Estado, disputas políticas e articulação socioespacial do Rio de Janeiro. Rio de Janeiro: Gramma, 2013–2014. 2 v.: bibl., ill., maps.

This innovative study of the establishment of railroads and roads in Rio de Janeiro state contains numerous oversize GIS-based maps showing the way that the railroad, first, disrupted existing transportation routes and then reshaped the city and its environs. [MAM]

1644 Brigagão, Clóvis and Trajano Ribeiro. Brizola. São Paulo: Paz & Terra, 2015. 287 p.: bibl., ill., index.

Leonel Brizola was a controversial politician. Brizola, the brother-in-law of João Goulart, had played a fiery role in the run-up to the 1964 coup. He stirred anxiety and violent emotion on the right when as governor of Rio Grande do Sul he claimed that he had guerrilla bands (*Grupos de Onze*) ready to defend the government. In fact, he did not—and the government fell. The authors take up the story with his self-imposed exile in 1977, first in the US and then in Portugal. The book provides insights into the development of amnesty that would be a major step toward creating a more open atmosphere in Brazil. It places Brazil more clearly into the complicated international scene of those years. [FDM]

1645 Cantarino, Geraldo. A ditadura que o inglês viu: documentos diplomáticos sigilosos revelam a visão britânica do Brasil desde o golpe de 1964 até o processo de abertura política em 1979. Rio de Janeiro: Mauad X, 2014. 199 p.: bibl.

Diplomatic records are often a quick way to make up for the inaccessibility of local national documentation. The coup and civil-military government after 1964 can easily be studied using the reports, dispatches, and analyses of foreign diplomats. They have the further advantage of often being opened to researchers before the local archives. In this book the author has assembled dispatches of British diplomats whose task was to explain to London what was happening in Brazil. Often their sources are well informed and could name names. And because the British were less culpable in the Vietnam conflict their sources might have been less emotional and less ideologically involved. The book's chapters follow a chronological order from 1963 through 1979. Very useful. [FDM]

1646 Carta de chamada: relatos da imigração judaica em São Paulo de 1930 até 1942. Organização de Marilia Levi Freidenson e Núcleo de História Oral Gaby Becker do Arquivo Histórico Judaico Brasileiro. São Paulo: Arquivo Histórico Judaico Brasileiro: Annablume, 2014. 407 p.: bibl., ill., index.

This book is an oral history testimony of Jewish immigrants, their children, or grandchildren that provides a diverse and lively image of their lives in São Paulo. The full transcripts are open to research in the Arquivo Histórico Judaico Brasileiro. The interviews here are organized chronologically so that they provide individual views of the larger happenings. The chapters treat some lives before coming to Brazil, the 1930 "revolution" through the 1932 revolt. Stories related to the rise of Nazism and the decisions to flee Europe are followed by personal experiences adjusting to life in Brazil. Other testimony treated the fears engendered by Integralism and the Estado Novo. There are stories from Austria and Italy about the dangers of sea travel and about the anxieties of being cut off from family and friends. Brazil's entry into the war brought other tales to light. This is an important source for those interested in Jewish migration and more generally the 1930s and early 1940s. [FDM]

1647 Castro, Evandro Carlos Guilhon de. Tropeiros em Mariana oitocentista. Belo Horizonte, Brazil: Fino Traço Editora, 2014. 146 p.: bibl., map. (Coleção História)

Study of a rarely explored group of workers in the internal Brazilian economy, muleteers, who were responsible for most of the short- and long-distance hauling of export and domestic products alike. Based on postmortem inventories from the Minas Gerais gold region. [MAM]

1648 O censo de 1906 do Rio de Janeiro. Coordenação editorial por Anabela Paiva; Prefácio por Nelson Senra. Rio de Janeiro: Prefeitura da Cidade do Rio de Janeiro, Secretaria Municipal da Casa Civil, Instituto Pereira Passos, 2012. 399 p.

Reproduction of the 1906 census of Rio de Janeiro, very valuable for researchers. [MAM]

1649 Colóquio Comunistas Brasileiros: Cultura Política e Produção Cultural. Universidade de São Paulo, Departamento de História, 2011. Comunistas brasileiros: cultura política e produção cultural. Organização de Marcos Napolitano, Rodrigo Czajka e Rodrigo Patto Sá Motta. Belo Horizonte, Brazil: Editora UFMG, 2013. 362 p.: bibl., ill. (Coleção Humanitas)

Finally we have a book about communists that is not laden with heavy Marxist jargon. Its group of scholars has focused on the cultural efforts of communists in drama, painting, television, journalism, music, and song. There is an interesting comparative chapter on Chile and Brazil and another on the role of Nelson Werneck Sodré in trying to move the military to the left. The essays provide insights that will help to make communist resistance during the military years more understandable. [FDM]

1650 Costa, Dora Isabel Paiva da. Fronteiras nas Améqricas: povoamento e colonização no Brasil e Estados Unidos, século XIX. São Paulo: Alameda Casa Editorial, 2014. 320 p.: bibl.

Comparative history of the role of frontiers in economic development and democracy in Brazil and the US. [MAM]

1651 Costa, Edwaldo. Meia culpa: O Globo e a ditadura militar. Florianópolis: Editora Insular, 2015. 287 p.: bibl., ill.

This book examines the role that the Rio de Janeiro newspaper *O Globo* played during the military years. Recently the paper apologized for its editorial stance, but the author believes that was not enough to wipe away its ideological support for the 1964 coup. The head of *O Globo* during those years, Roberto Marinho, may not have benefitted materially, although there are suspicions, but he certainly colored negatively the image of the armed resistance. The principal objective of the book is to analyze the discussion *O Globo* used to support the regime and its gradual change of attitude. It promoted the idea that the communist threat was real and later that the military were the best prepared to bring democracy back. The author concludes that the paper "manipulated History, subverted values of those who opposed the military regime, omitted information and a few times . . . [violated] one of the requirements of journalism, which is to hear and explain all sides of a question or fact" (p. 269). [FDM]

1652 Costa, Rafael Maul de Carvalho. Escravizados na liberdade: abolição, classe e cidadania na Corte Imperial. Rio de Janeiro: Rio Prefeitura, Casa Civil: Arquivo Geral da Cidade do Rio de Janeiro, 2014. 219 p.: bibl.

This study of free workers in 19th-century Rio de Janeiro is based on extensive research in primary documents and adds free workers to the groups involved in Brazil's abolitionist movement. It reflects a new direction in Brazilian history, looking at "worlds of work" of both free and enslaved laborers. [MAM]

1653 Coutinho, Renato Soares. Um Flamengo grande, um Brasil maior: o Clube de Regatas do Flamengo e a construção do imaginário político nacionalista popular (1933–1955). Rio de Janeiro: 7Letras, 2014. 194 p.: bibl., ill. (Coleção Brasil republicano)

The author confronts the basic question of why Flamengo became the most popular futebol club in Brazil. Like many things in Brazil, it began in the 1930s. Under the leadership of its president, José Bastos Padilha (1933–37), the club shaped its image in an attractive manner at the moment when the Brazilian state was heralding nationalism and popular culture. Throughout the text the author raises a number of possible explanations. The press and the radio coverage were significant. [FDM]

1654 Cowan, Benjamin A. "Nosso terreno": crise moral, política evangélica e a formação da "Nova Direita" brasileira. (*Varia Hist.*, 30:52, jan./abril 2014, p. 101–125)

It is curious that evangelicals think that it is proper to involve their churches in partisan politics. Stranger still, in Brazil and the US, they have tied themselves firmly to the political right. This often puts them at odds with the Christian message. This article adroitly introduces the personalities and maneuvers that carried them rightward. The Baptists and Assembly of God members had supported the military regime and looked disfavorably on ecumenicalism, social justice schemes, and communism. They supported repression and denied that Brazil was under a dictatorship. More study is clearly needed and this is a useful starting point. [FDM]

1655 Cunha, Paulo Ribeiro da. Militares e militância: uma relação dialeticamente conflituosa. Prefácio por João Roberto Martins Filho. São Paulo: Editora UNESP, 2014. 295 p.: bibl.

Is there a leftist military? Military organization and mode of thought generally leans toward the right, rather than the left. Yet, in Brazil there was a persistent leftist current in the armed forces from the 1920s through the 1960s. Is it accounted for by the sharp inequality in the society that calls out for remediation? Did persecution strengthen the tendency by giving it recognition? The author's discussion of the thinking of Samuel Huntington, Nelson Werneck Sodré, Edmundo Campos Coelho, Alfred Stepan, Alan Rouquié, João Quartim de Moraes, and others will help students enter the debates. But perhaps it would be more profitable to spend more effort on archival research than in arguing theory. [FDM]

1656 d'Avila, Cristiane. João do Rio a caminho da Atlântida: por uma aproximação luso-brasileira. Rio de Janeiro: Contra Capa: FAPERJ, 2015. 237 p.: bibl.

This work provides a cultural history of Rio de Janeiro in the 20th century through the life trajectory of Brazilian writer João do Rio, especially the period between 1908 and 1920. Based on new sources (letters) found at the National Archives in Rio de Janeiro and the Real Gabinete de Leitura, the author presents a well-crafted analysis of the formational years of João do Rio when he developed nationalist feelings and language that came to characterize his literary production and career, culminating in the publication of the magazine *Atlântida*. [F. Prado]

1657 Dimensões e fronteiras do estado brasileiro no oitocentos. Organização de José Murilo de Carvalho e Lúcia Maria Bastos P. Neves. Rio de Janeiro: EdUERJ, 2014. 375 p.: bibl.

Important collection of essays by significant Brazilian scholars about the strengths, weaknesses and contours of the Brazilian state as seen through its relationships to the law, the economy, the press, and other factors. [MAM]

1658 Ditadura: o que resta da transição. Organização por Milton Pinheiro. São Paulo: Boitempo Editorial, 2014. 372 p.: bibl. (Coleção Estado de sítio)

This multi-authored collection focusses on the notion of class and the role it played in the civil-military regime installed in 1964. The extra-military role of the armed forces militarized the state apparatus. Unlike the Nazi-fascist totalitarianism in which the party controlled the political police, in the Brazilian case it was the army generals that controlled the political police (p. 91 ff). There is a fair amount of theory applied to politics in these essays. The coup aimed at crippling nationalist populism and over the next 21 years produced new social-economic reactions that will take decades to work out. [FDM]

1659 Dreher, Martin Norberto. 190 anos de imigração alemã no Rio Grande do Sul: esquecimentos e lembranças. 2a edição. São Leopoldo, Brazil: Oikos Editora, 2014. 248 p.: bibl.

Essays on German immigration to southern Brazil by a senior German-trained Brazilian historian of religion that includes reflections on push factors leading to German immigration to Brazil, the historiography of the Mucker revolt, the relationships between immigrants, Africans, and indigenous people, and other topics, including the Brothers Grimm as reading material among German-Brazilians. No bibliography. [MAM]

Dunn, Christopher. Contracultura: alternative arts and social transformation in authoritarian Brazil. See item **2887**.

1660 Estado e administração: a construção do Brasil independente (1822–1840). Organização de Dilma Fátima Avellar Cabral da Costa et al. Rio de Janeiro: Ministério da Justiça, Arquivo Nacional, 2015. 431 p.: bibl., index.

Valuable reference source on the organization of the Brazilian government in the early independence period, that includes informative essays and alphabetized entries by agency including enabling legislation and an outline of responsibilities over time. [MAM]

1661 Evangelista, Ana Maria da Costa.
Arroz e feijão, discos e livros: história do Serviço de Alimentação da Previdência Social, SAPS (1940–1967). Apresentação de Jorge Ferreira. Rio de Janeiro: FAPERJ, Fundação Carlos Chagas de Amparo à Pesquisa do Estado do Rio de Janeiro; Rio de Janeiro: 7Letras, 2014. 227 p.: bibl., ill. (Coleção Brasil republicano)

The Vargas era was rich in assistance to workers as demonstrated by the creation of the Serviço de Alimentação da Previdência Social in 1940. The SAPS established low cost restaurants in urban areas to provide decent, balanced meals. Soon libraries were added to the restaurants along with classes to teach reading and writing, and specialized courses in sewing and making clothes. These centers also promoted folk festivals, such as São João, to increase local sociability. They sent specialists in nutrition to make home visits to provide direct advice on how to improve family diets. A well-written work with fluid language. [FDM]

1662 Ferreira, Roquinaldo. Biografia como história social: o clã Ferreira Gomes e os mundos da escravização no Atlântico Sul. (*Varia Hist.*, 29:51, set./dez. 2013, p. 679–695)

Important article that joins a small group of pieces that trace biographies in the Atlantic world, in this case in Angola and Brazil. [MAM]

1663 Fraga, Gerson Wasen. Uma triste história de futebol no Brasil: o Maracanaço: nacionalidade, futebol e imprensa na Copa do Mundo de 1950. Passo Fundo, Brazil: Méritos Editora, 2014. 530 p.: bibl., ill.

The author notes that the text is very close to his doctoral dissertation of 2009. This is likely the best book I have seen on Brazilian futebol. It is not only good on the sport, it is good history. He takes readers back into the 19th century and sets the sport into the context of succeeding eras. No matter what a reader is primarily interested in, this book will capture, hold, and gently instruct. It should not be missed. [FDM]

1664 Fragoso, João Luís Ribeiro. Barões do café e sistema agrário escravista: Paraíba do Sul/Rio de Janeiro (1830–1888). Rio de Janeiro: 7Letras, 2013. 195 p.: bibl., ill., index.

An examination of the structure of agriculture and society in the west-center part of the state of Rio de Janeiro. This region was one of the most populous areas of the Paraiba Valley, important in the production of coffee in 19th century Brazil. The author looked at private, church, and public records to examine the social structure of the region. An important part of the study is a description of slavery in this region. This is a valuable study on economic issues connected to the abolition of slavery. This is a revision of the author's dissertation finished in the 1980s. [MG]

1665 Gertz, René Ernaini. De Otto von Bismarck a Angela Merkel: do "perigo alemão" ao "neonazismo" no Brasil. (*Hist. Quest. Debates*, 30:58, jan./junho 2013, p. 89–112)

German immigrants have long been objects of suspicion for Brazilians. Such suspicion reached a peak during WWII, but elements of concern have appeared from time to time since. Some have linked separatist movements in Rio Grande do Sul to German descendants.This article examines rumors, news reports, and statements by police and politicians to conclude that there is little to no reason to suspect such people of harboring neo-Nazi sentiments. [FDM]

1666 Godoy, Marcelo. A casa da vovó: uma biografia do DOI-Codi (1969–1991), o centro de sequestro, tortura e morte da ditadura militar: histórias, documentos e depoimentos inéditos dos agentes do regime. São Paulo: Alameda, 2014. 610 p.: bibl., ill., index.

The title of this book, "Grandma's House," is the name that agents of the repression applied to their place of "work." To use such a name was a sad cruel irony. Although some also called it the Açouge or Slaughterhouse. DOI are the initials of Destacamento de Operações de Informações. At Grandma's, army and police worked together to catch, interrogate, torture, and to kill. *Operação Bandeirante* (Oban) in São Paulo created the model that was later applied throughout Brazil. Some 66 Brazilians disappeared into the darkness after torture (p. 39) or from their wounds after a supposed shoot-out (p. 27). The author bravely interviews 25 men and women who were DOI agents, some of whom had been warned by Colonel Carlos Alberto Brilhante Ustra to stay silent. One can imagine the heaviness of the guilt they carry. This is an excellent book for those interested in research methods. Hopefully it will also be an antidote to the evil sickness that its pages reveal. [FDM]

1667 Gomes, Flávio dos Santos. Da nitidez e invisibilidade: legados do pós-emancipação no Brasil. Belo Horizonte, Brazil: Fino Traço Editora, 2013. 377 p.: bibl. (Coleção História)

Important set of articles that argues for breaking barriers between the historiography of enslaved and free labor and the pre- and post-abolition periods. Comprehensive bibliography. [MAM]

1668 Gonçalves, Carlos Barros. Até aos confins da terra: o movimento ecumênico protestante no Brasil e a evangelização dos povos indígenas. Dourados, Brazil: Universidade Federal da Grande Dourados—UFGD, 2011. 287 p.: bibl.

Research on rarely explored topic: the evangelization of indigenous people in Brazil by Protestant missionaries. [MAM]

1669 Gonçalves, Paulo Cesar. Mercadores de braços: riqueza e acumulação na organização da emigração europeia para o Novo Mundo. São Paulo: Alameda, 2012. 536 p.: bibl., ill.

Important new study of the transition from enslaved to free labor in Brazil, emphasizng Italian immigration to São Paulo and labor contractors in Italy. Based on extensive research in Italy. [MAM]

1670 Guerra literária: panfletos da Independência (1820–1823). Vol. 1, Cartas. Organização de José Murilo de Carvalho, Lúcia Bastos e Marcello Basile. Belo Horizonte, Brazil: Editora UFMG, 2014. 1 v.: bibl., ill., indexes (Humanitas)

The text is the first volume of an important four volume collection of pamphlets about Brazilian Independence circulated in Brazil, Portugal or the Cisplantine region between 1820 and 1823. Volume 1 is devoted to letters and includes a general introduction to the sources, a checklist of authors, a chronology of Independence, and an index of names. [MAM]

1671 Guerra literária: panfletos da Independência (1820–1823). Vol. 2, Análises. Organização de José Murilo de Carvalho, Lúcia Bastos e Marcello Basile. Belo Horizonte, Brazil: Editora UFMG, 2014. 1 v.: bibl., ill., indexes. (Humanitas)

The text is the second volume of an important four volume collection of pamflets about Brazilian Independence circulated in Brazil, Portugal or the Cisplantine region between 1820 and 1823. Volume 2 includes a wide variety of pamphlets analyzing the relationship between Brazil and Portugal at the time, an introduction to the volume, a detailed table of contents, and an index of names. [MAM]

1672 Guerra literária: panfletos da Independência (1820–1823). Vol. 3, Sermões, diálogos, manifestos. Organização de José Murilo de Carvalho, Lúcia Bastos y Marcello Basile. Belo Horizonte, Brazil: Editora UFMG, 2014. 1 v.: bibl., ill., indexes (Humanitas)

The text is the third volume of an important four volume collection of pamphlets about Brazilian Independence circulated in Brazil, Portugal or the Cisplantine region between 1820 and 1823. Volume 3 is devoted to sermons, dialogues and manifestos and includes an introduction to the sources, a detailed table of contents, and an index of names. [MAM]

1673 Guerra literária: panfletos da Independência (1820–1823). Vol. 4, Poesias, relatos, Cisplatina. Organização de José Murilo de Carvalho, Lúcia Bastos e Marcello Basile. Belo Horizonte, Brazil: Editora UFMG, 2014. 1 v.: bibl., ill., indexes. (Humanitas)

The text is the fourth volume of an important four volume collection of pamphlets about Brazilian Independence circulated in Brazil, Portugal or the Cisplantine region between 1820 and 1823. Volume 4 is devoted to poems, articles of various types, and material from the Cisplantine region and includes an introduction to the documents in the volume, biographical notes about the principal names in the pamphlets, a list of documents in the Oliveira Lima Library that were not included, and an index of names. [MAM]

1674 **Heinsfeld, Adelar.** A geopolítica do Barão: as ações de Rio Branco e seus reflexos na Argentina. Curitiba, Brazil: Editora Prismas, 2015. 386 p.: bibl., maps.

The text revisits the efforts by the Baron of Rio Branco to establish Brazil's borders, but emphasizes the impact that said efforts had on Brazil's relationship with Argentina. The research is significantly based on Argentine sources as well as Brazilian ones. [MAM]

1675 **História da escola dos imigrantes italianos em terras brasileiras.** Organização de Terciane Ângela Luchese. Caxias do Sul, Brazil: EDUCS, 2014. 285 p.: bibl.

A history of elementary schools created by Italian immigrants in seven Brazilian states and the role of Italian foreign policy in creating the schools. The essays are written by scholars of education and history and are based on primary sources and extensive bibliography. [MAM]

1676 **História das mulheres e do gênero em Minas Gerais.** Organização de Cláudia Maia y Vera Lúcia Puga. Ilha de Santa Catarina, Brazil: Editora Mulheres, 2015. 552 p.: bibl., ill.

From this book it is possible to assert that Women's Studies are alive and energetic in Brazil, or at least in Minas Gerais. In four conferences (2006, 2008, 2010, and 2012) of ANPUH-MG sessions devoted to Women's Studies revealed the rich trove of research that has been gathered in this volume. The topics inspire curiosity and a desire to read. The papers are organized into four sections: transgressors and insubordinates; feminine knowledge and tasks; marriage and motherhood; education. Some of the topics that stand out deal with teachers, concubines of priests, abolition, insanity, violence, the Sertão, midwives, Pentecostal churches, 17th-century divorce, Congado, marriage and politics. [FDM]

1677 **História dos homens no Brasil.** Organização de Mary del Priore e Marcia Amantino. São Paulo: Editora UNESP, 2013. 415 p.: bibl., ill.

Collection of important articles on the history of masculinity in Brazil by historians and anthropologists. Among the groups examined are African and Brazilian slaves, priests, soldiers, and elites. Themes include gender, sexuality, fashion, and sport. Extensive bibliography. [MAM]

1678 **História e memória das ditaduras do século XX.** Organização de Samantha Viz Quadrat e Denise Rollemberg. Rio de Janeiro: FGV Editora, 2015. 2 v.: bibl.

These essays collectively seek to broaden the discussion of dictatorship beyond Brazil by looking to Argentina, Chile, Uruguay, Spain, Italy, Germany, and Vichy France. The authors find memory to be malleable and perhaps not the best source for historical accuracy. History and memory all too easily can clash. The essays will stimulate and provoke as they push the discussion forward. It is notable that Brazilian government funding (CNPQ) underwrote some of the research. [FDM]

1679 **História militar: novos caminhos e novas abordagens.** Organização de Fernando da Silva Rodrigues, Francisco Ferraz e Surama Conde Sá Pinto. Jundiaí, Brazil: Paco Editorial, 2015. 433 p.: bibl. (Coleção Escritos acadêmicos. Série Estudos reunidos; 2)

Moving beyond distaste for things military, which had grown as a reaction to the post-1964 regime, scholars are forthrightly studying military history to better understand what happened in Brazil. These wide-ranging essays are well worth reading. While each has a particular focus that provides considerable depth, taken together they reach farther back into the past than is usually the case. The first essays delve into the colonial era examining Portuguese military policy in Europe and in America. The topics include French commentary on the military, barracks life, and the Paraguayan war in the 19th century, the convergence of military and diplomacy in the fleet revolt of 1910, and the first five years of the Escola Militar do Realengo. Other essays examined political-military interactions in the First Republic, the historiography of the FEB, repression of officers after the coup of 64 and a useful comparative look at the Revolution of Carnations in Portugal 1974. Well done. [FDM]

1680 **História urbana: memória, cultura e sociedade.** Organização de Gisele Sanglard, Carlos Eduardo Moreira de Araújo e José Jorge Siqueira. Rio de Janeiro: FGV Editora, 2013. 367 p.: bibl.

Collection of essays by major Brazilian historians about various aspects of the urban experience in Minas Gerais and Rio de Janeiro from the colonial period through the 20th century. Topics include sociability and conflict, workers, civil society, public health, and cultural history. Relatively new topics under discussion include deindustrialization in late 20th-century Rio, the construction of monuments on the Praia do Flamengo and the development of images of the *sertanejo* in São Paulo. [MAM]

1681 **Histórias do Maranhão em tempos de República.** Organização de Antônio Evaldo Almeida Barros *et al*. São Luis do Maranhão, Brazil: EDUFMA; Jundiaí, Brazil: Paco Editorial, 2015. 806 p.: bibl., ill.

Articles by three generations of historians of Maranhão exploring the state's history during the Republican period. Themes include popular culture, politics, economic and social history, religion, women, and historical memory. [MAM]

1682 **Os intelectuais e a nação: educação, saúde e a construção de um Brasil moderno.** Organização de Karoline Carula, Magali Gouveia Engel e Maria Letícia Corrêa. Textos de Alessandra Frota Martinez Schueler *et al*. Rio de Janeiro: Contra Capa, 2013. 316 p.: bibl.

A collection of articles that looks at the role of intellectuals in education and public health in the development of postcolonial Brazil. Up-to-date bibliography and methodology in the history of ideas. [MAM]

1683 **Jean, Martine.** "A storehouse of prisoners": Rio de Janeiro's correction house (Casa de Correção) and the birth of the penitentiary in Brazil, 1830–1906. (*Atlan. Stud. Global Curr.*, 14:2, 2017, p. 216–242, bibl.)

Excellently researched and documented study of race and imprisonment in 19th-century Rio de Janeiro, with extensive notes and bibliography. [MAM]

1684 **Joffily, Mariana.** O socialismo na França e no Brasil durante a II Internacional Socialista (1889–1918). São Paulo: Alameda, 2012. 211 p.: bibl.

Revised Sorbonne PhD thesis placing the introduction of socialist ideas to Brazil in the context of the development of socialism in France. The work is based on extensive research in socialist documents and publications of the period. [MAM]

1685 **Lamounier, Maria Lúcia.** Ferrovias e mercado de trabalho no Brasil do século XIX. São Paulo: EDUSP, 2012. 287 p.: bibl. ill.

The text is a comparison of the construction of railroads by English companies in Brazil's sugar and coffee export regions, including extensive discussion of labor in the period covering the Empire and the Old Republic, based on research in Brazil and England. Extensive bibliography and notes. [MAM]

1686 **Lima, Oliveira.** O reconhecimento do Império: história da diplomacia brasileira. Introdução por Leslie Bethell. 2a edição. Rio de Janeiro: Topbooks, 2015. 224 p.: bibl.

The text is a new edition of the classic history of Brazilian diploimacy by historian Oliveira Lima, first published in Rio de Janeiro in 1902. The introduction by Leslie Bethell, historian of Brazilian foreign relations, provides a brief biography of the author and a discussion of the importance of the text. [MAM]

1687 **Lochery, Neill.** Brazil: the fortunes of war: World War II and the making of modern Brazil. New York: Basic Books, 2014. 345 p., 8 unnumbered p.: bibl., ill., index.

This is a well-written account that mines the secondary literature and archival holdings to highlight the important impact that WWII had on Brazilian development. Lochery keeps Vargas at the center of the story, which is useful and accurate. He is very good at setting scenes and drawing out the personalities of the main actors. The book is a fast read and well worth the time of researchers and general public interested in the era. [FDM]

1688 Lopes, Maria-Aparecida. Struggles over an "old, nasty, and inconvenient monopoly": municipal slaughterhouses and the meat industry in Rio de Janeiro, 1880–1920s. (*J. Lat. Am. Stud.*, 47:2, May 2015, p. 349–376, bibl., graphs, map)

This article confronts an important question, namely what did people eat and where did they get the food. The item in this case was meat, mostly beef. Rio's supply system passed through three stages: long-existing clandestine slaughtering; a centralized and partially regulated public abattoir system; and lastly meat-packing companies. The author also researched how each stage affected per capita meat availability. As Rio grew from a 270,000 population in 1872 to 1,080,000 in 1920, supply often proved inefficient in satisfying the demand. The public abattoir system worked well until the turn of the century providing a steady supply of meat at foreseeable prices. World War I and the onset of a refrigerated meat industry opened export markets for Brazil's low-grade frozen beef. The exports grew so intense that there were fears for the internal supply. Overall, the article is useful for clarifying some issues related to "the complex transition between a traditional system of food provisioning and the industrial slaughterhouse" (p. 375). [FDM]

1689 Marques, Teresa Cristina de Novaes. A cerveja e a cidade do Rio de Janeiro: de 1888 ao início dos anos 1930. Jundiaí, Brazil: Paco Editorial; Brasília, Brazil: Editora UnB, 2014. 341 p.: bibl.

Social and economic history of until now understudied topic, the history of the Brahma and Antartica beer companies in Brazil, with an emphasis on the acquisition of credit, based on primary source research in Brazil, England, and Germany. [MAM]

1690 Martins, Marcelo Thadeu Quintanilha. A civilização do delegado: modernidade, polícia e sociedade em São Paulo nas primeiras décadas da República, 1889–1930. São Paulo: Alameda, 2014. 337 p.: bibl.

Extensively researched study on the formation of the civil and military police in São Paulo focusing on their relationship to the modernization of the city and the state during the Old Republic. [MAM]

1691 Melo, José Evando Vieira de. O açúcar no vale do café: Engenho Central de Lorena (1881–1901). São Paulo: Alameda, 2012. 275 p.: bibl. (Coleção História econômica)

A study of the sugar economy of the São Paulo county of Lorena and the implantation of industrial sugar production in the last two decades of the 19th-century that contributes to the development of knowledge about internal consumption in Brazil. The research contributes to arguments that even where coffee cultivation for export was most intense, assumptions of monoculture are overblown. [MAM]

1692 1964: 50 anos depois: a ditadura em debate. Organização de Grimaldo Carneiro Zachariadhes em colaboração com Alessandra Carvalho *et al.* Aracaju, Brazil: EDISE, 2015. 579 p.: bibl.

It is worth remembering that many civilians in Brazil supported the coup in 1964 and the government that resulted. Some of these essays raise the important question, "what kind of a country do Brazilians want?" The authors agree that to respond they must first know what happened. What did those 21 years mean? The responses in this collection of essays are important and may provide useful guideposts on the journey to the future. [FDM]

1693 1964: do golpe à democracia. Organização de Angela Alonso e Miriam Dolhnikoff. São Paulo: Hedra, 2015. 419 p.: bibl., ill.

It was very strange that a government as weak as that of João Goulart could have been seen as such a threat that it had to be overthrown. The central question has been since then, to whom was it a threat? Truly in 1963 there was radicalization of both the left and the right. But it was the right that had the army and hence the guns to ensure its control. The essays focus on two periods: the time before the coup and its immediate aftermath and then the later process of redemocratization and today's democracy. The authors are connected to the *Centro Brasileiro de Análise e Planejamento* (Cebrap) in São Paulo. In between analytical chapters there are first-hand accounts by key participants in the events. [FDM]

1694 **Monteiro, Marcelo.** U-93: a entrada do Brasil na Primeira Guerra Mundial. Prefácio por João Barone. Porto Alegre, Brazil: BesouroBox, 2014. 321 p.: bibl., ill. (Jornalismo front verso)

Journalist's account of Brazil's participation in World War I based on primary sources. [MAM]

1695 **Otovo, Okezi T.** Progressive mothers, better babies: race, public health, and the state in Brazil, 1850–1945. Austin: University of Texas Press, 2016. 273 p.: bibl., ill. (Joe R. and Teresa Lozano Long series in Latin American and Latino art and culture)

An exploration of motherhood and the development of a maternalist ideology from the mid-19th century to the middle of the 20th, which contributes to the history of public health, medicine, and race and gender. [MAM]

1696 **Pimenta, João Paulo G.** A independência do Brasil e a experiência hispano-americana (1808–1822). São Paulo: Hucitec Editora: FAPESP, 2015. 492 p.: bibl. (Estudos históricos; 100)

Extensively researched study of the independence process in Spanish America from the perspective of Brazil that then places Brazilian independence in the broader context of independence in the Americas. Unusually, the text addresses bibliography in Spanish and English as well as Portuguese. [MAM]

1697 **Políticas da raça: experiências e legados da abolição e da pós-emancipação no Brasil.** Organização de Flávio Gomes e Petrônio Domingues. São Paulo: Selo Negro Edições, 2014. 415 p.: bibl.

Important collection of articles by junior and senior scholars of post-emancipation Brazil that contextualizes questions of race, labor, politics, and citizenship. [MAM]

1698 **Presos políticos e perseguidos estrangeiros na era Vargas.** Organização por Marly de Almeida Gomes Vianna, Érica Sarmiento da Silva e Leandro Pereira Gonçalves. Textos por Alexandre Ribeiro Samis *et al.* Rio de Janeiro: Mauad X: Faperj, 2014. 263 p.: bibl., ill.

This is another multi-authored book. This one based on the archives of state and federal secret police. The targets are familiar anarquistas and union organizers, Italians involved in anti-fascist movements, the Galego center in Rio de Janeiro, Integralistas, Nazis, Armenians, Japanese, and Jewish families from Russia. The chapter on the archives of the Brazilian political police is likely the most important for those beginning research on political repression. [FDM]

1699 **A província fluminense: administração provincial no tempo do Império do Brasil.** Organização de José Edson Schümann Lim. Pesquisa por Anderson Fabrício Moreira Mendes *et al.* Rio de Janeiro: Governo do Rio de Janeiro, Arquivo Público Estado do Rio de Janeiro, 2012. 351 p.: bibl., index.

Important reference book on government administration in the province of Rio de Janeiro during the 19th century, includes essays describing development and responsibilities of provincial governments, as well as organizational charts and brief biographies of provincial presidents. Essential reference for historians of 19th-century Brazil. [MAM]

1700 **Relações internacionais do Brasil: antologia comentada de artigos da Revista do IHGB (1841–2004).** Organização de Luiz Felipe de Seixas Corrêa. Brasília: Fundação Alexandre de Gusmão, 2016. 498 p.: bibl. (História diplomática; 765)

The text is a collection of essays and articles based on primary research about Brazilian foreign relations between 1841 and 2004, that includes contributions by important historians of an earlier generation, including Pedro Calmon and Wanderley Pinho. [MAM]

1701 **Ribeiro, José Iran.** O Império e as revoltas: Estado e nação nas trajetórias dos militares do Exército imperial no contexto da Guerra dos Farrapos. Rio de Janeiro: Ministério da Justiça, Arquivo Nacional, 2013. 331 p.: bibl. (Prêmio Arquivo Nacional de Pesquisa—2011)

Prizewinning study in the new military history tradition that examines the role of the imperial army in Farrapos revolt, based on extensive research in regional and national archives and contextualized in extensive bibliography. [MAM]

1702 **Ribeiro, Renilson Rosa.** O Brasil inventado pelo Visconde de Porto Seguro: Francisco Adolfo de Varnhagen, o Instituto Histórico e Geográfico Brasileiro e a construção da ideia de Brasil-Colônia no Brasil-Império, 1838–1860. Cuiabá, Brazil: Entrelinhas, 2015. 442 p.: bibl.

Well written and argued analysis of the legacy of Varnhagen in the development of Brazilian historiography. [MAM]

1703 **Rostoldo, Jadir Peçanha.** A cidade republicana na Belle Époque capixaba: espaço urbano, poder e sociedade. Jundiaí, Brazil: Paco Editorial, 2014. 269 p.: bibl.

Extensively researched revised USP PhD dissertation on the 19th- and 20th-century capital of Espírito Santo state, a topic that has received little attention until now. [MAM]

1704 **Sales, Tadeu José Gouveia de.** José Mariano e seu tempo, 1850–1912: o tribuno do Recife e a utopia da liberdade durante o Império e a República. Recife, Brazil: Cepe Editora, 2013. 301 p.: bibl., ill.

Readable and accessible biography of relatively unknown José Mariano Carneiro da Cunha, one of the leaders of the popular abolitionist movement in Pernambuco, by prizewinning journalist. [MAM]

1705 **Santiago, Luís.** O mandonismo mágico do sertão: corpo fechado e violência política nos sertões da Bahia e de Minas Gerais, 1856–1931. Pedra Azul, Brazil: Luís Carlos Mendes Santiago, 2015. 543 p.: bibl., index.

This text, winner of the 2014 Silvio Romero price of CNFCP/Iphan, addresses a rarely addressed topic: magical beliefs around the concept of the "corpo fechado" and their relationship to rural political power in the Brazilian sertão from the middle of the 19th century through the death of Colonel Horácio Mattos. The bibliography is extensive, as is the research, and the book includes complementary texts helpful for understanding the author's arguments. [MAM]

1706 **Santos, Eugénio dos.** D. Pedro: imperador do Brasil e rei de Portugal. São Paulo, Brazil: Alameda, 2015. 415 p.: bibl.

A unique biography of the founder of Brazil's independence, Dom Pedro I. The author is a retired professor of history from the Universidade do Porto (Portugal). The book provides a psychological examination of Dom Pedro, attempting to determine the motives and reasons for his actions. Offers useful considerations of Pedro from both the Brazilian and Portuguese perspective. The appendix includes copies of selective letters written to his family mentioned in the study. [MG]

1707 **Schulze, Frederik.** Auswanderung als nationalistisches Projekt: "Deutschtum" und Kolonialdiskurse im südlichen Brasilien (1824–1941) [Emigration as national project: Germanness/Being German and colonial discourses in Southern Brazil]. Köln, Germany: Böhlau Verlag, 2016. 426 p.: bibl., indexes. (Lateinamerikanische Forschungen; 46)

Emigration from Germany to Brazil started in 1824 mainly attracting peasants eager to colonize the Brazilian south. When mass emigration arose at the end of the 19th century, the number of Germans migrating to Brazil increased. Colonialization societies, Church administrations, and state institutions in Germany thought that these emigrants should maintain their Germanness ("Deutschtum") for the benefit of their mother country's international foreign policy. However, most of the emigrants did exactly the contrary. They assimilated, learned to speak Portuguese (maintaining their German within the family and among German social groups), and accepted their new home country. Nationalist groups did exist among emigrants, for instance in the era of National Socialism, but these groups would never represent the vast majority. In 1941 due to the nationalist policies of Getúlio Vargas and Brazil's rapprochement with the US and their war allies, every German activity in Brazil, such as teaching German to immigrants and the formation of cultural societies were forbidden by law. The study examines how the nationalist discourses of "Deutschtum" worked in Brazil. [F. Obermeier]

Seminario Internacional Diálogos entre Brasil y Argentina: Historia e Historiografía, *Mariana, Brazil, 2013*. Historia, poder e instituciones: diálogos entre Brasil y Argentina. See item **1041**.

1708 Seminário Nacional 100 Anos da Guerra do Contestado, *Florianópolis, Brazil, 2012*. 100 anos do Contestado: memória, história e patrimônio. Coordenação por CEAF, Memorial MPSC. Organização por Arno Wehling *et al.* Florianópolis, Brazil: MPSC, Ministério Público, Santa Catarina, 2013. 449 p.: bibl., ill.

This collection of essays brings together presentations at two major conferences organized in Rio de Janeiro in conjunction with the centenary of Santa Catarina's Contestado rebellion, between 1912 and 1915. The authors, who include historian José Murilo de Carvalho, reflect on various aspects of the revolt in hopes off "problematizing the acquired image" of the revolt. The essays cover a number of factors related to the rebellion, including geography, legal issues, social history, religious history, anthropology, and collective memory. Most of the essays are short, but none the less reflect serious research. Moving photos. [MAM]

1709 Silva, Aldo José Morais. Instituto Geográfico e Histórico da Bahia: origem e estratégias de consolidação institucional, 1894–1930. Feira de Santana, Brazil: UEFS Editora, 2012. 308 p.: bibl.

Institutional history of one of the most important historical societies in Brazil based on primary research that includes an analysis of membership and financial conditions. Research relates the development of the Instituto to efforts to modernize Bahia, and particularly Salvador. [MAM]

1710 Silva, José Bento Rosa da. Cenas da escravidão e pós-abolição no Brasil meridional: SC: 1791–1891. Itajaí, Brazil: Editores Casa Aberta; Rio de Janeiro: Biblioteca Nacional, 2015. 207 p.: bibl.

Collection of 12 "scenes" drawn from research in never-before examined archive of the Courthouse of Tijucas that examines the day-to-day experiences of Africans and their descendants in Santa Catarina. [MAM]

1711 Silva, Wellington Barbosa da. Entre a liturgia e o salário: a formação dos aparatos policiais no Recife do século XIX (1830–1850). Jundiaí, Brazil: Paco Editorial, 2014. 250 p.: bibl.

Political, administrative and social history of a rarely-studied topic in Brazil, the formation of the police, in this case in Recife. Study based on extensive research in primary sources that engages a broad bibliography on the topic. [MAM]

1712 Sousa, Avanete Pereira. Poder político local e vida cotidiana: a Câmara Municipal da cidade de Salvador no século XVIII. Vitória da Conquista, Brazil: Edições UESB, 2013. 139 p.: bibl.

A study of the Municipal Council of Salvador and its relationship to labor organization, public health, education and the Catholic Church during the 18th century. [MAM]

1713 Summerhill, William Roderick. Inglorious revolution: political institutions, sovereign debt, and financial underdevelopment in imperial Brazil. New Haven: Yale University Press, 2015. 342 p.: bibl. (Yale series in economic and financial history)

Deeply researched economic history of Brazil that asks why, if the Brazilian Empire had the confidence of foreign banks sufficient to obtain loans, the nation did not develop economically. Some familiarity with economics is required to fully appreciate the text. [MAM]

1714 Terra, Paulo Cruz. Cidadania e trabalhadores: cocheiros e carroceiros no Rio de Janeiro (1870–1906). Rio de Janeiro: Arquivo Geral da Cidade do Rio de Janeiro, 2013. 305 p.: bibl.

This book based on prizewinning Ph.D. dissertation as part of the Research Group on Worlds of Labor at the Federal Fluminense University in Rio de Janeiro, is a study of the social history of transportation in Rio that explores the relationships between free and enslaved laborers. [MAM]

1715 Toledo, Roberto Pompeu de. A capital da vertigem: uma história de São Paulo de 1900 a 1954. Rio de Janeiro: Objetiva, 2015. 582 p.: bibl.

Broad overview of the history of the city of São Paulo emphasizing the expansion of the city, architecture and infrastructure development, population growth, and politics. Very readable. [MAM]

1716 **Torres, Rosane dos Santos.** Filhos da pátria, homens do progresso: o Conselho Municipal e a instrução pública na Capital Federal (1892–1902). Rio de Janeiro: Arquivo Geral da Cidade do Rio de Janeiro, Rio Prefeitura Cultura 2012. 188 p.: bibl., ill., map.

Prizewinning monograph examining the role of politicians in the development of education in Rio de Janeiro between the Empire and Republic. [MAM]

1717 **Turin, Rodrigo.** Tessituras do tempo: discurso etnográfico e historicidade no Brasil oitocentista. Rio de Janeiro: EDUERJ, 2013. 267 p.: bibl.

A cultural analysis of 19th-century ethnographic studies of Brazil and their relationship to the construction of a national historical identity. Particular foci are the Instituto Histórico e Geográfico Brasileiro, Varnhagen, and the Museu Nacional. [MAM]

1718 **Witt, Marcos Antônio.** Em busca de um lugar ao sol: estratégias políticas: imigração alemã, Rio Grande do Sul, século XIX. 2a edição ampliada e revisada. São Leopoldo, Brazil: Oikos Editora: Editora Unisinos, 2015. 391 p.: bibl., ill. (Coleção Estudos Históricos Latino-Americanos; 19)

Intensely researched and contextualized social and economic history of how German immigrants in Rio Grande do Sul achieved political integration. [MAM]

1719 **Woitowicz, Karina Janz.** Imagem contestada: a Guerra do Contestado pela escrita do *Diário da Tarde* (1912–1916). Ponta Grossa, Brazil: Editora UEPG, 2014. 327 p.: bibl.

This study examines the reporting of and the role in the construction of the image of the Contestado of Paraná's most important newspaper at the time, the *Diário da Tarde*. More than a study of historical representation, it also explores the organization of and audience for newspapers in Brazil at the beginning of the 20th century. The study is based on extensive research by scholar of journalism. [MAM]

LITERATURE

SPANISH AMERICA
Colonial Period

AMBER BRIAN, *Associate Professor of Spanish and Portuguese, University of Iowa*

THE PUBLICATIONS FROM 2012–2016 reviewed for *HLAS 74* include monographs, anthologies, translations, and editions, published in Spanish and English in Latin America, the US, and Europe. As a whole, they are representative of trends in the field where we see new approaches to established objects of study and new paths for research through newly discovered materials. Three key elements characterize the scholarship under review: first, as has been the trend, scholars are continuing to locate significant manuscripts or understudied colonial imprints that further the collective understanding of colonial letters and cultural production; second, scholars are continuing to demonstrate the critical importance of translations and editions; third, scholars are continuing to engage with and adapt methodologies and studies from other disciplines, particularly history, art history, and anthropology.

Three noteworthy monographs are Raquel Chang-Rodríguez's *Cartografía garcilasista* (item **1722**), Regina Harrison's *Sin and Confession in Colonial Peru* (item **1725**), and Anna More's *Baroque Sovereignty* (item **1728**). Each of these scholars delves into primary texts with sophisticated theoretical analyses and rigorous textual analyses. Chang-Rodríguez has studied colonial Peru and specifically Inca Garcilaso for decades. Her book reveals that deep knowledge of and intimacy with the material as she outlines, or "maps," the key thematic trends in Inca Garcilaso's writings. Harrison's study of Spanish-Quechua penitential texts is also the product of many years of study and a broad-ranging knowledge of early modern religious culture and native Andean Catholicism. Harrison's study highlights how problematic binaries are in colonial studies, as she underlines the ways in which Catholic tradition interacted with native customs and language in the context of native Catholic practice. More's deeply researched analysis of the Creole archive and early modern political thought establishes her book as a must-read on Sigüenza and 17th-century New Spain. It also models opportunities for further scholarship relating close textual analysis with larger theoretical questions.

Two noteworthy, yet distinct, examples of editions and translations are Janet Burke and Ted Humphrey's version of Bernal Díaz del Castillo's *True History, The Essential Díaz* (item **1744**) and Beatriz Mariscal Hay's edition of Patricio Antonio López's *Mercurio yndiano poema histórico* (item **1746**). Providing the first-person perspective of the foot soldier, Bernal Díaz's *True History* is one of the most readable and influential Spanish accounts of the conquest of Mexico. Burke and Humphrey's new text with its fresh translation provides a selection of chapters that make this edition very useable for the classroom. Mariscal Hay's edition of the historical poem written by an 18th-century Zapotec cacique from Oaxaca, *Mercurio yndiano*, brings to the attention of students and scholars the work and story of a late colonial native intellectual. Countering the impression that native scholarly production ended in the century after the deaths of figures like Inca Garcilaso de la Vega (1539–1616) and Fernando de Alva Ixtlilxochitl (c. 1578–1650), this fascinating text by Patricio Antonio López—found in manuscript form at the Bancroft Library at the University of California, Berkeley—reminds us that native people engaged in scholarly reading and writing well into the 18th century. Further, the inclusion of the letter from the descendant of Huayna Capac raises the possibility that a network of natives in New Spain and Peru shared materials related to claims of their elite native ancestry.

Two noteworthy examples of the wide range of studies explored in anthologies are Claudia Parodi, *et al*.'s *La resignificación del Nuevo Mundo* (item **1749**) and Fernando Cervantes and Andrew Redden's *Angels, Demons, and the New World* (item **1739**). These volumes highlight the wealth of sources, themes, and methodologies that inform our understanding of colonial society and cultural production. *La resignficación del Nuevo Mundo* underlines the ways in which sociolinguistic analysis can provide novel insights into colonial texts. Particularly remarkable in this volume is the essay by Natalie Operstein, "Afro-Hispanic Villancico in Spain and Spanish America: Linguistic and Sociocultural Aspects." Her meticulous examination of the language used in these early modern religious song-forms reveals African-inflected Spanish and illuminates the lived experiences of African slaves and freedmen in Spanish America. With nine essays by esteemed historians and anthropologists, Cervantes and Redden's volume on angelology and demonology points to the interconnectedness among fields of colonial study with literary scholars, historians, and anthropologists generously sharing methods of textual analysis and analysis of colonial society to the benefit of all. Of particular note is the essay by renowned Peruvian anthropologist Ramón Mujica Pinilla, who looks at angels, demons, Hispanic cosmology, and political theology in the context of viceregal Peru. Through a close study of a range of materials, including paintings, the published works of Inca Garcilaso and Bartolomé de las Casas, and the extraordinary manuscript cum line drawings by Guaman Poma de Ayala, Mujica Pinilla concludes that "Andean angelic and demonological iconography was used as a visual argument of re-vindication" (p. 210). Mujica Pinilla reminds us that native peoples, through various media, articulated a voice of resistance as they maintained their cultural knowledge in the face of the imposition of Spanish cultural, linguistic, and political norms. And, Operstein's work shows us that we can also locate the voice of African-descendant inhabitants of viceregal New Spain and Peru.

The works described here underline the central importance of interdisciplinary research for the field of colonial studies and point to the need to continue searching for new materials, bringing these and other understudied texts to the attention of fellow scholars and students, while also returning to known texts with fresh lenses. The colonial period offers a treasure trove of primary materials and secondary studies that shed light on early modern processes of cultural interaction, imperialism, and resistance that are foundational to other periods of Latin American literary and cultural production. Scholars, as we see in these studies, continue to produce groundbreaking and critically incisive works that help guide our understanding of the colonial period.

INDIVIDUAL STUDIES

1720 Alatorre, Antonio and **Martha Lilia Tenoria.** Serafina y sor Juana, con tres apéndices. Segunda edición. México: El Colegio de México, 2014. 193 p.

This second edition of a study first published in 1998 has been corrected and expanded. It addresses a manuscript letter known as the *Carta de Serafina de Cristo* that has been attributed by some to Sor Juana Inés de la Cruz. The authors argue, basing their conclusion on careful paleographic and philological study, that it is not hers. The 1998 publication was very influential though also polemical, and the second edition addresses some of the concerns that arose. This is an important work for scholars of Sor Juana, *sorjuanistas*, but also for academics more broadly who are invested in productive scholarly debate.

1721 Boturini Benaducci, Lorenzo. Idea of a new general history of North America: an account of colonial native Mexico. Edited and translated by Stafford Poole. Foreword by Susan Schroeder. Norman: University of Oklahoma Press, 2015. 288 p.: bibl., ill., index.

Poole makes available for the first time in English translation the writings of Lorenzo Boturini Benaducci, an Italian who moved to Spain and then New Spain, where he became fascinated with Mesoamerican cultures. Poole also translates Boturini's *Catálogo*, an annotated list of the works that he had collected in New Spain. Boturini learned Nahuatl and collected and copied indigenous texts, which he used to write a history of Mexico. The Spanish Crown ultimately confiscated and dispersed his collection and writings. Boturini rewrote the history from memory, completing the work in 1746. Poole's erudite annotations explain Boturini's references to mythology, classical antiquity, humanist writings, ecclesiastical texts, and legal sources, and define terms in Nahuatl, Spanish, Latin, and Italian. Poole's book is a most valuable contribution to the fields of history, ethnohistory, and literature of the Americas. For additional comment, see item **198**.

1722 Chang-Rodríguez, Raquel. Cartografía garcilasista. Prologo de Carmen Ruiz Barrionuevo. Alicante, Spain: Universidad de Alicante, 2013. 285 p.: bibl., ill. (some col.), index. (Cuadernos de América sin nombre, 32)

This important study of Inca Garcilaso de la Vega (1539–1616) by an eminent scholar attempts to provide a "cartography" or mapping of the major thematic threads found in the work of the mestizo author from Peru. Before the study itself, the author includes a detailed chronology of significant events related to the life and works of Garcilaso Inca. The study, rigorous in its analysis of text and context, is built around three of Garcilaso Inca's works: *Relación de la descendencia de Garci Pérez de Vargas* (1596), *La florida del Inca* (1605), and *Comentarios reales* (1609; 1617). *Relación* is a manuscript that relates the genealogy of a distant Spanish relative of Garcilaso Inca, while the other two texts were published.

1723 Cortés Koloffon, Adriana. Cósmica y cosmética: pliegues de la alegoría en sor Juana Inés de la Cruz y Pedro Calderón de la Barca. Pamplona, Spain: Universidad de Navarra; Madrid: Iberoamericana; Frankfurt am Main: Vervuert, 2013. 266 p.: bibl., ill. (Biblioteca Aurea hispánica; 81)

This engaging study looks at two theatrical works: Sor Juana Inés de la Cruz's *El Divino Narciso* and Pedro Calderón de la Barca's *Eco y Narciso*. The *loa* to *El Divino Narciso* is often considered an independent text because of its distinct dramatic structure as well as the theme it addresses—the conquest of America—and the author treats it as a stand-alone piece. The study opens with an informative chapter on theater in the early modern period. The author explores deeply the allegorical meanings associated with each theatrical piece, looking at not just textual elements but also oral, aural, and visual elements. This study would be of special interest to early modern literary scholars.

1724 González Boixo, José C. Letras virreinales de los siglos XVI y XVII. México: UNAM, 2012. 548 p.: bibl. (Estudios de cultura iberoamericana colonial)

This book provides a panoramic study of the state of the field. Opening with a chapter that addresses reality and fiction in the narrative discourse of Christopher Columbus and concluding with two essays on key Baroque Spanish American poets—Peruvian Juan de Espinosa Medrano and Mexican Sor Juana Inés de la Cruz—the volume's expansive scope is especially useful for the generalist reader. The author also includes a useful bibliography of important works that is divided by text and includes editions and significant studies.

1725 **Harrison, Regina.** Sin and confession in colonial Peru: Spanish-Quechua penitential texts, 1560–1650. Austin: University of Texas Press, 2014. 310 p.: bibl., ill., index. (Joe R. and Teresa Lozano Long series in Latin American and Latino art and culture)

Drawing from works in Spanish and Quechua, this rigorous and insightful study addresses how Catholic confession was implemented among the indigenous population in colonial Peru. Native people were taught the practice of confession in their native language, in this context Quechua. Harrison studies a wide range of colonial Andean texts, including Bartolomé de Las Casas's *Avisos y reglas para confesores* (1552) and Quechua-language *Doctina christiana* (1584), and a series of 16th-century Spanish-Quechua dictionaries. The bilingual doctrinal texts produced to facilitate the practice of confession, Harrison argues, leave traces of ancient practices of Quechua-speaking cultures. These texts also provide a window to the larger issues related to colonialism, including land ownership; the evangelical enterprise; and, the imposition of European norms regarding sexuality, labor, and property.

1726 **López de Mariscal, Blanca.** La escritura y el camino: discurso de viajeros en el Nuevo Mundo: artículos reunidos. México: Bonilla Artigas Editores; Monterrey, Mexico: Tecnológico de Monterrey; México: CONACYT, Consejo Nacional de Ciencia y Tecnología, 2014. 218 p.: bibl., ill. (Memoria, literatura y discurso; 2)

This compelling study addresses the topic of travel and writing with a focus on three categories of travelers: the Spaniard whose goal is to conquer, the religious whose goal is to proselytize, and the woman who has no choice but to travel for her husband. The author both looks at canonical texts, such as Hernando Cortés's letters, and less studied materials, such as the *Relación del espantable terremoto* (1541), an early imprint from Mexico City that addresses the 1541 earthquake in Guatemala. Through the study of such topics as text and image, publication permissions, and gold and hunger, López de Mariscal probes these early colonial texts for what they reveal of the traveler's engagement with new peoples and new surroundings.

1727 **Marrero-Fente, Raúl.** Poesía épica colonial del siglo XVI: historia, teoría y práctica. Spain: Universidad de Navarra; Madrid: Iberoamericana; Frankfurt am Main: Vervuert, 2017. 280 p.: bibl., index. (Biblioteca Indiana; 45)

This book provides a comprehensive overview of colonial studies through the lens of 16th-century epic poetry. The author makes an effective case for both how central this genre should be to studies of the early colonial period and for how marginal it has become in the field. Seeking to remedy that, through analysis of form, context, and theme, Marrero-Fente presents thorough studies of nine epic poems. He explores variations on key themes, such as conquest, discovery, violence, and lament. Included in the 10 chapters are studies of canonical works such as Alonso de Ercilla's *La Araucana,* Juan de Castellanos's *Elegías de varones ilustres de Indias,* as well as less studied texts, such as Antonio Saavedra Guzmán's *El peregrino indiano.*

1728 **More, Anna Herron.** Baroque sovereignty: Carlos de Sigüenza y Góngora and the Creole archive of colonial Mexico. Philadelphia: University of Pennsylvania Press, 2013. 350 p.: bibl., index.

This extraordinarily well-researched and well-written study takes as its centerpiece the works of Sigüenza y Góngora (1645–1700), a Creole scholar who was born and died in Mexico City. More probes the works of Sigüenza for what they reveal of the response in late 17th-century New Spain to Spanish imperial decline. She argues that as a whole, his works give the clearest articulation of "how issues of governance, history, and citizenship combined to form a discourse of Creole patriotism" (p. 16). This discourse would continue to grow in influence in the century leading up to the war of independence. In a nuanced analysis, More addresses the role of the Creole archive, Creole antiquarianism, Creole governance, and Creole citizenship.

1729 Peña Núñez, Beatriz Carolina. Fray Diego de Ocaña: olvido, mentira y memoria. Prólogo de Elena Altuna. Alicante, Spain: Publicaciones de la Universidad de Alicante, 2016. 455 p.: bibl., ill., index, maps. (Cuadernos de América sin nombre; 38)

This book addresses the work of Fray Diego de Ocaña (c. 1570–1608). A Hieronymite friar from Cáceres, Ocaña traveled through vast parts of the Viceroyalty of Peru and spent the final part of his life in Mexico City, where he died. Ocaña produced a *Relación*, where he noted observations and comments, in text and image, related to his travels. Peña Núñez offers a comprehensive study of this text, the original manuscript of which is preserved at the University of Oviedo in Spain. She also addresses Ocaña's *Comedia de Nuestra Señora de Guadalupe y sus milagros*.

1730 Pérez, Mirzam. The comedia of virginity: Mary and the politics of seventeenth-century Spanish theater. Waco, Tex.: Baylor University Press, 2012. 173 p.: bibl., index, maps.

This innovative study looks at multiple approaches to representing the Virgin Mary in *comedia*, or works of theater, from 17th-century Spain. Pérez develops a deep analysis of the context in which the plays were written and performed, demonstrating for the reader the important ways in which the staging of theatrical pieces always occurred in dialogue with the political exigencies of the moment. The final chapter, a transatlantic study, about *Santa Rosa del Perú* (1669), is of greatest interest to the student and scholar of the Americas. Completed one year after her beatification, this play praises the virtues that Rosa of Lima, who would go on to become the first American saint, embodies for a 17th-century Spanish audience.

1731 Rodilla León, María José. "Aquestas son de México las señas": la capital de la Nueva España según los cronistas, poetas y viajeros (siglos XVI al XVIII). Madrid: Iberoamericana; Frankfurt am Main: Vervuert; México: Universidad Autónoma Metropolitana, 2014. 409 p.: bibl. (Parecos y australes; 12)

Divided into five parts that present the city through five different lenses—the indigenous, the Creole, the festive, the sacred, and the allegorical—the book offers a detailed study of representations of Mexico City from Hernando Cortés's arrival in 1519 through the period of the Bourbon Reforms in the 18th century. Rodilla León studies a wide range of primary texts, including chronicles, letters, poetry, and archival documents. Provides an excellent overview of key texts and themes related to Mexico City that will be especially useful to advanced undergraduates and graduate students.

1732 Rovira, José Carlos. Miradas al mundo virreinal: ejemplos en la literatura hispanoamericana y recuperaciones contemporáneas. México: UNAM, 2015. 324 p.: bibl., ill. (Estudios de cultura iberoamericana colonial/Coordinación de Humanidades, Programa Editorial)

The author locates a thread of continuity from the prehispanic and colonial periods through the contemporary period. The chapters address specific figures who embody the process of resignification that is the focus of the study. Rovira opens with the 15th-century Tetzcoca leader Nezahualcoyotl who, himself revered as a poet, is the object of adoration by the turn-of-the-century *modernista* poet Rubén Darío and other authors before the 20th century. In this chapter and the following, the author traces the readings and rereadings of the figure in question. Other historical figures include the 16th-century poet and conquistador Gutierre de Cetina, the 17th-century Spanish Baroque poet Luis de Góngora, and the 17th-century Cuban poet Silvestre de Balboa.

1733 Schmidhuber de la Mora, Guillermo and **Olga Martha Peña Doria.** Sor Juana: teatro y teología. México: Bonilla Artigas Editores: Universidad del Claustro de Sor Juana, 2016. 187 p: bibl., ill. (some color). (Colección Novohispana; 2)

This volume offers a meticulous study of Sor Juana Inés de la Cruz's three *autos sacramentales*, religious and allegorical theatrical pieces that would have been presented inside and outside the convent. The authors provide a detailed introduction to the theatrical works of Sor Juana, which is followed by studies dedicated to *El mártir del Sacramento, San Hermenegildo, El cetro de Joseph*, and *Auto del Divino Narciso*. There are various supplementary essays, the final and longest of which argues that Sor Juana should be understood as the first female theologian of the Americas. Given the topic, this volume will be of most interest to specialists.

1734 **Tenorio, Martha Lilia.** El gongorismo en Nueva España: ensayo de restitución. México: El Colegio de México, 2013. 291 p.: bibl., index. (Biblioteca Novohispana. Estudios; 2)

Tenorio's study looks at colonial poetry from New Spain that was inspired by the quintessentially Baroque verse of the Spanish poet from Córdoba, Luis de Góngora y Argote (1561–1627). Tenorio resists any characterization of the Mexican poets as simple imitators of Góngora. Rather, her study emphatically highlights the ways in which Mexican poets of the 17th and 18th centuries drew inspiration from Góngora's approach to poetic language, which was liberated and flexible in both syntax and lexicon while aspiring to maximal musicality and lyric economy. Present is the most prized and studied New Spanish Gongorist, Sor Juana Inés de la Cruz. Tenorio, however, also draws the reader's attention to less studied examples of *gongorismo* in New Spain.

1735 **Turner, Guillermo.** Los soldados de la Conquista: herencias culturales. México: Ediciones el Tucán de Virginia: Instituto Nacional de Antropología e Historia, 2013. 242 p.: bibl. (Colección Batallas de Conquista)(Ensayo)

This study focuses on the Spaniards who accompanied Hernando Cortés during the conquest of Mexico. The author draws heavily from *The True History of the Conquest of New Spain* by Bernal Díaz del Castillo, but he also studies Cortés' letters and works by Francisco de Aguilar and Andrés de Tapia. Turner's interest is in capturing the experience of the Spanish conquistadors, looking specifically for ways in which the texts register manners of speech, emotions, injuries, illnesses, and beliefs. An innovative study of well-known texts, this book would be of special interest to literary scholars and historians.

1736 **Valdez Garza, Dalia.** Libros y lectores en la Gazeta de literatura de México (1788–1795) de José Antonio Alzate. México: Bonilla Artigas Editores; Nuevo Léon, Mexico: Instituto Tecnológico y de Estudios Superiores de Monterrey; Madrid: Iberoamericana, 2014. 266 p.: bibl., facsimiles. (Memoria, literatura y discurso; 4)

José Antonio Alzate (1737–99) established in Mexico City the influential *Gazeta de Literatura*, a literary journal active in the final decades of the 18th century. Valdez Garza's study situates the journal in the cultural, political, and historical context in which it was published and consumed. A fascinating study, this book by an emerging scholar offers a window onto literary production during the Enlightenment in New Spain. The work will be of special interest to advanced graduate students, literary scholars, and historians.

1737 **Valero Juan, Eva María.** Ercilla y "La Araucana" en dos tiempos: del Siglo de Oro a la posteridad. Sevilla, Spain: Iluminaciones, 2016. 194 p.: bibl. (Iluminaciones; 114)

This insightful and thoroughly researched study of Alonso de Ercilla's epic poem *La Araucana* (1569) is organized in two parts. The three chapters in the first part put *La Araucana* in dialogue with other early modern works that address travel, navigation, and greed; Miguel de Cervantes's *Don Quijote* (1605, 1615); and the work of Inca Garcilaso de la Vega. Each of these comparative discussions offers an innovative reading of *La Araucana*. The second part opens with a study of the Andrés Bello's 19th-century work on *La Araucana*, followed by a study of unpublished work by Gabriela Mistral on the 16th-century poem, and concludes with chapters addressing Pablo Neruda's and Raúl Zurita's engagement with Ercilla. Of great interest to literary scholars.

1738 **Volek, Emil,** La mujer que quiso ser amada por Dios: Sor Juana Inés en la cruz de la crítica. Madrid: Editorial Verbum, 2016. 257 p.: bibl. (Verbum Ensayo)

This polemical volume opens with the broad statement that "[p]ractically all the information that circulates among readers about the Mexican poet, the nun Sor Juana Inés de la Cruz, is, in fact, erroneous . . ." (p. 11). Volek proposes that his approach to Sor Juana's work through genetic criticism renders a more faithful analysis of her work. Though his conclusions vary from those of other scholars of Sor Juana, his emphasis on the textual, contextual, and intertextual approach to studying her work is representative of trends in Sor Juana studies.

TEXTS, EDITIONS, ANTHOLOGIES

1739 **Angels, demons and the New World.** Edited by Fernando Cervantes and Andrew Redden. Cambridge: Cambridge University Press, 2013. 318 p.: appendix, bibl., ill., index, map.

This illuminating volume explores the many and varied ways in which the significance of angels and demons is reconfigured in the colonial New World context. The anthology is divided into three sections, with three essays in each by established historians. Essays in the first section address sources from Europe as well as the ways in which religious in the New World were forced to reimagine angelology and demonology in their interactions with native peoples and prehispanic cultures. The second section looks closely at indigenous Christian cultures and how native peoples responded to angels and demons. The third section looks at the ways in which angels and demons figure into literary and visual arts from the 17th and early 18th centuries.

1740 **Balbuena, Bernardo de.** Grandeza mexicana. Edición, introducción y notas de Luis Íñigo-Madrigal. Madrid: Biblioteca Nueva, 2013. 395 p.: bibl.

This facsimile of the 1604 publication of the epistolary poem about Mexico City is accompanied by a concise introduction and excellent notes. The quality of the reproduction is very good. *Grandeza mexicana*'s representation of the capital of New Spain in the early 17th century is essential reading for students of colonial Mexico, colonialism, and also global history. In addition to his vivid descriptions of inhabitants and daily life in Mexico City, Balbuena addresses the circulation of goods from Asia through New Spain and then on to Europe. This is be an eminently usable edition for a range of readers from undergraduate and graduate students to specialists.

1741 **Coloniality, religion, and the law in the early Iberian world.** Edited by Santa Arias and Raúl Marrero-Fente. Nashville: Vanderbilt University Press, 2014. 280 p.: bibl., ill., index.

Divided into three parts of four essays each, this anthology focuses on three realms in which colonial institutions played a role in the production of coloniality: "politics," "religion," and "law." The first section focuses on how Spanish officials and clergy sought to impose colonial order and how native leaders and intellectuals resisted the logic of possession. The second section addresses ways in which the colonizers both exerted influence on the colonial enterprise through Catholic practices and how they were impacted by native sacred practices. The final section focuses on the relationship between early ethnography, humanistic discourses, and ethnic and racial identity on the law. As a whole, these essays offer very timely insight into processes around coloniality.

1742 **Congreso Internacional "La Tradición Clásica en la América de los Siglos XVI y XVII,"** *Madrid, 2014.* Clásicos para un nuevo mundo: estudios sobre la tradición clásica en la América de los siglos XVI y XVII. Edición de Laura Fernández *et al.* Bellaterra, Spain: Centro para la Edición de los Clásicos Españoles, Universidad Autónoma de Barcelona, 2016. 505 p.: bibl., index.

This anthology includes a selection of papers presented at the international conference "La tradición clásica en la América de los siglos XVI y XVII," held at the Fundación Juan March in Madrid, May 8–10, 2014. The 25 essays provide studies of a wide range of topics and authors, all related to the rich and significant study of the influence of classical traditions, texts, and languages on colonial writings. Noteworthy are essays on Vasco de Quiroga, Juan de Espinosa Medrano, and Inca Garcilaso. Economical and accessible, the essays in this volume are of particular interest to advanced undergraduates and graduate students.

1743 "Diario de la navegación hecha por José Antonio Vázquez": contribución al conocimiento náutico de la ruta entre Filipinas y la Nueva España. Edición de María Luisa Rodríguez-Sala con la colaboración de Dante Guillermo Celis Galindo e Ignacio Gómezgil R. México: UNAM, Instituto de Investigaciones Sociales: Instituto de Geografía, UNAM, 2013. 62, 324 p.: bibl., ill.

In the late 18th century, a pilot serving in the Royal Spanish Armada, José Antonio Vázquez, documented his travels and travails in a diary kept during the journey from Manila to San Blas. The document was found in the archive of the Naval Museum in Madrid and is published for the first time in this volume. The text itself is preceded by a useful introductory study that addresses the social and historical context in which the diary was written as well as maps that detail the route. The diary will be of interest to students and scholars of maritime history, navigation, history of science, and the Hispanic Enlightenment.

1744 Díaz del Castillo, Bernal. The essential Díaz: selections from the *True history of the conquest of New Spain.* Edited and translated, with an introduction, by Janet Burke and Ted Humphrey. Indianapolis: Hackett Publishing Company, Inc., 2014. 203 p.: bibl.

The publication of this abridged edition and original translation of Bernal Díaz del Castillo's important first-person narrative of the Spanish conquest of Mexico is timely, given that 2019 marks the 500th anniversary of Hernando Cortés' arrival in Yucatán. A foot soldier for Cortés, Díaz's *True History* is a staple for courses that address the conquest and early colonial period. The editors have selected 14 sequences from Díaz's lengthy text, to which they have added two short but useful introductory essays, a list of prominent figures in the text, a timeline, suggested further readings, and notes. The edition is informed by recent scholarship and the translation is fresh and very readable. This is an excellent choice for undergraduate students.

1745 Ilarione, da Bergamo, fra. El viaje a México de Hilarión de Bérgamo: paleografía, traducción, estudio introductorio y notas. Edición de Martín Clavé Almeida. Traducción de Manuel Martín Clavé Almeida. México: Universidad Autónoma Metropolitana, Azcapotzalco: ADABI, 2013. 247 p.: bibl., color ill.

A first-ever translation from Italian to Spanish of an 18th-century travel narrative written by a friar from Bergamo, in northern Italy, who traveled to Mexico in 1762. His detailed narrative gives a first-person view of the transatlantic voyage, stops in Cuba and Puerto Rico, and journeys throughout the Viceroyalty of New Spain. The text is accompanied by color illustrations from the original manuscript of native fruits, vegetables, plants, trees, dwellings, and maps of the region. This fascinating text is accessible and will be of interest to both students and scholars.

1746 López, Patricio Antonio. Mercurio yndiano: poema histórico. Edición, estudio y notas de Beatriz Mariscal. México: El Colegio de México, 2014. 166 p. (Biblioteca novohispana; XI)

This is an edition of an extraordinary 18th-century manuscript found at the Bancroft Library at the University of California, Berkeley, a historical poem authored by a self-named "cacique of the Zapotec nation in the Valleys of Oaxaca" and written in honor of the arrival of the 39th viceroy of New Spain in 1740. The text is accompanied by a well-researched and informative introduction and helpful notes. In the tradition of erudite 17th-century writings by native intellectuals such as Inca Garcilaso de la Vega or Fernando de Alva Ixtlilxóchitl, this is a highly unusual text for the 18th century. Following the poem is a letter titled "Letter that Father Bernardo Ynga wrote," presumably a letter authored by a descendant of Huayna Capac.

1747 Manuscript cultures of colonial Mexico and Peru: new questions and approaches. Edited by Thomas B.F. Cummins, Emily A. Engel, Barbara C. Anderson, and Juan M. Ossio A. Los Angeles, Calif.: Getty Research Institute, 2014. 199 p.: bibl., index. (Issues & debates)

This anthology includes five essays on colonial Peru and three essays on colonial Mexico by established scholars of art history, book history, and anthropology who address ways in which a new manuscript culture, which drew from local cultural practices, took hold in the Andes and Mesoamerica in the 16th and 17th centuries. Many essays rely on the work of interdisciplinary teams and innovative research techniques, such as the use of fiber-optic light to study folios, comparison of illustrations with textiles, and the recreation of 16th-century New World pigments. The volume offers enlightening studies of, among others, the following extraordinary illuminated colonial manuscripts: the *Florentine Codex* and two Martín de Murúa manuscripts—the Galvin Manuscript and the Getty Manuscript.

1748 Oviedo, José Miguel. Historia de la literatura hispanoamericana. Vol. 1, De los orígenes a la emancipación. Madrid: Alianza Editorial, 2012. 1 v.: bibl., indexes.

A new edition of a 1995 publication, this history of Spanish American literature provides a comprehensive descriptive survey of texts from the prehispanic period through the 19th century, from Mexico to Chile. The annotations are brief yet informative, and are followed by suggestions for further reading. Examples of texts included in the study are the *Popol Vuh*, Cabeza de Vaca's *Naufragios*, works by Inca Garcilaso, Guaman Poma, and Sor Juana, as well as Bolívar and Bello. This would be useful as a reference for undergraduate and graduate students studying early literature from Spanish America. For comment on the 1995 publication, see *HLAS 58:3472*.

1749 La resignificación del Nuevo Mundo: crónica, retórica y semántica en la América virreinal. Edición de Claudia Parodi, Manuel Pérez y Jimena Rodríguez. Madrid: Iberoamericana; Frankfurt am Main: Vervuert, 2013. 254 p.: bibl., ill.

This volume of 11 essays written in Spanish and English by scholars located in the US, Europe, and Latin America is organized in three sections dedicated to broad topics associated with colonial studies: chronicle, rhetoric, and travel; cultural semantics and ideology; and, art and festival. Essays include analyses of linguistic phenomena examined in the processes of "Indianization" and "Hispanization" of language in bilingual contexts and a sociolinguistic study of Afro-Hispanic villancicos. Essays also include studies attentive to literary and historical language, such as one on a little studied 16th-century work by Martín Fernández de Enciso that deals with New World geography, and a set of villancicos dedicated to the Virgin of Guadalupe sung in the cathedral in Mexico City from 1694–1728.

1750 Signs of power in Habsburg Spain and the New World. Edited by Jason McCloskey and Ignacio López Alemany. Lewisburg, Penn.: Bucknell University Press, 2013. 246 p.: bibl., ill., index.

Transatlantic in its focus, this anthology includes essays that address Spain and the viceroyalties of New Spain and Peru. The central theme is relevant to studies of the colonial period and two of the essays directly take up materials from the New World—John Slater's "Tampering with Signs of Power: Juan de Palafox, Historiography, and the Limits of Heraldry" and José A. Cárdenas Bunsen's "*Ius gentium* and Just War: The Problem of Representation in Inca Garcilaso's Royal Commentaries." The bishop of Puebla from 1639–1649, Palafox modified the crest of Philip IV in a retable of the Habsburg kings created for the cathedral in Puebla. Cárdenas Bunsen studies how Garcilaso incorporated the theme of just war throughout his *Royal Commentaries* (1609,1617).

1751 Tres crónicas mexicanas: textos recopilados por Domingo Chimalpáhin. Paleografía y traducción de Rafael Tena. México: Dirección General de Publicaciones del Consejo Nacional para la Cultura y las Artes, 2012. 359 p.: bibl., indexes. (Cien de México)

This volume presents editions of texts associated with the colonial Nahua intellectual don Domingo de San Antón Muñón Chimalpahin Cuauhtlehuanitzin, who collected documents and wrote histories in 17th-century New Spain. Each text is found in volume 3 of a set of manuscripts that until 2014 belonged to the British and Foreign Bible Society, but in that year was purchased by Mexico and is now housed in the Instituto Nacional de Antropología e Historia in Mexico City. These works are an important part of Mexico's cultural patrimony and Tena's translations from Nahuatl to Spanish

1752 Valle y Caviedes, Juan del. Guerras físicas, proezas medicales, hazañas de la ignorancia. Edición, estudio preliminar y anotación de Carlos Fernando Cabanillas Cárdenas. Madrid: Iberoamericana; Frankfurt am Main: Vervuert, 2013. 755 p.: bibl, index. (Biblioteca indiana; 34)

This impressive tome presents an extraordinarily well researched critical edition of the poetry against physicians in Lima written by Juan del Valle y Caviedes (1645–98), a prominent Baroque poet. Cabanillas Cárdenas provides a nearly 200-page introduction to the text, which addresses the biography of the author, key historical references for the period, and a close analysis of the poems themselves, followed by an extensive bibliography. The 300-page edition of *Guerras físicas* is heavily annotated. The third and final section provides a catalog of variants found in the 10 known manuscripts of the text. This publication will be a tremendous resource to researchers studying a range of topics related to 17th-century viceregal society, from Baroque poetry to history of medicine.

make them more accessible to a wider reading public. This book will be of interest to literary scholars and historians.

21st Century Prose Fiction
Mexico

RYAN LONG, *Associate Professor of Spanish and Portuguese, University of Maryland*

MANY OF THE OUTSTANDING WRITERS of 2014–2017 demonstrated significant stylistic accomplishments, including a careful consideration of the relationship between text and image. The quality of Mario Bellatin's publications in this regard is as surprising as their quantity. *Jacobo reloaded* (item **1759**) and *El perro de Fogwill* (item **1760**) present text and image side-by-side whereas *Retrato de Mussolini con familia* (item **1761**) is divided between a section comprised of text and another of image. Zsu Szkurka illustrates all three books, which, taken together, challenge readers to consider whether it is the text or image that imposes the esthetic or narrative order. The space of tension created between these media corresponds with Bellatin's thematic interest in who has the authority to tell stories about the past, who defines what communication is and does, and how rules and customs tilt toward the reproduction of violent social and political structures. Communication is the central theme of a fourth book by Bellatin, *Carta sobre los ciegos para uso de los que ven* (item **1758**), which is about two blind and deaf siblings who rely on prosthetic devices to interact through words. Another author who combines text and image, Verónica Gerber Bicecci, includes drawings in *Conjunto vacío* (item **1768**) that map out an intermediate space in which the narrator struggles to understand herself and her relations with others. The experiences of loss and separation associated with living in Mexico as Argentine exiles outline the empty set of Gerber Bicecci's title, a space of potential and impossible relationality.

The diary form is used effectively by other works, giving readers of contemporary Mexican fiction the sense that the literary present is a moment of introspection, rather than one of action. Tedi López Mills' *La invención de un diario* (item **1775**) employs intertextuality, especially with respect to David Markson's *Wittgenstein's Mistress* (1988), to create a very slowly developing sensibility at the intersection of several different senses, locations, and moments. The isolation that pervades Gerber Bicecci's book finds an echo in the loneliness of Brenda Lozano's diarist in *Cuaderno ideal* (item **1776**), a text whose metafictional elements recall Bellatin's work. Metafiction also effectively organizes Celene Guzmán's *Días de chicle* (item **1770**), a diary-based narrative about a writer afraid to publish her work, which humorously criticizes a masculinist literary establishment.

Structure is one strong point of Laia Jufresa's beautiful portrayal of the impact of trauma on multiple generations in *Umami* (item **1773**). The text alternates among five different characters who speak from different moments presented in reverse chronological order from 2004 to 2000. Like López Mills' text, Jufresa's achieves an exquisite degree of sensuousness. Although less accomplished in terms of narrative than form, Aura Xilonen's *Campeón gabacho* (item **1798**) constructs a voice that moves almost seamlessly between interiority and often violent action, using a unique blend of slang, neologism, and Spanglish.

Standing out among the well-established writers who continue to address a broad range of topics with stylistic aplomb are Ana García Bergua, David Toscana, and Jorge Volpi. García Bergua's *Fuego 20* (item **1766**) is a fantastical novel that, like many contemporary texts—including those by Héctor Aguilar Camín (item **1753**), Coral Aguirre (item **1754**), Daniel Espartaco (item **1763**), and Marxitania Ortega (item **1780**)—returns to the 1970s or 1980s for its setting. García Bergua centers her exploration of subjectivity and critique of corruption around a portrayal of the 1982 fire that destroyed the Cineteca Nacional. Toscana's *Olegaroy* (item **1796**) relies upon its author's unmatched ability to work with irony, humor, and poignancy to tell a tale about the apparent dangers of reading in a strange take on the murder mystery. Volpi's choral testimonial novel, *Las elegidas* (item **1797**), is comprised of a collection of poems that navigate a complicated mix of genres and that represent a sex-trafficking network in equally mythic, historical, and documentary terms.

The genres of crime fiction and the historical novel continue to be well represented. Significant contributions of the former include Bef's *Azul cobalto* (item **1765**), an installment of the Andrea Mijongas series that adopts a historical perspective. Two historical novels stand out: Pedro Ángel Palou's *Tierra roja: la novela de Lázaro Cárdenas* (item **1786**), with its fine portrayal of an investigative journalist; and Vicente Quirarte's novel about Benito Juárez and the French Intervention, which takes place largely in New York City, *La isla tiene forma de ballena* (item **1788**).

Excellent short-story collections include those by Gabriela Juaregui (item **1772**), Daniela Bojórquez (item **1762**), Jonathan Minila (item **1778**), and Palou (item **1785**). Juaregui's *La memoria de las cosas* draws on its author's experience as a poet to provide fascinating and socially critical portrayals of common objects and their global itineraries. Palou's *Demonios en casa* rounds off the stylistic accomplishments of the contemporary period by perfecting a way of writing that is at once enigmatic, clear, symbolic, and spartan.

PROSE FICTION

1753 Aguilar Camín, Héctor. Toda la vida. México: Penguin Random House Grupo Editorial, 2016. 134 p.

A novelist and historian, Aguilar Camín is adept at writing compelling, though occasionally heavy-handed, fiction that explores the gray areas where different forms of storytelling overlap. Serrano, the first-person narrator and protagonist of *Toda la vida* is writing the history of a 1920s state-perpetrated massacre as he experiences the consequences of the murderous abuses of power by the Mexico City police. Agents of the historical and now defunct División de Investigaciones para la Prevención de la Delincuencia (DIPD), notorious for its use of torture and extrajudicial killings, alternately assist and menace Serrano when he investigates the circumstances of a murder that took place in the late 1970s and involved his lover's sister. Writing about the murder years later leads Serrano to learn more about his own desires and flaws than about any reasonable explanation for the violence and impunity that persists within Mexican security forces.

1754 **Aguirre, Coral.** El resplandor de le memoria. Monterrey, Mexico: Universidad Autónoma de Nuevo León, 2014. 294 p. (Narrativa)

A follow-up to her 2008 novel, *Los últimos rostros, El resplandor* continues developing the topics of insurgency and counterinsurgency, primarily in Mexico but also in relation to the author's native Argentina. An insurgent leader attempts to return to a semblance of normalcy following years of exile and clandestine living. Others from his militant group struggle to reconcile their 30-year old goals with contemporary forms of resistance. Particularly interesting is the contrast between the insurgency, when an identifiable group fought in the name of a cause, and the contemporary drug war in Mexico, with its emphasis on money and revenge. The novel's slow, fragmentary, polyphonic, and almost obfuscated development gradually comes to fruition and attests to Aguirre's ability to organize a complex narrative structure. Here she succeeds in telling a convincing, interesting, and complex story.

1755 **Aridjis, Homero.** Carne de Dios. México: Alfaguara, 2015. 218 p.: bibl., index.

This novel takes place primarily in the 1950s and 1960s in the Oaxacan city of Huautla de Jiménez, and is focused on the real life figure of María Sabina, who became famous worldwide for her healing sessions, which featured singing, poetry, and psychotropic mushrooms. The novel juxtaposes the stories of several different visitors to Huautla, including a fictionalized version of Albert Hoffman, who invented LSD, as well as John Lennon and Juan Rulfo. Testimonial elements include songs and poems by Sabina, whom Aridjis remembers in the book's acknowledgements. Aridjis' story considers the many forms of human exploration, including chemical, poetic, and sexual.

1756 **Arreola, Guillermo.** Fierros bajo el agua. México: Joaquín Mortiz, 2014. 166 p.

In 1985, Leonardo, a young gay man, leaves his parents' unaccepting home in Mazatlán for Tijuana. His life in Tijuana is precarious and threats to his safety abound. His friend Cas is brutally murdered and another friend, Sebastián, drowns in the Pacific. More than 20 years later, Leonardo returns to Tijuana to write about Danielle Gallois, the actual French-born painter who spent most of her life in Tijuana. While there, Leonardo becomes determined to discover who murdered Cas. He seeks information from a number of sources, including journalists, police officers, and old acquaintances. Uncertainty prevails in this fragmentary, polyphonic text, especially as episodes from Leonardo's past overlap with his present-day return to Tijuana. The novel's title refers to metal bars under the ocean's surface which mark the US-Tijuana border, a symbol of danger that pertains to the threat that the past poses for the present.

1757 **Arriaga Jordán, Guillermo.** El salvaje. Barcelona: Alfaguara, 2017. 694 p. (Narrativa hispánica)

This is the first novel in more than 15 years from the screenwriter perhaps best known for his films with Alejandro González Iñárritu, including *Amores perros* (2000) and *Babel* (2006). The novel's clipped sentences and complex structure share with those films an emphasis on violence, interlacing narratives, and non-linear chronology. Juan Guillermo is an adolescent left alone in his apartment in Mexico City following the deaths of his parents and brother. His story jumps backward and forward in time from this moment, recounting formative events and tracing them to their different conclusions. The novel is interesting for its portrayal of precarious teens in the years after 1968 and for its initially successful construction of a suspenseful narrative. The parallel story of an Inuit hunter and a wolf creates a point of contrast between the wilderness and Mexico City. At first a page-turner, the novel eventually unravels because of its excessive length and overwrought organization.

1758 **Bellatin, Mario.** Carta sobre los ciegos para uso de los que pueden ver. Barcelona, Spain: Alfaguara, 2017. 90 p. (Narrativa hispánica)

Two siblings, blind and deaf since childhood, are abandoned by their parents and forced to live unofficially in a section of the Colonia de Alienados Etchepare, an institution for sufferers of dementia, which is surrounded by packs of wild dogs. The narrator's cochlear implant allows her to hear, and a cable connecting her computer to her brother Isaias's braille-registering device enables the siblings to communicate with one another. In the form of one continuous paragraph, the narrator recounts events to Isaias, including a visit to the Colonia by a writer who speaks to the blind about photography. This example, which the novel treats seriously and ironically, encapsulates Bellatin's exploration of how the senses, prosthetic devices, and language work or fail to work together. The novel's meditation on communication and shared experience includes tales that the siblings invent. These tales blur boundaries of gender as much as the novel blurs boundaries of sensory perception and language.

1759 **Bellatin, Mario.** Jacobo reloaded. Ilustraciones de Zsu Szkurka. México: Sexto Piso, 2014. 216 p.: ill. (Narrativa Sexto Piso)

Illustrated with maps and itineraries, this novel-within-a-novel features an apocryphal intertext called *La frontera* by the Austrian writer Joseph Roth. Bellatin's narrator reads the novel and recalls childhood conversations with his grandfather who, like a character in *La frontera*, shared experiences of friendship and exile. This spiral of stories that travels from Russian pogroms to the US and Mexico generations later is typical of Bellatin's metafiction. The novel maintains an extraordinary balance among thematic elements of rescue, camaraderie, fear, contemplation, and irony.

1760 **Bellatin, Mario.** El perro de Fogwill. Ilustraciones de Zsu Szkurka. Montevideo: Criatura Editora, 2015. 101 p.: ill.

Individual expression and the stability of meaning are explored in this beautifully illustrated parable about rules, purity, sacrifice, and desire. Bellatin critiques the association of authorship and possession through a portrayal of an encounter with the real life Argentinian author Rodolfo Enrique Fogwill. The novel juxtaposes text with Zsu Szkurka's drawings, and acknowledges the value of impurity and distance and the danger of purity and identity. The most dramatic account of possession appears in the novel in the figure of the Saluki, a dog whose sacredness limits its circulation, leading to its sacrifice. Dogs and words must be allowed to move about freely.

1761 **Bellatin, Mario.** Retrato de Mussolini con familia. Illustraciones de Zsu Szkurka. México: Alfaguara, 2015. 1 vol. (unpaged): ill. (some color).

In this illustrated collaboration, Bellatin and Szkurka place words and images in separate sections, both of which share the book's title. This dual structure reinforces the book's critique of the desire for comprehension and culmination, portrayed in the text as an erotic union between a dying man and the priest who performs his last rites. This desire for order coincides with a mother and father's concern about the chaos that defines their existence after the death of the book's eponymous dictator. Bellatin's text appears as typescript on fragments of paper that appear to be stapled into the book's pages, thereby turning text into an image, which, in turn, leads to a question: How do you know you're done reading an image? Is it as easy or difficult to determine as the end of a sentence, or a book?

1762 **Bojórquez, Daniela.** Óptica sanguínea. México: Consejo Nacional para la Cultura y las Artes, Dirección General de Publicaciones: Tumbona Ediciones, 2014. 93 p.: ill. (chiefly color).

A visual artist and a writer, Bojórquez combines images and short, fragmentary texts in this collection of often metafictional reflections on a range of topics, including memory, technology, surveillance, and unease. Photographs, official documents, paintings, and even proofreader's marks accompany the texts. Two discussions of memory stand out. The first tells of a recollection which is supplanted by a photograph, and the second has a narrator who seeks information on Google about her dead mother and finds it difficult to separate her mother's life from the chaotic assortment of hits that the search produces. The book succeeds in producing convincing, unsettling, and consistently voiced interior monologues that express almost paralyzing sensations of alienation and isolation.

1763 Espartaco, Daniel. Memorias de un hombre nuevo. México: Penguin Random House Grupo Editorial, 2015. 108 p.

This novel connects childhood with leftist politics and state socialism, both relegated to a past more distant than the number of years between it and the present would suggest. Born to a Mexican mother in the Central European socialist country of Ruritania, which no longer exists, David, the novel's protagonist, writes about the fading memories of his early childhood and his difficulties maintaining connections with his parents, friends, and lovers while an adolescent and young adult in Mexico. This novel is especially effective at communicating loss and disorientation through a motif of evidence of lives past, which appears in multiple forms, including the memories of a photographer in Ruritania, a typescript written by David's father, and contemporary images of a war that has laid waste to Ruritania's capital city. Fear of violence in Mexico leads a friends to lament that he feels like David because the Mexico where he was born, like Ruritania, does not exist anymore either.

1764 Esquinca, Bernardo. Carne de ataúd. México: Almadía, 2016. 290 p. (Narrativa)

Esquinca's first two novels in the Casasola series take place in the present. This third installament features Eugenio Casasola, the grandfather of the series' original protagonist. Both men are crime reporters who find themselves in peril while investigating serial murders. *Carne de ataúd* takes place mostly between 1908 and 1910, when journalists opposed to Porfirio Díaz, Casasola the grandfather among them, faced persecution. His initial investigation into the return of the murderer who killed his lover in 1888 leads this Casasola to understand the violence and corruption of the Díaz regime. Spiritualism emerges as a central motif, underscoring the influence of the past on the present. The prose and characterization are occasionally clumsy, but the historical backdrop with its emphasis on the dangers threatening journalists are compelling and relevant.

1765 Fernández, Bernardo (Bef). Azul cobalto. Mexico: Editorial Oceano de Mexico, 2016. 314 p.

The most recent installment of the Andrea Mijongas series takes its readers back to David Alfaro Siqueiros's attempt to assassinate Leon Trotsky in 1940. As the novel portrays it, after the attempt and while in hiding, Siqueiros only has access to industrial-grade paints and surfaces. When his assistant suggests that the materials are perfect for proletarian art, Siqueiros begins to work with the tools he originally disdains. More than 70 years later, Bef's appealing villain, Lizzy Zubiaga, begins trading Siqueiros' paintings, both the originals and the forgeries she commissions. Mijongas is hired to investigate illegal art trafficking, and Bef intertwines her story with Zubiaga's. Foils of one another, Mijongas and Zubiaga ostensibly stand on different sides of the law, a boundary whose edges are blurred by the corruption and impunity Bef's novel critiques with humor, insight, and a mastery of orality and wordplay.

1766 García Bergua, Ana. Fuego 20. México: Ediciones Era, 2017. 306 p. (Biblioteca Era)

This fantastical tale returns to a deadly and mysterious 1982 fire that destroyed Mexico City's Cineteca Nacional and with it, an important film archive. The fire serves the point of intersection for the stories about the novel's main characters, Arturo, who, despite his father's wishes would rather not study medicine, and Saturnina, who studies art history and mourns her beloved uncle's recent death. Both protagonists wish they could be someone else, and the novel's deft portrayal of alter-egos, ghosts, and a sinister seducer offers a varied and insightful look at the benefits and risks of such a desire. The intertwined narratives of this excellent book offer a critique of corruption and the abuse of power. Intertexts, such as Fernando del Paso's *Palinuro de México* (1977), help bring the 1980s to life.

1767 García Bergua, Ana. La tormenta Hindú. México: Textofilia Ediciones: Consejo Nacional para la Cultura y las Artes, Dirección General de Publicaciones, 2015. 192 p. (Colección Lumía. Serie Narrativa)

The title story recounts an unexpected series of events with humor, tenderness, and a sense of the absurd, qualities shared by the other stories in García Bergua's sixth collection. A disclosed secret at the end of "Visita a las muchachas" exemplifies how unacknowledged motivations and repressed feelings underlie and undermine apparently placid lives. A master of describing the uncanny, the author presents fantastical occurrences, such as the eruption of paper from the title character's body in "El notario," directly and with a flat tone. The stories' tense interplay between surface and depth drives seemingly trivial events to dangerous, if not deadly heights, as in the violent revenge fantasies that obsess a married couple in "Las almohadas del Doctor Nijinsky," and the fear of reprisals suffered by the judges of a dance competition in "La entrega del Terpsícore."

1768 Gerber Bicecci, Verónica. Conjunto vacío. México: Almadía, 2015. 215 p.: ill. (Narrativa)

Readers initially do not learn the name of this novel's first-person narrator and, ultimately, do not learn it from her. Her name, Verónica, appears instead in a letter written by another character. This gradual and relational way of identifying and developing characters corresponds with the novel's portrayal of human interaction in mathematical terms, announced by its title. Families and friendships grow closer, more distant, and closer again across the space and time defined by exile, in this case between Argentina and Mexico. Verónica's mother's empty house stands as a concrete, container-like symbol, a set, that conveys loss, decay, alienation, and separation, and that functions significantly within the narrator-protagonist's attempt to organize painful experiences abstractly. The novel emphasizes relationality in formal terms through its interplay of narration, letters, and drawings. For comment on *Empty set*, the English-language version of this novel, see item **2643**.

1769 González, Mariño. Pésimas personas. Guadalajara, Mexico: Arlequín, 2014. 85 p. (Cuento)

Literary and musical traditions, especially the picaresque and punk rock, serve as reference points for these short stories and the characters who inhabit them. The disdainful, intelligent narrative voice in "Yo ladrón" succeeds in surviving through theft (including the theft of ideas), but cannot escape his own self-loathing. The characters in "Guía del pequeño vacacionista" find themselves trapped in an existence defined as much by songs and films as by repetition, absurd coincidences, and surveillance. González demonstrates his effective and grotesque sense of humor in "Nuestro punk," a story about a couple who bring home a punk rocker as a pet.

1770 Guzmán, Celene. Días de chicle. Culiacán, Mexico: Programa de Estímulos a la Creación y el Desarrollo Artístico de Sinaloa, 2014. 101 p.

This ironic and sympathetic portrayal of early adulthood takes the form of a diary. The entries span one summer in the life of a young woman struggling to maintain her nascent independence. The protagonist tries to define herself on the page while simultaneously trying to establish her own space. The narrator's room of her own is an apartment with a balcony overlooking the ocean in her hometown of Mazatlán. Her parents and friends help the narrator overcome her fears about entering a writing contest. The novella comments humorously on the way gender shapes expectations with its portrayals of self-satisfied male writers. Colloquial language and multiple references to popular culture enhance the convincing first-person voice.

1771 Hiriart, Hugo. El águila y el gusano: acción en prosa. México: Literatura Random House, 2014. 348 p.

The novel's subtilte "Acción en prosa," explains its drama-like structure—at least to the extent that it connects dialogue with action. Hiriart's work emphasizes the power of political and social discourse, even, or especially, discourse that does not signify anything beyond itself. The book's comic, baroque, and well-crafted dialogue is nothing if not prolix, a quality that emphasizes both the emptiness of words and their destructive power. Characters and settings share a vacuous absurdity and lack of apparent connection. The reader experiences the fragmentation and instability that correspond to the precarity and chaos of the characters' lives.

1772 Jauregui, Gabriela. La memoria de las cosas. México: Sexto Piso, 2015. 125 p. (Narrativa Sexto Piso)

Twenty-three stories across four sections recall the game of 20 Questions (Vegetalia, Mineralia, Animalia, Artificilia). The mostly very short texts provide readers with surprising trajectories about familiar objects. Trees move thousands of kilometers. Avocados thrive in California due to theosophy. Bronze mollusks change hands from trash collectors in Mexico City to Somali pirates. A guiding tension between knowledge and imagination provides another point of organization for the collection. In one story, a father learns more about gummy bears than he ever thought possible, while his son dreams of being glue so that he can stick with his friends. The stories imagine the past and possible futures of various objects based on knowledge of current and historical events, especially those related to global commerce and exploitation.

1773 Jufresa, Laia. Umami. México: Random House Mondadori, 2015. 234 p.: ill.

Alfonso is an anthropologist who studies the flavor that gives the novel its title and amaranth, an ancient Aztec staple. He owns a private *vecindad* that consists of five houses, named acid, bitter, sweet, salty, and umami. Five characters from the *vecindad* provide different perspectives on the events that affect them over a five-year period, which the novel traces backward, from 2004 through 2000. This spatial, temporal, and narrative regularity seems schematic. However, the novel's convincing development of different voices, ranging from a young girl, Luz, to Alfonso, who is also an aging widower, develops a strong, complex counterpoint. Themes of loss, trauma, mourning, and loneliness emphasize the attractiveness of order while revealing its fragility. The novel's sensory character, appropriate to its title, is one among its many strengths. Examples include the smell of a swing's rusty chain, the sight of light moving across newly painted walls, the taste of mushrooms, and the sound of words, a topic the novel develops through neologism and malapropism, an outstanding example of which is the child's transformation of camouflage into *camuflash*.

1774 Lara Zavala, Hernán. Macho viejo. México: Alfaguara, 2015. 150 p.

A documentary novel about the so-called old man of Puerto Escondido, based on an earlier book by Roberto Cortés Tejeda, Lara Zavala's book is an elegiac, fairy-tale like portrayal of the widower and local wise man Ricardo Villamonte, better known as the Macho Viejo. A doctor, Villamonte treats patients in the small town where he lives and in the surrounding rural community. His travels into the countryside provide the narrator with opportunities to describe the abundant and sometimes threatening jungle and the ocean, and to develop one of the novel's plots, a love story from the doctor's earlier years. The novel is a song of praise for a region and for an antiquated, regionalist style, which is appropriate for a story on aging that is also a meditation on how to tell such a story.

1775 López Mills, Tedi. La invención de un diario. México: Almadía, 2016. 315 p. (Narrativa)

From January 1 to December 31, 2013, López Mill's diarist writes clear and aphoristic entries that present the intersection between a receptive mind, a series of books, a group of friends and acquaintances, and a world observed with insight, tenderness, trepidation, fear, anger, and indignation. The diarist gradually and enigmatically brings the reader into a sensibility, a place at the meeting point of one's own words and the words of others, that is shaped by seeing, listening, and responding to events near and far, both geographically and temporally. Central intertexts include David Markson's *Wittgenstein's Mistress* and Fray

Bernardino de Sahagún's *Historia general*. These and other texts lead the diarist to formulate questions about subjectivity, citizenship, and the stubborn effects of colonial violence.

1776 Lozano, Brenda. Cuaderno ideal. México: Alfaguara, 2014. 226 p.

This novel's title recalls the doubling characteristic of metafiction, the genre it practices. An ideal notebook is one that allows the person writing in it to comprehend the company of others by way of private thoughts. Ideal is also the brand name of a notebook that the novel's first-person narrator and protagonist treasures. One episode typical of the novel's occasional sardonic humor is the infomercial for Ideal notebooks that the narrator imagines. A critique of the marketing of the self is more pervasive and subtly rendered throughout the novel by the narrator's emphasis on open-ended and ambiguous transformations, those that resist the coherency of the transactional logic of self-fashioning. The gradually unfolding and aphoristic qualities of the narrator's diary entries reflect the narrator's concluding observations about relationality and totality in a book about the world's rivers. How do her entries relate to one another? What book do the words create by running across its pages? Beautifully written, the novel's brief passages have a rythmic quality, creating a vital alternation between life and language.

1777 Malpica Cuello, Antonio. #MásGordo ElAmor. Ilustraciones de Bernardo Fernández (Bef). México: CONACULTA, Dirección General de Publicaciones: GranTravesía, 2015. 432 p.: ill.

Compelling, funny, and tender (reminiscent of the film *Stand by Me*, Rob Reiner's adaptation of Stephen King's "The Body"), Malpica's novel juxtaposes middle age with adolescence, centering its story around Simón, a somewhat pathetic figure whose failed adult relationships lead him to seek out his first love. The narrative moves back and forth between the 1980s and the present, providing opportunities for equal doses of disappointment and nostalgia. In addition to the effective use of a best friend as a narrative foil, the novel is complemented by the occasional insertion of comic strips illustrated by Bef, which are attributed in the novel to Simón.

1778 Minila, Jonathan. Lo peor de la buena suerte. México: Consejo Nacional para la Cultura y las Artes, Dirección General de Publicaciones, 2015. 133 p. (Fondo Editorial Tierra Adentro; 532)(Cuento)

This collection of seven short stories showcases its author's ability to combine interiority with perspectivism within a range of genres, including fantastical and dystopian fiction. "Perorata de un desaparecido," for example, develops the topics of friendship, security, and anonymity by telling the story of a man whose body gradually disappears, but whose voice remains. "Siguiente estación" is a brilliant tale of suspense about a group of strangers whose disturbing experience on a subway train brings them together. A journalist living in a Mexico City of the not-so-distant future where crime is the only story to be reported, the protagonist of "Insomnio inducido" is unable to wrest himself from a particularly pervasive form of surveillance. Overall, the collection attests to Minila's ability to write thought-provoking and compelling stories.

1779 Norte: una antología. Compilación de Eduardo Antonio Parra. México: Ediciones Era; Monterrey, N.L.: Fondo Editorial de Nuevo León; Culiacán, Sinaloa: Universidad Autónoma de Sinaloa, 2015. 329 p.: ill.

Short-story writer and novelist Parra compiles 49 texts by as many writers in this anthology that spans the period from the first quarter of the 20th century to the present. Useful for general readers and scholars alike, the volume provides a panorama of texts by canonical writers, including José Revueltas, Alfonso Reyes, Martín Luis Guzmán, and Inés Arredondo. Several recent writers stand out, including Liliana Blum, Cristina Rascón Castro, and Luis Jorge Boone. Their stories are about respectively, a pair of friends coming to terms with a mutual friend's death, undocumented immigrants in Nogales, Arizona, and the perils experienced by young medical students who hitchhike at night. These and other writers combine dialogue, description, and references to other media well in their evocations of life and landscape in northern Mexico.

1780 **Ortega, Marxitania.** Guerra de guerrillas. México: Jus, 2014. 273 p.

Paris is a space strangely shared by a father and his daughter in this novel about the personal consequences of armed resistance movements in Mexico in the 1970s and 1980s. Antonio is exiled to Paris and his daughter studies there years later. The novel's representation of the disorientation and alienation of exile is heightened by the generational gap experienced by Sara, whose father was absent for much of her childhood. In a novel that focuses on feelings, it is not surprising, but still somewhat disappointing, that interiority is executed more effectively than dialogue and action.

1781 **Ortiz, Salvador.** Los últimos días de la fotografía. México: Siglo Veintiuno Editores: UNAM: El Colegio de Sinaloa, 2016. 133 p.: bibl. (La creación literaria)

An isolated young man seeks company and erotic pleasure through music and photography. While trying to figure out how he can share feelings and memories with others, he meets a cruel and decadent artist who challenges his staid and detached approach to life and work. The novel's clear realist style makes especially stark the painful separation it establishes between thought and feeling, and action and physical encounter. The novel's title refers to a condensed and erotically charged manifestation of this separation, in the protagonist's desire to separate the bodies he desires from the light reflected off of them. The novel's predominantly male point of view about sex becomes somewhat tiresome.

1782 **Ortuño, Antonio.** Méjico. México: Océano, 2015. 235 p.: bibl. (Hotel de las letras)

Ortuño's quickly unfolding sentences convey effectively the fear and brutality associated with violence. His readers share his characters' uncertainty, as they struggle to comprehend how brutality and trauma pass from one generation to the next as if genetically. The novel's intertwining plots take place in multiple spaces and across several different years, not presented chronologically. The text begins in Guadalajara in 1997, then jumps to Veracruz in 1946, before introducing new chronotopes, such as Madrid in 1923 and Santo Domingo in 1945, and returning to those it has already established. The novel's imagery is often grotesque, contributing to its socially critical stance. Its multiple voices and perspectives are not always successfully rendered.

1783 **Ortuño, Antonio.** El rastro. México: FCE, Fondo de Cultura Económica, 2016. 166 p. (A través ojepse led)

Billed as *literatura juvenil*, this novel reads more like a thriller aimed at an adult audience. The first-person narrative is more convincing and coherent than the multi-vocality that characterizes his previous novel, *Méjico* (see item **1782**) and shows Ortuño's promise. The novel's humor is another welcome addition to Ortuño's style. Ortuño's ability to keep his readers' interest through a fragmentary chronology helps adds suspense to the novel's story of a kidnapping in rural northern Mexico.

1784 **Palabras mayores: nueva narrativa mexicana.** Selección de Guadalupe Nettel, Cristina Rivera Garza y Juan Villoro. Barcelona: Malpaso, 2015. 300 p.: ill.

Rivera Garza frames this anthology by explaining that the 20 works by writers under the age of 40 attempt to portray the current moment defined as it is by cruel neoliberalism and to demonstrate the need for an active civil society to take over from a state in crisis. Stories and selections from novels by a range of young authors—Pergentino José Ruiz, Eduardo Ruiz Sosa, Brenda Lozano, Fernanda Melchor, and Valeria Luiselli among them—address work, abandonment, disappearance, family, and literature, among other topics. "La pierna era nuestro altar," by Laia Jufresa, stands out for its beautiful expression of loneliness and community. It takes place at a pool where the first-person narrator observes her fellow swimmers, rather than interacting with them, no matter how much she might prefer the latter.

1785 **Palou, Pedro Ángel.** Demonios en casa. Xalapa, Mexico: Universidad Veracruzana, Dirección Editorial, 2015. 180 p. (Colección Ficción)

Demonios consists of seven stories, six of which are divided into chapters. The first and longest story, at about 30 pages, is "El emboscado." Framed by a diegetic narrator speaking to an unknown audience, the story recounts a man's attempt to survive after being banished to the woods as punishment for murdering his wife. The man begins to call himself *el Autócrata*. More than a story of survival, "El emboscado" is about the impossibility of starting over. *El Autócrata* attempts to reduce experience and thought to basic principles that he symbolizes in runes, such as, perception requires memory. The narrator's revelation that runes ultimately cover the walls of the cabin illustrates the man's failure to forge a humane existence. Several of the condensed and cyptic stories in this collection read like runes themselves. Their metafictional tendencies complement their meditations on writing and its relation to lived experiences, such as the tales of forbidden love in a medieval kingdom in "El corazón y sus especias"; desire and wartime persecution in "Exterminio"; and the death and anxiety at the heart of "Un pequeño mundo cerrado."

1786 **Palou, Pedro Ángel.** Tierra roja: la novela de Lázaro Cárdenas. México: Editorial Planeta Mexicana, 2016. 370 p.: ill. (Autores españoles e iberoamericanos)

Characterized by a clear and detailed style, Palou's novel presents Lázaro Cárdenas as a leader struggling to balance the political demands of the presidency with the moral demands of the promise of the Mexican Revolution. The novel opens with an impressive synopsis of the period from 1912 to 1932, as the future president comes to terms with the ongoing damage of revolutionary violence and the consequent difficulty of remaking Mexico. The detached, descriptive approach to the title character contrasts with the intimate, dialogue-driven representation of the contentious collaboration between a journalist for the *nota roja*, the historical figure Eduardo Téllez, and a police officer, whose name, Filiberto García, is a nod to *El complot mongol* (1969) (see *HLAS* 72:2734), Rafael Bernal's classic thriller. By pairing journalism about crime and fiction about crime in this excellent historical novel, Palou ironically suggests the difficulty of discerning truth from artifice—let alone revolutionary promise from political disillusion.

1787 **Peña, Hilario.** Págale al diablo. México: Nitro/Press, 2016. 111 p.: ill.

In this, his fourth crime novel, Peña tells the story of a woman, her lover, her husband's life insurance policy, multiple betrayals, murder, and a burning desire to get away from it all. The complicated plot almost becomes a parody of the hard-boiled tradition it convincingly manipulates. There is much more focus on criminals than crime fighters, and the protagonist's story, especially his past, is as difficult to trust as his voice is consistently and compellingly crafted. Peña capably uses pastiche, tongue-in-cheek imitation of generic conventions, and a range of intertexts whose most prominent examples are *Moby Dick* and the film, *The Princess Bride*. The result is an impressive example of how the *novela negra* continues to benefit from stylistic and thematic innovations.

1788 **Quirarte, Vicente.** La isla tiene forma de ballena. México: Seix Barral, 2015. 236 p. (Biblioteca breve)

This historical novel takes place during two wars in two countries, the Second French Intervention in Mexico and the Civil War in the US. Benito Juárez, Mexico's president, is on the run, travelling through the country he might lose, trying to elude capture, while his family is exiled in New York City. The novel succeeds in offering a personal perspective on historical events by combining letters, diary entries, and third-person omniscient narration. The incorporation of apocryphal letters from Margarita Maza de Juárez to her husband provides the most concise and poignant combination of personal and historical topics. Also compelling are the novel's spy narrative and its intertextual references to Edgar Allen Poe and the detective story.

1789 **Ramos, Agustín.** Justicia mayor. México: Literatura Random House, 2015. 341 p.

Ramos dedicates his ninth novel to writers Fernando del Paso and Jorge Aguilar Mora, among others. Their dense style, characterized by word play, polyphony, and fragmentary structure, are reflected in this portrayal of a corrupt colonial administration's repression of the 1769 indigenous rebellion in the mountains of Tutotepec, in what is now the state of Hidalgo. Ramos' primary narrator compiles his story years after the fact from documents and tales others have told him, focusing on Don Pedro José de Leoz, who becomes the mayor of the city of Tulancingo in the years leading up to the rebellion. Another narrator presents events with more immediacy. *Justicia mayor* is a novel that succeeds in portraying the ambition, greed, and venality that often characterize politics, while refusing to grant itself clear narrative authority.

1790 Ramos Revillas, Antonio. Los últimos hijos. México: Consejo Nacional para la Cultura y las Artes, Dirección General de Publicaciones: Almadía, 2015. 259 p. (Narrativa)

The actions of the first-person narrator and protagonist in Ramos' third novel test the limits of the reader's sympathy and comprehension. Alberto goes to great lengths to compensate for a devastating personal loss he and his wife Irene have suffered. Dissatisfied with one solution, and angered and unsettled after experiencing a disturbing burglary, Alberto takes a form of revenge that compels him and Irene to separate themselves absolutely from whatever sense of belonging they still managed to sustain. With a detached tone and a storyline that flirts with dark science fiction, *Los últimos hijos* presents alienation and frustration as the only possible outcomes to family issues, parenthood, crime, and impunity. Particularly effective is the depiction of the stubbornly lingering consequences of grief.

1791 Rangel, Joselo. One hit wonder. México: Almadía, 2015. 179 p. (Narrativa)

The lead guitarist and vocalist of the Mexican rock band Café Tacuba (Café Tacvba) offers 20 short stories in this collection. Characterized by humor and cleverness, the stories include a tale of a band that never performs after decades of delays involving rehearsal time, finding the perfect name, the quality of their demo, and aging; a convincing break-up story told from the point of view of a woman who has only been married for a week; and the ingenious title story, which explains that one-hit wonders are actually all by the same band, lost in time travel and unable to find the present-day. The relatively long story titled, "Rockstar" is an effective representation of adolescent desires for love, fame, and mobility, and the disillusionment that comes with the gradual awareness of how naiveté tends to shape such longing.

1792 Sánchez, Josué. En el pabellón de las dieciséis cuerdas. México: Consejo Nacional para la Cultura y las Artes, Dirección General de Publicaciones, 2015. 91 p. (Fondo Editorial Tierra Adentro; 527)(Cuento)

The author's first book, this collection of 15 very short stories (usually less than six pages) exhibits an impressive style that is detached, visual, and melancholy. As the title suggests, boxing is one of its topics, which extends to other activities and venues where there are intense alternations between action and reflection, even if that reflection only occupies a few seconds. Sánchez succeeds especially well in describing the body in motion. Literary, cinematic, and musical references—Ray Bradbury, David Lynch, and David Bowie—help round out the collection's character development. One character's question about whether science fiction is meant for gringos enhances the collection's critical awareness of cultural asymmetry in a time of globalization.

1793 Sánchez Mota, Marcela. La otra piel. México: La Cifra Editorial, 2014. 292 p.: ill. (La otra parte. Novela)

In a bewildered but clear first-person voice, the protagonist addresses her recently deceased father, who confessed to her on his deathbed that the woman who raised her was not her mother. The search for answers about a life that now feels alien takes the protagonist through different moments of political resistance, including the anarchist activity before and during the Revolution and the Student Movement of 1968. Most interesting is the novel's focus on Monte Verità, in Arcona, Switzerland, the commune where the protagonist's origins appear to lie. The blurred boundaries between memories, dreams, and visions add elements of mystery to the novel's otherwise overly descriptive and verbose style.

1794 Silva Márquez, César. La balada de los arcos dorados. Oaxaca de Juárez, Mexico: Almadía, 2014. 224 p. (Negra)

Part thriller and part whodunit, Silva Márquez's novel tells parallel stories of a crime reporter and a police officer who investigate a series of murders in Ciudad Juárez. Many killings are drug-related and bear the signs of gang violence, which also threatens both main characters. The novel develops a mystery about revenge killings told in the form of interrelated narratives from different points of view, and which implicate a broader circle of characters, including the members of a support group for women whose loved ones have joined Juárez's grim ranks of femicides. The novel combines references to crime fiction and historical serial murders, including Cormac McCarthy's *No Country for Old Men* (2005) and the Manson killings, juxtaposing entertainment and morbid fascination to the consequences of contemporary violence. Silva Márquez proves especially adept at establishing a frightening and melancholy atmosphere.

1795 **Solorio Reyes, Víctor.** Artillería nocaut. México: Consejo Nacional para la Cultura y las Artes, Dirección General de Publicaciones: Joaquín Mortiz; Querétaro, Mexico: Instituto Queretano de la Cultura y las Artes, 2014. 192 p.

Eleuterio Marto is a talented boxer who throws matches and splits the winnings with his manager. When his friend's daughter, Esperanza, implores him to investigate her father's fate, Eleuterio tries to make up for the bad behavior he exhibits inside and outside of the ring. In this generally well-written thriller about murder, drugs, and high-level government corruption, the Mexican military and private security firms also play a role. The first half of the novel is especially good, but once the reasons for Esperanza's father's murder become clear, the novel devolves into a somewhat convoluted and clumsy revenge story.

1796 **Toscana, David.** Olegaroy. Barcelona: Alfaguara, 2018. 312 p. (Narrativa Hispánica)

Toscana's well-developed and longstanding detached, ironic style strengthens, by contrast, the affective power of several moments that punctuate this unusual meditation on the complicated relationships among language, fiction, the truth, and lived experience. The novel's title character dedicates himself to compiling news reports of accidental deaths in order to complete his *Enciclopedia de la desgracia humana*. The novel takes place in the spring of 1949, and references to real-life tragic events from that period, including Kathy Fiscus' death after falling into a well and the airplane crash that killed Turin's soccer team, add confounding import to Olegaroy's concerns about the inability to distinguish between the veracity of his life and the stories he reads. A murder mystery aids the novel's character development, in shocking and often darkly comic ways, and underpins its treatment of posterity, legacy, life, and death.

1797 **Volpi Escalante, Jorge.** Las elegidas. México: Alfaguara, 2015. 143 p.

Volpi's account of a sex-trafficking network centered around the strawberry industry in San Ysidro, California—which brutalized girls and young women primarily from Tenancingo, Mexico—takes the form of 100 poems comprising a book divided into three parts: "La tierra prometida," "Los enviados," and "El sacrificio." The novel's incorporation of biblical references, suggested by the titles of parts one and three, is clearest in the text's refiguration of the story of Abraham, Sarah, and Isaac, especially Abraham's insistence that Sarah pretend she's his sister and his near sacrifice of his only son. In the novel, the son's name is Ulises, whose association with return places in relief the displacement and alienation that the novel's victims suffer: they are exploited by male family members from their home town, a cruel irony encapsulated by the novel's title. Volpi's short poems elaborate distinct voices, including the story told to a police officer by a girl fortunate enough to escape, which provides a monovocal contrast to the text's generally choral structure. The poems are predominantly visual, which creates strong, distinct impressions of the patriarchy's violent reproduction of itself and of the destruction that ensues.

1798 **Xilonen, Aura.** Campeón gabacho. México: Literatura Random House, 2015. 332 p.

Campeón is told from the first-person perspective of Liborio, a young man recently arrived from Mexico to the US. His defense of a young woman's honor lands him in violent trouble and sets in motion the story that concludes with Liborio's having found a community by reading and training to be a boxer. Liborio's struggle to move beyond his circumstances is reflected in the novel's accomplished style, which reads like a constant conflict between description and narration, dialogue and reflection, and English and Spanish. Written Spanish surprises the reader for its orality. Especially in the novel's first half, while Liborio still struggles to find a home, sentences read like small, spiral-shaped journeys, the slang and neologisms that comprise them understood only looking back from the period, a vantage point affording just enough comprehension for the reader to continue learning more about and enjoying Liborio's complex perspective.

LITERARY CRITICISM AND HISTORY

1799 **Sheridan, Guillermo.** Toda una vida estaría conmigo. Oaxaca de Juárez, Mexico: Almadía, 2014. 391 p.: bibl.

Reading Guillermo Sheridan can be frustrating. He is an insightful, incisive, funny writer who is capable of developing a voice so clear and consistent that readers can almost hear him speaking. The range of topics he addresses is also impressive. Some of the best pieces in this collection of short, frequently autobiographical essays and musings, are about seemingly trivial things, like the train set in Sheridan's grandparents' basement, the terrible fate of his grandmother's dachshund, and a curmudgeon's defense of cigarettes. When Sheridan writes on topics of apparently more public interest, like his encounters with Juan Rulfo and García Márquez, he is less successful because he fails to balance his admiration for such figures with his ambition to be considered among them. In one outstanding essay, Sheridan writes about the death of his cousin Dení, who was killed in the 1970s, a victim of Mexico's dirty war and, according to Sheridan, of the so-called revolutionaries who misled her into taking up arms. With this affecting piece, Sheridan demonstrates his ability to engage readers and defend his convictions, even if readers may disagree with his conclusions.

Central America

YVETTE APARICIO, *Professor of Spanish and Chair of Latin American Studies, Grinnell College*
ERIN FINZER, *Associate Professor of Spanish and Associate Vice Chancellor for Academic Affairs, University of Arkansas at Little Rock*
with the assistance of TIFFANY D. CREEGAN MILLER, *Assistant Professor of Spanish, Clemson University*
FRANCES JAEGER, *Associate Professor of Spanish, Northern Illinois University*
FRANCISCO SOLARES-LARRAVE, *Associate Professor, Northern Illinois University*

GUATEMALA

GUATEMALA HAS ALWAYS been a country of storytellers. While there are well-respected poets who grace its literary history (such as the Romantic José Batres Montúfar, *modernista* Rafael Arévalo Martínez, and *guerrillero* Otto-René Castillo, as well as Ana María Rodas and Margarita Carrera), Guatemalan literature still speaks in short stories and novels.

Of these two genres, the short story has been always a favorite of Guatemalan authors. In fact, a history of Guatemalan literature is a history of its short story writers; even some of those who were known as poets, such as Arévalo

Martínez, dabbled in the short story. It is interesting, however, to see how there has been a significant shift towards the novel in the last decades. In fact, even the *microcuento* or *microrrelato* trend that emerged in the 90s has faded, and in its place one sees a number of novels dealing with themes that range from historical fiction to crime (related and unrelated to the civil war years), literature by and about women, and the plight of immigrants abroad.

One probable reason for this resurgence of the novel is the appearance of more literary prizes that also offer publication of winning entries. While Guatemala used to have two well-established literary contests—the *Certamen Permanente Centroamericano 15 de septiembre* and the *Juegos Florales Hispanoamericanos de Quetzaltenango*—beginning in the late 90s others came to light, with the intention of promoting genres, like the novel, that had been "abandoned." Thus, the *Premio de Novela Mario Monteforte Toledo*, created by writer Mario Monteforte Toledo (himself a prolific novelist), was aimed at promoting the writing of novels, and it gave rise to a young generation of new novelists. Then followed the *Certamen Letras BAM* (sponsored by the Banco Agrícola Mercantil), which also has affected other literary genres because it alternates its awards between the short story and the novel. Events like FILGUA (Feria Internacional del Libro en Guatemala) also enhance the production and distribution of books and literature in Guatemala. In fact, FILGUA deserves a special mention for having been active uninterruptedly since the year 2000, attracting academics, writers, and other personalities every year, and being the site for panels and conference cycles on literature, workshops for young authors, and other literacy activities.

In addition to these prizes and events, large international publishers have demonstrated a growing interest in Guatemalan literature. Fondo de Cultura Económica, Grupo Editorial Norma, Alfaguara, and Santillana, for instance, have opened offices that satisfy the local market by publishing established writers or winners of literary contests, and bringing back older, classic books for the textbook market. Publishers like these have created competition, and as a result there is a healthy number of local publishing houses that may not be able to print a large number of copies, but still manage to cover a particular niche. The most important, even if it is not small, is F&G Editores, whose catalog encompasses academic and popular fiction. Among the smaller publishers, *Letra Negra*, *Sophos*, and *Magna Terra* are stand outs. The government-run *Editorial Cultura* continues to be the publishing outlet for official contest winners, and it too has built a catalog of quality authors in the past years.

Historical novels—or fiction of a historical nature—seem to dominate the literary production of the past two years. The novels by Oswaldo Salazar (item **1855**) and Víctor Muñoz (items **1839** and **1840**) address different periods of Guatemalan history (Salazar's with a definitive literary history bent as well), whereas Maria Elena Schlesinger's novel (item **1857**) deals with what could be termed literature about women by women, but framed in a different historical period (in this case, during the Estrada Cabrera dictatorship and later years). Anabella Schloesser de Paiz's novel (item **1858**) differs from the others in that it centers on her family history, and attempts to explain the German diaspora in Spanish America and Guatemala.

Literature of a more existential type was not very popular in the past, but recent years have brought a noticeable production of texts like the one by Maurice Echeverría (item **1814**), an heir to writers who emerged on the scene in the late 90s with the "transgressive literature" of *Editorial X*. His novel depicts a nuanced environment that includes social media, computers, and other types of technology. Denise Phé-Funchal (item **1845**) follows this pattern, although her contribution also can be seen as a partial attempt to move away from the constant reminders of the civil war towards a more contemporary register that deals with human relationships. In a way, Carol Zardetto does both things at the same time; while her *Ciudad de los minotauros* (item **1865**) focuses on the problems experienced by those who leave the country, it also explores cultural differences in a land that is alien to all. With this text, multiculturalism enters the realm of Guatemalan literature.

The short stories by Martín Díaz (item **1812**) and Javier Mosquera Saravia (item **1836**) represent the forefront of an experimental trend in Guatemalan narrative. Even though this tendency is constant, these two authors offer innovative contributions. Alas, that is not the case of Leo de Soulas (item **1859**), Luis Emilio Morales Barrios (item **1836**), and Axel Javier Moreira Mazariegos (item **1837**), whose texts represent a return to the *indigenista* narrative of the 30s and 40s.

Interestingly enough, while crime fiction has been a hot commodity elsewhere, the Guatemalan production (except for Dante Liano's and Rodrigo Rey Rosa's books) has not been as voluminous. Amidst this scarcity of crime fiction, Gerardo Guinea Diez's novel merits attention: Although *La mirada remota* (item **1825**) presents a fairly original premise, it does not deliver fully as the *noir* it intends to be. Nevertheless, it is a good effort from a seasoned writer who has written many other novels and short story collections.

Ending this list of contemporary Guatemalan literature is what we could term a professional memoir by Ana María Jurado G. (item **1829**). This text represents a collection of experimental poems and photographs, a series of essays on different works by Miguel Ángel Asturias, and a gathering of psychological case studies written in an informal, anecdotal style. Still, it is worth mentioning that Jurado chose to focus her work on the narrative, rather than the analytical side, and that her book reads as a collection of stories instead of an attempt to reproduce Freud's *Psychopathology of Everyday Life*.

In short, the production of narrative prose in Guatemala appears to be shifting slowly towards the novel. In fact, the whole Guatemalan cultural landscape is intense, active, and productive. While the emergence of the novel is a new, unexpected development, probably favored and fueled by publishers, it remains to be seen how firm this trend may be, because the short story tradition is still very strong in this country. [TCM and FSL]

HONDURAS

The dearth of reviews of Honduran titles can be attributed to a number of factors. The economic and political obstacles that the country faced as a result of the 2009 coup continue to present challenges for Honduran authors and the country's literary establishment. In the face of social and political instability, authors have responded with uneasiness, cynicism, or in some cases, silence. Moreover, narrative continues to be a less dominant genre than poetry. Recognizing the limited options and opportunities within the country for publishing their texts, many authors have decided not to work with traditional presses, opting instead to disseminate their work online through social media or blogging. Finally, within the Honduran book market, winning a literary prize remains one of the most certain ways for authors to gain visibility for their work, as is the case with Jorge Medina García's *El viento que sopla los carbones apagados del amor*, which was originally released as *Romance del Secuestrado*, and awarded the Premio Único de Novela

Corta Centroamericana 2012 (item **1832**). In this context, Tegucigalpa remains the center of the Honduran literary scene, with all six of the texts reviewed here published in the nation's capital through a variety of presses. The novels and short stories included here demonstrate a continued influence of an esthetic of cynicism and an emphasis on quotidian realities particular to Honduras, such as Miguel Acosta's short stories in *Un día como cualquiera* (item **1800**), Francisco Barralaga de Olancho's *El sisimite: novela antropológica* (item **1804**), Boris Lara's *El Inquilino y otros cuentos* (item **1830**), and Antonio Ramos's *Pintura y aguarrás: cuentos de arriba y de abajo* (item **1850**). [TCM]

EL SALVADOR

In the narrative texts by Salvadoran writers included here, the strongest trend is the revisiting and reconfiguring of the meanings and consequences of the Salvadoran Civil War (1980–92). This reevaluation of the daily realities of the war and the wounds it wrought, for instance in Nora Méndez's novel (item **1834**) or in Claudia Hernández's text (item **1826**), is both a reckoning with the damage done by the guerrillas to the country in general and to women in particular. Unlike fiction on the war written by men, women in the novels by Méndez and C. Hernández are full-fledged guerrillas, not only *compañeras* who inspire male guerrillas to fight. Méndez's interior monologues reveal an urban guerrilla's commitment, as well as her struggle to remain resolute under torture. C. Hernández's novel traces the life of "ella," a poor rural woman who joins the guerrillas as do her father and brothers. She births four daughters during and after the war and, after the death of her last *compañero* and the signing of the peace accords, continues to fight for the right to a better life for herself and her daughters. This novel gives voice to the women who fought beside men in the war and then confronted a postwar in which they were expected to fall back into traditional gender roles.

These two novels offer an interesting counterpoint to Ricardo Hernández's *testimonio* (item **1828**), whose retelling of the narrator's years in the *cerro*, echoes the genre's characteristic texts. Like Méndez, R. Hernández narrates his integration into the guerrilla forces and his struggle to remain strong. He also directly criticizes some of the *comandantes'* decisions to discipline cadres and the FMLN's (Frente Farabundo Martí para la Liberación Nacional) destructive, cruel internecine fighting both in El Salvador and among US-based activists. The internal struggles of the Salvadoran and Latin American left is also a key element of David Hernández's fictional biography of Roque Dalton (1935–75) (item **1827**). In the novel, Dalton's virtues as a poet are secondary to his representation as an alcoholic, womanizing, unreliable revolutionary. Dalton, in this sense, resembles his less critical, more orthodox comrades. In another text centered on a male guerrilla, Horacio Castellanos Moya's narrator is in exile in Mexico City and navigates the Salvadoran left's landscape in an attempt to return to his country to take part in recently begun peace negotiations (item **1807**).

In a less clearly leftist reading of the civil war (item **1818**), Jorge Galán reconstructs the events surrounding the November offensive (1989), the November 16 assassination of the Jesuits and two women at the UCA (Universidad Centroamericana—José Simeón Cañas), and the subsequent investigation into the crime and search for justice. Unlike the guerrilla texts discussed above, Galán's novel attempts to come to terms with the violence unleashed by the military on the Salvadoran citizenry as a whole, and to show the struggle against impunity and injustice.

Among the reviewed fictional texts, only one does not directly address the civil war: Jacinta Escudos' novella (item **1817**). But it is set in an urban space that recalls unhappy postconflict Central American cities with clear class divisions and isolated, distrustful protagonists.

The two literary criticism collections included here consider important moments in Salvadoran history: the founding of cultural institutions and cultural journals in the 19th century (item **1870**) and the cultural politics of General Hernández Martínez's regime (item **1867**). Although the texts and events discussed precede the civil war, both critics draw links between their texts and more contemporary history. [YA]

NICARAGUA

At the time of writing (August 2018), Nicaragua is entering its fifth month of state-sponsored terrorism and violent oppression in reaction to national protests that began on 12 April after the Ortega government failed to respond to the devastating fire that consumed over 12,000 acres of the delicate Indio Maíz Biological Reserve. When social security reforms and reduced pension benefits for the elderly were announced one week later, the protests grew, as did the Ortega government's brutal repression in the form of paramilitary bands, murders, torture, and disappearances. These protests did not occur overnight. Resentment towards Daniel Ortega's government has been mounting over the past few years, likely due in part to both a slight economic downturn as Venezuela's petro-investments have waned and an increased awareness of the corruption and totalitarianism in the Ortega administration. In contrast to *HLAS 72*, which included no novels or short stories expressing political messaging or ideology, five of the eight texts annotated for *HLAS 74* express disillusionment with the present official iterations of Sandinismo, referred to in recent months as Orteguismo. Erick Blandón Guevara (item **1805**), Arquímedes González (item **1821**), Mario Urtecho (item **1863**), and William Grigsby Vergara (item **1823**) unabashedly criticize the Ortega government for its corruption, hypocrisy, and betrayal of core Sandinista values. Silvio Páez's and Juan Centeno's historical short stories are more nuanced (items **1809** and **1842**), but still critical of the current regime.

Related to its broad "structure of feeling" (a term coined by Marxist theorist Raymond Williams) of discontent in Sandinista politics, recent Nicaraguan prose fiction also participates in the esthetic of cynicism that has predominated Central American narrative of the past two decades. The characters in González's *Dos hombres y una pierna* (item **1821**) and in Páez's short stories (item **1842**) face total despair. Grigsby's narrator in *Mecánica del espíritu* writes with bitterness about Managua's privation with respect to social justice and gender equality, but his love for art and literature, and his shows of humanism ultimately eschew any cynicism in this deeply original and melancholic novel (item **1823**).

Gender also figures heavily into the overarching issues of three books with strong criticisms of machismo and patriarchy. Grigsby's male narrator consciously falls in love with intellectual, feminist women, and he dedicates multiple pages to denouncing the machismo that continues to plague 21st-century Nicaraguan culture. Juan Pablo Gómez (item **1866**) examines how discourses and assertions of masculine power in early 20th-century conservative writers helped to undergird the cultural legitimacy of the Somoza García dictatorship. Insofar as social and popular media are now portraying Ortega as a dictator equal to or worse than Somoza, Gómez's gendered approach to examining power and dictatorship could be extended to future studies. In contrast to these more progressive texts, Urtecho's detective novel, *Mala casta* (item **1863**), falls into problematic gendered stereotypes that demonstrate the persistent cultural reality of gender inequality and machista pretension.

Historical fiction has predominated postwar Central American fiction and this continues to be true in the current Nicaraguan literary scene. In addition to Gómez's literary history, Blandón, Centeno, González, and Páez all negotiate 20th-century Nicaraguan history in an attempt to shed light on the present. Blandón reveals the hypocrisy and corruption of Sandinista leadership in the early days of the revolution (item **1805**). Páez and Centeno (items **1809** and **1842**) draw uneasy parallels between the Somoza dictatorship and current government corruption, underdevelopment, and social injustice. González calls for a revival of Sandino's values to cure the social sickness caused by Ortega's contamination of Sandinismo (item **1821**).

It goes without saying that as events continue to unfold in Nicaragua against the Ortega dictatorship, literary production will be impacted. At present, all of the universities are closed and occupied with students in resistance. Thousands of young people and intellectuals are fleeing the country as political exiles. With the exception of the Centro Nicaragüense de Autores, all of the bookstores in Managua have closed due not only to the economic impact of the political unrest, but also due to the violence. In June, a worker at Librería Hispamer was wounded by a stray bullet, and evening literary events and readings have been suspended because it is impossible to be in the streets at night. With the closure of El Literato, Sergio Ramírez tweeted on June 22, "Mueren asesinados nicaraguenses que pertenecían al futuro y muere también la cultura con el cierre de @literatotienda Los Robles" [Fallen Nicaraguans who belonged to the future die and culture also dies with the closure of @literatotienda in Los Robles][1]

Editorials are also out of production as intellectuals grapple with the political situation. As writers respond to the violence with *testimonio*, it will be the cultural work of narrative and poetic texts to reimagine Sandinismo and Nicaraguan national identity beyond Ortega. [EF]

COSTA RICA

Costa Rican prose fiction writers continue to produce narratives that challenge the official national myth of the country as the "Switzerland of Central America." Three detective novels by Víctor Alba de la Vega (item **1802**), Fernando Durán Ayanegui (item **1813**), and Warren Ulloa Argüello (item **1862**) confront government corruption, human trafficking, and the drug trade. Luis Chacón's dystopic science fiction novel presents a hollowed country addicted to virtual realities and internet connections (item **1810**). A number of other novels, especially those by Chacón, Fernando Durán Ayanegui, Juan Ramón Rojas (item **1853**), Benjamín Campos Chavarría (item **1806**), and Abril Gordienko (item **1822**), wrestle with the bourgeois status quo of Costa Rica that contributes to a vacuum of national culture, values, and identity in the early 21st century.

Despite a predominant dissatisfaction with the contemporary national reality, Costa Rican narrative appears to be moving away from the cynical esthetic, in that only two texts conclude in despair: Chacón's futuristic novel and Rojas' ficti-

---

1. Aguero, Arnulfo. "Librería Literato cerrará su local y clausura eventos impactada por crisis en Nicaragua." *La Prensa* 22 June 2018. Web.

tious memoir about a young Costa Rican university student who joins the Frente Sandinista, only to have his life and dreams devastated when he returns home a paraplegic. As if narrated by the idealistic son of Rojas' wounded narrator, Campos Chavarría's novel features another idealistic university student who confronts his depression and disillusionment with Costa Rica through literature and travel, assuming a Latin American identity, which places him in solidarity with the region's long tradition of producing intellectuals and revolutionaries.

As in the novels of Durán Ayanegui, Alba de la Vega, and José Ricardo Cháves (item **1811**), both Rojas and Campos Chavarría portray narrators who are pretentious in their knowledge of Hispanic literature and assert themselves as part of this literary tradition. Campos Chavarría even provides his readers with an appendix with biographical and bibliographical information about all the writers mentioned in the novel. Through abundant literary allusion, these novels indicate how they would like to be read: as legitimate participants in the Latin American literary canon.

In addition to the themes described above, Costa Rican authors continue to produce narratives that readily lend themselves to ecocritical approaches. Dorelia Brahona Rivera's anthology of short stories dedicated to Yolanda Oreamuno features a story by Oreamuno and another by Anacristina Rossi, known for her environmental novels, that together create sensual landscapes portraying their protagonists' sentimental lives (item **1860**). Geography and climate also figure forcefully in Tatiana Lobo Wieboff's *El puente de Ismael* (item **1831**), which explores the consequences of the neoliberal economic system and underdevelopment. Finally, in Roxana Pinto's nostalgic *Ida y vuelta* (item **1847**), a Costa Rican artist in Paris confronts artifice and mass production in her tropical floral paintings before abandoning the concrete city to return to her Costa Rican forests.

Several novels also featured LGBTQ protagonists or secondary characters. In Cháves' *Espectros de Nueva York* (item **1811**), a Costa Rican historian follows the footsteps of theosophist Madame Helene Blavatsky in a journey that links spiritual enlightenment and homoerotic encounters. Michelle Roe's collection of short stories feature lesbian protagonists struggling with and accepting their sexuality (item **1852**). As if contesting this progressive inclusion of LGBT identities in Costa Rican literary culture, short story writer María Pérez-Yglesias presents four didactically heteronormative portraits of middle class couples (item **1844**). Other writers, such as Gordienko and Alba de la Vega, question the patriarchal, machista culture, which has been the norm in Costa Rica. Collectively, these gendered themes demonstrate the extent to which Costa Rica is participating in more LGBTQ and feminist international movements. [EF]

PANAMA

Throughout its history, Panama has been at the crossroads of global trade. From the era of Spanish colonialism to the present, Panama's geographic position has guaranteed that more people pass through the isthmus than settle in it. In addition to the transitory nature of its population, the printing press arrived relatively late to Panama (1820). As a result, literary production evolved more slowly than in other Central American countries and Colombia. Despite its marginalized status in the Latin American canon, Panama has produced writers who have reached international fame, such as Rogelio Sinán and Enrique Jaramillo Levi. With an intriguing mix of native, African, and immigrant communities, Panama offers a complex culture on which to base a national literature. While publication of literature is less widespread than other Latin American countries, the Ricardo Miró literary awards provide a venue for new writers to submit their work and gain attention and publication. As a general rule, Panamanian writers who have established themselves as full or part-time writers have been its recipients. One of the works reviewed for *HLAS 74*, Rogelio Guerra Ávila's *La puerta de arriba* (item **1824**), was the 2016 winner of the Ricardo Miró prize in the novel category.

While novels are regularly read and published, the short story is the dominant genre of Panamanian literature. Notably, the workshops conducted by Enrique Jaramillo Levi (item **1869**) have given young writers a space to develop their craft and ultimately publish. In an effort to expand opportunities for writers and expand the reading public, Jaramillo Levi has joined forces with Carolina Fonseca to found Foro/Taller Sagitario Ediciones, which published *Puente levadizo* (item **1849**) and *Escenarios y provocaciones* (item **1816**). Both collections include many representatives of the Panamanian literary canon and are therefore excellent introductions to the nation's literature. As is typical in Panama, most of these writers are also poets, novelists, and playwrights.

While the short story remains the most popular literary genre and is cultivated extensively in literary workshops, the novel is a better vehicle for capturing the complexity of Panamanian society. For example, the genre of the canal novel offers a wide canvas on which to explore a complex national identity heavily influenced by the demands of the global marketplace and the US occupation of the Canal Zone. In an effort to promote literacy and Panamanian literature, all high school students are assigned readings from national writers, many of whom came to prominence due to the Ricardo Miró award. *Alquiler fatal* (item **1815**) and *Ni un golpe más* (item **1848**) are evidence of a national consciousness that more novels need to be published that will reach younger readers. In other words, there is a concerted effort to use national authors to promote literacy in Panama.

Literary criticism in Panama is part of an effort to promote national writers and their work. *Nuevas iluminaciones* (item **1869**), with its evaluation and recognition of the importance of Enrique Jaramillo Levi's poetry and prose, exemplifies such efforts and should be required reading for those seeking to broaden their understanding of Panamanian literary culture. [FJ]

PROSE FICTION

1800 Acosta, Miguel. Un día como cualquiera. Tegucigalpa: subVersiva, 2014. 74 p.: ill.

This collection of short stories presents characters that could be any one of us on any day (as the title indicates). A woman rushes to arrive on time to a wedding, a man contemplates suicide to escape life's monotony, and another man struggles to read with concentration in the unbearable heat. As the characters move through the urban sprawl of Tegucigalpa, they listen to the traffic, smell the city's aroma, and take in the sensorial stimuli typically associated with large cities. [TCM]

1801 Aguirre Arango, José Pedro. Zafiros refulgentes: novela. Guatemala: Sonibel, 2012. 190 p.

Zafiros Refulgentes is Aguirre Arango's first novel, which takes place over the course of three days—from Saturday, Jan 30th to Monday, Feb. 1st—with specific times noted throughout the chapters. The attention to marking the passage of time in the narrative contributes to the elements of suspense in a crime. The novel begins with the thoughts of the narrator, René, who plans on killing his enemy as an act of vengeance. René believes his brother-in-law killed his sister to collect on the life insurance policy, which leads to the death of his mother from grief. This novel posits an underlying critique about the ineffectiveness of the judicial system which destroys evidence, does not catch the bad guy, and generally fosters a lack of trust in the police. [TCM]

1802   Alba de la Vega, Víctor. La ausencia del mal. San José: Ediciones Lanzallamas, 2013. 261 p. (Colección Dedalus; 5)

A washed-up detective fiction writer maintains a diary of his love affair with Mercedes. With strong overtones of Pedro Salinas and filled with poetic allusion and metafiction plays, the narrator implicates himself in the murder of Mercedes' husband in an effort to assert his masculinity and cavalier agency in an age of government and corporate corruption that perpetuates violence against women, particularly in sex trafficking. [EF]

1803   Argüello Mora, Manuel. Margarita; Elisa Delmar; La trinchera; Esbozo del novelista, sus artículos en la prensa y apéndice ilustrativo. Edición de Fernando Herrera. Pérez Zeledón, Costa Rica: Ediciones Chirripó, 2014. 144 p.: bibl., ill. (Clásicos costarricenses)(Colección Letras patrias)

As part of the Colección Letras Patrias of Ediciones Chirripó, this anthology of Argüello Mora's foundational fictions includes stories and memories of the author (1834–1902) from the days of the early republic under President Juan Rafael Mora and the wars against William Walker. The narration carries a sense of its own future historical merit and is characterized with both *costumbrista* descriptions of 19th-century Costa Rica and nationalist romances. [EF]

1804   Barralaga de Olancho, Francisco. El sisimite: novela antropológica. Ilustraciones de Fernando Mencias. Tegucigalpa: Ediciones Guardabarranco, 2012. 124 p.: ill.

Emphasizing rural cultures and their indigenous roots in Honduras, the novel's title appeals to the legend of the "Sisimite" (similar to the North American Big Foot), which is believed to capture women from surrounding villages. With pencil sketches interspersed throughout the text, the novel recounts the daily experiences in the life of the protagonist, who is a man from a small town regularly visiting the city to further his education. It is not until the concluding pages that the narrator insinuates that he may be a descendant of the *Sisimites*, who have evolved over centuries into judges, mayors, and other public officials with a general disdain for working. [TCM]

1805   Blandón Guevara, Erick. Vuelo de cuervos. México: Alfaguara Infantil, 2017. 112 p.

A disenchanted Sandinista intellectual writes his *testimonio* of an ill-fated march to the Miskito coast shortly after the 1979 triumph to forcibly relocate indigenous and Afro-Caribbean communities to model communities. The impending journey and mission on the Atlantic Coast are marked with post-traumatic stress, fear, hunger, and a growing uncertainty about the corrupt upper echelons of Sandinista leadership. The novel climaxes in a cultural event broadcast to the nation meant to unite the hearts of the Miskito communities with revolutionary ideology. With Sandinista dignitaries and foreign celebrities in the audience, the Miskitos combine local folklore, satire, and war symbolism in the dance of *El Zopilote*, only to vanish at the end of the spectacle as they join their folk hero, Cotón Azul, in another realm. This fantastic inclusion of magical realism questions the boundary between novel and *testimonio*. Completed in 1997, the 2017 publication date corresponds with the growing dissatisfaction towards Ortega that resulted in the Nicaraguan Spring of 2018. The novel's critical commentary on early Sandinista leadership may have contributed to its international publication, as a Nicaraguan press would have likely not have been able to risk its printing. [EF]

1806   Campos Chavarría, Benjamín. El abismo asoma en un bosque de palabras. Heredia, Costa Rica: EUNA, 2015. 136 p.: bibl.

A precocious university student writes a multi-genre narrative recounting his travels through Central America and Mexico in an attempt to pull himself out of his suicidal depression and make sense of his bourgeois life filled with sex, drugs, and Latin American literature. This solipsistic road novel lacks the political consciousness of Ernesto Che Guevara's diaries, turning instead to a pantheon of Latin American writers for guidance and inspiration in a postmodern world divested of meaning and purpose. Upon his return to San José, the narrator realizes that he does not belong in Costa Rica, but rather in a city of "metros and editors" (126). Understanding through his favorite authors, primarily Bolaños, that "los latinoamericanos no tienen patria," he will likely return to Mexico City. Although San José represents a cultural vacuum to the narrator, as a Costa Rican he embraces a meaningful existence as a Latin American. The text concludes with an appendix with biographic and bibliographic information on all of the writers alluded to in the novel. [EF]

1807 **Castellanos Moya, Horacio.** El sueño del retorno. Barcelona: Tusquets Editores, 2013. 178 p. (Andanzas; 799)

In this novel, the well-known and sometimes controversial Salvadoran writer reprises characters and story lines from previous Civil War novels. In this case, the narrator, Erasmo Aragón—a committed urban guerrilla but unreliable, womanizing husband and father, living in México, D. F.—plans his return to El Salvador. Despite his fear of counterinsurgent repression and of his own comrades, his need to flee his Mexican wife and their child to participate in peace negotiations is overwhelming. These plans are complicated by hypnosis sessions he undergoes in search for a cure to his physical and emotional problems. Before completing treatment and finding out what he divulged under hypnosis, his doctor returns to El Salvador leaving Aragón in a state of panic. [YA]

1808 **Castro Celada, Estuardo.** La noche de los espíritus ciegos. Guatemala: F&G Editores, 2014. 189 p.

Taking the reader back to the 90s of the postwar period following the armed conflict (1960–96), Castro's novel focuses on the experiences of a group of college students in a band called, "Los Espíritus Ciegos" (The Blind Spirits). The narrator fondly recalls his experiences as a percussionist in the band, playing their first live show at La Libertad, a popular nightclub, and eventually rising to fame to play alongside well-known Guatemalan rock bands, such as Los Buitres Santos and Los Ponchos. Given the musical theme of the novel, Castro includes numerous musical references to international musical icons, including Pink Floyd, Led Zeppelin, and Garth Brooks. Driven by sex, drugs, and rock n' roll, the young musicians' adventures take them from one party to the next, until their popularity as Los Espíritus Ciegos eventually declines, and the individual members of the band go their separate ways. [TCM]

1809 **Centeno, Juan.** Más allá de la fantasía. León, Nicaragua: Promotora Cultural Leonesa, 2012. 99 p.

Centeno frames his collection of short stories with a "prólogo autobiográfico de última hora," in which he writes, "En 2000 descubrí la política surrealista nicaragüense [. . .] En 2012 muchas historias se han repetido" (p. 6–7). Following suit, portraits of daily life set against the backdrop of 21st-century Nicaragua include tales of love, seduction, magical realism. At times funny and at others banal or sad, these often *costumbrista* stories establish continuity between the years of Somoza dictatorship, civil war, and Sandinista rule. Several stories feature a Nicaraguan protagonist visiting Cuba, subtly revealing an underlying humanist approach to revolutionary ideology that rejects totalitarian government and celebrates individuality and relationship. [EF]

1810 **Chacón, Luis.** Ciudad radiante. San José: Uruk Editores, 2015. 243 p. (Colección Sulayom)

This dystopic science fiction novel contains first-person narrations of various characters, all interrelated and living in a decadent San José of the near future that is marked by traffic jams, mediocrity, addiction, sex, social media, and fallen dreams. Playing on themes of connectivity and disconnection, the characters are addicted to the illegal drug L30, which allows their brains to connect directly to the Internet, allowing them to be part of Google and experience intense and personal virtual realities of pornography, consumerism, and social media. Like zombies, the characters in this novel come to embody not individual subjectivities, but computer chips that spread viruses like sexually transmitted infections. [EF]

1811 **Chaves, José Ricardo.** Espectros de Nueva York. San José: Editorial Costa Rica, 2015. 227 p.

A Costa Rican biographer of the great 19th-century theosophist, Madame Blavatsky, travels to New York and Tibet to trace the mystic's footsteps and find inspiration in the spaces she inhabited. In his journeys, which blend a past and present of mysticism and sexuality, Blavatsky apparently channels the biographer, who develops visionary gifts after visiting Cagliostro, still living as a Mexican shaman. Foreseeing the events of September 11 but not understanding them, the narrator perishes in the terrorist attacks. Although the novel references a handful of early 20th-century Central American theosophists (all men) and ponders the impact of ancient Meso-American religions on Blavatsky, it fails to document the notable extent to which theosophy influenced Latin American intellectuals, particularly women, throughout the late 19th and early 20th-century. [EF]

1812 Díaz, Martín. Escolopendra. Martín Díaz Valdés. Guatemala: Editorial Cultura, 2014. 189 p. (Narrativa)(Colección Narrativa. Serie Augusto Monterroso; 46)

This volume gathers 35 stories, all printed in small type and what looks like single space. In short, the book design appears dense, tight, and nearly impenetrable. The content of the stories mirrors this appearance and design. In fact, Díaz Valdés has managed to present a collection of quirky, unpredictable stories on topics that range from failed drug deals to the (fictional) death of God, to whether porn stars feel pain while they have intercourse. All of this in stories that share a direct, precise language that offers a portrayal of contemporary culture (slang expressions, language from online forums, use of English and other languages). In short, Díaz Valdés strays from some of the trends that had dominated Guatemalan short narrative, such as the "microcuento," urban violence and the civil war, and offers a genuinely innovative proposal that is, oddly enough, cerebral and passionate at the same time. [FSL]

1813 Durán Ayanegui, Fernando. La desconocida: novela. San José: Ediciones Guayacán, 2015. 143 p.

This novel is an abridged version of an unedited 500-page manuscript left by the author, who was killed in an automobile accident, and includes characters named after the author's girlfriend and son, who also perished. In this sleepy political thriller, a literature professor turned speech writer for Costa Rica's fictitious socialist president, is placed in danger when he discovers a family secret that would stain the reputation of the president. This novel resonates with contemporary Costa Rican narratives that represent the corruption and potential for violence within the country's bourgeois ruling class. [EF]

1814 Echeverría, Maurice. Un rencor puro y perfecto. Guatemala: Alas de Barrilete Editorial, 2015. 91 p.

Echeverría's novel has been described as existential and even absurd. Written in an intense language that is both disturbing and lyrical, its main character describes his life in an apartment building, and offers cruel descriptions of the tenants that share it with him. Echeverría's fiction attempts to break all conventions in terms of chapter organization, style, and content. He mentions and uses social networks, events drawn from the news and recent history (one of the tenants has a sinister obsession with guns and massacres), and alludes to figures from politics, rock and history. [FSL]

1815 Ehlers S. Prestán, Sonia. Alquiler fatal: novela. Segunda edición. Panamá: Fuga Editorial, 2014. 159 p.

This novel purports to be a thriller about illegal trafficking with a focus on Arab and Indian communities in Panama. While the subject matter is intriguing and the setting promising, the meandering pace lacks the action of a traditional thriller. Even though there is some exploration of the closed worlds of these immigrant communities, the narrative perspectives remain on the margins of the illicit activities, thereby making this novel slow-moving. Moreover, the author elects to detail bureaucratic tasks rather than delving into the action, which is relegated to the background. In the hands of a more skilled writer, the setting and the subject matter would have resulted in a very exciting novel. Interestingly enough, the discussion questions at the end of the book make it clear that it aims to serve a pedagogical purpose. [FJ]

1816 **Escenarios y provocaciones: mujeres cuentistas de Panamá y México 1980-2014.** Antologizado por Carolina Fonseca y Mónica Lavín. Panamá: Foro/taller Sagitario Ediciones, 2014. 280 p. (Colección "Convergencias")

As a contribution to the X Feria Internacional del Libro celebrated in Panama and dedicated to Mexico in 2014, Foro/Taller Sagitario Ediciones decided to organize this binational anthology around contemporary women short story writers in Panama and Mexico. While this very eclectic collection includes works by well-established writers who have written in multiple genres, as well as newer authors, it limits itself to works published after 1980. Although not all stories are set in Panama, the current collection of 15 authors is a solid introduction to contemporary women writers in the country. Among the fine short stories included here, Giovanni Benedetti's "Un olor a violetas" deserves special mention because of its innovative structure, Rosa María Britton's "El jardín de Fuyang" recounts the mass suicide of Chinese laborers during the construction of the Panamanian railroad, and Consuelo Tomás Fitzgerald's "De reinas y maestras" pokes fun at beauty pageants with sly humor. Danae Brugiati Boussounis's "La estrella del jenízaro" and Lissette E. Lanuza Sáenz's "Cerveza, beer" are set outside of Panama with non-Panamanian protagonists. Contemporary women themes such as emotionally and physically abusive domestic relationships are explored in Ana Luisa Herrera's "Lisaduvilda," Isabel Herrera de Taylor's "La vida es un trío en mi menor," Melanie Taylor Herrera's "Tiempos acuáticos" and Amparo Márquez's "El hombre en la telaraña." Local setting and color are most prominent in Maribel Wang González's "El paso de las Máquinas," Bertalicia Peralta's "Encore," Moravia Ochoa López's "Una noticia de impacto," Marisín González's "Manuela," Isabel Burgos's "El profesor Theodoridis" and Alondra Badano's "El músico." [FJ]

1817 **Escudos, Jacinta.** El asesino melancólico. México: Alfaguara, 2015. 95 p.

This short novel, written in precise language but set in an imprecise location, narrates the story of a reluctant murderer. The nameless narrator—we only learn his and the other character's name at the end—works as a parking attendant. He is a lone man without any expressed wants or desires, a failure in his own eyes. His life begins to change when a middle class woman repeatedly parks her car in his lot and asks him to kill her. She tries to "seduce" him by writing him notes trying to convince him to get her out of her misery. Her husband left her and she feels there is no reason to live. She eventually traps him into the crime and he ends up imprisoned. Here, as in *Crónicas sentimentales* for example, Escudos fashions a slim, poetic narrative about human loneliness and the lengths to which we go to find and to lose companionship. [YA]

1818 **Galán, Jorge.** Noviembre. México: Planeta Editorial, 2015. 255 p.

In this novel, Galán, a poet and writer who began publishing after the Civil War ended, reconstructs the events of November 16, 1989: the assassination of six Jesuit priests, a female housekeeper, and her daughter at the UCA (Universidad Centroamericana José Simeón Cañas). The novel is divided into seven mostly untitled parts. While Galán includes a section told from the perspective of a soldier, the majority of the novel is told from the point of view of a surviving Jesuit, José María Tojeira, with an "interviewer" as the interlocutor. The last three sections of the novel describe and lament the "sinuoso camino hacia la justicia," as the Jesuits, led by Tojeira, attempt to find openings in the Salvadoran government and the armed forces to confront the military elite and negotiate justice. [YA]

1819 **Gálvez Suárez, Arnoldo.** La palabra cementerio. Guatemala: Prisa Ediciones: Editorial Santillana, 2013. 182 p. (Punto de lectura ; 566/1. Narrativa)

La palabra cementerio is a collection of six short stories. The title story, "La palabra cementerio," follows a group of high school students from the capital who attend a local Opus Dei school in 1999, just before Y2K and the technological uncertainties of the new millenium. Despite the religious emphasis of their education, the group of friends escapes the city for an excursion to Panajachel for a weekend of drug-induced sexual fantasies with gringas to the soundtrack of corridos by Los Tigres del Norte.

When the adolescents meet a group of party-seekers on Calle Santander, their adventures take a dark turn, leading to the rape of one of their friends and irreversible bloodshed. [TCM]

1820 **Gasteazoro, Eva.** Todos queríamos morir. Managua, Nicaragua: Ánama Ediciones, 2015. 79 p.

Mariagracia, a Nicaraguan living in New York, learns she is dying of cancer. Mixing first and third-person perspectives with past and present, the narrative delves into a heartrending family history and recounts Mariagracia's very personal experience of grief, fear, desire, and ultimately ability to find agency in her choice to submit to dying. [EF]

1821 **González, Arquímedes.** Dos hombres y una pierna. Panamá: Editorial Tecnológica, Universidad Technológica de Panamá, 2012. 186 p.

This destabilizing, postmodernist narrative artfully evokes Salvador Mendieta's *La enfermedad de Centroamérica* (1934) and other early 20th-century naturalist writings that sought to diagnose social ills through positivist causes. Unlike Mendieta's three-volume essay, which suggested that Unionism would cure Central America's problems of classism, racism, and oppression at the hands of fragmented criollo elites, González offers no remedy, instead condemning the Sandinista government for years of corruption and hypocrisy that have resulted in the shared misery of her characters. Set in a Managua hospital, the narrative jumps among horrifying patient histories determined by generational poverty and abuse. Startlingly scatological and hopeless (in the style of El Salvador's Jacinta Escudos), the cynical narrative indicts Ortega for neglecting and disdaining his people while purporting to take care of them. [EF]

1822 **Gordienko, Abril.** Negra noche en blanco. San José: Uruk Editores, 2016. 339 p. (Colección Sulayom)

Raymundo, an abusive father, lies dying while his son, Manuel, cares for him. During his final days, Manuel and Raymundo reflect individually on their traumatic childhoods, both traumatized by generational abuse. In this tender narrative, the family serves as a metaphor for the nation, ruled for generations by a bourgeois elite that is reinforced by patriarchal oppression and abuse. The novel ends with Raymundo's death, which is briefly investigated as a patricide. Manuel, ridden with guilt for resenting his father his entire life, also questions whether or not he may have killed his father. [EF]

1823 **Grigsby Vergara, William.** Mecánica del espíritu. Managua, Nicaragua: Anamá Ediciones, 2015. 144 p.

In this poignant novel set in contemporary Managua, an overweight, 30-something graphic design professor at the Universidad Centroamericana (UCA) reflects on history, art, and sex. With echoes of Galeano and García-Canclini, he laments that while he once enjoyed wandering through Cuba and Europe, walking the streets of Managua only reminds him of the city's underlying machismo and its underdevelopment. He feels incapacitated by the lack of social and political justice in Nicaragua but finds refuge in his art, which also makes him feel like an accomplice to the neoliberal machine. He is devastated when his favorite student throws himself from a third-floor building—one of the few multi-story structures in Managua due to earthquakes—at the UCA (in 2018 this scene also reads as an eerie foreshadowing of the student-led movement against Ortega). Although the narrative flirts with an esthetic of cynicism, the narrator repeatedly finds beauty and freedom in national art and culture, revolutionary rhetoric, and the undefiled promise of young people. Ultimately, the novel delivers a particularly tender critique of the neoliberal evisceration of Sandinista values. [EF]

1824 **Guerra Ávila, Rogelio.** La puerta de arriba. Panamá: Editorial Mariano Arosemena, Instituto Nacional de Cultura (INAC), 2017. 311 p. (Colección Ricardo Miró. Novela; 2016)

Winner of the 2016 Premio Nacional de Literatura Ricardo Miró in the novel category, *La puerta de arriba* opens with an intriguing conversation between a writer and an investigator in paranormal activities. After raising a series of mysteries in the first chapter, the novel proceeds to recount the history of two families who owned a large house with a mysterious door. Alternating between 1989–90 and the mid-19th century, certain parallels between the women in the family emerge. Also, the modern-day occupants of the house are tormented by unexplainable noises and the ghostlike appearance of a small boy. When tragedy strikes and their baby is taken hostage, an unusual circumstance revealing time-travel through the mysterious door develops. In the climatic ending, Sofía Villalaz, the mother of the disappeared baby in 1990, confronts a dying 96-year old man, who was stolen by the eldest son of the Usaga family and lived his entire life as an Usuga in another time. [FJ]

1825 Guinea Diez, Gerardo. La mirada remota. Guatemala: F&G Editores, 2014. 236 p. (Colección premio nacional de literatura; 7)

In this novel, the main character, Santiago Merino, is a lawyer who has returned to Guatemala after a long stay in Spain, studying criminology, after the death of his lover Oralia, a woman from Honduras who was murdered by the Guatemalan government. Upon his return, he starts working for the Guatemalan attorney general's office, and is tasked with writing a report on femicides dating back 10 years before the start of the story. This novel departs from others dealing with civil war crimes in that it is concerned with contemporary crime in Guatemala and offers a harsh criticism of the corruption and posturing behind the justice system. In literary terms, this novel attempts to be high literature at times, while at others it reads like a *noir* novel, and in the end, it is neither. However, the plot, story, and characters offer some originality that make the novel worth reading. [FSL]

1826 Hernández, Claudia. Roza, tumba, quema. Bogotá: Editorial Kimpres, 2018. 347 p.

In characteristic fashion, the characters in this Claudia Hernández novel are nameless, resilient, and caught in a world of daily cruelty and inhumanity. Unlike her best-known short stories, in this novel the spatial and temporal settings are named and precisely plotted. The narrator refers to characters through pronouns and circumlocution: the protagonist is simply "ella," her mother is "la madre," and her daughters, for example, "la tercera de las hijas que se crió con ella." Ella is an ex-guerrillera and lives on the land she and her dead third partner received at the end of the war. She struggles to survive the post-conflict era as a single mother with four daughters, one that was put up for adoption by nuns without her consent and lives in Paris, and three others who grow up with her. The title refers to the protagonist's willingness to make any and all sacrifices necessary for her daughters so that they have a place to return to when necessary. This is a complex, perceptive novel about the violence and economic and gender conflicts that persist after peace in El Salvador. [YA]

1827 Hernández, David. Roquiana. San Salvador: DPI, Secretaría de Cultura de la Presidencia, Dirección de Publicaciones e Impresos, 2014. 255 p. (Colección Ficciones; 25)

This is a fictional biography of Roque Dalton and the Salvadoran left. It is divided into three sections: Roque, Enroque, Desenroque. In it, Hernández reimagines Dalton's milieu in the international left as well as in relation to Cuba and its influence on the Central American revolutions of the 1960s and 1970s. Dalton's persona emerges through various narrators involved in direct revolutionary action as well as in the Cuban and Chinese intelligence service, for instance. Including well-known moments of Dalton's life, such as his stays in Havana and Prague and his imprisonment, Hernández plots Dalton's actions, literary and political production, and his comrades' reactions and perspectives about him. The "mythical" Roque who escaped prison, wrote eloquently, and died for his commitment, is countered by an alcoholic, womanizing, unreliable *compañero* who "needed" to be eliminated for the good of the Salvadoran left. Besides offering the reader a more complete image of El Salvador's most influential 20th-century poet, Hernández paints a vivid portrait of the Salvadoran left and its place in Latin America. [YA]

1828 Hernández, Ricardo. Cerro negro. Managua: Anamá Ediciones, 2014. 398 p. (Colección Visiones Anamá)

In this *testimonio*, Hernández retells the experiences of an ex-guerrillero, member of the BPR (Bloque del pueblo revolucionario), one of the revolutionary groups comprising the FMLN (Frente Farabundo Martí para la Liberación Nacional). The reader will note similarities between Ricardo, the testimonio's narrator, and Omar Cabezas in *La montaña es algo más que una gran estepa verde* (1982, 1985). Both narrators describe their developing social consciousness and involvement in their revolutionary group's student organizations before entering the urban guerrilla group and going on to the war in the "mountain." Further, women's roles are similar—as sexual partners and sentimental anchors. Even as he is involved with various *compañeras* and fathers children, Ricardo pines for Raquel. In fact, it is news of her that compels Ricardo to share his *testimonio*. In contrast to other war testimonial texts, Hernández's also narrates the cruelty of some of his superiors' disciplinary decisions and the FMLN's strategic choices. We also learn about the ideological differences of the FMLN's political organizers and activists in the US as Ricardo spends time in the US as an organizer before returning to the "front" and then immigrating permanently to the US. [YA]

1829 Jurado G., Ana María. La lucidez de la locura: relatos clínicos. Guatemala: F&G Editores, 2014. 109 p.

The author, Ana María Jurado, is an analyst, and in this book she narrates a series of clinical cases in an anecdotal style that still preserves some medical and technical terms. She admits to having conceived the idea for the book long before writing it, and she only decided to write after "achieving maturity as a writer of fiction." The 12 stories (or cases) illustrate different psychological diagnoses, all told from the perspective of the analyst and revealing minimal information about the patients' social and personal circumstances. [FSL]

1830 Lara, Boris. El inquilino y otros cuentos. Tegucigalpa: [publisher not identified], 2015. 105 p.

The realism in this collection of 12 short stories is reminiscent of Edgar Allen Poe and Horacio Quiroga's work. The short story "El inquilino," takes place in Tegucigalpa during a suffocating summer of unmanageably high temperatures. Without the relief of air conditioning in an office building in the nation's capital, the narrator, along with the other staff, succumbs to heat-induced naps. Disturbingly, the narrator is unable to recall the details of his slumber, finding himself in a bed presumably following sexual relations. The narrator soon realizes that during these episodes, he is not the agent of his actions, but rather at the mercy of his body who identifies as "Diego" during these out-of-body-experiences. With detailed descriptions of his nightlife adventures, the narrator invites the reader to accompany him on these escapades that eventually lead the narrator to realize that he has forever lost control to Diego, and will henceforth be merely a tenant in his own body. [TCM]

1831 Lobo Wiehoff, Tatiana. El puente de Ismael. San José: REA, 2014. 147 p.

Ismael, an 11-year old boy with mental disabilities, dies in the middle of the night, having mysteriously fallen through the decayed railing of a 100-year-old bridge that connects the towns of Providencia and Providencia Abajo. The bridge is destroyed, and Providencia Abajo is cut off until a new bridge, donated by the Chinese government, replaces it several months later. The novel draws the reader into the lives of the various inbred, underdeveloped, complex characters of the town of isolated Providencia Abajo, all of whom—with government and neoliberal structures—share the blame for Ismael's death. [EF]

1832 Medina García, Jorge. El viento que sopla los carbones apagados del amor. Tegucigalpa: Ediciones Yolotl, 2014. 265 p.

This novel, originally released as *Romance del Secuestrado*, was awarded the Premio Único de Novela Corta Centroamericana 2012. It was subsequently published under a new title after the Secretaría de Cultura, Artes y Deportes (SCAD) of Honduras failed to publish the 2012 text, as they are required to do given the stipulations of the literary prize. The author altered the title, but not the content of the novel. In it he describes the kidnapping of two characters: Rania, who is the daughter of Ricardo Kattán Cassiomanelli, and "El Pollón" (Arquímedes Cabrera), a mechanic in Turkish Afif Ramsés Salomón's car repair shop. Through an eloquent narrative boasting an abundance of adjectives and adverbs, the omniscient narrator details the confrontations of these characters with their captors: Cantalicio, whose nickname is "Caralimpio" (Cleanface), and Olegario, who is known as "La Nutria" (The Otter). [TCM]

1833 Mejía, Carlos A. Cuentos del invisible: cuentos por ser cuentos. Tegucigalpa: [publisher not identified], 2013. 84 p.

Accompanied by computer-generated images in color, this collection brings together short stories that have been previously recounted by an invisible person, as the narrator reveals in the collection's brief introduction. In the first short story, the narrator elaborates on the nuances of meaning of the term "invisibility." In a quest to determine whether they are invisible, the narrator says "hello" to see if people return the greeting and seeks people they know as possible tests to determine whether they are invisible to others. After philosophical musings, rationalizing that if one thinks, they must exist, a young boy wakes up the narrator who has fallen asleep in a church—which serves as a testament to his visibility. Everyone saw his shameless slumber, but as the narrator leaves the church, they look away, pretending not to see him/her. Visibility as a construction of self-perception in relation to exterior reaffirmation is implicit in the other short stories in the collection. [TCM]

1834 Méndez, Nora. De seudónimo Clara. Guatemala: Letra Negra Editores, 2013. 167 p. (Narrativa centroamericana; 95)

In this venture into narrative, Méndez, a poet and cultural activist, presents the reader with the story of the capture of an urban guerrilla. In autobiographical interior monologues, Méndez's narrator reveals her illegal, revolutionary actions, her ideological doubts, and the internal debates within her faction. Much of the narrative focuses on the narrator's uncertainty about what she may have revealed while being tortured and her certainty that her actions for the revolution have harmed loved ones. Similar to her poetry, in this testimonial novella, Méndez discusses politics directly and locates the narrative in specific locations in San Salvador during the Civil War (1980–92). [YA]

1835 Montejo, Victor. Pixan: el cargador del espíritu. Guatemala: Editorial Piedra Santa, 2014. 221 p.

This satirical novel written by a Jakaltek Maya survivor of the armed conflict (1960–96) details the struggle to maintain an indigenous identity in postwar Guatemala. Specifically, it addresses the postwar recovery and reconstruction efforts, as well as the Maya legend of the *pixan*, which says that for each native baby, a companion animal is born. Montejo situates postwar Maya as negotiating their future in dialogue with a saturation of NGOs in Guatemala. In many cases NGOs are sponsored or founded by international entities, however Maya in Guatemala often occupy positions of leadership in these organizations. As Maya rise to high-ranking positions, they begin to "ladinizarse," or lose their Maya roots and cultural cosmovision. Montejo centers the narrative on the character Juan Kiej, who finds himself in this situation after becoming the president of his NGO, COPODER (Consejo Posmoderno de Desarrollo Rural). [TCM]

1836 Morales Barrios, Luis Emilio. Por culpa de la Calandria! Guatemala: Editorial Universitaria, Universidad de San Carlos de Guatemala, 2015. 109 p. (Colección Literaria/narrativa)

In style, language, setting, and characters, this novel is a throwback to the traditional narrative of the 30s and 40s. In fact, the *calandria* of the title (which is Spanish for a type of lark) is a young woman with whom the two main characters, *el Canche* and *Campeón*, are in love. Although the events take place in the aftermath of the overthrow of Jacobo Arbenz Guzmán's government, this does not seem relevant to the plot, even though some characters' political allegiances are part of their (long) descriptions. The language is stilted and, at times, formulaic and unoriginal, but the structure offers something evocative of García Márquez's narrative, which is the announcement of a death in a small town from the perspective of a number of different characters. Despite these shortcomings, the fact that the action occurs in 1955, and the author plays out the contrasting backgrounds of the two main characters make it an interesting novel to read. [FSL]

1837 **Moreira Mazariegos, Axel Javier.** Retoños de tronco viejo. Guatemala: Letra Negra Editores, 2011. 67 p. (Colección Narrativa Centroamericana; 69)

This book contains 15 very uneven short stories, which range from experimental narrative styles ("La hormiga y yo," "El libro del día y de la noche") to the anachronistic ("La iglesia de La Merced y el padre Gancho," "¡El potro blanco!"). [FSL]

1838 **Mosquera Saravia, Javier.** Una manzana peligrosa en el último día perfecto. Ilustraciones de María Fernanda Estrada Muralles. Colonia Centro América, Guatemala: F&G Editores, 2015. 200 p.: ill.

The 16 stories in this collection are playful yet cerebral, self-referential yet descriptive. In some stories, the author acknowledges his admiration for Julio Cortázar; in another, he tries to seduce women in exchange for owning a first edition of Benedetti's novel, *La tregua*. The biggest joke (or laugh at the reader's expense) is the story titled "El insospechado problema de la existencia," in which he describes the apparent non-existent text on p. 64 of an upcoming book of his . . . and then, on p. 64 of this same book, there is a blank page. Mosquera Saravia deliberately blurs the lines between reality and art, to play with our perceptions and question our beliefs. His stories are original and well written. [FSL]

1839 **Muñoz, Víctor.** La noche del 9 de febrero. Guatemala: Prisa Ediciones, 2013. 161 p. (Punto de lectura; 593/1)(Narrativa)

Víctor Muñoz became known early in his literary career as author of satirical, humorous pieces in the pages of *El Imparcial*. His subsequent short stories and novels followed in the same vein until 1995, when he published the somber, satirical novel *Todos queremos de todo*. With *La noche del 9 de febrero* Muñoz has definitely abandoned his youthful, irreverent humor and embraced a theme common to most Guatemalan writers: the civil war. However, Muñoz resorts to a character from his previous work, Bernardo Santos, and instead of presenting him as a comic and pathetic figure, he appears as the father of Ernesto Santos, a 19 year-old student who was "disappeared." The novel, carefully written and structured, describes the journey that Bernardo and his wife undertake in order to find their son, and presents the people they meet in the process. In careful and measured language Muñoz inserts biographical details of Bernardo Santos that illuminate the political and social circumstances of the plot. Despite the theme, Muñoz's writing is highly readable. The novel is reminiscent of García Márquez's *El coronel no tiene quien le escribe* in that the trip is more important than the destination. [FSL]

1840 **Muñoz, Víctor.** La reina ingrata: cuentos. Guatemala: Ministerio de Cultura y Deportes, Editorial Cultura, 2013. 131 p. (Colección Cuento. Serie Augusto Monterroso; 14)

This collection of 11 short stories won the highly coveted Premio Nacional de Literatura "Miguel Ángel Asturias" in 2013. Featuring colloquial, vernacular language, the short stories represent the lives of middle-class Guatemalans. The titular story, "La reina ingrata," relates the trials and tribulations of a married couple and their only daughter, La Carlota. The family lives paycheck to paycheck, with barely enough to make ends meet, despite the fact that their daughter attended school and is employed at a bank. In a turn of events, Carlota is chosen to be the "reina del banco" in the company beauty pageant, but loses everything when they are unable to make the payments to the bank. In the end, academic studies and professional achievements are squandered for the harsh reality of beauty contests in which merits are vain and superficial. Ultimately, the family is disillusioned, recognizing their inescapable destiny of living in poverty and destitution. [TCM]

1841 **Narrativa guatemalteca: antología.** Segunda edición. Guatemala: Alfaguara, 2012. 179 p. (Serie roja)

This collection of short stories reflects the complex heritage of Guatemalan literature, with transatlantic influences from Spain and the Americas. The anthology begins with a selection from the anonymous manuscript, "Título de la casa de Ixcuin-Nehaib," which features the first known literary reference to the Guatemalan national heroe, Tecún Umán. Also from colonial times, the anthology features a selection of Bartolomé de las Casas's *Brevísima relación de la destrucción de las Indias,* in which the Dominican friar documents his observations in Guatemala. Moving more or less chronologically, the anthology features an example of the *cuadro de costumbres* from 19th-century José Milla y Vidaurre, which describes the Feria de Jocotenango. Other 19th-century authors are featured, such as Enrique Gómez Carillo and Rafael Arévalo Martínez. Early 20th century canonical authors include Miguel Ángel Asturias, Alfredo Balsells Rivera, Mario Monteforte Toledo, and Francisco Méndez. More contemporary examples exemplify the Latin American "boom" such as Augusto Monterroso's piece. Among the selections representative of the late 20th century, the anthology features "La Miss," a short story by Luis de León, a Kaqchikel Maya author who was kidnapped and disappeared during the armed conflict (1960–96). [TCM]

1842 Páez, Silvio. El debutante. Managua: Centro Nicaragüese de Escritores, 2014. 111 p. (Colección Narrativa)

In these stories of underdevelopment, Páez combines irony and humor to recount the hopeless histories of a handful of mid-century Nicaraguans. In the title story, "El debutante," a gifted young singer's talent is neglected by his oppressively religious parents. His death deprives the world of his exquisite voice. In "La Galería," set after the 1972 earthquake, the narrator revives the plans of his dead girlfriend to establish a national art gallery. After working for months to collect a number of significant pieces, his plans are shattered because all the building permits are limited to commercial endeavors, and the artwork remains stored with no place to share them. The final story of the collection, "Bienvenida Miss Clairol," features Felicita, a young woman full of aspirations who, inspired by Hollywood movie stars, dyes her hair blonde. Her story ends in desperation, as she resists planting a tree in her patio fearful that her son will hang himself from it. [EF]

1843 Pensamiento Velasco, Juan. PerZONA. Guatemala: Ministerio de Cultura y Deportes, Editorial Cultura, 2014. 48 p. (Colección Cuento guatemalteco. Serie Augusto Monterroso)

This novel is comprised of chapters, which are numerically titled for the zones of Guatemala City (though with 21 zones in total, the novel has more zones than the actual city). Each chapter presents the daily life and struggles of a series of working class characters in the urban sprawl of the Guatemalan capital. Chapter 1, "zonaUNO," presents the daily routine of an elderly woman on a public bus, passing through the city, seeing the same faces each day. In a later chapter, a woman makes the journey to the electricity company to have her power turned back on (after not paying the bill), while another chapter details the life of a nurse working in a hospital who is able to obtain illegitimate work taking newborns and offering them in clandestine adoption circuits for gringo families. This novel provides the reader with a window into the trials and tribulations of working class families. In each chapter, the narrator underscores the unpleasant and disgusting aspects of quotidian life, reminiscent of Beatriz Cortez's conceptualizations of the esthetic of cynicism in the context of Central American neoliberalism. [TCM]

1844 Pérez-Yglesias, María. Anclas sin poema. San José: EUNED, Editorial Universidad Estatal a Distancia, 2015. 188 p.: ill.

This collection of four love stories features proudly educated, middle-class, heterosexual Costa Rican couples and celebrates their commitment to love and long-term relationships. [EF]

1845 Phé-Funchal, Denise. Ana sonríe. Colonia Centro América, Guatemala: F&G Editores, 2015. 249 p.

Guatemalan Denise Phe-Funchal is an award-winning writer of fiction (short stories and novels), and has also done work as screenwriter. In *Ana sonríe,* she displays a very sensitive, evocative style, and a particularly poetic language to express the inner struggles of Ana, a woman who, along with her sisters Loretta and Lucrecia, tells a story of strength and desperation. The novel is structured in chapters that alternate between the narratives of each sister, and even though Phe-Funchal does not offer any clues about the setting (chronological or geographic) of her novel, one can ascertain that it is contemporary Guatemala. The unexpected ending may be controversial, especially if one wants to see this novel as feminist literature. However, the tone, characters, and sensitive depiction of emotions and events are a remarkable achievement in a literary landscape that tends to portray women in stereotypical ways. [FSL]

1846 **Pierson, Pierre.** La fuerza del azar. Managua: Mar Dulce, 2015. 331 p.

Álvaro, a young Spaniard inspired by the Age of Enlightenment, embarks for the New World with ideals of justice and abolition. When his young wife dies under mysterious circumstances after wandering away from home, Álvaro explores the Caribbean, chronicling encounters with pirates, early signs of independence struggles in Nueva Granada, and, like Álvaro Cabeza de Vaca, living among the indigenous communities, who heal his fevers and depression with traditional remedies. In addition to promoting racial justice and Latin American autonomy, the novel takes on feminist overtones when Álvaro is saved from prison by an Argentinian opera singer who once broke his heart. [EF]

1847 **Pinto, Roxana.** Ida y vuelta. San José: Uruk Editores, 2016. 234 p. (Colección Sulayom)

Anadí, an artist, has lived and worked in Paris for years, where she mass-produces decorative floral paintings for a commercial art distributor. Inspired by the Mexican muralists, she dreams of painting a botanical mural in Paris, and her dreams come true when she is commissioned to paint a tropical forest on the Rue de Commerce. Anadí's floral subject matter reflects her nostalgia and longing for the forests of Costa Rica, and the book offers an eco-critical approach through Anadí's preoccupations of deforestation and biodiversity from the concrete city of Paris. At the novel's end, a homesick Anadí returns to Costa Rica, where she is surprised by her Costa Rican boyfriend whom she had left in Paris. [EF]

1848 **Puello Ch., Ricardo A.** Ni un golpe más. Panamá: [publisher not given], 2012. 225 p.

With the specific aim of offering young people moral models, this novel sticks to its didactic mission. Set in the home of an alcoholic single mother being taken in by a human trafficker on a street corner where sellers hawk their wares daily, the novel explores themes of domestic violence, dysfunctional families, poverty, alcoholism, and human trafficking. While the novel does offer an insider's view of the closed society of street sellers, the result feels forced. For example, the main protagonist is an adolescent girl, but her dialogue does not sound like that of a 15 year old, and at times the action lacks believability. Also, a skilled copy editor would have improved the novel. While the subject matter and the settings are promising, the result falls short of its potential. [FJ]

1849 **Puente levadizo: veinticuatro cuentistas de Panamá y España.** Antologizado por Enrique Jaramillo Levi y Pedro Crenes Castro. Panamá: Foro/taller Sagitario Ediciones, 2015. 184 p. (Colección "Convergencias"; 3)

As the title indicates, this anthology of Panamanian and Spanish short stories seeks to establish a bridge between writers in the two nations. Given the very productive exchange between Spanish and Panamanian writers in the Festival Eñe in 2014, Foro/Taller Sagitario Ediciones sought to extend this fruitful collaboration with the present publication. The resulting collection aims to introduce readers to an eclectic representation from each country, and works to fulfill that mission by including writers from three distinct Panamanian generations. Among the representatives from the established generation of short story writers (Justo Arroyo, Pedro Rivera, Moravia Ochoa López, Dimis Lidio Pitty and Enrique Jaramillo Levi), Arroyo's haunting "El jardín de Urbano" and Pitty's dark humor in "Carta del Ministerio" deserve special attention. The second generation is represented by Consuelo Tomás Fitzgerald, whose Cortazaresque "Laberinto" should be highlighted, and the relative newcomer Dimitrios Gianareas. The third generation (born in the 1970s) are

Carlos Oriel Wynter Melo, Melanie Taylor Herrera, Pedro Crenes Castro, Isabel Burgos, and Roberto Pérez-Franco. Brugos's Borgeian "El profesor Theodoridis" and Taylor Herrera's transgender tale "Agenesia" are notable contributions to the genre. As is to be expected in an anthology of this type, the styles, settings and themes are very diverse. Nonetheless, this anthology is an excellent introduction to the contemporary short story in Panama. [FJ]

1850 Ramos, Antonio. Pintura y aguarrás: cuentos de arriba y de abajo. Tegucigalpa: Design & Print, 2013. 111 p.

This collection of short stories features brief texts, some occupying just a few lines on the page, while others span a few pages. The book itself is divided into three sections: "Nivel humano," "Nivel de la tierra," and "Nivel del cielo." Ramos's literary style and language reveals a heavy influence of Honduran mannerisms, forms of speech, and experiences that will likely be recognizable even to the novice reader. For example, in one of his stories, Ramos describes the unique sandals that Honduran women wear, giving them a flirty appeal, while in another text, he addresses a more sober theme, the love a migrant has for Honduras, even if s/he feels the need to leave the country in search of a better life in the US. [TCM]

1851 Relatos de mujeres nuevas. Edición de Guisela López. Guatemala: Seminario de Literatura Feminista y Ciudadanía, 2011. 67 p.

The 17 short stories in this collection address the exclusion and general marginalization of women in society. The authors are diverse, representing a variety of ages, degrees of education, professions, ethnic groups, and nationalities. Invoking different aspects of female experiences in their stories, the authors promote women's human rights through their writing, addressing issues such as the right to be, to have a name, identity, good treatment at home, education, citizenship, freedom of expression, bodily autonomy, the right to vote, the right to own property, the right to live free of violence, and the right to join the military. Beyond these general issues of gender equality, Amalía Jiménez Galán's piece, "Mi radio de acción no tiene límites," addresses the politics of indigenous language use, given that in addition to Spanish there are 22 Mayan languages currently spoken in Guatemala. [TCM]

1852 Roe, Michelle. Mujer alada pero rota no vuela. San José: Uruk Editores, 2016. 219 p. (Colección Sulayom)

This collection of short stories is linked by the shared sense of liberty and fulfilled identity of its openly lesbian protagonists. Documenting LGBT history and culture in Costa Rica from the 1970s to the present, this text individualizes and humanizes the long, often painful and fearful road to an increased acceptance of homosexuality in Costa Rica today. [EF]

1853 Rojas, Juan Ramón. Los últimos días. San José: Uruk Editores, 2015. 317 p. (Colección Sulayom)

An ideological Costa Rican university student, Julio, recounts his decision to join a clandestine political organization, the Movimiento Auténtico Revolucionario, in 1978 in order to join the Frente Sandinista de Liberación Nacional (FSLN) in overthrowing Anastacio Somoza in Nicaragua. Wanting to represent Costa Rica in the revolutionary struggles that defined Latin America during the 1970s, as well as to reclaim Costa Rica's communist and revolutionary legacy of the early 20th century, Julio alienates his loved ones and sacrifices his own autonomy after he is wounded and paralyzed just before the 1979 Sandinista triumph. This fictitious *testimonio*, which is marked by rich historical details, ends in cynicism and despair as the narrator documents his simple hope that someone will find his memories interesting enough to read. [EF]

1854 Salazar, Braulio. Comandante Sombra. Guatemala: Letra Negra Editores, 2013. 195 p. (Narrativa centroamericana; 94)

This novel centers on Johana Aparicio, a Guatemalan scientist living in the US. The product of her indigenous mother's rape by the coffee plantation owner where she worked, Johana was the only survivor of her village after it was massacred during the armed conflict (1960–96). Later adopted by a colonel and his wife, Aníbal Aparicio and Amanda Arriaza, Dr. Johana Aparicio returns to Guatemala to clear her father's name of charges of genocide. While she feels sympathetic to the victims of the genocide, she refuses to believe that her adoptive father was the Kaibil soldier known as Comandante Sombra, who massacred entire indigenous communities, including women and children. As Johana reads the documentation and evidence against her father detailing the horrific brutalities of the armed conflict, the narrative structure features flashbacks recounting the violence in her biological mother's village. [TCM]

1855 Salazar, Oswaldo. Hombres de papel. México: Alfaguara, 2016. 354 p.: bibl.

This genre-challenging work is marketed as a novel, but it is also a fictionalized biography of Guatemalan writer Miguel Ángel Asturias (Nobel Prize for literature winner) and his son, Rodrigo Asturias (also known as Gaspar Ilom among the guerrilla combatants he joined in his youth). Salazar presents both men as complementing, not opposing each other. In fact, Rodrigo tells his father that in joining the rebel forces he will bring to life all the books he wrote. Then, in chapters that alternate between the two characters, and from one timeline to another, Salazar portrays the personal, familial, and intellectual dynamics between Asturias the writer, and Asturias the *guerrilla* member, and, in the process, drops allusions, turns of phrase, and names of people and places whose significance will not escape those who know the work of Asturias. Even the title is a pun on one of Asturias' best known novels, *Hombres de maíz*. While using a conventional language and structure, this novel is vast in scope, and even though a knowledge of Spanish American literary history is not required, it is helpful to understand all the allusions in the text. [FSL]

1856 Sánchez Quesada, Leonel. Cuentos y sentencias. Compilación por Ricardo Rosabal Conejo. San José: EUNED, Editorial Universidad Estatal a Distancia, 2015. 199 p.

This posthumous collection of unedited short stories and sayings features an omnipresent narrator who inserts himself with commentary in the oral tradition of storytelling. The stories presented here are diverse anecdotes of country life in Costa Rica, with themes ranging from the tragic choices and consequences of poverty, abusive bosses, free trade, legends, family conflicts, love, death, and aging. [EF]

1857 Schlesinger, María Elena. Aída la bella. México: Alfaguara, 2015. 150 p.

Schlesinger's stories have been published in newspapers for a long time, and their themes, characters, and topics deal with an idealized Guatemalan past: that of the early 20th century, on or around the dictatorship of Manuel Estrada Cabrera. Her stories portray, in a respectful and genteel way, the ways and habits of Guatemalan old *bourgeoisie* through a particular style that seems nostalgic and romantic, but also reveals practices and ideas prevalent at the time. Women like Aída in "Aída la bella," and María in the series "Pluma de ganso," appear as victims of society, only to emerge vindicated in the end. To a certain extent, one could argue that these stories continue the tradition of the 19th-century vignettes known as "cuadros de costumbres," but instead of observing and critiquing their circumstances, as the previous writers did, Schlesinger seems to demystify the past by giving the characters and faces in old family photos a truly human soul. In short, in addition to reviving the genre of the vignette, Schlesinger modernizes it, thus making it relevant to contemporary readers. [FSL]

1858 Schloesser de Paiz, Anabella. Asuntos de familia. México: Alfaguara, 2016. 246 p.

This is an historical novel, which narrates the life of the author's family, with specific focus on their migration from Germany (during the 1920s and 30s) to Central America. The style and characters are fairly traditional, although the narrative structure is organized in a more experimental manner, with chapters that go back and forth between the past and the present, and among the different family groups portrayed in the story. [FSL]

1859 Soulas, Leo de. Al borde del precipicio. Guatemala: Letra Negra Editores, 2012. 146 p. (Narrativa Centroamericana; 88)

The six short stories collected here are unexpectedly long, and could even be called *novellas*. While their style is not innovative and the narrative language is rather traditional, the settings vary from one to the next, and some even sound like the work of *indigenista* writers. [FSL]

1860 **13 ficciones del país sin soldados.** Selección y prólogo de Dorelia Barahona Riera. México: Coordinación de Difusión Cultural, Dirección de Literatura/UNAM, 2015. 212 p. (Textos de difusión cultural. Serie Antologías)

In recent years, Yolanda Oreamuno's (Costa Rica, 1916—Mexico, 1956) work has been recovered and revalorized as foundational to Costa Rican contemporary fiction. Taking Oreamuno as a source of inspiration, Brahona Rivera's prologue promises a collection of contemporary Costa Rican short stories in which, as in Oreamuno, characterization seems driven by a sumptuous sense of place rooted in climate, landscape, and sensuality. In Oreamuno's lead story, "Valle alto," the protagonist finds herself stranded overnight with a man on a scorching dirt road in Mexico. When it rains unexpectedly, the environment becomes an extension of the protagonist's own sexuality—or she is an extension of the environment—and daybreak brings green foliage and flowers to the landscape that was parched the day before. With the exception of Anacristina Rossi's bewitching "Marea alta," other authors of the collection—who include Daniel Quirós, Uriel Quesada, and Rodrigo Soto—fall outside of Oreamuno's esthetic, but their original fictions do not fail to please. [EF]

1861 **Ugarte, Diego.** Yo, artista. Guatemala: F&G Editores, 2013. 141 p.

This novel is based on the lives of El Gordo and Alfonso, with each chapter named after one of the two characters. El Gordo is an aspiring author, who submits essays to local newspapers and publishes on his Facebook page the poetry he finds online by unknown poets. Alfonso is also an aspiring artist, but he has dedicated his career to being a film director and scriptwriter. His artistic career, however, has not taken off, so even though he is in his 30s, Alfonso still lives with his dad. Though their stories never cross, both are examples of frustrated artists desperately trying to make a living from their work. [TCM]

1862 **Ulloa Argüello, Warren.** Elefantes de grafito. San José: Uruk Editores, 2015. 437 p. (Colección El cuervo)

In 437 pages of delinquency and corruption, Ulloa has mastered the detective genre in his second novel. An international web of crime unfolds when a cultural attaché to the US Embassy is found dead. A police artist and his journalist lover expose a world of sex, drugs, and arms trafficking connected by the dark web with Costa Rica's Oficina de Investigaciones Judiciales at the center of the action. [EF]

1863 **Urtecho, Mario.** Mala casta: novela. Managua: Impresión Comercial La Prensa, 2014. 178 p.

In perhaps the first modern Nicaraguan detective novel, Sandinista and corporate corruption is revealed by Granada's Afro-Caribbean police chief, La Capitana. When rising business star and ruthless oligarch, Eugenia, is charged with laundering money from narco and human trafficking rings, her scandalous sexual affairs are also publicized. Government officials involved in the human trafficking inexplicably go free at the time of the 2011 presidential elections. When Eugenia goes to jail, condemned to death by the Mexican cartel bosses, her cuckolded boyfriend steals away to Menorca with La Capitana, who has retired. The novel is problematic from a gendered perspective: although all characters in the novel are guilty of infidelity to varying degrees, the narration seems to fetishize La Capitana, while relishing in Eugenia's harsh punishment for being a sexually assertive business tycoon. Nevertheless, it is notable that the narrative's criticism of the Sandinista government demonstrates cultural resistance to the Ortega regime three years before the violent oppression of student movements began in April 2018. [EF]

1864 **Vásquez Bonilla, Vicente Antonio.** La casa de los trece gatos: novela. Guatemala: Editorial El Arco, 2012. 184 p.: col. ill.

The opening of the novel launches directly into a scene of violence in La Antigua, with the death of a *marero*, who was assassinated for having kissed one of the rival band members' girlfriends on a bus (she was also killed). The plot centers on the lives of gang members as they move through the city, so Chapters 2–12 read as travel literature, referencing real-life places and streets in Antigua. Throughout the novel, the narrator constantly juxtaposes the experiences of tourists who visit the colonial city with those of gang members, who turn to gangs not out of a love for violence, but as a survival mechanism to escape poverty. Violence is justified not only as self-preservation when confronting a lack of options, but as the narrator repeats, "Mejor coger que ser cogido." If you are not the violent one, then someone else will harm you. As the violent escapades of the gang members are detailed, the novel implicitly critiques the ineffectiveness of the justice system: the delinquent youth get away with everything since people do not want to confront gang members. [TCM]

1865 Zardetto, Carol. La ciudad de los minotauros. México: Alfaguara, 2016. 300 p.

Felipe Martínez, a Guatemalan self-exiled former engineer, abandons his life and family and goes to New York in order to fulfill his dream of becoming a screenwriter. In the process, he confronts not only the otherness of a strange and, at times, hostile culture, but also discovers his own past and rediscovers his own culture after a series of chaotic and convoluted experiences with his fellow classmates in New York. *La ciudad de los minotauros* earned a mild, yet positive critical reception in Guatemala, and most of the praise echoed notions about culture shock, the woes of globalization, and the struggle of those who leave their country and find themselves in between two cultures, but belonging to none. While this novel is ambitious and intends to present the dilemmas and problems that Guatemalan immigrants go through in the US, it does not present anything new in terms of insights or views. In fact, it is difficult to sympathize with Felipe because, unlike other Guatemalans, he is not running away from violence and poverty, but is rather having an existential crisis. Despite his claims of poverty, Felipe manages to secure a shared apartment with a woman called Toni Lacrosse, and makes friends with his classmates at the nameless academy in which he studies screenwriting. His musings occupy chapters of heavy prose, interwoven with the real work of two anthropologists whose work he quotes, as well as dropping names and references to multiple authors and works from the Spanish American canon. The discursive alternation that appears throughout the text, between Felipe's own autobiographical narrative and other sources, probably the author herself, working as a kind of readerly reverberation chamber is the novel's chief innovation. [FSL]

LITERARY CRITICISM AND HISTORY

1866 Gómez, Juan Pablo. Autoridad, cuerpo, nación: batallas culturales en Nicaragua (1930–1943). Managua: Instituto de Historia de Nicaragua y Centroamérica de la Universidad Centroamericana, IHNCA-UCA, 2015. 239 p.: bibl., ill.

Masterfully combining literary criticism and cultural history, this text offers a fresh, discerning analysis of the Nicaraguan literary vanguard's Movimiento Reaccionario in shaping national ideology and culture in the early 20th century. Inserting themselves in contentious dialogue with the more progressive Latin American intellectuals of their day, these writers, chiefly Pablo Antonio Cuadra, effectively solidified the rule of Anastasio Somoza García by nostalgically defending the Nicaraguan oligarchy as heir to the victorious Catholic conquistadors whose right to authority extended to the present in the guise of masculinist, fascist ideology, which they framed as a strategic response to North American imperialism and as justification for oppressing indigenous populations. This study will be foundational in years to come in Nicaraguan literary and historical scholarship, and its analysis of consolidating power and dictatorship will instruct comparisons of Ortega to Somoza. For comment by historian, see item **757**. [EF]

1867 Lara Martínez, Rafael. Del silencio y del olvido, o, Los espectros del patriarca: cinco seis ocho ensayos salarruerianos. San Salvador: Fundación AccesArte, 2013. 333 p.: bibl., ill.

Readers of this author will recognize this collection's writing style and interest in conjoining Salvadoran literary history and cultural context to specific major writers. In this case, the focus is on Salarrué and Gen. Maximiliano Hernández Martínez's regime and its cultural politics. The author's main contention is that researchers have chosen to ignore primary sources of the period that prove that cultural elites, including Salarrúe, were tightly allied to Martinez's modernizing projects and shared his theosofic beliefs as well as his views of the indigenous, rural, and poor. The majority of Lara Martinez's sources are literary, for instance, Salarrúe's narrative and contemporary cultural journals, or from the visual arts. His use of some sources is problematic because he fuses fragments from different authors together without clearly marking authorship. Overall, these essays offer readers interested in the *martinato* and the period's intellectuals a rich resource. [YA]

1868   Morales, Mario Roberto. Estética y política de la interculturalidad: el caso de Miguel Ángel Asturias y su construcción de un sujeto popular interétnico y una nación intercultural democrática. Guatemala: Editorial Cultura, 2017. 167 p.: bibl. (Colección Ensayo. Serie Luis Cardoza y Aragón; 60)

Mario Roberto Morales, once known as the *enfant terrible* of Guatemalan literature thanks to his groundbreaking experimental novel *Los demonios salvajes* (1977), is now a respected (albeit often controversial) opinion writer and political commentator. As a former academic (he has a PhD in literature from the University of Pittsburgh), he has authored a number of articles and books on various academic topics. Here he addresses one of his chief concerns: multiculturalism and its depiction. In this book, Morales has gathered a series of essays on Asturias's works, ranging from *El señor presidente* to *Hombres de maíz*, including *Mulata de tal* and *Leyendas de Guatemala*, in order to propose how Asturias attempted to formulate what Morales calls "a popular, interethnic subject." His arguments are based on theories by Homi Bhabha and René Prieto, among others. His essay on *El señor presidente* stands out for being the one that attempts to link this particular novel with the elements of interethnicity and interculturality found in other works; Morales finds a solution in Asturias' portrayal of the dictator as a figure directly drawn from the *Popol Vuh*, and demonstrates how the chapters that show the lionization of Estrada Cabrera (the dictator presumably described in this novel) are associated with depictions of Kukulkan and Tohil. [FSL]

1869   Nuevas iluminaciones: la larga trayectoria literaria de Enrique Jaramillo Levi. Compilación por Fernando Burgos Pérez, Fátima R. Nogueira. Panamá: Editorial Tecnologica, Universidad Tecnológica de Panamá, 2016. 213 p.: bibl.

This volume includes 14 essays, one of which is an extensive interview between Fernando Burgos Pérez and Enrique Jaramillo Levi, with the aim of providing a critical evaluation of the Panamanian writer's poetry and prose. Among the goals of the collection is to offer a critical evaluation of the works of Panama's most international recognized writers. Jaramillo Levi's output of 24 collections of short stories, 12 volumes of poetry and 10 essays on literature justify this extensive critical review of his work. A second goal is to offer this volume as an homage to a writer who has been active for 55 years, a university professor for 20, and a tireless cultural promotor. A recurring theme in the 14 essays is the metaliterary nature of Jaramillo Levi's prose. Most of the essays focus on his short stories. [FJ]

1870   Roque Baldovinos, Ricardo. El cielo de lo ideal: literatura y modernización en El Salvador (1860–1920). San Salvador: UCA Editores, 2016. 276 p.: bibl., ill.

These essays focus on Salvadoran literary history during the late 19th and early 20th centuries. While the essays have been published before, this collection gives readers easier access to well-researched work on Salvadoran cultural history and politics. The book is divided in three sections: literature and Salvadoran Liberal projects, Salvadoran *modernismo* and its place in Latin American letters, and Salvadoran literature and the creation of a mestizo nation. This an excellent addition to a little-researched, and often idealized, period of Salvadoran culture. [YA]

Hispanic Caribbean

DIANA ÁLVAREZ AMELL, *Associate Professor of Spanish, Seton Hall University*
MYRNA GARCÍA-CALDERÓN, *Associate Professor of Spanish, Syracuse University*

CUBA
WHILE THE MEDIA SPECULATES about Cuba's future regarding possible social and political changes, Cuban writers direct their gaze, obsessively it seems, inwardly, and, to a great extent, towards the past. Addressing the present, the themes center around Cuba's troubled social and political issues, such as censorship and the effects of sexual tourism on Cubans. These themes, both the historical and the broken present, are reflected in three narratives from internationally recognized writers: Abilio Estévez, Zoé Valdés, and Wendy Guerra. Of the three texts, Estévez's *Archipiélagos* (item **1886**) is the most ambitious novel in its overarching historical themes, and the most complex in its narrative structure. Estévez, an exiled writer currently living in Barcelona, has recreated in this novel the troubled and violent Depression-era dictatorship of Gerardo Machado. Estévez chooses a particularly difficult period for the country as the historical setting for his novel. The Depression hit Cuba hard after the economic boom of the 20s—the euphoria that had preceded it was called "The Dance of the Millions." Many immigrants settled on the island during that time, and this novel reflects this history in the immigrant background of some of its characters. The "machadato," as Gerardo Machado's dictatorship is called, was a moment of extreme economic and political difficulty that ultimately sparked a violent revolt against the government. While *Archipiélagos* is an historical novel evoking the problems of dictatorship and political violence, and introducing the themes of immigration, far from taking the traditional form of the genre, the author subverts the linear narrative of the historical novel. Estévez disrupts and blurs the plot line with a multiplicity of voices that challenge the reader and the concept of history in fiction.

Successful and popular women writers are responsible for the two other significant texts. Zoé Valdés is a long-time resident of Paris, and Wendy Guerra lives in Cuba, but is permitted to travel extensively. Although both works are autobiographical with a first-person narrator, the narratives are very different in structure. Valdés' text integrates a fragmented autobiography with the form of the essay, while Guerra's novel is conventional in its structure. Valdés, in *La Habana, mon amour* (item **1916**), writes a very personal account, intermingling the autobiographical with the historical as the text meanders through the streets and landmarks of the capital city. While Valdés draws a literary and historical urban landscape of Havana, she mixes the exposition with episodic accounts of her own life. At times it is highly confessional—she tells of her erotic initiation and romantic affairs, although without naming names. The story of her own troubled family life is also part of the narrative. Her personal ethnic ancestry is drawn from the city's past, from her Irish grandmother to her Chinese grandfather. She recounts, at times with detail, the historical and cultural past of the city, although always in relation to her personal connection with places. Her text incorporates historical facts about the city's past, its churches, buildings, and neighborhoods. It includes the everyday popular places that the author remembers visiting, such as theaters and movie houses—at one time Havana had more movie theaters per capita than New York City. Those popular sites that the author remembers have been brought down in ruins or disappeared during her lifetime. The author reminisces about well-known urban characters and historical artists. These urban memories are interspersed with allusion to her own personal romantic mishaps while growing into a premature sexual maturity. The narrator also evokes cultural figures from the city's past. She dreams, for example, of running into the celebrated 19th-century Afro-Cuban classical composer Claudio Brindis de Sala. She describes her visits to the house where the poet and independence leader José Martí was born, explaining the significance of those visits in her life. However, although the reader might first imagine otherwise from the title—at times the prose is lyrical in its urban descriptions—it is a curiously unsentimental text. While it is a personal tribute to the city of her birth, it is far from nostalgic or emotional. She takes pains to point out that she does not indulge in nostalgia. Hers was not the formerly legendary city known for its bright nightlife. She matter-of-factly emphasizes that her birthright is the impoverished urban landscape that she roamed. She stresses that the city in which she was born and raised, where her mother and her daughter were also born, is a landscape of ruins. This text is part confessional and part essay. It is an unsentimental love story to the Cuban capital, as the title indicates. The title is borrowed from the celebrated French film *Hiroshima, mon amour*, where two lovers meet and talk after the catastrophic destruction of a city. Valdés' text is at most a melancholic and wry remembrance of a love story among the ruins.

Wendy Guerra's straightforward autobiographical novel *Domingo de revolución* (item **1890**) follows some basic facts from the author's life. The protagonist is a young writer who received an international literary award. Her global acclaim does not change her depression nor loneliness after a parent's death. Nor does it change her anonymity in her own country where her books are not published. She lives in a big house where her parents used to live. It is a rambling home where, despite her solitude, privacy is impossible since state security forces have installed hidden bugs and cameras. There is a love story with an international actor that ends in failure and there is also an element of political thriller as the protagonist slowly discovers hidden facts about her own past.

Anna Veltfort contributes an autobiographical graphic novel about her time in Cuba (item **1919**). The subtitle could well be "How I Became Cuban and Then Had to Leave the Island." Veltfort was born in Germany and became an American citizen; she went on to be raised partly in Cuba after the Revolution. Her American stepfather, a radical leftist, moved to Cuba in the 60s with his family. Veltfort's graphic novel, drawn in color, tells the story of her life in Havana as a teenager who grows into an adult. It chronicles the rapid changes in the country. During that time, Havana had become a place frequented by many international intellectuals and artists who the Cuban government invited to participate in cultural events. The graphic novel contrasts the glittering intellectual world that foreign visitors experienced with the increasingly harsher realities that Cuban citizens faced. Veltfort's graphic novel—far from being a sentimental journal as the title might suggest—is more of a *bildungsroman*. The journey is one of evolving consciousness, a growing awareness of the self and of political realities. Veltfort discovers herself and her own sexuality, and the repression that she must confront while studying at the university. The book addresses political repression, especially of gays, and the increasing constraints placed on the social and material world of her Cuban friends and classmates due to surveillance, censorship, and increasing food shortages. Such restrictions are contrasted to the privileged lives of Communist foreign intellectuals, such as her stepfather, who worked for the

Cuban government. He and other revolutionary tourists were granted benefits that were rarely accessible to Cubans.

Several short story anthologies were published during this review period. The collection of short stories in Alberto Garrandés' *Aire de luz: cuentos cubanos del siglo XX* (item **1872**) provides a panoramic sampling of this literary form presented in a traditional chronological order. As the title points out, it gathers in one volume the most iconic and best-known short stories written in Cuba during the last century. This anthology includes the work of some of the most outstanding writers who went into exile in the 60s. Until very recently, these writers were not only omitted from state publications, but had been erased from the country's literary history. In the prologue, Garrandés points out that the exclusion of two writers, Guillermo Cabrera Infante and Norberto Fuentes, was due to their refusal to be published in Cuba. While undoubtedly true, at least in the case of Cabrera Infante, it is a somewhat skewed representation of state policies toward the work of dissidents or exiled writers and artists whose work has been suppressed.

The collection of homoerotic tales, *Mañana hablarán de nosotros* (item **1898**) is a more personal anthology. As with Garrandés' volume, this collection, published in Spain, includes writers who live on and off the island. The theme of gay love is seen through the Cuban prism: there is a story of the lonely exiled gay young man who is living by himself in Barcelona. The issue of gay sexual tourism is evident in Cuban characters who prostitute themselves to subsist in the country. Another collection of texts gathered around a specific theme is Enrique del Risco's *El compañero que me atiende* (item **1883**). The main theme is the effect and repercussions on the lives and works of writers who face surveillance and state censorship. These stories explore the state's long shadow on literary production, the subtle and not so subtle ways that Cuban state controls and actively manipulates what is written and published. The irony of the title is in fact historically accurate. After the Revolution, the term used to express human solidarity, *compañero,* became an imposed form of speech that took the place of traditional forms used to address others. The discarded forms "señor" and "señora" were deemed to be middle class. The state-imposed form for social interaction "compañero" may appear to have a deceptively innocuous connotation, as does the verb "attender," which implies to serve and to see to someone. However, the meaning of the phrase is sinister within the Cuban context where the phrase transforms into the opposite of the apparent meaning. The "compañero" is the enemy who looks after the writer not to serve, but to persecute and harass the writer into submission. The short volume *Escenas del yo flotante* (item **1885**) addresses writers who no longer live on the island and are literally left adrift. This too is an unsentimental exploration of the condition of exiles. It incorporates tales of writers who were born after 1960, and whose only reality was revolutionary Cuba, unlike previous writers who left the country at the beginning of the Revolution. They have become flotsam, floating adrift, cast off not only geographically, but also ideologically.

The Cuban prerevolutionary literature of the *Origenista* group has received attention from current writers who grew up at a time when these writers were either exiled or banned on the island. Aguilera Chang's book on the dissenter of the *Origenistas,* Lorenzo García Vega (item **1937**), and Pio Serrano's anthology of essays written by the important poet and man of letters Gastón Baquero (item **1878**) highlight this renewed interest in Cuba's literary past. García Vega and Baquero are very different writers in terms of their literary style, esthetics, and political points of view. However, both left the country in the early 60s. Baquero went to Spain, and García Vega ended up in Miami. Despite these differences, the two writers shared the cultural world of Havana in the 50s and were associated with the *Origenistas*. Given the dispersal that continues to be a major factor in Cuban literary production, these books constitute an act not only of cultural continuity, but also of cultural recovery.

Finally, some publications incorporate essays that appeared originally in cultural magazines and are now gathered in book form. The novelist José Manuel Prieto ponders the Cuban situation in *La revolución cubana explicada a los taxistas* (item **1912**). Prieto's life reflects and is a result of the many ideological twists and turns of 20th-century Cuba. Raised in Cuba, the son of parents who were true believers, although his father now lives in Miami, he was sent to study in the former Soviet Union, only to end up exiled first in Mexico and now in the US. This book offers a personal account of his political legacy and ideological coming of age. Reconciling his past as he takes stock of his political perspective reveals an ambiguity: while recognizing the failures of the Cuban system, he considers that the way towards healing and reconciliation is to accept the Revolution as the Mexicans have accepted theirs. While not defending the status quo, Prieto contends that there were accomplishments, such as health care and education—repeating the points often made by those unwilling to denounce the current political system in Cuba. This same ideological tightrope seems to be the balance struck by Carlos Manuel Álvarez. He was chosen as one of the 2017 Latin American writers under 30 by the Bogotá 39 list. Álvarez, who started out as a journalist, and who writes for international publications, is also involved in the digital review *Estornudo*, currently banned in Cuba. Nevertheless, he too is the son of a father who enthusiastically favored the Revolution, a medical doctor trained by the revolutionary government, but who ended up living in Miami, making ends meet in menial jobs. Álvarez's short slice-of-life texts in *La tribu: retratos de Cuba* (item **1874**) express an ideological no man's land, and the bewilderment of former true believers, left adrift and dazed in the Cuban economic collapse where daily life is untenable. While Prieto and Álvarez are from different generations, both try to make sense of the confusion. Both now live outside of Cuba: Prieto in the US and Álvarez in Mexico. [DAA]

DOMINICAN REPUBLIC
Violence and dictatorship are the main themes in both fiction and literary criticism in Dominican literature. The theme of immigration is also increasingly present. Most of the published fiction of note has been promoted with literary awards. The prolific writer Roberto Marcallé Abréu's work addresses political corruption and street violence in his short story collections, *Bruma de gente inhóspita* (item **1899**) and *En la oscuridad de la habitación* (item **1900**). Several writers address ethnic tensions that erupt because of immigration. Vladimir Tatis Pérez's award-winning short story *Con la misma moneda* (item **1915**) addresses ethnic strife and violence in the interaction between two minorities in Spain: a Dominican and a gypsy. Rey Andújar also writes about a Dominican immigrant in Spain in *Los gestos inútiles* (item **1875**). Osiris Vallejo's short story "¿Volver a casa?," included in his book *Dimensiones del espejo* (item **1917**), also registers the misunderstandings between two ethnic minorities, a Dominican immigrant and an African American, this time in the US. These writers provide accounts of the Dominican immigrant experience. Laureano Guerrero's *La sentencia* (item **1891**)

deals with an interesting ethnic confrontation between Dominicans and the Haitian immigrants who cross the border that divides the island into two nations. While the immigrant experience has marked the Dominican Republic's society and its literary experience, the country itself has been at times the reluctant recipient of immigrants who cross the border from Haiti. Guerrero's story addresses the often hostile encounters between people from the two countries.

The character of the *caudillo* is pervasive in Spanish-language literature. The literature from the Dominican Republic is no exception. One of the first notable Dominican novels written on the island is Tulio Cestero's *La sangre: una vida bajo la tiranía* (item **1882**). Considered the author's most important novel, the plot is set during the rule of the 19th-century strongman Ulises Heureaux. Heureaux was killed eventually by a member of the political opposition. Another historical novel that addresses the same period is Manuel Salvador Gautier's *Gregorio y su mundo perfecto: una saga antillana del siglo XIX* (item **1889**). In her critical study *En la piel de las mujeres: reescrituras de la dictadura trujillista en la ficción dominicana en los años 90* (item **1926**), Giulia de Sarlo addresses critically important works of fiction that deal with the effects of Rafael Trujillo's dictatorship. In the study, she analyzes some of the novels written about this traumatic period such as those by Haitian-American Edwidge Danticat, Peruvian Mario Vargas Llosa, Dominican-American Julia Álvarez, and Spaniard Manuel Vazquéz Montalbán. De Sarlo's work highlights the impact of this violent and repressive time in 20th-century Dominican history and how it transcended and has been interpreted in international fiction. [DAA]

PUERTO RICO

Es inevitable comenzar estas notas con una referencia temporal que marca un momento crucial de la historia puertorriqueña: 20 de septiembre de 2017, fecha del peor desastre natural en la historia del país. Cuando el Huracán María desató su furia sobre el archipiélago de Puerto Rico, su devastación no solo afectó la infraestructura, la economía, la educación y los sistemas de salud, por mencionar los servicios más vitales para cualquier sociedad, el huracán obligó a los habitantes de la isla a comprender lo que significa vivir a la intemperie. En la colección de ensayos de Eduardo Lalo titulada precisamente *Intemperie* (item **1931**) y publicada un año antes del huracán, asistimos a una reflexión profunda sobre el papel de la literatura y el arte en una sociedad en donde se han venido abajo los modelos y las reglas, las normas, preceptos y principios con que se regían la conducta social y humana del país. Este y otros textos puertorriqueños recientes aquí comentados reflexionarán de maneras directas e indirectas sobre esta crisis.

Las propuestas estéticas aquí son múltiples, sin embargo, ciertas afinidades y coincidencias permiten extrapolar algunas visiones más amplias acerca de la producción reciente isleña. Una serie de poemarios premiados por el Instituto de Cultura Puertorriqueña muestran la vitalidad de la producción poética y la importancia del aparato editorial en apoyar y mantener robusta la aparición de textos poéticos. La serie Literatura Hoy del Instituto de Cultura ha apoyado esa producción como puede observarse en seis de los siete poemarios presentes en esta muestra. *Mantras* (item **2148**), por ejemplo, nos remite a lo sonoro de la lengua, a sus elementos más fundamentales: sílabas, palabras, fonemas que pueden o no tener un sentido literal o sintáctico. La invitación a mirar y sentir las imágenes representadas es central a la colección. La variedad formal muestra un aparato lingüístico maleable y ágil en manos de Echevarría Pagán. *Ventriloquus* (item **2149**) reflexiona sobre el gesto de emitir sonidos de manera espectacular a través de *otro* cuerpo. Las múltiples referencias al *poeta* en tercera persona hacen pensar en la representatividad de uno que habla por otros. Irónicamente, la práctica de la ventriloquia se realiza típicamente a manera de un diálogo pero que toma la forma de vocalización disimulada, controlada. *Oratorio* (item **2154**), por su parte asume la palestra sugerida por el título para explorar lo público y lo privado, lo íntimo y lo distante. Los poemas de *Siglo de pájaros* (item **2157**) son poemas de intimidad que hablan de presencias y ausencias; de viajes, naturaleza, memoria, nostalgia, mapas, despedidas, regresos. La poeta logra conectar estos poemas individuales a través de transiciones fluidas. Por su parte, *Ultramar* (item **2167**), invita a pensar en un *aquí* y un *allá*. En este mundo de mar, tierra, islas y naturaleza, los poemas se detienen a mirar el mundo de los afectos, de las pequeñas ceremonias familiares, de los recuerdos. Se trata de una poesía clara, directa, esencial. Por su parte *Larga jornada en el trópico* (item **2174**) también privilegia el espacio isleño, su inmediatez, su belleza así como sus trampas. Por último, la colección titulada *Set* (item **2168**) antologa textos escritos entre 1973 y 1998. Importa no solo el gesto de reunir una suerte de *summa poética* del autor, sino el hecho de que esta reedición de poemas escritos décadas atrás recurre a la traducción al inglés de los textos originales, abriendo el acceso de los textos a un público más amplio. Algo que aúna a todos estos poemarios es la materialidad de su escritura, los ejercicios de la memoria y la espacialidad de donde emergen.

Los ejemplos narrativos toman varias formas. Las doce novelas comentadas asumen inflexiones genéricas, lenguajes, extensión y estructuras diversas. Escritores como Cabiya (item **1880**), cuyas novelas anteriores se han caracterizado por un acercamiento lúdico e irreverente de los géneros literarios sorprende en *Reinbou* con su narración de corte más realista, dejando atrás el género gótico y la ciencia ficción de textos anteriores para acercarse a un tema de corte más político. Fuster Lavín (item **1888**) mezcla en su novela algunos aspectos de lo gótico con temáticas y problemáticas afines a la literatura juvenil. Esa narración de tipo realista aparece también en las novelas de Mattos Cintrón (items **1902** y **1903**), Pagán Vélez (item **1909**), *Azábara* de Rabelo (item **1913**), y *Dicen que los dormidos* de Gutiérrez (item **1892**). Pero las restantes novelas incluidas en esta reflexión ofrecen interesantes experimentaciones. Por ejemplo, *Mar de Azov* de Bauzá (item **1896**) hace excelente uso de la parodia; Lozada Pérez (item **1897**) mezcla el género policial con la fantasía, Materyn (item **1901**) narra su novela en diez distintos monólogos, recordándonos un poco el recurso usado por Rosario Ferré en su novela *Maldito amor* de 1986.

De este grupo de novelas tres merecen mención especial. *El capitán de los dormidos* de Montero (item **1905**) incluye una mezcla de sicología, novela gótica, intriga y folletín junto a referentes históricos reales. Utilizando con destreza la estrategia textual de alternar las dos voces narrativas de los personajes Andrés Yasín, viequense y propietario de un hotelito en la llamada Isla Nena, y John Timothy Bunker, un norteamericano de Maine, aviador y el capitán al que se refiere el título de la novela, Montero cuenta desde el discurso de la ficción, un episodio central para el destino de la isla de Vieques. Esto le permite tejer una historia íntima alrededor de episodios históricos de importancia vital: la presencia militar norteamericana en la isla, una rápida modernización y alteración de patrones sociales, culturales y económicos que redefinen la isla, así como la intervención norteamericana en los movimientos de resistencia isleña, especialmente la lucha de los nacionalistas.

El marco temporal del texto de Montero se ubica a mediados del siglo XX pero es inevitable conectarlo con las luchas viequenses de finales del siglo XX y principios del XXI. El asesinato de David Sanes Rodríguez, víctima de una bomba lanzada por un avión militar de Estados Unidos en el área de tiro utilizada por la Marina en Vieques en donde éste trabajaba, precipitó una de las luchas sociales más importantes en la historia moderna de Puerto Rico, en demanda por la desmilitarización y el cese de los bombardeos en la Isla Nena. Sanes Rodríguez se convirtió en la alegoría de la vieja lucha de los viequenses, que llevaban décadas empujando a la Marina estadounidense fuera de sus tierras. La lucha de un frente amplio de puertorriqueños en respuesta a este evento logró la retirada de la Marina de Vieques. Si bien la novela no pretende narrar esa historia concreta, sí logra 16 años más tarde mantener viva la discusión sobre Vieques a través de una historia muy íntima y humana de los distintos personajes involucrados en este conflicto.

Gutiérrez (item **1892**), por su parte, ofrece en *Dicen que los dormidos* una instantánea desgarradora de la violencia sin sentido que muchas poblaciones urbanas a nivel mundial sufren todos los días. Su acierto es la manera tan normal con que presenta una historia personal de la violencia tal y como suele suceder, unos maleantes vinculados con el narcotráfico disparan de carro a carro. En este caso, ficticio, han confundido el vehículo. La víctima queda en coma y despierta cuatro años más tarde. El siguiente fragmento muestra como este joven escritor, de 26 años al momento de aparición de la novela, representa esa violencia sin sentido, aceptada como pan de cada día: *Porque por cada tiro que te dieron, por cada balazo estallando en tu cuerpo, por cada pedazo de material indispuesto quebrando tu epidermis, dermis, etcétera., te halaron a ti y a los tuyos a un mundo de vómito y diarrea y mierda por todos lados. Un mundo que está encima y está debajo y está al lado y adentro y entre medio y por encima. Y me hablarás de todo menos de lo que te dice el hombre . . .* (p. 63) Esta novela detectivesca sin detectives, como la llama el autor, plasma de manera eficaz, esa violencia cotidiana, ese desfase urbano, una historia personal de la violencia, tal y como suele suceder, es uno de los mayores logros de esta narración. La brevedad, rasgo de muchos de los textos aquí incluidos, junto a una oralidad creíble y convincente hace de esta una novela memorable.

Posiblemente la más intrigante de las novelas de esta muestra lo sea *La troupe Samsonite* de Font Acevedo (item **1887**). Ya su libro anterior *La belleza bruta* le valió un reconocimiento especial por parte de críticos y lectores, gracias a la delicada artesanía con la que el autor construyó la historia y la fuerza de sus imágenes, que representan un universo urbano caribeño hecho único por su diversidad de voces y registros sociales. En *La troupe Samsonite* nos encontramos ante una historia aún más atrevida que desafía los modelos convencionales de escritura y lectura. Para crearlo, el autor ha diseñado un aparato narrativo caracterizado por el flujo de conciencia, la evocación y la dislocación de la voz narrativa. Todo esto se logra a través del vértigo impreso en esta historia por la característica principal de sus protagonistas: una familia de circo. La novela está estructurada en capítulos cortos, y en cada uno encontramos el punto de vista de un personaje diferente; Mirko, por ejemplo, nos habla de un episodio en particular, mientras que Tanya asume el control en el siguiente. Estos cambios en el punto de vista llegan al lector sin previo aviso, por lo que el proceso de lectura debe ser aún más atento. En varios puntos, solo podemos decir quién nos está hablando por un proceso de eliminación, por los ojos a través de los cuales vemos a los otros como compañeros en la acción. Con esto en mente, la calidad de la escritura de Font Acevedo se vuelve clara cuando nos damos cuenta de que, a través de esta complicada opción narrativa, sus personajes se desarrollan completa y naturalmente en la historia; no hay desequilibrio entre sus partes, ya que el autor describe cuidadosamente el desarrollo de la historia y sus protagonistas.

Aparte de las novelas mencionadas, vale señalar que la narrativa breve aparece representada a través de cuentos, crónicas de actualidad y otros géneros híbridos. La prolífica escritora Arroyo Pizarro continúa su exploración del cuerpo femenino a través de la colección *Menorragia: histerias de octubre* (item **1877**). Mediante una serie de situaciones sociales que cuestionan muchas expectativas tradicionales y problemáticas con relación a la mujer, estos cuentos hurgan en visiones construidas sobre *lo perverso*, las sexualidades, el deseo, la violencia y la hipocresía social. También hablan de la solidaridad y de la justicia social. Estas fluidas narraciones muestran a una escritora en absoluto control de su arsenal narrativo. Por su parte Caleb Acevedo (item **1881**) y Rabelo Cartagena en su libro *2063 y otras distopías* (item **1914**) desafían los límites del género cuentístico tradicional. En el caso de Rabelo Cartagena resulta interesante su uso del micro relato. Rabelo también juega desde el título mismo con la noción de la distopía. Si al tratar de retratar los males de una sociedad ficticia los relatos distópicos se caracterizan por contraponer lo *real* con lo *irreal* para así poder describir estados sociales y/o políticos ilusorios o imaginados, no es sorprendente que en la colección estén plagados de ironía.

Los ejemplos de crónica urbana están excelentemente representadas por tres colecciones de Guillermo Rebollo Gil. Si la tradición de la crónica urbana en Puerto Rico ha contado con importantes productos culturales en las últimas décadas, especialmente la prolífica pluma de Edgardo Rodríguez Juliá, observador y crítico atento de la realidad puertorriqueña, sin lugar a dudas la producción de Rebollo Gil reclama su espacio como observador incisivo y escritor agudo de la realidad puertorriqueña. Sus textos híbridos muestran nuevas formas de comunicación marcadas por las diversas plataformas electrónicas que inciden en el día a día de la vida contemporánea. Con mirada escrutadora, prosa fluida y facilidad de entender y representar todo tipo de discurso, incluyendo jergas particularizadas, este sociólogo y abogado de formación ofrece en sus escritos algunos de los retratos más lúcidos de la realidad puertorriqueña actual.

La ensayística y los estudios académicos también aparecen representados con fuerza. Dos textos en particular, *Cartas viajeras: Julia de Burgos, Clarice Lispector: versiones de sí mismas* (item **1935**) y *Tapia: el primer puertorriqueño* (item **1940**) son investigaciones profundas sobre figuras centrales de la literatura puertorriqueña. Evaluaciones críticas de autores conocidos como *Para devorarte otra vez: nuevos acercamientos a la obra de Luis Rafael Sánchez* de Barradas (item **1922**) y la crítica de nuevas voces, discursos y medios de representación discutidos por La Fountain-Stokes en *Escenas transcaribeñas* (item **1930**) muestran las necesarias conversaciones entre los diferentes discursos críticos. Volúmenes como el de Centeno Añeses (item **1923**), buscan enfatizar la importancia y pertinencia de géneros como el del ensayo. Finalmente, la hermosa memoria *Inventario con retrato de familia* de Barradas (item **1879**) subraya la fuerza y límite de fijar las cambiantes realidades del país a través de relatos que combinan discursos, historias, cultura material y cultura popular.

Tres textos merecen una mención especial. En su libro *PR 3 Aguirre* (item **1876**) la autora, Aponte Alsina, crea un relato híbrido en donde combina la narración novelesca con toda otra serie de discursos: documentos, historia, diarios, informes, artículos periodísticos, entrevistas y fotografías. En su exploración de las relaciones coloniales entre Puerto Rico y los Estados Unidos se detiene en el estudio de la genealogía de las familias privilegiadas norteamericanas que vienen a la isla a explotar la industria de la caña. Su relato se detiene en todo un tramo de la carretera PR 3 entre los pueblos de Guayama y de Salinas donde ese pasado cañero ha dejado un rastro de silencios y ausencias. Al retornar a esas voces del pasado, de un mundo laboral y explotación que creó trabajo y muchos conflictos obreros, Aponte Alsina ofrece una profunda reflexión acerca de las ruinas modernas y una poderosa meditación sobre el proyecto histórico del país que llamamos Puerto Rico.

Intemperie, de Lalo (item **1931**), cuestiona con incisiva mirada crítica un espacio caribeño en donde las representaciones culturales y literarias desde los que se armaron muchas de las ideas de la alta cultura en la civilización occidental se han derrumbado. Esto ha obligado a todos los creadores conscientes a cuestionar fundamentos esenciales de la creación, tanto las prácticas discursivas como la ética de la escritura. Su mirada profunda, transeúnte convoca a los lectores a hurgar con mayor profundidad y urgencia el acto de la escritura, los silencios y las borraduras, la voz y sus límites, los cuerpos y sus ausencias, los textos y las ideas que estos convocan.

Tanto la propuesta de Aponte Alsina como la de Lalo coinciden con el gesto de ruptura presente en el libro de Duchesne Winter, *Caribe, Caribana: cosmografías literarias* (item **1927**). Este texto busca producir un conocimiento y sentido más profundo y amplio de la cuenca caribeña, uno en donde las relaciones de cuerpos, ideas e imaginarios caribeños se desborden más allá de los límites artificiales y articulen un pensamiento más amplio y más profundo sobre la zona.

Al cerrar estas notas es necesario redirigir la mirada a la crisis profunda económica y el impacto del desastre natural que han intensificado el asalto a algunas de las instituciones culturales más importantes de Puerto Rico. Las universidades, especialmente la Universidad de Puerto Rico, han sido objeto de recortes presupuestarios que atentan contra la existencia misma del primer centro docente. El efecto de la crisis ha impactado a importantes centros culturales, bibliotecas, librerías y editoriales. Los textos aquí comentados son solo una muestra de la pujante producción literaria de la isla en los peores tiempos de crisis. Y, sí, la producción literaria y cultural sigue pujante, contra viento y marea. [MGC]

PROSE FICTION

1871 Acosta, José. Un kilómetro de mar. La Habana: Fondo Editorial Casa de las Américas, 2015. 103 p.

This novel depicts a roadtrip of two Dominican teenagers who leave their home in the mountains to view the sea for the first time. It is, of course, a story of initiation and self-discovery as well. The author, a novelist and poet, received the 2015 Casa de las Américas Award for this brief novel. [DAA]

1872 Aire de luz: cuentos cubanos del siglo XX. Edición de Alberto Garrandés. La Habana: Ediciones Cubanas, ARTEX 2014. 651 p.

This ambitious anthology of Cuban short stories includes what the editor Garrandés, writer and former editor of the state publishing house Letras Cubanas, considers the most significant of this literary form written on the island. It encompasses narratives from the beginning of the 20th century to contemporary writers. Included are such writers as Jesús Castellanos, Alfonso Hernández Catá, and Enrique Serpa, who wrote in the first decades of the 20th century. Important mid-20th-century writers, such as Carlos Montenegro and Lino Novás Calvo, are represented here. Alejo Carpentier's very well-known "Camino de Santiago" is also included. The list of writers is impressive: Virgilio Piñera, José Lezama Lima, Enrique Labrador Ruiz, Calbert Casey, etc., which highlights a fault line in Cuban literature: the writers in this anthology represent all political points of view. Such distinguished writers—distinguished also for their opposition to the government—as Lino Novás Calvo and Reinaldo Arenas are represented alongside Abel Prieto, a state cultural functionary, and Rubén Martínez Villena, a member of the Cuban Communist Party in the thirties, and Antón Arrufat. Many writers who are currently in exile are part of this anthology, such as Amir Valle, José Lorenzo Fuentes (who died in December 2017), and the dissident Ángel Santiesteban. Short stories from some recent contemporary writers have been added to the collection: Yoss (José Miguel Sánchez), Ronaldo Menéndez, Anna Lidia Vega, and Eduardo del Llano. In the prologue written in 1998, Garrandés points out in a footnote that Guillermo Cabrera Infantes and Norberto Fuentes had refused to have their work included in this collection. For a review of the first edition published in 1999, see *HLAS 60:3467*. [DAA]

1873 Almánzar Rodríguez, Armando.
Enigma; Alicia. Santo Domingo: Dirección General de la Feria del Libro, 2014. 353 p.

Two nouvelles, *Enigma* and *Alicia* by Armando Almánzar Rodríguez, the novelist and noted film critic who died in July 2017, are published here in one volume. The writer received the highest literary recognition in the Dominican Republic, the Premio Nacional de Literatura (National Literary Prize), in 2012. In interviews, Almánzar Rodríguez pointed to Gabriel García Márquez as his main literary influence. Mostly known for his short stories, he explores obsession in *Alicia* and crime in *Enigma*. *Alicia* is the story of the inexplicable obsession of one man for the face of an unknown woman, glimpsed from afar. In this first-person narration there is an uncertain frontier between the lived and the imagined experiences of the protagonist. *Enigma* is a crime thriller that explores the apparent suicide of a young man who falls from the roof of a building. [DAA]

1874 Álvarez, Carlos Manuel. La tribu: retratos de Cuba. Prólogo de Martín Caparrós. México: Sexto Piso, 2017. 257 p. (Sexto Piso realidades)

This book of chronicles comes with acclaim from some notable critics. The Argentine writer and journalist Caparrós in his prologue praises highly Álvarez's writing style. The journalist and American writer Jon Lee Anderson writes that this is a must-read book for anyone who is Cuban or who has feelings for the country. The themes of decadence and a certain understated hopelessness characterize the life stories of the well-known, real-life Cuban personalities who Álvarez interviews. For example, and most poignantly, Álvarez follows the life of a former Tropicana cabaret dancer who now survives from the refuse in a dumpster. He ponders what the salsa group Bam Bam meant to generations of Cubans. The theme of cultural repression is also prominent in his interview of the elderly poet Rafael Alcides, who died in June 2018. The author found him living in a garage converted into an apartment, ostracized and censored. In another chronicle, he tells of his father's attempt to survive in Miami by picking coconuts to sell to a processing company. His father had been a doctor in Cuba, and a former supporter of the Castro government. Despite the drama inherent in these chronicles, Álvarez shuns the pathetic or the melodramatic in a restrained style of storytelling. [DAA]

1875 Andújar, Rey Emmanuel. Los gestos inútiles. Santo Domingo: Ediciones Cielonaranja, 2016. 175 p.

The brief novel was awarded the Premio Latinoamericano de Novela Alba Narrativa for 2015. This literary award was created in 2010 by Cuba in conjunction with Venezuela to promote the work of younger writers. Andújar's fictional world is one of dispersion and immigration, political corruption and drug trafficking. The plot centers on the days spent on the island when a Dominican psychologist who lives in Barcelona makes a return trip for family reasons. [DAA]

1876 Aponte Alsina, Marta. PR 3 Aguirre. Cayey, Puerto Rico: Sopa de Letras, 2018. 365 p.

Relato híbrido que combina narración novelesca, textos históricos, documentos, informes, diarios, selecciones de prensa y entrevistas para desarrollar la historia del poblado de Aguirre en Salinas, municipio en la parte sur de Puerto Rico. Hablar de Aguirre implica hablar de las relaciones coloniales entre Puerto Rico y los Estados Unidos y el rol de los inversionistas norteamericanos venidos de Boston a desarrollar y explotar la central azucarera a finales del siglo XIX y principios del XX. Al explorar ese mundo descubrimos la historia física, el encuentro con el otro, las diferencias sociales culturales y económicas, así como las luchas obreras representadas en el texto, particularmente las huelgas obreras de 1905. Producto de una cuidadosa investigación y marcada por una fina observación de la espacialidad y la temporalidad representadas, el texto aparece narrado con sutileza y maestría. [MGC]

1877 **Arroyo Pizarro, Yolanda.** Menorragia: histerias de octubre. San Juan: Instituto de Cultura Puertorriqueña, 2014. 115 p.

Esta colección de narraciones recibió el primer premio de la categoría cuento en la premiación literaria del Instituto de Cultura Puertorriqueña del año 2015. El libro consta de 17 relatos breves divididos en cuatro secciones: "Histerias de iniciación," "Histerias históricas," "Histerias perversas," y "Histerias del cuerpo." La autora maneja muy bien la construcción de personajes, creíbles todos. Logra incorporar efectivamente consideraciones de raza y sexualidades múltiples y diversas. Los referentes históricos de la segunda parte aparecen plasmados con originalidad y gran humanidad. Las historias perversas y las del cuerpo hurgan en zonas incómodas y necesarias de la mente de los lectores. [MGC]

1878 **Baquero, Gastón.** Ensayos selectos. Madrid: Editorial Verbum, 2015. 430 p.: bibl., index. (Verbum Ensayo)(Serie Biblioteca cubana)

This work presents an important collection of essays by one of Cuba's leading poets and intellectuals in the 20th century. Most of the essays appeared originally in newspapers in Cuba and from 1959 onward in Spain, where the writer lived until his death in 1997. In his introduction, Pío Serrano highlights the singularity of Baquero, who was born into a very poor family in 1914. This circumstance meant that he worked from a very young age. He was biracial, which also meant that he encountered racial prejudice. Neither circumstance, poverty or race, deterred him from becoming an important poet who belonged to the celebrated "originista" group led by José Lezama Lima. Furthermore, after accepting a position in the fifties offered to him by the dictator Fulgencio Batista, he became a problematic figure in intellectual and social circles in Havana. This collection of essays chosen by Serrano reveals the breadth and depth of Baquero's cultural and historical knowledge as well as his intellectual acumen. The essays are divided into three categories: the first deals with essays about poetics, the second about the arts and history of Cuba. The last section brings together essays about the poetry of international writers. Baquero wrote extensively about poetry; his essays address the writings of such poets as Emily Dickinson, Rainer Maria Rilke, Vicente Huidobro, Paul Claudel, Goethe, César Vallejo, and Gerardo Diego. The essay, "El negro en Cuba," deals precisely with human racial prejudice, and is an even-handed and intellectual treatise on the consequences of human interaction. This book is a good resource for some of his essays, especially those addressing the esthetics of poetry. [DAA]

1879 **Barradas, Efraín.** Inventario con retrato de familia. San Juan: Ediciones Callejón, 2018. 103 p. (Colección Litoral. Literatura)

Los 23 escritos que componen este libro cristalizan la intencionalidad y resumen la importancia de fijar esas aparentemente evanescentes historias de todos los días, aquella famosa *pequeña historia* que explica lo que la otra con frecuencia excluye, nubla o menosprecia. En el libro, Barradas recupera su historia familiar mientras se da a la tarea de limpiar y cerrar la casa de sus padres, la casa en la que se ha criado. Este inventario detallado y muy humano de su historia familiar, tan única y personal resulta también representativa de la historia puertorriqueña amplia. Ofrece, además, una mirada detallada de los espacios representados, especialmente el de pueblos como Aguadilla donde comunidad e historia ofrecen una óptica más amplia del Puerto Rico de los siglos XX y XXI. [MGC]

1880 **Cabiya, Pedro.** Reinbou. New York: Zemí Book, 2017. 287 p. (Zemí book; 6)

Reconocido por sus ficciones *Historias tremendas* (1999), *Historias atroces* (2003), *La Cabeza* (2005) *Trance* (2007) y

Mala Hierba (2011), todos textos bastante alejados de la ficción realista, *Reinbou* es la historia de Ángel Maceta, un niño soñador que cree en la magia de los arcoíris y que está en busca del padre que nunca conoció en tiempos de la Guerra Civil dominicana de 1965. Se trata de su primera novela de tema político o que deliberadamente se ocupa de plasmar una región territorial. La novela toma lugar en las calles de Santo Domingo. Tiene mucho de folklor, mitología caribeña, farmacopea pero polifónica. También tiene la complejidad textual a la que Cabiya ha acostumbrado a sus lectores. [MGC]

1881 **Caleb Acevedo, David.** Historias para pasar el fin del mundo. San Juan: Trabalis; Bayamón, Puerto Rico: Ediciones Aguadulce, 2015. 94 p. (Colección Cuir)

Esta colección de narraciones imagina que es el siglo XXII y una plaga convierte a todas las personas en homosexuales promiscuas. No hay manera de lograr la inseminación artificial, debido a que los espermatozoides mueren al exponerse al aire, y se espera que la humanidad llegue a su fin. La trama se narra desde el punto de vista de ocho personajes que cuentan su vida, o más bien, sus aventuras sexuales, sean heterosexuales u homosexuales, antes de la plaga. También se trabaja su presente dentro de la historia. Los ocho personajes están emparentados, se trata de unos ex-esposos y sus dos hijos, que comparten, junto a la pareja de cada cual, en una cabaña en Inglaterra. Durante esta reunión familiar, los ocho discuten y sostienen relaciones sexuales y hasta incestuosas entre sí, en anticipación del final de la humanidad. [MGC]

1882 **Cestero, Tulio Manuel.** Narrativa completa. Introducción y notas de Miguel D. Mena. Santo Domingo: Cielonaranja, 2016. 342 p.: bibl. (Biblioteca de literatura dominicana)

Considered one of the Dominican Republic's first important novelists, Cestero was also a diplomat. He died in Chile in 1955. His literary career began with the historical novel *La sangre: una vida bajo la tiranía*, which takes place during the dictatorship of Ulises Heureaux at the end of the 19th century. *La sangre*, his most important work of fiction, was first published in 1913. It remains significant in Dominican literature, and it is the last work included in this anthology of his work. It denounced, as the subtitle clearly indicates, the conditions under Heureaux's violent rule. However, this compilation begins with *El jardín de los sueños* (1909), short vignettes written in the Spanish American "modernista" style of prose, filled with allusions to classical and exotic themes. [DAA]

1883 **El compañero que me atiende.** Edición de Enrique del Risco. Middletown, Del.: Editorial Hypermedia, 2017. 471 p.

Kafka's *Process* (*The Trial*) annotated, explained, expanded, and exemplified in the tropics might give a reasonable account of the multiple voices of Cuban writers about state surveillance. Nevertheless, the editor, historian Enrique del Risco, assures the reader through the analysis of well-known cases that the multiple testimonies and short stories included in this anthology are far from being simply a weepy list of grievances. This body of work constitutes a needed statement about the impact of censorship, harassment, and surveillance on the personal and creative lives of Cuban artists. In some instances, the writer has been a privileged member, closely "attended" by the state agent assigned to monitor him or her. The texts are arranged chronologically, not just based on the writer's age, but because, according to Del Risco, surveillance and other methods of control implemented by the totalitarian regime have evolved. In the first phase, from 1959 to 1971, writers were either jailed or driven into exile. Along with the consolidation of power came a more nuanced type of vigilance—just in case the writer should "slip up." Some texts deal with perhaps the most internationally known case, the "Padilla Affair," when the poet Heberto Padilla was interned in Villa Marista, the school turned into a feared and infamous detention center for state security. The book includes the texts of contemporary writers such as Ahmel Echevarría, Orlando Luis Pardo Lazo, and the science fiction writer Yoss. In Echeverría's brief microstory, the "comrade" who comes to detain him, and whose screeching car wheels can be heard from his top floor apartment, is the same person who advised him to be careful as they kissed in a previous goodbye. Pardo Lazo expounds on the case of the political activist Oswaldo Payá, whose death—

explained by the state as a car accident—has been denounced as a state execution by his family members. In the introduction we learn that the title of this anthology comes from Leonardo Padura's novel *El hombre que amaba a los perros* about Ramón Mercader, Trotsky's assassin, who lived his last years in Havana. Del Risco explains that the title is an ironic phrase used as a metaphor for the insidious totalitarian control over the private lives of Cuba's citizens. [DAA]

1884 Cuba on the verge: 12 writers on continuity and change in Havana and across the country. Edited by Leila Guerriero. New York: Ecco, an imprint of HarperCollinsPublishers, 2017. 285 p.: ill.

As the subtitle indicates, this collection brings together 12 essays about contemporary Cuba. Six are written by Cuban writers and actors: Carlos Manuel Álvarez, Wendy Guerra, Leonardo Padura, the art critic Iván de la Nuez, and Vladimir Cruz, the actor who played one of the protagonists in the well-known film *Strawberry and Chocolate*. The other essays are by non-Cubans who have written about the island in the past, such as American novelist Francisco Goldman and journalist Jon Lee Anderson. The editor and author of the introduction is an Argentine journalist. The essays are of uneven quality. Some incur the seemingly unavoidable clichés of tropical sensuality, the Tropicana club with its chorus girls, and gay sexual tourism. [DAA]

1885 Escenas del yo flotante: Cuba: escrituras autobiográficas. Edición de Carlos A. Aguilera y Idalia Morejón Arnaiz. Leiden, The Netherlands: Bokeh Press 2017. 143 p.: ill. (Narrativa)

This anthology is comprised of six brief texts from contemporary artists. The brief texts include a poem from Néstor Díaz de Villegas, a text on the work of visual artist Sandra Ramos, narratives about exiles in Rome from Omar Pérez López and images of Germany by Carlos Aguilera, and a brief poignant account of child abuse by Idalia Morejón Arnaiz. In her prologue to this edition, Adriana Kanzepolsky points out that the "I" represented as a "floating" identity has as much to do with the condition of being born on an island as with the drama of migration: the exiles and "inxiles" (*insilios*), the term applied to those who, while still living in Cuba, are disconnected and in discord with their surroundings. Kanzepolsky points out that although the six writers included in this edition are all in exile, there seems to be no nostalgia for the reality recreated in some of these texts. This distancing emphasizes the "floating" quality of the personal identity represented in these texts. [DAA]

1886 Estévez, Abilio. Archipiélagos. Barcelona: Tusquets Editores, 2015. 461 p. (Colección Andanzas; 866)

Estévez's novel takes place during the troubled Depression era of the thirties under the dictator Gerardo Machado, known in Cuban history as the "machadato." On the one hand, this historical novel recalls the ambitious scope of 19th-century fiction. The author's initial two-page presentation of characters would seem to confirm this intent. However, it simultaneously reveals the deliberate distancing in its fragmentation of the fictional whole. It shows slyly its double-edged intention, for how could a reader be helped at the beginning of the novel by the presentation of a long list of characters with fragmentary remarks about their lives? The historical grounding is accomplished by inserting historical state crimes committed by the Machado regime, but the flow of consciousness of the different first-person narrators assaults the reader with indeterminacy. The novel begins with a tragically well-known episode of a crime committed by the state: a mass murder in Havana. A rumor had spread on the radio that the dictator Machado had left the country. Crowds gathered in the streets of Havana to celebrate. But Machado's chief of police was waiting for them; it had been a false rumor. The police machine-gunned the people, killing many unarmed civilians. The Havana in this novel is populated with characters who are historically grounded. The fictional and historical-based characters reveal the immigrant composition of the city. The characters come (or are the children of people) from the Canary Islands (Spain), China, or Yucatán (Mexico). There are also the reverse migrations of Cubans who return to the island. Some of these characters were born, for example, in Paris, because their parents had sought refuge there during the

19th-century Cuban wars. The novel offers a broad historical panoramic view of a society represented, inversely, in a fragmentary novelistic discourse with a chorus of voices that destabilizes the narrative flow. The first-person narration alternates with the third person. At the beginning of the novel, the romantic German writer Heinrich von Kleist is cited. In one of his most famous essays, "On the Marionette Theater," von Kleist developed a complex argument about the concept of self-consciousness in artistic creation. It is a pertinent insight in Estévez's rewriting of the traditional literary genre of the historical novel. [DAA]

1887 **Font Acevedo, Francisco.** La troupe Samsonite. San Juan: Folium, 2016. 195 p. (En babia. Narrativa)

Sin duda uno de los escritores de prosa más interesantes de los últimos años en la isla y en toda América Latina. Sus dos primeros libros, *Caleidoscopio* (2004) y *La belleza bruta* (2010) (véase HLAS 62:2301) le abrieron un espacio en la escena literaria. Su tercera oferta *La troupe Samsonite* lo consolida como una de las voces más importantes en la literatura puertorriqueña. En la *La troupe Samsonite* nos encontramos ante una historia aún más atrevida que desafía los modelos convencionales de escritura y lectura. Para crearlo, el autor ha diseñado un aparato narrativo caracterizado por el flujo de conciencia, la evocación y la dislocación de la voz narrativa. Todo esto se logra a través del vértigo impreso en esta historia por la característica principal de sus protagonistas: son una familia de circo. De particular interés y efectividad es la manera en que el texto asume el tropo circense para auscultar los espacios urbanos precarios. La fuerza lírica y profundamente humana con que este texto representa a los artistas que laboran al margen es una de las muchas fortalezas de este libro. [MGC]

1888 **Fuster Lavín, Ana María.** Mariposas negras: novela. San Juan: Isla Negra Editores, 2016. 253 p. (Colección La montaña de papel)

Esta novela participa de varias tradiciones escriturarias: ficción juvenil, peripecias afines al género gótico, sexualidad, violencia, intriga. En sus cuatro partes la novela se adentra a distintas capas del tejido social. La primera sección está marcada por una seria crítica social, urbana, humor negro, reflexión sobre las rutinas, la apatía social ante los "otros", y siempre, la soledad, la falta de solidaridad, la falta de equidad. La segunda sección, más experimental, es un cuento gótico-sicológico-erótico (dividido en micro-cuentos), sobre una mujer que ha enloquecido. La tercera parte está construida a base de micro-cuentos que reflexionan acerca del acto de escribir, sobre la creatividad, también son líricos, góticos, eróticos, divertimentos. La cuarta y última parte regresa a la atmósfera de la primera con pinceladas también de las dos anteriores, trata el lado cruel del ser humano, mucho humor negro. [MGC]

1889 **Gautier, Manuel Salvador.** Gregorio y su mundo perfecto: una saga antillana del siglo XIX. La Esperilla, Dominican Republic: Santuario, 2016. 237 p.: bibl.

The novel is based on the historical character of Gregorio Riva, who introduced the first railroad to the island. The author claims that this novel is a fictional recreation of the Dominican progressive entrepreneur. The character of the Puerto Rican 19th-century nationalist Ramón Betances (the men were classmates) also appears in the story, which takes place during the government of strongman Ulises Heureaux at the end of the 19th century. See also item 1882. [DAA]

1890 **Guerra, Wendy.** Domingo de Revolución. Barcelona: Anagrama, 2016. 224 p. (Narrativas hispánicas; 563)

This is the most recent novel from the author who won the 2006 Bruguera Prize for her first novel, *Todos se van* (*Everybody Leaves*), a semi-autobiographical account of growing up in Cuba. A movie version of that novel with the same title came out in 2013. *Domingo de Revolución* appears to be another semi-autobiographical account, this time with a female protagonist who is a successful writer abroad, but who is not published in her own country. Living alone in an old mansion, she is under constant surveillance by state security forces, who have installed hidden cameras and microphones. A family secret and a brief affair with a Hollywood actor of Latin background collide in this tale of a silenced writer. Guerra claims that she is unknown in her own country. Nevertheless, the writer is well-connected in cultural circles: she dedicates her novel to "Gabo," the Colombian writer Gabriel García Márquez, who was a mentor. The character of the foreign actor seems to be a veiled reference to Benicio del Toro, who was the protagonist in the Hollywood film *Che*. Guerra was involved in writing the script for that movie. The intrigue about her own background and state secrets is part of the novel's plot that is ultimately a tale of a writer who faces censorship at home and success abroad. [DAA]

1891 **Guerrero, Laureano.** La sentencia: novela. La Esperilla, Dominican Republic: Editorial Santuario, 2015. 168 p.

The social and political conflicts between the Dominican Republic and Haiti are laid bare in this brief novel that addresses the ethnic and racial tensions felt by Dominicans towards the Haitian immigrants living on the Dominican side of the border that divides the island. While exposing the hardships and poverty of the Haitians' living conditions, the novel also explores the conflicted feelings towards this minority group in the Dominican Republic through the characters of a Dominican family that initially tries to improve the Haitians' living conditions. [DAA]

1892 **Gutiérrez Negrón, Sergio.** Dicen que los dormidos. Segunda edición. San Juan: Instituto de Cultura Puertorriqueña, 2015. 149 p.

Segunda novela de Gutiérrez que le mereció el primer premio de este género en el certamen del Instituto de Cultura Puertorriqueña del 2015. Hermosa, breve y lírica narración que narra la violencia urbana y sus secuelas. El texto cuestiona lo que le sucede a una familia cuando uno de sus miembros se ausenta mental y físicamente tras haber sido víctima de la violencia y tras su vuelta a su *cotidianeidad* se ve obsesionado por la venganza. Uno de los logros más acertados es la cuidadosa y delicada representación de la relación entre los dos hermanos. [MGC]

1893 **Hacer y deshacer el amor: 7 narradores cubanos contemporáneos.** Selección y prólogo de Alex Fleites. La Habana: Ediciones Unión, 2015. 180 p.: portraits.

The editor points out in her brief preface that this is a collection, not an anthology, based both on the common theme of the human feeling of love and on the quality of the fiction. For Fleites, the writers in this personal selection are the best Cuban contemporary fiction writers. The 14 short stories come from the pen of seven well-known Cuban writers: Leonardo Padura, Senel Paz, Arturo Arango, Luis Manuel García Méndez, Francisco López Sacha, Reinaldo Montero, and Miguel Mejides. Each writer is represented with two short stories. [DAA]

1894 **Jovine Bermúdez, Federico.** Vuecencia: novela. Santo Domingo: Ediciones Alambique de Letras, 2015. 238 p.

The poet, novelist, and translator Jovine Bermúdez (d. January 2017) offers in this novel a pessimistic view of his country's early colonial past. The island, the first seat of Spanish colonial power in the New World in the 16th century, became a forgotten and impoverished outpost by the 17th century due to its geographic location, far from the maritime transatlantic commercial route. This historical novel recreates the early colonial society dominated by the power of the Church that implemented the Inquisition and thus controlled oppressively the early settlements. [DAA]

1895 **Llano, Eduardo del.** Omega 3. La Habana: Editorial Letras Cubanas, 2015. 362 p. (El cuento)

One of the film scriptwriters for the subversive 1991 comedy *Alice in Wondertown* (*Alicia en el pueblo Maravilla*), Llano is also known for his satiric shorts, some of which can be found on YouTube about his character Nicolas O'Donnell. *Omega 3* is a seeming narrative bric-a-brac of many short stories that include science fiction. Underneath the literary banter is an undercurrent of political satire, as in the story "Un cuento gótico." The leftist who stays in an apartment where there have been sightings of Marx, Lenin, and even Stalin and Mao, later is unsure of what he saw, whether it was the fleeting apparition of Karl Marx or Charlie Manson. The story "Fucking Lennon" is the tale of two sisters: one is a member of the Communist Party who ends up in London married to a British taxidermist, and the other, the sister, is a diehard rocker. The sister who lives in London brings a tube filled with Lennon's semen so her sister can be impregnated and have his child. The absurd, the ludicrous, and the improbable collude in this plot that invites a not-so-nonsensical reading of Cuban realities. [DAA]

1896 **López Bauzá, Juan.** El mar de Azov. San Juan: Libros AC, 2016. 331 p.

Esta tercera novela de López Bauzá está centrada en un individuo solitario, un tal Martín León Mercado, que narra, sin aparente destinatario, su historia. El texto está dividido en capítulos, agrupados en cuatro secciones, donde se juega con el tiempo y, posiblemente, las fronteras entre lo real y la fantasía. Escuchamos la voz del protagonista a lo largo de sus 22 capítulos y de tres de los cuatro fragmentos que inician cada una de las secciones en las que se divide el relato. Se trata de una novela paródica que gira en torno a un supuesto castillo en el pueblo de Guayanilla, localizado en el sur. Las claves que estructuran la novela son el misterio, la fantasía, la parodia y la caricatura. A pesar de que la trama puede resultar un tanto complicada, la novela seduce por su hábil caracterización y ágil escritura. [MGC]

1897 **Lozada Pérez, Hiram.** Los muertos se visten de blanco: novela policíaca. San Juan: Isla Negra Editores; Santo Domingo: Isla Negra Editores, 2015. 122 p. (Colección La montaña de papel)

En esta nueva novela de Lozada Pérez, su tercera, el escritor puertorriqueño incursiona en el género policíaco en una narración que une los elementos que típicamente se relacionan con el género (una masacre, un enigma y una investigación) junto a lo fantástico, lo poético y lo que podría llamarse una galería de antihéroes. La novela está escrita en 21 capítulos y narrada en múltiples voces. La misma cuenta la historia de la vida de un corrillo en el residencial Villa Flores. Allí seis amigos, Andy, Pello, Rey, Rafa, el Gordo y Antonio, celebran lo que el dinero fácil, adquirido por vías ilícitas, les puede ofrecer en el mundo precario en que se mueven. El Gordo traiciona el grupo, lo que da paso a una horrible matanza, donde mueren todos. En muchos aspectos el texto reflexiona acerca de la precariedad, la violencia y las múltiples desigualdades. [MGC]

1898 **Mañana hablarán de nosotros: antología del cuento cubano.** Prólogo de Norge Espinosa. Recopilación de Michel García Cruz. Madrid: Dos Bigotes, 2015. 280 p.

In his prologue to this collection of short stories that incorporate the homoerotic experience, Espinosa provides the literary background of this theme throughout 19th-and 20th-century Cuban literature. Published by a Spanish editorial house that specializes in LGBT literature, this anthology includes short stories by recent Cuban writers living both on the island as well as abroad. Ahmel Echevarría's *Esquirlas* (*Splinters*) incorporates the experiences of the writer with the erotic—and the homoerotic—within the boundaries of the unavoidable surveillance in a police state. The short story "El día de cada día" ("Day After Day") delves into the psychological consequences of scarcity and prostitution in today's Havana. While some of these writers reside in Cuba, which has a history of political gay repression, José Félix León, who lives in Barcelona, encounters the traumatic experience of gay sex with a perfect stranger in "Dolor" ("Pain"), which serves to underscore the isolation of living far from home. This is a collection of short stories written by Cubans born mostly in the seventies and eighties. Abilio Estévez, Carlos Pintado, Ahmel Echevarría, Anna Lidia Vega, Raúl Flores Iriarte, and Luis Yuseff are some of the well-known writers who contribute to this anthology of gay fiction. [DAA]

1899 **Marcallé Abréu, Roberto.** Bruma de gente inhóspita; novela. Dominican Republic: Biblioteca de Roberto Marcallé Abreu, 2015. 403 p.

The author, who was awarded the 2015 Premio Nacional de Literatura in the Dominican Republic, continues exploring the themes of political corruption and social violence in this novel. The political class is involved in criminal activities and the greed is uncontrolled. For some Dominican literary critics, the sinister chaos in the higher spheres of power represented in this novel are very close to actual current events on the island. [DAA]

1900 **Marcallé Abréu, Roberto.** En la oscuridad de la habitación: historias. Dominican Republic: MC Editorial, Biblioteca Roberto Marcallé Abreu, 2014. 154 p.

This prolific writer's background as a newspaperman is evident in these 11 mostly crime stories. The extreme street violence is a principal theme in this collection. For example, in the short story "Excúsenme, no era mi intención," a gang member's discourse is an apologetic explanation for a robbery gone violent: the victim, an invalid, ends up hacked to death with a machete. The first-person narrator gives voice to the perpetrator who nevertheless reveals the grisly nature of the violence while trying to explain it away. [DAA]

1901 **Materyn, Diego.** Frenesí del conejo universal. Buenos Aires: Mansalva, 2015. 74 p. (Colección poesía y ficción Latinoamericana; 116)

Esta inusual novela está narrada en la forma de monólogos de 10 alumnos de secundaria que reflexionan en voz alta en turnos separados. El texto ofrece una instantánea distinta y peculiar de los que se piensa que es el lenguaje deformado, entorpecido o intervenido de muchos jóvenes. En lugar de narrar anécdotas el lector se enfrenta a lo que podría verse como presagios, incluso estragos. Totalmente distinta a la literatura que narra este tipo de literatura juvenil el texto deviene una suerte de texto silente, un texto que se niega a hablar. Escrita con gran imaginación, al alejarse a los modelos tradicionales de la literatura juvenil para darle peso y solidez a sus personajes. [MGC]

1902 **Mattos Cintrón, Wilfredo.** El Evangelio según Luzbel: novela. San Juan: Ediciones La Sierra, 2015. 240 p.

En esta enigmática novela Luzbel, al ser expulsado del cielo, decide regresar a la tierra a predicar su evangelio en la encarnación de Jesús de Galilea. En esta versión, gracias a Luzbel, Jesús atraviesa múltiples avatares que le permiten enfrentar en carne propia el dolor de los humanos. Enigmática, complicada y sugerente historia, la novela pretende reflexionar acerca de los orígenes del los seres humanos, de dónde venimos y hacia adónde vamos. [MGC]

1903 **Mattos Cintrón, Wilfredo.** La vida es una enfermedad sexualmente transmisible: novela. San Juan: Ediciones La Sierra, 2014. 220 p.

Una de las características que distingue a esta novela es su representación de la interacción de dominicanos y puertorriqueños dentro de este relato policial escrito con imaginación y con soltura. La anécdota es bastante típica. Describe cómo el asesinato de Aparicio Malverde, un conocido hombre de negocios, divide a la comunidad dominicana de la que formaba parte. Miña Toral, una joven dominicana, esclavizada en un terrible burdel, le pide ayuda su familia a través de un mensaje escrito en un pedazo de papel y que dice: "¡Sáquenme de aquí!" Dos casos mezclados le revelan a Isabelo Andújar a un perverso personaje conocido como El Maestro, importador de mujeres y niños dominicanos para trata humana. En medio de todo eso aparece una historia de amor marcada por la tragedia. Es importante la manera humana con que se crean estos personajes así como la representación de ambos extremos de la realidad socioeconómica de la comunidad dominicana emigrada. [MGC]

1904 **Michelena, José Antonio.** Cuba: memoria y desolvido. Prólogo de Leonardo Padura. Madrid: Ediciones La Palma, 2015. 188 p.: bibl., ill. (Colección Cuba; 1)

While the writer and journalist Michelena published a book about the Cuban novelist Leonardo Padura, in this edition Padura obliquely returns the favor, writing the prologue to Michelena's book. This collection brings together newspaper chronicles that were first published in the Cuban review *Cultura y Sociedad.* Michelena's columns appeared as a standard feature in a section titled: "Cuba, más acá del olvido." Padura links Michelena's historical chronicles to the 19th-century tradition of *costumbrismo* that appeared in Cuban periodicals of that period. Michelena's articles are an assortment of researched historical curios: from the 16th-century Cuban pirate who once sailed with Sir Francis Drake ("Piratas en La Habana") to investigating the historical truth behind a famous incident attributed to the French 19th-century actress Sarah Bernhardt, who reputedly called Cubans "Indians in frock coats" when she first performed in Havana. According to Michelena's "Sarah Bernhardt, Mazantini y los toros," the French actress, when asked about it much later, said she did not recall her words, but was sure that she never "said anything about frock coats" (p. 96). These brief vignettes are narrated by intertwining historical facts with amusing anecdotes, from Edith Piaf's visit to Havana to urban legends about the city's streets, movie houses, and former town criers. [DAA]

1905 Montero, Mayra. El capitán de los dormidos. San Juan: Ediciones Callejon, 2015. 219 p. (Coleccion litoral)

El capitán de los dormidos, mezcla diversos intereses e intenciones: política, psicológica, gótica, de intriga, caribeña, folletinesca. Mayra Montero escribe el relato con fluidez, con deliberada ambigüedad, manteniendo la intriga hasta la última página. Armada con un trama compleja y diversa, Montero sitúa la acción principal en 1950, cuando las tropas estadounidenses se entrenan en Panamá e invaden la pequeña isla de Vieques. La presencia norteamericana en la Isla Nena coincidirá con el año del fracasado intento de revuelta nacionalista en el que participará el padre de Andrés, hijo de los dueños de un hotelito en la isla, y en la que morirá Roberto, el amante de su madre. La complejidad de acciones y tiempos es considerable. Los referentes históricos son manejados con acierto. Para comentario sobre la primera edición, véase *HLAS 60:3505*. [MGC]

1906 Morelli, Rolando D.H. Cuentos argentinos de Cuba para un editor español. Madrid: Editorial Verbum, 2017. 104 p. (Biblioteca cubana)

Although reduced mostly in the popular imagination to Che Guevara, the relationship between Cuba and Argentina had many other connections. In the sixties, Cuba received and at times invited several left-wing visitors from this and other South American countries who relocated to the island in search of a promised political utopia. Later there would be exiles from the right-wing Argentine military dictatorship. The fate of some of these confused, displaced, and disenchanted characters—fictional but based on personal experience according to the author—is narrated in these short stories. These escapees of one dictatorship end up trapped in another. The loss of ideological innocence is one of the main themes of these short stories. [DAA]

1907 Pablo en Bohemia. Textos de Pablo de la Torriente Brau y otros autores. Compilación, prólogo y notas por Leonardo Depestre Catony. La Habana: Ediciones La Memoria, Centro Cultural Pablo de la Torriente Brau, 2015. 272 p.: bibl., ill. (Palabras de Pablo)

Pablo de la Torriente Brau was a Puerto Rican-born Cuban journalist and left-wing activist who died in 1937 fighting on the side of the Spanish Republic during the Spanish Civil War. According to the web site of the Fundación Cultural Miguel Hernández, the Spanish poet Hernández, who fought at times alongside Torriente Brau, was one of the men who carried his corpse (which was never sent back to Cuba). Torriente Brau was an intellectual as well as a political activist who moved in Cuban literary and political circles. Jailed during the Machado dictatorship, he later went into exile in New York City with his wife, Teté Casuso, a Cuban writer and political activist. This book presents a collection of some of his writings that appeared in the influential Cuban magazine *Bohemia*. Not all of these writings were political; "Guajiros en Nueva York" ("Cuban Hillbillies in New York") is a chronicle about an art exhibit at a New York gallery of the Cuban artist Antonio Gattorno. In the article, Torriente Brau offers a defense of the negative stereotypes associated with the Cuban rural population. The other half of the book includes several articles written about him by prominent political and literary figures such as Raúl Roa, Agustín Acosta, and more recently Jaime Sarusky and Víctor Casaus. The book concludes with several historical photographs. [DAA]

1908 Padura Fuentes, Leonardo and Laurent Cantet. Regreso a Ítaca. Barcelona, Spain: Tusquets, 2016. 202 p. (Andanzas; 881)

This book is a novelized version of the coauthored script from the 2014 movie of the same title directed by French screenwriter Laurent Cantet. The film is about a gathering of middle-aged *habaneros* who revisit and rehash their past. Unavoidably the hopes, dreams, and aspirations of their youth collide with an implacable present. The theme of exile or immigration is also evident, since they meet when one of the members of their group makes a return trip to Havana after many years of living in Spain. [DAA]

1909 Pagán Vélez, Alexandra. Amargo. San Juan: La Secta de los Perros, 2014. 199 p.: ill.

Amargo se divide en tres partes, cada una introspectiva y compleja. Las secciones se titulan *Locura, Deseo, Mito*. Estos relatos cotidianos muestran la capacidad narrativa de una escritora que logra plasmar personajes creíbles con quienes nos identificamos absolutamente, a la par que crea un perfil sicológico que le da peso y vitalidad a la historia. El manejo de situaciones cotidianas y la cristalización de los espacios en donde se mueven estos personajes es particularmente encomiable. [MGC]

1910 Pereira, Manuel. El beso esquimal. México: Textofilia, 2015. 183 p. (Colección Lumía; 33. Serie Narrativa)

The slogan of the student movement from the sixties, "the personal is political," takes on a dizzyingly sinister meaning when referring to Cuban personal lives. Oppressive and divisive politics are mirrored in the personal lives of the characters in this novel about a Cuban exile who returns to Havana after 12 years living abroad. The protagonist's tale of the four days and three nights spent in the city gives structure to this narrative of the return of the prodigal son. He returns to see his ailing and elderly mother who had refused to visit him because "she was afraid of flying." Her Alzheimer's prevents her from recognizing her own son, while he is torn with guilt for having left her behind. At one point later in the novel, he explains to his sister that he "had to leave" to build his life in spaces of freedom. His arrival to the island is marked by the fear of not being allowed to leave afterwards. The prose is peppered with sarcasm about Cuban daily life: the taxi driver who picks him up at the airport is really a mechanical engineer; the Havana Chinatown, emptied out of the Chinese who were driven out by the Revolution. By then, used to living in democratic societies, he sometimes forgets that it is dangerous to openly criticize the government on the island of Mirages ("Isla de Espejismos"), as he calls Cuba. At times, he is asked whether he is a foreigner. To the very end of his trip, he is tormented with feelings of remorse, for having been a coward and leaving his mother behind. [DAA]

1911 Pogolotti, Graziella. En busca del unicornio. La Habana: Ediciones Unión, 2015. 211 p.

The op-ed articles included in this book first appeared in the Cuban state publication *Juventud Rebelde* between 2006 and 2015, and were written by this well-known official literary critic. The opinion short pieces express the official point of view. In some instances, they highlight prominent figures such as Raúl Roa, Che Guevara, and Miguel Díaz-Canel, the current president of the island. [DAA]

1912 Prieto González, José Manuel. La revolución cubana explicada a los taxistas. México: Editorial Planeta Mexicana, 2017. 213 p.: ill.

In most cases, for people to say in public that they are Cuban is not a neutral statement. To identify oneself as being from the island transforms an individual into someone else's case study. Therefore, it is no surprise that the experience of the casual conversation with a taxi driver from anywhere in the world serves as the starting point for this part memoir, part political coming-of-age story of a Cuban writer whose parents enthusiastically collaborated with the revolutionary government, only to end up exiled much later in Miami. Prieto studied in the former Soviet Union, and ended up penniless in Mexico City with a family to support and looking for ways to make a living. In this book, he comes to terms with his own life story, which is overwhelmingly affected by the political situation in Cuba. Excerpts from the book were published in the Mexican cultural review *Letras Libres*. Prieto is duly pessimistic. In his opinion, nothing can truly change, so he reaches several polemical conclusions. He agrees with the revolutionary government's debatable claim that education and health have been accomplishments. Cubans, he advises, should come to terms with their own history and accept the Revolution in the same way that Mexicans have. At the same time, he recognizes the social, economic, and cultural impoverishment that the Cuban Revolution has brought to the country. Is it possible to attribute this divided and contradictory political consciousness to what has been termed postmemory? [DAA]

1913 Rabelo Cartagena, José A. Azábara: novela. San Juan: Isla Negra Editores, 2015. 155 p. (Colección La Montaña de Papel)

En la botánica *azábara* se refiere a una planta similar al áloe que tiene propiedades medicinales. En esta novela es el nombre de una isla que se hunde. Las causas para el hundimiento son desconocidas. Las reacciones de varios actores sociales dentro de Azábara resultan ser diversas y perplejas. Una galería de personajes muy bien delineados reaccionan de maneras diversas a esta inminente catástrofe. Todo esto lleva al lector a entender que el naufragio de Azábara es la metáfora de un país que zozobra entre los males contemporáneos: la corrupción de sus líderes, la apatía de sus ciudadanos, el mal uso de los recursos naturales y humanos. Esta novela, en apariencia *sencilla*, está narrada con gran acierto y control narrativo. También participa de un particular tono apocalíptico que veremos en *2063 y otras distopías* (véase item **1914**). [MGC]

1914 Rabelo Cartagena, José A. 2063 y otras distopías. San Juan: Isla Negra Editores; Santo Domingo: Isla Negra Editores, 2018. 196 p.

Colección de cuentos y micro-relatos escritos con un lenguaje preciso que relatan historias sorprendentes para un lector activo. Si el término *distopía*, presente en el título, designa un tipo de mundo imaginario, recreado en la literatura o el cine, que se considera indeseable y que suele contrastar con su opuesto: *utopía*, sirva el título de advertencia de lo que el lector encontrará entre las tapas. Los temas y personajes son variados: el poder le es devuelto a las mujeres, la presencia de imágenes futuristas ya anticipadas en el título; también los inevitables eventos apocalípticos, así como la presencia de un muy particular tipo de zombis. [MGC]

1915 Tatis Pérez, Vladimir et al. Con la misma moneda y otros cuentos. Santo Domingo: Editorial FUNGLODE, 2015. 89 p. (Premios Funglode/GFDD 2013. Cuento)

This brief collection leads with Vladimir Tatis Pérez's short story "Con la misma moneda" that received the first prize of the 2014 Premio Funglode de cuento Juan Bosch. The five additional stories are by writers who received honorable mentions for the award. Tatis' story, set in Madrid, deals with immigration, violence, and ethnic violence. In the past few decades, immigrants from different Latin American countries have settled in Spain, and their acceptance has been uneven. In this short story the protagonist is a "sudaca," a pejorative term for South Americans that is used in Spain. He has a violent past and is a wife-beater. After leaving a brothel filled with South American prostitutes, he meets a violent death at the hands of a Spanish gypsy, with whom he had had a minor altercation. (Gypsies are an ethnic minority in Spain as in other parts of Europe.) This is a well-written story by a new author who is a Dominican immigrant in Spain. The other authors included in this collection are Keiselim A. Montás, Olivier Batista Lemaire, José Beltrán, Omar Messón, and José Fernández Caminero. [DAA]

1916 Valdés, Zoé. La Habana, mon amour. Barcelona, Spain: Stella Maris, 2015. 173 p. (Ciudades y letras; 1)

Here Valdés gives us lyrical musings about the Cuban capital city. The title comes from Alain Resnais' well-known French New Wave film, *Hiroshima, Mon Amour*. The stories offer a mix of personal childhood and adult memories with evocations of historical landmarks of Havana, the novelist's birthplace. Valdés places her texts within the literary tradition of many other Cubana writers since the 19th century who have made of the city a literary motif and topos. The three initial epigraphs recall this literary tradition, since they are taken from the writings of the Countess of Merlin, Guillermo Cabrera Infante, and Reinaldo Arenas. They also ground the narrative from the point of view of Cubans who have seen Havana from the perspective of the émigré. This duality is a peculiarity of Cuban literature. Since the 19th century, many of its best-known writers have not lived in the country. Part memoir, the dedication grounds the narrative in the personal; Valdés dedicates her texts to her grandmother, her mother, and her daughter, who all hail from Havana. [DAA]

1917 **Vallejo, Osiris.** Dimensiones del espejo. Santo Domingo: Editora Nacional, 2015. 66 p.

This brief collection of 11 short stories received the 2014 Premio Letras de Ultramar de Cuentos awarded by the Dominican Cultural Commission in New York. The initial epigraph which quotes Jorge Luis Borges serves to introduces the themes of the fantastic, the confusion created by reflections, the loss of parents, and manuscripts. These themes are all recurrent in the author's literary production. Several of the short stories take place in New York City with characters who are Dominican immigrants. In ¡Volver a casa!, the character attempts to bridge a cultural gap: while an African-American insists that he is denying his "African" side, the Dominican tries to explain that he is from "an island in the Caribbean," which means he has another cultural identity. [DAA]

1918 **Veloz Maggiolo, Marcio.** El sueño de Juliansón: novela. La Esperilla, Dominican Republic: Editorial Santuario, 2014. 127 p.

Ostensibly this short novel is the story of an archeologist named Juliansón Omelet who is working in an ancient precolumbian archeological site not far from the present-day town of Santiago de los Caballeros. The plot serves as a starting point in a meandering tale peppered with many literary quotes about the power of myth and the substratum beneath the layers of civilizations. [DAA]

1919 **Veltfort, Anna.** Adiós mi Habana: las memorias de una gringa y su tiempo en los años revolucionarios de la década de los 60. Madrid: Verbum, 2017. 233 p.: bibl., ill. (Narrativa Verbum)(Biblioteca cubana)

This autobiographic graphic novel tells the story of the 10 years the German-born American artist spent in Havana. As a teenager, brought to the island by her American left-wing father, she integrates herself into the Havana lived by Cubans and doesn't remain confined to the privileged state-financed bubble created by the revolutionary government for foreign sympathizers who came to live or work on the island, principally in the sixties. The book is in color and, notably, is written in Spanish since Veltfort came to see herself as "aplatanada" (Cuban slang for a foreign-born individual who feels and becomes "Cuban"). She explains her parents' comfortably privileged existence and describes her encounters with many of the international artists and intellectuals who visited Havana in the sixties. As a Cuban, she witnessed the progressive scarcity of food and the deteriorating living standards of Cuban nationals that was not apparent within the enclave for foreigners who had access to goods that were forbidden to Cuban citizens. While studying at the Universidad de La Habana, she experienced ideological and sexual surveillance and censorship. The discovery of her own sexuality, when she had to hide she was gay, also made her aware of state repression. In the end, her family opted for leaving the island. [DAA]

LITERARY CRITICISM AND HISTORY

1920 **Álvarez Álvarez, Luis** and **Ana González Mafud.** De José Lezama Lima a Severo Sarduy: lenguaje y neobarroco en Cuba. Santiago de Compostela, Spain: Universidade de Santiago de Compostela, 2014. 253 p.: bibl. (Biblioteca de la Cátedra de Cultura Cubana 'Alejo Carpentier' de la USC; 11)

Neo-Baroque was a major stylist creation associated with some of the most prominent writers of 20th-century Cuban literature. This study examines that manifestation in José Lezama Lima, Alejo Carpentier, and Severo Sarduy. The book also includes a chapter dedicated to the work of poet Nicolás Guillén, which is arguably problematic since it stretches the concept of this literary movement. However, as defined broadly by these critics, the Neo-Baroque is a movement that incorporates the linguistic aspects of Spanish as spoken on the island. [DAA]

1921 El Atlántico como frontera: mediaciones culturales entre Cuba y España. Edición de Damaris Puñales Alpízar. Madrid: Editorial Verbum, 2014. 339 p.: bibl. (Verbum ensayo)

This collection of essays analyzes the cultural exchanges—not just demographic or political, although both factors are important—between Cuba and Spain. The different critics address such obvious figures as Gertrudis Gómez de Avellaneda, José Martí, and for the 20th century, Cubans such as Lydia Cabrera, Virgilio Piñera, and the origenistas' personal and cultural relations with Spanish writers—exiles from the Spanish Civil War—María Zambrano, Juan Ramón Jiménez, to the relatively unknow Catalan poet José María Fonollosa, who lived in Cuba in the fifties and composed "Romancero de Martí," included in this edition, dedicated to the poet and hero of Cuban independence. [DAA]

1922 Barradas, Efraín. Para devorarte otra vez: nuevos acercamientos a la obra de Luis Rafael Sánchez. Santo Domingo: Cielonaranja, 2017. 251 p.: bibl. (Letras de Puerto Rico en Ediciones Cielonaranja)

En el 1981, Barradas publicó un volumen crítico titulado *Para leer en puertorriqueño: acercamiento a la obra de Luis Rafael Sánchez*. Los siete capítulos de aquel libro exploraban varias texturas de la obra de Sánchez: teatro, cuento, novela, ensayo. Este nuevo libro contiene muchos ensayos que fueron publicados posteriormente en revistas y periódicos, junto a otros textos que originaron como presentaciones en congresos académicos. El libro estudia la casi totalidad de la obra de Sánchez hasta el presente. Mira, además, aspectos poco explorados del autor como, por ejemplo, su faceta como escritor académico. Los enfoques teóricos usados por Barradas también son múltiples: desde la estética neobarroca hasta las reflexiones sobre el travestismo físico y cultural. El texto también sostiene una importante conversación con otros críticos. [MGC]

1923 Centeno Añeses, Carmen. Intelectuales y ensayo. Río Piedras, Puerto Rico: Publicaciones Gaviota, 2017. 262 p.: bibl.

La tarea del análisis crítico es reflexionar, discutir y, en su caso, desmontar los dispositivos simbólicos e institucionales, reflexionando públicamente sobre los procesos y las prácticas culturales. El discurso privilegiado y camaleónico del ensayo ha asumido esa función desde sus orígenes. Este volumen se acerca de manera enjundiosa al ensayo político y cultural producido en Puerto Rico por figuras como Eugenio María de Hostos, Nilita Vientós Gastón, Edgardo Rodríguez Juliá, Aureamaría Sotomayor y Marta Aponte Alsina, entre otros. Para la autora, este género ha sido el discurso por excelencia para la interpretación de lo nacional e identitario. El libro interpela las voces e ideas de los ensayistas mencionados. [MGC]

1924 Chevalier, Nan. Pasión analítica: apuntes sobre escritores dominicanos e hispanoamericanos. Santo Domingo: UNAPEC, Universidad APEC. 2016. 437 p.: bibl., index.

Some of the major Latin Americans writers, from the "boom" to more contemporary writers, are analyzed in their literary context. The book's first chapter delves into Julio Cortázar's influence in Dominican literature. Subsequent chapters are dedicated to Mario Vargas Llosa, José Donoso, and Juan Carlos Onetti, and additional chapters focus on more recent writers such as the Peruvian Santiago Roncagliolo and Sergio Ramírez from Nicaragua. The rest of the book is dedicated to Dominican writers, among them the noted intellectual Juan Bosch and Virgilio Díaz Grullón, among others. [DAA]

1925 De Ferrari, Guillermina. Community and culture in post-Soviet Cuba. New York: Routledge/Taylor & Francis Group, 2014. 218 p.: bibl., index. (Routledge Interdisciplinary Perspectives on Literature; 23)

The critic applies contemporary neo-Marxist theories to the post-Soviet Cuban cultural production. Using Alain Badiou's concept of an "event," Cuba's 1959 Revolution represented a moment of "hopeful liberation" and as such "truth-process" that gives meaning to an epoch (p. 97). With the fall of the Soviet Union, Cubans must recognize the failure. For De Ferrari, cultural theorists such as Jean Baudrillard, Badiou, and Slavoj Žižek provide the conceptual framework to understand Cuban writers who address the debacle—social as well as ideological, such as Iván de la Nuez, Ena Lucía Portela, and Wendy Guerra, for example. This book addresses the work of writers of previous generations from different political persuasions such as Jesús Díaz, Leonardo Padura, Abel Prieto, and Abilio Estévez. Additional chapters are dedicated to the work of Pedro Juan Gutiérrez, Antonio José Ponte, and Guillermo Rosales. [DAA]

1926 De Sarlo, Giulia. En la piel de las mujeres: reescrituras de la dictadura trujillista en la ficción dominicana de los años 90. Madrid: Consejo Superior de Investigaciones Científicas; Sevilla, Spain: Universidad de Sevilla: Diputación de Sevilla, 2016. 366 p.: bibl. (Colección Americana; 55)

The period known as the *trujillato* continues to cast a long shadow over the Dominican Republic. De Sarlo presents the situation of women in this traumatic national period and considers its effect on fiction. The study includes writers who are not necessarily Dominican, and it is not exclusively about novels written by women, as the title might seem to suggest. Rather, the author analyzes how the violence of this period has been interpreted in fiction. She examines the novel by Spaniard Manuel Vázquez Montalbán, *Galíndez* (1990), that deals with the well-known story of the Spanish citizen who opposed Trujillo. The historical Galíndez was purported to have been abducted while living in New York and killed by assassins sent by Trujillo. The novel *The Farming of Bones* (1998) by the Haitian-American Edwidge Danticat is also included. Danticat's novel takes place with the backdrop of Trujillo's massacre of Haitians. De Sarlo also examines Mario Vargas Llosa's well-known novel about the period, *La fiesta del chivo* (2000; see *HLAS 58:3691* for the Spanish and *HLAS 62:3306* for the English translation). In another chapter, De Sarlo addresses the very well-known novel by the Dominican-American writer Julia Álvarez, *In the Time of the Butterflies* (1994). This book does not limit its analysis to literary criticism; rather, it offers a cultural and sociological study of the feminine condition during this period and how it has been represented and interpreted in fiction. [DAA]

1927 Duchesne Winter, Juan. Caribe, Caribana: cosmografías literarias. San Juan: Ediciones Callejón, 2015. 312 p.: bibl. (Colección En fuga. Ensayos)

Con rigor académico y gran originalidad este libro se replantea las nociones de *Caribe*. El uso de la palabra *cosmografía* en el título adelanta la manera en que este estudio erudito combina en su reflexión características físicas y culturales que combinan mapas, astronomía, elementos de la geografía a lo que el autor se refiere como "el rastreo del sentido del territorio." Ese sentido se hurga más allá de lo que típicamente se define como *espacio* caribeño. También amplía las nociones de lo que suele designarse como pensamiento caribeño, ofreciendo una reflexión que incorpora de manera certera el pensamiento amerindio y ampliando la discusión sobre nociones territoriales. Incorpora el pensamiento *Watunna*, la importancia del animismo en las culturas de la zona, reflexiones sobre el ser desde posturas indígenas y modos de organización social y política que van más allá del marxismo tradicional. Producto de una investigación y reflexión profundas, este provocador acercamiento abre una discusión importante sobre territorios, cultura, sociedad y pensamiento caribeños. [MGC]

1928 Harrison, Osvaldo di Paolo. Noir boricua: la novela negra en Puerto Rico. San Juan: Editorial Isla Negra, 2016. 171 p.: bibl. (Colección Visiones y cegueras)

Noir Boricua estudia no solo este género popular dentro de la tradición literaria puertorriqueña, sino que lo hace desde un ángulo muy preciso. El libro explora con incisivo detalle la variedad de fusiones genéricas que el investigador estudia en minuciosamente. Esa combinación incluye otros géneros populares como la novela rosa, detectives gay o fuera del armario, mujeres detectives, autobiografía, novela de auto-formación y ciencia ficción, entre otros. También presta atención a una serie de temas que dinamizan las actividades de estos detectives y que visibilizan algunos de los males sociales que aquejan a Puerto Rico: el narcotráfico, la violencia, los barrios marginales, el abuso sexual, la homosexualidad, el poshumanismo, la ecocrítica y la denuncia global, entre otros. Libro académico producto de una sólida investigación. [MGC]

1929 Hernández Salván, Marta. Mínima Cuba: heretical poetics and power in post-Soviet Cuba. Albany, N.Y.: SUNY Press, 2015. 262 p.: bibl., index, photos. (SUNY series in Latin American and Iberian Thought and Culture)

How did the rhetorical imaginary of the revolutionary sixties fare with what Hernández Salván finds as a trope that "functions as a signifier at three different levels that determine each other: as national subjectivity of Cubanness . . . as a rhetorical ethos (social realism and melodrama) and as a form of affect melancholy"? It seems not to have prospered. This study looks at the aftershocks of the nineties, during the *Período especial* ("Special Period in Time of Peace") in Cuba. The author analyzes the work of writers who became dissenters: Antonio José Ponte, the group Diáspora(s), Rolando Sánchez Mejías, and Iván de la Nuez, among others such as Carlos A. Aguilera and Pedro Márquez de Armas. She also explores the so-called revival in the interest about José Lezama Lima. The book concludes that in the work of these writers, as well as in that of others, the idea of literature as part of a project of social emancipation is discarded. [DAA]

1930 La Fountain-Stokes, Lawrence. Escenas transcaribeñas: ensayos sobre teatro, performance y cultura. San Juan: Editorial Isla Negra, 2018. 292 p.: bibl. (Colección Visiones y cegueras)

Escenas transcaribeñas es una compilación de ensayos, entradas de blog, columnas de periódicos y conferencias sobre teatro, performance, literatura, televisión y artes visuales, publicados en diversas fuentes (como *Claridad, El Nuevo Día, 8ogrados*) en Puerto Rico y otros lugares entre 1996–2017. Incluye traducciones del inglés al español, con un enfoque en temas LGBT y asuntos relacionados con masculinidades contemporáneas en Puerto Rico, México, y entre Latinxs en los EEUU. Este libro de crítica cultural combina de manera eficaz la interseccionalidad necesaria al estudiar representaciones culturales contemporáneas. También documenta la producción de piezas, eventos e intervenciones espontáneas o de limitada duración en escenarios. [MGC]

1931 Lalo, Eduardo. Intemperie. Buenos Aires: Corregidor, 2016. 140 p. (Archipiélago Caribe; 8)

El título de esta colección de ensayos o reflexiones en voz alta plasmadas en la página no podría ser más acertado. El vocablo *intemperie* se refiere a ambientes o entornos de tipo atmosférico que se consideran como una variante o también a la inclemencia del tiempo que afecta progresivamente a sitios, lugares, objetos o elementos que no están cubiertos o protegidos. Los ocho escritos incluidos en la colección reflexionan acerca de lo que significa vivir a la intemperie en ese entorno caribeño contemporáneo, tan diverso y tan cambiante. Implícito en los textos está nuestro lugar en el mundo, el de nuestro cuerpo físico, así como el de nuestra imaginación. ¿Qué hacer con nuestros cuerpos y nuestra geografía? ¿con las presencias y las ausencias? ¿con los excesos y las identidades? ¿Qué espacio le corresponde al mundo de la imaginación y de la creación en un mundo desarticulado? En el texto el cielo abierto, el deambular por la ciudad y la oscuridad de la noche sirven de marco para esta fina reflexión sobre el artista, el arte y los diversos espacios posibles para la creación. [MGC]

1932 Lucien, Renée-Clémentine. Requiem por la utopía en *Muerte de Nadie*, de Arturo Arango, y *El hombre que amaba los perros*, de Leonardo Padura. (*in* Iconofagias, distopías y farsas: ficción y política en América Latina. Madrid: Iberoamericana; Frankfurt am Main, Germany: Vervuert, 2015, p. 49–60)

This study of two Cuban novels by Arango and Padura concludes that they embody a requiem for a utopian vision transformed into dystopia. The failure of utopia is a recurrent theme in Cuban fiction written since the 90s. According to the critic, there is also often a demystification of the figure of the charismatic leader, as is the case in both of the novels analyzed. [DAA]

1933 Martínez Carmenate, Urbano. Milanés: las cuerdas de oro. Matanzas, Cuba: Ediciones Matanzas, 2013. 294 p.: bibl., ill., portraits. (Biografías)

The second version of the biography of the legendary poet José Jacinto Milanés was published as part of the commemoration of the 19th-century romantic poet's death in 1863. Milanés was part of the cultural circle of Domingo del Monte and was an important poet and playwright. His descent into madness—attributed to an unhappy love affair—and his support for his country's independence, have made him the prototype of the legendary romantic figure. His life seems to embody that of the romantic hero, with its mélange of a tragic love, irrationality, and his dedication to liberty. Martínez Carmenate's title is taken from verses dedicated to Milanés written by José Martí. This well-researched biography offers a more prosaic interpretation of the poet's life, disputing the romantic version of Milanés' mental illness with historical facts. [DAA]

1934 **Martínez-San Miguel, Yolanda.** Spanish Caribbean literature: a heuristic for colonial Caribbean studies. (*Small Axe*, 20:3, No. 51, Nov. 2016, p. 65–79)

This article offers a theoretical approach to propose the concept of "Spanish Caribbean" as a "functional category" to "understand better the colonial and postcolonial terrain of the region." The author bases the usefulness of this category on colonial "relaciones," the early accounts during the Spanish colonization of the region, and the travel narratives from the 16th century. According to this study, the area has been part of the "Spanish and US American empire." For a review of the full journal issue, see item **809**. [DAA]

1935 **Merced Hernández, Grisselle.** Cartas viajeras: Julia de Burgos, Clarice Lispector: versiones de sí mismas. San Juan: Nubedeletras Editorial, 2015. 408 p.: portraits.

Este denso estudio sobre el epistolario de Julia de Burgos y Clarice Lispector está sustentado en una documentación rigurosa de fuentes primarias y secundarias a la par de un aparato crítico y teórico sofisticado y pertinente. Esto le permite a Merced interpelar la escritura íntima de estas dos figuras monumentales de las letras latinoamericanas con herramientas teóricas que ayudan a ampliar el conocimiento de los textos estudiados. De particular interés es el análisis del epistolario de las hermanas Julia y Consuelo. La autora tuvo acceso a papeles personales de la familia de Burgos, cartas hasta hace muy poco inéditas. [MGC]

1936 **Nuez, Iván de la.** Iconofagia: los mitos de la revolución en la literatura actual latinoamericana. (*in* Iconofagias, distopías y farsas: ficción y política en America Latina. Madrid: Iberoamericana; Frankfurt am Main, Germany: Vervuert, 2015, p. 199–208)

This essay by the Cuban-born art critic and curator who currently lives in Spain is part of a book that gathers essays from different Spanish-speaking countries. All the essays explore the relationship between fiction and politics in contemporary literature. Nuez's starting point is Alejo Carpentier's exploration of revolutionary violence in the historical novel *El siglo de las luces (Explosion in a Cathedral)*. The novel's plot centers on the impact of the French Revolution in the Caribbean. Nuez points out that although Carpentier held an important cultural post in the Cuban Revolution, it took several years for the novel to be published. He compares the Revolution as a theme in other contemporary Latin American literature with three recent novels from Cuban writers whom he calls the "grandchildren" of Carpentier: Ahmel Echevarría Peré in *Días de entrenamiento* (2012); Jorge Enrique Lage's *Carbono 14: (una novela de culto)* (2010; see *HLAS* 72:2036), and José Antonio García Simón's *En el aire* (2011). For Nuez, the peculiarity of the topic in recent Cuban literature is that it is marked by a sensation of having lived in a permanent state of transition bereft of any future (p. 207). [DAA]

1937 **La patria albina: exilio, escritura y conversación en Lorenzo García Vega.** Edición de Carlos A. Aguilera. Leiden, Netherlands: Almenara, 2016. 196 p.: bibl.

García Vega was a disaffected member of the legendary *Orígenes*, the most important Cuban cultural magazine that published important Cuban and foreign writers from Virgilio Piñera, Gastón Baquero, and Eliseo Diego, to the translated work of Albert Camus and the artwork of Wifredo Lam. At the end of the seventies, already living outside the country, García Vega penned a scorched-earth account of the cultural group. In this book, he deconstructs the literary aura of the group and especially of José Lezama Lima, who by then had gained international renown for his novel *Paradiso* (see *HLAS* 44:5324). In a 2009 conference in Madrid, García Vega recounted his reasons for his love-hate relationship with the writer whom he called "Maestro," a parody that, like all parody, implies an homage despite the obvious derision. García

Vega's "Maestro por penúltima vez" closes this book that includes several critical essays from international writers and scholars about this self-proclaimed *enfant terrible* of *Orígenes*. His dismantling or deconstruction of *Orígenes'* national and literary *grand récit* became a cult book—as an exile his work had become practically inaccessible in Cuba—for a new generation of writers who created the literary magazine *Diáspora(s)*. Aguilera, the book's editor, belonged to the neovanguard group of writers. The essays explore such works by the author as "El oficio de perder" and "Rostros del reverso," among others. García Vega's texts are based on notions of the fragmentary and often seem to be incoherent collages.

His esthetic mode stood in direct contrast to the master discourse sought by the *Orígenes*. In addition to Aguilera's piece, the essays of several other well-known writers and critics, Cuban and foreign, are included in this critical assessment of García Vega, who died in Miami—a city he mocked as "playa albina"—in 2012. [DAA]

1938 La patria organizada . . . : (antología de narrativa del nacionalismo puertorriqueño). Edición de Reynaldo Marcos Padua. San Juan: Los Libros de la Iguana, 2015. 297 p.: bibl., ill.

El tema del nacionalismo en Puerto Rico ha sido motivo de varios volúmenes de investigación, historia, política y creación literaria. No se trata de un corpus particularmente amplio pero sí desempeña una función discursiva importante en distintos momentos de la historia del país. Este volumen recopila trabajos de ficción, testimonios y ensayos sobre el tema escritos a partir de la década de 1950. La recopilación tiene un valor como referencia sobre el tema. También contribuye a la visibilidad e historia de las discusiones sobre el nacionalismo en Puerto Rico. [MGC]

1939 Pérez Firmat, Gustavo. La Habana de Wallace Stevens. (*Cuba. Stud.*, 44, 2016, p. 214–229, bibl.)

Pérez Firmat analyzes the Cuban reception of Wallace Stevens' 1923 poem "Academic Discourse at Havana." The American poet had briefly visited the Cuban capital. The Cuban cultural publication *Revista de Avance* published a translation in its 1929 edition. When Stevens sent his book of poems, *Ideas of Order*, to José Rodríguez Feo, the latter responded by praising precisely that poem. Citing that incident, Pérez Firmat argues that Stevens' poem influenced one of José Lezama Lima's most important poems, "Una oscura pradera me convida," from his 1941 book *Enemigo rumor*. Pérez Firmat also delves into the meaning of the tropics and argues that it includes the duality between North and South, the concept of exotic in Stevens' poem. Lastly, Pérez Firmat points out the irony that by the time Stevens' book was published, the very popular Cuban song "El manisero" ("The Peanut Vendor") had been composed. "The Peanut Vendor" is from 1927 and Stevens' poem "Academic Discourse at Havana" was written in 1923, so the verse in his poem "a peanut parody/For peanut people" could not have been a reference to the popular tune. Although Pérez Firmat argues, as others have done previously, that the poem has very little to do with Havana, notwithstanding the title, the episode serves to highlight the cultural exchanges between important literary 20th-century American and Cuban modernist poets. [DAA]

1940 Ramos-Perea, Roberto. Tapia: el primer puertorriqueño: tratado biográfico sobre el dramaturgo y escritor puertorriqueño Don Alejandro Tapia y Rivera (1826–1882). San Juan: Publicaciones Gaviota, 2015. 995 p.: bibl., ill., facsimiles, portraits.

Estudio monumental de 995 páginas que documenta la biografía personal y literaria de Alejandro Tapia y Rivera, reconocido como el iniciador de lo que podría llamarse literatura puertorriqueña. Este tratado biográfico y filológico detalla la vida y la obra de Tapia y a través de ellas la historia misma de la literatura puertorriqueña. Este trabajo de erudición y paciencia estuvo gestándose por más de una década. Ramos Perea, destacado dramaturgo, director de teatro y promotor de la cultura y las letras, ofrece una obra imprescindible a todo aquel que se interese por la historia social, cultural, literaria y de las ideas de Puerto Rico. [MGC]

1941 Rebollo-Gil, Guillermo. Amigos en todas partes: en defensa de los agitadores. Cabo Rojo, Puerto Rico: Editora Educación Emergente, Inc., 2016. 140 p: bibl.

Este libro de Rebollo Gil continúa su exploración de la cotidianeidad puertorriqueña auscultada con lente incisivo en volúmenes previos. Publicado en el 2016, el libro recoge no solo la instantánea, la descripción del estado de cosas, sino que claramente establece la importancia de la acción social, en cualquiera que sea la forma en que se presente. Nuevamente muestra un oído aguzado que le permite representar las voces de una generación cuyas plataformas y altoparlantes están destinados a redirigir los discursos sociales. [MGC]

1942 **Rebollo-Gil, Guillermo.** Todo lo que no acontece igual: crónicas y comentarios. Cabo Rojo, Puerto Rico: Editora Educación Emergente, 2015. 170 p.

La vitalidad de la nueva crónica urbana y de textos híbridos que emulan nuevas formas de comunicación inmediata como los *tuits*, así como una definición muy personal de la forma e intención de los ensayos es lo que este texto propone a sus lectores *Todo lo que no acontece igual* en sus 33 entradas. Producto de una generación que ha tenido que enfrentar la disolución de un particular tejido social, una intensa crisis económica y devastadores desastres naturales, no es extraño que a lo largo de las páginas de este libro se hable de corrupción, crímenes, inestabilidad, falta de solidaridad, junto a imperceptibles actos de heroísmo cotidiano que nos recuerdan que no todo acontece igual. Los temas son variados y los ensayos breves y plagados de una libre asociación buscan interpelar a los lectores en busca de una reacción. [MGC]

1943 **Rebollo-Gil, Guillermo.** Última llamada. Carolina, Puerto Rico: Ediciones UNE: Biblioteca Jesús T. Piñero, Centro de Investigación Social, 2016. 204 p.: bibl., ill.

La función típica de un altoparlante es servir de amplificador de la voz. Suele relacionársele con un intento de alzar la voz, y por extensión, darle una voz más amplia a quien típicamente no la tiene. En *Última llamada*, Rebollo Gil le ofrece un altoparlante a espacios poco convencionales como videos de Youtube, comentarios publicados en medios sociales por los sujetos más oprimidos junto al discurso, al parecer, omnipotente, de las reacciones de los más privilegiados en la sociedad puertorriqueña y de los medios de comunicación. Según el propio autor su "palabra quiere convocar al sujeto que llama, grita, dice, y que, colocado detrás de un altoparlante, piensa que la voz no se borra del todo en la escritura." Este gesto lo lleva a alzar la voz a través de su literatura para visibilizar la violencia cotidiana y sistemática por género y raza; la estrecha relación entre la ley, el poder, la ética y la escritura; los límites de los discursos, entre ellos el literario; y la violencia del nombre y de la ley. [MGC]

1944 **Sankhé Adebowale, Maimouna.** Presencia del negro en la novela vanguardista hispanoamericana: tiempo y contratiempo. Madrid: Editorial Pliegos, 2016. 273 p.: bibl. (Pliegos de ensayo; 249)

The brief fourth chapter in this survey of *Negrismo* in vanguard prose in Latin America is dedicated to the often-overlooked Cuban writer Lino Novás Calvo. Although originally an immigrant from Spain, Novás Calvo's representations of Afro-Cuban culture in his short stories are mentioned. The study addresses the cultural elements, although curiously Novás Calvo's novel *El negrero*, about a slave trader, is not part of this analysis. Fernando Ortiz, the Cuban anthropologist, is a reference in this book. [DAA]

Andean Countries

JOSÉ CARDONA-LÓPEZ, *Regents Professor of Spanish, Texas A&M International University*
CÉSAR FERREIRA, *Professor of Spanish, University of Wisconsin-Milwaukee*

COLOMBIA AND VENEZUELA

LA NOVELA COLOMBIANA tiene ahora como referente inmediato de sus realidades narrativas la historia contemporánea y la actualidad, no la sociedad del siglo

XIX y otros anteriores, como ha sucedido en otros años. En *Cadáveres de papel*, Jairo Andrade recrea la memoria reciente del país a partir de la explosión de un avión que volaba de Bogotá a Cali en noviembre de 1989 y las circunstacias de corrupción que en la investigación posterior han rodeado a este crimen (item **1968**). De las últimas décadas de la violencia colombiana en el siglo XX se testimonia literariamente en *Como una melodía* de Juan Sánchez Cuervo (item **1986**). *La reina y el anillo* de Luis González Sarmiento es una novela negra en la que se explora creativamente un escándalo en las cúpulas de la policía nacional, lo que llevará a mostrar de nuevo la corrupción y falta del surgimiento de la necesaria verdad en procesos judiciales (item **1979**). Lo social y las luchas de sectores oprimidos de la población encuentran su voz novelada en *Rebelión de los oficios inútiles* de Daniel Ferreira (item **1976**), que trata sobre la toma de una tierra baldía por parte de unos campesinos y las acciones de paramilitares para desalojarlos. Flor Romero de Nohra en su *No me mates: ¡Te amo!*, construye historias en las que siempre la mujer es la víctima de maltrato, abuso sexual y asesinato (item **1984**). Son narraciones que unidas por una voz conforman la novela y muestran cómo la mujer es víctima en diversos países, no solo en Colombia. Las consecuencias de una sociedad desigual y de pocas opciones para una vida digna y con futuro se presentan al nivel de lo individual en *¿De donde flores si no hay jardín?* de Alonso Sánchez Baute (item **1985**). En *Regresos* de Luis Fayad de nuevo actores de la clase media se enfrentan a una sociedad cerrada y agobiante, en esta opotunidad a partir de un profesional que regresa a su país luego de vivir en el exterior por varios años (item **1975**). En la narrativa breve sobresale la novela corta *Juego de niños* de Guido Tamayo, la memoria de un grupo de hermanos se interna en la infancia que compartieron (item **1988**). En *El infinito se acaba pronto* de Joseph Avski se logra una excelente fusión entre narrativa y el mundo de las matemáticas y la filosofía (item **1969**). En cuento destacan *Cosas peores* de Margarita García Robayo y *Los papeles de Dionisio* de José Luis Díaz Granados (items **1972** y **1977**). La *Tercera antología del cuento corto colombiano* de Guillermo Bustamante y Harold Kremer es una abundante muestra del alegre y saludable estado del minicuento en el país (item **1989**).

En Venezuela su novela visita dos fragmentos de la realidad en el tiempo. En uno de ellos la creación literaria refiere mundos bajo las dictaduras que este país tuvo en el siglo XX, como la de Juan Vicente Gómez que tiene presencia en *Reportero en resistencia: la tinta indeleble de la libertad*, de Elizabeth Valarino de Cemboraín y la de Marcos Pérez Jiménez en *El circo*, de Michaelle Ascensio (items **2058** y **2074**). Ambas aparecen como miradas por el espejo retrovisor de la historia para referir, por elusion y alusión, el estado actual de este país. El otro fragmento de realidad en el tiempo es una recreación de la Venezuela de hoy, con todas sus desgarraduras sociales y políticas. *La mala racha* de Fernando Martínez Mottola muestra las inconveniencias de un hogar en el que el padre ha perdido su trabajo y la madre quiere irse del país, tal como sucede hoy en día con tantas familias que se ven conminadas a buscar asilos en otra parte (item **2067**). Pero la escritura trasciende a mundos de anticipación o de otra parte imaginada y conlleva en su quehacer una realidad narrativa que no escapa a lo que sucede en la sociedad venezolana actual. En *La cabalgata tenebrosa* de Otrova Gomas un sicario es contratado para ejecutar a un grupo grande de personas comprometidas en actos de corrupción en la capital de un país imaginario (item **2063**). La novela negra continua dando muestra de su mayoría de edad. De nuevo Inés Muñoz Aguirre en *A los vecinos ni con el pétalo de una rosa* despliega su gran capacidad para tejer situaciones e intrigas con un crimen al fondo (item **2068**). *Muerte en el Guaire* de Raquel Rivas

Rojas es otra novela negra de gran riqueza en el lenguaje coloquial (item **2071**). Entre las novelas cortas publicadas destacan *Vieja verde* de Alicia Freilich de Segal (item **2062**), narración de mucho humor situada en la Venezuela de finales del siglo XX y los proyectos politicos que se impusieron desde el gobierno. *Limbo* de Gabriel Jiménez Emán presenta un mundo de anticipación en una Venezuela de 2050 que arrastra los mismos inconvenientes de la tecnología deshumanizada y una ética de gobierno a medias o inexistente que tanto impera en el mundo (item **2065**). En colecciones de cuentos mereen especial mención *Cronicuentos de última página* de Igor Delgado Senior, el asesinato salta de la calle y sus noches para entrar a la página roja de diarios y revistas, por lo que en estos cuentos abunda la forma y tono de la crónica (item **2061**). *Trampa-jaula* de Liliana Lara y *Lo irreparable* de Gabriel Payares son cuentos costruidos a partir de la recreación de la condición humana expresada en fatales situaciones, siempre con la violencia en sus centros (items **2066** y **2069**). [JCL]

BOLIVIA, ECUADOR, PERU
En este entrega, destacan una serie de libros en la narrativa boliviana reciente que hurgan en el pasado histórico de ese país a partir de ambiciosos relatos de escritores como Enrique Ipiña Melgar (item **1957**) y Gabriela Ovando (item **1960**), Carlos Mesa Gibert y Verónica Ormachea Gutiérrez (item **1959**). Estos últimos nos ofrecen versiones interesantes sobre la conquista española y la Segunda Guerra Mundial, respectivamente. Ambos acontecimientos son revisados bajo una óptica local, vale decir, su impacto en la realidad boliviana. Destaquemos, asimismo, el buen momento del que goza el género del cuento gracias a los aportes de Adolfo Cárdenas Franco (item **1953**), Guillermo Ruiz Plaza (item **1964**), Paul Tellería, Manuel Vargas (item **1967**) y Edmundo Paz Soldán (items **1961**, **1962**, y **1963**). Este último, junto con Rodrigo Hasbún (item **1956**), figura entre los narradores bolivianos de mayor proyección internacional. En el campo de la crítica, conviene tener en cuenta el estudio de Willy Muñoz sobre la novela boliviana (item **1945**).

En el Ecuador, la novela y el cuento gozan de buena salud a partir de nuevos títulos publicados por Gabriela Alemán Salvador (item **1990**), Sandra Araya (item **1993**) y Mónica Ojeda (item **2002**), todas escritoras con buena proyección internacional. También conviene subrayar los aportes en el cuento de María Fernanda Ampuero (item **1991**). Finalmente, destacan dos magníficas novelas escritas por Diego Araujo Sánchez (item **1992**) y Raúl Vallejo Corral (item **2004**), respectivamente, que hurgan en la figura de Jose María Velasco Ibarra, cinco veces presidente del Ecuador.

En la narrativa peruana reciente, es indudable el protagonismo adquirido por escritoras de gran talento. Conviene tener presente los nombres de Katya Adaui Sicheri (item **2007**), María José Caro (item **2016**), Alina Gadea (item **2024**), Mayte Mujica (item **2034**), Jennifer Thorndike (items **2048** y **2049**) y Nataly Villena Vega (item **2019**), entre otras. En líneas generales, la novela peruana sigue manteniendo un gran nivel narrativo gracias a nuevos títulos y reediciones de escritores consagrados como Edgardo Rivera Martínez (item **2043**) y a la aparición de nuevos nombres como los de Marco García Falcón (item **2028**) y Diego Trelles Paz (item **2051**). El cuento sigue gozando de grandes cultivadores, entre los que destacan Pedro Llosa Vélez (item **2032**) y Karina Pacheco (items **2038** y **2039**). Asimismo, el ensayo crítico sigue explorando los muchos matices que ofrece la vasta obra de Mario Vargas Llosa a través de nuevos estudios de Jorge Coaguila (item **1947**) y Efraín Kristal (item **1949**). [CF]

LITERARY CRITICISM AND HISTORY

Bolivia

1945 Muñoz, Willy Oscar. Territorios, razas y etnias en la novela boliviana (1904–1952). Cochabamba, Bolivia: Grupo Editorial Kipus; 2016. 299 p.

Colección de ensayos en la que se analiza la novela boliviana de la primera mitad del siglo XX. El motivo del viaje vincula a varias de las novelas objeto de estudio de este libro. Bolivia es representda como un territorio desconocido, de modo que la travesía realizada, ya sea por bolivianos o extranjeros, llega a ser un descubrimiento sorprendente. [CF]

Peru

1946 Arámbulo López, Carlos and **Jorge Valenzuela Garcés.** Narración, 50 años después. Lima: Universidad Ricardo Palma, Editorial Universitaria, 2018. 67 p.: bibl.

Ensayo que consta de dos estudios en torno al grupo *Narración*, una generación de escritores surgida en los años 60 y 70 en el Perú. El primer ensayo realiza una aproximación a la revista alrededor de la cual se articularon escritores peruanos como Miguel Gutiérrez, Oswaldo Reynoso o Antonio Gálvez Ronceros. El segundo es un análisis de las crónicas sociales producidas desde esta instancia grupal que abogaba por la praxis literaria y política como actividades conjuntas. [CF]

1947 Coaguila, Jorge. Vargas Llosa: la mentira verdadera. Lima: Revuelta Editores, 2017. 220 p.: bibl., ill.

Libro que pasa revista a todas las novelas del autor: sus personajes, los temas que bordan y los contextos en los que ocurren los elementos de la trama. Asimismo, se recuerda qué pasaba con el autor mientras Vargas Llosa escribía cada uno de sus libros. También se revisa los ensayos y la dramaturgia del Nobel. Se incluye una larga entrevista de Coaguila con el autor. [CF]

1948 Güich Rodríguez, José. Universos en expansión: antología crítica de la ciencia ficción peruana: siglos XIX–XXI. Lima: Universidad de Lima, Fondo Editorial, 2018. 436 p.

Ambiciosa antología sobre la ciencia ficción en las letras peruanas. Guich da cuenta de la tradición del género en el Perú desde 1843, año de la publicación de *Lima de aquí a cien años*, de Julián del Portillo, y traza su afianzamiento a través de cultivadores del género como Abraham Valdelomar, Ventura García Calderón, Clemente Palma, José B. Adolph y Enrique Prochazka, entre otros. [CF]

1949 Kristal, Efraín. Tentación de la palabra: Arte literario y convicción político en las novelas de Mario Vargas Llosa. Lima: Fondo de Cultura Económica, 2018. 494 p. (Lengua y Estudios Literarios)

Estudio que abarca la totalidad de las novelas de Vargas Llosa—desde *La ciudad y los perros* (1963) hasta *Cinco esquinas* (2016)—diferenciando tres momentos fundamentales en la trayectoria novelística del Nobel peruano. En ellos se advierten importantes transformaciones en sus contenidos literarios en directa correspondencia con sus convicciones políticas y su concepción sobre la relación literatura y vida. [CF]

1950 La narrativa de Jorge Eduardo Benavides: textos críticos. Edición de César Ferreira y Gabriel T. Saxton–Ruiz. Lima: Universidad Ricardo Palma, Editorial Universitaria, 2018. 216 p.

Conjunto de ensayos que revisa la narrativa de este importante escritor peruano. Las aproximaciones críticos aquí incluidas examinan tanto la vasta obra novelística de Benavides, así como su producción cuentística. También se incluye una entrevista con el autor en la que reflexiona sobre su obra. [CF]

1951 Valenzuela, Jorge. La ficción y la libertad: cuatro ensayos sobre la poética de la ficción de Mario Vargas Llosa. Lima: Cuerpo de la Metáfora Editores, 2017. 147 p.: bibl.

Importante ensayo que reúne cuatro textos sobre el quehacer ficcional de Mario Vargas Llosa. En el primero de ellos, Valenzuela examina el carácter politico de la novelística vargasllosiana. El segundo opta por una mirada antropológica sobre su universo ficcional. El tercer reflexiona sobre el génesis de la ficción de muchos de sus libros. El último capítulo examina la relación entre el teatro y la novela en la obra del Nobel peruano. [CF]

1952 **Vargas Llosa, Mario** and **Rubén Gallo.** Conversación en Princeton. Barcelona: Alfaguara, 2017. 287 p.

Volumen que transcribe una serie de conversaciones mantenidas por Vargas Llosa en la Universidad de Princeton durante un seminario sobre su ficción. En medio de una conversación espontánea y fluida con estudiantes, Vargas Llosa desmenuza la importancia de la novela decimonónica en su propia obra o reflexiona sobre la amenaza del terrorismo islámico del siglo XXI. Asimismo, comparte detalles sobre la elaboración de *Conversación en La Catedral* o sobre las exigencias que supuso escribir las memorias de *El pez en el agua*. Este libro es una gran puerta de entrada al vasto quehacer ficcional del escritor peruano. [CF]

PROSE FICTION
Bolivia

1953 **Cárdenas Franco, Adolfo.** Opera rockocó: cuentos reunidos 1979–2008. La Paz: Editorial 3600, 2014. 374 p.

Relatos de este importante narrador boliviano que destacan por su uso del humor y la ironía, así como un fino uso de la parodia; asimismo, el uso de un lenguaje donde se funden la realidad y la ficción, lo oral y lo escrito, lo paceño y lo universal; finalmente, la creación de un lenguaje mutante, con temas cotidianos y finales sorprendentes. [CF]

1954 **Carvalho, Homero.** Pequeños suicidios: microcuentos. La Paz: Editorial 3600, 2016. 109 p. (Colección Narrativa)

Esta obra del celebrado narrador y poeta paceño presenta una serie de mini-narraciones desde astutas hasta profundas. En ellas el autor contempla nuestra existencia incluyendo los discursos culturales que la informan. Hay una serie de intertextualidades que incluyen menciones a la Biblia, *El Quijote, La metamorfosis, Cien años de soledad*, la poesía de Neruda, la narrativa de Cortázar, etc. La invocación de leyendas, historias e historia reconocidas sirven como fuente de las observaciones del autor. El resultado es una amena lectura, a veces humorística, a veces mordaz, que sirve para exponer la picardía y sabiduría de su creador. [J. Ballesteros]

1955 **Chávez Camacho, Benjamín.** La Indiferencia de los patos. La Paz: Editorial 3600, 2015. 126 p.

Novela que narra las aventuras de una joven deseosa de olvido y que emprende un accidentado viaje hacia La Paz. Tras una gran fiesta en el Cuzco y ante un bloqueo de caminos, debe atravesar a pie la aridez del altiplano escrutando el lago Titicaca. La vasta geografía retratada en el relato invitan a la reflexión y autoconocimiento de la protagonista. [CF]

1956 **Hasbún, Rodrigo.** El lugar del cuerpo. 2. ed. La Paz: Editorial El Cuervo, 2018. 108 p.

Novela breve cuya trama gira en torno a la vida de Elena, una escritora que ha llegado a la vejez llena de recuerdos de diversa índole, frutos de una vida desenfrenada, signada por el amor, las drogas y los recuerdos familiares. Y, sobre todo, por un acontecimiento infausto producido durante su niñez. [CF]

1957 **Ipiña Melgar, Enrique.** La duda del caminante: últimos días de un soldado de la guerra del Chaco. La Paz: Vínculos, 2012. 368 p.

Novela histórica que abarca una época decisiva en la formación de la moderna nación boliviana, entre la posguerra del conflicto con Chile a fines del siglo XIX, la Guerra del Chaco y la revlución de los años 50 en el siglo XX. La vida de Ignacio Camino, el protagonista, sirve de marco para comprender el desarrollo histórico y social boliviano y las tribulaciones más personales del personaje. [CF]

1958 **Mesa Gisbert, Carlos D.** Soliloquio del conquistador. San Andrés Cholula, Mexico: Universidad de las Américas Puebla; Puebla, Mexico: EDAF Editorial, 2014. 212 p.

Novela que se narra a partir del pensamiento ininterrumpido de Herán Cortés. Se evoca su conquista de nuevas tierras para la corona Española, su astucia aventurera, así como su avaricia y uso de la fuerza. El monólogo cortesiano se une con la conquista del Perú y figuras como Pizarro, Atahualpa y Manco II buscando desentrañar la dimensión de ese momento decisivo de la historia latinoamericana. [CF]

1959 **Ormachea Gutiérrez, Verónica.** Los Infames. La Paz: Editorial Gisbert, 2015. 296 p.

Novela que narra la Segunda Guerra Mundial desde una óptica boliviana. Relato de corte cosmopolita, este transita entre Varsovia, Auschwitz, La Paz, Nueva York y Londres. Sus personajes están atrapados en conflictos y contradicciones como en el caso de Dr. Moritz (Don Mauricio) Hochschild, una suerte de Schindler boliviano. Así, judíos y nazis conviven en un territorio boliviano lleno de intrigas y contrastes. [CF]

1960 Ovando, Gabriela. Los mellizos de Nápoles. La Paz: Plural Editores, 2014. 172 p. (Colección Narrativa)

Novela histórica que recrea los primeros años del reinado de Carlos III y los comienzos del Virreinato del Río de La Plata. Se cuenta la vida de Francisco de Paula Sanz, Gobernador de Buenos Aires, desde que partió de Nápoles hasta su ejecución en Potosí en 1810, en los inicios de la Guerra de Independencia argentina. [CF]

1961 Paz Soldán, Edmundo. Los días de la peste. Barcelona, Spain: Malpaso, 2017. 325 p.

Novela que se adentra en un duro microcosmos, una cárcel en la que conviven el horror con la cotidianidad, un reflejo distorsionado y exacerbado de la sociedad actual, es decir, una alegoría de la corrupción endémica, la estructura de poder y sus abusos. [CF]

1962 Paz Soldán, Edmundo. Tiburón: una antología personal. México: Almadía, 2016. 208 p. (Narrativa)

Las particularidades de esta antología de la narrativa breve del autor son dos: por un lado, es una recopilación que abarca los 27 años de producción del autor y, por otra, haber sido el seleccionador de los 21 relatos incluidos en el libro. Desde el ya clásico "Dochera" hasta "El próximo movimiento", pasando por "El acantilado", el imaginario de Paz Soldán abarca su infancia boliviana y la ciencia ficción hasta arribar a las crisis políticas recientes en los E.E.U.U. [CF]

1963 Paz Soldán, Edmundo. Las visiones. Madrid: Páginas de Espuma, 2016. 166 p. (Colección Voces; 229. Literatura)

Catorce cuentos ambientados en la realidad futurista (y opresiva) de la ciencia ficción. Todos los relatos están interconectados con personajes y situaciones de *Iris*, una novela anterior del autor (ver *HLAS 70:1652*). Un juez "ve" a quienes ha condenado; una niña tiene revelaciones de lo que podría ser el porvenir; un médico decide poner a prueba sus experimentos con armas químicas; un soldado enloquece, con resultados insospechados. [CF]

1964 Ruiz Plaza, Guillermo. Sombras de verano. La Paz: Editorial 3600, 2016. 181 p. (Colección Narrativa)

Relatos que nacen de esa turbadora y desconocida zona que son las relaciones familiares. Ruiz Plaza es dueño de un estilo limpio con diálogos certeros y finales contundentes que dan cuenta de complejas relaciones humanas que transitan entre la cultura, los sentimientos soterrados y las reconciliaciones. [CF]

1965 Tellería Antelo, Paul. El acto de agua. La Paz: Editorial 3600, 2015. 363 p.

Volumen de relatos en los que el elemento del agua es utilizado como una alegoría de transparencia pero también de una súbita violencia. Temas como la violencia de género, el abuso doméstico y el horror desfilan en un libro duro, cargado de emociones, donde la prepotencia de la sociedad patriarcal se erige como un asunto capital. Tellería construye realidades siempre complejas y ambiguas que intrigan, inquietan y, en definitiva, dejan un gran malestar en el lector. [CF]

1966 Urquiola Flores, Rodrigo. El sonido de la muralla. Cochabamba, Bolivia: Gobierno Autónomo Municipal de Cochabamba: Casa de la Cultura: Grupo Editorial Kipus, 2015. 290 p.

Novela que narra, desde la voz de una niña convertida en anciana, una saga familiar. Un día, al retornar de un viaje, una familia descubre que ha perdido su casa a manos de unos invasores desconocidos. Novela sobre la espera, este relato es también una novela sobre la memoria como ente independiente, un espacio donde todo puede suceder. [CF]

1967 Vargas, Manuel. Recuento de daños. La Paz: Editorial 3600, 2015. 187 p.

Libro de cuentos en los que sus personajes se detienen para ver hacia atrás y revisar sus logros y sus fracasos. Así, su hilo conductor es la evocación de un pasado para narrar lo acontecido que incluye la evocación de momentos que, en su mayoría, dirigen a la derrota y a las cicatrices que esta dejó en su conciencia. [CF]

Colombia

1968 Andrade, Jairo. Cadáveres de papel. México: UNAM: Siglo XXI Editores; Culiacán, Mexico: El Colegio de Sonora, 2015. 135 p. (La creación literaria)

Novela ganadora del XII Premio Internacional de Narrativa que se otorga en México cada año. Es una novela corta construida a partir del atentado terrorista que contra un avión en pleno vuelo de Bogotá a Cali, en noviembre de 1989, cometió el llamado cartel de Medellín. Si bien este hecho da ocasión para la novela, luego ella trasciende a otros espacios, en los que la corrupción no deja de hacer sus fiestas, tal como en efecto ocurrió con el atentado mismo y la investigación que se hizo de los hechos. Antonio Cervantes, Yoana Moungolo y un editor de proyectos artísticos son los personajes principales que circulan en cada una de las tres partes que componen la novela, misma que para el lector es presentada como un rompecabezas. [JCL]

1969 Avski, Joseph. El infinito se acaba pronto. Buenos Aires: Emecé Colombia, 2015. 140 p. (Fuera de colección)

Novela corta o *nouvelle* cuyos eventos narrados transcurren en Montería, ciudad del autor. Marco Lyons Pupo es el protagonista de la novela, un joven matemático obsesionado con el concepto del infinito. Paralelo a las visicitudes del protagonista, en la obra también se narran pasajes de la vida de Georg Cantor, matemático alemán. Joseph Avski, seudónimo de José Palacios, aparece como personaje. El objeto de esta obra es contar de la llegada a la locura que Lyons Pupo y Cantor tienen a raíz de las obsesiones de ambos con el infinito, expresión del tiempo que, en contravía con una de las paradojas de Zenón de Elea, no acude a la subdivisión infinita sino a la multiplicación infinita, según se sugiere al promediar la narración. [JCL]

1970 Castro García, Óscar. Sola en esta nube y otros cuentos. Medellín, Colombia: Sílaba Editores, 2016. 173 p.: colored ill. (Mil y una sílabas)

Trece cuentos en los que los asombros, hallazgos y fatigas de la vida cotidiana conducen a elaborar tramas con un misterio declarado o escondido tras las palabras de un discurso muchas veces cargado de poesía y juegos con el lenguaje. En "Sola en esta nube" una prostituta cumple 70 años y levanta las hojas de su memoria para recordar paisajes esenciales de su vida, los que a la vez corresponden a una zona particular de Medellín, el barrio Guayaquil. Ella espera en su cumpleaños la visita de algunos hombres a quienes ha servido en su oficio, a quienes añora y aún desea. "Encuentro" es una narración que avanza en sus regodeos de intentos para empezar a ser contada, mostrando diferentes y atractivas formas de empezar una historia. [JCL]

1971 Cepeda Samudio, Alvaro. Obra literaria. Coordinación de Fabio Rodríguez Amaya y Jacques Gilard. Córdoba, Argentina: Alción; Poitiers, France: CRLA-Archivos, 2015. 613 p.: bibl., ill. (Colección Archivos "Nueva serie"; 8)(Colección Archivos; 66)

Antología crítica de la obra intensa y breve de un autor definitivo en la literatura colombiana que va de la segunda mitad del siglo XX hasta nuestros días. Se reúnen *Todos estábamos a la espera* (cuentos, 1954), *La casa grande* (novela corta, 1962) y *Los cuentos de Juana* (cuentos, 1972). La compilación y edición crítica ha sido hecha por Fabio Rodríguez Amaya y Jacques Gilard, ya fallecido. En esta labor colaboraron otros 18 conocedores de la obra de Cepeda Samudio, entre los que destacan Gerald Martin, Álvaro Medina, Julio Olaciregui y Jorge Rufinelli. La edición está acompañada por un extenso y bien documentado estudio de la obra del autor por parte de Rodríguez Amaya. [JCL]

1972 Díaz Granados, José Luis. Los papeles de Dionisio: cuentos 1968–2012. Bogotá: Collage Editores, 2015. 156 p. (Colección Caribe adentro)

Diez cuentos y dos textos de largo aliento que son novelas cortas se reúnen en esta colección. En ella leemos sobre el aprendizaje de vida y de escritor que el autor, ficcionalizado en las páginas, ha tenido. El barrio Palermo de Díaz-Granados, sus años de adolescencia, sus jornadas como burócrata, otras como escritor y las bellas e infaltables sobre el amor, en este libro son resultado de la realidad vivida, ahora recuperada con la palabra creadora. La presencia del padre y otros seres definitivos en la vida del narrador, casi siempre en primera persona, cobran esencia en varios de los cuentos. También el mundo literario, musical, artístico, social y politico. El cuento "Los papeles de Dinosio" llega a ser una confesión de los años y mundo de aprendizaje del autor. [JCL]

1973 Escobar Giraldo, Octavio. Cuentos. Medellín, Colombia: Fondo Editorial Universidad EAFIT, 2015. 108 p. (Debajo de las estrellas; 2)

Nueve cuentos, la mayoría, escritos con una prosa vertiginosa, que recrean espacios urbanos, muchos de ellos de Manizales, ciudad donde siempre ha vivido del autor. La cultura popular en diversas expresiones, como la musical y el cine, tienen gran presencia en sus textos. Las narraciones gozan de virtudes de la crónica, y así se da cabida a algunos signos de los tiempos de Colombia, como el narcotráfico y la violencia. Hay ironía, como en el cuento "La murte de Dioselina." Rodrigo, tío de Julio, un adolescente, se le adelanta a éste en una conquista de amor y deseo. Luego de haber planeado cómo iba a lograr sus objetivos, al final tendrá que consolarse con la primera cerveza de su vida, a la que lo invita su tío. [JCL]

1974 Escobar Velásquez, Mario. Chofer de taxi. Medellín, Colombia: Sílaba, 2015. 197 p. (Colección Medellín entre líneas)

Alaín, el personaje narrador, toma nota de lo que la vida le ofrece desde la calle y los asientos de pasajeros en su taxi. Nutrida su imaginación con esos apuntes, una voz predominantemente en primera persona, a veces muy íntima, avanza en su escritura con un lenguaje que escudriña la palabra misma, la altera, la inventa para acentuar sus efectos sonoros, fiel al principio del narrador de que la literatura nace y se nutre de la vida al desnudo. Destacan en lo narrado lo referente a Blanca Rodríguez, una joven drogadicta, y a Malena, el amor de Alaín. Ellas se manifesitan con fuerza mediante

monólogos. La narración está acompañada de reflexiones sobre la literatura y el proceso de escritura. [JCL]

1975 Fayad, Luis. Regresos. Bogotá: Literatura Random House, 2014. 324 p.

De nuevo el mundo que siempre este autor ha sabido recrear con tanta maestría. Personajes de clase media, cargados de esperanzas y planes para cruzar al otro lado de la semana; edificios y casas en que la duela chirria entre olor a mugre y cera y bajo los pies de sus habitantes; oficinas, ventanillas y la eterna burocracia que muele al ser y sus ilusiones. El personaje principal es Ernesto Gonzaga, un antropólogo que luego de haber vivido por 20 años en Montreal regesa a Colombia porque le han prometido un excelente trabajo en un ministerio. Pisa de nuevo el país y comienzan sus avatares porque la sociedad ya no es la misma, todo ha cambiado y la vida ahora es más difícil. Novela escrita con prosa fina, muy pulida para hallar siempre la expresión más adecuada, unida también a un humor e ironía sin estridencias. [JCL]

1976 Ferreira, Daniel. Rebelión de los oficios inútiles. Bogotá: Penguin Random House Grupo Editorial, 2015. 293 p. (Alfaguara)

Esta obra mereció el premio Clarín de Novela 2014, de Argentina. Se narran eventos y pormenores de la toma de un terreno baldío por parte de un grupo de campesinos sin tierra y las acciones de unos paramilitares para luego desalojarlos. Los personajes principales, y en quienes recae los principales hilos de la narración, son Ana Larrota, lideresa de la toma; Simón Alemán, hombre adinerado venido a menos y dueño del terreno, y el periodista Joaquín Borja. Todo transcurre en los años de la década del 70 del siglo pasado, tiempos de permanente estado de sitio y que correspondieron al desmonte del Frente Nacional, 16 años de gobierno que empezaron en 1958 y que se caracterizaron por la represión a toda manifestación de protesta social, así como de cierre a cualquier vía de expresión que no fuese las de los dos partidos tradicionales. La voz narrativa de Joaquín Borja, expresada en largos párrafos que llenan páginas sin una pausa, actúa como una conciencia de lo que se narra. [JCL]

1977 **García Robayo, Margarita.** Cosas peores. La Habana: Fondo Editorial Casa de las Américas, 2014. 99 p.

Colección que mereció el premio Casa de las Américas (cuento) en 2014. Si bien la expresión "Hay cosas peores" surge en nuestras vidas como para darnos consuelo ante nuestros infortunios, García Robayo nos pone en palabras y papel algo de esas cosas peores en las que los personajes están hundidos en situaciones límites: engordar de manera incontrolada, los arañazos del cáncer, un aborto no deseado, la muerte de un ser querido. Y lo peor está en las consecuecias que estas inconveniencias ocasionan en el entorno de los personajes comprometidos de manera directa con la situación, por lo general sus propias familias, las que acaba por ser un lugar demasiado incómodo para vivir. El lenguaje es directo, en manos siempre de un narrador en tercera persona omnisciente. [JCL]

1978 **Gómez, Santiago Andrés.** La caminata. Medellín, Colombia: Fondo Editorial Universidad EAFIT, 2015. 139 p. (Coleccion Becas a la creación. Cuentos)

Doce cuentos en que se relata situaciones y circunstancias en las que la generocidad y solidaridad se manifiestan ante el otro, ante los otros y sus tantas vidas. Medellín, sus calles y sus habitantes nutren los escenarios de los cuentos, en los que la voz narrativa registra con palabras de un lenguaje sencillo lo que sucede, lo que percibe y decide transformar en texto con destino literario. La sencillez comienza desde los títulos de los cuentos, un artículo y un sustantivo concreto o abstracto como "La nevera," "La caminata," "El grado," igual que los nombres de las tarjetas de un juego de lotería. Y así, al final el lector logra llenar su tablero de cartón y gana al sentir el regusto de una buena lectura. [JCL]

1979 **González Sarmiento, Luis.** La reina y el anillo. Bogotá: Literatura Random House, 2016. 299 p.

Novela negra ambientada en una Colombia violenta y de muertes arrumadas en archivos de juzgado, de los que nunca surge la verdad como mínimo reparador entre familiares y otros deudos. Sindy Correa, cadete de la policía se ha involucrado en la investigación de un caso de homosexualidad en esa institución, y por ello la asesinan. En la imagen de muerte atroz que muestra su cadáver todavía ella conserva su belleza, mas no el anillo de diamante que llevaba en su mano izquierda y que se lo gabía regalado su novio, otro cadete. Gracias a la intervención de Constanza, madre de Sindy, la investigación sobre lo sucedido avanza, entre sorpresa y sorpresa. Los capítulos son breves, con mucha presencia de diálogo, y siempre conservando un tono de texto policiaco y crónica periodística. [JCL]

1980 **Montt, Nahum.** Hermanos de tinta. Bogotá: Alfaguara, 2015. 221 p.

Shakespeare y Cervantes coinciden en Valladolíd. Todo trascurre a comienzos del siglo XVII, siglo en que el pícaro que se recrea en algunas obras de Cervantes y contempráneos, estaba en la calle. Muchos de estos pícaros han salido de las páginas de Cervantres y hacen su vida en el mundo real y objetivo. El desempeño de Cervantes que recrea el autor en esos espacios de vida dura aparece muy humanizado. Con motivo de las celebraciones para la rectificación del tratado de paz entre España e Inglaterra en 1605, en Valladolid se va a presentar *Hamlet* de Shakespeare, lo que ocasionará que el autor inglés visite la ciudad y luego, ya casi al final de la novela, se conozca con Cervantes. "Siempre supe que tenía un hermano de tinta. Lo que nunca imaginé es que fuera español," le dice Shakespeare a Cervantes compartiendo copas de ron. El lenguaje de la novela no corresponde al español de España sino al de Hispanoamérica. Con esta virtud Cervantes y Shakespeare, así como la lengua española, de nuevo legitiman y afirman su existencia universal. [JCL]

1981 **Noriega, Luis.** Razones para desconfiar de sus vecinos. Bogotá: Literatura Random House, 2015. 304 p.

Nueve cuentos que, en ambientes urbanos, recrean situaciones cargadas de violencia y humor. En el cuento que da título al libro, en un edificio de apartamentos los inquilinos han escuchado un grito, del que no se sabe origen, causa y consecuencia. No obstante, ese grito es la llave que abre con fuerza la desconfianza, envidia, inquina y maledicencia que puede haber entre unos vecinos. De nuevo la metáfora de la condición humana en las brasas de las anomalías del alma muestra al desnudo los personajes que podemos llegar a ser al estar en situaciones límites. En algunos de los demás cuentos destacan escritores y seres de la vida académica, que por una u otra razón acaban por caer en manos de la violencia y el crimen. Este libro de cuentos mereció el "Premio de cuento Gabo" en 2016. [JCL]

1982 Paredes, Julio. Encuentro en Lieja. Bogotá: Taller de Edición Rocca, 2016. 186 p.

Una novela negra en la que hay dos víctimas, una de ellas está en estado de coma en un hospital y allá va Lucien Renchon, el narrador. En el hospital un día Lucien encuentra a George Simenon y de esta manera el narrador entra al mundo novelesco de este autor. Leyendo a Simenon, Lucien va a hallar muchas similitudes de la realidad ficticia con su propia realidad objetiva, sobre todo la de su mundo interior. Al final el lector se entera que Lucien ha sido el victimario. Narración muy bien construída con el recurso de la metaficción que logra crear atmósferas y tonos muy propios de la novela negra, siempre desde la perspectiva de quien ha cometido el crimen. [JCL]

1983 Pérez Gaviria, Lina María. El mismo lado del espejo. Medellín, Colombia: Sílaba Editores, 2016. 191 p. (Colección Trazos y sílabas)

Antonia, es una enamorada del arte y pinta. Sus obras las presenta en una galería bajo el nombre de Antonio Talero. Con esta argucia su imaginación cobra mucho vuelo y en actitud mitómana se aprovecha de las tantas mentiras que debe inventar siemrpe. Las dueñas de una galería donde ha desjado sus cuadros quieren conocer a Talero, pero Antonia siempre se vale de inteligentes evasivas para seguir encubriendo su verdadera identidad. Se narran años de juventud de Antonia, con mucha memoria de los encantos que para ella significaba la ciudad de hierro. Al cabo de varios años precisamente un conocido suyo de la ciudad de hierro descubre el secreto de Antonia. Al final el secreto no se descubre. Es una novela narrada en primera persona por la protagonista, con un lenguaje coloquial en el que sobresalen imágenes de mucha fuerza. [JCL]

1984 Romero de Nohra, Flor. No me mates: ¡te amo!: relatos. Bogotá: Flor Romero, 2015. 216 p.

Veinticinco narraciones sobre el maltrato y opresión de la mujer a través de los tiempos se unen para conformar esta novela de título tan conmovedor. Cada narración actúa a manera de capítulo de la novela y cuenta de mujeres maltratadas y hasta asesinadas por hombres. El hilo conductor que da unidad a los relatos es Purificación, quien es secuestrada por Espósito, un empleado del padre de ella. Purificación, a manera de Scherazada, para que su secuestrador no la maltrate, le lee o cuenta aquellas historias. Los maltratos y femicidios que suceden en los relatos están situados en diversos países, como corresponde a lo universal de esta fatalidad social e histórica tan presente hoy en día. [JCL]

1985 Sánchez Baute, Alonso. ¿De dónde flores, si no hay jardín? Bogotá: Alfaguara, 2015. 263 p.

Tres narraciones independientes conforman este libro. Los protagonistas habitan márgenes sociales adonde han sido llevados bien por sus orígenes o porque poco a poco fueron conducidos a la orilla. A Jackson Sobrado, un jíbaro o vendedor callejero de droga, a Gema Almendrales una prostituta y a un deportista fracasado corresponden las narraciones. Textos escritos con dinámica prosa propia de la crónica, forma literaria y periodística que el autor conoce muy bien. Lo que lee el lector es la vida difícil de unos personajes inscritos en realidades narrativas que muestran las llagas sociales y humanas de una sociedad de grandes y profundas desigualdades. [JCL]

1986 Sánchez Cuervo, Juan Mario. Como una melodía. Medellín, Colombia: Sílaba, 2015. 316 p. (Colección Trazos y sílabas)

Bello título para una novela en que circulan los años de la violencia colombiana del ultimo tercio del siglo XX, cuyos agentes principales fueron guerrillas, paramilitares, narcotráfico y fuerzas del estado. Mario, el narrador y mismo autor de la novela, cuenta de Ramón y las difíciles circunstancias a las que se ven enfrentadas dos familias, los Restrepo Restrepo y los Sánchez Cuervo. Ambas están unidas por el vínculo entre

Rosa y Ramón, también por la tragedia y el perdón. Ramón es uno de los tantos muertos de cuyas vidas el lector se entera, todos víctimas de la violencia de aquellos años. Los hechos narrados ocurrieron en la vida real, y la crudeza y atrocidades pasan por el filtro creativo del autor mediante un lenguaje terso, elaborado con la cadencia de lo poético. [JCL]

1987 **Shaves-Ford Dunoyer, Robert.** Hilos de fuego: novela. Ibagué, Colombia: Caza de Libros, 2013. 107 p. (Colección Caza de Libros—Club de lectores; 27)

Conmovedora novela corta que relata sobre la vida de Kurt Crünwel, enlistado en el ejército alemán, mientras padece la Segunda Guerra Mundial y sus espantos. Durante la ocupación de Francia, luego de que los alemanes han sido atacados por gente campesina de la población de Mieux, a lo que siguen las consecuentes retaliaciones del ejército invasor, el horror que debe presenciar Kurt lo llevará a perder la sensibilidad de su cuerpo. En el capítulo X el narrador pregunta "¿Puede un cuerpo dimitir de la realidad? . . . ¿Puede un cuerpo olvidarse de sí mismo?" (p. 42). Kurt responde afirmativamente a esas preguntas perdiendo la sensibilidad. En Londres el amor le deparará alivios en su vida. [JCL]

1988 **Tamayo, Guido Leonardo.** Juego de niños. Bogotá: Literatura Random House, 2016. 139 p.

Fernando, un chico que padece una enfermedad que le impide participar de los juegos propios de la infancia, se refugia en su apasionamiento por la palabra y hace crucigramas. Los otros niños de la familia a la que Fernando fue dado en adopción siempre lo han visto a él como un hombre mayor. Es una bella novela corta mediante la cual la palabra ayuda a la memoria de un grupo de personajes a levantar una especie de cartografía esencial de la infancia que compartieron, con sus alegrías y desencantos, y siempre en el centro de la memoria está Fernando, quien un día muere cayendo al vacío. Varias voces participan en la narración, la que procede mediante la fragmentación, y así poco a poco se construye una historia de infancia en la que los niños se ven enfrentados al amor y la muerte, entre algunas otras esencialidades de la vida. Los crucigramas de Fernando aparecen en el texto y llegan a ser otros fragmentos de la novela, mismos que aparecen como una metáfora de la que lee el lector. [JCL]

1989 **Tercera antología del cuento corto colombiano.** Compilación de Guillermo Bustamente y Harold Kremer. Cali, Colombia: Editorial Universidad de Valle, 2016. 217 p.

De nuevo los autores de la antología entregan una muy extensa selección de cuentos cortos colombianos. Esta es una forma narrativa que en la presente literatura hispanoamicana es muy frecuentada por sus autores y goza de muy buena salud. Para llegar a este estado cabe recordar que en su genética el minicuento en Hispanoamérica ha tenido grande cultores, piénsese en Julio Torri, Rubén Darío, Juan José Arreola, Edmundo Valadés, Jorge Luis Borges y Augusto Monterroso. En Colombia hay también un muy buen desarrollo de esta forma narrativa, el que posibilita la entrega de textos que saben impactar entre la brevedad y lo leve, bien sea con la sorpresa o la prisa morosa que esconde el desenlace. [JCL]

Ecuador

1990 **Alemán Salvador, María Gabriela.** Humo. Bogotá: Literatura Random House, 2017. 204 p. (Seix barral. Biblioteca breve)

Novela que cuenta la historia de Gabriela, una mujer que tras abandonar Paraguay 17 años atrás decide regresar y evocar la vida que allí vivió. Trae consigo el cuaderno de su difunto amigo Andrei y a través de lo que que allí está escrito repasará historias privadas y sociales de América Latina. Se trata de una novela cautivante y ambiciosa que hurga en el pasado a nivel individual y colectivo. [CF]

1991 **Ampuero, María Fernanda.** Pelea de gallos. Madrid: Páginas de Espuma, 2018. 115 p. (Colección Voces. Literatura; 255)

Primera colección de relatos de esta escritora guayaquileña. En ellos se traza algunos temas de vasto alcance latinoamericano: violencia, clasismo, machismo, abuso de menores, hipocresía social, precariedad, insensibilidad ante el maltrato—físico, psíquico, humano, animal—sexualidades reprimidas, tensión entre amo y esclavo, imposibilidad de limpieza o inocencia, supercherías e ignorancias, o el peso de un sentimiento religioso que termina siendo castrante. [CF]

1992 Araujo Sánchez, Diego. Los nombres ocultos. Quito: Rayuela Editores, 2016. 136 p.: bibl.

Novela de corte detectivesco que se inicia en febrero de 1935, cuando Antonio Leiva, chofer del presidente Velasco Ibarra, muere tras un accidente de tránsito. Estamos ante una narración que tiene todo: intriga, suspenso, historias bien elaboradas que se entrecruzan en momentos cumbres de la trama. En la trama se entrecruzan tres historias y tres vidas diferentes: la del infortunado chófer, la del presidente Velasco y la de Manuel Romero, un periodista caído en desgracia a quien se le mete entre ceja y ceja descubrir una sola gran incógnita: ¿quién mató al chofer del Presidente Velasco? El relato todo es una mirada crítica sobre el mundo del poder en el Ecuador. [CF]

1993 Araya, Sandra. Orange. Quito: Antropófago, 2014. 181 p.

Novela en la que ha muerto Beatriz Donoso, la cabeza de una familia signada por la maldición. Los relatos intimistas de cada personaje van develando un pasado ominoso que marcará el destino de la familia. Entre secretos y pesadillas, el relato se nutre del thriller, la novela negra y el relato psicológico. [CF]

1994 Arcos Cabrera, Carlos. Memorias de Andrés Chiliquinga. Quito: Editorial Santillana, 2014. 207 p. (Colección Alfaguara)

Novela de corte autobiográfico que explota con maestría la correlación entre la tradición literaria ecuatoriana y la historia, al revisar de manera irónica la novela *Huasipungo* (1934), de Jorge Icaza. A través de los ojos de Chiliquinga, músico otavaleño homónimo del inmortal personaje de *Huasipungo*, nos embarcamos en un viaje de estudios a los E.E.U.U. en el que Andrés descubre su historia, su cultura y su identidad. [CF]

1995 Benítez Torres, Milton. El niño que mataba por amor. Quito: Editorial El Conejo, 2013. 245 p. (Colección Narrativa selecta)(Novela)

Novela de marcado realismo social que aborda temas como la marginación social, la pobreza, la discriminación y la influencia religiosa en la existencia humana. Se trata de un relato de sólida línea argumental pero que también apela por momentos al uso de elementos fantásticos. [CF]

1996 Castro R., Juan Pablo. Los años perdidos. Quito: Alfaguara, 2013. 345 p.

Novela que cuenta la historia de Faustino Alcázar, un personaje que divide su tiempo entre ser profesor universitario en una universidad de Quito, vivir oscuras aventuras con amigos de dudosa calaña y escribir novelas interminables que nunca publicará. No obstante, Faustino recuerda una y otra vez una época pasada de su vida en Lisboa. Ese momento de felicidad incide en su manera de encarar el presente. Bien leído, el libro de Castro Rodas es una compleja exploración del yo con momentos cargados de delirio y excesos vitales. [CF]

1997 Cuerpo adentro: historias desde el clóset. Edición de Raúl Serrano Sánchez. Quito: Ministerio de Cultura y Patrimonio, 2013. 301 p. (Colección Letras-cultura-patrimonio)

Volumen que reune 30 cuentos de escritores ecuatorianos del siglo XX y XXI. Con diversas estrategias narrativas, estos textos dan cuenta de la sexualidad humana y sus muchas manifestaciones personales. Este compendio se remonta a autores canónicos como Pablo Palacio y Pedro Jorge Vera e incluye autores más recientes como Lucrecia Maldonado, Raúl Vallejo y Esteban Mayorga. [CF]

1998 Espinosa Ochoa, Francisco. La búsqueda. Quito: CCE Benjamín Carrión Casa de la Cultura Ecuatoriana, 2014. 128 p. (Colección Casa Nueva; 13)

Novela que narra un tema recurrente en la literatura latinoamericana: la búsqueda del padre y los orígenes de una identidad personal. El anónimo protagonista de Espinosa Ochoa va en busca de su padre, un hombre sexagenario que desapareció súbitamente. El protagonista viaja entre Estados Unidos, Italia y el Ecuador para rastrear las huellas de su progenitor. Su largo recorrido tendrá un final feliz y le dará la paz existencial que anhela. [CF]

1999 Estrella, Ana. La curiosidad mató al alemán: y otros cuentos. Quito: Pontificia Universidad Católica del Ecuador, 2013. 87 p.

Conjunto de cuentos que ponen sobre el tapete una variedad de conflictos personales y sociales irresueltos. Por ello nos encontramos con personajes como un canadiense poco aventurero, una escritora cuya batalla creativa la lleva a dudar de su oficio o un médico cuyas tribulaciones vitales lo llevan a experimentar la traición. El humor y la ironía matizan una serie de situaciones insólitas. En el relato que le da título al volumen, el más logrado, destaca la representación de una crisis de identidad que es producto de un dilema nacional mayor en el Ecuador: la identidad. [CF]

2000 Hermosa Mantilla, Hernán. Los dueños de la perinola: el caso de los verdes y colorados en un pueblito de jurisdicción no delimitada. Quito: Ediciones Abya Yala: Universidad Politécnica Salesiana, 2015. 277 p.

Novela ambientada en el trópico ecuatoriano donde no existe jurisdicción territorial definida, volviéndolo tierra de nadie y lugar para quienes buscan riqueza y prosperidad sin límites. La Perinola seguirá creciendo hasta convertirse en un centro de desarrollo, pero sus conflictos llevan al Congreso Nacional a emitir un decreto poniendo a todos sus protagonistas fuera de combate. [CF]

2001 Macías Huerta, Adolfo. Las niñas. Bogotá: Editorial Planeta Colombiana, 2016. 248 p. (Seix barral. Biblioteca breve)

Volumen compuesto de cinco relatos que se entrecruzan y forman un universo cerrado con reglas propias. En estos cuentos, Macías Huerta construye personajes condicionados por un eje fundamental: el azar. A todos sus protagonistas los une conductas guiadas por la venganza, el dolor, la maldad y, en definitiva, una existencia abismal que, unida a una pasión desbocada, los lleva a una temeraria relación con la muerte. [CF]

2002 Ojeda, Mónica. Mandíbula. Barcelona, Spain: Editorial Candaya, 2018. 285 p. (Candaya narrativa; 49)

Novela ambiciosa y de aristas múltiples que, en principio, puede ser descrita como una novela de iniciación pero con elementos pertenecientes al thriller de horror. En ella se cuenta la historia de Fernanda, una joven adolescente que es secuestrada a una cabaña en el bosque por Clara, su maestra de Literatura en un colegio exclusivo del Opus Dei. Allí, ambas mujeres comparten y viven grandes historias de terror. Tiempo atrás, Fernanda y Annelise, su mejor amiga, iniciaron a un grupo de compañeras en historias de horror y un rito sadomasoquista. Dentro de la complejidad del relato, destaca la destreza discursive de esta buena escritora. [CF]

2003 Romero, Fausto. Los rieles del tamarindo: el tiempo del cóndor. Quito: Editorial El Conejo, 2015. 257 p.: bibl.

Novela de corte histórico que recrea la vida de Eloy Alfaro, conocido como "El Viejo Luchador." El relato evoca las circunstancias políticas y sociales que dieron lugar a la Revolución Liberal liderada por Alfaro en el Ecuador en el siglo XIX y comienzos del siglo XX. Para ello, Romero utiliza la metáfora del ferrocarril como alegoría del paso del tiempo y muestras las luchas que llevaron a Alfaro al poder en diversas ocasiones a través de levantamientos militares. Una nueva vuelta de tuerca a un personaje legendario de la historia ecuatoriana. [CF]

2004 Vallejo Corral, Raúl. El perpetuo exiliado: novela collage. Bogotá: Literatura Random House, 2016. 439 p.

Novela que evoca la figura del dictador ecuatoriano José María Velasco Ibarra, cinco veces presidente de la república. Se retrata al politico de carne y hueso, al idealista y represor, facilitador del poder olígárquico, así como al hombre enamorado de la poeta Corina Parral, la mujer que lo acompañó en sus exilios. [CF]

2005 Vásconez, Javier. Cuentos reunidos. Quito: USFQ Press, 2018. 423 p.

Libro que reúne toda la producción cuentística de este importante escritor ecuatoriano. El volumen incluye textos clásicos del autor como su excelente "Angelote, amor mío," acaso su relato más antologado, y otros cuentos inéditos como "Corrupción o la fama de un poeta." El libro se abre con un esclarecedor prólogo de Pedro Angel Palou y se cierra con una bibliografía de los cuentos del autor. En muchos relatos se dialoga y se rinde homenaje a una serie de autores canónicos latinoamericanos, europeos y e ingleses. [CF]

Peru

2006 Adaui Sicheri, Katya. Aquí hay icebergs. Lima: Literatura Random House, 2017. 124 p.

Conjunto de cuentos en los que destacan temas que ya forman parte del universo literario de esta escritora: el pasado familiar, los lazos afectivos que se rompen, las cicatrices que deja el pasado en los personajes. Se trata de un libro que destaca por una prosa cargada de emociones que se expresan a través de una escritura arriesgada y audaz. [CF]

2007 Adaui Sicheri, Katya. Nunca sabré lo que entiendo. Lima: Planeta, 2014. 66 p. (Autores españoles e iberoamericanos)

Primera novela de esta importante escritora. En medio de una escritura aparentemente desprovista de estructura, Adaui explora con buenos recursos expresivos y una prosa bien trabajada la vida de Ana, una mujer que evoca su vida luego de abandonar a Tomás, su esposo durante cinco años. Se trata de un viaje físico en tren, pero sobre todo de un viaje introspectivo e intimista en el que la protagonista evalúa su vida, sus deseos, sus logros y sus fracasos. Destaca en este libro un gran tono confesional y una prosa con una gran carga emocional. [CF]

2008 Ampuero, Fernando. La bruja de Lima. Lima: TusQuets Editores, 2018. 104 p. (Colección Andanzas)

Novela que recrea la vida de un hombre—alter ego del autor—que ha sido diagnosticado con una muerte rápida debido a un cáncer. Sin nada que perder, el protagonista acude donde Hilda, una bruja limeña que lo ayuda a reconciliarse consigo mismo y a comprender mejor todo el entorno peruano que lo rodea durante la década de los años noventa. Sin duda uno de los relatos más personales de Ampuero. [CF]

2009 Ampuero, Fernando. Lobos solitarios. Lima: Peisa, 2017. 71 p. (Serie del río hablador)

Novela que recrea la vida de Edmundo de los Ríos y Xavier Ugarriza, dos periodistas de la revista limeña, *Caretas*. Ambos personajes, tan disímiles entre sí, comparten no solo el mismo oficio, sino también la misma pasión: la literatura. Esa es la fuente de las diversas emociones y desencuentros que experimentan ambos durante el relato. [CF]

2010 Arámbulo López, Carlos. Quién es D'Ancourt. Lima: Alfaguara, 2017. 289 p. (Narrativa hispánica)

Novela de claro corte metaliterario. En la Lima de fines del siglo XX, cuando la sociedad peruana está inserta en la gran violencia política de los años 80 y 90, un profesor trata de descifrar los versos de un joven poeta llamado D'Ancourt. El relato es un retrato de época, donde la música, la literatura y las drogas son un refugio ante la violencia social imperante para sus jóvenes personajes. Al mismo tiempo, el texto dialoga y rinde homenaje a artistas como Pound, Mozart, Borges, Nabokov y Bolaño. [CF]

2011 Baudry, Paul. El arte antiguo de la cetrería. Lima: PEISA, 2017. 141 p. (Serie del río hablador / PEISA)

Primer libro de cuentos de este joven escritor. Los cuatro relatos de este volumen examinan momentos históricos claves del siglo XX peruano. El poder y sus estructura serán cuestionados en cada situación planteada. Así, el autor examina figuras importantes del pasado peruano (Haya de la Torre, María Reiche, por ejemplo), al tiempo que explora ideas como el cosmopolitismo, las relaciones entre América Latina y Europa y diversas experiencias de aprendizaje. [CF]

2012 Beleván, Harry. La piedra en el agua. 3a ed. Lima: Animal de invierno, 2017. 132 p.

Reedición de un clásico del género fantástico peruano publicado originalmente en 1977. Se trata de un libro breve pero arriesgado en sus formas. Cuenta la historia de una madre y su hija universitaria cuando ambas se mudan a la que fuera la casa de un escritor. Ahí, en la biblioteca, hallarán una novela que provocará una serie de trasvases entre la realidad y la ficción. [CF]

2013 Benavides, Jorge Eduardo. El asesinato de Laura Olivo. Madrid: Alianza Editorial, 2018. 323 p. (Alianza literaria)

Novela detectivesca que cuenta la vida del Colorado Larrazabal, un expolicía peruano que se instala en Madrid en los años noventa. Larrazabal es negro pero de origen vasco y ha abandonado su Lima natal tras haberse enfrentado a un caso de corrupción en la época de Fujimori. En Madrid, instalado en Lavapiés, trabaja como detective privado. Allí su casera le pide investigar el el caso de su sobrina, una joven periodista a la que señalan como sospechosa de la muerte de una célebre agente literaria, Laura Olivo. Larrazabal hurga en el mundo editorial español, gracias al cual lector el relato recrea un divertido mundo de escritores ególatras y desencantados. La novela es también un gran retrato de la sociedad española de nuestros días que le da la bienvenida a migrantes de muchas partes del mundo. [CF]

2014 **Bustamante Petit, Armando.** Constelación. Lima: Animal de Invierno, 2017. 226 p. (Colección La Jauría. Novela)

Abordados desde esquinas separadas, los personajes de esta novela conforman, sin embargo, una familia. El acercamiento a ellos que realiza Bustamante Petit es lento, bien contenido, pues jamás se apresura en traar de sobreexponer tramas o psicologías, y eso le permite lucir una gran destreza descriptiva, una recreación de situaciones de muy buen oficio. Los protagonistas coinciden en desnudar su soledad, persistir en un estado de aislamiento que solo se resuelve con pequeñas fugas como la lectura y algún que otro súbito arrebato emocional. La separación de estos hombres y mujeres se subraya justamente por el cosmos de padres, madres, hermanos, abuelos o amigos que nunca son una seguridad de compañía sino un punto de referencia cruel para aquellos incómodos con su entorno. [CF]

2015 **Cáceres, Grecia.** Mar afuera. Lima: Fondo Editorial Universidad César Vallejo, 2017. 228 p.

Novela en la que una escritora llamada Miranda se muda a París. Con ella van sus dos hijos mellizos. La vida complicada de Lima y la muerte de su esposo quedan atrás, pero con la mudanza la protagonista no se desligará fácilmente de su pasado peruano. Padeciendo los embates del desarraigo, Miranda buscará cumplir sueños, pero también reconciliarse con su ciudad y su doloroso pasado. [CF]

2016 **Caro, María José.** ¿Qué tengo de malo? Lima: Alfaguara, 2017. 96 p. (Narrativa Hispánica)

Partiendo de su debut literario con un libro llamado *La primaria*, Caro entrega un conjunto de relatos al que añadió cinco cuentos nuevos y un orden cronológico. Así, acompañamos a Macarena desde la primera infancia hasta las turbulencias de la adolescencia. Crecer supone cuestionar la familia, el entorno social, el colegio y el amor, entre otros temas. [CF]

2017 **Castañeda, Luis.** Mi madre soñaba en francés. Lima: Alfaguara, 2018. 361 p. (Narrativa hispánica)

Novela cuyo tema central es la maternidad y las compleja relación madre-hijo. Los poemas de César Moro sirven como una guía vital de los personajes, así como el dilema de un padre ausente o la imposibilidad de comunicarse pese a hablar varios idiomas, como sugiere el título. [CF]

2018 **Cisneros, Renato.** Dejarás la tierra. Lima: Planeta, 2017. 338 p.: ill. (Autores Españoles e Iberoamericanos)

Novela que hurga en los orígenes de la familia Cisneros, una familia de patricios en la sociedad peruana. Al hacerlo, el auor hurga en la historia del Perú, con sus tragedias y ambiciones, doscientos años atrás. Detrás de un relato largo y ambicioso, donde el autor rastrea a sus antepasados, se revela un pasado familiar hecho de secretos y falsas mascaras. En definitiva este es un libro que hurga en el tema de la identidad, un asunto recurrente en la obra de este talentoso autor. [CF]

2019 **Como si no bastase ya ser: 15 narradoras peruanas.** Selección de Nataly Villena Vega. Lima: PEISA, 2017. 213 p. (Serie del río hablador)

Quince narradoras nacidas entre 1966 y 1986 ofrecen a través de relatos diversos una singular mirada a temas como la emancipación, la familia, la relación amorosa, la maternidad, el rol social, el viaje, la migración, el secreto, la incomunicación, todo lo que implica ser mujer. [CF]

2020 **Cortázar Velarde, Juan Carlos.** Cuando los hijos duermen. Lima: Animal de Invierno, 2016. 166 p.

Novela que explora la problemática de la identidad sexual en medio de los rígidos códigos de una sociedad patriarcal. Sus personajes son César y Adrián, dos personajes adultos que tienen hijos y viven relaciones heterosexuales. Un día, ambos personajes se conocen y viven muchas peripecias para poder vivir existencias clandestinas como pareja. [CF]

2021 Cueto, Alonso. La segunda amante del rey. Lima: Literatura Random House, 2017. 285 p.

Novela en la que Cueto hurga nuevamente en el mundo de la clase alta peruana con un relato de corte detectivesco. En un exclusivo mundo limeño se dan la mano un empresario exitoso, la esposa de este y su amante. Asimismo, un prostituto argentino y una detective privada enviada por la esposa del empresario para hurgar y luego destruir su aventura amorosa. En medio de una trama muy eficaz, destaca el uso de una mirada femenina en un mundo de falsedades, pocos escrúpulos y muchas traiciones. [CF]

2022 Dughi, Pilar. Puñales escondidos Lima: Cocodrilo Ediciones, 2017. 136 p.

Nueva edición de una novela que cuenta la historia de una poderosa banquera a quien una repentina enfermedad la obliga a pensar en la jubilación. Mientras tanto, aparecen en su contra acusaciones de turbios manejos financieros en un mundo donde el poder patriarcal y la avaricia prevalecen. Con ingredientes de un buen thriller, esta novela puede ser leída como una fina crítica al mundo del dinero con no pocos personajes femeninos dignos de ser cuestionados. [CF]

2023 Dumett, Rafael. El espía del inca. Lima: Lluvia Editores, 2018. 775 p. (Colección: Felipe Guamán Poma de Ayala)

Novela que se inicia con la secreta misión de dejar libre a Atahualpa, el último inca, tras ser apresado por los conquistadores españoles a su llegada al Perú. Utilizando elementos de la novela detectivesca, Dumett urde tres tramas que se entrecruzan a través de las peripecias de un futuro espía devenido en un gran contador de historias. Los quipus aparecen en el relato como plataforma para recrear los diversos puntos de vista de los personajes, mientras el texto dialoga con la novela negra y el relato histórico. [CF]

2024 Gadea, Alina. Destierro. Lima: Emecé Cruz del Sur, 2017. 112 p.

Tercera novela de esta novelista en la que se cuenta la intimidad de una mujer en proceso de separación. Con una prosa finamente trabajada, Gadea se sumerge en un registro privado y su novela se lee como el atractivo diario de la soledad de una mujer en un doloroso trance en su vida. [CF]

2025 Galarza, Sergio. Algún día este país será mío. Lima: Alfaguara, 2018. 239 p. (Narrativa hispánica)

Novela que cuenta la historia de un amigo, Zeta, pero que también es la historia del autor. Sin dejar de ser una obra que roza la biografía del autor, se retrata a la sociedad peruana en su desmoronamiento moral tras el fujimorismo. [CF]

2026 García, Luis Eduardo. Señor Cioran. Trujillo, Perú: CEA, 2016. 216 p.

Novela de época que recrea el Perú de los años 80 y 90. Sus protagonistas son cuatro jóvenes universitarios que apuestan por la revolución como un medio de cambio. Su juventud e ingenuidad los lleva a utilizar la figura emblemática del filósofo rumano Emil Ciorán para sus actividades clandestinas. La violencia de Sendero Luminoso y una crisis institucional generalizada pondrá en entredicho su idealismo y su lucha por la justicial social. [CF]

2027 García Falcón, Marco. Esta casa vacía. Lima: PEISA, 2017. 139 p. (Serie del Río Hablador)

Novela que cuenta la historia de Giovanni Perleche, un sujeto en crisis. Utilizando la escritura como terapia y catarsis, el personaje evoca su vida de conviviente, el remoridimiento que supone la infidelidad matrimonial, los descalabros familiares y financieros y la pérdida de un hijo enfermo a manos de su pareja. Al mismo tiempo, este libro es un comentario sobre la escritura, vale decir, sus retos y las bondades liberadoras que ella ofrece. [CF]

2028 García Falcón, Marco. La luz inesperada. Lima: PEISA, 2018. 115 p. (Serie El Río Hablador)

Novela que cuenta la historia de Bruno Gózar, un publicista próspero que vive años en Nueva York. Para reencontrarse con un pasado feliz, organiza una fiesta para reunir a sus compañeros de colegio, pero la fiesta será un revés que lo confrontará más bien con los fantasmas de un pasado doloroso. [CF]

2029 **Hinostroza, Rodolfo.** Cuentos incompletos. Lima: Lustra Editores, 2009. 277 p. (Biblioteca Rodolfo Hinostroza)

Libro que reúne los cuentos de este renombrado poeta en dos grandes grupos. En *Cuentos casuales*, Hinostroza ubica a sus personajes en diversas ciudades del mundo, mostrando un claro aire cosmopolita. Así, sus personajes deambulan por París, Deyá, México o los Estados Unidos, teniendo siempre a Lima como escenario de referencia. En ellos el mundo musulmán aparece como un mundo lleno de dramas existenciales y no pocos absurdos, mientras sus personajes viven experiencias fantásticas no exentas de un sabor local. En *Cuentos de Extremo Occidente*, la presencia de Borges se vuelve un referente obligado para muchos de los relatos y las experiencias fantásticas de sus protagonistas. [CF]

2030 **Incendiar el presente: la narrativa peruana de la violencia política y el archivo (1984–1989).** Edición, estudio, y suplemento testimonial por Enrique E. Cortez. Lima: Campo Letrado, 2018. 349 p.: ill.

Antología de cuentos que examina el conflicto armado en el Perú de los años 80. Los cuentos escogidos transitan con acierto entre la experiencia individual y colectiva de sus muchos personajes en un momento para la historia peruana cargado de violencia y trauma. Se incluyen textos de 15 autores: Pérez Huarancca, Rosas Paravicino, Zorrilla, Nieto Degregori, Ninapayta, Dughi, Valenzuela, entre otros. [CF]

2031 **Jara Jiménez, Cronwell.** Faite. Lima: ARSAM, 2016. 157 p.

Novela en la que Jara recrea el mundo del *fighter* o peleador callejero. Su protagonista es un sujeto a medio camino entre el héroe popular y el delincuente común. Piurano de nacimiento, es un personaje pintoresco, algo ególatra y muy sentimental. No solo es amante de Los Panchos y Nat King Cole, sino autor de poemas a una mujer perdida. Destaca el uso de la jerga popular y el retrato humano que hace Jara de los barrios populares peruanos. [CF]

2032 **Llosa Vélez, Pedro José.** La medida de todas las cosas. Lima: Emecé Cruz del Sur, 2017. 284 p.

Libro de cuentos que incluye seis relatos donde una serie de personajes se enfrenta a temas vinculados al mercado y a la economía y donde la vida pública se entrevera con lo privado. Todo ello da lugar a luchas de poder y a la crítica de una cuestionable intelectualidad. [CF]

2033 **Martínez Arias, Jack.** Bajo la sombra. Lima: Estación La Cultura, 2014. 94 p.

Un joven científico de origen peruano especializado en prótesis humanas es convocado por una antropóloga puertorriqueña como parte de un trabajo de campo sobre los latinos en el Midwest estadounidense. Esta relación es el tronco de una novela breve que transita por varios espacios geográficos para tratar temas como la mentira, el peso de la herencia, la migración, las carencias afectivas y las mutilaciones físcas y morales. [CF]

2034 **Mujica, Mayte.** Una ciudad para perderse. Lima: Animal de Invierno, 2018. 108 p.

Primera novela de esta escritora que se desenvuelve en dos espacios: el familiar y el político. Por un lado, narra la ruptura de un matrimonio y, por otro, una historia que transcurre a finales de los años 30 en Europa, donde el abuelo es un exiliado aprista. El contrapunto de estas dos vidas, así como una bien dosificada prosa intimista y lineal son dos elementos dignos de destacar. [CF]

2035 **Neyra Magagna, Ezio.** Pasajero en La Habana. Lima: Emecé, 2017. 116 p. (Emecé cruz del sur)

Novela sobre las carencias de la capital cubana golpeada por el militarismo, las construcciones accidentadas en los barrios y la influencia de los mares sobre el estado de ánimo de su gente. Se cuenta la historia de un joven escritor a quien su estancia en varias partes de Cuba ha determinado sus relaciones amorosas, su trabajo y hasta su capacidad de escribir. Finalmente, decidirá establecerse en un solo lugar, donde descubrirá el porqué de tanto cambio. [CF]

2036 Ollé, Carmen. Halo de la luna. Lima: PEISA, 2017. 77 p. (Serie Del río hablador)

Novela breve que cuenta la historia de Samantha, una hermosa chica que va a morir, pero no sin antes conocer el placer por deseo expreso de sus padres. Estos encargan a un ama la búsqueda de un amante. El relato se sostiene en el equilibrio entre lo erótico y lo tanático, la búsqueda del placer y el afán de poseer en una rara combinación de historia negra con vuelo poético. [CF]

2037 Otero, Diego. Días laborales. Lima: Literatura Random House, 2018. 137 p.

Primera novela de este poeta peruano. En ella se narra la vida de un protagonista que, tras ser despedido de su trabajo, se encuentra envuelto en un enredo criminal del cual no saldrá bien librado. Destaca en el relato el uso de referencias al cine, lo que le otorga al texto una gran imaginación visual. Otra virtud es su gran economía de recursos narrativos, producto del oficio del poeta del autor. [CF]

2038 Pacheco, Karina. Lluvia. Lima: Seix Barral, 2018. 108 p. (Biblioteca Breve)

Libro que nos ofrece nueve relatos, donde siguen presentes el erotismo, la violencia y la presencia de la naturaleza. Esta última desde una visión mítica o conflictiva. El uso de un estilo depurado de frases cortas, la impronta poética y una resolución más directa dan como resultado historias contundentes. Estos cuentos nos muestran a personajes inmersos en relaciones pasionales—personales o sociales—donde la naturaleza emerge como escenario en el que estos conflictos estallan. [CF]

2039 Pacheco, Karina. Las orillas del aire. Lima: Editorial Planeta Perú S. A. Bajo su sello Seix Barral, 2017. 248 p. (Seix Barral Biblioteca breve)

La extraña desaparición de una mujer en la selva da pie a la evocación de diversos pasajes de la historia del Perú del último siglo. En esta novela, Pacheco nos sitúa en un ambiente de activismo político y crisis sociales. A lo largo de sus páginas se realiza un recorrido por diferentes ambientes peruanos, en especial la selva y la sierra. Y es por este cruce de geografías que pesa tanto la fuerza natural en la prosa de Pacheco.

Además de ello está la historia de Rada, la arqueóloga que azarosamente se topa con una atronadora verdad sobre el pasado, específicamente el de su abuela, Aira. [CF]

2040 Pérez, Julián. Anamorfosis. Lima: Banco Central de Reserva del Perú, 2017. 229 p.

Novela de gran maestría verbal ganadora del Premio Julio Ramón Ribeyro-Banco Central de Reserva del Perú. En el relato, los personajes pertenecieron, cuando eran jóvenes, a un grupo literario de pretensiones revolucionarias. Al producirse la insurgencia ayacuchana, se comportaron de manera muy diversa. El uso de un lenguaje irónico y carnavalizador desnuda las deficiencias académicas y culturales de Ayacucho; y se conjuga con una pluralidad de perspectivas (incluyendo la real-maravillosa de un muerto convertido en *qarqacha*), cada una deformando anamórficamente lo ocurrido. [CF]

2041 Pimentel, Jerónimo. Estrella solitaria: canciones escritas para ser cantadas por Nacho Vegas. Lima: Fondo de Cultura Económica, 2016. 68 p. (Colección Tierra Firme)

Novela corta que evoca la época juvenil de la Lima de los años 80 y 90. La escritura de Pimentel destaca por sus muchas referencias metaliterarias en medio de un realismo que por momentos cae en lo violento y grotesco. La rebeldía con que se recrea la etapa juvenil de los protagonistas va de la mano con el retrato urbano de un mundo desencantado y hostil. En el relato abundan las referencias eruditas junto a elementos pertenecientes al mundo popular limeño. [CF]

2042 Ríos, Edmundo de los. Los juegos verdaderos. Primera edición en Surnumérica. Arequipa, Perú: Surnumérica, 2017. 281 p. (Clásicos & contemporáneos; 1)

Nueva edición de una novela premiada y admirada cuando se publicó por vez primera. El protagonista evoca en el relato su infancia y adolescencia en Arequipa, una ciudad entre señorial y taciturna en ese momento. Luego, su juventud universitaria, donde las inquietudes revolucionarias son portadoras del idealism de un sujeto que cree que el cambio social es posible. Finalmente, la madurez de la vida adulta con su pesada carga de desencanto y soledad. [CF]

2043 Rivera Martínez, Edgardo. Soliloquios/Ciudad de fuego. Lima: Debolsillo, 2018. 197 p.

Volumen de cuatro novelas cortas. Tres de ellas pertencen a *Ciudad de fuego*, obra reeditada del autor que se concentran en una Lima neblinosa y nostálgica (ver *HLAS 60:3598*). La cuarta es "Soliloquios", relato que es una suma de recuerdos dentro de recuerdos, pues la protagonista, Laura, también reflexiona sobre la memoria de quienes la rodearon y expande su mundo íntimo sobre la base de sus lecturas. Otro punto de interés es el nexo de esta limeña con el mundo andino que le mostraron las personas que trabajaron en su hogar y algún romance de antaño. [CF]

2044 Robles, Juan Manuel. No somos cazafantasmas. Lima: Editorial Planeta Perú S.A., 2018. 249 p. (Seix Barral Biblioteca breve)

Conjunto de cuentos con ecos de ciencia ficción. Robles hurga en la memoria personal y los mecanismos a través de los cuales se jerarquizan aquellos eventos significativos. Sin embargo, en estos siete relatos, la mayor sorpresa es la perspectiva desde la que nos presenta sus historias, una ficción distópica que nos muestra las diversas formas en que la tecnología se usa para manipular nuestros recuerdos. "Memorias de la China" y "No somos cazafantasmas" plasman mejor esta propuesta. [CF]

2045 Rodríguez, Gustavo. Madrugada. Lima: Alfaguara, 2018. 237 p. (Narrativa hispánica)

Novela que cuenta la historia de Trinidad, una mujer luchadora que, puesta en la necesidad extrema, debe contactar con su padre que ignora su existencia. Danny es un pícaro noble, mujeriego y bipolar que se gana la vida cantando temas del recuerdo. Además del tema de la paternidad, esta es una novela sobre Lima y sus tribulaciones sociales: el racismo, la violencia omnipresente, el machismo, el clasismo y otras taras en la sociedad peruana. [CF]

2046 Sánchez Flores, Miguel Antonio. Secta Pancho Fierro. Lima: Planeta, 2017. 166 p. (Autores españoles e iberoamericanos)

En un viaje de amor, pasión y nostalgia se enrumba el profesor Miguel Fontana para develar el enigma escondido entre los pincelazos del pintor Pancho Fierro. La novela pone sobre el tapete las andanzas de ladrones, falsificadores y verdugos, quienes accionan en el marco de una gran conspiración camuflada detrás del arte. [CF]

2047 Sumalavia, Ricardo. No somos nosotros. San Isidro, Peru: Editorial Planeta Perú S.A, Seix Barral, 2017. 137 p. (Seix Barral Biblioteca breve)

Novela que narra las peripecias de un hombre que estuvo ausente del Perú por 10 años. Su residencia en Francia le ha creado una serie de problemas de pertenencia con su país. Su espacio de refugio son los libros, siendo estos su puerta de escape a otros universos para vivir muchas vidas. Destaca en el relato la gran exploración de un sólido "yo" narrativo. [CF]

2048 Thorndike, Jennifer. (Ella). 3 ed. Lima: Debolsillo, 2017. 120 p.

Nueva edición de la novela debut de Thorndike, una auscultación de los resquicios más desagradables de la humanidad, en particular aquellos que se fisuran dentro de la esfera familiar. La relación entre madre e hija en esta historia es desagradable y cruel, por la vileza con que la primera busca tener el control de la segunda, y la desoladora forma en que esta última se somete por largo tiempo a los maltratos y las humillaciones, hasta que la tolerancia llega a un límite y los traumas estallan, con la correspondiente onda expansiva que suelen originar los desastres. Todo hilvanado por una poderosa y meticulosa narración. [CF]

2049 Thorndike, Jennifer. Esa muerte existe. Lima: Literatura Random House, 2016. 159 p.

Novela que cuenta la historia de la Larva, una muchacha que sobrevivió a un terrible accidente que ha confinado a sus padres a un hospital, mientras ella y su hermana ciega son acogidas por su abuelo, quien las explota y maltrata sin ninguna clemencia. Distintas peripecias provocarán que finalmente Larva asesine a su hermana y sea condenada a la pena capital. Se trata de un relato que hurga en los bajos fondos del alma humana, plagado de violencia, humillaciones y vejaciones. Todo ello en medio de una prosa tensa que no claudica. [CF]

2050 Tola, Raúl. La noche sin ventanas. Lima: Alfaguara, 2017. 426 p. (Narrativa Hispánica)

Ambiciosa novela que cuenta dos historias. La primera es la vida de Madeleine, quien luego de perder a sus progenitores parte a París. Allí vivirá los horrores de la ocupación alemana e ingresará poco después a formar parte del mundo clandestino de la Resistencia. La otra es la historia de Francisco García Calderón. En compañía de su hermano Ventura y de Víctor Andrés, El Arequipeño, todos ellos fundadores de la Generación del 900, Francisco vivirá las vicisitudes de la guerra y pondrá a prueba sus convicciones ideológicas. [CF]

2051 Trelles Paz, Diego. Adormecer a los felices. Lima: Planeta, 2015. 138 p.

Libro de cuentos en el que el autor construye personajes que deambulan por el mundo en busca de una revelación que cambie sus vidas o alguna aventura trivial y cotidiana le dé repentinamente sentido a una existencia anodina. Destaca el tono melancólico de algunos relatos, así como un fino uso del humor. [CF]

2052 Trelles Paz, Diego. La procesión infinita. Barcelona, Spain: Editorial Anagrama, 2017. 215 p. (Narrativas hispánicas; 588)

Novela que narra el Perú tras el fin de la dictadura de Alberto Fujimori en el año 2000. Se recrea una sociedad en la que convive la imposibilidad del verdadero amor y la amistad duradera. Los personajes viven la secuela de un mundo enrarecido, corroído y enfermo. En medio de un gran despliegue narrativo, este es un gran retrato generacional del autor. [CF]

2053 Vega Jácome, Selenco. El japonés Fukuhara. Lima: Asociación Peruano Japonesa, Fondo Editorial, 2017. 155 p.

Conjunto de cinco relatos que abordan, entre otros tópicos, las complicadas relaciones familiares y de pareja. Tampoco está ausente la historia de cuando los colegiales humillaban a cualquier japonés por representar el mal absoluto en los años de la Segunda Guerra Mundial ni la violencia política con la violencia política durante la dictadura fujimorista. Destaca también el epónimo que le da título al volumen, una bella nouvelle sobre el horror y los silencios largos. [CF]

2054 Villena Vega, Nataly. Nosotros que vamos ligeros. Lima: Animal de Invierno, 2018. 121 p.

Conjunto de cuentos que tiene como tema central la experiencia del exilio. Por ello, los viajes que viven sus personajes son tan físicos como afectivos. En ellos vemos retratadas experiencias como los muchos sentimientos que despierta vivir entre dos mundos y la escisión psicológica del sujeto; el mito de París y su desencanto; o la búsqueda de una madre por una hija perdida en Europa. Cada personaje de Villena se pregunta por un sentido de pertenencia que el terruño extranjero otorga o quita. [CF]

2055 Yrigoyen, José Carlos. Orgullosamente solos. Lima: Literatura Random House, 2016. 155 p.

Novela en la que se hurga en el pasado familiar y aristocrático del autor para enfrentarse a una dura verdad: su abuelo, un conocido hombre público, había sido también un defensor del fascismo en el Perú y practicó una doble vida que terminó impactando en los suyos. El libro funciona como una fábula del Perú del siglo XX. [CF]

2056 Yuen Cárdenas, Hugo Antonio. El laberinto de los endriagos. Lima: PetroPerú, Ediciones COPÉ, 2018. 368 p.

Novela que reelabora la geografía amazónica, concretamente la de Madre de Dios, su trayectoria histórica (con especial atención a la labor misionera del padre Apaktone y a la minería informal) y la cosmovisión mítica de sus etnias. Se trata de un relato en el que se fusiona el humor y la intensidad poética y donde se entrelaza lo económico con lo erótico y lo ecológico con lo chamánico. [CF]

2057 Yushimito, Carlos. Las islas. Lima: SIC Libros, 2006. 159 p. (Colección Breve)

Nueva edición de este primer libro de Yushimito. En sus ocho cuentos destaca la presencia de un estilo denso, singular y sorprendente. Sus relatos ocurren en territorios que vagamente pueden ser el Brasil, un país imaginado donde lo narrado siempre está puesto en entredicho. Aunque aparecen figuras de narcos, bandoleros y muchos pobres diablos, todos ellos son como fantasmas que viven en un mundo nebuloso y un permanente desasosiego. De todos los relatos, destaca "Seltz". [CF]

Venezuela

2058 **Ascencio, Michaelle.** El circo. Caracas: Editorial Alfa, 2015. 196 p. (Colección Orinoco; 66)

Novela en tres capítulos que retrata la vida y el mundo no como un teatro, tal ha sido tradicional verlos y estar en ellos, sino como un circo. Sea lo uno o lo otro, al final un espectáculo, una actuación. Y el espectáculo es nada menos que los años de Venezuela que van del golpe de estado militar contra Rómulo Gallegos en 1948 hasta 1952, cuando luego de descaradas y aviesas maniobras electorales asume el poder Marco Pérez Jiménez y se instaura su dictadura. Los personajes muestran de sí lo que en el fondo es la sociedad venezolana de entonces, una socieda fracturada desde los mismos niveles de la familia. El texto es narrado por dos personajes, Floriana y Yolanda, y lo hacen desde las entrañas de lo cotidiano, de la vida que discurre a pesar de los afanes y dificultades que impone la historia de su país. [JCL]

2059 **Cuentos memorables venezolanos.** Compilación de Ednodio Quintero. Caracas: Editorial Planeta Venezolana, 2015. 412 p. (Colección Planeta lector. Contemporáneo)

Ednodio Quintero, cuentista mayor de las letras venezolanas, hace una selección de 33 cuentos que se iluminan desde su memoria de lector, iniciada a muy temprana edad. Casi un siglo de narrativa venezolana en forma de cuento se expone en estas páginas. Según se desprende de las palabras de Quintero, su visión inicial de antólogo de cuentos propios de su region, Mérida, ahora se ha ampliado a una más general y abarcadora en tiempo y espacio. De esta manera, en narraciones en las que sobresale lo cotidiano, Venezuela transcurre en muchos de sus registros sociales e históricos. Como acto de ayuda y cortesía con el lector, en el prólogo Quintero da una lista de los argumentos de cada uno de los 33 cuentos. [JCL]

2060 **De qué va el cuento: antología del relato venezolano 2000–2012.** Compilación de Carlos Sandoval. Caracas: Editorial Santillana, 2013. 516 p.: bibl.

Selección extensa de cuentos publicados en 12 años recientes de ese país, son predominantemente urbanos y en ellos aparece la sociedad venezolana actual. Una fotografía de la creación literaria de Venezuela, y a la vez de su historia contemporánea, pero todo hecho y dicho en tempo de cuento, forma narrativa breve de gran desarrollo en ese país. Son 40 los autores convocados en sus páginas, entre los que destacan por su trayectoria Roberto Echeto, Sonia Chocrón, Enza García Arreaza, Fedosy Santaella y Eduardo Febres, acompañados por otras voces de gran valía. [JCL]

2061 **Delgado Senior, Igor.** Cronicuentos de última página. Caracas: Editorial Lector Cómplice, 2016. 174 p. (Colección La noche boca arriba)

Con un lenguaje eficaz, de periodismo, que va directo a lo que se quiere narrar, en el que predomina el afán por ser una crónica, el autor entrega 46 cuentos de poca extensión, suficiente para que cada uno quepa en los espacios de los diarios y revistas destinados a la página roja. Los nombres corresponden a los usados para dar una noticia sobre un crimen o un delito. De esta manera, en la colección se narra sobre hechos en los que siempre hay una víctima del crimen, bien sea en Venezuela o cualquier otro país de América Latina. Venganzas, ajustes de cuentas, atracos, celos, secuestros, y muchos otros, son los motivos y esencias de las narraciones. Al final del libro, el autor propone cien posibes títulos de otros posibles cronicuentos, con lo que la abundante labor de imaginación del autor puede continuarse, ya quizá en manos del lector. [JCL]

2062 **Freilich de Segal, Alicia.** Vieja verde. 2da edición. Caracas: Editorial Eclepsidra, 2015. 137 p. (Colección El falso cuaderno. Narrativa)

Novela corta o *nouvelle* dividida en cuatro partes, en cuya estructura predomina la fragmentación. Es una narración cargada de humor, signos de la cultura popular y refiere la Venezuela de finales del siglo XX. La fragmentación señalada da lugar a la presencia de pasajes de la historia más reciente de Venezuela, a los excesos y demagogias de los nuevos gobernantes pero iguales promeseros de un bienestar que nunca llega. De toda esta situación es testigo Fulgencia, una mujer de edad quien debe ver y sentir el derrumbe de unas castas políticas y la llegada de otras con idéntico destino. El deslave de Vargas de 1999, conocido también como la Tragedia de Vargas, es el evento que contiene y resume la disolución de las esperanzas hacia la Revolución Bolivariana. La narración fluye rápido, en la que no falta la dinámica del relato policial. [JCL]

2063 Gomas, Otrova. La cabalgata tenebrosa. Caracas: Ediciones Oox, 2016. 188 p.: ill.

En Luxaria, la capital de un país imaginario, se descubre un cuantioso desfalco. Kurlo, un hijo rebelde que se ha ido de casa, es contratado como sicario para asesinar 20 políticos comprometidos con actos de corrupción. Sus estrategias y planes para cometer los asesinatos son muy ingeniosas, valiéndose de increíbles tretas cargadas de muchas sofistiquerías al servicio del crimen. Kurlo cumple a cabalidad con sus misiones y el grupo que lo ha contratado, llamado el Octeto, está muy satisfecho, por lo que él recibe instrucciones para continuar con el asesinato de otras personas. En el futuro, la limpieza asesina contra la corrupción habrá de continuar y Kurlo propone quedarse al frente de las operaciones, las que serán ejecutadas por sicarios del extranjero. La narración sostiene su fuerza seductora en los actos y maniobras de Kurlo para llevar a cabo sus ejecuciones. [JCL]

2064 Hurtado Lores, Camilo. Los delirios de Julio Pineda. Península de Paraguaná, Venezuela: Ediciones del Cerro, 2011. 224 p.

Julio Pineda ha sido líder estudiantil en la secundaria y ya en la universidad se vincula a un grupo del partido oficial de gobierno. De Pablo Arnáez él escucha que para no fracasar en la política se debe atacar al adversario sin compasión. Esta recomendación le recuerda otras del mismo tenor que su padre le dijera. En forma rápida Julio asciende en el partido y regresa a su pueblo de origen, en donde valiéndose de acciones criminales logra ser elegido alcalde. Todo empieza a derrumbarse en su vida gracias a las investigaciones que se hacen sobre su fortuna, hasta que debe salir huyendo, ahora sin siquiera su esposa, quien lo ha abandonado. Al final, solo y sin dinero, se consuela pensando en que el tiempo pasará y él podrá volver a sus aviesas acciones de político. [JCL]

2065 Jiménez Emán, Gabriel. Limbo. Caracas: Fundación Editorial el Perro y la Rana, 2016. 148 p.: index. (Colección Páginas venezolanas. Serie Contemporáneos)

Novela corta de anticipación. A partir de una Venezuela imaginada de 2050, el autor parte de las circunstancias actuales del mundo, en buena parte comandadas por la tecnocracia, para llevar al lector a leer unas páginas en que discurre la intolerancia y otras inconveniencias de la humanidad. Ante esa sociedad del futuro se impone y se opone una ética para vivir y convivir, encarnada por organizaciones ambientalistas de diversos países. Al final, a pesar de todos los esfuerzos por conducir a una vida más ajustada a los elementales valores de la ética, el mundo es destruido mediante una lluvia ácida y aquellos que habitaron el planeta pasan en masa a la eternidad, a la espera de que se les dé "una segunda oportunidad" (p. 147). [JCL]

2066 Lara, Liliana. Trampa-jaula. Caracas: Editorial Equinoccio, Universidad Simón Bolívar, 2015. 149 p. (Colección Papiros. Serie Narrativa)

Siete cuentos que merecieron ser finalistas del Premio Equinoccio de Cuento Oswaldo Trejo 2012. La Venezuela en sus crisis de comienzos del siglo XXI es el telón de fondo de estos cuentos, en los que algunos personajes transitan de uno a otro, buen ardid literario con el que se logra dar continuidad y contigüidad entre las historias que se cuentan. El fatal comportamiento humano es signo de la brutalidad social en la que los personajes están atrapados, brutalidad que asciende a la bestialidad y es subrayada con la presencia de animales que juegan un papel importante en algunos cuentos. Así, destaca la presencia de un perro emasculado, culebras, pirañas y pájaros. En el cuento de igual nombre al libro, se narra sobre el emprendimiento de un proyecto vial para unir un pueblo con el mar, es un proyecto interminable que es acometido por el hijo de un padre que también lo había intentado. [JCL]

2067 **Martínez Mottola, Fernando.** La mala racha. Caracas: Fundavag Ediciones, 2015. 292 p. (Colección Nueva palabra; 20)

Novela desgarradora sobre la situación actual de Venezuela. Matías Romero ha perdido su trabajo y ama Venezuela. Helena, su esposa, quiere irse del país con sus hijos. Surge pues, en Matías, el dilema de irse del país o quedarse. Tal dilema se expone y potencia mediante las preguntas que dan título a cada uno de los capítulos de la novela. Y cada pregunta es una de las tantas que puede llegar a hacerse un ciudadano, con familia o no, que reflexiona sobre el caos económico y político que padece y lo asfixia. Escrita en un lenguaje sencillo, brinda una especie de retrato hablado de la vida, pensamientos e intimidad de un profesional que ve derrumbarse país y sueños suyos. [JCL]

2068 **Muñoz Aguirre, Inés.** A los vecinos ni con el pétalo de una rosa. Caracas: Ediciones B, 2014. 369 p. (Vértigo. Novela negra)

Novela negra que narra la ambientación social y humana de los habitantes de un edificio del Chacao, zona importante de Caracas, y cuya normalidad de sus vidas se ve interrumpida y desviada por un crimen. Un día cualquiera Ana Luisa va a visitar a su madre y la encuentra sangrando en la alfombra del apartamento, ya muerta. Todos los inquilinos de los 12 apartamentos son sospechosos de haber cometido el crimen, y a medida que avanza la narración ellos muestran de sí sus bajezas y miserias. Los detectives Carolina Larotta y Wilfrido Pérez, que ya habían aparecido en otra novela de la autora, serán quienes adelanten la investigación del crimen. La narración avanza rápido, ágil, sin soltar al lector, entre capítulos en los que destacan las fichas de los interrogatorios de vecinos del edificio, el ultimo será el de la autora del crimen, la misma hija de la mujer asesinada. [JCL]

2069 **Payares, Gabriel.** Lo irreparable. Caracas: Ediciones Puntocero, 2016. 174 p. (Colección Ficción; 38)

Ocho cuentos en los que el amor y la violencia circula en el mundo de las realidades narrativas y los personajes. Casi todos los cuentos suceden en Caracas y dos de ellos en Argentina. Las narraciones avanzan en un lenguaje que explora lo subjetivo, circunstancia en buen parte amparada por la frecuencia del narrador en primera persona. En "Los payasos" un hombre y sus compañeros de ancianato esperan la visita de unos payasos. La situación es motivo para que el hombre piense con una mezcla de nostalgia y amargura sobre su situación actual. La amargura se impone en todo el relato y al final concluye que los payasos tienen como misión "imponernos una larga resaca a cambio de pocos, poquísimos, minutos de fiesta" (p. 88). [JCL]

2070 **Reyes Hernández, Luis Angel.** 48 horas de vida: un diálogo increíble. Maracaibo, Venezuela: Fondo Editorial Universidad Nacional Experimental Rafael María Baralt, 2013. 108 p. (Colección El dorado. Serie Phoebus)

Novela que el lector puede relacionar con el bello y triste cuento "El milagro secreto" de Jorge Luis Borges. En este caso, antes de ser ahorcado a Paulo Fernando Lenz se le brinda la gracia, que proviene de lo humano y no de lo divino, de contarle a un escritor los episodios más esenciales de su vida como criminal y traficante armas. También la desgracia final suya proviene de lo humano, él mismo decidió y solicitó ser ahorcado. La narración avanza en forma de diálogo entre Lenz y el escritor, y toda ella trascurre en las últimas 48 hora de vida del condenado. [JCL]

2071 **Rivas Rojas, Raquel.** Muerte en el Guaire. Caracas: Ediciones B, 2016. 156 p. (Vértigo, novela negra)

Novela negra que trata de las indagaciones alrededor de siete cadáveres de hombres jóvenes que aparecen en el río Guaie, cinco de ellos desmembrados. Sere es la narradora y le cuenta a Olga, una amiga de Londres, sobre las investigaciones que dirige Patricia, una periodista. La novela se centra en los casos de los dos cadáveres completos. Estos cadáveres corresponden a personas cuya vida y circunstancias que surgen en las investigaciones van a conectar los objetivos de las pesquisas con el gobierno venezolano. Los capítulos no tienen numeración y cada uno está escrito con un lenguaje coloquial, propio de un epistolario. Esta enunciación provoca una familiaridad e intimidad en la que el diario vivir emerge y contribuye a atenuar la dureza que suele aparecer en textos policiacos. [JCL]

2072 Sánchez, Manuel Gerardo. Sangre que lava. Caracas: Ediciones Puntocero, 2016. 142 p. (Colección Ficción; 39)

Once cuentos separados en tres secciones dan cuenta de situaciones en las que los personajes muestran de sí anomalías y miserias de la condición humana, para retratar así una sociedad puesta en la escena de ostentaciones y oropeles. Los personajes exhalan melancolía y aburrimiento tras las máscaras con que tratan de continuar una vida que se va diluyendo poco a poco con la llegada de los nuevos agentes de cambio social. Así la Venezuela actual de nuevo es el telón de fondo para las narraciones. Justamente el cuento que da título al libro muestra parte de lo que es el régimen que hoy gobierna. Algunos cuentos son ambientados en escenarios catalanes. Son textos narrados con una prosa que juega a ser de crónica social, que cae alegremente en el humor y la ironía. [JCL]

2073 Socorro, Milagros. Cuentos guajiros. Caracas: Alfaguara, 2011. 87 p. (Serie roja)

El universo e imaginario de las poblaciones indígenas que pueblan el estado Zulia, la parte venezolana de la península de la Guajira, es el componente primordial de estos siete cuentos. En ellos, sobre todo, la narración se enfoca en presentar voces infantiles y adolescentes de diversas comunidades indígenas y de la sociedad venezolana no indígena. De esta manera se da cabida a la mirada del ser sobre el otro, pero desde una visión todavía no tan contaminada por los prejuicios sociales. El cuento "La triste viuda añú" es una hermosa narración en la que la niña Isabelita escucha a varios ancianos que cuentan un mito fundacional de su cultura, la del caballo Apañakai. [JCL]

2074 Valarino de Cemboraín, Elizabeth. Reportero en resistencia: la tinta indeleble de la libertad. Caracas: Ediciones B Venezuela, 2015. 263 p.

Novela basada en hechos reales ocurridos durante los años de la dictadura de Juan Vicente Gómez (1908–35), y que al lector le sugiere muchas similitudes con el regimen actual. Al igual que ahora, en los tiempos de "El Benefactor" también fueron los estudiantes quienes desde la calle clamaban y exigían cambios, luego lo harán desde la prisión con su resistencia. Aparecen elementos propios de la vida de la autora, cuyo padre, Nerio Aquiles Valarino, murió envenenado en La Rotunda, prisión emblemática de torturas y muertes en la sociedad venezolana. [JCL]

2075 Vall de la Ville, Keila. Los días animales. Caracas: Oscar Todtmann Editores, 2016. 209 p. (Colección Hoy la noche será negra y blanca . . .)

Una mujer, Julia, que ha mantenido una relación muy difícil con Rafael y cuya madre acaba de morir, viaja por muchos lugares del mundo, hasta llegar a Katmandú y luego volver a su Venezuela. La mujer escala paredes de piedra, colgando de una cuerda mientras a punta de esfuerzo y vértigo sus faenas de alturas le lastiman las manos y forjan fortalezas. Su andar por el mundo termina por recrear de nuevo la metáfora del viaje como un tránsito esencial hacia el interior del ser. Es una novela de 23 capítulos que a su vez se dividen en fragmentos, todos narrados por Julia. La prosa avanza lenta, construyendo a la vez una especie de poesía del ascenso luego de car y caer entre los vértigos del viaje y la vida. [JCL]

River Plate Countries

CLAIRE EMILIE MARTIN, *Professor of Spanish, California State University, Long Beach*
LAURA R. LOUSTAU, *Associate Professor of Spanish, Chapman University*
GIOVANNA URDANGARAIN, *Associate Professor of Hispanic Studies, Pacific Lutheran University*

ARGENTINA
PUBLICADAS ENTRE 2013 Y 2016, las obras incluidas en este volumen siguen varias pautas temáticas que podemos clasificar en seis vertientes específicas.

Algunas de estas obras pertenecen a más de una de estas clasificaciones, pero hemos elegido agruparlas de acuerdo a criterios generales que se ajustan lo más cercanamente posible al tipo de narrativa que representan.

La clasificación más nutrida corresponde a obras que se sitúan en el presente de la Argentina para evidenciar trágicas y absurdas realidades en términos económicos, ético-morales y políticos. Muchas de estas narrativas están ambientadas en diferentes entornos laborales, en círculos de criminalidad, o entre ámbitos profesionales en el conurbano bonaerense y en las provincias. La Triple Frontera, zona geográfica de exuberancia natural y de criminalidad consolidada, se convierte en marco de la novela de Oliverio Coelho, *Bien de frontera* (item **2083**). El protagonista, un joven talentoso jugador de ajedrez, desemboca en una encrucijada vital en la cual pierde su rumbo y se adhiere a la jungla humana de estafadores, corruptos y criminales. *Los perros* de Víctor Heredia (item **2091**) pinta con trazos realistas la vida de los niños y jóvenes (los denominados perros) quienes viven, trabajan y mueren en los basurales del conurbano. La luz de la esperanza toma forma de libros rescatados entre las basuras por el protagonista, El Sabio, quien narra la trágica vida y muerte de su hermano menor, y alude a la digna pobreza de su familia. Emilio Di Tata Roitberg, en *González Catán* (item **2085**) da voz a las historias de personajes marginales de la barriada pobre bonaerense. Entre la parodia, el humor, y la visión despiadada de la realidad, los personajes continúan la lucha dispar por la sobrevivencia. La novela de Luis Gusmán, *Hasta que te conocí* (item **2089**) nos interna por el mundillo sórdido de un stripper y fisioculturista asesinado y los personajes imbricados en su vida. Las peleas de pitbuls y la corrupcion de una zona marginada, sintetizan el fracaso individual al mismo tiempo que marcan el desgarramiento de una clase social que se mueve en la periferia. La incertidumbre y la desolación de la familia burguesa en la novela de Marina Mariasch, *Estamos unidas* (item **2101**) hacen contrapunto a la temática de las novelas comentadas anteriormente desde la perspectiva femenina de una clase holgada en la década de los 90, pero que se encuentra sin timón moral frente a una sociedad cada vez más abiertamente consumista y poco comprometida con su realidad a nivel nacional. Gonzalo Unamuno relata en *Que todo se detenga* (item **2111**) la desesperada apatía de un joven en caída libre hacia la droga, la desidia, la humillación del cuerpo en el marco de una sociedad indiferente al sufrimiento. En *La mala fe* (item **2086**), Romina Doval retrata la desilusión, la falta de principios, la inseguridad a todo nivel de dos jóvenes amigas de la infancia ante las limitaciones impuestas por un país en franca desintegración. La vena existencialista de esta novela se ve reflejada en las decisiones de los personajes abandonados a su propia suerte y presente también en las novelas discutidas. El ámbito del periodismo y de los trabajadores de oficina son explorados en dos novelas: *Las noticias* de Hernán Arias (item **2079**) y *La fusión: memorias de oficina* de José María Gómez (item **2088**). En ambas, la cotidianidad del trabajo encierra las pequeñeces humanas, los conflictos entre profesionales, el vacío de una existencia marcada por los ritos, la conveniencia y la ausencia de escrúpulos.

Una segunda vertiente de la narrativa actual hace referencia concreta a la historia nacional reciente y trata de rescatar las voces del olvido; esta narrativa intenta recuperar y lograr justicia para aquellos que ya no están. Algunas pretenden desenterrar el pasado literalmente como en *Chicas muertas* (item **2076**) de Selva Almada, historia de varios actos de femicidio que la autora recuerda desde su infancia. Estos actos de violencia contra la mujer han quedado impunes, y Almada se propone exhumar esas voces para hacer un llamado a la justicia, a la conciencia de un país patriarcal y sexista que ha enterrado literalmente sus crímenes contra la mujer. En *Los manchados* (item **2078**) de María Teresa Andruetto, la protagonista, Julieta, entrevista personas del pasado familiar en su pueblo de origen, Tama. A partir de archivos, una novela y entrevistas, la historia oral de la familia comienza a construirse a la par de la historia nacional que aparece en breves pinceladas para contextualizar el exilio, la búsqueda por la identidad, el perdón y la culpa. *Todos éramos hijos* (item **2100**) de María Rosa Lojo de Beuter utiliza el apodo inusual de una colegiala llamada Frik durante los años 70 para darnos una voz narrativa peculiar e inteligente. Frik y sus amistades descubren en sus padres, hermanos y allegados los elementos constitutivos del país: el inmigrante económico, el exiliado político, el intelectual soñador, el militante intransigente, el noble ideólogo, el joven comprometido y el alienado. *El refugio en el telar* (item **2112**) de Damián Verduga reconstruye la historia en una novela testimonial en la cual la voz narrativa dialoga con una sobreviviente de la llamada "Noches de las corbatas" acontecida en Mar del Plata y Neuquén en julio del 1977.

Finalmente, otras voces marginalizadas por la sociedad se revelan en la novela de Bernarda Pagés, *La fauna divina* (item **2103**). Perla, la narradora de su propia historia vuelca el odio y la impotencia de aquellos que sufrieron como ella las consecuencias espeluznates de la talidomida, causante de terribles deformaciones en los recién nacidos.

Una serie de relatos fusionan historias autobiográficas con trazos ficcionales y aspectos sicológicos en las que se describen estados de ánimo, pasiones y conflictos internos. En varios casos, la narración coexiste con representaciones artísticas para abordar experiencias personales desde una mirada sensible e intimista. En *Encuentro con Munch* (item **2092**) de Sylvia Iparraguirre, la presencia omnisciente del pintor noruego Edvar Munch le permite a la narradora, desde Oslo, Noruega, reflexionar sobre el desarraigo, la extranjeridad y la cotidianidad. Por otro lado, la pintura, la poesía y el cuento forman parte de la trama de los relatos en *Vestidos de colores: poemas, cuentos, pinturas* (item **2113**) de Olga Zamboni, Trini Álvarez, y Tito Busse. Estos artistas de la provincia de Misiones emplean imágenes y colores para organizar los cuentos y poemas que en su mayoría reconstruyen memorias de la infancia y de la juventud. En otro relato autobiográfico, *El sol detrás del limonero* (item **2105**), Ángela Pradelli presenta una conmovedora historia en la cual los versos, las cartas y los relatos pintan una historia familiar de destierros, miserias y desencuentros. Otros textos, aunque no son necesariamente autobiográficos, dialogan íntimamente con la música y otras literaturas, como es el caso de la novela *Pequeña flor* (item **2090**) de Iosi Havilio, en la que el personaje principal comparte la pasión por el jazz, y sus intérpretes, especialmente por Sidney Becket, y por los novelistas rusos. Desde una perspectiva autobiográfica, la segunda novela del escritor Osvaldo Bossi, *Yo soy aquel* (item **2082**), presenta un relato veraz sobre la amistad y las vivencias de la niñez, que nos marcan y acompañan a lo largo de nuestras vidas. También se trata la importancia de la amistad durante los años formativos en la novela titulada *El invierno con mi generación* (item **2098**) de Mauro Libertella la cual rememora la juventud en un colegio secundario bonaerense y pone énfasis en las relaciones personales que se forjan entre la primera juventud y la edad adulta. Otra voz infantil que recrea un ambiente ominoso y por momentos fantástico es *La habitación del presidente* (item **2108**) de Ricardo Romero cuya narrativa incursiona en una suerte de viaje real y metafórico por su propia casa y por el vecindario creando una serie de idas y vueltas entre lo real y lo fantástico, entre lo contemplativo y lo inquietante. En la vertiente de la novela de autoficción, podría ubicarse *Estamos unidas* (item **2101**), relato en primera persona el cual intercala una voz intimista con experiencias sociales y políticas de los años 90. Predominantemente ante la presencia de mujeres que viajan entre EE. UU., Europa y Buenos Aires, se intenta evocar un mundo de apariencias y ausencias donde el personaje principal parece hundido en una especie de cuestionamientos sicológicos. Así mismo, en *El secreto de Irina* (item **2096**), se enfatiza la caracterización interior de la protagonista al descubrir que lo inesperado y lo absurdo pueden afectar su alma cansada.

Dentro del corpus de los textos reseñados, cabe destacarse el género de novela histórica. Una de las principales características de estas novelas es la preparación documental de los autores quienes para recrear ambientes de las épocas referenciadas evidencian un amplio conocimiento crítico de los hechos históricos así como de sus habilidades narrativas. En *Monteagudo: anatomía de una revolución* (item **2109**) de Marcos Rosenzvaig se documenta a través de un cuaderno íntimo de un médico forense las conversaciones con Monteagudo las que humanizan a las figuras históricas de la época de la independencia. En *Peones de ajedrez: otra partida* (item **2093**) de Marcelino Iriarnni, se noveliza la historia decimonónica de la frontera entre Tandil y Azul donde se representan las tensiones diarias entre las tribus del lugar, los estancieros y el ejército. En *Madre de la patria: capitana de Belgrano, María Remedios del Valle* (item **2110**) de José Luis Thomas, se visualiza la figura de María Remedios, una mujer de raza negra que peleó, cuidó y acompañó a Manuel Belgrano durante la campaña al Alto Perú. A través de esta novela histórica, Thomas le da voz a una luchadora incansable, excluida de la historia oficial y en el proceso retrata la discriminación, las vejaciones y la exclusión que padeció una verdadera heroína que luchó por la patria. En *Evita, una vida apasionada* (item **2084**) Helen Davis noveliza la vida de Eva Perón. Tomando como referencia una variedad de documentos históricos de la época, Davis intenta humanizar la figura de la legendaria Evita.

Como parte de las novelas de corte experimental, especialmente en cuanto al empleo de las tecnologías digitales o su referencia y a la innovación en las técnicas empleadas, se incluyen *La menor* (item **2107**) de Daniel Riera y *Las constelaciones oscuras* (item **2102**) de Pola Oloixarac. En la primera un escritor recibe una oferta para escribir una novela que se pueda enviar por mensaje de texto. Así comienza el experimento de una novela menor que se caracteriza por el empleo tanto de formas como de contenido creativo e innovador. En la segunda novela, por su parte, se entrelazan espacios de la biología, la tecnología y la ciencia ficción en una narrativa que presenta tres ejes temporales a lo largo de tres siglos. La innovación narrativa se recrea tanto en las técnicas literarias como en el contenido de la novela.

Algunas de las obras con rasgos biográficos que se destacan en los textos reseñados incluyen aquellas que presentan un balance entre la historia del siglo XX y los datos sobre el autor biografiado. Por ejemplo *Galeano: apuntes para una biografía* (item **2137**) de Fabián Kovacic se basa en textos, archivos, videos y entrevistas que recrean tanto la vida literaria del escritor uruguayo Eduardo Galeano como su comprometida participación en la historia del siglo XX latinoamericano. Por su parte, el libro *La forma inicial* (item **2132**) de Ricardo Piglia, se aleja del contenido y el tono formal de la inclusión de la historia para dar lugar a un texto que favorece el carácter conversacional representado en entrevistas, reseñas sobre libros y cine así como en ensayos sobre su propia relación con la lectura y la escritura. A través de esta biografía literaria y personal de Piglia, el lector logra acercarse al extraordinario pensamiento del escritor argentino. Otro texto marcado por una exhaustiva investigación sobre el autor y su obra es aquel titulado, *Adolfo Bioy Casares. Obra completa III (1972–1999)* (item **2081**) cuya edición se encuentra a cargo de Daniel Marino. Esta obra reúne por primera vez todos los escritos publicados por Bioy Casares entre 1972 y 1999 además de aquellos textos que no fueron recogidos en ningún volumen. El cuidadoso trabajo de Marino aporta referencias y anotaciones literarias, históricas y lingüísticas sobre la obra del Bioy Casares, esenciales para ahondar en los variados mundos íntimos y literarios del autor argentino.

Finalmente, en la categoría de cuentos, micronarrativas y relatos cortos, resaltan las historias de la infancia, las vivencias personales y se gravita en torno a temáticas humanas de cariz universal. La mayoría de estos cuentos quedan casi siempre enmarcados en el contexto histórico de la narración y en la realidad cotidiana de la ciudad o del pueblo de provincia. Selva Almada, en *El desapego es una manera de querernos* (item **2077**) recoge cuentos publicados a partir del 2003 donde los personajes de provincia emanan autenticidad en su manera de amar, de recordar y de odiar. Almada invita a sus lectores a dialogar con estas creaciones que nos asombran y nos enriquecen. Otra recopilación de cuentos publicados muy anteriormente al presente se encuentra en la colección *El reconocimiento y otros cuentos* (item **2094**) de Amalia Jamilis. Hay un intento de recuperación de esta cuentística quizás no muy valorada en su época (los años 60). Andrea Candia Gajá, compila 22 cuentos de escritores argentinos exiliados—al menos por un periodo— en México. Los cuentos de *Relatos del exilio: escritores argentinos en México* (item **2106**) giran en torno al dolor inenarrable del exiliado, sus ansias de pertenencia, la ilusión del regreso y la certidumbre de no poder cumplir con el sueño del retorno. En manos de Humberto Costantini, Juan Gelman, Mempo Giardinelli y Tununa Mercado, el exilio se vuelve un grito desgarrador. María Rosa Lojo de Beuter, recopila cuatro colecciones de microcuentos en *Bosque de ojos: microficciones y otros textos breves* (item **2099**). Ejemplo de la prosa poética, Lojo se regodea en un lenguaje preciso y evocador para resaltar cómo ve el artista al mundo y cómo descubre una realidad siempre escondida y revelada a medias. La primera colección de cuentos de Alejandra Kamiya, *Los árboles caídos también son el bosque* (item **2095**) exploran con un lenguaje depurado las relaciones entre sus dos culturas: la argentina y la japonesa. La extranjeridad, el desarraigo y la pertenencia constituyen el meollo temático de esta talentosa voz narrativa. *Se vende o se alquila: cuentos* (item **2087**), es una colección de 24 relatos de Olga Ferrari la cual maneja una serie de personajes dispares y atrayentes que van tejiendo historias personales en donde se reflejan las pasiones humanas. [LRL y CEM]

URUGUAY
El corpus reseñado, cuya fecha de publicación corresponde en su mayoría al 2016, retiene rasgos generales presentes en la producción literaria del trienio anterior. Se constata una prevalencia de textos de autoría masculina, una producción—menor en número pero canónica—dentro de las creaciones en el campo de la ficción histórica así como una presencia estable del subgénero de la novela negra. La mayoría de los autores cuentan con una obra reconocida en el país (Roberto Appratto, Juan Carlos Mondragón y Hugo Burel son los casos más notables) pero esto también define aquellos casos de escritores cuya obra se sitúa en un espacio único, tanto por el tono como por el estilo que han cultivado en su práctica escritural (lo que puede afirmarse en términos de la obra de Leo Maslíah y Gustavo Espinosa).

Una de las novelas históricas de más peso en la producción literaria de este periodo, aunque publicada en Argentina, es *El loco: luces y sombras de Domingo Faustino Sarmiento* de Mercedes Vigil (item **2130**). Si el título advierte de la intención de mantener el retrato alejado de la idealización, la novela va más allá. La apertura y la clausura del texto están a cargo de la voz de quien fuera la pareja de Sarmiento, Aurelia Vélez Sarsfield y no de su mujer. En un gesto que podría calificarse de feminista, Vigil le otorga a este personaje el poder de establecer los parámetros temporales dentro de los cuales pintar la vida del protagonista. Aurelia inaugura la narración recordando un Sarmiento ya muerto y la culmina, anciana, recordando el momento en que se conocieron en Montevideo, durante la visita sarmientina a los exiliados antirrosistas que allí residían. Se podría decir que la vida de Sarmiento que importa, en esta novela, es la que empieza con el encuentro con Aurelia y la que termina con los recuerdos que ella guarda de él.

Desde el punto de vista estrictamente temático y trascendiendo subgéneros, en esta producción reciente se pueden identificar dos temas: el de la soledad y el de la identidad. En algunos casos el primero se erige en el catalizador mismo del argumento. Hugo Burel, cuyo texto *Montevideo noir* (item **2121**) constituye un ejercicio metaliterario dentro del género de la novela negra, profundiza en la creación de un protagonista quien, enfrentado a una viudez repentina a edad aún temprana y a la ausencia de un hijo que migra al otro extremo del mundo, halla en la literatura un sucedáneo de la vida. Con *Solo para ti*, Gladys Franco (item **2124**) en tono intimista y desde la creación de una voz narrativa en tercera persona, al alinearse con los pensamientos y emociones de una niña que lucha con la complejidad de su identidad como hija adoptiva—eje de la historia—construye eficazmente la psique solitaria protagónica. Por su parte en *Taxi* (item **2119**), Sergio Altesor yuxtapone ambos temas en el contexto de una reflexión poco común sobre la memoria del llamado pasado reciente en Uruguay. De hecho, se puede decir que la novela resignifica la categoría "pasado reciente". Para el protagonista este es ahora sinónimo del periodo mismo del exilio y no necesariamente de los hechos o del periodo uruguayo que lo llevaron a emigrar a Suecia en los años 80. Desde este punto de vista, el énfasis se coloca en el dilema de resituar su experiencia de inmigrante (otra vez) en el marco más amplio de las exclusiones sociales y económicas del presente. Al representar la transformación política de la otrora generosa Suecia para con los exiliados cono-sureños y al hacer de su protagonista un testigo de algún modo privilegiado de esa historia, Altessor introduce el tema de una memoria diferente, no la del exilio—de la que la literatura uruguaya tiene ejemplos—sino de la del retorno fallido a Uruguay y de la de la aceptación de la identidad post-retorno y nueva emigración. Con este eje narrativo, que se aparta de representaciones colectivas sobre el tema de la dictadura y del exilio uruguayos frecuentes en la producción literaria del pasado, Altessor invita a los lectores a explorar los efectos duraderos de la vida fuera de fronteras nacionales durante los años en que esa existencia se articulaba solamente en términos de provisionalidad. El desafío que enfrenta el protagonista es de doble carácter: se trata de reconocer como propias la vida y las relaciones forjadas en aquel exilio de los 80 pero también de deconstruir la romantización de un país adoptivo y del originario en la actualidad. Por último, la identidad y la experiencia de antiguos inmigrantes llegados a Uruguay después de la Segunda Guerra Mundial se visibiliza en los cuentos de Fritz Kalmar (item **2125**) y Raquel Zieleniec (item **2131**). El primero se centra en la representación de la alienación lingüística sufrida por un recurrente inmigrante austríaco en Bolivia y Uruguay. La segunda ficcionaliza experiencias diaspóricas judías en Montevideo. [GU]

PROSE FICTION
Argentina

2076 **Almada, Selva.** Chicas muertas. Segunda edición. Buenos Aires: Literatura Random House, 2015. 187 p.

Novela de corte testimonial, narra los tres asesinatos de jovencitas en diferentes provincias de la Argentina. Basada en parte en los recuerdos de infancia de la autora, en las crónicas de los periódicos, las entrevistas con parientes y conocidos de las víctimas, las emisiones radiales de la época en que ocurrieron los crímenes (en los años 80), la novela se va revelando en forma de rompecabezas hilvanando desparejamente las circunstancias particulares de cada una de las muchachas. El estilo distanciado, propio de algunas narrativas testimoniales, deja sin embargo vislumbrar la profunda empatía de la narradora hacia las víctimas del femicidio y de la injusticia de estos crímenes impunes, espejos de una sociedad patriarcal. [CEM]

2077 **Almada, Selva.** El desapego es una manera de querernos. Buenos Aires: Literatura Random House, 2015. 294 p.

Publicados entre 2003 y 2015, los cuentos de esta colección (revisada por la autora), contienen desde el germen de su escritura hasta los más recientes ejemplos de su desarrollo como narradora. La ambientación en la provincia, el calor humano que se despega de sus personajes, el lenguaje fiel a la realidad que retrata, las temáticas universales, los diálogos veloces y punzantes hacen de la narrativa de Almada, un repositorio viviente y auténtico de lo que significa ser humano. El amor, las rivalidades, los ritos de pasaje, la amistad, las desgracias familiares, forman una cadena de vivencias que despierta con su lectura el deseo de conocer más sobre estas vidas que tanto se asemejan a las nuestras. [CEM]

2078 **Andruetto, María Teresa.** Los manchados. Buenos Aires: Literatura Random House, 2015. 188 p.

La reconstrucción de la historia nacional y, en particular, del noroeste del país desde fines del siglo XIX hasta las últimas décadas del XX está a la base de la novela de Andruetto. La protagonista, Julieta, plasma las versiones de la historia familiar a medida que va encontrando personajes del pueblo de Tama que de alguna manera van a completar el rompecabezas de su familia. Bajo el pretexto de hacer investigación para una tesis doctoral en Alemania, Julieta descubre en esas voces, en una novela escrita por Milagros Linares, y en los archivos que consulta la confusión de su propio linaje y los vestigios de la memoria colectiva de una región empobrecida por la avaricia y la corrupción y orgullosa de su historia mantenida de boca en boca por la tradición oral. [CEM]

2079 **Arias, Hernán.** Las noticias. Córdoba, Argentina: Editorial Nudista, 2014. 104 p.

Este periodista cultural cordobés presenta en esta corta novela lo que podría considerarse una novela de redacción periodística. Es un retrato de la cotidianidad de un grupo de periodistas que trabajan en un semanario porteño, el que publica todo tipo de noticias. El narrador es parte del suplemento *Cultura*, el cual entrevista a escritores y publica reseñas de libros. Organizada en capítulos cortos y escrita en frases escuetas, la novela se centra en ciertas notas requeridas, tales como la visita de Máxima Zorreguieta a la Argentina y una entrevista a un "figurón local" de las letras. La narración alude al trabajo que se lleva a cabo en la redacción como un oficio burocrático y muchas veces impuesto. Como indica el narrador, casi a modo de manifiesto: "Las noticias también se inventan. Donde no había nada, algo debe aparecer". [LRL]

2080 **Bilbao Richter, José.** Juan Bautista Túpac Amaru y el misterio de la Orden del Sol. Buenos Aires: 1884 Editorial, Círculo Militar, 2014. 338 p. (Colección Novela histórica; 2)

Novela histórica que recupera del olvido a un personaje de la historia sudamericana: el indio Juan Bautista Túpac Amaru. La novela recrea la trágica vida del protagonista en un entorno racista, discriminatorio y extremadamente cruel. Juan Bautista, así bautizado por los españoles, se convirtió en un inca revolucionario quien tuvo que pagar su rebelión contra la corona española con muchos años de cárcel, exilio, esclavitud y vejámenes, siguiendo los pasos trágicos de su hermano mayor, José Gabriel Noguera Túpac Amaru II, quien fue descuartizado en 1781. A través de un exhaustivo trabajo de investigación, Bilbao Richter reconstruye en 14 capítulos los viajes de Juan Bautista, sus cautiverios en Perú, España, África y la Argentina y su peregrinaje de Cusco hasta Buenos Aires. El autor entrelaza sus amplios conocimientos de la historia con sus habilidades como novelista al crear un personaje llamado Américo quien narra y al mismo tiempo es testigo tanto de la cotidianidad del mundo quechua y aymara como de las despiadadas crueldades e injusticias a la que fueron sometidos. [LRL]

2081 **Bioy Casares, Adolfo.** Obra completa. Vol. 3, 1972–1999. Edición al cargo de Daniel Martino. Buenos Aires: Emecé, 2014. 1 vol.: ill.

El presente volume reúne por primera vez los escritos de Bioy Casares (1914–99) aparecidos entre 1972 y 1999. Se incluyen obras como *Dormir al sol* (1973), *El héroe de las mujeres* (1978), *La aventura de un fotógrafo en La Plata* (1985), *Historias desaforadas* (1986), *Unos días en el Brasil (Diario de viaje)* (1991), *Un campeón desparejo* (1993), *Una magia modesta* (1997), *De un mundo a otro* (1998) y *De las cosas maravillosas* (1999), así como "Obra del período no recogida en volumen" y una cuidada sección dedicada a notas a los textos junto a una bibliografía. Este volume a cargo de Daniel Marino, quien anteriormente había preparado numerosos trabajos sobre la obra de Adolfo Bioy Casares, aporta minuciosas explicaciones y aclaraciones sobre las referencias literarias e históricas que aparecen en los cuentos, creando un caudal de anotaciones precisas. Vale aquí destacar la ardua tarea de Martino que en este volumen revela la exhaustiva investigación y el profundo conocimiento sobre la obra de Bioy Casares. [LRL]

2082 **Bossi, Osvaldo.** Yo soy aquel. Córdoba, Argentina: Editorial Nudista, 2014. 109 p.

Yo soy aquel es la segunda novela del poeta y escritor Osvaldo Bossi. Desde una perspectiva autobiográfica, se relata de la infancia de Os, un niño de nueve años que vive con su familia en una barrio pobre del conourbano bonaerense. La novela se inicia poniendo énfasis en la imaginación del niño: "¿Soy un árbol o soy un niño?" El niño desde la ventana de la humilde casilla mira la luna y juguetea con los insectos que pasan zumbando a su lado. Es finales de la década de los 60 y aparecen Neil Amstrong y la llegada del hombre a la luna. A pesar de la pobreza y de la presencia de un padre abusador, se normalizan los comportamientos de la madre que hace torta fritas y las reparte entre los vecinos y el del padre que sale en su carro de botellero junto a su caballo Tornado. El niño acompaña a su padre por las calles de otros vecindarios y vive la experiencia con entusiasmo, como una aventura. Lo anecdótico se presenta en las relaciones de amistad entre los varones, algunos sensibles y honestos, como el niño San y otros que lo acusan de ser un niño "raro". En general, es un relato noble y fresco sobre la amistad y las vivencias de la niñez que nos marcan y nos acompañan durante toda la vida. [LRL]

2083 **Coelho, Oliverio.** Bien de frontera. Buenos Aires: Seix Barral, 2015. 254 p. (Biblioteca breve)

Dividida en tres partes, la novela de Coelho narra la vida y muerte de un tal Sauri, campeón de ajedrez cuando joven, quien se convierte en un estafador en serie en la zona de la Triple Frontera en un futuro cercano (termina en 2019). El protagonista usa su inteligencia y astucia para engatusar a incautos personajes que confían en él. El único vestigio de su vida pasada está en su hija, Malena, a quien busca infructuosamente luego de viajar con ella hasta la zona de las tres fronteras antes de dar a su vida un cambio radical. [CEM]

2084 **Davis, Helen R.** Evita, una vida apasionada. Buenos Aires: Libros En Red, 2015. 313 p.

La licenciada norteamericana Helen Davis escribe una novela sobre la vida de Eva María Duarte de Perón. Narrada en primera persona, el texto recrea desde una perspectiva personal las relaciones íntimas, sociales y políticas de la legendaria figura. Basándose en una variedad de documentos históricos relativos tanto a Eva como a su esposo, el general Juan Domingo Perón, Davis narra la relación simbiótica aunque complicada que existió entre Evita y Perón, quien fuera presidente de Argentina en tres oportunidades. A través de la voz de Evita y de los diálogos con Perón, allegados, seguidores, descamisados y con figuras públicas nacionales e internacionales, tales como Eleanor Roosevelt, se alude a la incansable dedicación a los descamisados, a los pobres y al Partido Peronista Femenino. También la novela se refiere, aunque soslayadamente, al carácter controvertido de su persona. Odiada, insultada y despreciada por las clases sociales favorecidas, la figura de Eva Perón es un personaje complejo y difícil de definir. La novela intenta retratarla más humana sin santificar su ya mítica figura. [LRL]

2085 Di Tata Roitberg, Emilio. González Catán. Buenos Aires: Clarín: Alfaguara, 2015. 382 p.

Los barrios más empobrecidos del conurbano bonaerense sirven no solo de marco para ambientar la historia, sino también son personajes de esta novela hecha de voces del pueblo. Olga, Javi, los niños de Olga, Teo, Marquitos, y una amplia gama de gente que representa la cara humana de estas zonas conocidas más que nada por el crimen que sale en las noticias. No obstante, la novela da espacio para profundizar en las vidas de estos seres limitados por la circunstancias: trabajadores honestos, inmigrantes que se mueven entre policías corruptos, narcotraficantes y vagos. Los personajes creados adquieren una realidad avasalladora en su búsqueda por la felicidad, la amistad, la venganza y la ilusión del éxito cada día más alejado. Los diálogos nos suenan veraces, con giros cómicos o rudos, desprovistos de las buenas maneras de la clase media, pero empapados de una humanidad que los ennoblece aun entre las inmundicias que los rodean. [CEM]

2086 Doval, Romina. La mala fe. Buenos Aires: Bajo la Luna, 2016. 275 p. (Buenos y breves; 58)

Ambientada a principios del siglo XXI, dos amigas de la infancia, Victoria y Paulina comparten un departamento y afrontan la precariedad económica de dos egresadas del secundario sin esperanzas de un futuro estable y cómodo en los turbulentos años que preceden la crisis económica. La historia de las amigas es narrada en dos tiempos en un constante vaivén entre un narrador en tercera persona desde el presente y los recuerdos de la escuela primaria en los años 80 y la secundaria en los 90, narrados en primera persona por Victoria. Este cuadro de la vida de dos jóvenes que intentan independizarse se complica con un personaje extraño pero atrayente, Soren, con quien discuten sin tregua en términos existenciales. El robo en los supermercados adquiere repercusiones profundas a partir de una lucha interna entre la educación recibida y parcialmente rechazada, las realidades económicas del momento, y las frustraciones de una juventud donde el compas ético-moral se halla atascado. [CEM]

2087 Ferrari, Olgar. Se vende o se alquila: cuentos. Buenos Aires: Georges Zanun Editores, 2011. 123 p. (Colección Tusitala; 2)

Esta colección de 24 relatos breves tiene como temática principal el misterio de la vida humana. Los personajes, sumamente diversos, desde un psicópata hasta una inmigrante ya anciana, revelan en forma concentrada las huellas de su paso por el mundo. En estos personajes se encierran dolores, crímenes, desilusiones, alegrías, misterios que nos toman de sorpresa y nos dejan como un eco del destino que les tocó vivir y del cual somos testigos por medio de la lectura. [CEM]

2088 Gómez, José María. La fusión: memorias de oficina. Buenos Aires: Interzona, 2015. 140 p.

Desde la agudizada conciencia del yo narrador, el mundo banal y a la vez misterioso de las oficinas emerge inexorablemente para traducir el lenguaje codificado minuciosamente por los que las habitan. El protagonista va desmadejando la compleja trama de relaciones, de pequeños odios y de miedo al fracaso, de deseos incumplidos y de profundas traiciones a sí mismo y a los que circulan en este ambiente sofocador y fríamente brutal. [CEM]

2089 Gusmán, Luis. Hasta que te conocí. Buenos Aires: Edhasa, 2015. 289 p. (Novela)

En esta novela se investiga el asesinato de Silvio, un stripper, fisioculturista esnob, estudiante de portugués, que un día aparece muerto. Al comienzo de la novela, aparece Lucero González, una muchacha que dice estar embarazada de un hijo de Silvio. Por diferentes caminos se cruzan

Walensky, ex pesista cuidador del gimnasio donde asistía Silvio, Bersani un inspector de policía que investiga el asesinato del stripper y Clara, una mujer veterinaria, casada y que había sido amante de Silvio. Aunque el asesinato y el embarazo de Lucero le da impulso a la novela, no se podría considerar ésta, una novela ni totalmente policial ni de amor. Por el contrario, el texto trata sobre espacios y personajes urbanos marginados, corruptos y fracasados. El perro de Silvio, un pitbul de pelea, lleva a algunos de los personajes a adentrarse en el mundo sórdido, cruel y corrupto de las peleas de perros pitbuls. Ese espacio inmoral y perverso representado en la novela, de alguna manera, dialoga con el sinsentido y la desconfianza que prevalece entre los personajes y las situaciones dentro de la novela. [LRL]

2090 **Havilio, Iosi.** Pequeña flor. Buenos Aires: Literatura Random House, 2015. 122 p.

En esta novela corta, de un único párrafo se relata en primera personal la historia de José, un joven que al perder su trabajo se ve obligado a quedarse en su casa con su pequeña hija mientras su esposa Laura sale a trabajar. La oración inicial, "Esta historia empieza cuando yo era otro" es reveladora de los hechos fortuitos que acontecerán. Al visitar a su vecino, Guillermo, con quien comparte la pasión por el jazz, lo mata (o cree matarlo) con una pala de jardín. A partir de ese momento, José se hunde en un mundo de inquietudes y de inseguridades, el cual se complica con la frágil relación con su esposa. Empleando múltiples alusiones a la literatura rusa (Dostoievski, Chéhov, Tolstoi) y al jazz norteamericano (Sidney Bechet), la novela alude a la muerte y a la resurrección real y metafórica de personajes y a la persistencia de situaciones inesperadas. [LRL]

2091 **Heredia, Víctor.** Los perros. Buenos Aires: Editorial Planeta, 2015. 203 p.

Entre los desperdicios del basural, las vidas de Matías, jovencito llamado El Sabio por su interés en leer y en escribir, y de su familia, revelan a retazos, los misterios de la vida entre una población de indigentes que busca su humanidad a pesar de las indignidades que sobrellevan cada día. El odio, la venganza, la pequeñez de los habitantes de estas laderas de escombros e inmundicias, parecen ser el motor de aquellos que trabajan de sol a sol para ganarse unos pesos o que se pierden en el humo de las drogas. Sin embargo, se vislumbra en el personaje principal, Matías, en su padre Evaristo, su madre, Silvia, su tía Miranda, y en la prostituta Sandra la entereza, la fortitud de los que no se dejan tumbar, los que esperan un futuro mejor, y una dignidad merecida. [CEM]

2092 **Iparraguirre, Sylvia.** Encuentro con Munch. Buenos Aires: Alfaguara, 2013. 195 p.

En este relato se fusionan elementos autobiográficos, ficción y crónica. El centro de la narrativa es ocupado por una narradora quien es a su vez la misma autora recordando un episodio de su vida en el año 2000. Invitada para ser madrina de un flamante navío, viaja a Oslo y Bergen en Noruega para la ceremonia. Es en Oslo que vive su mejor amiga, ausente en ese momento a causa de unas vacaciones muy necesarias para recuperarse luego de un cáncer. Son, sin embargo, las reflexiones sobre el desarraigo, el encuentro con el otro, las máscaras usadas en el trato cotidiano y la presencia apremiante del pintor noruego Edvar Munch que llevan adelante la narrativa. En parte somos testigos del proceso de recordar, de leer, de ver y de asociar que nos deja presenciar mediante la lectura esta escritora talentosa. [CEM]

2093 **Irianni, Marcelino.** Peones de ajedrez: otra partida. La misma historia. Tandil, Argentina: Universidad Nacional del Centro de la Provincia de Buenos Aires, 2013. 328 p.

Doctor en historia y oriundo de Tandil, Argentina, Marcelino Irianni escribe una novela histórica que tiene lugar a mediados del siglo XIX en la frontera sur de la provincial de Buenos Aires, entre Tandil y Azul. Aparecen representadas las tensiones y los peligros diarios entre indios, estancieros, negros y el ejército ocupado en pelear contra la Confederación. A través de un lenguaje detalladamente descriptivo y por momentos poético, se exponen las inclemencias del tiempo, el arraigo a las tradiciones del lugar y los múltiples personajes que conforman el relato. Así, se entrelazan experiencias de aquellos tribus que perdieron sus tierras y sus lugares sagrados en medio de tratados y acuerdos ajenos a sus derechos. La novela subraya las alianzas y las traiciones como la del viejo cacique Catriel que se ve obligado a aliarse con los criollos y milicos por el temor al poderío de los otros caciques. [LRL]

2094 Jamilis, Amalia. El reconocimiento y otros cuentos. Córdoba, Argentina: Eduvim, 2015. 323 p. (Narradoras argentinas)

El volumen recoge los dos primeros libros publicados por Jamilis, *Detrás de las columnas* (1967) y *Los días de suerte* (1969)". La colección Narradoras Argentinas tiene como misión reconocer el talento de las escritoras argentinas mediante la publicación de una obra quizás olvidada o poco valorada en su época. Se ha añadido a estas dos colecciones un cuento inédito, "El reconocimiento," el cual explora, desde la perspectiva de Estela Botti—cuyo hijo se ha exiliado en Montevideo—la violencia de la dictadura y sus consecuencias. [CEM]

2095 Kamiya, Alejandra. Los árboles caídos también son el bosque. Buenos Aires: Bajo la Luna, 2015. 120 p.: bibl. (Buenos y breves; 56)

Este es la primera colección de cuentos de la autora, aunque individualmente varios de los cuentos incluiqdos en esta colección fueron anteriormente publicados y premiados. En su conjunto, los cuentos de *Los árboles caídos también son el bosque* retratan la herencia japonesa y la argentina, el lado de acá y el de allá, mundos que coexisten en los cuentos. En los 12 cuentos de la colección aparecen espacios domésticos, rurales y urbanos. Kamiya se adentra en la problemática de la extranjeridad tanto geográfica como existencial. En "Desayuno perfecto", una mujer japonesa le prepara un último desayuno a su familia antes de suicidarse; en "Arroz", la narradora come con su padre japonés quien con gestos y silencios le da una lección de vida sobre su propia cultura; en "Tan breves como un trébol", se relata la desesperación de una madre al presenciar el accidente de su pequeño hijo. Con un lenguaje literario preciso y exquisito, Kamiya recrea una diversidad de mundos donde coexisten lo cotidiano, lo extraño y lo trágico, en donde los personajes humildemente observan, reflexionan y aprenden. [LRL]

2096 Kociancich, Vlady. El secreto de Irina. Buenos Aires: Tusquets Editores, 2016. 258 p. (Colección Andanzas)

Esta novela de 17 capítulos narra la historia de cinco amigos que deciden ir de vacaciones a la Costa Maya en México. Irina, la única que viaja sin pareja, acaba de divorciarse. Sus amigos esperan que el viaje pueda aliviarle la tristeza profunda en la que se ha hundido. En el hotel los días transcurren entre comidas, tragos, incursiones al mar y a la piscina. El momento decisivo en el relato es cuando el grupo decide ir a visitar un cenote, un pozo de agua manantial, con ríos subterráneos, cavernas y pasadizos. El cenote al que deciden visitar está aislado y es poco visitado por los turistas. En un momento Irina se aleja del grupo y queda atrapada sin que sus amigos se den cuenta de su ausencia. Así Irina, casi muerta, es rescatada por Zalazar, un maya de la región que junto a su esposa la cuidan. Al creerse a salvo, Irene descubrirá que lo inesperado y lo absurdo puede afectar un alma cansada, como la suya y como la de su propio rescatista. El secreto de Irina se va dilucidando a través de las diferentes voces de los personajes, los que de alguna manera tienen su propia visión de los hechos. [LRL]

2097 Laurencich, Alejandra. Las olas del mundo. Buenos Aires: Alfaguara, 2015. 377 p.

La protagonista de esta novela ubicada en los años 70, Andrea, es una jovencita de 13 años, soñadora e inteligente que inventa historias basadas en hechos verídicos, fantasías, nuevas amistades y cantantes famosos; entre ellos, los rockeros Mick Jagger y Luis Alberto Spinetta por quién siente una adoración sin límites. De familia clase media de inmigrantes italianos, Andrea, su hermano Fabián, los padres y la abuela constituyen un mundo seguro y cariñoso; sin embargo, la violencia de esta década comenzará a invadir la tranquilidad de sus vidas, y se infiltrará poco a poco hasta concluir con la partida de Fabián a Italia. Con el paso de los meses, las familias del barrio dejan o venden las casas; Andrea siente que el silencio, el misterio y la amenaza del mundo exterior la van acorralando; la duda y la culpa de un secreto revelado quizás por un error de ella misma, la harán cómplice de una tragedia. La reconstrucción de esa época salvaje desde la perspectiva de Andrea la adolescencia pura se enfrenta a la maldad, la traición y el sufrimiento en una trama que es encrucijada de historia amorosa, diario de una jovencita y thriller político. [CEM]

2098 **Libertella, Mauro.** El invierno con mi generación. Buenos Aires: Literatura Random House, 2015. 122 p.

El joven narrador rememora los años cruciales de su juventud en un colegio de Núñez en dónde conoce a unos pocos muchachos con quienes comparte gustos e intereses. La voz narrativa cuenta en un tono sosegado el descubrimiento de una amistad fuerte y duradera, los vaivenes de la amistad, y los inevitables cambios operados por las experiencias vitales de los muchachos que forman su grupo. Entre nostálgico y cerebral, el rito de pasaje de la primera juventud a la edad adulta, constituye el meollo de esta novela de iniciación. [CEM]

2099 **Lojo de Beuter, María Rosa.** Bosque de ojos: microficciones y otros textos breves. Buenos Aires: Sudamericana, 2011. 249 p.

Este volumen contiene cuatro colecciones de cuentos cortos o micro narrativas escritas en el curso de casi tres décadas, como lo anuncia la autora misma en "Una breve historia de *Bosques de ojos*" ensayo que concluye el libro. Las temáticas recurrentes se presentan en estas breves narraciones bajo diversos aspectos; se vuelven evidentes en los títulos de cada colección y de cada narrativa: "Historias del cielo," "Esperan la mañana verde," "Forma oculta del mundo," y "Visiones" son los titulares que encierran la prosa poética de Lojo. Cada una de ellas revela los temas que le interesan y que explora: echar una mirada que intenta ir más allá de la realidad, de lo que se palpa para entrever otro mundo, otra forma de ver y de entender. Signos, avatares, viajes, revelaciones, tránsitos se convierten en sustantivos de un lenguaje personal que la impulsa a sondear bajo la superficie de las cosas y de los seres. [CEM]

2100 **Lojo de Beuter, María Rosa.** Todos éramos hijos. Buenos Aires: Sudamericana, 2014. 249 p.

La época turbulenta y trágica de los años 70 cobra vida a través de la protagonista, apodada Frik. La novela se abre con el primer día de clases de la primaria en el colegio Sagrado Corazón de Castelar. Es este el inicio de su educación formal y de las amistades e influencias que determinarán en parte la vida de esta muchacha siempre perdida entre las páginas de un libro. De padres españoles quienes esperan encontrar en Argentina, tierra de promisión, la felicidad tranquila de una vida que aleje los fantasmas de la guerra civil española, Frik entabla amistades entrañables que se pondrán a prueba ya en la universidad o en la militancia. Los jóvenes quienes están en el centro de la narración, analizan sin comprender del todo la relación entre padres e hijos, entre posturas ideológicas, corrientes culturales, y sucesos históricos. Frik se convierte en memoria de los desaparecidos, de los exiliados que en su momento le dieron sentido a su vida. Las reflexiones y debates sobre la historia nacional de esa década constituyen una manera de querer comprender ese momento a través de las vidas de los jóvenes y de sus padres, y de alguna manera dejar constancia del destino trágico del país. [CEM]

2101 **Mariasch, Marina.** Estamos unidas. Buenos Aires: Mansalva, 2015. 75 p. (Colección Poesía y ficción latinoamericana; 117)

Relato breve en el que se narran los desencantos de una familia burguesa, compuesta por mujeres porteñas que viven entre EEUU, Europa y Buenos Aires. Son los años 90: época que se evoca en el texto como un mundo de apariencias y ausencias: un padre que abandona la familia por la secretaria, una hermana que se muda un tiempo a EEUU, una madre distante y fría que finge preocuparse por su familia y una abuela desubicada que se conecta muy poco con sus nietas. Con una prosa sencilla y breve, Mariasch retrata la incertidumbre de una época y la apatía de una sociedad consumista. La narración en primera persona mezcla el relato intimista con las experiencias sociales y políticas de una época. [LRL]

2102 **Oloixarac, Pola.** Las constelaciones oscuras. Buenos Aires: Literatura Random House, 2015. 239 p.: ill.

En esta segunda novela de la autora, se presentan tres ejes temporales: el de un naturalista decimonónico, Niklas Bruun, quien, con sus experimentos renovadores y escritos botánicos, traza pactos secretos entre especies oceánicas y terrestres; el segundo eje titulado "Cassio, 1983" retrata al joven Cassio Liberman-Brandão da Silva, un "hacedor de la serie de virus informáticos más violentos de la historia del país"; el tercer eje, "Piera 2024", se adelanta en el tiempo para presentar a Piera, una bióloga que llega a Bariloche, Argentina, para trabajar con un grupo de investigación tecnológico. Con un estilo único, la novela entrelaza espacios de la biología, la tecnología y la ciencia ficción, creando una narrativa sobre el control del Estado sobre las investigaciones científicas así como el control de la información y de los comportamientos humanos. [LRL]

2103 **Pagés, Bernarda.** La fauna divina. Buenos Aires: Interzona, 2014. 185 p. (Narrativa. Argentina)

Primera novela de la autora que obtuvo el premio del Fondo Nacional de las Artes a la Producción Literaria Nacional en el año 2012. La fauna divina relata la historia de vida de Perla, una joven que nace en los años 50 en Diamante, un pueblo de Entre Ríos, víctima de la talidomida, medicamentos que generaban deformaciones físicas. Al morir su madre, Perla decide irse a vivir al cotolengo San Miguel Febres donde se hace monja. Con una voz irónica, sarcástica, por momentos cruel, Perla cuestiona el sentido de su existencia y el de muchos otros jóvenes que nacen con terribles deformaciones. El cotolengo para Perla es una fauna creada por Dios, con el que vive una relación contradictoria entre la fe y el enojo. La novela se acerca y se aleja de lo políticamente incorrecto y desafía los perjuicios sobre la deformidad y los defectos físicos. [LRL]

2104 **Pauls, Alan.** Historia del dinero. Barcelona, Spain: Anagrama, 2013. 208 p. (Narrativas hispánicas; 514)

Esta novela cierra la trilogía sobre los años 70 junto a *Historia del llanto* (2007) e *Historia del pelo* (2010). Si bien ubicada en la sangrienta década de los 70, el joven personaje, sus padres y allegados parecen estar ajenos al drama que se está gestando a su alrededor. El dinero, los fajos de billetes que su padre lleva consigo a todas partes, las pequeñas fortunas que su madre dilapida, los verdes billetes que transitan por la novela adquieren una corporalidad acuciante. El joven acosado por el dinero perdido y recuperado no halla salida. La novela se vuelve una disquisición sobre le uso, el valor y la influencia del dinero sobre la vida humana, sobre el curso de la historia tanto nacional como individual. [CEM]

2105 **Pradelli, Ángela.** El sol detrás del limonero. Buenos Aires: Bien del Sauce, 2016 126 p.: ill., index.

En este conmovedor relato autobiográfico, la autora recupera parte de su historia familiar, la cual comenzó en las montañas de Peli, un pequeño pueblo ubicado en la provincia de Piacenza, en el norte de Italia. Desde ese pueblo, el abuelo de Pradelli parte hacia la Argentina y se radica en Burzaco, en el Gran Buenos Aires. Las cuatro partes que componen el texto, escritas en prosa y verso, retratan los vaivenes epistolares entre el abuelo y la familia italiana así como los viajes de la autora al pueblo de su padre con la intención de rescatar y compaginar una historia familiar de miseria, desarraigos y desencuentros. [LRL]

2106 **Relatos del exilio: escritores argentinos en México: Humberto Costantini, Juan Gelman, Mempo Giardinelli y Tununa Mercado.** Compilación de Andrea Candia Gajá. San Pedro de los Pinos, Mexico: Ediciones del Ermitaño, 2014. 164 p.: ill. (Colección Narrativa)(Minimalia. Cuento)

Esta colección de cuentos de escritores argentinos exiliados—que por un tiempo vivieron en México—remueve todo el dolor, la incomprensión, el olvido y la memoria que se evoca y que tortura en tierras ajenas. Veintidós narraciones (algunas muy breves) que nos invitan a mirar desde afuera a la patria y a los estragos de esa era sangrienta que fueron los años 70. Estas son páginas escritas desde y en el dolor profundo del exilio y en la certeza de lo irremediablemente perdido. Representan en su conjunto la necesidad de comunicación con el pasado, y la esperanza solapada de atreverse a soñar un mejor futuro. [CEM]

2107 **Riera, Daniel.** La menor. Buenos Aires: Galerna, 2015. 70 p. (Narrativa contemporánea)

Un escritor recibe una prometedora oferta de un hombre que fabrica contenidos de teléfonos celulares para escribir una novela que se pueda enviar por mensaje de texto. La premisa es que cada capítulo tiene que tener un máximo de 1000 caracteres, contener frases cortas y no sobrepasar 60 capítulos. Así el escritor crea una novela "menor" con cuatro personajes: dos hombres que suben al Himalaya nepalés, una mujer con la que tienen sexo y una pequeña nacida del fruto de esa relación triangular. La pequeña, de nombre Himalaya, es clave en la trama de esta novela lúdica y original, la cual aparece matizada con varias alusiones intertextuales y con entretenidas aventuras mesiánicas. Aparece Dios convertido en lombriz y se escucha a través del teléfono celular una canción de Rocky. Hacia el final el escritor de la novela "menor" se conecta con los cuatro personajes del Himalaya. La brevedad de la novela le permite al escritor y al lector crear y leer un texto ameno e inteligente. [LRL]

2108 Romero, Ricardo. La habitación del presidente. Buenos Aires: Eterna Cadencia Editora, 2015. 95 p.

En esta corta novela, un niño adolescente nos cuenta que en el pueblo donde vive él y su familia, todos los habitantes tienen una habitación del presidente. A través de la mirada contemplativa del niño se crea un ambiente ominoso y por momentos fantástico de la habitación del presidente que su propia familia ha amueblado y preparado. La novela comienza con una descripción detallada de la casa de dos pisos con un desván o "altillo," como prefiere llamarle el niño. Así, parte de la novela es el recorrido que el niño realiza física y mentalmente por su propia casa. En un momento, nos cuenta que su madre es la que más entra a la habitación del presidente porque es quien se encarga de limpiarla mientras él y su hermano miran la puerta de reojo pero nunca se atreven a entrar. A lo largo de la novela, el niño narrador tiene fiebre y en su delirio piensa en otras casas y habitaciones ajenas. El carácter ominoso en la novela está dado en la intriga de qué es y para quién es exactamente la habitación del presidente así como los peligros del afuera de la casa que contrastan con el interior. En una ocasión, el hermano menor se pierde por las calles del pueblo y no aparece por un día entero. El relato es una suerte de idas y vueltas entre lo real y lo fantástico, entre la contemplación y la perplejidad. [LRL]

2109 Rosenzvaig, Marcos. Monteagudo: anatomía de una revolución. Buenos Aires: Alfaguara, 2016. 184 p.: index.

En 1825, en la ciudad de Lima, es asesinado a los 35 años, el revolucionario Bernardo Monteagudo. Su historia reaparece junto con sus huesos—reclamados por las autoridades argentinas—en otra época sangrienta, octubre del 1917. El médico forense, Pascasio Romero, muere dos días después de recibir los despojos de Monteagudo y deja un cuaderno íntimo donde narra su conversación con el difunto y su viaje hasta "las puertas del paraíso". En el diálogo con Monteagudo, las figuras históricas de la época de las independencias revelan tanto su humanidad como su grandeza, y el doctor Romero recuerda sus amores y sus deseos para la nación fundamentados en una visión "de pureza sanguínea" y no hispana. [CEM]

Shellhorse, Adam Joseph. Anti-literature: the politics and limits of representation in modern Brazil and Argentina. See item **2541**.

2110 Thomas, José Luis. Madre de la patria: capitana de Belgrano, María Remedios del Valle. Córdoba, Argentina: Pirca Ediciones, 2015. 153 p.

Oriundo de Bell Ville, Córdoba, José Luis Thomas escribe una novela histórica sobre María Remedios del Valle, una heroína asiduamente excluida de la historia oficial argentina por ser mujer y por ser de raza negra, "parda" como se la denominaba entonces. María Remedios estaba casada y tenía dos hijos pero el afán por servir a la patria superó las obligaciones domésticas que se esperaban para una mujer de la época. Recorrió el norte argentino y llegó hasta el alto Perú a mediados del siglo XIX, cuidó y acompañó a Güemes y a Belgrano, quien la nombró Capitana del ejército. Fue tomada prisionera y azotada salvajemente por los realistas. Thomas recrea la figura de María Remedios utilizando un lenguaje escrito y sonoro propio del habla del personaje, haciendo una aclaración previa sobre los cambios fonéticos que se encuentran en el texto. De este modo, el personaje de María Remedios se presenta con su propia voz, además de la voz de un narrador en tercera persona, quienes recrean tanto las penurias y la discriminación que padeció la Capitana entre los soldados así como el extraordinario sentido de patriotismo que la llevó a servir al país incondicionalmente. [LRL]

2111 Unamuno, Gonzalo. Que todo se detenga. Buenos Aires: Galerna, 2015. 139 p. (Narrativa contemporánea)

Germán Baraja es un joven de 34 años que vive hundido en la desesperanza y la apatía. Encarna el derrumbe total de un ser humano (droga, abandono personal, desidia). Se autodefine al principio de la novela: "Soy, en esencia, un llorón, un hombre que razona y obra sin amor." Un tono cínico, patético e indiferente permea la voz de Germán que se rehúsa a ver a su madre enferma y le miente a su hermana sobre su condición física y mental. En esta novela generacional se alude al desencanto de los jóvenes de los 90 que cuestionan los cambios del nuevo siglo. Germán "piensa, piensa mucho" a lo largo del relato, piensa en lo que pudo ser y en lo que no será. Como lo define el narrador, el mundo de Germán es de un "virtuosismo estéril," vale decir la nula respuesta ante la existencia. [LRL]

2112 Verduga, Demián. El refugio en el telar: novela testimonio sobre la Noche de las Corbatas, el crimen de la dictadura en julio de 1977. Buenos Aires: Editorial Biblos, 2015. 112 p. (Narrativa)

Novela testimonial en cuatro partes que reconstruye los hechos del cruento episodio conocido como la Noche de las Corbatas, (de 13 de junio y el 13 de julio de 1977) en las ciudades de Neuquén y de Mar del Plata. La narración parte de los recuerdos de una de los sobrevivientes, Marta García de Candeloro cuyos recuerdos forman la base de la narración testimonial. La sucesión de eventos desde el secuestro hasta la salida se narran en forma lineal con pequeñas acotaciones en cursiva hechas por el autor quien trata de entender y de "sentir" lo que Marta ha vivido. La narrativa rinde homenaje a la generosidad y el valor de aquellos con quienes Marta compartió el dolor y la angustia de la detención. [CEM]

2113 Zamboni, Olga; Trini Álvarez; and Tito Busse. Vestidos de colores: poemas, cuentos, pinturas. Posadas, Argentina: Universidad Nacional de Misiones, 2011. 116 p.: ill.

En este libro tres artistas misioneros, dos artistas plásticos y una escritora presentan una colección de pinturas, epígrafes, poemas y relatos alusivos a diferentes colores. Cada color presenta infinitas posibilidades de vida y muerte. Las alusiones a sensaciones visuales y olfáticas reconstruyen las memorias de la infancia y la juventud en diferentes tiempos y espacios. En "Laguna negra," se narra la desintegración de una pareja que debe escapar de una persecución y acaban internados en un espacio selvático que los destruye física y emocionalmente. En "De verde," varias personas creen ver la imagen de una niñita, vestida "de verde" que avanza por la selva sin llegar a ningún lugar; de este modo, se representa una especie de duende selvático que intriga y sorprende a los lugareños, En "Doña Rita," la mención de un ramillete de flores moradas traídas por la anciana lavandera, es el disparador del cuento que rememora las tradiciones de Semana Santa en un pueblo misionero. Así, cada color actúa como un medio para iluminar o apagar el alma de los personajes de los cuentos, las ilustraciones y los poemas de este original texto. [LRL]

Paraguay

Alemán Salvador, María Gabriela. Humo. See item **1990**.

2114 Barreto, Maribel. Ciudad rebelde. Asunción: Servilibro, 2015. 272 p.

Novela que ficcionaliza por primera vez, en el panorama literario paraguayo, la llamada revolución del 47 o de *los pynandí* (pies descalzos en guaraní): la guerra civil que enfrentó a la capital con el resto del país, al ámbito rural con los sectores estudiantil, obrero y militar. En 46 breves capítulos y sobre la base de testimonios que recogió la autora en entrevistas que se mencionan manteniendo la confidencialidad de la identidad de los testimoniantes, Barreto reconstruye el conflicto a partir de voces femeninas de Concepción, da cuenta del exilio (en Argentina y en Uruguay) así como del impacto del conflicto en el microcosmos familiar. [GU]

2115 Colmán Gutiérrez, Andrés. El país en una plaza: la novela del Marzo Paraguayo. A 15 años de la gesta ciudadana. Asunción: Servilibro, 2014. 227 p.

Reescritura de la versión del 2004 sobre los hechos de violencia acontecidos en la capital paraguaya en 1999 a partir del momento en que el entonces vicepresidente Luis María Argaña fuera asesinado. La novela está enmarcada por la referencia a los ocho jóvenes mártires que perdieron la vida como consecuencia de la represión policial desplegada frente a los manifestantes. La nueva versión modifica el comienzo y el desenlace del texto original pero mantiene el desarrollo argumental que tuviera la primera versión. Hace explícita la génesis del texto: registrar los hechos ocurridos a pedido de quien como personaje femenino es identificada como Batichica tricolor (Andrea Soledad en la dedicatoria). Con esta novela, Colmán se suma al corpus de la novela histórica paraguaya más reciente. [GU]

2116 Gertopán, Susana. El fin de la memoria. Asunción: Servilibro, 2014. 162 p.

Una novela que conjuga la representación de múltiples traumas (silencios intrafamiliares, fracasos profesionales, soledades endémicas) y diversas migraciones (de los judíos europeos refugiados en Paraguay, de un opositor al régimen stronista exiliado en Londres, de una senegalesa discriminada en Europa). Los ghettos europeos y los conventillos paraguayos de ayer se reconocen en los espacios marginados de refugiados e inmigrantes de hoy. Una de las premisas centrales de la novela es que existe un propósito sanador en el discurso de la memoria y una responsabilidad colectiva para configurarlo. En el curso de dicho proceso, la identidad escindida del protagonista muerto (violinista, reparador de muñecas, exiliado) solo se recompone con los discursos ajenos y con ella, la de los que se cruzaron en su camino a lo largo de dos continentes y distintas fases de su vida. [GU]

2117 Gertopán, Susana. El Señor Antúnez. Asunción: Servilibro, 2015. 134 p.

En la que es su novena novela, la autora despliega tres universos narrativos que se superponen a modo de ejercicio metaescritural. Por un lado, existe la narración que tiene por protagonista a José Martínez, escritor paraguayo, sorpresivamente invitado a Buenos Aires para crear el desenlace de una novela ajena. Se trata del texto inconcluso de un escritor argentino (Dantón Antúnez) cuya propia novela se ha convertido en una carga insostenible y en una imposibilidad. Entre ambas se erige, interrumpida sistemáticamente, la historia que el propio Martínez aspira a escribir y que tiene por protagonista a una modista. Gertopán vuelve a incluir en esta nueva obra, aunque tangencialmente, los temas de la dictadura stronista, el impacto del tiempo y el valor de la libertad creativa. [GU]

2118 Pérez-Maricevich, Francisco. Los rostros del murallón. Asunción: Criterio Ediciones, 2015. 135 p.: bibl.

En esta colección de nueve relatos escritos en la década de los 70, se retratan fundamentalmente universos populares, tanto en lo que tiene que ver con la extracción social de sus personajes como por la clara relevancia de un colectivo protagónico en cada cuento. Las narraciones iluminan especialmente los procesos de socialización infantil y juvenil de sectores marginados. En el marco de la identidad híbrida presente a través del uso frecuente del jopara—combinación lingüística del guaraní y del español que según estudios recientes, constituye el modo más común de comunicación oral entre casi un 90 porcentaje de la población paraguaya—las y los desamparados de la Tierra, a medio camino entre mártires y bandidos, se revelan como la única cara de la solidaridad. [GU]

Uruguay

2119 Altesor, Sergio. Taxi. Fotografías de Urban Götling, Matts Husser y Elin Götling. Montevideo: Estuario Editora, 2016. 182 p.: ill.

Si la producción literaria que surgió de la experiencia del exilio uruguayo de los 70 y 80 en Suecia es en cierta medida conocida en el país, esta novela explora una representación menos común. Narrado en primera persona en forma de diario, el texto constituye una mirada al exilio después del exilio y un retorno a sitios y personas que presumiblemente debían quedar en el pasado. El protagonista emprende un viaje doble: recorre calles y recuerdos en un país que ya no es el que lo recibió como ex preso político y es forzado a reflexionar sobre el hombre que fue y sobre el hombre que es. Desde el espejo retrovisor de su nuevo espacio diario (el taxi), observa, interpreta y negocia la realidad de ser inmigrante nuevamente en la Suecia del presente. La forma narrativa seleccionada (diario) lo desafía así a indagar y definir su identidad. [GU]

2120 **Appratto, Roberto.** Mientras espero. Montevideo: Criatura Editora, 2016. 87 p.

Novela corta en la que las expectativas de acción narrativa que pueda generar el título devienen cavilaciones de un narrador en primera persona sobre el hacer de los otros y sobre la índole misma del acto de espera. Esta instancia (sea en una cola de cajero automático o en un consultorio médico) se convierte en una oportunidad para ficcionalizar la realidad creando un efecto de extrañamiento. La reflexión sobre el acto mismo de la creación literaria aunada al absurdo resultante de una realidad fragmentada (los pies y las voces que se descubren o imaginan detrás de una puerta desprendidas de un cuerpo que los identifique) ponen a los lectores en el sitio inamovible del testigo. [GU]

2121 **Burel, Hugo.** Montevideo noir. Montevideo: Alfaguara: Penguin Random House Grupo Editorial, 2015. 323 p.

El autor, ya consagrado en el terreno de la novela negra, construye una trama que por un lado, juega con la idea de la influencia (perturbadora) de la literatura en la vida, en un tipo de quijotización a la inversa (el lector/protagonista del género noir deviene villano, no héroe). Por otro lado, se trata de un texto que ficcionaliza la posibilidad de que cualquier ciudadano común, dadas las circunstancias, pueda convertirse en asesino. El marco temporal de los hechos que se narran es la década del 70, que sirve para establecer una complicidad con el lector quien puede interpretar la apariencia de normalidad que encubre crímenes, sospechas y traiciones como una metáfora del estado de erosión del tejido social y de la instalación de la duda y del miedo que definirieron la sociedad uruguaya de los 70 y 80. [GU]

2122 **Cynovich, Carolina.** El síndrome de las ciudades hermosas. Montevideo: Fin de Siglo Editorial, 2015. 125 p. (Colección ñ)

Novela ganadora del premio Gutemberg, una iniciativa conjunta de la editorial que publicó este texto con la Unión Europea y que convocó a narradores menores de 30 años que residieran en Uruguay o fueran uruguayos. Desde una voz narrativa masculina que conduce en forma ágil una trama fascinante, la mirada lectora es forzada a entrar y a salir, en forma constante, de las mútiples dimensiones que dan estructura al texto: del cine a la historia, de esta a la literatura para retornar una y otra vez, a una filmación en proceso. En el curso de este viaje sin destino final del que el lector, voyeurísticamente participa detrás del protagonista Molina, la novela se erige sobre el leit motif de la fluida frontera entre la realidad y la ficción con un tono que tiene mucho de cortazariano. [GU]

2123 **Espinosa, Gustavo.** Todo termina aquí. Montevideo: Hum, 2016. 179 p.

Ganadora del premio nacional Bartolomé Hidalgo del 2016, la cuarta novela de este autor—cuya voz narrativa se cita entre las más interesantes del panorama uruguayo de hoy—es a la vez un ejercicio y una provocación que se despliega a partir de diversos registros discursivos. A nivel formal, construye un universo de collage basado en ficticias crónicas pueblerinas, reseñas especializadas de música y literatura que son intervenidas, sin éxito, por cartas de ciudadanos comunes, resistentes y cuestionadores de la legitimidad de la narración central, formulada en primera persona. Es esta voz, la del outsider/voyeur de un Treinta y Tres literario (que por momentos evoca la Santa María onettiana) la que oscila entre la displicencia hacia el entorno y los sujetos que retrata por un lado y la desilusión y el afecto con que los inmortaliza por otro. [GU]

2124 **Franco, Gladys.** Solo para ti. Montevideo: Yaugurú, 2016. 111 p. (Narrativivas; 21)

En esta, su segunda novela, la autora construye, a través de una prosa escueta y sugestiva, un universo geográficamente impreciso (basta saber que todo ocurre en alguna región rural del país pero podría tratarse de otros en la región) dentro del cual y a través de una voz narradora en tercera persona, se da voz a una historia de adopción. El discurso narrativo (regalo/ofrenda al que se alude en el título) interioriza los pensamientos de su protagonista (niña adoptada por pareja de estancieros). La cuestión central de la identidad se simboliza en la caracterización de una figura central que carece de nombre y se define exclusivamente en base a su edad. La historia es un arco que nace y culmina en la partida a la ciudad para estudiar en un colegio de monjas. Esta separación traumática de lo único conocido y amado pero no necesariamente propio, augura la oportunidad de un crecimiento y una liberación. [GU]

2125 **Kalmar, Fritz.** Vivir entre dos mundos: cuentos de añoranzas de judíos y otros exiliados en Bolivia y Uruguay. Traducción del alemán austríaco por Raquel García Borsani. Montevideo: Ediciones Trilce, 2011. 150 p.

Conjunto de ocho relatos más un apéndice a la edición en castellano (del alemán austríaco) realizada por Raquel García Borsani. Es la primera traducción al español de uno de los trabajos escritos de Kalmar, quien residiera en Uruguay desde 1953 hasta el 2008 en que falleció (previa residencia de catorce años en Bolivia después de haberse autoexiliado como resultado de la anexión austríaca que efectuara Alemania). El resto de su obra publicada en Austria a partir del 1997 le deparó reconocimiento literario en su país de origen. En esta colección se recogen, en prosa ágil y tramas atrapantes, las experiencias diaspóricas poco estudiadas de los exiliados austríacos en América del Sur. En narraciones realistas cuyo tono oscila entre la nostalgia y el humor, se recrea la alienación lingüística, el dolor de la asimilación, la imposibilidad del regreso a las raíces. [GU]

2126 **Maslíah, Leo.** El bobo del pueblo y otras incorrecciones. Montevideo: Criatura Editora; Montevideo: Verbum, 2015. 188 p.

Se trata de una colección de textos que en tanto maslianos se definen por su eclecticismo y que confirman el carácter antitético de una obra a la que la crítica Anahí Barboza Borges (2013) situara en el espacio de lo que llama una "marginalidad canónica". Desde el punto de vista de estilo, prevalece el recurrir al extrañamiento lingüístico el que, en principio y en forma inmediata, conduce al humor. Un humor que sin embargo, funciona también en la mayoría de los casos, como metáfora de la incomunicación o como denuncia de lo absurdo-abyecto de la explotación o de la burocracia. Los mini-textos que a veces son en verso ("Noche antigua"), en forma dramática ("Debates televisivos") o siguen una fórmula narrativa tradicional nos obligan a mirar de cerca y compulsivamente una realidad que no tiene sentido o a cuestionar taxonomías inoperantes. [GU]

2127 **Mondragón, Juan Carlos.** El submarino peral. Montevideo: Yaugurú, 2016. 159 p. (Colección Narrativivas; 19)

En este, su décimo octavo libro en el género de la narrativa, el autor enlaza una colección de 11 cuentos por medio de la referencia que da título a uno de ellos: el torpedero submarino inventado por el ingeniero y navegante español, Isaac Peral y Caballero a fines del siglo XIX. Varios de los relatos se estructuran alrededor de—como en el caso histórico—la idea y la realidad del fracaso, las intrigas, los desentendimientos pero aún en los casos en que la presencia de Peral o la de su submarino no es explícita, las historias se hilan en torno al tropo del viaje (sea este la muerte, el amor o la soledad). [GU]

2128 **Polleri Sierra, Felipe.** La vida familiar. Montevide: Criatura Editora, 2016. 84 p.: ill.

En una serie de 10 relatos, de extensión y estilo variados, el autor pinta con lenguaje brutal múltiples manifestaciones de violencia (emergente e imperante en la institución familiar, síntoma de una erosión del tejido social en diversos planos, sintomática de soberanías que se revelan ya como inexistentes). Se presentan ilustraciones que imitan la estética infantil y contrastan con el tono de los textos que las acompañan. De la antítesis resultante, emerge un sentido de desacomodo para los lectores. La colección es homogénea en cuanto a la creación de una atmósfera hostil en la que protagonistas y lectores son forzados a ver en lo grotesco el síntoma de una decadencia contemporánea o al menos la advertencia de su advenimiento. [GU]

2129 **22 mujeres 3: 21 cuentistas y una proloquista.** Prólogo de Mercedes Rosende. Contribuciones de Magdalena de Torres *et al.* Uruguay: Irrupciones

Grupo Editor, 2014. 168 p.: ill. (Colección Excéntricos)

Por tercera vez se agrupan y publican textos aunados en torno a la común autoría femenina y la nacionalidad/residencia uruguayas, diversos en tema y en representación generacional bajo la reflexión breve e inaugural, en este caso, de una escritora conocida por su creación en el género de la novela negra. Como ocurriera en las antologías 1 y 2, esta serie de relatos presenta una visión panorámica y desigual sobre temas tales como relaciones de pareja, constreñimientos en torno al disciplinamiento del cuerpo femenino en la sociedad contemporánea, visiones fantásticas de un futuro deshumanizador, imágenes de mujeres como ejecutoras de violencia. Rosende justifica la nueva colección por lo que identifica como la permanencia de una doble escasez genérica en el ámbito literario uruguayo: la del cuento y la de textos escritos por mujeres. [GU]

2130 **Vigil, Mercedes.** El loco: luces y sombras de Domingo Faustino Sarmiento. Buenos Aires: Planeta, 2016. 252 p.

En su décimocuarta novela histórica, la autora reconstruye la vida del pedagogo y estadista argentino a partir de su rol en momentos clave de la política y la historia de su país durante la segunda mitad del siglo XIX. La vida sarmientina se narra desde su paisaje por el Uruguay de la Guerra Grande y culmina con la descripción de su muerte en el Paraguay. En este sentido, el Sarmiento de Vigil es antes que nada un exiliado. Esta decisión narrativa simboliza, en la estructura novelística, lo que el título anticipa: la identidad de *outsider* nunca dejó de definirlo. La otra estrategia que pone en juego el texto tiene un carácter correctivo de la historia. Aurelia Vélez Sarsfield (pareja de Sarmiento la mayor parte de su vida) a quien la sociedad finisecular argentina le negara su sitio en el duelo oficial y público de Sarmiento, es quien abre y cierra la novela. [GU]

2131 **Zieleniec, Raquel.** La frontera y otros relatos. Montevideo: Yaugurú, 2016. 109 p. (Narrativas; 20)

El cuento, cuyo título da nombre a esta colección, sitúa el eje del libro en un concepto que es más simbólico, a lo largo de todas las historias, que literal y que se despliega en dos dimensiones que se repiten. Se plantea la noción de frontera como distancia insalvable por un lado entre seres humanos y por otro, entre seres humanos y máquinas. En el primer caso se muestra cómo esos seres eligen y son capaces de mantener, en ocasiones hasta la muerte, una identidad inescrutable e insospechada aún para los más cercanos (tales como la del amigo/traidor o la de la pareja judía que nunca revela su identidad a su cónyugue). La brecha entre máquinas (usualmente autos) y seres humanos en cambio señala diferencias socioeconómicas y estas resultan en ejercicios fallidos de comunicación. [GU]

LITERARY CRITICISM AND HISTORY
Argentina

2132 **Piglia, Ricardo.** La forma inicial: conversaciones en Princeton. Edición a cargo de Arcadio Díaz Quiñonez y Paul Firbas. Madrid: Sexto Piso, 2015. 245 p. (Ensayo Sexto Piso)

Piglia advierte que este libro fue publicado en Chile, pero en esta edición él ha añadido cinco piezas más: "Tiempo de lectura", "Secreto y narración", "Aspectos de la nouvelle", "Volver a empezar", y "Las versiones de un relato". El subtítulo de la obra contextualiza el lugar donde las conversaciones y las reflexiones sobre estos temas fueron formadas. Piglia favorece el tono conversacional y conserva la fluidez del dialogo en su momento; al mismo tiempo, admite que hay una intención de improvisación a lo largo de la obra, fuente a veces de inspiración. El libro contiene ensayos, conversaciones, entrevistas que reflejan el pensamiento pigliano sobre el cine, la novela, la política. Cada una de estas piezas que componen el libro abordan de una manera u otra el espinoso tema de la lectura, de la relación entre texto y lector/a, del complejo proceso que se inicia en la primera página, de las influencias, de las mil maneras que un escritor se relaciona con su palabra y con sus interlocutores. El material contenido en este libro nos sumerge en el pensamiento de Piglia, en las entretelas de un intelectual cabal, de un artista con conciencia social, de un escritor que además de producir literatura, consume, digiere y ama la lectura. [CEM]

Paraguay

2133 Barreto, Maribel. El mundo de la novela en el Paraguay siglo XXI: 2000–2014. Asunción: Servilibro, 2014. 278 p.: bibl. (Colección Academia Paraguaya de la Lengua Española; 15)

Estudio publicado en el marco de la celebración de los 86 años de la fundación de la Academia Paraguaya de la Lengua Española. Reseña la obra de 22 novelistas incluyendo un prefacio que atiende, en primer lugar, a rasgos formales tales como uso del diálogo, lirismo, construcción discursiva y figura del héroe. Asimismo se describen dos subgéneros prevalentes en el periodo mencionado: la novela histórica, centrada en la representación del periodo dictatorial y la novela psicológica, de índole intimista. La primera se construye a partir de miradas situadas en los márgenes del régimen (la resistencia fallida de la guerrilla o la posición de la amante de Stroessner) mientras que la segunda modalidad emerge en torno a los tópicos de la familia, el amor, lo fantástico así como la memoria y la migración (tal es el caso de la recreación de la experiencia judío-paraguaya que aborda Susana Gertopán). [GU]

2134 El Guairá literario. Compilación de Ramiro Domínguez. Selección de textos por Ramiro Domínguez y Mirta Roa. Asunción: Servilibro, 2015. 251 p.: bibl., ill.

Antología de textos de índole diversa (antropológicos, literarios, entrevistas) que recorren la historia y la cultura del departamento paraguayo de Guairá. El libro está estructurado en un prólogo y cinco capítulos que abordan el periodo prehispánico, el colonial, el correspondiente a la independencia, el periodo moderno y el contemporáneo. La mayoría de los autores comparte su ciudad de origen (Villa Rica, capital departamental) o en el caso de los extranjeros, la residencia prolongada en dicha región. La compilación revela un conjunto ecléctico de textos y miradas que abarcan desde versiones bilingües (español/mbyá) de León Cadogan, único hombre blanco con el que la etnia mbyá compartió información sobre invocaciones y rituales comunitarios, una entrevista que da cuenta de la historia de Stephan Vysokolán, inmigrante ruso que participó de la Guerra del Chaco hasta poemas y relato del canónico Augusto Roa Bastos. [GU]

2135 Pérez-Maricevich, Francisco. El castellano del niño urbano y otros escritos. Asunción: Servilibro, 2014. 287 p.: bibl. (Colección Academia Paraguaya de la Lengua Española; 11)

Libro publicado en el marco de la celebración de los 85 años de la fundación de la Academia Paraguaya de la Lengua Española y como una de las 13 obras seleccionadas para conformar la "Colección Academia Paraguaya de la Lengua Española" que se editó como conmemoración de dicho hecho. Se trata de una compilación de textos críticos publicados por el autor a lo largo de tres décadas en torno a lo literario y lo lingüístico. En tanto dos de las secciones abordan el bilingüismo (español/guaraní) o las especificidades del castellano hablado en el ámbito urbano, las otras dos incluyen un estudio comprehensivo sobre la literatura paraguaya desde el periodo colonial hasta el 90s así como una extensa serie de prólogos y análisis de textos y autores particulares entre los que también se incluye la introducción a una breve historia del teatro paraguayo. [GU]

Uruguay

2136 Gregory, Stephen. El rostro tras la página: Mario Benedetti y el fracaso de una política del prójimo. Montevideo: Estuario Editora, 2014. 278 p.: bibl. (Ensayo)

This monograph is an intellectual study of one of Uruguay's most important literary figures of the 20th century, Mario Benedetti. This text studies the intellectual and political development of Benedetti and offers insights into who he was as an author and critic of society and politics. The text seeks to untangle how Benedetti presented himself to the world as a "human and citizen" (p. 44). The book will be of more interest to literary critics rather than historians (or even social scientists), as it offers little of the political context surrounding Benedetti's life. While the author demonstrates a formidable familiarity with Benedetti's work, it often fails to contextualize the works within a larger historical time frame. It should be noted that the text does draw richly from Benedetti's work. [B.M. Chesterton]

2137 Kovacic, Fabián. Galeano: apuntes para una biografía. Barcelona: Vergara, Grupo Zeta, 2015. 352 p., 8 unnumbered pages of plates: ill.

Trece secciones y una introducción forman parte de esta biografía sobre el periodista y escritor uruguayo Eduardo Galeano. En la introducción Kovacic explica que debió escribir esta biografía de Galeano sin el testimonio de primera mano del autor, convirtiendo ésta en un biografía no autorizada. Se basó entonces en textos, archivos, videos, fuentes en bibliotecas y entrevistas con otros escritores latinoamercanos para compaginar una cronología de la vida de Galeano. En el texto se mezcla lo personal con la historia de América Latina al retratar una variedad de temas, tales como el Uruguay social, económico y político en el que nace Galeano, los años de la revista *Marcha*, los primeros viajes y las primeras publicaciones, la influencia de la Revolución cubana en América Latina, la relación de Galeano con Argentina, el desarraigo, las dictaduras y la transición a la democracia, entre otros temas. Aunque se destaca más la historia y las ideas progresistas y de izquierda de Galeano, Kovacic entabla una conexión entre la vida del periodista y escritor uruguayo con la historia del siglo XX latinoamericano. [LRL]

Poetry

JOSÉ R. BALLESTEROS, *Professor of Spanish, St. Mary's College of Maryland*
MARÍA LUISA FISCHER, *Associate Professor of Romance Languages, Hunter College of the City University of New York*
ELIZABETH GACKSTETTER NICHOLS, *Professor of Spanish and Chair of the Language Department, Drury University*
RITA M. PALACIOS, *Professor of Spanish, Conestoga College*
JEANNINE M. PITAS, *Assistant Professor of English and Spanish, University of Dubuque*
JOSÉ RAMÓN RUISÁNCHEZ SERRA, *Associate Professor of Hispanic Studies, University of Houston*
CHRYSTIAN ZEGARRA, *Associate Professor of Spanish, Colgate University*

MEXICO

AUNQUE ESTÁ LEJOS DE SER la mejor de las antologías publicadas en estos años, *Arbitraria* es, sin lugar a dudas, útil como síntoma de algo que se venía esbozando de diferentes maneras en el campo literario mexicano (item **2142**). La aproximación entre poesía y ensayo ha llegado al punto en que resulta natural publicarlas en el mismo libro. Si bien todavía separándolas al alternar un texto de cada género. Esto es, sin llegar a la abolición de la diferencia entre los dos. En este sentido, no parece tan interesante la ya muy visitada posibilidad de lo híbrido, como la de una creciente afinidad entre la manera de escribir: una poesía como vehículo de pensamiento, un ensayo con una libertad cada vez mayor.

A esta luz, un libro mediano en la producción ensayística de Malva Flores, *La culpa es por cantar*, merece atención (item **2306**). Pues, aunque sus ensayos no llegan a la hondura de su excelente monografía sobre la revista *Vuelta*, hay, empero, una búsqueda de formas sostenida, que huye a los cánones académicos y apunta hacia posibilidades que, aunque no logra conquistar, sí explora. Un territorio intermedio donde la prosa reflexiva rehúye una dicción expositiva, y con frecuencia se convierte en verso. Un caso semejante, aunque menos logrado, es *Caída del búfalo sin nombre* de Alejandro Tarrab.

Una aproximación también interesante es la que se produce en dirección de las artes visuales. El ejemplo más obvio es la *Poesía visual* del también crítico de arte Alberto Blanco. Más arriesgado resulta *Box* de Ismael Velázquez Juárez. Pero encuentro en *Ondulaciones sobre el puente: zapping del horizonte* (item **2258**) el libro-objeto de la artista Aurora Noreña, el ejemplo más interesante de este diálogo, pues no sólo trabaja con materiales de las artes visuales—tanto propios, como citados de muy diversas fuentes—sino también practica la escritura de un ensayo lírico para formar este collage muy estimulante.

Finalmente, el tercer vector que debe ser pensado a partir del corpus producido recientemente, es el del renovado interés de la poesía por contar de manera clara—en éste ámbito deben considerarse los libros recientes de Eduardo Langangne, José Ramón Enríquez, A.E. Quintero, Juan Domingo Argüelles, y Margarito Cuéllar—con una dicción que es la de la voz lírica que desciende directamente del romanticismo o la flexión metalingüística, sino incluso llega cabalmente a la minificción, como en los textos brevísimos de Armando Alanís Pulido en *Narciso el masoquista*. En otros, casos, los poemas se permiten contar pero sin dejar de cantar, y pienso en los textos más notables de Balam Rodrigo o en las anchas secciones de lo que Francisco Hernández no deja de considerar su poesía, tanto las entradas en prosa de *Diario invento* como la narrativa en verso de *Soledad al cubo*, que aparecen en *En grado de tentativa* (item **2229**), la obra más importante de estos años.

Además este giro hacia la tercera persona, hacia un verso narrativo que si bien no intenta poemas épicos, sí apunta hacia la acumulación paulatina de un nosotros lírico, de la poesía reciente, también ilumina la importancia de una serie de reediciones y compilaciones: la gozosa de poesía popular, alburera y secreta de Juan Domingo Argüelles (item **2145**) que mucho le debe a la obra de Renato Leduc, compilada por Edith Negrín en el 2000 y recientemente reeditada (item **2239**); el robusto tomo que reúne la poesía de Abigael Bohórquez (item **2196**), el poeta sonorense que ha generado de manera póstuma un interés notable y muy justificado.

Finalmente, la publicación de la *Historia crítica de la poesía mexicana* (item **2296**) merece una mención, más allá de su poco imaginativa y, digámoslo todo, reaccionaria estructura liberal-romántica de ensayos dedicados a poetas, como radiografía del panorama de las posibilidades y limitaciones críticas presentes; esto es, como estado de la cuestión. Su índice ofrece una mezcla de críticos muy rica. Hay que subrayar, por ejemplo, que hay artículos que importan más como genealogías de los poetas que los firman (como los tres de Arturo Dávila) y otros que verdaderamente marcan nuevos rumbos de crítica (como los dos de Ignacio Sánchez Prado). [JRRS]

CENTRAL AMERICA

Over the past five years, Central America has seen an increase in the participation of new literary voices, particularly those of Indigenous and Afro-descendent poets whose work has been little known and seldom read. This flurry of activity is reflected in the poetry festivals celebrated throughout the isthmus that continue to thrive and reflect old and new literary incursions. Poetry is a genre that allows for the most access and experimentation, so perhaps it is not surprising that the voices that have been systemically ignored or silenced have readily found an outlet in poetry and a platform in small presses. For this and host of other reasons pertaining to literary creation in Indigenous languages, it is no surprise that Indigenous literatures see their most realized expression in poetry. Guatemala is perhaps where we can best appreciate an increased production of such poetry given the country's particular location and pre- and post-invasion history, as well as a significant Indigenous presence—not to mention the work of the pan-Maya movement in relation to linguistic preservation and cultural revitalization. Even so, these literatures face many obstacles and their recognition has not been easy, in great part because of the lack of government support. This new poetry is daring, confronting issues of discrimination, racism, class, ethnicity, as well as gender and sexuality. For these reasons, the work of small, independent presses is key: they fill a void, promoting work that would otherwise be ignored.

A small publishing outfit that has taken on this challenge is Metáfora, associated with the poetry festivals throughout the region and headed by Marvín García (Quetzaltenango, Guatemala). It has published collections that capture the work of poets whose approach is innovative and representative of the rich and diverse emerging voices in Central America. Metáfora's special collection, PoétiCA (Poetas por la integración centroamericana, *Poets for Central American Integration*) sets out to capture new poetic voices, particularly those of Indigenous, Xinca, and Afro-Caribbean writers. To date Metáfora has published five volumes (Guatemala, El Salvador, Costa Rica, Panama, and Honduras). Two are worth mentioning here: *Palabras para colgar en los árboles: breve selección de poesía guatemalteca* (item **2162**), the first installment, with poems from up-and–coming Maya writers, some of whom were previously unpublished; and *La voz que no marchita: breve selección de poesía costarricence* (item **2178**) with poetry by Afro-Caribbean and Indigenous writers. Other independent presses in Guatemala that provide a platform for new and daring voices include Catafixia, Tujaal ediciones, La maleta ilegal, and Editorial X.

Another important publishing project is Escénica/Poética, a collaboration between Catafixia and the Centro Cultural de España en Guatemala that sets out to reignite the connection that has long existed between poetry and performance. For Escénica/Poética, each author works alongside a playwright to bring their work to life both in print and on the stage. The years 2013 and 2014, respectively, saw the work of Cecilia Porras Sáenz and Manuel Tzoc (*El jardín de los infantes locos y la escafandra de oro*) (item **2267**) and Rosa Chávez and Camila Camerlengo (*Awas*) (item **2203**) come to life. These collaborations are of note because they feature performances by the artists themselves. This poetic performance is an important aspect of Tzoc and Chávez's oeuvre and is rooted in the Maya cultural tradition that poetry cannot be confined to the written word alone. With these performances, the public is presented with a contemporary Maya understanding of the world that is steeped in the clashes, contradictions, and the everyday dialogues of contemporary Guatemala. Other well-known Guatemalan poets who have participated in the Escénica/Poética project between 2013 and 2017 include Garífuna poet Wingston González, Maurice Echeverría, Vania Vargas, Javier Payeras, Julio Serrano Echeverría, and Carolina Escobar Sartí.

Recognizing the need for the dedicated study of literature written by Indigenous and Afro–descendent peoples in the region, FILGUA (Feria Internacional del Libro en Guatemala) 2019 will host its third annual Contemporary Central American Literature congress with a special focus on these literatures. The conference will be dedicated to renowned K'iche' poet Humberto Ak'abal, with Chiapas as the honorary guest. In North America, LASA (Latin American Studies Association) recently launched an Indigenous Languages and Literatures track which debuted in Boston in May 2019, and will be part of subsequent annual congresses. In addition, in April 2018, SUNY Press announced a new series: Trans-Indigenous Decolonial Critiques, edited by Arturo Arias.

Finally, despite numerous challenges and persistent attitudes, LGBTQI activism in Guatemala is growing and taking small but sure steps, something that is reflected in the cultural realm with the recent publication of the poetry collection *Anatomías del deseo negado: Antología LGBTIQ+* (item **2176**), zines, and the festival Queerpoéticas, which began in 2015 and continues to grow.

Elsewhere in Central America, we encounter a rich esthetic of urbanity, undeniably shaped by the sociocultural footprint of globalization in the region. These urban verses are filled with the cacophony of the city, the elusiveness of social media, the physical and spiritual ailments of 21st century life, and endless consumption. Costa Rica's urban poetry landscape is well represented by Jonatan Lepiz Vega and María Morales, among others (items **2240** and **2252**). In their poetry, these authors put urban life center stage, whether searching for love, understanding death, or dealing with the everyday.

Nicaragua for its part, lost one of its most beloved writers, Claríbel Alegría, in January 2018: we can expect to see many welcome retrospectives, studies, and tributes in the coming years. Some of the poetry of the past five years in Nicaragua continues with the tradition laid out by the greats, like Rubén Darío, while other poetry makes a sharp turn and carves out its own place, though not without acknowledging the past (item **2301**). Take for example, Daniel Ulloa's *Desde el espinazo de la noche* (item **2290**), which consists of a set of poems that together weave a narrative of a young man who moves through real and imagined spaces in the pulses and beats of existential dread, Jim Morrison, Pablo Neruda, and cyberspace. El Salvador, for its part, continues its tradition of observing a poetry that is political and *comprometida* (see *Ceniza enamorada: poetas salvadoreños de la resistencia*) (item **2146**), but like other Central American poetry, recent work is also shaped by globalizing forces. [RMP]

COLOMBIA AND VENEZUELA

Daily life and literary production for poets working in Venezuela and Colombia have changed significantly in the last two years. Economic collapse in Venezuela, a contentious border between the two nations, and increasing stability in Colombia have meant a widening gap between the neighbor-states that is reflected in the poetry produced in each nation.

While the political and economic situation in Venezuela at the time of *HLAS 72*'s publication seemed as dire as possible, conditions in the nation have further worsened in the 2016–2018 period. Currency devaluation, the contested reelection of President Maduro, food shortages, and inflation nearing 1,000,000 percent annually have resulted in a Venezuelan diaspora. Some estimate that as much as 20 percent of Venezuela's population had left the nation by 2018, a number which included many writers and poets. This crisis has had an understandably chilling effect on the production and publication of literature in the last two years.

When confronted with a stack of poetry collections, some published in Venezuela and some in Colombia, it is easy to tell the origin of the work without even looking at the author. Books published in Venezuela are made of materials of increasingly low quality, with faint printing, and rough, fragile paper. Books published by the Bolivarian government are of especially poor quality, with barely visible ink and frequent misprints. The few works by Venezuelan writers printed on higher quality paper were published in other nations, such as Spain or Ecuador.

The Venezuelan government, working with the publishing houses *El Perro y la Rana* and *Librerias del Sur*, continues to issue the work of pro–Maduro politicians and other friends of the socialist government. A new player in the Venezuelan poetry scene is Oscar Todtmann Editores which produced a series of works in 2016-2018 by dissident voices, using slightly higher quality materials.

In sharp contrast to the deteriorating situation in Venezuela, Colombian publishing and poetic production appear to be thriving under a more stable and viable central government, following the peace and disarmament agreements signed by rebel groups in 2017. A literary renewal seems to be underway across the nation as peace allows regional governments, university presses, and private editorials to devote more publishing space to literature. Several Venezuelan poets, such as the venerable Rafael Arraiz Lucca published with Colombian editorials in the past two years.

While narrative in Colombia still overshadows poetic production, poetry continues to thrive in such venues as at the Medellín Poetry Festival, which celebrated its 28th anniversary in 2018. The festival continues to grow in size and importance, while also embracing and providing a space for artists of color and indigenous and Afro-descended voices. The support for the festival and the yearly attendance of tens of thousands of citizens is a visible demonstration of the growing importance of poetry in Colombia.

In both Venezuela and Colombia, recent poetry publications reveal an increasing interest in the use of visual media and visual imagery to enhance poetic communication. Many poets from both nations (including those Venezuelan poets living and publishing abroad) are integrating drawings, photos, and paintings into their work (see items **2257** and **2269**). While this use of visual media is not completely new, the frequency with which it happens is markedly higher of late.

Also appearing frequently alongside visual imagery is sensorial description that covers all five senses, mixing and matching them in almost surrealist ways (for example, item **2230**). The venerable Juan Gustavo Cobo Borda includes a poem called "Cinco sentidos" in his latest work (item **2205**), and proposes the invention of "nuevos sentidos." In both Colombian and Venezuelan verse, sight, sound, touch, taste, and smell are often combined by the poets to create new and unexpected moments and experiences for the reader. [EGN]

BOLIVIA AND ECUADOR
Además de las obras de letrados establecidos, las publicaciones recientes de poesía boliviana se destacan por una valoración consciente de la diversidad y calidad de la poesía quechua y una celebración de sendas nuevas que apuntan hacia una nueva era de vanguardia andina. Esta labor se lleva a cabo con la publicación de la antología más amplia de poesía boliviana quechua hasta la fecha y la aparición de varios poemarios ganadores de certámenes de poesía. Ambos reconocimientos subrayan un interés en Bolivia de apoyar, promover y proyectar poesía que hace pocos años se hubiera considerado marginal sea por su idioma de origen o por su atrevimiento lingüístico.

Dentro de la obra de poetas hispanos ya establecidos, vale reconocer nuevamente el trabajo refinado del prolífico Homero Carvalho (*Pequeños suicidios: microcuentos*; item **1954**) y Mauro Bertero Gutiérrez. En los mejores momentos de su quinto poemario *Primaveras impuntuales* (item **2144**) Mauro Bertero crea una filosofía profunda sobre el amor y su contrapunto. Se trata de un libro sabio que explora el tema a fondo, no con la llama viva de la corporalidad tan presente en las primaveras de la poesía tradicional, sino desde un presente empoderado por la emoción madura causada por la ausencia. En un poema sin título que tiene como tema central el existencialismo de la voz poética ante la noche personificada, el poeta escribe: "Eres sollozo de cielos vencido/ consuelo encantado del instante detenido/ brisa filtrada de un todo clandestino, venganza tardía que no contiene nada, huella de una promesa rota" (p. 57).

Sin ninguna duda, la obra de mayor importancia para la poesía boliviana de los últimos años es la antología *Poesía quechua en Bolivia* (item **2164**) editada por el peruano Julio Noriega Bernuy quien en el 2011 ya había publicado una antología similar sobre la poesía quechua peruana. La antología recoge la poesía de más de 70 poetas nacidos entre el siglo XVIII y finales del siglo pasado. Los poetas incluidos en la antología incluyen desde voces ya celebradas como Ema Paz Noya y Fernando Villegas Villegas, hasta poemas escritos por jóvenes en centros de aprendizaje. Se trata de una obra monumental, no solo por la cantidad temática que cubre, ni solo por la calidad de los poemas en la obra, sino porque servirá como un texto literario fundacional para la formación de futuros letrados y poetas quechuas de la región.

La variedad de temas en el texto es vasta, pero surgen también algunos que se repiten. El uso de la naturaleza andina para expresar aspectos de la psicología de las voces poéticas es un una característica común de la poesía en casi todo el texto. Nótese el gran ejemplo del joven Emilio Corrales al final de "Yuyaska Sarachay": "Sarachay, pitaq qunqasunkiman,/ Munakuyki ñañitay,/Ama saquiwaychu, ñañitay/ Jallp'a jalllp'aman puñuchikusqayki,/ Yaku yakupi tusuchikusqayki" (p. 792). [Maíz, quién te puede olvidar,/ te quiero hermanita,/ no me dejes hermanita/ te haré dormir sobre arena/ te haré bailar sobre agua] (p. 793).

También hay ciertos tropos comunes como la geografía andina, la religión, la migración, el amor filial, la protesta ante los abusos del trabajo y la orfandad. Finalmente, hay poemas importantes sobre temas sociales contemporáneos incluyendo los derechos de la mujer y la destrucción del medio ambiente. La pluriculturalidad surge como uno de ellos por mano de la cochabambina Julieta Zurita Cavero (1953–) al escribir en la última estrofa de "Ymaimana ruka kanchik": "Tukuyniqpi runa kanchik/ may chhikata miranchik/ may chhiata rmanchik/ imaymana kawsayniyuk/ kaspa/ imaymana runa kanchik./Jinapis tukuypis kawsanchik/ Tukuypis mannanchik" (p. 630). ["Diversidad": En todas partes estamos hombres/ mucho nos multiplicamos/ muchas lenguas hablamos/ muchas formas de vida creamos/ pero todos sentimos/ todos amamos] (p. 631).

Finalmente destacan en los últimos años poemarios que participan de una experimentación lingüística que refleja la poetización del ser humano acosado y deshecho ante el poder de los fenómenos y discursos culturales que lo forman y deforman. Estos intentos de poetización delatan las fuerzas discursivas que acosan la identidad del ser del siglo XXI y las incorporan en sus versos. Una de las características de ese delato suele ser la experimentación lingüística que refleja la complejidad de nuestra existencia, pero a la vez que va creando imágenes sorprendentemente bellas. Los prólogos a varios de estos textos subrayan esta tendencia como "neobarroca." Sin embargo, los fenómenos culturales en nuestras sociedades globales surgen en velocidades y cantidades inimaginables hasta hace pocos años desde una perspectiva postmoderna. Por ello podría ser que un mejor término sea el de postbarroco.

El interés por un tipo de escritura que lidie con una interpelación tan eficaz por los fenómenos anteriores es notable si se considera la valoración de dichas obras por medio de premios de poesía nacional y regional. No sorprende entonces que el poemario ganador del Premio Nacional de Poesía Yolanda Bedregal, *El arte de la fuga* (item **2191**) de Vadik Barrón Rollano, refleje como uno de los temas principales la identidad del poeta ante el mundo como aniquilante por tantos discursos y medios. Barrón concluye en el poema que da nombre al texto que el único remedio es el poético mismo, o sea la escritura de nuestra actual o eventual invisibilidad al notar, "el escapismo final es la teletransportación,/ la desintegración de mis moléculas en el éter trémulo,/ la materialización de las palabras como aliento en los cristales" (p. 56).

Poetas cuyo primer libro debuta en la poesía boliviana por medio de premios literarios también reflejan estas ansiedades subrayando a la vez discurso y corporalidad. Luis Carlos Sanabria, ganador del VIII Concurso para Jóvenes Poetas Bolivianos, 2014 escribe en su obra *Disección* (item **2280**), "Ya no vivo yo, mas la teoría viven en mi[. . .]/mas la angustia vive en mí,/ no soy en nada diferente a la multitud de curiosos/ de profetas del conocimiento/ que tiene la patológica necesidad/ de conocerlo todo" 79. El caso es similar en la obra de una reinterpretación *queer* de la Eucaristía católica publicada a petición del desierto Segundo Concurso Municipal de Poesía "Edmundo Camargo" en Cochabamba en el 2014. En *Eucaristicón* (item **2288**) Edgar Soliz Guzmán recrea el rito católico como un acto espiritual sexuado donde se subraya continuamente el proceso discursivo y, por ende, poético de la misa al notar, "la mañana muere abandonada en el vértice de una lágrima ajada/ El horizonte se aferra al aniquilamiento de tus suspiros./ Olvidé que había olvidado escribir en tus labios, tu dedos y tu sexo" (p. 46–47). Esta mescla de angustia—"cierro tus ojos mordiendo la ansiedad en mis labios" (p. 49), llevan al poeta a un vacío silencioso donde percibe a su amante cuyas "manos heridas resuenan en la palabra escrita,/ en la memoria de la tierra que maldice sus gusanos/ en le deseo de esos dioses que devoran la otra carne" (p. 52).

La poesía boliviana publicada en los últimos años demuestra una gran intensidad y variedad. Es una poesía atrevida, profunda y pluricultural que apunta hacia la posibilidad de un futuro artístico muy productivo para el país.

Las publicaciones de poesía en el Ecuador durante los últimos años continúan un proceso de antologizar a voces importantes del siglo XX y XXI, pero además apuntan hacia un ímpetu por editoriales en exponer la escritura de autores de calidad que provienen de sectores típicamente marginados. Además, los poemarios ganadores de varios certámenes importantes se caracterizan por obras experimentales que entretejen la multiplicidad discursiva—la hipertextualidad de estos tiempos—con la expresión poética, dando como resultado obras de gran originalidad y complejidad.

Durante los primeros años de la segunda década del siglo XXI, las publicaciones poéticas en el Ecuador se caracterizan por una recopilación de las obras de varios autores por medio de antologías personales o generacionales. Uno de los importantes letrados contemporáneos del Ecuador, Xavier Oquendo Troncoso, se encargó de editar varias de esas antologías. Oquendo Troncoso aparece nuevamente en esta segunda mitad de la década como importante figura dentro del ámbito de las antologías poéticas al introducir, junto con Ana Cecilia Blum el texto *Modelo 1972: 12 poetas ecuatorianos: (con los ojos también maravillados)* (item **2161**). Esta antología recopila la importante obra de autores nacidos alrededor de dicha fecha incluyendo la de los autores de la introducción.

Otra antología importante que reúne la obra de varios autores es *Hatun taki: poemas de la madre tierra y los abuelos* (item **2152**), editada por Yana Lucíla Lema. La antología expone la obra de autores indígenas y afro-ecuatorianos de varias generaciones. La mayoría de textos han sido escritos en quichua y traducidos al español. Sobresale en la antología la obra de Esperanza de Lourdes Llasag Fernández de Cotopaxi, quien abarca a la vez los temas de la pluriculturalidad, el género sexual y la escritura misma en su poema "Mishki shimita kilkakuna" ["Poetisas"]. La poeta escribe que mujeres escritoras van a apareciendo de una en una para unirse, "Unas la cara pintada de alegría, teñidos los ojos de admiración,/ coloreados los labios de sonrisas,/ corazones matizados, puro coraje." [Wakinkunaka kushimanta, ñawi shuyushka rikurinkuna/ ñawi paktashka rikushkawan shuyushka/ asikunawan shimikunapash shuyushaka/ shunkukunapish ñutuyasha] (p. 76–77).

Actualmente las antologías personales de autores ecuatorianos incluyen poetas importantes que reflejan la diversidad cultural del Ecuador. Estas no se citan aquí simplemente por venir de sectores marginados, sino por su calidad, aunque en grupo demuestran que culturalmente el país está pasando por una época de apertura social que desea reconocer dicha variedad cultural. Tres obras importantes reflejan esta característica de una manera profunda e impactante. En *El habla del cuerpo: antología personal 1992–2015* (item **2179**) el cuencano Cristóbal Zapata elabora el tema erótico de una manera libre y apasionada, abarcando con tenacidad y belleza un espectro sexual amplio que incluye la bisexualidad. Un ejemplo impactante sucede en "El ciprés" donde Zapata escribe el encuentro erótico entre dos amigos jóvenes, "De chicos penetrábamos debajo del ciprés del Parque Central/ como si ingresáramos por una inmensa vulva a la perfumada entraña del árbol./ En su interior entre el laberinto de ramas,/ protegidos por su espesa copa,/ nos entregábamos a lo que propicia el secreto y la penumbra/ Pronto, las manos y bocas,/ hacían lo que ya habían aprendido a hacer" (p. 100–101).

Las antologías de los poetas afro-ecuatorianos Walter Jacinto González Tenorio y Antonio Preciado demuestran un deseo de reconocer la impactante poesía que se viene escribiendo en la provincia de Esmeraldas por mucho tiempo. En *Las huellas digitales de mi pueblo: antología poética* (item **2150**) la Casa de la Cultura Ecuatoriana en Esmeraldas celebra la obra de "Jalisco" González Tenorio con una publicación que expone más que todo su obra poética de política revolucionaria y justicia social. Desde una perspectiva cultural se destaca la última sección de texto que lleva el mismo título de la antología. En esta sección la poesía se vuelve más experimental, menos política, y el poeta aplica un léxico y ritmo regional para expresar cómo su ámbito cultural ha influenciado su vida como autor.

La publicación por El Angel Editor en Quito de la antología *De lo demás al barrio* (item **2268**) de Antonio Preciado demuestra que el interés actual por la poesía afro-ecuatoriana va más allá de los regionalismos tradicionales del país. En la antología se destaca la última sección que coincide con el texto anterior en su exposición de la cultura lingüística esmeraldeña y el efecto que esta tuvo en el autor. El autor representa el lenguaje con el que se crio y lo utiliza para representar a los seres de sus entornos. Nótense las primeras líneas de "Bochinche barriocalenteño con chillangua verbal" donde Preciado describe los amoríos de su barrio de antaño, "Al frequi de Eudalasio/ cambímbora,/ salido,/ puñetero,/ se le había metido un facufacu de cosario/ por la coquimba de María Luisa/ (que era volantusa,/ prespresuda/ que andaba por el barrio/ candongueando su conqué/ su alferí)/ queriendo empatiguarla/ y llevársela a un pandán/ a morder/ a janguear/ a jalar piola/ en el jurón de su calacú/ [. . .]" (p. 143).

Otra notable característica de los poemarios publicados recientemente es el reconocimiento por medio de premiaciones importantes a obras experimentales. Los poemarios más destacados son: *El designio de la espuma* (item **2190**) de Omar Balladares Rodríguez, finalista del concurso poético Paralelo Cero 2011–2012; *Cesado el nombre* (item **2223**) de Pablo Chávez Flores ganador del primer lugar de Poesía Latitud Cero del 2013; y *Registro de la habitada* (item **2209**) de Andrea Crespo Granda quién ganó el prestigioso premio nacional Aurelio Espinosa Pólit 2016. Hay que destacar aún más la obra *Fragmentos para armar una ciudad debajo de un asterisco* (item **2224**) de Luis Franco González ganadora del Premio Internacional de Poesía Gilberto Owen Estrada de La UAEM, 2015–2016. Es importante reconocer que aparte de Chávez Flores los poetas premiados provienen de litoral del país. Esto podría significar que en los últimos años la poesía que estos jóvenes poetas guayaquileños están escribiendo comienza a sobrepasar en reconocimiento a las obras serranas.

A pesar de sus diferencias estéticas individuales dichos poetas se caracterizan por poéticas que retan al público por su complejidad discursiva. Estos poetas se esmeran por representar las vastas posibilidades discursivas actuales promovidos por la reproducción de lenguaje e imagen por medios tradicionales y virtuales. Varios de los textos incluyen código de computación, enumeraciones, tablas, etc. Los poetas utilizan también un lenguaje rebuscado con una plétora intertextos para crear sus mundos poéticos. Nótese por ejemplo el siguiente segmento de Luis Franco González: "Esta ciudad mira su última pared bordada en la noche/ como un cuerpo hundido tras el rostro mestizo/ embebido en los matorrales y cosidos bajo la telaraña del último encefalograma/ en su mano izquierda muge un número que aún no distingo/ Chopin corre desnudo mientras me ahogo con el vestido de novia de mi madre/ [luminiscencia mudo&torpe&necia]/ [serendipia in vitro detrás de los párpados]/ mar cayéndose en mi espalada como si fuese una pasiva/ [=metáfora hecha de hambre]/ 01001110 01110101 01101110 01100011 01100001/ " (p. 37).

La publicación y reconocimiento nacional e internacional del valor de estas obras apuntan a que el Ecuador se perfila como una pequeña potencia en cuanto las tendencias vangüardistas actuales en la poesía latinoamericana. A la vez los poemarios publicados en el Ecuador durante los últimos años reflejan el deseo de celebrar la calidad pluricultural de sus creadores y creadoras. [JRB]

PERÚ

En un lapso de sólo dos años (entre 2015 y 2016) se puede verificar que ha habido una proliferación de ediciones antológicas y recopilatorias de influyentes poetas peruanos del siglo XX. Estas iniciativas, impulsadas generalmente por editoriales autodenominadas "independientes", valen la pena resaltarse debido a que, con la ilustre excepción de César Vallejo, las manifestaciones líricas que tienen cabida más allá de las fronteras peruanas se pueden contar con los dedos de una mano. Por esto, el hecho de que los sellos Casa de Cuervos y Sur Anticuaria, en un esfuerzo conjunto, hayan publicado la *Poesía reunida: 1949–2000* (item **2177**) de Blanca Varela (1926–2009), la poeta más relevante aparecida a partir de la segunda mitad del siglo pasado, es un acontecimiento mayor. Carlos Germán Belli (nacido en 1927) merecía, igualmente, un lugar protagónico para ampliar aún más el conocimiento de su poesía; así, el tomo *Miscelánea íntima: antología poética* (item **2143**), que se concibe como un muestrario personal del autor, es un gran acierto de Caja Negra Editores. Este volumen se constituye, desde ya, en una excelente oportunidad para monitorear los derroteros de un poeta dotado con un sobresaliente virtuosismo técnico.

En esta vena, la especialista uruguayo-italiana Martha Canfield, con el respaldo de Lustra Editores y Sur Anticuaria (otra vez), emprendió la titánica labor de editar en su totalidad la "poesía escrita" de Jorge Eduardo Eielson (1924–2006); el resultado, hasta la fecha, se resume en tres volúmenes publicados entre 2015 y 2016 (items **2214, 2215** y **2216**). Esta estudiosa divide la obra textual eielsoniana en una triada de "períodos-ciclos", organizados según décadas y ubicados en los centros urbanos—Lima, Roma y Milán—donde el autor de *Reinos* se afincó durante la mayor parte de su productiva existencia. De igual manera, el poeta tacneño Juan Gonzalo Rose ha sido reconocido con *Juan Gonzalo Rose: antología poética* (item **2169**). Esta selección incluye sus poemarios más celebrados, entre los que destaca *Informe al rey*, dedicado al cronista indígena Guamán Poma de Ayala, y que propone una lectura teñida de una ácida retórica descolonizadora, muy a tono con las disquisiciones traídas a colación en la política latinoamericana después del triunfo de la revolución cubana en 1959. Su poesía se empeña en restaurar cualidades humanas que puedan emplearse como contrapartida a los abusos cometidos en un universo flagelado por la injusticia. Cerrando este apartado sobre recopilaciones de autores consagrados en el Perú, mencionamos el caso particular de Raúl Deustua (1920–2004), quien había sido etiquetado por décadas como un escritor secreto—un poeta para poetas—o un autor de culto; por esto la edición de *Sueño de ciegos: obra reunida* (item **2212**), se vuelve imprescindible para que su poesía, de corte hermético y metafísico, sea asequible a un público más extenso.

Con el propósito de visibilizar voces significativas, pero a menudo desatendidas en muestras de poesía peruana contemporánea, el sello editorial de la Universidad Nacional del Altiplano viene realizando una encomiable labor de publicación de escritores provenientes del departamento de Puno. Según el Dr. Porfirio Enríquez Salas, rector de esta institución educativa: "[La Biblioteca Puneña] es un instrumento, un arma de guerra contra la indiferencia que sufre nuestra región y el sur peruano como sistema demográfico-político. Representa . . . un homenaje a los hombres que hicieron de Puno una región de tradición, inteligencia y grandeza cultural". En este ensayo destacamos las entregas antológicas, ambas publicadas en 2015, de dos de ellos: *Antología previa* de Omar Aramayo y *Más allá de mis ojos: antología poética* de Leoncio Luque Ccota (items **2141** y **2155**). El primero es oriundo de Yunguyo y pertenece, cronológicamente, a la promoción de 1960, la misma que integraron escritores capitalinos como Cisneros, Hernández y Heraud. Sus poemas, de arriesgado diseño formal, lo vinculan a vates puneños como Oquendo de Amat y Churata; su fuerza verbal, enraizada en una cosmogonía andina, se enfrenta a tendencias mercantilistas propias de la civilización occidental. Luque Ccota nació en Huancané en 1964 y, a pesar de haber recibido el Premio Copé de Oro en 2013, otorgado por Petro Perú, no goza del interés ni de la debida repercusión en los medios como otros poetas de su edad. Su obra cava nichos en lo profundo de la zona sureña y afirma la búsqueda de una identidad nacional de carácter mestizo y pluricultural.

En este sentido, es reconfortante notar que otros centros de enseñanza, como la Universidad Nacional Agraria La Molina, apoyen la publicación de volúmenes de poesía que tendrían inconvenientes de ser acogidos en los típicos canales editoriales. Así, llama la atención el poemario bilingüe, quechua y español, de William Hurtado de Mendoza Santander , titulado *Maskhaypa harawin = Harawi de la búsqueda* (item **2231**). Este libro otorga protagonismo a expresiones aborígenes para rescatar la herencia de una musicalidad silenciada por planteamientos alineados con escuelas europeas o norteamericanas. Asimismo, el Fondo Editorial de la Universidad San Martín de Porres sacó a la luz la obra agrupada (1994–2014) de Alfredo Pérez Alencart—poeta nacido en Puerto Maldonado y radicado en Salamanca—bajo el título *Los éxodos, los exilios* (item **2266**). Esta colección se organiza a semejanza de una bitácora de viaje escrita por un sujeto migrante quien, como un Ulises posmoderno, proclama, en el terreno de una Ítaca imaginaria, la madurez existencial que proveen décadas de caminos transitados. Además, es preciso realzar el mérito de ciertas instituciones gubernamentales, como la Municipalidad Provincial del Santa, cuya labor editorial ha concretado, en 2016, la salida de la obra poética completa, *Cosecha de otoño*, del poeta chimbotano Dante Lecca (item **2238**). Estos textos complejizan la vertiente estética de la poesía, al añadirle una dimensión ética, que incide en que es factible perfeccionar las facultades humanas del individuo; sobre todo las que se enfocan en la brega por construir un mundo menos injusto y enfrascado en tender lazos solidarios y fraternos.

De la reciente hornada poética queremos singularizar dos voces que, con un paciente y tenaz oficio literario, alejado de la celebridad del instante, han conseguido posicionarse en un punto expectante dentro del panorama lírico actual. Nos referimos a Antonio Sarmiento, poeta de Chimbote, con *La colina interior* (item **2285**), y Denisse Vega Farfán, natural de Trujillo, con *El primer asombro* (item **2291**). El arsenal literario de esta joven y cuajada escritora está compuesto de un variado registro temático, alimentado con una eficiente amalgama de referentes de la tradición libresca que entiende el ejercicio poético como una constante problematización de los roces entre el sujeto y el mundo habitable. Cada acto de lectura reside en la capacidad de asombrarse ante el privilegio de volver a tomar posesión de un espacio puro, visionado antes de la caída y el pecado original.

En esta época cada vez más surcada por la tecnología, cabe destacar la activa presencia, en el ciberespacio y redes sociales, de nuevos corredores de difusión digital que aprovechan el alcance masivo de estos medios para llegar con mayor rapidez al público lector; así como a aficionados a—y especialistas en—la poesía peruana. Dos ejemplos pertinentes ilustrarán esta situación. La Biblioteca Nacional del Perú mantiene una cuenta de Facebook que actualiza frecuentemente y donde sus seguidores encontrarán variada información sobre actividades literarias. Un recurso útil es una aplicación llamada "BNP Digital", que los usuarios pueden descargar en sus teléfonos móviles para acceder a cerca de 2000 libros que han sido digitalizados hasta la fecha; obviamente, no todos son de poesía, pero, dentro de este rubro, se hallan títulos valiosos como *Consejero del lobo* (Hinostroza) o *Poemas humanos* (Vallejo). Alternativamente, los lectores, si desean, pueden beneficiarse de esta opción si visitan el portal en línea de la Biblioteca: http://bibliotecadigital.bnp.gob.pe/. Por su parte, la Casa de la Literatura Peruana, institución dirigida por Milagros Saldarriaga, también se sirve de Facebook para anunciar semanalmente charlas, talleres, visitas guiadas, lanzamientos de libros o exposiciones—relativas a la poesía—que tienen lugar en sus instalaciones del centro de Lima. Recientemente, se inauguró la exposición permanente "Intensidad y altura de la literatura peruana", la cual "realiza un recorrido por la historia [literaria del Perú] teniendo como eje la construcción de las identidades [raciales y lingüísticas]". Esta propuesta interactiva, orientada a lectores, académicos y docentes, se presenta en múltiples plataformas: papel, audio y video. Con esto en mente, la Casa ha puesto a disposición gratuita de los interesados la Sala de Investigadores de su Biblioteca Mario Vargas Llosa, donde se pueden revisar unos 8000 libros y revistas, entre los que destacan numerosos volúmenes líricos y de crítica literaria. El catálogo virtual se encuentra en: www.casadelaliteratura.gob.pe/. [CZ]

CHILE

Al revisar las publicaciones recientes de poesía chilena se comprueba la vitalidad del género, y la presencia de una activa industria editorial que acoge los libros de poetas consagrados y de larga trayectoria, de nuevas voces fundamentales, así como de múltiples muestras de autoedición o subvencionadas de valor variable. Entre los títulos correspondientes a la modalidad de la autoedición o la subvención privada o estatal, es de interés anotar una gran variedad de lenguajes que demuestran el prestigio y difusión del discurso poético en el campo cultural chileno, desde el rubendarismo de los sentimientos y de la mística religiosa que persiste como molde de autoexpresión en *Mi última cena* de Carlos Hanssen Tallar, al que anota coloquial y confesionalmente la intimidad en *De moscas y mariposas* de Zulema Retamal, pasando por la expresión lírica-erótica de *Poemas al velador* de Rafael Vallvé, el haikú de *Ensenada* de Víctor Alegría e, incluso, la honesta poesía etnocultural en *Diáspora* de Jaime Araya Miranda (item **2186**).

Entre las antologías a destacar, *Obra poética* de Juan Marín (item **2158**), un poeta activo en los años 20 e incluído en el canónico *Índice de la nueva poesía americana* de 1926 a cargo de Borges, Huidobro e Hidalgo, completa el mapa de la actividad de las primeras vanguardias; su rescate en la presente edición pone a disposición del lector contemporáneo una obra relativamente desconocida. Del influjo sostenido del surrealismo es testimonio *Mujer en sueño y otros poemas* de Ludwig Zeller (item **2180**), poeta y artista gráfico activo desde los años 50 en Chile, Canadá y México, donde se publica el volumen. En *Al fin todo es un milagro: nueva antología personal* de Hernán Lavín Cerda (item **2153**) se entrega una creación fundamental y reveladora en la que confluyen y se sintetizan sutilmente lo mejor de la poesía chilena y latinoamericana, citas apócrifas y verdaderas, la reflexión filosófica, el jazz, el bolero, la ciencia actual. La obra de poeta exiliado en México desde 1973 merece destacarse para continuar reconectando las voces de las promociones poéticas dispersadas por la historia reciente. Asimismo, *Poesía completa* de Pedro Lastra (item **2235**), poeta y profesor universitario contemporáneo a Lavín Cerda, reúne en una bella edición con ilustraciones de Mario Toral, breves poemas de observación delicada de la palabra de otros, del día a día y de la irrealidad de la propia biografía. Si se busca aquilatar el contorno formativo de muchos de los poetas mencionados más arriba, así como la puesta al día y reelaboración de los lenguajes del surrealismo, se encontrará una vía en *El volcán y el sosiego: una biografía de Gonzalo Rojas* de Fabienne Bradu (item **2300**): en el volumen se documentan con precisión, por ejemplo, los influyentes Encuentros de Escritores y Escuelas de Verano que Rojas organizó mientras fue profesor de la Universidad de Concepción entre 1955 y 1967, eventos que permitieron conectar, en un anticipo de las sintonías hemisféricas y mundiales de los 60, a intelectuales y creadores chilenos con los del continente y el mundo. Por otra parte y en contraste, en la veta del romance y la lírica de corte popular, las más de 400 páginas de *Arte ingenuo: antología* de Griselda Núñez (item **2259**) hacen accesible una extensa obra que actualiza la lira popular; se incluyen tanto recopilaciones de la tradición oral del Valle Central de Chile a cargo de la Batucana, como creaciones propias de una importante cultora de la poesía popular y activa participante de la resistencia cultural a la dictadura militar en los años 80. Sus crónicas en décimas de eventos cruciales de ese momento, así como acerca de las duras condiciones que enfrentaban en el día a día los más pobres en la ciudad y el campo, contribuyen a la memoria de una historia todavía por escribirse.

El cuidado tomo de tapa dura de casi 1000 páginas *Poesía reunida: mi culpa fue la palabra* de Gabriela Mistral (item **2160**), entrega la voz de una poeta esencial, cuya obra y presencia continúa siendo objeto de gozo, estudio y reevaluación. En este sentido, la edición a cargo de la poeta y ensayista Verónica Zondek reordena radicalmente los libros de Mistral, tanto los póstumos como los publicados en vida, de acuerdo a categorías temáticas y formales que permiten reconocer, prescindiendo del ordenamiento cronológico habitual, "el conocimiento al que accede" y "las obsesiones que le inquietan" a la poeta Premio Nobel de Literatura.

Como heredera directa de Mistral, cruzada por las herencias de las neovanguardias y el experimentalismo, Soledad Fariña, una poeta activa desde los años 80 quien conoce el exilio y el retorno, escribe en *Yllu* en los bordes entre la poesía, el aforismo y las visiones en prosa (item **2221**). Su obra representa una variedad de lo que se dio en llamar la escena de avanzada en la cultura de resistencia antidictatorial, una influencia que ha sido fructífera en no pocas ocasiones en el campo de la literatura y cultura nacionales. La poeta y académica Kemy Oyarzún en *Tinta sangre* (item **2262**) aplica parcialmente las enseñanzas de la neovanguardia en un poemario temáticamente unitario que integra en visiones entrecortadas los fragmentos de experiencias de violencia de y hacia mujeres y niñas; es una poesía que habla en primera persona desde los cuerpos y la intimidad, así como desde inventarios de posesiones, documentos judiciales y crónicas de la prensa para denunciar y exponer los mecanismos a través de los cuales opera la violencia de género y de los discursos sociales.

En la ruta de la antipoesía, el poemario *Bitácora y otras cuestiones* de Juan Camerón (item **2197**), un poeta de la promoción de los 60 o de la diáspora, ofrece apuntes poéticos de la infancia y primera juventud que recobran, a través de escenas de cuidada factura, un tiempo ido de significados múltiples. Resultan de interés los poemas en que los retazos de la memoria se cruzan con el lenguaje de la última tecnología, así como los que escenifican pesadillas o sombras personales frente a frente a las de la historia y la actualidad. La poesía que investiga el lenguaje de la tribu como lo hace Nicanor Parra tiene un representante eminente en Claudio Bertoni Lemus, poeta contemporáneo a Camerón y Fariña. Adelgazando al máximo la elaboración poética, *No queda otra* (item **2193**) se presenta como los sucesivos cuadernos de notas o diario de un periodo depresivo como efecto de la enfermedad crítica, la vejez y los dramas de la política del presente. Bertoni Lemus alcanza en este libro, a través de un lenguaje que conjuga frases "oídas a la pasada", la confesión cruenta de la angustia, las iniquidades del cuerpo y la merma del deseo, una densidad que no se encontraba en el poeta callejero del voyerismo adolescente; se descubre de este modo una implacable forma de poesía confesional, minimalista y descarnada.

De la importancia de Raúl Zurita en la poesía actual que se escribe en castellano hablan dos preciosas y cuidadas reediciones: la mexicana del inaugural *Anteparaíso* (item **2181**)—en la que solo se echa de menos la referencia a la fecha de la primera edición en 1982—y *El paraíso está vacío* (item **2294**), un libro que había sido publicado en una edición artesanal semiprivada de apenas 65 ejemplares en 1984 y que ahora está al alcance del público debido al excelente trabajo de la editorial Alquimia de Santiago de Chile. En este último se encuentra ya la matriz del libro del Once del poeta, el monumental *Zurita* (2011): la imagen alucinada, que reúne la experiencia de la dictadura militar con el cosmos, expandiéndose en pequeñas fábulas y comprimiéndose en visiones que podrían entenderse como el apunte de una toma de un guión cinematográfico desarrollándose en la imaginación. Además, la extensa y completa *Tu vida rompiéndose: antología personal* (item **2295**) en conjunto con la compilación de estudios publicados con ocasión del Doctorado Honoris Causa otorgado al poeta por la Universidad de Alicante en España en marzo de 2015, *Raúl Zurita: alegoría de la desolación y la esperanza* a cargo de Carmen Alemany Bay, Eva Valero Juan y Víctor M. Sanchis Amat (item **2304**), permiten acceder a una visión de conjunto de una obra fundamental.

La juguetería de la naturaleza de Leonardo Sanhueza (item **2284**) es un ejemplo de lo mejor de la poesía de las promociones nacidas en los años 70. Escrito bajo el prurito de que "la vida no es realista / y funciona mucho mejor sobre las tablas", sus poemas se van hilvanando por ecos, resabios y claves para construir observaciones y reflexiones consumidas y amargas; sin embargo, la ferocidad del detalle y la precisión del lenguaje constituyen una señal de esperanza y afecto por el mundo. Se trata de una poesía a la vez enigmática y transparente. [MLF]

ARGENTINA, PARAGUAY, URUGUAY
Tengo el privilegio de compartir con ustedes los resúmenes correspondientes a 20 libros mencionados en esta parte de la bibliografía que contiene el presente volumen. Aunque la selección es inevitablemente limitada, he tratado de representar en ella la diversidad de voces poéticas de la región austral sudamericana. Los poetas incluidos aquí representan zonas urbanas y comunidades rurales; son religiosos y laicos; demuestran perspectivas optimistas e idealistas y también actitudes de cinismo, desilusión y crítica social; su poesía es lírica y antilírica, tradicional y experimental, sincera e irónica. Espero que esta selección pueda servir de ayuda a cualquier investigador que desee aprender más sobre la gran diversidad de culturas y perspectivas literarias que actualmente existen en Argentina, Uruguay, y Paraguay.

Al seleccionar los libros para este volumen, consideré importante asegurarme de que las voces de las mujeres recibieran tanta representación como las de los hombres. Hasta hoy, exceptuando algunos círculos de especialistas, la mayoría de los lectores del mundo anglófono (y aún algunos en el mundo hispanoparlante) no tienen mucha familiaridad con la gran diversidad de voces poéticas latinoamericanas. Esto es especialmente cierto si se trata de las voces de las mujeres. En esta selección de textos quería representar a tantas mujeres como a hombres, una tarea no muy difícil debido a la abundancia de excelentes poemarios que hay.

Esto es especialmente cierto en el caso del Uruguay, un país con una larga tradición en la educación de las mujeres desde principios del siglo XX hasta hoy. Es un gran gusto mencionar la nueva edición de las obras completas de la gran modernista Delmira Agustini (1886–1914) realizada por Alejandro Cáceres y publicada por Ediciones de la Plaza en 2014 (item **2184**). Del mismo modo he incluido un poemario nuevo de Circe Maia (item **2246**), una de las poetas uruguayas más prominentes del siglo XX que sigue escribiendo poemas interesantes y conmovedores; en este caso, una colección que explora el concepto filosófico del dualismo en la cultura occidental desde varias perspectivas. Mientras tanto, Claudia Rossi (item **2275**) y Andrea Arismendi Miraballes (item **2187**) representan las generaciones más jóvenes de uruguayas que siguen con esta cadena de voces. Esta abundancia femenina también se encuentra en Argentina con poetas como Lucila Févola (item **2222**), cuyos versos representan una búsqueda de la "piedra fundamental" de la existencia humana; Romina Olivero (item **2261**), que medita sobre la crisis ecológica que estamos enfrentando actualmente; y Luisa Peluffo (item **2264**), que explora varias cuestiones filosóficas orgánicamente ligadas a la fotografía.

También se encuentran muchas voces femeninas en Paraguay, un país que he deseado destacar en mi selección. En general, el caso del Paraguay es de especial interés cuando se trata de su literatura simplemente por la escasez de libros que pueden encontrarse; sin embargo, los que se mencionan en esta selección son de una calidad excelente. Paraguay es uno de los países más pobres de América del Sur con poca representación cultural en el exterior; hasta hoy, no se ha traducido ningún poemario paraguayo al inglés. Al contrario de Argentina y Uruguay, países que aparte de las dictaduras militares surgidas durante los 70 y 80, han sido tradicionalmente democráticos, Paraguay ha pasado la mayoría de su historia bajo gobiernos totalitarios; una realidad cuyo legado se siente en el país hasta hoy.

Adicionalmente, Paraguay se distingue por su identidad como nación bilingüe; en Asunción se oyen el castellano y el guaraní simultáneamente, a veces aún en la misma oración. Sin embargo, aunque esta mezcla de culturas indígenas e europeas está muy presente en la cultura del Paraguay, lo europeo todavía domina las letras. Esto es evidente en la antología organizada por M. Mar Langa Pizarro (item **2163**); aunque este volumen ofrece una introducción muy amplia y comprensiva de la poesía paraguaya del siglo XX y comienzos del XXI, la editora misma confiesa que solamente ha podido incluir a poetas que escriben en castellano. Sin embargo, algunos de los otros poemarios que he seleccionado por lo menos hacen referencia al idioma guaraní. En *Ñe'e paje: la magia de la palabra: cuenta, cuentos—tierravenada: leyendas, relatos, historia y poesía*, Margarita Miró Ibars busca inspiración en la cultura guaraní (item **2250**). "Cuenta tus cuentos, América," ruega la poeta, y esta exhortación tiene respuesta en la primera parte del libro, con su colección de cuentos basados en la sabiduría guaraní. Semejantemente, Tory Lubeka concluye su libro con una selección de canciones guaraníes traducidas al castellano (item **2244**).

Por lo general, he tratado de ofrecerles un panorama no comprensivo, pero sí representativo de la gran variedad de estilos poéticos que se abundan en Argentina, Uruguay y Paraguay. Aunque en muchos contextos la poesía puede parecer un arte perdido, o por lo menos perdiéndose. Pero cuando miramos los casos del Uruguay, donde hay una lectura de poesía en la capital cada noche de la semana, o Argentina, un país donde abundan editoriales pequeñas e independientes, y aún Paraguay, que a pesar de sus desafíos económicos sigue produciendo literatura de calidad, vemos otra historia. Espero que estas anotaciones sirvan para presentarles a la gran riqueza cultural del Sur de Sudamérica. [JMP]

ANTHOLOGIES

2138 Adet, Walter. 25 poetas argentinos contemporáneos: poesía de las provincias. Edición de Santiago Sylvester. Buenos Aires: Fundación Sales, 2015. 224 p.

Como el título sugiere, esta antología presenta a veinticinco poetas argentinos provenientes de las provincias, no de la capital. Tal vez sería más apropiado darle a esta antología el título "25 poetas argentinos del siglo XX" en vez de "contemporáneos," ya que muchos de los poetas representados aquí fallecieron hace bastante tiempo. De todos modos este libro es muy importante para revelar la abundancia de "esa poesía nacida, o desarrollada, más allá de la ciudad enorme, cosmopolita y devoradora que es

Buenos Aires: en nuestro país, no sólo una ciudad sino un problema" (p. 9). El editor menciona "las dificultades que tiene la poesía de las provincias para ser considerada como parte de la poesía argentina, tanto en antologías generales como en historias de la literatura" (p. 10). Este libro es parte de un proyecto editorial más amplio que busca llamar la atención sobre importantes poetas de las provincias. [JMP]

2139 **Alva-Viale, Harold.** La épica del desastre: antología poética 2000/2015. Lima: SUMMA, 2016. 136 p. (Serie Personae)

Poeta, editor, antólogo, son algunas facetas de este activo y prolífico escritor piurano. Esta antología resume 15 años de ininterrumpida producción literaria, desde *Libro de tierra* (2000) hasta *Cuaderno de maratón* (2015). Si bien predominan los textos sobre la sordidez, el caos o la enfermedad mental producto de la experiencia urbana—el autor formó parte del Movimiento Cultural Neón—también se puede percibir el derrotero del hablante por parajes rurales (acequias, cerros, quebradas) desde los cuales su palabra brota como alabanza de una encontrada comunión con una especie de torrente subterráneo cuyo recorrido se adhiere a la permanencia de un "alfabeto universal". Resaltan las composiciones que retratan escenas de un erotismo convulso; el encuentro con la amada se escenifica contra el telón de fondo de fenómenos naturales extremos, y se inscribe con metáforas alusivas a ceremonias de sacrificio donde los cuerpos se ofrecen al cosmos a ritmo de cuchillos afilados. [CZ]

2140 **Alva-Viale, Harold.** La hoguera desencadenada: antología poética del Movimiento Cultural Neón, 1990–2015. Lima: Summa, 2015. 296 p.

Fundado en 1990, el Grupo Neón reaccionó estéticamente, desde una postura que recuerda la imagen del poeta maldito, a la ruina económica de García y la violencia de Sendero Luminoso de los 80 y 90. Estos poetas exhiben sensaciones de alienación y "desencanto" al vivir en una sociedad posmoderna y en firme proceso de globalización. Como movida universitaria, el colectivo amalgamó diversas manifestaciones artísticas (video, música, *happenings*) en una propuesta contestataria contra la situación política imperante; por esto, en términos literarios, el grupo buscaba alcanzar una suerte de "lirismo integrador". Sobresalen las metáforas ancladas en vivencias citadinas, a menudo marginales, entre el concreto de las calles, la miseria de ciertas esquinas y el bullicio de callejones tugurizados; todo reproducido desde la óptica de locura iluminada del creador. Los poemas parecen máquinas veloces que surcan vías asfaltadas registrando testimonios verídicos y desgarradores de un momento critico de la historia peruana reciente. [CZ]

2141 **Aramayo, Omar.** Antología previa. Puno, Peru: Universidad Nacional del Altiplano, 2015. 263 p. (Biblioteca puneña; 101)

Escritor de Yunguyo (Puno) perteneciente a la generación del 60. Esta selección ofrece una muestra de sus más importantes poemarios, desde *Prohibido pisar el grass* (1968) hasta *La lluvia infinita* (2015). Una amplia variedad de temas y estilos convergen en estas páginas, donde se dan cita textos que recogen una mirada prístina hacia la armónica compenetración entre individuo, insectos, animales y otros elementos naturales (aire, piedras, metales) con poemas de corte vanguardista emparentados con poetas puneños como Oquendo de Amat y Churata. Aramayo teje una dimensión sacra de la existencia humana que radica en el contacto esencial con plantas y alimentos oriundos (quinua, "choclo de oro") para transmitir una vitalidad novedosa y edificante; así como en el vínculo del poeta—quien asume el rol de danzante cósmico y sacerdote oficiante de ritos milenarios—con poderes tutelares que operan como aliados para contrarrestar la organización utilitaria y pragmática del mundo occidental. [CZ]

2142 **Arbitraria: muestrario de poesía y ensayo.** Alejandro Albarrán *et al*. Ilustraciones de Rachel Levit. México: Ediciones Antílope, 2015. 180 p.: ill. (Presente)

Arbitraria conjunta 12 poemas y 12 ensayos de autores nacidos entre 1975 y 1988 (esto es, menores de 40 años en el momento de la publicación del libro). Como es de esperar, los textos de estos autores son de calidades diversas. En general, queda claro que, como poetas, muchos de estos autores (Sara

Uribe, Paula Abramo, Maricela Guerrero) ya han encontrado su voz, mientras que, en tanto ensayistas, aún prima el deslumbramiento frente a los textos que encuentran, con frecuencia en los seminarios de un posgrado, sobre su capacidad de verdaderamente conversar con ellos, de transformarlos mediante una lectura singular. Sin embargo, lo que resulta verdaderamente interesante es cómo el libro, sin mediar un prólogo, muestra la dirección o una de las direcciones importantes del campo. Aunque se supone que los textos se alternan, un poema sigue a un ensayo, en muchas ocasiones es obvio y productivo el descuadramiento genérico como en el fragmento del bestiario de Rafael Toriz, en el texto de Óscar de Pablo y o el ensayo gráfico de Pablo Duarte. [JRRS]

2143 Belli, Carlos Germán. Miscelánea íntima: antología poética. Lima: Caja Negra, 2015. 244 p.

Selección personal del autor, planteada como "archipiélago verbal", que incluye desde los celebrados poemas de la década de 1950 hasta textos recientes (aparecidos en 2015). Este volumen es una inmejorable ocasión para rastrear la evolución de un lenguaje virtuoso, aunque plagado de giros coloquiales y exuberante ironía, que se mueve en un contexto moderno. La poesía, a la manera de un "bolo alimenticio", debe digerirse lentamente para saborear su plenitud estética. Estos versos, escritos con rigor formal, adjudican un aliento fresco a la tradición clásica, a pesar de materializarse con los "defectos" del "verso cojo sin remedio". Con todo, escribir poesía produce la iluminación del espíritu al ser un instrumento musical que trae armonía a las tribulaciones de la carne y el alma. Se metaforiza la vida y la muerte como ciclos en retroalimentación, de la forma en que la serpiente uroboros une cabeza y cola en un rito infinito. [CZ]

2144 Bertero Gutiérrez, Mauro Alberto.
Primaveras impuntuales. La Paz: Plural Editores, 2015. 157 p.: ill.

El quinto libro del poeta cruceño es una extensa contemplación de la presencia/ausencia del ser amado. Bertero Gutiérrez habita los silencios solitarios de esta dualidad, y de allí dirige un lamento de donde brota una emocionalidad profunda, casi monumental—si los temas que trata no fuesen tan efímeros. Esta metafísica del amor yace en el contexto primaveral, a menudo presentado en la obra como parte de una indagación poético-filosófica sobre los temas del deseo, el amor, la ausencia y el olvido. La madurez del poeta logra crear una perspectiva nueva sobre la primavera como tropo poético. Esta termina siendo más frágil, más seria e intensamente sabia como representante de amor, de recuerdo y dolor. Son paisajes íntimos donde se celebra la esencia del ser amado sin los estorbos de la nostalgia o, peor aún, de la melancolía. [JRB]

2145 Breve antología de poesía mexicana: impúdica, procaz, satírica y burlesca.
Selección, prólogo y notas de Juan Domingo Argüelles. México: Océano Exprés, 2015. 353 p.: bibl., index. (Poesía)

Como su título anuncia, esta antología agrupa desde albures y pintas encontradas en baños de cantina (su deuda con Armando Jiménez es explícita) hasta composiciones en rigurosas formas cultas, como el soneto, debidas a plumas conocidas como las de Alfonso Reyes, Salvador Novo, Rodolfo Usigli y aun Sor Juana. La colección está subdividida en: Historia y política, Festiva y burlesca, De letrinas y retretes, De letras y letrados, Culta y erudita, Machista y homosexual. Al pie de cada poema hay una nota que aclara su contexto, las dudas posibles en cuanto a léxico, pero que a veces peca de excesivamente didáctica, explicando el chiste o, peor, tratando sin éxito de entrar a su tono. [JRRS]

2146 Ceniza enamorada: poetas salvadoreños de la resistencia. Edición de Otoniel Guevara. Villhermosa, Mexico: Universidad Juárez Autónoma de Tabasco, 2016. 165 p. (Colección José Gorostiza. Poetas del mundo)

This compilation, compiled by poet Otoniel Guevara, gathers the voices of seven poets who were involved in El Salvador's armed conflict and who lost their lives because of it. These include: Roque Dalton, Lil Milagro Ramírez, Alfonso Hernández, Arquímidez Cruz, Amílcar Colocho, Claudia María Jovel and Leyla Quintana. The poetry is raw, personal, and at times political, but most importantly, it constitutes a record of the country's violent history and an important chapter in its well-known *literatura comprometida* tradition. [RMP]

2147 **Dávila, Arturo.** Sátiras: Catulinarias, Poemas para ser leídos en el metro, La cuerda floja. Madrid: Editorial Hiperion, 2017. 226 p.

Este volumen compila dos libros anteriormente publicados—*Catulinarias y Poemas para ser leídos en el metro*—y les añade un inédito: *La cuerda floja*. Los tres comparten la vocación por la sonrisa mordaz, producto del cilicio satírico. Aunque a diferencia de sus modelos romanos, estos poemas no están dirigidos contra un individuo sino más bien contra un tipo, y nunca dejan de rozar al yo que los suelta como buscapiés. Dávila (Ciudad de México 1958) encuentra su mayor felicidad en la observación que pertenece simultáneamente a los dos mundos, al contemporáneo y al de la antigüedad latina: "Me aseguras, Octavio, / que tu mujer te adora / y te ama como a nadie amó en la vida. // No te engañes, amigo: / primero adora su propia figura, / después quiere a sus hijos, / a las joyas que guarda en el ropero, / luego al gato siamés, / al perrito faldero, / a su auto deportivo, / a su flamante amante, / y, finalmente, Octavio, /—no te engañes, amigo—/ te quiere mucho a ti." [JRRS]

2148 **Echevarría Cabán, Abdiel.** Mantras. San Juan: Instituto de Cultura Puertorriqueña, 2015. 34 p. (Serie Literatura hoy)

Colección de 28 poemas numerados. El primero está dirigido a la ciudad. En éste y otros poemas recurren varias imágenes: naturaleza, tierra, vida, muerte, dolor, tiempo, sexo, conexiones humanas, perpetuas interrogantes sin respuestas. Muchos poemas representan el mundo íntimo. Los versos muestran una poesía melodiosa, anclada en realidades internas y externas. El título usa una palabra que emana del sánscrito: *mans* = mente / *tra* = sinónimo de liberación, podría traducirse en este contexto como *pensamiento*; también como esa palabra sagrada que se recita como apoyo a la meditación o para invocar a la divinidad. [M. García Calderón]

2149 **González Ríos, Juanmanuel.** Ventriloquus. San Juan: Instituto de Cultura Puertorriqueña, 2015. 43 p.: portrait. (Serie Literatura hoy)

Publicado en la serie Literatura/Hoy del Instituto de Cultura Puertorriqueña, *Ventriloquus* revela su proyecto desde su título. Si el ventrílocuo, el que habla con el vientre, usa el arte de modificar la voz para imitar otras voces y sonidos, no es ni sorprendente, ni casual asociar esa voz al acto de representación poética. Los poemas son brevísimos, muchos de solo dos líneas. Un gran número de ellos hablan de "el poeta." Varios de los poemas muy breves están dedicados a poetas conocidos, vivos y muertos. Muchos de los textos están llenos de ironía y sarcasmo; otros de humor. Todos invitan al lector a pensar en lo que implica el gesto de hablar desde el vientre por otro. [M. García Calderón]

2150 **González Tenorio, Walter Jacinto.** Las huellas digitales de mi pueblo: antología poética. Esmeraldas, Ecuador: Casa de la Cultura Ecuatoriana "Benjamín Carrión," Núcleo de Esmeraldas, 2012. 121 p.

La antología incluye poemas de cuatro obras de González Tenorio incluyendo *Voces y raíces, A todo lo que más he querido, Camino hacia la luz con la sangre armada* y *Las huellas digitales de mi pueblo*. La obra cubre el desarrollo de la poética de "Jalisco" González desde la década de los 70 hasta los tiempos actuales. Esta trayectoria subraya casi siempre la denuncia y protesta social y el compromiso a los seres marginados de la sociedad esmeraldeña. El simbolismo relacionado con el socialismo es una de las características comunes de la obra del poeta sobretodo durante la década de los 80. Dentro de esa poesía existe también un llamado a la defensa armada revolucionaria a favor de los seres más vulnerables de la sociedad. La cuarta sección de la antología recopila obras cuyo vocabulario, ritmo y temática celebran poéticamente la cultura popular y artística afro-esmeraldeña. [JRB]

2151 **Guillén, Paul.** Aguas móviles: antología de poesía peruana (1978–2006). Lima: Perro de Ambiente, 2016. 193 p.

El criterio de selección de esta antología se restringe a poetas nacidos entre 1952–82, quienes publicaron su primer poemario entre 1978–2006. Guillén prefiere no ceñirse a la tradicional división de escritores por generaciones (60, 80, 90, por ejemplo); sino que plantea "una lectura de los flujos, variables y constantes de la poesía peruana" desde la segunda mitad del siglo XX en adelante. También se busca problematizar y ampliar las nociones imperantes de "heterogeneidad" y "hegemonía de la vertiente conversacional" para proponer, más bien, líneas de fuga colindantes entre propuestas poéticas, que se atraviesan siguiendo el movimiento de "espirales de composición" literaria. Los poetas antologados se agrupan de acuerdo a seis "sistemas" expresivos: coloquial, neobarroco a la peruana, lirismo, concretismo y post-concretismo, poesía escrita en lenguas aborígenes y poesía del lenguaje. Así, se diagnostica el estado de la poesía actual usando el concepto "copresencia de lo diferente" prestado de Morales Saravia. [CZ]

2152 **Hatun taki: poemas a la Madre Tierra y los abuelos.** Edición de Yana Lucíla Lema. Quito: Ediciones Abya-Yala, 2013. 77 p.

Esta antología de poesía indígena recoge las voces de 11 mujeres y cuatro hombres. Las nacionalidades representadas incluyen kichwa, afro-ecuatoriana, tsáchila, shuar e incluso "la urbe quiteña" (Rodas Morales). Hay dos poetas invitados del extranjero: una de Perú y otro colombiano. Considerando los poetas que incluyen fecha nacimiento en los datos biográficos, se trata de una antología de poetas nacidos entre 1955 y 1998. En la mayoría de los casos se observa una antología bilingüe escrita en quichua y español, aunque hay poetas cuya obra solo está en español. Generalmente no se encuentran apuntes en el texto sobre el proceso de escritura/traducción. Varios poetas ya han publicado y/o ganado certámenes literarios, para otros, es su primera publicación. [JRB]

2153 **Lavín Cerda, Hernán.** Al fin todo es un milagro: nueva antología personal. México: Secretaría de Cultura, Dirección General de Publicaciones, 2016. 225 p. (Práctica mortal)(Poesía)(Literatura)

Cuidadoso volumen en el que se sintetiza lo mejor de la poesía chilena y latinoamericana, citas apócrifas y verdaderas, la reflexión filosófica, el jazz, el bolero, la ciencia actual. La voz de "Vuestro Inseguro Servidor", quien va anotando las pérdidas del individuo y de la utopía, es fundamental a la hora de completar el mapa de la poesía chilena contemporánea. [MLF]

2154 **Luna, Herbert.** Oratorio. San Juan: Instituto de Cultura Puertorriqueña, 2015. 39 p.: portrait. (Serie Literatura hoy)

La palabra oratorio sugiere varios posibles significados. El primero de ellos es espacial: la parte de una casa o edificio público que dispone de un altar para orar y donde se puede celebrar misa. La segunda es discursiva: de la oratoria o relacionado con ella. Los múltiples temas de este breve poemario interpelan ambas posibles definiciones. Algunos de los poemas tienen temas religiosos, otros son simplemente ejercicios líricos. [M. García Calderón]

2155 **Luque Ccota, Leoncio.** Más allá de mis ojos: antología poética. Puno, Perú: Universidad Nacional del Altiplano, 2015. 180 p.

Poeta de Huancané (Puno), fundador del grupo Noble Katerba en la década de 1990 y ganador del Copé de Oro en 2013 con el libro *Igual que la extensión de tu cuerpo*, incluido en este volumen antológico; además, se reproducen otros cuatro poemarios anteriores. Se evidencia un parentesco literario con el poeta alemán Rilke, de quien se toma una famosa máxima que dota a la belleza de un terrible poder seductor. Estos versos testimonian las marcas y cicatrices que deja el paso veloz del tiempo en el cuerpo del hablante; asimismo, rasgan el velo que cubre la faz de algún ente sagrado que yace más allá de la aspereza de lo cotidiano. En plena madurez creativa, Luque diagrama una genealogía que hunde sus raíces en el altiplano ancestral, y que transmite una herencia nacional que uno de los miembros familiares declara con orgullo: "Soy peruano / por todos los poros". [CZ]

2156 **Marejada: antología de mujeres poetas del Magdalena.** Edición de Hernán Vargascarreño. Santa Marta, Colombia: Gobernación del Magdalena, 2014. 237 p.: bibl., portraits. (Colección dorada de autores del Magdalena; 16)

This important collection of female Colombian poets, published by a regional government, is evidence of the increased attention to poetry in the nation and the expanded possibilities for publishing in peacetime. The collection presents biographical sketches and a collection of poetic works by 21 women writing in Colombia from the 1950s to the present day. The youngest of these poets were born in the 1980s, and as such, this volume, the first such anthology of women published in the nation, represents an indispensable panorama of women's poetry in Colombia. [EGN]

2157 **María, Angélica.** Siglo de pájaros. San Juan: Instituto de Cultura Puertorriqueña, 2015. 53 p.: portrait. (Serie Literatura hoy)

Otro poemario de la serie Literatura/ Hoy del Instituto de Cultura Puertorriqueña. Se trata de breves y brevísimos poemas que hablan de presencia/ausencia, viajes, naturaleza, memoria, nostalgia, sentidos, mapas, despedidas y regresos. La colección incorpora transiciones que pretenden conectar el sentido de los poemas del volumen. Todos los textos comienzan con minúsculas para enfatizar este flujo. Esto sugiere un tipo de monólogo evocativo. La naturalidad de estas transiciones se ve con eficacia en algunos de los poemas que hablan de dolor, tristeza y separación. En dos ocasiones (p. 34–35) y (p. 47–48) se recurre al poema en prosa. La autora también hace uso de la cita (Jaime Sabines y otros). A lo largo del libro aparecen versos en varios poemas distintos en azul. Al leer estos en secuencia podrían verse como un poema independiente. Lírica limpia y clara. [M. García Calderón]

2158 **Marín, Juan.** Obra poética: Juan Marín. Edición de Francisco Martinovich y Cristóbal Gómez. Santiago: Editorial Cuarto Propio, 2014. 113 p. (En estado de memoria. poesía)

Incluído en el canónico *Índice de la nueva poesía americana* de 1926 a cargo de Borges, Huidobro e Hidalgo, la edición completa el mapa de las primeras vanguardias con una obra asaz desconocida. Se pone a disposición del lector contemporáneo *Looping* (1929) y *Aquarium* (1934). [MLF]

2159 **Melgar, Mariano.** Antología esencial. Arequipa, Perú: Aa. Aletheya, 2015. 135 p.: ill. (Antologías Esenciales; 01)

El arequipeño Melgar (1790–1815) fue prócer de la patria y poeta conocido mayormente por sus yaravíes, que son cantos de tono melancólico y temática amorosa— generalmente de amor no correspondido que causa sufrimiento por la crueldad tiránica de la amada—y cuyo origen se encuentra en la tradición oral quechua. Esta antología, que sigue a las ediciones publicadas en 1971 y 1997, reúne 175 composiciones, entre las que destacan 71 yaravíes y 11 fábulas. Según la editorial, este libro se propone como una "fuente refundadora de la poética melgariana", y contiene, además de lo mencionado, elegías, sonetos, décimas, glosas y odas. Se incorpora un útil anexo con tablas y cuadros que comparan la obra de Melgar reproducida en las dos ediciones anteriores. Destaca la famosa epístola "Carta a Silvia"; así como odas que transmiten un mensaje independentista, a favor de esclavos e indios, quienes "cautivos habéis sido en vuestro suelo". [CZ]

2160 **Mistral, Gabriela.** Poesía reunida: mi culpa fue la palabra. Edición y presentación de Verónica Zondek. Adición de Walter Hoefler. Santiago: LOM Ediciones, 2015. 950 p.: bibl.

El cuidado tomo de tapa dura entrega la voz de una poeta esencial cuya obra y presencia continúa siendo objeto de gozo, estudio y reevaluación. La edición reordena radicalmente los libros de Mistral según categorías temáticas y formales, lo que permite releer productivamente a la Premio Nobel de Literatura. [MLF]

2161 **Modelo 1972: 12 poetas ecuatorianos: (con los ojos también maravillados).** Granada, Spain: Valparaíso Ediciones, 2016. 111 p. (Colección Valparaíso de poesía; 76)

Esta obra recoge la poesía de varios poetas de la denominada "generación del nuevo desencanto" nacida al inicio del los años 70 del siglo pasado. Los prólogos subrayan la importancia del muro de Berlín, el fin del pensamiento utópico y la aceleración de la pobreza como características generacionales para estos autores. El poemario brinda homenaje e incluye el poema "1972" del autor boliviano Gabriel Chávez Cazasola. Los poemas incluidos datan desde los años 90 hasta la presente década. Las voces, temas y estilos son variados como es de esperarse, pero en comparación de generaciones más jóvenes se observan un lenguaje y estilos más asequibles, más directos. No hay deseo de ofuscar o reflejar los límites de la comunicación por medio de la complejidad lingüística como se observa luego en los poetas nacidos en la década de los 80 en el país. La obra incluye a los siguientes poetas nacidos entre 1971–73: Sandra de la Torre Guarderas (Quito), Pedro Gil (Manta), Juan Secaira Velástegui (Quito), Freddy Peñafiel Larrea (Quito), Xavier Oquendo Troncoso (Ambato), Franklin Ordóñez Luna (Loja), Ana Cecilia Blum (Guayaquil), Marialuz Albuja Bayas (Quito), Carlos Garzón Noboa (Quito), Julia Erazo Delgado (Quito), Gabriel Cisneros Abedrabbo (Latacunga) y Carmen Inés Perdomo Gutiérrez (Esmeraldas). [JRB]

2162 Palabras para colgar en los árboles: breve selección de poesía guatemalteca. Edición de Marvín García. Guatemala: Metáfora Editores, 2013. 89 p. (Colección Poética; 01)

This is the first installment of the PoétiCA series, with poems from six up-and-coming Maya writers, five of them born on or after 1980. The collection includes the work of writers like Manuel Bucup Tzoc (K'iche') and Pedro Chavajay (Tz'utujil) who are known in the literary scene, but also other important voices, such as Negma Janeth Coy (Kaqchikel), Wilson Loayes (Mam), and Oscar Boj (K'iche'). The poems are fresh, some appear alongside their corresponding Mam or Kaqchikel translations, and all offer an intimate look into what it means to be Maya in Guatemala today. Boj asks: "¿Qué es ser indio?, / me preguntaron. / Les respondí: caminar y caminar." [RMP]

2163 Poesía paraguaya: antología esencial. Edición de M. Mar Langa Pizarro. Madrid: Visor Libros, 2014. 621 p.: bibl. (Estafeta del viento; 15)

Este volumen es un recurso valioso para cualquier lector que busque una introducción comprensiva a la poesía paraguaya del siglo XX. Con mucho entusiasmo y cuidado, la investigadora Mar Langa Pizarro ha preparado una antología de 24 poetas que nos ofrecen una vista panorámica del siglo. Este libro es un gran recurso para investigadores y traductores. Desafortunadamente, la literatura de Paraguay ha sido frecuentemente ignorada por la academia estadounidense; ojalá que este volumen llame más atención a la poesía de este país multicultural y bilingüe. Una de sus virtudes es el esfuerzo de la editora por incluir las voces de mujeres; aunque solamente 40 por ciento de los poetas seleccionados son mujeres, este porcentaje es mejor que muchas antologías poéticas que se publican. Una tremenda falta de esta antología es la decisión de limitarla a poetas que escriben en castellano y no incluir a los que escriben en guaraní. Ojalá que futuras antologías poéticas de este país incluyan esta perspectiva indígena que es tan fundamental en la identidad cultural paraguaya. [JMP]

2164 Poesía quechua en Bolivia: antología. Edición de Julio Noriega Bernuy. Lima: Pakarina Ediciones: Facultad de Letras y Ciencias Humanas, Universidad Nacional Mayor de San Marcos, 2016. 804 p.: bibl.

Al igual que su antología *Poesía quechua escrita en el Perú* (1993), esta obra del catedrático andino es una importantísima contribución a la historia y presente literarios de la poesía quechua latinoamericana. La antología incluye poemas de más de 70 escritores de lengua quechua de Bolivia. La variedad de los poetas es vasta e incluye a poetas publicados, reconocidos y galardonados, así como aquellos cuyas obras eran inéditas hasta la publicación de la antología. El texto se divide en nueve secciones cuyos nombres explican la división del texto basado en las características de los autores: I. Legendarios, II. Apologéticos, III. Seudónimos, IV. Educadores, V. Activistas, VI. Premiados, VII. Compositores, VIII. Inéditos y IX. Centros de aprendizaje. Cada una de estas secciones está dividida cronológicamente con información biográfica y bibliográfica, cuando esta existe. El material que prologa la poesía presenta un resumen bibliográfico de las antologías anteriores de la poesía quechua en la región. Esta obra es fundamental para quienes estén interesados en la poesía quechua andina y seguramente será fundacional para lectores y escritores quechuas futuros interesados en cultivar la riqueza y variedad de las tradiciones literarias indígenas andinas. [JRB]

2165 Premio Mesoamericano de Poesía "Luis Cardoza y Aragón": diez años: antología. Guatemala: Editorial Cultural, 2015. 73 p. (Colección Premio

Mesoamericano de Poesía "Luis Cardoza y Aragón"](Poesía)

The winners of the first decade (2005 to 2015) of the prestigious Premio mesoamericano de poesía *"Luis Cardoza y Aragón"* form part of this anthology. The collection features poems from the winning tomes by Carlos Cortés (Costa Rica), Gerardo Guinea (Guatemala), Enrique Noriega (Guatemala), Klaus Steinmetz (Costa Rica), Rubén E. Nájera (Guatemala), José Landa (México), David Cruz (Costa Rica), and Ignacio Ruíz-Pérez (México). Overall, this is solid and illustrative of the caliber of the work of these poets though the voices of women are clearly missing from it, or perhaps more specifically, from the award. [RMP]

2166 Puertas abiertas: antología de poesía centroamericana. Edición de Sergio Ramírez. México: Fondo de Cultura Económica, 2011. 479 p.: bibl. (Tierra firme)

Of all the anthologies from Central America outlined here, this is perhaps the most complete though it consists of writers who are established, well-known, and who have long formed part of the poetry scene in the respective countries (Guatemala, El Salvador, Honduras, Nicaragua, Costa Rica, and Panama). To wit: out of the 42 authors, only four were born after 1980. Overall, the collection is well balanced and captures the most renowned voices (of both men and women) of the region of the 20th and 21st centuries, including a few Indigenous authors. [RMP]

2167 Ramos, Rubén. Ultramar. San Juan: Instituto de Cultura Puertorriqueña, 2015. 48 p.: portrait. (Serie Literatura hoy)

El título de este poemario convoca al lector a pensar en lo que significa el término *ultramar*: "País o territorio situado al otro lado del mar, considerado desde el lugar en que se habla." Desde el título, entonces, el sujeto interactúa con el mar, la tierra, las islas, la naturaleza. Dentro de un mundo de esencias y temporalidades desfilan por las páginas del libro imágenes de muerte, vida, comunidad, pequeñas ceremonias familiares. También vemos procesos y actividades: pesca, erosión, cambio, permanencia, así como los recuerdos y memorias sugeridos por lugares: el trópico, el Caribe, sol, calor, campo, ciudad. Escrito con gran musicalidad y naturalidad. [M. García Calderón]

2168 Rivera, Luis César. Set. Viejo San Juan, Puerto Rico: Ediciones Callejon, 2016. 97 p. (Colección de poesía El farolito azul)

Esta edición doble contiene una sección de textos originales escritos en español y una segunda parte con traducciones al inglés de los poemas. El volumen incluye tres colecciones: *Botones* (1973), *Latas* (1979) y *Cordeles* (1998). Poemas íntimos y profundos sobre variedad de temas: el amor, la cotidianeidad, la política, la ciudad, los recuerdos. La mayoría de los textos son muy breves. Muchos de ellos evocan gestos mínimos, tanto así que la mayoría sirven casi como instantáneas fotográficas. Un ejemplo sería la sección titulada "Río Piedras parece una ciudad" en donde los poemas observan de manera acuciosa un momento particular de la ciudad en gran detalle. [M. García Calderón]

2169 Rose, Juan Gonzalo. Juan Gonzalo Rose: antología poética. Selección de Gryzel Matallana Rose. Prólogo de Marco Martos. Illustraciones de Eunice Espinoza. Lima: Ediciones SM, 2015. 121 p.: color ill. (Colección Clásicos peruanos)

Poeta tacneño. Compilación dirigida a "jóvenes lectores" que incluye los libros más representativos del autor. Se nota una genuina preocupación por establecer lazos de solidaridad con el prójimo al protestar contra la represión de regímenes despóticos. El autor mismo fue desterrado a México en 1950 durante la dictadura de Odría. El contenido revolucionario plasma situaciones propicias al cambio social en el país, alimentado por las guerrillas de la década de 1960. El poemario *Informe al rey* se dedica a Guamán Poma de Ayala; el destinatario de estas cartas es una especie de monarca omnipotente que aplica programas de exterminio en el Perú, tierra de "indios, pobres y hechizados". Puede leerse como referencia anti-imperialista en contra de políticas neocolonizadoras provenientes de la rica zona norte. La poesía recupera una esencia humana modelada por la felicidad y el goce, contra las distorsiones de un mundo dominado por injusticias que promueven la deshumanización. [CZ]

2170 Santiváñez, Roger. Sagrado: poesía reunida (2004–2016). Lima: PEISA, 2016. 220 p.

Además de los libros publicados en el período consignado en el título, esta muestra incluye un poema de *Antes de la muerte* (1979) y el texto "Lauderdale", del mismo año, que fue escogido, pensamos, porque adelanta varios rasgos de la "poesía del lenguaje" que el fundador de Kloaka empezó a practicar en el siglo XXI. Para el autor, lo "sagrado", como sinónimo de poesía, "es una devoción y una mística y ascética disciplina". Esto se sustenta en un depurado estilo neobarroco de profundas raíces peruanas—jerga, lugares, referentes culturales—donde la sexualidad es siempre exploración de un cuerpo femenino que parece tocado por primera vez. Las aguas del río Cooper se transforman en símbolo que actúa como puente movedizo que liga visiones memorables de los Andes con el bucólico paisaje norteamericano. Santiváñez confirma sus dotes cromáticas y musicales que confieren un carácter personalísimo a los parajes descritos. [CZ]

2171 Segundo índice antológico de la poesía salvadoreña. Edición de Vladimir Amaya. San Salvador: Índole Editores: Kalina, 2014. 523 p.: bibl.

This anthology picks up where David Escobar Galindo's *Índice Antológio de la Poesía Salvadoreña* (1982) leaves off, taking on the difficult task of identifying leading poetic voices from the 1970s to 2011. Amaya's Nota Preliminar does a wonderful job of providing a clear snapshot of El Salvador's poetic landscape of the four decades following the first *Índice*. What is truly noteworthy, is the scope of the work: understanding the country's political history and what it has meant to Salvadorans, Amaya includes the literary production of diasporic writers as well. [RMP]

2172 Sinfonía de sal / Nunca cerrar los ojos. Escrito por Elsy Santillán Flor. / Escrito por Raquel Lanseros. Quito: El Ángel Editor, 2013. 72 p. (Colección 2 alas; 1)

Este doble poemario es el primero en la Colección 2 Alas que propone publicar a poetas ecuatorianos e españoles juntando "sensibilidades similares, que permita que dos poéticas se den la mano y traten de alcanzar al lector a través del vuelo cómplice de dos alas que crean a ese pájaro del poema." Este ejemplar expone la obra de la quiteña Santillán (1957–) desde su poemario *En las cuevas ajenas de la noche* (1997), pasando por *Aristas del tiempo nuevo* (2013), para aterrizar finalmente en un libro inédito titulado *Proscritas nimediades*. El otro "ala" se ve compuesta por poemas de cinco poemarios de Lanseros, nacida en Jerez de la Frontera en 1973. Los poemas fueron escritos entre 2005 y 2012. Sin quitar ningún valor a las obras, resulta complejo un análisis de contraste o comparación que no sufra de la misma subjetividad que incitó originalmente querer reunir estas voces sin que un editor pueda guiar al lector un poco más. Fuera de gran interés, por ejemplo, a futuro, ver cómo los mismos autores (o autoras como es el caso acá) se ven reflejados en la obra de sus homólogos. [JRB]

2173 Sombra roja: diecisiete poetas mexicanas (1964–1985). Selección y epílogo de Rodrigo Castillo. Madrid: Vaso Roto Ediciones, 2016. 266 p.: ill. (Vaso Roto poesía; 101)

En esta colección se reúne el trabajo de algunas de las autoras más experimentales de la reciente poesía mexicana. El libro es importante porque—aunque deja fuera a Tania Favela, quien es la mejor poeta de esta generación, y a María Rivera, quien sin duda es la más discutida y leída, y cuyos méritos líricos son muy superiores a muchas de las aquí convocadas, entre otras autoras necesarias—logra crea un retrato sumamente intelectual y exigente que desmiente muchos lugares comunes sobre la escritura de mujeres y sobre todo respecto a sus limitaciones; que muestra que este grupo está haciendo una buena parte de la poesía más radical del presente, incluyendo a dos autoras que trabajan de manera bilingüe en español y en lenguas originarias. Sin embargo pesan las exclusiones de textos provenientes de *peceras* de Maricela Guerrero y de *Antígona González* de Sara Uribe (los libros más logrados de estas autoras) y de muchos textos en los que además de la radicalidad en la experimentación hay felicidad en el verso (o en la prosa). Al final el retrato de grupo parece cristalizar sospechosamente en autorretrato del antólogo, quien no se atreve en su inepto posfacio—

una neblina de mala prosa que oculta la radical carencia de ideas—a confesar que ésta es su genealogía, el marco de su propio trabajo como poeta. [JRRS]

2174 Tavárez Vales, Amarilis. Larga jornada en el trópico. San Juan: Instituto de Cultura Puertorriqueña, 2015. 44 p.: portrait. (Serie Literatura hoy)

Los epígrafes en esta colección de poemas convocan la idea de "islas" físicas y personales. El referente físico es concretamente el Caribe. Los poemas hablan de mar, agua, horizontes, lugar, procedencia, distancia, archipiélagos. En la interacción de lo físico y lo personal aparecen muchas metáforas de movimiento, fuga, de correr, de la ideas de irse y volver y el llamado de la casa. También se habla de las enseñanzas de la tierra, los ciclos de la naturaleza, el trópico de sortilegios y cadenas, el clima y sus efectos, la memoria y los afectos. Para insistir en la igualdad de planos y de lo esencial de todos estos elementos aparece un sostenido uso de letras minúsculas a lo largo del libro. [M. García Calderón]

2175 Teatro bajo mi piel = Theatre under my skin. Edición de Tania Pleitez Vela, Alexandra Lytton Regalado y Lucia De Sola. San Salvador: Editorial Kalina, 2014. 290 p.: bibl., ill. (Poesía salvadoreña contemporánea = Contemporary Salvadoran poetry; 1)

Bilingual anthology of Salvadoran poetry of the last three decades, all poets included were born after 1960. The first half of the collection comprises the work of poets currently residing in the country. The second half, like Amaya's *Segundo Índice Antológico de la Poesía Salvadoreña*, acknowledges the Salvadoran exodus brought on by the war and it includes El Salvador-born writers who left the country, some of whom write in English. The collection opens with three brief essays, one of which is written by Ana Patricia Rodríguez and deals directly the Salvadoran diaspora. [RMP]

2176 Tzoc, Manuel and Cecilia Porras Sáenz Anatomías del deseo negado: antología LGBTIQ+. Edición de Manuel Tzoc. Guatemala: Editorial X, 2018. 76 p.: ill. (e/X; 96)

Manuel Tzoc Bucup gathers the literary voices (poetry and narrative) of Guatemala's queer movement who are very active at this time and whose activism has a rich and diverse cultural dimension. Some of the authors who appear in the anthology are also participants of the annual Queerpoéticas, where they explore concepts related to the body, sex and sexuality such as the *posporno* through visual art, video, literature and performance. [RMP]

2177 Varela, Blanca. Poesía reunida: 1949–2000. Lima: Casa de Cuervos, 2016. 296 p.: ill.

Este libro agrupa la obra de la autora, fallecida en 2009, desde *Ese puerto existe* (1959) hasta *El falso teclado* (2000). También incluye los poemas de "Puerto Supe" (años 40) que fueron excluidos de compilaciones anteriores. Ana María Gazzolo subraya la "actitud reticente" de Varela, quien se "entrega al silencio" como fuente primaria de inspiración. Este comentario sirve para comprender un proceso creativo de afirmación y autocrítica que desecha esos textos iniciales como no representativos de la voz que Varela desea proyectar en su escritura. Se percibe una incesante meditación acerca del vacío existencial, la desacralización del mundo, el derrumbe de roles asignados a la mujer por una sociedad patriarcal; en suma, una postura vital que cincela una estampa humana en un universo de faz absurda. Un erotismo descarnado se combina con reflexiones metapoéticas sobre la ineptitud del lenguaje para nombrar lo que debería permanecer en medio del desorden. [CZ]

2178 La voz que no marchita: breve selección de poesía costarricence. Edición de Marvín García. Guatemala: Metáfora Editores, 2014. 53 p. (Colección Poética; 4)

The fourth volume of the PoétiCA series includes poetry by Afro-Caribbean and Indigenous writers: Dionny Milena Palmer Brown, Mariana Lucrecia Bejarano Pérez, Severiano Fernández Torres, and Justo Avelino Torres Layant. The inclusion of Torres Layant's work in the original Bribri language (with Spanish translation) is of particular note given that up to date there have only been two other significant publications on Bribri poetry, *Poesía Bribri de lo cotidiano: 37 cantos de afecto, devoción, trabajo y entrenimiento* (2006) and *Poesía tradicional indígena costarricense* (1996) by Adolfo Constenla Umaña. [RMP]

2179 Zapata, Cristóbal. El habla del cuerpo: antología personal 1992–2015. Prólogo de Luis Antonio de Villena. Sevilla, Spain: Editorial Renacimiento, 2016. 144 p. (Calle del aire; 145)

Esta antología del poeta cuencano marca la trayectoria del tema erótico a lo largo de su obra. En la colección la carnalidad del ser humano y del yo poético masculino aparece emancipada de cualquier categorización o limitación inclusive de género. Por ello se trata de un obra queer. Aparecen cronológicamente ejemplos de los poemarios *Corona de cuerpos* (1992), *Te perderá la carne* (1999), *Baja noche* (2000), *No hay naves para Lesbos*, (2004), *Jardín de arena* (2009), *La miel de la higuera* (2012) y del libro inédito *El habla del cuerpo* (2014). En sus primeras páginas, el poeta lleva a sus lectores tras la cortina de amantes dentro de la literatura y arte clásicas y, aunque los contextos artísticos continúan a lo largo de la antología, existe un yo poético contemporáneo que nos va confesando sus deseos más íntimos y sus encuentros amatorios. Luego el poeta expone contextos más contemporáneos como lienzo para plasmar la carnalidad del hombre. [JRB]

2180 Zeller, Ludwig. Mujer en sueño y otros poemas. México: Almadía, 2015. 181 p. (Poesía)

El cuidado y pequeño volumen ilustrado, casi un libro-objeto, demuestra el influjo sostenido del surrealismo en la poesía chilena. Zeller es un poeta y artista gráfico activo desde los años 50 en Chile, Canadá y México. [MLF]

2181 Zurita, Raúl. Anteparaíso. México: Almadía, 2016. 189 p.: ill. (Poesía)

Bellísima reedición del inaugural e indispensable volumen de 1982 que recoge la disposición gráfica del original así como las fotografías de la escritura en el cielo. [MLF]

BOOKS OF VERSE

2182 Achugar, Hugo. Los pasados del presente: (2014–2016). Montevideo: Yaugurú, 2016. 60 p. (El Clú de Yaugurú)

¿Dónde podemos encontrar el significado de una vida sin ningún sentido aparente? Esta pregunta guía *Los pasados del presente*, un poemario y exploración filosófica sobre temas como la percepción del tiempo y el espacio, la memoria, la relación ambigua entre lo natural y lo artificial, y la búsqueda de un sentido cuando nos enfrentamos al absurdo. El libro se divide en tres partes. La primera postula la idea de la repetición pero también sugieren que el presente tiene varios pasados posibles que dependen de la perspectiva y la percepción. En la segunda sección, el poeta ofrece una serie de poemas narrativos muy oníricos y surreales que tratan de lo irracional, lo existencial y la inevitabilidad de la muerte. La última parte regresa al estilo de la primera parte, pero con más atención a los objetos mecánicos hechos por el ser humano. El poemario termina con la idea que esa repetición también contiene la posibilidad de variación, y aquí, en este caso con la promesa de algo nuevo, una "cesta vacía" que otra vez será llenada por un futuro que todavía no se ha convertido en ningún pasado. [JMP]

2183 Aguinaga, Luis Vicente de. Qué fue de mí. Guadalajara, Mexico: Mantis Editores 2017. 83 p. (Colección Terredades)

En este libro, de Aguinaga (Guadalajara 1971) justamente explora, desde una dicción muchísima más tersa que la de *Reducido a polvo*, por ejemplo (véase *HLAS 64:2138*), una lírica de la madurez, del paso del tiempo. Donde los amores son ya de matrimonio de muchos años. Donde las aventuras y desventuras físicas las tiene en vez del yo poético, Matías, su hijo. Donde, finalmente, ya asoma la muerte. Precisamente la combinación entre el paso del tiempo y su contemplación retrospectiva, mediante una manera de decir simplificada (pero nunca simplona) es lo que confluye en uno de los poemas más memorables del libro, y de estos tiempos: "Poca monta" del que cito una estrofa: "Ya nos avergonzábamos entonces / de los adultos que no éramos / aún, serios y horribles, / y al final nos burlábamos del alma / para vengarnos del cuerpo, / que se burlaba de nosotros". [JRRS]

2184 Agustini, Delmira. Delmira Agustini: poesías completas. Edición de Alejandro Cáceres. Edición del centenario. Montevideo: Ediciones de la Plaza, 2014. 639 p.: bibl., ill., indexes.

Con mucha devoción y compromiso, el investigador Alejandro Cáceres nos ha dado un gran regalo: una cuarta edición de los poemas completos de Delmira Agustini, una de los poetas más icónicos del Uruguay del siglo XX, publicada para el centenario de su muerte. Además de los cuatro volúmenes de poesía de Delmira Agustini, esta cuarta edición incluye otros materiales invaluables: reproducciones de algunas pinturas de Agustini, que también era artista visual; comentarios críticos acerca de la poeta que fueron publicados con *Astros del abismo*; poemas que ella escribió entre las edades de diez y quince años, publicados en varias revistas de la época; y otros importantes materiales relacionados con su vida y muerte, incluida una carta que su esposo—Enrique Job Reyes—le escribió a su madre antes del trágico asesinato-suicidio llevado a cabo por él, así como el informe policial que se escribió después del trágico suceso. Ojalá que este gran esfuerzo de Cáceres genere más atención sobre esta poeta legendaria. [JMP]

2185 **Alvarado, Jaime.** Tanto contigo. Lima: Caja Negra, 2016. 72 p.

Autor limeño radicado en Londres y que vivió en España por nueve años. Poemas dedicados al amor perdido o abandonado, pero no olvidado que, para mitigar sus secuelas negativas, se recurre al alcohol o a aventuras pasajeras. Prevalece una búsqueda de expresión honesta para no caer en la hipocresía de la corrección política imperante. Los poemas se rebelan contra las convenciones sociales que limitan el ejercicio del amor a la rigidez de un acuerdo contractual; por el contrario, se persigue la enteresa de afirmar una identidad en espacios extraños, alejados del país nativo. A pesar de que el hablante ha crecido entre situaciones deplorables (homofobia, violencia subversiva, discriminación) la patria continúa siendo un sitio entrañable al que se regresa para reconectarse con una sensación de pertenencia a la tierra. La poesía significa, por esto, una batalla contra comportamientos que oprimen a los desposeídos o estigmatizados por prejuicios raciales y clasistas. [CZ]

2186 **Araya Miranda, Jaime.** Diáspora. Mexico: Simiente, 2015. 131 p. (Colección Los rostros de Erató; 4)

Poemario de la identidad y la observación de los objetos que se aplica con un lenguaje transparente a la definición del yo y la nación desde el cosmogonía mapuche y el idioma mapudungun, cruzados por la presencia de hebras del presente y la Antigüedad. [MLF]

2187 **Arismendi Miraballes, Andrea.** Detalle de los bosques. Maldonado, Uruguay: TSE, Trópico Sur Editor, 2016. 61 p: ill.

El tema de este poemario es la relación entre la naturaleza humana e inhumana. En un libro hermoso, aunque también doloroso, Arismendi Miraballes expresa el deseo universal a acceder al conocimiento de una realidad trascendente. Esta meditación sobre la naturaleza recuerda los Románticos británicos que, enfrentados por los cambios traídos por la revolución industrial, buscaron aliento en la naturaleza. Sin embargo, un poeta como William Wordsworth rápidamente se da cuenta de que la naturaleza es bella pero también peligrosa; su sublimidad tiene un elemento de terror. Esa dualidad de sublimidad y belleza se captan en este poemario como un encuentro inesperado entre un "yo" incierto y un interlocutor que aparece en el bosque literal y el bosque metafórico de la mente inconsciente. El tono general de este poemario es de un lamento. El objeto de la búsqueda nunca se encuentra, algo que deja al yo poético en un estado de incomprensión y frustración, pero también de catarsis. [JMP]

2188 **Balam Rodrigo.** Libro centroamericano de los muertos. México: Fondo de Cultura Económica; Aguascalientes, Mexico: Instituto Nacional de Bellas Artes: Instituto Cultural de Aguascalientes, 2018. 141 p.: color ill. (Colección Poesía)

Con este libro Balam Rodrigo (Villa de Comaltitlán, Chiapas 1974) entrega el segundo volumen de una trilogía que escribe a su región y a sí mismo como partes de Centroamérica. Al haber ganado el 50 Premio Aguascalientes el libro alcanzará una visibilidad mayor que la primera entrega (véase item **2189**) con la que comparte algunos elementos, como el hecho de que los poemas vertebrados por el flujo narrativo sean superiores a los de la mera lírica del paisaje o del tránsito sobre la Bestia, el tren de carga que atraviesa México y que los migrantes aprovechan en su intento para llegar a los EEUU. Aunque el título remita a los textos de tránsito egipcios y tibetanos, en realidad sus bases intertextuales son otras: la *Brevísima relación* de fray Bartolomé de las Casas y la *Spoon River Anthology* de Edgar Lee Masters, que a su vez retoma la griega y Balam Rodrigo lee filtrada a través de Rulfo—a quien reescribe en su libro del 2012 *Cuatro murmullos y un relincho en los llanos del silencio*—y sobre todo de la *Chetumal Bay Anthology* del poeta quintanarroense Luis Miguel Aguilar. En el libro alternan las voces de los muertos: "Quise ser cantante de corridos, / pero ya no canto, migro sin descanso. // Sólo sé que soy mudo. // Lejos de Centroamérica, me quedé sin voz", con el "Álbum familiar centroaemericano: "Mi padre es el hombre de la extrema izquierda, arriba. // Se asoma entre el sombrero de Nicolás (hondureño) / y mi hermana Cisteil. Nicolás era afable, trabajador, / el filo de su sonrisa partía la dureza o los modos fieros / de cualquiera. Arriba también, cargando a mi hermana / Exa, justo en el medio, Orlando (hondureño); evangélico, / tranquilo, con esa paz de las reses que van al matadero. / Se quedó en la casa mayor tiempo que los demás." [JRRS]

2189 Balam Rodrigo. Marabunta. Montevideo: Yauguru, 2018. 120 p.

Esta es la primera entrega de una trilogía cuyo segundo volumen es *El libro centroamericano de los muertos* (véase item **2188**), en la que Balam Rodrigo (Villa de Comaltitlán, Chiapas 1974) a partir del gesto crucial de asumirse, en tanto chiapaneco, como centroamericano, canta pero sobre todo cuenta (el mejor registro de su poesía es de índole narrativa) más que la historia, las historias de la frontera sur de México, del incesante ir y venir, no sólo en dirección norte de los migrantes expulsados por la violencia, aunque desde luego están allí, sino también de los mexicanos que entran y salen de Guatemala, como el propio padre del sujeto poético: "Nos dijo el hombre en Frontera Talismán: / 'los espero del otro lado, cerca de los buses'. // Al llegar, una sonrisa. Es un hombre de palabra. / Veinticinco quetzales, su paga. Nos dividimos la mercancía. / Si los verdes preguntan de quién es, nada sabemos." Lo más importante de estos libros es que, por una parte no eliden la violencia de kaibiles, maras, zetas y policías de diferentes países, pero, a diferencia de lo que sucede en la vasta mayoría de las narrativas, no se explota la espectacularidad de la violencia, sino se crean estampas muy intensas donde lo que el verso logra es subrayar la singularidad humana. Por ejemplo el poema central del libro sobre un hombre, con un tatuaje con el nombre de su esposa en el brazo, "Mara Noemí Hernández Santis, mujer de Juan López", que le cuesta ser confundido como pandillero, encarcelado y, en la cárcel, golpeado hasta morir. [JRRS]

2190 Balladares Rodríguez, Omar. El designio de la espuma. Quito: El Ángel Editor, 2012. 85 p.: ill. (Colección Ópera prima)

Este es el primer poemario completo de Balladares Rodríguez (Guayaquil 1979) conocido como uno de los ganadores del concurso El Retorno (2003) y uno de los poetas del poemario *Trayecto Cero* (2013). El poemario actual se destacó como finalista del concurso poético Paralelo Cero 2011–2012. Al igual que otros poetas contemporáneos pertenecientes al litoral ecuatoriano, esta obra se caracteriza por una experimentación de tendencia neobarroca. El lenguaje directo y sencillo de generaciones anteriores se trueca por un lenguaje rebuscado, pero suntuoso. En la obra el mar es un escenario poético poblado de aventuras casi legendarias de los hablantes en los poemas. Se observan guerreros, ninfas, sirenas como habitantes de estos contextos cuyo efecto no sólo es contar varias historias con un tono casi épico, sino también de exaltar la vida interior del poeta hasta el nivel de mito. Se trata del deseo de usar la semiología relacionada con el mar para recrear la vida existencial de la voz poética. [JRB]

2191 Barrón Rollano, Vadik. El arte de la fuga. La Paz: Plural Editores, 2014. 58 p.

Este poemario, ganador del Premio Nacional de Poesía Yolanda Bedregal en el 2013, es la quinta obra escrita del autor y músico. Se trata de un poemario de desengaño. El texto, muy humano, sínico pero emocional, profundo pero ameno, atestigua la zozobra del ser contemporáneo ante la disonancia creada por todas las fuerzas discursivas que impactan nuestras vidas. Los mundos virtuales, los móviles, la programación reality, los telediarios, y el impacto de otros fenómenos contemporáneos como el avance tecnológico y el cambio climático son expuestos a lo largo del poemario como un contexto propicio para que el poeta cumpla su función de delatar. También se tratan los temas del deseo y el de la poesía misma. Dentro de estos poemas el autor asume una postura bastante irónica e irreverente, pero siempre con un humor muy honesto que termina causando carcajadas, pero también ternura. [JB]

2192 **Bello, Javier.** Los grandes relatos. Santiago: Editorial Cuarto Propio, 2015. 124 p. (En estado de memoria. poesía)

Poemas de lenguaje hermético y cifrado, combinando versos extendidos y poemas en prosa, en los que se entregan visiones de alta densidad figurativa. Bello, autor de por lo menos ocho poemarios e irremplazables estudios sobre poesía chilena reciente, escribe como si el castellano fuera una lengua hecha natural y únicamente de metáforas. [MLF]

2193 **Bertoni Lemus, Claudio.** No queda otra. Santiago: Editorial Cuarto Propio, 2014. 297 p. (Poesía)(Colección Uvas de la ira)

Cuadernos de notas o diario mínimo de un periodo depresivo como efecto de la enfermedad, la vejez y los dramas de la política del presente. Los materiales de estos apuntes son variados: mensajes de texto, reportes médicos, sueños, recuerdos, miedos, frases "oídas a la pasada". Heredero directo de la antipoesía, Bertoni entrega inesperadamente una implacable poesía confesional, minimalista y descarnada. [MLF]

2194 **Bescós, Roberto.** La ciudad que no es. Santiago: RIL Editores, 2015. 74 p.

Crónica poética de San Antonio, un puerto afantasmado de la memoria, el mito y de un presente marginal y desencantado en que se lucha por sobrevivir a las inclemencias del "progreso" neoliberal posdictatorial. Se utiliza el lenguaje bajo de la calle, con una ortografía incorrecta y maleducada. En páginas tituladas "Documentario", se incluye el manuscrito hológrafo de unas páginas arrancadas a un cuaderno para subrayar la pertenencia del objeto-libro a un mundo que no es ni tecnológico ni digital sino manual, precario y privado. [MLF]

2195 **Bezzubikoff Díaz, Evgueni.** Laponia. Líma: Hipocampo Editores, 2018. 56 p.

Una propuesta literaria inusual, debido a su cuidado lirismo desprovisto de cualquier intromisión extrapoética, en el panorama lírico peruano del momento. Leemos una historia de amor contada por medio de un ingenioso recurso epistolar—que alcanza niveles metadiscursivos—y que se desenvuelve entre extensos viajes en tren que parecen trasladar al amante hacia el remanso de su amada, quien se aloja en el gélido paisaje finlandés. Sobresale el énfasis en los detalles que se magnifican por la destreza verbal del autor, como cuando grafica el efecto de un minúsculo rayo de luz en una pelusa de polvo. En la lejanía del Círculo Polar, el amor se congela y adquiere la solidez del hielo macizo, para perennizarse en un instante que se pretende eterno: "Y he remado / dos mil años luego / para habitar este granizo". [CZ]

2196 **Bohórquez, Abigael.** Poesía reunida e inédita. Edición, estudio y notas de Gerardo Bustamante Bermúdez. Hermosillo, Mexico: Instituto Sonorense de Cultura, 2016. 697 p.: bibl. (Clásicos sonorenses; 1)

Bohórquez (Caborca 1936-Hermosillo 1995) es un poeta que, después de una vida precaria y sin cabal reconocimiento de su obra, goza de una fama póstuma y de un decidido interés tanto de la crítica académica como de un grupo creciente de lectores, sobre todo poetas jóvenes. Este volumen es la compilación definitiva, tanto de sus libros publicados en vida, como de sus colecciones póstumas y sus textos no coleccionados. Lo que este panorama revela es por una parte al poeta que incorpora a su dicción culta el léxico del desierto del noroeste de México: "—Adela, parece que te escucho—: / chicharra, bichicori, chora, calichi, péchicta, mochomo, / cholla, cachora, churea, chilicote, / chapo, sopichi, cochupeta, bichi, / apupuchi, chiriqui, cuitlacochi, / subterráneos imanes, dígitas soledades, sombra casi luz sólida"; por otra al poeta primero en incorporar la epidemia del sida en forma de una antología en el sentido griego en *Poesida*; pero también ahora se revela a un poeta que, aprovechando el vuelo narrativo de sus amores homosexuales, no cesa de hacer experimentos formales, pero no para enrarecer su poesía, sino para prestarle más voces a su habla: "G, pequeño de estatura, goloso, ratón tierno, / sensual, lacio de pelo, nálguido, moreno / lúbrico, indócil, buena onda / dionisiaco y alegre, / géminis y sanguíneo / cabrón, rechoncho, lampiño, bienmembrado, / ni duda cabe, lleva ventaja / que él me miró primero." Uno de los libros imprescindibles de estos años. [JRRS]

2197 Camerón, Juan, Bitácora y otras cuestiones. Quito: CCE Benjamín Carrion, Casa de la Cultura Ecuatoriana: El Ángel Editor, 2014. 69 p. (Poesía en paralelo)

El poeta de Valparaíso, integrante de la promoción de los 70 o de la diáspora, ofrece, con un lenguaje en que se divisa a Parra, Lihn y Tellier y se dibuja la memoria cultural de una generación, escenas de cuidada factura que recobran un tiempo ido de significados múltiples. El poemario recibió el Premio Internacional de Poesía Paralelo Cero 2014. [MLF]

2198 Cardenal, Ernesto. Noventa en los noventa: antología. Edición de Sergio Ramírez. México: Trilce Ediciones; Monterrey, México: Universidad Autónoma de Nuevo León, 2014. 382 p.: ill.

Compiled by his friend and fellow poet, Sergio Ramírez, this wonderful collection was published in 2014, in celebration of Ernesto Cardenal's 90th birthday. It comprises some of the poet's best work, and it includes great images of the poet and an introduction by Ramírez. [RMP]

2199 Carranza Gálvez, Doris. Flor de café. Lima: Editorial Bracamoros, 2015. 85 p.

Poeta de Jaén (Cajamarca), autora de libros de poesía infantil. Sus poemas expresan sentimientos de nostalgia que se matizan, afectiva y plásticamente, con la majestuosidad de los elementos naturales del paisaje andino, o con indestructibles centros prehispánicos (como Kuélap). Las ruinas arqueológicas dotan de permanencia y solidifican la potencia de la voz lírica para enfrentar la tristeza que sigue al abandono amoroso. Estas composiciones transitan entre la calidez e intimidad de los vínculos familiares, reflexionando acerca del alejamiento de los hijos o sobre la elocuencia que brota del mutismo de los parientes ancianos. Se busca definir una identidad propia de rasgos nativistas ("yaraví", "maracuyá") dentro del agitado ritmo de un medio ambiente multiplicado por agentes refractarios (luces, espejismos, porciones de tiempo); para esto se fabrica una estrecha conexión entre lo corpóreo y la naturaleza: "Y en mi sueño confundí / mi cuerpo y mis cabellos / con los arrozales". [CZ]

2200 Castellanos, Julio. Poesía reunida: 1983–2013. Córdoba, Argentina: Llantodemudo, 2014. 511 p. (Poesía)

La poesía de Julio Castellanos es una meditación sobre las grandes preguntas relacionadas con la vida y la muerte. En la tradición de Juan de la Cruz y Teresa de Ávila, Castellanos nos ofrece una poesía contemplativa—incluso mística—que explora los temas esenciales de la experiencia humana. Diálogos con el mito, la filosofía, y la ciencia se combinan con las experiencias cotidianas del amor y la amistad para crear una poesía que trasciende el tiempo y lugar para ir hacia alguna verdad universal. Un rasgo interesante es la consistencia que muestran la voz y el tono a lo largo de las catorce colecciones reunidas en este volumen. Desde *Umbrales*, su primer poemario, publicado en 1983, hasta los últimos poemas, vemos la misma búsqueda de conocimiento de una realidad última expresada formalmente de diferentes maneras, entre ellas es verso libre, sonetos, y poemas en prosa. Aunque las estrategias son múltiples, el viaje sigue sin interrupciones. Ojalá que a través de este gran tomo de su poesía, aquí reunida la escritura de Castellanos reciba la atención crítica que sin duda merece. [JMP]

2201 Chacón, Alfredo. Sin mover los labios. Caracas: Oscar Todtmann Editores, 2015. 53 p. (Poesía Oscar Todtmann Editores; 5)

This collection by the well-respected and prolific Venezuelan poet is a study in dissonance and lack of understanding. Many of the poems are short and written in a conversational tone, as if the reader were catching bits of dialogue without context. As the poetic voice of one of the poems states, "recojo los fragmentos," which seems to summarize the collection's esthetic of depicting of small spaces and tiny moments. These moments are expressed both in the short poems and in the busy little drawings interspersed among them throughout the work. In the poetry, there is a sense of darkness, absence, and loss at times tempered with a faint, subjunctive hope. [EGN]

2202 **Chaves, Raquel.** Un largo viaje juntos: textos elegidos. Asunción: Servilibro, 2016. 165 p.: ill. (Colección Academia Paraguaya de la Lengua Española; 18)

Raquel Chaves es una poeta de viajes en búsqueda de una realidad espiritual que no se ve fácilmente en la modernidad. Esta búsqueda la lleva a muchas partes, incluso a una fascinación con la cultura guaraní que—aunque tal vez problemática—forma una parte integral de la identidad cultural paraguaya. De todos modos, esta selección muestra una voz poética y muy conmovedora. El libro empieza con selecciones de *Todo es del viento: siete viajes* (1984). Como una especie de diario espiritual, esta sección lleva al lector en un recorrido que, según lo revela el discurso, será al mismo tiempo un viaje a la interioridad de la hablante. Esta búsqueda continúa en las selecciones de *Espacio sagrado* (1988). En *Partes del todo* (2000) vemos la fe de la poeta a pesar de la incertidumbre de la vida y la inevitabilidad de la muerte. La antología concluye con *La ciudad invisible*, una novela corta en prosa y verso sobre un joven que está preocupado por la crisis ecológica que afecta el planeta entero en el siglo XXI. Este tema se extiende por toda la obra de esta poeta, que responde al sufrimiento del mundo con amor y empatía. [JMP]

2203 **Chávez, Rosa** and **Camila Camerlengo.** Awas. Creación colectiva de Rosa Chávez y Camilla Camerlengo a partir de la obra poética de Rosa Chávez. Guatemala: Catafixia Editorial, 2014. 55 p.: ill. (Escénica poética; 4)

This is a collection of Chávez poetry that was adapted for the stage. *Awas* is a Maya Q'eqchi' concept that signifies both illness and cure, and here Chávez explores issues of Maya identity from the perspective of a Maya woman in Guatemala. The solo performance was presented at the IX Festival Nacional de Teatro in Guatemala in 2015. [RMP]

2204 **Chirinos Arrieta, Eduardo.** Siete días para la eternidad: homenaje a Odysseas Elytis. San Isidro, Peru: Librería Sur, 2015. 97 p.

Este poemario está diseñado como homenaje a la obra de Elytis—para hallar un "correlato mítico con la experiencia sensorial"—a la vez que lleva a cabo la tarea de reescribir el poema homónimo del poeta griego. Otros escritores invocados por Chirinos, en un afán por insertarse en una vertiente de parentesco literario, son Baudelaire, Neruda, Eliot, Seferis, por citar algunos nombres. Las jornadas de esta semana poética se ofrenda a alguna divinidad del panteón clásico (Marte, Venus, Zeus) y presenta los grandes temas de la poesía de todos los tiempos: la angustia ante la nada, el erotismo, el desamor, la violencia, la imposibilidad de conocer total y ciertamente la realidad; así como, también, y en nota positiva, la regeneración del orbe en cada amanecer. [CZ]

2205 **Cobo Borda, Juan Gustavo.** Poesía: última trinchera. Montevideo: Yaugurú, 2014. 57 p. (El Clú de Yaugurú)

This new collection from the esteemed Colombian poet continues the author's fine work in verse. The poems here are reminiscent of Neruda's later works in their meditations on small moments and in their playful tone. The works collected here use the five senses and visual references common in the poetry of the last few years to offer the poet's thoughts on love, loss, and mortality. Indeed, Cobo Borda's "Cinco sentidos" in this volume might be seen as an *arte poética* for the moment. [EGN]

2206 **Corcuera, Arturo.** Baladas de la piedra, del amor y de la muerte. Lima: Ediciones El Nocedal, 2016. 108 p.

Corcuera es autor del celebrado *Noé delirante* (see *HLAS 64:2162*). La voz poética modela una entidad indestructible que precede y sobrevive al nacimiento y la aniquilación al fusionarse con las "partículas" del universo. Versos breves, de efectiva imaginería e ironía, reinterpretan poemas famosos de la tradición literaria; como "Lo fatal" de Darío: "¿Y si la piedra sufre / y su más grande dolor / es no haber nacido / ser humano?". El estilo recuerda el halo misterioso y el sugerente cromatismo de Eguren, aunque dotado con un toque de humor, como la referencia a la sentencia promulgada por censores para quemar las cenizas del Ave Fénix, acusado de subversión. La triada de elementos del título se puede leer así: piedra (fundación y origen milenario), amor (erotismo y vida), muerte (envejecimiento y sufrimiento). El poeta es un "gallo de pelea", la poesía un acto de resistencia frente a los ataques de un mundo enemigo. [CZ]

2207 Corcuera, Marco Antonio. Trina el pájaro ciego: the trill of the blind bird. Trujillo, Peru: Cuadernos Trimestrales de Poesia, 2014. 161 p.

Edición bilingüe de este escritor oriundo de Contumazá (Cajamarca), fallecido en 2009. Este volumen antológico recoge textos de una docena de libros—desde Poemas del ayer lejano (1940) hasta Alba de cosecha (2009)—acompañados de un dossier fotográfico. El proceso poético se define como aprendizaje de una suerte de elevación hacia cuestas donde el espíritu pueda oxigenarse con un aire diáfano y se nutra de experiencias plenas. Igualmente, lo importante no es alcanzar una meta satisfactoria a corto plazo, sino que vale más el enriquecimiento personal que llega con el trajín de andar por un camino que se traza con cada paso al futuro. La escritura también obedece a una consigna ética: el hombre debe ponerse manos a la obra para traer justicia social al mundo, sin esperar alguna solución divina. Es palpable el genuino interés en representar a los habitantes andinos desterrando estereotipos asociados con un indigenismo de postal. [CZ]

2208 Cortés González, Alejandro. Sustancias que nos sobreviven. Bucaramanga, Colombia: Dirección Cultural, Universidad Industrial de Santander, 2015. 143 p.

This award-winning collection from the young Colombian poet is word-dense and packed with sensorial imagery. The poems here are conversational in tone, but read as fragments of a larger discussion. Cortés González uses his works to communicate his personal experiences of concrete and everyday items and events. The originality of the style, tone, and format of this young poet's works suggest that Cortés González is a poet to watch in the coming years. The publication of this collection by a regional and university press is again an indication of increased poetry publication in Colombia. [EGN]

2209 Crespo Granda, Andrea. Registro de la habitada: poesía. Quito: Centro de Publicaciones, Pontificia Universidad Católica del Ecuador, 2016. 115 p.

Este segundo poemario de la escritora guayaquileña ganó el prestigioso premio nacional de poesía Aurelio Espinosa Pólit 2016. Se trata de un texto extremadamente experimental y radical. La autora, con un léxico neobarroco de gran imaginación, hilvana intertextualidades con la música, el cine y otros medios de comunicación, para formar algo semejante a un diario interdiscursivo que proyecta nuevas imágenes para rescatar a la memoria. La importancia de la palabra en la creación de la memoria—imagen íntima hecha de lenguaje—se observa en la obra al resaltar plataformas textuales para el proceso creativo incluyendo poesía, prosa, epígrafes, guiones, acotaciones, coros y código de computación. Así, algo semejante a recuerdos aparecen poblados de los mismos personajes femeninos que se van desarrollando, proyectando, a través de varios medios de comunicación. El lenguaje íntimo e intensamente corporal humaniza la obra a la vez que el lenguaje religioso eleva a la corporalidad humana para crear una especie de experiencia espiritual semejante a un loop de transubstanciación donde la palabra se convierte en carne y la carne en palabra. [JRB]

2210 De la Fuente, Juan. Puentes para atravesar la noche. Lima: Paracaídas Editores, 2016. 62 p.

Estos textos se despliegan como armas provistas de un vocabulario intenso, descarnado, político (como en el poema dedicado a Mao Zedong): "Estas metáforas amenazan / con mostrar tus cicatrices". Se pretende ampliar el significado convencional de las costumbres mundanas para acceder a aquel otro lado que se atisba allende el contorno del lenguaje. El hablante transita por metrópolis extranjeras (París, Shangai, Nueva York, Londres) transformando su dolor en aullido por medio de la poesía; la actividad literaria le permite conectarse con las vivencias de sus semejantes, materializando una sensación de colectividad. Se escribe para refundar un origen que no divida el mundo en disociaciones antitéticas—se une paraíso e infierno, creador y creación—haciendo que el individuo se impregne de la vastedad de la naturaleza sin bordes precisos o impuestos. El final remite al comienzo de un ciclo que se muerde la cola en la inacabable rueda de los días. [CZ]

2211 Deltoro, Antonio. Rumiantes y fieras. México: Ediciones Era, 2017. 101 p. (Alacena bolsillo)

Esta colección está llena de seres vivos que van desde Dios hasta la animación de la arena "enterrada en sí misma", las aguas "que nunca fueron nubes", "que no se mueven" en el fondo del océano y la basura como naturaleza muerta. Aunque, como suele suceder en los libros de Deltoro, priman los árboles. Sin embargo, lo verdaderamente vivo de este libro es el juego, la chispa, la felicidad del arte menor. En "Infancia" por ejemplo: "Se fantaseaba perro, / un perro entre los perros, / no un perro solitario; / husmeando todos juntos; / amigos poco a poco / o de repente." Incluso en los poemas en los que el tema es melancólico "Talaron el encino / en su ausencia / le digo encino / a todo árbol", la dicción aligera lo dicho, pero no obliterándolo sino invitándonos a decirlo de nuevo, a meditarlo. [JRRS]

2212 Deustua, Raúl. Sueño de ciegos: obra reunida. Lima: Lápix Editores, 2015. 400 p.: bibl., ill.

Edición indispensable de este poeta poco difundido, debido tal vez a que se alejó del Perú a comienzos de la década de 1960 y murió en Ginebra en 2004. Sin ánimo de echar mano a etiquetas, esta poesía podría considerarse hermética—en la tradición de poetas italianos como Ungaretti o Montale—con tendencia a disquisiciones metafísicas que tratan de desentrañar el misterio y el destino último de la existencia: "Hay tal vez la señal de un dios absurdo / pero su verbo es enigmático". La amplitud del paisaje marino es un referente constante en esta obra, adquiriendo la figura de un inmenso lienzo donde se cruzan la música del viento, la solidez de las rocas, los naufragios cotidianos y el diseño geométrico del vuelo de las aves. El libro se completa con traducciones de Eliot y Catulo, textos críticos sobre poetas peruanos, entrevistas y la pieza de teatro inédita *Judith*. [CZ]

2213 Di Paolo, Rossella. La silla en el mar. Lima: PEISA, 2016. 83 p. (Serie Alma Matinal)

Poemario dedicado a dos personajes de Melville: Ahab (*Moby Dick*) y Bartleby, famoso por su frase "preferiría no hacerlo". La elección de caracteres opuestos genera un contraste entre la apuesta por la acción del primero frente a la inacción del segundo. Se retrata al individuo como sometido a la esclavitud del horario y a la burocracia kafkiana en oficinas de tono impersonal, en las que se sienta fijamente en una silla esperando que suceda algo que rompa la rutina. La capital del Perú se equipara al vientre blanco de una ballena, que destiñe el color paisajístico, otorgándole un aspecto infernal ("vade retro cielo de Lima"). En esta época hiperreal, los jóvenes ya no distinguen entre actividad y pasividad, porque ellos encarnan las dos situaciones a la vez: creen controlar sus actos, digitalizando todo desde sus aparatos electrónicos, pero, al mismo tiempo, son gobernados por un simulacro cibernético que los engulle. [CZ]

2214 Eielson, Jorge Eduardo. Poesía escrita. Vol. 1, Poeta en Lima. Edición de Martha Canfield. Lima: Lustra Editores, 2016. 1 vol., 180 p.: ill.

Una cuidada edición de Canfield, conocida especialista eielsoniana, de la "poesía escrita" del autor, que excluye sus experimentos visuales y concretos (como la colección Papel); es decir que no se incorporan las manifestaciones artísticas cimentadas en "lenguajes transverbales". Este proyecto comprende un total de cinco volúmenes, tres de los cuales se han publicado hasta la fecha. El criterio de la editora consiste en segmentar en "períodos-ciclos" la producción textual de Eielson. Estas fases se organizan por duraciones temporales y se ubican en lugares geográficos donde el poeta residió la mayor parte de su vida (Lima, Roma y Milán). Con esto se pretende visibilizar afinidades temáticas y técnicas entre las distintas etapas literarias. El resultado logrado hasta ahora es Vol. 1–3. Vol. I. *Poeta en Lima* abarca: *Moradas y visiones del amor entero* (1942), *Cuatro parábolas del amor divino* (1943), *Canción y muerte de Rolando* (1943), *Reinos* (1944), *Antígona* (1945), *Ájax en el infierno* (1945), *En La Mancha* (1946), *El circo* (1946), *Bacanal* (1946), *Doble diamante* (1947), *Primera muerte de María* (París, 1949), *Tema y variaciones* (Ginebra, 1950). Cabe notar que los poemarios publicados fuera del Perú mantienen correspondencias con el ciclo limeño. Destaca *Reinos*, un sobresaliente despliegue de virtuosismo estético y de amplio conocimiento de la tradición lírica de Occidente. Para comentario sobre volumen 2, *Poeta en Roma*, véase **2215**. Para comentario sobre volumen 3, *Poeta en Milán*, véase **2216**. [CZ]

2215 **Eielson, Jorge Eduardo.** Poesía escrita. Vol. 2, Poeta en Roma. Edición de Martha Canfield. Lima: Lustra Editores, 2016. 1 vol., 227 p.: ill.

El segundo volumen de un proyecto que comprenderá cinco volúmenes. *Poeta en Roma* contiene *Habitación en Roma* (1952), *La sangre y el vino de Pablo* (1953), *Mutatis mutandis* (1954), *Noche oscura del cuerpo* (1955), *De materia verbalis* (1957–1958), *Naturaleza muerta* (1968), *Acto final* (1959), *Ceremonia solitaria* (1964), *Pequeña música de cámara* (1965), *Arte poética* (1965). Se distingue la exploración de la cotidianeidad en *Habitación en Roma* y la exposición de los vericuetos de la carne y el recorrido metafórico por el interior corporal en *Noche oscura del cuerpo*. Para comentario sobre volumen 1, *Poeta en Lima*, véase **2214**. Para comentario sobre volumen 3, *Poeta en Milán*, véase **2216**. [CZ]

2216 **Eielson, Jorge Eduardo.** Poesía escrita. Vol. 3, Poeta en Milán. Edición de Martha Canfield. Lima: Lustra Editores, 2016. 1 vol., 217 p.: ill.

El tercer volumen de un proyecto que comprenderá cinco volúmenes. *Poeta en Milán* agrupa *Celebración* (1990–1992), *Sin título* (1994–1998), *Del absoluto amor y otros poemas sin título* (1990–1992). Textos dotados de ingeniosos juegos con la permutación y las posibilidades combinatorias de la lengua, creando sentidos inéditos, a menudo absurdos o paradójicos, que radiografían las consecuencias de la trivialización posmoderna. Para comentario sobre volumen 1, *Poeta en Lima*, véase **2214**. Para comentario sobre volumen 2, *Poeta en Roma*, véase **2215**. [CZ]

2217 **Espinosa, Rafael.** El vaquero sin agua en la cantimplora. Lima: Librería Inestable, 2017. 55 p.

Autor que declara abiertamente que escribe "poemas de la descomposición". Esto se nota en sus reflexiones abstractas y en descripciones del paisaje urbano miserable de Lima. Se dibujan, de preferencia, zonas empobrecidas del centro limeño (Jr. Torrico, Jr. Lampa) habitadas por personajes marginados—drogadictos, mendigos, minusválidos—que decoran un trasfondo de música de rock (David Bowie, Rolling Stones). Como varios poetas de su generación, la del 90, el poeta denuncia la alienación y despersonalización de los individuos producto de estar inmersos en un contexto hipertecnológico, convertidos en ridículos "juglares del iPhone", que ha reducido el esplendor de la naturaleza a niveles ínfimos. [CZ]

2218 **Esquinca, Jorge.** Cámara nupcial. México: Ediciones Era; Xalapa, Mexico: Instituto Veracruzano de la Cultura, 2015. 139 p.: 1 ill.

En este libro Esquinca (Ciudad de México 1957) usa a Emily Dickinson como pretexto, como interlocutora, como objeto textual y visual. El resultado es variable. En ocasiones, le permite acceder a un territorio intermedio, entre sus registros anteriores y el de la poeta de Amherst: "Hay aquí un *abejorro* distinto /a los que trae el verano—muy serio—/ una especie de galán de barrio bajo". Lo mejor del libro es cuando la voz poética se deja raptar por su propio estro y salta de los versos a una prosa desbocada, pienso especialmente en el poema "Se trata de un sueño dentro de un sueño" del que cito un fragmento: "yo preparé la infusión de plata el baño sagrado donde habrías de quedar retenida para siempre a tus dieciséis años a los ciento ochentaidós de tu nacimiento a los quinientos de la nieve que cae en el interior de tu recámara ahora que te miro a través de la lenta dijo Hamlet rodeada de flores dijo Emily nunca tan cierva tan dueña de tu propio sacrificio como en esta imagen nunca tan Ofelia entregada a las catástrofes de esta caja oscura donde apareces todas las noches." Un buen suplemento a este poemario es el texto ensayístico sobre Dickinson en *Breve catálogo de fuerzas* (véase item **2302**). [JRRS]

2219 **Etchevarren, Javier.** Fábula de un hombre desconsolado. Montevideo: Yaugurú, 2014. 58 p. (Todos los gallos estan despiertos. Segunda serie (poesía); 7)

En este poemario corto, el autor regresa a su niñez y el barrio pobre donde creció con dos hermanos y una madre soltera. Con honestidad, ironía, y humor Etchevarren logra evocar la miseria que experimentó y el trauma que ha marcado su vida como adulto. El lenguaje coloquial invita que el lector entre en el texto y que se identifique con el yo poético; mientras tanto, la repetición evoca el sentido de frustración de no poder escapar de la pobreza, de quedarse en el ciclo vicioso. Aunque este humor sardónico corre por el poemario entero, está acompañado de una sinceridad muy conmovedora. Mientras dice que su padre "murió solo, sin gloria / y ni siquiera tuve / interés en su cadáver," (p. 18) agradece a la madre que "tiene seis brazos. Así logró salvar a sus tres hijos de aquel incendio" (p. 15). En 2017, Action Books lo publicó como *Fable of an inconsolable man* en versión bilingüe, y ahora los lectores anglófonos ya pueden acceder a esta historia tan real y relevante. [JMP]

2220 **Falconí, Ana María.** Sobrevivir es un acto de invierno. Lima: Paracaídas Editores, 2015. 74 p.: ill. (Serie &nsular de poesía)

Poemario dividido en cuatro secciones referidas a meses sucesivos (junio, julio, agosto, setiembre). Las metáforas aéreas, bajo la tutela de Huidobro, describen la necesidad de liberar un cuerpo agrietado por cuyo interior se cuelan ráfagas de niebla difusa de aspecto fantasmal. Esto se concreta en versos etéreos que simulan ambientes atemporales. Las atmósferas irreales, solitarias o misteriosos remiten a Pizarnik: "ella dejas sus cabellos en el viento / como arbustos albos / que enredan pensamientos". El final del libro adquiere un tono apocalíptico—por eso los meses se encuentran tachados: junio, por ejemplo—donde aves blancas ("palomas") luchan contra pájaros negros ("cuervos") anticipando el "fin de los tiempos". Lo que permanece después de todo, y que puede comunicarse por la poesía, es la memoria de fuerzas naturales que brinda sensaciones de eternidad. La escritura encarna un ritual de sobrevivencia en medio de la incertidumbre y el castigo de lo temporal. [CZ]

2221 **Fariña, Soledad.** Yllu. Santiago: LOM Ediciones, 2015. 98 p. (Colección entre mares)

Poesía experimental de una voz de amplia trayectoria que se expresa en los bordes entre la poesía, la narración y las visiones en prosa donde se imaginan y van configurando el romance familiar y el lugar del yo. [MLF]

2222 **Févola, Lucila Beatriz.** Así seas. Buenos Aires: Ediciones del Dock, 2015. 66 p.

Es posible definir la poesía como un intento de decir lo indecible. Este intento es lo que más llama la atención en la poesía de Lucila Févola. En diálogo con varias figuras de la historia de la literatura y filosofía, este poemario intenta llevarnos en un viaje más allá de los límites del lenguaje. Con mucho juego de palabras, a veces este poemario tiende a la palabrería, donde nada tiene sentido. El ángel de Rainer Maria Rilke vuela por estos poemas, pero nosotros no lo podemos atrapar. El río de Heráclito sigue fluyendo. Un motivo que se repite en el poemario es el de la piedra fundamental (*lapis philosophorum*), que aparece en la imaginación como un espejismo pero nunca se encuentra). La búsqueda toma un carácter místico; tiene algo de profecía en su repetición de sabiduría antigua, una repetición con variación: "Buscar es convertirnos en lo que buscamos hasta encontrarnos en lo que nos busca" (p. 16). Aunque no podamos saber lo que es, hay algo que nos busca. De eso Févola está segura. [JMP]

2223 **Flores Chávez, Pablo.** Cesado el nombre. Quito: El Ángel Editor, 2013. 73 p. (Poesía en paralelo)

Este poemario celebra el primer lugar de Poesía Latitud Cero del 2013. Es el último de varios premios nacionales que ha ganado el joven poeta quiteño (n. 1988) cuya obra se ha publicado en México y en los EEUU. En la primera parte, Flores poetiza la esencia filosófica de varios pensadores. Los poemas se titulan con el nombre de Aristóteles, Kant, Echeverría, etc., y el poeta aplica un lenguaje bello y complejo que defamiliariza aunque eleva al nivel poético a la filosofía a la que apunta. En la segunda mitad del texto aparece el mismo lenguaje rebuscado—es un neobarroco existencial, intertextual e íntimo—para seguir poblandol las páginas con poemas relativamente cortos, pero complejos. Hay mucha inserción de múltiples textualidades que sirven como capas semióticas que llenan de seriedad canónica y de emoción existencial a los poemas. Los poemas no pecan por sentimentales, pero tampoco provocan ni compasión ni empatía por la voz poética. En esta poesía las cosas del mundo, los seres del mundo, sólo sirven como herramientas para poner en marcha un proceso de representación del desvelo artístico de los argonautas del discurso. [JRB]

2224 Franco González, Luis. Fragmentos para armar una ciudad debajo de un asterisco. México: SDC, 2016. 106 p.

El prolífico joven costeño (Santa Elena, 1988) añade un nuevo reconocimiento internacional a su carrera como poeta con esta publicación ganadora del Premio Internacional de Poesía Gilberto Owen Estrada de La UAEM, 2015–2016. Se trata de un canto nocturno que (de)construye contextos donde habitan seres refractados, pero siempre en un proceso de (re)creación cuya acción invita a contemplar cómo enfrentarnos a la multiplicación de realidades, comunidades y soledades de nuestros tiempos. La idea de lugar—el cuerpo, la ciudad, el mar, el cosmos, el mundo virtual—y la identidad van de la mano en esta obra, pero nunca como contexto para completar al ser sino para multiplicar las complejidades—los lenguajes, signos, códigos virtuales—que conforman su existencia. El ámbito espiritual cristiano, africano, y humanista, crea aún más contextos para las capas semiológicas en la obra. [JRB]

2225 Gelman, Juan. Hoy: Ciudad de México, 2011–2014. México: Literatura UNAM: Ediciones Era, 2014. 307 p. (Poesías en Ediciones Era)

Este poemario es la respuesta del gran poeta Juan Gelman (1930–2014) al juicio en 2011 de los que asesinaron a su hijo, Marcelo, que fue desaparecido durante la dictadura de Jorge Rafael Videla, y cuyo cadáver fue encontrado en el Río San Fernando en un barril lleno de cemento. Este libro—el último del poeta, escrito cuando tenía 83 años—culmina el proyecto de su vida entera: decir toda la verdad. Para Gelman, la violencia es inherente al ser humano y sólo la verdad nos puede redimir. Los poemas son un testigo y un lamento; navegan un espacio incierto entre esperanza y desesperanza, pero siempre buscan la belleza en el dolor. Sin embargo, la poesía es el remedio. Estos poemas demuestran la necesidad de revelar la verdad brutal del pasado y demostrar sus repeticiones atemorizantes en varios contextos. Pero Gelman no pierde la esperanza en la justicia, el amor, y la redención. [JMP]

2226 Gómez Migliaro, Willy. Pintura roja. Lima: Paracaídas Editores, 2016. 96 p.

Poeta de la generación del 90 que continúa publicando poemarios sólidos. Su consigna radica en escribir—o mejor pintarrajear—una poesía (con ribetes de incendio y sangre, de aquí el color rojo del título) que agite la pasividad y autocomplacencia de la institución literaria. Para esto, el cuerpo se disgrega en cada paso de su recorrido por los recovecos asfaltados de la urbe. Estos poemas están anclados en una temática social, donde la posición de clase del hablante organiza una visión del mundo en base a un sistema de acceso a más o menos privilegios; esta dinámica recuerda la máxima de Benjamin: politizar el arte. Estos versos, al configurarse en secuencias sin aparente ilación, pueden desconcertar al principio, pero una atenta lectura revela las pistas de su propuesta: la "negación del capitalismo" al liberar con rebeldía la fuerza interior de quien persigue el rumbo subversivo del fogonazo poético. [CZ]

2227 González, Wingston. Espuma sobre las piedras. Creación coreográfica de Alejandra Garavito Aguilar a partir de la obra poética de Wingston González. Guatemala: Catafixia Editorial: Centro Cultural de España en Guatemala, 2014. 69 p.: ill. (Escénica/poética; 3)

A booklet more than a book, *Espuma sobre las piedras* comprises a collection of short, evocative poems by Wingston González, along with photographs by Carlos Bernardo Euler Coy and Andrea Nathalie Vásquez. González's poetry is highly experimental, with forms that range from the structure of a film script to calligrams in the tradition of Guillaume Apollinaire. The concept behind the book is relatively original, as it attempts, according to the book presentation text, "to reunite two paths that have gone their separate ways: theater and poetry, or the body on the stage and the written word." The result is a quirky collection of interesting poems, photographs, and other texts that deal with problems such as the production of art and its place in life. [F. Solares-Larrave]

2228 **Guerrero, Victoria.** En un mundo de abdicaciones. Lima: Fondo de Cultura Económica, 2016. 122 p. (Colección Poesía)

Libro dividido en dos secciones: I) Un arte de la pobreza y II) Un arte de la incomplacencia (que es más bien una antología de poemas publicados anteriormente). La poesía se convierte en una suerte de "esposa" de la poeta, en un arma feroz—de aquí que abunde el vocabulario bélico: guerrilla, comuna, revolución, batalla—que se blande para hacer frente a un cambio de actitud generacional que se nota en el comportamiento de las "niñas" de hoy. Se propone una amalgama de términos entre vida, poesía y sobrevivencia; ya que ejercer lo poético significa un aprendizaje de la austeridad (o de lo frugal), un deber ético, en realidad, en un mundo dominado por la vanidad y lo superficial. [CZ]

2229 **Hernández, Francisco.** En grado de tentativa: poesía reunida. México: Fondo de Cultura Económica: Almadía, 2016. 2 vol. (v. 1: 568 p.; v. 2: 576 p.). (Poesía)

Habitualmente las obras completas tienen la desagradable capacidad de tornar ilegible el conjunto de los textos que reúnen. Aunque naturalmente, no se publican para eso, sino para volver a ofrecer libros que, dispersos en el tiempo, pueden resultar inencontrables; especialmente en el caso de poemarios, que a veces aparecen con tirajes muy breves en fondos editoriales con escasas ambiciones y posibilidades de distribución, o en casas que no duran lo suficiente como para reeditar un libro. Sin embargo, en este caso, los más de 20 libros que ha publicado Hernández (San Andrés Tuxtla 1946) a lo largo de su carrera, no sólo se dejan leer por separado—por ejemplo *Moneda de tres caras, Imán para fantasmas*, las simpatiquísimas composiciones de arte menor firmadas como Mardonio Sinta—sino, al leerse de corrido, forman un fascinante poliedro en el que los diarios en prosa de *Diario invento* e incluso sus intentos iniciales sobre artes visuales, se convierten en facetas de lo que su muy notable *Odioso caballo* cristaliza finalmente. Sería imposible citar la variedad de registros que recorren estas más de 1100 páginas, pero se suman, sin duda, en el libro del año en el campo de la poesía mexicana. [JRRS]

2230 **Herrera Gómez, Fernando.** Breviario de Santana. México: Ediciones Sin Nombre, 2016. 77 p. (Cuadernos de la salamandra)

This collection by the Colombian poet addresses the growing movement toward visual imagery by engaging verbally with the Colombian landscape. The poems in this volume are short meditations on traditional and non-traditional elements of the countryside. Written in a prose style that recalls an encyclopedia entry, the poet engages with a range of common sights of the country-pastoral, like farm animals and mountains, but also less traditional images, like irrigation systems and buckets. Each item or view is described in visual detail, often then adding textures, sounds and smells to the overall description. [EGN]

2231 **Hurtado de Mendoza Santander, William.** Maskhaypa harawin = *Harawi de la búsqueda*. Lima: Universidad Nacional Agraria La Molina, 2015. 173 p.

El diseño bilingüe del libro, que alterna páginas en quechua y español, usa estrofas cortas de tres versos, a la manera del haikú, aunque emparentadas mayormente con la poética andina proveniente de la tradición oral prehispánica, aquella del *harawi* o de su versión mestiza, el yaraví. Hay una marcada interrelación entre los dos idiomas: el español se mezcla con el quechua y viceversa. Sobresale la exploración del canto vernacular para desenterrar las raíces invisibilizadas de vertientes ancestrales. Asimismo, el radiante esplendor de la naturaleza, codificado en elementos minúsculos (insectos, semillas, pétalos), se refleja en el minimalismo de la forma poética, de versos brevísimos, cuya estructura en espiral desenreda una madeja de referentes nativos. Las imágenes acuáticas y de vuelo señalan un espacio-tiempo en flujo constante que se mueve hacia un territorio de libertad. [CZ]

2232 **Ildefonso, Miguel.** Diario animal. Lima: Hipocampo Editores, 2016. 62 p.: ill.

Sin duda el escritor más prolífico aparecido en la década de 1990. En este volumen, aves y animales de tradicional belleza (ruiseñores, gorriones, tigres) comparten su hábitat aéreo y terrestre con insectos repugnantes (pulgas, cucarachas, moscas); así como con otros organismos degradados por el imaginario poético (ratas o vampiros). En esta mezcla de imágenes disímiles, el autor continúa indagando en los pliegues de lo sórdido, lo cual certifica la complejidad de una obra esmerada en representar los vericuetos de un universo que se resiste a ser encasillado en cualquier dimensión unilateral de lo bello. La confluencia de situaciones hermosas y grotescas—un ángel caído emborrachándose con Dios en un bar del centro de Lima, o Rimbaud durmiendo intoxicado en una plaza decadente—afianzan el propósito del hablante, que consiste en revelar nuevas aristas estéticas en contextos sorpresivos o inexplorados, en ámbitos ubicados fuera de lo que comúnmente se considera poetizable. [CZ]

2233 Ildefonso, Miguel. El hombre elefante: y otros poemas. Lima: APJ. Asociación Peruano Japonesa, Fondo Editorial, 2016. 125 p.

Usando la figura de Joseph Merrick, este poemario explora el tema de la deformidad física como estigma en una sociedad banalizada por cánones tradicionales de belleza; lo que no encaja en el patrón estético dominante es expuesto al escarnio. En un ambiente kafkiano, los individuos ejercen un excesivo control de sus apariencias. En este mundo dominado por leyes del espectáculo, las desviaciones físicas se convierten en mercancías a la medida de espectadores condicionados para consumir imágenes que subliman sus ansias criminales y violentas. Los "monstruos" que pueblan esta galería del horror deambulan por calles diseñadas como telarañas laberínticas buscando algún resquicio de luminosidad. La ciudad es similar a un olimpo degradado donde habitan dioses caídos y héroes irredentos; pero se remarca una sacralidad alternativa: aquella compuesta por gestos de armoniosa convivencia entre seres marginales—prostitutas, niños vagabundos, vendedores ambulantes—que invaden espacios ignorados por las directrices del poder. [CZ]

2234 Iris, Manuel. Los disfraces del fuego. Monterrey, Mexico: Ediciones Atrasalante; México: Consejo Nacional para la Cultura y las Artes; Tuxtla Gutiérrez, Mexico: Consejo Estatal para las Culturas y las Artes de Chiapas, 2015. 61 p. (Colección Atrasalante poesía; 5)

Manuel Iris (Campeche 1983) muestra en este libro un considerable talento para el verso (y el versículo, a veces incluso la prosa) reflexivo, que asume como sus herencias voces que el resto de los poetas de su generación han dejado de lado: la de Octavio Paz y la de Alí Chumacero, y sobre todo el lugar donde ambas confluyen: el vértice en que el deseo hace arder a la razón. No el deseo realizado sino más bien el espacio para el deseo es lo que tensa a estos versos. Por ello, el silencio, la ausencia y la muerte son temas cruciales pero siempre como precondiciones de un futuro fuego. Por ejemplo: "Pero el olvido es otra forma de ocultarnos, de nacer". Es una dicción del ciclo, de la metamorfosis perpetua. [JRRS]

2235 Lastra, Pedro. Poesía completa. Ilustraciones de Mario Toral. Prólogo de Carlos Germán Belli. Posdata de Enrique Lihn. Valparaíso, Chile: Editorial UV de la Universidad de Valparaíso, 2016. 237 p.: ill. (Colección poesía)

El poeta y académico recoge y revisa su poesía leve y mínima que observa el día a día, la irrealidad de la propia biografía y el tiempo, deseando que esos "años y meses fantasmales / embellecidos por el viento, / vuelvan . . . por una vez / con lo perdido y olvidado." [MLF]

2236 Leal, Francisco. Mundos/Carne. Santiago: Editorial Cuarto Propio, 2014. 173 p. (Colección Uvas de la ira)(Poesía)

Poesía experimental de la violencia del lenguaje, el cuerpo y el mundo. [MLF]

2237 Lebron, Maybell. Ser: poesía completa. Asunción: Editorial Arandurã, 2015. 139 p.

Según señala Patricia Camp en el prefacio a esta colección de la poesía completa de Maybell Lebron, "[Esta] poesía [. . .] es un canto a la vida. A la existencia humana, completa, con sus momentos de gozo, su cotidianidad y también sus penas" (5). En esta obra la poeta argentina-paraguaya afirma la dignidad del ser humano y el milagro de nuestra capacidad de comunicarse y amarse uno al otro. Con su utilizaciónde la rima y un lenguaje barroco, Lebron a veces puede parecer sentimental; sin embargo, si la miramos con atención, vemos que su alegría es algo que se ha ganado después de conocer muy bien el dolor y el sufrimiento. Lebron es heredera de los modernistas y los posmodernistas latinoamericanos: la energía de Rubén Darío, Alfonsina Storni y Juana de Ibarbourou fluyen por estos versos, y en su totalidad los poemas forman una plegaria a este "alguien" que todavía viene a sanar un mundo que puede parecer roto. [JMP]

2238 **Lecca, Dante.** Cosecha de otoño: obra poética de Dante Lecca 1973–2015. Chimbote, Perú: Municipalidad Provincial del Santa, 2016. 406 p.: color ill.

Poeta chimbotano de formación autodidacta y dedicado al trabajo de construcción civil y otros empleos afines. En estos poemas, que recogen más de 40 años de actividad lírica, se nota una preocupación bifurcada en una doble vertiente: ética, es decir un compromiso con el mejoramiento de las capacidades humanas del individuo; y, estética, la cual vislumbra la poesía como vehículo que propicia el goce del arte y la literatura. Esta propuesta se evidencia desde el poema pórtico de este libro recopilatorio, "Sed de justicia", incluido en el volumen *Adolescere* (1973), que establece el propósito del hablante de bregar por un mundo equitativo donde se pueda vivir sin desigualdades. Estos versos fueron erigidos con la pericia de unas manos de albañil que alza edificaciones duraderas, cimentadas en la tierra fértil de la costa peruana, y que han sido decoradas con la milenaria vigilancia de las cabezas clavas de la cultura Chavín. [CZ]

2239 **Leduc, Renato.** Obra literaria. Compilación e introducción de Edith Negrín. Prólogo de Carlos Monsiváis. México: Fondo de Cultura Económica, 2016. 752 p.: bibl., ill. (Letras mexicanas)

Después de muchos años se reimprime el volumen con la obra de Renato Leduc (Ciudad de México 1897–1986), cuya parte más importante es la poesía. A lo que se había compilado en los años 40 y 60, se suman otros poemas no coleccionados en libro y, sobre todo, lo que la editora del volumen llama aún con pudor "poesía interdicta": sus exitosísimas parodias de la literatura griega. La más célebre de las cuales, "Prometeo sifilítico" marca el momento en que la poesía popular, habiéndose apropiado de las músicas del modernismo, las pone al servicio de un decir cotidiano igualmente alejado de las represiones del beletrismo porfirista, como del malditismo de Tablada o Rebolledo: "Si me hubiera tejido la puñeta / no sintiera el dolor de que taladre / mi canal uretral la espiroqueta". Aunque hoy algunos textos resultan incómodos por su machismo y su homofobia, el volumen es invaluable como documento de lo que estaba pasando con la poesía mientras se hacía la narrativa de la revolución en los años 30 y en paralelo con los experimentos más radicales de Novo en lo que José Emilio Pacheco llamó "la otra vanguardia". Los textos introductorios de Negrín y Monsiváis, algunas crónicas y las memorias, publicadas póstumamente, ayudan a comprender mejor la génesis de estos poemas. [JRRS]

2240 **Lépiz Vega, Jonatan.** El humo de las cosas. San José: EUNED, Editorial Universidad Estatal a Distancia, 2014. 93 p.

This wonderful collection by Costa Rican poet Jonatan Lepiz is divided into two sections, an A and a B side, much like a vinyl record. And as in a record, the poems are called ballads, some recalling 20th and 21st century musicians, like Glenn Gould, Kurt Cobain and Nick Cave, and others movie legends, like Humphrey Bogart, Marilyn Monroe and Sergio Leone. The poetry is fresh, inventive, and sometimes unexpected, but the language is clear and direct and Lepiz's poetic voice does not fail to demonstrate a deep appreciation for life's sharp turns. [RMP]

2241 **López Degregori, Carlos.** La espalda es frontera. Lima: Paracaídas Editores, 2016. 76 p. (some folded).

Poemas en prosa donde el narrador se posesiona, a manera de juego de máscaras, de varias personalidades literarias (Kafka, Shulz). Se constata la pluralidad del individuo, encarnada en otros semejantes: "El mundo está lleno de mundos". El hablante vive inmerso en una confluencia de planos espaciales y temporales, en un universo que refulge con luminosidad, a la vez que con desasosiego. También se advierte un experimento literario que se inmiscuye en situaciones paradójicas al meditar sobre el sentido del tiempo y la existencia. Si la espalda, metonimia del cuerpo, es el límite del ser humano, ésta se encuentra conectada con los objetos que la rodean. Es decir que lo corporal se simboliza como una frontera porosa, que derriba puertas y expande muros hacia la amplitud de lo abierto. Cada componente de la naturaleza está preñado de vida, como los huevos de las aves que contienen la potencialidad del vuelo. [CZ]

2242 **López Herrera, Luis Alberto.** Hijo de madre. Lima: Caja Negra, 2016. 73 p.

Poeta y docente universitario natural de Otuzco y radicado en Canadá. Se posiciona una voz descolonizadora, a manera de memoria colectiva, que afirma la presencia impostergable de grupos marginados ("El-Gran-Otro") por la negligencia de los gobernantes de turno, con el fin de visibilizar miles de historias sepultadas que pueden retratar afinidades grupales. Hay una apuesta por reconciliar a la víctima y al perpetrador para "deconstruir una injusticia". Con esto, se manifiesta la idea de que el individuo nunca nace aislado, sino que es parte de una "madre comunidad" que impone cierta responsabilidad con los otros para recordarles que vinieron a este mundo sin haber caído en la contaminación que produce la violencia que tiñe de sangre el curso de la historia. Las huacas (remanentes) prehispánicas son restos que atestiguan el peso fundacional de la madre andina, pero se debe superar la vergüenza de reconocerse herederos de esta herencia no occidental. [CZ]

2243 **López Méndez, Xel-Ha.** Crónicas de un nuevo siglo. Guadalajara, Mexico: Ámbar Cooperativa Editorial: Secretaría de Cultura, Gobierno del Estado de Jalisco, 2016. 61 p.: ill. (Colección 21)

López Méndez (Guadalajara 1991) presenta en este libro un intento para lidiar con la violencia, pero encuentra una dicción mucho más interesante que la mayor parte de la promoción joven: "cinco mil pesos quieren porque tiene muchas hermanas porque dicen que son más bonitas que mi novia chamulita y dice también su padre que me largue de su corazón tzotzil". Una dicción en que el horror deja de ser obvio y se funde con una contemplación ingenua que fluye mucho mejor en prosa o en versículos (los medios dominantes del libro) que en verso. [JRRS]

2244 **Lubeka, Tory.** De este río he de beber. Asunción: L&T Autoeditores, 2015. 167 p.

Con ironía y mucho humor, Tory Lubeka cruza las fronteras, entre el pasado y el presente, entre el español y el guaraní, entre la cultura "alta" y la popular, entre la poesía, la prosa y el teatro. El resultado es un vistazo lúcido y realista al mundo actual; como cada gran comediante, tiene un lamento detrás de cada broma. El tono se hace siempre más directo y sincero en las últimas partes del libro, donde el lamento se hace más aparente en una serie de haikus y otros poemas cortos. A través de esta obra es evidente que Lubeka bien sabe que viene de un país que no recibe mucha atención de los medios de comunicación globales, ni de los medios especializados del mismo mundo hispanohablante. Pero esta colección le recuerda a los lectores la importancia de esas partes del mundo que pueden parecer periféricas. Lubeka tiene algo importante que decir, y aquí lo dice de una manera impactante. [JMP]

2245 **Lucano, Juan Carlos.** El reino de las desolaciones. Lima: Ornitorrinco, 2016. 62 p.

Esta selección personal de este autor de Chimbote consiste de cuatro partes. Amparado en epígrafes de Rimbaud y Juan Ojeda, se perciben las tribulaciones de una existencia vivida al límite, al margen de las normas sociales y con un pie en el recinto atemorizante de la locura. Con una poética que roza la incertidumbre y la desesperación (a lo Vallejo o Adán), se explora la búsqueda de momentos reveladores en medio del ajetreo diario. Se sospecha sobre la utilidad del lenguaje convencional para descifrar los enigmas del mundo, ya que la palabra a menudo individualiza (en el caso del egocentrismo del poeta) y no da cabida a propuestas fraternales. Ante esto, el hablante se sumerge en la densidad de lo vital, incluso en experiencias no tradicionalmente literarias (de tipo obsceno o abyecto), para perseguir una especie de "redención" al expandir, o desarreglar, el terreno de los sentidos. [CZ]

2246 **Maia, Circe.** Dualidades. Montevideo: Rebeca Linke Editoras, 2014. 99 p.

Aunque se inspira de muchas fuentes, parece que la gran inspiración de este poemario es la famosa Alegoría de la Caverna de Platón, con su concepto de una realidad dual que se define entre formas permanentes y sombras impermanentes. Este libro nevega entre las dos percepciones—permanencia y cambio—pero siempre con una preferencia por el segundo. El libro se divide en dos partes: "Imágenes", que consiste en meditaciones sobre la naturaleza de la imagen y varios poemas ecfrásticos, y "Voces", que consiste en diálogos sostenidos algunas veces por dos sujetos, y otras veces entre la poeta y otros escritores. A través del poemario se ve también una dualidad en los temas; Maia explora oposiciones binarias como la memoria y el olvido, lo natural y lo artificial, o la necesidad y el azar. Pero estas oposiciones nunca son estables, y muchas "dualidades" no son nada más que una construcción de la imaginación humana. [JMP]

2247 **Maldonado, Bernardita.** Con todos los soles lejanos: poesía. Loja, Ecuador: CCE Benjamín Carrión, 2015. 133 p.

Este segundo poemario de la lojana cuya obra se ha publicado tanto en revistas ecuatorianas y españolas abarca como tema central el ser liminal. La migración como fenómeno emocional y el viaje a nuevas geografías son contextos importantes en el poemario. En la primera mitad de la obra surgen objetos poéticos—piedras, pájaros, luz, barro, barcazas, jacarandás—como elementos que reflejan la identidad de los hablantes de cada poema. El poemario marca varias veces un retorno por medio de las frágiles memorias de un lugar efímero en su totalidad, cuya desaparición se evita gracias a ser (re)poblado por los signos que lo habitan dentro del recuerdo. La poeta subraya un existencialismo geográfico y, por ende, cultural donde vale repetir la frase "en ninguna tierra podrás plantar tu casa". Luego el mar y el ser amado toman fuerza como límite de ese otro lugar, signo de otra serie de contemplaciones y de desencantos. [JRB]

2248 **Marín Sevilla, Desirée.** Almohada sin huella. Quito: El Ángel Editor, 2010. 74 p. (Colección Flor de ángel)

Tal como su título promete esta obra de Marín Sevilla (Quito, 1966-) abarca el tema del ser ante la ausencia del ser amado. Pero no se trata simplemente de un poemario que celebra el encuentro con el otro para luego poetizar un *ubi sunt* emocional. Es una profunda y honesta observación a los procesos sentimentales personales que logran empoderar a la voz poética como un ser que puede hasta autocriticarse con valor. El mundo de las cosas—naturales o no— aparecen no como clichés metafóricos, sino como puntos de referencia, guías en un mar donde el ser va zozobrando por las pérdidas que ha sufrido. Una taza de té, un ceibo, una panga, surgen como símbolos nuevos de gran calidad que dan un contraste casi chocante ante los laberintos interiores que crea la poeta. Existe una gran variedad de verso libre y sobresalen poemas cortos que surgen como suspiro intenso, como un destello psico-artístico. [JRB]

2249 **Martos, Marco.** Musas del celuloide. Lima: Caja Negra, 2016. 135 p.: ill.

Prolífico autor integrante de la generación del 60. Este libro retoma la confluencia entre cine y poesía en el Perú, que se manifiesta desde las décadas iniciales del siglo XX. La novedad de este volumen radica en dedicarse íntegramente a homenajear a actrices (de diversos matices raciales) consagradas del séptimo arte, entre las que se incluyen varias divas peruanas (Sánchez, Domínguez, Solier, Saba, Neyra) y latinoamericanas (Cepeda, Oreiro, Hayek, Félix). Se nota la fascinación del autor por el aura proyectada por las estrellas en el ecrán. Además de recrear secuencias clásicas, como el baño de Ekberg en la fuente de Trevi, estos poemas se internan más allá de la pantalla, para llegar a la memoria visual de millones de cinéfilos. La eficacia hipnotizadora de las celebridades se transmite a los espectadores quienes, desde sus butacas, en plena oscuridad, las elevan al pedestal de divinidades modernas. [CZ]

2250 **Miró Ibars, Margarita.** Ñe'e paje: la magia de la palabra: cuenta cuentos— tierravenada: leyendas, relatos, historia y poesía. Asunción: Servilibro, 2014. 183 p.: bibl., ill.

Este texto híbrido—que consiste con una sección de ensayos y relatos en prosa, y otra sección de poesía—es una celebración de América. Aunque la historia del hemisferio occidental es una de tragedia y brutalidad, la obra de Miró Ibars asevera que vale la pena celebrar la mezcla de culturas que ha florecido como resultado. Aunque se refiere a Paraguay, con su identidad bilingüe y multicultural, este texto tiene una visión amplia de una "América morena, blanca y negra / rica, pobre y desbastada / sana y enferma / joven y milenaria" (p. 95). La poesía, escrita de una manera muy coloquial y accesible, nos invita a viajar por América: a Nicaragua y Ecuador, los Andes y la región amazónica. El tono es de alabanza y celebración, tal como lo hicieron hace un siglo Rubén Darío y los modernistas. Miró Ibars afirma la riqueza cultural de América, pero de una manera que pone la identidad indígena al centro en vez de a la periferia. [JMP]

2251 **Morales, Andrés.** Esencial (1982–2014). Santiago: RIL Editores, 2015. 147 p. (ÆREA. Selección personal)

Poesía del decir despojado, la búsqueda metafísica y del lenguaje. Contra las efusiones del yo, poesía dedicada a los amigos poetas, a los libros, a la madre, al amor, la muerte y a Dios. Un yo testigo de ojos abiertos recicla la tradición poética chilena y utiliza fuentes clásicas, bíblicas y de los poetas nahuas para decir los quiebres privados. [MLF]

2252 **Morales C., María.** En el otro patio. San José: Centro Cultural de España: Ediciones Perro Azul, 2008. 79 p. (Poesía)

This collection by Costa Rican poet María Morales is composed of a series of short poems that revisit childhood songs ("Lullaby I" and "Lullaby II"), describe a breakfast made up of items in a medicine cabinet ("Continental Breakfast"), and offer a sober look at love in its many expressions ("Trans," "El falso inquilino," and "Ahogados en la ducha," to name a few). Overall, with its quirky introspection, *En el otro patio* is a pleasant examination of themes that would otherwise be dark and heavy. [RMP]

2253 **Morales Santos, Francisco.** Estación Florida. Guatemala: Editorial Cultura, 2014. 61 p. (Colección Tz'aqol; 3)

Morales Santos' *Estación Florida* is a collection of previously unpublished work, his first in almost two decades. The poet, well-known in literary circles, was one of the founders of the influential literary group Nuevo Signo in the late 1960s in Guatemala. *Estación Florida* consists of two poems; "Coronación de un sueño" and "Elogio del presente." In the first poem, Morales Santos turns his gaze to the past, tracing a sort of artistic genealogy, while in the second poem, he offers a reflection on life and death and on the notion of legacy. His verses are clear and direct, but also moving. The collection ends with an epilogue by Wingston González. [RMP]

2254 **Moscona, Myriam.** Ansina. Madrid: Vaso Roto Ediciones, 2016. 73 p. (Poesía; 91)

Este volumen colecciona de manera separada los poemas que aparecieron por primera vez formando parte de la novela autobiográfica *Tela de sevoya* (2012). Todos estos textos están escritos en ladino, el español que hablaban los judíos expulsos en el siglo XV, al que Moscona añade felizmente vocabulario para referirse a situaciones contemporáneas. A diferencia de otros libros escritos en esta variación arcaica del español, los temas no se limitan al exilio y al sueño del regreso, sino que permiten que los recorra el humor, sin que eso borre por completo la melancolía: "Eskrivo una kantika kada diya // *es mentira* // la dovlo en kuatro / i esos papeles / kon eskritura antikua / a la perra sirven para pishar en eyos: // *es verdad* // ansina se ambeza / a pishar en el mismo sitio". La combinación no solamente añade un capítulo a la poesía en ladino, sino que refresca desde estas maneras de decir, el panorama de lo publicado en México. Aunque las composiciones no aparecen traducidas al español contemporáneo, el libro cuenta con un glosario suficiente en su epílogo. [JRRS]

2255 **Najlis, Michele.** El viento que la sostiene. Managua: ANE-Noruega-CNE, 2015. 222 p.

A selection of poetry by Nicaraguan poet Michèle Najlis published works between 1963–2014. The selected poems provide an excellent overview of Najlis body of work, beginning with the militant, Sandinista verses of her first poetry collection that denounce the injustices and violence of the Somoza government. Her feminist outlook and the mysticism of later poetry also permeate the pages of *El viento que la sostiene*. [RMP]

2256 **Navarrete, Otilia.** Poesía. Lima: Edición de la autora, 2015. 203 p.

Compilación propia de la autora, de más de 20 años de escritura, que remarca el rol de la poesía como actividad que busca expiar un sentimiento de culpa que se padece como un malestar impuesto antes del nacimiento. La voz poética emite sentencias a las que se aferra en medio de la vorágine cotidiana y la incertidumbre. La existencia se compara a un flujo de aguas claras que van tornándose pantanosas conforme corre el tiempo; o se retrata a semejanza de un edificio con numerosas puertas cerradas, repletas de capas nebulosas y espesuras silentes, tras las que se espía esperando escuchar alguna revelación, o un llamado que tienda puentes salvadores desde la otra orilla del río de la vida. Abundan las metáforas que borronean los límites entre la vigilia y el sueño, dibujando atmósferas espectrales que siembran duda sobre la veracidad de lo visto con los ojos abiertos. [CZ]

2257 **Noguera Penso, Claudia.** Caracas mortal. Caracas: Oscar Todtmann Editores, 2015. 50 p.: ill. (Poesía Oscar Todtmann Editores; 9)

This politically anti-Chavista collection of narrative poetry recalls the city-centered 1980s, when many poets spoke to the alienation of life in the megalopolis. Taking its name from the work of a Venezuelan poet of that period, the collection presents visceral images of the decay of Caracas as it suffers through the economic crisis. One of the works that overtly combines visual imagery with written text, this collection uses art work showcasing lines of poetry floating over photos of the city, while also evoking the sounds and smells of Caracas. The relationship between poet and city is revealed as one of love and loathing, a desire to flee but a need to stay. The Venezuelan diaspora and the crumbling of society hover tangibly over this volume. [EGN]

2258 **Noreña, Aurora.** Ondulaciones sobre el puente: zapping del horizonte. México: Consejo Nacional para la Cultura y las Artes (CNCA), 2015. Caja con fichas emprease.

Estas fichas que incluyen en su mayoría materiales visuales y textos en prosa, tanto de la artista visual como, jugando con el formato físico, de otros autores que se fichan, comparten como punto de convergencia formal, una reflexión sobre el horizonte. Sin embargo, y de nuevo, el hecho físico de no estar encuadernadas ni numeradas (aunque sí fechadas) ayuda a prestarles la flexibilidad del azar. Se pueden leer en una infinidad de maneras, creando siempre distintos horizontes de interpretación, y sin llegar nunca a un cierre. De hecho, Noreña insiste que la caja permanece abierta a la intervención de otros autores. Me interesa que la enunciación, a pesar de estar en prosa, es, tanto en las citas como en la escritura propia, invariablemente de índole poética, sin dejar de asediar su tema ensayístico. Por ejemplo: "La diferencia entre el jardín y paisaje es que mientras en el jardín el horizonte puede no existir o ser un incidente más, en la puesta en escena del paisaje el horizonte tiene un papel protagónico". [JRRS]

2259 **Núñez, Griselda.** Arte ingenuo: antología. Santiago: Editorial USACH, 2013. 418 p.: ill. (Colección Germen)

Compilación que pone al día la lira popular a cargo de una brillante cultora de la poesía popular. Fue activa participante de la resistencia cultural a la dictadura militar en los años 80 y sus crónicas en décimas de eventos cruciales de ese momento contribuyen a completar la memoria de ese período. [MLF]

2260 **Ojeda, Gabriel.** Antología de la indiferencia: poemario. Asunción: Arandurã Editorial, 2014. 145 p.

El tema de esta colección es la decepción y desilusión que surgen cuando uno se da cuenta que vive en la decadencia social, el aislamiento inherente en la vida urbana, y la futilidad de política. La primera mitad del poemario consiste en cuatro poemas largos que se dividen en secciones muy cortas, aforismos que recuerdan el estilo de Nietszche. En la segunda mitad los poemas se alargan, pero los temas permanecen en el mismo ambiente. El consumismo que domina en una sociedad capitalista, la superficialidad de los medios de comunicación, la búsqueda de placeres transitorio, todo eso resulta en una actitud de indiferencia tanto al nivel social como personal. Sin embargo, a pesar del cinismo y el pesimismo de esta obra, Ojeda nos presenta una cosmovisión compleja y conmovedora; sus varias referencias a las tragedias de Shakespeare evocan un patetismo profundo, y en ciertos momentos, se ve, por lo menos, una posible esperanza. Por el lente de un realismo casi brutal, Ojeda mira la condición humana con compasión. [JMP]

2261 Olivero, Romina. Acá es así. Buenos Aires: El Suri Porfiado, 2016. 45 p. (Poesía)

Este breve poemario hace unas observaciones agudas acerca de nuestra sociedad actual. Como las mejores historias de ciencia ficción, la poesía de Romina Olivero abunda en comentarios sardónicos sobre la distopía que ya se está empezando a realizar. La fuerza insidiosa de la tecnología, el reino del capitalismo, la degradación ecológica, la dependencia total de sistemas industriales que no son justos, y la mirada indiferente de los medios de comunicación hacia la realidad del sufrimiento humano aparecen detrás de los chistes y la ironía presente en estos poemas. En yuxtaposición a los momentos de humor e inocencia, sin embargo, Romina contrapone recuerdos de las heridas más profundas de nuestra época, como el tratamiento cruel de los animales que comemos y la realidad constante de la guerra. La voz de Olivero es muy necesaria en estos momentos de cambios, catástrofes y preocupación por el futuro incierto del frágil planeta que habitamos. [JMP]

2262 Oyarzún, Kemy. Tinta sangre. Kemy Oyarzún. Santiago: Editorial Cuarto Propio, 2014. 153 p.

Interesante volumen temáticamente unitario que se adscribe a los lenguajes de la neovanguardia. Se recogen los fragmentos de experiencias de violencia de y hacia mujeres y niñas; se denuncian y exponen los mecanismos a través de los cuales opera la violencia de género y de los discursos sociales. [MLF]

2263 Paz, Juan Alberto. El alba de mi esperanza. Caracas: Fundación Editorial El perro y la rana, 2016. 105 p. (Colección Poesía venezolana. Caminos que andan)

This work is an example of the political poetry being produced in Venezuela under the Chavista government led by Nicolás Maduro. Politically popular poet, Paz has written numerous collections that have been published by the government. Of interest to scholars of folklore, protest, and political poetry, this collection presents works reminiscent of the songs of Ali Primera, with musicality and rhyme characterizing the poems. Divided into three parts, the collection seeks to represent different images of the strength and beauty of Venezuela: its women, its natural splendor and its fight against political injustice. [EGN]

2264 Peluffo, Luisa. Foto grafías. Buenos Aires: Gárgola Ediciones, 2014. 163 p.

Luisa Peluffo dice que para ella, estos poemas son "instantáneas / como fotos tomadas con palabras" (p. 7). Breves y sobrios, estos poemas son retratos de momentos, sentimientos y pensamientos fugaces. Podemos imaginarnos a la poeta captando oportunamente en estos poemas tales momentos. Así como un buen fotógrafo tiene siempre su cámara lista para registrar una imagen, la poeta mantiene siempre su pluma cerca. Al incluir la versión escrita a mano de cada poema al lado de la versión escrita a máquina, Peluffo también llama la atención sobre el aspecto visual de la escritura que, como ocurre con la fotografía ante la realidad captada, se convierte en una tecnología al servicio de la memoria. Algunos de los poemas más interesantes y conmovedores de la colección tratan sobre el arte mismo de la fotografía. Al mirar otras fotos familiares que muestran la migración de sus antepasados, desde Europa hasta América, medita sobre el tiempo y la muerte: "mirar viejas fotografías / es nadar contracorriente" (p. 115). [JMP]

2265 Pérez, Luis Marcelo. Ese agudo deseo. Montevideo: Antítesis Editorial, 2015. 171 p. (Signos de lira; 6)

Luis Marcelo Pérez, poeta, periodista, y gestor cultural uruguayo, nos entrega aquí una antología de autor que representa veinte años de su vida y su escritura. Este tomo contiene selecciones de siete poemarios, una pequeña selección de poemas inéditos, y una entrevista entre el autor y el crítico Jaime Clara. Una característica principal de estos poemas son su sencillez minimalista, con evidente habilidad para comprimir mucho sentido en pocas palabras. Otra es la exploración constante de lo erótico y la realidad carnal de la experiencia humana. "Arriba tu cuerpo / debajo el mío / prendidos / por fuera, por dentro / más cuerpo los cuerpos / los nuestros" (p. 61). Para Pérez, esta corporeidad es la base de nuestra existencia y nuestras preocupaciones intelectuales y espirituales; no hay dualismo cartesiano. Solamente se puede acceder a lo espiritual a través de lo físico. La mente nos puede engañar si la consideramos una entidad aislada; el cuerpo, en cambio, no miente. [JMP]

2266 **Pérez Alencart, Alfredo.** Los éxodos, los exilios: (1994–2014). Lima: Fondo Editorial Universidad de San Martín de Porres, 2015. 204 p.: ill.

Poeta de Puerto Maldonado y radicado en España, donde ejerce la docencia en la Universidad de Salamanca. Este volumen, compuesto por cinco "libros", puede leerse como la bitácora, escrita a lo largo de dos décadas, de un empedernido viajero y sujeto migrante (el poeta mismo desciende de inmigrantes españoles y brasileños): "Sé que en este viaje llevas el corazón hecho pedazos / y sé que vas diciendo / que ningún obstáculo te impedirá llegar a tu destino". Como en la metáfora de la Ítaca del poema de Cavafis, antes que arribar a la meta geográfica deseada, importa más el aprendizaje y la madurez vivencial que otorga el movimiento trazado al desplazarse por diversas instancias migratorias. Al final, se trata de encontrar un lugar al que uno pueda considerar su "patria", aunque éste no se ubique necesariamente en el lugar original de nacimiento. [CZ]

2267 **Porras Sáenz, Cecilia** and **Manuel Tzoc.** El jardín de los infantes locos y la escafandra de oro. Guatemala: Catafixia Editorial; Centro Cultural de España en Guatemala, 2013. 90 p. (Colección Escénica/Poética; 1)

Bucup's first formal exercises into poetic performance, and here we are confronted with a text that is largely autobiographical, in which the poetic voice explores what it means to be queer and Maya in Guatemala in the 21st century. [RMP]

2268 **Preciado, Antonio.** De lo demás al barrio. Quito: El Ángel Editor, 2013. 150 p. (Colección Entre nubes)

Este décimo tercero libro del celebrado poeta esmeraldeño refleja su deseo de representar a los seres que el poeta considera íntimos que ahora forman parte de su identidad. El contexto va de global a local pasando por Senegal, Cuba, Nicaragua, Ecuador, Esmeraldas y finalmente, su propio Barrio Caliente. Los personajes también marcan la misma variedad contextual desde Martí hasta sus mejores amigos de barrio. El poeta humaniza a los seres "históricos" mientras mitifica a personajes íntimos de su vida. El autor crea leyendas de su compadre, de sus amigos y futbolistas de barrio. El poemario inicia con un poema que describe un retrato hecho al poeta como caracterizado como un contenedor de los seres de su pasado y presente. Es decir que la función del artista es revelar en su propio sujeto los seres que han formado su identidad. El poemario concluye con poemas que exponen el contexto lingüístico de la infancia del poeta afro-ecuatoriano, celebrando la originalidad del lenguaje particular que ha nutrido la obra, o sea la identidad, del poeta. [JRB]

2269 **Quesada Vanegas, Gustavo.** Uno lleva su cuerpo. Obra pictórica de Leonardo Rodríguez Sirtori. Bogotá: Fundación Común Presencia, 2012. 70 p.: color ill. (Colección Los conjurados. Poesía; 55)

This work from Quesada Vanegas is an example of both the roots of the movement toward visual imagery in poetry and of the economic gap between Venezuelan and Colombian publishing. This collection of body-centered poetry is introduced in each section with a full-color plate by the Colombian artist Leonardo Rodríguez Sirtori. The collaboration between the two results in a work focused on both the human body and the landscape that surrounds it, what the poet calls "la ansiedad gloriosa de los cuerpos." Space, and the distance between objects, "midiendo la distancia" is a central theme of these works. [EGN]

2270 **Quila, Elizabeth.** Oblivion. Buenos Aires: El Suri Porfiado, 2016. 60 p. (El Suri Porfiado Ediciones)

La prolífera narradora y poeta guayaquileña presenta en la obra una serie de poemas que subrayan constantemente la dualidad presencia/ausencia como imprescindible al momento de recordar y (r)escribir sobre el ser amado. La autora nota que el escribir sobre el amor es una práctica de escribir sobre el cuerpo mismo. En muchos de los poemas, la carnalidad del acto amatorio se convierte en un portal hacia una soledad existencial pero sabia. Quila trabaja la corporalidad amatoria en los poemas con mucha confianza y los lectores son testigos de una voz poética empoderada libre para consumir o ser consumida hasta el oblivion. [JRB]

2271 **Roca, Juan Manuel.** Temporada de estatuas y: biblia de pobres (Biblia pauperum). México: Editorial Praxis, 2015. 184 p. (Poesía)

This collection brings together two works by the Colombian poet in one volume, one a consideration of statues and landscape, the other a meditation on love and hope in the face of poverty. Each is, at heart, about the transmutation of the physical into the metaphorical. The poems in each collection showcase Roca's linguistic playfulness, with neologisms and unusual vocabulary piled together. The works are playful, sad, and misanthropic by turns, grounding ideas in the real, to then suggest further metaphysical meaning. As with other works from Venezuela and Colombia, these collections are very visual, using images seen by the poet to anchor less tangible ideas. [EGN]

2272 **Rojas Guevara, Xiomara.** Láudano. Mérida, Venezuela: FUNDECEM, 2014. 58 p. (Colección Gilberto Ríos)

This collection, by the poet and dancer Rojas Guevara, presents a collection of body-centered sensual verse. The use of corporeal imagery here follows a strong tradition of erotic poetry and women's verse related to the body. While perhaps not completely original, this collection grounds itself in the tradition of poets such as Gabriela Mistral, María Auxiliadora Alvarez, and Yoldana Pantin, while presenting flashes of unique metaphor and sensual imagery that incorporates more than just sight and touch. The poet's body here is an object to be considered, evaluated, and enjoyed in turn. [EGN]

2273 **Rojas Salas, Luis Eugenio.** Poesía elemental. Lima: Hipocampo Editores, 2017. 80 p.: color ill.

Dividido en dos secciones (Preludios y Estancias) este poemario deslumbra por el trabajo de orfebre del poeta, por su minuciosa dedicación para labrar y pulir el idioma con el fin de que sólo enuncie lo estrictamente necesario—usando aquellas "simples / palabras" que a menudo ocupan por sí mismas la extensión de los versos—para retratar objetos, eventos, sentimientos. Como se constata en el poema titulado "Escritura": "Alineando / sonidos / claveteando / horizonte". En una época tendiente al derroche, la acumulación y la exagerada exposición mediática, el poeta da la espalda a toda pirueta de la vanidad para recuperar la belleza esencial de la vida, que todavía es factible de hallar si uno decide ver, oír o palpar las maravillas del mundo con la facultad primigenia de los sentidos. [CZ]

2274 **Roque, Randall.** Isla Pop. San José: REA, 2015. 222 p.: ill.

This is a book by Costa Rican poet Randall Roque, illustrated by artist Carlos Tapia. The images are rich and bright and they appear alongside verses that are at times humorous or mordant, at others times dark and defiant, and yet at others, erotic. Overall, the collection is well put together, the images complete the texts and the poetry itself in many ways is characteristic of 21st-century poetry in the region: whether he sets his verses in a mall, comments on the movements of a plastic bag, or recalls Andy Warhol and Alejandra Pizarnik, the marks of globalization are present, as are those of frustration and disenchantment. [RMP]

2275 **Rossi, Claudia.** Tiempo y vuelo. Punta del Este, Uruguay: Botella al Mar, 2015. 55 p. (Colección Alcázar)

El duelo es una realidad inevitable para cada ser humano. Cada uno tiene que lidiar con el cambio, la pérdida, y la muerte. *Tiempo y vuelo*, el primer poemario de la actriz uruguaya Claudia Rossi, es al mismo tiempo un lamento y una meditación sobre las etapas del duelo. Su tema central es el progreso de este duelo, con su vacilación entre momentos de desolación profunda e instantes de consuelo inesperado. Las líneas cortas de los versos permiten que el lector entre en el texto facilmente; sin embargo, detrás de esta sencillez de forma hay una gran complejidad de emociones e imágenes. Al pasar por las etapas del duelo—pero no de una forma lineal—estos poemas demuestran de una manera muy lúcida que la experiencia de la pérdida es simultaneamente particular y universal. [JMP]

2276 Ruisánchez Serra, José Ramón. Pozos. México: Literatura UNAM: Ediciones Era, 2015. 145 p.: ill. (some color). (Biblioteca Era)

Esta obra importante del novelista mexicano revela la contemplación íntima, intelectual y psicológica de un narrador incitado a la escritura, en parte, por su contacto con la gran diversidad de mundos discursivos que habita como un ser contemporáneo de occidente. Se trata de una obra a propósito fragmentada, con un narrador fragmentado también, a veces hasta poeta, que se lee como cuaderno íntimo de apuntes de un profesor de literatura, o filosofía, o arte, o psicología, etc. La mente va errando por los pasillos discursivos al alcance de los seres de nuestro siglo. La obra recoge a la par la manera en que nuestros encuentros amistosos forman también parte del canon crítico para quienes practican el análisis literario o cultural. Aparecen teorías culturales -filosóficas, literarias, lingüísticas, estéticas— reflejadas por los artistas que inspiran los pensamientos que terminan sobre el papel. Diderot, Benjamin, Zizek, Flaubert, Freud, Emiliy Dickinson, Vallejo, etc., aparecen juntos con entradas que recopilan conversaciones de los amigos del narrador. Los inter/con/textos varían entre obras de arte museo, de enciclopedias a Wikepedia, de novelas a poemarios a crítica literaria. Aparece Facebook también como contexto y las imágenes nos recuerdan a Instagram, a Pinterest. La obra remata con una dedicatoria a José Emilio Pacheco celebrando su influencia y amistad para con el narrador como otro ser quien logró representar de una manera muy presente y muy íntima la memoria cultural del tiempo que le tocó vivir. [JRB]

2277 Ruiz Pérez, Ignacio. Islas de tierra firme. México: Aldvs, 2015. 139 p. (Adlus)

En esta colección Ignacio Ruiz-Pérez (Tuxtla Gutiérrez 1976) escribe una poesía muy afinada, tanto en verso como en prosa. Al interior de las diferentes secciones del libro, los poemas presentan una continuidad trabajada más allá de el mero paraguas temático que hace más rica una lectura continuada de cada uno de los cuadernillos que la individual de cada obra. Esta lectura revela el intenso trabajo de asedio que propone Ruiz-Pérez. Sin duda las dos secciones más logradas, son las escritas en prosa: "Invernadero" y "Avíos de equitación" en las que las flores y las cosas le permiten lograr una densidad de observación que lo lleva al máximo brillo de su dicción. [JRRS]

2278 Ruiz Rosas, Alonso. Espíritupampa. Lima: Paracaídas Editores, 2015. 166 p.

Poeta arequipeño que reflexiona sobre la propiedad del espíritu como fenómeno en convulsión, equiparado al desborde de volcanes o torrentes. Una voz primigenia, carente de inicio y final, recorre estas páginas que abarcan la compleja totalidad de lo creado, que incluye también lo destruido: una poética del ser como sucesión recíproca de existencia y desintegración: "El mundo recomienza / en cada historia y en cada historia / acaba". Se hace *tabula rasa* del paisaje costero para examinar la particularidad del desierto como espacio colmado de piezas inexploradas que zanja nuevas sendas literarias. La poesía constituye una ofrenda a la "mamapacha" para que salve la vida de un planeta constantemente amenazado por la misma mano humana. Existe la necesidad de recuperar huacas e ídolos ancestrales, como semillas que visibilizan conexiones con un pasado precolombino que no ha podido ser sepultado por los discursos oficiales, ni por el pensamiento dualista occidental. [CZ]

2279 Ruiz Velazco, Víctor. El fin de la poesía. Lima: Paracaídas Editores, 2015. 56 p.: ill.

Uno de los escritores (y editores) jóvenes más relevantes y activos de la literatura peruana actual. Estos poemas en prosa—en la mejor senda de Baudelaire o Max Jacob—denuncian la mercantilización de la belleza, graficada en ecos fantasmales proyectados por una sociedad inmiscuida en la inmediatez, en la gratificación o satisfacción de lo fugaz. La referencia al "fin de la poesía" se puede leer como un diagnóstico, fácilmente comprobable, de que el trabajo lírico se ha divorciado de su correlato vital; ya que no vale la pena utilizar palabras vacuas sobre temas transcendentes (amor, muerte, existencia). Ante esto, se recupera una consigna, grata a las vanguardias históricas, cuyos postulados conectaban arte y praxis vivencial: "el poema que nunca acaba con la escritura del poema". Se aspira, así, a un proceso de aprendizaje de lo visto y lo oculto, de ausencia y presencia que resuma la integridad de la realidad. [CZ]

2280 **Sanabria, Luis Carlos.** Disección. La Paz: Editorial 3600, 2015. 95 p.: ill.

El primer poemario del escritor cochabambino (1987-) quién se ha hecho conocer ya por sus obras narrativas incluyendo cuentos y crónicas. *Disección* ganó el VIII Concurso para Jóvenes Poetas Bolivianos. El poemario presenta continuamente la imagen de un cuerpo siendo disecado. Mientras el bisturí va haciendo su trabajo, el poeta escribe versos que habitan existencialmente el descubrimiento de un espacio liminal entre la vida/muerte. La escritura va poblando esa frontera emocional entre la presencia y ausencia que la carnalidad que un cuerpo recién muerto motiva. El cadáver parece gemir pacientemente, con curiosidad y profundidad, su no ser. Dentro de esa morgue metafórica la contemplación (¿científica?¿objetiva?) del deseo, del amor, la compañía y de la soledad. [JRB]

2281 **Sánchez, Diego Alonso.** Pasos silenciosos entre flores de fuji. Lima: Paracaídas Editores, 2016. 39 p.: color ill.

Poeta que recibió el Premio José Watanabe Varas en 2013. La influencia de la poesía japonesa en el autor se evidencia desde su poemario *Por el pequeño sendero interior de Matsuo Bashí* (2009). Así, se privilegia la expresión llana, sin aspavientos, para que la palabra adquiera la ingrávida levedad de las plumas. Formalmente, estos poemas se construyen con un párrafo introductorio en prosa poética, seguido de un remate de versos breves que sintetizan emociones o afectos plurales. Los personajes del sujeto lírico ponen en escena facetas cambiantes, desde una poeta cortesana hasta un secretario de ministros en la esfera de influencia del Emperador. Se distingue una reformulación de la estructura del haikú—con estrofas de cinco versos en lugar de tres—para condensar esencias que ligan recíprocamente al individuo con la naturaleza. Estamos ante una poesía delicada que imprime sonoridad al silencio, a lo no aún expresado. [CZ]

2282 **Sánchez León, Abelardo.** El habitante del desierto. Lima: Paracaídas Editores, 2016. 66 p.

Poemas que acometen la tarea de buscar el revés de las experiencias abarrotadas, multitudinarias de la cotidianeidad urbana para, por el contrario, sumergirse en los linderos de la soledad, el silencio, la desnudez que yace bajo ropajes y posesiones materiales. Con esto se pretende hacer aflorar un aura divina en medio del páramo deshabitado. Con un "lenguaje parco, lacónico, introvertido" se rastrean las oleadas migratorias y los nuevos establecimientos de viviendas precarias en la franja del desierto, surcada por la extensión del mar. Pero, también, se reproduce la desolación que siente el individuo en la ciudad, la autosatisfacción de quien asiste en solitario a una función de cine erótico, y goza, agazapado en su butaca, como un fantasma en la bruma. El tránsito hacia la muerte se ejemplifica en el despojamiento de memorias familiares, enterradas en el arenal; como una especie de poética del vacío que abarca todo lo existente. [CZ]

2283 **Sandoval Bacigalupo, Renato.** Prooémium mortis. Lima: Ediciones Copé, 2016. 63 p. (Colección Obras ganadoras de la XVII Bienal de Poesía—Premio Copé 2015)

El objetivo de este autor es contrastar su propia "experiencia de la divinidad" con las definiciones de 24 filósofos del siglo XII. De esta constatación se desprenden estos poemas. Se parte de lo unitario para indagar acerca de las esferas de lo infinito o lo ubicuo, con lo que se describe una entidad de contornos abiertos, laberínticos, contradictorios o negativos. Lo divino se plantea como un origen sin comienzo, a la manera de una genealogía de la antítesis. Un lenguaje expansivo, de versos largos, se mueve por diversos niveles temáticos vinculados entre sí por el proceso recordatorio de la memoria. Por último, se anhela recuperar la continuidad entre individuo y totalidad sentida a la hora de nacer. [CZ]

2284 **Sanhueza, Leonardo.** La juguetería de la naturaleza. Saltillo, Mexico: Secretería de la Cultura del Gobierno del Estado de Coahuila de Zaragoza; Ciudad de México: LUMEN, 2016. 84 p. (Poesía)

El libro, que recibió el Premio Manuel Acuña 2015, es un ejemplo de lo mejor de la poesía de los poetas nacidos en los años 70. Los poemas se van hilvanando por ecos, resabios y claves para construir observaciones y reflexiones consumidas y amargas; sin embargo, la ferocidad del detalle y la precisión del lenguaje, a la vez enigmático y transparente, constituyen una señal de esperanza y afecto por el mundo. [MLF]

2285 Sarmiento, Antonio. La colina interior. Lima: Ediciones Copé, 2016. 86 p. (Colección Obras ganadoras de la XVII Bienal de Poesía <<Premio Copé 2015>>)

Poemas que hablan sobre el desenterramiento de unas sombras de 25 pulgadas de longitud, encontradas por arqueólogos dirigidos por el francés Le Chevalier en la zona de La Florida, una barriada cercana al mar en el departamento de Ancash, de donde proviene el autor. Hay referencias al terremoto del 31 de mayo de 1970, que asoló la región causando cerca de 60,000 muertos y 20,000 desaparecidos; así como al año de 1922, cuando nace la abuela del hablante, y que marca una fecha emblemática que da cuenta de una época de efervescencia experimental en Europa y Latino América, en términos literarios y artísticos. Por la coexistencia de referentes antiguos y modernos, pensada como ejercicio de excavación en las diferentes capas sedimentadas del lenguaje, se llega a palpar la vibración de su centro neurálgico. [CZ]

2286 Sarmiento, Sixto. Lágrimas sin sombras. Lima: Editorial Summa, 2016. 55 p.: ill. (some color).

Poeta ayacuchano premunido de una expresión sencilla, afectiva, esencial. Los campos semánticos que estos poemas construyen giran en torno a ejes como lágrima, herida, ceniza, sufrimiento, nostalgia, sueño. El enunciador lucha contra la precariedad de sus herramientas verbales para canalizar signos vitales en medio de la angustia producida por el dolor. Como toda situación, también se cantan situaciones positivas, como la belleza voluptuosa del cuerpo de la amada, simbolizada en el renacimiento de la luz o en el combate con la oscuridad. Los versos recuperan instantes de plenitud que han quedado grabados en la memoria de un pasado feliz. La mujer es, a fin de cuentas, aquel agente redentor que conecta al individuo con un atisbo de totalidad y complementariedad. [CZ]

2287 Siguas, William. Como errante que no quiere nada. Lima: Paracaídas Editores, 2016. 71 p.

Joven poeta de Cañete. El enunciador, asentado en el pueblo de Camatrana, en la provincia de Ica, medita sobre la relevancia del parentesco y de algunas creencias tradicionales (como el canto de lechuza que presagia alguna calamidad) que se usan para curar enfermedades. También se encuentran poemas de ambiente citadino que, lejos de la apacible vida pueblerina, retratan las peripecias de personajes viajeros y cosmopolitas, como Hunter S. Thompson. Estas composiciones semejan el diseño de cuadros fotográficos captados en "blanco y negro" que abren ventanas hacia el pasado entretejiendo vínculos familiares como nudos oscilantes que recorren un camino retrospectivo desde el ayer hacia el presente. Se enfatiza el papel de la poesía como experiencia—poniendo énfasis en el contacto con objetos cotidianos—y canto, antes que como maestría textual. Lo poético reside en aspectos inmateriales, como el olor que emana la permanencia de la tinta en un puñado de cartas amarillentas. [CZ]

2288 Soliz Guzmán, Edgar. Eucaristicón. Cochabamba, Bolivia: Gobierno Autónomo Municipal de Cochabamba: Casa de la Cultura, 2014. 52 p.

Esta obra es una de dos publicadas a petición de los jueces luego de haberse declarado desierto el Segundo Concurso Municipal de Poesía "Edmundo Camargo" en Cochabamba en el 2014. Edgar Soliz Guzmán, conocido por su programa de radio "Soy marica y qué" quien se ha declarado como "rojo, pobre, cholo y maricón" y miembro del Movimiento de Maricas de Bolivia, logra con este poema establecerse como una voz profunda y atrevida que intenta una reescritura queer de prácticas y discursos sacros de una manera que empodera a los seres marginados, justamente por las actitudes de los seguidores más conservadores de dichas prácticas. Apoyándose en un estilo neobarroco, el autor crea una nueva eucaristía donde la corporalidad masculina, tan importante en la ceremonia católica, se expresa por medio de una carnalidad existencial y espiritual en un contexto netamente homosexual y espiritual. De la lectura de esta obra surge un doble filo: uno que abre un espacio para que el deseo y amor (filial/paternal/sexual) homosexual se celebren, como una misa, a un nivel espiritual; y otro que subraya la carnalidad homoerótica ya existente dentro de la semiótica lingüística de la ceremonia eucarística. [JRB]

2289 Tasso, Alberto. Pasando el tiempo: poesía reunida 1959-2013. Santiago del Estero, Argentina: EDUNSE Editorial Universitaria, 2014. 301 p.: bibl. (Colección Convergencias)

Esta gran colección del poeta y sociólogo argentino representa cinco décadas, 17 poemarios, una gran variedad de estilos que incluye composiciones en verso libre, sonetos, formas muy cortas y sobrias, y poemas largos en prosa. El tono de esta poesía también demuestra una gran variación, desde la ironía y la parodia presentes en sus primeros poemas hasta el tono más serio—incluso melancólico—de su madurez, así como el retorno a la comedia en sus poemas más recientes. Tasso es así un poeta que sorprende. Aunque algunos rasgos—como su demostrado interés en la experimentación formal—permanecen constantes, ninguna sección de este libro se parece a otra. Nacido en la provincia de Buenos Aires pero radicado casi toda la vida en Santiago del Estero, Tasso toma en serio la importancia del espacio y el lugar. Pero el ambiente no es idílico. Aunque nunca menciona la política de una forma directa, la historia dolorosa de Argentina tiene una presencia constante en estos poemas. [JMP]

2290 Ulloa, Daniel. Desde el espinazo de la noche. Managua: Ediciones del Centro Nicaragüense de Escritores, 2014. 82 p.

Daniel Ulloa's daring poetry collection consists of 30 poems that weave together the story of Ishmael. The young man, the collection's poetic voice, moves through real and imagined spaces attempting to understand the realities created in and outside of mass media, in particular his solitude and search for love. Ulloa deftly navigates through classic and popular cultures to craft a series of innovative and sensual poems that despite their complexity are very accessible. [RMP]

2291 Vega Farfán, Denisse. El primer asombro. Lima: Paracaídas Editores, 2014. 85 p. (Serie Insular de poesía)

Joven poeta de Trujillo que evidencia una sorprendente madurez literaria. Bajo el sello de Blanca Varela, estos poemas hacen referencia al amor erótico como acto sacrificial dentro de contextos temporales ancestrales, como la cultura Mochica. Hay un arduo trabajo formal para que la poesía reproduzca un amplio registro de emociones sobre el mundo. Se asume la escritura como una perenne reformulación del contacto entre la voz lírica y los objetos, como una sorpresa que se actualiza en cada interacción con lo que la rodea. El "asombro" del título significa volver a ocupar aquel privilegiado espacio del ser humano que recorrió por primera vez la superficie de la tierra, para mirar con ojos nuevos la pulcritud de un paisaje incontaminado. La literatura se plantea como actividad regenerativa y curativa ante los malestares cotidianos. A pesar de expresarse con un lenguaje "insuficiente", la poeta se esmera en embellecer el lugar donde mora. [CZ]

2292 Vega Jácome, Roy. Muestra de arte disecado. Lima: Ediciones Copé, 2016. 67 p. (Colección Obras ganadoras de la XVII Bienal de Poesía <<Premio Copé 2015>>)

Textos que trazan una genealogía que rescata la sabiduría, y el halo divino, de los ancestros muertos. Ante la ausencia de estos parientes, la vida se percibe como falsa y vacía. Siguiendo la ruta de los derroteros coloquiales de Cisneros o Hernández, se enfatiza el aburrimiento ante la rutina de las vivencias diarias, en tanto "diminutas tragedias", que ejercen un crucial impacto en el futuro. El credo del autor radica en hacer que la poesía no sea solamente letra muerta o retórica inflada, sino que sea capaz de encender la pasión erótica arrolladora, siguiendo la vía surrealista de César Moro. La poesía se identifica con un animal disecado, "cuyos ojos—aparentemente muertos—/ perforan el aire y transforman lo real". [CZ]

2293 Villarreal, Minerva Margarita. Las maneras del agua. México: INBA, 2016. 81 p. (Coleccion Poesía)

En este libro, que ganó el Premio Aguascalientes 2016, Minerva Margarita Villarreal (Monterrey 1957) parte de una evocación de Teresa de Ávila, de sus visiones, de su obra y de su tiempo, para crear un diálogo con un aquí muy diferente. Un aquí donde hay jóvenes que intentan dejar sus adicciones, donde se produce una accidente automovilístico porque un hombre intenta tocar sexualmente a su hija, un aquí que puede ser un cuarto de hotel de cinco estrellas. Teresa, que en algunos versos se convierte en Tersa, es un tú que permite este ir y venir entre la visión y lo visto. [JRRS]

2294 Zurita, Raúl. El paraíso está vacío. Santiago: Alquimia Ediciones, 2016. 42 p.: bibl. (Colección Calles de mano única)

Se reedita la *plaquette* publicada en una edición artesanal de apenas 65 ejemplares en 1984. En su lenguaje experimental ya se identifica la matriz del libro del Once del poeta, el monumental *Zurita* de 2011: la imagen alucinada que reúne la experiencia de la dictadura militar con el cosmos, expandiéndose en pequeñas fábulas y comprimiéndose en visiones que parecen ser el apunte de una toma de un guión cinematográfico desarrollándose en la imaginación. [MLF]

2295 Zurita, Raúl. Tu vida rompiéndose. Santiago: Lumen, 2015. 590 p.: ill.

Un compendio sustancial de la obra del poeta del cosmos y el golpe. Las amplias secciones tituladas Del Mein Kampf, Purgatorio, Anteparaíso, El paraíso está vacío, La vida nueva, Poemas militantes, Inri y Zurita, reorganizan los libros publicados desde 1979 hasta 2011. Se incluye la obra visual del poeta. [MLF]

GENERAL STUDIES

2296 Historia crítica de la poesía mexicana. Coordinación de Rogelio Guedea. México: Fondo de Cultura Económica: Consejo Nacional para la Cultura y las Artes, 2015. 2 vol.: bibl. (Biblioteca mexicana)

Obra de consulta, supongo que tendrá muy pocos lectores que la recorran completa, desde el artículo inicial, dedicado al Neoclacisimo hasta el que la cierra, dedicado a Inti García Santamaría. Esto es normal pues está diseñada de modo enciclopédico, en un orden más o menos cronológico, en siete grandes apartados que abren con ensayos panorámicos, que sirven a su vez como pórtico a ensayos dedicados a autores individuales. Tres de los cuatro ensayos ensayos panorámicos del primer tomo son aptos—"Neoclacisimo" muy erudito y completo de Raquel Huerta Nava; "Romanticismo" en el que Carlos Oliva Mendoza tiene la brillante intuición, que por desgracia no agota, de pensar desde Bolívar Echeverría; "Modernismo" de Gabriel Bernal Granados, cuya comprensión de modernidad, en contraste con la de Oliva, parece rudimentaria—la excepción es el de Benjamín Valdivia que hubiera debido resumir de la primera vanguardia a Octavio Paz y Efraín Huerta, pero se limita a tratar de los Estridentistas. Los del segundo tomo son mucho más discutibles, pues ha habido menos tiempo para consagrarlos: es llamativo cómo sólo Armando González Torres adopta para su inteligente ensayo panorámico el título de la sección: "Neorromanticismo" que abarca las décadas del 50 y del 60. Tanto Alí Calderón que escribe de la poesía mexicana de 1960 a 1979—un ensayo curiosamente desconectado con el resto del contenido de la sección—como Israel Ramírez que escribe un trabajo muy informado de los 30 años que van de 1980 al 2010, sortean los rótulos Posmodernismo y Anfiguardismo [sic.] respectivamente. Aunque el seguir usando de manera automática la fórmula romántica-liberal aislando al escritor, elimina posibilidades de nuevas lecturas, hay algunos textos que vale la pena rescatar, como el de Eduardo Espina, gracias precisamente a que reúne en un solo texto a Marco Antonio Montes de Oca, Gerardo Deniz y el David Huerta de Incurable, o el de Jorge Ortega sobre Manuel Acuña, que logra enfrentarse con el lugar común que privilegia el "Nocturno" como su poema más importante. [JRRS]

SPECIAL STUDIES

2297 Aguinaga, Luis Vicente de. De la intimidad: emociones privadas y experiencias públicas en la poesía mexicana. México: Fondo de Cultura Económica, 2016. 131 p.: bibl., ill. (Sección de obras de lengua y estudios literarios)

En estos siete ensayos, Luis Vicente de Aguinaga (Guadalajara 1971) lee la poesía que le interesa no una intervención en la plaza pública, sino en "la plaza íntima"; esto es, privilegiando en la lírica de Enrique González Martínez, el padre Placencia, José Rosas Moreno, Luis G. Urbina, Octavio Paz, José Emilio Pacheco, Jorge Fernández Granados y Ángel Ortuño no lo que resulta único, sino lo que los reúne en la comunidad de un género, de una tradición, del trabajo sobre un tópico. Un muy buen libro, sobre todo en lo que se refiere a la relectura de los poetas del siglo XX de la región Occidental de México. [JRRS]

2298 Aparicio, Yvette. Post-conflict Central American literature: searching for home and longing to belong. Lewisburg, Pa.: Bucknell University Press, 2014. 169 p.: bibl., index.

A study of the literature written in the Central American region in the last three decades, centered around the notions of home and belonging. The focus is primarily on poetry and short fiction written in El Salvador, Nicaragua, and Costa Rica after 1990. Some of the poets examined include Ernesto Cardenal, Roque Dalton, Leonel Rugama, Claríbel Alegría, Marta Leonor González, Susana Reyes, María Cristina Orantes, and Luis Chaves. [RMP]

2299 Bradu, Fabienne. Permanencia de Octavio Paz. Madrid: Vaso Roto Ediciones, 2015. 126 p. (Cardinales; 7)

Uno de los libros escritos para conmemorar el centenario del nacimiento de Paz (1914–98), éste contiene 11 ensayos breves, de calidad dispar. Ejemplar y emocionante resulta el dedicado a la relación con la poesía chilena, obvio aunque no trivial el dedicado a la traducción, demasiado corto, un apunte que no se desarrolla, el dedicado a las mujeres a las que pensó Paz. Lo mejor del libro es la prosa tersa de Bradu (Francia 1954) y cómo enmarca ciertas citas, algunas raras, pues pertenecen a correspondencias que permanecen inéditas, varias claves, prácticamente todas muy brillantes y muy hermosas de Paz, a quien efectivamente invita a releer. [JRRS]

2300 Bradu, Fabienne. El volcán y el sosiego: una biografía de Gonzalo Rojas. México: Fondo de Cultura Económica, 2016. 486 p.: bibl., ill., index (Tierra firme)

Riguroso, documentado y ameno relato de la vida del poeta de Lebu nacido en 1916, y del humus cultural y artístico de su época. La estudiosa francesa afincada en México a quien se deben estudios fundamentales dedicados a la poesía de G. Rojas, ha escrito la biografía imprescindible del poeta y su tiempo. [MLF]

2301 Darío, Rubén. Del símbolo a la realidad: obra selecta. Edición conmemorativa. Madrid: Real Academia Española: Asociación de Academias de la Lengua Española: Alfaguara: 2016. 443 p.: bibl., index.

This is a selection of Rubén Darío's work, which includes *Prosas profanas y otros poemas* (1896), *Cantos de Vida y Esperanza: Los cisnes y otros poemas* (1905) and *Tierras solares* (1904). The volume was put together by la Real Academia Española and la Asociación de Academias de la Lengua in commemoration of the 100th anniversary of Darío's death and is accompanied by a number of studies about the author and his work. It also includes an excellent select bibliography on important editions of the poet's major work and on critical studies of his oeuvre. [RMP]

2302 Esquinca, Jorge. Breve catálogo de fuerzas: tentativas, conjeturas, vislumbres. Toluca, Mexico: Bonobos Editores; México: CONACULTA, Dirección General de Publicaciones, 2015. 160 p.: bibl., ill. (Colección Postemporáneos)

Este libro reúne los ensayos de Esquinca (Ciudad de México 1957) dispersos en prólogos, actas y publicaciones periódicas. El esfuerzo más sostenido se dedica a Octavio Paz. Otra parte importante autores fundamentales del occidente mexicano—Agustín Yáñez, Elías Nandino, Alí Chumacero. Otros ensayos los dedica a autores, como Vicente Quirarte, Francisco Hernández, que han llegado a una estación importante en sus carreras o en el caso de Guillermo Fernández, muerto. Un par a autores de su generación (Coral Bracho) o más jóvenes (Luis Vicente de Aguinaga). Una sección completa se dedica al ámbito extranjero: Bradbury, Michaux, Dylan Thomas, du Bouchet y, especialmente interesante como genealogía de su *Cámara nupcial* (véase item **2218**), Emily Dickinson. Esquinca es un muy agradable ensayista, aunque no se haya dado el tiempo de ampliar definitivamente sus textos de ocasión. [JRRS]

2303 Lima, Paolo de. Al vaivén fluctuante del verso: (cansancio/Mundo Arcano/Silenciosa Algarabía/Inéditos). Lima: Hipocampo Editores, 2012. 119 p. (Serie Katatay)

Miembro del Movimiento Neón. Esta compilación incluye tres libros publicados hasta la fecha: Cansancio (1995 y 1998), Mundo arcano (2002) y Silenciosa algarabía (2009), así como un breve grupo de textos inéditos. Un registro coloquial, repleto de jergas peruanas, es usado para constatar la apatía y el desdén posmodernos ante un mundo hueco. Conforme avanza su arte literario, el poeta demuestra mayor conciencia del inasible vuelo de la musicalidad del lenguaje, que oscila en coreografías que no se materializan, ni fijan, en el soporte de papel del libro. El tono reflexivo otorga nuevas capas de significado al abrupto coloquialismo del debut literario del autor. Se nota una sostenida madurez de la voz poética que apela a un lenguaje nómada, fluido, rizomático que testimonia aspectos fronterizos y movibles de la condición posmoderna. Es constante el hincapié en referencias anticapitalistas y anticonsumistas para constatar la vacuidad del paisaje hiperreal de nuestros días. [CZ]

2304 **Raúl Zurita: alegoría de la desolación y la esperanza.** Edición de Carmen Alemany Bay, Eva Valero Juan y Víctor Manuel Sanchis Amat. Madrid: Visor Libros, 2016. 490 p.: bibl., ill., maps. (Biblioteca filológica hispana; 182)

Útil compilación de más de 30 estudios inéditos consagrados a la obra de Zurita que se publican con ocasión del otorgamiento del Doctorado Honoris Causa por la Universidad de Alicante en España en marzo de 2015. [MLF]

MISCELLANEOUS

2305 **La flama del tiempo: testimoniales y estudios poéticos.** Coordinación de Maribel Urbina, Jocelyn Martínez Elizalde y Alejandro González Acosta. México: Universidad Autónoma Metropolitana: Academia para la Educación e Investigación en Ciencias, Artes y Humanidades, 2018. 194 p.: bibl., ill. (Molinos de viento; 168. Serie Mayor. Ensayo)

Más que un volumen crítico, esta compilación es un Festschrift que reúne varios textos de ocasión que se escribieron después de la muerte de Rubén Bonifaz Nuño en el año 2013. Decepciona que Josefina Estrada, que lo entrevistó largamente no haya aprovechado los materiales de su libro del 2008, así como el hecho de que, por pudor, varios de los textos memorísticos prefieren callarse algunas anécdotas que acaso no parecían adecuadas al momento de la muerte reciente del poeta, traductor y académico de la UNAM. De esto escapa el divertido texto de René Avilés Fabila. La parte más académica, incluye textos como el de Jocelyn Martínez o el de Manuel Iris, que leen de manera puntual algunos poemas de Bonifaz Nuño. Pero en general falta el filo crítico o incluso la posibilidad abarcadora de un ensayo como el que le dedicó en otro momento Jorge Fernández Granados a Bonifaz. [JRRS]

2306 **Flores, Malva.** La culpa es por cantar: apuntes sobre poesía y poetas de hoy. México: Literal Publishing: CONACULTA, Dirección General de Publicaciones, 2014. 121 p.: bibl.

Este libro es mucho menos denso que su notable *Viaje de Vuelta*, sobre la revista de Octavio Paz, además, a pesar de que para ser una polémica elide demasiado para identificar con qué pelea. Sin embargo, lo que me parece importante de este libro de Flores (Ciudad de México 1961) es su búsqueda formal. De hecho, en ocasiones es más arriesgada en estos textos breves en prosa que en sus propios poemas, que, como confiesa aquí mismo, son más bien de índole conservadora. Se trata de un libro que ayuda a trazar el perfil cada vez más nítido de un ensayismo lírico, muy libre, en el que incluso se insertan estrofas en verso de vez en cuando. [JRRS]

2307 **González, Wingston.** Four Poems. (*Asymptote (online)*, July 2018)

A collection of four of González's Afro-Caribbean poems, translated by José García Escobar, that appeared in the July 2018 issue of *Asymptote,* an online journal of world literature in translation. The poems were first published in *Microfé: poesía guatemalteca contemporánea* (2012) edited by Javier Payeras. Upon hearing González at a reading, García Escobar set out to capture the rhythms of his verses, complete with speech patterns of the inhabitants of Livingston. The result is a fabulous translation, particularly of one of the poems, "My Kimera, Black Faviola." [RMP]

Drama

PAOLA HERNÁNDEZ, *Professor of Spanish, University of Wisconsin-Madison*
ELAINE M. MILLER, *Associate Professor of Spanish, Christopher Newport University*

MEXICO, THE CARIBBEAN, AND CENTRAL AMERICA

MOST OF THE PLAYS recently published and annotated for this volume are written by established dramatists who were born during the 1960s and 1970s and have received international recognition like Conchi León and Alejandro Román from Mexico, Elizabeth Ovalle from the Dominican Republic, and Jorgelina Cerritos from El Salvador. Among these latest publications are anthologies with works by multiple authors: *Dramaturgia cubana contemporánea* (item **2325**), edited by Ernesto Fundora and including ten plays produced after 2000, and *Escribir las fuerzas* (item **2327**), edited by Enrique Mijares and consisting of eight works produced during a dramaturgical workshop that he directed in 2014 in Ciudad Juárez, Mexico. The list includes collections of works by single playwrights who are currently active, such as the Puerto Rican Roberto Alexander Pérez, as well as those who were well-known during the earlier part of the 20th century, such as Raúl Cáceres Careno (1938–2017) (item **2313**) and Elena Garro (1916–98) (item **2330**) from Mexico and the Cuban José Cid Pérez (1906–94) (item **2317**).

In Mexico, the Spanish-speaking Caribbean, and Central America, the trend toward greater cultural, geographic, and linguistic diversity remains. Notable examples in Mexico are the publication of works by playwrights from the country's northern and southern borders and a study about theater written and produced in the US-Mexican Borderlands (item **2359**). The plays tend to be set in these border regions and deal with issues affecting the people who live there. Most of the plays in the anthology *Escribir las fuerzas* (item **2327**) take place in Ciudad Juarez and all the plays by Conchi León in *Conchi León: dramaturga de la península* (item **2335**) are set in the Yucatan Peninsula. However, the themes resonate elsewhere in Mexico and around the world. In Alejandro Román's play *Muerte de la virgen* (item **2344**), the social subjugation experienced by three female characters in contemporary Ciudad Juárez, Mexico City, and 17th–century Italy is shown to be a key factor in femicides and violence. Raúl Cáceres' three plays in *Ritual maya* (item **2313**), which were written and produced in the later part of the 20th century, illustrate how the Maya were not the only civilization to confront foreign imperialism by incorporating references to modern-day US foreign intervention.

Many of the Caribbean plays are transnational such as Dominican Elizabeth Ovalle's *Por hora* and *Latinos* (item **2342**), featuring Latin American migrants living in New York, and Cuban Ulises Rodríguez Febles' *Huevos*, about a visit to the island by a character who had emigrated to the US during the Mariel boatlift (item **2325**). Some of these plays have been produced outside of the Caribbean like Puerto Rican Roberto Alexander Pérez's *¡Habla, Marica!* and *Noches de galería* (item **2343**), which premiered in New York and Buenos Aires, respectively. A transnational vision of what constitutes Cuban dramaturgy is evident in Mexican publisher Paso de Gato's anthology *Dramaturgia cubana contemporánea* (item **2325**). Compiler Ernesto Fundora, who resides in the US, includes plays written by dramatists living in the diaspora as well as on the island.

Recent Central American publications include plays from Costa Rica, El Salvador, and Nicaragua focusing on impunity and political corruption. Jorgelina Cerritos' *La audiencia de los confines* (item **2316**) addresses 20th-century occurrences of these damaging social and political problems that, sadly, continue to be relevant today. In the play, attempts to reclaim the historical memory of the Salvadoran Civil War are incomplete, suggesting that there has yet to be a full accounting of and response to the human rights abuses during the conflict. Melvin Méndez Chinchilla dedicates *Emergencia en el Castillo Azul* (item **2338**) to the memory of Parmenio Medina, a journalist who investigated corruption in Costa Rica, including a case involving a priest. The fictitious situation in the play in which religious leaders arrange the murder of those who threaten their financial status and authority clearly alludes to the real-life murder of Medina in 2001.

Another noteworthy trend in these publications is experimentation with dramatic structures and techniques. For example, the influence of detective fiction is evident in Cuban Abel González Melo's *Chamaco* (item **2325**) and Costa Rican Sergio Masís Olivas' *El silencioso vuelo del búho* (item **2337**). Both reveal secrets that the characters had been concealing from their families. González Melo's play consists of ten scenes structured as a police report about a murder in which the characters cross paths. After committing the crime, a male prostitute has sex with the victim's father, a widowed judge whose relationship with his adult children is disintegrating. In Masís' work, a homeless man invited to dinner on Christmas Eve by an upper-middle-class married couple assumes a detective-like role in solving the mystery of what really caused the death of their terminally ill adopted daughter, exposing in the process his own surprising connection to the family. Mexican Alejandro Román writes *Muerte de la virgen* (item **2344**) entirely in verse reminiscent of an epic poem in which three women speak about the violence surrounding them and Cuban Raúl Alfonso indicates in a note preceding the play that he uses verse in *El pie de Nijinski* (item **2325**) when the character Vaslav Nijinski speaks to capture the mythical dimension of the famous Russian ballet dancer.

Román's play also lacks stage directions, which is characteristic of many of the works from the US-Mexican border in the anthology *Escribir las fuerzas* (item **2327**) and the Cuban works *Huevos* by Ulises Rodríguez Febles and *Liz* by Reinaldo Montero in the anthology *Dramaturgia cubana contemporánea* (item **2325**). Rodríguez Febles explicitly states that he inserts spaces rather than didascalia in the script to give the director more creative freedom in staging it. In these examples, the absence of stage directions requires a close reading of the dialogue to determine how actors might perform the plays with lighting, scenery, props, sound, costumes and visual effects. Cuban Salvador Lemis' *La cebra*, published in the same anthology (item **2325**) with *Liz* and *Huevos*, adopts a different approach to stage directions. Some instructions about the actors' gestures and facial expressions appear in the playtext. However, Lemis includes more extensive directions at the end of each scene involving the use of curtains or screens to project shadows and cinematographic effects, such as aircraft dropping a variety of objects from the sky and an ambulance hitting pedestrians in the street.

An additional notable technique in the published plays is intertextuality. Susana Báez Ayala in *Tierra caliente* and Selfa Chew in *Los reyes de Guadalupe* from the US-Mexican Borderlands anthology *Escribir las fuerzas* (item **2327**) incorporate Mexican songs such as traditional rancheras and corridos and contemporary pop hits by Marco Antonio Solís and Juan Gabriel. This use of music either connects or contrasts the emotions expressed in the songs with the characters' brutal reality. In *Tierra caliente* a young woman is gang raped and a transgender person is physically assaulted while riding the freight train La Bestia to the US. In *Los reyes de Guadalupe* Chew also starts each scene with a Mexican proverb to preview its theme and emphasize how the characters, female members of the real-life Reyes Salazar family from the Juarez Valley who fought as activists against a proposed nuclear waste dump and criticized the government's drug war, are uprooted from their culture when they seek asylum in the US after their loved ones are murdered.

In addition to intertextual references to popular culture, Báez Ayala cites a fragment of the poem "La sangre derramada" by poet and dramatist Federico García Lorca. The recital in her play of the verses by characters who have become vigilantes fighting against the drug cartels links their wish not to witness the murder of their loved ones to the desire expressed in the poem not to see the blood from a friend gored to death during a bullfight. Other examples of intertextuality are *Ícaros* by Norge Espinosa and *Ifigenia* by Yerandy Fleites Pérez from the anthology *Dramaturgia cubana contemporánea* (item **2325**). Both not only present their own recastings of Greek mythology, but also insert metatheatrical references to plays previously written by Cuban dramatists such as Virgilio Piñera, Antón Arrufat, and Abelardo Estorino. These examples of intertextuality highlight the international relevance of the themes from these Mexican and Cuban plays. [EMM]

SOUTH AMERICA

Dentro de la variedad de publicaciones teatrales se encuentran algunos puntos en común que valen la pena resaltar. En especial, las publicaciones de Marcos Perearnau (item **2308**) se proponen exponer textos de dramaturgos que han tenido éxito en el escenario, la mayoría siendo ya reconocidos e importantes nombres (Vivi Tellas, Rafael Spregelburd, Beatriz Catani, Mariano Pensotti, entre varios otros). Sus tres volúmenes aportan importantes obras para el estudio del teatro argentino contemporáneo y cada uno es acompañado por un estudio preliminar que enfatiza la centralidad de estos trabajos. De similar manera, Ricardo Dubatti compila a nuevos dramaturgos, pero con la diferencia de que sus nombres, por su mayoría, son desconocidos (item **2341**). Este libro les brinda un espacio de acceso y visibilidad que extiende el éxito que hayan tenido en las tablas. A la vez, se percibe una intensidad en el valor de publicar antologías de dramaturgos de provincias. Ejemplos de esto se ven en las antologías creadas para autores serranos (Argentina) (item **2318**), antiqueños (Colombia) (items **2309** y **2333**) como también de diferentes regiones de Argentina que no son Buenos Aires (La Plata y Bahía Blanca, items **2326** y **2350**, respectivamente). El valor de estas publicaciones trae consigo una forma de descentralizar las formas dramáticas de las ciudades y de explorar las producciones que no llegan a tener la misma recepción. Por otro lado, varias publicaciones demuestran la fuerza dramática de algunos de sus autores: Patricia Suárez (items **2348** y **2349**), Néstor Caballero (item **2312**), Santiago Loza (item **2336**), Eduardo Rovner (item **2345**), Luis Cano (item **2315**), y Jorge Huertas (item **2334**). Un libro que llama la atención por su trabajo minucioso de investigación es el de Olga Cosentino (item **2355**) sobre el repertorio teatral del conocido Juan Carlos Gené. Dentro de sus varios roles como guionista, escritor, productor y director, se encuentra la fundación y trabajo con el Clú del Clown, grupo de los años 80 pionero en un tipo de teatro *under* argentino. Por último, Carlos Fos (item **2356**) brinda un estudio necesario de la historia del Teatro Municipal, su nacimiento, sus cambios y su centralidad hoy en día. Con acceso a los archivos del Teatro San Martín, este libro es una fuente obligatoria al estudiar las variaciones de la historia del teatro argentino. [PH]

PLAYS

2308 Antología de argumentos teatrales en Argentina 2003–2013. Edición de Matías Luque y Marcos Perearnau. Buenos Aires: Editorial Libretto, 2015–2016. 3 v.: bibl., ill.

Este trabajo emprendedor de Perearnau consiste en publicar obras que han sido importantes en las tablas argentinas, y en algunos casos, internacionales, y hacen hincapié en transformaciones culturales dentro de una variedad de procesos históricos, políticos, artísticos, y en especial, económicos, ya que varios de estos trabajos contestan de alguna manera a la crisis económica del 2001. En volumen 1, bajo el título "Formas de reconocimiento", se encuentran las obras *Cozarinsky y su médico* de Vivi Tellas; *Bizarra, una saga argentina* de Rafael Spregelburd; *Los muertos* de Mariano Pensotti y Beatriz Catani; y *Nada del amor me produce envidia* de Santiago Loza. En volumen 2, bajo el título "Modos de asociación", se publican las obras *Instrucciones para un coleccionista de mariposas* de Mariana Eva Pérez; *Adonde van los muertos* de Grupo Krapp; *Cineastas* de Mariano Pensotti; y *Las multitudes* de Federico León. Volumen 3, bajo el título "Circuitos y circulación", incluye *Una obra útil* de Gerado Naumann; *Paraná Porá* de Maruja Bustamante; *Pueden dejar lo que quieran* de Fernando Rubio; y *CMMN SNS PRJCT* de Laura Kalauz y Martín Schick. [PH]

2309 Antología de teatro de La Guajira. Edición de Leonardo Aldana de Hoyos. Riohacha, Colombia: Orígenes, 2015. 180 p. (Colección Guajira 50 años)

Con la celebración de los 50 años de existencia de la Colección Guajira, se presenta este libro con cuatro obras diferentes. *Las negativas* de Tomás Emilio Pichón es una obra decimonónica donde se enfoca en cómo embellecer un cementerio de la ciudad. Las demás obras son contemporáneas, y no existe una explicación para su publicación, excepto la obra *Gallinas indispuestas al sacrificio* de Fredy González Zubiría (Premio Casa de las Américas, 2012) y también de su autoría, *Diáspora en los cielos*. [PH]

2310 Assad Cuellar, José. Tribulaciones de un autor desconcertado, o, La saga del espejo constante. Bogotá: Universidad Nacional de Colombia, Sede Bogotá, Facultad de Artes, 2015. 87 p.: ill. (Colección Punto aparte)(Opera prima. Dramaturgia)

Obra que se remonta a William Shakespeare quien es convocado por tres brujas de su propia autoría a explicar las deudas y problemas que dejó en sus personajes. Así, se crea una divertida obra metateatral donde la ficción, la escritura y la recepción se mezclan entre el pasado y el presente de estos personajes. [PH]

2311 Beccar, Alejo. Tributo: tres piezas teatrales. Buenos Aires: EUDEBA, 2016. 107 p. (Colección Biblioteca Proteatro)

Alejo Beccar, director de teatro, dramaturgo y dueño de una sala de teatro independiente, publica tres de sus obras. Desde su óptica como productor, estas obras responden a un formato técnico de bajos recursos y compenetran a la audiencia a que con una incógnita inicial se genere un conflicto dramático hasta el final. Las primeras dos obras se componen desde el misterio, de gente que se reúne (o por primera vez como en *Simplemente sucede*, o como un grupo de amigos como en *Be Happy*). Ambas se crean desde lo desconocido para llevarnos hacia la cuestión de la proximidad humana. En *Sacudir la lanza* el hilo conductor es el debate de la autoría de Shakespeare para especular que Sir Francis Bacon fue el verdadero autor de las obras isabelinas. [PH]

2312 Caballero, Néstor. Piezas del adiós. Caracas: Alcaldía de Caracas: Gobierno del Distrito Capital: Fondo Editorial Fundarte, 2016. 299 p.: index. (Colección Mirando al tendido; 17)

Esta colección publica cuatro obras que son las más recientes del reconocido dramaturgo venezolano. *Desiertos del paraíso* expone una trama en distintos espacios de encierro, que a su vez simbolizan diferentes países latinoamericanos y sus políticas. *Hay que comerse a Rita* es una obra histórica que trata las rebeliones militares del 4 de febrero de 1992 y el golpe de estado del 11 de abril del 2002. *El despiadado reguetón de Candy Crush*, a través de una mirada desde el video juego, se exponen los temas de la dependencia económica en las tasas extranjeras y la deshumanización de los ciudadanos venezolanos. Por último *Baúles . . . del adiós* es un homenaje a diferentes dramaturgos venezolanos. [PH]

2313 Cáceres Carenzo, Raúl. Ritual maya: tres piezas de teatro épico. Ilustraciones en páginas interiores de Alfredo E. Lugo Domínguez. Mérida, Mexico: Gobierno del Estado de Yucatán, SEDECULTA, Secretaría de la Cultura y las Artes de Yucatán; México: Consejo Nacional para la Cultura y las Artes, 2013. 126 p.: bibl., ill.

This volume includes three plays linking the Spanish conquest of the Maya to the abuse of power familiar to 20th-century audiences, referencing US intervention abroad and the Franco dictatorship in Spain. *Ritual maya del dios desconocido*, originally published in 1963 and revised in 2003, presents the world's creation according to Maya cosmovision. In *Mestizaje: cruz de relámpagos*, originally performed in 1964 and developed into a new version in 1999, historical figures are characters, with Gonzalo Guerrero (16th-century Spanish sailor turned Maya warrior) notably being a symbol of resistance to imperialism. Accompanying *Canek: caudillo maya* is information about its 1988 staging and a critical study linking the Maya hero Canek's struggle to past, present, and future liberation movements. [EMM]

2314 Camilletti, Stella. El despertar de la ilusión. Buenos Aires: Prosa Amerian Editores, 2014. 94 p.

Dos obras de teatro, *El despertar de la ilusión* y *En tránsito*, se compenetran en el tema de la inmigración italiana a la Argentina. Los temas varían, pero en el vaivén de los viajes también se encuentran temas de la dictadura de Mussolini y la última dictadura militar argentina. La poética existente en ambas repercute en los textos, en la fluidez con la que los personajes hablan y en la sensación marítima de movimiento constante de estos viajes entre dos continentes. [PH]

2315 Cano, Luis. Se fue con su padre. Buenos Aires: Complejo Teatral de Buenos Aires: Losada, 2014. 64 p.: ill.

Una obra de intensidad emocional en la cual cuatro mujeres (una joven prostituta, su madre, su tía y su media hermana) se reúnen para compartir un terrible secreto. Con influencia del universo agobiante de August Strinberg, la trama teje crueles e intensos lazos de la relación humana. El libro contiene una entrevista al autor de José María Brindisi con fotografía de la puesta en escena. [PH]

2316 Cerritos, Jorgelina. La audiencia de los confines: primer ensayo sobre la memoria. San Salvador: Índole editores, 2014. 93 p. (Colección onda expansiva El Salvador; 6)

The first part in a trilogy by a dramatist who has won international awards, including the prestigious Casa de las Américas Prize, this allegorical play is about reclaiming historical memory of the Salvadoran Civil War (1980–92). As indicated by the word *ensayo* in the title, the play is a "rehearsal" or an attempt to remember the past of the characters and of El Salvador. Three characters represent Truth, Memory, and History in a metatheatrical scene. The darkness surrounding them as they await dawn is a metaphor for the silence that some Salvadorans hope to break about human rights abuses during the war. Sunlight never arrives in the play, suggesting that these atrocities continue being silenced. [EMM]

Chávez, Rosa and **Camila Camerlengo.** Awas. See item **2203**.

2317 Cid Pérez, José. Teatro selecto. Edición crítica por Lourdes Betanzos. Madrid: Editorial Verbum, 2014. 160 p.: bibl. (Verbum Teatro)

This work includes four previously unpublished plays by José Cid Pérez (1906–94) and three critical studies by Betanzos about their representation of important moments in Cuban history: the women's suffrage movement, the beginnings of socialist ideology, and Christopher Columbus' voyages. In the comedy *Cadenas de amor* a female character challenges gender norms by becoming a lawyer. The brief dramatic sketch *Justicia* and the series of vignettes *Estampas rojas* critique the concept of justice during the early republic. Both identify poverty as a root of crime and show the discrimination of the legal system against lower social classes. *Radio-episodios de la historia de Cuba*, an example of a genre aiming to educate and entertain radio listeners, humanizes Columbus by showing the obstacles that he faced. [EMM]

2318 **Confluencias: dramaturgias serranas: recopilación en torno a los encuentros del Proyecto Pluja.** Prólogo de Gabriela Borioli. Edición de Soledad González y Marcelo Márquez. Buenos Aires: Inteatro, 2013. 278 p. (El país teatral)

Este libro colecciona obras de jóvenes dramaturgos que compartieron encuentros en la residencia Pluja, en Córdoba entre los años 2004 y 2008 en homenaje a su fundador, el mendocino Jorge Díaz (1958–2003). Entre las obras se encuentran: *Pata-gonia*, creación colectiva; *Cuerpos de hielo* de Soledad González; *La desconfianza 3: matar al otro* de Rodrigo Cuesta; *La sexualidad de Sandra* de Maximiliano Gallo; *Maskin, capaz de solucionar todo* de Javier Ramírez; *Manos traslúcidas en fiebre de olvido* de Gabriel Fernández Chapo; *El club de los fracasados* de Luis Alejandro Pérez; *Habla él* de Leonel Giacometto, *Esotcolmo, la primavera de los llorones* de Emilio H. Díaz Abregú; *A la deriva* de Cristóbal Valenzuela y *Din* de Ariel Farace. [PH]

2319 **Cortés, Darío A.** Oliverio: la obra de teatro inspirada en textos de Oliverio Girondo. Buenos Aires: Aurelia Rivera Libros, 2015. 78 p.: ill.

Con evidente intertexto a la vida y obra de Oliverio Girondo, este unipersonal trabaja con la hipertextualidad poética por la cual se conoce su vida y obra. Sin embargo, a pesar de la complejidad del texto poético, la fuerza dramática permite que el público entre en esta historia sin necesidad de entender el contexto literario. El libro además aporta secciones como "Apuntes de 'Olveiro'" con información del estreno, "Prensa y Crítica" donde se recopilan varias reseñas de la puesta del 2013, como también una entrevista al autor. [PH]

2320 **Degiovanangelo, Guillermo.** En busca del rostro perdido. Canelones, Uruguay: Ediciones del Pescador, 2016. 122 p.

Tres obras dramáticas componen este libro: *En busca del rostro perdido* (Premio Nacional de Literatura, Dramaturgia Inédita 2015), una historia sobre el verdadero personaje Isidore Ducasse, Conde de Lautréamont; *Sabat* (2007), basada en la correspondencia entre Gabriela Mistral, Pablo Neruda y Carlos Sabat Ercasty; y *Las tres parcas, un encuentro con Shakespeare, Cervantes e Inca Garcilaso de la Vega*, homenaje a los tres escritores que fallecieron el 23 de abril de 1616. [PH]

2321 **Denis Molina, Carlos.** Teatro mitológico. Montevideo: Ediciones del Caballo Perdido, 2016. 130 p.: ill.

El reconocido poeta, dramaturgo y novelista uruguayo nos brinda dos obras de teatro, *El regreso de Ulises* (1948) y *Orfeo* (1951), obras que valoran el arte vanguardista de los años 30, así como también la influencia de los modelos dramáticos extranjeros a la dramaturgia del Uruguay de los años 40 y 50. [PH]

2322 **Di Mauro, Daniel.** Elementos en resistencia: obras para teatro de títeres. Caracas: Fondo Editorial Fundarte, Alcaldía de Caracas, 2016. 193 p. (Colección Mirando al tendido; 18)

Piezas para títeres componen este volumen donde las figuras históricas (o heroínas) de la ficción traen consigo una relación ecológica. Así, Doña Bárbara representa la tierra, María Lionza, el agua y Luz Caraballo, el viento. Incluye nueve obras cortas: *La psicovenganza de Doña Bárbara, La ecorrebeldía de la Diosa de Sorte, La errotribulación de Luz Caraballo, La colección del peregrino, Luz de Buría, Sabio de Todarivquivia, Juan Petróleo, La cabeza voladora* y *El árbol del universo*. Temas de leyendas venezolanas, como también un juego entre los mitos indígenas, creados desde la ficción, llevan a temas sobre la relación ecológica con los seres humanos de hoy. [PH]

2323 Díaz Bagú, Alberto. Diógenes al desnudo. Córdoba, Argentina: Letras y Bibliotecas de Córdoba, 2013. 108 p. (Voces en el centenario; 5)

Comedia dramática social que indaga en los temas de clase y política de 1975 dentro de la sociedad burguesa de la provincia de Córdoba, Argentina. La familia se convierte en una metáfora del país donde se entrelaza lo cómico, lo dramático y lo terrible de esta década de peso político. El prólogo aporta un contexto importante tanto por la temática de la obra, como también por la recepción que tuvo cuando se estrenó en 1975. [PH]

2324 Dramaturgia antioqueña, 1879–1963: antología. Edición de Felipe Restrepo David. Medellín, Colombia: Fondo Editorial Universidad EAFIT, 2014. 304 p.: bibl. (Colección Bicentenario de Antioquia; 84)

Una excelente antología con un estudio cabal sobre el teatro de Antioquia, Colombia, desde el siglo XIX hasta los años 60. Las 10 obras aquí publicadas son *Por el rey y por la honra* de Juan de Dios Uribe Restrepo; *Zoila Rosa* de Alejandro Vásquez Uribe; *Nosce te ipsum* de Juan José Botero; *Adiós, Lucía* de Salvador Mesa Nicholls; *Contra viento y marea* de Isabel Carrasquilla de Arango; *Roque Yarza* de Efe Gómez; *Lauro candente* de Alejandro Mesa Nicholls; *HK-111* de Gonzalo Arango; *Calle tal, número tal* de Regina Mejía de Gaviria; y *Prometea desencadenada* de Ciro Mendía. El objetivo de este volumen es dar a conocer la tradición teatral de esta zona, mientras que también explorar los diferentes estilos y temas que se propone cada autor o autora. [PH]

2325 Dramaturgia cubana contemporánea: antología. Compilación y prólogo de Ernesto Fundora. México: Paso de Gato, Toma, Ediciones y Producciones Escénicas y Cinematográficas: CONACULTA, 2015. 450 p.: bibl. (Serie Dramaturgia)

This collection includes 10 plays produced after the year 2000 by dramatists mainly born after 1960 and currently living in Cuba or in the diaspora. In Nilo Cruz's *Ana en el trópico*, a family embraces tradition while facing pressure to adopt new manufacturing methods in their cigar factory in Florida. Norge Espinosa's *Ícaros* and Yerandy Fleites Pérez's *Ifigenia (Tragedia ayer)* continue the rich tradition in Cuban dramaturgy of reconfiguring ancient Greek mythology to reflect contemporary concerns. In *Huevos* by Ulises Rodríguez Febles a character who left Cuba as a boy during the 1980 Mariel boatlift returns in 1993 to deal with the traumatic memory of repudiation by friends and neighbors. Abel González Melo's *Chamaco* shows the harsh reality of male prostitution in Havana. [EMM]

2326 Dramaturgias bahienses. Compilación de Nidia Burgos y Miguel Mendiondo. Bahía Blanca, Argentina: Editorial de la Universidad Nacional del Sur (EdiUNS), 2015. 229 p.: bibl., map. (Serie Extensión. Colección Creación literaria)

Con el objetivo de hacer notar el trabajo de dramaturgos del sur de Argentina, este volumen selecciona obras estrenadas entre 2011 y 2014 que tuvieron lugar en Bahía Blanca, Argentina. Los ocho textos dramáticos son de Leandro González, Guido Carlos Christensen, Silvana Seewald, Celeste Giraudo, Pablo Ariel Fiordelmondo, Miguel Mendiondo, Camila Rodríguez, Mariana Bordón, y Gonzalo San Millan. Además de sus obras, el volumen cuenta con un prólogo y una minuciosa introducción a cargo de Nidia Burgos. [PH]

2327 Escribir las fuerzas: taller de dramaturgia Juárez 2014. Edición de Enrique Mijares. Juárez, Mexico: Universidad Autónoma de Ciudad Juárez, 2016. 194 p.

This anthology of eight plays written during a workshop led by Enrique Mijares in Ciudad Juárez also includes an essay explaining the participants' process in creating works that address contemporary social issues along the US-Mexican border, such as gender violence and vigilantes fighting drug cartels in Susana Báez's *Tierra caliente*, human trafficking in Virginia Ordóñez's *El circo*, as well as metatheatrical commentary about dramaturgy in Ciudad Juárez in Blas García's *Aristófanes inbox*. All the works have a nonlinear structure, minimal stage directions, and a variety of perspectives presented by the characters within a single play. [EMM]

2328 Finzi, Alejandro. Tosco: (teatro), 2013. Córdoba, Argentina: Alción Editora, 2014. 78 p.

Una obra de valor histórico que se centra en la Masacre de Trelew y las ramificaciones políticas que tuvo la acción de Agustín Tosco entre 1970 y 1973 en Argentina. Sin embargo, la obra contiene un valor onírico y hasta mítico que le brinda una mirada perspicaz desde otras posibles miradas. [PH]

2329 **García Vilar, Carmen.** Y Miss Venezuela es . . . : (. . . o de cómo algunas mujeres vivieron los acontecimientos más importantes de la Venezuela contemporánea, especialmente desde Pérez Jiménez hasta el Caracazo . . .): comedia (algo oscura) en cuatro actos, para teatro. Caracas: Gobierno del Distrito Capital: Alcaldía de Caracas, Fondo Editorial Fundarte, 2013. 91 p.

Premio Nacional de Dramaturgia "César Rengifo," esta obra confluye el espacio doméstico con la historia del certamen de Miss Venezuela. A través de cuatro mujeres, de tres generaciones diferentes, las historias personales se mezclan con eventos históricos y sociales de Venezuela. Con humor y soltura, se exploran diferentes vicisitudes del mundo femenino, mientras que la intriga y la desconfianza desembocan en la ambivalencia de un crimen. [PH]

2330 **Garro, Elena.** Teatro completo. Prólogo de Jesús Garro Velázquez y Guillermo Schmidhuber de la Mora. Edición y nota editorial de Álvaro Álvarez Delgado. México: Fondo de Cultura Económica, 2016. 403 p.: bibl. (Letras mexicanas)

Researchers studying prominent 20th-century Mexican playwright Elena Garro will celebrate this anthology of all 16 of her dramatic works in their definitive versions resulting from the editor's examination of their previous publication in books and journals. The editor also corrects typographical errors from earlier versions and presents the plays in chronological order according to their original publication date. The prologue draws on information from Garro's nephew, who lived with her for more than 30 years, and letters that she exchanged with Mexican dramatist Guillermo Schmidhuber, to provide insight into the playwright's life and opinions. [EMM]

2331 **Guarín Salazar, Milkiades.** El escarabajo de oro. Bogotá: Universidad Cooperativa de Colombia, 2016. 72 p.: ill. (Colección General de divulgación)

Obra musical que incluye danza, bailes y canciones creadas como aporte al teatro para niños de la Universidad Cooperativa de Colombia. El tema traza una línea entre el mundo animal, lo mítico de un escarabajo de oro y la vida en una población costera en el Caribe colombiano. [PH]

2332 **Guebel, Daniel.** Pornografía sentimental. Buenos Aires: Interzona, 2015. 171 p. (Colección Zona de teatro)

Una obra dividida en cinco partes, o bien en cinco obras teatrales: "Matrimonio", "Divorcio", "Interludio romántico", "Reconciliación" y "Despedida". Como lo describe el mismo autor en el prefacio: "Puestas en escena, estas cinco piezas teatrales, unidas por los personajes y la cronología, configuran una pentalogía que puede leerse en sucesión o independientemente". Como describen los títulos, las obras exploran la intimidad de las relaciones de pareja de una manera cruda, directa y emotiva. [PH]

2333 **Hacia una dramaturgia nacional: cinco autores del Teatro Libre.** Compilación de Claudia Montilla y Ricardo Camacho. Bogotá: Facultad de Artes y Humanidades, Departamento de Humanidades y Literatura, Universidad de los Andes, 2013. 348 p.: bibl., ill.

El Taller de Dramaturgia de Teatro Libre celebra su 40o. aniversario con esta recopilación de obras de autores colombianos. Las obras aquí publicadas demuestran la variedad de la creación de este taller a través de los años. Ellas son: *Episodios comuneros* (1981) y *Un muro en el jardín* (1985) de Jorge Plata; *Sobre las arenas tristes* (1986) de Eduardo Camacho Guizado; *Algún día nos iremos* (2013) y *Gato por liebre* (1991) de Piedad Bonnett; *Los inquilinos de la ira* (1975) de Jairo Aníbal Niño; y *La agonía del difunto* (1977) de Esteban Navajas. [PH]

2334 **Huertas, Jorge.** Teatro reunido. Buenos Aires: Editorial Biblos, 2016. 316 p. (Teatro del siglo)

Trece obras de teatro demuestran la trayectoria de este reconocido dramaturgo, psicólogo, guionista de televisión y novelista. La variedad de las obras se encuentra tanto por sus fechas de escritura y estrenos (desde 1982 hasta 2010), hasta por los temas y conceptos que trata: la naturaleza del litoral argentino, los mitos perdidos, los grandes escritores argentinos, la memoria y la búsqueda de los nietos desaparecidos durante la última dictadura militar argentina. [PH]

2335 **León, Conchi.** Conchi León: dramaturga de la península. Compilación y prólogo de Enrique Mijares. Durango, Mexico: Siglo XXI: UJED: Espacio Vacío Editorial, 2013. 274 p. (Teatro de frontera; 29)

This work includes 10 of León's plays that reflect with humor and irony the speech and preoccupations of contemporary Yucatecans, such as prostitution, human trafficking, political corruption, immigration, and the patriarchal oppression of women. In her internationally renowned *Mestiza power* (2005), indigenous and mestiza women confront domestic violence, discrimination due to their economic status and ethnicity, exploitation by employers, and lack of access to education. *Las chancletas USA* focuses on family members who chose to stay in Mexico when their relatives immigrated to the US. In many of the plays included here, León interweaves the characters' daily lives with Maya traditions and explores female resistance to subjugation. [EMM]

2336 **Loza, Santiago.** Textos reunidos. Buenos Aires: Editorial Biblos, 2014. 271 p. (Colección Teatro del siglo)

Este excelente libro reúne 11 obras del consagrado dramaturgo Santiago Loza, entre ellas: *La vida terrenal, El mal de la montaña, Mau Mau o la tercera parte de la noche* y *Tu parte maldita*. El libro es acompañado por una introducción contundente de Jorge Dubatti en donde encuentra en sus textos teatrales "una definida personalidad, una poética identificable y de rasgos recurrentes". A la vez, el libro brinda una cronología de las obras, las puestas y la información sobre cada montaje. [PH]

2337 **Masís Olivas, Sergio.** El silencioso vuelo del búho. San José: Gráfica Litho Offset, 2015. 84 p.

Winner of a national prize in Costa Rica, this one-act psychological drama features three middle-aged characters who are hiding big secrets, one of which involves child euthanasia. Two of the characters are a married upper-middle-class couple who observe a unique tradition of inviting a different homeless person to Christmas dinner every year. In a plot twist, this year's male guest is not a stranger to one of the married couple. With characteristics of detective fiction, this work has many surprising revelations that are presented with dark humor and connected to contemporary social issues, two common elements in Masís' dramaturgy. [EMM]

2338 **Méndez Chinchilla, Melvin.** Ya lo pasado pasado: emergencia en el Castillo Azul. San José: SI Productores, 2014. 72 p. (Tinta en Serie. Dramaturgia costarricense contemporánea; 28)

These two one-act plays, which won a national prize in Costa Rica, are examples of Méndez's dramaturgy reflecting the speech and concerns of characters from lower social classes. Although the plays are connected by a newscast—the first play reporting an event from the second—each strongly denounces a different social issue. In the first work a father and son employed at a construction site disagree about complaining to their boss about unsafe working conditions. In the second play two shantytown residents make a living by claiming that one of them is a saint and selling miracles. Their actions threaten the financial status and authority of a corrupt Catholic priest and Protestant minister who order their murder. [EMM]

2339 **Miyashiro, Aldo.** La sangre del presidente. Lima: Titanium Editores, 2016. 112 p.

Obra que dirige su mirada a la política peruana contemporánea. Con un humor ácido, se retratan hombres y mujeres interesados en el poder. Con un lenguaje coloquial y hasta callejero, la obra denuncia de manera a veces sarcástica la situación política del Perú. [PH]

2340 **Modern, Rodolfo E.** Teatro completo. Vol. 6, La muerte y el pavo; Un entremés con caracú; Se busca trabajo; Consecuencias del chateo; El paraguas. Buenos Aires: Torres Agüero Editor: Editorial Nueva Generación: Prosa Amerian Editores, 2014. 1 v.

Cinco farsas cortas que combinan comedia y política a través de personajes vegetales, animales y de objetos. Para el comentario del vol. 2, ver *HLAS 60:4030*. [PH]

2341 **Nuevas dramaturgias argentinas: obras de autores nacidos entre 1981–1990.** Compilación de Ricardo Dubatti et al. Buenos Aires: EdiUNS, 2013. 180 p.

Dentro de los estudios del teatro argentino, Ricardo Dubatti sigue trazando un espacio para la publicación de obras teatrales de nuevos autores. De este modo, esta antología ofrece seis obras cortas para resaltar el valor del trabajo de estos jóvenes. Las obras son: *Piedra sentada, pata corrida* de Igancio Bartolone; *Niña con cara de jirafa* de Natalia Carmen Casielles; *Pollerapantalón* de Lucas Lagré; *Las casas íntimas* de Eugenia Pérez Tomas; *Potencialmente Haydée* de Patricio Ruiz, y *La fiera* de Mariano Tenconi Blanco. [PH]

2342 **Ovalle, Elizabeth.** Piezas por hora. Santo Domingo: Ministerio de Cultura, 2014. 310 p.

These 11 plays focus on the realities faced by urban and rural lower-class Dominican women living on the island and in New York. Ovalle's comedies, social realist pieces, and monologues reflect Dominican speech. *Por hora y a piece-work* and *Latinos*, which also includes Colombian, Venezuelan, Puerto Rican, and Cuban characters, offer negative views of migration. *Alerta roja* and *Vivencias campesinas* present the daily lives and traditions of women from rural areas on the island, one who has AIDS and another whose husband suffers from alcoholism. *A la espera* and *Contigo no*, set in urban areas on the island, address gender violence, with the first play denouncing human trafficking and the second domestic violence. [EMM]

2343 **Pérez, Roberto Alexander.** De mi placard: "triología de piezas teatrales sobre la diversidad, la identidad y la conciencia". San Juan: Instituto de Cultura Puertorriqueña, 2016. 235 p.: portrait.

The word *placard*, a closet, in the title and its association with the expression "coming out of the closet" allude to the sexualities that the characters conceal. *¡Habla, Marica!* is a comedy of errors set in Miami whose Cuban, Argentine, and Puerto Rican characters discover that two of them were romantically involved. In *Por culpa de Dios* a gay male couple deals with religious teachings about homosexuality. In *Noches de galería*, a group of people trapped in an art gallery express their normally hidden prejudices and desires. Pérez shows the social exclusion experienced by gays despite advances made in LGBT rights. [EMM]

2344 **Román, Alejandro.** Muerte de la virgen. Tamaulipas, Mexico: Gobierno del Estado: Instituto Tamaulipeco para la Cultura y las Artes, 2015. 83 p. (Colección Fortalezas)

Sharing the same title as the controversial Caravaggio painting of the Virgin Mary's death, this dramatic poem connects three female characters involved in murders and femicides across time and geographical space. Two of the women, a 17th-century courtesan who served as a model for the Italian artist and a young woman living in contemporary Mexico City, are victims killed by men who knew them intimately. The third woman from Ciudad Juárez, after being bullied at school, murders her adoptive parents. Clever references to music, art, clothing, and social media reinforce the connections between the characters and women in general, demonstrating their limited roles of being victims or victimizers. [EMM]

2345 **Rovner, Eduardo.** Teatro. Vol. 6, El hombre lobo; En tren de soñar; Los Velázquez; La sombra de Federico; Los peligros del turismo; Otras almas gemelas; Sueños de artistas. Buenos Aires: Ediciones de la Flor, 2014. 1 v.

Del reconocido y prolífico dramaturgo argentino, Eduardo Rovner, esta colección ofrece nuevas obras llenas del humor característico con la profunda inquisición en la mente y emociones humanas. En particular, *Otras almas gemelas* (nueva versión de su famosa obra *Compañía*) le propicia un espacio al género femenino no antes concebido. A la vez, *La sombra de Federico*, obra de base histórico del conocido poeta, dramaturgo y director Federico Lorca, expone el fracaso de la humanidad frente a la guerra. En *Los peligros del turismo*, Rovner se atreve a indagar el tema de la pobreza y de su objetivación como forma de nuevo turismo. Para el comentario del vol. 2, ver *HLAS 58:4255*. [PH]

2346 **Sáenz Andrade, Bruno.** Mitos, misterios. Quito: Casa de la Cultura Ecuatoriana Benjamín Carrión, 2015. 290 p. (Colección Tramoya de dramaturgia)

Una colección con varias obras inéditas que se enfocan en los clásicos mitos para abordar temas de las relaciones humanas, las dudas existenciales y la noción de muerte. Entre ellas se destacan *Dormición de Eurídice* y *Prometeo liberado* donde se expone un cierto lirismo poético, como también *La piedra de Cataluña*, donde a través de juegos teatrales se brinda una mirada paródica a la historia de Cataluña. [PH]

2347 **Silva Yrigoyen, Mariana.** Sobre lobos. Lima: Caja Negra, 2016. 116 p.

Con un enfoque en la psicología femenina de dos mujeres (una mujer de clase media y una vedette decadente) se exploran temas de vínculos emocionales y sinceros donde la violencia, la soledad y la marginalización llegan a ser centrales. [PH]

2348 **Suárez, Patricia.** De mujeres y de tragedias: textos dramáticos. Mendoza, Argentina: Jagüel Editores de Mendoza, 2016. 73 p.

Cuatro obras nuevas de la excelente dramaturga argentina que toma la imagen de la mujer de la Antigüedad Clásica. En este volumen, Suárez se remonta a mujeres como Helena de Esparta, Casandra de Troya, Fedra de Creta y Medea de Cólquita para contar sus historias de pasión, de guerra, de engaño, desde el ámbito contemporáneo. [PH]

2349 **Suárez, Patricia.** Teatro II: Marcela; El fruto; La vergüenza; La araña. Rosario, Argentina: Baltasara Editora, 2015. 262 p. (Teatro)

Este libro cuenta con cuatro obras que entablan un diálogo con temas de importancia como ser la violencia en el matrimonio y la familia, el antisemitismo y el aborto. En especial *La vergüenza* retoma el tema del médico nazi, Carl Vaernet, que se dedicó a experimentar en los campos de concentración con prisioneros homosexuales. Vaernet logró radicarse en Argentina donde instaló una clínica para "curas hormonales". [PH]

2350 **Urman, Andrea et al.** Futura: dramaturgias platenses. La Plata, Argentina: Malisia, 2014. 231 p.

Antología que reúne a seis autores de los últimos años, las cuales Dubatti determina como un "canon de la multiplicidad", donde se refiere a la variedad de temas y técnicas de cada una de estas obras. Los temas varían entre la memoria política, la prostitución, las dificultades de vivir dentro de la marginación económica, entre otros. Las obras son *La mujer que quería otra cosa* de Andra Urman; *Interferencia* de Alejandro D'Orto; *Tiempo despierto* de Diego Ferrando; *Cuero de chancho* de Patricia Ríos; y *Síndrome monoblock* de Ramiro Larrain. [PH]

2351 **Villarreal, Felipe.** Corruptocracia. Monterrey, Mexico: Universidad Autónoma de Nuevo León; Xalapa, Mexico: Universidad Veracruzana, 2017. 90 p. (Teatro)

This play critiques Mexican bureaucracy and political corruption as an engineer's bribery demand to grant permission for a well on communal lands is just one in a series of attempts to financially benefit from the decision. Following the petition as it moves from the state to the federal government, reaching the president, the play shows how even those with a certain level of power must submit to those occupying a higher political position. The stage directions, which suggest that the same actors play characters from different levels of political hierarchy, reinforce the unchanging nature of this unequal power dynamic. Villarreal includes an alternate ending, allowing the director or the audience to decide the president's fate. [EMM]

2352 **Vizcarra, Vanessa.** Ponemos tu obra en escena: 5to concurso de dramaturgia peruana 2014. Textos de Vanessa Vizcarra, Chiara Roggero y Federico Abrill. Lima: Asociación Cultural Peruano Británica, 2015. 221 p.

Las tres obras son las ganadoras de un concurso de dramaturgia que tuvo lugar en 2014. Dentro del jurado, la conocida dramaturga Mariana Althaus explica la fuerza de la obra ganadora: *Una historia original* ya que es sencilla, compleja y bella, que abre miles de posibilidades en escena sobre un cuento infantil que termina siendo una hermosa pesadilla. *Huracán*, la segunda obra, trata sobre un triángulo amoroso de unas personas que se encuentran en un departamento en Nueva York, atrapados mientras pasa huracán Sandy (2012). La tercera obra,

El año que perdí la fantasía, trata sobre el mundo imaginado de una niña que sueña con ganarse un viaje en medio de una crisis familiar. [PH]

2353 **Wilcock, Juan Rodolfo.** Teatro inédito. Estudio preliminar de Carina González. Buenos Aires: Ediciones Biblioteca Nacional, 2015. 140 p. (Colección Los raros; 50)

Quizás una mejor descripción de este libro sea entender el propósito de la colección Los Raros, donde explican que "se propone interrogar los libros clásicos argentinos que han corrido la suerte de la lenta omisión que traen el tiempo y el olvido de los hombres." El propósito de este libro es dar a conocer dos obras inéditas en español, olvidadas por el campo. Las dos obras originalmente publicadas en italiano en 1962 y 1982, respectivamente, *Dido* y *Elisabetta y Limón*, son contextualizadas por un excelente estudio preliminar donde permite al lector entender la vida y obra de Wilcock dentro y fuera de sus relaciones con escritores como Jorge Luis Borges y Silvina Ocampo. Más reconocido como narrador que como dramaturgo, este libro reconoce el valor de dos de sus obras inéditas en español: *Dido*, donde los intereses poéticos de los mitos clásicos prevalentes en el trabajo de Wilcock se repiten en las tablas, donde mundos fantasmagóricos aluden a la ficción del teatro y donde se percibe un interés por las técnicas brechtianas. El segundo texto, *Elisabetta y Limón*, es una obra más absurdista, donde la profanación de los rituales y la transgresión del luto encierran a los personajes en un mundo en ruinas. [PH]

THEATER CRITICISM AND HISTORY

2354 **Arroyo de Jesús, Frances.** Ángeles cuarteados: alegoría del prostíbulo en el teatro puertorriqueño. San Juan: Editorial Isla Negra, 2014. 241 p.: bibl., ill. (Colección visiones y cegueras)

This work examines how the brothel functions as an allegory of the Puerto Rican nation in four plays: Luis Rafael Sánchez's *Los ángeles se han fatigado* (1961), Myrna Casas' *Cristal roto en el tiempo* (1960), Juan González-Bonilla's *Palomas de la noche* (1992), and Roberto Ramos-Perea's *Miénteme más* (1992). This intriguing study situates its analysis in the context of the global origins of prostitution and historical studies about prostitution in Puerto Rico. The prostitutes in these plays, like the island they inhabit, are used by occupying forces with the complicity of some Puerto Ricans. In some works, the decadence of the brothel-nation is apparent, while in others the female characters assert power. [EMM]

Cid Pérez, José. Teatro selecto. See item **2317**.

2355 **Cosentino, Olga.** Mi patria es el escenario: biografía a dos voces de Juan Carlos Gené. Prólogo de Pablo Zunino. Buenos Aires: Corregidor, 2015. 205 p.: ill.

Si existen iconos del teatro argentino, Juan Carlos Gené es uno de ellos. Autor, director, traductor, guionista y gran actor, Gené es un hombre que dejó su impronta en las tablas del teatro latinoamericano. Como intelectual del teatro también llevó su arte al cine y a la televisión, promulgando programas de mejor calidad. Este libro recoge minuciosamente vida y obra de Juan Carlos Gené, enfocándose en las influencias de su arte en el teatro argentino, haciendo hincapié en el conocido grupo el Clú del Clown. Acompañado de fotos, entrevistas y una cronología, la vida del excepcional Gené se hace presente. [PH]

2356 **Fos, Carlos.** El viejo Municipal: el sistema de producción pública y su relación con el teatro independiente. Compilación y edición de Laura Rauch sobre textos de Carlos Fos. Buenos Aires: Editorial Nueva Generación, 2014. 262 p.: bibl., ill. (Colección Patrimonio histórico teatral argentino)

Un estudio minucioso sobre la historia del teatro argentino en torno a la construcción de espacios teatrales, en especial la historia del Viejo Municipal inaugurado en 1944, pasando por su relación con el Teatro del Pueblo que ocupó la sala que hoy le pertenece al Teatro Municipal. Además del enfoque sobre los edificios que sirvieron como teatros, los estudios de Carlos Fos brindan una narrativa histórica sobre el nacimiento y crecimiento del teatro independiente desde los años 30. [PH]

2357 **Fumero Vargas, Patricia.** El teatro de la Universidad de Costa Rica (1950–2012). San José: EUNED, Editorial Universidad Estatal a Distancia, 2017. 330 p.: bibl., ill. (Colección Historia cultural de Costa Rica; 17)

This book traces the history of theater at the Universidad de Costa Rica and its Teatro Universitario, showing its social impact as part of the university authorities' cultural policies to promote modernization and educate Costa Ricans. Fumero critically examines how the Teatro Universitario, rather than being an experimental venue to train students, has instead been controlled by small groups of theater professionals who also worked on independent productions in San José. This well-researched study provides information about public and private sector productions, making it an essential resource about Costa Rican theater in general. [EMM]

2358 Maldonado Toral, Consuelo. El grupo de teatro Malayerba y la poética de la diferencia. Quito: Fondo Editorial, Ministerio de Cultura y Patrimonio, 2013. 203 p.: bibl., ill.

El famoso y relevante grupo, Malayerba, concebido en el año 1979 bajo el trabajo colectivo liderado por tres artistas exiliados: María del Rosario Francés (Charo), Susana Pautasso y Arístides Vargas, es el protagonista de este libro. Con cuidadosa investigación histórica teatral, Maldonado compone las influencias tanto europeas como latinoamericanas que llevaron a que este grupo se convirtiera en uno de los ejes de la creación colectiva. A la vez, recrea una cronología necesaria del trabajo de dirección y escenificación del grupo, creando así un camino más abierto para mayores investigaciones académicas. [PH]

2359 Moreno, Iani del Rosario. Theatre of the borderlands: conflict, violence, and healing. Lanham, Md.: Lexington Books, 2015. 289 p.: bibl., index.

This study examines theater written and produced during the late 20th and early 21st centuries in the US-Mexican borderlands. It introduces key playwrights in this region such as Jorge Celaya, Virginia Hernández, Enrique Mijares, Víctor Hugo Rascón Banda, and Hugo Salcedo, and analyzes more than 30 of their works. Moreno provides a detailed overview of the history of the borderlands, focusing on its geography, economy, and culture as she explores how this theater addresses the identities of indigenous people, border crossings, heroes and folk saints, the cities of Tijuana and Juárez, femicides, and the violence associated with drug trafficking. [EMM]

BRAZIL
Novels

REGINA IGEL, *Professor of Spanish and Portuguese, University of Maryland, College Park*

THREE RECENT deeply researched studies will certainly become valuable sources of scholarly information: *Angústia* (item **2377**), an anthology of reviews about the first edition of the homonymous novel by Graciliano Ramos; *Érico Veríssimo, escritor do mundo* (item **2372**), by Carlos Cortez Minchillo, presents Veríssimo as a writer who incorporated topics and developed characters beyond the country's geographic frontiers during a time when Modernist authors were focusing almost exclusively on national themes; and *Clarice Lispector pintora: uma biopictografia* (item **2362**), by Marcos Antônio Bessa-Oliveira, who may have coined the word "biopictografia" for his comparative study about the author of *Água viva*, her literary life, and her painting. Marina Ruivo (item **2378**) studies two novels—one by Brazilian Carlos Eugênio Paz and the other by Angolan Pepetela—both of which fictionalize dire political upheaval and guerilla movements in their respective countries.

Detective novels, which were scarce for many years in the corpus of Brazilian literature, are starting to find a niche, as the following three narratives demonstrate: *Um lugar perigoso* (item **2365**), in which Investigator Espinosa, created by L.A. Garcia–Roza, attempts to figure out whether or not a crime took place; *Bellini e o labirinto* (item **2361**) is set in the state of Goiás, where Mr. Bellini, the investigator created by Tony Bellotto, goes to examine a radiological incident with Caesium-137; and *Alice: não mais que de repente* (item **2370**) by Bernardo Kucinski, a whodunit set at the Universidade de São Paulo, focusing on the poisoning of a female scientist and the efforts of two amateur investigators (a retired professor and a graduate student) to find the murderers. Though not a detective novel, Isabela Noronha's *Resta um* (item **2375**), is a mystery involving the vanishing of a teenager. It focuses on the mother's feelings as she tries to analyze her own crumbling life in the aftermath of the disappearance with the help of a sagacious neighbor.

Some novels are concerned with social issues, such as *Uma ladeira para lugar nenhum* (item **2363**), by Marco Carvalho, which follows a romantic relationship between a Catholic priest and an Afro-Brazilian woman while a mountain community of black citizens is being demolished in 1920s Rio de Janeiro. The gentrification of an area of Rio de Janeiro is addressed in *A casa cai* (item **2360**), by Marcelo Backes, as a former seminarian confronts the changes occurring in the city. The novel collects observations by a man who was going to be a priest until receiving his father's inheritance. He criticizes the local society made up of the "nouveau riche," which he escapes by traveling abroad and visiting museums and other cultural centers. The novel *A vida não tem cura* (item **2373**), by Marcelo Mirisola, presents a caustic picture of Brazilian urban society of the 1970–80s as a man and a woman pursue the meaning of their lives through orgies, exchange of raw language, etc., only to have one of them express a desire for atonement years later. The novel *CBA, Companhia Brasileira de Alquimia* (item **2367**), by Manoel Herzog, takes an ecological approach in its description of the deadly environment of a chemistry plant located in the city of Cubatão, São Paulo, where workers fight for clean air and struggle with horrific working conditions. The novel *Os ventos gemedores* (item **2371**), by Cyro de Mattos, takes place in Brazil's rural region. Mattos describes the ongoing struggles between cacao owners and their employees. The novel is one of the few dedicated to the country's backlands, since the majority are set in urban areas.

European territories make an appearance in a number of novels. *F* (item **2381**), by Antônio Xerxenesky, may attract movie buffs in particular, since the plot includes plans developed in Paris to have a Brazilian hit-woman kill Orson Welles and sprinkles in detailed analyses of some of his movies. In *O romance inacabado de Sofia Stern* (item **2380**), by Ronaldo Wrobel, we are introduced to a German grandmother who settled in Rio de Janeiro. Accompanied by her grandson, she traces her former life in a journey to Germany. That same country is a refuge of sorts for an anti-social Brazilian recluse from Santa Catarina who lives in Berlin (item **2379**).

Another work on seclusion is *Não tive nenhum prazer em conhecê-los* (item **2364**), by Evandro Affonso Ferreira, about a 90-year old writer who finds no pleasure in his life. Personal isolation also plays a part in *Matusalém de flores* (item **2374**), by Carlos Nejar, in which the protagonist has the company of his dog, at least, while his stream of thoughts on literature flows. Another novel related to solitude is *O amor dos homens avulsos* (item **2366**), by Victor Heringer, who died prematurely in 2018. The protagonist, Camilo, remembers the love he felt for Cosme, whom his father brought to their home when the boys were adolescents; a profound affection tied them together until Cosme's tragic death, as recalled by Camilo 30 years later.

The bounty of novels in the past few years, as selectively shown in this section, is eclectic in topic, ranging from solitude and individual conflicts to rebellion, alternating between national and international settings, revealing a dimension in diverse and pluralistic themes.

This is my final *HLAS* section on Brazilian novels after more than three decades as a Contributing Editor. These years have been a blessing, a privilege, and an honor for me, especially since, with each batch of books, I have been introduced to wonderful Brazilian novels. I share my profound gratitude for the late Dolores Martin, who invited me to be part of this outstanding group of editors, for the late professor Alexandre Severino, who preceded and recommended me for this task, and for the excellent staff of the Hispanic Division of the Library of Congress, always extremely dedicated to *HLAS*. All the best to the incoming Contributing Editor to whom I wish the same joys that I have experienced in reviewing novels.

2360 Backes, Marcelo. A casa cai: romance. São Paulo: Companhia das Letras, 2014. 425 p.

A former seminarian leaves his protective environment to start a new life when his father dies, leaving him a significant inheritance. Far away from his theology studies, the man observes the tumultuous and rapid gentrification of the "Zona Sul" (Southern district) of Rio de Janeiro, which he joins, unwilling or unable to find any other occupation. He the joins the world of the wealthy, sometimes partaking of it, while other times avoiding their idleness and futil escapes. He travels and visits museums and other cultural centers abroad, offering detailed reflections on the arts, artists, paintings, architecture, and many other matters involved with creativity. The novel becomes a repository of erudite explanations.

2361 Bellotto, Tony. Bellini e o labirinto. São Paulo: Companhia das Letras, 2014. 274 p.

This detective novel places investigator Bellini in Goiânia, where he will try to help a duo of singers, interestingly named Maron and Brandão. One of them was kidnapped and Bellini's job is to negotiate for his client's safety. As the author is a guitarist and composer, the narrative is much at home in the realm of these musicians. The detective is helped by Dora Lobo, chief and owner of a detective agency, and Gisela, his assistant in technology. These characters recur in Bellotto's novels. This time, the detective deals with the aftereffects of Caesium-137, the culprit of an accidental radioactive contamination in the same city of Goiânia in 1987.

2362 Bessa-Oliveira, Marcos Antônio. Clarice Lispector pintora: uma biopictografia. São Paulo: Intermeios Casa de Artes e Livros, 2013. 313 p.: bibl., ill.

The text is a witness to the specialization of the author, who holds a PhD in visual arts and is a university professor of drama and dance in Mato Grosso do Sul, Brazil. The volume presents an analysis of Clarice Lispector as an amateur painter, and examines the values she adopted as an artist/craftperson on canvas and in her literary work. The author asks whether or not there is a dialogue between Lispector's literary pages and her paintings. The critic presents the novel *Água viva* (see *HLAS* 38:7319 for the original and *HLAS* 68:2690 for the English translation) as the point of reference for the in-depth examination of Lispector's abilities as painter and writer, honoring her as a mortal being who has never died.

2363 Carvalho, Marco. Uma ladeira para lugar nenhum. Rio de Janeiro: Editora Record, 2014. 159 p.

Using straightforward language, almost devoid of qualifiers or other literary devices, the author brings poetic lyricism to the text along with the presence and words of an Afro-Brazilian woman, trapped in an unhappy marriage with a Portuguese man. She becomes involved with a Catholic priest and their impossible love story is interlocked with the removal of a mountain ("Morro do Castelo") in Rio de Janeiro in the 1920s. The mountain was destroyed to get rid of its dwellers, mostly destitute black people. This urban novel discloses the history of Rio from the times of the French invasion during the colonial period to the end of an era, as symbolized by the flattened mountain. Racial apartheid is also evident in this narrative. The protagonist, the son of the priest and the Afro-Brazilian woman, is forbidden from participating in a public event because of his skin color. The episode is a reference to a real event when black boys were forbidden from appearing in a choir during a visit of the Belgian king to Brazil. The author fictionalizes an old prejudice that lingers today. The novel reveals the brutality of city bureaucrats, who, in their intense desire to "beautify" the city, neglected and rejected a sizeable number of its citizens due to their skin color and social status.

2364 Ferreira, Evandro Affonso. Não tive nenhum prazer em conhecê-los. Rio de Janeiro: Editora Record, 2016. 367 p.

The author qualifies his book as a "mosaic novel." Indeed, it is comprised of hundreds of aphorisms, mostly in relation to death, stated by a 90-year-old writer. The nonlinear narrative, with short and reflective paragraphs, includes sentences by other authors and philosophers. With the voice of Billie Holiday providing a background, Ferreira exposes his thoughts about irony, noir humor, and sadness, all with an element of self-deprecation. His bitter taste for life at his old age may be summarized in one of his paragraphs: "Life is a garment that doesn't fit me well" (Vida é uma vestimenta que não me cai bem). With a hint of love, though, he remembers a woman who might have been part of his existence, the one "who will never return." With a sour taste in the selection of words, proverbs, and advice, the book is a portrait of someone who didn't revel in meeting humankind.

2365 García-Roza, Luiz Alfredo. Um lugar perigoso. Rio de Janeiro: Companhia das Letras, 2014. 262 p.

In this detective novel, Sheriff Espinosa tries to unravel clues which may (or may not) add up to a crime committed years ago. A retired university professor discovers among his old papers a page with 10 women's names written on it. One of the names is circled in ink: Fabiana. Suffering from Korsakoff syndrome, whose symptoms include forgetting recent and past activities, the professor imagines that perhaps he committed a crime against the women on the list or that he killed Fabiana. He doesn't remember any of these occurrences, the women, nor when he wrote their names. He seeks out Espinosa to solve the mystery. The detective is a recurring character in the author's many mystery novels. In this narrative, the search is not for a criminal, but for a crime.

2366 Heringer, Victor. O amor dos homens avulsos. São Paulo: Companhia das Letras, 2016. 155 p.: ill.

The author, who died at a young age (1988–2018), leaves an original literary legacy. His novel *Glória* received the Jabuti prize in 2013, and *O amor dos homens avulsos* was among the finalists in literary contests in Rio de Janeiro, São Paulo, and Portugal. This novel shares the memories of Camilo, a man who reminisces about his father, a medical doctor, who one day abruptly brings home Cosme, a boy a little younger than his own son, when both were adolescents. The boys develop a strong affection for one another, unfortunately cut short by Cosme's tragic death at a young age. That incident, which took place in Rio de Janeiro in the 70s, changed the life of Camilo who, 30 years later, remembers the reciprocal love he and Cosme had the brutality of life, he also recalls how sweet and tender it was to experience the love with Cosme, especially in the acts of giving and receiving. The novel is about the incongruities of life, as observed by the protagonist, in a rhythm that goes from fantasy to harsh descriptions, from poetry to realistic features. The text is enhanced by pictures, drawings, doodles, and sketches by the author.

2367 Herzog, Manoel. CBA, Companhia Brasileira de Alquimia. São Paulo: Editora Patuá, 2013. 423 p.

Awarded the 2012 Facult Prize in the city of Santos, this novel was a semifinalist for the 2014 Telecom Portugal Prize. The narrative is set in a chemical plant located in the industrial park in Cubatão, São Paulo, the author's hometown. Unrestrained irony and a scatological vocabulary appear in the narrator's depiction of life among the factory workers. Nicknamed "Poeta," the narrator debunks the capitalist regime and outlines the workers' pleas, which management summarily ignores. Coincidently, the factory was founded on 31 March, the same day the military regime took power in Brazil in 1964 and, in some ways, the narrative reflects the generals' utopian dreams for a better life in Brazil. The workers endure the worst possible conditions at their production site, in spite of their bosses' promises for improvements. The "Poet" describes the industrial unit as a place where nobody is a comrade or a friend, where each worker can attain a high position in the plant—by reputable means or otherwise. He also dreams of becoming a writer himself, demonstrating his knowledge of national icons of Brazilian and Portuguese literature (such as Machado de Assis and Fernando Pessoa). In his writing that became this novel, he recreates foreign words, giving them a phonetic spelling, and incorporates a coarse and rude vocabulary that he intends to be jargon typical of the workers' class.

2368 Izhaki, Flávio. Tentativas de capturar o ar. Rio de Janeiro: Rocco, 2016. 223 p.

The author applies the literary device of writing about a deceased person who did not leave behind any information about his life. In this case, the story is about a novelist who has passed away. Izhaki bases the story on discussions with the writer's son, interviews with his editor, and conversations with people who were his friends, in spite of his antisocial behavior and his selective choice of confidants. A letter he left for his son is a key element of the book's narrative. The novel's metaphorical title refers to the biographer's attempt to retain the essence of the art of writing, according to the late writer Antonio Rascal. Episodes related to that writer, his heir, and his biographer come together, resulting in a delicate pattern of multiple voices around one motif.

2369 Kirst, Marcos Fernando. A sombra de Clara. Porto Alegre, Brazil: Editora da Cidade, 2015. 160 p.

A journalist in Rio Grande do Sul state, Kirst is a daily newspaper columnist and the author of 16 books, including two novels, a children's book, and one of poems. *A sombra de Clara* won the Prêmio Açorianos for Long Narratives. It is an intriguing and admirable novel, which combines elements of a literary work with those of mystery fiction. Its narrator, Clara, is a journalist who has lost her job and whose family lives faraway. She has also broken up with boyfriend, César, and become acquainted with Tinho, a painter. Since her salary is gone, she poses for a fee. Tinho then recommends her to one of his male students, young Stefan, for whom she poses naked. Although female, she writes several times that she is not a woman. She explains that she has had previous lives and also will have future lives—as she is falling from the 10th floor of a building. By then the reader knows that she has murdered her old neighbor, Mrs. Morgana, as well as César and Stefan, and that Tinho has thrown her from the top of his building. She thinks she is a falling female angel with wings. [M.A. Guimarães Lopes]

2370 Kucinski, Bernardo. Alice: não mais que de repente. Rio de Janeiro: Editora Rocco LTDA., 2014. 189 p.

This detective novel addresses the sudden death of a scientist, a descendant of Japanese immigrants, at the Universidade de São Paulo where she worked as researcher. A chocolate lover, she was poisoned when she ate a piece of the candy. Set in the present, the narrative and dialogue expose a toxic atmosphere in academia that is filled with jealousy, anger, envy, treason, accusations of plagiarism, mistrust, and bullying, among other unpleasantness. Several renowned past professors in the departments of math and physics at that university are depicted in the text, although they are disguised as characters with different names. These characters try to help solve the crime puzzle. The discovery of the culprit startles the university.

2371 **Mattos, Cyro de.** Os ventos gemedores. Taubaté, Brazil: LetraSelvagem, 2014. 207 p. (Coleção Gente Pobre; 9)

The multiple award-winning author, lawyer, poet, journalist, and member of the Academia de Letras da Bahia introduces 12 parts in this novel, each with two to eight chapters. Set on a cacao plantation in the south of Bahia, the novel portrays the struggles of destitute people, half-slaves and half-employees of a despotic and cruel landowner. The narrative revolves around "colonels" (masters) and "jagunços" (gunmen), the latter led by Genaro, a man forced to become a warrior motivated by the insidious and sinister activities of local bosses. Some of the characters' names send a cryptic message, such as Vulcano Bras, which may be interpreted as a Brazilian volcano that is still roaring in that same area where other smaller "volcanos" are also spitting their justified anger against their merciless chiefs.

Merced Hernández, Grisselle. Cartas viajeras: Julia de Burgos, Clarice Lispector: versiones de sí mismas. See item **1935**.

2372 **Minchillo, Carlos Cortez.** Erico Veríssimo, escritor do mundo: circulação literária, cosmopolitismo e relações interamericanas. São Paulo: EDUSP, 2015. 314 p.: bibl.

Awarded the 2018 Casa de las Américas Prize, this sweeping study focuses on Veríssimo, the author of *Música ao longe* (see *HLAS 01:2224*) and 11 other novels, 12 books for children, four travel narratives, three books on Brazilian literature, and numerous articles for newspapers, magazines, and anthologies. According to Minchillo, this book-length essay in the field of cultural studies is the result of a convergence of intellectual history, an analysis of Veríssimo's critical practices, and a literary scrutiny of a selection of his works. He examines this "gaúcho" as a cosmopolitan and humanist author who geared his novels toward an international audience at a time when Brazilian writers were adamantly concentrating on their own country, all but neglecting the rest of the world. Starting in the second decade of the 20th century, Brazilian modernism emerged; the country's different regions and the diversity of their peoples, who had seldom been topics of a "truly Brazilian literature," began to stimulate writers. Veríssimo observed this trend, but also infused his narratives with universal conflicts and drama, as in the three novels addressed here: *Saga*, (see *HLAS 06:4388*), *O senhor embaixador*, and *O prisioneiro* (see *HLAS 30:4121*), in which foreign characters living in other countries filled his imaginative worlds. The book has four parts, a section on "Considerações finais," and an abundant bibliography.

2373 **Mirisola, Marcelo.** A vida não tem cura. São Paulo: Editora 34, 2016. 85 p.

This novel takes a cynical look at part of Brazilian urban society in the 1970–80s. Through such an approach, Mirisola introduces an allegorical portrayal of the union between Luis and Natacha, based on the purest love, affinities, and common dreams. They completed each other from the time she became a refined sadistic woman and he, a humiliated masochist, more a work-in-progress than a man. Both were involved in sexual orgies with others until the bubble exploded. The novel's style follows other publications by the author: the fast-paced plot includes raw scenarios of sexual perversions. The author offers a bit of an interlude through the love that the couple expresses towards their daughter, Clara. In an ironic twist, the protagonist seeks out one of the new religions or sects that settled in Brazil, trying to redeem himself of his sins.

2374 **Nejar, Carlos.** Matusalém de flores. São Paulo: Boitempo Editorial, 2014. 212 p.: ill.

The main characters of this allegorical novel are Matusalém and his beloved dog, Crisóstomo; they represent the eternal nature of literature via their spoken and unspoken interpretations of the world. According to the narrator (and by inference, to the author), fidelity, affection, loyalty, and other similar qualities are inherent to words and literature, as personified by Matusalém and the dog, who are compared to Quijote and his faithful right-hand Sancho (with the exception that Matusalém married, while Quijote did not). The narrative embodies biblical passages, and reverberates with extracts from works by iconic Brazilian and foreign writers, among other literary devices, such as legends and myths that are esthetically entangled in the sequence of events that Matusalém and his canine companion witness. The style is reminiscent of chivalry novels, poetry, and medieval *romanceros*. The author, a member of the Academia Brasileira de Letras, is also a translator and renowned poet.

2375 **Noronha, Isabela.** Resta um. São Paulo: Companhia das Letras, 2015. 301 p.

The plot involves the mysterious disappearance of Amelia, the teenage daughter of Jose and Lucia, while returning home from a party at a nearby house. The novel is set in São Paulo, where the mother is a math professor who wants life to be as clear and straightforward as a mathematical equation. The vanishing of her daughter creates mental chaos for her, dissolving all of the certainties she understood in life. Feeling guilty about how she raised her daughter, she shares her frustration, sadness, and impotence with a neighbor. The neighbor writes a sort of a diary about the challenging circumstances that Lucia—a mathematician whose marriage fell apart because of the tragic and unsolved loss of her child—faces. The mother experiences the full gamut of emotions. The elements of suspense, apprehension, tension, and anxiety place the narrative in the category of a mystery novel.

2376 **Peres, Ana Maria Clark.** Chico Buarque: recortes e passagens. Belo Horizonte: Editora UFMG, 2016. 234 p.: bibl. (Coleção Babel)

A scholarly and lively set of essays about the composer Francisco Buarque de Holanda, better known as Chico Buarque. These excellent essays provide a biography of sorts of a key figure in 20th-century Brazilian culture, examining his music, writing, involvement in Brazilian politics, and keen interest in soccer. Clark Peres provides biographical information, connecting it to Buarque's work. Chico Buarque started composing and writing songs at 21, but only in his early 50s did he write his five novels. Having studied the language since his childhood, he was influenced by French literature, as well as philosophy, linguistics, and other fields. His love of soccer, Brazil's national sport, is an important part of his personality. The work includes a conversation between Clark Peres and Chico Buarque. [M.A. Guimarães Lopes]

2377 **Ramos, Graciliano.** Angústia. Organização de Elizabeth Ramos. Edição comemorativa 75 anos. Rio de Janeiro: Editora Record, 2013. 382 p.

This dense volume gathers a collection of reviews published throughout Brazil at different times in celebration of the first edition of *Angústia* (1936; see HLAS 02:2942) by Graciliano Ramos (1892–1953). The novel's 4th edition, with the author's most up-to-date corrections, is reprinted in the book along with articles by such literary celebrities as Rachel de Queiroz, Ledo Ivo, Edison Carneiro, Dalcídio Jurandir, and Jorge Amado, among others. Otto Maria Carpeaux and Silviano Santiago penned post-scriptum notes. These scholars, like the book reviewers, point out the importance of the novel *Angústia* and its influence in the realm of psychological Brazilian fiction—despite being both realistic and lyrical, as projected by the reflections of Luís da Silva, the protagonist.

2378 **Ruivo, Marina.** Geração armada: literatura e resistência em Angola e no Brasil. São Paulo: Alameda, 2015. 291 p.: bibl.

This volume presents a comparative study of two writers and their works: *Viagem à luta armada* by Brazilian Carlos Eugênio Paz and *A geração da utopia* by Angolan Pepetela. While the former comprises fiction and historical facts, the latter deals with the disillusion that most Angolans felt after independence, mainly in the second half of the 20th century. Both authors were part of the guerrilla movements in their respective countries, although they followed different strategies. According to the scholar Marina Ruivo, their novels can be read as literary and artistic constructions as well as eyewitness and participant accounts of the conflicts in Angola and Brazil.

2379 Tiburi, Marcia. Uma fuga perfeita é sem volta. Rio de Janeiro: Editora Record, 2016. 601 p.

A prolific writer, philosophy professor, and active participant in Brazilian politics over the past 10 years, the novelist sends Klaus, the protagonist, to tell his story in *Uma fuga perfeita é sem volta*. The man, a Brazilian, returns to his hometown of Florianópolis, which he left some 40 years ago when he relocated to Berlin to start a new life. He remained in contact with his family (father and sister) through one phone call a year. Nobody asked him to return home for a visit, and he never invited anyone to his home in Germany, his father's birthplace. Klaus had difficulty speaking modern German because he grew up speaking a dialect typical of immigrants in the south of Brazil. Therefore, his verbal communication was mostly a failure. Moreover, he was a stutterer, causing him to withdraw from social interaction, except for his friendship with a blind man and a telephone operator, both colleagues in the museum where Klaus worked in the cloakroom. He did not like jokes; he was self-conscious because he was unable to understand them; and he had a hard time smiling. The author examines this secluded and private person through his personal problems and through his strong feelings that he had not escaped his family and country. After hearing of his father's death three months after it happened (through the phone call that opens the novel), he decides to write a letter to his sister, and this novel is the resultant letter.

2380 Wrobel, Ronaldo. O romance inacabado de Sofia Stern. Rio de Janeiro: Editora Record, 2016. 255 p.

Sofia Stern was born in Germany during the Holocaust and relocated with her family to Brazil at a young age. With this book, her grandson Ronaldo enters her life both through research and through her own fragmented memories and stories. Stern escaped fascist Germany after receiving a visa from Aracy de Carvalho Guimarães Rosa—wife of intellectual and diplomat João Guimarães Rosa—who worked at the Brazilian Consulate in Hamburg. (Aracy de Carvalho helped many Jews emigrate and was later awarded the title Righteous Among the Nations by Israel for her humanitarian efforts during WWII.) After living in Rio de Janeiro for many years, Sofia Stern receives a phone call from Germany, which her grandson Ronaldo answers. The caller explains that a judicial process in Germany may result in the family receiving a huge sum of money. Ronaldo travels to Germany to learn more about his grandmother, who is now suffering from dementia. The narrative, mostly in the first person, is a mix of thriller and auto-fiction. Once the young man and his grandmother reach Europe, inconsistencies present challenges to her long-told stories. Some of the narrative twists may startle readers.

2381 Xerxenesky, Antônio. F. Rio de Janeiro: Rocco, 2014. 239 p.

The title of this novel, *F*, is so well disguised on the cover and on the first page that few readers will be able to see it. "F" refers to Orson Welles' movie *F for Fake* (*Verdades e Mentiras*) and is a tribute to the late American film director. *Citizen Kane* and *The Third Man*, other Welles movies, are also part of the plot. An obscure group invites a 25-year-old Brazilian woman to kill Welles because of her past as a guerrilla warrior. To learn more about her target, she flies to Paris, where she screens several movies (mainly the three mentioned above). There, she receives instructions about the crime she is to commit. Paris in the 80s is the setting for episodes that are relayed like scenes of a movie, given the electrifying cast of people planning a murder. The novel will interest cinephiles, not only because it analyzes films in minutia, but also because the actions of the characters who meet the hypothetical hit-woman provide a kinetic structure to the narrative. The author warns his readers that if they intend to watch these movies, they should close the book immediately to avoid spoilers.

Short Stories

M. ANGÉLICA GUIMARÃES LOPES, *Professor Emerita of Literature, University of South Carolina, Columbia*

THE SHORT STORY CONTINUES to thrive in Brazil. Younger authors are often more daring than their predecessors in their choices of subject and language. There is no censorship in either, which may surprise and even shock readers. The stories reviewed for this *HLAS 74* are all worth reading for their competence and the wide variety of approaches and styles. Some of the writers experiment with the notion of fiction, including text in various formats and genres.

2382 **Andrioli, Luiz.** O laçador de cães. São Paulo: Grua, 2012. 109 p.

Andrioli's debut fiction collection includes "Um abraço" (A hug) which received a prize in the 2011 Miguel Sanches Neto National Short Story Contest in the author's home state of Paraná, where all these stories are set. The characters are generally socially marginalized and deal with authorities such as policemen and reporters, who are often unjust. However, a few of the characters show kindness, such as the hunter in the title story who spares very young and older dogs or the older reporter who dresses as Santa Claus at Christmas giving presents to children in the slums. Notwithstanding the realism of the characters and their attitudes, several stories offer meaningful surprises.

2383 **Bon, Henrique.** A última vez que vi meu pai. Rio de Janeiro: Vermelho Marinho, 2016. 185 p.

This impressive collection includes stories that are geographically and historically varied, set in France, Paraguay, Chile, and Argentina in different eras. As a literary work it honors major writers such as Borges and Guimarães Rosa. Some of the stories have an autobiographical quality as they feature French immigrants, like the author's grandfather, in Rio de Janeiro state, as well as in other countries. The stories are psychologically clear and very well written by a physician who is also a psychiatrist. His settings are as expressive as his characters and plots. Bon won the Paulo Setúbal Prize for short stories in 2010 and the Festival de Música e Poesia de Paranavaí (FEMUP) prize in 2012 and 2013.

2384 **Braga, Roberto Saturnino.** Ela e as vitrines do Rio. Rio de Janeiro: Editora Record, 2016. 159 p.

Excellent and varied collection named for Rio de Janeiro's shop windows (*vitrinas*) focuses on the daily emotions common to most of us, such as love, curiosity, jealousy, surprise, and wonder. Varied characters are shown in numerous situations: fighting schoolboys, philosophical candyseller, swimming teacher, and dying friend. Roberto Saturnino Braga has lived in the city of Rio de Janeiro for more than 80 years and knows it well. His knowledge extends to a public life of almost 50 years as mayor, city councilmember, and senator for the state of Rio de Janeiro.

2385 Brito, Ronaldo Correia de. O amor das sombras. Rio de Janeiro: Alfaguara, 2015. 219 p.

A somber collection offers excellent complex stories revealing a world of shadows and mystery in families and between friends, acquaintances, and even strangers. Literature has an important role in the stories: characters quote Shakespeare, Lope de Vega, Quevedo, Octavio Paz, and other writers. The author's experience is impressive. A medical doctor he was a writer-in-residence at the University of California, Berkeley in 2017. He is the author of children's fiction, plays, newspaper columns, short stories, and novels. His novel *Galateia* won the São Paulo Literary Prize and was translated into Spanish, French, Italian, and Hebrew. Stories take place in England, North African countries, and Brazil. They deal with children, some of whom are Jewish or Near Eastern immigrants to Brazil, and all of whom are in difficult situations.

2386 Cabral, Astrid. Alameda: contos. Presentação de Leyla Leong. Estudo crítico por Antônio Paulo Graça. 3a edição. Rio de Janeiro: Ibis Libris, 2014. 99 p.

The poet, professor, and diplomat Astrid Cabral first published *Alameda* in 1963 in Amazonas state, but notwithstanding recognition and praise from eminent writers such as Carlos Drummond de Andrade, Fausto Cunha, and Octávio de Faria, the collection did not receive much public appreciation until many years later. *Alameda* is an admirable, elegant original collection in which characters are plants: flowers, trees, fruits that think and live very much like human beings with birth, life, and death.

2387 Cafiero, Flavio. Dez centímetros acima do chão. São Paulo: Cosac Naify, 2014. 154 p.

The short story collection entitled "Four Inches Above the Ground" requires a persistent readers to finish all 14 stories due to their peculiarities, starting with punctuation and sentences. The first story, "Recent Studies," starts with a lowercase word in an initial and incomplete sentence. The leitmotif is death, introduced by summer dangers about which the narrator talks to several "yous." The second story, "The Knife Thrower," follows the same pattern of no names and unknown characters. It also has three long explanations and nouns and adjectives modified by an inner "nh," which in Portuguese often suggests a diminutive. The story ends with the narrator threatening another with a knife. More usual stories are exceptions. One of them is "Dog" about good city dogs which are never mistreated. Syntactically this story is much more clearly developed than the majority. The other is "Handbook of the Weather Man," which takes place in snowy winter. Notwithstanding the lack of characters and places names, this story follows a more usual fiction pattern.

2388 Carrascoza, João Anzanello. Aquela água toda. Ilustrações de Leya Mira Brander. São Paulo: Cosac Naify, 2013. 93 p.: ill.

Although the collection's stories are very short, usually from three and a half to five pages long, they are deeply analytical in their examinations of the emotions and actions of families. Among the stories are the tales of the joy of a young boy and his parents on a sunny weekend morning; a boy's fear that he is unable to explain; and the sadness of an old man whose job is to pick up dead pets from their homes. In one moving and dramatic story a boy wins a basketball game after long and hard practice and delights in this triumph, but on his way home, he sees his brother get hit by a train. Carrascoza is a well-known writer. His first published book, *Hotel Solidão*, won the eminent National Short Story Prize of Paraná State. His work has also received the Radio France International Prize and the Brazilian Jabuti , and the Eça de Queiroz. His works has been published in anthologies in Italy, France, the US, Sweden, and Spanish America. Each story in this collection is illustrated by Leya Mirer Brander, an acclaimed artist whose works have been shown at the Museo de Arte Moderna in Rio de Janeiro and in galleries and museums in the US, Portugal, Switzerland, Germany, Cuba, and Colombia.

2389 Castro, Marcílio França. Histórias naturais: ficções. São Paulo: Companhia das Letras, 2016. 196 p.

In this collection, the author extends the limits of fiction. In the first story, "Roteiro para duas mãos," the narrator is a hand double for movie and television actors playing the role of pianists. It is an unusually long short story at 42 pages. França Castro is obviously familiar with history and the classics, as well as contemporary literature. In his stories, he mentions Eurípides, Gogol, Shakespeare, Balzac, Hemingway, and many others. He also shows his knowledge of cartography and soccer. The settings are varied and include his native Belo Horizonte and other Brazilian, European, and Asian cities. An ambitious collection, *Histórias naturais* deserves readers' interest and admiration. In 2012, França Castro received the Clarice Lispector Prize from the Fundação da Biblioteca Nacional for his short story collection *Breve cartografia de lugares sem nenhum interesse*.

2390 Cavalcanti, Geraldo Holanda. Os dedos de Norma. Rio de Janeiro: Editora Record, 2014. 207 p.

In several of these very fine stories, the narrators are septuagenarian intellectuals who quote poets and other writers such as Bioy Casares, Victor Hugo, and the Goncourt brothers. With significant details, the narrators reveal the mystery of looks exchanged between strangers or people who have not seen each other in decades. In "A nuca," a woman's nape with a dragon tattoo catches a man's interest. In other stories, the narrators' eyes are caught by those of unknown women. In "Desdemona," an old narrator recalls his youth when he loved the theater and thought of becoming an actor. In a Rio de Janeiro *Othello* production, he almost strangles Luciana in her Desdemona role and she then refuses to have anything to do with him. Some of the stories take place in Budapest and Rome. The author has himself spent time abroad as the Brazilian ambassador to Mexico, UNESCO, and the EU. He was general secretary of the Latin Union in Paris, and president of Brazil's Pen Club. His *Poesia reunida* received the União Brasileira de Escritores (UBE) Fernando Pessoa Prize, in 1998. His translating activity has been equally honored with the 1998 Premio Internazionale Eugenio Montale for translations of Montale's poems, and the next year, the Paulo Ronai prize from the Brazilian Biblioteca Nacional for his translation of Salvador Quasimodo's poems. He was one of the translators recommended for the Jabuti Prize of 2003 for Giuseppe Ungaretti's *A Alegria*. His debut work in fiction, *Encontro em Ouro Preto*, was a finalist for the 2008 Jabuti Prize.

2391 Dapieve, Arthur. Maracanazo e outras histórias. Rio de Janeiro: Alfaguara, 2015. 159 p.

A professor and journalist, Arthur Dapieve has written 11 books, including interviews and novels. One of these, *Black Music*, was published in France by Asphalte Editions in 2012. The story "Maracanazo" was also published in France by Folies d'Encre and presented at Paris Salon du Livre in 2015. *Maracanazo* was chosen as one of the best books in the fourth Jules Rimet Prize for fiction related to sports. "Maracanazo" is a pejorative for Rio de Janeiro's famous Maracanã stadium. In *Maracanazo* there are five stories, the last of which gives the collection its name. The first "Tempo ruim" is about a young man who enjoys the danger of swimming off Copacabana beach when the wind and currents are too strong. He almost dies. The next story, "Fragmentos de paisagem" takes place in Austria and Germany and includes historical characters and facts, such as Hitler and Mussolini, and the musicians Bruno Walter, and Mahler. It deals with the two World Wars. The second one is about to start and the narrators' parents will emigrate to Brazil. The third story, "Inverno, 1968," presents rock musicians in England. One, "a genius," is difficult to get along with. The fourth story, "Bloqueio" has a man in a wheelchair in a difficult situation. He has to go downtown for an appointment made seven months before, but is unable to get a taxi. The city is not named, but the narrator mentions a hill in the shape of a solitary tooth on top of which is a huge white concrete statue with open arms—a non-poetical description of Christ the Redeemer by someone fearful and lost. Victor, the Spanish narrator, hates Maracanã. His country had lost soccer games there in 1950, 2013, and 2014, some to Brazil, and now he is there for another major game. He mentions the present game: Chile 2 x Spain 0. A Chilean girl sits near him and kisses him. She will only explain why she did it much later. Although politically they are very different, they spend the night together. "Maracanazo" is an admirable story which recreates the atmosphere of the World Cup. With a length of 75 pages, one can understand why the French consider it a novel.

2392 Fantini, Sérgio. Silas. Natal, Brazil: Jovens escribas, 2011. 125 p.: ill.

This collection presents five stories about the character, Silas. The first one, "Belo Horizonte, 21 de agosto de 1986," is a letter by Silas's mother, Afonsina G. Fonseca, who is very worried about her son, "a very good boy" though imprudent. After he left home, she found a letter to the organizer of a "Young short stories contest" as well as a story, both of which she sends the editor, hoping to find her son. In a preface Fantini explains to readers that the son's letter to a suffering mother was actually a story by Silas which will be published as such. Other stories deal with a drunken Silas on the street during Mardi Gras and other disreputable characters in a bar. A realist, the author uses strong vulgar language, which some readers may find harsh, but does not diminish the quality of the writing. The stories in *Silas* were written over 25 years and some were previously published. In addition to his works of fiction, Fantini has had seven works of poetry published.

2393 Fernandes, Rinaldo de. Confidências de um amante quase idiota. Rio de Janeiro: 7Letras, 2013. 129 p.

Original, dramatic, often perplexing, and even mysterious, these stories are also daring, covering both quotidian encounters and vulgar, brutal, and generally forbidden topics. These are micro-stories, varying in length from a few sentences to half a page. Fernandes looks with compassion at the poor and the sick. He is recognized by critics as a "master of the short story" (Regina Zilberman), and "a great short story writer" (Luis Augusto Fisher). He has been compared to Dalton Trevisan. His story "Beleza" won the Nationl Paraná Short Story Prize in 2006. His novel *Rita no pomar* was a finalist for the São Paulo Literature Prize. "Duas margens," one of his stories, was made into an acclaimed movie in 2013.

2394 Freire, Marcelino. Amar é crime. 2a edição, revista. Rio de Janeiro: Editora Record, 2015. 146 p.

In the book's introduction, Ivan Marques remarks that "in every story we see the stain of crime covering a long gallery of pariahs." With their extreme reactions Marcelino Freire's characters demand the reader's attention because their "dramas" are common ones. In its 16 stories, *Amar é crime* exhibits not only a variety of characters, but also language matching each characters. Ignorant and vulgar characters think and speak in terms of their personalities and experiences. In the subtitle, the stories are introduced as being "about love and death or short novels." Indeed the characters and milieus are vastly different though these are dangerous loves often ending in crime or death. A successful collection.

2395 Fux, Jacques. Meshugá: um romance sobre a loucura. Rio de Janeiro: José Olympio, 2016. 195 p.

A brilliant and bold collection, *Meshugá* will surprise and even shock readers who admire Jews for their centuries of distinguished contributions to arts, sciences, business, and philanthropy in so many nations. Each chapter has a different title and deals with an eminent Jewish man or woman. Each chapter could be a short story. In an introduction, the author examines many of the myths pertaining to the historical people he is writing about. The author is always present as a narrator, but the reader is unable to tell whether he is a character or the voice of the writer of the book. Between each chapter on a real-life character, there is a short one on the general attitudes and thoughts expressed about Jews. Among the figures profiled are Canadian physician Sarah Hoffman, born in 1980, who became the Deputy Premier of Alberta, and its Minister of Health; Woody Allen, Ron Jeremy, Austro-Hungarian Otto Weininger, and Bobby Fischer.

2396 Gonçalves, Carlos Eduardo Soares. Pequenas estórias. Rio de Janeiro: 7Letras, 2015. 114 p.

A debut short story collection by a professor with a PhD in economics. The "little stories" are generally short and cover different situations, some realistic and others surreal—such as one in which a manuscript leaves a message to its writer. Some are hyperbolic like the one told by the brother of the huge baby whose birth almost kills their mother. As an adult, he eventually weighs 350 pounds and continues to depend on her, dying shortly after she does. Dreams in stories can become nightmares or carry another dream inside them in this strong and imaginative collection.

2397 Henriques Neto, Afonso. Relatos nas ruas de fúria. Rio de Janeiro: Azougue Editorial, 2014. 210 p. (Azougue para viagem)

Mystery is an important element in these stories, as is surrealism. There are no paragraphs in the pieces and all are presented as "fiction" except for three and one poem. In one, the narrator on Copacabana beach has thoughts and feelings that are not his. They come from a stranger who is with a prostitute he intends to kill. Other stories have an historical Latin American background. In "Hazard's Shards," a young man is tortured and killed after writing a letter about Argentina's military dictatorship. In another, the narrator saves a young man from the Brazilian military dictatorship. The variety and competence of the 30 pieces make this an admirable collection. Afonso Henriques Neto is also a poet, the author of 11 poetry collections between 1972 and 2012. His work appears in several anthologies and has been translated into French, Italian, and Spanish.

2398 Iriarte, Flávia. Todo homem naufraga. Rio de Janeiro: Oito e Meio, 2013. 94 p.

"Every Man Drowns," points out the vicissitudes of the lives of mostly male characters and a few female ones. Two of the stories have "man" in their title: "Homem" and "Homem de 67 anos" (67 Year-Old Man). The young "Homem" character feels he is not a child anymore when he meets Júlia, but only becomes a man when she leaves him. The 67-year-old man is wealthy, successful, and sexually active. Intelligent collection concentrates on characters' difficulties due to their own personalities and life around them.

2399 Jardim, Ana Teresa. A mesa branca. 2a edição. Rio de Janeiro: 7Letras, 2015. 92 p.

"The White Table" in the title story reminds the narrator of her past and present, like most of the others in this excellent collection. In general, the narrators are women dealing with husbands, children, lovers, friends, and others. The last story, with the English title "Perceptions," starts in Brooklyn. The author is indeed perceptive about herself and those around her, and also insightful about memories and dreams. As she writes, "perceptions can also connect different time periods." In this semi-autobiographical story, the narrator explains that she was born and raised in Copacabana, a few blocks from the beach. She also remembers a birthday with her mother, grandmother, and nannies. It is easy to understand why this book went into a second edition.

2400 Lísias, Ricardo. Concentração e outros contos. Rio de Janeiro: Alfaguara: Objetiva, 2015. 270 p.: ill.

The work of critically acclaimed Lísias has been translated into Spanish, English, Hebrew, Japanese, and German. His novels are *Cobertor de estrelas, Duas praças, O livro dos mandarins, e O céu dos suicidas*. He won the Brazilian Association of Art Critics best novel prize in 2012 with *Divórcio*, and was chosen by the journal *Granta* as one of the 20 best young Brazilian writers. Some stories in *Concentração* have real historical characters in fictional circumstances, such as Bolivian President Evo Morales and Argentina's Perón. The collection's title, "Concentration," is appropriate for the concise, imaginative, and well-told stories.

2401 Lispector, Clarice. O tempo de Clarice Lispector. Curadoria por Roberto Corrêa dos Santos. Rio de Janeiro: Rocco, 2014. 263 p.

The collection is the second one on Lispector by Corrêa dos Santos, a specialist on her work and the first to write a master's thesis based on Lispector. The title may convey both meanings of the word *tempo* in Portuguese: "time" and "weather." "O tempo," offers a series of quotations, sometimes short paragraphs separated by two- or three-line spaces, from eight of Lispector's works including five novels, journalism, and letters. These sentences exhibit Lispector's talent and shine like jewels. *O tempo* is a precious and practical collection of some of the numerous examples of Lispector's magnificent style. This book serves as a companion to Corrêa dos Santos' 2013 work *As palavras*, which collected quotations from Lispector's work.

2402 **Maceira, Rodrigo.** Até de repente. Rio de Janeiro: Oito e Meio, 2016. 203 p.

The long stories in this fine collection present young men and women who delve into popular music, electronics, journalism, and literature in Brazil (mostly in São Paulo) as well as in Argentina and Spain. They work, take classes, or teach together and are "the friends who left" to whom Maceira dedicates the book. In the introduction a mystery is mentioned as are the negative aspects of life and a long Francis Picabia quote, "It is like your hopes: nothing; like your paradise: nothing; like your idols: nothing; like your politicians: nothing; like your heroes: nothing; like your artists: nothing; like your religions: nothing."

2403 **Machado, Antônio de Alcântara.**

António de Alcântara Machado: antologia de contos: com os livros *Brás, Bexiga e Barra Funda, Laranja da China, Mana Maria*; e o conto avulso O Mistério da Rua General Paiva. Organização e apresentação de Orna Messer Levin. Estabelecimento de texto e notas de Danielle Crepaldi Carvalho. São Paulo: Lazuli Editora: Companhia Editora Nacional, 2012. 255 p.: bibl.

This anthology presents almost the complete works of Alcântara Machado, a major figure of Brazilian modernism. It is a successful scholarly endeavor. In addition to updating the spelling to reflect current Portuguese, the collection includes historical notes and biographical notes about Machado.

2404 **Melo, Rômulo César.** Dois nós na gravata. Recife, Brazil: Companhia Editora de Pernambuco, 2015. 148 p.

This collection was one of the winners of the second Pernambuco Literature Prize for short fiction. Well-developed stories vary in style, setting, location, and time. The first one, "The First Cut in Van Gogh's Flesh," deals with hominids. Drawings by Van Gogh, "the madman," and Gauguin, "the warrior," in a paleolithic cave are studied by modern day archeologists. Author is ironic in his use of the names of famous modern painters for his paleolithic ones. Several of the other stories are sad and even tragic, like the man in "Estrela" who wanted to be a famous musician and ends up drowning with his wife and their five children in a hurricane. Ironically, he becomes famous for a completely different reason. In another story, the son of unhappily married parents contemplates suicide after his mother's death, which the reader assumes was not a suicide, but murder. In "Fire Eyes," a jealous lawyer kills his lover and has to work in a zoo where he is killed and partly devoured by a monkey. Other stories are equally tragic, though "A Rose for Keké," about a generous and obedient young boy in the slums who believes in Santa Claus, is sweet and pleasant to read.

2405 **Mendonça, Martha.** Filhas de Eva. Rio de Janeiro: Editora Record, 2016. 127 p.

"Daughters of Eve" first offers Eve herself in Eden and then 16 other stories of different women. There is a certain chronology as the first stories deal with young girls as the major character or the only one, and the other stories have older characters. "Morta" is the last one and as indicated by the title, has a dead narrator. Well written, imaginative, psychologically accurate and often dramatic, the collection is a first-rate work by a journalist.

Merced Hernández, Grisselle. Cartas viajeras: Julia de Burgos, Clarice Lispector: versiones de sí mismas. See item **1935**.

2406 **Moscovich, Cíntia.** Essa coisa brilhante que é a chuva. Rio de Janeiro: Editora Record, 2012. 140 p.

Woody Allen's epigraph "Life doesn't imitate art; it imitates bad television," suggests the nature of the stories in this collection. Moskovich is a realist with a powerful imagination who examines daily events, as well as extraordinary moments in life. Readers will note an ironic touch in these stories that mostly deal with family, friends, and neighbors. Notwithstanding sad and tragic events, Moskovich allows a certain optimism to appear at the end of several stories. Thus the "shiny rain" in the title and the stars in the story "O brilho de todas as estrelas" are more than decoration. Moskovich is a well-known novelist and also a journalist. She has received major literary prizes, including the Jabuti and three Açorianos. Her fiction is in anthologies in Portugal and Brazil and has been translated into English and Catalan.

2407 Nascimento, Elomar. Contos de plenilúnio. Rio de Janeiro: 7Letras, 2015. 126 p.

These "Full Moon Stories" offer a variety of characters, situations, and perspectives. They are usually short and extremely well written. Some are realistic, dealing with everyday facts, and others are dreamlike, such as "The Little Christmas Pine Tree" in which trees have feelings and talk to each other and "New Friends" in which the figures in museum paintings leap from the canvases in order to play with a young boy. Stories can be dramatic, like "The Farce" in which a wife discovers her husband's betrayal, and tragic like "The Governess," in which babies are drowned by their caretaker. Author's introduction to the collection is poetic: "Night becomes day. The moon rises over the shadows. It's full moon."

2408 Nascimento, Evando. Cantos profanos: (contos). São Paulo: Editora Globo, 2014. 147 p.: bibl. (Biblioteca azul)

Imaginative and well-written, these "profane songs" propose parallel biblical stories in which there is no God and evil reigns. The "Cantos" are the first part of the book. The other sections are "Profanações" and "Vestigios," also parallel to the Bible in a negative way. In the story, "Demo" the devil explains himself and his importance. "I preach evil's universality," "my true challenger is reason's sensitivity," he says. And further, "I proclaim the New Gospel. Amen to all of you." This erudite collection offers numerous quotations, often in their original language, and others translated by author: Shakespeare, Baudelaire, Carlos Drummomd de Andrade, Edgar Allan Poe, Lewis Carroll, Thomas Mann, Jean Genet, and Paul Valéry. A brilliant, original, and at times depressing collection by an author recognized as one of the best in contemporary Brazilian letters.

2409 Norões, Everardo. Entre moscas. Rio de Janeiro: Confraria do Vento, 2013. 179 p. (Os contemporâneos)

Strong, elegant stories that often deal with mystery and abstractions, and that are often disturbing. The stories are set in Brazil, Portugal, France, and Arab-speaking countries. Real writers, philosophers, and artists are mentioned. "Among Flies," the story for which the collection is named, is characteristic of the others included here. The focus is on a fly on the narrator's dining room ceiling which at dusk, at the end of the story, he confuses with himself. In "The Cold Blade," the narrator realizes that a cousin he spent time with in childhood is now a professional killer. Norões' poems have been translated into several languages. He is also a newspaper columnist, translator, and organizer of anthologies of contemporary Peruvian, Italian, and French poetry. His work appears in several Brazilian and foreign anthologies, and he is the author of a dozen books.

2410 Parisio, João Paulo. Legião anônima: contos. Recife, Brazil: Cepe Editora, 2014. 124 p.

A variety of characters, backgrounds, and perspectives make this "Anonymous Legion" a splendid, though often pessimistic, collection. The first story's ironic title "The Good Action" has a poor man falling on the street then being spat upon and hit. He had grown angel wings and risen from the ground and the crowd around him had attacked him, stolen everything he carried, and left him naked. Several stories deal with unhappy children and adolescents who feel unappreciated. Adults can be equally unhappy. However "Camelia's Monologue" has a female narrator who sings the glories and usefulness of her profession—prostitution—which the ignorant middle class despises. Brilliant story "Natal nos trópicos" is different as it tells of a boy who wants to give a bicycle to a poor boy as a Christmas present.

2411 **Pimenta, Gabriel.** À sombra do centauro e outros contos. Belo Horizonte, Brazil: Editora Letramento, 2016. 107 p.

In this collection, the strong, well-written stories often have elements of horror, such as characters returning home to be met by police officers who find a woman's head on top of the refrigerator, and another story in which a man kills a couple while they are making love. Often stories do not reveal major aspects of physical descriptions that the author leaves for reader to imagine. Some of the images could be metaphors such as the narrator's description of himself and others in a group as "phantoms invisible as they wander." Another surprising element is the live rhinoceros in the title story, which the author finds in his building when he returns home. The centaur is a large statue near the building where the narrator and colleagues are having a major business meeting.

2412 **Polesso, Natália Borges.** Amora: contos. Porto Alegre, Brazil: Não Editora, 2015. 255 p.

Collection's epigraph, "Aos amores e às amoras" establishes a major theme with a pun since "amores" is "loves" and "amoras" is "mulberries." The two parts of the book develop the parallel, the first part is "large and juicy" with 26 longer stories, while the second part is "small and tart," with six much shorter stories. "Amora" could also be read or interpreted as "love" in the feminine with the addition of the "a," the final letter that in Portuguese indicates the feminine noun or adjective. Homosexuality is a major theme in the collection, mostly between young women. Polesso is a strong literary writer who mixes her elegant style with careless, misspelled colloquial speech. The stories convey happiness marred by fear, and even death, as part of usually forbidden sexual relationships.

2413 **Ribeiro, Ana Elisa.** Meus segredos com Capitu: livros, leituras e outros paraísos. Natal, Brazil: Editora Jovens Escribas, 2013. 166 p.

The title page of this book informs the reader that the collection focuses on "books, reading, and other paradises," thus revealing author's enthusiasm for literature. These 30 columns written for the blog, *Digestivo Cultural* (www.digestivocultural.com), are varied, often both poetic and realistic. The title suggests another important ingredient of the collection: Capitu, a major character in Machado de Assis's *Dom Casmurro*. The mystery connected to Capitu—did she betray Bentinho or not?—is an essential element in Ribeiro's book. The varied and interesting essays owe much to Ribeiro's concern with literary aspects that might escape many readers' attention: handwriting, different kinds of bookstores and bookstands, and careless or ignorant readers.

2414 **Rodrigues, Alexandre Marques.** Entropia. Rio de Janeiro: Editora Record, 2016. 302 p.

Starting with its complex thermodynamic title, the collection offers quite a few challenges. Classified as a novel by the publisher who also notices an autobiographical aspect, the book offers several stories in geographical order as happening in Trafalgar, Moscow, Leipzig, and Waterloo, but which do not take place in those locations. Sexuality is a major ingredient often described in vulgar words. A female character tells a man, "You have never understood women." A strong and exciting book by the author of *Parafilias* (see item **2415**).

2415 **Rodrigues, Alexandre Marques.** Parafilias. Rio de Janeiro: Editora Record, 2014. 158 p.

By the author of *Entropia* (see item **2414**), this collection shares with her other work an almost mysterious title, as well as literary worth. The Greek word "parafilia" (in Cyrillic script also) is explained to the reader as "beyond or away from love; deviation; perversion." An impressive collection, each of its stories examines disturbed or even criminal sexual encounters, generally heterosexual. Most female and male characters are strangers to one another. Narrators can be impersonal or one of the examined couple. In the brilliant "Quartos" (Bedrooms), the narrator is an intelligent and well-read young man who cleans rooms in a brothel. He has been forced to take on the work because his father has all the family's money. During the night, the young man reads or remembers works by Tolstoy, Chekov, and others.

2416 Rodrigues, Marcus Vinicius. A eternidade da maçã. Rio de Janeiro: 7Letras, 2016. 117 p.

This collection of stories received the 2016 Prêmio Nacional ABL. It covers a disturbing era of brutal military government in Brazil (1964–78), and each story is set in a specific year. Several stories deal with characters accused of communism who were tortured and often died. However, courage and kindness are also features of some of the stories. A young man who had fled and escaped death realizes when he comes back home years later that his girlfriend had not told authorities where he was and was therefore tortured herself. In another story, a banana vendor not only hides a young revolutionary, but also offers him a job selling fruit. Soldiers working for the government find the man they were looking for, but take him to his girlfriend's house instead of prison. Rodrigues is also a successful poet.

2417 Sant'Anna, Sérgio. O homem-mulher: contos. São Paulo: Companhia das Letras, 2014. 183 p.

Sergio Sant'Anna is one of the most significant Brazilian short story writers of the second half of the 20th century. With a thematic focus on sexuality and old age, this fine collection examines several aspects of life not usually treated in literature, including the title story which explains that men who want to dress as women are not homosexuals, but just comfortable with their feminine side. Another unusual story, "Lencinho" (Small Handkerchief) ends with Manoela attending her husband's funeral with her lover. In "Madonna," a thief in a museum analyzes Munch's pictures. Sant'Anna's stories have been translated into German, French, Spanish, and Italian. Some have been made into films. He received the Jabuti prize four times, as well as the APCA Prize.

2418 Silva, Cidinha da. Sobreviventes! Rio de Janeiro: Pallas Editora, 2016. 131 p.

Forty-two short columns on Afro-Brazilians examine their present day lives. These characters are both "viventes" (living) and "sobreviventes" (survivors) because, notwithstanding four centuries of slavery and mistreatment, Afro-Brazilians have had a tremendous impact on Brazilian society in the arts, music, sciences, medicine, literature, and sports, especially soccer. Silva's perception is as sharp as her writing. An important collection as a literary and journalistic work.

2419 Silvestre, Edney. Welcome to Copacabana & outras histórias. Rio de Janeiro: Editora Record, 2016. 351 p.

The English title suggests the international appeal of Copacabana beach and district. However, Copacabana and Rio de Janeiro are not the only settings for these stories. The book has three parts: "In Rio," "Beyond Rio," and "Back to Rio," which guide the reader geographically. Although most of the stories deal with everyday life of family and friends, some are disturbing and difficult to read with cruel actions such as beating, raping of children, and young and old women—sometimes told with people laughing. The mission of mysterious Zak of the eponymous story is the destruction of the planet, which is described in the first sentence of its narrative. Families are the center of some stories with births, diseases, surgeries, and deaths, and changes wrought by these events. Characters can be unusual, like Madame K, a palm reader found dead in her apartment and Sílvio ("Sílvio trabalha"), a male prostitute. Although extremely talented, the journalist Silvestre can frighten and shock his readers. A powerful fiction writer he is recognized as such by the Jabuti prize and São Paulo's 2010 Best Novel. He is also one of the most translated contemporary Brazilian fiction writers with novels published in France, England, Germany, Holland, Portugal, Italy, and Serbia.

2420 Sperling, Rafael. Um homem burro morreu. Rio de Janeiro: Oito e Meio, 2014. 130 p.

Undeniably talented, Sperling presents a combination of originality and vulgarity in 25 stories, the last one having the book's title, "A Stupid Man Died." The author's everpresent irony goes from amusing to grotesque. In "Eles eram muitos cavalos," for example, horses invade a town and kill all the people there. The "stupid man" dies of disappointment when he sees he cannot have his toast because he had forgotten to plug in the toaster. In a shocking interpretation, and certainly not historical, Dante Alighieri and family are dressed in dirty clothes and there is garbage all over their house. Several babies on the floor are hit by others and killed without disturbing the family. A musician and composer, Sperling published his first book, a short story collection, in 2011. His fiction has been published in newspapers and reviews in Austria, Germany, Spain, and the US. Many of them were also translated into English, Spanish, French, Basque, and Catalan.

2421 Tavares, Zulmira Ribeiro. Região: ficções etc. Posfácio de Augusto Massi. São Paulo: Companhia das Letras, 2012. 354 p.

Região presents Tavares' literary work in chronological order, from 1970 onward. It includes not only stories, but also essays, columns, and poems. Most of them have been published previously, and as Augusto Massi notes in his "Posfácio," the work includes fiction, essays, and poems. The first section of this work is made up of stories from Ribeiro Tavares' *Termos de comparação* for which she won the 1974 Associação Paulista de Críticos de Arte prize. The second section of *Região, etc.* includes stories from *O japonês de olhos redondos*, first published in 1984. The next section has essays from *O mandril*, first published in 1988, and also the poems from *Torre de Pisa*. Three columns on "O tio paulista," first published in 1988, make up the fourth section, and the story "Região" is the fifth section. The sixth section is "Dois narizes—um estudo," written in 2007. Ribeiro Tavares writes fiction, essays, and poetry with ease. It can be said that she writes like a Paulista, a native of São Paulo, who are characterized by other Brazilians as being practical, civilized, and clever.

2422 Trevisan, Dalton. O beijo na nuca. Rio de Janeiro: Editora Record, 2014. 143 p.

One of the best-known late 20th-century Brazilian fiction writers, Trevisan is the author of 41 books. His style is very elegant. As an example, the story "Chuvinha" (Drizzle) shows his admirable mixture of reality and surrealism from the first line: "A white spider with one thousand legs covers the town. . . with a sticky web." Besides Brazil, his stories take place in European countries such as Germany, Austria, Spain, France, and Italy. His characters are as varied as his settings: an apparition of Mary, the mother of Jesus, in the rain; little girls at the end of a Catholic mass; and prostitutes in brothels. An intellectual author, Trevisan also mentions Mozart, Van Gogh, Cocteau, and Rimbaud in his excellent stories.

2423 Tudo o que não foi: coletânea literária. Organização por Deborah Kietzmann Goldemberg. Cuiabá, Brazil: Carlini & Caniato, 2014. 111 p.

"Everything That Wasn't" is an anthology of 15 stories dealing with automobile and motorcycle accidents. Its purpose is to expose the high rate of accidents in Brazil and encourage government enforcement of penalties for guilty drivers, especially drunken ones. The authors belong to the group "Não Foi Acidente" (It was not an accident), which seeks support from the Ordem dos Advogados do Brasil (Brazilian Bar Association) for a five-year minimum prison term for drunk drivers. The 15 stories are diverse and well told.

2424 Viana, Antonio Carlos. Jeito de matar lagartas. São Paulo: Companhia das Letras, 2015. 147 p.

Very fine stories focus on older characters, their bodies, and changes in their lives; several of them are widowers. Sometimes they remember their distant childhoods and youth, thinking about what was different then and what might have been different in their lives. Realistic stories at times introduce a bit of romanticism which is then almost ironically erased. The book's title comes from one story of the cruel actions of a boy who enjoys jumping on lizards until they burst. A collection by a writer who is also a translator and who won the Associação Paulista de Críticos de Arte prize for his *Cine Privê*.

2425 Villa-Forte, Leonardo. O explicador. Rio de Janeiro: Oito e Meio, 2014. 86 p.

"O explicador," the title of both the collection and one of its stories provides the thematic opening to the book, as it suggests making a person, an idea, or an object clear to the reader. Here this element is almost always associated with a negative attitude. In one story, the "explicator" character annoys his audience that becomes hostile and whom he calls "brainless worms . . . with a corroded mind." He ends by shooting and killing one of them. Stylistically, the collection is impressive. As the critic Gonçalo M. Tavares wrote, "its language is dry, and straight to the subject, without unnecessary and useless lateral beauty." *O explicador* also includes poems. It is Villa-Forte's first published book and has received the Off FLIP Short Story Prize. Several of his stories have been published in Brazilian anthologies, newspapers, and magazines, and translated into English in British reviews.

Crônicas

DÁRIO BORIM JR., *Professor of Portuguese and Luso-Brazilian Literature and Culture, University of Massachusetts, Dartmouth*

WITHIN THIS CORPUS of 33 works of Brazilian crônicas, most of which were published between 2014 and 2016, we find writers whose other jobs and occupations vary quite substantially. The majority of works, though, are written by journalists (items **2428, 2431, 2438, 2446, 2447, 2449, 2453,** and **2454**) and poets (items **2427, 2428, 2431, 2432, 2434, 2435, 2436,** and **2450**). Others are bloggers (items **2436, 2445,** and **2447**), college professors (items **2427, 2429, 2440, 2449, 2455, 2457,** and **2458**), novelists (items **2428, 2432,** and **2433**), painters (items **2429** and **2450**), a politician (item **2439**), a priest (item **2430**), a restoration expert (item **2429**), translators (items **2428** and **2431**), short story writers (items **2427** and **2432**), and scriptwriters (items **2435, 2449,** and **2451**).

Personal lives and current affairs dominate thematically. The vicissitudes of living alone (item **2428**), coming of age (items **2427, 2429,** and **2432**), marriage (item **2431**), and family history (item **2429**) are some examples. Stories on neurological illnesses (item **2440**), the metabolic and emotional benefits of crying (item **2445**), curiosities of contemporary sex life across the globe (item **2441**), early aging (item **2451**), pains and glories of parenting babies and young children (item **2451**), self-deprecation (item **2444**), plus poverty and child labor (items **2454** and **2455**) also appear.

One of the most captivating books dealing with growing up is award-winning novelist Luiz Ruffato's first book of crônicas (item **2454**). Several of his pieces describe pivotal moments in the author's personal growth and professional development. "Minha primeira vez" (My First Chance), the book's title piece, is an autobiographical crônica in two parts that ruminates on the amazingly transformative impact that books can have on people's lives. Bullied by his classmates, Ruffato found refuge in a quiet room, which turned out to be the school library. A librarian helped him to become a voracious reader. In hindsight, it was probably his "first chance" to move up the social ladder. He asserts ironically that he "had been contaminated by the reading virus" (p. 86).

A second group of books emphasizes lifestyles and atmospheres in different cities and towns within Brazil and abroad. Rio de Janeiro, arguably the birthplace of the Brazilian crônica in the 19th century, is just one among many cities portrayed. Other state capitals appearing in this current batch of crônica books, apart from Brasília, the Federal District's capital, are Belo Horizonte, Curitiba, Porto Alegre, Recife, São Luiz, and São Paulo. Many smaller cities and towns are also profiled or serve as the setting for a crônica Araxá (MG), Cataguases (MG), Juiz de Fora (MG), Peabiru (PR), Ponta Grossa (PR), Santo Anastácio (SP), and São João del Rei (MG), among a few others. Cities outside Brazil also appear: Dublin, Havana, Krakow, Macau, Madrid, Mexico City, Moscow, and St. Petersburg, among them.

Vivid city and town images depict, for example, the peculiar lifestyles on the periphery of São Paulo (items **2428** and **2432**), the bohemian and legendary districts, apart from gentrified favelas, in Rio de Janeiro (items **2433**, **2434**, and **2435**), exploits in the red light districts and churches of Araxá, Rio de Janeiro, and Recife (items **2429, 2443**, and **2454**). One also reads much about the cultural and intellectual life of large cities like Curitiba (items **2439, 2447, 2448**, and **2458**), Recife (item **2442**), and and Belo Horizonte (item **2446**). Humorous and bittersweet accounts of odd behavior in public by anonymous individuals, such as the homeless, prostitutes, the sick and the lonely, and the mentally ill come alive in items **2442, 2444, 2447, 2448, 2456**, and **2457**. Conversations among strangers at bars and restaurants are overheard in São Paulo (item **2432**) or Curitiba (items **2439, 2447**, and **2448**). Amazon region's villages' colors and sounds are counterpoints to street fruit vendors in Araxá (item **2429**), Cataguases (item **2454**), and Recife (item **2442**), as well as to roaming cats and singing birds in the streets of Paraná's capital (items **2447** and **2448**).

Cities and towns set up, likewise, the stage for humor, which abounds in multiple volumes, for example items **2428, 2431, 2432, 2440, 2444**, and **2446**. Urban life fosters hilarious interactions between unexpected parties, such as those of a world leader and a humble but defiant snack seller (item **2454**). In reality, the sting of an author's humor can fall on himself/herself. This is what happens to Mentor Muniz Neto, a resentful balding man, who fears dental treatment, struggles with unpleasant diets, and has a hard time finding clothes that fit him because he is overweight (item **2444**).

Direct or indirect activism in support a wide range of causes is explored in crônica writing. This is the case with a plea for more reading (items **2427** and **2454**), mental illness awareness (item **2427**), religious freedom (item **2430**), socialism (item **2430**), Liberation Theology (item **2430**), the opening of parks, entertainment centers and schools on the periphery of large cities, as well as the creation of rehabilitation centers for underaged criminal (item **2433**). Crônicas can also take the form of satirical letters to local authorities requesting improvement in hospitals and schools (item **2434**), advocate for the use of animals in the health care of individuals with mental disabilities (item **2435**), and tell amusing and educating stories in order to defend animals' rights and preservation (item **2437**).

Many narratives and discussions on violence and other crimes permeate the crônicas of this period. Some of these texts deal with domestic disputes and abuses (items **2427** and **2449**), death and disease of indigenous populations (item **2426**), pros and cons of capital punishment (item **2433**), and evils of machismo and rape (item **2454**). Questions of ethics and prejudices behind the choices of reporting small crimes (item **2427**), detective stories (item **2448**), lack of ethics in capitalism (item **2430**), and manifestations of racism (item **2433**) set the tone of numerous crônicas.

Perhaps it is in the realm of politics that we find the largest number of texts dealing with crimes and prejudices. One will find stories and opinions on street protests, opposing political regimes and ideologies, the 2014 presidential elections in Brazil, metallurgical workers' strikes, and the phony love of the bourgeoisie for the poor. The mistakes of the extremes in politics, and, especially, the mega corruption and organized crime schemes involving the three branches of power in Brasília play a major thematic role, too. In particular, we read numerous pages on the criminal or unethical deeds by the four consecutive PT presidential administrations, from Lula to Dilma Rousseff, in partnership with large companies' greedy scoundrels.

Just slightly less controversial are the texts in this corpus that address Brazil's national passion, soccer. Mário Filho's book (item **2453**) addresses the topic almost exclusively. His 1940s and 1950s sports crônicas detail the onset of professional football, as the world outside the US calls it. Creative and stylistic crônicas on the global sport and its connections with corruption in Brazil are relevant in Décio Pignatari (item **2450**). Brazil's ludicrous and scandalous loss 1–7 to Germany in the 2014 World Cup does not escape Antonio Prata's body of crônicas (item **2451**).

The arts also have a voice in these 33 books. Painters emerge in items **2429** and **2436**; moviemakers, in items **2428**, **2436**, **2440**, and **2454**; and television, in items **2427**, **2428**, **2432**, **2437**, **2449**, **2451**, and **2457**. Music themes arise through texts on Bob Dylan (item **2432**), Antonio Carlos Jobim (item **2432**), Leonard Cohen (item **2436**), João Gilberto (item **2444**), Caetano Veloso (item **2449**), and remarkable animal musicians (item **2437**).

Linguistics and literature occupy the minds of a large number of cronistas. One comes across, for example, Guimarães Rosa's informant Manuelzão's speech patterns (item **2426**) and the penchant for word curiosities (items **2443**, **2444**, and **2450**). Poetry is quite often the object of praises and explanations (items **2427**, **2428**, **2431**, **2435**, **2436**, **2440**, **2450**, and **2452**). Some texts elaborate on specific literary trends, styles and special topics, like the Concrete and Neo-Concrete poetry movements (item **2450**), the presence of animal characters in literary works (item **2435**), or the legendary encounters of canonical authors and artists in Recife (item **2442**). Nobel laureates, such as José Saramago and Gabriel García Màrquez, inspire some discussions (item **2430**). Other texts will debate or incorporate as characters a plethora of writers, like Sophia de Mello Breyner Andresen (item **2436**), Lima Barreto (item **2433**), Simone de Beauvoir (item **2445**), Jorge Luis Borges (item **2440**), Clarice Lispector (item **2454**), Ana Martins Marques (item **2440**), Betty Milan (item **2426**), Edgar Allan Poe (item **2445**), Zulmira Ribeiro Tavares (item **2440**), and Lygia Fagundes Telles (item **2426**).

The last subject to highlight here is the genre crônica itself, a favorite topic among so many crônica writers of all times. This type of journalistic-literary mix keeps evolving through the passing of time, of course, and one more step in that direction is Mentor Muniz Neto's material: a collage of humorous and irreverent FaceBook entries (item **2444**). While the oldest style of Brazilian crônica is also part of this review, through the publication in book form of the newspaper columns written by 19th century canonical poet Antônio Gonçalves

Dias (item **2434**), there are several other writers whose pieces contribute to a better understanding of the crônica's historical development to the present day. Thoughts on the crônica as a genre, with its open potentials for innovation and multiple constraints, emerge in items **2438**, **2445**, **2447**, **2448**, and **2458**, among others.

2426 Antologia UBE. Organização de Joaquim Maria Botelho. São Paulo: Global Editora, 2015. 287 p.

With 25 crônicas by 25 different authors, along with 25 poems and 25 short stories, this project gathers works selected among thousands of others submitted by São Paulo state writers. Edited by the União Brasileira de Escritores (Brazilian Writers' Union) President Joaquim Maria Botelho, this book features both young writers and well-known authors, like Antonio Candido, Betty Milan, Lygia Fagundes Telles, and Frei Betto. Some pieces address serious issues, like death or the troubles of indigenous populations. Others carry a lighter tone on a disparate set of topics, while discussing, for example, the surprising insights and speech patterns of João Guimarães Rosa's informant Manuelzão, the life and work of James Joyce and the Bloomsday celebrations in Dublin, and former President Jânio Quadro's father's penchant for horsemeat.

2427 Balbino, Evaldo. Apesar das coisas ásperas: crônicas. Rio de Janeiro: Imprimatur, 2016. 123 p.

Cronista, essayist, poet and short story writer from Resende Costa, Minas Gerais, Balbino holds a Ph.D. in Comparative Literature from the Federal University of Minas Gerais, where he teaches Portuguese and literature. His volume presents undated pieces, some previously published. Childhood memories, social interactions in a provincial small town, and reflections on art and literature constitute the thematic core of the volume. A self-declared evangelical, Balbino advocates for reading, in general, and the contemplative beauty of poetry, in particular. He discusses mental illness in society and the importance caring for animals. Domestic violence and the ethical dilemmas of daily life, such as whether to denounce non-paying bus riders, also appear in his crônicas.

2428 Barbara, Vanessa. O louco de palestra: e outras crônicas urbanas. São Paulo: Companhia das Letras, 2014. 193 p.

Journalist, novelist, poet, and translator Vanessa Barbosa, who writes regularly for the international edition of the *New York Times* and *Folha de São Paulo*, is a Jabuti award-winning author. In this collection of texts divided into three thematic sections, she chronicles colorful daily life in Mandaqui, a northern district of São Paulo, where she was born and raised. All the texts indicate when and where they were previously published. The collection includes humorous and intellectual narratives sometimes resembling the style of Paulo Mendes or Rubem Braga. Babara discusses political street protests, tiny domestic pets, inner-city bus rides, as well as covering literary festivals, the Olympics, and television programming, among other topics.

2429 Barreto, Fernando. Sob o céu de Araxá: crônicas. Montevideo: aBrace Editora, 2011. 319 p. (Coleção Palavra viva)(Coleção Palavra)

Professor, painter, and art restoration expert Fernando Barreto wrote most of these pieces in his 80s, after becoming visually impaired. They tell stories of his childhood and adolescence spent in Araxá, Minas Gerais, between 1929 and 1947. He affirms that his crônicas are "simply testimonials," since they are all "related to the times of early years and my early learning about life" (p. 6). Several passages allude to the importance of cinema in the daily life of Araxá. The historical presence of Brazil's president Getúlio Vargas at the grand opening of a large, up-scale hotel and casino in town also draws the memoirist's attention. Other stories narrate exploits in Araxá's red light district and quaint scenes of children and teens playing in the main square's bandstand, street fruit-sellers, and domestic servants, including one whose parents were slaves. Barreto was a child who played sax and travelled with his middle-school band, sold jewelry at his parents' store, and helped at his church as an altar boy. Occasionally, Barreto assumes a more professorial tone to comment on the 1929 New York stock market crash, the history of professions, or on the origins and development of coconut trees.

2430 Betto, Frei. Paraíso perdido: viagens ao mundo socialista. Rio de Janeiro: Rocco, 2015. 525 p.: bibl.

One of the most articulate spokespersons for human rights, socialism, and Liberation Theology in Brazil, Carlos Alberto Libânio Christo, aka Frei Betto, is a Dominican friar with a resounding literary career. Among many other distinguished merits, he has received the Jabuti, Brazil's most prestigious prize for literature, for his 1982 memoir book *Batismo de sangue* (Blood Baptism) and the Juca Pato, from the União Brasileira de Escritores (Brazilian Writers' Union), for his 1985 book of interviews, *Fidel e a religião* (Fidel and Religion). This global bestseller has been published in 32 countries and translated into 19 languages. Many details of the conversations between the Cuban dictator and the Brazilian priest (the content of the successful book) appear in some of the 80 texts of this volume, whose title in English could be "Lost Paradise: Travels to the Socialist World." Frei Betto's crônicas are travel narratives interspersed with commentaries about religious practices in the "real" socialist world, which is apparently the "lost paradise" of the volume's title. He paints a very gloomy picture of the draconian authoritarianism, corruption, and the educational brainwash in Eastern Europe, but demonstrates an enormous amount of admiration for Cuba's social and political model. For him, a regime of a supposed harmony among popular collectives and governmental leaderships works better than a democracy sustained by free voting. Frei Betto contends that one should not assess a nation's democracy "by the ways in which there is rotation among people in power, but rather by the rights and benefits earned by its citizens" (p. 160). His writing sheds some light on the political transition from Lula to Dilma Rousseff in Brazil. In a conversation with Castro, Betto says: "My opinion was that [Lula], for sure, would have preferred to indicate Antônio Palocci or José Dirceu as his successor." Dilma, adds Frei Betto, "was the third option. She was the one because the other two people fell under suspicion of corruption" (p. 499). Politics and religion inform *Paraíso perdido*, but there is much more in this captivating book. One learns, for example, about St. Petersburg, a city of 4 million people, where there are 2,500 libraries. The author also shares a family recipe for *bobó de camarão*, a cassava-based shrimp-in-palm-oil stew of fine zest and piquancy (p. 121). Frei Betto has pedigree, after all. His mother, Maria Stella Libanio Christo, wrote a classic culinary book, *Fogão de lenha: 300 anos de cozinha mineira* ("Wood Stove: 300 Hundred Years of Minas Gerais Culinary").

2431 Campos, Paulo Mendes. De um caderno cinzento: crônicas, aforismos e outras epifanias. Organização, apresentação e notas de Elvia Bezerra. São Paulo: Companhia das Letras; 2015. 234 p.

Born in Belo Horizonte, Minas Gerais, Paulo Mendes Campos (1922–91) had a long and successful writing career as translator of world literary classics, journalist, essayist, and most of all, master of the crônica genre. Among the well-preserved 55 notebooks found in his personal archives, where he entered quotes and multiple ideas for future writing projects, there were two gray ones. According to the Elvia Bezerra, the researcher who has edited the present volume, Campos used those two notebooks as "test tubes" for the texts that he would write and publish in Rio de Janeiro's newspaper *Diário Carioca* and the national magazine *Manchete*. Crônicas, social commentaries, prose poems, short dialogues, and aphorisms are among various types of writing in the notebooks. Irony and sarcasm dominate here. He writes, for example, "marriage is a slow surgical operation that has the power to separate two creatures cruelly and keep them desperately tied together" (p. 23). But he also offers advice for young poets: "What is necessary in poetry writing is to learn not to need the qualities that one does not possess" (p. 184). And self-deprecatingly, targets himself in a critique of Brazil's provincialism: "Brazil is a country where even a man like me can be seen as intellectual" (p. 35).

2432 Corsaletti, Fabrício. Ela me dá capim e eu zurro. São Paulo: Editora 34, 2014. 157 p.

In his first book of crônicas, the Paulista novelist, poet, and short story writer Fabrício Corsaletti is most of all a conversationalist and frequenter of bars, cafés and restaurants, a stroller and people watcher in airports, markets, and multiple streets and squares in the São Paulo city districts of Liberdade, Pinheiros, and Pompéia. Most of the 59 undated texts were previously published in either 2010 or 2014 in a magazine that accompanies the newspaper *Folha de São Paulo*. On the book jacket, Augusto Massi points out three themes: a sentimental topography of the city of São Paulo, the social act of sitting at a table and talking, and a writer's interest in food and drink. Through his stories, the day-to-day life of a writer takes many forms and colors, whether it is a visit to a used books store, an afternoon at an art gallery, or a cup of coffee at a corner bakery. Corsaletti also discusses the use of television sets in bars and restaurants that could easily survive financially without them. (He currently leads a campaign to make their use in those venues illegal.) He is likewise opinionated about literature, music, and painting. For him, Julio Cortázar, Bob Dylan, William Faulkner, Tom Jobim, Amedeo Modigliani and a few others are heroes of talent and grace. He describes his childhood in the town of Santo Anásticio (in the western side of the state of São Paulo), his college years in Vila Mariana, and his teaching experiences at high school level. He shares his pain when his cat is killed in the street, and his regret at not reacting with equal kindness to a stranger in Ouro Preto, Minas Gerais, who claimed to be a fan of his books.

2433 Costa Filho, Odylo. Odylo Costa, filho. Seleção e edição de Cecília Costa Junqueira e Virgilio Costa. Prefácio de Cecília Costa Junqueira. Introdução de Virgilio Costa. São Paulo: Global Editora; Rio de Janeiro: Academia Brasileira de Letras, 2015. 528 p.: bibl. (Coleção Melhores crônicas)

Recommended by a handful of masters of Brazilian literature, including Carlos Drummond de Andrade, Manuel Bandeira, and Rubem Fonseca, Odylo Costa Filho's writing has been critically well received. These crônicas by the Maranhense author, dating from 1938 through 1979, were originally published in the Rio de Janeiro newspapers *Diário de Notícias*, *O Jornal do Comércio*, *A Tribuna*, e *Folha Carioca*. Chronologically sequenced in this volume without thematic divisions, they cover a wide scope of topics, from political discussions to literary analyses. The cronista's penchant for sociopolitical issues is evident and he does not avoid controversy. He has ironic and often humorous comments on the different manifestations of prejudice and hatred, including a short piece on racism practiced in Brazil and the US. He writes that in Brazil, we "have always had prejudice, yes, against blacks and *mestiços*. Why do we deny it?" (p. 137). He also decries capital punishment and calls for more attention to be paid to those who live on city's geographic and economic peripheries.

2434 Dias, Antônio Gonçalves. Crônicas reunidas: folhetins teatrais, crítica literária e de artes plásticas e crônica urbana. Estudo, organização e notas de Luís Antônio Giron. Rio de Janeiro: Academia Brasileira de Letras, 2013. 572 p.: bibl. (Coleção Afrânio Peixoto; 100)

Better known today as a poet, rather than a cronista, Antônio Gonçalves Dias was actually a prolific *folhetinista*, the term applied to crônica writers in the middle of the 19th century. In his long and rigorous study introducing the volume, Luís Antônio Giron argues that Gonçalves Dias "pre-established the terms of the fin-de-siècle crônica developed by Machado de Assis and João do Rio" (p. 3), helping to establish a literary genre that acquired very strong Brazilian characteristics (p. 3). The poet from São Luiz moved to Rio in 1846, where he started working as a lawyer and writing for local newspapers. His crônicas often exhibit a light and ironic tone, a playful take on daily deeds and serious matters alike. He interacts with his readers while hiding his own identity by mixing and blending pen names. Through this subterfuge, he comments on significant political matters without risking his job or compromising his network of supporters. In his newspaper columns, for example, Gonçalves Dias would write and publish multiple satirical letters addressed to local authorities, such as hospital, police and school district directors, in order to denounce ethical absurdities or advocate for changes and improvements.

2435 Gullar, Ferreira. A alquimia na quitanda: artes, bichos e barulhos nas melhores crônicas do poeta. São Paulo: Três Estrelas, 2016. 287 p.

Born and baptized José de Ribamar Ferreira in São Luis, Maranhão, in 1930, this canonical poet and plastic artist lived in Rio de Janeiro most of his life. Not long after moving to the *cidade maravilhosa*, then the country's capital, in the early 1950s, he joined the vanguard group that revolutionized Brazilian poetry, the *concretistas*. His rebellious nature led him to break with the concretistas to pioneer a new movement called neoconcretism, which strove for connections between his former colleagues' esthetics and a wider sociopolitical engagement. Affiliated with the Brazilian Communist Party, he was jailed for his political views in 1968 and later forced into exile in Chile and Russia. In the early 21st century, he became one of the rare intellectuals and artists to speak out about the abuses perpetrated by the socialist PT (Workers' Party). These 124 short texts are rooted in politics. Besides Lula and the PT, Gullar writes about the two couples who ran Argentina (Perón and Kischner), the death of the former president of Brazil, Getúlio Vargas, the rise of Barak Obama, and the creation of Plano Real (the economic package that saved Brazil from mammoth inflation, recession, and unemployment, in 1993). Of course the title of this collection would be misleading (The Alchemy at the Market: Arts, Animals and Noises in the Poet's Best Crônicas), if the texts focused on politics alone. In clever, humorous, and sensitive pieces, Gullar writes about animals, the plastic and performing arts, the complexities of poetry, the gentrification of favelas, the inscrutable links between intelligence and sexuality, and racism in Brazilian literature and music. Ferreira Gullar shows himself to be another master of the crônica.

2436 Ianelli, Mariana. Breves anotações sobre um tigre: crônicas. Desenhos de Alfredo Aquino. Prefácio de Ignácio de Loyola Brandão. Porto Alegre, Brazil: Ardotempo, 2013. 111 p.: ill., index.

Born in São Paulo in 1979, the author has published five books of various genres, some of which have have been winners or finalists in prestigious award contests, such as the Jabuti and the Casa de las Américas. Ianelli's pieces "run like prose that is more like poetry, and reality that is more like fiction," in the words of acclaimed novelist Ignácio Loyolla de Brandão (p. 14). Ianelli's crônicas focus on literary and artistic works, and on the writers and the filmmakers, musicians, painters and writers who create them. She writes about artistic predicaments, anonymity, and an oeuvre influenced by tragic news. She shares her insights about Sophia de Mello Breyner Andresen, Leonard Cohen, Francisco Goya, Rainer Maria Rilke, Andrei Tarkovsky, and many others.

2437 Kaz, Roberto. O livro dos bichos: a ararinha repatriada, o macaco candidato, o camundongo que foi para o espaço e outras reportagens. Ilustrações de Audrey Furlaneto. São Paulo: Companhia das Letras, 2016. 243 p.: ill.

Some of the informal, personable, empathetic, and humorous crônicas gathered here were previously published in the daily newspapers *O Globo* and *Folha de São Paulo* and the magazines *Piauí* and *Nautilus*. With pieces that are longer and more thematically cohesive than conventional crônicas, six thematic sections divide the total corpus of 21 texts, all of them focusing on famous or unknown animals. On the book jacket, João Moreira Salles contends that those who read this volume "will know how to place themselves in the shoes of a serpent or a bull and will better understand what is like to be an animal." This is "a book that moos, shrieks, barks, meows, peeps, clucks, and neighs." Sometimes, "it is out of pleasure, very often, out of pain," adds Salles. He informs the readers that there are animals there who "speak, crawl and play the piano." Some are cosmonauts, prehistoric, and "even inorganic, made out of cloth and Styrofoam."

2438 Kepp, Michael. Um pé em cada país: crônicas. Porto Alegre, Brazil: Tomo Editorial, 2015. 184 p.: ill.

A former freelance journalist who wrote for *Time and Newsweek* magazines, this American ex-pat living in Brazil since 1983 is now publishing his third book of crônicas. The author's preference for humor is evident in the titles of his first two volumes, *Sonhando com sotaque* (Dreaming with an Accent), from 2003, and *Tropeços nos trópicos* (Tripping in the Tropics), 2011. He writes lightly and creatively in Portuguese. At the same time, he remains American enough to maintain an entertaining critical distance from Brazil's reality and to see what many time Brazilians do not. The 73 crônicas are divided into five sections entitled, "Confidences," "Opinions," "Cultural Comparisons," "Travel," and "Contemplations."

2439 Lerner, Jaime. Quem cria, nasce todo dia. Curitiba, Brazil: Travessa dos Editores, 2014. 204 p.: ill.

A three-term mayor of Curitiba, Jaime Lerner surprises his readers with an uconventional life and equally unconventional writing. He campaigned for the office of mayor for a mere 12 days and won the election in one of the most important state capital cities of Brazil. Born to a family of Jewish immigrants from Poland, Lerner studied urbanism in France. His travels there and elsewhere are reflected in his writing, and so is his touching gesture of gratitude to his family. His short texts (rarely running more than two pages) are interspersed with his own handwritten notes and sketches of buildings, gardens, and much more. The book's short introduction notes that Lerner's writing reads like "sessions of generous friendship" (p. 6). Funny and emotional moments on his trips to China, Holland, Israel, Mexico, among other places, add color and laughter to his narratives. After enjoying a long life of challenges and discoveries, Lerner wants his writing, like other aspects of his life, to have a positive impact on people. In one of the last crônicas in this book, a man in the last phase of life is very serious about some advice: "Without poetry, there is no audacity . . . lose your fear of the ridiculous, and enjoy the best of what you see around you. Celebrating is a must" (p. 202).

2440 Maciel, Maria Esther. A vida ao redor: crônicas. Belo Horizonte, Brazil: Scriptum, 2014. 277 p.: ill.

A former Federal University of Minas Gerais professor in literary theory, Maria Esther Maciel has published several books of poetry, essays, and fiction. This work is a compilation of approximately 90 crônicas published in the cultural section of the daily *Estado de Minas* between July 2011 and April 2014. The crônicas address travel, animal care, life styles, art, cinema, and literature, among other topics. Her poetic sensibilities emerge in essays on the linguistic competence of bird species and street names in Brazil and Portugal. Maciel's writing shifts in tone and becomes more professorial when approaching topics such as the difference among irony, sarcasm, and debauchery. Interestingly, the *cronista* becomes more personable in a third-person narrative when she describes her own medical condition, a neurologic illness that prevented her from writing her weekly pieces for months.

2441 Moraes, Reinaldo. O cheirinho do amor: crônicas safadas. Rio de Janeiro: Alfaguara, 2014. 264 p.

The book's title says it all. While not easy to translate, one version in English could be "Little Smells of Love: Dirty Tales." Rather than "dirty," other choices would also be apt: "shameless," "naughty," "mischievous," or even "barefaced." The 37 well-written stories of this collection all have something to do with sex. They cover a wide spectrum of topics associated with sexuality, human and non-human alike. Written between March 2011 and May 2014 for the nationally circulated monthly magazine *Status*, these crônicas address cultural policies, the farce of orgies, blockbuster movies, and wild sex adventures, or the prudish hypocrisy in the Vatican to scandals in the political arena outside Rome.The humorous and the picaresque are also on display. One of the most entertaining, lightweight, yet educational pieces (fit, let's say, for study-abroad candidates) is the piece that explores the perceptions of American writers living in Brazil, like *New York Times* journalist Seth Kugel and crônista Matthew Shirts, about dating and kissing the Brazilian way.

2442 Mota, Urariano. Dicionário amoroso do Recife. Ilustrações de Leonardo Filho. Anagé, Brazil: Casarão do Verbo, 2014. 338 p.: ill. (Dicionário Amoroso)

The city of Recife, with its famous characters and unknown heroes, is the protagonist of this journalist and novelist's undated crônicas. Presented in alphabetical order, these 26 texts bring to life one of the most fascinating state capitals of Brazil, its rich history, and pioneering efforts in the arts, sciences and politics. The series, as its editors explain, is a way of exploring the well-known and secret spaces of Brazil's state capitals. Mota describes and reflects on the lives of Recife-born or Recife-adopted poets, sculptors, and another master of the crônica, Antonio Maria. Legendary venues like the Bar Savoy, a favorite spot for poet João Cabral de Melo Neto and sociologist Gilberto Freyre, are also described. In "Clarice Lispector e o frevo" (Clarice Lispector and Frevo), Mota evokes a 1976 visit of the acclaimed novelist to the house where she grew up and witnessed the growth and glory of frevo dance and music. Lesser-known people, like a homeless man who studied on his own and passed a qualifying exam for a desirable career at the Banco do Brasil are also part of this collection. Historical events, too, have a place in this volume, as we learn about mesmerizing Catholic Churches and their leaders, like Dom Helder Câmara, a steadfast defender of human rights and political freedom during the military governments. We also read about the first two synagogues ever built in the Americas, Kahal Zur Israel and Maguem Abraham, in the coastal city known as the Venice of the Tropics (p. 152). Mota details the history of the still-existing synagogue, Kahal Zur Israel, as described in a 1657 document cataloged in the Netherlands (p. 156). Mota also discusses the role of 23 of its faithful, who left Recife for what would become New York City on January 26, 1654, the day before the Dutch in Pernambuco surrendered to Portuguese forces after 24 years of occupation. Those 23 men, women, and children were among the first groups of Jewish immigrants to arrive in New Amsterdam. Mota describes a variety of documents on the subject, including verses by Sefardi poet Daniel Levi de Barros (p. 155).

2443 Moutinho, Marcelo. Na dobra do dia: crônicas. Rio de Janeiro: Rocco, 2015. 225 p.

In keeping with a long tradition of crônica writing Moutinho devotes this book to life in the city of Rio de Janeiro. Among Moutinho's undated pieces are descriptions of the streets of Barra da Tijuca, Copabacana, Lapa, Madureira and other neighborhoods. Bar scenes, the run-abouts of eccentrics, movie-house inconveniences, Carnaval rehearsals, flooding dramas, lack of males, samba jams, strange street names inform his crônicas. Moutinho's topics range more widely, though, as he continues another tradition of the crônica: writing about words and writing about writing, especially the perils and pleasures of writing crônicas. He also discusses, with good humor, the value of intimate and long-lasting friendships, and the call for the saideira (the last the beer bottle for the table, the one "for the road" that is never really the last one).

2444 Muniz Neto, Mentor. Proibido estacionar e outras histerias urbanas. São Paulo: Dash Editora, 2016. 221 p.

"The first slap I took in life was from the doctor, when I had just been born. The second one was when people started calling me by this name of mine" (p. 113). This self-portrait illustrates the author's joking attitude toward the world, at large, and his writing, in particular. The marketing manager shares his good humor and playful creativity when he addresses any or all of his 120,000 followers on FaceBook. Yes, this book collects entries initially posted on that global social media outlet. Continuing the tradition among cronistas of playing and questioning words, Muniz Neto not only picks on his own name, but also reveals his disgust at some old-fashioned and some contemporary linguistic uses. His fake pretentiousness urges him to declare that when he becomes president of the world, he will compose and publish *The World's Writing and Oral Language Manual*. One of his texts is a preview of that long book to come. This volume, whose title translates into English as "Parking Prohibited and Other Urban Hysterias," is the second book published by the São Paulo-native. Presented in chronological order, its short pieces seem to result, most of all, from the funny or unexpected small deeds and creative observations of daily life in a big city. His attitude shifts and an ironic vein flares when he tells the story about the smile he got at a traffic light stop from a man with a machine-gun in his lap: "I am happy to know that in this city where I waste my life away there still are strangers who smile at a stranger" (p. 137).

2445 Nahas, Ana Laura. Quase um segundo: crônicas. Vitória, Brazil: Cousa, 2013. 140 p.

Originally from Ribeirão Preto, state of São Paulo, the author released her first book of crônicas, *Todo sentiment*, in 2009. She has previously published these undated pieces in her own blog. Unrelated themes emerge, such as the meaning of the Day of the Dead, in Mexico, the nature of stuck-up people, and the tough days faced by cronistas with a deadline to meet but without a subject to write on. Some of Hahas' concerns are philosophical, like the origin and development processes of new ideas, the pleasure of small things, and the value of friendships. Nahas occasionally inserts quotes from other cronistas and from novelists and poets, such as Carlos Drummond de Andrade, Simone de Beauvoir, Rubem Braga, Gilberto Gil, Herman Hesse, and Clarice Lispector.

2446 Navarro, Walter. Creme e castigo: 100 crônicas escolhidas e ilustradas, 1996–2011. Belo Horizonte: Editora C/Arte, 2011. 281 p.: ill. (some color).

This visually appealing volume, with more than 100 images (50 of which were commissioned from 50 different plastic artists) contains 100 crônicas written by Walter Paraíso Ribeiro de Navarro Filho, aka Walter Navarro, between 1996 and 2011. Most of the entries were part of the author's column in the Belo Horizonte daily *O Tempo*. The book's title, "Cream and Punishment," is an obvious pun on *Crime and Punishment*, by Russian novelist Fyodor Mikhail Dostoevsky. The author's note of gratitude on the opening page is an ironic jab at the Brazilian government. He thanks the Ministério da Cultura (aka MinC, an agency within Brazil's federal executive branch of power assigned to culture), which sponsored the sophisticated edition of his book. Under tight control by the Workers' Party (PT), Navarro says that MinC would not have approved the expensive publication (on glossy pages with more than 100 images in color), had anyone in that office read the manuscript. Otherwise, "I am completely wrong and this country's government is democratic, accepts criticism, and does not practice censorship" (p. 4). Nearly all crônica's titles express some joking spirit, whether it is through sarcasm, puns, or other types of wordplay. A good number of Navarros' jokes and spoofs, here and there interspersed with serious comments, are aimed at politicians, especially those associated with the Workers' Party, in particular, Luiz Inácio Lula da Silva. The former president's alleged hypocrisy, vanity, insincerity, rudeness, and obscene or uneducated speech points are all noted by Navarro. Navarro's language itself is a mix of pop and erudite lexicons, a zigzag of x-rated and sophisticated wording.

2447 Pellanda, Luís Henrique. Asa de sereia. Porto Alegre, Brazil: Arquipélago Editorial, 2013. 207 p. (Arte da crônica)

A former journalist of the daily newspapers *Gazeta do Povo* and *Primeira Hora*, Luís Henrique Pellanda is one of the most respected cronistas of contemporary Brazil. This volume includes 44 dated pieces of regular length (2–3 pages) and a series of 19 vignettes under the label "Meus vizinhos, seus amigos, teus irmãos e o diabo" (My Neighbors, Their Friends, Your Sibblings and the Devil). The web site *Vida Breve* has published most of the pieces. Others have appeared in the magazines *Topnews*, *Opete-Mercado*, and *Mediação*. A few more have come out in the newspapers *Gazeta do Povo* and *Suplemento Pernambuco*. As an observer of the city of Curitiba for 11 years, Pellanda describes poetic and prosaic scenes, such as conversations with the homeless or taxi drivers, clowns, drunkards, lunatics and prostitutes. He is interested in listening to other people's conversations in the streets. An old couple fighting on the sidewalk or a widow reminiscing at a cemetery, these make up the fabric of his crônicas. Urban developments and climatic changes, with their consequences on both the city dwellers' life quality and the trees and flowers' overall health, also interest him. He writes, for example, that "frosting is like art, magical but useless" (p. 101). He can be philosophical, too. Pride requires nothing but smoke, he implies after witnessing a young man recover from a fall on the street (p. 61). From a café's window, the cronista and a fellow writer, Luiz Ruffato, see the teenager wake up from the alcohol-induced nap that followed his tumble. Though the contents of his backpack were stolen and gone by now, all that the youngster needed was to light up a cigarette he got from a passer-by to feel all right again (p. 61).

"People out there say that writers are good at observing the world and mapping out its shortcomings, that they have eyes in the back of their necks, antennas in their souls, and three golden hearts in their chests," says Pellanda (p. 59). That is nonsense, he counter-argues: "We see nothing, only the invisible, some gaps, at best." The pains we "pretend to feel," though, are truly ours, he adds, paraphrasing Portuguese bard Fernando Pessoa (p. 59).

2448 Pellanda, Luís Henrique. Detetive à deriva. Porto Alegre, Brazil: Arquipélago Editorial, 2016. 223 p. (Arte da crônica)

In the author's note closing this volume, Luís Henrique Pellanda alludes to the quotation by Raymond Chandler's private detective Philip Marlowe opens his third book of crônicas: "It looked like a good neighborhood to cultivate bad habits" (p. 7). As critic Alvaro Costa e Silva explains, this book is a series of discoveries. Maybe the best of them is the connection between a flâneur and a detective, the same as that between cronistas and mystery writers. "It is day-to-day mysteries told through some leads that only the author sees," adds Costa e Silva. For Costa e Silva, the detective "was above all a sentimental guy. [And] Pellanda, [is] a lyrical tough-guy." Lyricism does abound in this gathering of 68 dated short texts, most of which were previously published in the Curitiba daily *Gazeta do Povo*. Urban life in all its complexities, whether violent or endearing, is raw material for Pellanda's pen. The city's scenes and sounds provide inspiration. They may include odd, subtle or extremely bizarre behavior of unknown individuals in the streets, like prostitutes, vendors, or mentally ill folks. Pellanda's eyes are also inquisitive and compassionate when he ponders animal and vegetable life. He is uninhibited about his love for trees of all kinds, for example. The writer's ears are keen on birdcalls and their potential to suggest forebodings, but he also creates poetic lines out of construction noises and the fragmented stories he hears on a city bus.

2449 Pena, Felipe. Beijo na testa é pior do que separação: crônicas do fim de tudo. São Paulo: Primavera Editorial, 2013. 177 p.

Having published 14 books so far (novels, biographies, essays, and short stories), Felipe Pena is a versatile professional with significant experience as journalist, psychologist, college professor, television program director, and school administrator. The central theme, which runs through most of the pieces, is separation, not only romantic, but also separation between writers and readers, politicians and voters, intellectuals and the masses. Pena employs a self-labeled unpretentious tone in pieces that tell stories about famous or unknown individuals. Despite that central theme of separation, his crônicas range widely in their topics. Written in first–or third-person, those pieces may be about a middle-class woman's love affair with a drug-lord or a fable about solitude and fear through the interactions of a grasshopper and a butterfly. A confessed ex-supporter of the Workers' Party, Pena bitterly assesses the role of Lula in the country's corruption schemes. He is similarly unsparing when sarcastically addressing a crônica-letter to the music superstar Caetano Veloso, making fun of the musician's faith in the role of artists within the nation's political landscape.

2450 Pignatari, Décio. Terceiro tempo. Cotia, Brazil: Ateliê Editorial, 2014. 120 p.

In his introductory essay, Antero Greco reminds us of how Décio Pinatari's "creative disquiet has illuminated Brazil's national culture on various fronts, as translator, poet, essayist, professor, playwright, and communications theoretician" (p. 7). Like few others, he adds, Pignatari has been able "to combine erudition and simplicity, depth and grace, seriousness and lightness" (p. 7). In this volume, we find Pignatari's short texts on soccer. Originally published in his column "Terceiro tempo" (Third Time), in *Folha de São Paulo*, between February and March, 1965, his crônicas appear here in chronological order without thematic separation. The book's design follows some of esthetic patterns of the concrete poetry movement, such as geometric forms and enlarged lettering fonts of book covers, posters, panels, paintings, etc. A declared fan of São Paulo's soccer club Corinthians, Pignatari writes during a period in which the nation's best team was

Santos, from the neighboring coastal city where Pelé unquestionably reigned as the world's greatest player. The cronista creates mythic conversations between soccer players, mixing the stylized narrative voice of the *Iliad* with tropes and mannerisms of sports commentators. The poet in Pignatari rereads the commonplace in the world of soccer's jargon and other communicative behavior. The soccer lover in him mingles that world with the world of plastic artists, and the semiotician analyzes the symbolic rites of the sport. The politicized columnist also focuses on the legal issues involving players and clubs, as well as on the ties between soccer and Brazil's political discourse at large. The cronista's task-at-hand, however, is not easy. Pignatari confesses that he struggles to keep a balance between the straightforward expectations of many of his readers, like those of an uneducated taxi driver or the neighborhood bakery manager, and the demands for sophistication from the newspaper editors.

2451 Prata, Antonio. Trinta e poucos. São Paulo: Companhia das Letras, 2016. 226 p.

Originally published in the daily *Folha de São Paulo*, these undated pieces by a television scriptwriter cover a wide range of topics without a thematic or chronological sequence. Topics can be a heart-warming conversation on a taxicab ride, the nearly surreal dream of seeing the aurora borealis, the impairing addiction to procrastination, or the curious differences between Christmas and Halloween traditions. Prata's crônicas may also concern the process of aging, the shock of a page of newspaper with your own article being used to wrap fish at a street market, and the hardship of changing diapers in the middle of the night. Several of texts narrate the pains and joys, or the magic and the dullness of parenting babies and little children. The funny side of daily life comes alive on those pages, too. That is the case when the cronista narrates his awkward experience of brushing his teeth right next to a stranger who does the same at a restroom at work, and then meeting that person minutes later at a formal interview. Several these crônicas narrate the ups-and-downs of the World Cup for a passionate soccer fan like him and millions of other Brazilians, including the historically infamous game in which the Cup's 2014 host nation, Brazil, mysteriously and shamefully loses to Germany, 1 to 7. On the serious side of the collection, the author comments on a biography of acclaimed cronista Rubem Braga. Prata confesses his profound admiration for him and writes a few pieces that address their intellectual and personal affinity. He also fictionalizes an encounter between them that never happened.

2452 Prêmio UFES de Literatura, 2nd, Vitória, Brazil, 2013-2014. Coletânea de contos & crônicas. II Prêmio UFES de Literatura. Vitória, Brazil: EDUFES, 2014. 204 p. (II Prêmio UFES de Literatura; 6)

Out of a pool of submissions from 223 writers, 10 received the opportunity to publish their crônicas or short stories in this volume organized by the official press of the Federal University of Espírito Santo. It is the second volume in a collection that started in 2010. According to an official statement in the book, the contest "aims at fomenting good literature, promoting Brazil's literary production, and revealing new talents" (p. 5). Essayists, journalists, poets, college professors, and short story writers are some of the contributors to this anthology (six males and four females). They represent each of the states of the country's Southeast region, except Minas Gerais.

2453 Rodrigues, Mário. As coisas incríveis do futebol: as melhores crônicas de Mário Filho. Apresentação de José Trajano. Organização de Francisco Michielin. São Paulo: Ed. Ex Machina, 2014. 199 p.: ill.

In newspaper columns, *crônicas*, and books, Mário Rodrigues Filho, aka Mário Filho (brother of famed playwright Nelson Rodrigues), created much of the language used to describe Brazil's greatest passion, soccer. So influential was he that after his death, the offical name of Maracanã, then world's largest soccer stadium, was changed to Estádio Jornalista Mário Filho. The 28 selected pieces included in this compilation are arguably some of the very first in a crônica subgenre created by him, the sports crônica. (According to some critics, the Mario Filho is also a pioneer of what has been called "the New Journalism," whose proponents were Gay Talese, Norman Mailer and Tom Wolfe, among others, thanks to his piece "A paixão do futebol" (The Passion of Soccer), originally published in the Rio newspaper *O Globo Sportivo* on May 13, 1949.) These crônicas were initially released in the 1940s and 50s, when "crônicas in Brazil produced quite a splash and constituted the topics of much conversation at public agencies, cafés, schools, factories, and stadiums," according to the introductory essay by José Trajano (p. 11). One of the most significant contributions of these texts is their descriptions of the origins of soccer phenomena such as the *jogo bonito* (beautiful flair), or the highly creative, playful, and tricky style that characterizes Brazilian soccer. Mário Filho presents numerous tales about soccer's mythic proportions, the individualism of Brazilian soccer players, and the superstitions of fans and coaches. His crônicas also document how certain expressions of soccer jargon developed.

2454 Ruffato, Luiz. Minha primeira vez. Porto Alegre, Brazil: Arquipélago Editorial, 2014. 189 p. (Arte da crônica)

After dozens of novels and short story releases, the prolific and internationally hailed novelist Luiz Ruffato has launched his first book of crônicas. Most of these texts, which date from 2008–2014, were previously published in the Angolan magazine *África 21* and in the Brazilian edition of *El País*, the Spanish daily for which the Mineiro writer has been writing weekly since 2013. Ruffato tells us that "[his] crônicas result from reflections on manifestations of life, and the most profound of them are born out of friendly and undemanding conversations" (p. 9). He introduces himself in a piece titled, "Sabe com quem está falando?," which, in Brazil, is an expression of class arrogance or social status, meaning "Do you know whom you are talking to?" Rather than claiming any upper-class heritage, Ruffino does the opposite. He asserts his humble origins and rejects the mantle of truth-bearer. Ruffato's mother, a washerwoman, and his father, a popcorn vendor, were barely literate. He himself began working for money as a child. Nonetheless, he was able to gain an education and began working as a journalist until he realized that literature, not news, was his mission. Ruffato also claims to see himself as a constant learner without any answers, somebody who continues to dream of a more just society (p. 13). Brazil's economic abyss and rampant violence are a running theme in Ruffato's crônicas. Other evils of Brazilian society, like domestic violence, machismo, and rape, also impel him to write. The intellectual side of the cronista appears as he discusses the attitudes of the Brazilian intelligentsia, the successes of Brazilian writers Clarice Lispector and Fernando Pessoa, the vicissitudes of the book market in Brazil, as well as the inspirational lives and legacies of Frei Betto, Humberto Mauro, Marcos Bagno and Maria Valéria Rezende, among many others profiled in the book.

2455 Sanches Neto, Miguel. Cidades alugadas: crônicas reunidas. Ponta Grossa, Brazil: Container Edições 2014. 206 p.

A novelist who has 30 published works, Santos Neto is also a college professor with a PhD in literary theory from University of Campinas. Dated, but not arranged in chronological order, these crônicas span a period of 12 years, from 2001 to 2013. The volume closes with a biography of the author with an emphasis on the eight cities and towns where he has lived, a life characterized by frequent moves as reflected in the book's title: *Cidades alugadas* (Rented Cities). A number of these texts appear to have been published in Curitiba's daily paper *Gazeta do Povo* and the national, high-profile magazine *Bravo!*, among other venues. Several of Santos Neto's crônicas are openly autobiographical. As a child in a family of very modest resources, he worked as a shoeshine, carpenter, barber, and bricklayer. He mingles his private trajectories with accounts of the places he has lived and visited, such as Rio de Janeiro, São João del Rei, Brasília, Madrid and Havana. We learn about the local culinary and the nightlife of bars and other places of entertainment. He also travels and writes about different cities and towns within his home state, Paraná, with its innumerable immigrant communities, and the distance he perceives between people engaged in cultural practices and people who prosper or just survive through agricultural exploits (p. 175–177). He also discusses social phenomena, such as the rural exodus caused by the coffee farming mechanization and the growing number of new inhabitants in rural towns. He critiques "pseudo-development," a process responsible for environmental problems and socioeconomic shortcomings. In other pieces, he is deeply personal, describing, for example, the angst of a broken heart, "Nove de Agosto" (August Ninth).

2456 Serafini, Breno. Millôres dias virão. Porto Alegre, Brazil: Libretos, 2013. 211 p.: bibl., ill. (Libretos universidade)

Humor and irony characterize the crônicas signed by Millôr Fernandes according to blogger and poet Bruno Serafini. Here Serafini analyzes 524 pieces written by Fernandes between March 1983 and April 1993 for the national magazines *Istoé* and *Istoé/Senhor*. The Gaúcho writer places Fernandes' work within a historical context, explaining that from 1983–1993, Brazil experienced one of its most acute social and economic crises. He labels Fernandes' oeuvre, "anarchic humanism." Many of his pieces expose the vices of public figures and reveal the strategies that ordinary people use to survive their day-to-day struggles. Serafini pays particular attention to Fernandes' use of sarcasm, including the evident fictionalization of history through historical research. The book's title is a pun on the author's name, playing with the notion that, with Millôr Fernandes' help, better (*melhores*, in Portuguese) days are coming. Serafini ends his book with a joke between Fernandes and one of his readers. Fernandes had asked if readers could tell him the difference between a politician and a thief. One reader replied, "one I choose, and the other chooses me" (p. 198). Delighted, Fernandes answered, "You are a genius. Nobody else was capable of telling me one single difference" (p. 198).

2457 Soares, Wellington. O dia em que quase namorei a Xuxa. Teresina, Brazil: Quimera Eventos, Cultura e Editoração, 2013. 162 p.

A light humorous tone and thematic variety mark this collection, the third book of crônicas by a short story writer, literature professor, and cultural agent from Piauí. A number of the texts reproduced here are from the author's column in the cultural section "Vida," of Teresina's daily *Meio Norte*, and/or in the magazine *Revestres*.

In his introduction, Ignácio de Loyola Brandão notes that the book is a mix of "naughtiness, sadness, humor, irony, and cruelty, plus charm and poetry" (p. 5). There are digressions on literary quandaries, such as Capitu's doubtful adultery in Machado de Assis' novel *Dom Casmurro*, or the enlightenment offered by African-Brazilian authors Cruz e Souza and Lima Barreto, Rio Grande do Sul novelist Moacyr Scliar, and German author Johann Wolfgang von Goethe. Moving and heartfelt pieces about the author's friends and family are also present in the collection, including one about the premature death of his brother to drug abuse and another about his daughters' dream of seeing him date the television superstar Xuxa.

2458 Tezza, Cristóvão. A máquina de caminhar: 64 crônicas e um discurso contra o autor. Rio de Janeiro: Editora Record, 2016. 191 p.: ill.

Selected by the volume's editor, who also compiled Tezza's first book of crônicas, *Um operário em férias* (see HLAS 72:2574), the 64 short texts of *A máquina de caminhar* (The Treadmill) were previously published in Curitiba's daily *Gazeta do Povo* between April 1, 2008 and Nov. 4, 2014. A native of Lages, in the southern state of Santa Catarina, Tezza was 46 years old and well into his literary career, with 14 published books, when the Curitiba newspaper invited him to write a weekly crônica column. His work is experimental, and with a PhD and several years of experience teaching college literature, he often questions the writing process. His short texts in this volume are between 2,800 and 2,900 characters (title included), as they meticulously follow the precise specifications established by the newspaper editors. His crônicas do not break the trend of meta-writing. In "A imaginação" (The Imagination), for example, he supports William Faulkner's notion that three dominant impulses are necessary and orient the writing process: imagination, experience, and observation. Just one of them, though, a writer's imagination, can make up for the absence or low level of the other two impulses. "It is an interesting triad for us to think how life recreates itself in writing; in some ways, entire literary corpuses articulate themselves within the balance or unbalance of those qualities" (p. 37). In "Um discurso contra o autor" (A Lecture against the Author), the fascinating essay that closes the book (not a crônica itself), Tezza reflects on the differences between writing fiction and the short newspaper pieces. For him, writing crônicas is like "a state of permanent exposure" (p. 170). It is like, "writing aloud," whereas writing novels is like, "writing in low voice" (p. 165). Other pieces in the book are ethnic, cultural and political debates mainly about Brazil, such as the so-called *preguiça brasileira* (Brazilian laziness), and the dueling forces of Brazilians' cordiality versus savagery. The remnants and consequences of slavery, the nuances of cultural production for export versus those of mainstream consumption, the political polarization of the last five or six years, and the rhetoric of leftist populism and political correctness, are likewise, subjects of several pieces. He also muses about other writers and their work, such as science fiction by Julio Verne and Ray Bradbury, to the life and work by Mikhail Dostoevsky, the mysteries of comedy in Dante Alighieri, influences from Carlos Drummond de Andrade and Millôr Fernandes, and the legacies of Stefan Zweig.

Poetry

CHARLES A. PERRONE, *Professor Emeritus of Portuguese and Luso-Brazilian Literature and Culture, University of Florida*

TO CLOSE THE second decade of the 21st century, the principal observations about the genre of lyric made in *HLAS* 72 remain true and applicable, above all the continuity of poetic enterprise in publishing (both university and trade presses), public events, and useful virtual domains, which, overall, may have even expanded (e.g., poesia.net). Of recent note in criticism are volumes with multiple segments concerning individual poets, both contemporary (item **2483**) and historical (item **2540**). A salient edited volume concerns the 1970s (item **2520**). The concept of "contemporary," and accompanying notions of "plurality," concern Marcos Siscar, a present-day analyst (item **2546**); he also contributes a volume on the grand figure of poet-theorist Haroldo de Campos (item **2547**), whose presence is reaffirmed yearly at the Hora H program at the Casa das Rosas in São Paulo. Exciting new North American studies (item **2541**) also examine Haroldo de Campos' inimitable work. For his part, Augusto de Campos (who was a highlight of this section in *HLAS* 72) is also a continuing subject of critical inquiry (item **2552**). The acknowledged dean of national lyric, Carlos Drummond de Andrade, has been studied anew in international venues (item **2526**) and by leading national critics (item **2539**), as has João Cabral de Melo Neto (items **2480** and **2540**). Other collected papers include at least one volume dedicated to myth criticism (item **2530**). Inter-American poetics orients a series of wide-ranging studies across borders (items **2470, 2525, 2526, 2527,** and **2528**), while back matter in tomes of collected poems offer substantial critical material (especially as in item **2462**).

The new volumes of complete poems that most merit attention (whether reprints or first editions) are those of Oswald de Andrade (item **2462**), Hilda Hilst (item **2499**), and Adélia Prado (item **2532**). Other similar publications honor productive local writers (items **2481, 2497,** and **2514**). Collected verse of two leading names of the *poesia marginal* phenomenon appeared, one having published consistently since the 1970s (item **2479**) and one returning at an advanced age (item **2524**). Antonio Carlos Secchin, a poet-professor now active in the ABL (Academia Brasileira de Letras), has published a particularly elegant volume (item **2538**). The current crop of authors includes many other men and women whose poetic vocation parallels employment in academia (items **2463**, **2488**, **2490**, **2460**, **2469**, **2482**, **2523**, and **2511**). While only one reprint of an absolute classic emerged (item **2464**), several notable active voices issued new collections (items **2475**, **2509**, and **2467**), especially Salgado Maranhão (items **2513** and **2512**) and Rodrigo Garcia Lopes (item **2505**), both of whom have experience in the US. Besides them, numerous other poets participate in a geocartographic paradigm including voyage and travel (items **2504, 2493, 2515, 2484, 2536, 2534,** and **2466**). International articulations also include the employment of haiku (item **2496**) and a trans-American approach (item **2513**). Within Brazil, regional-interest items include verse-histories and nuclei in Goiania (item **2519**), Pernambuco (items **2503**, **2545**, and **2522**) and Maranhão (items **2501**, **2535**, and **2514**). Other identitarian items have appeared, such as one concerning Afro-Brazilian heritage (item **2486**) and another on the emerging topic of "peripheral literature" (item **2551**). In some works, the greatest attraction may not be its theme or author, but the vehicle itself, alternative media or modes of presentation other than a standard print book (items **2544, 2554, 2494, 2473,** and **2492**).

In other instances, links with the other arts are a prime feature. In Brazil the always engaging topic of music and poetry endures, with studies of famous collectives (item **2548**) and landmark composers (item **2525**), and titles of singer-songwriters who also edit/write (items **2473, 2478, 2485,** and **2517**). In this realm, one must include a superb affective anthology of Vinícius de Moraes (item **2516**), since it brings together many song texts by the dean of Bossa Nova lyrics. He also wrote sensual verse, so he was included in a colossal anthology of erotic poetry that covers all centuries of national letters (item **2465**). Both elder and younger poets have published in the circle of verse that is openly preoccupied—in title, theme, imagery, symbols, lexicon—with the bodily, the corporeal, the sensual, the sexual (items **2460, 2463, 2481, 2482, 2532,** and **2554**). Among the most noted of these is some late-career work of Hilda Hilst (item **2499**), one of several female writers gaining deserved greater attention. To repeat an assertion mentioned in *HLAS* 72, although numerous observers believe that the goal of gender-neutral equity has been accomplished in parts of the realm of poetry, one can still document the vigor of women's poetry (lyric by female authors), such as a feminist feature in a bilingual international issue (item **2459**) and publications in series around Brazil (items **2474, 2486, 2487, 2493, 2502, 2504, 2511, 2530, 2532, 2533, 2535,** and **2536**), with or without accompanying critical apparatus.

In any honest assessment of poetry in Brazil, in any period, the dominant practice is personal lyric of experiential navigation, but affiliate concerns persist. In the second half of the 2010s, given controversial governmental (executive, legislative, and judicial) occurrences, historical and participatory factors became more intense (see, for example, items **2491** and **2555**). Social media has been used to disseminate political matter—announcements and messages as well as chapbooks, books, and editorials. Poetry files (virtual and print) and collective endeavors include protests of police violence against teachers (Paraná), accounts of high school occupations (São Paulo), and above all an anthology in support of former president Lula da Silva (item **2506**), which includes three visual poems by Augusto de Campos (Instagram #poetamenos), one a reprint of a 1967 popcreto during the early years of the authoritarian military regime. An opening session of the 2018 FLIP (Festival Literário de Paraty), "Poesia e Resistência," explored how lyric in all its forms can respond to objectionable circumstances. Whether as committed verse or non-normative language, poetry fulfills its function as an antidote to the ordinary and as an instrument of expression of the human condition.

2459 Alba: culture in translation. Vol. 8, March 2017, Contemporary feminist Brazilian poetry. Edited by Virna Teixeira and Jessica Pujol. London: Carnaval Press.

This special issue features seven poets, some discursive segments, two stories, and abundant illustrations. The poetry is varied, from blatantly discursive free verse to prose poems and experimental Neo-Baroque passages. The most notable translator is the award-winning Idra Novey. This title, naturally, is apt for gender approaches to literature, but also for transatlantic studies.

2460 Alves-Bezerra, Wilson. Vertigens. São Paulo: Iluminuras, 2015. 71 p. (Poesia)

This sequence of 29 page-long texts (identified with Roman numerals, I–XXIX) provides a vertiginous experience in a seeming mix of oneiric and real-life sources. Intertextuality is prominent here, as the poet-professor includes an abundance of literary references, some obvious and others not as much. Stylistically there many different ingredients: symbolist, Beat, marginal, Neo-Baroque, among others. Corporeal and erotic imagery are frequent in the delirium of a lyrical self (narrator) with no set compass.

2461 Andrade, Mário de. A lição do amigo: cartas de Mário de Andrade a Carlos Drummond de Andrade, anotadas pelo destinatário. Apresentação por Carlos Drummond de Andrade. Posfácio por André Botelho. São Paulo: Companhia das Letras, 2015. 437 p.: bibl.

While this volume is officially categorized as correspondence, it is fully relevant to this section on Poetry as the author of the two decades of epistles is no less than the "pope" of Brazilian modernism and the recipient is the universally acknowledged doyen of national poetry. The annotations by the latter should be considered as part of the book's critical apparatus, as should the opening presentation (from the original 1982 publication) and the afterword that confirm the main value of the collected letters as a source to study the esthetic education of *modernismo*. While some of the letters are two-liners with little artistic interest, many of Mário's letters are long and replete with material for biographers, literary historians, aficionados, apprentice poets, or anyone who appreciates well-crafted prose.

Andrade, Mário de. O turista aprendiz. See item **2859**.

2462 Andrade, Oswald de. Poesias reunidas. Coordenação editorial por Jorge Schwartz e Gênese Andrade. São Paulo: Companhia das Letras, 2017. 321 p.: bibl., ill., index.

This reprint edition of the collected verse of one of the heavy hitters of Brazilian modernism includes novelties: two dozen previously unpublished poems. The critical apparatus and back matter number nearly 100 pages, including a brief self-presentation by the poet himself, a letter by Drummond, and reprints of two indispensable essays, one by Mário da Silva Brito, the best known chronicler of *modernismo*, and the landmark study of Oswald's radicality by Haroldo de Campos, to this day the single most indispensable analysis of this poetic corpus. For a review of the original 1945 edition, see *HLAS 11:3425*.

2463 Andrade, Paulo. Corpo Arquivo. São Paulo: Patuá, 2014. 96 p.

A poet-professor known for studies of Torquato Neto and Sebastião Uchoa Leite (see *HLAS 72:2580*), both of whom inspire textual dialogues, Andrade has divided his own book of verse into six sections: archive, dramatic bodies, ethereal bodies, ex/centric bodies, camera obscura, and minimal poisons. Bodies here are literal—the vessel of human life, erotic instruments, sites of experience, and more conceptual—bodies of knowledge, textual corpora, figures. A sharp preface by fiction writer Fernando Fiorese develops the notion of duality between *physis* and *logos* in these poems, which can be deceptively simple or simply abstract.

2464 **Anjos, Augusto dos.** EU e outras poesias. Edição comemorativa dos 100 anos do EU. João Pessoa, Brazil: Academia Paraibana de Legras; Brasília: Senado Federal, 2012. 252 p.: ill.

There have been many reprint editions of this landmark book of imaginative premodernist verse, but this one stands out for the timing (centenary celebration), critical choice (reprint of courageous 1920 editorial presentation), and iconography (mostly photos). For the review of a 1982 edition, see *HLAS 46:6191*.

2465 **Antologia da poesia erótica brasileira.** Organização de Eliane Robert Moraes. Desenhos de Arthur Luiz Piza. Cotia, Brazil: Ateliê Editorial, 2015. 499 p.: bibl., ill.

Nearly 150 poets—from the 17th to the 21st century, and representing all schools and esthetic trends—are included in this grand undertaking, fruit of long and rigorous textual research. The verses can be sensual in allusive fashion or obscene in outright ways. The addition of numerous anonymous items complements the collection. The substantial critical introduction adds to the scholarly utility of the volume.

2466 **Autran, Lúcio.** Fragmentos de um exílio voluntário. Rio de Janeiro: Editora Bookess, 2016. 96 p.

This book brings together three dozen linked poems by a respected author who debuted in 1985 and who has published regularly since then. Rather than a gathering of varied lyrical instances, this collection comprises a sequence, a sort of poetic voyage—mental and physical—from a space of disillusionment and anguish to an inland abode where family and contemplation of the arts are possible. The poems are rarely short, as the self-imposed "exile" prompts a lot of thought and image-laden responses. The last entry refashions fragments (parts/pieces of the preceding poems) in a grand effort to unify the whole.

2467 **Azevedo, Carlito.** Livro das postagens. Rio de Janeiro: 7Letras, 2016. 73 p.

This is the first book since 2009 (see *HLAS 66:3065*) by this well-known poet-translator who debuted under the sign of innovation in the 1990s. This slim volume comprises just two poems. In the first, "Livro do cão," a (canine?) voice imprisoned in a cube addresses a possible audience with constant reference to an author who "should be there." The intertextual, metaliterary exercise expands in the titular second text, a sort of collage of private thoughts mixed with citations, paraphrases, words overheard, and snippets of emails. A sense of frustration can be culled from both long poems.

2468 **Barros, Manoel de.** Menino do mato. Rio de Janeiro: Alfaguara, 2015. 112 p.

The author (1916–2014) went from an obscure rural writer to one of the most celebrated poets of the late 20th century. This reprint edition has two parts; the first titular one, composed of six lyrical instances, recalls childhood and contact with nature, and the second contains 36 brief utterances, from one-line aphorisms to half-page utterances of an adult longing for the days of innocence and apprenticeship. The very brief preface does not make a clear argument to justify the new edition from a critical point of view.

2469 **Bastos, Alcmeno.** Poemenos. Rio de Janeiro: Editora Batel, 2016. 130 p.

Bastos, a poet-professor who has written extensively about both fiction and poetry, divides this collection of poems into six untitled sections. The groupings, however, have thematic cohesion. The first is craft-oriented and metaliterary, the second is amatory, the third is lyrico-spatial, the fourth is self-concerned, the fifth is temporally driven, and the sixth can be seen as a combination of the preceding divisions. The title inevitably echoes Augusto de Campos' *Poetamenos* (see *HLAS 40:7509*) but there is no sense whatsoever of the verbivocovisual esthetic of concrete poetry.

2470 **Bittencourt, Rita Lenira de Freitas.** Guerra e poesia: dispositivos bélico-poéticos do modernismo. Porto Alegre, Brazil: UFRGS Editora, 2014. 244 p.: bibl., ill.

Like so many academic publications, this book is based on a thesis intent on implementing an abundant theoretical apparatus. Yet the analytical proposal is unusual and intriguing. The point of departure for regionally inflected socioesthetic readings is the historic turning point that was the War of Paraguay (1865–70) pitting Brazil, Argentina, and Uruguay against their disturbingly successful land-locked neighbor. The author first considers sambas and folk quatrains that mention the war, especially those that reflect subjectivities concerned with the construction of national identity. The main corpus is modernist poetry (vanguardia in the case of the Argentine texts employed) in which bellicosity is both literal and a figuration of avant-garde impulses. The literary material is complemented with readings of painting and sculpture. Given the transnational configurations in the text, this original study merits appreciation by inter-American studies as well.

2471 Bresciani, Alberto. Sem passagem para Barcelona. Rio de Janeiro: José Olympio Editora, 2015. 106 p.

This is the second book of personal, often disenchanted free verse by an author approaching his 60th year and aware of time gone by and multiple manifestations of lack. The title connotes an absence of passage, poems with falls, voids, tears, pain, ashes, survival, and other signs that might be tagged as existentially anguished.

2472 Britto, Paulo Henriques. Nenhum mistério. São Paulo: Companhia Das Letras, 2018. 70 p.

A short but dense and penetrating collection of fresh poems by a leading voice of present-day poetry. The author deploys fixed forms with rare talent and sharp wit. He also writes in English: "there's no second chance: this is the end."

2473 Caderno de poesias. Seleção de textos e concepção do espetáculo por Maria Bethânia. Idealização do projeto por Maria Bethânia, Heloisa Maria Murgel Starling, e Wander Melo Miranda. Direção do vídeo e projeto gráfico por Gringo Cardia. Belo Horizonte, Brazil: EDUFMG, 2015. 274 p.: bibl., ill. (some color), index.

This multimedia volume is meticulously prepared and exquisitely produced. Based on a 2009 show, the famed vocalist selected and sequenced 75 literary items, mainly poems, most of which were matched with reproductions of geomusically themed works of art. The accompanying DVD contains visual treatments of the musical numbers. The book also includes critical assessments, brief artistic biographies of the chosen authors (poets, lyricists, and creative prose writers), and a bibliography. As in previous musico-literary experiences, the singer-connoisseur selects both texts of artists of her own generation (e.g., Caetano Veloso, Waly Salomão) and classics of Luso-Brazilian letters (e.g., Fernando Pessoa, Clarice Lispector—the main voices of Brazilian modernism). A truly gratifying spectacle.

2474 Caiafa, Janice. Patchwork. Rio de Janeiro: 7Letras, 2016. 58 p.

The author is better known as an urban anthropologist with several monographs to her credit. Simultaneously she has published half a dozen short books of personal, cosmopolitan free verse informed by keen perception and intertextuality across discursive genres and borders: Europe, North America, South America, modern poetry, fine arts, song, essays, and her own repertory. The title of this latest book dovetails with a poem named "Crazy Quilt," a metaphor for the creative process at work here.

2475 Carpinejar. Todas as mulheres. Rio de Janeiro: Bertrand Brasil, 2015. 109 p.

The author is one of the nation's most prolific across genres. This work adds to his repertory of lyric poetry; it comprises a hundred linked instances (without titles) that form a single long poem driven by the recurring question "Who will be my widow?" Thus "all the women" (todas as mulheres) of the title refers not to the wide range of feminine possibility but to the narrator's own self-circumscribed affective world. While some of the contemplations and images reach beyond an essentially romantic enclosure, the language is scarcely innovative.

2476 Carvalho, Hermínio Bello de. Meu zeppelin prateado: poemas. Rio de Janeiro: Folha Seca, 2015. 86 p.

Having debuted in the early sixties, this well-regarded poet-lyricist-author of crônicas issues his sixth collection of personal free verse marked by the prevalence of emotivity over any intellectual operator. The best image of this collection is indeed the title itself, drawn from the opening poem.

2477 **Castro, Flávio.** For mar (1999–2014). Rio de Janeiro: 7Letras, 2016. 103 p.

In his third collection of ultramodern verse, this linguistically obsessed word-artist distributes his fragmented experiments into five sections: "for mar" (an ambivalent splicing), "ideogramas" (alphabetic one-liners, in a clear nod to the criticism and practice of the concrete poets of São Paulo), "braille" (an effective cummings-esque tactile figuration), "côdea" (single word with echoes of code, coda, and modifiers), and "ravinas" (a spatial conceit of fracture). The author calls the inner divisions of his compostions "esthetic blocks," and the concern for artistry and architecture, as opposed to any sort of discursivity, is patent. Very clear debt to 20th-century (neo)avant-garde. See *HLAS 72:2601* for his similar previous book.

2478 **César, Chico.** Versos pornográficos. Ilustrações de Sári Szántó. Rio de Janeiro: Confraria do Vento, 2015. 45 p.: ill.

With a helpful preface exploring the distinction between the erotic and the pornographic, this chapbook, in effect, offers rather sexually explicit verse with an occasional thought-provoking observation. One of its selling points, transgeneric, is that the author is a successful singer-songwriter.

2479 **Chacal.** Tudo (e mais um pouco): poesia reunida (1971–2016). São Paulo: Editora 34, 2016. 407 p.: bibl., index.

Collected poems of one of the principal voices of the so-called *poesia marginal* of the 1970s and early 1980s (see *HLAS 70:2172*). In addition to the decades of chapbooks and short books of informal, experiential verse, this title includes the text of a recent collective autobiographical performance, adding creative perspective to critical understanding of the generational phenomenon and attitudes toward literary practice.

2480 **Costa, Ricardo Ramos.** Poéticas da visualidade em João Cabral de Melo Neto e Joan Miró: a poesia como crítica de arte. Jundiaí, Brazil: Paco Editorial, 2014. 222 p.: bibl., ill., index.

Originally a doctoral thesis, this monograph qualifies as criticism in comparative literature on two counts, the transnational focus (Brazil, Spain) and the cross-genre approach (literature and plastic arts). Cabral's fascination with the Spanish landscape is well known, and his engagement with painters and sculptors is also intense and revealing, another way to innovate lyric in the late modernist decades. This work examines the visual-critical in the poet and the critical-poetic in the artist. The figures, unfortunately, are flat black-and-white; they illustrate but do not illuminate.

2481 **Coutinho, Araripe.** Obra poética reunida: 1989–2013. 3a edição revisada. Aracaju, Brazil: Gráfica e Editora J. Andrade, 2013. 598 p.: ill.

Though born in Rio, this flamboyant poet-journalist (1968–2014) made his career in the tiny state of Sergipe. He published 10 books of personal, often sensual or tormented, verse, collected in 2010. The present volume reprints all of those and adds one new segment, "Chopin's Heart, Ashes for an Epitaph," an eerie foreshadowing of the artist's early death. This new edition does bibliographically conscious readers no favors, as it has no table of contents, index, or chronology, and the back-flap afterword is dark to the point of illegibility. As for thematic interests, many items are relevant to corporeality, inter-arts (I-Ching and jazz figures), and intertextuality, texts per se and interesting epigraphs. For a review of the second edition, see *HLAS 70:2144*.

2482 **Cunha, Rubens da.** Curral. Florianópolis, Brazil: Editora UFSC, 2015. 68 p.: ill.

Second title (extended chapbook, in effect) by a poet-professor concerned with the body, aging, and the vagaries of memory. The verse is terse, even curt, reminiscent of late modern experiments without being experimental.

2483 **Daniel, Claudio.** Pensando a poesia brasileira. São Paulo: Lumme Editora, 2018. 268 p.

This volume is composed of 48 "think pieces," almost all previously published in arts periodicals. Each of these concise critical assessments concerns a maker of literarily informed lyric, mostly contemporary poets (first book between 1975 and 2015). The main exception is Augusto de Campos, still active (see *HLAS 72:2595* and *2596*). The poet-critic has a unique talent for reading his peers honestly, without concern for canons or anti-canons, and for synthesizing their strong points and notable characteristics. Very useful collection for anyone seeking to grasp the current breadth of mature talent in national verse.

2484 David, Sérgio Nazar. Tercetos queimados. Rio de Janeiro: 7Letras, 2014. 91 p.

Third brief book of lyric by this author of Lebanese descent, working in Portugal, airs of which are present here alongside other non-Brazilian sites (Beirut, Cairo, Mediterranean, Biblical scenes). As for structures, the four internal divisions (I, II, III, IV) have no titles or given orientation, and other strophic forms are included in addition to the titular tercets. Themes are conventional: time, solitude, senses of self.

2485 Dolabela, Marcelo Gomes. Acre, ácido, azedo. Belo Horizonte, Brazil: Scriptum, 2015. 57 p.

The author (b. 1957) is better known for his publications in popular music, especially national rock, but he has issued collections of verse over the years. Here the main attraction is the abundance of postmodern sonnets (a curiously abiding manifestation in Brazilian lyric). Another thematic identifier is the city of Belo Horizonte.

2486 Duarte, Drika. Negra Onawale. Natal, Brazil: Offset Editora, 2014. 122 p.: ill.

Thematically driven verse by a young specialist in dramatic arts, which is palpable in the performable texts. The poems reflect Afro-descendant culture—geneaology, capoeira, candomblé, folk verse, etc.—while recalling painful and shameful histories. The ethical thrust is wholly antiracist and fraternal.

2487 Emmer, Denise. Poema cenário e outros silêncios. Ipanema, Brazil: 7Letras, 2015. 102 p.

The award-winning author has published three novels in addition to 13 previous books of poetry, for which she has gained the admiration of establishment figures. The prime presence in this latest collection is the father figure, from the opening dedication to the concluding triad of instances, called "O pai."

2488 Espínola, Adriano. Escritos ao sol: antologia. Rio de Janeiro: Editora Record, 2015. 143 p.

A gratifying selection of the most compelling poems/passages from four previous books by this deservedly recognized (retired) poet-professor: *Praia provisória* (see *HLAS 66:3091*), *Beira-sol* (1997, inspiration for the present title); *Trapézio* (*Haicais*) (see *HLAS 68:2587*); and the expansive lyrical epic *Táxi*. Other books should be covered in a follow-up anthology.

2489 Fernandes, Ronaldo Costa. O difícil exercício das cinzas. Rio de Janeiro: 7Letras, 2014. 91 p.

This is the seventh collection of well-tempered verse by this award-winning author of fiction and poetry. The title of one of the new poems, "Exame médico-existencial," reflects the ethos and pathos of the collection; the poems concern health, being-in-the-world, body, soul, relations, surroundings, and temporal consequences.

2490 Ferraz, Eucanaã. Escuta: poemas. São Paulo: Companhia das Letras, 2015. 129 p.

This is the seventh book of poetry (with several prizes earned) by this active poet-professor, also known as an editor of leading national authors (Caetano Veloso, Vinícius de Moraes, Carlos Drummond de Andrade), contact with whom has spilled into the varied voices of this collection. Poetic spaces are vast and multiple, geographically—Rio de Janeiro, the Brazilian interior, Portugal, Africa—and psychically. The simple title itself suggests breadth: *escuta* can be a familiar second-person imperative (imploring to be heard) or a noun for listening or spying (implying an observer of the world).

2491 Fortuna, Felipe. O mundo à solta: poemas. Rio de Janeiro: Topbooks, 2014. 108 p.: ill.

Sixth book of late modern poetry by Fortuna, a poet-diplomat who is not afraid to let the exposure to affairs he is granted by virtue of his profession leak into his verbal art, as suggested in the title "O diplomata alerta" and verified in multiple poems of observance of a "world turned loose," violent and perplexed, from favelas to the streets of London, from drones to jet liners.

2492 **Fróes, Elson.** Viajo com os olhos: poesia visual. Bragança Paulista, Brazil: Urutau, 2018. 102 p.: ill.

Each of these consistently entertaining visual poems has a gloss by the author on a facing page. The majority of these pieces (as early as 1984) predate the rise of the internet and on-line lyric. Since c. 2000 the author has distinguished himself as an editor of virtual/digital poetry.

2493 **Garcia, Marília.** Engano geográfico. Rio de Janeiro: 7Letras, 2012. 49 p.

A single expansive poem of free verse constructing a travel poem (Barcelona, France, et al.) of self-searching with clear transatlantic and inter-American gestures. The author is one of the editors of an internationally oriented e-periodical: revistamododeusar.blogspot.com.

2494 **Gonçalves, André.** Coisas de amor largadas na noite. Letras, fatos, textos de André Gonçalves. Papéis, cores, tipos, garatujas de Josélia Neves. Teresina, Brazil: Quimera Eventos, Cultura e Editoração, 2014. 1 portfolio (54 loose leaves): ill.

Each of these witty 54 loose leaves (c. 5″ x 7″) contains an illustrated text of some sort: lyrics, mini-stories, creative long dictionary entries, prose poems, fragments, etc. The work has airs of Oswald de Andrade, Sebastião Nunes, Glauco Mattoso, visual poetry, and album art. Great item for the study of inter-arts and alternative media.

2495 **Gullar, Ferreira.** Autobiografia poética e outros textos. Belo Horizonte, Brazil: Autêntica, 2015. 155 p.: ill.

One of the principal voices of the late 20th and early 21st centuries, Gullar (1930–2016) was productive until the end of his life. Here he offers a self-story of poetry and reprints two of his best long interviews, as well as three studies of poets he admired (Rimbaud, Pessoa, Vallejo). This volume is a must-read for scholars of this key figure.

2496 **Haicai do Brasil.** Organização e ilustrações por Adriana Calcanhotto. Rio de Janeiro: Edições de Janeiro, 2014. 151 p.: bibl., ill.

This anthology of nationally produced haiku (and haiku-like mini-texts) qualifies as a fine-press book; the print pages are top quality, and each of the 33 poets selected merits an illustration by the volume editor, herself a successful singer-songwriter and producer. The critical segments are not lengthy, but they are well conceived and valuable to the task of considering the Brazilian uses of this Japanese form in the domain of comparative literature. Selections include principal *modernistas* and 20th-century names such as Paulo Leminski and Alice Ruiz, who still conducts haiku workshops. One glaring omission is Adriano Espínola (see item **2488**).

2497 **Hecker Filho, Paulo.** Paulo Hecker Filho: poesia reunida. Organização por Alexandre Brito e Celso Gutfreind. Porto Alegre, Brazil: Corag, Companhia Rio-grandense de Artes Gráficas: Instituto Estadual do Livro, 2014. 410 p.: bibl., ill.

This book brings together the collected poems of a prolific author (1926–2005) of Rio Grande do Sul state across all literary genres. Hecker Filho published some 18 titles of lyric with character ranging from youthful disquiet to quiet contemplations of an elder statesman. The verse is varied, both free and fixed form, and largely conventional, concerned with classic themes (love, sensuality, time, books themselves) and communicability. An important publication for the literary history of the state, which sponsored the project.

2498 **Herik, Helder.** Rinoceronte dromedário. Recife, Brazil: Cepe, Companhia Editora de Pernambuco, 2015. 82 p.

This charming short book won the second state (Pernambuco) literary prize. As the title suggests, the abiding spirit is inspiration in animal life. A childlike fascination with flora and fauna drives the minimalist and brief lyrical project, which is reminiscent of modernists such as Oswald de Andrade and favorite son Manuel Bandeira.

2499 **Hilst, Hilda.** Da poesia. Ilustrações por Hilda Hilst. Estabelecimento de texto por Leusa Araujo. São Paulo: Companhia das Letras, 2017. 581 p.: bibl., ill., index.

The author (1930–2004) was the featured name at the 2018 FLIP (Festival Literário de Paraty), a well-deserved recognition given the lack of critical attention relative to the quality and quantity of her literary output, which also includes prose fiction, drama, and crônica. Although not indicated in the title, this admirably produced volume comprises her complete poetry (in chronological order), including assorted items not collected in previous volumes. The back matter is substantial, valuable for readers and scholars alike. Her poetry is vast (20 titles) and versatile, ranging from songlike medieval lyrics, odes, and other fixed forms, to inventive late-modern contemplations, even a series of "obscene" or "pornographic" texts that mark a conscious break with "official literature." As a whole, this book will be the indispensable source to study this poetic corpus.

2500 *Hoblicua.* No. 4, 2017, Uma certa distância: especial Paulo Henriques Britto. Teresina, Brazil: Revista Hoblicua.

Fourth in a series of nicely produced periodical specials by local (Teresina, Piauí) arts enthusiasts, this one dedicated to the outstanding contemporary poet and translator of Rio de Janeiro, Paulo Henriques Britto, who also writes short stories. The volume opens with a lengthy interview that touches on all the arts and ends with a brief biography. A well-deserved recognition of the importance of this author. See also the last segment in item **2540**.

2501 Leão, Ricardo. No meio da tarde lenta. Jundaí, Brazil: Paco Editorial, 2012. 139 p.

This is the third book of lyric by Leão, an academic and native of São Luis do Maranhão, the subject of this urban lyrical outing—a sometimes sad elegy upon the city's 400th anniversary. Originally written in the early 1990s, this long poem was retooled for publication decades later, though youthful daring remains clear. There are airs of Pessoa (heteronym Alvaro de Campos) and Ferreira Gullar (*Poema sujo*) in this expansive text, which adds to the local municipal repertory and to the Brazilian set of city poems, usually lyrical epics.

2502 Lima, Angélica Torres. O nome nômade. Rio de Janeiro: 7Letras, 2015. 103 p.

This is the fifth book of lyric by Lima, a fixture in the poetry scene of Brasília, just one of the poetic spaces in this nomadic experience of places—including Berlin, Havana, San Francisco, Rio de Janeiro—and variegated psychic situations. The author annotations let readers know that some of the poems were originally composed in the 1970s and 1980s, but the overall sensation is considerably more current, with affective and political overtones.

2503 Lima, Samarone. O aquário desenterrado. Rio de Janeiro: Confraria do Vento, 2013. 82 p.

This short book by a Northeastern journalist won two literary prizes in Brasília and the admiration of poetry critics. Though memory, family, life events, and real geography (Recife and the surrounding region) are constants in this personal free verse, there is no bothersome confessionalism but rather an achievement of density with simple words and engaging diction.

2504 Lisboa, Adriana. Parte da paisagem. São Paulo: Iluminuras, 2014. 119 p.

Lisboa, an award-winning prose-fiction writer (b. 1970) and one of the notable names of her generation, issues here an impressive collection of mood-modulating late modern lyric with clear modernista debts (cf. her own afterword) and cosmopolitan content, textual spaces including Africa, Asia, Europe, and the US, where she resides, creating a poetic "I" who aspires to become, per the title and geometaphorical titular poem, "part of the landscape." The presentation by Princeton University professor Pedro Meira Monteiro is also figuratively eventful.

2505 Lopes, Rodrigo Garcia. Experiências extraordinárias. Londrina, Brazil: Kan Editora, 2014. 102 p.

The author (b. 1965) is one of the notable names of his generation for reliably informed and creative poetic projects (five collections) as well as editorial labor and singer-songwriting. These *experiências extraordinárias* (extraordinary experiences) do not pretend to be modest; rather, they are daring, varied, and imaginative. The first of four sections riffs on the pun of "Idade Mídia" with serial ironies about the current globalized age. The second section features a Nipo-Brazilian heteronym and haikus, while the third includes "dialogues"—intertextual explorations with authors of all ages and continents. The fourth titular section presents the lyric poems per se, from extended fragments to quatrains and sonnets, which are searching, penetrating, gratifying.

Overall, a multitoned collection with much to offer.

2506 Lulalivre*Lulalivro. Organização por Ademir Assunção e Marcelino Freire. São Paulo: Fundação Perseu Abramo, Partido dos Trabalhadores, 2018. 188 p.: ill., photos.

Ninety artists from throughout Brazil, the majority of whom are poets, participate in this anthology in support of the freedom of former President Lula (Luiz Inácio da Silva), whose jailing is characterized by the editors as a "juridical-political-media aberration." The English-language press release states: "the purpose of the book is to create yet another important act of protest, from writers, poets, and cartoonists taking a stand to join the national and international movement against the farce of the ex-president's imprisonment—and the anti-democratic coup that represents his exclusion from the 2018 elections when Brazil will choose its new president." Contributors include Augusto de Campos, Alice Ruiz, Chico Buarque, and many other prominent figures. The self-published print version was launched in several cities in August 2018, and the virtual version is available at https://www.xpeduca.com.br/LulaLivreLulaLivro/.

2507 Luz, Rogerio. Escritas. Goiânia, Brazil: Editora UFG, 2011. 159 p. (Coleção Vertentes)

The author (b. 1936) has published as a film and art critic in addition to poetry. The present volume contains 76 (LXXVI) poems, mostly free verse, and a verse memorial to Walter Benjamin. The overarching concern is with lyric discourse itself: utterance, words, voice, forms, genre, sound, gestures, texture. A notable item for the study of metaliterary preoccupation.

2508 Macedo, Dimas. Guadalupe: 45 poemas. Fortaleza, Brazil: Edições Poetaria: Imprece, 2012. 60 p.

Eighth book by this poet of Ceará state, the title of which is the symbolic Mexican virgin who forms part of the opening sequence of brief place poems, "Alfabeto" (though only eight letters of the alphabet appear). The remaining items are grouped as a nominative "Suite" in which each poem explores a single noun, and as "poems and songs," also with meaning-laden nouns to contemplate.

2509 Machado, Nauro. O baldio som de Deus. Desenhos por João Sánchez. Rio de Janeiro: Contracapa, 2015. 1 v. (unpaged): ill.

The author (1935–2015) is the nation's leading sonneteer and a literary institution in São Luis do Maranhão. The present collection of 240 sonnets is his eighth book wholly dedicated to the revered form.

2510 Machado, Nauro. Percurso de sombras. Desenhos por Pedro Meyer. Rio de Janeiro: Contra Capa, 2013. 216 p.: ill.

In addition to eight books of sonnets (see item **2509** for the most recent one), the author published 30 other books of verse, largely dominated by serious tones and metaphysical concern. As he is so partial to metrification and convention, he represents an extension of the Generation of '45. This antepenultimate title uses strophes with folkloric rings to continue a characteristic elevated diction.

2511 Malufe, Annita Costa. Um caderno para coisas práticas. Rio de Janeiro: 7Letras, 2016. 101 p.

Another poet-professor with strong lyrical impasses, Malufe has four previous collections. Nearly two hundred annotations comprise this notebook with no internal titles or punctuation, thus the sensation of automatic writing or stream of consciousness broken into bits and pieces. The instances range from two liners to entire pages, all utterances of a voice in search of organization and sense who refers to unidentified others as well. The linguistic trip is worth the effort.

2512 Maranhão, Salgado. O mapa da tribo. Rio de Janeiro: 7Letras, 2013. 101 p.

This decorated poet has published 12 collections of verse since the early 1980s, and a few have earned him well-deserved literary prizes. His image-driven work can be understood variously as modern, late modern, ultramodern, postmodern, and neomodern. Poet and art critic Ferreira Gullar once described his brilliance with the word "synergy," the ability to combine a word-oriented poetry with a deep grasp of the real, even if beyond the logic of discourse.

The present collection has five internal divisions. The overall title of the collection is derived from the lead poem of the last group, in which "map" is not just geographical space but also historical heritages and "tribe" is actually plural: indigenous peoples, forced African immigrants, and the legacies of the Portuguese language.

2513 Maranhão, Salgado. A sagração dos lobos. Rio de Janeiro: 7Letras, 2017. 97 p.: bibl., ill.

In this latest book by one of the leading voices of current Brazilian poetry, Maranhão pays careful attention again to external structure; there are four interrelated sections. The overall epigraph summarizes a sage Cherokee legend, and the first section has the same title as the book; the mythical inspiration qualifies as an inter-American gesture as well. The second section, "Larvas da fratura," is the closest to anything experiential, though its abstractions range wide. The third section, "A Deusa Bárbara," is clearly metatextual, though emotion is palpable as well. The fourth section, "Como um rio," is a dense elaboration on the titular simile. Two useful critical segments appear in the front and back of the book; both affirm the career continuity and depth of this lauded author. See also item **2512**.

2514 Maranhão Sobrinho. Poesia reunida. Edição por evocativa do Centenário da morte de poeta, e organizada e promovida por Jomar Moraes. São Luís, Brazil: EDUFMA, 2015. 383 p.: color ill.

Upon the centenary of the passing of this accomplished symbolist poet of Maranhão state, the local university sponsored this celebratory edition, which brings together the three books he published in his short life (1879–1915) and all the periodical items of lyric. An informative critical segment by volume organizer Jomar Moraes, encouraged by Augusto de Campos, and two other evaluative segments, cement the value of this volume for the expanded study of symbolism in Brazil.

2515 Marques, Ana Martins. O livro das semelhanças. São Paulo: Companhia das Letras, 2015. 108 p.

This is the third book by Marques, a critically recognized poet of Minas Gerais with original diction. External structure impinges on interpretation in this book. The first section, "Livro," is a witty set of short poems about the book vehicle itself, while the second, "Cartografias," has literal maps and psychic configurations. The third section, "Visitas ao lugar comum," ironically undoes commonplaces, while the longest, the titular fourth section, displays varieties of figured language—simile, metaphor, signs, and countersigns—in sensitive moods.

2516 Moraes, Vinícius de. Todo amor. Organização e apresentação por Eucanaã Ferraz. São Paulo: Companhia das Letras, 2017. 276 p.: bibl., ill., index.

While this gorgeous, thematically organized volume contains stories and other prose pieces, the main attraction is the amorous and amatory poems and song lyrics. The illustrated chronology at the end is well-designed and useful. The selection is based, with one exception, on the new editions of the author's work issued by this same publisher. Clearly a must for all Vinícius scholars and aficionados. See also item **2525**.

2517 Moreira, Moraes. Poeta não tem idade. Rio de Janeiro: Numa Editora, 2015. 211 p.

At the age of 70, the singer-songwriter of Novos Baianos fame and solo career here gathers his quatrains, *cordel*-like sextains, and other folk-toned strophes. The approach is straightfoward and unpretentious. Many of the items are related to music itself and to real-life musicians. The author even refers to himself as the "Cole Porter of *carnaval* in Bahia." Certainly relevant to the broad theme of poetry and song.

2518 Morgado, Flávio. Uma nesga de sol a mais. Rio de Janeiro: 7Letras, 2016. 68 p.

This is the second short book by Morgado, a young *carioca* with cosmopolitan interests and largely fractured style. An abiding concern with expressivity runs through this brief collection of personal lyric.

2519 Nascente, Gabriel José. A biografia da cinza. Goiânia, Brazil: Kelps, 2013. 233 p.

This prolific author is primarily known in his home state of Goiás. He has written more than 50 books across all literary genres, two-thirds of which are poetry. The present title is divided into two books. The first is the titular section and the second is subdivided into four parts, from classical to ultramodern sets. The posing poet self-describes the whole as a "tearing out of crazy poems" designed to free him from metaphysical torment, but there is a wide range of expression in the energetic and effusive collection.

2520 Neste instante: novos olhares sobre a poesia brasileira dos anos 1970. Organização por Viviana Bosi e Renan Nuernberger. São Paulo: Humanitas: FAPESP, 2018. 450 p.: ill.

Thirteen critical segments (plus organizers' introduction), each on an individual work or poet active in the 1970s. Outstanding poets analyzed include Augusto de Campos, Waly Salomão, Paulo Leminski, and Ana Cristina César. Contributors include advanced students at USP and colleagues from other universities. Admirable edited volume.

2521 Oliani, Luiz Otávio. Entre-textos. vol. 3. Porto Alegre, Brazil: Vidráguas, 2016. 104 p.

This is the third volume of a collection of poetic dialogues, poems by the lead author written in response to poems sent to him on social media (Facebook, WhatsApp, etc.). Each volume has more than 40 participants, about 10 percent of whom are established or recognized names. Thus the project shows the vitality of lyric in the virtual age and an original creative spirit on the part of the organizer, who appealed to peers in almost all the states of Brazil. Excellent example of a possible and productive exercise for a writing workshop anywhere in the world.

2522 Onofre, Jonatas. Opusfabula. Recife, Brazil: CEPE Editora, 2015. 76 p.

This brief book has an explanatory introduction and a single quasidiscursive lyrico-epical text of 56 fragments. The topic is foundational myth. In 1530 the Portuguese defeated local natives and founded Igarassu; centuries later locals venerated the history. The young poet of Pernambuco contemplates indigenous and European worldviews in the construction (key, recurring word) of this representative place.

2523 Oseki-Dépré, Inês. Paula Glanadel. Rio de Janeiro: EdUERJ, 2014. 110 p.: bibl. (Coleção Ciranda da poesia)

It is pleasing to witness the continuity of this series; this particular issue is about a local poet-professor with a solid reputation based on four collections of condensed cosmopolitan lyric. The Paris-based critic is concerned with situation, sources, and, above all, diction, the intricate making of the poems.

2524 Peixoto, Charles. Supertrampo: (poesia reunida—1971–2014). Prefácio por Eucanaã Ferraz. Rio de Janeiro: 7Letras, 2014. 193 p.

The author (b. 1948) was one of the recognized voices of *poesia marginal* in the 1970s. All of the chapbooks from that period are reprinted here alongside subsequent poetic publications, including a book of mature free verse issued after a more-than-two-decade absence from the literary scene. The presentation by Eucanaã Ferraz is short but useful.

2525 Perrone, Charles A. Bons tons diversos versos: o compositor, célebres letristas e a poética da Bossa Nova. (*in* Maestro soberano: ensaios sobre Antonio Carlos Jobim. Organização de Luca Bacchini. Belo Horizonte, Brazil: Editora UFMG, 2017, p. 81–104, bibl.)

While several of the studies in this edited volume ponder textual issues, this commissioned segment specifically addresses the poetry of song in the Jobim songbook, fortified by the large presence of Vinícius de Moraes and Chico Buarque, and capped by the composer's own masterpiece "Aguas de março." For a review of the complete volume, see item **2920**.

2526 Perrone, Charles A. Carlos Drummond de Andrade. (*in* Cambridge companion to Latin American poetry. Edited by Stephen Malcolm Hart. London: Cambridge University Press, 2018, p. 152–162)

The 18 segments of this very useful edited volume are divided into three sections: History, Six Key Figures, Diversity and Heterogeneity. This entry is the only chapter wholly dedicated to Brazilian poetry, specifically to the multifaceted work of the universally recognized national master of the genre. Several other chapters include Brazilian authors, most notably that of A.J. Shellhorse, who presents Brazilian *modernismo* alongside Spanish American avant-gardes.

2527 Perrone, Charles A. Recepção e circulação de poesia(s) brasileira(s) na América do Norte. (*in* Poesia na era da internacionalização dos saberes: circulação, tradução, ensino e crítica no contexto contemporâneo. Organização por María Lúcia Outeiro Fernandes, Paulo Andrade, e Charles A. Perrone. São Paulo: Cultura Acadêmica, 2016, p. 17–34)

This paper identifies and evaluates the attention that Brazilian poetry and poets have received in North America since the 1920s in literary histories and anthologies (both bilingual and translation only, all documented in a useful appendix). Even with increased activity since the 1990s, the principal reference remains the landmark collection edited by Elizabeth Bishop and Emanuel Brasil in 1972 (see *HLAS 36:7043* and *HLAS 40:7830*).

2528 Perrone, Charles A. Shared passages: Spanish American-Brazilian links in contemporary poetry. (*in* Beyond Tordesillas: new approaches to comparative Luso-Hispanic studies. Edited by Robert Patrick Newcomb and Richard A. Gordon. Columbus: Ohio State University Press, 2017, p. 162–172, bibl.)

A follow-up study to chapter five of *Brazil, Lyric, and the Americas* (see *HLAS 66:3121*) focusing on thematic and linguistic links between present-day Spanish and Portuguese-language poetry. In this chapter the main attraction is the musically driven work, in both tongues, of Edimilson de Almeida Pereira.

2529 Plástico bolha: antologia de poesia. Organização por Lucas Viriato. Rio de Janeiro: OrganoGrama Livros, 2014. 121 p.: bibl., index.

A selection of over 70 of the best poems from the literary journal of the same name, which had previously published an anthology of the best prose pieces to appear in the journal since its inception in 2005 as the product of a writers' workshop at PUC-Rio de Janeiro. Most of the poets included in the collection are college-age writers, though a few elder or established local poets have also contributed, notably Paulo Henriques Britto and Claudia Roquette Pinto. The editorial process has filtered and distilled a solid selection that demonstrates the variety of tone and diction in current urban verse.

2530 Poesia com deuses: estudos de Hídrias, de Dora Ferreira da Silva. Organizado por Enivalda Nunes Freitas e Souza e Alva Martinez Teixeiro. Rio de Janeiro: 7Letras; Belo Horizonte, Brazil: FAPEMIG, 2016. 196 p.: bibl.

A year before her passing, the feted poet won a third national book award (Prêmio Jabuti) for *Hídrias* (2004; see *HLAS 64:2407*), contemplations of 10 Greek deities. The 15 studies in this edited volume consider that book and Silva's work as a whole from the vantage points of mythology, psychology, and philosophy. Other approaches include tracing images of the feminine.

2531 Poesia na era da internacionalização dos saberes: circulação, tradução, ensino e crítica no contexto contemporâneo. Organizado por Maria Lúcia Outeiro Fernandes, Paulo Andrade, e Charles A. Perrone. São Paulo: Cultura Acadêmica, 2016. 237 p.: bibl., ill. (Série Estudos literários; 17)

This edited volume brings together reworked papers from a 2014 academic conference at UNESP Araraquara and subsequent submissions that are pertinent to the overarching theme. Seven of the 12 segments deal with Brazilian poetry. As others treat North American topics, there is a simultaneous inter-American interest. Following the keynote address (see item **2527**), there is a statement by featured poet Salgado Maranhão (see items **2512** and **2513**) and a pair of essays relevant to native and ecopoetics. Virtual access (free download) is available via e-books/Série Estudos Literários at www.fclar.unesp.br/laboratorioeditorial.

2532 Prado, Adélia. Poesia reunida. Rio de Janeiro: Editora Record, 2015. 543 p.

The author (b. 1935) did not make her poetic debut until the mid-1970s, but since then her reputation and critical fortune have grown steadily. This impressive and indispensable volume brings together her eight full books of verse (not counting those of previous collected poems) and substantial back matter: an admiring critical appraisal, the author's complete bibliography (including other genres), an account of national criticism (including many theses), and international items. Prado is a sui generis figure studied for her place in the letters of Minas Gerais, including intertextuality; as a prominent voice in Latin American women's literature; as a poet of sensuality; for the spiritual elements (Catholic) in her repertory; and as a late modern fount.

2533 **Rebuzzi, Solange.** O riso do inverno. Rio de Janeiro: 7Letras, 2018. 62 p.

Poems 2014–2018 by a critic and creative writer who explores love, laughter, lamentable situations (social reality) and the ever-present themes of nature.

2534 **Rêgo, Josoaldo Lima.** Carcaça. Rio de Janeiro: 7Letras, 2016. 127 p.

This is the third book of verse by a poet-geographer who teaches in Maranhão but is attentive to the mapimundi. The temptation to read these quick lyric instances (some as short as a single line) via his discipline is strong, as toponyms, accidents, cardinal points, and voyages all figure into the intriguing and entertaining imaginary at play. A justifiable paradigm of comparison would be the *Poesia Pau-Brasil* of Oswald de Andrade (see item **2462**).

2535 **Sá, Lenita de.** Pincelada de Dalí e outros poemas. São Luís do Maranhão, Brazil: Aquarela Gráfica e Editora, 2015. 76 p.

The author has published in all literary genres and won the state award for poetry in 2010 with this book. In the preface, the poet laureate of Maranhão, Ferreira Gullar, calls it "impetuous, vibrant and communicative." There is indeed an emotional lyrical engagement with everyday life and things, with artistically inspired turns of language (cf. the titular reference to the surrealist Dalí).

2536 **Sant'Anna, Alice.** Pé do ouvido. São Paulo: Companhia das Letras, 2016. 61 p.

This book, the third by Sant'Anna, a young poet of Rio de Janeiro (b. 1988), is written in two nonstop streams titled simply "Part One" (50 p.) and "Part Two" (5 p.), forming a long travel log and a brief note of return. In this wandering search for significance, the international elements at play are US American and Japanese. The intimate unfolding scene verges on the dramatic.

2537 **Scott, Paulo.** Mesmo sem dinheiro comprei um esqueite novo. São Paulo: Companhia das Letras, 2014. 75 p.

With four books of fiction and a previous book of poetry to his credit, the author (b. 1966) hails from Porto Alegre but resides in Rio de Janeiro, marks of which are frequent in this collection of colloquial personal verse, as are his narrative impulses.

2538 **Secchin, Antonio Carlos.** Desdizer e antes. Rio de Janeiro: Topbooks, 2017. 211 p.

This volume comprises seven sections, the first of which is the title segment (poems 2003–2017) and the rest ("e antes"/"and before") reprints of books/chapbooks of lyric published since 1969. The author is best known as a careful literary critic, especially of national poetry (see, for example, items **2539** and **2540**) and as an innovative member of the new-look ABL (Academia Brasileira de Letras), but he is also an accomplished poet, if not particularly prolific, in his own right. He prefers fixed forms over free verse, though he is comfortable with any modern mode. His verse is typically rigorous, dense, and prone to the paradoxical. An insightful review by Nelson Ascher is available at https://www1.folha.uol.com.br/ilustrada/2018/03/obra-reunida-de-secchin-brilha-em-seu-apego-aos-paradoxos.shtml.

2539 **Secchin, Antonio Carlos.** Papéis de poesia: Drummond & mais. Goiânia, Brazil: Martelo, 2014. 159 p.: bibl. (Coleção Ideia e memória; 02. Série Litterae)

This is the fourth collection of critical pieces this respected teacher-scholar has published since 1996. In the preface, Antonio Cicero confirms his ABL colleague's peculiar ability to conduct criticism almost as if it were in the voice of the writer under scrutiny. Five of the studies in this volume concern Carlos Drummond de Andrade (see also item **2526**) and another 15 cover a range of subjects from infamous errata to the poetry of the late Ferreira Gullar (who passed away in 2016). This book is best consulted with another of the author's works (item **2540**), with which there is some overlap.

2540 Secchin, Antonio Carlos. Percursos da poesia brasileira: do século XVIII ao século XXI. Belo Horizonte, Brazil: Editora UFMG, 2018. 367 p.

This volume is an auto-anthology of criticism. The author has selected (and in some cases revised) two statements of principle and over 40 studies he has done of national poets, or groups of poets (in three cases), from the 18th century to the present. The entries have appeared in five previous books (see, for example, *HLAS 70:2190* and item **2539**); here they are organized not by original date of publication but by the dates of the poets under review. A few previously unpublished items are included as well. As a set, the segments, none too lengthy, elaborate a sort of "informal history" of Brazilian poetry, from the Arcadians of Minas Gerais through romanticism and modernism to outstanding current voices, e.g., Paulo Henriques Britto and "some contemporaries." The studies are both academic and general-public, both conjunctural (sociohistorical) and close readings, consistently elegant. Aside from their purely critical qualities, Secchin's essays are notably valuable as teaching tools. Each piece fundamentally answers the question "Why read this poet?"

2541 Shellhorse, Adam Joseph. Anti-literature: the politics and limits of representation in modern Brazil and Argentina. Pittsburgh, Pa.: University of Pittsburgh Press, 2017. 258 p.: bibl., ill., index. (Iluminations: cultural formations of the Americas series)

Five of the six chapters in this enthusiastically reviewed monograph concern Brazilian letters, especially poetry, in particular the experimental work of the Noigandres poets who invented *poesia concreta*. In establishing his complex notion of "anti-literature," the critic examines the poetics of Oswald de Andrade in concrete poetry, the post-concrete Neo-Baroque of Haroldo de Campos, and a sui generis post-utopian political poem of his. "Anti-literary" modes of writing are seen both textually and in subversive light, as reactions to political and cultural conditions in contemporary frames (since c. 1955). The whole is heavily informed by post-structuralist literary theory and by theoretical Latin Americanism. As a whole, this work represents a remarkable contribution to the study of Latin American literature; the specific treatment of aspects of Brazilian poetry is fresh and profound.

2542 Silva, Luiz Roberto Nascimento. Sim: (2008–2014). Rio de Janeiro: Bem-Te-Vi Produções Literárias, 2016. 93 p. (Coleção Canto do Bem-te-vi)

The author (b. 1952) has published several books of verse, as well as fiction and essays. Three interesting aspects are present in this slim book: using Twitter as a pretext for updating one's language, the recurrence of scenes in Rio de Janeiro, and a sequence of instances built on the word *sim*, including Joyce's famous "yes" in *Ulysses*.

2543 Silvestrin, Ricardo. Metal. Porto Alegre, Brazil: Artes e Ofícios Editora LTDA, 2013. 134 p.

This active author (b. 1963) of Porto Alegre adopts a nearly conversational tone in this multitude of individual utterances, most of which have no title or are in a numbered series of "landscapes" or "canvasses." Observation of the world can lead to disillusioned expression, but an abiding musicality provides a countercurrent.

2544 Silvestrin, Ricardo. Typographo. São Paulo: Patuá Editora, 2016. 145 p.

This is the 10th book of poetry by this writer-musician of Porto Alegre who manages to ponder the grand themes of lyric tradition in measured light verse (one hundred items) with little pretense to experimentalism. The archaic spelling of the title suggests an interest in print culture of previous centuries, which the author takes all the way back to classical Greece. Typography, or the maker who is the typographer, as a conceit or figure of language is not developed until the very last entry, which is printed on purple pages. The poet of the 21st century and digital age still makes "subtle revolutions" with fonts and abiding structures. See also (item **2543**).

2545 Siqueira, João Batista de Cancão. Musa sertaneja: Flores do Pajeú: Meu Lugarejo: poemas inéditos. Recife,

Brazil: Cepe Editora, 2013. 347 p. (Letra pernambucana)

During his lifetime (1912–1982), this poet of the backlands published three books of popular verse (mostly *décimas*), which are reprinted here along with dozens of previously unpublished items. The compositions are decidedly popular (folk), attending to an outback muse, admiring local flora, and expressing a beloved place. Four short presentations locate the author in the pantheon of state verse-makers.

2546 **Siscar, Marcos.** De volta ao fim: o "fim das vanguardas" como questão da poesia contemporânea. Rio de Janeiro: 7Letras, 2016. 237 p.: bibl.

This notable collection of essays is divided into two parts; the first concerns Brazilian poetry in the post-vanguard period (since the 1970s) and the second addresses the more universal "other crises of verse," which are applicable to Brazil. The principal focus of the lead essays are the epoch-making "post-utopian" theories and post-concrete poetry of Haroldo de Campos, whom the critic is not afraid to challenge in attempting to comprehend plurality in late-century lyric. Other essays look at the controversial Bruno Tolentino and the celebrated Ana C. (Cristina César), whose postmortem critical fortune surpasses her actual literary production. The critic is well versed in contemporary theory and well regarded as a present-day poet in his own right, thus his perspective is widely appreciated.

2547 **Siscar, Marcos.** Haroldo de Campos. Rio de Janeiro: EdUERJ, 2015. 97 p. (Coleção Ciranda da poesia)

Another in this well-regarded collection of personal selections and critical appraisals of select national authors. The analysis in this work focuses on the ultra-cosmopolitan and frequently intertextual "post-utopian" poetry of the world-renowned poet-critic Siscar beginning in the 1980s. Valuable 21st-century vantage of a fellow poet-professor.

2548 ***Suplemento literário de Minas Gerais.*** Nov. 2017, A poesia musical do Clube da Esquina. Belo Horizonte, Brazil: Biblioteca da Faculdade de Letras.

This 10-segment illustrated special edition of the long-standing state cultural periodical is dedicated to the lyricists of the famed popular-music collective, the Clube da Esquina, most active in the 1970s-1980s. Includes interviews, short memoirs, and critical appreciations. Nice contribution to the topic of music and poetry, such a lively theme since the 1960s.

2549 **Trevisan, Armindo.** Adega imaginária: seguido de, O relincho do cavalo adormecido. Porto Alegre, Brazil: L&PM Editores, 2013. 203 p.

The prolific author of Porto Alegre (b. 1933) has issued over a dozen titles in poetry and at an advanced age offers this pair of books with items ranging from aphorisms and epigrams to ironic shots at present-day life and more effusive mood pieces.

2550 **Trigo, Luciano.** Separação. Rio de Janeiro: 7Letras, 2016. 75 p.

The author's previous books include film studies, literary criticism, and one of poetry. The present collection is emotive, experiential, confessional, and often melancholic.

2551 **Vaz, Sérgio.** Flores de alvenaria. Apresentação por Chico César. São Paulo: Global Editora, 2016. 177 p. (Literatura periférica)

With an introduction by Chico César (see item **2478**), this short book is an excellent example of so-called peripheral literature (outskirts of São Paulo) with multiple short poems, longer lyrics, prose poems, actual prose pieces, and more. Urban experience and literary preoccupations are present throughout.

2552 **Vieira, Fábio.** A anti-retórica do menos, leituras sobre Augusto de Campos. Natal, Brazil: Caule de Papiro, 2016. 146 p.

Originally an academic thesis, this book first reviews the critical reception of concrete poetry and its tendency to engage in cultural dialogue. The central part includes analyses of non-linearity and concision using a sort of reader-response method mixed with semiotic close reading. The most satisfying subheading is the treatment of "todos os sons," with its mix of music and typography.

2553 **Weintraub, Fabio.** Treme ainda. São Paulo: Editora 34, 2015. 92 p.

The author studied both psychology and letters, which is reflected in his creative work. He has issued three previous books of personal lyric, all of which were well received. His short verses of relaxed diction communicate caustic observations and varying tones and attitudes of disquiet or lament.

2554 Young, Fernanda. A mão esquerda de Vênus. São Paulo: Editora Globo, 2016. 327 p.: ill.

The author is known for her work in television and film, and she has penned eight works of fiction. This is her second book of poetry, but more than a collection of lyric the unique volume is a two-headed multimedia monster: the 45 texts are printed in red ink in the back part, while the fully illustrated front presents the texts in notebooks with all sorts of formats and reproductions: manuscripts, typescripts, cards, photos of pages and bodies, pen and ink drawings, watercolors, tattoos, etc. Thus the vehicle is more compelling than the self-absorbed words, though some thematic interests, notably the body and the erotic, do emerge.

2555 Zular, Roberto. Encaroçada de estrelas: alguns poemas de Paulo Henriques Britto e a transição democrática. [*Lua Nova*, 96, sept./dic. 2015, p. 15–37, bibl.)

Zular, an academic at USP selects several turn-of-the century poems by Britto, the duly recognized poet of Rio de Janeiro (see items **2472** and **2500**) and a trio of postmodern cultural theorists to speculate on a certain indeterminate dimension in the political domain (vestiges of nondemocratic operations) during the still on-going "transition" from authoritarian military rule to a technically democratic regime. The analysis of aspects of *polis* in poetical enunciation is certainly unusual, though the argument will be better received by humanistic readers than social-science constituencies. The publication date of the article, a year before the parliamentary coup d'état of 2016, is curious if not ironic.

Drama

ISADORA GREVAN DE CARVALHO, *Assistant Professor of Portuguese, Rutgers University*

THE PUBLICATIONS ON BRAZILIAN THEATER selected for this section follow a number of different directions, but most show a preoccupation with historical archival research and the registration of visual documentation to be accessible to the public. The publications of contemporary plays favor authors from the Rio de Janeiro-São Paulo theater circuit, especially authors that work directly with theater groups of either popular or critical acclaim in these regions.

A number of scholarly publications expand on the concept of performance and theater to investigate the sociopolitical impact of these practices in different milieus. Books that aim to explore the role of Afro-Brazilian cultural specificity in places such as the state of Bahia, associated with the group *Olodum* (item **2578**), is a trend that continues with strong vitality, complemented by a beautiful visual historiography documenting the presence of Afro-Brazilians on stage (item **2581**) and the development of new theater educational models in the poor communities of Rio de Janeiro (item **2576**). This arc of preoccupation with the marginalized and the intersections between the city spaces and theater is complemented by the study of Artur Azevedo's writings as they connect and respond to the world around him, within and beyond the theater (item **2583**). Moreover, this thematic focus also appears in the book about *reisado* (item **2572**), a folk traditional itinerant theater from the Northeast, complemented by ethnographic research and visual documentation.

Books that explore the political dimensions of theatrical criticism, writings, and performance follow an interest on the impact of repressive regimes on Brazil's theater scene, at the same time both productive and stultifying. Thus, two studies on the impact of the Getúlio Vargas administration on the theater scene (items **2573** and **2575**) are published together with a more thorough analysis of Augusto Boal's career on theater (item **2571**). Vargas' persona and propaganda machine along with his government's censorship apparatus are explored in well-researched detail, contributing to the historiography on the role of censorship and propaganda in molding texts and performances during repressive political regimes. Furthermore, the collection of articles about Augusto Boal could spearhead a trend on academic research on the author beyond the theater of the oppressed, which remains an unexplored area.

A scholarly analysis of Plínio Marcos' theater (item **2570**), with a focus on the presence of violence in two of his plays, adds to the grouping of books on the political dimensions on Brazilian theater during the dictatorship and beyond. Furthermore, the publication of Sábato Magaldi's theater criticism during a period of 22 years (item **2579**) provides an immense contribution to the study of Brazilian theater, specifically the São Paulo theater scene. It also adds to the historiography of theater during the dictatorship.

Three books shine for their beautiful visual documentation, including a study of Cacilda Becker's theatrical career (item **2586**), a history of the São Paulo Municipal Theater (item **2574**), and an analysis of the presence of Afro-Brazilians on stage and beyond (item **2581**). Though visually appealing and valuable for its archival documentation, the book on Cacilda Becker would benefit from more thorough academic rigor and diversity of viewpoints from a variety of theater critics as opposed to presenting the view of just one author. The book on the Theatro Municipal de São Paulo is a bilingual edition, but a translation would need revision in order to reach an English-speaking audience.

Anthologies of lesser-known female playwrights such as Maria de Lourdes Nunes Ramalho (items **2564** and **2565**) and Maria Ribeiro (item **2566**) reflect a renewed interest in examining the theater canon. Though an important contribution, without an arc of scholarly publications with a focus on those same female authors, it is hard to imagine that they would gain the visibility needed. The publications focusing on female authorship are complemented by works of new contemporary playwrights such as Pedro Kosovski (item **2563**), Daniele Avila Small (item **2567**), Jô Bilac (items **2558** and **2559**), Atílio Bari (item **2557**), Luiz Britto (item **2560**), Paulo Henrique Alcântara (item **2556**), Paulo Jorge Dumaresq (item **2562**), Sérgio Thales (item **2568**), and Fernando Caruso (item **2561**). Though most of these playwrights work for theater groups in the Rio-São Paulo circuit, many explore topics that go beyond the region, with plays taking place in the Northeast or addressing the themes of migration and economic hardship that citizens living in other parts of Brazil face.

The works reviewed in this section demonstrate a continuous preoccupation for new contemporary playwrights as well as a renewed interest in women authors. Additionally, we see important contributions to the study of Brazilian theater, specifically the study of the impact of marginalized groups, especially the presence and influence of Afro-Brazilian culture on performance. The publication of original plays by contemporary playwrights continues, highlighting new theatrical groups that work in tangent with playwrights to develop original material to be put on stage. However, critical and thorough analysis should accompany these texts to make them more accessible to different theatrical groups and readers. Due to the association of various texts with particular groups, such as Kosovski's (item 2563), Small's (item 2567), Bilac's (items 2558 and 2559) and Caruso's (item 2561), and the lack of related in-depth critical analysis, for example, these plays could end up being overlooked as important contributions.

ORIGINAL PLAYS

2556 Alcântara, Paulo Henrique. Partiste. Salvador, Brazil: FGM, Fundação Gregório de Mattos, 2015. 79 p. (Selo literário João Ubaldo Ribeiro; I)

This play shows the day-to-day life of five characters from the same family: the mother, her three children, and an old aunt, who live in a northeastern Brazilian city in the interior of the state of Bahia. In their daily lives, they await the letters of Jairo, the eldest son who left for São Paulo. But it is the news of the death of the father that instigates a whole set of new motivations and changes within the family dynamics. Furthermore, the play is about the impact of Brazilian migration and longing, precipitated by economic hardships, but made more difficult by strong family ties.

2557 Bari, Atílio. Julgamento no velho Chico. Goiânia, Brazil: Editora UFG, 2015. 78 p. (Coleção Vertentes)

Partly musical and partly poetic, this play develops a satirical absurdist rendition of historical figures from the Northeast of Brazil, such as Padre Cícero and Virgulino. The six characters that appear on stage are either dead or statues, which Bari uses as a way to revisit the official history and make the stories from books come alive.

2558 Bilac, Jô. Infância, tiros e plumas. Rio de Janeiro: Cobogó, 2015. 92 p. (Coleção Dramaturgia)

This satirical play revolves around the meeting of nine people on a flight to Disney World, triggering a series of incidents. The conflicts between the characters intensify with the altitude and the turbulence of the flight, putting their relations to the test, taking the passengers and the crew to the limit, throwing questions about the decadence of human relations in a society without a set of common morals. The piece is part of the repertoire of Cia OmondÉ.

2559 Bilac, Jô. Os mamutes. Rio de Janeiro: Cobogó, 2015. 82 p. (Coleção Dramaturgia)

This play presents the trajectory of Leon, who is in search of a job in a fast food multinational restaurant that produces hamburgers from human flesh. To get the job in the *Mamutes* Food market, Leon must shoot down a mammoth: a person considered worthless. A multitude of characters cross his path, instigating questions about this society, marked by an exaggerated consumerism. Leon's dilemma slowly builds up in his head, whether to become a relentless hunter or to resist in the name of his principles. Presented in Bilac's satirical style, the piece is part of the repertoire of Cia OmondÉ.

2560 Britto, Luiz. A mansão Marquês de Berimbau: (versão teatral). Salvador, Brazil: Prova do Artista, 2013. 143 p.: ill.

This four-act play satirizes the class, gender, and racial conflicts present in the city of Salvador, Bahia. Britto presents the citizens in conflict with one another, often in absurd and exaggerated ways, through the invasion of a luxurious building in the city's wealthy neighborhood.

2561 Caruso, Fernando. Z.É: zenas escrevinhadas. Organização por Bernardo Jablonski. Rio de Janeiro: Editora Caravansarai, 2011. 197 p.: ill.

This collection brings together a number of short sketches used for warm up, introduction, and centering of themes before improvisational comic pieces. This publication stems from an extremely successful improvisational live theater show, partially inspired by Mad TV and Saturday Night Live, composed of four permanent members (Fernando Caruso, Gregório Duvivier, Marcelo Adnet, and Rafael Queiroga), a featured director, and an invited actor for each performance.

2562 **Dumaresq, Paulo Jorge.** Repouso do Adônis; Bocas que murmuram: 1991–1992. Natal, Brazil: FJA, 2011. 97 p. (Coleção Cultura potiguar; 08)

This publication brings together the author's first two plays. The first play, *Repouso do Adônis*, is a northeastern comedy set in a decadent brothel in the interior of Rio Grande do Norte state, providing an array of rich diverse characters stemming from the Brazilian Northeast. The second piece, *Bocas que murmuram*, takes an ironic stance about the press, which is explored with a critical look at the ways corruption and manipulation take center stage in this environment.

2563 **Kosovski, Pedro.** Cara de cavalo. Com a colaboração de Marco André Nunes e Aquela Cia. de Teatro. Rio de Janeiro: Cobogó, 2015. 66 p. (Coleção Dramaturgia)

This play by Kasovski was written in collaboration with Marco André Nunes and *Aquela Cia. de Teatro* theater group. The play is based on the trajectory of the famous criminal from 1960s Rio de Janeiro, Manoel Oliveira, popularly known as "Horse Face." The dramaturgy structure is divided into four planes of reality: it begins at Skeleton Hill favela, where Horse Face was a bandit without great pretensions, living off the exploitation of prostitutes and the animal game; in the second moment, the characterization of the conduct of the case after the murder of the police detective Le Coq is explored; the following section includes an interview with the last survivor of the men that worked with an organized criminal group to kill Horse Face. Throughout the play, video projections mixing fiction and reality are featured as well images of Helio Oiticica's artwork based on the criminal.

2564 **Ramalho, Maria de Lourdes Nunes.** Teatro (quase completo) de Lourdes Ramalho. vol. 1. Organização, fixação dos textos, estudo introdutório e notas de Valéria Andrade e Diógenes Maciel. Maceió, Brazil: EdUFAL, 2011. 1 v.: bibl.

A collection of four plays that mix the poetic structures of the Cordel poetry leaflets of the Northeast and the theatrical modes of Iberian dramaturgy configured in a dramatic hybrid way through the words of playwright Lourdes Ramalho. The two volumes aim to acknowledge the work of Ramalho and other female writers and playwrights from areas of Brazil beyond Rio de Janeiro and São Paulo, particularly because their work is usually excluded from studies of the history of Brazilian theater.

2565 **Ramalho, Maria de Lourdes Nunes.** Teatro (quase completo) de Lourdes Ramalho. vol. 2. Organização, fixação dos textos, estudo introdutório e notas de Valéria Andrade e Diógenes Maciel. Maceió, Brazil: EdUFAL, 2011. 1 v.: bibl.

This second volume of plays features six texts that explore an antipatriarchal and emancipatory project for women. They highlight the most diverse range of plays to provide the reader with a look at Lourdes Ramalho's depiction of gender and regional issues. For a review of Vol. 1, see item **2564**.

2566 **Ribeiro, Maria.** Teatro quase completo. Organização, estabelecimento de texto, ensaio introdutório, bibliografia e notas de Valéria Andrade. Ilha de Santa Catarina, Brazil: Mulheres, 2014. 261 p.: bibl.

A collection of texts from Brazilian dramaturgy by female writers, this book retrieves part of an extensive work produced by a playwright in 19th-century Brazil whose original oeuvre had been mostly lost to a fire, *Liceu de Artes e Ofícios* (Rio de Janeiro). The author, along with Alencar, Quintino Bocaiúva, Machado de Assis, and others, was part of a group of playwrights committed to the renewal of the Brazilian theater in the mid-19th century. Although Maria Ribeiro wrote many texts for theater, she published very little and had little recognition because of her gender.

2567 **Small, Daniele Avila.** Garras curvas e um canto sedutor: peça para Raymond Carver. Rio de Janeiro: Cobogó, 2015. 77 p. (Coleção Dramaturgia)

This publication presents a play inspired by the short story "Cathedral" by the American author Raymond Carver, accompanied by three theater reviews. The plot develops from the arrival of Robert—a blind man who has just lost his wife—at the house of Marina and João, raising several questions that interfere in the life of the couple. The play is part of the repertoire of the collective Double Complex Theater research group.

2568 **Thales, Sérgio.** Teatro de Sérgio Thales. São Paulo: Giostri Editora LTDA., 2011. 231 p. (Dramaturgia brasileira)

Sérgio Thales' four plays are published by Giostri Editora as part of their *Dramaturgia Brasileira* collection featuring works by new authors of Brazilian theater, which have been written and staged in recent years, in an effort to foster a new generation of playwrights. "O Resgate . . ." is geared towards children, exploring environmental concerns, while "Deasarme" is geared towards a young audience, dealing with urban violence and war. "Hotel Pi-Addas" is a comedy with vaudevillian tones, while "A Dona da Casa" explores the social issues of the profession of maids, with tones of dark humor.

THEATER CRITICISM AND HISTORY

2569 **Antropologia e performance: ensaios Napedra.** Organização de John C. Dawsey *et al.* São Paulo: Terceiro Nome, 2013. 499 p.: bibl., ill. (Antropologia hoje)

This book provides a collection of texts from the work of the Center for Anthropology, Performance and Drama (Napedra; Onthestone), a group that brings together anthropologists in search of knowledge associated with the performing arts and art researchers interested in anthropology. In the academic and artistic fields, the concept of performance has acquired a multitude of interpretations; according to the introduction by the organizers of the book, more than a circumscribed type of academic discipline or even an interdisciplinary field, performance studies configures, for some authors, a kind of antidiscipline. Thus, this book provides a valuable contribution to the field of performance studies in Brazil, giving the reader a wide array of fields from which to discuss it, including theater, the performing arts, cinema, anthropology, sociology, psychoanalysis, linguistics, folklore, and gender studies.

2570 **Araújo, Gessé Almeida.** A violência na obra de Plínio Marcos: Barrela e Navalha na carne. Salvador, Brazil: Edufba, 2015. 187 p.: bibl.

Plínio Marcos, an author from São Paulo, used to call himself "a reporter of bad times" for making theater based on the life of the marginalized. Guided mainly by the dramaturgical texts "Razor in the flesh" and "Barrela", this study analyzes the presence of violence in the work of Marcos, paying special attention to how extreme forms of violence are used to criticize the construction of Brazilian society, marred by inequality. The author also looks at the sociocultural context in which the playwright is inserted, and reflects upon Plínio Marcos' esthetic innovation and contributions.

2571 **Augusto Boal: arte, pedagogia e política.** Organização de Zeca Ligiéro, Licko Turle e Clara de Andrade. Rio de Janeiro: Mauad X, 2013. 224 p.: bibl., ill.

This book provides an important addition to the study of Augusto Boal's oeuvre as a whole through a collection of articles from a diverse group of scholars and theater practitioners. It aims to expand the interest in his work by highlighting not just his most well-studied and known methodology of "theater of the oppressed," but also his playwriting, political activism, and pedagogical contributions. The volume also aims to provide research articles that investigate his career trajectory in its entirety, from its inception to his death, looking at the ways his personal life had an impact on his philosophical framework.

2572 **Barroso, Oswald.** Teatro como encantamento: bois e reisados de caretas. Fortaleza, Brazil: Amazém da Cultura, 2013. 422 p., 14 unnumbered pages: bibl., music.

The book, adapted from the author's PhD dissertation, is also the result of 35 years of research on traditional Brazilian folk theater traditions undertaken by the author as a reference for his work as an actor, author, mentor, and theater critic. This study follows the book on Congo Kings, published in 1996. The author surveys a total of 177 groups of *bois e reisados* (loosely translated as bulls and kingdoms) tradition of travelling theater, with detailed ethnographic documentation and recording of 82 of these groups, throughout the interior of Ceará state. This study provides invaluable resources for readers interested in the folk traditions of this region and beyond.

2573 **Camargo, Angélica Ricci.** A política dos palcos: teatro no primeiro governo Vargas (1930–1945). Rio de Janeiro: FGV Editora, 2013. 147 p.: bibl. (FGV de bolso. Série História; 27)

This book analyzes the construction of a governmental policy for the development of Brazilian theater during the first Getúlio Vargas administration, focusing on the work of the Comissão de Teatro Nacional (National Theater Commission), created in 1936, and its successor, the Serviço Nacional de Teatro (National Theater Service), established in 1937. Following the main discussions and initiatives promoted by the two bodies, the author highlights the participation of artists, authors, and organizations of theatrical professionals in this process and points out the different interests at stake in transforming theater problems into government problems. The study thus brings to the fore relevant issues in the history of the relationship between state and culture in Brazil that coincide with the emergence of a Brazilian national theater.

2574 **Camargos, Marcia.** Theatro Municipal de São Paulo: 100 anos: palco e plateia da sociedade paulistana. Organização de Carlos Eduardo Martins Macedo. Ensaio fotográfico por Cristiano Mascaro. Tradução para o inglês de Anthony Doyle = São Paulo Municipal Theater: 100 years: stage and seating of São Paulo society. Edited by Carlos Eduardo Martins Macedo. Photographic essay by Cristiano Mascaro. Translation into English by Anthony Doyle. São Paulo: Dado Macedo Edições, 2011. 190 p.: bibl., ill. (some color).

This book celebrates the 100-year history of the Theatro Municipal de São Paulo. The project originated in 1973 with Luciano Cerri, who had been an editor for the theater's brochure publishing company. This beautiful edition includes photos, brochures, drawings, and periodic news that record and illustrate the history of the theater. In addition to pictures of the theater's interior, the book also features city views following its long history. It is divided into chapters such as "Paradigm Shift" and "Vanguard Steps," for example, giving us a glimpse, not just of the theater groups, but also of the history of Brazil's cultural effervescence of the Modern Art Week. This bilingual publication features an English version of the text.

2575 **Casadei, Eliza Bachega.** Getúlio Vargas e o teatro: comunicação, poder e censura na construção simbólica do imaginário Varguista (1930–1954). São Paulo: Grupo Editorial Scortecci, Fábrica de Livros, 2011. 150 p.: bibl.

Based on extensive archival research in the Miroel Silveira Archive of the School of Communications and Arts of the Universidade de São Paulo, this book explores aspects related to the way Getulio Vargas' imagery was captured, constructed, and reconfigured in the national theater scene during his government. In addition, this study also shows the role of censorship in the national theater and seeks to demonstrate which images were vetoed in the São Paulo Theater due to this controversial politician.

2576 **Coutinho, Marina Henriques.** A favela como palco e personagem. Rio de Janeiro: FAPERJ; Petrópolis, Brazil: DP et Alii, 2012. 231 p.: bibl., ill.

Adapted from the author's PhD dissertation, this work deals with the relationship between theater and community in the realm of performances developed by *favela* groups in the city of Rio de Janeiro, such as the well-known group *Nós do Morro* (Vidigal). Furthermore, the study explores the concept of applied drama in marginalized communities both theoretically and historically.

2577 **Encontro: São Paulo, 2013.** Organização de Cristina Espírito Santo, Eleonora Fabião e Sonia Sobral. São Paulo: Itaú Cultural, Rumos Itaú Cultural, 2013. 148 p.: color ill.

This publication presents the results of a semester-long interaction among 12 theater groups in all parts of Brazil. The institution Itaú Cultural offers a semester-long stipend in support of these groups for them to find ways to create a dialogue, links, and experiment so they can learn from one another. The culmination of this project is meant to increase interaction and experimentation, not to be a final performance. The groups are also asked to create a blog, narrating the experience along the way, which is the main source of this book.

2578 **Lírio, Vinícius da Silva.** Bença às teatralidades híbridas: o movimento cênico transcutural do Bando de Teatro Olodum. Salvador, Brazil: Quarteto Editora, 2014. 246 p.: bibl., ill.

Adapted from the author's MA thesis, this study provides an investigation of the esthetic theatricality of *O Bando de Teatro Olodum*, an Afro-Brazilian theatrical group in Bahia, through the study of the performance of the play *Bença* (a colloquial expression for the word "blessing"), directed by Marcio Meirelles in 2010. The study shines when exploring the notions of transcultural esthetics and hybrid theatricalities from the disciplines of cultural and theater studies to look at the ways the play affirms and problematizes the Afro-Brazilian body on stage and beyond.

2579 **Magaldi, Sábato.** Amor ao teatro. Pesquisa, seleção e organização de Edla van Steen. Assessoria, José Eduardo Vendramini. São Paulo: Edições Sesc, 2014. 1223 p.: bibl. (Coleção críticas)

This book provides an important contribution to the history of theater criticism in Brazil, particularly the work of one of the most well-known theater critics, Sábato Magaldi. It was organized by Edla Van Steen, his then wife, a couple of years before Magaldi's passing. It is mostly a reference book, providing a collection of 783 theater criticism texts written for *O Jornal da Tarde* from São Paulo, published between 1966 and 1988. Moreover, Magaldi wrote for this newspaper for 20 years, giving the book's readers a theatrical panoramic view of an important period; it is a historical period of violence during which innovation and resistance were impacted by censorship, with the slow path to democratization reflected in the critic's later texts from this collection.

2580 **Oliveira, Reinaldo.** O palco da minha vida. Recife, Brazil: Edições Bagaço, 2013. 344 p.: ill.

This book documents the 71-year history of the *Teatro de Amadores de Pernambuco* through the author's personal recollection, supported by archival research and interviews. Though unusual in its format due to the groupings of personal and historical accounts, this work provides invaluable resource for future generations of researchers of the Northeastern theater scene.

2581 **Santos, Joel Rufino dos.** A história do negro no teatro brasileiro. Rio de Janeiro: Novas Direções, 2014. 254 p.: bibl., ill. (chiefly color), portraits (chiefly color).

Joel Rufino dos Santos provides a much-anticipated contribution to the study of the presence of Afro-Brazilians in Brazilian theater. The author investigates Afro-Brazilians as writers, characters, objects, and types—both onstage and off. In addition to offering an overview of the role of race in the history of Afro-Brazilian theater and drama, the book also contains many invaluable images that illustrate and add insight to the written pages. The work begins the much-needed work of filling a gap in critical studies of Brazilian theater.

2582 **Santos, Klécio.** Sete de Abril, Pelotas, Rio Grande do Sul, Brasil: o teatro do imperador. Pelotas, Brazil: Libretos, 2012. 191 p.: bibl., ill. (some color).

This profusely illustrated book describes the Theatro Sete de Abril in Pelotas, Rio Grande do Sul, since its inauguration in 1834. The study includes informative chapters on its construction, visits of the Imperial family and João Caetano's theater company, carnaval balls, local playwrights and actors, zarzuela, opera, and instrumental music. Relatively useful for scholars interested in 19th-century theater in Brazil. [R. Budasz]

2583 **Siciliano, Tatiana Oliveira.** O Rio de Janeiro de Artur Azevedo: cenas de um teatro urbano. Rio de Janeiro: Mauad X: FAPERJ, 2014. 336 p.: bibl., ill.

Based on detailed archival research on Azevedo's life, chronicles, and plays, the author investigates the development of the city of Rio de Janeiro, the capital of Brazil in the 19th century. Through the critical eye of Azevedo and his cultural milieu, we see a city that is transformed. This work serves as a fundamental reference on the life in the city of Rio de Janeiro at the turn of the 19th to the 20th century, without any pretense of objectivity.

2584 **A terra do não-lugar: diálogos entre antropologia e performance.** Organização de Paulo Raposo *et al.* Florianópolis,

Brazil: Editora UFSC, 2013. 388 p.: bibl., ill. (chiefly color). (Coleção Brasil plural; 2)

This book brings together many of the papers presented at the *NoPerformance's Land?* international meeting (Lisbon, 15–17 April, 2011) which brought together 23 researchers and 14 performers from various countries. The volume aims to explore the communalities and possible intersections between the social sciences, most prominently anthropology, and performance studies.

2585 Vannucci, Alessandra. A missão italiana: histórias de uma geração de diretores italianos no Brasil. Belo Horizonte, Brazil: FAPEMIG, Fundação de Amparo à Pesquisa do Estado de Minas Gerais; São Paulo: Istituto Italiano di Cultura San Paolo; São Paulo: Perspectiva, 2014. 335 p.: bibl., index. (Estudos; 318. Teatro)

This well-researched study describes the origins of some of the principle directors of the Italian and Italian-Brazilian theatrical generation who gave a new impetus to the Italian theater in the mid-20th century and who also crossed the Atlantic and staged these innovative ideas in Brazil, leaving a lasting legacy. Adolfo Celi, Ruggero Jacobbi, Luciano Salce, Gianni Ratto, Flaminio Bollini Cerri, and Alberto D'Aversa joined the entrepreneurial spirit of the culture and artistic talents of Franco Zampari and Ciccilo Matarazzo, among others, using well-known Brazilian actors and directors of the time, such as Cacilda Becker and Ziembinski.

2586 Vargas, Maria Thereza. Cacilda Becker: uma mulher de muita importância. São Paulo: Imprensa Oficial, Governo do Estado de São Paulo, 2013. 160 p.: bibl., ill. (Coleção Aplauso teatro Brasil)

This book investigates the 30-year career of actress Cacilda Becker through brief autobiographical descriptions, while also highlighting some of her most well-known contributions with critical commentaries. Cacilda staged 68 plays in Rio de Janeiro and São Paulo, made two films and a telenovela, and participated in other television productions. The author emphasizes that Cacilda Becker inaugurated the Municipal Theater of São Carlos with the piece *Waiting for Godot* in the beginning of 1969. The study shines by providing beautiful, high quality photographs in a visually appealing format for both the general public and academics.

TRANSLATIONS INTO ENGLISH FROM THE SPANISH AND THE PORTUGUESE

MARÍA CONSTANZA GUZMÁN, *Associate Professor, School of Translation, Department of Hispanic Studies, Glendon College, York University*
ÉLIDE VALARINI OLIVER, *Professor and Director of the Center for Portuguese Studies, University of California, Santa Barbara*
STEVEN F. WHITE, *Professor of Spanish and Portuguese, Chair of Modern Languages and Literatures, St. Lawrence University*

TRANSLATIONS FROM THE SPANISH

AT THE END of the second decade of the 21st century, it is still early to settle on conclusive statements about Latin American writing in our time. Nevertheless, publications in these past few years show Latin American literature in translation unfolding in ever-increasing variety. This biennium the section covered mostly novels, and some of the trends observed in previous years continue. A number of publishing houses—mostly academic and independent—demonstrate a steady commitment to publishing Latin American fiction, and more publishers are embarking on translations of both new works and works by established, never-before translated 20th-century writers. This phenomenon is analogous in Latin America, where independent publishers are playing an increasingly focal role and bookstores, festivals, and fairs are becoming more common. Although the numbers have not changed so significantly, according to Chad Post, 2018 was "a great year" for translation into English, and Spanish was the most translated language.[1]

US publishers continue to issue a wide array of high-quality translations from a diverse set of writers.

About one third of the works reviewed this year were written by women writers; these include the Dominican Rita Indiana (item **2644**), the Argentinian Samanta Schweblin (item **2660**), the Bolivian Liliana Colanzi (item **2631**), and others. Several works deal with loss, death, and memory (items **2638**, **2643**, **2659**, and **2656**, among others). Also common are stories of dystopian realities and those foregrounding the digital/machine-human interface. Some authors focus on the interplay between the personal and the political as relates to recent history—as is the case with Héctor Abad Faciolince and Santiago Gamboa vis-à-vis Colombia (items **2635** and **2642**, respectively). A number of publishing houses are committed to translating works from specific regions and genres. Restless Books, for instance, has been steadily publishing Cuban sci-fi (items **2655** and **2658**). Given the current prominence of comics and graphic novels, this genre was included in this section for the first time, featuring a late-50s Argentinian cult classic, *El eternauta* (item **2647**). Although few comics are available in English translation, there appears to be a growing recognition of a long-standing Latin American comics tradition, and we can expect more translations in years to come.

Commercial considerations continue to play a critical part in what gets translated into English and barriers to translation remain. Measures to support translated literature, such as country-specific awards, help overcome these barriers and make a difference when it comes to numbers of titles published; one such case continues to be the Argentine Programa Sur which is run by the Ministerio de Relaciones Exteriores y Culto and funds literary translations. Despite the more encouraging and dynamic panorama, certain voices remain less visible. Translations and Afro-Latin American writing are scarce. In this volume of *HLAS*, we include Ecuadorian Velasco Mackenzie's 1949 novel *Drums for a Lost Song* (item **2661**). Also scarce are works by LGBTQ authors. Moreover, we have no evidence of a publishing house committed to publishing translations of Latin American indigenous writing. These writings may circulate in magazines and other periodical publications, but are practically absent in English in book form. One laudable initiative is the translation and retranslation of a number of foundational works that were largely bypassed by US publishers during the Latin American Boom years. Now academic houses are issuing annotated, scholarly editions of these works, making them available to a wider audience. *La vorágine* (1924), by José Eustasio Rivera, first translated in 1935, and recently retranslated and published by Duke University Press in 2018 (item **2653**), is a fine example of this resurgence of interest in classic literary works from Latin America.

It is worth noting that while we strive to include as many translation titles as possible in this section, these reviews do not constitute a comprehensive collection of translated Latin American literature. Rather, in addition to highlighting a number of titles, the reviews are an overview of a select number of high-quality translations and serve as an indicator of general trends in the literary translation

---

1. Post, Chad. "The Plight of Translation In America." *Publishers Weekly*. 1 March 2019.

world. It is also important to note that Latin American and Latino writing often defies categorizations—as does most writing—and this also applies to language choice. Writers around the world write in several languages; bilingual and multilingual authors in the US and in Canada often write in more than one language—Valeria Luiselli and Daniel Alarcón write in English and in Spanish, for example. The question of language in a world in which writers are increasingly multilingual and embody multiple identities is a relevant variable for researchers working on Latin American writing at large.

As pointed out in the introductions to this section in *HLAS* 70 and 72 (Guzmán and Pollack), the 21st century has brought forth new writers as well as a new generation of translators—some of whom are becoming quite well-established. The number of Latin American writers whose works in translation have been nominated for or awarded literary prizes is illustrative of the current high standards for literary translations. Among the recent awardees are Rodrigo Fresán (item **2640**) and Samanta Schweblin.

The number and visibility of online translation fora, articles, blogs, and the presence of translators in the media continues to grow, largely due to excellent digital journals and portals that began in the last decade. Two of these, *Words Without Borders* and *Three Percent*, continue to feature reviews, news, blogs, and in the case of *Three Percent*, a podcast and a translation database, now hosted by *Publisher's Weekly*. These resources have established an ongoing conversation about translation-related matters, moving beyond the sporadic article or review prompted by the recent publication of a title of translated fiction. Journals focusing on Latin American literature available online, such as *Latin American Literature Today (LALT)*, are increasingly publishing translations and featuring bilingual editions. Translations have also gained greater visibility due to authors themselves being more visible and active online and in social media (via Facebook, Twitter, and their own blogs), thus increasing their participation in intellectual life. In addition, translations appear in venues focusing on culture and society at large that feature works and artists (for example, Daniel Alarcon's *Radio Ambulante* podcast and the three *New Yorker* podcasts devoted to literature).

Finally, institutions continue to play a role in the dissemination of and awareness about translation as a cultural and intellectual practice and a field of knowledge. Associations such as MLA and NeMLA have for years included sessions on translation in their annual conferences. The American Literary Translators Association (ALTA) remains critical in educating translators about the publishing industry, granting visibility to translated works, and contributing to the translation into English of works from all languages, including lesser translated languages, writers, and regions. In 2018, ALTA held its 41st meeting at the University of Indiana in Bloomington. One highlight of the conference was the opportunity to visit the Lilly Library, the university's fantastic rare books, manuscripts, and special collections library, which, under the leadership of translator Breon Mitchell, has for a few years now been building a collection of translation-related documents—the first of its kind in North America. Researchers and visitors can consult collections of well-known translators such as Suzanne Jill Levine, Edith Grossman, Cola Franzen, John Felstiner, Clifford Landers, and other translators of Latin American literature. These archives will doubtless help shed new light on the transmission of Latin American writing in North America and beyond. [MCG]

TRANSLATIONS FROM THE PORTUGUESE

THE PERCEPTION that Brazilian works are not translated into English often enough is widespread. In this case, perception is reality. Only three percent of the books published in the US are translations and only one percent of these are literary fiction and poetry. Despite Portuguese being the sixth most-spoken language in the world, the percentage of Brazilian works translated into English is, indeed, minimal.

The Encyclopedia of Literary Translation into English by Heloísa Golçalves Barbosa and Maria Lúcia Santos Daflon Gomes (see *HLAS 60:4361*) provides a detailed table of writers whose works have been translated into English up to the year 2004. More recent data about Brazilian translations into English can be accessed from digital databases, publishers' websites, and book fairs. *Publisher's Weekly,* for example, hosts a translation database formerly compiled and hosted by the University of Rochester's *Three Percent* website. The database documents all translations published in the US each year.

Machado de Assis, the greatest and perhaps the most recognized Brazilian writer, has been receiving more attention through new translations of his works and through studies by Brazilian scholars written in or translated into English. For a writer of Machado de Assis' importance however, there is still much to be done, both in terms of better translations of his works, and in terms of original scholarship on Assis—two centuries worth!—that still awaits translation from Portuguese. *Machado de Assis em linha* (http://machadodeassis.fflch.usp.br), an online journal from the Brazilian Literature Department of the Universidade de São Paulo, offers a diverse selection of studies on Machado in Portuguese which await translation and dissemination. *Machado de Assis: tradutor e traduzido* edited by Andréia Guerini, Luana Ferreira de Freitas and Walter Carlos Costa (item **2672**) already has some articles written in English and would be an excellent work to translate in full.

More translations of Machado de Assis' works are fundamentally important given the inherent difficulties of his literary style, his irony and tone, the diversity of range and voice, as well as the nuances of his rich vocabulary. The competing existing translations never quite succeed in conveying these elements. There is, however, a recent translation by Margaret Jull Costa and Robin Paterson of Machado de Assis' short stories, which is a welcome addition: *The Collected Stories of Machado de Assis* (New York and London: Liverlight Publishing Corporation, 2018; to be reviewed in a future volume of *HLAS*).

Another important Brazilian writer, João Guimarães Rosa, also deserves more attention from translators. Guimarães Rosa is considered Brazil's greatest writer of the 20th century. Unfortunately, clumsy translations have buried the originality and uniqueness of his writing. His novel *Grande sertão: veredas* (see *HLAS 20:5389*), along with his short stories, garnered him a permanent place in France, Germany, and Italy and in Spanish-speaking countries due to careful, and in most cases masterful, translations of his works. However, the translation, or rather adaptation of his novel in the US, titled *The Devil to Pay in the Backlands* (see *HLAS 26:2008*) is riddled with inadequacies, mistakes, and disregard for vocabulary, style, and tone. Consequently, Rosa's work never received the acknowledgment and reputation it deserves in the US and other English-speaking countries.

Brazilian Modernismo, which culminated in Modern Art Week of 1922, includes luminaries such as the writers and poets Mário de Andrade, Oswald de

Andrade, Manuel Bandeira, Cecília Meireles, as well as Carlos Drummond de Andrade and João Cabral de Melo Neto. All deserve to be better known among English readers. One hopes that the relatively recent publication of a translation of a classic of Brazilian literature, *The Athenaeum*, by Raul Pompéia (item **2671**) will pave the way for a retranslation of *Os sertões*, by Euclides da Cunha, as well as a critical edition of the works of Lima Barreto. Given its importance as a study of the roots of Brazil's formation *and* its iconic status as the best scholarship produced by the second wave of Modernism, a new translation of *Raízes do Brasil* by Sérgio Buarque de Holanda is long overdue.

The discovery of Clarice Lispector by the publishing industry in the US is a mixed blessing because the translations of her work are constrained by the American cultural context (involving gender and identity). US translations of her work tend to distort her ability to be simultaneously a universal and a local writer—which was the way she wanted to be viewed by her reading public—and obscure her place within Brazil's unique cultural and literary chronology. Lispector was part of a generation of fiction writers working in Rio de Janeiro after the second wave of Modernism. Her works act as a guide to the significant cultural events that Lispector witnessed in Rio. Understanding and conveying this context, instead of reframing her culturally for an American audience in accordance with today's politicized sensibilities, would better serve readers and would support serious scholarship.

The late Jorge Amado (item **2673**) and the prolific Paulo Coelho (items **2666** and **2667**) are likely the Brazilian writers best known to US audiences. Amado wrote many bestselling novels and Coelho is Brazil's best-selling writer of all times. Despite their obvious mass appeal, neither writer has a secure position within the Brazilian literary canon.

A select number of writers from Brazil's literary canon have seen their works translated into English. Among those who have had at least one of their works translated, mostly during the 1980s, are Antonio Callado, Autran Dourado (see *HLAS* 46:6477 and 52:5307), Lêdo Ivo, Lygia Fagundes Telles (see *HLAS* 50:4308 and 4324 and 68:2701), João Ubaldo Ribeiro (see *HLAS* 52:5044, 56:4625, and 68:2697), Moacyr Scliar (see *HLAS* 50:4306–4307, 50:4319–4321, 52:5031, 52:5045–5047, 58:469, and 68:2699–2700). Unfortunately, it can now be difficult to find these editions in bookstores. From the 1990s onward, there were translation of Lya Luft (see *HLAS* 56:4623), Nélida Piñon (see *HLAS* 52:5043 and 54:5081), Adélia Prado (see *HLAS* 52:5028 and *HLAS* 70:2325), Milton Hatoum (see *HLAS* 56:4621, 60:4352, and 66:3295–3296), Edla Van Steen (see *HLAS* 44:6331, *HLAS* 54:5071 and 5082, 58:4707, and 60:4348), and João Gilberto Noll (see *HLAS* 58:4367 and 4688), among others. We can add the recent translations of Michel Laub's *A Poison Apple* (item **2670**) and Roberto Drummond's *Hilda Hurricane* (item **2668**) to the list of acclaimed Brazilian writers whose works are available in English.

The US art world, too, has shown recent significant interest in Brazilian figures. Exhibitions at the Whitney Museum of Art and the Met Breuer in 2017 called attention respectively to the works of Hélio Oiticica and Lygia Pape. In 2018, MOMA hosted a retrospective on Tarsila do Amaral, one of the artists at the forefront of the Modernist movement. There was also a renewal of international interest in the Italian architect Lino Bo Bardi, who lived and worked in Brazil and the landscape artist and architect Roberto Burle Marx. These artists and architects are recognized cultural figures in Brazil and there is an extensive body of literature about them in Portuguese. Currently, however, there is a gap in the existing English-language literature on these and other significant Brazilian cultural figures. Addressing these lacunae through translations of existing works or the production of original scholarship in English would be of great value.

Literary translations are essential to help an international audience understand Brazil's cultural context: the historical trends, the character of the regions, the make up of the Brazilian population, and the structure of social and political hierarchies. For centuries, Brazilian writers have created stories about Afro-Brazilians and indigenous Brazilians; explored the vast ecological landscape of the nation; commented on dictatorship, democratization, social inequalities, and economic development; mourned the rise of urban violence; and watched evangelical Protestantism find a foothold in a country long Catholic. The translation of literary works is not a mere exercise in word play, translation is the lens that enables English readers to see and understand Brazil through the eyes of its writers. Each year a small number of Brazilian literary works continue to find their way to translators. We look forward to reviewing these works in forthcoming volumes of *HLAS*. [EVO]

ANTHOLOGIES

2587 **América invertida: an anthology of emerging Uruguayan poets.** Edited by Jesse Lee Kercheval. Albuquerque: University of New Mexico Press, 2016. 286 p. (Mary Burritt Christiansen Poetry Series)

Jesse Lee Kercheval has selected 21 Uruguayan poets (brought into English by an equal number of translators), born between 1976 and 1989, for this bilingual collection of emerging writers. Kercheval's introduction is exactly what the English-speaking reader needs to enter this world of South American poetry in a country that has produced outstanding writers that include Isidore Ducasse, Julio Herrera y Reissig, Juana de Ibarbourou, Delmira Agustini, Mario Benedetti, Marosa di Giorgio, Circe Maia as well as the 2018 winner of Spain's Cervantes Prize Ida Vitale. In addition to a discussion of this rich literary tradition, Kercheval also makes reference to certain key moments of recent Uruguayan history, such as the military dictatorship (1973–1985), though she makes it clear that "the younger poets' work is a response, not to history, but to what it is like to live in Uruguay now." One noteworthy poet, Agustín Lucas, in Kercheval's translation, chronicles the lives of the homeless in Montevideo: "The transients sleep, children of the street, with one eye obviously open, the proprietors of the stairs and of the railing, of the glass, of the bottle, of the remains of noodles and the heels of bread, of the blanket and the flip-flops, of the size extra large, of the toes sticking out. Prisoners of winter, free of the calendar and of the clock, heroes of the tranquility, friends of the dogs." [SFW]

2588 **Asymmetries: anthology of Peruvian poetry.** Bilingual edition. Bloomington, Ind.: Cardboard House Press, 2014. 304 p.: bibl.

Paul Guillén, editor of the formidable cultural journal Sol negro and someone who has the deepest and broadest knowledge of poetry from Peru imaginable, has assembled a thoroughly responsible and useful bilingual anthology of Peruvian poetry written by authors born between 1924 and 1960. Here they are (14 men and 2 women. Oops! What happened to Carmen Ollé and her amazing *Noches de adrenalina*?): Jorge Eduardo Eielson, Blanca Varela, Carlos Germán Belli, Pablo Guevara, Rodolfo Hinostroza, Antonio Cisneros, Juan Ojeda, Luis Hernández, José Watanabe, Juan Ramírez Ruiz, Enrique Verástegui, Mario Montalbetti, Miguel Ángel Zapata, Roger Santiváñez, Eduardo Chirinos and Mariela Dreyfus. It took a team of eighteen translators to do the job in this bilingual edition, though there seem to have been some technical difficulties getting the en face part of the format to line up correctly, a problem that should have been eliminated by the publisher at the proofing stage. Especially noteworthy is Gary Racz's English versions of poems by Eduardo Chirinos, who passed away in 2016 and is sorely missed: "They say the river is life and the sea death./Here is my elegy:/a river is a river/and death an affair that shouldn't concern us." [SFW]

2589 **Autores baianos: um panorama = Bahianische autoren: ein panorama = Bahian authors: a panorama = Autores bahianos: un panorama.** Bahia, Brazil: P55 Edições, 2013. 1 vol.: ill.

This book, funded by the Cultural Foundation of the state of Bahia, FUNCEB, is an anthology of poems, short pieces, and book chapters, all already published elsewhere, by contemporary authors from that state of Brazil. The intention is to showcase Bahia's literary production. The sampling is uneven and random, and the presentation is confusing. The texts selected are translated respectively into German, English and Spanish. The selection comprises the following authors: Adelice Souza, Aleilton Fonseca, Allex Leilla, Antonio RIsério, Carlos Ribeiro, Daniela Galdino, Florisvaldo Mattos, Hélio Pólvora, João Filho, Karina Rabinovitz, Katia Borges, Lima Trindade, Luís Antonio Cajazeira Ramos, Mayrant Gallo, Myrian Fraga, Roberval Pereyr, Ruy Espinheira Filho, Ruy Tapioca. Despite the miscellany, there are interesting individual samples within the volume, although the literary level is uneven. The quality of the translations vary, as well, from the passable to the good. [EVO]

2590 **Buenos Aires noir.** Edited by Ernesto Mallo. Brooklyn, NY: Akashic Books, 2017. 219 p. (Akashic noir series)

As part of the wonderful—now more than 60 volume—Noir series published by Akashic books, comes out Buenos Aires Noir, edited by Argentinian journalist and author Ernesto Mallo—who organizes the festival BAN! Buenos Aires Negra, the city's international noir literary festival. The volume includes stories set in different neighbourhoods of Buenos Aires, a city that has a long-standing noir literary tradition. The collection is divided into four parts: "How to get away with . . . ", "Crimes? Or Misdemeanors?" "Imperfect Crimes" and "Revenge". Featured authors are Inés Garland, Inés Fernández Moreno, Ariel Magnus, Alejandro Parisi, Pablo De Santis, Verónica Abdala, Alejandro Soifer, Gabriela Cabezón Cámara, Enzo Maqueira, Elsa Osorio, Leandro Ávalos Blacha, Claudia Piñeiro, María Inés Krimer, and Ernesto Mallo himself. In his three-page introduction, Mallo notes that in the stories that make up the volume "we can glimpse what Buenos Aires really is: distinctive points of view, as well as the narrative potential of a city that has reinvented itself many times over. This collection highlights the relations between the social and economic classes—from the tensions, from their cruelties, and also from their love. Deep inside, inhabitants of Buenos Aires live this contradiction". All pieces were translated by John Washington and Cristina Lambert (Washington translated the introduction with John Granger). [MCG]

2591 **Earth, water and sky: a bilingual anthology of environmental poetry.** Edited by Jesse Lee Kercheval. Montevideo: SARAS, South American Institute for Resilience and Sustainability Studies, 2017. 149 p.

In her introduction to this anthology of ten contemporary poets from Argentina and Uruguay, Jesse Lee Kercheval explains how the volume came into being: "These poets responded to a call I sent out for the SARAS (South American Institute for Resilience and Sustainability Studies) Prizes in Poetry. The judge for the competition, Chilean poet Marcelo Pelligrini, selected the prize winners [. . .] Since 2010, SARAS has held an annual conference in Maldonado, Uruguay. Last year's conference, "Imagining resilience: Art-Science collaboration for sustainability" was an example of how SARAS seeks to integrate art with science, disciplines that have been historically separate." In her first-prize poem "Otter," as translated by Seth Michelson, Natalia Romero says: "But one morning/after the moon/ the otter had returned./A resurrection/deep in the hills,/a secret act/that would be an omen:/ he had to cleanse his body/of evils,/ give himself to water/after letting go of land." [SFW]

2592 **Oy, caramba!: an anthology of Jewish stories from Latin America.** Edited by Ilan Stavans. Albuquerque: University of New Mexico Press, 2016. 333 p.: bibl.

Translation of an anthology of Jewish-Latin American authors from several countries. The stories included were originally published in various countries in either Spanish, Brazilian Portuguese, or English. The volume is divided by country and includes pieces by authors from Argentina, Colombia, Chile, Peru, Mexico, Uruguay, Venezuela, Cuba, Guatemala, and Brazil. The collection includes stories by Ana María Shua, Ariel Dorfman, Isaac Goldenberg, Clarice Lispector, Moacyr Scliar, and others. It opens with a substantial (41-page) introduction by Stavans, in which he talks about the genesis of the project, frames it, and discusses Jewish writing in Latin America in relation to demographics, common themes, and intellectual debates, as well as the contribution of individual authors. Stavans notes that some of the stories were published in an earlier collection entitled *Tropical Synagogues: Short Stories by Jewish-Latin American Writers* (see *HLAS 56:4530*), and acknowledges the debt to other earlier publications about Latin American Jewish writing in translation. According to Josh Hanft, the anthology is a "critical sourcebook" as in it Stavans places "each writer in their historical and geographical context" (Jewish Book Council review). The volume concludes with an appendix entitled "The Mythical Jew of Jorge Luis Borges," which includes Borges' stories "Emma Zunz," "Death and the Compass," and "The Secret Miracle." [MCG]

2593 Ramos Sucre, José Antonio. Selected works. Translated by Guillermo Parra. Prologue by Francisco Pérez Perdomo. New Orleans, La.: Uno Press, 2012. 181 p. (Engaged writers series.)

José Antonio Ramos Sucre (1890–1930) is considered one of Venezuela's most distinguished literary voices. This anthology contains 129 poems in a bilingual format selected from *La torre de Timón* (1925), *Las formas del fuego* (1929) (see *HLAS 52:4164*) and *El cielo de esmalte* (1929). In a prologue, Francisco Pérez Perdomo affirms that "Ramos Sucre is a poet who feels a hypnotic fascination for the dark and for the abysses [...] a hallucinating poet who suffers in his solitude." It is difficult to understand why a publisher would not understand the crucial importance of publishing a bilingual edition so that the reader can appreciate the text that underlies the translation of this poetry from Spanish into the English language. Many readers would relish the chance to accompany the Venezuelan poet in his own language on his linguistic travels as rendered by translator Guillermo Parra: "To enter the kingdom of death I advanced through the bronze portico that interrupted the sinister ramparts. The shade rested on them perpetually like a vigilant monster." [SFW]

2594 Sekou, Lasana M. Corazón de pelícano: antología poética = Pelican heart: an anthology of poems. Selección, introducción y notas de Emilio Jorge Rodríguez. Traducción de María Teresa Ortega. Selection with introduction and notes by Emilio Jorge Rodríguez. Translated by María Teresa Ortega. Philipsburg, St. Martin: House of Nehesi Publishers, 2012. 420 p.

Pelican Heart is an anthology of poems selected from 10 published works in English by Lasana M. Sekou, who was born Harold Hermano Lake in 1959 in San Nicolás, Aruba with family connections in St. Martin. Renowned Cuban literary critic Emilio Jorge Rodríguez provides ample bio-and bibliographical information on this writer whose work is translated here into Spanish in a dual language edition by María Teresa Ortega, who also has created Spanish versions of works by Caribbean authors George Lamming, Jan Carew, James Carnegie, and Mark McWatt. Rodríguez maintains that "dialogue with Caribbean literature, culture and history, past or present, is inherent to the production of this author." A good example of this consciousness can be found in the poem "Boats" from *Mothernation* (1991): "and ven boats didn't tek back tobacco/dey tek cotton and sugar/dey tek salt/den dey tek us, salt of the earth, again." [SFW]

2595 Zurita, Raúl. Sky below: selected works. Translated from the Spanish and with an introduction by Anna Deeny Morales. Bilingual edition. Evanston, Ill.: Curbstone Books, Northwestern University Press, 2016. 267 pages: bibl., ill.

Raúl Zurita, born in Santiago, Chile in 1950, is one of Latin America's foremost literary figures. Anna Deeny Morales, who teaches at the Center for Latin American Studies at Georgetown University, follows in the footsteps of accomplished translators of Zurita's work, such as Jack Schmitt, Jeremy Jacobson, William Rowe, and others to offer this anthology with poems chosen from all the Chilean poet's major publications. In her introduction, "Zurita: on the Disappeared and Beloved," the translator writes: "Across his extraordinary oeuvre, Zurita continues to rework the representational axes along which we understand language, power, religion, history, and love." This is certainly the case in "Song for His Disappeared Love," in which a voice laments: "Oh, love, broken we fell and as I fell I wept looking at you. It was blow after blow, but the last ones weren't necessary. We barely managed to drag ourselves among the fallen bodies to stay together, to stay one next to the other." [SFW]

TRANSLATIONS FROM THE SPANISH
Poetry

2596 **Aquino, Alfonso D'.** Fungus skull eye wing: selected poems of Alfonso D'Aquino. Translated by Forrest Gander. Port Townsend, Wash.: Copper Canyon Press, 2013. 75 p.

Alfonso D'Aquino, born in Mexico in 1959, writes poetry, according to Forrest Gander in his introduction, "as exploration of the relationships between nature and culture, body and feeling, language and perception." It is clear in this anthology of poems drawn from perhaps 10 different works published originally in Spanish, that the author has a deep, underlying ethnobotanical knowledge. In "Spores," there are references to "Dehiscent verse" and "Sessile rhyme." In "Networks," the poet clarifies his personal sense of place: "below my plant skin/below my animal face/below my stone bones//below my flesh which is earth." Gander, who has done a formidable job translating D'Aquino's challenging poetry, speaks of the difficulties of "trying to find new arrangements for his orchestrations of sound." [SFW]

2597 **Aridjis, Homero.** Tiempo de ángeles = A time of angels. Version en inglés = English version by George McWhirter. Ilustraciones = Illustrations by Francisco Toledo. Cuarta edición bilingüe. México: Fondo de Cultura Económica; San Francisco: City Lights Books, 2012. 122 p.: ill.

Suitable for collectors, this dual language edition of renowned Mexican writer and eco-activist Homero Aridjis is a stunning example of collaboration at the highest level that brings what is perhaps Aridjis's most important work, *Tiempo de ángeles*, to English-speaking readers with suggestive illustrations by Francisco Toledo from Oaxaca, and the excellent translations by George McWhirter, who also translated Aridjis's *Solar* poems. In his introduction, J.M.G. Le Clézio calls *A Time of Angels* "a book filled with grace and light as the air" that "also bears the weight of anger and the bitterness of experience." There will be an angel here for every reader, including the ecological angel who bears witness to the destruction of Amazonia, where "the morning was a paradise in ruins." [SFW]

2598 **Ballesteros, Cacayo.** Polvo enamorado = Lovedust. Los Angeles: Izote Press, 2013. 144 p.

Ecuadorean poet José R. Ballesteros teaches at St. Mary's College of Maryland and is also director of Zozobra Publishing, which recently published the bilingual anthology *Knocking on the Door of the White House: Latina and Latino Poets in Washington, D.C. Lovedust* is presented in a bilingual format, English translations done by the poet, who publishes under the name Cacayo. It is a personal anthology of poetry written over a decade from 2002–2012. [SFW]

2599 **Baranda, María.** Nightmare running on a meadow of absolute light. Two poems translated by Paul Hoover. Bristol, England: Shearsman Books, 2017. 92 p.

In his introduction, translator Paul Hoover informs the reader that Mexican poet María Baranda is one of the most prominent voices in a generation of writers born in the 1960s. He says that he selected her long poem "Nightmare Running on a Meadow of Absolute Light" for translation due to its "force of language, dreamlike power, and connection to the poetry of Sor Juana Inés de la Cruz, whose words, taken from "First Dream," are embedded and scattered through sections of Baranda's poem." Was it for monetary reasons that Hoover and Shearsman Books decided not to include the original Spanish text? Did the poet knowingly agree to publish this book of experimental poetry that may remind some readers of Huidobro's *Altazor* without the benefit of a bilingual format? In any case, the compelling poetry in English included here will motivate readers to seek more of her work: "You briefly switch on a galaxy and touch your childhood sea. The world is a dark road where night is the voice of what you say." [SFW]

2600 **Cáceres, Omar.** Defense of the idol. Brooklyn, N.Y.: Ugly Duckling Presse, 2018. 61 p. (Lost literature series; 23)

According to the brief biographical information provided by this edition, Omar Cáceres (1904–1943) is considered "a cult poet in the Chilean avant-garde," which explains why his only book of poetry had an introduction by Vicente Huidobro. For the author of *Altazor*, Cáceres "always seems to be examining the beyond with a stethoscope." *Defensa del ídolo* was originally published in Santiago, Chile in 1934, but, unfortunately, had so many typographical errors that the poet attempted to burn the entire edition. As one might expect, there are resonances of Neruda and Vallejo in this poetry presented in a bilingual format: "The water! . . . Who does the water look for, numerous?/Inside clouds, its contortion tightens;/in the meantime, as if heralds of life,/the rain's steps go on—singing,/awake in the dream." [SFW]

2601 **Cádenas, Rafael.** Gestiones: dealings. Traducción por Rowena Hill. Mérida, Venezuela: Universidad de Los Andes, Dirección General de Cultura y Extensión: Ediciones Actual, 2011. 179 p.

Gestiones, by Venezuelan poet Rafael Cadenas, originally appeared in 1992 and earned the author the Pérez Bonalde International Poetry Prize. In his homage "Rilke," Cadenas speaks about journeys that are simultaneously linguistic and historical, akin to writing itself: "Journeys/were a way of listening. Coming and going/between languages/the sure hand/sought/the true stroke/far from the ruins/of the age,/the sober calligraphy/that goes beyond lamenting." [SFW]

2602 **Cádenas, Rafael.** Intemperie: exposure. Traducción por Rowena Hill. Mérida, Venezuela: Universidad de Los Andes, Dirección General de Cultura y Extensión: Ediciones Actual, 2011. 89 p.

Venezuelan poet Rafael Cadenas, born in 1930, is perhaps the most distinguished voice of the Generation of 1958 and won his country's National Literature Prize in 1985. He has published numerous collections of poetry and also has translated Whitman. *Intemperie* was first published in 1977, and, according to the introduction of this bilingual volume, constitutes "the reality, changing, unstable, fluid and enigmatic, of existence itself." The force of the poetry draws on these ontological conflicts: "It's so short, the distance between us and the abyss,/almost non-existent, a slight indulgence. We just/have to stop and there it is. We are that." [SFW]

2603 **Calveyra, Arnaldo.** Letters so that happiness. Translated from the Spanish by Elizabeth Zuba. Brooklyn, N.Y.: Ugly Duckling Presse, 2018. 62 p.: photo

This bilingual edition of poetry by Argentine Arnaldo Calveyra (1929–2015) is accompanied by a useful "Translator's Note" that provides appropriate biographical and historical information to orient English-speaking readers who are not familiar with his work. His exile in France began in 1961, and, according to translator Elizabeth Zuba, Calveyra "was warned not to return to Argentina—the intellectual left was being targeted by right-wing death squads." In his adopted country in 1999, Calveyra was awarded France's highest national medal for contributions to the arts—Commander of the French Order of Arts and Letters. It was in Paris that he became close friends with Julio Cortázar and many other international literary luminaries. Zuba had the advantage of meeting Calveyra in 2010 and, subsequently, closely working with him (as well as his son) on her translations of poems marked by the peculiarities of "the Argentine-specific landscape and nuances of the Entre Ríos dialect," which no doubt include the following references: "pampero winds quack-quack in the through-rush." [SFW]

2604 **Carlo, Elias.** Parterre. Translated by Robin Myers. Foreword by Luis Armenta Malpica. Toronto: Quattro Books; Jalisco, Mexico: Mantis editores, 2012. 115 p.

Elías Carlo was born in Monterrey, Mexico in 1975, and currently lives in Guadalajara. The title of this collection, *Parterre*, refers to a technique for designing a formal garden with an ornamental arrangement of flowerbeds. In his introduction "Words with (Greenhouse) Effect," Luis Armenta Malpica says that Elías Carlo is a poet who eschews perfume: "For him, sweat, the various smells of the night, the patience with which the poet irrigates a text, the sickle he uses to clear it, the kind of intelligence that doesn't grow in pots, these are enough for him." This is hardly a collection of eco-poetry, and yet, there are certain transcendent moments that invoke the natural world in the lovers' bedroom: "the leaves/unhurriedly/return/from autumn/to the sunlit tree/gardens abandoned by nostalgia/to arm its tanks/inside your veins/faces diluting in the foliage/the whole world shakes." [SFW]

Corcuera, Marco Antonio. Trina el pájaro ciego: the trill of the blind bird. See item **2207**.

2605 **Di Donato, Dinapiera.** 2001–2011 colaterales. Brooklyn, N.Y.: Akashic Books, 2013. 127 p.

Dinapiera Di Donato was born in Venezuela in 1957 and has been in Manhattan since 1999, where she teaches Spanish and French. This collection won the National Poetry Series' Octavio Paz Prize. The back cover informs the reader that the poems in this bilingual gathering "were written during days spent clearing river debris while living along the Hudson River" and "speak of the wanderings of a nomadic subject who erases and rewrites in an imaginary landscape." In his introduction, Víctor Hernández Cruz says that "her poetry as prayer pleads for the full disclosure of a mystery, and her minimalist work breathes life into the obvious and the occult." And these mysteries tell a story, even when the message is truncated: "Death arrived/and found me busy /with your lips/found you drawn with henna on your skin/where we would be/death and myself/chasing ourselves blindly through the forest/until you drew me/the eye of the gazelle/and her/a lion of the desert/and in the palm of your hand/the name of Allah/an arrow to the heart's tissue." [SFW]

2606 **Di Giorgio, Marosa.** I remember nightfall. Translated by Jeannine Marie Pitas. Brooklyn, N.Y.: Ugly Duckling Press, 2017. 318 p.

This bilingual collection of poetry by Uruguayan writer Marosa Di Giorgio (1932–2004) is composed of the following four volumes: *Historial de las violetas* (1965), *Magnolia* (1965), *La guerra de los huertos* (1971) and *Está en llamas el jardín natal* (1971). These are poems linked to the landscape of Salto, where the poet spent much of her life, specifically the family farm, on which, according to the translator, "all of nature assumes a dreamlike, erotically-charged quality that signals danger as well as beauty." This is especially evident in the prose poems from Magnolia: "We came again to the foot of the stone. The ritual was completed in an instant. The knife swung. It went from hand to hand. The heads fell. All of them. The chicken's head, the mouse's head, the hare's head. And the head of the child." [SFW]

2607 **Echavarren, Roberto.** The Virgin Mountain. Translated by Donald Wellman. New Orleans, La.: Diálogos Books. 2017. 101 p.

Uruguayan Roberto Echavarren was born in 1944 and is a well-known poet writing in a Neo-Baroque style that also characterizes the work of Néstor Perlongher, Osvaldo Lamborghini, Coral Bracho and others. Translator Donald Wellman affirms in his prologue that "in *The Virgin Mountain* different threads include exploration of landscape and engage the forms of homoeroticism most crucial to the poet's experience of our twenty-first century modernity." Here is an example of these poetics of erotic flow: "The new open field/exposed the earthly curve,/a perfect place for affection/impersonal floating on the whole;/the ink spot has expanded/and a pure fluid in a free state/falls over an alien body." The book opens with the complete English translation, which is then followed by the unbroken text in Spanish. [SFW]

2608 Girondo, Oliverio. In the more marrow: en la mas medula. Translated by Molly Weigel. Notre Dame, Ind.: Action Books, 2012. p.

Argentine Oliverio Girondo (1891–1967) is a major figure of avant-garde Latin American poetry, and this volume, the poet's last, is frequently praised on the same level as Vallejo's *Trilce* and Huidobro's *Altazor*. Molly Weigel characterizes the poems she translated as "passionate, nihilistic [and] profoundly multivalent." She says, "I needed to take apart the already taken-apart Spanish and let it be multiple in Spanish and English, then let it reform in English as a new but related unstable entity." This pushes things about as far as they have gone in the Spanish language, and it can make for a frustrating but, ultimately, fruitful, reading experience. Readers will no doubt enjoy the experience of Girondo sending them to his dogs: "Shadowhounds/pregargoyles bloodlettings/ extralachrymose hounds/ between bastard contelluric frictions of so absent margins." [SFW]

2609 Girondo, Oliverio. Poems to read on a streetcar. Translated by Heather Cleary. New York: New Directions Books, 2014. 64 p.: bibl. (New Directions poetry pamphlet; 11)

This brief volume of poems by Oliverio Girondo, who was born in Buenos Aires in 1891 and died in the same city in 1967, attempts to represent all six books that the Argentine author published during his lifetime. Heather Cleary, in a Translator's Note, says that "the works selected for this pamphlet are meant to reflect this breadth, as well as the conceptual and symbolic depth, of his creative production." Strangely, and with no ready explanation, the book is only partially bilingual, beginning with the poems from *The Persuasion of Days*. If the reader has never been to Venice, Girondo will be happy to be a guide based on his 1921 journey there: "I doubt that, even in this sensual city, there exist phalli more attractive or with more sudden erections than the clappers in St. Mark's campanile." [SFW]

2610 Goldemberg, Isaac. Dialogues with myself and my others = Diálogos conmigo y mis otros. Translated by Jonathan Tittler. Bloomington, Ind.: Cardboard House Press, 2016. 103 p.: ill.

Peruvian Isaac Goldemberg, who was born in 1964 and is a longtime resident of New York City, draws frequently on his Jewish heritage in *Dialogues with Myself and My Others*. Sometimes these others, as in "The Jews in Hell," include Marx, Freud, Spinoza, Einstein, and Kafka: "The fable tells us/that the Jews bought for themselves/a private place in hell . . . /In the sixth circle/Noah is drunk, riding on a zebra./In between the holes of rocks/Einstein searches for atoms./In the last circle,/tilting a telescope,/Kafka laughs like crazy." Translator Jonathan Tittler, who is perhaps best known for his translation of *Changó, the Biggest Badass* by Afro-Colombian author Manuel Zapata Olivella, does especially effective work in "Funeral Oration," which is set in Goldemberg's native Chepén, Perú: "The desert is my exile and my home./A mother who is time, fragments of thread and bones,/encounter, identity, rhythm./We both still wander there among the tall dunes." [SFW]

2611 Kozer, José. Tokonoma. Translated by Peter Boyle. Exeter, England: Shearsman Books, 2014. 132 p.

Prolific and innovative Cuban poet José Kozer was born in 1940 and left Cuba in 1960 to live in New York, where he taught at Queens College until 1997, before retiring and moving to Florida. His work won the Pablo Neruda Latin-American Poetry Prize in 2013. *Tokonoma*, on topics related to the Zen contemplative tradition, was first published in Spain in 2011. The poetry in this bilingual volume is full of glimpses of enlightenment, or, as Kozer puts it, "a kind of satori, or its cheap imitation." But there it is, nonetheless, in all its simple, everyday glory captured in the poetry: "The milk is boiling in/the saucepan: see it/doesn't evaporate, The/coffee is ready, the sugar/bowl contains two/measures of brown sugar/(I'm pleased as punch): I/catch a glimpse, (glancing/back) I catch the/conflagration, the dying/ash's break-even point still/red-hot coals." [SFW]

2612 Laguna, Fernanda and Cecilia Pavón. Belleza y felicidad. Selected writings of Fernanda Laguna and Cecilia Pavón.

Translated by Stuart Krimko. Key West, Fla.: Sand Paper Press, 2015. 267 p.

Fortunately, Stuart Krimko provides a Translator's Introduction that explains how he met Argentines Fernanda Laguna (b. 1972) and Cecilia Pavón (b. 1973), who, together, form the writing and visual arts duo known in Buenos Aires as Belleza y Felicidad, ironic pseudonyms for two people who began disseminating their work around the time that the economy of Argentina collapsed in 2001 and the country experienced severe general hardship. Fernanda also publishes under the name Dalia Rosetti. Krimko says that "the alchemy generated by their first conversations eventually led to the desire to create a spatial dimension for the writing and art they were making, [which] quickly took shape as a physical location, a storefront gallery and art-supply store in the neighborhood of Almagro." Over time, Krimko develops a friendship with Belleza y Felicidad based on what he calls an "ideological and aesthetic kinship." The work included here chronicles and celebrates the urban Argentine underground of self-liberating experience. Fernanda writes of "liberation through a combination of colors and materials" and her desire "to be a plant/and live in a city/surrounded by human beings." In "Annihilation," Cecilia says, "The only thing Fernanda and I do/ is talk about everyone else." There are all kinds of characters in these poems. [SFW]

2613 Lima, Chely. What the werewolf told them: lo que les dijo el licantropo. Translation by Margaret Randall. Edited by Lynne DeSilva-Johnson. Brooklyn, N.Y.: Operating System, 2017. 240 p.

Margaret Randall, legendary founder of *El corno emplumado*, chronicler of the Cuban and Nicaraguan revolutions and tireless translator of Cuban poets over the decades, brings us English versions of work by Chely Lima, who was born in Cuba in 1957. In her introduction, Randall provides important biographical information about the "gender-transgressive" identity of this writer: "I knew the poet first as a young woman, [and] I have followed his work for 35 years—thrilling to its extraordinary unfolding—and, as I believe Chely Lima is primarily a poet of place, because beginning in this way allows me to speak of his progression through a number of physical locations as well as through the places imprinted upon or reinvented on his body." The opening poem is especially poignant: "You will be confused/by your body, your voice trained to sound sweet,/inoffensive. But you are you are you are you:/A solitary man who lives between two worlds." [SFW]

2614 López Amaya, Zurelys. Flocks = Rebaños. Translated by Jeffrey C. Barnett. Bilingual edition. Chico, California: Cubanabooks, 2016. 161 p.

According to Daniel Díaz Mantilla in his brief introduction to *Flocks* (originally published in Spanish in 2010), Zurelys López Amaya, who was born in Havana in 1967, describes how "to be a flock is to abdicate one's selfhood, one's individual liberty, one's personal traits and principles, in order to sink into a malleable mass open to manipulation." Translator Jeffrey C. Barnett praises the book's "poignant socio-political insight" and affirms that "the vision and imagery of the extended metaphor lead the reader to consider disturbing questions about modern-day Cuba." López Amaya writes: "In my thoughts I see the actions of men and I go out into the street so I can remember we are still sheep on a hill, that silently we look at the other side of the ravine without seeing, without crossing into the unknown for fear of not coming back to our usual place, where everyone resembles each other." [SFW]

2615 Mattos, Martín Barea. Never made in America. Translated by Mark Statman. Introduction by Jesse Lee Kercheval. New Orleans, La.: Diálogos Books, 2017. 289 p.

In Mark Statman's vivid and personal introduction fits well with the informal poetics of Uruguayan Martín Barea Mattos. The translator characterizes the poet in the following way: "He is a dynamic individual, passionate, funny, as comfortable singing with his rock band as he is talking about Dante or critiquing capitalism. He is decidedly not academic, has little interest in the academy, and would much rather organize an anarchic international poetry festival (which he has) than a well-oiled poetry conference (which he has not)." Statman, who is perhaps best known for his translation of Lorca's *Poet in New York* published by Grove Press, appreciates the chance he had to work with Barea Mattos directly, beginning in a café in Montevideo. The texts gathered here are from two works in Spanish, *Por hora, por día, por mes* (2008) and *Made in China* (2016). Pick up the book, open it anywhere, and just jump in: "computers in the water/mailmen fish/a box with a letter at the bottom/of an attic with the heel of a giant/that travels with a message." Strange journey guaranteed! [SFW]

2616 **Minga, Ana.** Tobacco dogs = Perros de tabaco. Translated from the Spanish by Alexis Levitin. Fayetteville, N.Y.: Bitter Oleander Press, 2013. 95 p.

Ana Minga, an Ecuadorean poet born in 1983, has published several books, including *A espaldas de Dios* (2006), from which all the poems in this bilingual edition of *Tobacco Dogs* are drawn. Alexis Levitin, who is best known for his translations of Brazilian and Portuguese poets, writes in a preface that "Ana Minga is always on the side of the beaten, the down-trodden, the marginalized, all beings threatened by dissolution and death, whether mongrel dogs or incarcerated lunatics." About these street denizens, Minga says, "We search for what does not exist/like humans seeking signs of God/like ingenuous dogs/who believe that on the next street/the sun is shining." [SFW]

2617 **Moscona, Myriam.** Negro marfil = Ivory black. Translated by Jen Hofer. Los Angeles: Figues Press, 2011. 149 p. (TrenchArt; 6/1. Recon series; 2)

Myriam Moscona is a Mexican poet and journalist of Bulgarian Sephardic descent who was born in 1955. Jen Hofer's translation of *Negro marfil*, first published in Spanish in 2000 (see HLAS 60:3879), won both the Harold Morton Landon Translation Award from the Academy of American Poets as well as the PEN Award for Poetry in Translation from the PEN American Center in 2012. This dual language edition includes an introduction by Francine Masiello from UC Berkeley, brief remarks from Moscona herself and, finally, an insightful piece by Hofer entitled "The Mobile Speaker: Translator's Notes." Hofer believes that, given the challenges of the original, "perhaps translation itself is a kind of reflexive verbal action; decisions are made and unmade and remade, never quite settling and never sounding entirely right in any case." There are indeed many challenges in this unsettling protean text with Biblical resonances: "Ivory Black/We will be an echo in your shares/Only fragments/Lack/Here the hearts/Like the head of John/And I: Awake." [SFW]

2618 **Neruda, Pablo.** Sublime blue: selected early odes of Pablo Neruda. Translated and introduced by William Pitt Root. San Antonio, Tex.: Wings Press, 2013. 83 p.

The poems in this collection by Nobel-winner Pablo Neruda are from the first group of *Odas elementales* published in 1954. William Pitt Root in his introduction recognizes that other translators have created English versions of these odes, but criticizes Margaret Sayers Peden, who translated *Selected Odes of Pablo Neruda* (see HLAS 54:4975), because, he says, "she has avoided altogether the more politically oriented works and such selection serves to domesticate a body of work as deliberately gnarly and behorned in some aspects as it is luminously tender in others." For William Pitt Root, Neruda in these odes "works as the universe itself works, building out of elemental materials those increasingly profound structures in which may live and breathe the astonishing and mysterious varieties of the human spirit." Sublime Blue includes "Ode to Wine," in which the Chilean poet says, "Wine the color of day,/color of night,/wine with purple feet/or topaz blood,/wine,/star-child/of earth." [SFW]

2619 **Neruda, Pablo.** Venture of the infinite man. Translated by Jessica Powell. Introduction by Mark Eisner. San Francisco: City Lights Books, 2017. 120 p.

As a way of characterizing this experimental poem that Pablo Neruda first published in 1926 (between *Veinte poemas de amor* and *Residencia en la tierra*), Mark Eisner says that the Chilean poet "describes the fantastic, nocturnal voyage of a melancholic Infinite Man who sets off on a quest to rediscover himself, to reach a state of pure consciousness." The edition is bilingual, first the English translation in its entirety, followed by the Spanish original. Both texts attempt to reproduce typographically some of the peculiarities of the original publication. The untamed surrealism that Neruda would learn to channel in his landmark *Residencia* blossoms here: "star suspended between the thick night the days of tall sails/as between you and your shadow uncertainties lie down to sleep/dock of doubts dancer on a string you held up twilights/you had in secret a dead man like a lonely road." [SFW]

2620 **Parada Ayala, Carlos.** La luz de la tormenta = The light of the storm. Hyattsville, Md.: Zozobra Publishing, 2013. 112 p.

In his editor's note, José R. Ballesteros says that *The Light of the Storm* is the first book by US Latino poet Carlos Parada Ayala, who was born in El Salvador in 1956 and currently lives in the Washington, DC metropolitan area. His work has been anthologized in *Al pie de la Casa Blanca: poetas hispanos de Washington, DC* and also won the Washington, DC's Commission on the Arts Larry Neal Poetry Award. In "Day of the Dead," the poet addresses the importance of keeping certain cultural traditions alive: "Now I rise with my head held high,/ carrying my country in the deepest part of my chest,/a sanctuary for my people, red and beating,/drumming ancestral rhythms,/on the Day of the Dead." [SFW]

2621 **Perednik, Jorge Santiago.** The shock of the lenders and other poems. Translated by Molly Weigel. Notre Dame, Ind.: Action Books, 2012. 107 p.

Argentine poet Jorge Perednik (1952–2011) founded the influential literary journals *XUL* and *Deriva* in Buenos Aires, and also translated Eliot, Cummings and Olson. *El shock de los Lender*, a long experimental poem based on a murder case in Argentina, was first published, partially, in April 1983, the last year of Argentina's military dictatorship and the end of the Dirty War. According to translator Molly Weigel, "Perednik wants English-speaking readers of *The Shock of the Lenders and Other Poems* published in *XUL* during the dictatorship to be able to use this information to read more deeply and widely, to be able to go down many paths." This is hermetic poetry written out of necessity, not exempt from self-censorship, as a means of surviving the threat of imprisonment, torture, and exile under state terrorism: "CHORUS (intellectuals if possible)/The electrical charges called shocks/can be caused when the wires corrode." [SFW]

2622 **Pizarnik, Alejandra.** The most foreign country. Translated from the Spanish by Yvette Siegert. Introduction by Cole Heinowitz. Brooklyn, N.Y.: Ugly Duckling Presse, 2017. 39 p. (Lost literature series; 14)

La tierra más ajena by Argentine poet Alejandra Pizarnik (1936–72) was first published in 1955. Translator Yvette Siegert says in her introduction that in these poems "we witness a poet driven by an insatiable thirst for communion, even if it can only be reached through estrangement and uncertainty." Unfortunately, the publisher decided not to print the original Spanish. Thus, the reading experience is truncated and allows for only a partial appreciation of the author's work: "Reading my own poems/ printed sorrows the daily transcendences/ proud smile forgiven misunderstanding/it's mine it's mine it's mine!!" [SFW]

Rivera, Luis César. Set. See item **2168**.

2623 **Rodriguez Iglesias, Legna.** Miami Century Fox. Translated by Eduardo Aparicio. Brooklyn, N.Y.: Akashic Books, 2017. 121 p. (The national poetry series' paz prize for poetry)

Legna Rodríguez Iglesias, born in Camagüey, Cuba in 1984, won the prestigious Casa de las Américas Prize for a theatrical work in 2016 and has published a collection of short stories as well as several volumes of poetry. In this dual language edition, which won the 2017 Paz Prize for Poetry, *Achy Obejas* describes this book's formal qualities: "a book of sonnets on the thoroughly contemporary topics of immigration, adaptation and assimilation, resistance and identification (and, of course, love); sonnets sprinkled with such fine humor and a little dash of English now and again." For this task, translator Eduardo Aparicio attempts to replicate the Petrarchan model in English. Here is how the poet begins her description of a trip from Miami to Providence to visit the tomb of an old friend: "Frost on my head, at five degrees./My legs and butt so cold they're blue./My gums and nipples are painful too./I think my teeth are about to freeze." [SFW]

2624 **Santibáñez, Julia.** Everyday poems. México: The Ofi Press, 2017. 13 p.

This slight bilingual volume by Mexican poet Julia Santibáñez, born in 1967, was originally published in Spanish as *Versos de a pie*. In one of these short poems that describe everyday life, "Unemployed," the poet writes: "You didn't die. You took a break, like the metro workers who strike one day to show how nothing works without them and they convince everyone. You can return now." [SFW]

2625 **Selva, Salomón de la.** An unknown songster sings: Salomon de la Selva's collected poems, 1915–1958 = Un bardo desconocido canta: poemas recolectados de Salomón de la Selva, 1915–1958. Compilation, prologue, and annotations by Luis M. Bolaños-Salvatierra. Translation by Luis M. Bolaños-Salvatierra, Guillermo Fernández-Ampié, and Moisés Elías Fuentes. Managua: Academia Nicaraguense de la Lengua, 2015. 529 p.

Salomón de la Selva (1893–1959), an iconic and controversial figure in Nicaraguan literature, was a bilingual author, who lived for a number of years in the US prior to WWI and attempted to create a Pan-American dialogue that would unite English–and Spanish-speaking writers who resided in New York City. Bolaños-Salvatierra has tracked down a wealth of poems in English by de la Selva that the Nicaraguan poet published in a wide variety of literary journals from that effervescent time of cultural exchange and has translated them into Spanish. The subtitle of the anthology, *Collected Poems: 1915–1958*, is, unfortunately, something of a misnomer since subsequent research by Professor Peter Hulme of the University of Essex in *The Dinner at Gonfarone's: Salomón de la Selva and his Pan-American Project in Nueva York, 1915–19* has unearthed substantial new material that is not included in *An Unknown Songster Sings*. Hulme, more importantly, also definitively disproves the following assertion made by Bolaños-Salvatierra in his introduction to this volume: "Although De la Selva's entire World War I fighting experience simmered down to less than a month (roughly from October 21st to November 11th 1918), the short time he spent in the warfront was inspiration enough to write his seminal poetic work, 'El soldado desconocido.'" This is now known to be false. A letter written by De la Selva on November 14, 1918 from Felixstowe proves beyond a shadow of a doubt that the Nicaraguan poet never experienced active combat in WWI and remained throughout the war in an English training camp. [SFW]

2626 **Taniya, Kyn.** Radio: poema inalámbrico en trece mensajes y dos poemas no coleccionados = Radio: wireless poem in thirteen messages & uncollected poems. Translated from the Spanish by David Shook. Graphics by Daniel Godínez-Nivón. Bloomington, Ind.: Cardboard House Press, 2016. 61 p.: ill. (SVR Avant-Garde Series)

From David Shook's Translator's Note the reader learns that the avant-garde work *Radio* (that first appeared in 1924) by Kyn Taniya (the pseudonym of Luis Quintanilla -1900–80) (see *HLAS* 72:2364) is part of the *estridentismo* Mexican avant-garde movement. The poet, who lived in France as a child and, like Huidobro, wrote part of his oeuvre in French, beckons the reader to join him in this linguistic journey: "Cross with caution/the diaphanous currents of space/don't let your soul be wounded against the light/Ascend slowly/vertically/and please leave a trail/SO THAT I CAN FOLLOW YOU!" [SFW]

2627 **Vallejo, Cesar.** Against professional secrets. Edited by Joseph Mulligan. New York: Roof Books, 2011. 100 p.

In a helpful introduction to this English version of *Contra el secreto profesional* by Peruvian poet César Vallejo (1892–1938), translator Joseph Mulligan explains that this unfinished "book of thoughts" was composed in 1923–24 and 1928–29 during Vallejo's "outright conversion to Marxism" but was first published in Spanish by the poet's widow Georgette in 1973. For Mulligan, this text presented in a bilingual format "possesses a seeming transparency, a kind of gleam or finish, but we must not be fooled. Beneath that shiny surface, elaborate and complex turns of language await the tenacious reader, and these are as poetic as any line in his four volumes of verse." Perhaps this affirmation can be borne out in the following fragment from "Sound of a Mastermind's Footsteps": "I don't know who let there be light again. The world once more crouched down in its worn out skin:

yellow Sunday, ash Monday, humid Tuesday; judicious Wednesday, scheming Thursday, somber Friday, raggedy Sunday. The world appeared as usual, at rest, sleeping, or pretending to be asleep. A hair-raising spider, with three broken legs, came out of Saturday's sleeve." [SFW]

2628 **Viel Temperley, Héctor.** The last books of Héctor Viel Temperley. Translated by Stuart Krimko. Key West, Fla.: Sand Paper Press, 2011. 97 p.

Argentine Héctor Viel Temperley (1933–87) is the author of *Crawl* (1982) and *Hospital británico* (1986), the two books that constitute this bilingual volume translated for the first time into English by Stuart Krimko. In the introduction, Krimko maintains that "especially in his later books, Viel Temperley's spirituality was the engine for highly innovative, even idiosyncratic, poetic forms." This is especially true in the case of the poems from *Crawl*, each of which have the same opening line: "I come straight from communion and I'm in ecstasy, brothers/ on mirrored days that held two seas./Vestry with wheat of nudes listening/to an altar of beehives. Singular shadow./Planks." Also included in this volume is a translation of an interview conducted by Sergio Bizzio shortly before the poet's death in which Viel Temperley says, "I'm not the author of *Hospital británico* like I was the author of *Crawl*. *Hospital británico* is something that was in the air. I did nothing more than find it." [SFW]

2629 **Vizcaíno, Santiago.** Destruction in the afternoon = Devastación en la tarde. Translated by Alexis Levitin. New Orleans, La.: Diálogos Books, 2015. 106 p.

Ecuadorian poet Santiago Vizcaíno, born in Quito in 1982, published the original Spanish text of *Devastación en la tarde* in 2008. The bilingual edition from Diálogos Books with translations by Alexis Levitin, who is known best for his work with writers from Portugal and Brazil, includes some biographical information on the author, but no introduction that would situate Vizcaíno for the English-speaking reader in the literary history of his country and that of Hispanic America. In the hallucinatory world of these unforgiving landscapes of the unconscious mind, the poet affirms: "And yet, I still have things to dream,/still find flowers amongst the carrion." [SFW]

2630 **Yanez, Mirta.** The visits and other poems = Las visitas y otros poemas. Edited by Nancy Alonso, Robert Lesman, and Sara E. Cooper. Chico, Calif.: Cubanabooks, 2016. 135 p.

Veteran translator of Spanish-language poetry Elizabeth Gamble Miller says in her foreword to this dual language edition of work by Mirta Yáñez, born in Havana in 1947, that her "desire to translate the writings of Mirta Yáñez has been constant since meeting her at her home in Cojímar in 2001." The heart of this selection, *Las visitas*, was first published in 1971 and won the Premio del Concurso "13 de Marzo." In some brief introductory remarks, Yáñez states: "In writing poetry, the anecdote is of utmost importance to me, like meandering through my city in "The Visits," and personal experiences related to literary practice, as in 'Class Notes.'" For José Antonio Portuondo, *The Visits* is a book that "constitutes a spiritual journey that gives back to the visited city its latent life as life evoked and shared in convivial remembrance." Ultimately, what reigns in these poems is the poetics of space: "For those who don't know about these things/I can tell you/that fear/lives in a particular street in Vedado." [SFW]

Brief Fiction and Plays

2631 **Colanzi Serrate, Liliana.** Our dead world. Translated by Jessica Sequeira. First Dalkey Archive edition. Victoria, Tex.: Dalkey Archive Press, 2017. 105 p.

Nuestro mundo muerto (2016) is the second short-story collection by the Bolivian Liliana Colanzi (b. Santa Cruz, 1981), winner of the Concurso nacional de microrrelato (2004) and the Aura Estrada International Literary Prize (2015) and considered one of the most promising Latin American fiction writers today. The collection, which was a finalist for the Gabriel García Márquez short-story award, is the first of her books to be translated into English. The novel is titled after an Ayoreo song, which is cited in the epigraph: "This is the trunk of all stories, it tells about our dead world". *Our Dead World* is a short novel in eight chapters, set in multiple locations—from small towns and the streets of urban centers to Mars—and straddles realism, horror, and the fantastic, and the tension between tradition and modernity. "Stories of mental breakdown, maternal cruelty, child death, indigenous slavery and suicide make up the meat of this collection [...] Colanzi has an eye for the darker side of life" (*A Year of Reading the World* blog review, Ann Morgan, 31 October 2017). Other books by Colanzi include *Vacaciones permanentes* (2010) and *La ola* (2014). Colanzi is a writer, journalist, and editor, and currently lives in Ithaca, NY, and is visiting Assistant Professor at Cornell. She has written for *El País*, *Letras Libres*, *Americas Quarterly* and other periodical publications. This translation is published as part of Dalkey Archive's Bolivian Literature Series. [MCG]

2632 Di Benedetto, Antonio. Nest in the bones: stories. Translated from the Spanish by Martina Broner and Adrian West. First Archipelago Books edition. Brooklyn, N.Y.: Archipelago, 2017. 275 p.

Translation into English of short stories by Argentine Antonio Di Benedetto (1922–86), an author who was highly admired by major writers such as Borges and Saer. The collection "showcases his short stories' development from sparse and experimental into melancholic, deeply affecting fables [...] These stories bolster Di Benedetto's reputation as a visionary talent" (*Publisher's Weekly*). This English publication follows the belated and welcome translation of the author's critically acclaimed historical novel *Zama* (published in 2016 by New York Book Review Classics)—"A neglected South American masterpiece" (*The New Yorker*, 23 Jan 2017) on which the film (directed by Lucrecia Martel)—was based. Di Benedetto has been hailed by other critics and authors, including Roberto Bolaño, as "one of the greatest writers of Latin America" and, although his oeuvre spanned over 60 years, it is only now that his works are becoming available to an English-speaking audience. A beautiful, carefully crafted edition by Brooklyn's Archipelago Books. [MCG]

2633 Enriquez, Mariana. Things we lost in the fire: stories. Translated by Megan McDowell. London; New York: Hogarth, 2017. 202 p.

This translation of *Las cosas que perdimos en el fuego* is the English-language debut by current Argentine literary sensation, Buenos Aires-based columnist, non-fiction, and fiction writer Mariana Enriquez (b. 1973). The author narrates, in a dark, powerfully honest, at once eerie and down-to-earth style, 12 seemingly mundane stories of contemporary characters, mostly women, living on the city's social fringes and encountering life's darkest corners. She renders them with a mix of historical fiction, everyday-life narrative, and the supernatural. Engaging questions of class and gender and placing readers in unsettling ethical positions, the author complicates common-sense narratives of early 21st-century urban life. Enriquez's poignant narratives are eloquently rendered by Megan McDowell who, in her four-page translator's note states that Enríquez's "particular genius catches us off guard by how quickly we can slip from the familiar into a new and unknown horror" (p. 202). In an interview with NPR's Lulu García-Navarro, Enríquez describes herself as part of the Argentine short-story tradition dealing with both sociohistoric and fantastic elements, and recounts that she has always been drawn to the macabre, in fact, in her lonely childhood, she found the dark world of fiction comforting. Speaking of her relationship with the Argentinian past, she says: "I'm a bit older than the children of the disappeared, but not all of them [...] what always haunted me once I knew the stories of these children is that there's a question of identity. I mean, I went to school with children that I don't know if they were who they were, if their parents were who they were, if they were raised by their parents or by the killers of their parents, or were given by the killers to other families. So there is a ghostly quality to everyday life. So it's almost like something is floating in the air—something that is not resolved. And there is a fear, a real fear, that was in the air that kind of got through my skin" ("In 'Things We Lost,' Argentina's Haunted History Gets A Supernatural Twist," NPR interview 19 Feb 2017). [MCG]

2634 Zambra, Alejandro. My documents. Translated from the Spanish by Megan McDowell. San Francisco, Calif.: McSweeney's, 2015. 241 p.

Translation of the first short story collection by critically acclaimed contemporary Chilean writer Alejandro Zambra (b. 1975 in Santiago) and the author of several short stories and novels, including *The Private Life of Trees* (see *HLAS 64:2034*), *Bonsai* (see *HLAS 64:2033*) and *Ways of Going Home* (see *HLAS 70:2318*). These 11 short stories, mostly set in Chile both before and after Pinochet and featuring Zambra's distinct, carefully crafted, and powerful style, are a fine introduction to Zambra's work. "In this excellent collection, as in all his work, memory is put under a microscope, and the division between author and characters is never certain ... Zambra's stories are always—or always allege to be—acts of remembrance, and the care he takes to let his readers know that suggests something distinctive about his method" (Chris Power, *The Guardian*, 2 May 2015). The collection was praised in *The New Yorker* by James Wood, who says that in it "Zambra returns to the twin sources of his talent—to his storytelling vitality, that living tree which blossoms often in these pages, and to his unsparing examination of recent Chilean history" (22 June 2015). Junot Díaz also praised it as a "dynamite collection of stories [. . .] but what I love most about the tales is their strangeness, their intelligence, and their splendid honesty." Zambra remarked, "I think that writing is more like telling the truth than lying. Or at least it's more like revealing the tricks, the weaknesses, the masquerade. Or it's a territory where honesty takes on a greater value, and it's is no longer about 'confessing,' but about showing a greater nakedness, the nakedness that no clothes could cover. The mere fact that a reader is willing to go along with that ambivalence of fiction makes fiction more productive. The most deceitful genre imaginable is autobiography; in fiction you are closer to the truth, because everything you say is, from the start, arguable. Because you are also speaking from uncertainty, from doubt, from arbitrariness." (A *McSweeney's* Books Q&A with Zambra, 25 August 2015). *My Documents* was a *The New York Times* Editors' Choice selection and was shortlisted for the Frank O'Connor International Short Story Award. [MCG]

Novels

2635 Abad Faciolince, Héctor Joaquín. The farm. Translated from the Spanish by Anne McLean. First Archipelago Books edition. New York: Archipelago Books, 2018. 375 p.

This is the second English-language translation of a work by Colombian Abad Faciolince (b. 1958), who gained renown with his memoir *Oblivion* (see *HLAS 70:2319*). Against the backdrop of Colombia's troubled 20th-century history, *The Farm* tells the story of three siblings who are the last heirs of a farm located in the mountains of Antioquia, which has been in the family for several generations. The siblings talk about their memories and lives as they face a decision regarding the future of the family property, and their intertwined voices shape the narrative. *The Farm* won the Cálamo Prize in Spain and was shortlisted for the Mario Vargas Llosa Prize. Kevin Canfield called the novel a "sweeping, satisfying tale about the interplay of family life and national history" and noted that the author is, in a sense, "like some of the characters in *The Farm*, doubling back to a piece of land that he knows extremely well" (*World Literature Today* review, March 2018). Abad Faciolince has worked as a university lecturer and translator, and is a columnist for the Colombian newspaper *El espectador*. Anne McLean is a prolific translator; her translations include works by Javier Cercas, Evelio Rosero, Carmen Marín Gaite, Julio Cortázar and others. She was awarded the Cruz de Oficial of the Order of Civil Merit in 2012 in recognition of her contributions to Spanish literature. [MCG]

2636 Aridjis, Homero. The child poet. Translated from the Spanish by Chloe Aridjis. First Archipelago Books edition. Brooklyn, N.Y.: Archipelago Books, 2016. 153 p.

Translation of *El poeta niño* (Fondo de Cultural Económica, 1971) by the Mexican poet Homero Aridjis (b. Michoacán, 1940). This is the memoir of a childhood that was interrupted by an accident Aridjis had at 11 years old, when he accidentally shot himself in his family home. This accident changed his life; he claims that afterward, he became a poet. "Throughout the memoir, Homero proves to have a febrile, discerning sensitivity, alert to the town's emotional atmosphere and the emotions of those around him [. . .] His childhood isn't cleaved neatly in two halves by a shotgun shell. "The Road to Toluca" is significant—it was a near-death experience, after all—but Aridjis allows its weight to remain mysterious, its effect on him not entirely knowable. That's childhood.... When we try to make sense of childhood and adolescence as adults, the puzzle pieces never quite fit neatly; there's always a few missing; the puzzle we've filled in doesn't look like what's on the box. *The Child Poet* lets those missing pieces stay missing, and for childhood to remain as fragmentary and incomplete as it is in our memories" (*The Quarterly Conversation* review, Walter Biggins, 13 June 2016). The translator of this memoir was the author's daughter, Chloe Aridjis. She delivers a beautiful version which renders well the poetic quality of the original. There is a two-page translator's introduction in the volume, in which she explains how significant the writing of the book was for her father as a means of retrieving memories that he thought had been lost. [MCG]

2637 **Barón Biza, Jorge.** The desert and its seed. Translated from the Spanish by Camilo Ramírez. Afterword by Nora Avaro. New York: New Directions, 2018. 218 p.

This novel is based on the tragic real-life story of the Argentine writer Jorge Barón Biza (1942–2001), whose father, the writer Raúl Barón Biza, threw acid on Jorge's mother, the historian Clotilde Sabattini, in 1964, and shot himself hours later. The novel is told from the perspective of 23-year-old Mario Gageac, the son—who is the protagonist. It begins right after the attack happens, when he and his mother are on their way to the hospital in a taxi. Describing the publication process, Ratik Asokan notes that "After jobbing as an art critic and copy editor at various publications, [Jorge Barón Biza] wrote *The Desert and Its Seed*, his only novel, in 1995. Rejected by publishers, it was ultimately self-published, in 1998—three years before Biza, too, committed suicide [. . .] The book, originally something of an underground hit, found a much wider audience when it was reissued in Argentina in 2013." ("A Cult Hit in Argentina, This Novel Evokes and Evades Malignant Machismo" *The New York Times Book Review*, 26 May 2018). Initially narrating with painstaking detail the months and years following the crime and Mario's accompanying his mother in the process of recovery, as it advances the novel increasingly moves toward Mario's psychological process, including his intimate ambivalent emotions and moral dissonance. [MCG]

2638 **Bosco, María Angélica.** Death going down. Translated by Lucy Greaves. London: Pushkin Vertigo, 2016. 151 p.

Translation of the 1955 thriller *La muerte baja en ascensor* by the Argentinean María Angélica Bosco (1909–2006), one of the first women to make a name for herself in the crime-fiction genre in Argentina (*Latin American Women Writers: An Encyclopedia*, Routledge, 2008). *Death Going Down* is set in post-WWII Buenos Aires. After Frida Eidinger's body is found in an elevator, an apparent suicide, Inspector Eircourt and his colleague look for clues in the building where she lived, piecing together the unreliable accounts of its residents. The first novel by Bosco, it was published in the prestigious Argentinian crime-fiction series Séptimo Círculo and won the Emecé novel award in 1954. Pushkin Vertigo is a crime fiction publisher currently publishing crime writing from across the world in the series Pushkin Vertigo Originals. [MCG]

2639 **Castagnet, Martín Felipe.** Bodies of summer. Translated from the Spanish by Frances Riddle. First Dalkey Archive edition. Victoria, Tex.: Dalkey Archive Press, 2017. 105 p.

Translation into English of *Los cuerpos del verano*, a debut novel by Castagnet (b. La Plata, 1986) and winner of the Saint-Nazaire MEET Young Latin American Literature Award. The novel is a sci-fi reflection on technology, gender, sex, identity, and the limits of what it means to be human in the 21st century. The central question of *Bodies of Summer* (as summed up by J. David Osborne's review in *World Literature Today*, May 2017) is "What if, after death, your consciousness [were] uploaded to the Internet, where you could either float around with other disembodied souls or choose to 'burn' yourself into a new body?" Published as part of Dalkey Archive's Argentinian Literature Series, the novel has been published into other languages. Castagnet is currently associate editor of *The Buenos Aires Review*. His short story "Bonsai" (trans. George Henson) was published bilingually online in *Latin American Literature Today* under speculative fiction. [MCG]

2640 **Fresán, Rodrigo.** The bottom of the sky. Translated from the Spanish by Will Vanderhyden. Rochester, N.Y.: Open Letter, 2018. 266 p.

This is the second Fresán novel translated by Vanderhyden and published by Open Letter, following the success of the award-winning novel *The Invented Part* (see item **2641**). Considered an homage to science, *The Bottom of the Sky* features Fresán's fragmented, metafictional and multi-referencial style—from the epigraph page we have quotes from Bioy Casares, Nabokov, Proust, Philip K. Dick, Vonnegut, Banville, and Cheever, and there are countless references to other, chiefly male, writers and artists. Divided in three parts, the novel opens with two Jewish cousins, Isaac Goldman y Ezra Leventhal, living in New York, who become immersed in sci-fi. It has multiple narrators—including an alien. It "deals with space travel, science-fiction factionalism, Philip K. Dick, the September 11 attacks, the US invasion of Iraq, Jewish-American identity formation, Kabbalah, suicidal widowers, awkward adolescents, snowball fights, alien invasion, time travel, the apocalypse, the Manhattan Project" and is written, "to use Fresán's description, as a clump of simultaneously broadcast messages, like a storyline that wants nothing but to be a succession of marvelous moments seen at one time [. . .] It withholds resolution until the reader just about wants to give up—but then he delivers." (Joey Rubin "The Gluttonous Genre Mutations of Rodrigo Fresán," *LA Review of Books*, 13 April 2018). Edmundo Paz Soldán described *El fondo del cielo* as an unconventional love story, more mystical than erotic, a cosmic solitude (*Letras libres*, Edmundo Paz Soldán, 31 de diciembre de 2009). [MCG]

2641 **Fresán, Rodrigo.** The invented part. Translated by Will Vanderhyden. Rochester, N.Y.: Open Letter, 2017. 552 p.

After his 2006 English-language debut *Kensington Gardens* (see HLAS 64:2525), this translation of *La parte inventada* (2014) is the second work to appear in English by the Argentinian Rodrigo Fresán (b. 1963), critically acclaimed best-selling author of *Historia argentina* and recently the recipient of the Roger Caillois award. Part of a novel series (which includes *El fondo del cielo*, and *La parte recordada*) and referencing Canciones Tristes, an imaginary city that appears recurrently in Fresán's works, this novel—labelled psychological fiction—is a metafictional narrative about writing, literary culture, and being a writer. It centers around the mind and world of an aging, disillusioned writer—Fresán's alter ego—and his existential diatribes and anxieties as he tries to write his own story. It is "literature set in the process of dying and someone who continues to write so as to postpone death" (*El cultural*, 7 August 2018). Fresán blends memory with Western music and literature—in the form of a soundtrack and a library—in a fragmented, digressive, and "kaleidoscopic" style. Enrique Vila Matas described the novel's prose as written for readers from a different, past time, the good old times when a writer could just keep writing, perfecting a style and a voice (Vila Matas, "Una vida de ventrílocuo", *El País*, 11 March 2014). Positive reviews hailed it "A tour de force," "charting a course from confusion to confusion and back again," "an exemplary postmodern novel that is both literature and entertainment" (*Kirkus Reviews*, March 2017). Will Vanderhyden's translation—partially funded by an NEA grant—received the Best Translated Book Award (2018). [MCG]

2642 **Gamboa, Santiago.** Return to the dark valley. Translated from the Spanish by Howard Curtis. New York: Europa Editions, 2017. 461 p.

Another novel by Colombian Santiago Gamboa (b. 1965, novelist, short-story writer, and journalist) to be published by Europa editions, this is the translation of *Volver al oscuro valle*, (Random House, 2017). This 460-page novel is similar to previous novels by prolific, award-winning Gamboa—such as *Necropolis* (2012) (see HLAS 70:2280) and *Night Prayers* (2016)—in that all are lengthy narratives set in multiple cities and concerned with global political and social problems. Divided into two parts and with an epilogue, the narrative moves from Europe to Latin America and Africa and features multiple female and male characters at the crux of moral and political tensions and contradictions. Among them are Juana and the Consul—characters also present in *Night Prayers*. Curtis's translation captures nicely the novel's tone and its colloquial range and richness. In her review article "Hell Can Be Beautiful" (*NYT Review of Books*, 19 July 2018) Silvana Paternostro provides the context of the novel in relation to the contemporary political situation in Colombia and remarks on the importance of the novel as preserving memories during the ongoing process of peace and reconciliation in the country. According ot Paternostro, "Gamboa's mixture of monologue, news analysis, rumination, world history, philology, philosophy, and tabloid scoop is, certainly, a new way of writing fiction about Colombia." [MCG]

2643 Gerber Bicecci, Verónica. Empty set. Translated by Christina MacSweeney. Minneapolis, Minn.: Coffee House Press, 2018. 209 p.

Translation of the critically acclaimed novel *Conjunto vacío* (see item **1768**) by the Mexican writer and visual artist Verónica Gerber Bicecci (b. 1981), winner of the Aura Estrada Prize for Literature in 2013. Set in Mexico in 2003, the novel is told from the perspective of the young narrator, Verónica, after a break up. She has to return to her family home, where she had lived with her mother and brother when their mother disappeared seven years earlier. Alone in the house, using the logic of set theory, she tries to make sense of her relationships and the loss of her boyfriend Tordo and of her mother, who in turn had experienced the losses of exile with Verónica's father as they fled Argentina's dictatorship. Gerber's first novel is ghostly, enigmatic, and structurally experimental. Dana Hansen describes it as "a Rubik's Cube in the best possible way: there may be an elegant solution, but this puzzle of a story doesn't make it easy to find. The head-scratching challenge of deciphering the messages and meanings hidden in the combination of Gerber Bicecci's spare words and enigmatic diagrams is one of the most appealing aspects of this unusual narrative" (*Chicago Review of Books*, 8 March 2018). Praising her writing, Francisco Goldman remarked that Gerber "writes with a luminous intimacy; her novel is clever, vibrant, moving, profoundly original. Reading it made me feel as if the world had been rebuilt." At the end of the novel there is an afterword by award-winning translator MacSweeney, who earned the 2016 Valle Inclán Translation Prize for her translation of *The Story of My Teeth*; her translation of *Among Strange Victims* was a finalist for the 2017 Best Translated Book Award. [MCG]

2644 Indiana, Rita. Papi: a novel. Translated by Achy Obejas. Chicago: University of Chicago Press, 2016 152 p.

This is the awaited English-language debut of contemporary Dominican artist, musician, and award-winning literary sensation Rita Indiana (b. Santo Domingo 1977). Practically since the publication of the Spanish-edition of this first novel, Rita Indiana became an outstanding figure in contemporary Latin American and Caribbean letters. She is known for her fast-paced, spoken-word-style filled with music, street speech, and pop culture references. The coming-of-age novel is a first-person portrait of the inner-life of the narrator, the eight-year-old daughter of an absent father. While he is away and living a gangster-life-style, she waits—for days, months, maybe years— and tells imagined stories of her dad's soon-to-happen triumphant returns with wealth and gifts. The girl "repeats 'Papi' like a mantra, spell, or rosary. His name takes on a supernatural power; it represents his daughter's immense belief in him no matter the length of his absences [. . .] Papi's invincibility is a blanket of comfort and denial for the narrator, as she is unable to demonize Papi no matter what promises or laws he breaks" (Marilyse V. Figueroa review *World Literature Today*, November 2016). In her narrative of her idolized father, he is both "larger than life" and "cocky and brash" [. . .] "Although the child clearly loves her dad and is thrilled to be part of his entourage, she has also had to reckon with the fact that Papi can be irresponsible, conniving, and cutthroat. Furthermore, she knows that he treats women badly and has herself been on the receiving end of his broken promises and blatant lies" (*Kirkus* review, March 22 2016). In her poignant novels, Indiana is able to tackle gender, class, and racial inequalities with sharpness, humour and wit. As she does in *Nombres y animales* (2013) and *La mucama de Omicunlé* (2015), in *Papi* she takes on, without romanticism and with dark humour and her characteristic vertiginous mix of registers and genres, the world and subjectivity of women in a patriarchal society and the violence of the intimate space. [MCG]

2645 **Jodorowsky, Alejandro.** Albina and the dog-men: a fantastical novel. Translated from the Spanish by Alfred MacAdam. Illustrations by François Boucq. Brooklyn, N.Y.: Restless Books, 2016. 207 p.

Translation of *Albina y los hombres perros* (2002), a novel by actor, film-maker, author, and "psychomagical guru", the Jewish Chilean artist and cult-figure Alejandro Jodorowsky (b. 1929). Set in Chile and Peru and at once a horror story and a humorous tale, this short surreal novel, filled with fantastical creatures, centers on the sexy amnesiac giantess Albina and her effects on men, who become wild dogs in her presence. Albina travels with Crabby (la Jaiba), a woman who saved her from threatening monks, and together they search for a magic healing cactus. The novel is divided into three parts and the English edition features an excerpt of *Where the Bird Sings Best* (see *HLAS* 72:2751). The novel "seems to be all imaginable things at once: a fable and a folktale, a Western, a tragedy, a lewd comedy" (Benjamin Russell, *Americas Quarterly* review, 2016). As Juan Vidal notes, "The setting is fertile ground for Jodorowsky to unleash a fantastical and genre-defying parable of love and friendship." [. . .] Throughout this dark dream of a novel, Jodorowsky's writing is comic and occasionally mesmerizing. It is also ripe with horror and philosophical questions about what it means to belong, everywhere and nowhere" (Juan Vidal, "Madness And A Search For Healing In 'Albina And The Dog-Men" NPR review, 14 May 2016). Distinguished translator and literary scholar Alfred MacAdam has translated works by Carlos Fuentes, Mario Vargas Llosa, Jorge Volpi and many other Latin American writers, as well as Jodorowsky's *Where the Bird Sings Best*. [MCG]

2646 **Nettel, Guadalupe.** After the winter. Translated by Rosalind Harvey. Minneapolis, Minn.: Coffee House Press, 2018. 264 p.

Translation of young and prolific award-winning Mexican author Guadalupe Nettel's third novel *Después del invierno* (Anagrama, 2014). Centering around the everyday lives of two immigrants, *After the Winter* recounts the first-person stories of Cuban-born Claudio, a middle-aged man who lives in New York City and can barely tolerate people, and Mexican-born Cecilia, a graduate student living in Paris who spends most of her time at the Père-Lachaise cemetery. From their alternating narratives, which foreground their pathos, the reader can see that both Claudio and Cecilia experience the city in its fullness, while knowing they are outsiders and meditating on their sense of alienation within a grim existence. "Nettel writes with compassion for her flawed, unhappy characters and the isolation they feel within their adopted cities. As they navigate life's losses and disappointments, both gradually integrate more fully into humanity" (*Kirkus Reviews*, 1 Aug. 2018). Nettel (b. 1973) is also author of short story collections and other novels and of the memoir *The Body Where I Was Born* (see *HLAS* 70:1558), which with Nettel's characteristic "unsparing" and "candid, unaffected prose" delivers, "somewhere between religious confession and secular disclosure [. . .] a sharp sense of a woman's harrowing girlhood" (Amy Rowland, *New York Times Book Review*, 2 July 2015). [MCG]

2647 **Oesterheld, Héctor Germán.** The eternaut. Drawn by Francisco Solano López. Seattle, Wash.: Fantagraphics Books, 2015. 362 p.: bibl., ill.

A welcome translation of a Latin American graphic novel classic, the Argentine *El eternauta*, originally published serially from 1957-59. Journalist and graphic novel writer Oesterheld (1919-?) and comics artist and illustrator Solano López (1928–2011), both Argentine, collaborated to bring this project to life. Oesterheld was "disappeared" during the military dictatorship and Solano López continued his career in exile as a comics artist until his death in 2011. In Argentina and with the Cold War as the backdrop, in this over 350-page sci-fi graphic narrative, the protagonist Juan Salvo, his friend Professor Favalli, and an array of other characters face nuclear threats, monsters, robots, alien invasions, Argentine everyday life, and space and time travel. While *El eternauta* has enjoyed cult-status in Argentina and among Latin

American comics artists and lovers, "Until the long-overdue arrival of this beautiful, highly gift-worthy slipcased edition" Oesterheld's "gritty and ruminative series" was "practically unknown in the broader comics world." "Lopez's noirish black-and-white art [. . .] cleverly highlights both Oesterheld's moody philosophizing and the high-octane action scenes. The complicated twists and existential bleakness deliver a richly mysterious experience" (*Publisher's Weekly*). The beautiful English edition, with supplemental texts by translator Erica Mena and scholar Martin Hadis, and specifically Mena's translation, have been highly praised. According to *World Literature Today's* review "There's a treasure trove of Spanish-language comics south of the border lost to English-only readers" and with the publication of this "epic odyssey" Fantagraphics Books has "changed comic book history" [. . .] "Erica Mena's translation beautifully captures the wondrous syntax and choice of words in the Spanish original. She finds just the right turns of phrase for the mix of linguistic registers [. . .] conveying the Eternaut's school and street smarts. The careful choice of a wide variety of forms of linguistic expression also importantly frees up the voices of each character, making their thoughts and dialogue uniquely their own" (Frederick Aldama, *World Literature Today*, March 2016). The Eternaut was the winner of the Eisner Award for Best Archival Collection/Project—Strips! [MCG]

2648 Oloixarac, Pola. Savage theories.
Translated by Roy Kesey. New York: Soho, 2017. 291 p.

Teorías salvajes (2008) is the first novel by contemporary Argentinian essayist and novelist Pola Oloixarac (b. 1977), and also the first to appear in English translation. Centering around the Buenos Aires academic milieu and entwined with the thinking of various theorists and authors, from Wittgenstein to Bolaño, the novel follows Rosa Ostreech's life as a graduate student, from her sex life to her readings and struggles with writing her thesis. Told in parallel are the stories of a Dutch anthropologist doing research in Africa, and a series of characters exploring the underground scene of Buenos Aires. The novel has been critically acclaimed in Argentina and abroad, mainly for its theme and use of language: "Dark and humorous in turns, the tone is wry, erudite, raunchy, and the text is sprinkled with references to politics, philosophy, anthropology, and pop culture and the occasional illustration. Academic posturing is mocked [. . .] While there are echoes of Borges and Bolaño here, the synthesis of ideas and the manic intelligence are wholly new" (*Kirkus Reviews*, 10 Jan. 2017). Of the translation, David Varno notes that, "the perversions of language is one of Oloixarac's central themes, and this, along with the nuanced references to Argentina's Dirty War and the country's political history following Peronism, plus the characters' tenuous interpretations of various philosophers expressed in murky academic syntax, must have made the book particularly challenging to translate. Roy Kesey succeeded in creating a text that is immersive, multilayered, sensual, and cerebral, and it captures Oloixarac's wicked brand of humor, which often triggers bark-like laughs followed by pangs of guilt" (*Words Without Borders*, January 2017). At the time of writing *Teorías salvajes*, Oloixarac was herself working on her doctorate at Stanford University. The author's novels—including *Teorías salvajes* and *Constelaciones oscuras* (see item **2102**) have been translated into several other languages. For literature specialist's comment on *Constelaciones oscuras*, see item **2102**. [MCG]

2649 Padura Fuentes, Leonardo. Heretics. Leonardo Padura. New York: Farrar, Straus and Giroux, 2017. 528 p.

Translation into English of *Herejes* (see *HLAS* 70:1620), one of the latest novels by renowned, award-winning Havana-based Cuban writer Leonardo Padura (b. 1955). An author of fiction and non-fiction and considered by many Cuba's best living writer, Padura is known for his detective novel series and, most recently, for the historical fiction master work *The Man Who Loved Dogs* (see *HLAS* 70:2292). Combining historical and detective fiction, *Heretics* narrates events surrounding the experience of Jewish refugee families in Havana during and after WWII. It centers on the disappearance of a Rembrandt painting—a portrait of Christ—brought to Cuba by one of the families travelling on the *S.S. Saint Louis* in 1939 to seek asylum in Cuba, and the search for it by Elías, son of Daniel Kaminsky and one of the relatives who succeeded in settling in Cuba. For this search, he hires detective Mario Conde, protagonist of several of Padura's novels, who aids Kaminsky in the search throughout Cuba and all the way to an auction house in London. This handsome hardcover edition of the over 500-page work is described as an epic novel and also as "the story of modern Havana, a lost family history, and the origins of a notorious painting." Critically acclaimed, "this rich and brilliant evocation of Jewish history will only burnish the already extraordinary reputation of the author of the acclaimed *The Man Who Loved Dogs*" (Elizabeth Fifer, *World Literature Today*, September 2017). Remarking on the feat that is the translation of this novel, Jason Sheehan praises Anna Kushner's rendition given the challenges of "committing to the page these beautifully complicated thoughts, these gorgeously convoluted lines." He notes how carefully she renders Padura's sentences, "all of them are just as lovely. Just as weirdly sticky. Just as packed with meaning and sculpted with such care" (NPR book review, "Rum-Soaked, Bloody, Sprawling *Heretics* Is A Romp Through Centuries," 19 March 2017). [MCG]

2650 Paula, Romina. August. Translated by Jennifer Croft. New York: The Feminist Press at CUNY, 2017. 199 p.

Agosto (2009) is the first of a series of novels by contemporary Argentinian author—playwright, director, and actor—Romina Paula (b. Buenos Aires, 1979) and the first to be translated into English. This fast-paced, intimate, self-deprecating, second-person narrative reads like a confession of a woman, 21-year-old Emilia, to her best friend, whom she lost to suicide. The story centers around her trip from Buenos Aires to the town in Patagonia where they grew up together and to which Emilia travels to scatter her friend's ashes. "Paula's English-language debut is almost impossible to put down: moody, atmospheric, at times cinematic, her novel is indicative of a fresh and fiery talent with, hopefully, more to come." (*Kirkus Reviews*, February 2017). This is an accomplished translation by award-winning Jennifer Croft, translator from Polish, Spanish, and Ukranian, and the recipient of the Michael Henry Heim Prize. Croft is also founding editor of *The Buenos Aires Review*. [MCG]

2651 Piglia, Ricardo. The diaries of Emilio Renzi: formative years. Translated by Robert Croll. Introduction by Ilan Stavans. Brooklyn, N.Y.: Restless Books, 2017. 448 p.

This is the translation of the first volume of the *Diarios*, a long-awaited work by one of the most important Argentinian, and Latin American, writers of the 20th century. Piglia (1941–2017) is the author of critically acclaimed novels such as *Artificial Respiration* (see *HLAS 56:4591*), *The Absent City* (see *HLAS 60:4304*), and others, and during his lifetime he was awarded prestigious prizes—including Rómulo Gallegos, Casa de las Américas, and José Donoso. As Adam Thirlwell noted, "In the long history of novelists and their doubles, doppelgängers, and alter egos, few have given more delighted attention to the problem of multiplicity than the Argentine novelist Ricardo Emilio Piglia Renzi" ("Imaginary Conspiracies" *New York Review of Books*, 19 July 2018). That relationship is at the heart of the three-volume *Diarios* of his long-standing fictional alter ego Emilio Renzi—who is also the detective in some of Piglia's novels. Piglia wrote this first volume, "Formative years", corresponding to the period between 1957 and 1967 in the first and third person in a span of almost 60 years—until 2015. Taken from 327 notebooks, the volume includes everyday notes, quotations, comments on writing, literary life and the print media world, and include interspersed pieces of fiction and non-fiction. Their overall autobiographical narrative—chiefly a literary life—tells of coming of age, family, reading, writing, and life in Argentina, and Latin America. It features references and close-reading notes to countless authors, from Borges, Onetti, and Cortázar to Beckett and Pirandello, and, as in Piglia's oeuvre, fiction and non-fiction blend with history and politics: "In Argentine history," Piglia once wrote, "politics and fiction . . . are two simultaneously irreconcilable and symmetrical universes" and literature "maintains coded relationships with the machinations of power." (Piglia quoted in "Imaginary Conspiracies" *New York Review of Books*,

July 19, 2018). The introduction to the English edition, written by Ilan Stavans, frames and contextualizes the book. [MCG]

2652 Piñeiro, Claudia. Betty Boo. Translated by Miranda France. London: Bitter Lemon Press, 2016. 315 p.

Translation of the thriller *Betibú* (see *HLAS 70:1819*) by the Argentinian, journalist, playwright, and script and fiction writer Claudia Piñeiro (b. 1960), "dubbed the Patricia Highsmith of Argentina" (*Globe and Mail*, 3 June 2016). It tells of the protagonist Nuria Iscar—also known as Betty Boo—who is covering the story of the murder of a wealthy Buenos Aires industrialist for the editor of a national newspaper who is also her former lover. The novel fits well in a genre which enjoys high prestige in Argentina. It is "definitely not a 'donkey at the Grand National'," as one critic once described crime fiction in relation to literature."If you like elegantly written mysteries with an international flavour, then the work of the award-winning Argentine writer Claudia Piñeiro is just the ticket" (*The Crime Warp*, 25 June 2016). Bitter Lemon Press previously published Piñeiro's *Thursday Night Widows* (2009, winner of the Clarín Prize for Fiction), *All Yours* (2011, winner of the German Literaturpreis), and *A Crack in the Wall* (2013). [MCG]

2653 Rivera, José Eustasio. The vortex: a novel. Translated and with an introduction by John Charles Chasteen. Durham, N.C.: Duke University Press, 2018. 240 p.: bibl.

A welcome publication, this is the English retranslation of the 1924 critically acclaimed Colombian classic *La vorágine* written by lawyer and writer José Eustasio Rivera (1888–1928)—the first English translation, by E.K. James, was published in 1935. Set circa 1900–20, the novel follows the trip of the protagonist, Arturo Cova—a young poet and an elite, educated urbanite—from Bogotá to the Amazon rainforest. Partly based on Rivera's own travels, the narrative is structured as Cova's diary, found after his disappearance, which is then transcribed to be submitted to the Minister of Foreign Relations. A testimony of the tragic human conditions lived at the time in this multi-nation region, *The Vortex* is "a powerful denunciation of the exploitation of the rubber gatherers in the upper Amazon jungle" (*Encyclopedia Britannica* entry for Rivera). As such, it also narrates the complex process toward modernity in Latin America in the early 20th century. This nice scholarly edition from Duke University Press features a map of the area where the novel takes place and an introduction by the translator, historian Chasteen. In the introduction, Chasteen describes his approach and the ways in which his version differs from the first English translation; he says he "endeavored to preserve more of the unconventional edginess of Rivera's prose and the naturalness of his dialogue" (p. xi). The translator also frames the novel in light of Ángel Rama's argument, in *The Lettered City*, about the role of *letrados* in the construction of national imaginaries, and mentions the importance granted to *La vorágine* soon after its publication, with translations into numerous languages and an edition in the prestigious Latin American collection Biblioteca Ayacucho (p. x). [MCG]

2654 Rojas, Agustín de. The year 200. Translated by Nicholas Caistor and Hebe Powell. Brooklyn, N.Y.: Restless Books, 2016. 644 p.

This is the second translation into English of a book by Cuban science-fiction master Agustín de Rojas (Santa Clara, Cuba, 1949–2011) translated by Nick Castor and Hebe Powell and published by Restless Books. The third of de Rojas' sci-fi trilogy, *The Year 200* (first published in Spanish in Havana, by Letras Cubanas, in 1990) followed the critically praised *A Legend of the Future* (see *HLAS 72:2763*). Over 600 pages long, the latter novel, considered socialist sci-fi, was published at the start of Cuba's so-called Special Period and sold over 40,000 copies in Cuba. In *The Year 200*, the Communist Federation has defeated the capitalist Empire but society is divided. In his enthusiastic review, Geoff Shullenberger notes that this "riveting narrative of espionage and political turmoil" has the "potential to reintroduce English-speaking readers to the suppleness, complexity, and productive ambiguities of the left-utopian tradition in science fiction. *The Year 200* speaks the language of cybernetics [. . .] and reveals some of the ways in which it did and did not anticipate our present dilemmas. De Rojas's lucid fictional world intersects with many of our contemporary technological obsessions but charges them with remarkably distinct political valences" (*Los Angeles Review of Books*, 20 July 2016). Agustín de Rojas was a biologist by training, practiced sport medicine and then dedicated his life to teaching theater and to writing, leaving behind an extensive and eclectic oeuvre (*The Encyclopedia of Science Fiction* entry). According to the Restless Books presentation of the writer, "while he was heavily influenced by Ray Bradbury and translated Isaac Asimov into Spanish, de Rojas aligned himself mostly with the Soviet line of socialist realism defined by brothers Arkady and Boris Strugatsky and Ivan Antonovich Yefremov." After the fall of the Soviet Union, he stopped writing science fiction. [MCG]

2655 **Ronsino, Hernán.** Glaxo: a novel. Translated from the Spanish by Samuel Rutter. Brooklyn, N.Y.: Melville House, 2016. 91 p.

Translation of the 2009 novel by the Argentine Ronsino (b. 1975 in Chivilcoy), and his English-language debut, *Glaxo* is set in a small and hauntingly calm town in the Argentine pampas. Opening with an excerpt from Rodolfo Walsh's *Operation Massacre* (see *HLAS 70:2323*), the novel is a mystery structured around the stories of a group of friends and told in multiple voices. It is divided into small vignettes, each of which reads somewhere between a witness testimony and a personal diary. The narrative unfolds in fragments and is structured in four parts, each with a name of a different character—one of whom has just been released from jail—and dated in different years (1973, 1984, 1966, 1959). "Allusive and reserved, as if peeking out at the scene of the crime from behind drawn curtains, Ronsino's short novel has an almost claustrophobic feel to it; if the only way to escape the place is to be imprisoned or drafted, the only way to get out of the narrative is to see people at their indifferent worst" (*Kirkus Reviews*, 15 Oct. 2016). Other works by Rosino, who is a sociologist and teaches at University of Buenos Aires, include *La descomposición* (Eterna cadencia, 2014) and *Lumbre* (Eterna cadencia, 2013). [MCG]

2656 **Saccomanno, Guillermo.** Gesell dome. Translated by Andrea G. Labinger. Rochester, N.Y.: Open Letter, 2016. 616 p.

Translation into English of Saccomanno's 2013 novel *Cámara Gesell* (see *HLAS 70:1824*)—winner of the 2013 Hammett award. This 600-page novel is set in a popular seaside vacation town called Gesell—which is a real Argentinian coastal city north of Mar del Plata—in the off-season months. The narrative, which opens with a teen's suicide and a stabbing, is filled with grim, tragic events of murder, surveillance, torture, rape, and all manners of abuse, and unfolds amidst a bleak atmosphere that is labyrinthine, oppressive, and claustrophobic. Saccomanno (b. 1946 in Buenos Aires) suffered first-hand the "Dirty-War" years, which are the backdrop of the novel. Although it is set in present-day Argentina, the years of the dictatorship are fresh in the country's memory and "its bruised ghosts are a haunting legacy" (Kim Fay, "Looking and Looking Away", *LA Review of Books*, 8 January 2017). The translator's introduction describes the process and challenges of translating this lengthy novel and mentions, among other things, some of the influences on the author, including Dante, Faulkner, and Dos Passos. She notes that *Gesell Dome* is "an abundant novel" and that although it is "by no means a tale for the squeamish [. . .] its humor, brutal honesty and the tenderness concealed in its murky heart make it irresistible" (p. xi). Other novels by Sacommano—a writer, cartoonist, journalist and screenwriter—include *Prohibido escupir sangre* (1984), *El buen dolor* (see *HLAS 62:2646*)—winner of the 2000 National Literature Award in 2000—and *El oficinista* (2010)—winner of Seix Barral's 2010 Biblioteca Breve award. [MCG]

2657 **Saer, Juan José.** The clouds. Translated from the Spanish by Hilary Vaughn Dobel. Rochester, N.Y.: Open Letter, 2016. 160 p.

Translation into English of *Las Nubes*, a 1997 novel by critically acclaimed Argentinian writer Juan José Saer (1937–2005). The son of Syrian immigrants, author of 20 novels, among them *The Event* (see *HLAS 56:4595*) and *The Witness* (see

HLAS 54:5045), as well as several volumes of essays and short stories, Saer is one of the most important Argentinian authors of the late 20th century. *The Clouds* is told in the form of a pseudohistorical narrative based in present-day Paris. The protagonist is Pichón Garay, a graduate student who receives a manuscript recounting a 19th-century trip by a doctor who is bringing a group of mental health patients to Casa de la Salud, a newly built asylum on the outskirts of Buenos Aires. This tragicomic novel features Saer's praised style and recurrent themes of madness and exile. Winner of Spain's Nadal prize in 1987, *The Clouds* is one of five novels by Saer published by Open Letter. As Lorna Scott Cox notes, "Saer was hailed by his friend and compatriot Ricardo Piglia as 'one of the best writers of today in any language'"; his importance and critical acclaim make "Saer's virtual absence from the literary radar, even within Latin America, remarkable" ("Possible Humans: On Juan José Saer," *The Nation*, 23 March 2011). [MCG]

2658 **Sánchez, José Miguel.** Super extra grande. Brooklyn, N.Y.: Restless Books, 2016. 160 p. (Cuban science fiction)

After the well-received *A Planet for Rent* (see *HLAS 72:2773*), *Super Extra Grande* is the translation of the second novel by contemporary Cuban writer Yoss (b. 1969), a heavy-metal rocker considered the most prolific and important science-fiction author in Cuba today. *Super Extra Grande* is set in a distant future, a time when space travel is a fast, everyday occurrence. Its protagonist, Dr. Jan Amos Sangan Dongo, a veterinarian who specializes in treating enormous alien animals—e.g., a giant amoeba—has to set off on a mission as a result of a colonial conflict threatening the galaxy. The novel is funny, linguistically playful, and parodic. Frye's translation renders this quality well, including the Spanglish of one of the novel's characters. "The give and take between Sangan Dongo and his lab assistant Narbuk, a member of a reptilian class called Laggoru, speaks to a highly probable future in which jumbled English and Spanish is an embraced universal dialect" (NPR Books, 11 June 2016). Like *A Planet for Rent* and other sci-fi Cuban writing, *Super Extra Grande* has received critical attention. Critics see it as an imaginative work by a master of the genre who is serious, committed, and capable of delivering a sharp critique of our times—vis-à-vis both Cuba and the world. As Juan Vidal commented in his review of the novel for NPR, for Yoss "Science fiction is the only literature today capable of capturing not only the decisions we're making in the present, but also the consequences these decisions can have on our future" (NPR Books, 11 June 2016). [MCG]

2659 **Saravia, Alejandro.** Red, yellow, green. Translated from the Spanish by María José Giménez. Windsor, Ontario: Biblioasis, 2017. 195 p. (Biblioasis international translation series; 20)

Translation into English of the novel *Rojo, amarillo y verde* by contemporary Bolivian poet and fiction writer Alejandro Saravia. Set in Montreal, this multi-genre novel tells of the experiences of exiles who meet in a global metropolis—specifically of the relationship between a Bolivian former soldier and a Kurdish freedom-fighter. Away from their homes, the characters grapple with memory, history, and identity. Cora Siré's review notes that "The book's structure stretches the boundaries of novelistic form. Delivered in two sections of segmented prose, there are no chapters, just short breaks to separate the scenes. The language of the novel is faithful to its subject, Alfredo's inner workings, simulating the convoluted, associative, and fragmented nature of the human mind and memory" ("History vs. Oblivion," *Montreal Review of Books*, 14 Sept. 2017) Saravia published *Rojo, amarillo y verde* in Spanish for the first time in Canada (Éditions Art-Fact/Ediciones de la enana blanca, Montreal, 2003), and both the English and the French translations were published by Canadian presses (Biblioasis's International Translation Series and Éditions Urubu respectively). An excerpt of the novel was published online by the Center for the Art of Translation (Issue 26, Spring 2017). [MCG]

2660 **Schweblin, Samanta.** Fever dream: a novel. Translated by Megan McDowell. New York: Riverhead Books, 2017. 183 p.

This translation of *Distancia de rescate* (2014), the English-language debut of award-winning Argentinian-Spanish author Samanta Schweblin (1978), was nominated for the Man Booker Prize. Schweblin is best known for her short-story collections, including *Pájaros en la boca* (see *HLAS* 68:2185) for which she received, among other awards, the Casa de las Américas prize. In this haunting psychological novel, Amanda lies dying in a hospital bed, a boy, David, is sitting next to her, and they are talking. Their relationship is unclear and the narrative unfolds in that ambiguity. The novel has received critical praise, e.g., *The Guardian* called it "terrifying but brilliant" (Chris Power, *The Guardian*, 24 March 2017). In a *New Yorker* interview, Schweblin remarked that, for a young Latin American author such as herself, being translated into English "is a kind of prize; in the eyes of Spanish-speaking critics and readers, it's almost a consecration. And this [. . .] has given [the novel] an unexpected push, which likewise led to translations into other languages. If the book had remained in the Spanish-speaking world only, it would have been difficult for it to reach so many readers. So I feel very grateful for and happy about everything that has happened since the book's English translation." (Interview by Deborah Treisman, *The New Yorker*, 22 May 2017). Translations into English of Schweblin's short stories have appeared in *The New Yorker*, *Granta* and other publications. [MCG]

2661 Velasco Mackenzie, Jorge. Drums for a Lost Song. Translated by Rob Gunther. Brooklyn, N.Y.: Hanging Loose Press, 2017. 193 p.

Translation of *Tambores para una canción perdida* (see *HLAS* 50:3384), the second novel by the Ecuadorian Jorge Velasco MacKenzie (b. 1949), which tells the story of a runaway slave during Ecuador's colonial period. As the author notes in the introduction, the novel "weaves a fantastical tale of the 19th-century runaway slave, José Margarito, the Singer, into the very real historical texture of the formative years before and just after Ecuador's independence" (p. 11). It is set against the historical backdrop of Gran Colombia, "(the vast short-lived republic [1819–30], roughly comprising present-day Colombia, Venezuela, Panama, Ecuador, and parts of Peru, Guyana, and Brazil), [during which] the slave trade was alive and well, though its legacy is often overlooked amidst the striking cultural diversity of today's Ecuador" (p. 11). Velasco is known as "the most accomplished and powerful writer of the 'Generación of Guayaquil' of the 1980s [. . .] his works show a profound knowledge of the multiple social textures of his native city: the world of the marginal and the excluded" (entry on Velasco in the *Encyclopedia of Twentieth-Century Latin American and Caribbean Literature*, p. 591) The novel opens with a preface by the translator, who briefly explains his personal reasons for translating the book and comments on its relevance as a historical referent and its value for an English-speaking audience. This is a welcome historical narrative about an Afro-Ecuadorian, and about Latin American life and history. Other works by the author include *El rincón de los justos* (see *HLAS* 52:3750) and *El ladrón de la levita* (1990) (see *HLAS* 54:3992). [MCG]

Essays, Interviews, and Reportage

2662 Cortázar, Julio. Literature class, Berkeley 1980. Translated by Katherine Silver. New York: New Directions Publishing, 2017. 303 p.

A lesser known, non-fiction piece by Julio Cortázar (1914–84), and first published in Spanish in 2013 as *Clases de literatura: Berkeley 1980*, this is the translation of the edited volume of the lectures that Cortázar delivered at the University of California in 1980. The volume, edited by Álvarez Garriga, keeps the tone and flavor of the oral lecture. It is divided into seven thematic sections, some of which are specific to the writing of his works. It also includes two additional, well-known essays based on lectures that Cortázar delivered elsewhere, namely "Latin American Literature Today" (an edited version of *Argentina: años de alambradas culturales*, 1984) and "Reality and Literature: With Some Necessary Inversions of Values" (an edited version of "About Gladiators and Children Being Thrown in the River," published in *Obras completas*). In a review essay, Dustin Illingworth describes each piece in detail and comments on the way they range from the more esthetically—to the more politically focused. Cortázar's "suspicion of grand narratives—both in literature and in life—informs much of *Literature Class* [. . .] The unifying through line is Cortázar's abiding insistence on the elasticity of literary art, the better to capture what he saw as a fleeting, contentious, and ever-fluid reality" [. . .] Illingworth notes that, "taken together, they comprise the enormously enjoyable subtext of *Literature Class*: the ambivalence of a great writer who seeks to interrogate the efficacy of a weapon he has no choice but to use" [. . . .] For Julio Cortázar, reality was just that: a question without need of an answer, an endless conversation, the breathless plunge when solid ground gave way to something falling, something freeing" ("The Subtle Radicalism of Julio Cortázar's Berkeley Lectures" *The Atlantic*, 28 March 2017). This is a rich and welcome publication, and the translation in Katherine Silver's expert hands is carefully done and captures nicely the oral delivery of the original pieces. Several works by Cortázar, including *Hopscotch* (see *HLAS 42:6628*) and *A Manual for Manuel* (see *HLAS 42:6629*) are available in English in outstanding translations. [MCG]

2663 Guerriero, Leila. A simple story. Translated by Frances Riddle. New York: New Directions Publishing, 2017. 107 p.

Translation of *Una historia sencilla* (Anagrama, 2018), a chronicle centred on a man's preparation for the national competition of the traditional, athletic malambo dance in the small town of Laborde (Córdoba, Argentina). *A Simple Story* was written by renowned Argentinian journalist Leila Guerriero (b. 1967), a weekly columnist for national and international newspapers whose chronicles have been published in book-length form. Guerriero followed a malambo dancer, Rodolfo González Alcántara, for one year as he prepared for the competition (which he won in 2012). "In the space of 150 pages of workmanlike prose that occasionally rises to lyricism, the Buenos Aires journalist Leila Guerriero tells a fascinating triple story: of a grassroots art form, of one man's pursuit of his dream, and of modern working-class Argentina." (*Times Literary Magazine*, Feb. 19 2016). "*A Simple Story* is about an expression of a culture that, unlike tango, has been passed over, neglected or forgotten by all but a few devotees, for whom it is an obsession. Its obscurity, this book suggests, is its salvation." ("Dancing in the Dark" *The Economist*, 12 Dec. 2015). [MCG]

2664 Poéticas de la traducción. Compilación de Francia Elena Goenaga Olivares. Bogotá: Universidad de Los Andes, Facultad de Artes y Humanidades, Departamento de Humanidades y Literatura, 2012. 158 p.

This volume is a compilation of articles that were presented at the Seminar on the Poetics of Translation, which was organized by Francia Elena Goenaga, who is a member of the faculty at Colombia's Universidad de los Andes. The conference was held at the country's National Library November 18–20, 2008. The book is divided into two sections: the first treats translation in relation to specific Colombian authors; the second deals with translation as it manifested itself in the Colombian literary journals *Eco* (1960–84), *Mito* (1955–62), and *Espiral* (1944–78). Contributors to this collection include: Doris Castellanos Prieto, Francia Elena Goenaga, Jairo Hoyos, Alvaro Rodríguez Torres, Michael Sisson, Nicolás Suescún, Tatiana Arango, María José Montoya, Melisa Restrepo, Gabriel Rojas, and Óscar Torres Duque. [SFW]

TRANSLATIONS FROM THE PORTUGUESE
Brief Fiction and Theater

2665 Lispector, Clarice. The complete stories. Translated from the Portuguese by Katrina Dodson. Introduction by Benjamin Moser. Edited by Benjamin Moser. New York: New Directions, 2015 645 p.: bibl.

The celebrated Brazilian author Clarice Lispector receives deserved attention in English with this collection of stories. The book has an introduction by Benjamin Moser, "Glamour and Grammar," an appendix titled "The Useless Explanation," a translator's note by Katrina Dodson, a bibliographical note, and final acknowledgments. The selection includes stories from *First Stories, Family Ties, The Foreign Legion* (including "Back of the Drawer"), *Covert Joy, Where Were You at Night, The Via Crucis of the Body, Vision of Splendor* and *Final Stories*. A demanding and difficult author to translate, Clarice Lispector deserves to be better known outside Brazil. The present volume takes credit for making an attempt, but the translations are uneven. The introduction's point of view overemphasizes aspects more recognizable to contemporary American cultural sensibilities, resulting in a kind of distortion that renders Lispector less recognizable from a Brazilian perspective. A better grasp of the literary contexts of the times would better serve both author and readers. [EVO]

Novels

2666 Coelho, Paulo. Love: selected quotations. Translation by Margaret Jull Costa. London: Michael O'Mara Books Limited, 2015. 128 p.: color ill.

A compilation of quotations from books and articles written by best selling writer Paulo Coelho. The chosen quotations are interspersed with colored illustrations by Catalina Estrada. "Love is a force that is here on earth to make us happy. To bring us closer to God and to our fellow creatures." All the other sententious thoughts are equally innocuous. The book itself is a pretty thing, though. [EVO]

2667 Coelho, Paulo. The spy: a novel of Mata Hari. Translated from the Portuguese by Zoë Perry. First Vintage International edition. New York: Vintage International/Vintage Books, a division of Penguin Random House LLC, 2017. 176 p.: ill.

In this novel Paulo Coelho purports to retell the life of Mata Hari, the famous spy. The novel is told in the first person and is loosely based on real events. The Dutch dancer was executed by the French at the end of WWI, accused of being a double spy. Paulo Coelho researched newspapers and letters in order to write his story. It also has all the markings of Paulo Coelho's other works: mysticism, self-help, and mystery as well as a clichéd and simplified view of Mata Hari. The work banks the easy money to be made on the current fashion for female victimhood literature: "her only crime was to be a free woman." [EVO]

2668 Drummond, Roberto. Hilda Hurricane: a novel. Translated from the Portuguese by Peter Vaudry-Brown. Austin: University of Texas Press, 2010. 268 p.

This novel, originally published in 1991, tells the story of Hilda Furacão (Hilda Hurricane), an urban myth from the city of Belo Horizonte, in the state of Minas Gerais. Her gold swimsuit, which she wore at the pool of the best club in town, got her the nickname. Born to one of the best families in the city, rich and beautiful, she disappears into the bohemian side of the city, becoming a prostitute. Along with the story of Hilda, there are also many other characters, based on people Drummond knew, set against the backdrop of the cultural and political climate of the 60s. Did Hilda really exist? She disappears without a trace into the world of legend. This translation captures the ironic, quick, colloquial verve of the original. [EVO]

2669 Gusmão, Alexandre de. The story of the predestined pilgrim and his brother reprobate: in which, through a mysterious parable, is told the felicitous success of the one saved and the unfortunate lot of the one condemned. Composed by Father Alexandre de Gusmão of the Company of Jesus in the province of Brazil. Translated with an introduction and index by Christopher C. Lund. Tempe: Arizona Center for Medieval and Renaissance Studies, 2016. 137 p.: bibl., ill., index. (Medieval and Renaissance texts and studies; 489)(Medieval and Renaissance Latin America; 2)

Published in 1682 by Alexandre de Gusmão, a Jesuit priest, this work is allegorical and didactical, probably serving the pedagogical needs of the Society of Jesus in its educational mission. Written at the zenith of the Baroque, this work is a Counter-Reformation summary of the doctrine of Catholicism, as well as its reaffirmation against the threats of the Reformation. Framed as a pilgrim's voyage from Egypt to Jerusalem, the reader follows both the predestined protagonist as well as the reprobate one in a travel that allegorizes both virtues and vices. [EVO]

2670 Laub, Michel. A poison apple. Translated from the Portuguese by Daniel Hahn. London: Harvill Secker, 2017. 1 vol. (unpaged).

A young man's memoir dealing with contemporary life in Brazil. It starts with a Nirvana show in São Paulo, passes through the author's conscription in the army, his studies at the university, his romantic involvements, his nascent career as a journalist and hints of reflections on death. The year is 1993 and the author is a guitar player in the city of Porto Alegre, capital of the state of Rio Grande do Sul in Brazil. Due to his conscription, the protagonist cannot leave the headquarters, but travels to São Paulo to watch the Nirvana show, risking prison. The author reflects on death, focusing on Kurt Cobain's suicide (the leader of Nirvana) and the Rwanda genocide. This is the second volume of a trilogy meditating on the individual effects of history. The first volume focused on the 1980's and is titled *Diário da queda*. [EVO]

2671 Pompéia, Raul. The Athenaeum: a novel. Translated from the Portuguese by Renata R. Mautner Wasserman. Introduction by César Braga-Pinto. Evanston, Ill.: Northwestern University Press, 2015. 230 p.: bibl. (Northwestern world classics)

One of the masterpieces of Brazilian literature, *The Athenaeum* is a novel, a memoir, and a bildungsroman all at once. It narrates the formative years of Pompeia's alter ego, Sérgio, as a student at the famous boarding school, the Athenaeum, with its purported modern education. Written in 1888, the novel is also known for its scathing satire, in which some see an allegory of the wider world of Brazilian institutions, the last days of the Brazilian Empire and the social and political upheavals that followed. Pompeia's style, with its baroque imagery, his masterful grip of rhetorical devices, and his immense vocabulary, demands a lot of translators. Pompeia presents readers with a miniature Rabelaisian world. It is a good to see the book translated, but more translations would be welcome given the many layers to be explored in the book: parody, satire, humor. The volume's introduction is titled: "Darwinism, Max Norday and Raul Pompeia's Struggle for Existence." The book also offers a translator's note at the end. Pompeia deserves a good fully annotated scholarly translation into English to do him justice. [EVO]

Essays, Interviews, and Reportage

2672 Machado de Assis: tradutor e traduzido. Organização de Andréia Guerini, Luana Ferreira de Freitas e Walter Carlos Costa. Florianópolis: PGET/UFSC; Tubarão: Copiarti Editora, 2012. 159 p.: color ill.

A selection of articles on Machado de Assis as translator, as well as critical assessments on the translations of his works into English, Italian, French and Spanish. The contributions are largely informative and focused. The book comprises the following chapters: "Machado nacional e internacional" by Andréia Guerini, Luana Ferreira de Freitas and Walter Carlos Costa. "Uma feliz coincidência, ou confluência: John Gledson e Machado de Assis" by João Hermesto Weber. "Traduzindo Machado de Assis: 'Dona Paula'" by John Gledson (article itself translated by Luana Ferreira de Freitas). "Uma vocação em busca de línguas: as (não) traduções de Machado de Assis" by Hélio de Seixas Guimarães. "Machado tradutor de teatro" by João Roberto Faria. "Tradução e intermediação: textos dramáticos franceses traduzidos por Machado de Assis" by Helena Tornquist. "Dom Casmurro em inglês: tradução, visibilidade e crítica" by Luana Ferreira de Freitas. "Domestication and foreignisation in two translations of 'A cartomante' by Machado de Assis" by Robert Coulthard. "Machado de Assis in Italia" by Anna Palma. "Traducciones de Machado de Assis al español" by Pablo Cardelino Soto. [EVO]

2673 Tooge, Marly D'Amaro Blasques.
Traduzindo o *Brazil*: o país mestiço de Jorge Amado. São Paulo: Humanitas: FAPESP, 2011. 237 p.: bibl. ill. (some col.)

Tooge analyzes the internationally known Brazilian writer, Jorge Amado, within the context of his translations into English in the US. The book offers a good analysis of Amado's success both in Brazil and abroad as he became a best-selling phenomenon. The details of Amado's dealings with his US publisher, Alfred Knopf, are presented with a critical overview of America's cultural policies: Good Neighbor agenda, followed by a renewal of its principles adjusted to the realities of the Cold War and the Cuban Revolution. The author also delves into useful details about the style of the translators themselves and their knowledge (or lack thereof) of the Portuguese language: Samuel Putnam, Harriet de Onís, James Taylor and William Grossman, and Barbara Shelby. For the author, *Brazil* is a rewriting of Brasil with a great alteration of its meaning. [EVO]

MUSIC

GENERAL

2674 Bitrán Goren, Yael. Perspectivas y desafíos de la investigación musical en Iberoamerica: memorias del Coloquio Iberoamericano sobre Investigación Musical Ibermúsicas 2015. Coordinación de Yael Bitrán Goren y Cynthia Rodríguez Leija. México: Centro Nacional de Investigación, Documentación e Información Musical "Carlos Chávez," 2016. 235 p.: bibl., ill.

Proceedings of the 2015 Ibermúsicas conference held in Mexico City, with the participation of scholars from Argentina, Brazil, Chile, Colombia, Costa Rica, Mexico, Paraguay, Peru, and Uruguay. The 13 chapters cover music topics from these nine countries. [J. Koegel]

2675 Canção romântica: intimidade, mediação e identidade na América Latina. Organização de Martha Tupinambá de Ulhôa e Simone Luci Pereira. Rio de Janeiro: Folio Digital: Letra e Imagem, 2016. 172 p.: ill.

This publication brings together a collection of essays on the Latin American romantic ballad. The volume includes chapters by Martha Ulhôa on Roberto Carlos and by Simone Pereira on bolero audiences among Brazilians and Cuban immigrants in São Paulo. While other essays (by Alejandro Madrid, Carolina Spataro, and Danuel Party) cover the *canción romántica* in Mexico, Chile, and Argentina, they also discuss transnational flows that include Brazil. The authors focus on performance, gender identity, sexuality, and male violence, but avoid easy dichotomies to speak more in terms of mediations and ambiguities. This timely publication covers a widely popular genre and is full of uneasy angles and topics often avoided by scholars, as noted in Pablo Semán's preface. [R. Budasz]

2676 Cantos de guerra y paz: la música en las independencias iberoamericanas (1800–1840). Edición de Begoña Lolo y Adela Presas. Madrid: Ediciones Universidad Autónoma de Madrid, 2015. 439 p.: bibl., ill., index, music. (Música y musicología; 3)

This important and varied collection of 22 essays by scholars from Spain and throughout Latin America covers disparate topics relating to the struggles for independence by Spain's American colonies and how those movements were reflected in numerous ways in music. The chapters are organized into five main categories: music and identity, religious music, musical theater in Spain and Latin America, identity through dance, and women in independent art. This most useful and attractively produced book, which is also notable for presenting multiple views from both sides of the Atlantic, will spark studies on related topics. (Mexico is the country that is best represented in this valuable book, with 10 of the 22 chapters covering various topics relating to Mexican music and independence.) Unusually for similar Latin American collections of musically related essays, it includes a detailed, helpful index. [J. Koegel]

Encuentro Iberoamericano de Jóvenes Musicólogos, 3rd, Sevilla, Spain, 2016. Actas: musicologia criativa. See item **2888**.

2677 Historia de la música en España e Hispanoamérica. Vols. 1–8. Dirección y coordinación editorial de Juan Ángel Vela del Campo. Madrid: FCE, 2009–2018. 8 v.: bibl., ill., index.

This important 8-volume work provides a narrative history of music in Spain from the middle ages to the present day, and of Latin American music from the time of

European colonization in the late 15th century onward. The collection is a worthy and useful successor to the magisterial 7-volume *Historia de la música española* (Madrid: Alianza Editorial, 1983–1985, Pablo López de Osaba, general editor), but now includes substantial sections and two separate volumes on Latin America—unlike its predecessor, which focused only on the Iberian peninsula. Leading scholars from Latin America and Spain edited the individual installments in the series, and the volumes include contributions by many prominent specialists in the diverse areas and topics included. Volume 1 focuses on medieval music in Spain. Latin America is not included in this volume, because although medieval liturgical practices were imported into Spanish America, Spanish colonization of the Americas only began in the Renaissance. Volumes 2–4 cover Spain and Latin America in the 16th through 18th centuries. Volumes 5 and 7 specifically examine Spanish music in the 19th and 20th centuries, and Volumes 6 and 8 entirely emphasize Latin American music of the 19th and 20th centuries. The volumes are organized thematically, by genres, repertories, composers, and other topics. This series represents the most significant inclusion of Latin American music history in a peninsular Spanish musicological or lexicographical context, other than the pioneering 10-volume *Diccionario de la música española e hispanoamericana* (Madrid: Sociedad General de Autores de España, 1999–2002, Emilio Casares Rodicio, general editor; see HLAS 60 for several entries from the publication). A major resource, beautifully produced, commissioned and published by the Spanish branch of Mexico's prestigious, government-supported academic publisher, the esteemed Fondo de Cultura Ecónomica. [J. Koegel]

2678 **International Association for the Study of Popular Music. Rama Latinoamericana. 10th, Córdoba, Argentina, 2012.** Actas. Vol. 1, Enfoques interdisciplinarios sobre músicas populares en Latinoamérica: retrospectivas, perspectivas, críticas y propuestas. Recopilación de Herom Vargas et al. Montevideo: Asociación Internacional para el Estudio de la Música Popular (IASPM), Rama Latinoamericana, 2013. 986 p.: bibl., ill., music.

This volume contains the complete text of the papers presented at the 2012 IASPM-AL conference in Córdoba, Argentina, emphasizing interdisciplinary approaches in the study of popular music. About 40 papers, out of a total of 88, focus on Brazil, with topics ranging from genre studies (rock, choro, samba, guarânia, etc.), gender, independent labels and alternative transmission, popular music in 19th-century Rio, competing samba narratives (São Paulo, Porto Alegre), and the spectacularization of traditional music, among others. The papers are available electronically at http://iaspmal.com/index.php/2016/03/02/actas-x-congreso/. [R. Budasz]

Kunstmusik—Kolonialismus—Lateinamerika. See item 2911.

2679 **A Latin American music reader: views from the south.** Edited by Javier F. León and Helena Simonett. Urbana: University of Illinois Press, published in collaboration with the Society for Ethnomusicology, 2016. 449 p.: bibl., ill., index, music.

This long-awaited and important volume compiles translated essays by leading music scholars from Latin America. First proposed by the Latin America Section of the Society for Ethnomusicology, whose members (including the author of this entry) did most of the translations, the book was conceived to bring important works first written in Spanish and Portuguese into scholarly conversations in the English-speaking world. Helena Simonett's expansive introduction is itself an important contribution to scholarly understanding of the region, providing a remarkably thorough overview of a century of writing about music in Latin America, from the evolutionist and *indigenista* works of the early 20th century to the diverse and divergent approaches of scholars working in the early 21st. Simonett's co-editor, Javier León, offers specific introductions to each of the volume's three main parts, which include an initial section on academic lineages and musical historiography, a second section on popular music and genre, and a final section on "alternate genealogies, marginal ontologies, and applied ethnomusicology." An incredibly useful volume for anyone wishing to learn more about—or to expose their students or colleagues to—the rich variety of music scholarship from Latin America, it is also an essential book for specialists in music from this region, who will find both well-known essays and little-known gems within its pages. Some individual essays are reviewed separately: see *HLAS 72:2780* for Raúl Romero's chapter on the history of Latin American music scholarship; item **2875** for José Jorge de Carvalho's piece on the appropriation of Afro-Brazilian cultural heritage; item **2916** for Angela Lühning's contribution on Brazilian ethnomusicology; and item **2903** for Rodrigo Cantos Savelli Gomes and Maria Ignez Cruz Mello's discussion of female bands in Brazil. [J. Ritter]

2680 Made in Latin America: studies in popular music. Edited by Julio Mendívil and Christian Spencer Espinosa. New York, N.Y.: Routledge, 2016. 182 p.: bibl., ill., index. (Routledge global popular music series)

This important new collection on popular music in Latin America is primarily by Latin American music scholars whose work has not been widely available in English. Editors Julio Mendívil and Christian Spencer frame the volume in their introduction as a critical engagement with the concept of "musical scene" in Latin America, as a way to circumvent and problematize more traditional associations between genre and class/race/ethnicity/nation. Divided into five parts, the book addresses: 1) historical scenes in Mexico and Latin America broadly; 2) identity and politics in music from Ayacucho (Peru) and Chile; 3) cumbia in Argentina and Ecuador; 4) "global flows" in music scenes as disparate as *merengue típico*, queer tango, and Otavalan (Ecuador) music in Japan; and 5) a critique of the scene concept itself through critical readings of the work of Fernando Ortiz and others. The book concludes with a translated interview by the authors with Susan Baca, the famed Peruvian singer and former minister of culture, that underscores some of the volume's themes regarding globalization, world music, race, and identity. For reviews of two entries in the book, one on Ayacucho and another on Chile, see *HLAS 72:2858* and *HLAS 72:2896*. [J. Ritter]

2681 Moya, Fernanda Nunes. Francisco Curt Lange e o americanismo musical nas décadas de 1930 e 1940. (*Faces Hist.*, 2:1, jan./junho 2015, p. 17–37)

This is a good summary of Curt Lange's writings and initiatives related to his cultural project of *americanismo musical*. The author argues that Curt Lange's close connections with artists and institutions in the US in the 1940s weakened his influence among Latin American intellectuals. [R. Budasz]

2682 La verdad: an international dialogue on hip hop Latinidades. Edited by Melissa Castillo-Garsow and Jason Nichols. Columbus: The Ohio State University Press, 2016. 317 p.: bibl., index. (Global Latin/o Americas)

In this edited volume, several international scholars examine the widespread dissemination and importance of hip hop throughout Latin America and the US, "highlighting in new ways the participation of women, indigenous peoples, and Afro-descendants in a reimagined global, hip hop nation." This essay collection also demonstrates the spread of hip hop with Latino/a or Latin American influences well beyond the Americas-Chicano rap in Taiwan, for example. The work establishes that "Latino hip hop is a multilingual expression of gender, indigeneity, activism, and social justice." A major study. [J. Koegel]

MEXICO

JOHN KOEGEL, *Professor of Musicology, California State University, Fullerton*

MUSIC IN NEW SPAIN and 20th-century music in Mexico are the best represented topics in the scholarship on Mexican music published in the most current biennium. However, important studies of topics involving indigenous music and 19th-century Mexican music have appeared alongside this larger body of scholarship. Relatively few studies of popular music appeared during this period, however. Luisa Vilar-Payá's magisterial article on Puebla Cathedral, Bishop Palafox, and composer Juan Gutiérrez de Padilla, is not only a seminal study that explores all aspects of its topic, but it is also a model of impeccable scholarship (item **2766**). The second installment in the valuable continuing series of thematic catalogs of the large Mexico City Cathedral music archive, ably edited by Lucero Enríquez Rubio, Drew Edward Davies, and Analía Cherñavsky, also appeared during the biennium (item **2708**). Spanish musicologist Javier Marín López has continued to publish a regular series of articles examining musical life in Nueva España and its connections with peninsular Spanish practices. He also organizes the annual Festival de Música Antigua Úbeda y Baeza, in the Renaissance-era towns of Úbeda and Baeza in Andalucia, which also sponsors a related annual scholarly conference. In connection with the 2017 festival, Marín López moderated the international conference *De Nueva España a México: el universo musical mexicano entre centenarios (1517–1917)*, at the Universidad Internacional de Andalucía, Sede Antonio Machado, in Baeza, with many presentations by scholars from Mexico, elsewhere in Latin America, Spain, and the US. An extensive conference proceedings volume is forthcoming.

Mexican musicologist Ricardo Miranda published a substantial survey of the 19th-century musical scene in Mexico in *Historia Mexicana*, one of the leading historical journals in the country. Miranda's lengthy review of the important essay collection *Los papeles para Euterpe: la música en la Ciudad de México desde la historia cultural; siglo XIX* (see *HLAS* 72:2801) compellingly insists on the centrality of the 19th century in Mexican national musical life (item **2747**). Luis de Pablo Hammeken's excellent book on opera and politics examines the popular reception of and political connections to the performance of Italian opera in 19th-century Mexico (item **2754**).

While a multitude of extremely diverse film music topics has attracted strong international interest among researchers in recent decades, and a large corpus of work has been published, the scholarly study of Mexican and Latin American film music is not as far advanced at this time. However, Jacqueline Avila, the leading scholar of Mexican film music, has published a number of important studies of this topic in recent years, including three articles included in this section (items **2695**, **2696**, and **2697**). The Mexican journal *Pauta*, directed by composer Mario Lavista, recently celebrated its 35th anniversary. The journal continues to publish important scholarship on Mexican music on a regular basis, alongside studies, chronicles, and reviews of music from outside Mexico. Commendably, it follows an on-time publication schedule and receives widespread distribution throughout Mexico. *Pauta* is also known for illustrating the articles it publishes in inventive and evocative ways. Among the most important articles that have appeared on its pages in recent years are those by Ana R. Alonso-Minutti on various aspects of the music of Mario Lavista (items **2687**, **2688**, **2689**, and **2690**). Also in the same journal, Alejandro Barceló Rodríguez's exhaustive two-part study of the composition studio of Carlos Chávez and Hector Quintanar at the Conservatorio Nacional and its influence on a generation of Mexican composers serves as an excellent model for future studies (items **2698** and **2699**). The Mexican national musical research center in Mexico City, the Centro Nacional de Investigación, Documentación, Información y Difusión Musical "Carlos Chávez" (CENIDIM), celebrated its 40th anniversary with a special conference held in Santa Cruz, Tlaxcala, in July 2015, which featured the work of its many staff researchers.

CENIDIM also issued a substantial volume of proceedings from that conference in 2016, spearheaded by CENIDIM director Yael Bitrán Goren (item **2732**).

Two important publications that position Mexican music in a Latin American and Iberian context were published in the current biennium: the essay collection *Cantos de guerra y paz: la música en las independencias iberoamericanas (1800–1840)* (item **2676**) and the eight-volume joint history of Spanish and Latin American music, the *Historia de la música española e hispanoamericana* (item **2677**) (Brazil is not included, however).

Numerous studies of Mexican indigenous music traditions and popular music repertories have been published in recent decades, although the period under review saw fewer publications on these areas. While a number of articles about the 19th century in Mexico appear in essay collections, some of which are included in this section under the collective title, fewer journal articles on 19th-century Mexican music have appeared lately. Since some books and articles on Mexican music have limited distribution, some publications may have eluded detection. One hopes that a greater level of scholarly activity in these particular areas will be undertaken in the future. In sum, however, the state of publication on the tremendous diversity of Mexican musical traditions, repertories, genres, and styles is in good shape.

2683 Abe, Marié. Reimagining Oaxacan heritage through accordions and airwaves in the San Joaquin Valley, California. (*J. Pop. Music Stud.*, 27:3, Sept. 2015, p. 304–327, bibl., ill., maps)

Oaxacan farmworkers toil in California's Central Valley and also dance to new versions of the traditional *chilena* accompanied by the accordion. Abe provides an ethnographic analysis of cultural and musical practices of the indigenous migrant Oaxacan community in California.

2684 Actores del ritual en la Catedral de México. Edición de Marialba Pastor Llaneza y Lucero Enríquez Rubio. México: UNAM, Instituto de Investigaciones Estéticas, 2016. 110 p.: bibl., ill.

This collection of six essays addresses music in the Mexico City Cathedral in the viceregal period. Topics include establishing the musical infrastructure in the cathedral in the early 16th century, the musical *capilla* during the time of Archbishop Juan Pérez de la Serna (1613–24), music in Counter Reformation-era New Spain, reform of the *capilla* in 18th century, and the copying and illumination of 18th-century choir books (*libros de coro*).

2685 Agrasánchez Jr., Rogelio. Viaje redondo: el cine mudo mexicano en los Estados Unidos 1900–1930. Prólogo de Rodolfo Quilantán Arenas. Harlingen, Tex.: Agrasánchez Film Archive, 2013. 312 p.: bibl., ill.

This work provides a fascinating and detailed history of Mexican silent films exhibited in the US based on extensive transcripts of US Spanish-language newpaper coverage and reviews, which often mention music and musical accompaniments to these films. The study focuses especially, but not exclusively, on Los Angeles, Calif., and San Antonio, Tex., since those two US cities had the largest Mexican populations in this period. (The US English-language daily press usually ignored developments in US Spanish-speaking communities during this period, including music, theater, and motion pictures.)

2686 Almeida, Jaime. Un siglo de historia musical. México: CONACULTA: Milenio Diario, S.A. de C.V., 2015. 311 p.: ill. (chiefly color).

Ten brief sections cover the period between 1920 and 2014 in Mexican popular music, visually illustrated. A popular treatment of the topic.

2687 Alonso-Minutti, Ana R. La "destrucción renovadora" de la Quanta. (*Pauta/México*, 32:130, abril/junio 2014, p. 22–34, bibl.)

In 1970 Mexican composer Mario Lavista (b. 1943), along with several other young nonconformists, established the group Quanta, which stressed collective musical improvisation and represented a symbol of resistance against a repressive Mexican government. (Quanta was also involved with the contemporary dance scene.) Although writings on 20th-century Mexican art music affirm that Quanta was an experimental musical collective, Alonso-Minutti finds that this group did not fit neatly within the experimental music mold, especially as it then existed in Mexico. She also shows that Quanta received the support from a seemingly unlikely patron, Emilio Azcárraga Vidaurreta, head of Telesistema Mexicano (now Televisa), one of Latin America's largest and most powerful television chains. Visually illustrated with evocative images of the group Quanta and its time.

2688 Alonso-Minutti, Ana R. Escuchando la pintura, pintando la música: intertextualidad musical y pictórica en la obra de Mario Lavista. (*Pauta/México*, 34:139/140, julio/dic. 2016, p. 85–105, bibl.)

The leading scholar on the music of Mexican composer Mario Lavista contributes this outstanding article. The study analyzes his many connections with the visual art world. Detailed attention is paid to works by Lavista and their visual inspirations such as *El pífano* (inspired by Édouard Manet's *Le Fifre*), *Las músicas dormidas* (after Rufino Tamayo's painting of the same title), and *Danza de las bailarinas de Degas* (suggested by Edgar Degas' *L'étoile*). The author shows how, for Lavista, painting has an "acoustic quality" and how he establishes webs of connections between image and musical sound.

2689 Alonso-Minutti, Ana R. Espacios imaginarios: *Marsias* y *Reflejos de la noche* de Mario Lavista. (*Pauta/México*, 131/132, 2014, p. 99–122, bibl., ill., music)

This study examines Mario Lavista's composition *Marsias* (1982) for oboe and crystal glasses, the contributions of Lavista's performer-collaborators such as Mexican oboist Leonora Saavdra, and the physical space necessary to achieve the composer's goals in terms of performance practice and audience reception. Alonso-Minutti presents a detailed musical analysis and an explanation of the background to this pathbreaking work. She also discusses Lavista's work *Reflejos de la noche*.

2690 Alonso-Minutti, Ana R. Espejos de un orden superior: la música religiosa de Mario Lavista. (*Pauta/México*, 32:134, abril/junio 2015, p. 67–82, ill., music)

Although Mario Lavista is not a practioner of any religion, he has nevertheless composed a number of important works that are inspired, relate to, or suggest religious belief and consolation. Along with providing a detailed list of these compositions, Alonso-Minutti analyzes these works in terms of their musical content and religious or spiritual connections, and places them in the context of Lavista's career, musical *oeuvre*, and time.

2691 Alonso-Minutti, Ana R. Gatas y vatas: female empowerment and community-oriented experimentalism. (*in* Experimentalisms in practice: music perspectives from Latin America. Edited by Ana R. Alonso-Minutti, Eduardo Herrera, and Alejandro l. Madrid. New York, N.Y.: Oxford University Press, 2016, p. 131–160, bibl.)

Alonso-Minutti examines the annual Gatas y Vatas experimental music festival in Albuquerque, N.M., that emphasizes local musicians and supports female empowerment. Musical activities by local performers "foster a feminist ideal rooted in a Hispanic connection."

2692 Alonso-Minutti, Ana R. The "here and now": stories of relevancy from the borderlands. (*J. Music Hist. Pedagogy*, 7:2, 2017, p. 106–111)

With an emphasis on the US-Mexico Borderlands region, the author discusses how the study of music history is and can be relevant to students, music teachers, and scholars through an examination of experimental music repertories and traditions.

2693 Alonso-Minutti, Ana R. *Simurg* y el canto de los pájaros. (*Pauta/México*, 32:129, enero/marzo 2014, p. 18–28, bibl., music)

Although Mario Lavista's main instrument is the piano, according to Alonso-Minutti, up to 2013 he had not shown a marked predilection for this instrument in a solo context, although he did write about a dozen works for solo piano. Therefore, his

Simurg for piano (1980), written for pianist and composer Gerhart Muench (1907–88), who premiered the piece, takes on special significance. The author emphasizes the intertextual relationships between the inspiration for the work, poetry, and Muench's personality and own compositions.

2694 Avila, Jacqueline. *Chin Chun Chan*: the zarzuela as an ethnic and technological farce. (*in* Oxford research encyclopedia of Latin American history. Oxford, England: Oxford University Press, 2018, http://latinamericanhistory.oxfordre.com)

The stereotyped Chinese-themed, somewhat racist, and wildly popular Mexican zarzuela *Chin Chun Chan*, with a musical score by Spanish composer and Mexican resident Luis G. Jordá and Mexican librettists José F. Elizondo and Rafael Medina, took Mexico City by storm in 1904 and later swept the Mexican countryside and Mexican theaters in the US, in live performances, sheet music sales, recordings, and various commercialized tie-ins. *Chin Chun Chan* initiated a new era in Mexican popular theater, providing an alternative to the imported Spanish *zarzuelas*, *revistas*, plays, and European operas then dominating the boards in the Mexican capital. *Chin Chun Chan* used Mexican national popular character types, music, and dialogue to represent national themes on stage in the capital city, and later elsewhere.

2695 Avila, Jacqueline. *El Fantasma* and Tin Tan: genre hybridity and musical nostalgia in Fernando Cortés's *El Fantasma de la opereta* (1959). (*Opera Q.*, 34:2/3, Spring/Summer 2018, p. 187–200)

This study appears in a special, pathbreaking issue of the musicological journal *Opera Quarterly* devoted to diverse film and musical representations and adaptations of Gaston Larue's ever-popular *The Phantom of the Opera*. Avila deftly focuses on musical borrowings in Tin Tan's (Germán Valdéz) madcap star musical film vehicle *El Fantasma de la operetta* (1959), directed by Fernando Cortés. Avila finds that sources for the film include the *teatro de revista* (musical revue) tradition of the early 20th century, foreign theatrical importations, and melodies reused from previous theatrical works, which were adapted to accommodate a Mexican national vernacular style in the process of "Mexicanization." *El Fantasma de la operetta* presents a mix of "comedy and suspense" and "nostalgia and cosmopolitanism," all centered around Tin Tan's comic and musical persona. An excellent article.

2696 Avila, Jacqueline. *México de mis inventos*: salon music, lyric theater, and nostalgia in *cine de añoranza porfiriana*. (*Lat. Am. Music Rev.*, 38:1, Spring/Summer 2017, p. 1–27, bibl.)

In this seminal study by the leading scholar of Mexican film music, Avila examines the musical, theatrical, and cultural meanings in the *cine de añoranza porfiriana* (films of Porfirian longing) of the 1940s, set during the Porfiriato, the time period of Porfirio Díaz's dictatorship (1876–1911). She gives particular attention to Juan Bustillo Oro's *En tiempos de don Porfirio* (1939) and *México de mis recuerdos* (1944), representative of the romantic film comedy genre. These musical films include excerpts from *zarzuelas*, the *teatro de revista*, and salon music of the Porfiriato. These two films also "expose the social contradictions of Porfirian culture, particularly concerning women's roles."

2697 Avila, Jacqueline. Musicalizar la muerte en el cine mexicano durante los años treinta. (*Balajú*, 3:2, agosto/dic. 2016, p. 48–60, bibl., ill.)

Avila examines the musical scores of two iconic Mexican films from the 1930s, *La mujer del puerto* (released 1934), directed by Arcady Boytler, and *Janitzio* (released 1935), directed by Carlos Navarro. She shows how the representation of death—in sound, music, and image—in these two films suggests an opposition to and critique of Mexico's national culture. Specifically, "cinematic death highlighted the consequences of acting against the predominant beliefs of society."

2698 Barceló Rodríguez, Alejandro. El taller de creación musical Carlos Chávez y Héctor Quintanar: 1960–1974, florescencia de un árbol plantado en el Conservatorio, primera parte. (*Pauta/México*, 34:139/140, julio/dic. 2016, p. 110–161, bibl., ill.)

This profusely illustrated major study and narrative history is presented in two lengthy parts that chart the history and long-lasting influence of the compositional studio of Carlos Chávez and Hector Quintanar in the Conservatorio Nacional in Mexico City from 1960 through 1974. Barceló Rodríguez highlights the many leading contemporary Mexican composers who received their training in this studio and discusses the place of this composition studio in the history and hierarchy of the national conservatory. He also investigates the activities and importance of the Laboratorio de Música Electrónica in the Conservatorio Nacional, established in 1970, and its connections to other electronic music studios at that time, such as the Princeton-Columbia Electronic Music Center. For the citation to the second part of the study, see item **2699**.

2699 **Barceló Rodríguez, Alejandro.** El taller de creación musical Carlos Chávez y Héctor Quintanar: 1960–1974, florescencia de un árbol plantado en el Conservatorio (segunda y última parte). (*Pauta/México*, 35:141/142, enero/junio 2017, p. 125–152, bibl., ill.)

See item **2698** for comments on the complete study.

2700 **Barrón Corvera, Jorge.** Clementina Maurel, cantante. (*Pauta/México*, 126, abril/junio 2013, p. 45–57, ill.)

This study examines the life and career of singer Clementina Maurel, wife of Mexican composer Manuel M. Ponce, his muse and helpmate, who enjoyed her own substantial musical career, in addition to supporting that of her famous husband. Visually illustrated with evocative photographs of the couple.

2701 **Barrón Corvera, Jorge.** Escritos en torno a la música mexicana. Zacatecas, Mexico: Universidad Autónoma de Zacatecas; México: MAPorrúa, 2014. 236 p.: bibl., ill., music. (Serie Las ciencias sociales. Tercera década)

This collection brings together separate essays by Barrón Corvera about diverse aspects of 20th-century Mexican music, including the works of Manuel M. Ponce and Rodolfo Halffter. Some of these studies stem from the author's previously published work on Ponce.

2702 **Bauer, Erin.** Beyond the border: meaning and authenticity in the adoption of Texas-Mexican conjunto music by international artists. (*Lat. Am. Music Rev.*, 37:1, Spring/Summer 2016, p. 34–64, bibl.)

Texas-Mexican *conjunto* music (accordion-led ensemble) is now internationally known. Bauer discusses issues of identity, musical authenticity, construction of repertories, familial connections, and personal belonging in *conjunto* music.

2703 **Bergman, Ted L.L.** *Jácaras* and *narcocorridos* in context: what early modern Spain can tell us about today's narco-culture. (*Roman. Notes*, 55:2, 2015, p. 241–252, bibl.)

This study compares the 17th-century Spanish *jácara* ballad tradition with the Mexican and US-Mexico Borderlands *narcocorrido* (the illicit drug-related corrido, or narrative ballad).

2704 **Bitrán Goren, Yael.** De la invisibilización al canon: mujeres en la academia, el rock y la sala de concierto en México en la segunda mitad del siglo XX. Con la asistencia de Paulina Molina y Gabriela Rivera. (*in* **Coloquio Iberoamericano sobre Investigación Musical Ibermúsicas, 3rd, Santiago, Chile, 2017.** Música y mujer en Iberoamérica: haciendo música desde la condición de género; actas. Edición de Juan Pablo González. México: CENIDIM, 2017, p. 92–110, bibl.)

This paper details the contributions to Mexican national musical life of numerous Mexican women musicians, composers, and scholars active in a variety of musical fields, genres, and styles since the early 20th century.

2705 **Brennan, Juan Arturo** and **Arón Bitrán.** Discografía integral del Cuarteto Latinoamericano. (*Pauta/México*, 128, oct./dic. 2013, p. 86–102, ill.)

This article presents a discography of 30 years of recording activity of the Cuarteto Latinoamericano, Latin America's leading string quartet, on LP album, compact disc, and DVD. The group has recorded a very wide range of repertory from around the world, most especially of Latin American music. See also *HLAS 64:2626*.

2706 **Bringas, Alfredo.** Tambuco para seis percusionistas de Carlos Chávez. (*Pauta/México*, 35:141/142, enero/junio 2017, p. 40–55, bibl., ill.)

This study focuses on the percussion ensemble piece *Tambuco* (1964), by Carlos Chávez, and its place in the contemporary percussion repertory.

Cantos de guerra y paz: la música en las independencias iberoamericanas (1800–1840). See item **2676**.

2707 **Cardona Ishtar** and **Christian Rinaud.** Son jarocho entre México y Estados Unidos: definición "afro" de una práctica transnacional. (*Desacatos*, 53, enero/abril 2017, p. 20–37, bibl., ill.)

The authors make connections between the performance of *son jarocho* from Veracruz and other areas in Mexico and the US; they also examine the Afro-Hispanic roots of the tradition. The study covers the interactions between Mexican *jarocho* musicians and performers active in Chicano/a-Latino/a music scenes in the US.

2708 **Catálogo de obras de música del Archivo del Cabildo Catedral Metropolitano de México.** Vol. 2, Vísperas, antífonas, salmos, cánticos y versos instrumentales. Edición de Lucero Enríquez Rubio, Drew Edward Davies y Analía Cherñavsky. México: UNAM, Instituto de Investigaciones Estéticas, 2016. 540 p.: ill., music.

The second volume in an ongoing series of important catalogs of the Mexico City Cathedral's very extensive music archive. A critical apparatus is accompanied by detailed entries, with musical incipits, of each of the works in the following genres represented in this very significant archive: vespers settings, antiphons, psalms, canticles, and instrumental *versos*. For a review of Vol. 1, see *HLAS 72:2787*.

2709 **Celebración y sonoridad en las catedrales novohispanas.** Coordinación de Anastasia Krutitskaya y Édgar Alejandro Calderón Alcántar. México: UNAM, 2017. 282 p.: bibl., ill.

This important collection of 16 essays covers a wide range of topics about music, rite, and ritual in cathedrals in New Spain. The preface by José López Calo, a founder of modern Spanish musicology, pays homage to two pioneering North American musicologists specializing in Latin American and Spanish early music—the late Robert M. Stevenson (former long-time *HLAS* music contributing editor for all of Latin America) and the late Robert Snow. Volume chapters cover Sor Juana and music, various aspects of the *villancico*, Portuguese chapelmaster Gaspar Fernandes (1566–1629) and his now-well-known *cancionero*, music in Morelia and Guadalajara cathedrals, indigenous musicians, music for Corpus Christi services, and viceregal organs.

2710 **Chávez, Alex E.** Sounds of crossing: music, migration, and the aural poetics of Huapango Arribeño. Durham, N.C.: Duke University Press, 2017. 425 p.: bibl. (Refiguring American music)

Chávez studies Mexican (im)migrant life in the US through the medium of the dance and song form of the *huapango arribeño*, which in recent years has spread throughout a wide geographic territory, from its origins in north-central Mexico, to other locations in the country, to various regions in the US. He stresses the importance of improvisational performance in this genre, and how the *huapango arribeño* relates to transnational musical performance, politics, and migration.

2711 **Chávez, Alex E.** Southern borderland: music, migrant life, and scenes of a "Mexican South." (*South. Cult.*, 28:3, Fall 2015, p. 35–52, bibl., ill.)

This photographic essay and text from an anthropological perspective examines Mexican popular music in immigrant communities in the US South.

2712 **Coloquio La Presencia Africana en la Música de Guerrero, 4th, Chilpancingo de los Bravos, Mexico, 2011.** La presencia africana en la música de Guerrero: estudios regionales y antecedentes histórico-culturales. Coordinación de Carlos Ruiz Rodríguez. México: Instituto Nacional de Antropología e Historia, 2016. 214 p.: bibl., ill., maps. (Colección Historia. Serie Memorias)

This volume presents the proceedings of a 2011 conference on the African presence and influence in Mexico, especially in the state of Guerrero. The book includes several valuable musical case studies.

2713 **Conformación y retórica de los repertorios musicales catedralicios en la Nueva España.** Coordinación de Drew

Edward Davis. Edición de Enríquez Rubio. Ciudad Universitaria, Mexico: Instituto de Investigaciones Estéticas, UNAM, 2016. 184 p.: bibl., ill., music.

These valuable essays address various aspects of music in New Spain, including Juan de Zumárraga, first bishop of Mexico, and his connections with music; composer and *maestro de capilla* Gaspar Fernándes' *cancionero*; music in Puebla Cathedral; *villancicos* by Antonio de Salazar and others; 18th-century responsories, and operatic waltzes preserved in the Mexico City Cathedral music archive.

2714 Correa Rodríguez, Alejandro. Danzas catalanas en la Nueva España. (*in* Cataluña e Iberoamérica: investigaciones recientes y nuevos enfoques. Coordinación y edición de Montserrat Galí Boadella *et al.* Barcelona: Asociación de Catalanistas de América Latina, Fundació Casa Amèrica Catalunya, 2016, p. 101–112, bibl., music)

The author establishes musical concordances between works in the important Eleanor Hague Manuscript (Autry Museum of the American West, Los Angeles, Calif.), a Mexican musical collection of 18th-century dances of various origins, and manuscript M741/22 of the Biblioteca Nacional de Catalunya, which preserves a similar repertory.

2715 Correa Rodríguez, Alejandro. Instrumentos y piezas musicales de un noble novohispano: inventario del marqués de Jaral. (*in* Encuentro Iberoamericano de Jóvenes Musicólogos, 3rd, Sevilla, Spain, 2016. Actas: musicologia criativa. Edição de Marco Brescia e Rosana Marreco Brescia. Sevilla, Spain: Tagus-Atlanticus Associação Cultural, 2016, p. 216–226)

The 1782 inventory of the estate of Miguel de Berrio y Saldívar, Conde de San Mateo de Valparaíso and Marqués de Jaral (d. Mexico City, 1779), reveals that this leading figure in the history of New Spain was a music lover, able violinist, and musical patron. At his death the Marqués de Jaral left a large collection of musical instruments and scores, which were lost, lamentably. Correa Rodríguez discovered this unknown inventory in the Archivo Histórico del Banco Nacional de México (Archivo Histórico Banamex, Citibanamex), located in Berrio y Saldívar's own Mexico City palace. The inventory highlights the varied *novohispano* and European musical repertory that circulated at that time. For a review of the full conference proceedings, see item **2888**.

2716 Correa Rodríguez, Alejandro. Locatelli y Leclair en la Nueva España: dos sonatas para violín en la Catedral de México. (*Rev. Cat. Musicol.*, 10, 2017, p. 121–148, bibl., music)

Although instrumental music composed in Europe and New Spain was well known in the viceroyalty in the 18th century, few instrumental musical manuscripts or imprints have survived to the present day in Mexico. Thus this identification and examination by Correa Rodríguez of two violin sonatas by the European composers Pietro Locatelli and Jean-Marie Leclair, in the Mexico City Cathedral Archive, is significant. The author also sheds light on instrumental performance practice there.

2717 Cuarenta años de investigación musical en México a través del CENIDIM. Coordinación de Yael Bitrán Goren, Luis Antonio Gómez y José Luis Navarro. México: Secretaría de Cultura, INBA, CENIDIM, 2016. 417 p.: bibl., ill.

These conference proceedings, covering a wide range of Mexican music topics, were presented at the *coloquio interno* of CENIDIM in Santa Cruz, Tlaxcala, in July 2015, in honor of the 40th anniversary of the founding of the Centro Nacional de Investigación, Documentación, Información y Difusión Musical "Carlos Chávez" (CENIDIM), the leading Mexican national music research institute in Mexico City.

2718 De la Garza, Armida. *Sobre las olas*, waltz and films: classical music and Mexican identity. (*in* Film music in "minor" national cinemas. Edited by Germán Gil-Curiel. New York; London: Bloomsbury Academic, 2016, p. 25–43, bibl., ill.)

This book chapter discusses the use and meaning of the world-famous waltz *Sobre las olas* by Mexican composer Juventino Rosas (1868–94) in the film biographies of the same composer and title (released in 1933 and 1950, respectively), the second of which stars the film *ídolo* and popular singer Pedro Infante as Rosas.

2719 **de la Torre, Ricardo.** El influjo de Julián Orbón en el pensamiento musical de Eduardo Mata. (*Pauta/México*, 133, enero/marzo 2015, p. 22–33, ill.)

This study charts the influence of Spanish-Cuban composer Julián Orbón (1925–91), also a resident of Mexico, on Mexican composer and conductor Eduardo Mata (1942–95).

2720 **De música y cultura en la Nueva España y el México independiente: testimonios de innovación y pervivencia.** Vol. 2. Coordinación y edición de Lucero Enríquez Rubio. México: Instituto de Investigaciones Estéticas, UNAM, 2017. 197 p.: bibl., ill. (some color), music.

This collection of six essays by leading Spanish and Latin American scholars covers music in viceregal Spain, with some representation of music in early independent Mexico. Topics include Sor Juana Inés de la Cruz and music, Mexico City chapelmaster Antonio Juanas, and music in Puebla Cathedral, among others.

2721 **Díaz Frene, Jaddiel.** A las palabras ya no se las lleva el viento: apuntes para una historia cultural del fonógrafo en México (1876–1924). (*Hist. Mex./México*, 66:1, julio/sept. 2016, p. 257–298, bibl., ill.)

This very important study establishes and analyzes the history of the use of the phonograph and sound recording technology in Mexico, from the late 19th century through the 1920s. The author discusses the importation, sale, and dissemination of phonograph machines and recordings from Europe, and describes the beginnings of a national Mexican recording industry through reportage in the daily press and other sources. The paper positions the growth of the phonograph industry in Mexico within the context of other contemporary technological developments.

2722 **Durán Moncada, Cristóbal Margarito.** La escoleta y la capilla de música de la Catedral de Guadalajara 1690–1750. Guadalajara, Mexico: Universidad de Guadalajara, Centro Universitario de Ciencias Sociales y Humanidades, 2014. 215 p.: bibl.

This study looks at the choir school and musical *capilla* (musical establishment) in the Guadalajara Cathedral between 1690 and 1750, through reference and examination of significant documentation in the cathedral archive. The author places music in the cathedral in the context of daily life in the city.

2723 **Estrada Valadez, Tania; Patricia de la Garza Cabrera; and Thalía Edith Velasco Castelán.** Los libros de coro copiados por fray Miguel de Aguilar: un primer acercamiento al studio de su encuadernación en la Nueva España. (*Intervención/México*, 5:10, julio/dic. 2014, p. 54–66, bibl., ill.)

This paper presents a detailed codicological study of musical choirbooks from New Spain currently held in the Museo Nacional del Virreinato in Tepozotlán, belonging to the Instituto Nacional de Antropología e Historia. (The entire collection originates from various cathedral, parish, and conventual collections.) The authors also discuss the restoration process for these choirbooks, which were copied by fray Miguel de Aguilar between 1700 and 1719.

2724 **Etnorock: los rostros de una música global en el sur de México.** Coordinación de Martín de la Cruz López Moya, Efraín Ascencio Cedillo y Juan Pablo Zebadúa Carbonell. Chiapas, Mexico: Universidad de Ciencias y Artes de Chiapas; San Cristóbal de Las Casas, Mexico: Centro de Estudios Superiores de México y Centroamérica; México: Juan Pablos Editor, 2014. 155 p., 32 unnumbered pages of plates: bibl., ill. (some color), portraits (some color).

This work examines cultural manifestations of rock music for indigenous peoples in three locations in southern Mexico: Veracruz, Guerrero, and Chiapas. The contributions address indigenous rock music, youth, and identity, among other topics.

2725 **Faudree, Paja.** Between aspiration and apathy: shifting scale and the "worlding" of indigenous Day of the Dead music. (*Pop. Music Soc.*, 39:3, 2016, p. 359–374, bibl.)

Faudree gives a close reading of indigenous festivities and music in Mazatec culture during Day of the Dead ceremonies.

2726 **Garcia, Cindy.** Salsa crossings: dancing latinidad in Los Angeles. Durham, N.C.: Duke University Press, 2013. 182 p.: bibl., index. (Latin america otherwise: languages, empires, nations)

Salsa clubs in Los Angeles, California, serve as the site for the examination of race, class, gender, and nationality among Latino/a dancers in the US, and how dance music and choreographies represent social aspirations.

2727 **Gaytán, Marie Sarita** and **Sergio de la Mora.** Queening/queering *mexicanidad*: Lucha Reyes and the *canción ranchera*. (*Fem. Form.*, 28:3, Winter 2017, p. 196–221, bibl.)

Gaytán and De la Mora present an expert, sensitive study of early *música ranchera* queen Lucha Reyes' (1906–44) life and career, and an analysis of her importance to Mexican popular music and audiences during her lifetime and continuing today, on both sides of the US-Mexico border. They also discuss how Reyes violated Mexican gender norms in her performances and how she "queered the ranchera genre, and challenged the heteronormative contours of *mexicanidad*." An essential article.

2728 **Glover, Andrew.** Three new Mexican flute works. (*Pan/London*, 34, Sept. 2015, p. 36–39, music, photos)

This article covers flute works by three Mexican composers—Joaquín Gutiérrez Heras, Mario Lavista, and Carlos Sánchez-Gutiérrez; however, the "new" in the title does not refer to new flute compositions, but rather to works that were new in 2015 to members of the British Flute Society.

2729 **Guzmán Bravo, José Antonio.** La música ceremonial mexica. (*Anu. Music.*, 73, 2018, p. 37–52, bibl., ill.)

This outstanding article covers music in Mexica ceremony, ritual, and culture. Dances dedicated to specific Mexica deities follow the prescribed ceremonial calendar *cempoalapohualli*; for example, musical destiny is dicated by the divinatory calendar *tonalpohualli*.

2730 **Guzmán Bravo, José Antonio.** Los primeros órganos tubulares en México. (*Anu. Music.*, 70, 2015, p. 43–62, bibl., photos)

This study deals with the construction, shipment, and installation of organs in early New Spain, in cathedrals, monastic and conventual settings, parishes, mission establishments, and other ecclesiastical centers. The author discusses the role of indigenous musicians as builders and players of organs and wind instruments. He also provides substantial technical information about organ construction.

2731 **Guzmán Bravo, José Antonio.** Proporciones, alegorías, ángeles músicos y ejecución históricamente informada en los órganos gemelos de la Catedral Metropolitana de México. (*Anu. Music.*, 71, 2016, p. 101–122, bibl., photos.)

This work details the construction, materials, maintenance, and architectural proportions and placement of the historic twin organs in Mexico City Cathedral, which date from the colonial era. The author emphasizes the need for continued documentation regarding restoration work and future needs of these historic instruments. See also item **2730**.

2732 **Koegel, John.** La investigación musical en México en el siglo XXI. (*in* Cuarenta años de investigación musical en México a través del CENIDIM. Coordinación de Yael Bitrán Goren, Luis Antonio Gómez, y José Luis Navarro. México: Secretaría de Cultura, INBA, CENIDIM, 2016, p. 25–39)

This conference paper reviews current scholarship in various areas of Mexican music, suggests new avenues of research and research resources, and promotes an inclusive view of Mexican music history that also encompasses Mexican music and musicians outside Mexico—especially in the US. For a review of the full conference proceedings, see item **2717**.

2733 **Koegel, John.** Mexican musical theater and movie palaces in downtown Los Angeles before 1950. (*in* Tide was always high: the music of Latin America in Los Angeles. Edited by Josh Kun. Oakland: University of California Press, 2017, p. 46–75, ill.)

This chapter presents a history of Mexican musical theater in Los Angeles, Calif., from 1900 to about 1950, with an emphasis on the Mexican *revista* (musical revue) as presented by local and touring Mexican theatrical troupes. The author foregrounds the work of performer, impresario, and librettist Romualdo Tirado, whose *revistas* championed the Mexican immigrant experience in Los Angeles' *México de Afuera*.

2734 **Koegel, John.** Non-English language musical theater in the United States. (*in* Cambridge companion to the musical. Edited by William A. Everett and Paul R. Laird. 3rd edition. Cambridge, England; New York, N.Y.: Cambridge University Press, 2017, p. 51–78, ill.)

This entry provides an interpretive history of non-English-language musical theater, based in immigrant communities in the US, with an emphasis on Spanish-language (especially Mexican) traditions, practices, and histories.

2735 **Kohl, Randall.** Octaviano Yáñez, guitarrista orizabeño olvidado del porfiriato. (*Pauta/México*, 134, abril/junio 2015, p. 49–61, ill.)

This brief study examines the life and music of the leading Mexican guitarist of his time, Octaviano Yáñez (1865–1927), the first Mexican guitarist to make commercial recordings (for the Edison Company).

2736 **Lamadrid, Enrique R.** Cautivos y criados: cultural memories of slavery in New Mexico. (*in* Linking the histories of slavery: North America and its borderlands. Edited by Bonnie Martin and James F. Brooks. Santa Fe, N.M.: School for Advanced Research Press, 2015, p. 229–256, bibl.)

This chapter explains the importance of captivity narratives as told in song by Native Americans living as *criados* in Hispanic New Mexico. The research is illustrated through reference to numerous song texts and translations.

2737 **Marín López, Javier.** Asistencia social, identidad peninsular y devoción mariana en una cofradía novohispana de músicos de mediados del siglo XVII. (*Resonancias/Santiago*, 21:41, julio/nov. 2017, p. 13–33, bibl.)

Spanish composer Fabián Pérez Ximeno founded the pious Congregación de Nuestra Señora de la Antigua in the Mexico City Cathedral in the 1640s for the professional cathedral musicians active there. This is one of the few *cofradías de músicos* (musical confraternities) in New Spain about which we currently have detailed information. Marín López discusses this confraternity's constitution, organization, and activities, and shows how it projected a Spanish peninsular identity through its emphasis on Marian devotions.

2738 **Marín López, Javier.** Constituciones de la congregación de Nuestra Señora de la Antigua de la Catedral de México. (*Resonancias/Santiago*, 21:41, julio/nov. 2017, p. 165–176)

This study, a companion to (item 2737), includes a transcription of the constitution of the Congregación de Nuestra Señora de la Antigua.

2739 **Marín López, Javier.** Mecenazgo musical e identidad aristocrática en el México Ilustrado: Miguel de Berrio y Zaldívar, Conde de San Mateo de Valparaíso (1716–1779). (*Lat. Am. Music Rev.*, 39, Spring/Summer 2018, p. 1–29, ill.)

This study expands on the 2016 work of Alejandro Correa Rodríguez on Miguel de Berrio (1716–1779), the Marqués de Jaral, and his estate inventory and musical activities (see item **2715**). Marín López finds that Berrio became famous for his musical gatherings at his palace in Mexico City, in which he participated, and that his interest in musical entertainment was, at least in part, motivated by a desire for self-promotion and the projection of his aristocratic identity.

2740 **Marín López, Javier et al.** Aportaciones al estudio de la música en la Santa Capilla de San Andrés de Jaén durante el siglo XVI: dos juegos de versos para ministriles de Gil de Ávila (Fl. 1574–1597). (*Anu. Music.*, 72, 2017, p. 51–96 bibl., ill., music)

Instrumental *versos* by the itinerant chapelmaster Gil de Ávila (fl. 1574–97) preserved in Puebla Cathedral in Mexico have a connection to the music performed in the parish church of San Andrés in Jaén, Spain, and its *cofradía* of La Inmaculada Concepción (known as Santa Capilla), established there in 1515. (Ávila was associated with Santa Capilla.) This study examines the musical exchange between Spanish institutions and their American counterparts, and includes a musical transcription of Ávila's *versos*.

2741 **Martínez-Hernández, Laura.** Música y cultura alternativa: hacia un perfil de la cultura del rock mexicano de finales del siglo XX. Puebla, Mexico: Universidad Iberoamericana Puebla: Instituto Tecnológico de Estudios Superiores de

Occidente, 2013. 229 p.: bibl., ill. (Lupus inquisitor)

This work examines the place of rock music in Mexican society at the end of the 20th century and reflects on its future.

2742 **Mauleón, Gustavo** and **Edward Charles Pepe.** Fuentes para el estudio del órgano histórico de la parroquia de Santa Inés Zacatelco (Tlaxcala, México). (*Anu. Music.*, 72, 2017, p. 97–122, ill.)

The organ in the parish church of Santa Inés Zacatelco, in Tlaxcala, is one of the most important instruments of its kind in Mexico. It was built by Seferino Agustin Castro, from a family of organ builders, during the first half of the 19th century, and is comparatively large for a parish church.

2743 **Mauleón, Gustavo** and **Edward Charles Pepe.** Vislumbres de Cabezón: algunas reflexiones y recepción novohispana de *Obras de Música*. (*Anu. Music.*, 69, 2014, p. 277–294, bibl., ill., music)

This article discusses the reception of Spanish composer Antonio de Cabezón's important published collection *Obras de música para tecla, arpa y vihuela* in New Spain in the 16th century. See also *HLAS* 70:2388.

McDowell, John H. "Surfing the Tube" for Latin American song: the blessings and (curses) of YouTube. See item **2807**.

2744 **Mendoza Huerta, Yasbil Yanil Berenice.** La influencia de la lingüística en la etnomusicología en México. México: Instituto Nacional de Antropología e Historia, 2013. 217 p.: bibl., indexes, music. (Colección Lingüística. Serie Interdisciplinaria)

This book emphasizes the importance of applying linguistic theories to music, especially in a Mexican ethnomusicological context.

2745 **Mercado Villalobos, Alejandro.** La educación musical en Morelia 1869–1911. Mexico: Universidad Michoacana de San Nicolas de Hidalgo, 2015. 169 p.

Music instruction was offered in 19th-century Morelia, Michoacán, to students at the Colegio de San Nicolás de Hidalgo, Escuela de Artes y Oficios, and the Academia de Niñas. This study gives a detailed view of the music curriculum, pedagogical methods, and instruments taught at these schools, as well as their importance to the city's cultural life.

2746 **Mercado Villalobos, Alejandro.** Lo europeo frente a lo mexicano en la música: el caso de *Euterpe*, revista de música, literatura y variedades, 1892–1894. (*Trans (online)*, 19, 2015, p. 1–16, bibl.)

The Mexican musical and cultural journal *Euterpe*, published in Morelia, Michoacán, in the 1890s, promoted European music as the model that Mexican society should follow.

2747 **Miranda, Ricardo.** Musicología e historia cultural: a propósito de *Los papeles para Euterpe*. (*Hist. Mex./México*, 61, 2016, p. 359–401, bibl., ill., music)

This major, penetrating, and polemical study reviews the entire condition of Mexican musical life in the 19th century, in the form of a detailed review and reflection on *Los papeles para Euterpe: a música en la Ciudad de México desde la historia cultural; siglo XIX* (see *HLAS* 72:2801). This contribution marks an important milestone in Mexican musical historiography.

2748 **Miranda Nieto, Alejandro.** Musical mobilities: son jarocho and the circulation of tradition across Mexico and the United States. Abingdon, England; New York, N.Y.: Routledge, an imprint of the Taylor & Francis Group, 2018. 140 p.: bibl., ill., index, maps. (Routledge advances in ethnography; 20)

This work examines the transnational dissemination of the Mexican *son jarocho* tradition and repertory in Mexico and the US. Based extensively on ethnographic research.

2749 **Morales Abril, Omar.** A presença de música e músicos portugueses no vice-reinado da Nova Espanha e na província de Guatemala, nos séculos XVI–XVII. (*Rev. Port. Musicol.*, nova série, 2:1, 2015, p. 151–174)

This article emphasizes the importance of Portuguese music and musicians in the Viceroyalty of New Spain, including the province of Guatemala, in Puebla and Santiago de los Caballeros de Guatemala, during the 16th and 17th centuries.

2750 **Música indígena y contemporaneidad: nuevas facetas de la música en las sociedades tradicionales.** Coordinación de

Miguel Olmos Aguilera. Tijuana, Mexico: El Colegio de la Frontera Norte; México: INAH, 2016. 295 p.: bibl., ill. (chiefly color), maps.

Indigenous communities in Mexico's northwest have embraced cumbia, rock, rap, ranchera, música tropical, and other national and international musical genres and styles, in order to find new forms of esthetic expression at the same time that they have sought to preserve their oral traditions.

2751 **Música vernácula de Chiapas: antología.** Coordinación de Thomas Arvol Lee Whiting y Víctor Manuel Esponda Jimeno. Chiapas, Mexico: UNICACH, 2014. 271 p.: bibl., ill. (some color), music. (Colección Selva Negra)

This anthology brings together previously published studies on vernacular and indigenous musics of Chiapas, including contributions by prominent scholars such as Henrietta Yurchenco and Francisco Domínguez.

2752 **Música y catedral: nuevos enfoques, viejas temáticas.** Coordinación de Raúl H. Torres Medina. México: UACM, Universidad Autónoma de la Ciudad de México, 2016. 207 p.: ill.

This collection of separate essays by leading scholars demonstrates how far research into music in New Spain has advanced in breath and depth of coverage and intellectual sophistication. Chapters cover such topics as indigenous musicians, parish musical life, cathedral music, music in provincial centers, and enslaved musicians, among others. The volume brings together the proceedings of a conference held in 2009.

2753 **Pablo Hammeken, Luis de.** Ópera y política en el México decimonónico: el caso de Amilcare Roncari. (*Secuencia/México*, 97, enero/abril 2017, p. 140–169, bibl.)

This study examines the role of opera in 19th-century Mexico, especially in relation to Italian opera impresario Amilcare Roncari, who ran afoul of Mexican politics—as did his productions. Roncari was jailed for a time because of financial difficulties tied to hotly blowing political winds and the vagaries and dangers of operatic touring. For Mexican historian's comment, see item **589**.

2754 **Pablo Hammeken, Luis de.** La república de la música: ópera, política y sociedad en el México del siglo XIX. Presentación de Clara E. Lida. México: Bonilla Artigas Editores, 2018. 257 p.: bibl., ill. (Pública histórica; 9)

This book provides an excellent social, political, and cultural history of the performance of European (mostly Italian) opera in mid 19th-century Mexico.

2755 **Peza, Carmen de la.** El rock mexicano: un espacio en disputa. México: Universidad Autónoma Metropolitan, 2013. 238 p.: bibl., discography. (Colección Tendencias)

According to the author, rock music is a sociocultural and political phenomenon and complex in which performers and spectators participate in public spheres and discourses. This study examines the rock scene in Mexico through the prism of class, race, genre, and generational divides.

2756 **Poder y privilegio: cabildos eclesiásticos en Nueva España, siglos XVI a XIX.** Coordinación Leticia Pérez Puente y Gabino Castillo Flores. México: IISUE, UNAM, Instituto de Investigaciones sobre la Universidad y la Educación, 2016. 395 p.: bibl., ill. (La Real Universidad de México Estudios y textos; XXXIV)

This volume covers a wide range of topics related to cathedral establishments in New Spain. Two of the 13 chapters examine music: Ruth Yareth Reyes Acevedo's study of musician-*prebendados* in Mexico City Cathedral and Antonio Ruiz Caballero's work on music in Valladolid (Morelia) Cathedral.

2757 **Pulido Llano, Gabriela.** Claves de la música afrocubana en México: entre músicos y musicólogos, 1920–1950. (*Desacatos*, 53, enero/abril 2017, p. 56–73, bibl., photos)

Pulido Llano interrogates the ideas of Cuban and Mexican musicologists who have written on African influences on Cuban and Mexican popular forms, such as the *danzón* and mambo. She pays particular attention to the music of Dámaso Pérez Prado.

La resignificación del Nuevo Mundo: crónica, retórica y semántica en la América virreinal. See item **1749**.

2758 **Rincón Serratos, Jazmín.** El verso instrumental entre la Nueva España y el México independiente. (*Anu. Music.*, 73, 2018, p. 201–214, ill., music)

Instrumental *versos* replaced in alternation choral and solo vocal psalm verses, hymns, and chants during the liturgical year. The author pays particular attention to the *versos* by Mexican composers José Manuel Aldana and Manuel Delgado in the Mexico City Cathedral.

2759 **Rodriguez, Alberto** and **Rene Torres.** John Lomax's southern states recording expedition: Brownsville, Texas, 1939. (*J. Tex. Music Hist.*, 16, 2016, p. 8–21, ill.)

Folklorist and English professor John Lomax, the father of folklorist Alan Lomax, collected and recorded popular and folk songs sung by Mexican and Mexican American residents of the Rio Grande Valley (Río Bravo) region of South Texas in the late 1930s. Rodriguez and Torres define Lomax's collection (in the American Folklife Center, Library of Congress) as a reflection of regional culture, ethnic and racial tensions, economic disparities, and Tejano/a identities. The article includes song texts and translations.

2760 **Roubina, Evguenia.** El tololoche en las artes de México o la virtud de llamar las cosas por su nombre. (*Cuad. Iconogr. Mus.*, 3:2, nov. 2016, p. 104–128, bibl., ill.)

This article examines the presence and use of the *tololoche* in New Spain and 19th-century Mexico. The *tololoche* was a bass string instrument that took many forms in the viceregal period in Mexico—bass guitar, string bass of various sizes, etc. (Today the term is usually used to refer to a stand-up string bass used in Mexican popular music.) An important organological and iconographical study.

2761 **Sánchez Novelo, Faulo M.** Documentos para la historia de las bandas de música del estado de Yucatán (siglos XIX y XX). Mérida, Mexico: Secretaría de la Cultura y las Artes de Yucatán, 2015. 159 p.: bibl., ill.

Military and civic wind bands have long had an important presence in Mexico and elsewhere in Latin America, although music scholars have only recently begun to study their histories and repertories systematically and value their contribution to the musical history of the region. (Many Mexican towns, cities, and states place a high value on their local bands today, however.) Happily, numerous recent publications have countered that scholarly lacuna. The state of Yucatán has been especially hospitable to wind bands, and Sánchez Novelo presents a plethora of documentary riches that demonstrate the importance of these ubiquitous ensembles to Yucatecan society in the 19th and 20th centuries. He includes information about band instrumentation, band repertory, pay schedules, and other topics.

2762 **Saucedo Estrada, Alán Saúl.** The influence of Carlos Prieto on contemporary cello music. Lanham, Md.: University Press of America, Inc., 2014. 124 p.: bibl.

The prominent Mexican cellist Carlos Prieto has long been a proponent of contemporary composition for his instrument. Saucedo Estrada examines his life and musical accomplishments and includes a detailed catalog of 72 compositions dedicated and/or dedicated to Prieto.

2763 **Spanish American music in New Mexico: the WPA era: folk songs, dance tunes, singing games, and guitar arrangements.** Compiled and edited by James Clois Smith Jr. Foreword by Jack Loeffler. Santa Fe, N.M.: Sunstone Press, 2017. 222 p.: bibl., ill., music.

The 1930s Works Progress Administration (WPA)-sponsored folk song gathering activities in New Mexico resulted in several publications, including this collection of Hispano-Hispanic New Mexican folk songs (here called Spanish American folk songs, as was the custom of the time). This valuable reprint edition brings this important repertory to general public attention again.

2764 **Varanasi González, Julieta.** La música en Xalapa entre 1824 y 1878. Veracruz, Mexico: Gobierno del Estado de Veracruz: Instituto Veracruzano de la Cultura, 2014. 195 p.: bibl., ill., index. (Colección Voces de la tierra)

This comprehensive book-length study examines the history of music in the city of Xalapa in the state of Veracruz in the 19th century. The work is based on primary research in civic archives and private collections in Xalapa, as well as on careful examination of newspaper reportage on musical activities. The author begins with the immediate postindependence period and ends with the onset of the Porfiriato, a time when Xalapa and its musical life benefited from improved communications with other Mexican cities and foreign centers.

2765 Vargas Cetina, Gabriela. Beautiful politics of music: trova in Yucatan, Mexico. Tuscaloosa: University of Alabama Press, 2017. 203 p.: bibl., discography, ill., index.

Vargas Cetina studies the beloved *trova yucateca,* the early 20th-century romantic song genre, in which residents of the state of Yucatán still take great pride. She also investigates Yucatecan patronage of the form, based on her own intimate knowledge of the form as a performing *trovadora,* and her extensive fieldwork in the state of Yucatán. She positions the performance of *trova yucateca* in the context of theories of modernity and cosmopolitanism.

2766 Vilar-Payá, Luisa. Lo histórico y lo cotidiano: un juego de libretes de coro para la consagración de la Catedral de Puebla y la despedida del Obispo Palafox (1649). (*Rev. Musicol./Madrid,* 40:1, enero/junio 2017, p. 135–176, music)

One of the most important articles on music in New Spain published to date, this study examines musical, liturgical, and political meanings of works composed by the *insigne maestro de capilla* Juan Gutiérrez de Padilla (ca. 1590–1664), held in the Puebla Cathedral music archive, with an emphasis on the now well-known *Missa ego flos campi.* Vilar-Payá carefully parses Antonio Tamariz y Carmona's (1617–83) well-known chronicle of the dedication of the Puebla Cathedral on 18 April 1649, *Relación y descripción del templo real de la ciudad de la Puebla de los Ángeles en la Nueva España, y su cathedral* (published 1650). On 6 May 1649, Bishop Juan de Palafox y Mendoza (1600–59) left the city to return to Spain, motivated by a complicated political situation. Vilar-Payá brilliantly connects Palafox's last months in Puebla, Tamariz y Carmona's chronicle, and Gutiérrez de Padilla's music to demonstrate how religious ritual, musical composition, and ecclesiastical power and politics were intricately intertwined. A seminal study of the topic. See also *HLAS 70:2404.*

2767 Vilar-Payá, Luisa and Ana R. Alonso-Minutti. Estrategias de diferenciación en la composición musical: Mario Lavista y el México de fines de los sesenta y comienzos de los setenta. (*Rev. Arg. Musicol.,* 12/13, 2012, p. 267–290, bibl., music)

This study positions Mario Lavista, the leading Mexican contemporary art music composer, in the context of the American (of all the Americas) and European musical avant-garde. Vilar-Payá and Alonso-Minutti emphasize Lavista's early works, from the 1960s and early 1970s, written at a time when the composer used atonal musical languages and extended performance techniques, and rethought the role of the performer in his music. The authors find that the components that were present in Lavista's early works still have relevance for his current compositional language. An important study.

2768 Voces de la sierra: marimbas sencillas en Chiapas. Textos de Juan Alberto Bermúdez Molina *et al.* Coordinación de Helmut Brenner, José Israel Moreno Vázquez y Juan Alberto Bermúdez Molina. Chiapas, Mexico: Universidad de Ciencias y Artes de Chiapas; Graz, Austria: Universidad de Música y Arte Dramático de Graz, 2014. 239 p.: bibl., ill. (some color), music. (Sonidos de la tierra: estudios de etnomusicología; 1)

This work presents a Mexican-Austrian binational ethnological and musical study of the *marimba sencilla*—the diatonic marimba usually played by several performers—based on fieldwork in the Mexican state of Chiapas, with the essential contributions of 21 *chiapaneco* practitioner-collaborators (who are identified in the book).

2769 Williamson, Emily. The fandango and shared music making among Mexican immigrants in the son jarocho community of New York City. (*Am. Music Rev.,* 46:2, Spring 2017, p. 1–6, ill.)

This study looks at Mexican *son jarocho* among Mexican musicians and in Mexican immigrant communitites in New York City. The article includes song texts and translations along with coverage of various dance types practiced in the fandango, or dance fiesta.

CENTRAL AMERICA AND THE CARIBBEAN

ALFRED E. LEMMON, *Director, Williams Research Center, The Historic New Orleans Collection*

THE PUBLISHED RESEARCH concerning the Caribbean and Central America in *HLAS* 74 reflects several consistent themes of prior years—the African diaspora, music as a reflection of social and political issues, the multicontinental musical history, and the American fascination with the Caribbean. Together they demonstrate the importance of music in understanding cultural heritage. In prior *HLAS* volumes, oral history was notably important as a source of information for ethnomusicologists. With this volume of *HLAS*, attention must be drawn to electronic media as a powerful means of sharing information within the scholarly community. Many of the works examined here are available to subscribers of MUSE, JSTOR, Newspapers.com or other database services. As a result, there are increasingly rich and creative resources available for the study of the region's music.

For *HLAS* 74, just over 30 works were reviewed. As in previous years, studies concerning Cuban music are the most numerous. The studies focused on Caribbean music outnumber those on Central American music. The majority of the works are in English and it is unusual that there are no works in French.

A number of significant biographical studies were issued in recent years, including works on Pablo Hernández Balaguer (Cuba, 1928–66) (item **2788**), Ignacio Cervantes (Cuba, 1847–1905) (item **2791**), Edgardo Martin Cantero (Cuba, 1915–2004) (item **2789**), Danilo Orozco (Cuba, 1944–2013) (item **2796**) and Rufus Callendar (Trinidad, 1910–76) (item **2772**). Moore's contribution on the prolific and multi-talented Fernando Ortiz (Cuba, 1881–1969) is exceptional (item **2793**). Robin D. Moore has repeatedly produced well-researched books and articles. Here he and several contributors present Ortiz's writings in English translation. Ortiz's pioneering work and methodology drew on a number of disciplines, including ethnography, history, music, law, lexicography, and sociology. It follows that Ortiz has long been the object of fascination among scholars from a wide range of fields. Emily Maguire's *Racial Experiments in Cuban Literature and Ethnography* (see *HLAS 68:1993*) and Stephen Palmié's "Fernando Ortiz and the Cooking of History" (*Ibero-amerikanisches Archiv*, Neue Folge, Vol. 24, No. 3/4 (1998)) are but two examples. The availability of selections of Ortiz's work in English likely will inspire a new group of scholars.

Art music drew the attention of a number of scholars. Chief among these are Solomon Gadles Mikowsky's study of Ignacio Cervantes (item **2791**) and Ricardo R. Guridi's examination of Edgardo Martin (item **2789**). Iván César Morales Flores (item **2792**) illuminates the work of younger Cuban composers such as Ileana Pérez Velázquez, Edoardo Morales-Caso, Neyla Orozco, Ailem Carvajal and Louis Aguirre. Likewise Christine Gangelhoff and Cathleen LeGrand (item **2774**) have provided a distinct service by preparing a guide to musical resources for art music of other Caribbean nations. One hopes that these studies will lead to updated versions of reference works such as Hoover's *A Guide to the Latin American Art Song Repertoire: An Annotated Catalog of Latin American Art Song Repertoire* (see *HLAS 68:2712*).

All researchers face the challenge of access to resources, both secondary and primary. The efforts to draw attention to earlier journals such as *Guitarra*

(1940–45) (item **2795**) and *Boletin Música* (Casa de Americas) (1970–90) (item **2798**) are especially critical. Again, the importance of their availability is paramount. In the case of *Guitarra*, the Órgano Oficial de la Sociedad Guitarrística de Cuba, WorldCat lists four institutions that hold copies. *Música* is available online at www.casadelasamericas.org/boletinmusica.php (accessed 8/18/2018). In their article, Mary Jo Zeter and Mary Black Junttonen (item **2799**) describe the Alfred Levy Archive of Cuban Music at Michigan State University. The acquisition of the archive is an excellent example of how cooperation between US and Cuban scholars provides public access to critical resources. The papers of John Alden Mason (1885–1967) at the Archives of Traditional Music (Indiana Unviersity—Bloomington) were astutely interpreted by Viera-Vargas (item **2784**). However, the vast majority of the personal archive of this important and multi-talented anthropologist awaits scholars at the American Philosophical Society Library in Philadelphia (John Alden Mason Papers, Mss.B.M384). Mary Caton Lingold (item **2777**) draws particular attention to pre-1900 travel narratives. The narratives she highlights are listed in an earlier publication that continues to be valuable resource for scholars: Robert Stevenson's "Caribbean Music History: A Selective Annotated Bibliography" (see *HLAS 46:7024*). Stevenson's bibliography lists 26 pre-1800 publications and 17 from the 19th century that await detailed musical examination. Indeed, Lingold's work should serve as an invitation to scholars to thoroughly study such accounts.

The American fascination with Caribbean music found expression in Edgar Hernández Collazo's work (item **2790**) on the efforts to teach Cuban music performance practice in the US and Andrew Martin's study of the US Navy Steel Band (item **2780**).

With a land mass of 92,541 square miles and a population of slightly more than 44 million, the Caribbean represents merely .58 percent of the estimated world population. Yet the exceptional number of publications on Caribbean music this biennium reflects the enormous impact of the region's music on the world.

THE CARIBBEAN (EXCEPT CUBA)

2770 Aponte-Ledée, Rafael. Las mieles del alba: Conservatorio de Música de Puerto Rico: dichas y desdichas. San Juan, Puerto Rico: Editorial Tiempo Nuevo, 2015. 290 p.: bibl., ill.

Rafael Aponte Ledée (b. 1938) studied in Spain with Cristóbal Halffter and later in Buenos Aires with Alberto Ginastera. Returning to Puerto Rico in 1968, he began a career as a professor at the Conservatorio de Música and formed, with Francis Schwartz, Fluxus to promote new music. As director of the Fundación Latinoamericana para la Música Contemporánea, he was responsible for performances of contemporary music. At the same time, he has been a prolific composer. As a result of such diverse activities, he is uniquely qualified to trace the development of musical life in Puerto Rico and, in particular, the Conservatorio de Música. In this work, he places Puerto Rican music within a global context (especially for the 19th century), which is essential for an understanding of Caribbean musical history. The volume provides important documentation on the Casals Festival as well as 20th-century musical repertoire in Puerto Rico.

2771 Berrian, Brenda F. Un peu de bonheur: Jocelyne Béroard and her lyrics about love. (*Lat. Am. Music Rev.*, 36:1, Spring/Summer 2015, p. 94–115, bibl., discography)

Berrian's contribution continues her long-standing interest in the French Caribbean as testified to in *Awakening Spaces: French Caribbean Popular Songs, Culture, and Music* (University of Chicago Press, 2000) and in her 1999 contribution "Zouk Diva: Interview with Jocelyne Béroard"

(MaComère; 2:1, 2011). Béroard (b. 1954), a singer of zouk and member of the music group Kassav (established in 1979), is the first "woman zouk singer from Martinique to perform and sing her own songs." The article includes a thorough biographical sketch and an analysis/summary of the various topics (Creole, love, maternal love patriotism)

2772 Eldridge, Michael. Caresser's dominion: race, nation, and calypso in postwar Canada. (*Small Axe*, 47, July 2015, p. 29-55)

An examination of the Canadian career of Rufus Callender (1910-76), better known as Lord Caresser. Like several other exponents of calypso, he recorded in New York during the 1930s. He relocated to Montreal in the 1940s and appeared regularly in nightclubs and radio broadcasts. The article examines the role of the Canadian Broadcasting Corporation's International Service in establishing Canada's world image after WWII and the increasing trade and tourism relation with the West Indies in the same period. Eldridge examines the popularity of Lord Caresser in terms of the growing West Indian population of Montreal (40 percent of the black population). The welcome extended to black performers was considered an example of Canada's progressive civil rights stance. At the same time, performers indicated that the initially welcoming attitude made it easier for Canadians to conceal "their unfriendliness" and that prejudices "although subtly applied, are nonetheless real."

2773 Fiol-Matta, Licia. The great woman singer: gender and voice in Puerto Rican music. Durham, N.C.: Duke University Press, 2016. 291 p.: bibl., index, photos. (Refiguring American music)

The primary focus of Fiol-Matta's scholarship is Latin American cultural studies, women's and gender studies, and music. In the current volume, she examines the careers of the multifaceted (singer, entertainer, entrepreneur) Myrta Silva; the "naturally virtuosic" and "household name" Ruth Fernández; Ernestina Reyes ("La Calandria"), who achieved fame as a singer of *música campesina* on radio and television; and the beautiful, musically gifted Lucecita Benítez. The biographies set a standard for future works on musicians.

2774 Gangelhoff, Christine and **Cathleen LeGrand.** Art music by Caribbean composers. (*Int. J. Bahamian Stud.*, 19:2, 2013, p. 3-76)

Christine Gangelhoff is assistant professor of the Music Faculty at the University of The Bahamas. She has also performed and published extensively and is active in arts administration. Cathleen LeGrand has served as the librarian of the Royal Thimphu College, Bhutan and the librarian, Lyford Cay International School, The Bahamas. Gangelhoff and LeGrand have provided the scholarly community with an excellent road map for future studies of Caribbean art music. The rich repertoire is inviting for both scholar and performer. However, due to the difficulty in locating materials, the topic has not been properly explored. The current volume includes composers who were born in the Caribbean and those who reside there. The volume contains information on scores, sheet music, recordings, and web sites. Also, included is a highly useful bibliography and list of relevant research institutions. The islands covered include: Antigua and Barbuda, Aruba, Barbados, Bonaire, Curaçao, Dominica, Grenada, Martinique, St. Kitts and Nevis, St. Lucia, St. Vincent and the Grenadines, Trinidad and Tobago,

2775 Hutchinson, Sydney. Tigers of a different stripe: performing gender in Dominican music. Chicago: The University of Chicago Press, 2016. 279 p.: bibl., ill., index, music. (Chicago studies in ethnomusicology)

Sydney Hutchinson's *Tigers of a Different Strip* reveals her exhaustive background in a variety of fields. A winner of numerous awards and prizes, she is experienced as a dancer, curator of exhibitions, and a writer of both popular and scholarly contributions. Her work in community outreach is significant. In the current volume, she expands our knowledge of Caribbean music by focusing on women. The result of more than a decade of research in both the Dominican Republic and New York, she examines the traditional Dominican Republic merengue típico and in particular, the role of the woman who often serve as instrumentalists and bandleaders as opposed to singers, as in many other Caribbean genres. It is an examination of the female version (*tíguera*) of the *tíguere* (a "street smart "tiger"). A *tíguera* may look like a woman, but "often plays and sings like a man." Her command of the topic ranges from a "Movement and Gesture Analysis of Fefita la Grande Performing 'La Chiflera'" to references to Pedro Francisco Bonó's 1856 novelette concerning *monteros* (backwoods huntsmen) and on to the "Historical Roots of Dominican Transvestism."

2776 **LeGrand, Cathleen.** "The isle is full of noises": C Force and musical life in the Bahamas. (*Int. J. Bahamian Stud.*, 20:2, 2014, p. 4–7)

C Force is a faculty trio ensemble of the College of The Bahamas and is comprised of piano, flute and euphonium. Through a variety of activities, the musical ensemble strives to foster music education (in the broadest sense of the term) and to promote the lesser known art music repertoire of The Bahamas and the Caribbean.

2777 **Lingold, Mary Caton.** Peculiar animations: listening to Afro-Atlantic music in Caribbean travel narratives. (*Early Am. Lit.*, 52:3, 2017, p. 623–650, bibl., facsims.)

More than 40 years have passed since Robert M. Stevenson's paper "A Guide to Caribbean Music History" was read at the 1975 Annual Meeting of the Music Library Association in San Juan, Puerto Rico (see *HLAS 46:7024*). The current author provides a detailed examination of two of the works referenced in Stevenson's 1981 contribution: Hans Sloan (p. 72) and John Gabriel Stedman (p. 73–74). The work is an indication of the significant amount of material awaiting scholars who "focus" on a detailed examination of items noted in Stevenson's bibliography. The in-depth exploration of travel accounts will inevitably help to place the current musical scene within a greater historical perspective.

2778 **Manuel, Peter.** Tales, tunes, and tassa drums: retention and invention in Indo-Caribbean music. Urbana: University of Illinois Press, 2015. 268 p.: bibl., graphs, ill., index, photos.

Astutely observing the current prominence of "syncretic popular music" in scholarship, the author notes that the themes of "identity, hybridity, and resistance" and "commercial popular music" have posed a challenge to studies of "traditional and neotraditional music." In the current volume, he traces the journey of musical practices from North India to the Caribbean. Professor of Ethnomusicology at John Jay College and the Graduate Center of the City University of New York, Manuel succeeds in bringing to life the richness of Caribbean music, while highlighting the contribution of the Indian diaspora. His discussion of the tassa drumming is particularly important and draws attention to the sophistication of such traditions.

2779 **Manuel, Peter** and **Michael Largey.** Caribbean currents: Caribbean music from rumba to reggae. Third edition. Philadelphia, Pa.: Temple University Press, 2016. 336 p.: bibl., ill., index, maps, music.

The authors provide an exceptionally useful service by tracing how the "Old Word music cultures" (Europe and Africa) met in the Caribbean. They place the impact of Caribbean musical culture in perspective by noting that the "sarabanda" and "chacona" achieved enormous popularity in Spain and eventually became basic musical forms of the Baroque period.The merging of European, African, and Amerindian music resulted in a musical phenomenon.The authors seek to answer how a region with only one percent of the world's population has had such a sustained impact on music globally. The volume succinctly traces the musical development of the Caribbean in a highly readable fashion that is inviting for both the musicologist/ethnomusicologist and student/amateur.

2780 **Martin, Andrew R.** Steelpan ambassadors: the US Navy Steel Band, 1957–1999. Jackson: University Press of Mississippi, 2017. 249 p.: bibl., ill., index. (Caribbean studies series)

Martin presents an exceptionally fine study of the development of the US Navy Steel Band. Noting that it was born during the "anxieties and tensions of the impending Cold War," it illustrates the impact of this musical organization on the popularity of Caribbean music in the US. Tracing the history of the Steel Band, Martin begins with Admiral Daniel Gallery, the band's creator. He relates how the early members, all trained musicians, were sent to Trinidad to study with steelpan experts. The impact of Admiral Gallery extended beyond the creation of the band. A master of public relations, within a relatively short period, Gallery had the band performing on the Ed Sullivan Show. Gallery corresponded with folk singer Pete Seeger, who was so captivated by the steel drums that he wrote a how-to-play manual, and together the two devised a repertoire and shared their enthusiasm for bringing steel drums to the US.Their collaboration, which occurred even as Seeger was under investigation by the House Un-American Activities Committee (HUAC) and effectively blacklisted, demonstrated a mutual respect that overcame political differences. The history of the band is indeed a "story of how a Caribbean tradition was adapted to suit an American sensibility."

2781 A reader in African-Jamaican music, dance and religion. Edited by Markus Coester and Wolfgang Bender. Kingston: Ian Randle Publishers, 2015. 735 p.: bibl., maps, photos.

A highly useful, masterful compilation of 42 articles by the following contributors: Aviodun Adetugbo, Ive Baxter, Martha Warren Beckwith, Judith Bettelheim, Kenneth M. Bilby, Fu-Kiau Kia Bunseki, Hazel Carter, Barry Chevannes, Ashley Clerk, Adina Henry, Donald Hogg, Walter Jekyll, Ilive Lewin, Elliot Leib, Douglas R. A. Mack, Patrick O'Gorman, Elizabeth Pigou, Hazel Ramsey, Erena Reckord, Helen H. Roberts, Cheryl Ryman, Monica Schuler, Edward Seaga, George Eaton Simipson, Laura Tanna, Maureen Warner-Lewis, Garth White and Sylvie Wynter. The selected articles were originally published between 1907 and 1999. The informative and highly readable Foreword by Laura Tanna chronicles the historiography and lists resources. She rightfully begins by paying homage to the Institute of Jamaica. Established in 1879, it is the "oldest centre of learning in the English-speaking Caribbean." She describes the development of the institution and its impact upon scholarship.

2782 Richards Mayo, Sandra. A sound legacy: the making of Jamaican music at the Alpha Boys' School and Home. (*Caribb. Q./Mona*, 59:1, June 2013, p. 50–69, photos)

An examination of the impact of Alpha Boys' School and Home (established in 1880 and known originally as Alpha Cottage) on Jamaican musical life. It is the intention of the author to show how the school is a "relic of Britain's imperial legacy" and a force within Jamaican "cultural history." In a summary of Jamaican popular music, the author examines the role of the school in the "popular music explosion" of Jamaica. Particular attention is paid to Sister Mary Ignatius (1921–2003) of the school. Known for her music collection, she played a pivotal role in music education and nurtured the talent of several leading Jamaican musicians. Working from interviews, the author notes the impact of the school through piano instruction from Sister Bonaventure, while other nuns such as Sister Marie Therese encouraged the students to explore music. Floyd "Lloyd" Seivright, a graduate of the school and currently the founder/owner of Tropic Entertainment and Recording Enterprises, recounts how he learned to be a "DJ" from the legendary Sister Ignatius. The author demonstrates how the former students have been able to utilize their "classical" training to develop Jamaican popular music.

2783 Schultz, Anna. Bollywood *bhajans*: style as "air" in an Indian-Guyanese twice-migrant community. (*Ethnomusicology Forum*, 23:3, 2014, p. 383–404, bibl.)

Schultz is associate professor of music at Stanford University. The current contribution is a reflection of her interest in Indian music and in particular the Indo-Caribbean diaspora. Here, she examines the devotional songs of the Indian-Guyanese Hindu temples in Minneapolis. The article grew out of a music ethnography class that the author offered in the Fall of 2007 when teaching at the University of Minnesota (2006–2010). Tracing the migrations, first to Guyana and subsequently to Minnesota, the article focuses on the "sacred," rather than "profane" or "secular," music influenced by the film industry. It clearly demonstrates the relation between music and religion and how it, in turn, reflects larger issues facing an immigrant community.

Sellers, Julie A. The modern bachateros: 27 interviews. See item **943**.

2784 **Viera-Vargas, Hugo René.** A son de clave: la dimensión afrodiaspórica de la puertorriqueñidad en la musica popular, 1929–1940. (*Lat. Am. Music Rev.*, 38:1, Spring/Summer 2017, p. 57–82, bibl., graphs, ill.)

In this article, the author focuses on the musical interactions between Puerto Rico and Cuba at the dawn of the 20th century. Based heavily on the papers of John Alden Mason (1885–1967) housed at the Archives of Traditional Music (Indiana University, Bloomington), it is testimony to the importance of the documentary record for the examination of the current popular music of the region. In addition, the author made extensive use of the Archivo Nacional de Cuba (Fondo Secretaría de Estado y Gobernación).

CENTRAL AMERICA

2785 **Bell, Elizabeth R.** "This isn't underground; this is the highlands": Mayan-language hip-hop, cultural resilience, and youth education in Guatemala. (*J. Folk. Res.*, 54:3, 2017 p. 167–197, bibl., map, photos)

Assistant Professor of Spanish at Ball State University, Bell's research focus is the Kaqchikel-Maya and indigenous self-expression. The article, based largely on experiences of the Maya in the vicinity of Lake Atitlán, demonstrates how hip-hop songs educate youth about their cultural history and identity and illustrates how it is part of a literary/poetic tradition seen in the *Popul Wuj* and *Chilam Balam*. The hip-hop movement addresses the need for identity education, necessary to combat discrimination and promote advancement.

2786 **Greene, Oliver N.** Music, healing, and transforming identity in *Lemesi Garifuna* (the Garifuna Mass). (*Caribb. Q./Mona*, 60:2, June 2014, p. 88–109, music, photos)

An examination of the adaptation of the Roman Catholic mass as witnessed in Belize (2007, 2010, 2012) and Los Angeles (2008) by the Garinagu, people of African and native South American ancestry. The author shows how the use of ancestor rituals enrich them as "Christians but also as Garifuna Christians." Placing his observations within the realm of the Spanish, French, and English Caribbean. The work is particularly rich in terms of bibliography, and as such is exceptionally useful. Examples demonstrate the belief that "ancestor veneration rituals restore physical health and family solidarity." An especially important part of the work is the examination of the existing bibliography

Singer, Deborah. Música colonial: otredad y conflicto en la Catedral de Santiago de Guatemala. See item **734**.

CUBA

2787 **Díaz Ayala, Cristóbal.** Oh Cuba hermosa!: el cancionero político social en Cuba hasta 1958. Charleston, SC: CreateSpace Independent Publishing Platform, 2012. 2 v.: bibl., discography.

Contains biographical sketches and a review/evaluation of a group of composers/singers/bandleaders comprised of Antonio Machín (1903–77), Arsenio Rodríguez (1913–70) and Julio Cueva (1897–1975). In addition to a brief biographical sketch, an analysis of song texts is included. Particularly important is an annotated discography of recordings of Cuban bands. Another highly useful section is "Teatro Lírico Cubano." Basically an annotated checklist of Cuban musical theater, it gathers together information about several hundred musical productions. Other topics covered in a similar fashion are "Negritud," "Religiones Afrocubanos," and "Política Social."

Fajardo Estrada, Ramón. Yo seré la tentación: María de los Ángeles Santana. See item **901**.

2788 **Fernández, Bertha.** Documenta musicae: rescatistas del legado musical cubano. (*Sinc. Habanero*, 3:1, 2018, p. 14)

Summary of activities of musicologist Pablo Hernández Balaguer concerning 18th-century Cuban composer Esteban Salas. Notes the continuation of Balaguer's work by Miriam Escudero.

2789 **Guridi, Ricardo R.** Edgardo Martín: vida y pensamiento musical. La Habana: Ediciones Museo de la Música, 2012. 247 p.: bibl., ill., music.

The diverse activity of Edgardo Martin Cantero (1915–2004) a multi-talented musician, composer, educator, and essayist is clearly outlined in this contribution. His life was testimony to the diverse activity of 20th-century Cuban music. As a composer, he published works such as Fugues for String Orchestra, Seis Preludios (piano), Variaciones para Guitarra, Concerto for Horn and Orchestra. As an writer, he penned *Panorama histórico de la música en Cuba* (1971). His musical output has been detailed by Ela Galvani, *Catálogo de obras musicales de Edgardo Martin* (1981). His work continues through the Festival Concurso de Guitarras "Edgardo Martín" held in Cienfuegos, Cuba. His inclusion on the recently released CD Piano Music of Cuba by Alexandre Moutouzkine (Steinway and Sons, 2017) illustrates how a young, international generation is continuing to discover his work as a composer. The present work is a biography as seen through Edgardo Martin's own writings. With excellent footnotes, this is an indispensable work.

2790 **Hernández Collazo, Edgar.** The three driving powers in Cuban music. North Charleston, S.C.: CreateSpace Independent Publishing Platform, 2018. 28 p.

A practicing musician, the author has written this slim volume specifically to help instruct students in the composition/performance style of Cuban music. The current volume, and other works by the author, should provide guidance to practicing musicians. Other contributions include *El arte de hacer música cubana* (s.l.: CreateSpace Independent Publishing Platform, 2017), *Los tres poderes de la música cubana, The three rhythmic powers within cuban music: sistema para arreglar, componer e interpretar* (s.l.: CreateSpace Independent Publishing Platform, 2017), and *Morfologia del tumbao: para piano* (s.l.: CreateSpace Independent Publishing Platform, 2017.)

2791 **Mikowsky, Solomon Gadles.** Ignacio Cervantes and the XIX-century Cuban danza. New York: Lambert Academic Publishing, 2016. 273 p.: bibl., music.

An updated version of pianist/pedagogue Salomón Gadles Mikowsky's 1973 doctoral dissertation, this is a study of the music, in particular the danza, of Ignacio Cervantes (1847–1905). Cervantes, arguably one of Cuba's more important, if not most important, 19th-century composers, enjoyed a period of training in France and Spain. He associated with musical personalities such as composers Gounod, Liszt, and Rossini. Returning to his homeland in 1870, he did not leave Cuba except for visits to the US and Mexico. The work examines Cervantes preferred musical form—the danza. He places the danza within the context of Cervantes' life, including the social history and European origins of the form. While clearly examining the French, Spanish, and English influences on the danza, he also examines the impact of African, Haitian, and French musical influences. The work includes a highly useful appendix of music by Cervantes and his contemporaries. For a comment on a 1988 edition of this publication, see *HLAS 54:5228*.

2792 **Morales Flores, Iván César.** Música, identidad y diásporo: jóvenes compositores cubanos en el cambio de siglo (1990–2010). (*Rev. Musical./Madrid*, 38:2, 2015, p. 748–756)

A summary of the author's doctoral dissertation at the Universidad de Oviedo, it examines the compositional activity of five recent students of the Instituto Superior de Arte de la Habana. Each graduate continued their studies in another country after earning a degree from the Instituto Superior. The students, and respective country of study after graduation are: Ileana Pérez Velázquez (US), Eduardo Morales-Caso (Spain) Keyla Orozco (Holland), Ailem Carvajal (Italy) and Louis Aguirre (Denmark).

2793 **Ortiz, Fernando.** Fernando Ortiz on music: selected writing on Afro-Cuban culture. Edited and with an introduction by Robin D. Moore. Philadelphia, Pa.: Temple University Press, 2018. 294 p.: bibl., ill., index, music. (Studies in Latin American and Caribbean music)

Fernando Ortiz, a pioneering scholar in Afro-Cuban studies, taught and influenced a generation of scholars. His contributions took full advantage of archival resources and were enriched by other disciplines such as ethnography. His works are important not only to scholars of Afro-Cuban studies, but also to scholars interested in Cuban intellectual history. Moore, a highly prolific scholar at The University of Texas at Austin, presents a comprehensive anthology, including examples of Ortiz's early works and contributions from the 1940s and 50s. This work is an enormous service to non-Spanish-speaking scholars and introduces the work of Ortiz to a new generation of scholars.

2794 Perry, Marc D. Negro soy yo: hip hop and raced citizenship in neoliberal Cuba. Durham, N.C.: Duke University Press, 2015. 284 p.: bibl. (Refiguring American music)

The author, a cultural anthropologist (Ph.D., University of Texas at Austin, Cultural Anthropology, 2004) is an assistant professor of anthropology at Tulane University (since 2010). He has been recognized for his work by the Ford Foundation and is a recipient of the Arnold O. Beckman Award for Distinguished Research at the University of Illinois, Urbana-Champaign. The current contribution reflects his wide experience in documentary filmmaking and broadcast journalism. The volume documents the changes experienced in Cuba and hip-hop as the island transitions from the economics of the post-Soviet era to a more liberal, tourism-friendly environment. Perry successfully argues that the Cuban hip-hop movement is decisively Afro-Cuban with its roots firmly based in the island's history. For comment by sociologist, see *HLAS* 73:2099.

2795 Pons, Joe Ott. Mirando al interior de una *Guitarra*. (*Sinc. Habanero*, 3:1, 2018, p. 9–12)

Summary of the activities of *Guitarra*, the official publication of the Sociedad Guitarrística de Cuba that was published between 1940 and 1945. During that period, more than 102 articles were published in the six issues of the journal. The journal was important for documenting the guitar in Cuba and throughout Latin America. The present article is a summary of the author's thesis (Colegio Universitario San Gerónimo de La Habana, 2011).

2796 Ruiz Zamora, Agustín. Entre Alto Cedro y Marcané: breve semblanza de Danilo Orozco (Santiago de Cuba, 17 de julio, 1944—La Habana, Cuba, 26 de marzo, 2013). (*Rev. Music. Chil.*, 70:226, dic. 2016, p. 85–105, ill.)

Danilo Orozco (1944–2013) was a Cuban musicologist and holder of a doctorate from Humboldt University. His methodology was marked by an emphasis on musical processes rather than on the broader social or cultural context. A central theme of his work was the music of the peasants, especially those in the Oriente province. One indication of his renowned scholarly work and dedication are the numerous invitations he received during his life to teach specialized courses in Brazil, California, Chile, Panama, Russia, Spain, and Venezuela.

2797 Saunders, Tanya L. Cuban underground hip hop: black thoughts, black revolution, black modernity. Austin: University of Texas Press, 2015. 356 p.: bibl., ill., index.

The author has a PhD in Sociology from the University of Michigan, Ann Arbor, and a Master of International Development Policy from the Gerald R. Ford School of Public Policy. In addition, she was a 2011–2012 Fulbright scholar to Brazil. The current volume is a reflection of her interest in examining ways that the African Diaspora has promoted social change. She is currently on the faculty of the University of Florida, Center for Latin American Studies. In this particular work, Saunders examines a wide range of topics beginning in 1998 and ending in 2006. Among the topics discussed are Cuba's racial history (and the Americas in general), contemporary Cuban life, and the role of Afro Cubans. The link between the topics is the Cuban hip-hop musical scene and its role in social movements. The work is an examination of music as a means of political activism.

2798 Souto Anido, Carmen. Un testigo de la historia: *Música*, boletín de Casa de las Americas. (*Sinc. Habanero*, 3:1, 2018, p. 3–8)

A summary of the author's thesis at the Colegio Universitario San Gerónimo de La Habana, 2011, it analyzes the content of the journal *Música* published by the Casa de las Américas between 1970 and 1990. The article is particularly useful as it gives information about the tenure of various individuals associated with the journal. It pays particular attention to the musical resources of the Casa de las Américas. Of exceptional importance was the documentation of 64 contemporary Cuban composers.

2799 **Zeter, Mary Jo** and **Mary Black Junttonen.** Alfred Levy Archive of Cuban music at Michigan State University. (*Fontes Artis Music.*, 62:3, 2015, p. 277–278)

Appearing in an issue devoted to the theme of "Archives as Evidence," this brief essay is devoted to the papers of Cuban composer and pianist Alfredo Levy Nadal (1914–99). Establishing his conservatory in 1947, he performed and championed the music of Cuban composers, accompanied opera singers, and served as choral director of the Teatro Musical de La Habana from 1970–76. Dr. Ricardo Lorenz of Michigan State University and Dr. Miriam Escudero (Director of Musical Patrimony of the Office of the Historian of the City of Havana) worked on behalf of the acquisition by the Special Collections Division of the library of Michigan State University to guarantee its preservation and access to scholars. With more than 1,000 scores, manuscripts, and correspondence, it will be a major source of study of Cuban music.

ANDEAN COUNTRIES

JONATHAN RITTER, *Associate Professor of Ethnomusicology, University of California, Riverside*

RECENT SCHOLARSHIP on music in the Andean region continues several now well-established trends. Urban popular music remains the dominant topic for research, reflecting not only popular tastes and market share but also these urban genres' broad impact on regional politics, economies, and cultures. Peru continues to be the source or the subject of the majority of scholarly work, though relevant and important publications continue to appear within the scarcer output from other countries in the region. As with previous review cycles, several important new books question national or nationalist frameworks, moving fluidly across national and even continental borders in their geographic scope and analysis. Kirstie Dorr's "performance geography" of South American music is a case in point (item **2809**), tacking back and forth between places (Peru and the US), genres (Andean folklore and Afro-diasporic forms), and disciplines (cultural studies, geography) to argue that place itself is sonically constructed and contested.

Among the recent transregional studies, two seminal collections—each with a Peruvian coeditor—stand out for their contribution to music scholarship in the Andes and Latin America. *A Latin American Music Reader: Views from the South* (item **2679**), edited by Peruvian ethnomusicologist Javier León amd Swiss ethnomusicologist Helena Simonett, makes the work of more than a dozen Latin American scholars available in English for the first time, including several essays by Peruvian and Colombian authors. The product of years of discussion and support from the Latin America Section of the Society for Ethnomusicology, the volume spans decades, topics, and regions, and has already become a staple of US-based undergraduate and graduate courses about Latin American music. Likewise, *Made in Latin America: Studies in Popular Music* (item **2680**), edited by Peruvian ethnomusicologist Julio Mendívil and Chilean musicologist Christian Spencer Espinosa, contains more than a dozen essays on diverse musical topics by Latin American scholars working in popular music scenes, including several from Peru,

Ecuador, and Colombia whose works have typically been published only in Spanish. Together, these two books form a substantial and important addition to the literature on Latin American music available in English translation, and particularly so for the Andean region.

As already noted, music scholarship in Peru was especially robust during this review cycle. Studies of contemporary urban popular music in the country, and particularly in Lima, continue to flourish in both number and scope. Carlos Torres Rotondo's study (item **2825**) provides the first new substantial history of Peruvian rock in more than 15 years, joining Pedro Cornejo's earlier work (*HLAS* 64:2726) in tracing the genre's birth and development in Lima in the 1960s and 70s. In prose both punkishly profane and philosophically provocative, North American anthropologist Shane Greene explores the underground world of *subte* music in Lima during the political violence of the 1980s and 90s (item **2812**), offering the first book-length study of Peruvian punk music in the process. José López Ramírez Gastón and Guiseppe Risica Carella (item **2813**) do the same for heavy metal in their joint memoir and reflection on the metal scene in Lima during the identical period. Peruvian journalist José Vadillo Vila (item **2826**) covers a very different form of urban popular music, painting an intimate portrait of the lives and music of eight prominent Andean folk and fusion music performers of the mid- and late 20th century. Ethnomusicologist Pablo Molina Palomino's analysis of the rise and fall of *nueva canción* in Lima in the 1970s and 80s (item **2817**) is an especially important contribution to Peruvian popular music history, ethnographically recovering the story of a once-influential song movement in Peru that has languished in scholarly obscurity for several decades.

Criollo music in Peru, long associated with dominant social classes on the coast, but paradoxically ignored by scholars in comparison with Andean musical traditions, has emerged over the last decade as a significant subject in a new body of interdisciplinary research. That new attention to *criollo* traditions is represented here in several publications, including two new books by Peruvian historian Fred Rohner (items **2820** and **2821**) which upend many of the (mis)conceptions about the class and racial dynamics that gave rise to *criollo* music in Lima in the early 20th century. Rodrigo Sarmiento Herenciaf's study (item **2824**) of musical style in the works of Felipe Pinglo—the "immortal bard" of the *vals limeño* and most prominent of *criollo* songwriters of the early 20th century—is also quite revelatory in uncovering new influences in his well-known works, as well as clarifying claims for his authorship in the contested catalog of popular *criollo* songs. These books, together with Raú Romero's chapter on the iconic singer-songwriter Chabuca Granda (item **2822**) and a recent memoir by the singer and folklorist Alicia Maguiña (item **2814**), provide a much-expanded view for comprehending the history of *criollo* music in Peru, and belong on a shelf with classic works on the topic by authors like Gerard Borras, Rodrigo Chocano, and José Llorens.

Though the role of Afro-Peruvian musicians in the development and performance of *criollo* music is well-documented in the literature just mentioned, the history of Afro-Peruvian and African diasporic music itself has also received significant attention recently. In addition to the Spanish translation of Heidi Feldman's award-winning study of the Afro-Peruvian revival (item **2810**), the publication of a richly illustrated catalog of musical instruments held by the Museo Afroperuano de Zaña in Chiclayo, on Peru's northern coast, makes an important contribution to scholarly understanding of Afro-Peruvian musical history beyond the usual focus on Lima and Chincha (item **2819**). A very different and more recent history of African diasporic influences in Peru is offered in Juan Saldivar Arellano and Juan Pablo Anticona Cebrián's study of Afro-Cuban immigration to Lima beginning in the 1980s (item **2823**), and the intertwined popularity of both salsa music and the santería religion in the neighborhoods in which they settled.

The relative paucity of research on Andean musical traditions during this review cycle is striking, given the long history and prior dominance of such studies in the region. Exceptions include several chapters on Andean folk or popular music in the aforementioned edited volumes on Latin American music (items **2679** and **2680**), Adil Podhajcer's article on *sikuri* music among Bolivian migrants in Buenos Aires (item **2800**), Simón Palominos Mandiola's study of music and dance as forms of knowledge contained in the 18th-century *Trujillo Codex* (item **2818**), and Kirstie Dorr's book on the transnational circulation of Andean musics in the 20th century (item **2809**). The disparity between these few publications and the prior centrality of "Andean music" to scholarship in the region is underscored by Julio Mendívil's monumental new monograph, *Cuentos fabulosos: a invención de la música incaica y el nacimiento de la música andina como objeto de estudio etnomusicológico* (item **2815**), a deeply theorized and broadly informed new history of music scholarship in Andean South America in the 20th century. Included here is what Mendivil terms the "invention" of Incan music and the "birth of Andean music" as a subject for scholarly inquiry, which should be essential reading for anyone with an interest in the intellectual history of the continent.

Though Bolivian publications were few in number during this review cycle, they made a significant and novel contribution to the scholarly understanding of popular music in that country. In particular, Bolivian sociologist Mauricio Sánchez Patzy's *La ópera chola: música popular en Bolivia y pugnas por la identidad social* is a revelation: at nearly 500 pages with a focus on rock and cumbia as well as neo/folklore, and an extensive epilogue on Aymara rap and other musical developments since the election of Evo Morales in 2006, this book truly rewrites and re-imagines the history of Bolivian popular music (item **2801**). Verónica Tejerina Vargas' more focused but ethnographically rich study of hip hop in El Alto and La Paz (*No somos rebeldes sin causa, somos rebeldes sin pausa*) (item **2802**) also extends scholarly knowledge of a popular music scene which has received very little attention to date. Both books, notably, were first drafted as theses for the Universidad Mayor de San Simón in Cochabamba.

Research on music in Colombia, Ecuador, and Venezuela was particularly light, though each country has at least one notable entry. In Colombia, Juan Sebastián Ochoa's critical genealogy of *cumbia* music (item **2804**) quite literally rewrites the genre's history, questioning the periodization and presumed influences that mark popular understanding and even much of the scholarly literature about its origins and development during the early 20th century. In Ecuador, Wilman Ordoñez Iturralde explores the music of the Montubio people of coastal Ecuador in two books (items **2806** and **2808**), introducing musical traditions which have never been substantially researched or written about previously. Though intended primarily as a theoretical intervention for the folkloric study of online performance, John McDowell's article on Latin American music on YouTube (item **2807**) also includes a rare examination of Quichua rap from Otavalo, Ecuador. Finally, Katrin Lengwinat (item **2827**) provides the first critical overview of ethnomusicological research in Venezuela in decades. She traces developments from initial publications to the well-known institution-building efforts of Isabel Aretz and Felipe Ramon y Rivera in the mid-20th century, to a summary of contemporary scholars and university programs today. Published by the Universidad Nacional Experimental de las Artes in Caracas, as part of a larger volume of essays dedicated to research on traditional musics in the country, the article suggests that there is a larger body of Venezuelan ethnomusicological research that is not yet reaching international audiences.

Finally, several articles and books contributed to the long-standing interest in the composition and performance of Western art music in the Andes. Cecilia Wahren (item **2803**) analyzes the changing notions of "Indianness" expressed in nationalist and *indigenista* works from Bolivia in the early 20th century; Raúl Romero (item **2822**) discusses the tensions between nationalism and universalism in the works of German-Peruvian composer Rodolfo Holzmann, including his impact on Peruvian art music and other composers of the mid-20th century; while Renzo Filinich Orozco (item **2811**) traces the institutional influences on Peruvian avant-garde composers of the 1960s and the ultimate impact those cultural and political environments made on their esthetic choices. Last, Tricia Tunstall and Eric Booth (item **2828**) follow up on Tunstall's earlier book about El Sistema in Venezuela (see *HLAS 70:2519*), offering an equally celebratory, but more didactic and prescriptive account of the pedagogical and social goals of the program, and how it is being exported to different locations around the globe.

BOLIVIA

2800 Podhajcer, Adil. Sembrando un cuerpo nuevo: performance e interconexión en prácticas musicales "andinas" de Buenos Aires. (*Rev. Music. Chil.*, 69:223, junio 2015, p. 47–65, bibl.)

A semiotic analysis of *sikuri* panpipe performance, emotion, and embodiment in Buenos Aires. Building on the author's doctoral research on Andean *sikuri* music in Argentina (see also *HLAS 68:2920*), Podjacer traces how musical performance itself plays an important role in creating intercultural experiences and relationships between Argentine participants, Bolivian migrants, and their descendants. Drawing on frame analysis, performance studies, psycho-sociological concepts like flow and *communitas*, as well as Peircian semiotics, Podjacer argues that close ethnographic attention to musical codes and embodied performance details in *sikuri* performances reveals a complex play of shifting meanings and symbols for this music among its varied performers and audiences in Buenos Aires. For comment on a version of this study published in English, see item **2838**.

2801 Sánchez Patzy, Mauricio. La ópera chola: música popular en Bolivia y pugnas por la identidad social. Lima: Instituto Frances de Estudios Andinos; La Paz: Plural Editores, 2017. 454 p.: bibl., ill. (Colección "Travaux de l'Institut français d'études andinas"; 347)

An ambitious and far-reaching study of popular music in Bolivia during the latter half of the 20th century. First written as a sociology thesis in 1999 at the Universidad Mayor de San Simón in Cochabamba, *La Ópera Chola* presents several distinct genre histories—folklore/neofolklore, rock, and cumbia—in order to address broader questions about cultural identity in Bolivia. The chapters on rock and cumbia are especially illuminating, given the scant scholarly attention given to these genres and their audiences in Bolivia to date. An extensive epilogue addresses musical and political developments in the country since the election of Evo Morales in 2006, including the rapid growth of Aymara rap and the revindication of indigenous themes and music(s) as part of nationalist expression.

2802 Tejerina, Verónica. "No somos rebeldes sin causa, somos rebeldes sin pausa": raptivismo: construyendo prácticas de ciudadanía artístico cultural, interculturalidad y educación desde el movimiento hip hop de El Alto y La Paz. La Paz: UMSS Universidad Mayor de San Simón: PROEIB Andes, 2014. 192 p.: bibl., ill.

A rare and long-overdue study of hip-hop culture in Bolivia. Written originally as a master's thesis at the Universidad Mayor de San Simón, the book focuses on rap scenes among youth in the cities of La Paz and El Alto, and ways in which notions of citizenship, interculturality, and education are transformed within them. Drawing on interviews, focus groups, ethnographic fieldwork, and analysis of song lyrics, Tejerina Vargas argues that rap simultaneously creates "urban tribes," providing working class youth with a locus for personal identity formation as well as a social support network, while also opening avenues for political and social activism (i.e. "raptivismo"). As such, hip-hop is a source of new forms of cultural citizenship that break with prior norms in Bolivia.

2803 Wahren, Cecilia. Sonoridades de lo autóctono: la reconfiguración de la indianidad en la construccion de la música folklórica boliviana. (*ANDES Antropol. Hist.*, 1:28, 2017, p. 1–15)

An overview of works by several prominent Bolivian art music composers and *indigenista* folklorists in the early 20th century. Focusing on the music and writings of Antonio González Bravo, Eduardo Caba, and Teófilo Vargas, the author traces how notions of "Indianness" were transformed at this time, incorporated into the nationalist project and its artistic expressions for the first time, but simultaneously marginalized as premodern and "authentic" only insofar as indigenous peoples remained rural, subordinate to other racial and social groups, and perhaps most importantly, anchored in the distant past.

COLOMBIA

2804 Ochoa, Juan Sebastián. La cumbia en Colombia: invención de una tradición. (*Rev. Music. Chil.*, 70:226, dic. 2016, p. 31–52, bibl.)

A critical genealogy of cumbia in Colombia, arguing that a mythologized history of the genre has been constructed to fit with nationalist, political aims of celebrating the country's tri-ethnic, mestizo heritage. Ochoa sketches that various ways that the term "cumbia" has been deployed—often well beyond reference to a single genre—that complicate any single historical narrative about it in the country. He then traces the ways in which this history has nevertheless been reduced and creatively reimagined into a founding myth of cumbia as the "foundational genre of music in the Colombian Caribbean region": one that originated in *gaita* and *flauta de millo*, music of primarily black and indigenous communities, respectively; then passed in a process of musical *mestizaje* to broader, multiracial audiences in the region early in the 20th century via *bandas pelayeras*, small wind ensembles featuring clarinets; and finally moving on to modern dance bands by the mid-20th century when the genre took on national and international importance. Ochoa documents the scarce evidence for this chain of events, and in fact notes that the historical record and logic contradict the first of these links between *gaitas/flauta de millo* music and that of the *bandas pelayeras*. Drawing on theories of collective memory and nationalism, particularly Anderson's notion of "imagined communities," Ochoa argues that the wide acceptance of this mythologized history is rooted in political concerns over the country's racial identity as expressed in both the Constitution of 1886 and its revision in 1991.

2805 Pinto Garia, Maria Elisa. Music and reconciliation in Colombia: opportunities and limitations of songs composed by victims. (*MAIA*, 4:2, 2014, p. 24–51, bibl., map, table)

An insightful study of the possibilities and limitations of peace-building and communal reconciliation via musical composition and performance, based on research conducted in Colombia in 2010. The author argues that music composed by victims of the Colombian conflict played an important and positive role in recovery and reconciliation by enabling singers and audiences to reconstruct and disseminate memories of the conflict, express deeply felt emotions related to the violence, and build new identities and communities of trust in the wake of the conflict. At the same time, songs that addressed controversial topics or promoted memories of the conflict at odds with those of some listeners raised the possibility of inciting revenge and deepening, rather than healing, social divides. The author concludes by noting that grassroots-level musical initiatives for peace and reconciliation merit further study, in Colombia and beyond, but should be approached with both their possibilities and potential limitations in mind. Includes appendices with interview protocols and song lyrics.

Reina Rodríguez, Carlos Arturo. Rock and roll en Colombia: el impacto de una generación en la transformación cultural del país en el siglo XX. See item **1132**.

ECUADOR

2806 Amorfino: canto mayor del montubio.
Introducción, compilación e investigación de Wilman Ordóñez Iturralde. Quito: Casa de la Cultura Ecuatoriana Benjamín Carrión, 2014. 239 p.: bibl. (Colección Yachana saberes; 2)

A longer and more substantial volume than the author's earlier overview of Montubio musical practices from Ecuador's central coast (see item **2808**), this book focuses on a single genre known as the *amorfino* (see also item **2821** for more on this genre in Peru). The first chapter, by Ordóñez Iturralde, offers a general history of music and other oral traditions among the Montubio. Several shorter chapters by other Ecuadorian authors follow, each exploring a different facet of the *amorfino* genre and collectively tracing its development through the 20th century, primarily through the analysis of its lyrics. Roughly half of the book, more than 100 pages, consists of an anthology of *amorfino* song texts.

2807 McDowell, John H. "Surfing the Tube" for Latin American song: the blessings and (curses) of YouTube. (*J. Am. Folk.*, 158:509, 2015, p. 260–272, bibl.)

Using examples from the author's research on *corridos* in Mexico's Costa Chica as well as contemporary Quichua rap in Otavalo, Ecuador, McDowell proposes several new ideas for considering YouTube videos within folklore research. He argues that YouTube videos constitute three different "communicative modalities": an archival modality, in which videos are gathered, stored, and accessed in reference to events that exist beyond the internet site; an "interdependent modality," in which YouTube serves to further the circulation of expressive culture in symbiosis with its offline presence; and a "YouTube-native modality," in which content is generated explicitly for internet diffusion. McDowell further notes that there is an epistemological side of YouTube performances that merits folklorists' attention, particularly the metadata about who uploads content and why, and—especially via the comments sections—who is consuming this media and what they say about it. A short but provocative article for thinking about the role that the online dissemination of expressive culture is playing in Latin America and beyond.

2808 Ordóñez Iturralde, Wilman. Alma montubia: de la música y el baile en el Litoral ecuatoriano. Chimborazo, Ecuador: Casa de la Cultura Equatoriana Benjamín Carrión Núcleo del Chimborazo; Almargen, Ecuador: Shamán Editores, 2012. 87 p.: bibl., music. (Cucayo; 18)

Written and collected by an Ecuadorian scholar, journalist, and dancer, this short book includes normative descriptions of traditional music genres from the Montubio peoples of the central Ecuadorian coast. An appendix contains musical transcriptions of select songs.

PERU

2809 Dorr, Kirstie A. On site, in sound: performance geographies in América Latina. Durham, N.C.: Duke University Press, 2018. 241 p.: bibl., index. (Refiguring American music)

An important new study of Andean music and its transnational flows in the later 20th century, particularly between Peru and the US. Drawing on theoretical literatures from cultural geography, ethnic studies, feminism, and gender studies, Dorr presents four main case studies: the history of the iconic "El Condor Pasa" suite from Peruvian composer Daniel Alomia Robles' 1913 *zarzuela* and its peregrinations to the US and Europe over the century that followed; the rise of Andean subway bands and the "Andean music industry" all over the world in the 1980s and 90s, particularly bands active in California during the author's research; Afro-Peruvian music and the cultural and political activism of prominent performers from the 1950s to the present that include Susana Baca, Victoria Santa Cruz, and Katherine Dunham; and finally, an ethnographic chapter focused on music and political activism at "La Peña del Sur" in Berkeley, California, during a fraught period for Latino/a immigrant rights in the state. Dorr's emphasis on place-making and geography via musical sound, and the social networks such moves entail, is especially novel and will interest scholars from a variety of disciplines across the humanities and social sciences.

2810 **Feldman, Heidi Carolyn.** Ritmos negros del Perú: reconstruyendo la herencia musical africana. Lima: Instituto de Etnomusicología, Pontificia Universidad Católica del Perú: IEP Instituto de Estudios Peruanos, 2009. 343 p.: bibl., ill. (Arte y sociedad; I)

A Spanish translation of Feldman's award-winning *Black rhythms of Peru: reviving African musical heritage in the Black Pacific* (see *HLAS 64:2728*).

2811 **Filinich Orozco, Renzo.** Ta[p]chas: references to indigenous traditions in Peruvian electroacoustic composition of the 1960s. (*Leonardo Music J.*, 27, 2017, p. 93–97, ill., photos)

A brief but useful overview of the esthetic choices, and political and cultural contexts that informed them, made by Peruvian electro-acoustic composers in the mid-20th century. The author highlights the importance of the Centro Latinoamericano de Altos Estudios Musicales in Buenos Aires, where Peruvian composers Edgar Valcárcel and César Bolaños were offered fellowships and composed some of their most important works in the mid-1960s, working alongside some of Latin American's most prominent avant-garde composers. The author also notes the complicated relationship between "revolutionary" and "indigenous" themes these composers' works during the Velasco military government in Peru (1968–75).

2812 **Greene, Shane.** Punk and revolution: seven more interpretations of Peruvian reality. Durham: Duke University Press, 2016. 235 p.: bibl., index

A provocative, profane, and subversively brilliant study of punk music in Peru during and following the Shining Path conflict of the 1980s and 90s. Structuring the book as a dialogue with—or perhaps more accurately, a riff on—Peruvian writer and socialist activist José Carlos Martiategui's seminal *Seven Interpretive Essays on Peruvian Reality* (1928), Greene adopts a punk "voice" to trace the history of Lima's *subte* ("underground") music scene through seven unorthodox chapters. The book is richly illustrated with photos, song lyrics, reproductions of zines, flyers, and other underground publications, as well as Greene's own riotous ethnographic prose rooted in long-term participation in this punk scene. The final chapter dispenses with academic pretense altogether and presents the story of Peruvian punk as a fictional short story, featuring dialogue between characters named "José Carlos" and "Mikhail," who debate the *subte* music scene's distinctive Peruvian origins and flavors while passing by its iconic sites in Lima. Highly recommended, both for the history of an arcane Peruvian musical and cultural phenomenon and for a narrative form that reflects its content.

2813 **López Ramírez Gastón, José Ignacio** and **Guiseppe Risica Carella.** Espíritu del Metal: la conformación de la escena metalera peruana (1981–1992). Lima: Sonidos Latentes Producciones and Discos Invisibles, 2018. 140 p.: ill.

A brief history of heavy metal music in Peru, focused primarily on Lima in the 1980s. The authors, a journalist and professor of music, were both part of the heavy metal scene at the time, and the book is written primarily from their own experiences and for other fans of the genre. Eschewing the conventions of a more academic approach—the book does not include a bibliography, citations, or other evidence of archival or ethnographic research—the authors nonetheless root their history and analysis in bigger questions about class, nationalism, and popular culture at a distinct juncture in Peruvian history. As such, the book goes well beyond mere description, and makes a useful contribution to the growing literature on Peruvian rock. The authors' observations on how class distinctions and political schisms within this largely unknown subgenre played out in the midst of the violence that shattered Peru during the period under discussion are especially noteworthy.

2814 Maguiña, Alicia. Mi vida entre cantos. Lima: Fondo Editorial Universidad San Martín de Porres, 2018. 301 p: ill., photos

A richly illustrated memoir by one of Peru's most acclaimed singers and songwriters. Replete with hundreds of photographs, song texts, musical transcriptions, facsimile reproductions of press articles, quotes from notable Peruvian musicians and scholars, and her own memories of a fascinating artistic life that bridged many of Peru's cultural and social divides beginning in the late 1950s, the book documents Maguiña's unusual career as a performer and composer of both *criollo* and Afro-Peruvian music as well as Andean genres.

2815 Mendívil, Julio. Cuentos fabulosos: la invención de la música incaica y el nacimiento de la música andina como objeto de estudio etnomusicológico. Lima: PUCP, Instituto de Etnomusicología, 2018. 307 p. (Estudios etnográficos; 10)(Travaux de l'Institut français d'études andines; 354)

A rigorous, engaging, and important study of the early history of Andean music scholarship. Drawing on the theories and methods of critical historiography, particularly that of Hayden White and Michel Foucault, Mendívil positions the emergence of scholarship about "Incan music" and debates over its purported pentatonicism within the cultural and political context of central Andean countries (Bolivia, Ecuador, and most prominently, Peru) where it emerged in the late 19th through the mid-20th centuries. Putting this scholarship in conversation with international developments in comparative musicology and early ethnomusicology, Mendívil traces the discursive use of *lo incaico* (the "Incan") through several discrete phases: evolutionist perspectives at the turn of the century; diffusionist theories in the 1930s; nationalist and *indigenista* writings by the mid-century; and finally the turn to more empirically grounded work in the 1960s that separated ethnographic work from historical inquiry into precolonial music. Mendívil's close reading of this scholarship, at once critical and sympathetic, makes this an essential reference work for anyone seeking to understand the development of music scholarship within South America. The author's broader arguments about how history itself is constructed—the "wondrous stories" that historians tell, from tragedies to satires, heroic epics to romances—make it a compelling read for everyone else.

2816 Mendívil, Julio. En contra de la música: herramientas para pensar, comprender y vivir las músicas. Buenos Aires: Gourmet Musical Ediciones, 2016. 221 p.: bibl., index.

An unusual, compelling, personal, and at times polemical book of more than 30 short essays, some just a few pages long, on a wide variety of topics related to music, culture, politics, history, commerce, technology, and more. Written by Peruvian ethnomusicologist Julio Mendívil and drawing on a deep knowledge of more than a century of music scholarship across three continents, the book offers an unorthodox history and explanation of the field of ethnomusicology and what it might contribute to thinking about music in the broadest terms today; it aims to "pluck ethnomusicology from university hallways and take it to a wider public" (p. 18). As such, Mendívil writes "against" music (as the title states) as a static object or universal category, but very much "for" music as a human activity that can help us understand and celebrate the diversity of peoples and cultures in the world. An enjoyable read for anyone who listens to music, and a thought-provoking read for everyone who studies or writes about it.

2817 Molina Palomino, Pablo. Los límites de lo latinoamericano: distinción e identidad en la configuración de un circuito de Nueva Canción en Lima. (*in* Vientos del pueblo: representaciones, recepciones e interpretaciones sobre la Nueva Canción Chilena, Santiago: LOM Ediciones, 2018, p. 327–362, bibl.)

A long-needed research article on the development of *nueva canción* in Peru in the 1970s and 80s. As Peruvian ethnomusicologist Pablo Molina notes in his introduction, research on the song movement has overwhelmingly focused on Cuba and the Southern Cone, to the detriment of understanding its diffusion, history, and impact elsewhere in Latin America. For the Peruvian case, Molina documents the tensions between the predominantly academic, middle-class musicians and audiences for *nueva canción* in Lima, and the working class, Andean migrants they often purported to represent. Case studies of Celso Garrido-Lecca and his Talleres de la Canción Popular (1975–79) in the National Conservatory, the rise of *peñas* catering to this music in the city center in the 1980s, and the 1986 "Week of Latin American Cultural Integration." Molina describes the latter event, which brought many of *nueva canción*'s biggest international artists to Peru, as the moment that also led to the genre's decline and disappearance within the country.

2818 **Palominos Mandiola, Simón.** Entre la oralidad y la escitura: la importancia de la música, danza y canto de los Andes coloniales como espacios de significación, poder y mesitzajes en contextos de colonialidad. (*Rev. Music. Chil.*, 68, julio/dic. 2014, p. 35–57, bibl.)

A deeply theoretical exploration of music and dance as alternate forms of memory and knowledge during the Spanish colonial period in the Andes. Framing the article in relation to coloniality, *mestizaje*, and Derridean *differance*, the author reviews indigenous and mestizo performance practices in the early colonial era before focusing on music, dance, and song genres discussed in Martínez Compañón's *Trujillo Codex*, written in Peru in the late 18th century. Palomino notes the co-presence of indigenous Andean, African, and European influences in the practices detailed in the codex, providing not only evidence for the profound process of *mestizaje* underway in the region, but also the play of power and memory in performances that blurred the boundaries between orality and writing.

2819 **Rocca Torres, Luis; Figueroa, Evelyn; and Sonia Arteaga.** Instrumentos musicales de la diáspora africana y museología: la experiencia del Museo Afroperuano de Zaña. Chiclayo, Perú: Museo Afroperuano, 2012. 169 p.: bibl., ill., photos

Well-illustrated history of Afro-Peruvian musical instruments, and the role of the Afro-Peruvian Museum in Zaña on the northern coast of Peru (Lambayeque department) in the revival of certain instruments and cultural practices in 2012. Chapter 1 presents a concise but quite extensive organology of the African diaspora in Latin America. Chapter 2 narrows the focus to Peru, documenting instruments present historically that have since disappeared, as well as those still extant today; the second half of this chapter presents a historical essay on Afro-Peruvian music, emphasizing the creativity and flourishing cultural world during the slave/colonial era, the "rupture" with traditional practices in the late 19th century through about 1950, listing more than a dozen distinctive Afro-Peruvian instruments that ceased to be made and used during this period, and the revival of Afro-Peruvian music beginning in the 1950s that included both revival of older Peruvian idiophones and the adoption of instruments from elsewhere in the African diaspora. Chapter 3 focuses on local black history in Zaña (much less discussed than Lima and Chincha in the literature on Afro-Peruvian populations), and the role of the Afro-Peruvian Museum, which launched in 2005, in researching instrument history and reconstructing extinct instruments, including drums and a marimba and the checo (gourd), and reinserting them into local musical practices. The concluding chapter by Evelyn Figueroa of the Smithsonian Institute, a consultant for the Zaña Museum, describes the conception and development of the project.

2820 **Rohner, Fred.** La guardia vieja: el vals criollo y la formación de la ciudadanía en las clases populares: estrategias de representación y de negociación en la consolidación del vals popular limeño (1885–1930). Lima: Instituto de Etnomusicología PUCP, 2018. 463 p.: bibl., ill. (Estudios etnográficos; 9)

A monumental new study of the early development of the Peruvian *vals criollo*. Written by Peruvian cultural historian Fred Rohner, originally as a doctoral dissertation for the University of Rennes (France), this book makes a major contribution to the recent body of new research on *música criolla* in Peru. Though certainly a book about music and musical history, it is also a study of class struggle, popular culture, social history, poetics, and Peruvian modernity at the dawn of the 20th century. Among the book's principal conclusions and contributions, Rohner argues that the *vals criollo*'s "old guard"—often mystified as an anonymous collective of working-class musicians—was in fact much more heterogenous in terms of class, ethnicity, and age, and it was in fact their mutual affinity for the *vals* that created new public spaces for musical exchange, from the street to the theater. Rohner further argues that elite musical practices, including the publication of sheet music for salon performance on the piano, was crucial for the genre's popular spread to brass bands and newly introduced *estudiantinas* (string bands), where it was more likely to be heard and played by working class audiences. Most importantly, and distinct from the *vals'* trajectory in other parts of Latin America at the time, the genre opened a space for working class composers and performers to position themselves as patriotic, modern, and culturally sophisticated in a way that would eventually be recognized by the country's elite, who re-adopted the genre first through recordings in the early 20th century, and later through its promotion as the quintessentially *criollo* and Peruvian genre.

2821 Rohner, Fred. Las tradiciones musicales de abajo del puente: una aproximación al universo musical del distrito del Rímac (1850-1950). Lima: Estruendomudo, 2017. 160 p.: bibl., ill.

A large-format, well-illustrated book documenting the musical history and practices associated with the urban Rimac District in Peru's capital city. The author celebrates Rimac as a quintessentially *criollo* or *mestizo* neighborhood in Lima, but one also defined since the 19th century by the presence of Afro-Peruvian and Andean/indigenous practices that constitute an important historical legacy of its *mestizaje* (cultural and racial mixture). Divided into three large sections, the book addresses: 1) the "Afro-Peruvian universe," including a summary history, illustrations, and select musical transcriptions of genres such as Son de los Diablos, *décimas, amorfino, landó, festejo*, and *panalivio*; 2) the "*criollo* universe," including a lengthy discussion of the *zamacueca/marinera* as well as the *vals*; and 3) the "Andean universe," focused exclusively on the *yaravi*, which is surprisingly revealed as among the most popular genres performed in Lima at the turn of the 20th century. The author concludes by noting that Rimac has long been a site of encounter between distinct peoples, cultures, and musical traditions, and thus multicultural from its very origins. Some of the arguments here are expanded in more academic form in Rohner's longer history of the *guardia vieja* (see item **2820**).

2822 Romero, Raúl R. Todas las músicas: diversidad sonora y cultural en el Perú. Lima: Instituto de Etnomusicología PUCP, 2017. 296 p.: bibl. (Estudios Etnográficos; 8)

A collection of 10 essays, written over a period of 30 years, by one of Peru's most insightful and influential scholars of music. Though all the chapters were previously published, their inclusion here in one volume makes several important contributions to music scholarship in and about the country. First, the collection gathers together essays that originally appeared in different languages and in diverse publications, many now long out of print, and puts them back in circulation, in an easily accessible volume that enables students and scholars to appreciate the trajectory of Romero's career. The initial chapters are especially interesting in this regard, consisting of three essays on the history of music scholarship in Peru—first published in 1986, 2002, and 2012—and thus tracing more than a quarter century of music research in the country. The second and third sections of the book, "Identidades y globalización" and "Agentes y lugares," offer seven case studies that illustrate the breadth of Romero's research interests, as well as a fine example of the overlapping interests of music criticism, musicology, and ethnomusicology in much of Latin America. These include essays on traditional and popular music in Peru's central Mantaro Valley, genre histories and ethnographies of cumbia music in Peru, seminal articles on Afro-Peruvian music and the beloved *criolla* singer Chabuca Granda, and even a final chapter on Western art music and nationalism in the country. The book confirms Romero's place not only as an important figure in the cultural affairs of the country—founder of the Instituto de Etnomusicología, the largest and most active archive of traditional music in the Andean region, and founding director of the Escuela de Música at the Pontificia Universidad Católica del Perú, as well as its recently launched graduate program in musicology—but also one of its keenest and most critical scholars. Highly recommended.

2823 Saldivar Arellano, Juan Manuel and **Juan Pablo Anticona Cebrián.** ¡Que viva Changó! Música y religiosidad afrocubanas en el Perú en tres décadas (1980–2010). (*Rev. Cienc. Soc./San José*, 149:23/29, 2015, p. 23–39, bibl.)

A brief history of Cuban cultural, religious, and musical influences in Peru, focused on the intertwined popularity of salsa music and the *santeria* religion since the 1980s. After noting the long presence of Cuban popular music throughout Latin America in the 20th century, the authors trace the impact of successive waves of Cuban migration to the country, beginning with the political crisis in Cuba in 1980 that brought the first significant group of exiles to Peru under government sponsorship. By the early 2000s, these Cuban migrants and their successors had established several *santeria* houses in Lima, which increasingly appealed to both Cuban migrants as well as the Peruvian middle and upper classes, and extended the popularity of salsa music in the Peruvian capital. The authors position these developments in terms of identity formation informed by both migration and transculturation.

2824 Sarmiento Herencia, Rodrigo. Felipe Pinglo y la canción criolla: estudio estilístico de la obra musical del Bardo Inmortal. Lima: Universidad Nacional Mayor de San Marcos, Fondo Editorial: Universidad Nacional Mayor de San Marcos, Facultad de Letras y Ciencias Humanas, 2018. 235 p.

Initially written as a thesis for the Universidad Nacional Mayor San Marcos, this is the first scholarly study of famed *criollo* songwriter Felipe Pinglo's musical style. In the introduction and first chapter, Rodrigo Sarmiento offers a concise history of how Pinglo's music and life have been studied, mythologized, promoted, and more, since his untimely early death in 1936. Later chapters closely analyze Pinglo's music, and the ways in which he set his texts. Close reading allows Sarmiento both to affirm Pinglo's refined poetic sensibility, as well as his affinity for adopting new musical influences, including those from North American popular music, while also questioning the attribution of some songs to Pinglo given the ways in which they depart from his established style. The second half of the book, more than 100 pages, constitutes a single appendix containing Pinglo's complete song lyrics.

2825 Torres Rotondo, Carlos. Demoler: el rock en el Perú 1965–1975. Lima: Planeta, 2018. 395 p.: bibl., ill.

The "definitive edition" of Peruvian journalist and music critic Carlos Torres' early history of rock music in the country, first published in 2009. While the introduction narrates the arrival of rock music to Lima in the late 1950s and early 60s with a focus on the lives and careers of the first pioneer performers, most of the book focuses on the years 1965–75. Divided into two long sections—"Garage y Beat" (p. 63–182) and "Psicodelia, Rock Pesado y Fusión" (p. 183–374)—Torres' narrative consists primarily of oral histories and interview excerpts with individual bands. In the conclusion, he notes that the left-leaning Velasco dictatorship (1968–75) created a difficult environment for rock music fans and musicians in Peru, given the nationalist/populist tenor of the government and its consequent distrust of "Western" and "alienating" music like rock.

2826 Vadillo Vila, José. APUS musicales: héroes de la canción andina peruana. Vol. 1. Lima: Artífice Comunicadores, 2018. 233 p.: bibl., ill., photos.

Written for a broad audience by Peruvian journalist José Valdillo, *Apus Musicales* offers chapter-length biographies of eight prominent Andean musicians in Peru. The selection of artists is intriguing, including "titans" of Peruvian folklore who made their fame in the mid-20th century like Jaime Guardia and Raúl García Zárate, more recent figures who continue to draw large audiences and broad attention to contemporary Andean music in Peru, including the Dúo Gaitán Castro, Amanda Portales, William Luna, and Pelo D'Ambrosio, and popular fusion artists such as Lucho Quequezana and the saxophonist Jean Pierre Magnet. With the exception of Guardia and García

Zárate, the emphasis is primarily on living, well-established, and commercially successful musicians who contribute in different ways to what the author refers to as the *novoandino* (new Andean) sound.

VENEZUELA

2827 Lengwinat, Katrin. Etnomusicología en Venezuela: desarrollo histórico y retos emergentes. (*in* Historia y desafios de la investigación de tradiciones musicales Caracas: Universidad Nacional Experimental de las Artes, 2017, p. 7-21.)

A concise and much-needed overview of the history of ethnomusicology in Venezuela. Lengwinat begins with the first scholarly studies of indigenous music in the country published by Ramón de la Plaza in the late 19th century, through the seminal research, publication, and institution-building work of Isabel Aretz and Luis Felipe Ramón y Rivera in the mid-20th century, ending with a summary of contemporary scholars and their research at various universities in the country today. A final section of the article notes the impact of the political environment in the country since the election of Hugo Chávez in 1999, and the new emphasis on applied research since that time.

2828 Tunstall, Tricia and **Eric Booth.** Playing for their lives: the global El Sistema movement for social change through music. New York: W.W. Norton & Company, 2016. 408 p.: bibl, ill., index

A celebratory account of the rise and spread of Venezuela's El Sistema movement for music education, arguing for its success, not only as an institution and approach for teaching music, but also as a force for creating positive social change in the world. The book is divided into three main sections: the first (chapters 1-3) traces the history of the movement from founder José Abreu's first rehearsal in 1975 in Caracas to its spread throughout Latin American and much of the world in the last few decades; the second (chapters 4-10) explains some of the key features of El Sistema as a pedagogical approach to teaching music and effecting social change; and finally, the third (chapters 11-15) discusses how the model has been adapted to different circumstances around the globe, in terms of community needs, funding sources, and more. The appendices include an international directory of El Sistema-inspired programs, pedagogical and other resources, and a brief set of parameters for defining El Sistema's approach.

SOUTHERN CONE

MICHAEL O'BRIEN, *Assistant Professor of Ethnomusicology, College of Charleston*

MUSIC MAKING IN THE SOUTHERN CONE continues to generate interest among scholars working in a variety of disciplines, including musicology and ethnomusicology, anthropology and sociology, and history. While such disciplinary distinctions are often important in scholars' institutional homes, what is increasingly clear is that interdisciplinarity and theoretical and methodological cross-pollination inform an ever greater number of scholarly approaches to the music of the region. Historical musicologists, even those working in the colonial period, bolstered their analyses by drawing insights from contemporary ethnographic work (item **2852**), and an important "life and works" analysis of contemporary Chilean composer León Schidlowsky (item **2846**) profited from ethnographic interviews with the composer and several disciples. Theoretical frameworks informed by a Deleuzean interest in affect were applied to a variety of musical practices in rural and urban Argentina in a larger and geographically more wide-ranging volume edited by Pabo Vila (items **2831** and **2838**), while a coauthored volume on Peronist political culture in Argentina demonstrated how the history of the senses and sound studies can enrich historiography (items **2829** and **2830**). The latter chapter also reflected the "new materialist" interest in the humanities, which ethno/musicologists in the Southern Cone and elsewhere have used, centering musical instruments and their social lives. Notable examples from the past few years include Adamovsky's aforementioned study of the *bombo peronista*, a new consideration of the importance of the harp in colonial Chile (item **2848**) and Alejandro Vera's intriguing argument for the connection between the colonial *guitarra barroca* and the contemporary Chilean *guitarrón* (item **2852**). Several works grapple with the ramifications of cultural patrimony and the intersection of interests ranging from UNESCO and national cultural heritage projects, the commercial music industry, and individual musicians, both in Argentina (item **2835**) and Uruguay (item **2853**).

Scholarly disciplines were not the only boundaries crossed in this corpus of work. Indeed, perhaps the most unifying trend of the last several years' work is the increasing attention to musical transnationalism in the Southern Cone, and Southern Cone musicians as transnational subjects. In the former category are works that illustrate the ways that even local music cultures in Chile and Argentina are often shaped by international trends and industries (items **2836**, **2842**, **2849**, **2850**, and **2851**). In the latter category are several important studies that focus on individual musicians, demonstrating the ways that Argentine musicians have navigated intra- and international boundaries, developing cosmopolitan and labile identities and esthetics in dialogue with the varied publics that they courted (items **2833**, **2839**, **2840**, and **2841**).

Argentina and Chile continue to have lively and productive, if small, book publishing industries committed to documenting and celebrating their national popular music industries and stars. These volumes are often valuable to scholars, but aimed at a more general audience. In Argentina, Ediciones Disconario has been a prolific source of such volumes, and two recent examples (items **2832** and **2837**) serve as fine examples of what they do best: short, synthetic, readable introductions to some of the most influential *rock nacional* artists, in which those artists themselves participate as interlocutors. In Chile, the Sociedad Chilena del Derecho de Autor has in recent years sought to fill a similar role; a recent biography-in-interviews of Pepe Fuentes (item **2845**) is an illustrative case of the genre. Gourmet Musical Ediciones in Argentina continues to pursue an ambitious and wide-ranging publication schedule encompassing books by and for scholars, journalists, and musicians themselves. The press's books have been widely read and cited by scholars within Latin America, but until recently they have had undeservedly limited distribution in the Anglophone world. One recent volume, Berenice Corti's 2015 *Jazz argentino* (see *HLAS 72:2873*) was awarded the 2017 prize for best non-English language book by the International Association for the Study of Popular Music. One hopes this marks the beginning of a wider audience for this author and this important press.

This gap between the publication output of Southern Cone authors (and Latin American authors more generally) and Global North/Anglophone audiences continues to be a topic of discussion and concern for scholars in and of the region. In a lengthy debate this past year on the e-mail discussion list of the Latin American branch of the International Association for the Study of Popular Music (IASPM-AL), the region's largest professional organization devoted to the topic, many scholars reported struggling with the disconnect between publishing in languages and forums that would be most accessible and relevant to their disciplinary interlocutors, and publishing in formats and venues that are more highly rewarded by their institutional evaluation schema. Ironically, many institutions use ranking systems that incentivize Latin American scholars to publish articles in pay-walled, often prohibitively expensive high-prestige English- language journals rather than in formats (books, open-source digital platforms) and languages (Spanish and Portuguese) that are more accessible to readers in their own countries.

Given this perverse incentive system, it is notable and laudable that several of the highest-profile music journals in the region have maintained a commitment to open-source or Creative Commons digital platforms instead of or in addition to print. In Chile, *Revista Música Chilena* and *Resonancias: Revista de Investigación Musical* both offer this resource, supported by their publishers/host institutions (the Universidad de Chile and the Pontificia Universidad Católica de Chile, respectively). In Argentina, *el oído pensante* is similarly open-source and, in their sixth year of publication, increasingly influential. The journal is supported by CONICET-CAICYT, Argentina's state-funded organization supporting research in the social sciences and humanities. It is with some trepidation, then, that this editor looks toward the immediate future of musical research in Argentina in particular, where since the election of a strongly neoliberal government at the end of 2015, national budgets for research, publication, and teaching have been subject to increasingly brutal cutbacks. The region has been home to innovative, productive scholars of urgent importance to the international scholarly community, and institutional support for their continued success remains both crucial and threatened.

ARGENTINA

2829 Adamovsky, Ezequiel. El bombo peronista. (*in* Marchita, el escudo y el bombo: una historia cultural de los emblemas del peronismo, de Perón a Cristina Kirchner. Edición de Ezequiel Adamovsky y Esteban Buch. Buenos Aires: Planeta, 2016, p. 235–367, bibl.)

A cultural history of the *bombo peronista*, the rope-tuned bass drum that is one of the only symbols of affinity with the Peronist political party to have been adopted "from below" rather than imposed by the party leadership. Adamovsky traces how Peronists gravitated toward the instrument, originally associated mainly with Carnival ensembles (*murgas*) and popular protest and disorder independent of party. The chapter examines several competing claims to having originated the use of bombos in Peronist circles, and offers new evidence, through interviews with a surviving participant, supporting the claims of a *murga* from the southern suburb of Berisso. During the postdictatorship 1980s, the bombo's identity became less partisan as competing political entities also embraced it as a sonic and visual icon of a populist identity.

2830 Buch, Esteban. La marcha peronista. (*in* Marchita, el escudo y el bombo: una historia cultural de los emblemas del peronismo, de Perón a Cristina Kirchner. Edición de Ezequiel Adamovsky y Esteban Buch. Buenos Aires: Planeta, 2016, p. 75–234, bibl.)

A cultural history of *Los muchachos peronistas*, popularly known as "*la marchita*" (the little march) by followers of Juan D. Perón's Justicialist party. Buch traces the song's uncertain origins and evolution through various lyrical and musical transformations, from the melody's probable origin in the fan club of a local soccer team, to its consecration in the iconic recording by Hugo del Carril, to its proscription during the dictatorship to its rebirth and memeification during the Kirchner administrations. A welcome, detailed analysis of an understudied and crucial piece of Argentine musical and political culture.

2831 Citro, Silvia and **Adriana Cerletti.**
The embodiment of *gozo*: aesthetics, emotion, and politics in the indigenous song-dances of the Argentine Chaco. (*in* Music, dance, affect, and emotions in Latin America. Edited by Pablo Vila. Lanham,

Md.: Lexington Books, 2017, p. 39–68, bibl., ill.)

An analysis of two round dances of the indigenous Toba/Qom people of the Argentine Chaco: the *nmi*, a courting dance popular among the youth prior to the introduction of evangelical Christianity in the early 20th century, and the *rueda*, an evangelical dance. Although contemporary community elders reject the *nmi* because of its connection to pre-Christian shamanism, Citro and Cerletti argue that the two dances are connected not only in their formal musical choreographic and musical structures, but also their association with the experience of *gozo*, or pleasure. Furthermore, the *rueda* dance became the field for a generational dispute between the church leaders and the Toba youth, for whom the *rueda* functioned as a way to contest their power relationship with their elders.

Citro, Silvia and **Soledad Torres Agüero.** Las músicas amerindias del Chaco argentino entre la hibridación y la exotización. See *HLAS 73:371.*

2832 **Dente, Miguel Angel; Gaguine, Daniel;** and **Matías Recis.** 50 años rock: 50 bandas argentinas fundamentales. Buenos Aires: Ediciones Disconario, 2016. 1 vol: ill.

A rock critic's introduction to the most important bands in Argentine rock history, presented chronologically. Part of a series that otherwise focuses on soloists, this slender volume features the most important album or albums by a rock band for each year from 1967 to 1985. In each case, the authors present a brief history of the band, list of significant performances, and discography. Most interestingly, they also include contemporary interviews with members of each featured ensemble, allowing compelling glimpses into personal biography and the context in which these iconic albums were created. Most likely to be of use to casual readers and non-specialists as an introduction to the genre.

2833 **Karush, Matthew Benjamin.** Musicians in transit: Argentina and the globalization of popular music. Durham: Duke University Press, 2017. 268 p.: bibl., ill., index.

Separate chapters trace the creative output and reception of seven of Argentina's most popular musicians on the world stage, examining the ways in which international markets and various forms of identity formations (local, national, regional, ethnic, and racial) shaped audience expecations for Argentine musicians making music in an international context over the course of the 20th century. Karush examines jazz musicans Oscar Alemán, Lalo Schifrin, and Gato Barbieri, folk singer Mercedes Sosa, tango iconoclast Astor Piazzolla, *balada* star Sandro, and the genre-hopping producer/composer/guitarist Gustavo Santoalalla. Taken together, their varied careers tell a compelling and coherent story about the shifting valence of *argentinidad* in the global culture industry.

Kerber, Alessander. Carlos Gardel e Carmen Miranda: representações da Argentina e do Brasil. See item **2910**.

2834 **Liska, María Mercedes.** El arte de adecentar los sonidos: huellas de las operaciones de normalización del tango argentino, 1900–1920. (*Lat. Am. Music Rev.*, 35:1, Spring/Summer 2014, p. 25–49, bibl.)

During the first two decades of the 20th century, the tango underwent substantial changes in its lyrical and choreographic practices, which correspond to tango's growing acceptance among Argentina's middle and elite classes. While these processes, through which the tango became "decent," (acceptable to the bourgeoisie) have been well studied, this article addresses the more typically overlooked changes in the musical practices of tango that occurred during the same time. In keeping with the nation-building processes obsessed with bodily excess as an anti-hygenic practice, tango music gravitated toward norms that were less conducive to ebullient and particularly erotic bodily performance. Specifically, tempos became slower and muscians sought to eliminate the practice of musical breaks, which encouraged especially scandalous movements such as *cortes* and *quebradas*.

2835 **Luker, Morgan James.** The tango machine: musical culture in the age of expediency. Chicago; London: The University of Chicago Press, 2016. 218 p.: bibl., index. (Chicago studies in ethnomusicology)

Effectively an ethnographic account of tango's intersection with the national and international culture industries, this work seeks to account not so much for what tango is, as what tango is good for. Luker casts a wide net, examining a number of key players, producers, and gatekeepers in the early 21st-century tango scene in Buenos Aires: nonprofit arts organizations, the metropolitan government, influential bands seeking to reframe tango as a contemporary, anti-commercial music of the people, and UNESCO, who recognized tango as part of the intangible cultural heritage of humanity in 2009.

Menezes, Andreia dos Santos. Pandeiros e bandoneones: vozes disciplinadoras e marginais no samba e no tango. See item **2924**.

2836 Palomino, Pablo. The musical worlds of Jewish Buenos Aires, 1910–1940. (*in* Mazal Tov, amigos! Jews and popular music in the Americas. Edited by Amalia Ran and Moshe Morad. Leidon: Brill, 2016, p. 25–43)

Drawing mainly on archival sources at the Idisher Visnshaftlejer Institut in Buenos Aires, Palomino paints a portrait of various facets of musical life among the Jewish populations in Argentina during the early 20th century. The article stretches from the private music studio of a teacher in rural Entre Rios province to the Jewish musical associations of the capital city. The documents tell a story of a population that is thoroughly cosmopolitan. Even in the isolated agricultural *entrerriano* piano teacher's studio, one finds that students mainly learned an international repertoire of songs published by North American Hebrew music publishers, themselves an agglomeration of Eastern European immigrants. The musical associations in Buenos Aires sought to bring musical culture to the local Jewish people, but did not restrict themselves to strictly Jewish repertoire. Rather, they "disseminated a musical ideology that was at once nationalist, universal, and populist" including European art music, and both high- and lowbrow productions of music from the New World.

2837 Petruccelli, Alejandro. Miguel Cantilo, huellas luminosas. Buenos Aires: Ediciones Disconario, 2016. 183 p.: discography, ill. (Portarretratos)

A conversational volume that bridges the gap between biography and autobiography, the author engages Miguel Cantilo, founder of the Argentine rock band Pedro y Pablo in a series of reminiscences that range from his childhood musical influences to the personal circumstances under which the influential band wrote and recorded their work. Petruccelli provides a structure and framing set of questions that elicit a candid and engaging portrait of the artist in his own words. Likely to be of interest mainly to fans of the band and scholars of Argentine rock music.

Podhajcer, Adil. Sembrando un cuerpo nuevo: performance e interconexión en prácticas musicales "andinas" de Buenos Aires. See item **2800**.

2838 Podhajcer, Adil. Traditional sonorous poetics: ways of appropriation and perception of "Andean" music and practices in Buenos Aires. (*in* Music, dance, affect, and emotions in Latin America. Edited by Pablo Vila. Lanham, Md.: Lexington Books, 2017, p. 69–86, bibl.)

This chapter, based on ethnographic particpant-observation among five *bandas de sikuris* (indigenous panpipe ensembles) in Buenos Aires, examines the ways in which groups of participants with different socioeconomic and ethnic identities ("traditionalists," typically indigenous working class migrants, and "hippies," predominantly white university students) understand the practice of ensemble playing to iconically represent and produce a utopian "Andean" community. For comment on a version of this study published in Spanish, see item **2800**.

2839 Ran, Amalia. Tristes alegrías: Jewish presence in Argentina's popular music arena. (*in* Mazal Tov, amigos! Jews and popular music in the Americas. Edited by Amalia Ran and Moshe Morad. Leidon: Brill, 2016, p. 44–59)

Unlike the companion piece in the same volume (see item **2836**), Ran's chapter focuses not on Jewish musicians' activity within the Jewish community, but rather on Jewish musicians active in the wider sphere of Argentine popular music. The chapter summarizes the already well-documented influence of Jewish musicians in the early decades of the tango, where they were one of many marginalized communities who participated in its development. More unique in the literature, though, is the lengthy discussion of Isaco Abitbol, a Sephardic Jew born in Corrientes province who became known as the "patriarch of chamamé." Abitbol, became an influential participant as the local genre rose to national prominence as mass-mediated folklore and rural populations alike enjoyed the support of the Perón regime from 1945–55.

2840 **Viladrich, Anahí.** More than two to tango: Argentine tango immigrants in New York City. Tucson: University of Arizona Press, 2013. 250 p.: bibl., ill.

Less a study of tango per se than a sociological analysis of an immigrant community in New York for whom working as tango dance teachers or musicians provides a crucial form of social capital. Vildarich examines the ways in which tango provides entrée into everything from income to free or low-cost medical care, but also considers the ways in which other factors ranging from phenotype, regional accent, age, and legal status shape the kinds of access and limitations that this population faces. While this work engages only peripherally with the musical practices of tango, it provides a fascinating ethnographic window into a key node in the tango diaspora that is both crucial and often overlooked in the literature.

2841 **Wohl, Lillian M.** Gypsy, cumbia, cuarteto, surf, blah blah blah: Simja Dujov and Jewish musical eclecticism in Argentina. (*in* ¡Mazal Tov, amigos! Jews and popular music in the Americas. Edited by Amalia Ran and Moshe Morad. Leiden: Brill, 2016, p. 171–187)

Wohl examines the career and musical output of Simja Dujov, an Argentine singer, multi-instrumentalist and DJ of Jewish descent, exploring the ways in which Dujov's work crosses boundaries of genre, ethnicity, and nationality depending on the context. Dujov at times chooses to embrace postnational, cosmopolitan musical esthetics: at times he, as a public figure, and his music are audibly and visibly marked as Jewish; at other times his Jewishness recedes to become irrelevant. Likewise, his identity as a Latin American is prevalent in some, but not all contexts. This subject-centered ethnography illustrates a canny and articulate musician who is flexibly able to deploy a wide variety of identities and a wide variety of musical resource, to a diverse and international range of audiences and contexts.

CHILE

2842 **Álvarez Hernández, Orlando.** Ópera en Chile: ciento ochenta y seis años de historia, 1827–2013. Santiago: Aguilar Chilena de Ediciones, 2014. 597 p.: bibl., index.

A careful compilation of data tracing the performance of opera in Chile, from the first traveling troupes of Europeans who performed excerpts in Valparaíso, to the founding of the Teatro Municpal in Santiago, through the year of the author's death. The work is unapologetically celebratory and nationalistic, the work of a devoted music enthusiast and critic better known as a legal scholar and jurist. Future researchers will find especially valuable the appendices, which include an exhaustive list of the repertoire and main performers organized by year from 1830 to 2013.

2843 **Cantos Cautivos.** Compiled and edited by Katia Chornik. Santiago: Museo de la Memoria y los Derechos Humanos, s.d. <https://www.cantoscautivos.org/en/index.php>

An ambitious, bilingual multimedia website dedicated to documenting the lives of political prisoners during Chile's military dictatorship (1973–90). The site includes oral history testimonies from more than 100 survivors of detention centers. Many of the testimonies are centered around the role of music and music-making in the lives of the imprisoned. Each testimony is accompanied by in-line streaming audio or video; while these recordings are not generally from the camps themselves, but rather period commercial recordings, they demonstrate the ways in which folk, popular, and other musical recordings, even if only accessible through memories, played an integral part in prisoners' survival and resistance.

2844 **Carreño Bolívar, Rubí.** Av. Independencia: literatura, música e ideas de Chile disidente. Santiago: Editorial Cuarto Propio, 2013. 242 p.: bibl. (Ensayo/Literatura)

An intensely personal book, celebrating and evaluating what the author identifies as dissident works by Chilean musicians and other artists since the mid-20th century, particularly during the Pinochet dictatorship. The first chapter focuses primarily on works by Violeta Parra and Diamela Eltit, noting how broader communities of resistance were formed and strengthened through their artistic work. A second chapter highlights the role of pleasure in work and dissidence, tracing how political action took place alongside and within cultural practices in Chile that included singing, dancing, and listening to genres like the urban *cueca* or *cumbia*, as well as emblematic works of *nueva canción* like Luis Advis' *Cantata Popular de Santa Maria de Iquique*. The third chapter focuses on exile and displacement, highlighting academic, literary, and artistic work that happened abroad during the dictatorship, as well as activities and artistic work by non-Chileans in solidarity with those living under the Pinochet regime. A brief portion of this chapter also addresses the contemporary Mapuche movement and their historical displacement. The final chapter examines artistic practices of memory today, including student marches, literature, and recent popular music. [J. Ritter]

2845 Fuentes, Pepe. A la pinta mia: versos, viajes y memorias de la música chilena. Entrevistas y edición de David Ponce. Santiago: Sociedad Chilena del Derecho de Autor (SCD), 2014. 199 p.: bibl., ill. (Colección nuestros músicos)

Music journalist David Ponce has organized a sort of dialogic autobiography, weaving together selections of interviews between Fuentes and many of his musical collaborators. Fuentes' musical career is wide-ranging in chronology and genre. He is perhaps best known as a guitarist of the influential *música típica* ensemble Fiesta Linda during the 1950s, and later as leader of Los Pulentos de la Cueca, one of the groups responsible for the urban cueca revival of the 1980s, but Fuentes also had a very active, and lesser known, career as a sideman, session musician, and producer. This volume is a finely grained and personal glimpse into that multifaceted and influential career.

2846 Fugellie, Daniela. León Schidlowsky, Premio Nacional de Artes Musicales 2014: perspectivas de su trayectoria artística en Chile, Israel y Alemania. (*Rev. Music. Chil.*, 69:224, dic. 2015, p. 11–36, bibl.)

The most general and wide-reaching of a number of articles in a special journal issue dedicated to the prolific Chilean composer León Schidlowsky on the occasion of his being named recipient of the Premio Nacional de Artes Musicales. Informed by interviews with the composer and with several of his students, Fuglielle traces the biographical contour of his life and works, from his formative years in Chile, including the influence of expressionism, pan-Latin American experimentalism, and leftist Zionist political ideology, to his tenure as one of the first avant-garde composers in the burgeoning art music scene in 1960s Israel to his later years in Germany, where like his expressionist forbears he also began experimenting with the plastic arts.

2847 González R., Juan Pablo. A mi ciudad: esucha crítica en la construcción simbólica del Santiago de 1980. (*Rev. Music. Chil.*, 70:226, dic. 2016, p. 9–30, bibl.)

Focusing on the first and best-known popular song about the city of Santiago written in the 1980s, González demonstrates how popular songs create meaning intertextually. "A mi ciudad," by Luis Lebert and Santiago del Nuevo Extremo, is a song that contributed to the popular imaginary of the city as alienated and suffering through both a repressive military dictatorship and neo-liberalism. The song's anti-hegemonic message is legible not mainly through its lyrics, but rather through a consideration of a variety of "texts" including the song's harmonic and formal design, the visual texts that accompanied its publication and dissemination (the song was published as a series of lyrics and chords in a popular magazine two years before the album's release, partially to circumvent censors). A valuable contribution not only as a case study for scholars of Chilean popular music, but as an example of a contemporary theoretical and methodological approach to popular musicology.

2848 Martínez García, Gonzalo and José Miguel Ramos. Nuevos antecedentes para el estudio del arpa en la periferia colonial chilena. (*Rev. Music. Chil.*, 69:224, dic. 2015, p. 125–141, bibl.)

Recognizing and attempting to correct for Chilean musicology's historical bias toward studying predominantly the musical life of its capital city, the authors build a case for understanding rural Chile during the colonial period as full of musical life as well. Recognizing the substantial obstacles that such a project entails (a dearth of archives in the rural regions, losses due to natural disasters, lower degree of literacy during the colonial period, etc.), the authors build a strong case through archival records of churches and landowners, demonstrating that the harp played an important role in the musical lives of the elites both in church and domestic settings throughout the colonial period, and suggest, furthermore, that it may have offered a means of upward social mobility for lower-class musicians.

2849 Mularski, Jedrek. Mr. Simpático: Dean Reed, pop culture, and the Cold War in Chile. (*Music Polit.*, 8:1, Winter 2014, bibl.)

This article traces the reception in Chile of American pop singer Dean Reed. During the early 1960s, the pop icon was widely beloved by middle-class Chilean youth culture, and the popularity of his songs, largely apolitcal and about young love, cut across political boundaries. By the early 1970s, Reed had become more outwardly political in both his private and personal life, critcizing the US involvement in Vietnam and expressing sympathy for President Salvador Allende's Undidad Popular government. As a result, the Chilean right abandoned and harshly criticized Reed, while leftists had a more lukewarm and skeptical response. For the Chilean left, Reed's claims of affinity for socialism were inextricably at odds with the commercially friendly, North American pop stylings of his musical output.

2850 Purcell Torretti, Fernando and **Juan Pablo González.** Amenizar, sincronizar, significar: música y cine silente en Chile, 1910–1930. (*Lat. Am. Music Rev.*, 35:1, Spring/Summer 2014, p. 88–114, bibl.)

This article traces the changing practices of live musical accompaniment to silent film during the early decades of the 20th century. While the authors focus primarily on the urban centers of Chile, they observe that the practices were strongly influenced by the similarly evolving industry in the US. In the first two decades of the 1900s, the newly emergent art form of silent moving pictures demanded new practices on the part of its audiences, and a new cultural consensus over appropriate behavior in public space. During this period, music served primarily to cover other more disruptive forms of audience noise, and to discipline audiences toward silent listening, an unusual practice in the consumption of other media. By the late 1910s, music became a more central part of the moviegoing experience, and film showings "enlivened" by popular musicians became a key strategy by which competing theaters were able to attract audiences. During the 1920s, the Chilean film industry embraced the growing importance of specific music composed for the film in question, which demanded not only new repertoire, but also new forms of distribution, such as cue sheets designed to assist live musicians in synchronizing their performance with a recorded film. The authors trace the particular importance of a 1924 manual for theater musicians by the Hungarian composer/pianist/director Erno Rapée in shaping the ways Chilean musicians learned to make thematically appropriate choices regarding repertoire and performance not only in order to "enliven," but to communicate meaning through the music.

2851 Sánchez Mondaca, Maximiliano. Thrash metal: del sonido al contenido: origen y gestación de una contracultura chilena. Santiago: RIL Editores, 2014. 168 p.: ill.

A sociological study, based largely in a Gramscian theoretical framework, of the emergence of a local thrash metal scene in Chile during the last years of the Pinochet regime. Sánchez Mondaca argues that, in the context of a repressive military dictatorship which actively, and even violently, supressed any expressions that challenged the hegemonic cultural order, the concept of *counterculture* is more appropiate than the more common *subculture* to understand the risky and inevitably political venture of creating thrash metal. The author traces the history of related antecedent genres including punk and heavy metal, and considers the constitutive elements of the genre, including not only sonic and lyrical content, but the performative elements of fan culture.

2852 **Vera, Alejandro.** La música entre escritura y oralidad: la guitarra barroca, el guitarrón chileno y el canto a lo divino. (*Rev. Music. Chil.*, 70:225, junio 2016, p. 9–49, bibl.)

Vera draws on archival sources, formal analysis of song texts, and secondary ethnographic sources to examine the relationship between the *guitarra barroca*, an instrument of five double courses of strings that was widely distributed in both rural and urban areas in Chile during the colonial period, and the 25-string Chilean *guitarrón*, used today to accompany both sacred and secular poetry (*canto a lo divino* and *canto a lo humano*, respectively). Vera proposes a new hypothesis to account for both the design of the guitarrón and the performance practices of *canto a lo divino*, in which non-metred modalism predominate. Earlier work argued that the guitarrón's additional strings, a novelty among colonial instruments, could be attributed to the influence of indigenous musical esthetics, which favored complex timbres and dense harmonics, while the modalism could be understood as a retention of Renaissance practices. Vera suggests that both factors are more intuitively explained by the evidence that the guitarrón was developed out of the guitarra barroca in order to accompany psalmodic recitation in liturgical contexts. The additional strings would have produced a timbre more similar to that of the organ, and the prevalence of mixolydian mode and particular melodic tropes in *canto a lo divino* mirrors the melodic practices of psalmody.

PARAGUAY

Otaegui, Alfonso. Le tamis triste des chants: sur les traductions altérées des événements chez les Ayoreo du Chaco paraguayen. See *HLAS 73:386*.

URUGUAY

2853 **Patrimonio vivo de Uruguay: relevamiento de Candombe.** Edición y corrección de Helvecia Pérez. Montevideo: UNESCO, Organización de las Naciones Unidas para la Educación, la Ciencia y la Cultura, Comisión Nacional del Uruguay para la UNESCO: Ministerio de Educación y Cultura-MEC, 2015. 264 p.: bibl., ill. (Patrimonio vivo de Uruguay)

A study commissioned on the occasion of candombe's recogntion as Intangible Cultural Heritage of Humanity in 2009, this multi-authored work provides a wide-ranging snapshot of the practices of contemporary candombe in both its historical birthplace of Montevideo and throughout the nation. A first section, drawing largely on the work of Lauro Ayestarán, provides an excellent synthesis of the historiography of candombe, while later chapters draw on more than 100 group and individual ethnographic interviews with candombe dancers, musicians, and directors. The authors identify crucial issues involving the changing social context and significance of candombe in the present, including the role of identity politics and Afro-Uruguayan cultural practices in national narratives, the influence of formalized competition, and the diffusion of local styles outside of their historical neighborhoods.

BRAZIL

ROGÉRIO BUDASZ, *Professor of Music, University of California, Riverside*

IN THE MIDST of never-ending political turmoil, scholarly research on Brazilian music continues to display vitality. This review includes publications from 2014 to 2017 that demonstrate originality, relevance, and depth. A number of publications from previous years have also been included in this section to address important omissions. Only a handful of the many journalistic biographies released during this period are listed, and the selection of scholarly journal articles on Brazilian music is particularly stringent. Because of the large number of articles published in recent years, I approach a number of full journal issues as individual entries, enticing readers to explore these venues on their own. Summarizing the coverage of ethnomusicology and popular music studies, more research appeared on *samba* than on funk, rap, and Northeastern styles. In musicology we see more interest in Villa-Lobos and nationalism than in avant-garde or even 19th-century music. Areas or fields that, although not really booming, remain attractive for researchers include *choro* and *sertanejo*, along with issues of national representation. Approaches or methods that are slowly but steadily growing include gender studies, applied or public scholarship, history and memory, and historical ethnomusicology—the latter often overlapping with the musicology of early popular and traditional music. This essay highlights texts that reveal some trends in the scholarly research on the music of Brazil, published either in Brazil or abroad. These texts emerge primarily from the disciplinary fields of ethnomusicology, musicology, and popular music studies—the latter also including perspectives from language studies, literature, sociology, and history.

In 2015, the publishing house Cosac & Naify released a long overdue Portuguese translation of Anthony Seeger's 1987 study on Lowland indigenous music of South America (item **2947**). Updated with two texts addressing the reception of the book and the multidimensional changes that occurred since 1987, this superb publication also includes a DVD with audio and video files. Another landmark for Brazilian ethnomusicology is the special edition of the journal *The World of Music* (item **2957**), which published an almost simultaneous Portuguese version in book format (item **2892**). These works contain multi-authored essays on a number of collaborative projects and urge ethnomusicologists to continue developing decolonizing methods. Research on the music of indigenous peoples of Brazil has produced a number of intriguing texts that focus on the body as a vector in strategies of listening and performing (items **2923** and **2927**), including, but not restricted to, contexts of spirit possession. This approach also resonates with research on Afro-Brazilian practices (items **2854** and **2900**), including black Catholicism (item **2908**) and *samba de roda* (item **2905**). Suzel Ana Reily demonstrates how the articulation of memory, esthetics, and community engagement creates a space of resistance against the homogenizing policies of the Catholic Church (item **2939**). This chapter is part of a landmark publication that Reily has organized with Javier F. León, *The Oxford Handbook of Music and World Christianities*, which also includes a focused chapter by Glaura Lucas on drumming in Catholic festivals supported by historical sources and theoretical considerations (item **2915**). One aftereffect of the work by Reily, Lucas, Iyanaga, and Alge (items **2857** and **2858**) is the effective way in which bridges and overlaps are being created between the fields of ethnomusicology and historical musicology. Conversely, ethnomusicologists and other humanities scholars have explored the symbiosis between culture industry and Northeastern and Amazonian traditions (items **2883**, **2890**, and **2898**), while *capoeira* has been scrutinized with music-theoretical tools (item **2884**) and Brazilian lullabies analyzed from a sociocultural perspective (item **2917**).

The proceedings of an international conference cosponsored by the CESEM/Universidade Nova de Lisboa and Universidade de São Paulo include original perspectives of early 19th-century musical practices and artists of both Brazil and

Portugal (item **2881**). Likewise, a number of papers delivered at a pioneering conference on music iconography, which took place in Salvador, have been published in book format (item **2891**). Among the most innovative studies on the so-called colonial music of Brazil is Paulo Castagna's intriguing study on the reception of André da Silva Gomes (item **2877**). Diósnio Machado Neto provides two convincing takes on rhetorical devices in the music of José Maurício Nunes Garcia (items **2918** and **2919**), and Mariana Portas de Freitas has published an excellent study on irreconcilable differences between theorists and performers as they surface in a polemic in 18th-century Bahia (item **2897**). Using a strongly theoretical foundation, Norton Dudeque analyzes the selective incorporation of Wagnerian techniques by Leopoldo Miguéz on a work inspired by republican ideals (item **2886**), while Ana Luiza Martins offers a fresh look at another nationalist composer and also a Wagnerian, Alberto Nepomuceno, in a study on the social, musical, and even political polarization of the *modinha* in Fortaleza (item **2921**). Two excellent texts that also address this vibrant space between "art" and "popular" music are Denise Fonseca's work on musical theater in São Paulo c. 1880–1910 (item **2896**) and Carlos Pereira's pioneering study on music in silent film in Rio de Janeiro (item **2934**).

An important development in Brazilian musicology during the past five years has been the consolidation of a field of Villa-Lobos studies, encompassing a range of theoretical and esthetic approaches, cultural phenomena, political issues, and ethnic considerations. Several Villa-Lobos scholars are active around the country; two competing Villa-Lobos conferences are celebrating their third iteration in São Paulo and Rio de Janeiro (items **2950**, **2951**, and **2952**); and an excellent reader has been just released (item **2956**). Moreover, accompanying the development of the discipline of musicology, scholars have reformulated questions (item **2861**) and used new methods (item **2936**) to convey a better understanding of the meaning and significance of Villa-Lobos in Brazilian culture. Updated and contextualized perspectives on Villa-Lobos and other figures of 20th-century Brazilian music have also been presented at recent conferences of the American Musicological Society, regional and international meetings of the International Musicological Society, and an international conference in Spain (item **2888**). A renewed interest on musicologist Francisco Curt Lange stimulated important studies of his ideology and interactions with nationalist intellectuals and artists (items **2864**, **2872**, **2681**, and **2911**). Likewise, Mário de Andrade returns to center stage with a critical and beautiful new edition of his *O turista aprendiz* (item **2859**), in addition to three articles in a special issue of a significant Danish journal of Brazilian Studies (item **2871**). Hopefully signaling a new reality, rather than just a trend, a number of prestigious Brazilian journals in the humanities have been particularly generous in their coverage of popular music (items **2840**, **2841**, **2962**, and **2963**).

Issues of nation and representation also permeate a number of studies in urban popular music. These include texts on foundation narratives and competing historiographies of samba (items **2868**, **2882**, **2912**, **2922**, **2928**, **2931**, and **2932**), representations of *sertão* (items **2913** and **2948**), and of regional and ethnic types in samba and tango (items **2910** and **2924**). Mainstream and regional variants of *choro* are explored in studies of early recordings (item **2860**), Garoto (item **2880**), Canhoto (item **2889**), Porto Alegre (item **2870**), and Curitiba (item **2935**). Politics and censorship during the military rule set the tone for a number of studies of *bossa nova* (item **2925**), *clube da esquina* (item **2885**), Wilson Simonal (item **2895**), and 1960s counterculture (item **2887**). Scholarship on Tom Jobim, and by extension *bossa nova*, gained new insights with two exceptional volumes of collected essays edited by Italian scholars Stefano La Via, Claudio Cosi, and Luca Bacchini (items **2920** and **2869**). Issues of race and ethnicity, although not completely absent from reviewed texts on samba and *choro*, are central to studies of the 1970s Black Rio movement (item **2933**), *pagode baiano* (item **2937**), rap (item **2953**), and funk (items **2868** and **2954**). Likewise, issues of gender guide discussions on Carmen Miranda (items **2867** and **2904**), female bands in Florianópolis and Rio de Janeiro (item **2902**), and the Latin American romantic ballad (item **2675**).

2854 Afolabi, Niyi. Ilê Aiyê in Brazil and the reinvention of Africa. New York: Palgrave Macmillan, 2016. 288 p.: bibl., index. (African histories and modernities)

Following the trajectory of Salvador's most influential *bloco afro*, the author argues that Ilê Aiyê deploys *carnival* as a "critical agency for advancing black pride and dignity." The book also explores contradictory discourses that emerge from the group's initiatives, such as the production of beauty pageant contests to advance an ideal of black beauty. Chapter 7 covers the politics of Afro-carnival music, describing Ilê Aiyê's various ensembles, analyzing the sociopolitical and educational content of their songs, and examining their interaction with the music business. The author takes a more critical stance in the last chapter, arguing that Afro-Brazilian Carnival should focus on the ultimate goal of gaining political power rather than solely resorting to cultural cosmetics and symbolic mediation (p. 228).

2855 O alcance da canção: estudos sobre música popular. Organização de Luís Augusto Fischer e Carlos Augusto Bonifácio Leite. Porto Alegre, Brazil: Arquipélago Editorial, 2016. 391 p.: bibl., ill.

Collected essays on popular song by authors from Rio Grande do Sul. Chapters cover early samba, bossa nova, Gal Costa, Caetano Veloso, manguebeat, and various genres of *gaucho* music, mostly from the perspective of literary criticism. Some authors develop a more integrated approach, taking into account text, music, performance, and production. Leandro Ernesto Maia delivers a multifaceted analysis of Caetano Veloso's song "O quereres," Carlo Pianta explores João Gilberto's technique and interpretive style, and Caroline Soares de Abreu discusses Gal Costa's performance of Chico Buarque's "Folhetim." Concentrating on production and distribution, Katia Suman examines the role of *jabá* (payola) in the formation of audiences during the past four decades. Closing the book, Luciana Prass brings an ethnomusicologist's perspective on the integration of popular music in academia.

2856 Alexandre, Ricardo. Cheguei bem a tempo de ver o palco desabar: 50 causos e memórias do rock brasileiro (1993–2008). Porto Alegre, Brazil: Arquipélago Editores, 2013. 255 p.: index.

Journalist Ricardo Alexandre tells 50 short stories on the rise and fall of Brazilian rock of the 1990s and early 2000s. The "falling stage" mentioned in the title is both a reference to an actual event and a metaphor to the shrinking relevance of the genre and the dismantling of the recording industry during the period. A useful index complements the book.

2857 Alge, Barbara. Kolonialmusik aus Minas Gerais als Ideologem. (*in* Musikwissenschaft: die Teildisziplinen im Dialog. Edited by Ruth Seehaber. Halle, Germany: Martin-Luther-University, 2016, p. 1–9, music)

This short essay revisits a number of narratives constructed around *Mineiro* music (i.e., *barroco, colonial, mulato*), following a revisionist trend that has gained traction in recent years. Applies Bakhtin's concept of ideologeme (as adapted by Jameson) to explain the universe of practices, representations, and politico-institutional initiatives that converge around the idea of *música colonial mineira* ultimately to "promote certain values and support the claim to power of certain social groups." See also *HLAS 70:2705*.

2858 Alge, Barbara. Música nos tempos coloniais: um olhar a partir da prática musical em Minas Gerais hoje. (*Música Contexto*, 11:1, out. 2017, p. 143–171, bibl.)

This article is partly new, and partly an expansion of the author's 2016 article on *Mineiro* music, without explicitly resorting to the ideologeme argument. The author adds her impressions from field work in Caeté, as a participant of the Festival of Nossa Senhora de Nazareth, and as a singer with an ensemble in Morro Vermelho. The second part of the article presents an original examination of how the Morro Vermelho community develops a sense of identity through music and the interaction with surrounding communities and their own narratives. Concludes by urging musicologists to examine current vernacular practices in order to better understand the musical practices of colonial Minas Gerais.

2859 Andrade, Mário de. O turista aprendiz. Edição de texto apurado, anotada e acrescida de documentos por Telê Ancona Lopez e Tatiana Longo Figueiredo. Com a colaboração de Leandro Raniero Fernandes. Reedição. Brasília: IPHAN, 2015. 461 p.: bibl., ill., CD-ROM, DVD.

This is a revised and annotated edition of Mário de Andrade's 1927–28 travel diaries, first published in 1976. It covers Andrade's 1927–28 trips in the northern and northeastern regions of Brazil and contains numerous descriptions and commentaries on musicians and musical practices. Provided source material for a number of Andrade's literary and scholarly texts. Accompanies a CD-ROM with 900 pictures and additional material that would be used for a planned second part of the book, and a DVD of the documentary "A casa do Mário."

2860 Aragão, Pedro de Moura. Entre polcas, quadrilhas e sambas: processos de mudança musical no choro a partir de análises comparativas entre gravações fonográficas no século XX. (*Claves/João Pessoa*, 10, 2014, p. 61–80, bibl., ill., music)

Analysis of the transformation of *quadrilha* and *polka* in choro recordings of the 20th century. The author argues that *polka* and *quadrilha* are "not just sound practices that change through time, but complex structures that entail discourses around identity, belonging, concepts of nationality and authenticity." Contends that these discourses define and justify continuity and change in choro.

2861 Arcanjo, Loque. Heitor Villa-Lobos: os sons de uma nação imaginada. Belo Horizonte, Brazil: Editora Letramento, 2016. 263 p.: bibl.

A critical and in many aspects original biography of Villa-Lobos. The author argues that, rather than a clear nationalist modernist, Villa-Lobos was a composer of multiple, often fragmentary identities, forged by his approximation and distancing with social and audience networks, and reflected in his numerous narratives about his own life and works (including his notorious "corrections" in the dates of his compositions), which ultimately determined how he imagined the Brazilian nation through music. The second part of the book examines Villa-Lobos' approximation with North-American musical circles and his suspicion towards Curt Lange's *Americanismo musical* and Koellreutter's *Música Viva* movements. The book is an outgrowth of the author's 2013 doctoral dissertation in history.

2862 *ArtCultura*. Vol. 19, No. 34, jan./junho 2017, Dossiê "Música folclórica: entre o campo e a cidade." Organização de Tânia da Costa Garcia. Uberlândia, Brazil: Universidade Federal de Uberlândia, Departamento de História, Núcleo de Estudos em História Social da Arte e da Cultura.

This special issue of a leading arts research journal focuses on the uses and appropriations of traditional music by the culture industry, linked or not to representations of national and ethnic identities. Juliana P. González discusses mutual influences between country and city in her analysis of early recordings of *caipira* music in São Paulo and the diffusion of gramophone recordings in rural areas of São Paulo state during the 1920s. Tânia C. Garcia explains that the legitimating of Rio's samba as Brazil's main tradition was a process that involved multiple agents and institutions, from the 1930s to the early 1970s. This issue also includes articles on "folk" music of Argentina, Chile, and the US.

2863 ArtCultura. Vol. 20, No. 36, jan./ junho 2018, Dossiê "Fora do cânone: história & música popular." Organização de Adalberto Paranhos. Uberlândia, Brazil: Universidade Federal de Uberlândia, Departamento de História, Núcleo de Estudos em História Social da Arte e da Cultura.

This special issue of *ArtCultura* explores noncanonical genres of Brazilian music. Maria Cristina P.F. Magalhães argues that the hybrid mixtures between rap and local styles in Goiânia and Aparecida de Goiânia reveal strategies of belonging and representation of regional identities. Lígia Nassif Conti explains that efforts to construct an image of São Paulo based on industrialization and modernization resulted in the obliteration of a black memory from local samba practices. The volume also includes articles by Roberto Camargos on rap, João Augusto Neves on funk, and Francisco G.C. do Nascimento on 1980s breakers Chico Vulgo and Jorge dü Peixe as predecessors of Mangue Beat in Pernambuco.

2864 Aubin, Myrian Ribeiro. Francisco Curt Lange e sua atuação nos meios musical e político em Belo Horizonte: constituição de uma rede de sociabilidades. (*Opus/Porto Alegre*, 22:1, junho 2016, p. 299–338)

This well-researched study discusses music and politics in Belo Horizonte during the 1940s. The author examined letters and newspaper articles to understand the role of Francisco Curt Lange in energizing a network of cultural and political agents with the purpose of developing institutions and promoting composers, performers, and repertories.

2865 Barbosa, Juliana dos Santos. Nelson Sargento e as redes criativas do samba. Curitiba, Brazil: Editora Appris, 2014. 190 p.: bibl., ill.

The author uses methods from genetic criticism and cultural studies to examine the creative process in samba culture, highlighting the role of social and creative networks, including, but not restricted to the practice of collaboration among samba composers. Originally and effectively, the author contextualizes Nelson Sargento's biography within the Mangueira samba school, examines his sketches and annotations, reveals connections and dialogues between his sambas and his paintings, and finds parallels between his identity as a sambista and his work as an actor and writer. This is an outgrowth of the author's 2013 doctoral dissertation in Language Studies.

2866 Barros, Rubem Rabello Maciel de. Poéticas de fragmentos: história, música popular e cinema de arquivo. São Paulo: Alameda, 2014. 262 p.: bibl., filmography.

This original study examines the production of full-length documentaries on popular music. The author focuses on two movies, *A voz e o vazio: a hora e a vez de Vassourinha* and *Cartola, música para os olhos*, to outline distinct methods of creating a filmic narrative based on a musicobiographic topic. The author demonstrates that, although both films deploy "found footage," their use of such material diverges greatly (e.g., historical source versus material for artistic expression). The third chapter examines how each film-maker constructed their narrative (postmodern/open/fragmentary versus traditional/truth-finder/linear), echoing well-known debates in the disciplines of history and musicology.

2867 Bishop-Sanchez, Kathryn. Creating Carmen Miranda: race, camp, and transnational stardom. Nashville, Tenn.: Vanderbilt University Press, 2016. 290 p.: bibl., ill., index.

More than a biography of Carmen Miranda, this essential book focuses on the construction of the popular culture icon, engaging with a number of discourses and controversies that permeate Brazilian and American culture of the first half of the 20th century. Reviews by Lisa Shaw (*LAMR*, 38:2, 2017, p. 246–247), Dário Borim Jr. (*LBR*, 54:1, 2017, p. E8-E10), and Andrea Matallana (*HAHR*, 98:2, 2018, p. 342–343).

2868 Bocskay, Stephen. Undesired presences: samba, improvisation, and Afro-politics in 1970s Brazil. (*LARR*, 52:1, 2017, p. 64–78, bibl., photos)

This article discusses Candeia's role in denouncing the modernization of samba during the military regime and explores the contradictions of his initiatives in promoting a revival of *partido alto*. The author argues that by stressing the authenticity of a certain type of samba and casting it in national tones, Rio's samba community prevented any engagement with Pan-Africanism. For a complementary perspective, see item **2933**.

2869 **Bossa Nova canção: prospettive teoriche e analisi poetico-musicali.** Testos di Stefano La Via e Claudio Cosi. Lucca, Italy: Libreria musicale italiana, 2017. 304 p.: bibl., index. (Grooves; 6)

A significant study on bossa nova by two leading Italian scholars. Although the music of Tom Jobim is always at the foreground, the authors also examine the poetry of Vinicius de Moraes and the performance style of João Gilberto. With two chapters by Stefano La Via, the book opens with an examination of the context and cultural roots of bossa nova, as well as its esthetic and musico-theoretical basis. This chapter is followed by a fine, 70-page, threefold analytical essay on Moraes' poetry, Gilberto's recording, and Jobim's music of "Chega de saudade." The second part includes four chapters by Claudio Cosi, beginning with modernism in Brazil before 1950, followed by three chapters on the music of Tom Jobim. Cosi brings useful information on Jobim's formative years and early career (up to the "Sinfonia do Rio de Janeiro"), when he transited between erudite and popular idioms, following with a chapter on Jobim's transition to bossa nova and his collaborations with Vinicius de Moraes and Newton Mendonça (with analytical insights and many musical examples). The book concludes with deeper considerations of Jobim's complex harmonic language in relation to his economic use of melodic cells.

2870 Braga, Reginaldo Gil. **Memória e patrimônio musical do choro de Porto Alegre: tensões e intenções entre tradição e modernidade.** (*Música Cult.*, 9, 2014, p. 1–14, bibl., music)

This musical ethnography of choro in Porto Alegre discusses the processes of creation, transmission, and performance among different generations in relation to memory, heritage, urban life, and transnational flows. The author examines the increasing role of online archiving and broadcasting in recent musical exchanges, as well as dialogues with other genres, notably Argentine tango. A good survey of a musical scene of which Yamandú Costa is currently the most visible exponent.

2871 *Brasiliana: Journal for Brazilian Studies.* Vol. 4, No. 1, 2015, The world of syncopation: dynamics in music and culture. Aarhus, Denmark: Aarhus University: The Royal Danish Library. <https://tidsskrift.dk/bras/issue/view/3273>

This special issue on Brazilian music includes papers selected from the 2014 BRASA conference in London and a 2015 seminar at UFRJ, Rio de Janeiro. The texts approach syncopation as a rhythmic feature and a metaphor for dislocations and disjunctures in musical scholarship, creation, and performance. The volume includes articles by Bryan McCann on Victor Ramil's "aesthetics of the cold," Débora Costa de Faria on *funk nacional*, and Dylon Robbins on polyrhythm. The collection also presents three articles on Mário de Andrade: Jean Carlo Faustino writes about the syncopated moda de viola, Enea Zaramella discusses syncopation, politics, and religion, and Maurício H. Vega Jr. analyzes Andrade's unfinished "Na pancada do ganzá."

2872 Buscacio, Cesar Maia. **Americanismo e nacionalismo musicais na correspondência de Curt Lange e Camargo Guarnieri, 1934–1956.** Ouro Preto, Brazil: Editora UFOP, 2010. 275 p.: bibl., ill.

This well-researched study examines the imbrications and frictions between Curt Lange's project of *americanismo musical* and Camargo Guarnieri's *nacionalismo* as they surface in letters exchanged between the two from 1934 to 1956. The author analyzes the approximation of Lange and Guarnieri with politicians and state officers in their attempts to promote musical institutions and initiatives. Winner of the Prêmio FUNARTE de Producão Crítica am Música. The book is an outgrowth of the author's doctoral dissertation and is freely available on the publisher's website: http://www.repositorio.ufop.br/handle/123456789/4582. See also item **2681**.

Canção romântica: intimidade, mediação e identidade na América Latina. See item **2675**.

2873 **Caneppele, Ismael.** A vida louca da MPB. São Paulo: Leya, 2016. 271 p.: bibl., ill.

This work presents short biographies of 17 figures of MPB (música popular brasileira), mainly focusing on their physical traits, unconventional habits, and Bohemian lifestyle (generally following a predictable narrative that also includes law, family, and health issues), punctuated with anecdotes of uneven quality. The entries are more informative and accurate than the average publication of this genre.

2874 **Carvalho, Hermínio Bello de.** Taberna da Glória e outras glórias: mil vidas entre os heróis da música brasileira. Organização de Ruy Castro. Rio de Janeiro: Edições de Janeiro, 2015. 223 p.: ill.

Organized by Ruy Castro on the 80th birthday of Hermínio Bello de Carvalho, this volume contains chronicles that the poet and cultural producer published in books, newspapers, album covers, and CD booklets during the 1980s and 90s. The study unveils Carvalho's role as a producer and coauthor in the field of popular music, and as a mediator between popular artists and the recording industry and cultural institutions. Although partly fictional, the book is quite entertaining and relatively useful as a primary source.

2875 **Carvalho, José Jorge de.** Metamorphosis of Afro-Brazilian performance traditions: from cultural heritage to the entertainment industry. (*in* Latin American music reader: views from the south. Edited by Javier F. León and Helena Simonett. Urbana: University of Illinois Press, in collaboration with the Society for Ethnomusicology, 2016, p. 406–429)

This entry represents a shortened English-language version of a highly relevant, although controversial essay originally published in 2004. The author offers an exposé of cultural appropriation disguised as mediation, as practiced by Brazilian white elites—namely cultural producers, media artists, and scholars. He provides guidelines for researchers as they approach intangible cultural heritage-bearing communities. Much of its polemical content lies in Carvalho's pessimistic view of the spectacularization of traditional culture, dismissing claims of empowerment and playing down the agency of traditional artists and communities in this process. A lively debate on the subject is currently taking place in the field of applied ethnomusicology. For a review of the entire volume, see item **2679**.

2876 **Carvalho, Pedro Henrique Varoni de.** A voz que canta na voz que fala: poética e política na trajetória de Gilberto Gil. Cotia, Brazil: Ateliê Editorial; Aracaju, Brazil: Editora Universitária Tiradentes, 2015. 358 p.: bibl., ill.

This book version of the author's PhD dissertation in linguistics (UFSC) aims at explaining how Gilberto Gil has transferred a particular discourse on *brasilidade*, from his enunciative position as a popular musician and key figure of the *tropicalismo* (as a discursive place) to his speeches and actions as a state minister of culture. The author combines Foucault's concept of archive (in Gil's case, the "archive of Brazilianness") with the analytical approach to popular song developed by Tatit and Wisnik, particularly their discussion on the potentialization of the speaking voice that lies within the singing voice. Inverting Tatit and Wisnik's paradigm, the author argues that Gil's voice as a minister was inevitably linked to the intensity and effectiveness of his singing voice.

2877 **Castagna, Paulo.** André da Silva Gomes (1752–1844): memória, esquecimento e restauração. (*Rev. Digit. Música Sacra Bras.*, 2, fev./abril 2018, p. 7–141, appendices, bibl., ill., tables)

This excellent study on reception follows the trajectory of André da Silva Gomes (1752–1844) throughout the 19th and 20th centuries in São Paulo, until his works became part of the Brazilian music canon by the 1970s. The author examines different prerogatives and contexts that conditioned the preservation, forgetting, and recreation of memories related to the composer during this period. The article is followed by five appendices reproducing the 1844 obituary, an 1866 article on Gomes' music for the Holy Week, an 1898 article on the continued performance of his works, and a 1909 article on his role in the orchestration and performance of D. Pedro's *Hino da Independên-*

cia. The fifth appendix contains a critical commentary on the edition of Gomes' "Ave Maris Stella," which is discussed earlier in the article and printed on p. 143–159.

2878 Castro, Ruy. Chega de saudade: a história e as histórias da bossa nova. Projeto gráfico de Hélio de Almeida. 4a edição revista, ampliada e definitiva. São Paulo: Companhia das Letras, 2016. 502 p.: bibl., ill. (some color), index.

This is the fourth edition of Castro's referential book on bossa nova, originally published in 1990 (2000 in English; see *HLAS 62:3577*). In addition to punctual revisions, Castro softens the evaluation of bossa nova as a reformist movement, arguing that a somewhat unified proposal only happened during 1958–61, after which artists followed the more or less steady development of Brazilian popular music (particularly samba), marked by continuities more than ruptures. In the about 100 pages of new material, there is a three-part survey of 600 songs, including pre-1958 songs that were influential to the movement, as well as songs that were recorded during and after the movement. The book closes with a useful index, a bibliography, and a discography of bossa nova.

2879 Castro, Ruy. A noite do meu bem: a história e as histórias do samba-canção. Projeto gráfico de Hélio de Almeida. São Paulo: Companhia Das Letras, 2015. 510 p., 32 unnumbered pages of plates: bibl., ill., index, maps.

Ruy Castro delves deeply into Rio's 1940s-60s nightlife, revisiting from a different perspective many of the issues and artists he covered in his previous books. The focus here is on *samba canção*, from the more "authentic" ones to the bolero and foxtrot overlaps. Yet, rather than telling a history of the genre, the author uses it as the main thread for dozens of short chronicles and anecdotal accounts about Rio's rich and famous. Some of these stories do offer backstage insights and valuable information on the creation and production of a genre that for many years was the quintessential romantic song of Brazil. A meticulous *cançãografia* (i.e., a list of songs), chronological list of nightclubs, discography, filmography, and index partially compensate for Castro's notorious lack of referencing. An essential counterpart to *Chega de saudade* (item **2878**).

2880 Choros de Garoto. Organização de Jorge Mello, Henrique Gomide, e Domingos Teixeira. São Paulo: IMS: Edições SESC, 2017. 220 p.: ill.

This generous publication contains a preface by Paulo Belinatti (p. 9–10) and a biographical sketch by Jorge Mello (p. 13–30). The main section includes 67 *choros* in lead-sheet score edited by Henrique Gomide and Domingos Teixeira (p. 31–165). This selection provides a good overview of Garoto's development as a composer from 1936 to 1955, although the reader should be aware that some pieces are based on more than one source, such as late recordings with more elaborate harmonizations than the respective manuscripts or printed editions, as explained in the contextual notes by Jorge Mello (p. 170–202). The book closes with a list of compositions (p. 204–220).

2881 Congresso Internacional "Música, Cultura e Identidade no Bicentenário da Elevação do Brasil a Reino Unido," São Paulo, 2015. Actas. Organização de Ruthe Zoboli Pocebon. Lisboa: CESEM-FCSH, Universidade Nova de Lisboa; Ribeirão Preto, Brazil: Laboratório de Musicologia, FFCL-USP, 2016. 393 p.: bibl., ill., music.

This volume publishes the proceedings of an international symposium on music in Brazil and Portugal organized by the CESEM/Universidade Nova de Lisboa and Universidade de São Paulo, Ribeirão Preto. The book contains the text of 28 papers presented at the event, ranging from sacred and theatrical music, archives and institutions, composers and musical analysis, to performance practice. Not all of the texts adhere to the symposium's theme. The e-book is freely available online.

2882 Couto, Caroline Peres. O samba serpenteia com o Escravos da Mauá: uma nova perspectiva sobre o Porto do Rio de Janeiro. Rio de Janeiro: Mórula Editorial, 2016. 179 p.: bibl., ill., map.

This urban ethnography of Rio's harbor district focuses on the *rodas de samba* promoted by members of the *bloco de carnival* Escravos da Mauá. The author discusses how samba practitioners helped to enhance the visibility of the area and to increase the circulation of aficionados, leading to what she calls a "spontaneous revitalization" of that then-neglected neighborhood. Addressing issues of history and memory, community and body, the author shows that the emergence of *blocos* and *rodas de samba* during the 1990s and early 2000s is helping to feed a number of discourses of Cariocas around that highly symbolic area—once the largest port of entry of African slaves in Brazil and inevitably connected with a number of foundation narratives.

2883 **Cruz, Danielle Maia.** Maracatus no Ceará: sentidos e significados. Fortaleza, Brazil: Edições UFC, 2011. 350 p.: bibl., color ill.

This ethnography of performances and participants of Maracatu Iracema, in Fortaleza, argues that *maracatu* is an energetic instrument of identity affirmation and a space for the construction of black identity. The study brings new light to the discussion on a controversial blackface tradition. An outgrowth of the author's MA thesis in sociology.

2884 **Diaz, Juan Diego.** Between repetition and variation: a musical performance of *malícia* in capoeira. (*Ethnomusicology Forum*, 26:1, April 2017, p. 46–68, bibl., ill., music, photos)

While *malícia*, or cunning, is one of the basic features of capoeira, the author demonstrates that it can also be found in the music that accompanies the game, as in variations and deviations from patterns that work as a form of concealed communication between musicians and *capoeiristas*.

2885 **Diniz, Sheyla Castro.** ". . . De tudo que a gente sonhou": amigos e canções do Clube da Esquina. São Paulo: Intermeios: Fapesp, 2017. 290 p.: bibl., ill. (some color).

A fascinating study of Clube da Esquina, a musical movement that emerged as a counterpoint and alternative to bossa nova and *tropicalismo*. Diniz discusses its consolidation as a sociocultural formation as well as its esthetic and politico-ideological underpinnings, as they surface in interviews, lyrics, censors' reports, album covers/visual material, and music (using a combination of analytical approaches).

Outgrowth of the author's MA thesis in sociology.

2886 **Dudeque, Norton.** *Prométhée* op. 21 de Leopoldo Miguez, considerações sobre o poema sinfônico, seu programa e a forma sonata. (*Opus/Porto Alegre*, 22:1, junho 2016, p. 9–34, bibl., music)

Analysis of Miguez's tone poem *Prométhée* as an example of the German influence in Brazilian music during the last decades of the 19th century. The study describes its formal structure as an adapted sonata form and detects a Wagnerian influence in the use of a floating tonal center and sequences. However, the author also notices the lack of German-influenced processes of thematic transformation and argues that the subject matter reflects the composer's republican ideals.

2887 **Dunn, Christopher.** Contracultura: alternative arts and social transformation in authoritarian Brazil. Chapel Hill: The University of North Carolina Press, 2016. 256 p.: bibl., index.

This original study of 1970s counterculture in Brazil dissects the concept of *desbunde* as a form of pacific-hedonistic resistance against the military regime, the militant left, and the conservative middle class (the *caretas*). The book shows the pervasiveness of *desbunde* in the *cultura marginal* throughout the decade, finding consistent links between more or less organized cultural phenomena (hippies and *bichos* in Bahia and Rio de Janeiro, alternative press, avant-garde art, black Rio, *movimento gay*), which opened new ways of understanding and expressing freedom, race, and sexuality. Examines the impact of issues discussed in the author's *Brutality Garden* (see *HLAS 62:3580*).

2888 **Encuentro Iberoamericano de Jóvenes Musicólogos, 3rd, Sevilla, Spain, 2016.** Actas: musicologia criativa. Edição de Marco Brescia e Rosana Marreco Brescia. Sevilla, Spain: Tagus-Atlanticus Associação Cultural, 2016. 864 p.: ill., music.

The proceedings of the third Ibero-American conference of young musicologists focus on a variety of Spanish, Portuguese, and Latin American topics. Papers on Brazilian themes include a study on H.-J. Koellreutter's pedagogy (by Tecla Alencar de Brito and Camila Costa Zanetta), Villa-Lobos' String Quartet no. 9 (Adriana Lopes Moreira and Allan Medeiros Falqueiro), musical archives in Goiânia (Fernanda Vasconcelos Furtado), Luso-Brazilian clarinetist José Cardoso Botelho (Gabriel Gagliano), Ciríaco Cardoso and late 19th-century musical theater in Rio de Janeiro (Filipe Gaspar), and Fernando Lopes-Graça and his interviews with six Brazilian composers in 1958 (Guilhermina Lopes). The e-book is freely available online.

2889 Estephan, Sérgio. Abismo de rosas: vida e obra de Canhoto. São Paulo: Edições SESC, 2017. 164 p.: bibl., ill., music.

This long overdue book focuses on the remarkable guitar composer and performer Luís Américo Jacomino (1889–1928), nicknamed Canhoto. The first part examines his early career in São Paulo, as a circus artist, in theater revues, and finally as soloist in national tours. The second part discusses Canhoto's performance style, compositional process, and addresses issues of transcription and edition (Canhoto did not read standard music notation, and during his lifetime his music was published in piano scores). The remainder of the book, although still relevant, is a little fragmented and outdated, overlooking recent research on the six-string guitar in late 19th- and early 20th-century Brazil. Yet, for its first chapter and most of the second, the book is a valuable addition to the literature on the Brazilian guitar. It also includes 11 compositions by Canhoto transcribed from early recordings or rescored for the guitar by Henrique Gomide and Ricardo Yoneta.

2890 Estrada, Chris. Talking pretty and kicking up dust: modernity and tradition in maracatu de baque solto of Pernambuco. (*Lat. Am. Music Rev.*, 38:2, Fall/Winter 2017, p. 212–245)

More recent and less known than the urban maracatu de baque virado (or de nação), Pernambuco's maracatu de baque solto (or rural) enjoys an increasing interest from both media and academia. This thoughtful article examines how the branching of maracatu into presentational and participatory modalities reflects persistent polarizations in Brazilian culture (erudite versus popular, intellectual elite versus media and culture industry), showing that maracatuzeiros are able to navigate in diverse spheres, reflecting or subverting concepts of tradition and authenticity, and shifting from participatory to presentational styles, while mobilizing technology and resources to promote their agendas.

2891 Estudos luso-brasileiros em iconografia musical. Organização de Pablo Sotuyo Blanco. Salvador, Brazil: EDUFBA, 2015. 280 p.: bibl., col. ill.

This is the most significant publication on musical iconography in Brazil since Mercedes Reis Pequeno's 1974 *Tres séculos de iconografia da música no Brasil* (see *HLAS 38:9075*), which is the focus of the introductory essay by Beatriz M. Castro. This compilation brings together 12 studies on topics that range from musician soldiers in 18th-century paintings of the Batalha dos Guararapes (Mary A. Biaison) to posters of rock festivals in Pelotas in the 1990s (Daniel R. Medeiros and Isabel P. Nogueira). The volume includes texts on musical subjects in or around 18th-century Catholic temples in Bahia (Pablo S. Blanco, Wellington M. Silva Filho, and Rosana M. Brescia), the 1920s ceiling paintings by João Batista de Deus in the 1699 Cathedral of São Luís (Alberto P. Dantas Filho), and the use of photographs to forge the visual identity of the Conservatório de Música de Pelotas (Isabel P. Nogueira et al.) and the Grupo de Compositores da Bahia (Pablo S. Blanco). Also on Brazilian themes, two essays discuss the social and politico-cultural uses of music imagery in newspapers and magazines in the state of São Paulo between 1860 and 1930 (Diósnio Machado Neto and Ozório B.P. Christovam). The e-book is freely available online.

2892 Etnomusicologia no Brasil. Organização de Angela Lühning e Rosângela Pereira de Tugny. Salvador, Brazil: EDUFBA, 2016. 323 p.: bibl., ill., map.

Portuguese version of the special number of *The World of Music* (new series), Vol. 5, No. 1, 2016 (see item **2957**).

2893 Faour, Rodrigo. Angela Maria: a eterna cantora do Brasil. Rio de Janeiro: Editora Record, 2015. 839 p.: bibl., ill. (some color), index.

A comprehensive, but mostly uncritical biography of Brazil's most popular singer during the second half of the 20th century. Examines Angela Maria's role in the shift from radio to TV as the most prestigious venue for Brazilian popular music during the period, as well as Angela Maria's migration to the so-called *samba-brega* style in the 1970s, which propelled her career even further. Based on extensive research in newspapers and magazines and, to a lesser extent, interviews and archival sources.

2894 Ferreira, Gustavo Alves Alonso.
Cowboys do asfalto: música sertaneja e modernização brasileira. Rio de Janeiro: Civilização Brasileira, 2015. 559 p., 24 unnumbered pages of plates: bibl., color ill., index.

Examines the transformations of *sertanejo* music from the 1950s to the 1980s, focusing on the pervasiveness and inconsistency of the dichotomy of authenticity versus modernization during this period. Explores controversies around esthetic paradigms, foreign influences, political allegiances, and the role of the culture industry in the shaping of *caipira, sertanejo*, and *sertanejo universitário* music. The author carried out archival research on newspaper and media sources and interviewed several artists. The book includes an album of 24 pages of color pictures and is enhanced with careful references and an index. The study is an outgrowth of the author's PhD dissertation in history.

2895 Ferreira, Gustavo Alves Alonso.
Quem não tem swing morre com a boca cheia de formiga: Wilson Simonal e os limites de uma memória tropical. Rio de Janeiro: Editora Record, 2011. 471 p.: bibl.

From bossa-nova star to populist hero of the *pilantragem* (rascality) cultural movement, Wilson Simonal has become a fascinating subject for social, racial, and political analyses, with more or less emphasis on music. This book alternates chapters of biographical content with discussions on the cultural debates of each period (particularly chapter 3, on race issues) and Simonal's ostracism during the 1970s and 80s. The author states that rather than finding individual scapegoats, his goal is to examine the role of Brazilian society in Simonal's demise, particularly those who were indifferent to the military dictatorship. The book contains an original analysis of *pilantragem* as a musical and esthetic project. Thoroughly referenced.

2896 Fonseca, Denise Sella. Uma colcha de retalhos: a música em cena na cidade de São Paulo: do final do século XIX ao início do século XX. São Paulo: SESI-SP Editora, 2017. 235 p.: bibl., ill.

An original and well-accomplished study on musical theater in the city of São Paulo from the 1880s to the 1910s. Covers zarzuelas, operetas, and a number of hybrid theatrical genres comprised within the generic denomination *teatro de revista*. Surveys a number of theatrical companies fom Brazil and abroad that visited the city and examines local productions of theatrical texts and musical scores. Discusses the privileged space of theater in the creation and dissemination of popular music, examining in depth the role of lyricist Arlindo Leal. The last section is an insightful study on the disciplining forces aimed to control artists, playwrights, composers, and audiences. Musicologists may complain about the little space given to the discussion of actual music, but the author offers numerous clues for further studies.

2897 Freitas, Mariana Portas de. Polémicas musicais entre "Practicos" e letrados: a dúvida entre Caetano de Melo de Jesus e Gregório de Sousa e Gouveia (Vila da Cachoeira, Recôncavo da Baía, 1760). (*Rev. Bras. Música/Rio de Janeiro*, 29:1, jan./junho 2016, p. 17–43, bibl., facsims., ill., music)

The author discusses the last section of the theoretical treatise by Caetano Melo de Jesus, chapel master of Bahia's cathedral, in which he tried to dismiss a practical question posed by Gregório Gouveia, former music director of the Santa Casa de Misericórdia and current music director in Cachoeira. The experienced Gouveia cornered the chapel master into explaining what a music director should do about musical instruments with keys or frets, which are unable to play the same pitches as singers trained in the Pythagorean system when they are performing together. The article demonstrates that the argumentation of each author was grounded on incompatible premises. Followed in the same volume by a transcription of the original text of this discussion (p. 45–66), and annotations, also by Freitas, on the musical instruments mentioned in the document, along with each author's respective argumentation (p. 67–88).

2898 Gabbay, Marcello Monteiro. Comunicação poética e música popular: uma história do carimbó no Marajó. Curitiba, Brazil: Appris Editora, 2017. 323 p.: bibl., ill. (chiefly color). (Coleção Educação e direitos humanos: diversidade de gênero, sexual, étnico-racial e inclusão social)

The book opens with a genealogy of *carimbó* masters and ensembles in Marajó Island during the 20th century, followed by a discussion on poetic communication and community value. More useful for music scholars are chapters 4 and 6, with a few ethnographic insights on the ritualistic dimension and local narratives of *carimbó*, and chapter 5, titled "the political dimension," which explores the dichotomies memory/history, regional/global, and modernity/tradition. Outgrowth of the author's 2012 PhD dissertation in communication.

2899 Garcia-Solek, Hélène. Sampling as political practice: Gilberto Gil's cultural policy in Brazil and the right to culture in the digital age. (*Volume/Bordeaux*, 11:2, 2015, p. 51–63)

Addresses Gilberto Gil's attempts to institutionally legitimize musical cultures involving sample and remix, and to clarify a redefinition of musical authorship and intellectual property in the context of a musical digital culture. Examines the *pontos de cultura* as alternative models of cultural production that enhance sustainability, allowing digital communities to acquire international visibility while remaining committed to the local.

2900 Gidal, Marc. Spirit song: Afro-Brazilian religious music and boundaries. New York: Oxford University Press, 2016. 220 p.: bibl., ill., index, maps, music.

This original study on spirit-mediumship rituals among Afro-Gaucho communities in Porto Alegre examines differences and similarities in which practitioners of Umbanda, Quimbanda, and Batuque use music to reinforce or blur boundaries, encourage innovation, or promote preservation. Reviewed by Patricia Barker Lerch (*Nova Religio*, 21:1, August 2017, p. 124–25), Kariann Goldschmitt (*Music & Letters*, 98:2, May 2017, p. 331–33), and Steven Engler (*Reading Religion*, http://readingreligion.org/books/spirit-song).

2901 Gomes, Antonio Henrique de Castilho. A [re]configuração do discurso do samba. Curitiba, Brazil: Editora CRV, 2014. 153 p.: bibl. (Coleção Pesquisa aberta)

The author argues that forging links with the state, the academy, and the culture industry was an intentional strategy of survival of *escolas de samba* in a process similar to the 1930s malandro rehabilitation. These alliances not only assured the continuity of samba-school carnaval as a space of transgression, but also as a place of speech of Rio's subaltern classes (that is, in a polyphonic texture through which those elite groups also speak).

2902 Gomes, Rodrigo Cantos Savelli. MPB no feminino: notas sobre relações de gênero na música brasileira. Curitiba, Brazil: Appris Editora, 2017. 188 p.: bibl. (Coleção Ciências sociais)

This important collection of essays focuses on gender in popular music. The first section looks at rock bands, samba, hip hop, and traditional music in Florianópolis and its surrounding. Less ethnographic than the first, the second section contains critical analyses of texts and narratives of early samba in Rio de Janeiro. Throughout the book, the author argues that gender analyses in popular music should take into account additional intersections, such as race, class, ethnicity, and generation.

2903 Gomes, Rodrigo Cantos Savelli and **Maria Ignez Cruz Mello.** Gender and Brazilian popular music: a study of female bands. (*in* Latin American music reader: views from the south. Edited by Javier F. León and Helena Simonett. Urbana: University of Illinois Press, in collaboration with the Society for Ethnomusicology, 2016, p. 318–330)

This entry provides an English translation of a pioneering study of music and gender in Brazil, originally published in 2007. The authors examine how the presence of women in popular music groups (rock, samba, pagode, and hip-hop) has challenged and transformed traditional gender roles, established dialogues with feminist organizations, and, in a number of ways, also influenced the development of new musical subgenres. For a review of the entire volume, see item **2679**.

2904 González García, Mónica. Eros imperial: Carmen Miranda y los "cuerpos imaginados" de la Buena Vecindad. (*Cine Cub.*, 201, 2017, p. 60–65, ill.)

Relevant and critical analysis of Hollywood's remaking of Carmen Miranda into an overly erotic feminine version of the good savage, feeding the imperialist fantasies about Latin American peripheries eagerly wanting to be conquered. See also item **2867**.

2905 Graeff, Nina. Os ritmos da roda: tradição e transformação no samba de roda. Salvador, Brazil: EDUFBA, 2015. 164 p.: bibl., ill., music.

Comprehensive and multifaceted study of *samba de roda*, of Bahia's *recôncavo* region, based on fieldwork and theoretical analysis carried on during 2010–2014. Chapters address the origins of the genre, spectacularization and folklorization trends, general features and regional styles, rhythmic structure, role of musical instruments, voice and dance, performance, and concludes by tracing parallels with Rio's samba (*bossa nova* and *partido alto*. Theoretical basis drawn from works by Gerhard Kubik and Tiago de Oliveira Pinto, relying on spectrogram and TUBS notation to visually represent sound and time events. The author states that the valorization of the particularities and variants of *samba de roda*, as well as its legitimating as a musical and choreographic genre, neither as "mere 'roots' of other sambas nor as their primitive version" (p. 152). Yet, in the introduction the author acknowledges that *samba the roda* has "a history that goes back centuries" and reveals her intention of "using musical and social analysis to help clarify vestiges of its history and its influence on other forms of expression of Brazil" (p. 16).

2906 Hess, Hans. Black Orpheus. (*in* Film music in "minor" national cinemas. Edited by Germán Gil-Curiel. New York; London: Bloomsbury Academic, 2016, p. 45–70, bibl.)

This essay considers the role of Brazilian music and the depictions of Afro-Brazilian life in the French film *Black Orpheus*. The author attempts to situate the movie within Guattari's concept of minor cinema (the subject of the book) and Latin American "Third Cinema," as a liberating film, free from capitalist and colonialist expectations. Yet, the author falls into a trap when he argues that "Camus did 'strike a chord' about Brazilian identity by depicting the effortless music manifestation of the country," a well-known stereotype with multiple ramifications. On the musical side, the chapter traces interesting parallels between *samba-canção* (or *samba-lírico*) and troubadour songs, along with a more obvious connection between the narrative of the movie and Greek theater and rhetorics. Contains a detailed analysis of the soundtrack.

2907 Idéias: Revista do Instituto de Filosofia e Ciências Humanas. Vol. 8, No. 2, 2017, Música popular e interdisciplinaridade. Campinas, Brazil: Instituto de Filosofia e Ciências Humanas da Unicamp.

Special edition of the journal *Idéias*, with sociohistorical perspectives on popular music. Opens with two articles on popular music in São Paulo, the first one on the tension between avant-garde and pop in Arrigo Barnabé's 1984 album *Tubarões Voadores* (by José Adriano Fenerick), followed by a discussion on Adoniran Barbosa's critique of progress and development in the metropolis (by Thiago F. Franco et al.). In his article on Wilson Simonal, Carlos E.A. de Paiva's argues that the singer's downfall should be understood in the context of a dictatorship that promoted the myth of a racial democracy and a society structured around racial tensions and hierarchies. Two additional articles on Leci Brandão and the Quinteto Armorial complement the issue. Available online at https://periodicos.sbu.unicamp.br/ojs/index.php/ideias/issue/view/1416/showToc.

International Association for the Study of Popular Music. Rama Latinoamericana. 10th, Córdoba, Argentina, 2012. Actas. See item **2678**.

2908 Iyanaga, Michael. Why saints love samba: a historical perspective on black agency and the rearticulation of Catholicism in Bahia, Brazil. (*Black Music*

Res. J., 35:1, Spring 2015, p. 119–147, bibl., ill., photo)

This fascinating and essential study contests views of Afro-Catholicism as a passive assimilation of European culture or a creative concealing of African beliefs and rituals. Instead, the author stresses the agency of black Catholics in Brazil, who resignified and rearticulated Catholic saints as samba-loving gods, instilling into the religion of the oppressor forms and esthetics rooted in Central Africa. The author also points out that racialized modes of celebration created solidarity among black subjects from different ethnicities, while samba itself was articulated simultaneously in the context of *calundus* and Catholic brotherhoods.

2909 Júnior, Gonçalo. Quem samba tem alegria: a vida e o tempo do compositor Assis Valente. Rio de Janeiro: Civilização Brasileira, 2014. 657 p., 16 unnumbered pages of plates: bibl., ill. (some color), index, portraits.

One of the most successful composers during the "radio days" in Brazil, Assis Valente lived a life that is full of obscure corners and unsolved mysteries. In this massive volume, journalist Gonçalo Júnior provides some answers, although not all of them are convincing (for example, when discussing his multiple suicide attempts and the numerous allusions to homosexuality in his songs). Yet the book is based on solid research and presents useful reference material and helpful details on the dynamics of the recording industry, radio, and carnival production during the 1930s–50s.

2910 Kerber, Alessander. Carlos Gardel e Carmen Miranda: representações da Argentina e do Brasil. Porto Alegre, Brazil: UFRGS Editora, 2014. 223 p.: bibl.

The author analyzes and compares the construction of national identities in Argentina and Brazil from the perspective of music, visual representation, and performances of Carlos Gardel and Carmen Miranda. He identifies a similar pattern of resignification of ethnic, regional, and popular types (Italian, Portuguese, *gaucho*, *baiana*, *compadritos*, and *malandros*) into national identities. The study examines different ways in which culture industry and authoritarian governments determined the artists' strategies of mediation.

2911 Kunstmusik—Kolonialismus—Lateinamerika. Edited by Barbara Alge. Essen, Germany: Verlag Die Blaue Eule, 2017. 181 p.: ill. (chiefly color), music, 1 DVD. (Rostocker Schriften zur Musikwissenschaft und Musikpädagogik; 4)

Five of the nine chapters of this book are on Brazilian themes. Marcos Holler discusses the influence of Jesuits in the music of colonial Brazil, Barbara Alge and Jan Phillip Sprick bring ethnomusicological perspectives to the study of *Mineiro* archives, and the chapter by Mary A. Biason and Guilherme M. da Silva describes the organization and cataloging of the Museu da Inconfidência/Casa do Pilar archive. Edite Rocha's chapter on the sources of the Lundum de Monroy/Marruá, although technically a Portuguese subject, has important Brazilian ramifications. In a very original chapter, Christian Storch examines music and theater practices in the German settlement colonies along the Itajaí river, Santa Catarina, during the second half of the 19th century. Storch sees these practices as a transcultural phenomenon that belongs to both German and Brazilian music histories, being influenced at different times by Pan-Germanism and by Vargas' *Campanha de Nacionalização*. The accompanying DVD contains video files of a concert that took place during the event that originated this book, with 18th- and 19th-century music from Brazil.

2912 Lima, Giuliana Souza de. Almirante, "a mais alta patente do rádio", e a construção da história da música popular brasileira (1938–1958). São Paulo: Alameda, 2014. 297 p.: bibl., ill.

This study discusses the trajectory of Henrique Foreis Domingues, nicknamed Almirante (1908–80) as a popular music performer, composer, critic, producer, researcher, and radio host. In addition to Almirante's writings, published on a variety of venues and formats, the author analyzes extant recordings and scripts of radio shows, concluding that he mixed the attributions of chronicler and historian, while providing his listeners with a diversified musical experience. The author also stresses Almirante's legacy in raising awareness to the sociohistorical relevance of urban popular music and shaping a new phase of popular culture studies in Brazil.

2913 **Lisboa Junior, Luiz Americo.** Da modinha ao sertão: vida e obra de Catulo da Paixão Cearense. São Luís, Brazil: Instituto Geia, 2016. 622 p.: bibl., index, DVD.

This is the most comprehensive biography of notable poet, singer, composer, and guitarist Catulo da Paixão Cearense, key figure in the manneristic development of late *modinha* and in the beginnings of a *sertanejo* (countryside) trend in urban popular music. Clarifies a number of chronological questions and contains a candid discussion on his collaboration with João Pernambuco and the ensuing controversy around "Luar do sertão." Essential for scholars interested in the six-string guitar in Brazil (in both "art" and popular music contexts, with many insights on class and gender) and in Brazilian popular music, particularly those working with issues of authenticity, national identity, the beginnings of the recording industry, and early copyright controversies. Accompanied by a DVD-ROM with 114 recordings from 1902 to 1937, and a comprehensive iconography.

2914 **Lopes, Israel.** Pedro Raymundo e o canto monarca: uma história da música regionalista, nativista e missioneira. Porto Alegre, Brazil: Letra&Vida Suliani Editora, 2013. 239 p.: bibl., ill.

Less a history than an almanac of *música regional* of Rio Grande do Sul, this publication contains short biographies, contextual information on various albums and songs, definitions of musical genres, and trivia. The author focuses on the figure of accordionist, composer, singer, and radio host Pedro Raymundo (1906–73).

2915 **Lucas, Glaura.** Drums in the experience of black Catholicism in Minas Gerais, Brazil. (*in* Oxford handbook of music and world Christianities. Edited by Suzel Ana Reily and Jonathan M. Dueck. New York: Oxford University Press, 2016, p. 163–186, bibl., ill., music)

This entry focuses on the role of drums in the process of reinterpretation and recreation of Catholic faith and symbols in Minas Gerais, particularly in the Reinado de Nossa Senhora do Rosário, or *congado*. The author associates the drums and drum beating of *congado* and *candombe* with the beginnings of the devotion to Our Lady of Rosary, showing that black Catholicism blended the meanings of Rosary and ngoma drums, while continues to provide an unbroken link between devotees and their ancestors. The author uses historical records, interviews, and musical analysis to show how, in the context of this tradition, drums function as mediators between humans and gods, the living and the dead, Africans and Portuguese, and among diverse black ethnicities.

2916 **Lühning, Angela.** Brazilian ethnomusicology as participatory ethnomusicology: anxieties regarding Brazilian musics. (*in* Latin American music reader: views from the south. Edited by Javier F. León and Helena Simonett. Urbana: University of Illinois Press, in collaboration with the Society for Ethnomusicology, 2016, p. 379–392)

The author urges Brazilian ethnomusicologists to rethink the responsibilities and obligations that come from their interactions with the bearers of traditional knowledge. More than a local version of Euro-American applied ethnomusicology, Lühning proposes a more participatory and engaged ethnomusicology, with the potential to reshape of our notion of science and its social commitments. This approach would aim at higher levels of translatability and understandability between traditional communities, academia, and Brazilian society as a whole, and result in the forging of more symmetrical partnerships between scholars and traditional musicians, allowing the latter to effectively act as agents, rather than research objects. Originally published in Portuguese in in 2006 in the book *Músicas africanas e indígenas no Brasil*, this text is still highly relevant. For a review of the entire volume, see item **2679.**

2917 **Machado, Silvia de Ambrosis Pinheiro.** Canção de ninar brasileira: aproximações. São Paulo: Edusp, 2017. 307 p.: bibl., ill. (some color), 1 audio disc.

This innovative study is divided into three thematic sections—the ox, the owl, and the frog—each one discussing the origins and features of well-known Brazilian cradle songs. The author draws intriguing connections between these songs and indigenous beliefs, religious practices, socioeconomic systems, phonetic and acoustic elements, and rhythmic structures. She also examines cultural aspects of infant caregiving among ethnic groups in Brazil, and parallels between cradle songs, Catholic hymns, and incantation formulas.

2918 Machado Neto, Diósnio. A arte do bem morrer: o discurso tópico na Sinfonia Fúnebre de José Maurício Nunes Garcia. (*Rev. Port. Musicol.*, nova série, 4:1, 2017, p. 33–66, bibl., ill., music)

A rhetorical/topical analysis of José Maurício Nunes Garcia's *Sinfonia Fúnebre*. The author examines Garcia's use of rhetorical figures of opposition and troped topics and finds parallels between this work and the ideas of orator Frei Antonio Redovalho. He argues that the composer was influenced by precepts of his rhetoric professor, Manuel Inácio da Silva Alvarenga.

2919 Machado Neto, Diósnio. A *commedia* na música religiosa: kyries como ouvertures em três missas de José Maurício Nunes Garcia. (*Rev. Bras. Música/Rio de Janeiro*, 29:1, jan./junho 2016, p. 149–164)

This article examines the Kyrie of three masses by José Maurício Nunes Garcia (1767–1830)—Missa de Nossa Senhora da Conceição, Missa Pastoril, and Missa de Santa Cecília—demonstrating the composer's awareness of up-to-date discursive practices of European music, as well as the circulation of musical styles between sacred and theatrical contexts. The author convincingly argues that the Kyrie acquired the function of opera overture, introducing the affective content of the drama embedded in the liturgical act.

2920 Maestro soberano: ensaios sobre Antonio Carlos Jobim. Organização de Luca Bacchini. Belo Horizonte, Brazil: Editora UFMG, 2017. 328 p.: bibl., ill., indexes.

This collection of essays proposes a critical and interdisciplinary reflection of Jobim's works. With a primary focus on his songs, there are essays on experimentalism and tradition (by S.C. Naves and P.H. Britto), on updating the esthetic paradigms of samba (F.G. Poletto), on the making of "Águas de Março" (W. Garcia), and on how a number of sketches provide hints on the genesis of "Matita Perê" (C.L. Chaves). Essays by C. Perrone (see item **2525**) and H.M.M. Starling discuss Jobim's poetics and contact points with Brazilian literature. On Jobim's passion for nature, A.R.L. Haudenschild examines his texts through the lens of W. Benjamin's theory of experience, and P.H.F. Lima demonstrates how notions of space, house, and nation converge in the lyrics of "Chapadão," and L. Bacchini concludes the volume extracting valuable insights on Jobim's creative process from a short message on a postcard. Scholars will benefit also from G.A. Cruz's description of the history, structure, and current activities of the Instituto Antonio Carlos Jobim.

2921 Martins, Ana Luiza Rios. Entre o piano e o violão: a modinha em Fortaleza e os dilemas da cultura popular (1888–1920). São Paulo: Alameda, 2016. 288 p.: bibl., ill., music.

This is a study of *modinha* as a conveyor of polarized views of race and nation in Ceará after the abolition of slavery and during the first decades of the republic. The author shows that the sentimental and nostalgic *modinhas* that originated in elite circles were accompanied at the piano and depicted a romanticized view of the rural and lower classes, implicitly portraying miscegenation as key to cultural and racial unity (i.e., whitening) of the nation. On the other hand, working-class *modinhas* accompanied on the guitar were satirical and irreverent, addressed social problems, and were critical towards the upper classes. The book sheds a new light on Alberto Nepomuceno's formative years and is a good addition to the existing literature on regional variants of *modinha*.

2922 Martins, Luiza Mara Braga. Os Oito Batutas: história e música brasileira nos anos 1920. Rio de Janeiro: Editora UFRJ, 2014. 213 p.: bibl. (História, cultura e idéias)

Examines the historiography of the musical group Os Oito Batutas produced since the 1930s by memorialists, musicologists, sociologists, and journalists. The third chapter examines the racial polemic fueled by the Brazilian press during the 1910s-30s. The fourth and last chapter compares these constructions and polemics with statements and interviews by members of the group. Central to the book is the process of construction of memories that legitimized ideological positions about race, music, and nation along the 20th century.

2923 **Meneses, Juan Diego Diaz.** Listening with the body: an aesthetics of spirit possession outside the *terreiro*. (*Ethnomusicology/Champaign*, 60:1, Winter 2016, p. 89–124, bibl., ill., music)

This case study focuses on how *candomblé* practitioners in Bahia experience preliminary stages of spirit possession when listening to ritual music outside of the ceremonial context, specifically when attending performances of the band Rumpilezz. The author proposes a form of embodied esthetics based on sensations, mythological imagination (linked of not to discourses of black empowerment and religious secrecy) to clarify how practitioners are able to transpose certain esthetic and religious experiences to secular contexts. Includes helpful musical examples of *candomblé toques* and timelines, as well as techniques of recontextualization in the music of Rumpilezz.

2924 **Menezes, Andreia dos Santos.** Pandeiros e bandoneones: vozes disciplinadoras e marginais no samba e no tango. São Paulo: Editora UNIFESP, 2017. 298 p.: bibl.

A comparative study on the role of samba and tango in the processes of nation representation and identity construction in Brazil and Argentina. The book examines how narratives around national characters and symbols became associated with distinct genres of popular music, accompanying and propelling the development of the phonographic industry in both countries around the same time. The author compares the *compadrito* and *malandro* characters in tangos and sambas during the 1910–40 period, and argues that these poetico-musical constructions reflect the processes of urbanization and industrialization in each country.

2925 **Merhy, Sílvio.** 20 Comando Operação Bossa-Nova: a edição de 2009 e o aniversário da Bossa-Nova na Ilha de Villegagnon. (*Claves/João Pessoa*, 10, 2014, p. 23–45, bibl., ill., music)

This insightful essay on history and memory focuses on a 2009 replay of a bossa nova show sponsored by the navy in 1959. While the show took place at the same auditorium and featured the same repertory, the author shows how and why the audience perceived and reacted on a widely different way than their counterparts (in some case themselves) of 50 years before. As the author explains, decades of military rule, the naturalization of a musical repertory, the absence of specific esthetic polarizations, a different perspective on authenticity and tradition, as well as a generally commemorative tone imbued the 2009 event with a sense of nostalgia that was absent in 1959. Concludes with relevant considerations on musical and cultural analyses of popular music.

2926 **Molina, Sergio.** Música de montagem: a composição de música popular no pós-1967. São Paulo: É Realizações Editora, 2017. 197 p.: bibl., ill., index.

Discusses sound layering processes in the composition of popular song after 1967. Very useful for popular music scholars interested in understanding a number of compositional and recording techniques and conveying more precision to their analytical vocabulary. Detailed analyses of songs by Milton Nascimento and Gilberto Gil (in addition to Beatles, Sting, and Björk) are illustrated with musical examples and spectrograms. Outgrowth of the author's 2015 PhD dissertation in music.

2927 **Montagnani, Tommaso.** Corpos sonoros: instrumentos e donos na prática musical dos Kuikuro do alto Xingu. (*Rev. Antropol./São Paulo*, 59:1, jan./junho 2016, p. 201–223)

This study examines the use of the instruments *kagutu* (flute) and *atanga* (double flute) and *takwara* (clarinet) in the belief system and ritual practices of the Kuikuro (southwestern Xingu). The author argues that these instruments function as living beings, experiencing a life cycle and working as mediators between humans and spirits, as they receive offers of food and water from the humans and convey the voice of the spirits. The study describes the various "owners" or ritual actors that intervene along the stages of existence of the instruments and how these instruments affect their lives.

2928 **Moraes, José Geraldo Vinci de.** Lúcio Rangel comendo "ovos quentes com Noel Rosa": a invenção de uma historiografia da música popular. (*Rev. Bras. Hist./São Paulo*, 38:77, 2018, p. 125–145, bibl.)

This informative article considers the role of journalist Lúcio Rangel in the construction of a memory of urban popular music in Rio de Janeiro during the 1950s and 1960s. The author describes how the critic morphed into a chronicler and a historiographer of popular music, particularly as editor of the *Revista de Música Popular* (1954–56). He argues that by emphasizing concepts such as originality, authenticity, and roots, Rangel infused "social and cultural relevancy to urban popular music, making possible its artistic and musical sublimation, while distancing it from simple entertainment and commercialism." This article is also presented in English translation by David Rodgers.

Moreira, Moraes. Poeta não tem idade. See item **2517**.

2929 **Música.** Organização de Marcos Lacerda. Textos de Acauam Oliveira et al. Rio de Janeiro: Fundação Nacional de Artes, FUNARTE: Edigráfica, 2016. 406 p.: bibl. (Coleção Ensaios brasileiros contemporâneos)

Contains 20 influential essays on Brazilian popular music published from the 1990s to 2015, some of which have been previously reviewed in *HLAS*. Authors include L. Mammì, V. Ramil, A. Risério, R. Schwartz, L. Tatit, J.M. Wisnik, among others. The book includes new essays by G. Alonso Ferreira on the origins of *música sertaneja* (partly addressed in his *Cowboys do asfalto* (see item **2894**)) and P.C. Silva on Jorge Ben Jor. A number of texts were revised and/or expanded for this excellent compilation.

2930 **Naves, Santuza Cambraia.** A canção brasileira: leituras do Brasil através da música. Seleção e organização de Frederico Coelho et al. Rio de Janeiro: Zahar, 2015. 202 p.: bibl., index.

Reading Brazil through music is the aim of this volume of collected texts by anthropologist/sociologist Santuza Cambraia Neves. Through 11 short chapters published over the past two decades, the author discusses the role of Brazilian music (mostly popular) as a source of commentary, bolstering, and questioning of sociopolitical developments and the cultural environment in the country since the 1930s. The book focuses on samba, bossa-nova, tropicália, rock nacional, and rap, but also discusses briefly nationalism in concert music.

2931 **Neto, Lira.** Uma história do samba. Vol. 1, As origens. São Paulo: Companhia Das Letras, 2017. 344 p.: bibl., ill., index.

One of Brazil's foremost biographers casts an iconoclastic look at the development of samba in Rio de Janeiro from about 1890 to 1930. With a good balance between scholarship and storytelling, this thoroughly referenced biographical history consists of short stories involving samba's main agents, which unfold in lively fragments that overlap and complement each other, making for a very pleasant read. The author emphasizes the role of lesser-known figures, like Hilário Jovino Ferreira, and downplays the importance of others, like Fred Figner. The narrative is punctuated by contextual information on cultural practices and political events, but shies away from tackling social and race issues. One notable exception is the description of urban reforms in Rio, tracing parallels between the process of hygienization of the space and the domestication of samba. On the other hand, if the author's myth-debunking zeal is laudable, it generally focuses on narratives already debunked by a number of scholars (e.g., Raphael Menezes Bastos, Marc Hertzman, Carlos Sandroni, Hermano Vianna, and others). This is the first volume of a trilogy that will also include a volume on the "Época de ouro" (1930–1945), and a last one stretching the narrative up to the present time.

2932 **Nogueira, Carlos.** Samba, cuíca e São Carlos. 2a edição. Rio de Janeiro: Oito e Meio, 2014. 227 p.: bibl., ill.

Cultural geography of the São Carlos hill (Estácio district), birthplace of Rio's first *escola de samba* in 1928. Based on memory accounts of notable *sambistas*, the author alternates interviews with short stories of places, practices, and historical events, Selected samba lyrics provide the main thread for the contextualizing narrative.

2933 **Peixoto, Luiz Felipe de Lima** and **Zé Octávio Sebadelhe.** 1976 Movimento Black Rio. Rio de Janeiro: José Olympio, 2016. 253 p., 92 unumbered pages of plates: bibl., ill.

An in-depth examination of the Black Rio movement, from the early 1970s (with Tim Maia, Toni Tornado, and Wilson Simonal), to the late 1970s, with the agency of band and producer Dom Filó, and up to the bailes funk of the early 1980s. The authors argue that the movement emerged partly out of a discontentment with the coopting of samba by radio and media. They discuss the controversies around ethnicity, authenticity, and a perceived imported racism, some fueled by intellectuals, others by sambistas (particularly Candeia). The book also considers the role of Waltel Blanco in bringing the black groove to the soundtrack of Globo telenovelas. See also item **2868**.

2934 **Pereira, Carlos Eduardo.** A música no cinema silencioso no Brasil. Rio de Janeiro: Museu de Arte Moderna, 2014. 127 p.: bibl., ill.

Pereira offers an excellent introduction to an intriguing subject. Although short, the study brings a wealth of information on the type of music that accompanied early silent films in Rio de Janeiro. The book contains chapters on the transition from theater with music to the cinematographer and from the adaptation of existing music to the composition of original soundtracks. The author also covers performers, orchestras, music publishing houses, copyright, and the transition to the sound era. The book provides many cues for future research.

Perrone, Charles A. Bons tons diversos versos: o compositor, célebres letristas e a poética da Bossa Nova. See item **2525**.

2935 **Peters, Ana Paula.** Nas trilhas do choro. Curitiba, Brazil: Maquina de Escrever, 2016. 100 p.: bibl., ill. (chiefly color).

A beautiful and unpretentious history of choro in Curitiba. Initial chapters focus on early and new venues (theater, radio, private houses, public spaces, festivals, bars and cafés), with their performers and ensembles. The last two chapters cover practices of *roda de choro* in Curitiba and the local choro repertory. Profusely illustrated.

2936 **Piedade, Acácio Tadeu de Camargo.** The city and the country in Villa-Lobos's Prelude to the *Bachianas Brasileiras no. 2*: musical topics, rhetoric and narrativity. (*Rev. Port. Musicol.*, nova série, 4:1, 2017, p. 83–100, bibl., music)

This article demonstrates some ways in which Villa-Lobos created nationalist narratives in the *Bachianas Brasileiras no. 2* using a lexicon of musical topics representing musical practices and genres, regional characters, ethnicities, urban life, and the nature. The author stresses the pervasiveness of some of these topics in Brazilian literature and imagination, providing an effective example of blending cultural analysis and musical analysis.

2937 **Pinho, Osmundo.** "Tiroteio": subjetificação e violência no pagode baiano. (*in* Antinegritude: o impossível sujeito negro na formação social brasileira. Organização de Osmundo Pinho e João Vargas. Cruz das Almas, Brazil: Editora UFRB; Belo Horizonte, Brazil: Fino Traço Editora, 2016, p. 121–144, bibl.)

This book chapter discusses a controversial episode involving a *trio elétrico*, street performance of pagode baiano artist Igor Kannário in São Francisco do Conde, Bahia, during which a shooting took place. Kannário's attitudes and representations provide material for the author to examine the "creation of 'cultural personas' in the context of 'pagode baiano,' as a proxy for a process of subjectivização and the definition of structures of feeling, masculine and racialized identities, with a particular focus on the ways in which violence and the 'shooting' are part of this elaboration." The author traces an interesting connection with studies on narcocorridos.

2938 **Quelé, a voz da cor: biografia de Clementina de Jesus.** Textos de Felipe Castro *et al.* Rio de Janeiro: Civilização Brasileira, 2017. 384 p., 20 pages of plates: bibl., ill. (some color), index.

One of the common perceptions about Clementina de Jesus (1901–87) is that she represented one of the last living connections with the music once performed by former slaves, which was in fact the case with a number of her relatives and acquaintances in Valença, upstate Rio de Janeiro. This first biography of Clementina de Jesus was the achievement of a team of college students, who unveiled details on Clementina's childhood in Valença and her early career in Rio. Among other things, they highlight her active role in Rio's carnaval since the 1920s, first with the samba school Unidos do Riachuelo, then with Portela and Mangueira, all of this before being "discovered" in 1963. The authors also provide details on landmark recordings and shows from the 1960s-80s and her uneasy relationship with the recording industry. The bibliography provides detailed entries of hundreds of newspaper articles. Contains an insert with 20 unnumbered pages of photos.

2939 Reily, Suzel Ana. Local music making and the liturgical renovation in Minas Gerais. (*in* Oxford handbook of music and world Christianities. Edited by Suzel Ana Reily and Jonathan M. Dueck. New York: Oxford University Press, 2016, p. 315–339, bibl., ill., music)

Based on fieldwork in the city of Campanha, this essential study examines the effects of shifting policies and ideologies of the Catholic Church in the musical practices of a community in Minas Gerais during the 20th century. The author explains how the promotion of music of a more participatory and vernacular character after Vatican II produced esthetically unsatisfactory results by reducing the importance of traditional choir groups and music once promoted by lay brotherhoods. The article includes valuable descriptions of musical practices representing the paradigms of liturgical renovation and genres now considered to be elitist. The entry includes a deeper analysis of the Holy Week festival, reminiscent of the pre-Vatican II period, which is still sponsored by the community as a source of local pride, a symbol of their Baroque legacy, and a way to counteract a perceived threat against their esthetic sensibilities and local traditions.

2940 Revista do Instituto de Estudos Brasileiros. Vol. 70, 2018, Dossiê "Samba, sambas: uma encruzilhada de conflitos (1917–2017)." Organização de Walter Garcia e Gabriel S.S. Lima Rezende. São Paulo: Instituto de Estudos Brasileiros da Universidade de São Paulo.

Coinciding with the 100th year of the recording of "Pelo telefone," this special issue of the journal of the Institute of Brazilian Studies of the Universidade de São Paulo examines samba at the crossroads between the historic constructions of national identity, local belongings, and transnational ethnic identities. The articles cover various topics such as sambas by Bide and Marçal (Claudia N. de Matos), samba as a rhythm of black resistance (Amailton M. Azevedo), parallels between the jazz drumset and batucada (Leandro Barsalini), Central-African patterns in 1933–78 urban sambas (Enrique V. Menezes), sambas de Orfeu (Marina B. Malka and Carlos Augusto B. Leite), the crisis of modernization in "Chega de saudade" (Gabriel S.S. Lima Rezende), the disjunctive sambas of Tom Zé (Christopher Dunn), Candeia and the anti-racist militancy of the 1970s (David Treece), sociability and associativism in youth samba schools of Rio (Ana Paula A. Ribeiro), and the relationship between samba and rap in the periphery of São Paulo (Walter Garcia).

2941 Revista USP. Vol. 111, 2016, Dossiê "Música popular brasileira na USP." Organização de Ivan Vilela. São Paulo: Universidade de São Paulo, Coordenadoria de Atividades Culturais.

Ivan Vilela introduces this special issue of the *Revista USP* with a provocative argument in favor of a greater inclusion of Brazilian popular music in the university—not as subject for research, as it already is, but in the curriculum of music programs. In this volume, Luiz Tatit discusses songwriting techniques as described in a number of statements of famous Brazilian artists, while Chico Saraiva uses a similar approach with guitar composers and Sérgio Molina uses a more technical language to classify and scrutinize some of those techniques. Alberto Ikeda examines the transculturation of *ijexá* rhythmic formulas into a genre of popular music; Ivan Siqueira analyses Djavan's compositional techniques; Gil Jardim focuses on Rogério Duprat's arrangement of "Construção" to highlight overlaps between arranging and composing; Walter Garcia and Eduardo Vicente write on diverse aspects of record production. On a more sociohistorical tone, José Geraldo Vinci de Moraes discusses the work of Ary Vasconcelos, Celso Favaretto summarizes some specificities of song production in *tropicália*, and Ivan Vilela concludes the volume by bringing attention to the process of canon formation in Brazilian popular music.

2942 Revista Vórtex. Vol. 6, 2018. Curitiba, Brazil: Universidade Estadual do Paraná: Escola de Música e Belas Artes do Paraná. <http://vortex.unespar.edu.br/>

Now in its sixth volume, the academic journal of the Universidade Estadual do Paraná (UNESPAR) has enjoyed a steady increase in quality and relevance among music scholars in Brazil. The main focus is still on performance practice and music theory/analysis, but articles of a more humanistic emphasis do make an impact once in a while. To mention a few examples, Vol. 3, No. 2, 2015, offers timely essays on music and street protests in Rio (2013–2015) by D.M. Martins; music in the context of the so-called pacification of Rio's favelas by the research group Musicultura; and war, predation, and alliances in the musical system of the Tikmu'un by R.P. de Tugny. Focusing on musicological perspectives, Vol. 5, No. 1, 2017, contains original articles on the pedagogical activity of Luis Alvares Pinto (1719–89) by L.F. de Matos and L. Câmara, the esthetic and pedagogical ramifications of Hermeto Pascoal's Jabour School by R.F. da Silva, Villa-Lobos' guitar music by L.J.R.S. Lima, and the amateur-professional dynamics in the São Paulo jazz scene by M.V.S.R.M. de Almeida.

2943 Samba, cultura e sociedade: sambistas e trabalhadores entre a "questão social" e a questão cultural no Brasil. Organização de Marcelo Braz. São Paulo: Editora Expressão Popular, 2013. 246 p.: bibl., ill. (Coleção Arte e sociedade)

The first section of this book sets the theoretical basis (mostly Marxist) for the study of the social and cultural questions in relation to the working class struggles. The second part articulates these two dimensions with historical, racial, and conceptual aspects of samba. The third part approaches samba as the sociocultural expression of subaltern groups, as they navigate issues of modernity, resistance, and tradition, with individual studies on Noel Rosa, Bezerra da Silva, and three Portela composers—Paulo da Portela, Candeia, and Paulinho da Viola.

2944 O samba e a filosofia. Organização de Renato Noguera, Ronie Alexsandro Teles da Silveira, e Sérgio Schaefer. Curitiba, Brazil: Editora Prismas, 2015. 292 p.: bibl., ill.

This book brings together collected essays on the philosophical dimension of samba. Most texts gravitate around some type of philosophical analysis of songs and practices or the proposition that making samba is doing philosophy. As expected, Noel Rosa's "A filosofia" and Candeia's "Filosofia do samba" are used to support varied arguments in different chapters, from conveying a hedonistic philosophy (Marcos Carvalho Lopes), to enabling subjects to think with their bodies (Leonardo Davino de Oliveira), or providing metaphysical consolation (João Coviello). Other sambas explore the dichotomy between mind/reason and body/will, as it emerges in Pascal, Descartes, and Schopenhauer (Wilson Coelho). Other essays approach samba as a communal practice, or even a school (Renato Noguera), while comparing issues of displacement or alienation among presocratic philosophers and the early creators of samba de morro (Norberto Perkoski and Ana Luiza Martins). One essay addresses samba as a rhetorical exercise (Claudia Helena Alvarenga and Tarso Bonilha Mazzotti), and offers a discussion of samba's exchange value, from a Marxist perspective.

Santos, Klécio. Sete de Abril, Pelotas, Rio Grande do Sul, Brasil: o teatro do imperador. See item **2582**.

2945 Saraiva, Chico. Violão canção: diálogos entre o violão solo e a canção popular. São Paulo: Edições Sesc São Paulo, 2018. 244 p.: bibl., ill., music.

This beautiful, original, and highly informative ethnographic study covers the compositional processes of some of the most important Brazilian guitar composers. The author interviewed Sérgio Assad, Paulo Belinatti, João Bosco, Elomar, Guinga, Marco Pereira, Paulo César Pinheiro, and Luiz Tatit. Generous musical examples illustrate their conversations. Topics include rhythmic, harmonic, and melodic matrices, lyrics, levels of interaction with the instrument, classical and popular guitar, from improvising to writing, and many others. Essential for guitar scholars.

2946 Satomi, Alice Lumi. Dragão confabulando: etnicidade, ideologia e herança cultural através da música para koto no Brasil. Curitiba, Brazil: Editora Prismas, 2018. 253 p.: bibl., ill.

This original study focuses on the music of Japanese immigrants in Brazil, particularly from Okinawa, and the diffusion of *koto* and its music (and of Japanese classical music in general) in the country. Based on fieldwork in Japanese-Brazilian associations, the book discusses issues of preservation and diffusion, socialization, teaching and learning, and the sociocultural meanings of musical resistance.

2947 Seeger, Anthony. Por que cantam os Kisêdjê: uma antropologia musical de um povo amazônico. Tradução de Guilherme Werlang. São Paulo: Cosac Naify, 2015. 159 p.: bibl., ill., index, 1 DVD.

Originally published in 1987, Seeger's essential book *Why Suyá sing* finally receives a Portuguese translation by anthropologist Guilherme Werlang. In addition to grammatical revisions of some Kisêdjê words, the book also contains a preface and a postface by the author on the changes that researcher, researched community, and the academic field itself experienced since 1987. Accompanied by a DVD with audio files of Seeger's 1972 recordings and video files of two realizations of the Festa do Rato (1996 and 2012). Reviewed by Rafael Nonato (*Mana*, 21:3, 2015, p. 675–678), Evandro de Souza Bonfim (*Espaço Ameríndio*, 11:2, jul./dez. 2017, p. 401–407), and Luciana Prass and Marília Stein (*El oído pensante*, 4:1, 2016).

2948 Seminário "Imaginação da Terra: Memória e Utopia na Canção Popular e no Cinema Brasileiro," Belo Horizonte, Brazil, 2008. Imaginação da terra: memória e utopia na moderna canção popular brasileira. Organização de Heloisa Maria Murgel Starling e Bruno Viveiros Martins. Belo Horizonte, Brazil: Editora UFMG, 2012. 242 p.: bibl. (Origem)

Collected essays on narratives and alegories of land and land issues in popular song. Opens with an insightful chapter by Elizabeth Travassos (1955–2013) on different ways in which urban artists have represented the *sertão* (countryside) and its people throughout the 20th century, from satire to nostalgic idealization, to parody and sampling. Chapters by Mauro Braga, Marcelo Ridenti, and Paulo César Araújo, address nostalgia and utopia in the context of the ideological polarization and political repression of the 1930s-40s and 1960s-70s. Includes chapters by three expert performers on Brazilian regional styles, Ivan Vilela, Paulo Freire, and Siba, each one balancing critical views with personal experiences.

2949 Simpósio Nacional de Musicologia da UFG, 5th, Pirenópolis, Brazil, 2015. Anais: V Simpósio Nacional de Musicologia da UFG e VII Encontro de Musicologia Histórica da UFRJ, Pirenópolis, 2015. Pirenópolis, Brazil: EMAC/UFG, UFRJ, 2015. 318 p.: bibl., ill., music.

Over the past the few years, the School of Music and Drama of the Universidade Federal de Goiás (UFG) organized three conferences of the series Simpósio Internacional de Musicologia. The 5th iteration (2015), in conjunction with UFRJ, took place in Pirenópolis, and the 6th and 7th (2016, 2017) in Goiânia, in collaboration with the Universidade Nova de Lisboa (CESEM-Núcleo Caravelas). The proceedings include papers on historical musicology (mostly on Brazilian and Portuguese topics), sociology of music, music education, analysis, and performance. All of the volumes of the proceedings since the 2011 edition are freely available on the conference website: https://www.musicologiaemac.org/anais.

2950 Simpósio Nacional Villa-Lobos, 1st, Rio de Janeiro, 2015. Obra, tempo e reflexos: anais. Rio de Janeiro: Sarau Agência de Cultura, 2015. 182 p. <http://www.festivalvillalobos.com.br/2015>

Conceived as a means to add an academic dimension to the Villa-Lobos Festival, in existence since 1961, this symposium provides a common ground for dialogue between scholars from different backgrounds interested in the Brazilian composer. These 15 papers provide perspectives from esthetics, reception (VL in Tom Jobim and Almeida Prado, VL's guitar music, VL's Choros no. 1 performed by *regionais*), historically informed performance (cuíca in VL's time, and the original scoring of *Quinteto em forma de choro*), and semiotics (topic theory [the canto de Xangô topic], Nattiez's semiology, and Tarasti's existencial semiotics).

2951 **Simpósio Nacional Villa-Lobos, 2nd, Rio de Janeiro, 2016.** Práticas, representações e intertextualidades: anais. Rio de Janeiro: Sarau Agência de Cultura: PPGM-UFRJ, 2017. 172 p. <http://www.festivalvillalobos.com.br/>

The second iteration of the Simpósio Nacional Villa-Lobos is organized in collaboration with the Universidade Federal do Rio de Janeiro. The 12 conference papers published in these proceedings explore a narrower range of topics than the previous symposium (Villa-Lobos in Paris, in the US, interactions with choro, and nationalism). For a review of the proceedings from the first conference, see item **2950**.

2952 **Simpósio Villa-Lobos, 3rd, São Paulo, 2017.** Novos desafios interpretativos: anais. Organização de Paulo de Tarso Salles et al. São Paulo: ECA-USP, 2017. 402 p.

Although coinciding with the 3rd edition of a Villa-Lobos symposium that takes place in Rio de Janeiro, this is a different event, organized by the Universidade de São Paulo and with previous editions in 2009 and 2012. The 22 papers published in the third volume of proceedings scrutinize the life and works of Villa-Lobos by means of biographical and historical contextualizations (5 papers), semiotics and topic theory (5), formal, harmonic, and processual analysis (5), editing (1), interactions with urban popular music (3), and performance practice (3). Within the first group, in addition to Latin American modernist nationalism, there is an interesting connection with Italian nationalist neoclassicism. Although the title is similar, there is no duplication with item **2956**.

Suplemento literário de Minas Gerais. See item **2548**.

2953 **Teperman, Ricardo Indig.** Se liga no som: as transformações do rap no Brasil. São Paulo: Claro Enigma, 2015. 177 p.: bibl., ill., index. (Coleção Agenda brasileira)

This is a good historical summary of rap in Brazil from its origins in disco and soul music in the 1970s until the most recent hybrid mixtures and technologies of production and distribution. Individual chapters examine how sociopolitical and ethnic issues shaped the development of rap music in Brazil, while the genre itself was being transformed by market forces.

2954 **Trotta, Felipe.** O funk no Brasil contemporâneo: uma música que incomoda. (*LARR*, 51:4, 2016, p. 86–101, bibl.)

Rejecting both the intellectuals' romantization and the media condemnation of funk and *rolezinhos,* Trotta points out to the positive effects of the 2013–14 controversy. He argues that, through its boasting lyrics, invasive sound, and explosive performances, funk (particularly São Paulo's funk *ostentacão*) synthesizes the social discomfort of *rolezinhos* as a political action aimed at questioning the cultural and social hierarchies of the country.

2955 **Vicente, Eduardo.** Da vitrola ao iPod: uma história da indústria fonográfica no Brasil. São Paulo: Alameda Casa Editorial, 2014. 268 p.: bibl., 1 ill.

This book discusses the transformations of the recording industry in Brazil in the last decades of the 20th century. Despite the title, the only mention of digital distribution of music is in the first chapter, which addresses international business models, the main recording labels, and the polarization of the industry in majors and indies. Chapter 2 examines the consolidation of the large international labels in Brazil during the 1960s and 70s and their influence on local performance standards and on the stratification of the market. Chapters 3 and 4 focus on the 1980s and 90s, explaining how the economic context and new recording technologies allowed segmentation and growth of the industry. The last chapter illustrates the previous discussions with tables and descriptions of musical genres or segments, recording labels, and their associations.

2956 **Villa-Lobos, um compêndio: novos desafios interpretativos.** Organização de Paulo de Tarso Salles e Norton Dudeque. Curitiba, Brazil: Editora UFPR, 2017. 491 p.: bibl., ill. (some color). (Série Pesquisa; 331)

This essential compendium identifies and tackles "new interpretative challenges" posed by the unavoidable Villa-Lobos. While most of the authors in this book do so by submitting specific works to a variety of analytical approaches, others engage with broader cultural issues. Among the latter, the two opening articles, by Leopoldo Waizbort and Pedro P. Salles, offer diverse yet complementary assessments of Villa-Lobos' use of ethnographic recordings in his appropriation of indigenous music. Flávia Toni and Manuel A. Corrêa do Lago unveil the role of Mário de Andrade, Di Cavalcanti, and Adolph Bolm in Villa-Lobos' ballet project *Carnaval das Crianças*. Pedro Belchior discusses the role of Museu Villa-Lobos in constructing and reinforcing certain memories of the composer and the nation, while in the following chapter Lutero Rodrigues argues that the composer's so-called discovery of Brazil was a slower process, which began much earlier than his epiphany in Paris, as suggested by Peppercorn, Tarasti, and Guérios. If Acácio T.C. Piedade also discusses Villa-Lobos' modernist nationalism, his theoretical approach allows him to identify and explain the use, in the *Bachianas* no. 2, of a number of topics from urban popular music. Sílvio Ferraz's chapter on *Rudepoema* shows how sketch studies (another analytical approach that became a field itself) can shed new light on a well-known piece. The remainder of the book is more theoretical in nature, with essays on gestuality in the 1945 String Trio (Norton Dudeque), on the series *Prole do Bebê* (Nahim Marun), chamber songs (Achille Picchi), symmetrical structures and processes (Allan Falqueiro, Walter Nery Filho, Joel Albuquerque, Ciro Visconti), representational strategies and harmonic collections in the *Choros* (Gabriel Ferrão Moreira), and pentatonism in the Guitar Concerto (Rodolfo Coelho de Souza). The book concludes with a dense chapter on sonata form in the string quartets, by the leading Villa-Lobos scholar Paulo de Tarso Salles.

2957 *World of Music (new series).* Vol. 5, No. 1, 2016, Ethnomusicology in Brazil. Edited by Angela Lühning and Rosângela Pereira de Tugny. Göttingen, Germany: Department of Musicology, Georg August University, 2016.

Special issue edited by Angela Lühning and Rosângela Pereira de Tugny, focusing on the discipline of ethnomusicology in Brazil. All articles are multi-authored (ranging from three to 10 authors), emphasizing the importance of research groups and collective efforts within the field in Brazil. The two opening articles discuss the discipline's engagement with social, political, and cultural issues, and the presence of ethnomusicologists not only in academia, but also in the public sector. One article describes the role of ethnomusicologists in the large-scale Sound Documentation Project, which currently works with six groups (Tikmũ'ũn, Guarani Kaiowa, Guarani-Mbyá, Enawene Nawe, Baniwa, and Krahô), enjoying the collaboration of indigenous and non-indigenous researchers, and aiming at documenting, analyzing, and discussing sound practices as they relate to diverse modes of being and acting in the world. Two articles explore intersections between ethnomusicology and music education, emphasizing the need for decolonizing strategies. Concludes with a study on recent changes in *forró* music and São João festivals, focusing on the organization of such activities and the increasing presence of professional musicians and practitioners who attend a formal music school. For a Portuguese translation of this important publication, see item **2892**.

PHILOSOPHY: LATIN AMERICAN THOUGHT

SUSANA NUCCETELLI, *Professor of Philosophy, St. Cloud State University*

GIVEN A BROAD UNDERSTANDING of Latin American philosophy, many studies qualify for inclusion in this chapter provided they satisfy two conditions. First, any qualifying work must fall within what admits classification as philosophy, broadly construed in order to include thinkers who have managed to raise significant philosophical questions without having had any formal training in philosophy—for example, Sor Juana Inés de la Cruz, Simón Bolívar, and José Martí. Second, the work must bear some relation to Latin America, whether by its topic, approach, or geographical origin. Although all publications selected for inclusion satisfy both conditions, most of them qualify as Latin American philosophy merely because they satisfy the geographical origin requirement. This phenomenon is consistent with works reviewed in previous years. In the past, most of the works included in the *HLAS* Philosophy section were published in Argentina, Chile, Colombia, Mexico, Peru, or Uruguay. The works reviewed for *HLAS 74* suggest that these countries continue to be the leaders in terms of total number of publications that qualify for this branch of philosophy. With this volume, however, it is apparent that countries which to date have had a lower record of qualifying publications might soon remedy this shortfall and catch up with the chief producers. Among them are Bolivia, Cuba, Ecuador, and Venezuela, as well as Spain and the US. Consider first Spain, a country that during the 20th century seems to have had little interest in Latin American philosophy, as shown by its very low record of publications in this area. That Spain's interest is now on the rise is suggested, for example, by two monumental reference works recently published in that country. Published in 2009 by Cátedra (Madrid), *El legado filosófico español e hispanoamericano del siglo XX*, edited by Manuel Garrido, Nelson R. Orringer, Luis M. Valdés and Margarita M. Valdés is not reviewed here because it falls outside the dates of inclusion for this volume. The other, *Enciclopedia iberoamericana de filosofía*, saw its first volume published in 1992. The final volome of this vast encyclopedia, issued in two parts, and edited by Reyes Mate, Osvaldo Norberto Guariglia, and León Olivé, is reviewed here (items **2965** and **2966**). This and other volumes of the *Enciclopedia* make clear that the editors mostly sought contributions written from the analytic perspective in philosophy, a 20th-century school that originated in the English-speaking world, but now seems to be taking root in other parts of the world, including some Spanish-speaking countries. Another work in that tradition reviewed for this issue of the *Handbook* is Verónica Zárate Toscano's journal article on the linguistic turn in Mexican philosophy (item **2995**), which occurred during the late 1960s and early 1970s.

Several countries are exhibiting a noticeable boom in their publications in Latin American philosophy, including Bolivia, Cuba, Ecuador, and Venezuela. The philosophical works from Bolivia reviewed in this edition of the *Handbook* feature topics and methods from some of the major Western idioms of philosophical thinking and also from some schools that have distinctively Latin American features. Prominent among the first group are the Frankfurt School, French philosophy, Marxism, and German phenomenology; among the second group, liberation philosophy, liberation theology, and feminist philosophy. Although we can detect numerous instances of cross-pollination between these groups, by and large these publications exhibit a preference for topics and methods of one or the other group (for example, see items **3018**, **3020**, **3021**, **3022**, and **3023**). Similarly marked preferences are evident in three publications from Ecuador (items **3008**, **3009**, and **3019**) and two publications from Venezuela (items **3001** and **3002**). Cuba is represented here by only one publication (item **3000**) that exemplifies a criss-crossing between Western philosophical schools and a distinctively Cuban topic. After all, it takes from the first group a Marxist theoretical framework and from the second group a focus on the future of socialism in Cuba.

Note that some of the publications from these countries tend to have their philosophical quality undermined by a heavy reliance on unargued metaphysical or ideological assumptions. As duly noted in the reviews, readers may fail to find in many of them the critical analysis expected as standard in a work of philosophy. Only when signs of improvements in this respect become available might we develop any optimistism about the prospects of philosophy in, say, Bolivia or Venezuela. However, a similarly dogmatist tendency is also noticeable in some of the publications from elsewhere in Latin America: for example, in some works from Argentina (items **2978**), **3033**, **3038**, and **3042**) and in a work from Colombia (item **2962**).

But not all of the works reviewed here, which mostly engage social and political philosophy as well as the history of philosophy, have a dogmatic tendency. Some of them successfully engage in reasoned argument—especially those that can be classified within the philosophy of race, an area in which authors generally argue for or against the so-called mestizaje (mix-of-races) view of Latin American identity (items **3001**, **2958**, **3029**, **2984**, and **2985**). The most persuasive authors look closely at the writings of historical figures who famously endorsed that view, such as Simón Bolívar, José Martí, José Carlos Mariátegui, and José Vasconcelos.

The works selected for review also suggest that there is another promising line of research concerning the history of philosophy and, more broadly, the history of philosophical ideas. Most publications in this area are essays and monographs focused on either a philosophical thinker or a doctrine that has had an impact on the philosophical thought of the subcontinent. Historiographical questions of either kind have the longest and most varied tradition in Latin America. So it is not surprising that the essays and monographs asking them tend to have a higher scholarly quality. When their focus is a figure, the relevant questions involve thinkers as dissimilar as Bartolomé de Las Casas (item **3016**), José Artigas (item **3032**), Pedro S. Zulen (item **3017**), and many others—while when their focus is a doctrine, they show a clear preference for exploring the ideas of the political left in Latin America, as illustrated by a number of works devoted to the political philosophy of anarchism (items **2961**, **2967**, **2997**, and **3028**).

Finally, judging from the publications reviewed for *HLAS 74*, we can say that other areas of Latin American philosophy show signs of progress. Supporting this conclusion are a relatively encouraging number of writings devoted to the philosophy of the Andean native peoples (items **3008**, **3012**, and **3014**); a vast reference work entirely devoted to religion in Latin America, which also includes essays on the religious practices of the native peoples of the region (item **2960**); and several works focused on meta-philosophical issues which have been central to Latin American philosophy since the mid-20th century. They concern the very nature and foundations of this discipline (items **2970**, **2977**, and **2982**, among others).

GENERAL

2958 Afro-Latin American studies: an introduction. Edited by Alejandro de la Fuente and George Reid Andrews. Cambridge, England: Cambridge University Press, 2018. 641 p.: bibl., ill., index. (Afrolatin america)

De la Fuente and Andrews have included in this edited volume 14 essays devoted to various aspects of the rising field of Afro-Latin American studies. The essays are arranged topically in four parts: "I. Inequalities," "II. Politics," "III. Culture," and "IV. Transnational Spaces." Parts I and II are the most closely related to philosophy since the essays raise questions of the philosophy of race and feminism. In particular, they challenge the mestizaje view of Latin American identity, which has enjoyed a long and varied acceptance in Latin America. Given their common objection, the mestizaje view implies that there must be "racial democracy" in the region. But since it does not exist, the objectors conclude that the mestizaje view is false.

Álvarez-Uría, Fernando. El reconocimiento de la humanida: España, Portugal y América Latina en la génesis de la modernidad. See item **354**.

2959 Anthology of Spanish American thought and culture. Edited by Jorge Aguilar Mora, Josefa Salmón, and Barbara C. Ewell. Gainesville: University Press of Florida, 2016. 427 p.: bibl., ill., index, map.

This anthology collects some of the key primary sources in Latin American thought. It construes this field broadly since it includes selections from thinkers who would not strictly be considered philosophers given current academic standards in the West—for example, selections from the writings of modern explorers, literary figures, religious thinkers, and political leaders. The result is a comprehensive volume that effectively introduces students and general readers to Latin American thought.

2960 The Cambridge history of religions in Latin America. Edited by Virginia Garrard-Burnett, Paul Freston, and Stephen C. Dove. New York: Cambridge University Press, 2016. 1 v.: bibl., index.

This comprehensive reference volume collects 49 essays on the different religions and religious practices in Latin America, from the precolumbian period to the present. The editors have made a serious effort at combining essays focused on historical and philosophical issues associated with the volume's main topic. In addition to essays on Catholicism, Latin America's mainstream religion, they have included essays on other religions and on religious practices with roots in precolumbian and Afro-Caribbean cultures and religions such as Judaism, Islam, Protestantism, and some non-Protestant forms of Christian fundamentalism that are now practiced on the subcontinent.

2961 Cappelletti, Angel J. Anarchism in Latin America. Translated by Gabriel Palmer-Fernández. Introduction by Romina Akemi and Javier Sethness-Castro. Chico, Calif.: AK Press, 2017. 429 p.: appendices, index.

In this historical and political study, Argentinian philosopher Angel Cappelletti offers a detailed account of the emergence and development of anarchism in Latin America. Cappelletti puts his vast knowledge of the history of ideas in Latin America at the service of producing a rigorous account of a revolutionary movement that was the subject of interesting twists when transported to Latin America. He also includes useful summaries of the development of anarchism in most Latin American countries.

2962 El Che en la psicología latinoamericana. Coordinación de Edgar Barrero Cuellar, Eduardo Viera, Marco Eduardo Murueta, Manuel Calviño y Mario Flores Lara. Bogotá: ALFEPSI Editorial, 2014. 224 p.: bibl., ill.

In addition to a lengthy introduction, this edited volume contains essays about Che Guevara's life and doctrines by Edgar Barrero Cuellar, Eduardo Viera, Marco Eduardo Murueta, Manuel Calviño, and Mario Flores Lara. These authors set themselves the task of celebrating this legendary figure of guerrilla movements in Latin America, while at the same time promoting his revolutionary doctrine. As a result, the book lacks the standard critical approach expected in a scholarly publication.

2963 Curcó Cobos, Felipe. Latin American political thought as a response to discourse ethics. (*LARR*, 50:4, 2015, p. 69–87, bibl.)

In this article Curcó Cobos argues that liberation philosophy raises a challenge for the so-called discourse ethics of the Frankfurt School, a German school of philosophy that attracted considerable attention in Latin America during the last part of the 20th century. His article might be of interest to scholars working in liberation philosophy, the Frankfurt School, or the relationship between these philosophical positions.

2964 Deconstrucción y genealogía del concepto de dignidad de los pueblos originarios en el pensamiento latinoamericano. Coordinación de Ana Luisa Guerrero Guerrero. México: Bonilla Artigas Editores: UNAM, Centro de Investigaciones sobre América Latina y el Caribe, 2015. 318 p.: bibl. (Colección Filosofía e historia de las ideas en América Latina y el Caribe; 21)

This edited volume contains 11 new essays plus an introduction by the editor. Prompted by the Zapatista uprising of the 1990s, the volume aims at addressing issues of multiculturalism and democracy in the pluri-national countries of Latin America. Of particular interest are three essays offering critical discussions of Luis Villoro's concept of "participative democracy."

2965 Filosofía iberoamericana del siglo XX. Vol. 1, Filosofía teórica e historia de la filosofía. Edición de Reyes Mate, Osvaldo Guariglia y León Olivé. Madrid: Trotta: Consejo Superior de Investigaciones Científicas, 2015. 1 v.: bibl. (Enciclopedia iberoamericana de filosofía; 33)

This volume of the *Enciclopedia* contains essays written mostly from the perspective of analytic philosophy. The authors look closely at developments in ethics, philosophy of history, philosophy of law, esthetics, and political philosophy in Latin America. Largely absent is the important issue of whether these disciplines in Latin America have something distinctive or merely form part of Western philosophy. However, the volume does include some essays that consider the contributions of the so-called Latin American essayists to the philosophy of the region. For a review of vol. 2, see item **2966**.

2966 Filosofía iberoamericana del siglo XX. Vol. 2, Filosofía práctica y filosofía de la cultura. Edición de Reyes Mate, Osvaldo Guariglia y León Olivé. Madrid: Trotta: Consejo Superior de Investigaciones Científicas, 2015. 1 v.: bibl. (Enciclopedia iberoamericana de filosofía; 33)

This is the second volume in a multivolume reference work devoted to philosophy in Spain and the countries that grew out of Spain's colonies in Latin America. It features new essays on the chief branches of philosophy cultivated in Latin America written by some emerging experts in those fields, which include metaphysics, philosophy of science, epistemology, philosophy of mind and language, ancient philosophy, medieval philosophy, and modern philosophy (in Spain). The articles provide abundant bibliographical information, but they are weak in the critical evaluation of the materials at hand.

2967 Garay, Gerardo. La vida es un arma: el pensamiento anarquista de Rafael Barrett y Luce Fabbri. Montevideo: Alter ediciones, 2015. 189 p.: bibl. (Biblioteca de Walter; 03)

In this monograph, Gerardo Garay makes a brief but solid contribution to the study of anarchism in Latin America. He focuses on the ideas developed by Spanish-born Rafael Barrett and Italian-born Luce Fabbri, both European thinkers whose ideas developed in Latin America (in Paraguay and Uruguay, respectively). Garay plausibly argues that their philosophical identity was not European but instead Latin American, owing to the fact that their thought was shaped by their experiences on this side of the Atlantic.

2968 González, José Eduardo. Appropriating theory: Ángel Rama's critical work. Pittsburgh, Pa.: University of Pittsburgh Press, 2017. 232 p.: bibl., index. (Illuminations: cultural formations of the Americas series)

This monograph traces the intellectual evolution of a 20th-century literary figure, Ángel Rama. González looks closely at Rama's life and his views on the chief tasks for literary criticism. He also offers an assessment of Rama's position on the value of technology, an issue that is of interest because of an ongoing debate in Latin America on that topic.

2969 Graff Zivin, Erin. Beyond inquisitional logic, or, toward an anarchaeological Latin Americanism. (CR, 14:1, Spring 2014, p. 195–211, bibl., photos)

This article argues against an essay, "For a Left with No Future," by art historian and leftist author T.J. Clark (New Left Review, Vol. 74, March/April 2012, p. 53–75). Graff Zivin's main objection to the article seems to be that it implies a pessimistic view that might have negative consequences for the Latin American left. To support this objection, he invokes some theoretical frameworks popular in current French philosophy, namely, the "Derridarian" and the "Levinasian" perspectives.

2970 Guía Comares de filosofía latinoamericana. Edición de Rafal Fornet-Betancourt y Carlos Beorlegui. Granada, Spain: Editorial Comares, 2014. 324 p.: bibl. (Colección Guía Comares de; 5)

This book presents a selection of essays in Latin American philosophy that were written at different periods, beginning with the precolumbian period and ending with current Latin American philosophy. It also introduces readers to Fornet-Betancourt's style of philosophy, the so-called intercultural philosophy. The result is an anthology that will be of interest to historically minded readers of Latin American philosophy as well as to instructors willing to introduce this subject at the undergraduate level and up.

2971 Hatfield, Charles Dean. The limits of identity: politics and poetics in Latin America. Austin: University of Texas Press, 2015. 158 p.: bibl., index. (Border Hispanisms)

In this study, Hatfield takes issue with a dichotomy that has dominated contemporary debates about the identity of Latin American thought: namely, the tension between universalism and Latin Americanism. Hatfield examines how that dichotomy is perceived in the writings of, among others, José Martí and José Carlos Rodó.

2972 Historicidad dialéctica: espacio y tiempo en nuestra América. Coordinación de Horacio Cerutti-Guldberg. México: UNAM, 2015. 209 p.: bibl. (Colección Filosofía e historia de las ideas en América Latina y el Caribe; 23)

Edited by one of the major figures in the liberation-philosophy movement, this collection offers 10 new essays on a variety of topics of political philosophy, esthetics, history of ideas, and literature in Latin America. Their common theme appears to be that all authors share the postulates of liberation philosophy.

2973 Ideas que cruzan el Atlántico: utopía y modernidad latinoamericana. Coordinación de Daniel Abraldes. Madrid: Escolar y Mayo, 2015. 342 p.: bibl., ill. (Euroamericana)

The new essays collected in this volume generally aim at either determining the collective identity of Latin Americans today or establishing how their identity was constituted throughout the region's history. They seek to achieve one or the other of these two goals by examining topics such as the morality of the Iberian conquest and the nature of Latin America's current relations with Europe and North America. The contribution by Abraldes offers an account of the conflict that arose between farmers and the government in 2008 in Argentina and thus hardly fits the general aims of the book.

2974 **Identidad y pensamiento latinoamericano.** Dirección de Oscar Mejía Quintana. Edición de Ivonne Patricia León y Pablo Ignacio Reyes Beltrán. Bogotá: Universidad Nacional de Colombia-Sede Bogotá, Facultad de Derecho, Ciencias Políticas y Sociales, Instituto Unidad de Investigaciones Jurídico-Sociales "Gerardo Molina"-UNIJUS, 2013. 219 p.: bibl., ill. (Colección Gerardo Molina; 36)

This edited volume, which lacks a table of contents listing all chapters and authors, contains four essays. Each editor and an outside author contributed these essays. Cohesion to the volume is given by two factors: (1) all essays discuss the collective identity of Latin Americans; and (2) all contributors favor the liberation-philosophy approach to that topic. Of special interest are the most historically minded contributions—namely chapters 3 and 4, which explore, respectively, Latin American identity during the Spanish colonial rule and during the national organization after the wars of independence in the 19th century.

2975 **El imaginario antiimperialista en América Latina.** Coordinación de Andrés Kozel, Florencia Grossi y Delfina Moroni. Buenos Aires: Ediciones del CCC, Centro Cultural de la Cooperación Floreal Gorini, CLACSO, 2015. 420 p.: bibl., ill.

Sponsored by the Consejo Latinoamericano de Ciencias Sociales (CLACSO) and the Centro Cultural de la Cooperación Floreal Gorini, this edited volume contains new essays that explore the notions of imperialism and anti-imperialism in recent Latin American political thought. In particular, the essays look closer at the use of these notions by contemporary figures such as Hugo Chávez and Juan José Arévalo. This collection will be of interest to readers seeking an update on a debate that has figured prominently in Latin American political thought since at least the 1970s.

2976 **Injusticias de género en un mundo globalizado: conversaciones con la teoría de Nancy Fraser.** Coordinación de María Antonia Carbonero Gamundí y Silvia Levin. Rosario, Argentina: Homo Sapiens Ediciones, 2014. 210 p.: bibl. (Colección Politeia)

The editors of this volume, both trained in the social sciences, invoke the "de-colonizing" framework of feminist philosopher Nancy Fraser to account for pervasive inequities that Latin American women face. To support this claim, they review the results of their empirical studies. One of the editors, Carbonero Gamundí, comments on her surveys of Latin American cleaning women in Spain. In her view, the work of these women is under-recognized and underpaid, but some remedies to these problems are available. The other editor, Levin, looks closely into the injustices that women in Argentina have faced since that country's return to democracy in the mid-1980s. Two essays by other authors, also included in the volume, invoke Fraser's framework to examine how the welfare state and globalization raise issues of justice for Latin American women.

2977 **Llorente, Renzo.** Gracia on Hispanic and Latino identity. (*J. Spec. Philos.*, 27:1, 2013, p. 67–78, bibl.)

In this journal article, Llorente argues that Jorge Gracia's well-known view about the identity of both Latin America and Latin American philosophy faces an inconsistency problem.

2978 **Lovisolo, Jorge.** Trastornos: filosofías políticas en la literatura. Buenos Aires: Ediciones Biblioteca Nacional, 2015. 346 p.: bibl.

This monograph offers an unusual approach to the study of the work of some prominent literary figures from both Latin America and Europe. Among them are Borges, Bioy Casares, Cortázar, Beckett, Kafka, Joyce, and a few others. Lovisolo combines elements of literature from these authors with notions of psychoanalysis from Peronism. The result is a series of claims about those figures based on very thin evidence.

2979 **Maduro, Otto.** Maps for a fiesta: a Latina/o perspective on knowledge and the global crisis. Edited and with an introduction by Eduardo Mendieta. New York: Fordham University Press, 2015. 181 p.: bibl., index.

Opening with an introduction by Mendieta, this book discusses Otto Maduro's theory of knowledge, which he developed by adapting the general framework of liberation philosophy. In doing so, Maduro set for himself a quite ambitious task since liberation philosophy lacks an account of subjects such as theory of knowledge and epistemic justification. In fact, Maduro rejects all Western epistemology, developing as an alternative his own epistemology. As a result, this book might be of interest only for those curious about how (or whether) liberation philosophy could be extended to include a theory of knowledge.

2980 **Millán, Elizabeth** and **Amy A. Oliver.** Toward an appreciation of Latin American philosophy: Jorge J.E. Gracia's recovery mission. (*CR*, 14:1, Spring 2014, p. 245–258, bibl.)

Mostly exegetical, this journal article is devoted to examining the impact in philosophy of the work of Cuban-American philosopher Jorge Gracia. It may be of interest to those who wish to learn about Gracia's ideas as a historian of Latin American philosophy, a literary critic, a metaphysician, or a Francisco Suárez scholar.

2981 **Moreiras, Alberto.** We have good reasons for this (and they keep coming): revolutionary drive and democratic desire. (*CR*, 14:1, Spring 2014, p. 213–243, bibl.)

This essay examines some recent publications on the prospects of communism and neocommunism, thus falling within the province of political philosophy in Latin America. It will be of interest to scholars in this discipline as well as to anyone curious about the future of communist movements around the world.

2982 **Orosco, José Antonio.** The philosophical gift of brown folks: Mexican American philosophy in the United States. (*APA News. Hisp. Latino Phil.*, 15, Spring 2016, p. 23–28)

In this essay, Orosco contends that Mexican American and Latin American philosophy can both have great prospects in the US provided they devote themselves to philosophical inquiry into questions concerning Latino identity, power, and citizenship.

Podetti, José Ramiro. Cultura y alteridad: en torno al sentido de la experiencia latinoamericana. See item **3041**.

2983 **Ramos, Juan G.** Sensing decolonial aesthetics in Latin American arts. Gainesville: University of Florida Press, 2018. 254 p.: bibl., index.

This book proposes a critical reevaluation of antipoetry, *nueva canción*, and third cinema in relation to decolonial theory and contemporary esthetic inquiries. A prime objective of the book is to bring these separate art forms into dialogue with each other as collectively contributing to an archive of decolonial art forms.

2984 **Segato, Rita Laura.** La crítica de la colonialidad en ocho ensayos: y una antropología por demanda. Buenos Aires: Prometeo Libros, 2015. 293 p.: bibl., ill.

Segato tells the readers of this monograph that she approaches the issues first as an anthropologist and second as a continental philosopher. But her philosophical perspective strongly interferes with her scientific perspective, especially when she accounts for the mestizaje view of Latin American collective identity. She discusses this issue in the course of examining various forms of discrimination based on race or gender in Latin America. The book will be more attractive to continental philosophers than to anthropologists seeking objective analyses of empirical data on the interesting issues addressed by Segato.

2985 **Simon, Joshua David.** The ideology of Creole revolution: imperialism and independence in American and Latin American political thought. Cambridge, England: Cambridge University Press, 2017. 284 p.: bibl., index. (Problems of international politics)

In this book, Simon looks closely at the national organization that followed colonial rule in the Americas. He seeks to establish some major commonalities and differences between the conceptions of nation-builders such as Alexander Hamilton in the US, Simón Bolívar in Gran Colombia, and Lucas Alamán in Mexico. His research reveals not only some illuminating factual information, but also concepts that can explain, at least in part, the complex relations between the countries in the Americas after the abolishment of colonial rule.

2986 **Socolow, Susan Migden.** The women of colonial Latin America. Second edition. New York: Cambridge University Press, 2015. 259 p.: bibl., ill., index. (New approaches to the Americas)

The Women of Colonial Latin America offers a historically minded account of the situation of women of different socioeconomic status in Latin America, especially during the colonial period. This second edition adds data on rural, native, and slave women. Socolow conducts a solid investigation that will be of interest to academic and non-academic readers wishing to learn about this part of Latin America's history. For a review of the first edition, see *HLAS 60:1060.*

2987 **Tolerancia: sobre el fanatismo, la libertad y la comunicación entre culturas.** Coordinación de Miguel Giusti. Lima: Fondo Editorial, Centro de Estudios Filosóficos, PUCP, 2015. 300 p.

This collection of 22 essays discusses the virtue of tolerance from a number of philosophical perspectives. It includes essays by some well-known figures of the Spanish-speaking world such as Oscar Nudler (Argentina), León Olivé (Mexico), Ernesto Garzón Valdés (Spain), Javier Muguerza (Spain), Humberto Giannini (Chile), and the editor Miguel Giusti (Peru). The scholarly quality of the essays is uneven: some express the author's personal opinion about the value of tolerance, while others conduct a more substantial philosophical inquiry. The issue of tolerance has gained significant attention in Latin America after the creation of truth-and-reconciliation commissions in countries that transitioned from military rule to democracy during the last decades of the 20th century.

2988 **Vistas cruzadas: los estudios latinoamericanos en Estados Unidos en los 90, vistos desde el Sur; un diálogo interdisciplinario.** Coordinación de Gustavo Remedi. Montevideo: Zonz Editorial, 2015. 267 p.: bibl.

This collection offers eight essays mostly devoted to investigating the perception in the US of some social sciences and humanities cultivated in Latin America. They include Latin American philosophy, anthropology, literature, feminism, and cultural studies. The contributions to the volume look closely at how these disciplines have developed in the US. Of particular interest for Latin American philosophy are Alejandra Umpiérrez's essay on Latino philosophy and Marisa Ruiz's essay on Latin American and Latino feminism.

MEXICO

2989 **Aguilar Rivera, José Antonio.** Después del consenso: el liberalismo en México, 1990–2012. (*Rev. Mex. Cienc. Polít. Soc.,* 58:218, mayo/agosto 2013, p. 19–52, bibl.)

This historically minded essay examines the re-emergence of liberalism in Mexico between 1990 and 2012. An informative article for scholars interested in political movements in contemporary Mexico such as liberalism, Indianism, and populism.

2990 **Democracia, otredad, melancolía: Roger Bartra ante la crítica.** Coordinación de Mabel Moraña y Ignacio M. Sánchez Prado. México: Fondo de Cultura Económica: Consejo Nacional Para la Cultura y las Artes, 2015. 390 p.: bibl. (Vida y pensamiento de México)

This edited volume offers 13 previously unpublished articles on the social thought of contemporary Mexican sociologist and essayist Roger Bartra. The contributions address Bartra's views on nationalism and populism, the political right and left, globalization, and the symbolic representation of the native peoples of Mexico.

2991 **Francisco Xavier Clavigero, un humanista entre dos mundos: entorno, pensamiento, y presencia.** Coordinación de Alfonso Alfaro, Iván Escamilla, Ana Carolina Ibarra y Arturo Reynoso. México: Fondo de Cultura Económica: UNAM, Instituto de Investigaciones Históricas: Universidad Iberoamericana; Tlaquepaque, Mexico: ITESO, 2015. 364 p.: ill., maps. (Sección de obras de historia)

This edited volume is devoted chiefly to some salient aspects of the life, work, and philosophical context of Francisco Xavier Clavigero. This leading Jesuit intellectual of the colonial period, like other members of the Society of Jesus, was forced to leave Spanish America in 1767. Among the essays discussing the reasons for their expulsion are contributions by Miguel León Portilla and each of the editors.

2992 Labastida, Jaime. ¡Pueden las aves romper su jaula? Iztapalapa, Mexico: Siglo Veintiuno Editores, 2016. 391 p.: bibl., ill., maps. (Teoría)

The topics of this monograph fall within the intersection of philosophy and literature. They generally bear on the issue of which property or properties, if any, are constitutive of Mexican identity. Labastida challenges this way of thinking about Mexican identity in terms of properties. He outlines the chief views at stake in ways that are accessible to readers who might not have a background in Mexican philosophy. Labastida also includes some chapters that may be attractive to readers interested in Sor Juana Inés de la Cruz, Inca Garcilaso de la Vega, Felipe Guaman Poma de Ayala, and other historical figures of Latin American thought.

2993 Sánchez, Carlos Alberto. Contingency and commitment: Mexican existentialism and the place of philosophy. Albany: State University of New York Press, 2016. 161 p.: bibl., index. (SUNY series in Latin American and Iberian thought and culture)

This monograph discusses existentialism in Mexico, the identity of Latinos in the US, and the quality of Mexican philosophy. Although Sánchez produces credible accounts in the three areas, his best contribution to Latin American philosophy is his treatment of existentialism in Mexico. His book is highly recommended for those interested in this topic as well as in the role of the Grupo Hiperion in Mexican philosophy.

Van Young, Eric. De una memoria truncada a una historia majestuosa: el caso de Lucas Alamán. See item **616**.

2994 Vinson, Ben. Before mestizaje: the frontiers of race and caste in colonial Mexico. New York: Cambridge University Press, 2018. 284 p., 8 unnumbered pages of plates: bibl., ill. (some color), index, maps (some color). (Cambridge Latin American studies; 105)

Vinson's monograph provides ample evidence of racial and ethnic categorizations—together with some associated forms of discrimination—that prevailed in Spanish America during the colonial period. Equipped with data gathered principally from contemporary sources in today's Mexico, Vinson offers solid analyses of the processes of mestizaje and mulataje that took place during the colonial period. For colonial historian's comment, see item **526**.

2995 Zárate Toscano, Verónica. La historia intelectual en México y sus conexiones. (*Varia Hist.*, 31:56, maio/agôsto 2015, p. 401–422, bibl.)

This journal article is devoted to a particular development in 20th-century Mexican philosophy: "the linguistic turn," a movement in the analytic tradition that gained some currency during the 1960s. The article will be of interest to historians of contemporary Mexican philosophy, especially its analytic variety.

CENTRAL AMERICA

2996 A grammar of justice: the legacy of Ignacio Ellacuría. Edited by J. Matthew Ashley, Kevin F. Burke, S.J., and Rodolfo Cardenal, S.J. Maryknoll, N.Y.: Orbis Books, 2014. 283 p.: bibl., index.

This edited volume is an important source for anyone interested in the ideas of Ignacio Ellacuría, and more broadly, of Liberation Theology. It offers new essays by experts on the life and work of this Liberation Theologian of the second half of the 20th century, whose contribution to Liberation Theology is now considered significant. The volume also features a classic essay by Ellacuría and a letter on martyrdom that he sent to Óscar Romero, a Catholic priest who like Ellacuría himself, was one of the several Liberation Theologians murdered by paramilitary groups in Central America during the final decades of the 20th century.

2997 Rodríguez Cascante, Francisco. Imaginarios utópicos: filosofía y literatura disidentes en Costa Rica (1904–1945). Costa Rica: Editorial UCR, 2016. 287 p.: bibl.

This collection of new essays addresses a wide variety of subjects. Some are focused on topics of philosophy, religion, and literature, while others discuss topics of theosophy, pseudoscience such as spiritism, and political doctrines such as anarchism and socialism. The volume will be attractive to scholars interested in Costa Rica's intellectual and cultural developments during the first half of the 20th century.

THE CARIBBEAN

2998 Freedom, power and sovereignty: the thought of Gordon K. Lewis. Edited by Brian Meeks and Jermaine McCalpin. Kingston: Ian Randle Publishers, 2015. 220 p.: bibl. (Caribbean reasonings)

Freedom, Power and Sovereignty includes 10 new essays devoted to the analysis of the political thought of Gordon K. Lewis. This Caribbean (by adoption) intellectual has written extensively on issues of Afro-Caribbean philosophy, rights, and identity. Of special interest are the essays devoted to his publications in these areas. For comment by political scientist, see *HLAS 73:1113*.

2999 Minaya, Julio. Pedro Francisco Bonó: vida, obra y pensamiento crítico. Santo Domingo: Editora Centenario, 2014. 410 p.: bibl., index. (Archivo General de la Nación; CCVI)

At 410 pages, this is an extensive monograph on a subject little known even within Latin American philosophy, except of course among the experts in Afro-Caribbean thought. That is precisely the main appeal of Minaya's book, which, although devoted to the study of Pedro Francisco Bonó, also offers a substantial introduction to the history of Latin American philosophy.

3000 Suárez Salazar, Luis. Updating Cuban socialism: a utopian critique. Translated by Mariana Ortega Breña. (*Lat. Am. Perspect.*, 41:4, July 2014, p. 13–27, bibl.)

This journal article analyzes the status of Cuba's socialist system today. It also provides some recommendations for that system's improvement, which according to the author may occur, provided improvements are made in the areas of democratic participation, freedom of the press, and the acquisition and enhancement of moral values. Whether or not one shares the author's optimism, the book offers a window into Cuba's political system today.

VENEZUELA

3001 Bolívar-Martí: pensamiento, vigencias y convergencias: antología. Compilación y prólogo por Alberto Rodríguez Carucci. Mérida, Venezuela: Fundación para el Desarrollo Cultural del Estado Mérida, FUNDECEM, 2013. 239 p.: bibl. (Colección Campaña admirable)

The articles commissioned for this edited volume address a well-known thesis: that José Martí vindicates the mestizaje view of Latin American identity previously theorized by Simón Bolívar. The thesis is interesting and deserves more attention than the book's contributors are willing to pay to it. Undermining their efforts is the book's tendency to put Bolívar and Martí at the service of advancing the prevailing ideological agenda in Venezuela today.

3002 Duno Gottberg, Luis. La política encarnada: biopolítica y cultura en la Venezuela bolivariana. Venezuela: Editorial Equinoccio, 2015. 431 p.: bibl., ill. (Colección Plural)

This edited volume offers 14 essays and an introduction by the editor. The essays are written from the perspective of contemporary French philosophy. In particular, they endorse the theory of Alain Badiou which, according to the authors of these essays, emphasizes the philosophical significance of bodies. But the essays do not address the fundamental questions of why Venezuela must be regarded as a body, and how Badiou's approach might contribute to an understanding of the political and socioeconomic crisis affecting the country.

COLOMBIA

3003 Aportes a la construcción del país: selección de pensadores antioqueños. Presentación a cargo de Héctor Quintero Arredondo. Bogotá: Editorial Universidad del Rosario, 2013. 367 p. (Colección Memoria viva, bicentenario Antioquia)

Quintero Arredondo has selected for this book 10 essays on some cultural and intellectual developments associated with the department of Antioquia in Colombia. The topics vary widely, from political and economic projects affecting the department (as well as some other parts of Latin

America) to issues of bioethics, art criticism, literature, and philosophy. Of special interest for those seeking an understanding of Latin American philosophy during the 19th century is a chapter on Andrés Bello by Marco Fidel Suárez.

3004 **Ávila Martínez, Alexander.** Esbozos del pensamiento latinoamericano: del pensamiento amerindio al siglo XX. Bogotá: Universidad Cooperativa de Colombia-sede Bogotá, 2011. 73 p.: bibl. (Colección Investigación)

In this short monograph, Ávila Martínez intends to trace the evolution of Amerindian thought in Colombia from the conquest to the present. But he delivers only a sketchy historical account confined to the thought of some Amerindian groups in the region. Thus the reader looking for anything relevant to Amerindian philosophy will be disappointed. Among the colonial thinkers considered by Ávila Martínez are Bartolomé de las Casas (especially his *Brevísima relación de la destrucción de Indias*) and Francisco Bilbao (especially his *El evangelio americano*).

3005 **Identidad cultural colombiana: visiones de filósofos y pensadores en tiempos del bicentenario.** Investigación principal por Franklin Giovanni Púa. Texto por Grupo Calibán y Juan Carlos Ruiz et al. Bogotá: Programa de Licenciatura en Filosofía, Universidad de San Buenaventura, sede Bogotá, 2017. 195 p.: bibl. (Serie Filosófica; 30)

This edited volume explores issues concerning Colombian national, racial, and ethnic identity. It includes contributions by members of the Grupo Calibán (Jhon Jairo Losada Cubillos, Juan Carlos Ruiz, Luis Alexander Aponte, and Nelson Fernando Roberto Alba) and other scholars. Some contributors approach the nature of Colombian identity by examining the work of 20th-century thinkers of the caliber of Germán Arciniegas. Other contributors are concerned with a specific type of identity, such as the identity of the native peoples of Colombia.

3006 **Losada Cubillos, Jhon Jairo.** Ontología y poder colonial: claves analíticas a propósito de la colonialidad del ser. Bogotá: Universidad de San Buenaventura, Facultad de Filosofía, 2014. 149 p.: bibl., ill. (Serie Filosófica; 26)

This monograph explores theories of coloniality and postcoloniality. Written from the perspective of liberation philosophy, it also invokes this perspective for the analysis of some historical examples of colonial thinkers. At points, the mixed conceptual framework undermines the clarity of the book.

Mesa Chica, Darío. Miguel Antonio Caro: el intelectual y el político. See item **1118**.

3007 **Rondón Almeida, Carlos Enrique.** La teoría de la dependencia como marco interpretativo y de acción frente al conflicto social en Latinoamérica. Bogotá: Ediciones USTA, 2013. 122 p.: bibl., ill. (Colección Summa cum laude)

This monograph investigates theories of dependence and peace that were at the center of heated debates in Latin America during the last part of the 20th century. The author approaches these topics from the perspective of French hermeneutics and liberation philosophy. Of special interest are his analyses of the Medellín statement that triggered the Liberation Theology movement and of the guerrilla movement known as the Fuerzas Armadas Revolucionarias de Colombia (FARC).

ECUADOR

3008 **Estermann, Josef.** Más allá de occidente: apuntes filosóficos sobre interculturalidad, descolonización y el vivir bien andino. Quito: Abya-Yala, 2015. 234 p.: bibl., maps.

In this monograph, Estermann aims at contrasting some standard conceptions of the good life in the West with the conception he ascribes to the native peoples of the Andean region. Estermann argues that Andean philosophy is more sustainable, and thus, more conducive to human flourishing. In his view, Andean philosophy should be understood as being neither a postmodern nor a postcolonial philosophy; it is instead a post-Western philosophy.

3009 **La estética del suspenso: epistemología para una historia compartida, a partir de la obra de Walter Benjamín: lecturas latinoamericanas.** Compilación de

Eloy Alfaro. Quito: Ediciones Abya-Yala: Universidad Politécnica Salesiana, 2013. 193 p.

In *La estética del suspenso*, Alfaro offers an eclectic collection of new and previously published essays. Although the leading concern in most of these essays is the literary and art criticism of Walter Benjamin, some of the contributions explore this German thinker's work as a political philosopher.

PERU

3010 Campuzano Arteta, Álvaro. La modernidad imaginada: arte y literatura en el pensamiento de José Carlos Mariátegui (1911–1930). Prefacio de Michael Löwy. Madrid: Iberoamericana; Frankfurt am Main: Vervuert, 2017. 329 p.: bibl. (Colección Nexos y diferencias; 46)

La modernidad imaginada offers a detailed analysis of the views of José Carlos Mariátegui on an area of inquiry rarely addressed by his commentators: namely, his views on esthetics. Of special interest to Campuzano Arteta are Mariátegui's writings on modernism, Latin American poetry, and Soviet neorealism.

3011 Marín Benítez, Ciro. Filosofía tawantinsuyana: una perspectiva epistémica. Lima: Juan Gutemberg Editores Impresores, 2015. 262 p.: bibl., ill.

This book promises to deliver a much needed account of the thought of the original peoples of South America. It focuses on a group related to Inca culture: the Tawantinsuyu. After dividing the history of these peoples into two periods, before and after the European expansion, the author argues that in spite of numerous Western attempts at destroying Tawantinsuyana culture during the second period, its philosophy survived and has been transmitted to the Tawantinsuyu of today. The philosophy consists of some distinctive views about the relationship between humans and the cosmos. But weak evidence (mostly from images) and extremely poor editing undermine the book's appeal.

3012 Mazzi Huaycucho, Víctor. Inkas y filósofos: posturas, teorías, estudio de fuentes y reinterpretación. Lima: Víctor Mazzi Huaycucho, 2016. 423 p.: bibl., ill.

This book surveys major sources for the study of philosophy among the Inca people during both precolumbian times and after the Spanish conquest. Since little is known about those sources, this book has the potential to become a mandatory reading for scholars investigating not only precolumbian philosophy, but also the origins of Latin American philosophy.

3013 Pérez Garay, Carlos Alberto. Liberalismo criollo: Ricardo Palma, ideología y política, 1833–1919. Lima: Universidad Ricardo Palma, Editorial Universitaria, 2015. 392 p.: bibl., ill.

This extensive monograph covers the life and work of Peruvian writer Ricardo Palma. It will be of interest to anyone curious about the intellectual history of the subcontinent, especially during the period marked by the rise and fall of positivism in Latin America.

3014 Portocarrero Maisch, Gonzalo. La urgencia por decir "nosotros": los intelectuales y la idea de nación en el Perú republicano. Lima: Fondo Editorial, Pontificia Universidad Católica del Perú, 2015. 359 p.: bibl., ill.

This monograph explores the conceptions of nationality that have been proposed by major Peruvian thinkers during the 19th and 20th centuries, including Pancho Fierro, Ricardo Palma, José Carlos Mariátegui, and José María Aguedas. One chapter is dedicated to the Huarochirí manuscript, a less commonly analyzed work of Quechua religious thought. The book will be of interest to those wishing to gain knowledge about either traditonal Andean thought or the nature of Latin American identity.

3015 Torres, Camilo. Camilo Torres Restrepo, profeta de la liberación: antología (teológica) política. Compilación de Lorena López Guzmán y Nicolás A. Herrera Farfán. Buenos Aires: CFU Colectivo Frente Unido: Editorial El Colectivo, 2016. 334 p. (Colección Pensamiento latinoamericano)

In this anthology, the editors offer a selection of writings by one of the founders of Liberation Theology, the Catholic priest and revolutionary social and political leader Camilo Torres. The topics range from education and religion in Colombia to democracy and social justice in Latin America. All primary sources are preceded by the editors' substantial introductions. These documents generally provide significant information about Torres and his connection to some of the early figures of the Liberation Theology movement.

3016 Zegarra Medina, Raúl Eduardo. La subversión de la esperanza: diálogo contemporáneo entre teología de la liberación, filosofía y opción por los pobres. Lima: Fondo Editorial, Pontificia Universidad Católica del Perú: IBC, Instituto Bartolomé de Las Casas: CEP, Centro de Estudios y Publicaciones, 2015. 284 p.: bibl., ill. (CEP; 379)

This monograph focuses on Liberation Theology, the progressive movement and philosophical and religious position developed within the Catholic Church in Latin America during the second half of the 20th century. Zegarra Medina rightly establishes historical connections between this position and the practical philosophy of Bartolomé de las Casas, a Spanish Dominican priest who in the mid-1500s argued forcefully for the rights of the Amerindians. But the interpretation of las Casas' doctrines, as well as the doctrines of some contemporary liberation theologians such as Ignacio Ellacuría, is at points obscured in the book by the author's appeal to postmodern thought.

3017 Zulen, Pedro S. Pedro S. Zulen: escritos reunidos. Compilación de Rubén Quiroz, Pablo Quintanilla y Joel Rojas. Lima: Fondo Editorial del Congreso del Perú, 2015. 686 p.: bibl., ill.

In this edited volume, four well-known Peruvian philosophers offer a comprehensive compilation of the writings of another Peruvian philosopher, Pedro S. Zulen. Each of Zulen's works included in the collection is introduced by an essay by one of the book's editors. The book will be of interest to historians of early 20th-century philosophy in Peru as well as to general readers of Latin American thought.

BOLIVIA

3018 Bautista S., Rafael. Reflexiones des-coloniales. La Paz: Rincón Ediciones, 2014. 208 p.: bibl. (Colección Abrelosojos; 6)

Reflexiones des-coloniales aims at clarifying a variety of topics of political philosophy and ethics as they affect people around the globe, especially in Bolivia. But it delivers only the author's opinions about the central topics of the book. Under the vague label of "de-colonization," Bautista discusses some challenging issues (e.g., racism, environmental damage, and economic inequality in Latin America) without offering any textual evidence for the claims he makes.

3019 Mansilla, H.C.F. Fausto Reinaga y los dilemas del indianismo en Bolivia. (*Ecuad. Debate*, 93, dic. 2014, p. 81–98)

This essay connects the Indianism of Bolivian political thinker Fausto Reinaga (1906–94) with the recent movements in continental philosophy known as theories of decolonization and postmodernism. Although generally lacking sufficient clarity, the essay might be of interest to scholars working on current developments in Amerindian thought.

3020 Mansilla, H.C.F. Herencias culturales y prácticas sociales: ensayos en filosofía política. La Paz: Plural Editores, 2015. 327 p.: bibl.

In this collection, Mansilla brings together 15 of his previously published essays on topics of political philosophy. In his view, they are all relevant to social studies in Bolivia, and more generally, in Latin America. Among the topics are the effects of massive democratization on humanist conceptions of value, the critical assessment of the Frankfurt School of philosophy, and the nature of Bolivian political thought. Of special interest is chapter 14, where Mansilla speculates about what an intellectual figure of Bolivia, Salvador Romero, would like to say to another such figure, Alcides Arguedas.

3021 Mansilla, H.C.F. Una mirada crítica sobre el indianismo y la descolonización: el potencial conservador bajo el manto revolucionario. La Paz: Rincón Ediciones, 2014. 216 p.: bibl. (Colección Abrelosojos; 5)

This short monograph examines some competing doctrines of the collective identity of the Bolivian people, with special attention to Indianism and the theory of decolonization.

3022 Rodas Morales, Hugo. René Zavaleta Mercado: el nacional-populismo barroco. La Paz: Plural Editores, 2016. 499 p.: bibl.

Rodas Morales offers in this book an investigation of some major political events in Bolivia during the second part of the 20th century. He conducts a historical, sociological, and political inquiry heavily influenced by a Marxist conceptual framework. The central figure of his research is René Zavaleta Mercado, about whom Rodas Morales has consulted an impressive number of sources. His book might be attractive also to historians of nationalist movements in Latin America during the same historical period.

3023 **Rodríguez Leytón, Nivardo.** Un anarquismo singular: Gustavo A. Navarro, Cesáreo Capriles, 1918–1924. Sucre: Archivo y Biblioteca Nacionales de Bolivia: Fundación Cultural del Banco Central de Bolivia: Banco Central de Bolivia, 2013. 202 p.: bibl. (Colección noveles investigadores; 4)

Rodríguez Leytón published this monograph in a series that features new researchers in Bolivia. It is entirely devoted to developments of anarchism in that country during the 20th century. In particular, Rodríguez Leytón looks closely at the versions of this political philosophy developed respectively by Gustavo A. Navarro and Cesáreo Capriles. He also examines the network in which the "individualistic anarchism" of these thinkers circulated during the years 1918–24. His book provides a window into an insufficiently known aspect of Bolivia's political thought during the early 20th century.

CHILE

3024 **Alvarado Meléndez, Marcelo.** Manuel Astica Fuentes, el revolucionario utópico: biografía político-intelectual. Santiago: Editorial USACH, 2015. 296 p.: bibl., ill. (Colección Humanidades)

Alvarado Meléndez's monograph looks closely at the political thought of Manuel Astica Fuentes, a leader of the Chilean left who fought for social change in that country during the 1930s. As a result, he suffered persecution and imprisonment. Later in life, Astica Fuentes played a crucial role in the cultural resistance to the dictatorship of Augusto Pinochet. With a full mastery of historical details, the author succeeds in adding the political philosophy of Astica Fuentes to the list of significant utopias developed in Latin America during the 20th century.

3025 **Cristi, Renato.** El pensamiento conservador en Chile: seis ensayos. Segunda edición. Corregida y aumentada. Santiago: Editorial Universitaria, 2015. 203 p.: bibl., index. (Imagen de Chile)

The previously unpublished essays in this volume look closely at the emergence and consolidation of neoliberalism within the conservative movement in Chile, a phenomenon that according to the authors began to take place in the 1960s. Each of the essays focuses on a conservative thinker who illustrates either nationalism, corporativism, or neoliberalism. The latter view became the prevalent form of conservatism in the mid-1970s during the regime of Augusto Pinochet. Of particular interest to historians of political and economic ideas in Latin America are two appendices: one devoted to Jaime Guzmán's conservative interpretation of the social doctrine of the Church; the other devoted to the evolution of conservatism in Chile during the 19th century.

3026 **Giannini, Humberto.** Giannini público: entrevistas, columnas, artículos. Santiago: Universidad de Chile, Vicerrectoría de Extensión y Comunidades: Facultad de Filosofía y Humanidades, Universidad de Chile: Editorial Universitaria, 2015. 287 p.: ill. (Colección Maestros y maestras de la Chile)

Giannini público is intended as an homage to Humberto Giannini, a Chilean public intellectual whose academic training was in philosophy. After graduation, Giannini went on to have a celebrated career in Chile's institutions of government and higher education. The book features a number of interviews with Giannini that provide information about his positions on a number of topics, including the role of philosophy in public life.

3027 **Oliva, Elena.** La negritud, el indianismo y sus intelectuales: Aimé Césaire y Fausto Reinaga. Santiago: Editorial Universitaria, 2014. 166 p.: bibl. (Colección Tesis)

This monograph aims not only at accounting for the collective identities of Afro- and Indo-Latin Americans but also at undermining what Oliva considers Eurocentric conceptions of those identities. To this end, she examines the work of two prominent intellectuals of the 20th century, each of whom was rooted in one or the other group of Latin Americans. For Afro-Caribbean identity, Oliva analyzes the work of literary author and African rights activist Aimé Césaire (Martinique, 1913–2003). For Indo-American identity, she examines the work of political thinker Fausto Reinaga (Bolivia, 1906–94). This book will be attractive to those with an interest in either of these figures, as well as those interested in the nature of Latin America's ethnic and racial identity.

3028 Quesada Monge, Rodrigo. Anarquía: orden sin autoridad. Santiago: EUNA: Editorial Fleuterio, 2014. 448 p.: bibl., ill., index.

Quesada Monge offers a comprehensive introduction to the major theses of anarchism. He looks closely at the origin of anarchism in the 19th century, and traces its convergence with current antiglobalization movements. This book is arranged in 25 chapters, divided in two parts: one topical, the other historical. In part I, Quesada Monge covers the views of anarchism related to terrorism, education, property rights, the state, and other topics of social and political philosophy. In part II, he considers some particulars of anarchism in Costa Rica and more generally, in Latin America. He also outlines key events in major anarchist/socialist revolutions around the world, including the Spanish Civil War (1936–39) and the Mexican Revolution (1910–17).

BRAZIL

3029 Mitchell-Walthour, Gladys L. The politics of blackness: racial identity and political behavior in contemporary Brazil. Cambridge, England: Cambridge University Press, 2018. 266 p.: bibl., ill., maps. (Cambridge studies in stratification economics: economics and social identity)

In this monograph, Mitchell-Walthour provides data from some empirical studies of how Brazilian people regard their own ethnic and racial identity. She also examines data about their views on racial biases and affirmative-action programs. Her main argument is one familiar in Afro-Latin American studies: the mestizaje model of identity must be false because there is no racial democracy in Latin America.

URUGUAY

3030 Drews, Pablo. Nietzsche en Uruguay, 1900–1920: José Enrique Rodó, Carlos Reyles y Carlos Vaz Ferreira. Montevideo: CSIC, Universidad de la República Uruguay, 2016. 127 p.: bibl. (Biblioteca plural)

In this book, Drews investigates the reception of Nietzsche in Uruguay at the turn of the 20th century. Drews produces evidence to support his thesis that the so-called generation of the 1900s not only read Nietzsche avidly, but also incorporated his ideas in their own writings. Particularly provocative is his claim that Nietzsche had an impact on the writings of José Enrique Rodó.

3031 Gatto, Hebert. Los sueños de la razón: socialismo, democracia, totalitarismo. Montevideo: Editorial Fin de Siglo, 2013. 315 p.: bibl.

In this original monograph, essayist and social scientist Hebert Gatto sets out to defend liberal democracy against socialism and other forms of utopian thought. He objects to utopias that appeal to a prior, unsubstantiated, moral framework (e.g., the duty to pursue a common good or human happiness) in order to support their preferred form of policy. Gatto contends that a democratic state must adopt instead a "neutralist" or impartialist point of view about morality.

3032 Rodríguez Maglio, Leonardo Rafael. La filosofía popular y regeneradora del magnánimo José Artigas. Montevideo: L. Rodríguez Maglio, 2014. 285 p.: bibl.

This monograph looks closely at the political thought of Uruguayan independence leader José Artigas, who was also the country's most prominent nation-builder after the end of Spain's colonial rule. The author argues that Artigas' ideas amount to a political philosophy, although, like other leaders of Latin America's independence and national organization, Artigas did not articulate them in ways now standard in academic philosophy (that is, by means of books, articles, and the like).

ARGENTINA

3033 Bonet, María Teresa. Debates por la historia: peronismo e intelectuales: 1955–2011. Buenos Aires: Imago Mundi, 2015. 164 p.: bibl., index. (Colección Bitácora argentina)

In this monograph, Bonet looks closely at the development of Peronism in Argentina. Covering about half a century of the intellectual history of this populist sort of nationalism, she analyzes the reactions of intellectuals such as Romero, Germani, Frondizi, and many others to Peronism. Her book will be of interest to historians of political ideas in Argentina during the mid-20th century.

3034 Cerruti, Pedro. Genealogía del victimismo: violencia y subjetividad en la Argentina posdictatorial. Bernal, Argentina: Universidad Nacional de Quilmes Editorial, 2015. 431 p.: bibl. (Colección Comunicación y cultura)

This monograph analyzes two phenomena that have influenced politics in Argentina since the fall of military rule in the mid-1980s: uncontrolled inflation that led to the economic crisis of 2001 and the rise of "insecurity" (a euphemism used in Argentina to refer to the increasing levels of violent crime that followed that crisis). Cerruti's own account of these phenomena remains unclear. At points he appears to espouse a conspiracy theory according to which the media is responsible for Argentinians feeling like victims of insecurity and denouncing what they regard as widespread impunity in their country's judicial system.

3035 Cervera, Felipe Justo. Identidad nacional en el siglo XXI: ensayo histórico. Rosario, Argentina: Prohistoria Ediciones, 2013. 164 p.: bibl. (Colección Universidad; 31)

In this monograph, Cervera argues that since the 1960s Argentina has been facing a crisis of national identity. The author hypothesizes that previous identifying concepts related to the country's territorial integrity and its history, together with the symbols that represented them, have lost relevance due to a fragmentation of the country's national identity into a variety of interest-group factions. Although Cervera provides abundant historical and social data to support his hypothesis, he includes neither a list of references nor a bibliography that could be used to verify the accuracy of his data.

3036 Del pensamiento continuo: apuntes de/sobre Norberto Griffa. Compilación de Jorge Zuzulich. Buenos Aires: EDUNTREF, Editorial de la Universidad Nacional de Tres de Febrero, 2014. 258 p.: bibl.

This hybrid edited volume brings together new essays on the life and work of Argentinian philosophical thinker Norberto Griffa. The work also includes two long essays written by Griffa in which he provides a clear indication of his sympathies for the German school of phenomenology that was popular during the first half of the 20th century. The book may be attractive to readers interested in Griffa's thought, which falls into the intersection of art, culture, and philosophy.

3037 Finchelstein, Federico. El mito del fascismo: de Freud a Borges. Buenos Aires: Capital Intelectual, 2015. 132 p.: bibl. (De autor)

Finchelstein's monograph assumes the truth of Sigmund Freud's theory of repressed psychological contents and contends that both Freud and Jorge Luis Borges have been interested in discovering how such contents have shaped the symbology of fascism. In his analysis of this topic, Finchelstein combines history with semiotics, producing an account of fascist symbols that differ greatly from standard historical accounts.

3038 Forster, Ricardo. La subjetividad y sus laberintos: conversaciones con Ricardo Forster. Edición de Alberto Catena. Buenos Aires: Desde la Gente, Ediciones del IMFC, 2014. 127 p.: bibl. (Colección Argentina debate)

This book features Alberto Catena's interview with Ricardo Forster, an Argentinian philosopher who has played a leading role in public advocacy for the political program of Kirchnerism, the brand of Peronism led by expresidents Nestor Kirchner (in office 2003–2007) and his wife, Cristina Fernández de Kirchner (2007–2015). During the interview Forster speculates about the chief social, political, and intellectual challenges currenty facing Argentina.

3039 Graciano, Osvaldo Fabián. Prácticas académicas y producción de saber de los intelectuales de izquierda en la universidad argentina, 1900–1930. (*Secuencia/ México*, 92, mayo/agosto 2015, p. 113–138, bibl.)

This essay looks closely at the academic careers of three leaders of the Argentinian Socialist Party who were active during the first two decades of the 20th century: Alfredo Palacios, Enrique del Valle Iberlucea, and Enrique Moucher. By revealing some interesting aspects of their political thought, the author makes a modest but important contribution to the history of ideas in the subcontinent.

3040 Myers, Jorge. Clío filósofa: los inicios del discurso histórico rioplatense, 1830–1852. (*Varia Hist.*, 31:56, maio/agôsto 2015, p. 331–364, bibl.)

In this historically minded article, the author focuses on Romanticism, the philosophical movement that was influential among Argentina's intellectuals after the country declared its independence from Spain in 1810. Myers is narrowly focused on the leading claims of this movement as developed between 1820 and 1830 in Argentina. Although his article has a narrow scope, it contributes to an understanding of political philosophy in Argentina during that period.

3041 Podetti, José Ramiro. Cultura y alteridad: en torno al sentido de la experiencia latinoamericana. Buenos Aires: Ediciones CICCUS, 2015. 252 p.: bibl., ill.

The first edition of this book appeared in 2008 and received a prize from the Fundación Centro de Estudios Latinoamericanos Rómulo Gallegos of Venezuela. As orginally designed, it is divided into two parts. The first part contains nine chapters written by Podetti on topics concerning globalization, race, and ethnic identity in Latin America. Some of the chapters focus on a Latin American thinker relevant to the topic at hand, such as José Vasconcelos or José Enrique Rodó. The second part is devoted to commentaries by critics about different aspects of Podetti's philosophical thoughts. For many readers, the most instructive chapters of the book will be those focused on some classic figures of Latin American thought. The second edition contains some changes to the chapters on Rodó and Fernando Ortíz, together with commentaries about the first edition by some scholars in Latin American thought.

3042 Qué es el peronismo: una respuesta desde la filosofía. Edición de Jorge Bolívar, Rubén H. Ríos, y José Luis Di Lorenzo. Buenos Aires: Octubre Editorial, 2014. 377 p.: bibl.

This book features new essays by a number of 20th-century Argentinian thinkers who have had a varying degree of sympathy for Peronism. They attempt to explain this movement from many perspectives, including those of Dussel, Kusch, Cirigliano, Poratti, and Bolívar (one of the editors). In spite of the editors' effort to avoid falling into political propaganda, their collection clearly displays a political agenda.

3043 Schwarzböck, Silvia. Los espantos: estética y postdictadura. Buenos Aires: Cuarenta Ríos, 2016. 144 p.: bibl.

In this monograph, Schwarzböck constructs a narrative of some major political events in Argentina, from the dictatorship of the Junta in the 1970s to the return to democracy in the 1980s. But she takes these turning points for the country's institutions to be a mere inspiration for her fact-free commentary about political events of the period. At the end of the day, her casual approach to truth renders her book closer to literature than to history or political philosophy.

3044 Terán, Oscar. Discutir Mariátegui. Buenos Aires: Hilo Rojo Editores, 2017. 285 p.: bibl. (Colección Heteroglosias)

In this monograph, Terán, an expert on the history of ideas in Latin America, reconstructs the evolution of José Carlos Mariátegui's thought since his early days as a journalist. Terán also includes in this book a few lesser-known primary sources such as the paper Mariátegui read at a conference on literature, "El destino sudamericano de un moderno extremista." This book will be of interest to scholars of Mariátegui and more generally, of early Marxism in Latin America. For a comment on an earlier edition of this work, see *HLAS 50:4664*.

ABBREVIATIONS AND ACRONYMS

Except for journal abbreviations which are listed: 1) after each journal title in the *Title List of Journals Indexed* (p. 757); and 2) in the *Abbreviation List of Journals Indexed* (p. 763).

ALADI	Asociación Latinoamericana de Integración
a.	annual
ABC	Argentina, Brazil, Chile
A.C.	antes de Cristo
ACAR	Associação de Crédito e Assistência Rural, Brazil
AD	Anno Domini
A.D.	Acción Democrática, Venezuela
ADESG	Associação dos Diplomados de Escola Superior de Guerra, Brazil
AGI	Archivo General de Indias, Sevilla
AGN	Archivo General de la Nación
AID	Agency for International Development
a.k.a.	also known as
Ala.	Alabama
ALALC	Asociación Latinoamericana de Libre Comercio
ALEC	*Atlas lingüístico etnográfico de Colombia*
ANAPO	Alianza Nacional Popular, Colombia
ANCARSE	Associação Nordestina de Crédito e Assistência Rural de Sergipe, Brazil
ANCOM	Andean Common Market
ANDI	Asociación Nacional de Industriales, Colombia
ANPOCS	Associação Nacional de Pós-Graduação e Pesquisa em Ciências Sociais, São Paulo
ANUC	Asociación Nacional de Usuarios Campesinos, Colombia
ANUIES	Asociación Nacional de Universidades e Institutos de Enseñanza Superior, Mexico
AP	Acción Popular
APRA	Alianza Popular Revolucionaria Americana, Peru
ARENA	Aliança Renovadora Nacional, Brazil
Ariz.	Arizona
Ark.	Arkansas
ASA	Association of Social Anthropologists of the Commonwealth, London
ASSEPLAN	Assessoria de Planejamento e Acompanhamento, Recife
Assn.	Association
Aufl.	Auflage (edition, edición)
AUFS	American Universities Field Staff Reports, Hanover, N.H.
Aug.	August, Augustan
aum.	aumentada
b.	born (nació)
B.A.R.	British Archaeological Reports
BBE	Bibliografia Brasileira de Educação
b.c.	indicates dates obtained by radiocarbon methods
BC	Before Christ

bibl(s).	bibliography(ies)
BID	Banco Interamericano de Desarrollo
BNDE	Banco Nacional de Desenvolvimento Econômico, Brazil
BNH	Banco Nacional de Habitação, Brazil
BP	before present
b/w	black and white
C14	Carbon 14
ca.	*circa* (about)
CACM	Central American Common Market
CADE	Conferencia Anual de Ejecutivos de Empresas, Peru
CAEM	Centro de Altos Estudios Militares, Peru
Calif.	California
Cap.	Capítulo
CARC	Centro de Arte y Comunicación, Buenos Aires
CARICOM	Caribbean Common Market
CARIFTA	Caribbean Free Trade Association
CBC	Christian base communities
CBD	central business district
CBI	Caribbean Basin Initiative
CD	Christian Democrats, Chile
CDHES	Comisión de Derechos Humanos de El Salvador
CDI	Conselho de Desenvolvimento Industrial, Brasília
CEB	comunidades eclesiásticas de base
CEBRAP	Centro Brasileiro de Análise e Planejamento, São Paulo
CECORA	Centro de Cooperativas de la Reforma Agraria, Colombia
CEDAL	Centro de Estudios Democráticos de América Latina, Costa Rica
CEDE	Centro de Estudios sobre Desarrollo Económico, Univ. de los Andes, Bogotá
CEDEPLAR	Centro de Desenvolvimento e Planejamento Regional, Belo Horizonte
CEDES	Centro de Estudios de Estado y Sociedad, Buenos Aires; Centro de Estudos de Educação e Sociedade, São Paulo
CEDI	Centro Ecumênico de Documentos e Informação, São Paulo
CEDLA	Centro de Estudios y Documentación Latinoamericanos, Amsterdam
CEESTEM	Centro de Estudios Económicos y Sociales del Tercer Mundo, México
CELADE	Centro Latinoamericano de Demografía
CELADEC	Comisión Evangélica Latinoamericana de Educación Cristiana
CELAM	Consejo Episcopal Latinoamericano
CEMLA	Centro de Estudios Monetarios Latinoamericanos, Mexico
CENDES	Centro de Estudios del Desarrollo, Venezuela
CENIDIM	Centro Nacional de Información, Documentación e Investigación Musicales, Mexico
CENIET	Centro Nacional de Información y Estadísticas del Trabajo, Mexico
CEOSL	Confederación Ecuatoriana de Organizaciones Sindicales Libres
CEPADE	Centro Paraguayo de Estudios de Desarrollo Económico y Social
CEPA-SE	Comissão Estadual de Planejamento Agrícola, Sergipe
CEPAL	Comisión Económica para América Latina y el Caribe
CEPLAES	Centro de Planificación y Estudios Sociales, Quito
CERES	Centro de Estudios de la Realidad Económica y Social, Bolivia
CES	constant elasticity of substitution
cf.	compare
CFI	Consejo Federal de Inversiones, Buenos Aires
CGE	Confederación General Económica, Argentina
CGTP	Confederación General de Trabajadores del Perú
chap(s).	chapter(s)
CHEAR	Council on Higher Education in the American Republics

Cía.	Compañía
CIA	Central Intelligence Agency
CIDA	Comité Interamericano de Desarrollo Agrícola
CIDE	Centro de Investigación y Desarrollo de la Educación, Chile; Centro de Investigación y Docencias Económicas, Mexico
CIDIAG	Centro de Información y Desarrollo Internacional de Autogestión, Lima
CIE	Centro de Investigaciones Económicas, Buenos Aires
CIEDLA	Centro Interdisciplinario de Estudios sobre el Desarrollo Latinoamericano, Buenos Aires
CIEDUR	Centro Interdisciplinario de Estudios sobre el Desarrollo Uruguay, Montevideo
CIEPLAN	Corporación de Investigaciones Económicas para América Latina, Santiago
CIESE	Centro de Investigaciones y Estudios Socioeconómicos, Quito
CIMI	Conselho Indigenista Missionário, Brazil
CINTERFOR	Centro Interamericano de Investigación y Documentación sobre Formación Profesional
CINVE	Centro de Investigaciones Económicas, Montevideo
CIP	Conselho Interministerial de Preços, Brazil
CIPCA	Centro de Investigación y Promoción del Campesinado, Bolivia
CIPEC	Consejo Intergubernamental de Países Exportadores de Cobre, Santiago
CLACSO	Consejo Latinoamericano de Ciencias Sociales, Secretaría Ejecutiva, Buenos Aires
CLASC	Confederación Latinoamericana Sindical Cristiana
CLE	Comunidad Latinoamericana de Escritores, Mexico
cm	centimeter
CNI	Confederação Nacional da Indústria, Brazil
CNPq	Conselho Nacional de Pesquisas, Brazil
Co.	Company
COB	Central Obrera Boliviana
COBAL	Companhia Brasileira de Alimentos
CODEHUCA	Comisión para la Defensa de los Derechos Humanos en Centroamérica
Col.	Collection, Colección, Coleção
col.	colored, coloured
Colo.	Colorado
COMCORDE	Comisión Coordinadora para el Desarrollo Económico, Uruguay
comp(s).	compiler(s), compilador(es)
CONCLAT	Congresso Nacional das Classes Trabalhadoras, Brazil
CONCYTEC	Consejo Nacional de Ciencia y Tecnología (Peru)
CONDESE	Conselho de Desenvolvimento Econômico de Sergipe
Conn.	Connecticut
COPEI	Comité Organizador Pro-Elecciones Independientes, Venezuela
CORFO	Corporación de Fomento de la Producción, Chile
CORP	Corporación para el Fomento de Investigaciones Económicas, Colombia
Corp.	Corporation, Corporación
corr.	corrected, corregida
CP	Communist Party
CPDOC	Centro de Pesquisa e Documentação, Brazil
CRIC	Consejo Regional Indígena del Cauca, Colombia
CSUTCB	Confederación Sindical Unica de Trabajadores Campesinos de Bolivia
CTM	Confederación de Trabajadores de México
CUNY	City University of New York
CUT	Central Unica de Trabajadores (Mexico); Central Unica dos Trabalhadores (Brazil); Central Unitaria de Trabajadores (Chile; Colombia); Confederación Unitaria de Trabajadores (Costa Rica)

CVG	Corporación Venezolana de Guayana
d.	died (murió)
DANE	Departamento Nacional de Estadística, Colombia
DC	developed country; Demócratas Cristianos, Chile
d.C.	después de Cristo
Dec./déc.	December, décembre
Del.	Delaware
dept.	department
depto.	departamento
DESCO	Centro de Estudios y Promoción del Desarrollo, Lima
Dez./dez.	Dezember, dezembro
dic.	diciembre, dicembre
disc.	discography
DNOCS	Departamento Nacional de Obras Contra as Secas, Brazil
doc.	document, documento
Dr.	Doctor
Dra.	Doctora
DRAE	*Diccionario de la Real Academia Española*
ECLAC	UN Economic Commision for Latin America and the Caribbean, New York and Santiago
ECOSOC	UN Economic and Social Council
ed./éd.(s)	edition(s), édition(s), edición(es), editor(s), redactor(es), director(es)
EDEME	Editora Emprendimentos Educacionais, Florianópolis
Edo.	Estado
EEC	European Economic Community
EE.UU.	Estados Unidos de América
EFTA	European Free Trade Association
e.g.	*exempio gratia* (for example, por ejemplo)
ELN	Ejército de Liberación Nacional, Colombia
ENDEF	Estudo Nacional da Despesa Familiar, Brazil
ERP	Ejército Revolucionario del Pueblo, El Salvador
ESG	Escola Superior de Guerra, Brazil
estr.	estrenado
et al.	*et alia* (and others)
ETENE	Escritório Técnico de Estudos Econômicos do Nordeste, Brazil
ETEPE	Escritório Técnico de Planejamento, Brazil
EUDEBA	Editorial Universitaria de Buenos Aires
EWG	Europaische Wirtschaftsgemeinschaft. *See* EEC.
facsim(s).	facsimile(s)
FAO	Food and Agriculture Organization of the United Nations
FDR	Frente Democrático Revolucionario, El Salvador
FEB	Força Expedicionária Brasileira
Feb./feb.	February, Februar, febrero, febbraio
FEDECAFE	Federación Nacional de Cafeteros, Colombia
FEDESARROLLO	Fundación para la Educación Superior y el Desarrollo
fev./fév.	fevereiro, février
ff.	following
FGTS	Fundo de Garantia do Tempo de Serviço, Brazil
FGV	Fundação Getúlio Vargas
FIEL	Fundación de Investigaciones Económicas Latinoamericanas, Argentina
film.	filmography
fl.	flourished
Fla.	Florida
FLACSO	Facultad Latinoamericana de Ciencias Sociales
FMI	Fondo Monetario Internacional

FMLN	Frente Farabundo Martí de Liberación Nacional, El Salvador
fold.	folded
fol(s).	folio(s)
FPL	Fuerzas Populares de Liberación Farabundo Marti, El Salvador
FRG	Federal Republic of Germany
FSLN	Frente Sandinista de Liberación Nacional, Nicaragua
ft.	foot, feet
FUAR	Frente Unido de Acción Revolucionaria, Colombia
FUCVAM	Federación Unificadora de Cooperativas de Vivienda por Ayuda Mutua, Uruguay
FUNAI	Fundação Nacional do Indio, Brazil
FUNARTE	Fundação Nacional de Arte, Brazil
FURN	Fundação Universidade Regional do Nordeste
Ga.	Georgia
GAO	General Accounting Office, Wahington
GATT	General Agreement on Tariffs and Trade
GDP	gross domestic product
GDR	German Democratic Republic
GEIDA	Grupo Executivo de Irrigação para o Desenvolvimento Agrícola, Brazil
gen.	gennaio
Gen.	General
GMT	Greenwich Mean Time
GPA	grade point average
GPO	Government Printing Office, Washington
h.	hijo
ha.	hectares, hectáreas
HLAS	*Handbook of Latin American Studies*
HMAI	*Handbook of Middle American Indians*
Hnos.	hermanos
HRAF	Human Relations Area Files, Inc., New Haven, Conn.
IBBD	Instituto Brasileiro de Bibliografia e Documentação
IBGE	Instituto Brasileiro de Geografia e Estatística, Rio de Janeiro
IBRD	International Bank for Reconstruction and Development (World Bank)
ICA	Instituto Colombiano Agropecuario
ICAIC	Instituto Cubano de Arte e Industria Cinematográfica
ICCE	Instituto Colombiano de Construcción Escolar
ICE	International Cultural Exchange
ICSS	Instituto Colombiano de Seguridad Social
ICT	Instituto de Crédito Territorial, Colombia
id.	*idem* (the same as previously mentioned or given)
IDB	Inter-American Development Bank
i.e.	*id est* (that is, o sea)
IEL	Instituto Euvaldo Lodi, Brazil
IEP	Instituto de Estudios Peruanos
IERAC	Instituto Ecuatoriano de Reforma Agraria y Colonización
IFAD	International Fund for Agricultural Development
IICA	Instituto Interamericano de Ciencias Agrícolas, San José
III	Instituto Indigenista Interamericana, Mexico
IIN	Instituto Indigenista Nacional, Guatemala
ILDIS	Instituto Latinoamericano de Investigaciones Sociales
ill.	illustration(s)
Ill.	Illinois
ILO	International Labour Organization, Geneva
IMES	Instituto Mexicano de Estudios Sociales
IMF	International Monetary Fund

Impr.	Imprenta, Imprimérie
in.	inches
INAH	Instituto Nacional de Antropología e Historia, Mexico
INBA	Instituto Nacional de Bellas Artes, Mexico
Inc.	Incorporated
INCORA	Instituto Colombiano de Reforma Agraria
Ind.	Indiana
INEP	Instituto Nacional de Estudios Pedagógicos, Brazil
INI	Instituto Nacional Indigenista, Mexico
INIT	Instituto Nacional de Industria Turística, Cuba
INPES/IPEA	Instituto de Planejamento Econômico e Social, Brazil
INTAL	Instituto para la Integración de América Latina
IPA	Instituto de Pastoral Andina, Univ. de San Antonio de Abad, Seminario de Antropología, Cusco, Peru
IPEA	Instituto de Pesquisa Econômica Aplicada, Brazil
IPES/GB	Instituto de Pesquisas e Estudos Sociais, Guanabara, Brazil
IPHAN	Instituto de Patrimônio Histórico e Artístico Nacional, Brazil
ir.	irregular
IS	Internacional Socialista
ITESM	Instituto Tecnológico y de Estudios Superiores de Monterrey
ITT	International Telephone and Telegraph
Jan./jan.	January, Januar, janeiro, janvier
JLP	Jamaican Labour Party
Jr.	Junior, Júnior
JUC	Juventude Universitária Católica, Brazil
JUCEPLAN	Junta Central de Planificación, Cuba
Kan.	Kansas
KITLV	Koninklijk Instituut voor Tall-, Land- en Volkenkunde (Royal Institute of Linguistics and Anthropology)
km	kilometers, kilómetros
Ky.	Kentucky
La.	Louisiana
LASA	Latin American Studies Association
LDC	less developed country(ies)
LP	long-playing record
Ltd(a).	Limited, Limitada
m	meters, metros
m.	murió (died)
M	mille, mil, thousand
M.A.	Master of Arts
MACLAS	Middle Atlantic Council of Latin American Studies
MAPU	Movimiento de Acción Popular Unitario, Chile
MARI	Middle American Research Institute, Tulane University, New Orleans
MAS	Movimiento al Socialismo, Venezuela
Mass.	Massachusetts
MCC	Mercado Común Centro-Americano
Md.	Maryland
MDB	Movimiento Democrático Brasileiro
MDC	more developed countries
Me.	Maine
MEC	Ministério de Educação e Cultura, Brazil
Mich.	Michigan
mimeo	mimeographed, mimeografiado
min.	minutes, minutos
Minn.	Minnesota

MIR	Movimiento de Izquierda Revolucionaria, Chile and Venezuela
Miss.	Mississippi
MIT	Massachusetts Institute of Technology
ml	milliliter
MLN	Movimiento de Liberación Nacional
mm.	millimeter
MNC	multinational corporation
MNI	minimum number of individuals
MNR	Movimiento Nacionalista Revolucionario, Bolivia
Mo.	Missouri
MOBRAL	Movimento Brasileiro de Alfabetização
MOIR	Movimiento Obrero Independiente y Revolucionario, Colombia
Mont.	Montana
MRL	Movimiento Revolucionario Liberal, Colombia
ms.	manuscript
M.S.	Master of Science
msl	mean sea level
MST	Movimento Sem Terra; Movimento dos Trabalhadores Rurais Sem Terra
n.	nació (born)
NBER	National Bureau of Economic Research, Cambridge, Massachusetts
N.C.	North Carolina
N.D.	North Dakota
NE	Northeast
Neb.	Nebraska
neubearb.	neubearbeitet (revised, corregida)
Nev.	Nevada
n.f.	neue Folge (new series)
NGO	nongovernmental organization
NGDO	nongovernmental development organization
N.H.	New Hampshire
NIEO	New International Economic Order
NIH	National Institutes of Health, Washington
N.J.	New Jersey
NJM	New Jewel Movement, Grenada
N.M.	New Mexico
no(s).	number(s), número(s)
NOEI	Nuevo Orden Económico Internacional
NOSALF	Scandinavian Committee for Research in Latin America
Nov./nov.	November, noviembre, novembre, novembro
NSF	National Science Foundation
NW	Northwest
N.Y.	New York
OAB	Ordem dos Advogados do Brasil
OAS	Organization of American States
OCLC	Online Computer Library Center
Oct./oct.	October, octubre, octobre
ODEPLAN	Oficina de Planificación Nacional, Chile
OEA	Organización de los Estados Americanos
OECD	Organisation for Economic Cooperation and Development
OIT	Organización Internacional del Trabajo
Okla.	Oklahoma
Okt.	Oktober
ONUSAL	United Nations Observer Mission in El Salvador
op.	opus

OPANAL	Organismo para la Proscripción de las Armas Nucleares en América Latina
OPEC	Organization of Petroleum Exporting Countries
OPEP	Organización de Países Exportadores de Petróleo
OPIC	Overseas Private Investment Corporation, Washington
Or.	Oregon
OREALC	Oficina Regional de Educación para América Latina y el Caribe
ORIT	Organización Regional Interamericana del Trabajo
ORSTOM	Office de la recherche scientifique et technique outre-mer (France)
ott.	ottobre
out.	outubro
p.	page(s)
Pa.	Pennsylvania
PAN	Partido Acción Nacional, Mexico
PC	Partido Comunista
PCCLAS	Pacific Coast Council on Latin American Studies
PCN	Partido de Conciliación Nacional, El Salvador
PCP	Partido Comunista del Perú
PCR	Partido Comunista Revolucionario, Chile and Argentina
PCV	Partido Comunista de Venezuela
PD	Partido Democrático
PDC	Partido Demócrata Cristiano, Chile
PDS	Partido Democrático Social, Brazil
PDT	Partido Democrático Trabalhista, Brazil
PDVSA	Petróleos de Venezuela S.A.
PEMEX	Petróleos Mexicanos
PETROBRAS	Petróleo Brasileiro
PIMES	Programa Integrado de Mestrado em Economia e Sociologia, Brazil
PIP	Partido Independiente de Puerto Rico
PLN	Partido Liberación Nacional, Costa Rica
PMDB	Partido do Movimento Democrático Brasileiro
PNAD	Pesquisa Nacional por Amostra Domiciliar, Brazil
PNC	People's National Congress, Guyana
PNM	People's National Movement, Trinidad and Tobago
PNP	People's National Party, Jamaica
pop.	population
port(s).	portrait(s)
PPP	purchasing power parities; People's Progressive Party of Guyana
PRD	Partido Revolucionario Dominicano
PREALC	Programa Regional del Empleo para América Latina y el Caribe, Organización Internacional del Trabajo, Santiago
PRI	Partido Revolucionario Institucional, Mexico
Prof.	Professor, Profesor(a)
PRONAPA	Programa Nacional de Pesquisas Arqueológicas, Brazil
PRONASOL	Programa Nacional de Solidaridad, Mexico
prov.	province, provincia
PS	Partido Socialista, Chile
PSD	Partido Social Democrático, Brazil
pseud.	pseudonym, pseudónimo
PT	Partido dos Trabalhadores, Brazil
pt(s).	part(s), parte(s)
PTB	Partido Trabalhista Brasileiro
pub.	published, publisher
PUC	Pontifícia Universidade Católica
PURSC	Partido Unido de la Revolución Socialista de Cuba

q.	quarterly
rev.	revisada, revista, revised
R.I.	Rhode Island
s.a.	semiannual
SALALM	Seminar on the Acquisition of Latin American Library Materials
SATB	soprano, alto, tenor, bass
sd.	sound
s.d.	*sine datum* (no date, sin fecha)
S.D.	South Dakota
SDR	special drawing rights
SE	Southeast
SELA	Sistema Económico Latinoamericano
SEMARNAP	Secretaria de Medio Ambiente, Recursos Naturales y Pesca, Mexico
SENAC	Serviço Nacional de Aprendizagem Comercial, Rio de Janeiro
SENAI	Serviço Nacional de Aprendizagem Industrial, São Paulo
SEP	Secretaría de Educación Pública, Mexico
SEPLA	Seminario Permanente sobre Latinoamérica, Mexico
Sept./sept.	September, septiembre, septembre
SES	socioeconomic status
SESI	Serviço Social da Indústria, Brazil
set.	setembro, settembre
SI	Socialist International
SIECA	Secretaría Permanente del Tratado General de Integración Económica Centroamericana
SIL	Summer Institute of Linguistics (Instituto Lingüístico de Verano)
SINAMOS	Sistema Nacional de Apoyo a la Movilización Social, Peru
S.J.	Society of Jesus
s.l.	*sine loco* (place of publication unknown)
s.n.	*sine nomine* (publisher unknown)
SNA	Sociedad Nacional de Agricultura, Chile
SPP	Secretaría de Programación y Presupuesto, Mexico
SPVEA	Superintendência do Plano de Valorização Econômica da Amazônia, Brazil
sq.	square
SSRC	Social Sciences Research Council, New York
STENEE	Empresa Nacional de Energía Eléctrica. Sindicato de Trabajadores, Honduras
SUDAM	Superintendência de Desenvolvimento da Amazônia, Brazil
SUDENE	Superintendência de Desenvolvimento do Nordeste, Brazil
SUFRAMA	Superintendência da Zona Franca de Manaus, Brazil
SUNY	State University of New York
SW	Southwest
t.	tomo(s), tome(s)
TAT	Thematic Apperception Test
TB	tuberculosis
Tenn.	Tennessee
Tex.	Texas
TG	transformational generative
TL	Thermoluminescent
TNE	Transnational enterprise
TNP	Tratado de No Proliferación
trans.	translator
UABC	Universidad Autónoma de Baja California
UCA	Universidad Centroamericana José Simeón Cañas, San Salvador
UCLA	University of California, Los Angeles

UDN	União Democrática Nacional, Brazil
UFG	Universidade Federal de Goiás
UFPb	Universidade Federal de Paraíba
UFSC	Universidade Federal de Santa Catarina
UK	United Kingdom
UN	United Nations
UNAM	Universidad Nacional Autónoma de México
UNCTAD	United Nations Conference on Trade and Development
UNDP	United Nations Development Programme
UNEAC	Unión de Escritores y Artistas de Cuba
UNESCO	United Nations Educational, Scientific and Cultural Organization
UNI/UNIND	União das Nações Indígenas
UNICEF	United Nations International Children's Emergency Fund
Univ(s).	university(ies), universidad(es), universidade(s), université(s), universität(s), universitá(s)
uniw.	uniwersytet (university)
Unltd.	Unlimited
UP	Unidad Popular, Chile
URD	Unidad Revolucionaria Democrática
URSS	Unión de Repúblicas Soviéticas Socialistas
UNISA	University of South Africa
US	United States
USAID	*See* AID.
USIA	United States Information Agency
USSR	Union of Soviet Socialist Republics
UTM	Universal Transverse Mercator
UWI	Univ. of the West Indies
v.	volume(s), volumen (volúmenes)
Va.	Virginia
V.I.	Virgin Islands
viz.	*videlicet* (that is, namely)
vol(s).	volume(s), volumen (volúmenes)
vs.	versus
Vt.	Vermont
W.Va.	West Virginia
Wash.	Washington
Wis.	Wisconsin
WPA	Working People's Alliance, Guyana
WWI	World War I
WWII	World War II
Wyo.	Wyoming
yr(s).	year(s)

TITLE LIST OF JOURNALS INDEXED

For journal titles listed by abbreviation, see *Abbreviation List of Journals Indexed*, p. 763.

Afro-Asia. Universidade Federal da Bahia, Faculdade de Filosofia e Ciências Humanas, Centro de Estudos Afro-Orientais. Salvador, Brazil. (Afro-Asia/Salvador)

Alba. Carnaval Press. London. (Alba/London)

The American Historical Review. Indiana University at Bloomington. Bloomington. (Am. Hist. Rev.)

American Music Review. H. Wiley Hitchcock Institute for Studies in American Music. Brooklyn, N.Y. (Am. Music Rev.)

American Quarterly. Johns Hopkins University Press. Baltimore, Md. (Am. Q.)

The Americas: A Quarterly Review of Inter-American Cultural History. Catholic University of America, Academy of American Franciscan History; Catholic University of America Press. Washington, D.C. (Americas/Washington)

Anais do Museu Paulista: História e Cultura Material. Museu Paulista. São Paulo. (An. Mus. Paul.)

Anales de la Academia de Geografía e Historia de Guatemala. Academia de Geografía e Historia de Guatemala. Guatemala. (An. Acad. Geogr. Hist. Guatem.)

Ancient Mesoamerica. Cambridge University Press. New York; Cambridge, England. (Anc. Mesoam.)

ANDES: Antropología e Historia. Universidad Nacional de Salta, Facultad de Humanidades, Centro Promocional de las Investigaciones en Historia y Antropología. Salta, Argentina. (ANDES Antropol. Hist.)

Annales de la Fondation Fyssen. Ed. De l'Interligne. Paris. (Ann. Fond. Fyssen)

Anos 90: Revista do Programa de Pós-Graduação em História. Universidade Federal do Rio Grande do Sul, Programa de Pós-Graduação em História. Porto Alegre, Brazil. (Anos 90)

Anuario Colombiano de Historia Social y de la Cultura. Universidad Nacional de Colombia, Facultad de Ciencias Humanas, Departamento de Historia. Bogotá. (Anu. Colomb. Hist. Soc. Cult.)

Anuario de Estudios Americanos. Consejo Superior de Investigaciones Científicas, Escuela de Estudios Hispano-Americanos. Sevilla, Spain. (Anu. Estud. Am.)

Anuario de Estudios Centroamericanos. Universidad de Costa Rica. San José. (Anu. Estud. Centroam.)

Anuario Musical. Instituto Español de Musicología, Consejo Superior de Investigaciones Científicas. Barcelona. (Anu. Music.)

APA Newsletter on Hispanic/Latino Issues in Philosophy. The American Philosophical Association, University of Delaware. Newark. (APA News. Hisp. Latino Phil.)

The Art Bulletin. College Art Association of America. New York. (Art Bull.)

Art History. Blackwell Publishers. London. (Art Hist.)

Art in Translation. Taylor & Francis. Abingdon, England. (Art Trans.)

ArtCultura. Universidade Federal de Uberlândia, Departamento de História, Núcleo de Estudos em História Social da Arte e da Cultura. Uberlândia, Brazil. (ArtCultura/Uberlândia)

Asymptote. Lee Yew Leong. Taipei City, Taiwan. (Asymptote (online))

Atlantic Studies: Global Currents. Taylor & Francis. Abingdon, England. (Atlan. Stud. Global Curr.)

Balajú: Revista de Cultura y Comunicación de la Universidad Veracruzana. Universidad Veracruzana. Xalapa Veracruz, Mexico. (Balajú)

Black Music Research Journal. Fisk University, Institute for Research in Black

American Music. Nashville, Tenn. (Black Music Res. J.)
Boletín Cultural y Bibliográfico. Banco de la República, Biblioteca Luis-Angel Arango. Bogotá. (Bol. Cult. Bibliogr.)
Boletín de la Academia Chilena de la Historia. Academia Chilena de la Historia. Santiago. (Bol. Acad. Chil. Hist.)
Boletín del Museo Chileno de Arte Precolombino. Santiago, Chile. (Bol. Mus. Chil. Arte Precolomb.)
Brasiliana: Journal for Brazilian Studies. Aarhus University: The Royal Danish Library. Aarhus, Denmark. (Brasiliana/Aarhus)
Bulletin de l'Institut français d'études andines. Lima. (Bull. Inst. fr. étud. andin.)

Caravelle: Cahiers du monde hispanique et luso-brésilien. Université de Toulouse, Institute d'études hispaniques, hispano-americaines et luso-brésiliennes. Toulouse, France. (Caravelle/Toulouse)
Caribbean Quarterly: CQ. University of the West Indies, Vice Chancellery, Cultural Studies Initiative. Mona, Jamaica. (Caribb. Q./Mona)
Caribbean Studies. Universidad de Puerto Rico, Instituto de Estudios del Caribe. Río Piedras, Puerto Rico. (Caribb. Stud.)
Centro Journal. Centro de Estudios Puertorriqueños. New York. (Cent. J.)
Cine Cubano. Cinemateca de Cuba. La Habana. (Cine Cub.)
Claves. Universidade Federal da Paraíba, Programa de Pós-Graduação em Música. João Pessoa, Brazil. (Claves/João Pessoa)
Colonial Latin American Historical Review. University of New Mexico, Spanish Colonial Research Center. Albuquerque. (CLAHR)
Colonial Latin American Review. City University of New York (CUNY), City College, Department of Foreign Languages and Literatures, Simon H. Rifkind Center for the Humanities. New York; Carfax Publishing, Taylor & Francis, Ltd. Abingdon, England. (Colon. Lat. Am. Rev.)
CR: The New Centennial Review. Michigan State University, College of Science and Arts. East Lansing, Mich. (CR)
Cuadernos de Iconografía Musical. UNAM. México. (Cuad. Iconogr. Mus.)

Cuban Studies. University of Pittsburgh Press. Pittsburgh, Pa. (Cuba. Stud.)

Desacatos: Revista de Antropología Social. Centro de Investigaciones y Estudios Superiores en Antropología Social (CIESAS). México. (Desacatos)
Diplomatic History. Society for Historians of American Foreign Relations. Wilmington, Del. (Dipl. Hist.)

Early American Literature. University of North Carolina at Chapel Hill. Chapel Hill. (Early Am. Lit.)
Early American Studies. McNeil Center for Early American Studies. Philadelphia, Pa. (Early Amer. Stud.)
ECA. Universidad Centroamericana José Simeón Cañas. San Salvador. (ECA/San Salvador)
Ecuador Debate. Centro Andino de Acción Popular. Quito. (Ecuad. Debate)
Eighteenth-Century Studies. Johns Hopkins University Press for the American Society for Eighteenth-Century Studies. Baltimore, Md. (Eighteenth-Century Stud.)
Estudios Sociales: Revista Universitaria Semestral. Universidad Nacional del Litoral, Secretaría de Extensión, Centro de Publicaciones. Santa Fe, Argentina. (Estud. Soc./Santa Fe)
Estudios Sociológicos. El Colegio de México, Centro de Estudios Sociológicos. México. (Estud. Sociol./México)
Estudos Históricos. Fundação Getulio Vargas, Centro de Pesquisa e Documentação de História Contemporânea do Brasil. Rio de Janeiro. (Estud. Hist./Rio de Janeiro)
Ethnohistory. American Society for Ethnohistory. Columbus, Ohio. (Ethnohistory/Columbus)
Ethnomusicology. University of Illinois Press. Champaign. (Ethnomusicology/Champaign)
Ethnomusicology Forum. Routledge Taylor & Francis Group. Basingstoke, England. (Ethnomusicology Forum)

Faces da História. Universidade Estadual Paulista, Faculdade de Ciências e Letras de Assis, Programa de Pós-Graduação em História. São Paulo. (Faces Hist.)
Feminist Formations. Johns Hopkins University Press. Baltimore, Md. (Fem. Form.)

Film History: An International Journal. Indiana University Press. Bloomington. (Film Hist.)

Fontes Artis Musicae. Barenreiter-Verlag. Kassel, Germany. (Fontes Artis Music.)

Fronteras de la Historia. Instituto Colombiano de Antropología e Historia. Bogotá. (Front. Hist.)

Gender & History. Blackwell Publishers. Abingdon, England; Williston, Vt. (Gend. Hist.)

Hispanic American Historical Review. Duke University Press. Durham, N.C. (HAHR)

Historia. Pontificia Universidad Católica de Chile, Facultad de Historia, Geografía y Ciencia Política, Instituto de Historia. Santiago. (Historia/Santiago)

História Ciências Saúde: Manguinhos. Fundação Oswaldo Cruz, Casa de Oswaldo Cruz. Rio de Janeiro. (Hist. Ciênc. Saúde Manguinhos)

Historia Crítica. Universidad de los Andes, Facultad de Ciencias Sociales, Departamento de Historia. Bogotá. (Hist. Crít./Bogotá)

Historia Mexicana. El Colegio de México, Centro de Estudios Históricos. México. (Hist. Mex./México)

História: Questões e Debates. Universidade Federal do Paraná, Programa de Pós-Graduação em História, Associação Paraense de História. Curitiba, Brazil. (Hist. Quest. Debates)

Historia y Sociedad. Universidad de Puerto Rico, Departamento de Historia. Río Piedras. (Hist. Soc./Río Piedras)

History. Historical Association. London. (History/London)

Hoblicua. Revista Hoblicua. Teresina, Brazil. (Hoblicua)

Iberoamericana. Iberoamericana; Editorial Vervuert. Madrid. (Iberoamericana/Madrid)

Idéias: Revista do Instituto de Filosofia e Ciências Humanas. Instituto de Filosofia e Ciências Humanas da Unicamp. Campinas, Brazil. (Idéias/Campinas)

International Journal of Bahamian Studies. Office of Research, Graduate Programmes and International Relations, College of the Bahamas. Nassau. (Int. J. Bahamian Stud.)

Intervención: Revista Internacional de Conservación, Restauración y Museología. Escuela Nacional de Conservación, Restauración y Museografía-INAH. México. (Intervención/México)

Investigaciones Sociales: Revista del Instituto de Investigaciones Histórico Sociales. Universidad Nacional Mayor de San Marcos, Facultad de Ciencias Sociales. Lima. (Investig. Soc./San Marcos)

Journal de la Société des américanistes. Paris. (J. Soc. am.)

Journal of Africana Religions. The Pennsylvania State University Press. University Park. (J. Africana Relig.)

Journal of American Folklore. American Folklore Society. Arlington, Va. (J. Am. Folk.)

Journal of Anthropological Research. University of New Mexico. Albuquerque. (J. Anthropol. Res.)

The Journal of Caribbean History. University of the West Indies Press; University of the West Indies, Department of History. Mona, Jamaica. (J. Caribb. Hist.)

The Journal of Economic History. Economic History Association; University of Arizona. Tucson. (J. Econ. Hist.)

Journal of Folklore Research. Indiana University, Folklore Institute. Bloomington. (J. Folk. Res.)

Journal of Latin American Cultural Studies. Carfax Publishing. Abingdon, England. (J. Lat. Am. Cult. Stud.)

Journal of Latin American Studies. Cambridge University Press. Cambridge, England. (J. Lat. Am. Stud.)

Journal of Music History Pedagogy. American Musicological Society. Brunswick, Maine. (J. Music Hist. Pedagogy)

Journal of Popular Music Studies. Branch of the International Association for the Study of Popular Music. Iowa City. (J. Pop. Music Stud.)

Journal of Speculative Philosophy. George Knapp & Co. St. Louis, Mo. (J. Spec. Philos.)

Journal of Texas Music History. Institute for the History of Texas Music, Southwest Texas State University. San Marcos. (J. Tex. Music Hist.)

Journal of Women's History. Indiana University Press. Bloomington; Johns

Hopkins University Press. Baltimore, Md. (J. Women's Hist.)

Labor: Studies in Working-Class History of the Americas. Duke University Press. Durham, N.C. (Labor/Durham)

Latin American and Caribbean Ethnic Studies. Taylor & Francis. Colchester, England. (Lat. Am. Caribb. Ethn. Stud.)

Latin American Music Review (LAMR) = Revista de Música Latinoamericana. University of Texas Press. Austin. (Lat. Am. Music Rev.)

Latin American Perspectives. Sage Publications, Inc. Thousand Oaks, Calif. (Lat. Am. Perspect.)

Latin American Research Review. Latin American Studies Association; University of Texas Press. Austin. (LARR)

The Latin Americanist. Southeastern Council of Latin American Studies. Orlando, Fla. (Lat. Am./Orlando)

Leonardo Music Journal. MIT Press. Cambridge, Mass. (Leonardo Music J.)

Lua Nova. Centro de Estudos de Cultura Contemporânea. São Paulo. (Lua Nova)

MACLAS Latin American Essays. University of Delaware. Newark. (MACLAS Lat. Am. Essays)

Magallania. Instituto de la Patagonia, Universidad de Magallanes. Punta Arenas, Chile. (Magallania/Punta Arenas)

Memorias: Revista de la Maestría en Historia Social y Cultural de la UNAH. Universidad Nacional Autónoma de Honduras. Tegucigalpa. (Memorias/Tegucigalpa)

Memorias: Revista Digital de Historia y Arqueología desde el Caribe. Universidad del Norte. Barranquilla, Colombia. (Memorias/Barranquilla)

Mexican Studies/Estudios Mexicanos. University of California Press. Berkeley. (Mex. Stud.)

Millars: espai i història. Universitat Jaume I. Castelló de la Plana, Spain. (Millars)

Music & Politics. University of California, Santa Barbara. Santa Barbara. (Music Polit.)

Music and Arts in Action. Exeter School of Music Sociology. Exeter, England. (MAIA)

Música e Cultura: Revista da Associação Brasileira de Etnomusicologia. Universidade Federal da Paraíba, UFPB. Brazil. (Música Cult.)

Música em Contexto. Universidade de Brasília. Brasília. (Música Contexto)

New Mexico Historical Review. University of New Mexico; Historical Society of New Mexico. Albuquerque. (N.M. Hist. Rev.)

NWIG: New West Indian Guide/Nieuwe West Indische Gids. Royal Institute of Linguistics and Anthropology, KITLV Press. Leiden, The Netherlands. (NWIG)

Op. Cit.: Boletín del Centro de Investigaciones Históricas. Universidad de Puerto Rico, Facultad de Humanidades, Departamento de Historia. Río Piedras. (Op. Cit./Río Piedras)

The Opera Quarterly. University of North Carolina Press. Chapel Hill. (Opera Q.)

Opus. Universidade Federal do Rio Grande do Sul, Instituto de Artes. Porto Alegre, Brazil. (Opus/Porto Alegre)

Pan. British Flute Society. Purley, England. (Pan/London)

Pauta: Cuadernos de Teoría y Crítica Musical. Consejo Nacional para la Cultura y las Artes, Dirección General de Publicaciones, Instituto Nacional de Bellas Artes. México. (Pauta/México)

Popular Music and Society. Taylor & Francis Group, Routledge Press. London; New York. (Pop. Music Soc.)

Res. Harvard University, Peabody Museum of Archaeology and Ethnology. Cambridge, Mass. (Res/Cambridge)

Revista Argentina de Musicología. Asociación Argentina de Musicología. Buenos Aires. (Rev. Arg. Musicol.)

Revista Brasileira de História. Associação Nacional de História. São Paulo. (Rev. Bras. Hist./São Paulo)

Revista Brasileira de Música. Universidade Federal do Rio de Janeiro, Escola de Música. Rio de Janeiro. (Rev. Bras. Música/Rio de Janeiro)

Revista Catalana de Musicologia. Societat Catalana de Musicologia. Barcelona. (Rev. Cat. Musicol.)

Revista Complutense de Historia de América. Universidad Complutense de Madrid, Facultad de Geografía e Historia, Departamento de Historia de América I. Madrid. (Rev. Complut. Hist. Am.)

Revista de Antropologia. Universidade de São Paulo, Faculdade de Filosofia, Letras e Ciências Humanas, Departamento de Antropologia. São Paulo. (Rev. Antropol./São Paulo)

Revista de Ciencia Política. Pontificia Universidad Católica de Chile, Instituto de Ciencia Política. Santiago. (Rev. Cienc. Polít./Santiago)

Revista de Ciencias Sociales. Editorial Universidad de Costa Rica. San José. (Rev. Cienc. Soc./San José)

Revista de Economia Política = Brazilian Journal of Political Economy. Centro de Economia Política. São Paulo. (Rev. Econ. Polít.)

Revista de Historia. Universidad Nacional, Escuela de Historia. Heredia, Costa Rica; Universidad de Costa Rica, Centro de Investigaciones Históricas de América Central. San José. (Rev. Hist./Heredia)

Revista de História. Universidade de São Paulo, Faculdade de Filosofia, Letras e Ciências Humanas, Departamento de História. São Paulo. (Rev. Hist./São Paulo)

Revista de Historia de América. Instituto Panamericano de Geografía e Historia. Comisión de Historia. México. (Rev. Hist. Am./México)

Revista de Indias Consejo Superior de Investigaciones Científicas, Instituto de Historia, Departamento de Historia de América. Madrid. (Rev. Indias)

Revista de Musicología. Sociedad Española de Musicología. Madrid. (Rev. Musicol./Madrid)

Revista Digital de Música Sacra Brasileira. São Paulo. (Rev. Digit. Música Sacra Bras.)

Revista do Instituto de Estudos Brasileiros. Universidade de São Paulo, Instituto de Estudos Brasileiros. São Paulo. (Rev. Inst. Estud. Bras.)

Revista Española de Antropología Americana. Universidad Complutense de Madrid, Facultad de Geografía e Historia, Departamento de Historia de América II (Antropología de América). Madrid. (Rev. Esp. Antropol. Am.)

Revista Europea de Estudios Latinoamericanos y del Caribe = European Review of Latin American and Caribbean Studies. Center for Latin American Research and Documentation = Centro de Estudios y Documentación Latinoamericanos. Amsterdam. (Rev. Eur. Estud. Latinoam. Caribe)

Revista Mexicana de Ciencias Políticas y Sociales. UNAM, Facultad de Ciencias Políticas y Sociales. México. (Rev. Mex. Cienc. Polít. Soc.)

Revista Musical Chilena. Universidad de Chile, Facultad de Artes, Sección de Musicología. Santiago. (Rev. Music. Chil.)

Revista Portuguesa de Musicología. Sociedade Portuguesa de Investigação e Música. Lisboa. (Rev. Port. Musicol.)

Revista Resonancias. Pontificia Universidad Católica de Chile, Instituto de Música. Santiago. (Resonancias/Santiago)

Revista USP. Universidade de São Paulo, Coordenadoria de Comunicação Social. São Paulo. (Rev. USP/São Paulo)

Revista Vórtex. Universidade Estadual do Paraná: Escola de Música e Belas Artes do Paraná. Curitiba, Brazil. (Rev. Vórtex)

Romance Notes. University of North Carolina, Department of Romance Languages. Chapel Hill. (Roman. Notes)

Secuencia: Revista de Historia y Ciencias Sociales. Instituto de Investigaciones Dr. José María Luis Mora. México. (Secuencia/México)

El Sincopado Habanero: Boletín del Gabinete de Patrimonio Musical Esteban Salas. Oficina del Historiador de La Habana. La Habana. (Sinc. Habanero)

Slavery and Abolition. Taylor and Francis. Oxon, England. (Slavery Abolit.)

Small Axe: A Journal of Criticism. Ian Randle Publishers. Kingston. (Small Axe)

Social Sciences. MDPI. Basel, Switzerland. (Soc. Sci.)

Southern Cultures. University of North Carolina Press. Chapel Hill. (South. Cult.)

Studies in Latin American Popular Culture. University of Arizona, College of Humanities. Tucson. (Stud. Lat. Am. Pop. Cult.)

Suplemento Literário de Minas Gerais. Secretaria de Estado de Cultura de Minas Gerais. Belo Horizonte, Brazil. (SLMG)

Temas Americanistas. Universidad de Sevilla, Servicio de Publicaciones. Sevilla, Spain. (Temas Am.)

Titivillus. Publicaciones de la Universidad de Zaragoza. Spain. (Titivillus)

Trans: Revista Transcultural de Música. www.sibetrans.com/trans/; Sociedad de Etnomusicología. Barcelona. (Trans (online))

Tzintzun: Revista de Estudios Históricos. Universidad de Michoacán de San Nicolas de Hidalgo. Morelia, Mexico. (Tzintzun)

Umbrales. Universidad Mayor de San Andrés, Post Grado en Ciencias del Desarrollo. La Paz, Bolivia. (Umbrales/La Paz)

Universum. Universidad de Talca. Talca, Chile. (Universum/Talca)

Varia História. Universidade Federal de Minas Gerais, Faculdade de Filosofia e Ciencias Humanas, Departamento de História. Belo Horizonte, Brazil. (Varia Hist.)

Volume!: la revue des musiques populaires. Éd. Mélanie Séteun. Bordeaux, France. (Volume/Bordeaux)

The William and Mary Quarterly. College of William and Mary. Williamsburg, Va. (William Mary Q.)

The World of Music. Georg-August-Universität, Department of Musicology. Göttingen, Germany. (World Mus.)

ABBREVIATION LIST OF JOURNALS INDEXED

For journal titles listed by full title, see *Title List of Journals Indexed*, p. 757.

Afro-Asia/Salvador. Afro-Asia. Universidade Federal da Bahia, Faculdade de Filosofia e Ciências Humanas, Centro de Estudos Afro-Orientais. Salvador, Brazil.

Alba/London. Alba. Carnaval Press. London.

Am. Hist. Rev. The American Historical Review. Indiana University at Bloomington. Bloomington.

Am. Music Rev. American Music Review. H. Wiley Hitchcock Institute for Studies in American Music. Brooklyn, N.Y.

Am. Q. American Quarterly. Johns Hopkins University Press. Baltimore, Md.

Americas/Washington. The Americas: A Quarterly Review of Inter-American Cultural History. Catholic University of America, Academy of American Franciscan History; Catholic University of America Press. Washington, D.C.

An. Acad. Geogr. Hist. Guatem. Anales de la Academia de Geografía e Historia de Guatemala. Academia de Geografía e Historia de Guatemala. Guatemala.

An. Mus. Paul. Anais do Museu Paulista: História e Cultura Material. Museu Paulista. São Paulo.

Anc. Mesoam. Ancient Mesoamerica. Cambridge University Press. New York; Cambridge, England.

ANDES Antropol. Hist. ANDES: Antropología e Historia. Universidad Nacional de Salta, Facultad de Humanidades, Centro Promocional de las Investigaciones en Historia y Antropología. Salta, Argentina.

Ann. Fond. Fyssen. Annales de la Fondation Fyssen. Ed. De l'Interligne. Paris.

Anos 90. Anos 90: Revista do Programa de Pós-Graduação em História. Universidade Federal do Rio Grande do Sul, Programa de Pós-Graduação em História. Porto Alegre, Brazil.

Anu. Colomb. Hist. Soc. Cult. Anuario Colombiano de Historia Social y de la Cultura. Universidad Nacional de Colombia, Facultad de Ciencias Humanas, Departamento de Historia. Bogotá.

Anu. Estud. Am. Anuario de Estudios Americanos. Consejo Superior de Investigaciones Científicas, Escuela de Estudios Hispano-Americanos. Sevilla, Spain.

Anu. Estud. Centroam. Anuario de Estudios Centroamericanos. Universidad de Costa Rica. San José.

Anu. Music. Anuario Musical. Instituto Español de Musicología, Consejo Superior de Investigaciones Científicas. Barcelona.

APA News. Hisp. Latino Phil. APA Newsletter on Hispanic/Latino Issues in Philosophy. The American Philosophical Association, University of Delaware. Newark.

Art Bull. The Art Bulletin. College Art Association of America. New York.

Art Hist. Art History. Blackwell Publishers. London.

Art Trans. Art in Translation. Taylor & Francis. Abingdon, England.

ArtCultura/Uberlândia. ArtCultura. Universidade Federal de Uberlândia, Departamento de História, Núcleo de Estudos em História Social da Arte e da Cultura. Uberlândia, Brazil.

Asymptote (online). Asymptote . Lee Yew Leong. Taipei City, Taiwan.

Atlan. Stud. Global Curr. Atlantic Studies: Global Currents. Taylor & Francis. Abingdon, England.

Balajú. Balajú: Revista de Cultura y Comunicación de la Universidad Veracruzana. Universidad Veracruzana. Xalapa Veracruz, Mexico.

Black Music Res. J. Black Music Research Journal. Fisk University, Institute for Research in Black American Music. Nashville, Tenn.

Bol. Acad. Chil. Hist. Boletín de la Academia Chilena de la Historia. Academia Chilena de la Historia. Santiago.

Bol. Cult. Bibliogr. Boletín Cultural y Bibliográfico. Banco de la República, Biblioteca Luis-Angel Arango. Bogotá.

Bol. Mus. Chil. Arte Precolomb. Boletín del Museo Chileno de Arte Precolombino. Santiago, Chile.

Brasiliana/Aarhus. Brasiliana: Journal for Brazilian Studies. Aarhus University: The Royal Danish Library. Aarhus, Denmark.

Bull. Inst. fr. étud. andin. Bulletin de l'Institut français d'études andines. Lima.

Caravelle/Toulouse. Caravelle: Cahiers du monde hispanique et luso-brésilien. Université de Toulouse, Institute d'études hispaniques, hispano-americaines et luso-brésiliennes. Toulouse, France.

Caribb. Q./Mona. Caribbean Quarterly: CQ. University of the West Indies, Vice Chancellery, Cultural Studies Initiative. Mona, Jamaica.

Caribb. Stud. Caribbean Studies. Universidad de Puerto Rico, Instituto de Estudios del Caribe. Río Piedras, Puerto Rico.

Cent. J. Centro Journal. Centro de Estudios Puertorriqueños. New York.

Cine Cub. Cine Cubano. Cinemateca de Cuba. La Habana.

CLAHR. Colonial Latin American Historical Review. University of New Mexico, Spanish Colonial Research Center. Albuquerque.

Claves/João Pessoa. Claves. Universidade Federal da Paraíba, Programa de Pós-Graduação em Música. João Pessoa, Brazil.

Colon. Lat. Am. Rev. Colonial Latin American Review. City University of New York (CUNY), City College, Department of Foreign Languages and Literatures, Simon H. Rifkind Center for the Humanities. New York; Carfax Publishing, Taylor & Francis, Ltd. Abingdon, England.

CR. CR: The New Centennial Review. Michigan State University, College of Science and Arts. East Lansing, Mich.

Cuad. Iconogr. Mus. Cuadernos de Iconografía Musical. UNAM. México.

Cuba. Stud. Cuban Studies. University of Pittsburgh Press. Pittsburgh, Pa.

Desacatos. Desacatos: Revista de Antropología Social. Centro de Investigaciones y Estudios Superiores en Antropología Social (CIESAS). México.

Dipl. Hist. Diplomatic History. Society for Historians of American Foreign Relations. Wilmington, Del.

Early Am. Lit. Early American Literature. University of North Carolina at Chapel Hill. Chapel Hill.

Early Amer. Stud. Early American Studies. McNeil Center for Early American Studies. Philadelphia, Pa.

ECA/San Salvador. ECA. Universidad Centroamericana José Simeón Cañas. San Salvador.

Ecuad. Debate. Ecuador Debate. Centro Andino de Acción Popular. Quito.

Eighteenth-Century Stud. Eighteenth-Century Studies. Johns Hopkins University Press for the American Society for Eighteenth-Century Studies. Baltimore, Md.

Estud. Hist./Rio de Janeiro. Estudos Históricos. Fundação Getulio Vargas, Centro de Pesquisa e Documentação de História Contemporânea do Brasil. Rio de Janeiro.

Estud. Soc./Santa Fe. Estudios Sociales: Revista Universitaria Semestral. Universidad Nacional del Litoral, Secretaría de Extensión, Centro de Publicaciones. Santa Fe, Argentina.

Estud. Sociol./México. Estudios Sociológicos. El Colegio de México, Centro de Estudios Sociológicos. México.

Ethnohistory/Columbus. Ethnohistory. American Society for Ethnohistory. Columbus, Ohio.

Ethnomusicology/Champaign. Ethnomusicology. University of Illinois Press. Champaign.

Ethnomusicology Forum. Ethnomusicology Forum. Routledge Taylor & Francis Group. Basingstoke, England.

Faces Hist. Faces da História. Universidade Estadual Paulista, Faculdade de Ciências e Letras de Assis, Programa de Pós-Graduação em História. São Paulo.

Fem. Form. Feminist Formations. Johns Hopkins University Press. Baltimore, Md.

Film Hist. Film History: An International Journal. Indiana University Press. Bloomington.

Fontes Artis Music. Fontes Artis Musicae. Barenreiter-Verlag. Kassel, Germany.

Front. Hist. Fronteras de la Historia. Instituto Colombiano de Antropología e Historia. Bogotá.

Gend. Hist. Gender & History. Blackwell Publishers. Abingdon, England; Williston, Vt.

HAHR. Hispanic American Historical Review. Duke University Press. Durham, N.C.

Hist. Ciênc. Saúde Manguinhos. História Ciências Saúde: Manguinhos. Fundação Oswaldo Cruz, Casa de Oswaldo Cruz. Rio de Janeiro.

Hist. Crít./Bogotá. Historia Crítica. Universidad de los Andes, Facultad de Ciencias Sociales, Departamento de Historia. Bogotá.

Hist. Mex./México. Historia Mexicana. El Colegio de México, Centro de Estudios Históricos. México.

Hist. Quest. Debates. História: Questões e Debates. Universidade Federal do Paraná, Programa de Pós-Graduação em História, Associação Paraense de História. Curitiba, Brazil.

Hist. Soc./Río Piedras. Historia y Sociedad. Universidad de Puerto Rico, Departamento de Historia. Río Piedras.

Historia/Santiago. Historia. Pontificia Universidad Católica de Chile, Facultad de Historia, Geografía y Ciencia Política, Instituto de Historia. Santiago.

History/London. History. Historical Association. London.

Hoblicua. Hoblicua. Revista Hoblicua. Teresina, Brazil.

Iberoamericana/Madrid. Iberoamericana. Iberoamericana; Editorial Vervuert. Madrid.

Idéias/Campinas. Idéias: Revista do Instituto de Filosofia e Ciências Humanas. Instituto de Filosofia e Ciências Humanas da Unicamp. Campinas, Brazil.

Int. J. Bahamian Stud. International Journal of Bahamian Studies. Office of Research, Graduate Programmes and International Relations, College of the Bahamas. Nassau.

Intervención/México. Intervención: Revista Internacional de Conservación, Restauración y Museología. Escuela Nacional de Conservación, Restauración y Museografía-INAH. México.

Investig. Soc./San Marcos. Investigaciones Sociales: Revista del Instituto de Investigaciones Histórico Sociales. Universidad Nacional Mayor de San Marcos, Facultad de Ciencias Sociales. Lima.

J. Africana Relig. Journal of Africana Religions. The Pennsylvania State University Press. University Park.

J. Am. Folk. Journal of American Folklore. American Folklore Society. Arlington, Va.

J. Anthropol. Res. Journal of Anthropological Research. University of New Mexico. Albuquerque.

J. Caribb. Hist. The Journal of Caribbean History. University of the West Indies Press; University of the West Indies, Department of History. Mona, Jamaica.

J. Econ. Hist. The Journal of Economic History. Economic History Association; University of Arizona. Tucson.

J. Folk. Res. Journal of Folklore Research. Indiana University, Folklore Institute. Bloomington.

J. Lat. Am. Cult. Stud. Journal of Latin American Cultural Studies. Carfax Publishing. Abingdon, England.

J. Lat. Am. Stud. Journal of Latin American Studies. Cambridge University Press. Cambridge, England.

J. Music Hist. Pedagogy. Journal of Music History Pedagogy. American Musicological Society. Brunswick, Maine.

J. Pop. Music Stud. Journal of Popular Music Studies. Branch of the International Association for the Study of Popular Music. Iowa City.

J. Soc. am. Journal de la Société des américanistes. Paris.

J. Spec. Philos. Journal of Speculative Philosophy. George Knapp & Co. St. Louis, Mo.

J. Tex. Music Hist. Journal of Texas Music History. Institute for the History of Texas Music, Southwest Texas State University. San Marcos.

J. Women's Hist. Journal of Women's History. Indiana University Press. Bloomington; Johns Hopkins University Press. Baltimore, Md.

Labor/Durham. Labor: Studies in Working-Class History of the Americas. Duke University Press. Durham, N.C.

LARR. Latin American Research Review. Latin American Studies Association; University of Texas Press. Austin.

Lat. Am. Caribb. Ethn. Stud. Latin American and Caribbean Ethnic Studies. Taylor & Francis. Colchester, England.

Lat. Am. Music Rev. Latin American Music Review (LAMR) = Revista de Música Latinoamericana. University of Texas Press. Austin.

Lat. Am./Orlando. The Latin Americanist. Southeastern Council of Latin American Studies. Orlando, Fla.

Lat. Am. Perspect. Latin American Perspectives. Sage Publications, Inc. Thousand Oaks, Calif.

Leonardo Music J. Leonardo Music Journal. MIT Press. Cambridge, Mass.

Lua Nova. Lua Nova. Centro de Estudos de Cultura Contemporânea. São Paulo.

MACLAS Lat. Am. Essays. MACLAS Latin American Essays. University of Delaware. Newark.

Magallania/Punta Arenas. Magallania. Instituto de la Patagonia, Universidad de Magallanes. Punta Arenas, Chile.

MAIA. Music and Arts in Action. Exeter School of Music Sociology. Exeter, England.

Memorias/Barranquilla. Memorias: Revista Digital de Historia y Arqueología desde el Caribe. Universidad del Norte. Barranquilla, Colombia.

Memorias/Tegucigalpa. Memorias: Revista de la Maestri´a en Historia Social y Cultural de la UNAH. Universidad Nacional Autónoma de Honduras. Tegucigalpa.

Mex. Stud. Mexican Studies/Estudios Mexicanos. University of California Press. Berkeley.

Millars. Millars: espai i història. Universitat Jaume I. Castelló de la Plana, Spain.

Music Polit. Music & Politics. University of California, Santa Barbara. Santa Barbara.

Música Contexto. Música em Contexto. Universidade de Brasília. Brasília.

Música Cult. Música e Cultura: Revista da Associação Brasileira de Etnomusicologia. Universidade Federal da Paraíba, UFPB. Brazil.

N.M. Hist. Rev. New Mexico Historical Review. University of New Mexico; Historical Society of New Mexico. Albuquerque.

NWIG. NWIG: New West Indian Guide/ Nieuwe West Indische Gids. Royal Institute of Linguistics and Anthropology, KITLV Press. Leiden, The Netherlands.

Op. Cit./Río Piedras. Op. Cit.: Boletín del Centro de Investigaciones Históricas. Universidad de Puerto Rico, Facultad de Humanidades, Departamento de Historia. Río Piedras.

Opera Q. The Opera Quarterly. University of North Carolina Press. Chapel Hill.

Opus/Porto Alegre. Opus. Universidade Federal do Rio Grande do Sul, Instituto de Artes. Porto Alegre, Brazil.

Pan/London. Pan. British Flute Society. Purley, England.

Pauta/México. Pauta: Cuadernos de Teoría y Crítica Musical. Consejo Nacional para la Cultura y las Artes, Dirección General de Publicaciones, Instituto Nacional de Bellas Artes. México.

Pop. Music Soc. Popular Music and Society. Taylor & Francis Group, Routledge Press. London; New York.

Res/Cambridge. Res. Harvard University, Peabody Museum of Archaeology and Ethnology. Cambridge, Mass.

Resonancias/Santiago. Revista Resonancias. Pontificia Universidad Católica de Chile, Instituto de Música. Santiago.

Rev. Antropol./São Paulo. Revista de Antropologia. Universidade de São Paulo, Faculdade de Filosofia, Letras e Ciências Humanas, Departamento de Antropologia. São Paulo.

Rev. Arg. Musicol. Revista Argentina de Musicología. Asociación Argentina de Musicología. Buenos Aires.

Rev. Bras. Hist./São Paulo. Revista Brasileira de História. Associação Nacional de História. São Paulo.

Rev. Bras. Música/Rio de Janeiro. Revista Brasileira de Música. Universidade Federal do Rio de Janeiro, Escola de Música. Rio de Janeiro.

Rev. Cat. Musicol. Revista Catalana de Musicología. Societat Catalana de Musicología. Barcelona.

Rev. Cienc. Polít./Santiago. Revista de Ciencia Política. Pontificia Universidad Católica de Chile, Instituto de Ciencia Política. Santiago.

Rev. Cienc. Soc./San José. Revista de Ciencias Sociales. Editorial Universidad de Costa Rica. San José.

Rev. Complut. Hist. Am. Revista Complutense de Historia de América. Universidad Complutense de Madrid, Facultad de Geografía e Historia, Departamento de Historia de América I. Madrid.

Rev. Digit. Música Sacra Bras. Revista Digital de Música Sacra Brasileira. São Paulo.

Rev. Econ. Polít. Revista de Economia Política = Brazilian Journal of Political

Economy. Centro de Economia Política. São Paulo.

Rev. Esp. Antropol. Am. Revista Española de Antropología Americana. Universidad Complutense de Madrid, Facultad de Geografía e Historia, Departamento de Historia de América II (Antropología de América). Madrid.

Rev. Eur. Estud. Latinoam. Caribe. Revista Europea de Estudios Latinoamericanos y del Caribe = European Review of Latin American and Caribbean Studies. Center for Latin American Research and Documentation = Centro de Estudios y Documentación Latinoamericanos. Amsterdam.

Rev. Hist. Am./México. Revista de Historia de América. Instituto Panamericano de Geografía e Historia. Comisión de Historia. México.

Rev. Hist./Heredia. Revista de Historia. Universidad Nacional, Escuela de Historia. Heredia, Costa Rica; Universidad de Costa Rica, Centro de Investigaciones Históricas de América Central. San José.

Rev. Hist./São Paulo. Revista de História. Universidade de São Paulo, Faculdade de Filosofia, Letras e Ciências Humanas, Departamento de História. São Paulo.

Rev. Indias. Revista de Indias. Consejo Superior de Investigaciones Científicas, Instituto de Historia, Departamento de Historia de América. Madrid.

Rev. Inst. Estud. Bras. Revista do Instituto de Estudos Brasileiros. Universidade de São Paulo, Instituto de Estudos Brasileiros. São Paulo.

Rev. Mex. Cienc. Polít. Soc. Revista Mexicana de Ciencias Políticas y Sociales. UNAM, Facultad de Ciencias Políticas y Sociales. México.

Rev. Music. Chil. Revista Musical Chilena. Universidad de Chile, Facultad de Artes, Sección de Musicología. Santiago.

Rev. Musicol./Madrid. Revista de Musicología. Sociedad Española de Musicología. Madrid.

Rev. Port. Musicol. Revista Portuguesa de Musicologia. Sociedade Portuguesa de Investigação e Música. Lisboa.

Rev. USP/São Paulo. Revista USP. Universidade de São Paulo, Coordenadoria de Comunicação Social. São Paulo.

Rev. Vórtex. Revista Vórtex. Universidade Estadual do Paraná: Escola de Música e Belas Artes do Paraná. Curitiba, Brazil.

Roman. Notes. Romance Notes. University of North Carolina, Department of Romance Languages. Chapel Hill.

Secuencia/México. Secuencia: Revista de Historia y Ciencias Sociales. Instituto de Investigaciones Dr. José María Luis Mora. México.

Sinc. Habanero. El Sincopado Habanero: Boletín del Gabinete de Patrimonio Musical Esteban Salas. Oficina del Historiador de La Habana. La Habana.

Slavery Abolit. Slavery and Abolition. Taylor and Francis. Oxon, England.

SLMG. Suplemento Literário de Minas Gerais. Secretaria de Estado de Cultura de Minas Gerais. Belo Horizonte, Brazil.

Small Axe. Small Axe: A Journal of Criticism. Ian Randle Publishers. Kingston.

Soc. Sci. Social Sciences. MDPI. Basel, Switzerland.

South. Cult. Southern Cultures. University of North Carolina Press. Chapel Hill.

Stud. Lat. Am. Pop. Cult. Studies in Latin American Popular Culture. University of Arizona, College of Humanities. Tucson.

Temas Am. Temas Americanistas. Universidad de Sevilla, Servicio de Publicaciones. Sevilla, Spain.

Titivillus. Titivillus. Publicaciones de la Universidad de Zaragoza. Spain.

Trans (online). Trans: Revista Transcultural de Música. www.sibetrans.com/trans/; Sociedad de Etnomusicología. Barcelona.

Tzintzun. Tzintzun: Revista de Estudios Históricos. Universidad de Michoacán de San Nicolas de Hidalgo. Morelia, Mexico.

Umbrales/La Paz. Umbrales. Universidad Mayor de San Andrés, Post Grado en Ciencias del Desarrollo. La Paz, Bolivia.

Universum/Talca. Universum. Universidad de Talca. Talca, Chile.

Varia Hist. Varia História. Universidade Federal de Minas Gerais, Faculdade de Filosofia e Ciencias Humanas, Departamento de História. Belo Horizonte, Brazil.

Volume/Bordeaux. Volume!: la revue des musiques populaires. Éd. Mélanie Séteun. Bordeaux, France.

William Mary Q. The William and Mary Quarterly. College of William and Mary. Williamsburg, Va.

World Mus. The World of Music. Georg-August-Universität, Department of Musicology. Göttingen, Germany.

SUBJECT INDEX

Abandoned Children. Brazil, 1592.
Abila, Blas de, 728.
Abitbol, Isaco, 2839.
Abolition (slavery). Antigua and Barbuda, 865. Barbados, 813, 815, 857. Brazil, 1565, 1576, 1583, 1613, 1632, 1652, 1664, 1667, 1697, 1704, 1710. Caribbean Area, 813–814. Children, 842. Colombia, 968, 1103. Economic History, 1631. Frontier and Pioneer Life, 1583. Haiti, 878. Jamaica, 831, 840–842, 878. Law and Legislation, 815. Mexico, 612. Political Philosophy, 2985. Puerto Rico, 876. US, 612. *See Also* Freedmen; Slaves and Slavery
Abolitionists. Brazil, 1632, 1704.
Abstract Art. Art Exhibitions, 69. Brazil, 144. Cuba, 93. Mexico, 69, 86. *See Also* Conceptual Art.
Abused Children. *See* Child Abuse.
Academia Colombiana de Historia, 1099.
Ação Integralista Brasileira, 1642.
Acción Católica Mexicana, 466.
Acción Democrática (Venezuela), 1071, 1082.
Acculturation. Brazil, 182. Catholic Church, 34. Colombia, 273. Mexico, 32. Peru, 985, 1191, 2823.
Actors. Argentina, 2355. Brazil, 2867. Cuba, 901.
Actresses. *See* Actors.
Adolescents. *See* Youth.
Adoption. Brazil, 1606. Colonial History, 1606.
African-Americans. *See* Blacks.
African Influences, 376. Architecture, 176. Brazil, 176, 2486, 2854, 2875, 2884, 2890, 2900, 2916, 2923, 2943. Caribbean Area, 802, 889, 2779, 2998. Ethnic Identity, 2998. Family and Family Relations, 863. Gender Roles, 863. Mexico, 2712, 2757. Music, 2707. Musical History, 2822. Peru, 2819. Philosophy, 2998. Uruguay, 2853. *See Also* Africans; Candomblé (cult); Santería (cult); Umbanda (cult).
Africans. Brazil, 1710. Central America, 736. Costa Rica, 727. Cuba, 867. Paraguay, 1024. Slaves and Slavery, 1629.

Afro-Americans. *See* Blacks.
Agrarian Reform. *See* Land Reform.
Agricultural Colonization. Mexico, 556, 575. *See Also* Land Settlement.
Agricultural Development. Chile, 1262. Mexico, 539. *See Also* Economic Development; Rural Development.
Agricultural History. Puerto Rico, 871.
Agricultural Industries. *See* Agroindustry.
Agricultural Labor. Brazil, 1531. Central America, 743. Honduras, 746. Mexico, 440, 472.
Agricultural Policy. Chile, 1281. *See Also* Land Reform.
Agricultural Workers. *See* Agricultural Labor.
Agriculture. Ecuador, 970. Puerto Rico, 928.
Agroindustry. Costa Rica, 778.
Agrupación Nacional de Empleados Fiscales (Chile), 1240.
Aguilera y Roche, Teresa de, 495.
Aguirre, Félix de, 1403.
Agustini, Delmira, 2184.
Airlines. Brazil, 1560.
Alacaluf (indigenous group). Chile, 247.
Alamán, Lucas, 616.
Alberdi, Juan Bautista, 1342.
Albizu Campos, Pedro, 1938.
Albuquerque, New Mexico (city). Music, 2691.
Alcohol and Alcoholism. Mexico, 677.
Alem, Leandro Nicéforo, 1417.
Alemán, Miguel, 628.
Alfonsín, Raúl, 1424.
Alianza Libertadora Nacionalista (Argentina), 1372.
Alianza Popular Revolucionaria Americana. *See* APRA (Peru).
Allende Gossens, Salvador, 1245.
Almirante, 2912.
Alva Ixtlilxóchitl, Fernando de, 192, 195, 199–200, 223, 241, 245.
Álvarez, Juan, 1381.
Alvarez Mola, Alfredo, 954.
Alvear, Marcelo Torcuato de, 1410.
Alzate y Ramírez, José Antonio de, 1736.

Amado, Jorge, 2673.
Amatzinac River (Mexico), 468.
Ambassadors. Dominican Republic, 906.
American Influences. Brazil, 1544.
Amistad (schooner), 881.
Anarchism and Anarchists, 343, 2961, 2967. Argentina, 1353. Bolivia, 3023. Brazil, 1548, 1698. Caribbean Area, 2997, 3028. Education, 1548. Globalization, 3028. Sex and Sexual Relations, 1404. Women, 1404.
Andean Region, 276. Civilization, 276. History, 1200. Tourism, 1180.
Andes Region. *See* Andean Region.
Andrade, Carlos Drummond de, 2461, 2526, 2539.
Andrade, Mário de, 149, 2461, 2859, 2871.
Andrade, Olegario Victor, 1332.
Andrade, Oswald de, 2462.
Anecdotes. Argentina, 1374. Chile, 1235, 1249. History, 1374. *See Also* Folklore.
Ângela Maria, 2893.
Anglicans. Barbados, 857.
Animals. Art, 188. Brazil, 188. Paraguay, 1039.
Anjos, Augusto dos, 2464.
Anthropology, 2988. Art, 114. Methodology, 923. Peru, 114.
Anthropometry, 320. *See Also* Anthropology.
Anti-positivism. *See* Positivism.
Antigua, Guatemala (city). Colonial History, 714.
Antioquia, Colombia (city). Drama, 2324.
Antioquia, Colombia (dept.). Colonial Administration, 1137. Foreign Influences, 1114. Indigenous/Non-Indigenous Relations, 1137. Minerals and Mining Industry, 1114.
Antuña, José G., 1516.
Apostólico Colegio de Nuestra Señora de Guadalupe, 617.
Apparitions and Miracles. Viceroyalty of New Spain (1540–1821), 522.
APRA (Peru), 1163.
Arabs. Argentina, 1396. Immigrants, 1396.
Araucana, 1005, 1737.
Araucanian (indigenous group). *See* Mapuche (indigenous group).
Araucano (indigenous group). *See* Mapuche (indigenous group).
Arboleda Cuevas, Esmeralda, 1127.
Archeological Surveys. Mexico, 615.
Archeologists. Peru, 15.
Archeology. Andean Region, 15. Guatemala, 232. Mesoamerica, 215. Mexico, 242, 480. Peru, 15. *See Also* Artifacts.
Architects. Brazil, 169, 171, 173. Women, 173.
Architecture. African Influences, 176. Art History, 64. Brazil, 163, 166, 170, 172, 175, 1541. Conservation and Restoration, 165, 169. Dictatorships, 163. European Influences, 173. History, 174–175. Mexico, 39, 455, 540, 705. Nationalism, 163. Peru, 56. Urbanization, 1541.
Archives, 319. Cuba, 2799. *See Also* Libraries.
Arévalo, Juan José, 2975.
Argentine Influences. Nicaragua, 754.
Armaza, Mariano, 1197.
Armed Forces. *See* Military.
Armenians. Brazil, 1698.
Armijo, Manuel, 605.
Arms Control. Nicaragua, 772.
Arredondo, Joaquín de, 487.
Art, 65. Anthropology, 114. Colombia, 1092. Dictatorships, 117. Education, 84, 100, 103, 107, 112–113, 120. Elites, 112. Feminism, 63, 101. Flowers, 178. Gender Relations, 63. Government, Resistance to, 76, 93. Homosexuality, 101. Literature, 179. Massacres, 73. National Identity, 81. Nationalism, 81. Natural History, 178. Neoliberalism, 104. Philosophy, 98, 110. Political Conditions, 112, 119. Precolumbian Civilizations, 114. Universities, 84. Violence, 73.
Art Catalogs. Brazil, 139–140, 143, 155–156, 184, 186. Chile, 105. Costa Rica, 87. Cuba, 91, 94. Mexico, 76. Peru, 57. Uruguay, 116. Venezuela, 119.
Art Collections. Brazil, 140, 156, 184, 1593.
Art Criticism, 65. Argentina, 98, 3036. Bolivia, 102. Brazil, 123–124, 132, 138, 149–150, 153–154, 179, 187, 190. Chile, 104. Colombia, 108, 110–112, 3003. Cuba, 89–90. Decolonization, 2983. Feminism, 80. Gender Relations, 80. Interviews, 187. Mexico, 77, 80. Newspapers, 102. Philosophy, 3009. Social Conditions, 65. Uruguay, 116–117.
Art Exhibitions, 68. Abstract Art, 69. Bolivia, 102. Brazil, 139–141, 145, 149, 151, 153–154, 157, 168, 181, 184. Chile, 105. Colombia, 106. Costa Rica, 87–88. Cuba, 90–91, 94. Dictatorships, 189. Feminism, 78. Government, Resistance to, 189. Illustrations, 77. Massacres, 74. Mexico, 69, 74–75, 77–78, 86, 193. Military History, 189. Modern Art, 69. Nationalism, 157. Paraguay, 113. Peru, 54. Urbanization,

140. Uruguay, 116. Venezuela, 119. *See Also* Exhibitions; Museums.
Art History, 62, 64, 66. Architecture, 64. Brazil, 122–123, 126, 133, 137, 144, 147, 151, 162. British Caribbean, 47, 826. Caribbean Area, 92. Chile, 104. Collective Memory, 110. Colombia, 107–110. Costa Rica, 88, 2357. Cuba, 90. Cuban Revolution (1959), 97. Dominican Republic, 936. Essays, 66. Feminism, 62. Film, 97. Lithography, 82. Mexico, 71–72, 79, 444, 457. National Identity, 79, 81. Paraguay, 1495. Performing Arts, 70. Peru, 56, 60. Photography, 1315. Political History, 72. Prints, 71. Race and Race Relations, 92. Sexism, 62. Social Conflict, 82. Socialism and Socialist Parties, 93. Uruguay, 117. Venezuela, 120.
Art Museums. Colombia, 109. Costa Rica, 88. Cuba, 90. Peru, 57.
Art Schools. Brazil, 133, 137. Venezuela, 120.
Artifacts. Brazil, 1593. Mexico, 527, 615. *See Also* Archeology.
Artigas, Andrés, 1323.
Artigas, José Gervasio, 1030, 1503–1504, 1506, 1510, 1514, 1517, 3032.
Artigas, Manuel, 1510.
Artisanry. Colombia, 107. Economic Development, 107.
Artisans. Colombia, 107. Mexico, 458.
Artistic Culture. Brazil, 121–122, 125.
Artists, 417. Argentina, 99–100, 2113. Ayahuasca, 115. Books, 190. Brazil, 124, 135–136, 141, 145–146, 155, 2473. British Caribbean, 47, 826. Colombia, 106, 111. Colonial History, 35. Communism and Communist Parties, 689. Cuba, 1919. Diaries, 83. European Influences, 143. Feminism, 78. Interviews, 67, 85, 115, 136, 146. Labor Movement, 656. Mexico, 83, 85, 656, 687. Modern Art, 68. Paraguay, 113. Peru, 115. Uruguay, 116. Women, 63, 78, 100, 144, 185, 689.
Assassinations, 416. Dominican Republic, 924. Mexico, 702.
Assimilation. *See* Acculturation.
Astica Fuentes, Manuel, 3024.
Astronomy. Argentina, 1460. Scientific History, 1460. *See Also* Cosmology.
Asturias, Miguel Angel, 1855, 1868.
Asturias, Rodrigo, 1855.
Asturias, Spain (region). Emigration and Immigration, 1347.
Atlantic Coast (Nicaragua). *See* Mosquitia (Nicaragua and Honduras).

Atlantic Trade. Brazil, 1567, 1617, 1624. British Caribbean, 808. Caribbean Area, 798. Slaves and Slavery, 196, 825, 837, 881.
Audiencia of Caracas, 1064.
Audiencia of Charcas. Intellectual History, 998.
Audiencia of Quito. Political History, 971.
Authoritarianism, 408, 415. Argentina, 1366. Brazil, 2887. Dominican Republic, 950. Nicaragua, 757. Uruguay, 3031. *See Also* Dictatorships.
Authors. Brazil, 2461. Mexico, 211. Peru, 1952.
Automobile Industry and Trade. Argentina, 1392. *See Also* Transportation.
Autonomy. Argentina, 1030. Dominican Republic, 844. Puerto Rico, 899. Venezuela, 1086. *See Also* Sovereignty.
Ayahuasca. Artists, 115. Peru, 115.
Ayalá, Berne, 741.
Ayllus. Bolivia, 287. Painting, 1215.
Aymara (indigenous group). Education, 262.
Azevedo, Arthur, 2583.
Azoreans. Brazil, 1595. *See Also* Portuguese Influences.
Aztecs, 1751. Anthropology, 234. Calendrics, 3. Civilization, 3, 26. Clothing and Dress, 4. Dance, 2729. Economic History, 234. Elites, 29. Food, 7. Historiography, 231. Imperialism, 234. Mortuary Customs, 219. Music, 2729. Rites and Ceremonies, 7, 2729. Sculpture, 3. Sociology, 234. Spanish Conquest, 4, 27, 231. Warfare, 27.
Bahia, Brazil (city). Race and Race Relations, 1559. Social History, 1559.
Bahia, Brazil (state). Abolition (slavery), 1576. Cultural History, 1575. Dutch Conquest, 1600. Food, 1575. Military History, 1600. Modernization, 1709. Political History, 1600. Slaves and Slavery, 1576. Social Life and Customs, 1575.
Bahía Blanca, Argentina (city). Historiography, 1416. Peronism, 1416.
Baja California, Mexico (region). Colonial History, 473. Regional Development, 696. *See Also* Baja California, Mexico (state).
Baja California, Mexico (state). Diseases, 553. Public Health, 553. *See Also* Baja California, Mexico (region).
Baja California Norte, Mexico (state). *See* Baja California, Mexico (state).
Balaguer, Joaquín, 805, 885.
Balance of Trade, 434. *See Also* Commerce.
Balbín, Ricardo. Biography, 1471.
Balboa, Silvestre de, 1732.

Balboa, Vasco Núñez de, 383.
Banana Trade, 333. Central America, 743. Honduras, 746.
Banco La Caja Obrera (Uruguay), 1507.
Bandeiras. Brazil, 1584.
Bandits. *See* Brigands and Robbers.
Banking and Financial Institutions. Brazil, 1713. Education, 691. Mexico, 562, 602, 691. Paraguay, 1507.
Baptista de Acosta, Joseph, 274.
Bardi, Lina Bo, 173.
Baroque Architecture, 24. Bolivia, 55. Brazil, 127. Mexico, 43. Peru, 59.
Baroque Art, 24. Bolivia, 55. Brazil, 127. *See Also* Art History; Baroque Architecture.
Baroque Literature, 1724, 1734. Cuba, 1920. Mexico, 1728. *See Also* Literature.
Barrão, 135.
Barreto, Adriana, 136.
Barrett, Rafael, 2967.
Basic Christian Communities. *See* Christian Base Communities.
Basílica Catedral del Cusco, 59.
Basques. Cuba, 903.
Batres, Leopoldo, 533, 615.
Battle of Huamachuco (Chile, 1883), 1171.
Battle of Zacatecas (1914), 668, 681.
Bautista de Pomar, Juan, 223.
Beaterio de Colima, 531.
Becker, Cacilda, 2586.
Beer Industry. Brazil, 1689. Credit, 1689.
Belgrano, Manuel, 1031, 1355, 1391, 1430, 1447.
Beliefs and Customs. *See* Religious Life and Customs. *See* Social Life and Customs.
Belisário, Waldemar, 148.
Belo Horizonte, Brazil (city). Art History, 125. Modern Art, 125. Music, 2864.
Benavides, Jorge Eduardo, 1950.
Benedetti, Mario, 2136.
Benítez, Lucecita, 2773.
Bernardino, Minerva, 906.
Bernardino de Sahagún. *See* Sahagún, Bernardino de.
Béroard, Jocelyne, 2771.
Berrio y Saldívar, Miguel de, 2715, 2739.
Berro, Bernardo Prudencio, 1505.
Betancourt, Rómulo, 924, 1082.
Bibliography. Dominican Republic, 862. Ecuador, 1155. *See Also* Research.
Bibliotheca Mexicana, 500.
Bienal Internacional de São Paulo, 155.
Biography. Argentina, 1291, 1299, 1369, 1381, 1417–1418, 1437, 1447. Brazil, 128, 1552, 1555, 1569, 1662, 1706. Catholic Church, 1630. Chile, 1238, 1249, 1257. Colombia, 1120, 1127. Costa Rica, 729. Cuba, 1919. Dominican Republic, 806, 897, 951. Ecuador, 1158. Mexico, 465. Painters, 75. Presidents, 1555. Puerto Rico, 1940. Trinidad and Tobago, 914. Uruguay, 1503–1506, 1510, 1514, 1517. Venezuela, 1054, 1056, 1069. Women, 185.
Birth Control. Argentina, 1404. Peru, 1181, 1183.
Black Carib (indigenous group). Caribbean Area, 818. Music, 2786.
Blacks, 376. Argentina, 1435. Bahamas, 807. Barbados, 815. Brazil, 159, 168, 181, 1528, 1571, 1598, 1697, 1710, 2854, 2882, 2938, 3029. Caribbean Area, 96, 802, 853, 946. Central America, 736. Church History, 894–895. Clothing and Dress, 993. Colombia, 961, 1091, 1102–1103, 1126, 1140. Colonization, 392. Community Development, 1528. Cuba, 803, 849, 1944, 2793, 2797. Dominican Republic, 894–895. Ethnic Identity, 946, 3027. Folk Music, 2810, 2819. Geographical History, 1598. Jamaica, 852, 860, 863. Mexico, 520, 563, 629. Music, 2682, 2707, 2757, 2794, 2908. Musical History, 2804, 2810. Musicians, 2938. Oral History, 1571. Peru, 979, 993, 1191, 2810. Philosophy, 2958, 2999. Photographers, 96. Protestants, 894–895. Puerto Rico, 854. Race and Race Relations, 3027. Relations with Indigenous Peoples, 736. Religious Life and Customs, 833. Sex and Sexual Relations, 852. Social Life and Customs, 803. Soldiers, 827. Theater, 2578. Uruguay, 1515. Women, 629, 830.
Blavatsky, Helena Petrovna. Fiction, 1811.
Boal, Augusto, 2571.
Bogotá, Colombia (city). European Influences, 1125. Social Development, 1125.
Bolero (music). Brazil, 2675. *See Also* Popular Music.
Bolívar, Colombia (dept.). Educational Reform, 1116.
Bolívar, Simón, 1065, 1070, 1076, 1084, 2985, 3001.
Bolívar, Venezuela (state). History, 955.
Bonampak Site (Mexico). Murals, 6.
Boneo y Villalonga, Martín, 1016.
Bonifaz Nuño, Rubén, 2305.
Bonó, Pedro Francisco, 2999.
Book Lists. *See* Bibliography.
Books. Argentina, 1357. Brazil, 190, 1597. Colombia, 1122. Colonial History, 367,

1597. Illustrations, 180. Mexico, 1736, 1747. Peru, 1747. Sculptures, 190.
Bookselling and Booksellers. Colombia, 1122.
Border Disputes. *See* Boundary Disputes.
Borderlands, 365. Mexico, 209, 547, 653, 655. *See Also* Mexican-American Border Region.
Bordieu, Julia Elena, 1320.
Borges, Jorge Luis, 3037.
Bosch, Juan, 805, 941.
Botany. Brazil, 178. Illustrations, 178.
Boturini Benaducci, Lorenzo, 198, 1721.
Boundaries. Argentina, 403. Argentina/Chile, 1465. Belize/Mexico, 718. Brazil, 403, 1596, 1615, 1674. Brazil/Uruguay, 1040. Mexico/US, 586. Paraguay, 1499. *See Also* Boundary Disputes.
Boundary Disputes. Bolivia/Chile, 1199. Costa Rica/Nicaragua, 712. *See Also* Boundaries.
Bourbon Reforms. Brazil, 1617. Law and Legislation, 983. Mexico, 504. Viceroyalty of New Granada (1718–1810), 973. *See Also* Colonial History.
Bowman, Henry Edward, 1315.
Bracety, Mariana, 877.
Brasília, Brazil (city). City Planning, 174.
Brazil. Exército, 1639.
Brazilians. France, 1520.
Bribri (indigenous group). Poetry, 2178.
Bridgetown, Barbados (city). Social History, 832. Women, 832.
Brigands and Robbers. Bolivia, 1219. Mexico, 578, 580.
British. Barbados, 817, 821. Brazil, 1585. Caribbean Area, 788. Chile, 1249. Hispaniola, 819. Painters, 95. Suriname, 821.
British Influences. Argentina, 1025. Brazil, 1585.
Britto, Paulo Henriques, 2500, 2555.
Brizola, Leonel de Moura, 1644.
Brunias, Agostino, 47, 826.
Buarque, Chico, 2376.
Buccaneers, 362. *See Also* Pirates.
Buenos Aires, Argentina (city). Colonial History, 1038. Colonization, 1029. Cooperatives, 1463. Mass Media, 981. Military History, 1037. Slaves and Slavery, 359. Social History, 1035. Social Life and Customs, 1029. Social Movements, 1463. Socialism and Socialist Parties, 1463.
Buenos Aires, Argentina (prov.). Immigrants, 1343. Internal Migration, 1326. Migration, 1343. Modernization, 1426.

Peronism, 1326. Private Enterprises, 1426. Public Works, 1426. Railroads, 1426.
Bureaucracy, 330. Argentina, 1384.
Burgos, Julia de, 1935.
Burials. *See* Cemeteries. *See* Mortuary Customs.
Busch Becerra, Germán, 1217.
Bustamante, Alexander, *Sir*, 931.
Caballero y Ocio, Juan, 513.
Cabañas, Lucio, 667.
Cabezón, Antonio de, 2743.
Cabildos. Argentina, 1356. *See Also* Colonial Administration.
Caboclos. *See* Mestizos and Mestizaje.
Cabral de Melo Neto, João, 2480.
Cabrera, Luis, 633.
Cacao, 310. Brazil, 1522. Colonial History, 972.
Caciques. Andean Region, 977.
Caingua (indigenous group). Social Life and Customs, 264.
Caldera, Rafael, 1054.
Calderón de la Barca, Pedro, 1723.
Calderón Guardia, Rafael Ángel, 748.
California, US (state). Description and Travel, 725.
Calvo, Francisco C., 740.
Calypso. Caribbean Area, 2772.
Camagüey, Cuba (prov.). History, 850.
Campa (indigenous group). Indigenous Resistance, 298.
Campaña Nacional (Costa Rica), 765, 771.
Campanha, Minas Gerais (city). Musical History, 2939.
Campos, Haroldo de, 2547.
Candeia Filho, Antônio, 2868.
Candomblé (cult). Music, 2923.
Cantilo, Miguel, 2837.
Capitalism, 404. Bolivia, 1220. Costa Rica, 771. Ecuador, 970.
Captives. Tattooing, 202.
Caracas, Venezuela (city). City Planning, 1087. History, 1057–1058, 1061. Political Participation, 1087. Women, 1058.
Cárdenas, Lázaro, 654, 1786.
Cardoza y Aragón, Luis, 85.
Caresser, 2772.
Carib (indigenous group). Colonization, 792. Grenada, 792.
Carlota, *Empress, Consort of Maximilian, Emperor of Mexico*, 532.
Carnival. Brazil, 1544, 2854, 2882–2883, 2901, 2932. *See Also* Festivals.
Caro, Miguel Antonio, 1118.
Carranza, Venustiano, 674.

Cartagena, Colombia (city). Blacks, 1102. Elections, 1119. Political Development, 1119.
Cartography. *See* Maps and Cartography.
Cartoons. Mexico, 541.
Casa de Contratación (Spain), 329.
Casas, Bartolomé de las, 3016.
Caste War (1847–1855), 209, 547. *See Also* Indigenous Resistance.
Castellanos, Rosario, 649.
Castilian Influences. Brazil, 1616. *See Also* Spanish Influences.
Castillo, Máximo, 664.
Castro, Fidel, 784, 940, 945.
Castro, Rosalía de, 797.
Catalan Influences. Mexico, 2714. *See Also* Spaniards.
Catamarca, Argentina (prov.). Blacks, 1435. Historical Demography, 1435.
Catedral de Guadalajara (Mexico), 2722.
Catedral de México, 2684, 2708, 2715, 2731.
Catedral de Puebla, 2766.
Catedral de Santiago de los Caballeros de Guatemala, 734.
Cathedrals. Brazil, 130. Mexico, 2756. Peru, 59.
Catholic Church, 340, 370, 378, 512, 1739. Amazon Basin, 246. Andean Region, 246, 276, 342. Argentina, 1303, 1398, 1408, 1420, 1432. Brazil, 1543, 1579, 1601, 1626, 1630, 1637, 1712. Chile, 1233. Colombia, 1139. Colonial History, 23, 369. Guatemala, 708. Iconography, 21. Indigenous/Non-Indigenous Relations, 1174. Inquisition, 1579. Liberation Theology, 3016. Mexico, 28, 197, 246, 449, 465–466, 476, 481, 587, 591, 617, 2713, 2756. Minerals and Mining Industry, 53. Music, 2684, 2752, 2786. Peru, 50, 985, 987, 1174, 1178, 1725, 1730. Political Philosophy, 421. Portugal, 1601. Race and Race Relations, 379. Spanish Conquest, 1744. Students, 673. Venezuela, 1060, 1074. Women, 481, 708. *See Also* Catholicism; Christianity.
Catholic Foreign Mission Society of America, 1174.
Catholicism. Argentina, 1466. Blacks, 2908. Caribbean Area, 824. Children's Literature, 1466. Cultural History, 1408. Ecuador, 1152. Ethnic Groups and Ethnicity, 239. Mexico, 673. Music, 2915. Philosophy, 2960. Political Culture, 1363. Political Philosophy, 3015. *See Also* Catholic Church.

Cattle Raising and Trade. Brazil, 1535. Plantations, 1535. Slaves and Slavery, 1535. *See Also* Food Industry and Trade; Meat Industry.
Caudillos. Argentina, 1329, 1369, 1419. Biography, 1419.
Cearense, Catullo da Paixão, 2913.
Cemeteries. Brazil, 1585. British, 1585. *See Also* Mortuary Customs.
Censorship. Brazil, 2575. Cuba, 1883. Mexico, 682. *See Also* Freedom of the Press.
Censuses. Argentina, 1384. Belize, 706. Brazil, 1648. Economic History, 1384. Mexico, 531, 655. *See Also* Population Growth.
Central-Local Government Relations. Mexico, 460. *See Also* Regional Government.
Centro Nacional de Investigación, Documentación e Información Musical Carlos Chávez, 2717.
Ceramics. Indigenous Art, 10. Peru, 58. Precolumbian Art, 10.
Ceremonies. *See* Rites and Ceremonies.
Cervantes, Ignacio, 2791.
Césaire, Aimé, 3027.
Cetina, Gutierre de, 1732.
Ceto Sánchez, Pablo, 775.
Chaco, Argentina (prov.). Peronism, 1405.
Chaco, Argentina (region). Indigenous Peoples, 271.
Chaco War (1932–1935), 1225, 1446. Diaries, 1204. Fiction, 1957. Gender Roles, 1493. Indigenous Peoples, 1201, 1492. Nationalism, 1201, 1492.
Charca (indigenous group). Colonial History, 997.
Charcoal. Mexico, 701.
Chavez, Angelico, 499.
Chávez, Carlos, 2698–2699, 2706.
Chávez Frías, Hugo, 1055, 2975, 3002.
Chevalier, François, 636.
Chiapas, Mexico (state). Elites, 557. Folk Music, 2768. Insurrections, 576. Military History, 559. Musical History, 2751. Political History, 557.
Chicanos. *See* Mexican Americans.
Chicha. Colombia, 966.
Chichimecs (indigenous group). Catholicism, 239. Mesoamerica, 239.
Chiefdoms. Mexico, 203. *See Also* Kings and Rulers.
Child Abuse. British Caribbean, 861.
Child Development. Caribbean Area, 934. Chile, 1251.

Child Labor. Brazil, 1606. Colonial History, 1606. *See Also* Children.

Childbirth. Jamaica, 879.

Children. Argentina, 1461. Brazil, 1532, 1606. Colonial History, 1606. Paraguay, 1501. Peru, 1163. Slaves and Slavery, 842. Songs, 2917. *See Also* Child Abuse; Child Development; Child Labor; Family and Family Relations; Youth.

Children's Literature. Argentina, 1466. Mexico, 469.

Chinese. Cuba, 882. Cultural Identity, 659. Mexico, 445, 630, 659. Puerto Rico, 864. Racism, 630.

Chinese Influences. Mexico, 659. Peru, 1168.

Chiquito (indigenous group). Ethnic Identity, 282.

Chiriguano (indigenous group). Bolivia, 265. History, 293.

Chocó, Colombia (dept.). Local History, 1121.

Cholera. *See* Diseases.

Christian Base Communities. El Salvador, 759.

Christian Democracy. Chile, 1251.

Christianity. Conservatism, 1654. Political Left, 1551. Viceroyalty of Peru (1542–1822), 976. Youth, 2831.

Christiano Junior, 159.

Chroniclers. *See* Cronistas.

Chronicles. *See* Crónicas.

Chubut, Argentina (prov.). Colonial History, 1442. Germans, 1442. Immigrants, 1339. Photography, 1300. Welsh, 1339.

Chuquisaca, Bolivia (dept.). History, 998.

Church and State. *See* Church-State Relations.

Church Architecture. California, US (state), 36. Mexico, 41–44, 46, 206. Peru, 50.

Church History, 378, 512. Abandoned Children, 1592. Argentina, 1398, 1408, 1420. Barbados, 857. Brazil, 1601, 1618, 1621, 1626. Chile, 1271. Dominican Republic, 894–895. Guatemala, 708, 716. Honduras, 710. Mexico, 37, 204, 518, 581, 591, 2713, 2756. Portugal, 1601. Venezuela, 1060, 1074. Viceroyalty of New Spain (1540–1821), 506, 522.

Church Music. *See* Religious Music.

Church of Jesus Christ of Latter-day Saints, 452.

Church-State Relations. Argentina, 1408, 1420, 1456. Brazil, 1540, 1626, 1654. Chile, 1010, 1233, 1236–1237, 1265, 1271. Colombia, 1128, 1139. Intellectual History, 1540. Law and Legislation, 1540. Mexico, 449, 456, 465, 587, 591, 704. Nicaragua, 757. Peru, 985. Political Ideology, 1540. Venezuela, 1060, 1074.

Churches. Colonial Architecture, 59. Peru, 59.

Cid Pérez, José, 2317.

Cinchona. Colonial History, 361.

Cinema. *See* Film.

Cities and Towns. Argentina, 308. Colombia, 964. Colonial History, 503. Mexico, 308, 561. South America, 313. *See Also* City Planning; Urbanization.

Citizenship. Argentina, 1412. Bolivia, 1211. Brazil, 1561, 1697. Mexico, 563. Peru, 1175. Philosophy, 2982. Puerto Rico, 890, 930.

City Planning, 422. African Influences, 176. Brazil, 147, 164, 167, 170, 172, 174, 1537. Mexico, 8, 442, 705. *See Also* Cities and Towns.

Ciudad Juárez, Mexico (city). Drama, 2327.

Civil-Military Relations. Dominican Republic, 950. Venezuela, 1059, 1068.

Civil Rights. Caribbean Area, 814, 904. Chile, 1231. Mexico, 598. Saint Vincent and the Grenadines, 904. *See Also* Human Rights.

Civil War. Colombia, 1106. Costa Rica, 748, 766. El Salvador, 741, 751. Guatemala, 775. Paraguay, 2114. Peru, 1177, 1184. Rural Conditions, 1184.

Civilization, 353. Mexico, 514, 538.

Class Conflict. *See* Social Classes. *See* Social Conflict.

Clavigero, Francesco Saverio, 2991.

Clergy. Masculinity, 1677. Mexico, 591. Venezuela, 1060.

Clientelism, 371. Argentina, 1445.

Climate Change. Peru, 259.

Clothing and Dress. Chile, 1278. *See Also* Textiles and Textile Industry.

Clube da Esquina (musical group), 2885.

Coahuila, Mexico (state). Crime and Criminals, 607. Social History, 607. Urban Areas, 561.

Coal Mining. *See* Minerals and Mining Industry.

Cochabamba, Bolivia (dept.). History, 994, 1219. Police, 1219. Spaniards, 994.

Cocoa Industry and Trade. Ecuador, 972. Mexico, 972.

Codex Mexicanus, 29.

Codex Ramírez, 27.

Códice florentino, 35.

Códice Guillermo Tovar de Huejotzingo, 201.
Codices. Colonial History, 1747. Mexico, 5, 201, 243.
Coffee Industry and Trade. Brazil, 1531, 1538, 1635, 1664. Costa Rica, 768, 771. Cultural Development, 1538. Jamaica, 868. Labor and Laboring Classes, 1635. Poverty, 1635. Slaves and Slavery, 1531, 1664. Social Conditions, 1664.
Coins and Coinage. Colonial History, 715. Costa Rica, 713. Guatemala, 715.
Cold War, 408, 418, 424. Caribbean Area, 947. Diplomatic History, 432. Mexico, 673. Mexico/US, 649. Peru, 1176. Puerto Rico, 947. Venezuela, 1073, 1088.
Colegio de San Ildefonso (Mexico), 567.
Colegio "Sarah Ashhurst", 886.
Coleridge, William Hart, 857.
Colima, Mexico (city). Social History, 531. Women, 531.
Colla (indigenous group). Colonial History, 997.
Collective Memory, 319, 410, 435. Argentina, 1327, 1361. Art History, 110. Brazil, 122. Colombia, 110, 1134. Dictatorships, 1678. Dominican Republic, 941. Mexico, 461.
Colleges. *See* Higher Education.
Colonial Administration, 356, 360, 366, 377, 386. Andean Region, 977. Bolivia, 286. Brazil, 1607. Caribbean Area, 820, 846. Chile, 1002. Coins and Coinage, 715. Colombia, 290, 962, 1137. Commerce, 357. Guatemala, 714, 722, 726. Mexico, 485, 604, 1741. Peru, 990. Political Corruption, 371. Viceroyalty of New Granada (1718–1810), 963. Viceroyalty of New Spain (1540–1821), 516, 1744. Viceroyalty of Peru (1542–1822), 975, 978, 984. Viceroyalty of Río de la Plata (1776–1810), 1016, 1023, 1042. Violence, 986.
Colonial Architecture. Brazil, 128, 130–131, 1582. Churches, 59. Peru, 59. Uruguay, 48.
Colonial Art, 25. Brazil, 126, 131. Cuba, 91. European Influences, 51. Mexico, 32, 39. Peru, 51, 54, 60.
Colonial Discourse. Liberation Theology, 3006. Philosophy, 3006.
Colonial History, 306–307, 358, 369, 1729. Argentina, 1041, 1398. Barbados, 783, 821. Biography, 1442. Brazil, 1041, 1580, 1584, 1588, 1597, 1611, 1622. Chile, 1005, 2848, 2852. Cities and Towns, 1740. Colombia, 49, 1105. Costa Rica, 729. Diaries, 1573. Dominican Republic, 805. Dutch, 388. Economic Development, 1622. Ecuador, 970. Genealogy, 203. Grenada, 792. Guyana, 955. Historiography, 382. Iconography, 49. Indigenous Music, 2818. Landowners, 636. Mexico, 203–204, 212, 454, 514, 636, 1744. Musical Instruments, 2852. Nobility, 203. Peru, 1192. Philosophy, 2966. Political Leadership, 2985. Political Philosophy, 2985. Population Growth, 1622. Social Classes, 381. Suriname, 955. Waterways, 212.
Colonial Literature, 1724, 1732, 1742. Spanish America, 1748. Spanish Influences, 1734.
Colonial Music. Andean Region, 2818. Brazil, 2857–2858, 2911. Guatemala, 734. Mexico, 2709, 2715, 2723, 2737–2740, 2766. Portuguese Influences, 2749.
Colonial Painting. British Caribbean, 47, 826. Colombia, 19. Ecuador, 61. Mexico, 483.
Colonization, 353, 401, 491. Animals, 188. Argentina, 1020, 1442. Belize, 859. Bolivia, 994. Brazil, 1533, 2522. Caribbean Area, 788. Chile, 1011. Cuba, 909. Ecology, 188. Germans, 1442. Grenada, 792. Guatemala, 726. Historiography, 350. Jamaica, 819. Maps and Cartography, 859. Mexico, 539. Panama, 721. Peru, 978. Puerto Rico, 789, 851. Spain, 355. Uruguay, 1017.
Commerce, 360, 384, 434, 437. Brazil/Portugal, 1608. Cacao, 310. China, 1168. Colonial History, 387, 972. History, 357. Mexico, 539. Peru, 259. Spain, 386. *See Also* Balance of Trade.
Commercial Policy. *See* Trade Policy.
Common Markets. *See* Economic Integration.
Communication. Bolivia, 1202. Political History, 1497.
Communism and Communist Parties, 343, 409, 418, 420, 754, 912, 2981. Argentina, 1413. Artists, 689. Bibliography, 1521. Bolivia, 1209. Brazil, 1521, 1525, 1649. Chile, 1257, 1274, 1276, 1283. Ecuador, 1150. Mexico, 670, 689, 699. Peru, 1176. Psychoanalysis, 1483.
Community Development. Music, 2805.
Comparative Literature. Brazil, 2378.
Composers. Biography, 2376, 2814, 2824, 2846. Brazil, 2376, 2525, 2880–2881, 2886, 2888, 2909, 2913, 2918–2919, 2936, 2950–2952, 2956. Chile, 2846. Cuba,

2787, 2789–2792, 2798–2799. Mexico, 2688–2690, 2693, 2698–2699, 2701, 2706, 2718–2719, 2728, 2758, 2762, 2767. Peru, 2811, 2814, 2824. Puerto Rico, 2770. *See Also* Music.
Composers, Spanish. Mexico, 2743.
Comuneros. *See* Insurrection of the Comuneros (Paraguay, 1730–1735).
Conceptual Art. Brazil, 142, 150. Mexico, 76. Uruguay, 117. *See Also* Abstract Art.
Conductors (music). Mexico, 2719. *See Also* Composers.
Confessions. Peru, 1725. *See Also* Crime and Criminals; Law and Legislation; Religious Life and Customs.
Confraternities. Mexico, 2737.
Congresses. Argentina, 1401.
Conibo (indigenous group). Maps and Cartography, 261.
Conjunto Conventual Franciscano de Nuestra Señora de la Asunción de Tlaxcala, 46.
Conquest. *See* Portuguese Conquest. *See* Spanish Conquest.
Conquest and Exploration. *See* Discovery and Exploration.
Conservation and Restoration. Brazil, 166, 169, 172. Catholic Church, 30, 43. Church Architecture, 50. Colonial Architecture, 48. Mexico, 615, 703.
Conservatism. Argentina, 1345. Chile, 1233, 1275, 3025. Ecuador, 1152. Mexico, 697. Student Movements, 693.
Conservatorio de Música de Puerto Rico, 2770.
Conservatorio Nacional de Música (Mexico), 2698–2699.
Constitutional History, 321, 400. Argentina, 1342. Mexico, 537, 569, 611. Peru, 1189.
Constitutions, 321. Argentina, 1390.
Construction Industry. Brazil, 1539. Labor and Laboring Classes, 1539. Railroads, 1539.
Constructivism (Art). Brazil, 144, 152.
Consumption (economics). Colombia, 1124. Historiography, 348.
Contact. *See* Cultural Contact.
Contemporary Art. *See* Modern Art.
Contestado Insurrection (Brazil, 1912–1916), 1708. Newspapers, 1719.
Contraband. *See* Smuggling.
Contraceptives. *See* Birth Control.
Convento de San José de Gracia (Mexico), 37.
Convents. Mexico, 37. *See Also* Monasteries.
Conversion. *See* Evangelistic Work.
Conversos. *See* Marranos.

Cooke, John William, 1472.
Cooking, 331. Argentina, 1320. Colonial History, 372. Mexico, 550. *See Also* Food.
Cooperatives. Argentina, 1463.
Copper Industry and Trade. Bolivia, 1223.
Cora (indigenous group). History, 580.
Cordero Michel, Emilio, 786.
Córdoba, Argentina (prov.). Clientelism, 1445. Collective Memory, 1479. Colonial History, 1443. Demography, 1450. Historiography, 1479. Indigenous Peoples, 1443. Political Conditions, 1479. Political Development, 1445. Political History, 1345. Political Parties, 1445. Social Conditions, 1450.
Córdoba, Diego Luis, 1121.
Corocoro, Bolivia (city). Economic History, 1223.
Corporatism. Brazil, 1564. Chile, 3025.
Corridos. Drug Traffic, 2703. Mexican American Border Region, 2703.
Corrientes, Argentina (prov.). Cattle Raising and Trade, 1289. Economic Conditions, 1335. Geopolitics, 1454. Peronism, 1405. Political History, 1454. Regional Development, 1335.
Cortés, Hernán, 192, 231, 1958.
Cosío Villegas, Daniel, 622.
Cosmology. Peru, 305. *See Also* Astronomy.
Cost and Standard of Living. Peru, 1190.
Cotton Industry and Trade. Mexico, 440.
Coups d'Etat. Airlines, 1560. Argentina, 1354, 1385, 1393, 1410. Brazil, 1562–1563, 1570, 1644, 1692. Dominican Republic, 951. Ecuador, 1158. Interviews, 1563. Mexico, 646.
Courts. Chile, 1246. Colonial History, 724.
Crafts. *See* Artisanry.
Credit. Mexico, 562.
Creoles. Colombia, 1114. Mexico, 1728. Portraits, 47, 826. US, 221.
Crime and Criminals, 314, 320, 323. Argentina, 3034. Chile, 1263. Jamaica, 852. Mexico, 444, 471, 650. Urban Areas, 3034. Viceroyalty of New Spain (1540–1821), 504.
Criminals. *See* Crime and Criminals.
Criollismo. Cultural Identity, 500.
Criollos. Venezuela, 957.
Cristero Rebellion (Mexico, 1926–1929). Exiles, 704. Foreign Policy, 704.
Cromberger, Juan, 367.
Cromwell, Oliver, 819.
Crónicas. Peru, 268.
Cronistas, 380.
Cruz-Diez, Carlos, 85.

Cruzeiro, 1536.
Crypto-Jews. *See* Marranos.
Cuaca, Colombia (dept.). Indigenous Resistance, 1131.
Cuadra, Pablo Antonio, 757, 1866.
Cuarteto Latinoamericano (musical group), 2705.
Cuban Influences. Chile, 1256. Mexico, 2757. Peru, 2823.
Cuban Missile Crisis (1962), 420.
Cuban Revolution (1959), 801, 870, 932, 954. Argentina, 1371. Art History, 97. Film, 97. Mass Media, 945. Public Opinion, 940.
Cubans. Dominican Republic, 888.
Cueva, Julio, 2787.
Culiacán, Mexico (city). Economic Development, 676.
Cults. Brazil, 129.
Cultural Adaptation. *See* Acculturation.
Cultural Assimilation. *See* Acculturation.
Cultural Contact. Africa/Europe, 1608. Brazil/Africa, 1608.
Cultural Development. Argentina, 1336, 1431. Brazil, 121, 1538, 1558. Caribbean Area, 2997. Colombia, 1134, 3003. Communism and Communist Parties, 1649. Dominican Republic, 936. Mexico, 448, 467. Venezuela, 118.
Cultural History, 66, 418. Andean Region, 3008. Argentina, 1336, 1349, 1431, 1482, 2356, 2829, 3036. Brazil, 122, 126, 1558, 1680. Caribbean Area, 809. Chile, 1279, 2844. Colombia, 967, 1095, 1130. Cuba, 845, 901–902, 909, 1884, 1904, 1925, 2793. Dominican Republic, 800, 920, 936, 943. El Salvador, 1867, 1870. Food, 624. Guatemala, 2785. Haiti, 878. Hispaniola, 811. Honduras, 710. Jamaica, 841, 878. Mexico, 307, 461, 624, 692, 2695, 2697, 2747. Nicaragua, 1866. Puerto Rico, 893, 1940. Venezuela, 120, 957.
Cultural Identity, 2971, 2973, 3001. Argentina, 1317, 1412. Bolivia, 2803. Brazil, 133, 1530, 1613. Caribbean Area, 785, 1927. Colombia, 1095. Cuba, 2794. Dominican Republic, 781, 943. Mexican-American Border Region, 2702. Mexico, 79, 466. Music, 2794. Paraguay, 1494. Philosophy, 2977. Spanish Influences, 2974. US, 2993.
Cultural Pluralism. *See* Multiculturalism.
Cultural Policy. Brazil, 2573. Costa Rica, 2357. Puerto Rico, 893.
Cultural Property, 319. Brazil, 165. Mexico, 533, 615.
Cultural Relations, 417. Caribbean Area/US, 2780. Cuba/Spain, 787, 1921. Dominican Republic/Mexico, 805. Latin America/Soviet Union, 432. Mexico/Spain, 2740. Mexico/US, 2707, 2710.
Cultural Studies, 2988. Brazil, 1717.
Cumbia (music). Bolivia, 2801. Colombia, 2804.
Cunha, José Mariano Carneiro da, 1704.
Cunningham, John, 872.
Curitiba, Brazil (city). Music, 2935.
Currency. *See* Money.
Dagua Hurtado, Abelino, 288.
Dalton, Roque, 1827.
Dance. African Influences, 2853. Argentina, 2834. Brazil, 2884, 2944. Colombia, 2331. Cuba, 2791. Mexico, 2714, 2769. Music, 2905. Uruguay, 2853.
Darién, Panama (prov.). Expeditions, 721.
Darwin, Charles, 315, 542, 1406.
Darwinism. *See* Social Darwinism.
Dávalos, José Manuel, 979.
De Torres y Vergara, José, 37.
Death. Mexico, 2697.
Debt. *See* Public Debt.
Decentralization. Costa Rica, 749. Mexico, 460.
Decolonization, 2984, 3006. Andean Region, 3008. Argentina, 2976. Bolivia, 3018, 3021. Jamaica, 948. Mexico, 538. Philosophy, 2984, 3008, 3018. Political Philosophy, 3019.
Decorative Arts. Brazil, 126, 130, 175, 185. Mexico, 45. Peru, 14. Women, 185.
Deforestation. Mexico, 701.
Deira, Ernesto, 99.
Delgado Gonzalez, Trifonio, 1204.
Democracy, 438. Bolivia, 3020. Brazil, 1650. Chile, 104. Colombia, 1089, 1109. Mexico, 537, 598. Multiculturalism, 2964. Uruguay, 3031.
Democratization. Venezuela, 1052.
Demography. Argentina, 1450. Peru, 1183. Venezuela, 1057.
Demonstrations. *See* Protests.
Depression (1929). *See* Great Depression (1929).
Desaparecidos. *See* Disappeared Persons.
Description and Travel. Brazil, 2859. Colombia, 1143. Colonial History, 1726. Cuba, 95, 793. France, 1520. Mesoamerica, 198, 1721. Mexico, 573, 1729, 1745. Peru, 1729. South America, 997.
Despradel, Fidelio, 897.

Detective and Mystery Stories. Argentina, 2076, 2089, 2656. Brazil, 2361, 2365, 2369–2370, 2375, 2411. Costa Rica, 1862. Cuba, 2649. Dominican Republic, 1897. Ecuador, 1992. Mexico, 1753, 1756, 1765, 1787, 1794, 1796. Nicaragua, 1863. Paraguay, 2121. Peru, 2013. Puerto Rico, 1897, 1903, 1928. Venezuela, 2071.

Devil. Colonial History, 1739. Honduras, 710.

Diaries. Artists, 83. Bolivia, 1204. Brazil, 1569, 1574.

Dias, Maurício de Mello, 139.

Dias & Riedweg, 139.

Díaz, Porfirio, 613, 2696.

Díaz del Castillo, Bernal, 211, 1735.

Díaz Ordaz, Gustavo, 638.

Dickinson, Emily, 2218.

Dictators. Assassinations, 924. Dominican Republic, 885, 907. Nicaragua, 777.

Dictatorships, 410, 435. Argentina, 1287, 1328, 1457. Art, 117. Brazil, 189, 1524, 1645, 1658, 1666, 1678. Chile, 1234, 1247–1248, 1259, 1267, 1275, 2843, 2847. Collective Memory, 1327. Cuba, 937. Diplomatic History, 1645. Dominican Republic, 905, 910, 951. Foreign Policy, 1287. Historiography, 1678. Homosexuality, 1306. Music, 2844. Photography, 105, 1327–1328. Rock Music, 2851. *See Also* Authoritarianism.

Diego, de Ocaña, 1729.

Diet. *See* Nutrition.

Diplomacy. Argentina, 1446. Brazil, 1633.

Diplomatic History, 430. Bolivia, 1197, 1199. Bolivia/Paraguay, 1225. Brazil, 1645, 1686, 1700. Brazil/Vatican, 1543. Costa Rica/France, 747. Cuba, 835. Cuba/Mexico, 675. Cuba/US, 938. Dominican Republic, 806. Dominican Republic/Haiti, 880. Dominican Republic/US, 905. Mexico, 554, 592, 690. Mexico/Spain, 684. Paraguay, 1496. Uruguay, 1519. Venezuela, 1067.

Diplomats. Brazil, 1702. Costa Rica, 747. Mexico, 554. Panama, 739.

Directories. Colombia, 1099.

Dirty War (Argentina, 1976–1983), 1368.

Disappeared Persons, 416. Argentina, 410. Brazil, 410.

Disarmament. *See* Arms Control.

Discourse Analysis. Argentina, 1353.

Discovery and Exploration, 329, 364, 382–383, 1722, 1726. Brazil, 1615, 1619. Diaries, 1743. Panama, 721. Río de la Plata (region), 1027. US, 725. *See Also* Portuguese Conquest; Spanish Conquest.

Diseases. Brazil, 1603, 1634. Chile, 1269. Colombia, 1107. Jamaica, 855. Mexico, 206, 590, 663. Peru, 1166. Slaves and Slavery, 796. Social Classes, 663. *See Also* Epidemics.

Distribution of Wealth. *See* Income Distribution.

Divorce. Argentina, 1341. Law and Legislation, 1341.

Doctors. *See* Physicians.

Documentaries. Mexico, 457.

Documentation. *See* Bibliography.

Documentation Centers. *See* Libraries.

Domestic Animals. Colonial History, 510.

Dominicans. Guatemala, 737.

Dominicans (religious order). Brazil, 1618.

Drama. Anthologies, 2308–2309, 2313, 2317–2318, 2324, 2352. Argentina, 2308, 2311, 2314–2315, 2318–2319, 2323, 2326, 2328, 2332, 2334, 2336, 2340–2341, 2345, 2348–2350, 2353. Colombia, 2309–2310, 2324, 2331, 2333. Costa Rica, 2337–2338. Cuba, 2317, 2325. Dominican Republic, 2342. Ecuador, 2346, 2358. El Salvador, 2316. Mexican-American Border Region, 2359. Mexico, 2313, 2327, 2330, 2335, 2344, 2351, 2359. Peru, 2339, 2347, 2352. Puerto Rico, 2343, 2354. Uruguay, 2320–2321. Venezuela, 2312, 2322, 2329.

Dramatic Criticism. Argentina, 2319, 2350, 2353. Cuba, 2317. Ecuador, 2358.

Dress. *See* Clothing and Dress.

Droughts. Puerto Rico, 873. Venezuela, 1078.

Drug Traffic. Colombia, 1110. Fiction, 1795. Mexico, 471. Popular Music, 2703.

Drugs and Drug Trade. *See* Drug Traffic.

Duarte, Juan Pablo, 862, 1051.

Dujov, Simja, 2841.

Durango, Mexico (state). Economic History, 602.

Dutch. Brazil, 1593, 1624. Colonization, 1587. Diseases, 1603.

Dutch Conquest. Brazil, 1587, 1600, 1603.

Dutch Influences, 388.

Dwellings. Architecture, 42.

Dyes and Dyeing, 22.

Earthquakes. Venezuela, 1061.

East India Company, 816.

East Indians. Music, 2783.

Echeverría, Luis, 657.

Ecology. Brazil, 188. Puerto Rico, 873.

Economic Assistance, US. Bolivia, 1208.

Economic Conditions, 336, 366, 406. Argentina, 1350, 1377. Chile, 1240, 1250, 1272–1273, 1277. Colombia, 1135. Colonial History, 356. Ecuador, 1157. Mexico, 463, 662. Peru, 1166. Slaves and Slavery, 1578. Venezuela, 1062.

Economic Crises. Argentina, 3034. Chile, 1237, 1280. Costa Rica, 771. Venezuela, 3002.

Economic Development, 427. Argentina, 1289, 1292, 1392, 1421, 1436. Artisanry, 107. Audiencia of Quito, 970. Barbados, 783. Bolivia, 1208, 1220. Brazil, 1538, 1566, 1622, 1631, 1643, 1658, 1713. Caribbean Area, 830. Chile, 1236, 1262, 1266. Colombia, 107, 1100, 1125. Democracy, 1650. Dominican Republic, 891. Ecuador, 1161. Foreign Policy, 1566. Gold, 1614. Jamaica, 868. Mexico, 676. Nationalism, 1292. Paraguay, 1014. Peru, 1175. Silver, 1614. Women, 830.

Economic Growth. *See* Economic Development.

Economic History. Argentina, 1376. Brazil, 1602, 1631, 1650, 1713. British Caribbean, 825. Caribbean Area, 946. Chile, 1279. Colombia, 962, 965, 1111, 1146. Costa Rica, 749. Dominican Republic, 910. El Salvador, 752. Guatemala, 756. Jamaica, 834, 868. Mexico, 444, 463, 530, 562, 564, 570, 604, 622. Paraguay, 1014. Peru, 1185. Presidents, 1424. Puerto Rico, 883. Saint Vincent and the Grenadines, 904. Slaves and Slavery, 1578, 1602. Trinidad and Tobago, 913. Venezuela, 1062. Viceroyalty of New Granada (1718–1810), 960.

Economic Integration, 411, 425.

Economic Planning. *See* Economic Policy.

Economic Policy. Argentina, 1468. Brazil, 1581. Mexico, 584. Venezuela, 1062, 1081. *See Also* Political Economy.

Economic Reform. Brazil, 1564. Mexico, 465, 470. Puerto Rico, 917.

Economic Theory. Colombia, 3003. Mexico, 622.

Education, 312. Art, 84, 103. Brazil, 1548, 1675, 1682, 1712, 1716. Chile, 1230, 1258. Colombia, 1098, 1139. Costa Rica, 758. Cuba, 886. El Salvador, 779. Honduras, 710. Mexico, 84, 691, 695, 698. Peru, 274. Philosophy, 1085. Prisons, 647. Puerto Rico, 851. Social Change, 2828. Venezuela, 2828. Women, 698, 779. *See Also* Elementary Education.

Education and State. *See* Educational Policy.

Educational Policy. Argentina, 1418, 1467. Bolivia, 1213–1214. Colombia, 1116. Drama, 2357. El Salvador, 779. History, 1085. Peru, 1173. Puerto Rico, 949.

Educational Reform. Argentina, 1467. Colombia, 1116. Mexico, 449, 567.

Educators. Chile, 1230.

Ejército Guerrillero de los Pobres (Guatemala), 775.

Ejército Revolucionario del Pueblo (Argentina), 1379.

Ejército Zapatista de Liberación Nacional (Mexico), 576, 640.

Ejidos. Argentina, 1298. Mexico, 208.

El Palmar, Mexico (town). History, 503.

Election Fraud. Colombia, 1089.

Elections. Brazil, 1628. Chile, 1268, 1282. Colombia, 1119. Ecuador, 1160. Law and Legislation, 549. Mexico, 541, 549, 598. Political Participation, 699. Puerto Rico, 782. Venezuela, 1072. *See Also* Voting.

Elementary Education. Peru, 1173. *See Also* Education.

Elites, 397. Bolivia, 1213. Brazil, 1628. Costa Rica, 709. Food, 679. Honduras, 719. Jamaica, 816, 841, 872. Masculinity, 1677. Mexico, 679. Political History, 1311. Precolumbian Civilizations, 29. Slaves and Slavery, 872. Venezuela, 957.

Ellacuría, Ignacio, 759, 2996, 3016.

Emancipation. *See* Abolition (slavery).

Emblems. Argentina, 1415.

Emigration and Immigration. *See* Internal Migration. *See* Migration. *See* Return Migration.

Emperors. Mexico, 502.

Encomiendas. Argentina, 267. Peru, 255, 978.

Encyclopedias. History, 800.

Energy Consumption. Mexico, 701.

Energy Policy. Bolivia, 1228–1229. Venezuela, 1081.

Energy Sources. Mexico, 701.

Engineering. Mexico, 595. Teaching, 595.

Engineers. Venezuela, 956.

Engraving. Brazil, 143.

Enlightenment. Jamaica, 841.

Entre Ríos, Argentina (prov.). Federalism, 1329.

Entrepreneurs. Economic Conditions, 662. Mexican Revolution (1910–1920), 662. Mexico, 662.

Environmental Degradation. Argentina, 1291. Caribbean Area, 788. Mexico, 701. Peru, 1169.

Environmental History. Bibliography, 1534. Brazil, 1534. Peru, 1164. Puerto Rico, 873.
Environmental Policy. Bolivia, 1228–1229. Brazil, 1581. Mexico, 703.
Epidemics. Mexico, 206, 511, 571. *See Also* Diseases.
Episcopal Church. Cuba, 886.
Epistemology, 2966, 2979. *See Also* Philosophy.
Ercilla y Zúñiga, Alonso de, 1005, 1737.
Erotic Literature. Brazil, 2373, 2412, 2415, 2417, 2465, 2478, 2549. Costa Rica, 1860. Puerto Rico, 2148.
Esmeralda (battleship), 1149.
Esperanza, Argentina (city). Regional Development, 1334.
Espionage. Mexico, 669. Shipping, 669.
Espírito Santo, Brazil (state). Social History, 1703. Urban History, 1703.
Esthetics. Argentina, 98. Peru, 2811.
Estrada de Ferro Noroeste do Brasil, 1539.
ETA (organization), 409.
Ethics, 2965.
Ethnic Groups and Ethnicity. Argentina, 1024. Belize, 706. Brazil, 1594–1595, 1659. Catholicism, 239. Colonial History, 214. Dominican Republic, 791. Jamaica, 834. Merchant Marines, 1620. Mexican-American Border Region, 621. Mexico, 199, 208, 214, 445, 563. Paraguay, 258, 1024. Philosophy, 3041. Viceroyalty of New Spain (1540–1821), 519.
Ethnic Identity. African Influences, 2998. Andean Region, 989. Aztecs, 38. Bolivia, 265, 3021. Brazil, 182, 3029. Caribbean Area, 946, 2786, 2998, 3027. Colombia, 3005. Colonial History, 214. Cuba, 803. Dominican Republic, 791. Guatemala, 773. Jamaica, 860. Japanese, 1196. Mesoamerica, 239. Mexico, 445, 773. Music, 2783. Philosophy, 2977, 2982, 3027, 3029.
Ethnography. Brazil, 1717. Mexico, 441.
Ethnohistory. Chile, 1242. Guatemala, 232. Mexico, 195, 242, 244, 459. Precolumbian Civilizations, 244.
Ethnology. Brazil, 269.
Ethnomusicology, 2679. Andean Region, 2815, 2838. Argentina, 2838. Brazil, 2875, 2892, 2903, 2911, 2916, 2927, 2945, 2947, 2957. Chile, 2852. Dominican Republic, 811, 943. Haiti, 811. Mexico, 2694, 2724, 2744, 2748, 2750, 2768. Peru, 2816–2817, 2822. US, 2683. Venezuela, 2827.
Eugenics, 422. Brazil, 1557. Periodicals, 1557.

Eurocentrism. Colombia, 1098.
European Influences. Argentina, 1451. Brazil, 2522. Caribbean Area, 2779. Chile, 1252. Colombia, 1125. Colonial Art, 51. Mexico, 2746. Peru, 56.
European Literature. *See* Baroque Literature.
Euterpe, 2746–2747.
Evangelicalism, 342. Brazil, 1654. Chile, 1265. Peru, 1178. Political Parties, 1654.
Evangelistic Work, 385. Africans, 379. Brazil, 1668. Chile, 1003. Colonial History, 23, 488, 490. Llanos (Colombia and Venezuela), 959. Mexico, 216–218.
Evangelization. *See* Evangelistic Work.
Evita. *See* Perón, Eva.
Evolution, 315. Argentina, 1406. Mexico, 542.
Exhibitions. Natural History, 1593.
Exiles. Argentina, 1312. Chile, 1274, 1285. Dominican Republic, 951. Mexico, 678, 704. Uruguay, 2125. *See Also* Refugees.
Exiles, Dominican. Venezuela, 1051.
Exiles, Spanish. Guatemala, 774. Historiography, 641. Intellectual History, 642. Mexico, 641–642, 675. Scientific History, 642.
Existentialism. Mexico, 2993.
Expatriates. Mexico, 637.
Expatriates, Soviet. Mexico, 651.
Expeditions, 315. Brazil, 1584, 1615. Pictorial Works, 16. South America, 997.
Expeditions, English. Chile, 1009.
Exploration. *See* Discovery and Exploration.
Explorers. Brazil, 1584, 1615. Philosophy, 2959. Río de la Plata (region), 1027. Venezuela, 256.
Explorers, British. Central America, 730.
Explorers, Spanish. US, 725.
Expressionism. Argentina, 99. Chile, 2846.
EZLN. *See* Ejército Zapatista de Liberación Nacional (Mexico).
Fabbri, Luce, 2967.
Family and Family Relations, 318, 334, 363. Andean Region, 251. Argentina, 1022, 1035. Brazil, 1532. Caribbean Area, 934. Colonial History, 727, 980. Costa Rica, 727. Jamaica, 836, 863. Mexico, 498. Peru, 980. Slaves and Slavery, 879.
Family Planning. *See* Birth Control.
Farrapos Revolution (Brazil, 1835–1845), 1701. Bibliography, 1701.
Fascism. Argentina, 1368, 1370, 1372, 3037. Brazil, 1547, 1642. Mass Media, 1547. Propaganda, 1547.
Fashion. Brazil, 1558. Chile, 1278.

Favelas. *See* Squatter Settlements.
FDI. *See* Foreign Investment.
Federal Government. *See* Federalism.
Federalism. Argentina, 1018, 1316, 1329, 1403. Mexico, 606. *See Also* Central-Local Government Relations.
Felix, Nelson, 141.
Feminism, 2988. Argentina, 101, 1375, 1476, 2976. Art, 63, 101. Art Criticism, 80. Art Exhibitions, 78. Art History, 62. Artists, 78. Brazil, 1676, 2459. Chile, 1239. Colombia, 1127. Communism and Communist Parties, 670. Dominican Republic, 916. Mexico, 78, 600, 670. Music, 2691. Performing Arts, 62. Periodicals, 1375. Philosophy, 2976. Revolutionaries, 1469. Writers, 1476.
Feminists. Dominican Republic, 906.
Ferdinand VII, *King of Spain*, 732.
Fernandes, Millôr, 2456.
Fernández, Ruth, 2773.
Fernós Isern, Antonio, 899.
Fertility. *See* Human Fertility.
Festivals. Colonial History, 732–733. Guatemala, 732–733. Viceroyalty of New Spain (1540–1821), 20.
Fiction. Argentina, 2076–2113, 2656. Bolivia, 1953–1957, 1959–1967. Brazil, 2360–2361, 2363–2375, 2377, 2379–2425. Caribbean Area, 1901. Colombia, 1968–1989, 2001. Costa Rica, 1802–1803, 1806, 1810–1811, 1813, 1822, 1831, 1844, 1847, 1852–1853, 1856, 1860, 1862. Dominican Republic, 1880, 1897. Ecuador, 1990, 1996–2000, 2002–2004, 2009. El Salvador, 1807, 1818, 1821, 1826–1827, 1834. Guatemala, 1801, 1808, 1812, 1814, 1819, 1825, 1829, 1835–1841, 1843, 1845, 1851, 1854–1855, 1857, 1859, 1864–1865. Honduras, 1800, 1830, 1832–1833, 1850. Mexico, 1753–1754, 1780, 1816, 1858. Nicaragua, 1805, 1809, 1820, 1823, 1828, 1842, 1846, 1863. Panama, 1815–1816, 1824, 1848–1849, 1869. Paraguay, 2133, 2135. Peru, 2006–2008, 2010–2018, 2020–2043, 2045–2057. Puerto Rico, 1876–1877, 1879, 1881, 1887–1888, 1892, 1896–1897, 1902–1903, 1905, 1909, 1913–1914, 1922, 1928. Spain, 1849. Uruguay, 2125. Venezuela, 2058–2075.
Fierro, Pancho, 3014.
Filibuster War (Nicaragua, 1855–1860), 753.
Film. African Influences, 2906. Art History, 97. Brazil, 1568, 2934. Chile, 2850. Cuba, 97. Cuban Revolution (1959), 97. Dominican Republic, 905. Mexico, 2685, 2695–2697, 2718. Music, 2685, 2696–2697, 2718. Musical History, 2850. Propaganda, 72. World War II (1939–1945), 1568.
Film Criticism. Brazil, 2866.
Filmmakers. Brazil, 2866.
Finance. Argentina, 1377.
Financial Crises. *See* Economic Crises.
Financial Institutions. *See* Banking and Financial Institutions.
Fiscal Crises. *See* Economic Crises.
Fiscal Policy. Mexico, 485, 535.
Fish and Fishing. Peru, 250.
Florencia Inca, Alonso, 971.
Flores Magón, Ricardo, 618, 647, 660.
FMLN. *See* Frente Farabundo Martí para la Liberación Nacional (El Salvador).
Fogwill, Roberto Enrique, 1760.
Folk Art. Brazil, 157–158. Exhibitions, 157.
Folk Dance. Brazil, 2572, 2898.
Folk Literature. Brazil, 2545.
Folk Music, 2679–2680. Andean Region, 2826. Blacks, 2810. Bolivia, 2801, 2803. Brazil, 2905, 2917, 2935. Caribbean Area, 2778. Ecuador, 2806, 2808. Jamaica, 2781. Mexican-American Border Region, 2702. Mexican Americans, 2759. Mexico, 2707, 2710, 2712, 2748, 2750–2751, 2769. Peru, 2810, 2819, 2821. US, 2748.
Folklore. Andean Region, 2826. Bolivia, 2801. Social Media, 2807.
Folktales. *See* Folk Literature.
Food, 331. Mexico, 550, 624, 679. National Characteristics, 372. Rites and Ceremonies, 7. Social Classes, 381.
Food Industry and Trade. Brazil, 1688.
Food Supply. Mexico, 584, 652.
Forced Labor, 324. Guatemala, 756. Puerto Rico, 864.
Forced Migration. Colonial History, 501.
Foreign Affairs. *See* Foreign Policy.
Foreign Direct Investment. *See* Foreign Investment.
Foreign Influences. Argentina, 1441. Colombia, 1114.
Foreign Intervention, British. Cuba, 838.
Foreign Intervention, French. Mexico, 530, 532, 545, 555, 559, 599, 620.
Foreign Intervention, US. Cuba, 937. Dominican Republic, 884. Grenada, 942. Mexico, 579. Panama, 780. Puerto Rico, 892.
Foreign Investment. Puerto Rico, 949. *See Also* Investments.
Foreign Policy. Argentina, 1287, 1362, 1446, 1465, 1478. Bolivia, 1197. Brazil, 1551, 1633, 1639, 1674, 1686, 1700. Colombia, 1090. Cuba, 835. Dictatorships, 1287.

Dominican Republic, 858, 880, 898, 941. Ecuador, 1149. Mexico, 554, 603, 654, 669, 684. Venezuela, 1073, 1088. *See Also* International Relations.
Foreign Relations. *See* International Relations.
Foreign Trade. *See* International Trade.
Forests and Forest Industry. Brazil, 1581.
Forster, Ricardo, 3038.
Fortaleza, Brazil (city). Blacks, 2883. Musical History, 2921. Social Life and Customs, 2883.
Franciscans. Biography, 241. Brazil, 1618. Discovery and Exploration, 329. Evangelistic Work, 230. Higher Education, 378, 512. Honduras, 719–720. Mexico, 241, 518, 617. Missions, 236, 378, 512, 720.
Fraser, Nancy, 2976.
Free Blacks, 368. Brazil, 1652, 1667. Jamaica, 836. Law and Legislation, 836.
Freedmen, 368. Antigua and Barbuda, 865. Belize, 859. Brazil, 1565, 1571, 1652, 1710. British Caribbean, 848. Diseases, 855. Jamaica, 852, 855, 863. Liberia, 392. Oral History, 1571. Puerto Rico, 854. *See Also* Free Blacks.
Freedom. *See* Abolition (slavery).
Freedom of the Press. Mexico, 551, 596.
Freemasonry. Argentina, 1308. Costa Rica, 740. Uruguay, 1508.
French Influences. Architecture, 171. Brazil, 1520, 1684, 2546. Chile, 1238. Liberation Theology, 3007. Philosophy, 3007. Urban History, 171.
Frente Farabundo Martí para la Liberación Nacional (El Salvador), 745.
Frente Sandinista de Liberación Nacional. *See* Sandinistas (Nicaragua).
Freud, Sigmund, 3037.
Freyre, Gilberto, 1582.
Frontier and Pioneer Life. Argentina, 1324, 1358, 1400, 1455. Brazil, 1619. *See Also* Frontiers.
Frontiers. Brazil, 1554, 1596. Mexico, 209, 547. *See Also* Frontier and Pioneer Life.
Frugoni, Emilio, 1516.
Fruit Trade. Central America, 743.
FSLN. *See* Sandinistas (Nicaragua).
Fuentes, Carlos, 649.
Fuentes, Pepe, 2845.
Fuerza de Orientación Radical de la Joven Argentina, 1382.
Fujimori, Alberto, 1181.
Galeano, Eduardo, 2137.
Galicians. Cuba, 797.
Gallegans. *See* Galicians.

Gallery, Daniel V., 2780.
Gálvez, José de, 473.
Gálvez y Montes de Oca, Lucas de, 494.
Garavaglia, Juan Carlos, 1378.
Garcia, José Maurício Nunes, 2918–2919.
García Pimentel, Luis, 582.
García Vega, Lorenzo, 1937.
Gardel, Carlos, 2910.
Garifuna (indigenous group). *See* Black Carib (indigenous group).
Garoto, 2880.
Garro, Elena, 2330.
Gautherot, Marcel, 161.
Gazeta de Literatura, 1736.
Gender Relations, 2984. Argentina, 1433. Art, 63. Art Criticism, 80. Brazil, 1532, 1676. Colombia, 1138. *See Also* Sex and Sexual Relations.
Gender Roles. Argentina, 1294. Brazil, 1559, 1677. Caribbean Area, 810, 1930. Chile, 1278. Dominican Republic, 810, 2775. Jamaica, 863. Mexico, 33. Paraguay, 1493. *See Also* Sex Roles.
Gené, Juan Carlos, 2355.
Generals. Cuba, 875. Mexico, 555. South America, 1084.
Genocide. Caribbean Area, 818.
Geographical History. Argentina, 1043. Brazil, 1043, 1598, 1627. British Caribbean, 794. Mesoamerica, 215. Mexico, 212, 461, 696. Paraguay, 1043. *See Also* Historical Geography.
Geography. Colombia, 1094, 1104.
Geopolitics. Argentina, 1674. Bolivia, 1199. Brazil, 1674. Caribbean Area, 947. Colonial History, 722. Costa Rica, 768. Costa Rica/Nicaragua, 712. Cuba, 838. Puerto Rico, 947.
Gerchman, Rubens, 154.
German Influences. Brazil, 137, 1523, 2886. Peru, 1164, 1179.
Germans. Acculturation, 1718. Brazil, 1550, 1556, 1574, 1659, 1665, 1718. Discrimination, 1550. Jamaica, 833. Mexico, 546, 650. Travelers, 300.
Gerstmann, Robert, 1210.
Giannini, Humberto, 3026.
Gil, Gilberto, 2876, 2899.
Girondo, Oliverio, 2319.
Glenadel, Paula, 2523.
Globalization, 425, 427. Mexico, 2990. Musical History, 2833. Philosophy, 3041. Political Philosophy, 3028.
Gold. Brazil, 1599, 1614, 1619. Colombia, 1114. Money, 339.
Gomes, André da Silva, 2877.

Gómez, José María Leandro, 1508.
Gómez, Juan Vicente, 2074.
Gómez Campuzano, Ricardo, 106.
Góngora y Argote, Luis de, 1732, 1734.
González, Juan Pablo, 2850.
González Ortega, Jesús, 551, 555.
González Serrano, Manuel, 75.
González y González, Luis, 644.
Good Neighbor Policy. Dominican Republic, 905.
Goulart, João, 1562.
Government. *See* Bureaucracy.
Government, Resistance to, 407. Argentina, 1333, 1382, 1385, 1428, 1444. Art, 76, 93. Bolivia, 287. Brazil, 142, 189, 1524, 1526, 1562, 1638, 1649, 2506. Caribbean Area, 844. Chile, 1247, 1256, 1270, 1274, 1285, 2843, 3024. Colombia, 1110, 1123. Cuba, 932. Dictatorships, 1524. Dominican Republic, 897. El Salvador, 2996. Guatemala, 775. Mexico, 76, 472, 508, 666–667. Peronism, 1385. Photography, 105.
Government Publications. Dominican Republic, 862, 880, 898.
Governors. Argentina, 1437. Brazil, 1573. Colonial History, 1573. Genealogy, 203. Mexico, 195, 203.
Grassman, Marcelo, 143.
Grassroots Movements. *See* Social Movements.
Great Britain. West India Royal Commission (1938–1939), 934.
Great Depression (1929). Mexico, 626.
Griffa, Norberto L., 3036.
Grupo Proceso Pentágono (México), 76.
Guadalajara, Mexico (city). Musical History, 2722. Newspapers, 634. Religious Music, 2722. Women, 634. Women's Rights, 634.
Guadalajara, Mexico (state). Textiles and Textile Industry, 639.
Guairá, Paraguay (dept.). History, 2134.
Guajira, Colombia (dept.). Economic History, 1111. Merchants, 1111.
Guanajuato, Mexico (state). Catholic Church, 30.
Guano Industry. Peru, 1169.
Guarani (indigenous group). Indigenous/Non-Indigenous Relations, 257. Missions, 257, 490, 1013. Paraguay, 258. Social Life and Customs, 257.
Guarnieri, Camargo, 2872.
Guayama, Puerto Rico (city). History, 949.
Güemes, Martín Miguel, 1449.

Guerillas. *See* Guerrillas.
Guerrero, Mexico (state). Indigenous Peoples, 207. Music, 2712. Religious Life and Customs, 207.
Guerrero, Vicente, 619.
Guerrilla Warfare. *See* Guerrillas.
Guerrillas. Argentina, 1378–1379, 1413, 1444. Collective Memory, 1444. Colombia, 1110, 1113, 1123, 3007. Dominican Republic, 888. El Salvador, 741. Guatemala, 775. Interviews, 1379. Mexico, 640, 667. Peru, 298. Political Philosophy, 2962.
Guevara, Che, 912, 2962.
Guitar. Brazil, 2889, 2913, 2942, 2945. Chile, 2852. Cuba, 2795.
Guitarists. Biography, 2845. Brazil, 2880, 2889. Chile, 2845. Interviews, 2845. Mexico, 2735.
Guitarra, 2795.
Gullar, Ferreira, 2495.
Gutiérrez de Padilla, Juan, 2766.
Gutiérrez Gutiérrez, Mario R., 1199.
Gutiérrez Poma, Justo, 1165.
Gypsies. *See* Romanies.
Haciendas. Argentina, 1020. Bolivia, 1226. Mexico, 492, 582. Peru, 978. *See Also* Plantations.
Haiku, Brazilian, 2496, 2505.
Haitian Revolution (1787–1794). Brazil, 1567. Slaves and Slavery, 1567.
Haitians. Dominican Republic, 781, 791, 908. Genocide, 908.
Health Care. *See* Medical Care.
Henríquez Ureña, Pedro, 805.
Heredia, José Francisco, 1064.
Hernández Balaguer, Pablo, 2788.
Hernández Pico, Juan, 760.
Herrera, José Manuel de, 554.
Heureaux, Ulises, 858.
Hieroglyphics. *See* Writing.
Higher Education. Colombia, 1092, 1099, 1112, 1117–1118, 1138. Mexico, 462, 567–568. Venezuela, 958. *See Also* Universities.
Hispanic Americans. *See* Hispanics.
Hispanics. Social Conditions, 431.
Historia de la Nueva México, 1005.
Historia de las Indias de la Nueva España e Islas de la Tierra Firme, 27.
Historians. Argentina, 1349, 1378. Biography, 1378. Brazil, 1702. Colombia, 108. Dominican Republic, 786. Ecuador, 1148. Mexico, 199, 211.
Historic Sites. Brazil, 160, 165. Photography, 160.

Historical Demography. Argentina, 1022, 1045, 1435. Bolivia, 490. Costa Rica, 735. Mexico, 440–442, 490, 497, 525, 531.
Historical Geography. Central America, 730. Colombia, 1133, 1143. Paraguay, 1494. *See Also* Geographical History.
Historiography, 345, 351. Argentina, 1364–1365, 1429, 1441, 1452, 1462, 1479, 1485, 1487. Brazil, 1580, 1611, 1614, 1678, 1702. Caribbean Area, 809. Chile, 1241, 1244, 1247, 1266. Colombia, 1094, 1101. Costa Rica, 707. Dominican Republic, 786, 862. Ecuador, 1147–1148, 1155. Mexico, 200, 211, 443, 450, 454, 459, 462. Peru, 60, 2816. Trinidad and Tobago, 913. Uruguay, 1519. Venezuela, 1057, 1077, 2827.
Hochschild, Moritz, 1959.
Holanda, Sérgio Buarque de, 1533.
Homosexuality. Argentina, 101, 1306. Art, 101. Brazil, 1559, 1577. Caribbean Area, 810, 1930. Colombia, 1138. Costa Rica, 1852. Cuba, 1898, 1919. Dominican Republic, 810. Music, 2727. Women, 1577.
Hospital San Ignacio (Colombia), 1117.
Hospitals. Brazil, 1553. Psychiatry, 1553.
Hostos, Eugenio Maria de, 805.
Households. Mexico, 441.
Housing. Brazil, 167. Labor and Laboring Classes, 705. Law and Legislation, 1511. Mexico, 705. Uruguay, 1511.
Huamanga, Peru (prov.). Constitutional History, 1189. History, 1186.
Huancavelica, Peru (city). Colonial History, 990.
Huanchaco, Peru (city). Fish and Fishing, 250.
Huánuco, Peru (dept.). Precolumbian Civilizations, 255.
Human Ecology. Brazil, 1581.
Human Fertility. Peru, 1183.
Human Geography. Venezuela, 1057.
Human Rights. Argentina, 1457. Brazil, 1526. Peru, 1181. *See Also* Civil Rights.
Human Sacrifice. *See* Sacrifice.
Humanism, 354.
Humanities. Mexico, 462.
Hunting. Mesoamerica, 228.
Hygiene. *See* Public Health.
Iberians. *See* Basques.
Iconography. Brazil, 177. Colombia, 49. Colonial History, 49. *See Also* Precolumbian Art.
Iglesia Asunción de Nuestra Señora (Tlaxcala de Xicohténcatl, Mexico), 46.
Iglesia de San Mateo Chalcatzingo (Mexico), 41.

Ilarione, *da Bergamo, fra*, 1745.
Ilê Aiyê (organization), 2854.
Ilha do Governador, Brazil (island). History, 1530.
Illiteracy. *See* Literacy and Illiteracy.
Illness. *See* Diseases.
Illueca Sibauste, Jorge Enrique, 739.
Immigrants. Acculturation, 1318, 1718. Argentina, 1339, 1343–1344, 1347, 1387, 1395–1396, 1438, 2314. Brazil, 182, 1641, 1646, 1659, 1669. Caribbean Area, 785. Chile, 1261. Citizenship, 1412. Cuba, 787, 797, 887. Diaries, 182. Economic Conditions, 1317. Germans, 1659, 1665. Mexico, 444–445, 648, 659. National Identity, 1412. Photographs, 1339. Pictorial Works, 182. Puerto Rico, 864. Rural Development, 1438. Social Conditions, 1317, 1461. Social Life and Customs, 1646. Spanish Civil War (1936–1939), 1387. Tango, 2840. World War I (1914–1918), 1387. World War II (1939–1945), 1387. *See Also* Migration.
Immigrants, Portuguese. Peru, 988.
Immigration. *See* Migration.
Imperialism, 309, 322, 402. Brazil, 1529. British Caribbean, 825. Caribbean Area, 788, 927. Pacific Area, 1169. Political Philosophy, 2975. Political Thought, 2975. Spain, 26. US, 333.
Imperialism, US. Cuba, 804. Dominican Republic, 896. Peru, 1194.
Imports and Exports. *See* International Trade.
Imuro, Masao, 648.
Incas. Bolivia, 284. Chile, 294. Colonial History, 283. Cosmology, 260. Music, 2815. Musical History, 2815. Myths and Mythology, 253. Peru, 305. Philosophy, 3012. Religious Life and Customs, 253, 260. Rites and Ceremonies, 284.
Income. Colonial History, 356.
Income Distribution. Costa Rica, 771.
Indentured Servants. Barbados, 817. Caribbean Area, 824. Law and Legislation, 824.
Independence Movements, 346, 399, 401, 404, 1070, 1084. Argentina, 1030, 1047, 1330. Brazil, 1670–1673, 1696. Colombia, 389, 1091. Cuba, 797. Dominican Republic, 805. Ideology, 581. Jamaica, 931, 948. Mexican-American Border Region, 621. Mexico, 205. Peru, 982. Political Philosophy, 396. Río de la Plata (region), 393. Uruguay, 1012, 1519, 3032. Venezuela, 1048–1050, 1069, 1086. Writing, 1670–1673. *See Also* Wars of Independence.

Indianismo and Indianidad. Bolivia, 263, 3021.
Indians. *See* East Indians. *See* Indigenous Peoples.
Indigenous Art, 2, 10, 17. Brazil, 177. Ceramics, 10. Chile, 252. Colombia, 13. Ecuador, 13, 2806. Exhibitions, 1. History, 5. Myths and Mythology, 14. Peru, 14, 56. Textiles and Textile Industry, 52.
Indigenous Influences. Brazil, 2522. Caribbean Area, 1927. Food, 372. Popular Music, 2811.
Indigenous Languages. Books, 1725. Writing, 291.
Indigenous Literature. Colonial History, 1005.
Indigenous Music, 2679. Andean Region, 2815, 2818. Bolivia, 2803. Brazil, 2916, 2927, 2947. Caribbean Area, 2778. Colombia, 2804. Colonial History, 2818. Ecuador, 2806, 2808. Guatemala, 734. Mexico, 2709, 2725, 2729, 2750–2751. Peru, 2821. US, 2683. Venezuela, 2827.
Indigenous/Non-Indigenous Relations, 4, 17, 256, 264, 282, 296, 306, 324, 374, 377, 398, 1749. Andean Region, 977. Argentina, 271, 277, 1024, 1291, 1346, 1358, 1400, 1423, 1455, 1473, 1481. Bolivia, 1203. Brazil, 281, 300, 1588, 1594, 1629, 1637, 1668. Caribbean Area, 788, 818. Chile, 1003, 1242. Colombia, 290, 1098, 1126, 1131, 1137, 1143. Colonial History, 199, 490, 505, 507. Costa Rica, 713. Ecuador, 1151, 1157. Grenada, 792. Guatemala, 737. Jamaica, 819. Jesuits, 1604. Mexico, 195, 515, 672, 1741. Narratives, 1481. Nicaragua, 723. Orinoco River Region (Venezuela and Colombia), 1083. Paraguay, 1024, 1201, 1492. Peru, 270, 1725. Philosophy, 3004. Viceroyalty of New Spain (1540–1821), 1746. Viceroyalty of Peru (1542–1822), 984.
Indigenous Peoples, 365, 1749. Acculturation, 270, 281. Alcohol and Alcoholism, 1572. Andean Region, 275, 1200. Argentina, 1346, 1423, 1443. Art, 23. Art Exhibitions, 193. Artifacts, 193, 198, 1721. Artisanry, 23, 25. Belize, 859. Bolivia, 264–265, 1206, 1215. Brazil, 264, 269, 289, 1572, 1590. Catholic Church, 197, 239, 246, 1637. Chile, 275. Church Architecture, 206. Colombia, 273. Colonial Administration, 724. Colonial History, 192, 244, 726, 735, 1017. Colonization, 490. Cosmology, 272, 1590. Costa Rica, 215, 735. Cuba, 909. Cultural History, 1590. Cultural Identity, 282. Curriculum, 289. Demography, 735. Diseases, 206. Ecuador, 1159. Education, 274, 985. Epidemics, 206. Ethnic Groups and Ethnicity, 989. Ethnic Identity, 3005. Ethnohistory, 244. Evangelicalism, 1668. Festivals, 2725. Forced Labor, 286. Gender Relations, 237. Genocide, 818. Goldwork, 1. Government, Resistance to, 263. Hunting, 228. Independence Movements, 205. Insurrections, 672. Intellectual History, 353. Irrigation, 486. Land Tenure, 296, 544, 548. Land Use, 275. Language and Languages, 249. Law and Legislation, 277, 983. Liberation Theology, 640. Literacy and Illiteracy, 1213. Literature, 198, 1721. Lithography, 82. Local Elections, 205. Marriage, 237. Mesoamerica, 198, 207, 215, 239, 1721. Mexican-American Border Region, 621. Mexico, 31, 200, 204, 208, 216–218, 244, 450, 472, 480, 563, 1751, 2990. Migrant Labor, 661. Missions, 385. Musical History, 2838. Myths and Mythology, 225, 268. Nicaragua, 215, 723. Nobility, 210. Painting, 5. Paraguay, 264. Peru, 285, 291, 1188. Philosophy, 272. Political Participation, 598. Printing Industry, 213. Protests, 731. Public Schools, 985. Regional Government, 205, 220. Relations with Spaniards, 723. Religion, 304. Religious Life and Customs, 207, 228, 2725. Rites and Ceremonies, 272, 275, 344. Rock Music, 2724. Sex and Sexual Relations, 237. Silverwork, 1. Slaves and Slavery, 196, 285, 377, 672, 812–813, 818, 989, 1629, 2736. Social Control, 717. Social Life and Customs, 1, 17, 300, 514. Social Movements, 658. Songs, 2736. Spanish Conquest, 192, 374. Sports, 279. Traditional Medicine, 344. Treatment of, 971, 989. Wills, 226. Women, 237, 1572, 2986. Writing, 200, 213, 291, 373.
Indigenous Policy. Bolivia, 1203, 1213, 1226. Chile, 1006. Mexico, 548, 658. Peru, 984. Viceroyalty of New Spain (1540–1821), 505.
Indigenous Resistance. Andean Region, 986. Colombia, 1131. Colonial History, 992. Peru, 255, 270, 992. Viceroyalty of Peru (1542–1822), 975.
Industrial Policy. Ecuador, 1161.
Industrial Relations. Mexico, 558.
Industry and Industrialization, 404. Argentina, 1291. Bolivia, 1220. Brazil, 1691. Caribbean Area, 829. Dominican Republic, 891. Ecuador, 1161. Indigenous/Non-

Indigenous Relations, 1291. Mexico, 463, 639, 694. Paraguay, 1502. Venezuela, 1075.
Inequality. See Income Distribution.
Infant Mortality. Mexico, 497.
Informal Labor. See Informal Sector.
Informal Sector. Mexico, 666.
Information Resources. See Bibliography.
Inheritance and Succession. Colombia, 296.
Inquisition. Brazil, 1577, 1579, 1591, 1601, 1626. Chile, 1007. Confessions, 1591. Historiography, 370. Homosexuality, 1577. Peru, 987. Portugal, 1601. Racism, 1591. Sexism, 1591. Viceroyalty of New Spain (1540–1821), 506.
Instituto Cultural Itaú, 145.
Instituto de Cultura Puertorriqueña, 893.
Instituto Geográfico e Histórico da Bahia, 1709.
Instituto Histórico e Geográfico Brasileiro, 1702.
Instruments. See Musical Instruments.
Insurgency. See Insurrections.
Insurrection of the Comuneros (Paraguay, 1730–1735), 1015.
Insurrection of Tupac Amaru (1780–1781), 986, 992.
Insurrections, 409. Brazil, 1708. Colombia, 1113. Cuba, 844, 874. Dominican Republic, 874. Jamaica, 860. Paraguay, 1015. Peru, 266. Puerto Rico, 874. Slaves and Slavery, 397.
Intellectual History, 354, 367, 396, 1513. Andean Region, 3008. Argentina, 98, 1357, 1381, 1406, 1442, 1484, 3036. Brazil, 1540, 1549, 1557, 1564, 1682, 1709. Caribbean Area, 799, 2997. Chile, 1247, 1279. Church-State Relations, 1540. Colombia, 1118, 3003. Cuba, 89, 845, 902, 1878. Dominican Republic, 896. El Salvador, 1867. Jamaica, 841. Law and Legislation, 1540. Mexico, 84, 199, 641–642, 678, 1728, 1736. Paraguay, 1516, 2136. Peru, 1187, 3013, 3017. Philosophy, 2965, 2971, 2999. Political Ideology, 1540. Psychology, 1483. Trinidad and Tobago, 914. Uruguay, 1509. Venezuela, 1056.
Intellectuals, 423, 2681, 2987. Argentina, 1480, 3033. Biography, 1381. Brazil, 1682, 1709. Chile, 1241, 3024. Colombia, 108, 112. Conservatism, 697. Costa Rica, 758. Cuba, 845, 939. Indigenous Peoples, 1746. Interviews, 187. Mexico, 199, 450, 678, 697. Puerto Rico, 856, 1923. US, 940. Venezuela, 1054.
Intercultural Communication, 2970. Philosophy, 2970.

Internal Migration. Argentina, 1045, 1326.
International American Conference, 391.
International Economic Relations, 336, 404, 434. Africa/Europe, 1608. Argentina, 1334. Argentina/Great Britain, 1025. Bolivia/US, 1208. Brazil, 1713. Brazil/Africa, 1608. Caribbean Area/Europe, 839. Caribbean Area/Mexico, 798. Caribbean Area/US, 794, 798. Colombia, 1100, 1124. Costa Rica/Germany, 768. Latin America/Europe, 1617. Mexico, 570. Mexico/Germany, 463. Paraguay, 1201, 1492. Puerto Rico/US, 921–922. See Also International Trade.
International Migration. See Migration.
International Relations, 402, 413, 430. Argentina, 1312. Argentina/Brazil, 1489, 1491, 1674. Argentina/Chile, 395, 1465. Argentina/Cuba, 1906. Argentina/Germany, 1287. Argentina/Great Britain, 1025, 1362. Argentina/Nicaragua, 754. Argentina/Spain, 1367. Bolivia/Chile, 1167, 1199. Bolivia/Paraguay, 1201, 1225, 1492. Bolivia/US, 1228. Brazil/Dominican Republic, 1545. Brazil/Egypt, 1639. Brazil/Germany, 1556. Brazil/Great Britain, 1645. Brazil/Haiti, 1545. Brazil/Israel, 1639. Brazil/Italy, 1640, 1669, 1675. Brazil/Middle East, 1639. Brazil/Netherlands, 1593. Brazil/Portugal, 1656, 1670–1673. Brazil/Uruguay, 1515. Brazil/US, 1542, 1563, 1566. Caribbean Area, 811. Caribbean Area/Africa, 889. Caribbean Area/Ireland, 785. Chile/Colombia, 1241. Chile/Cuba, 1256. Chile/France, 1252. Chile/Peru, 1167, 1216. Colombia/Dominican Republic, 1133. Colombia/US, 1090. Colonial History, 722. Commerce, 433. Costa Rica/France, 747. Costa Rica/Nicaragua, 712. Cuba/China, 882. Cuba/Dominican Republic, 888. Cuba/France, 835. Cuba/Great Britain, 835. Cuba/Spain, 835, 846. Cuba/US, 94, 784, 804, 938. Dominican Republic/Haiti, 781, 811, 880, 1891. Dominican Republic/Mexico, 805. Dominican Republic/US, 806, 858, 898, 900, 905, 929, 941, 950, 952. Dominican Republic/Venezuela, 924. Ecuador/Japan, 1149. Ecuador/Peru, 1216. Ecuador/US, 1149–1150. England/Spain, 721. Great Britain, 355. Great Britain/Spain, 819. Guatemala/Spain, 726, 769, 774. Haiti/Jamaica, 878. Latin America/Europe, 2973. Latin America/Mexico, 654. Latin America/Soviet Union, 432. Latin America/Spain, 960. Latin America/US, 309, 322,

417, 420, 603. Mexican-American Border Region, 653. Mexico/Germany, 669. Mexico/Spain, 26, 467. Mexico/US, 471, 649, 655, 687–688, 690, 704. Panama/US, 780. Paraguay, 1499. Paraguay/Europe, 1496. Peru/Great Britian, 1194. Peru/Spain, 980. Peru/US, 1194. Portugal/Spain, 1522, 1596, 1616. Puerto Rico/Spain, 846. Puerto Rico/US, 789, 856, 953. Río de la Plata (region), 1489. South America/Great Britain, 866. South America/Spain, 311. Spain, 355. Uruguay/Spain, 1012. Venezuela/South Korea, 1067. Venezuela/US, 1073, 1088. See Also Foreign Policy.

International Trade, 437. Colombia, 1122. Ecuador/Mexico, 972. Mexico/Japan, 45. Mexico/US, 529. See Also International Economic Relations.

International Trade Relations. See International Economic Relations.

Interviews. Artists, 67, 85, 115. Brazil, 1666. Musicians, 67. Performing Arts, 70. Peronism, 3038. Philosophers, 3026, 3038. Poets, 67. Writers, 67.

Investment. See Investments. See Saving and Investment.

Investments. Bolivia, 1229. See Also Foreign Investment.

Irala, José, 1496.

Irigoyen, Hipólito, 1373.

Irish. Argentina, 1344. Caribbean Area, 785, 824.

Irrigation. Colonial History, 486.

Islam. Philosophy, 2960.

Islamic Influences, 419, 429.

Islands. Brazil, 1530.

Isnardi, Francisco, 1086.

Itaipú (power plant), 1502.

Italian Influences. Brazil, 137, 2585, 2919. Drama, 2353.

Italians. Argentina, 2314. Brazil, 1641, 1675. Chile, 1266. Cultural Identity, 1317. Mexico, 556, 575.

Itza (indigenous group). Religious Life and Customs, 717. Social Life and Customs, 717.

Ixil (indigenous group). History, 775.

Jacomino, Américo, 2889.

Jails. See Prisons.

Jalapa, Mexico (city). Food Supply, 652. Mexican Revolution (1910–1920), 652.

Jalisco, Mexico (state). Economic Development, 676. Federalism, 460. Political Development, 460. Regional Development, 460. Social History, 577.

Jamaica Progressive League, 948.

Jamaicans. Racism, 816.

Japanese. Bolivia, 1212. Brazil, 1698. Mexico, 648. Peru, 1196. Social Classes, 648.

Japanese Influences. Brazil, 2946. Mexico, 45.

Jazz. Argentina, 2833. Brazil, 2878, 2942.

Jesuits. Brazil, 1574, 1586, 1589, 1604, 1618, 1621. Central America, 760. Chile, 1003. Cultural History, 1589. Diaries, 1574. Economic History, 1621. Ecuador, 970. Education, 1589. El Salvador, 759. Mexico, 2991. Missionaries, 1586, 1604, 2991. Missions, 490, 959, 1013, 1083, 1586. Paraguay, 1015. Philosophy, 2991. Social Development, 1589. Venezuela, 1083.

Jesus, Caetano de Melo de, 2897.

Jesus, Clementina de, 2938.

Jews, 429. Acculturation, 1318. Argentina, 1296, 1318, 1357, 1395, 1438, 2836, 2839, 2841. Brazil, 1550, 1579, 1609, 1646, 1698, 2442. Chile, 1242. Colonial History, 987. Discrimination, 1550. Inquisition, 1579. Interviews, 1646. Musical History, 2836, 2839. Musicians, 2841. Peronism, 2839. Publishers and Publishing, 1357. Religious Life and Customs, 1609. Rural Development, 1438. Social Life and Customs, 1318. See Also Judaism.

Jiménez de la Espada, Marcos, 997.

Jobim, Antonio Carlos, 2525, 2869, 2920.

Johan Maurits, Prince of Nassau-Siegen, 1593.

Journalism. Brazil, 1605, 1636, 1651, 1694, 1719. Mexico, 464, 551, 566, 592. See Also Mass Media; Newspapers.

Journalists. Biography, 1096. Colombia, 1096. Dominican Republic, 786. Ecuador, 1157. Mexico, 596. Uruguay, 1517.

Journalists, US. Cuba, 945.

Juana Agripina, 876.

Juana Inés de la Cruz, Sor, 1720, 1723, 1733, 1738.

Juárez, Benito, 599, 1788.

Juárez, Mexico (city). See Ciudad Juárez, Mexico (city).

Judaism. Brazil, 1609. Philosophy, 2960. See Also Jews.

Judicial Process. Chile, 1246. Jamaica, 852.

Jujuy, Argentina (prov.). Church-State Relations, 1021. History, 1021.

Juvenile Literature. Caribbean Area, 1901. Puerto Rico, 1888.

Kahlo, Frida, 77.

Kaingang (indigenous group). Ethnic Identity, 248. Land Tenure, 248.
Kaingangue (indigenous group). *See* Kaingang (indigenous group).
Kalinya (indigenous group). *See* Carib (indigenous group).
Kannário, Igor, 2937.
Kearny, Stephen Watts, 605.
Kennedy, John Fitzgerald, 1090.
Keresan (indigenous group). Colonial History, 486.
Kings and Rulers. Mexico, 532. *See Also* Chiefdoms.
Kinship. Andean Region, 251.
Kruchin, Samuel, 169.
Kuikuru (indigenous group). Musical Instruments, 2927.
La Pampa, Argentina (prov.). Historiography, 1365. Peronism, 1290, 1365, 1409. Political History, 1290. Political Participation, 1409. Women, 1409.
La Paz, Argentina (city). Frontier and Pioneer Life, 1358. Indigenous/Non-Indigenous Relations, 1358.
La Paz, Bolivia (city). History, 995. Social History, 1221.
La Paz, Mexico (city). Commerce, 534. Economic History, 534.
La Plata, Argentina (city). Peronism, 1470.
La Rioja, Argentina (prov.). Indigenous Peoples, 267.
Labor and Laboring Classes. Argentina, 1305, 1389, 1392, 1397, 1411, 1459, 1468, 1475. Artists, 656. Automobile Industry and Trade, 1392. Brazil, 1531–1532, 1539, 1554, 1635, 1647, 1652, 1667, 1685. Caribbean Area, 824, 904. Chile, 1234, 1240, 1250, 1259–1260, 1267, 1272, 1280, 1284, 1286. Colombia, 1107. Construction Industry, 1539. Dominican Republic, 952. Guatemala, 756. Housing, 705. Interviews, 1305. Massacres, 657. Mexico, 458, 470, 656–657, 705. Musical History, 2817, 2820. Nationalism, 1468. Peru, 1188, 1191, 1193. Political Culture, 1389. Popular Music, 2820. Puerto Rico, 917, 919, 923. Radicalism, 1397. Railroads, 1539. Saint Vincent and the Grenadines, 904. Urban Areas, 1351. Urban History, 1525. *See Also* Migrant Labor.
Labor Movement. Argentina, 1331, 1397. Bolivia, 1220. Catholicism, 673. Dominican Republic, 900. Mexico, 470, 656, 673, 699. *See Also* Labor and Laboring Classes; Labor Policy.

Labor Policy. Argentina, 1411, 1475. *See Also* Labor Movement.
Labor Unions. *See* Trade Unions.
Ladinos. Colombia, 273.
Laet, Johannes de, 388.
Lagos Escobar, Ricardo, 1248.
Lagrange, Desiderio, 528.
Lame Chante, Manuel Quintín, 1131.
Land Ownership. *See* Land Tenure.
Land Reform. Bolivia, 1226. Colombia, 1144. Mexico, 544, 703. Peru, 1188. Puerto Rico, 928. *See Also* Agricultural Policy.
Land Settlement. Brazil, 1554. Chile, 1252. Jamaica, 834. Mexico, 208, 561. Spaniards, 737. US, 309. *See Also* Agricultural Colonization.
Land Tenure. Argentina, 1298, 1421. Bolivia, 263. Colonial History, 489. Conibo (indigenous group), 261. Mexico, 544, 548. Nicaragua, 772. Peru, 978, 1162.
Land Use. Argentina, 1298. Bolivia, 287. Peru, 1162.
Landi, António José, 130.
Landowners. Chile, 1262. Colonial History, 636. Insurrections, 82. Mexico, 498, 636. Peru, 978.
Lange, Francisco Curt, 2681, 2864, 2872.
Language and Languages. Argentina, 1337. Paraguay, 2135. Philosophy, 2966. Puerto Rico, 949. Spanish Conquest, 242.
Larrinaga, José Pastor, 979.
Latin American Influences. Art, 16. Europe, 16. US, 2988. *See Also* Hispanics.
Latin Americanists. Colombia, 1099.
Lavalle, Juan, 1437.
Lavista, Mario, 2687–2690, 2693, 2767.
Law and Legislation, 400. Argentina, 1341. Brazil, 1540, 1660. Chile, 1246. Church-State Relations, 1540. Colombia, 1108. Colonial History, 983. Dominican Republic, 898. Guatemala, 724. Labor Policy, 1475. Language and Languages, 724. Philosophy, 2965. Political History, 1540. Public Administration, 1660.
Le Corbusier, 422.
League of Nations, 684.
Lebanese. Mexico, 700.
Legislation. *See* Law and Legislation.
León Toral, José de, 702.
Leprosy. Brazil, 1634.
Levy Nadal, Alfredo, 2799.
Lewis, Gordon K., 2998.
LGBT. *See* Homosexuality.
Liberalism. Argentina, 1383, 1439, 1452, 1488. Brazil, 1529. Colombia, 1094, 1115,

1141. Costa Rica, 778. Ecuador, 1152. Mexico, 548, 579, 606, 611, 654, 660, 2989. Newspapers, 685. Peru, 3013. Revolutionaries, 660. Women, 916. *See Also* Political Theory.

Liberation Theology, 2963, 2972, 3006, 3015. Colombia, 3007, 3015. Colonial Discourse, 3006. Cultural Identity, 2974. El Salvador, 2996. Ethnic Identity, 2974. French Influences, 3007. German Influences, 2963. Mexico, 640. Peru, 1174. Philosophy, 2979.

Libraries, 319. Colonial History, 1597. Historiography, 1597. *See Also* Archives.

Lida, Clara Eugenia, 470.

Life Expectancy. Mexico, 497.

Lima, Oliveira, 1686.

Lima, Peru (city). Clothing and Dress, 993. Colonial History, 991. Commerce, 259. Education, 1173. Festivals, 982. Jews, 987. Mass Media, 981. Medicine, 979. Political History, 982. Social History, 993.

Linguistics. Mexico, 242, 2995. Philosophy, 2995.

Lisboa, Antônio Francisco, 128, 131.

Lispector, Clarice, 1935, 2362.

Literacy and Illiteracy. Bolivia, 1213. Chile, 1258.

Literary Criticism, 2980. Argentina, 2132, 2541. Brazil, 2372, 2378, 2525–2527, 2539–2541, 2546–2547. Caribbean Area, 1927, 1931. Colombia, 3003. Cuba, 1878. Decolonization, 2983. Dominican Republic, 805. Ecuador, 2005. El Salvador, 1867, 1870. Guatemala, 1868. Mexico, 1738, 2276. Nicaragua, 1866. Panama, 1869. Peru, 1948, 1951–1952, 3010. Philosophy, 2968, 3009. Poetry, 2983. Puerto Rico, 1923, 1935, 1938, 1941, 1943. Uruguay, 2184, 2968, 3030.

Literatura de Cordel, 2524. Brazil, 2517. *See Also* Popular Literature.

Literature. Peru, 1946. *See Also* Authors; Baroque Literature; Biography.

Literature, Baroque. *See* Baroque Literature.

Lithography. Brazil, 143. Insurrections, 82. Mexico, 82. *See Also* Printing Industry; Prints.

Living Standards. *See* Cost and Standard of Living.

Llanos (Colombia and Venezuela). Jesuits, 959, 1083. Missions, 959.

Lleras Camargo, Alberto, 1090.

Local Elections. Mexico, 205, 549.

Local History. Bolivia, 1227. Colombia, 1121, 1146. Mexico, 447. Peru, 1192. Puerto Rico, 949.

Lockouts. *See* Strikes and Lockouts.

Lomax, John, 2759.

Longoni, Eduardo, 1328.

López, Cándido, 1495.

López, Patricio Antonio, 1746.

López de Velasco, Juan, 380.

López Portillo, José, 690.

Lorena, Brazil (city). Industry and Industrialization, 1691. Sugar Industry and Trade, 1691.

Los Angeles, California (city). Dance, 2726. Labor Movement, 618. Music, 2726. Political History, 618.

Lozada, Manuel, 580.

Lubkov, Vasili, 1512.

Lula, 2506.

Lyricists. Peru, 2824.

Macció, Rómulo, 99.

Machado de Assis, 2672.

Machado y Morales, Gerardo, 937.

Machín, Antonio, 2787.

Machismo. *See* Sex Roles.

Madero, Francisco I., 646, 672.

Magalhães, Fernão de, 383.

Magic. Brazil, 1705.

Magón, Ricardo Flores. *See* Flores Magón, Ricardo.

Malaria. Colonial History, 361.

Malaspina, Alessandro, 383.

Malayerba (theater company), 2358.

Malnutrition. *See* Nutrition.

Mañach, Jorge, 933.

Manaus, Brazil (city). City Planning, 1537. Political Development, 1537. Urban Development, 1537.

Manumission. *See* Abolition (slavery).

Manuscripts. Mexico, 35, 1747. Peru, 1747.

Manuscrito Tovar, 27.

Maps and Cartography. Belize, 859. Central America, 730. Colombia, 1104, 1143. Paraguay, 1494.

Mapuche (indigenous group). Ball Games, 279. Colonial History, 1003. History, 280, 301, 1006. Indigenous Resistance, 1005. Relations with Spaniards, 1011. Religion, 1007.

Mar del Plata, Argentina (city). Immigrants, 1347. Photographs, 1347.

Maracaibo Lake Region (Venezuela). Art History, 120. Cultural History, 120.

Maragh, G.G., 915.

Marajó Island (Brazil). Music, 2898.
Maranhão, Brazil (state). Cacao, 1522. Collective Memory, 1681. Economic History, 1681. Political History, 1681. Popular Culture, 1681. Portuguese Empire, 1522. Slaves and Slavery, 1629. Social History, 1681. Spanish Influences, 1522. Women, 1681.
Marcos, Plínio, 2570.
Marginalization. *See* Marginalized Peoples.
Marginalized Peoples. Colombia, 1141. Ecuador, 1160. Mexico, 458.
Mariátegui, José Carlos, 3010, 3014, 3044.
Marimba. Mexico, 2768.
Marín, Luis Muñoz. *See* Muñoz Marín, Luis.
Marine Resources, 332. Mexico, 332.
Maritime History. Slaves and Slavery, 796. South America, 866. *See Also* Naval History.
Marketing. Colombia, 1093.
Markets. Colombia, 1093.
Marof, Tristán, 3023.
Maroons. Colombia, 961. Mexico, 482.
Marranos. Peru, 987.
Marriage, 334. Argentina, 1035, 1341. Ethnic Groups and Ethnicity, 363.
Martí, José, 402, 804, 849, 2971, 3001.
Martin, Edgardo, 2789.
Martín, *de Porres, Saint*, 976.
Martínez Nadal, Rafael, 935.
Marxism, 3044. Bolivia, 3022. Literature, 1925.
Mary, *Blessed Virgin, Saint*, 18, 21, 1730.
Masculinity. Alcohol and Alcoholism, 677. Brazil, 1677. Caribbean Area, 1930. Mexico, 677. Paraguay, 1502.
Masons. *See* Freemasonry.
Mass Media, 316, 426. Argentina, 1359, 1461. Brazil, 1547, 1636, 1651. Caribbean Area, 927. Colombia, 1108. Dictatorships, 1500. Dominican Republic, 941. Economic Development, 1636. Mexico, 541, 592, 603, 682. Narratives, 1636. Peronism, 1301. Political History, 1301. Soccer, 1653. Violence, 596.
Massacres. Argentina, 1309, 1354. Art, 73. Dominican Republic, 908. Guatemala, 769. Haitians, 908. Mexico, 73–74, 657.
Mata, Eduardo, 2719.
Mata Hari, 2667.
Material Culture. Mexico, 480.
Matienzo, Juan de, 285.

Mato Grosso, Brazil (state). Colonial History, 1043, 1627. Geographical History, 1043, 1627.
Mato Grosso do Sul, Brazil (state). Colonial History, 1043, 1627. Geographical History, 1043, 1627.
Maurel, Clementina, 2700.
Maximilian, *Emperor of Mexico*, 502, 532.
Mayas. Caciques, 210. Calendrics, 238. Captives, 202. Cosmology, 238. Cultural History, 232, 236. Drama, 2313. Epigraphy, 232. Ethnic Groups and Ethnicity, 191. Ethnohistory, 191, 232. Fire, 235. Food, 240. Guatemala, 2785. Hieroglyphics, 202, 240. Kings and Rulers, 6. Language and Languages, 493. Mexico, 392. Missions, 236. Mural Painting, 6. Myths and Mythology, 225, 230, 238. Origins, 230. Political Conditions, 240. Political History, 232. Political Leadership, 240. Popular Music, 2785. Religious Life and Customs, 238. Rites and Ceremonies, 235, 240. Sacred Space, 236. Sacrifice, 235. Tattooing, 202.
Mayors. Ecuador, 1153.
Mazatec (indigenous group). Music, 2725.
Mazatlán, Mexico (city). Economic Development, 676.
McCutcheon, John Tinney, 631.
Meat Industry. Brazil, 1688. *See Also* Cattle Raising and Trade.
Media. *See* Mass Media.
Medical Anthropology. Caribbean Area, 853. Colonial History, 524. Mexico, 524.
Medical Care. Colombia, 1117. *See Also* Medicine.
Medical Policy. Colombia, 1107.
Medicinal Plants. Colonial History, 361, 524. Paraguay, 1039.
Medicine. Brazil, 1695. Codices, 233. Colombia, 1117. Colonial History, 524. Peru, 979. *See Also* Medical Care.
Meireles, Cildo, 142, 150.
Memory. *See* Collective Memory.
Mendoza, Argentina (prov.). Historiography, 1316. Political Development, 1316. Social Classes, 1459. Wine and Wine Making, 1459.
Menem, Carlos Saúl, 1474.
Menéndez, José, 1291.
Mercedarians. Guatemala, 716.
Merchant Marines. Brazil, 1620. Spain, 357.
Merchants. Argentina, 1335. Brazil, 1617. Colombia, 1093, 1111. Dutch, 1624.

Jamaica, 839. Mexico, 666. Political Participation, 666. Puerto Rico, 871.

Mérida, Carlos, 85.

Mérida, Mexico (city). Colonial History, 525. Ethnic Groups and Ethnicity, 525. Slaves and Slavery, 478. Social Structure, 478.

Mérida, Venezuela (state). Political History, 1066.

Mestizaje. *See* Mestizos and Mestizaje.

Mestizos and Mestizaje. Andean Region, 373. Central America, 373. Colonial History, 475. Marriage, 363. Peru, 980. Viceroyalty of New Spain (1540–1821), 526, 2994.

Metal-Work. Peru, 12.

Metallurgy. Bolivia, 53. Peru, 12.

Metaphysics, 2966, 2980. Bolivia, 974.

Metropolitan Areas. *See* Cities and Towns.

Mexica. *See* Aztecs.

Mexican-American Border Region. Frontier and Pioneer Life, 621. Great Depression (1929), 626. Historiography, 560. History, 586. Migration, 586. Music, 2692. Popular Music, 2703. *See Also* Borderlands.

Mexican-American War (1846–1848), 479, 564.

Mexican Americans. Artists, 687. History, 560. Music, 2683, 2710. Philosophy, 2982. Political Participation, 618. Popular Music, 2711. Songs, 2710. Violence, 536.

Mexican Revolution (1910–1920), 664. Biography, 674. Cartoons, 631. Censorship, 682. Conferences, 623. Cultural History, 646, 692. Entrepreneurs, 662. Food Supply, 652. Foreign Relations, 683. Historiography, 683. Intellectual History, 697. Interviews, 645. Journalism, 631. Liberalism, 660. Literature, 538, 588. Local History, 692. Mass Media, 633, 682. Military History, 668, 683. Newspapers, 633, 685. Photography, 538. Political History, 623, 633, 644. Political Leadership, 674. Political Participation, 632. Social Development, 632. Social History, 632. US, 631. Women, 600.

Mexicans. Cultural History, 687. Philippines, 501. US, 626, 647, 649.

México, Mexico (city). Aztecs, 38. Catholic Church, 44. Colonial History, 497, 504. Cronistas, 1731. Description and Travel, 1731. Economic History, 484. Food, 584. Government, Resistance to, 523. Historiography, 1731. Inquisition, 510. Musical History, 2708, 2747, 2754. Painting, 40. Poetry, 1740. Political History, 523.

Public Health, 511. Public Works, 583. Religious Music, 2684, 2708. Social History, 510, 574.

México, Mexico (state). Political History, 606.

Mexico. Ejército, 585.

Michoacán, Mexico (state). Economic Development, 676. Ejidos, 208. Ethnic Groups and Ethnicity, 208. Indigenous Peoples, 208. Land Settlement, 208. Mexican Revolution (1910–1920), 644. Nahuas (indigenous group), 208. Political History, 644.

Michoacán de Ocampo, Mexico (city). Archeology, 242. Ethnohistory, 242. Indigenous Peoples, 242. Language and Languages, 242. Linguistics, 242. Spanish Conquest, 242.

Middle Classes. Musical History, 2817.

Migrant Labor. Mexico, 661. Puerto Rico, 918. US, 918. *See Also* Agricultural Labor.

Migrants. *See* Immigrants.

Migration, 328, 427. Argentina, 326, 1343. Brazil, 326. Family and Family Relations, 318. Historiography, 325. Mexican-American Border Region, 625, 655. Mexico, 625. Public Opinion, 431. South America, 311. Suriname, 911. *See Also* Forced Migration; Immigrants; Internal Migration; Return Migration.

Migration, Argentine. US, 2840.

Migration, Asturian. Argentina, 1347.

Migration, Basque. Argentina, 1344. Cuba, 903.

Migration, Bolivian. Argentina, 2800.

Migration, Caribbean. US, 794.

Migration, Chinese. Peru, 1168. Puerto Rico, 864.

Migration, Cuban. Peru, 2823.

Migration, English. Argentina, 1315.

Migration, German. Argentina, 1442. Brazil, 1718. Mexico, 546.

Migration, Guyanese. US, 2783.

Migration, Internal. *See* Internal Migration.

Migration, Irish. Argentina, 1344.

Migration, Italian. Argentina, 1317. Brazil, 1641, 1669, 1675. Mexico, 575.

Migration, Japanese. Bolivia, 1212. Mexico, 648. Peru, 1196.

Migration, Jewish. Argentina, 1318, 1395, 1438. Chile, 1242.

Migration, Latin American. US, 431.

Migration, Mexican. Music, 2711. US, 536, 625, 653, 655.

Migration, Portuguese. Brazil, 1595.

Migration, Puerto Rican. US, 918.
Migration, Russian. Paraguay, 1512.
Migration, Spanish, 317. Central America, 755. Cuba, 787, 887. Mexico, 484.
Migration, Welsh. Argentina, 1337, 1339.
Milanés, José Jacinto, 1933.
Militarism. Brazil, 1655. Dominican Republic, 950. Political Left, 1655.
Military. Nicaragua, 757.
Military Government. Brazil, 1570, 1666. Interviews, 1666.
Military History, 358, 365, 438. Argentina, 1028, 1037, 1046, 1313, 1324, 1328, 1380, 1388, 1437, 1443. Bibliography, 1701. Bolivia, 1000, 1166, 1197. Brazil, 1524, 1526, 1542, 1544, 1587, 1600, 1638, 1655, 1658, 1679, 1701. British Caribbean, 827. Chile, 1238, 1253. Colombia, 1123. Colonization, 1587. Costa Rica, 713. Cuba, 784, 838, 870, 925. Diplomacy, 1633. Diseases, 1603. Dominican Republic, 786, 888, 907, 929, 950. Ecuador, 973. Guatemala, 773. Jamaica, 790, 819. Mexico, 487, 515, 585, 668, 688, 773. Newspapers, 685. Nicaragua, 744, 750, 761. Paraguay, 1490, 1501, 1518. Peronism, 1385. Peru, 1166. Photography, 1328. Racism, 827. Río de la Plata (region), 1034. Uruguay, 1028, 1506, 1508. Venezuela, 1059, 1068, 1088. Women, 1253.
Military Intervention, British. Argentina, 1028, 1034, 1037. Uruguay, 1028, 1034.
Military Intervention, US. Dominican Republic, 884. Grenada, 942.
Military Occupation, US. Dominican Republic, 896, 900, 929, 950, 952. Mexico, 688.
Military Police. Brazil, 1690.
Military Policy. Venezuela, 1068.
Minas Gerais, Brazil (state). Architecture, 164. Baroque Art, 127. Blacks, 129. City Planning, 164. Cults, 129. Discovery and Exploration, 1619. Feminism, 1676. Frontier and Pioneer Life, 1619. Gender Relations, 1676. Gold, 1599, 1619. Historiography, 1611. Musical History, 2857–2858. Nationalism, 1599. Pottery, 158. Religious Music, 2858. Social Classes, 1625. Social Conditions, 1625. Urbanization, 1680. Women, 1676.
Minerals and Mining Industry. Bolivia, 53, 974, 1210, 1223. Catholic Church, 53. Chile, 1262, 1269. Colombia, 1114. Mexico, 558, 595. Peru, 990. Photography, 1210. Trade Unions, 558.

Mintz, Sidney Wilfred, 799.
Miracles. *See* Apparitions and Miracles.
Miranda, Carmen, 2867, 2904, 2910.
Miró, Joan, 2480.
Miró Quesada Laos, Carlos, 2055.
Misiones, Argentina (prov.). Political Leadership, 1403.
Miskito Coast (Nicaragua and Honduras). *See* Mosquitia (Nicaragua and Honduras).
Miskito (indigenous group). Colonial History, 736.
Missionaries. Argentina, 267, 1420. Brazil, 1574, 1586, 1604, 1668. Colonial History, 23. Diaries, 1574. Guatemala, 496. Indigenous Languages, 496. Jamaica, 833. Mexico, 452.
Missions. Architecture, 36. Bolivia, 490. Brazil, 1604, 1618. Catholic Church, 342. Colonial History, 1013. Economic Development, 1604. Honduras, 720. Mexico, 490. Paraguay, 258.
Mita. Bolivia, 286. Peru, 259.
Moctezuma Family, 203.
Modern Art, 68. Argentina, 99. Art Exhibitions, 69. Brazil, 121, 123, 134–136, 138–139, 141–142, 145–156. Colombia, 106, 109, 111. Costa Rica, 88. Cuba, 91. Mexico, 39, 69, 75–76, 86, 457. Paraguay, 113. Slaves and Slavery, 168. Venezuela, 118.
Modernism (art), 68. Brazil, 141, 148. Chile, 103. Venezuela, 118.
Modernism (literature). Brazil, 2403, 2461–2462, 2473. Caribbean Area, 1931. Peru, 3010. Philosophy, 3010. Puerto Rico, 1909, 2157.
Modernism (music). Chile, 2844. Peru, 2811.
Modernity. Argentina, 1336. Bolivia, 1221. Colonial History, 507. Guatemala, 756.
Modernization. Argentina, 1303, 1384, 1426. Bolivia, 1206. Brazil, 1542, 1690. Caribbean Area, 926. Colombia, 1097. Mexico, 565–566. Paraguay, 1507. Peru, 1180. Puerto Rico, 847. Social Classes, 1191. Sports, 1527.
Molinar, Diego Luis, 85.
Monagas, Julio Enrique, 944.
Monarchs. *See* Kings and Rulers.
Monasteries. Mexico, 46. *See Also* Convents.
Monasticism and Religious Orders. Brazil, 1618.
Monetary Policy. Colombia, 965.

Money. Colombia, 965. Colonial History, 715. Spain, 339.
Monteagudo, Bernardo, 2109.
Monterrey, Mexico (city). Mass Media, 528. Military History, 479.
Montevideo, Uruguay (city). Civilization, 1023. Housing, 1511. Political History, 1012. Slaves and Slavery, 359.
Montezuma II, *Emperor of Mexico (ca. 1480–1520)*, 231.
Monuments. Brazil, 1582. Cuba, 925. Mexico, 615.
Mora, Juan Rafael, 738, 767, 770.
Morales Córdova, Ángel, 951.
Morales Jorge, María, 775.
Morales Languasco, Carlos Felipe, 898.
Morals. *See* Ethics.
Morán, Francisco, 737.
Morant Bay Rebellion (Jamaica, 1865), 860.
Moravians. Jamaica, 833.
Morelia, Mexico (city). Music, 2745–2746.
Morelos, José María, 469, 572.
Moreno, Mariano, 1033, 1383.
Moreno, Nahuel, 1413.
Mormons. Mexico, 452.
Mortuary Customs. Mexico, 574. *See Also* Cemeteries.
Mosquitia (Nicaragua and Honduras). Description and Travel, 711. Discovery and Exploration, 711.
Mosquito (indigenous group). *See* Miskito (indigenous group).
Motherhood. Brazil, 1695. Caribbean Area, 934. Race and Race Relations, 934.
Motion Pictures. *See* Film.
Movimiento de Izquierda Revolucionaria (Chile), 1232.
Movimiento de Izquierda Revolucionaria (Venezuela), 1071.
Movimiento de Liberación Nacional (Uruguay), 1518.
Movimiento Revolucionario Túpac Amaru (Peru), 298.
Mulata de Córdoba (opera), 629.
Muleteers. Brazil, 1647.
Multiculturalism, 2964, 2987. Puerto Rico, 789.
Multinational Corporations. Mexico, 570.
Munguía, Clemente de Jesús, 591.
Muñoz Marín, Luis, 928, 953.
Muñoz Rivera, Luis, 795.
Museo de Arte de Lima, 57.
Museo Nacional de Colombia, 1126.
Museo Nacional de México, 527.
Museu de Arte do Rio, 168.
Museu de Arte do Rio Grande do Sul Ado Malagoli, 186.
Museum Exhibitions. *See* Art Exhibitions. *See* Museums.
Museums. Argentina, 1451. Brazil, 186, 1536, 1709, 1717. Mexico, 527, 533. *See Also* Art Exhibitions.
Music, 2675. African Influences, 2682, 2712, 2757, 2875, 2890, 2900, 2908, 2916. Bibliography, 2774. Brazil, 2884, 2906, 2908. Caribbean Area, 2774, 2779. Community Development, 2805. Confraternities, 2737. Cuba, 2777, 2793–2794. Cultural Identity, 943. Dictatorships, 2825. Dominican Republic, 943. Education, 2745, 2770, 2776, 2782, 2785, 2828, 2892, 2941, 2949, 2957. European Influences, 2746. Festivals, 2691. Film, 2934. German Influences, 2886. Iconography, 2891. Indigenous Influences, 2682. Jamaica, 2782. Japanese, 2946. Linguistics, 2744. Mexican Influences, 2763. Mexico, 2718, 2732. National Identity, 2747. Nationalism, 2681, 2872, 2951–2952. Peace, 2676. Research, 2679, 2732, 2916. Semiotics, 2744. Sex Roles, 2902. Social History, 2935. Spanish Influences, 2763. Technological Development, 2721. Theory, 2911. Venezuela, 2828. Violence, 2805, 2937. Women, 2691.
Music Criticism, 2674–2675, 2677. Andean Region, 2815. Brazil, 2548, 2855, 2857, 2860–2861, 2870, 2872, 2886, 2892, 2894, 2929, 2957. Colombia, 2805. Mexico, 2688, 2701, 2720, 2741, 2755. Peru, 2815–2817, 2822, 2824–2825.
Music Industry. Brazil, 2856, 2953, 2955. Mexico, 2705, 2721, 2747.
Música, 2798.
Musical History, 2674, 2676–2677, 2679–2680. African Influences, 2822, 2853. Andean Region, 2800, 2809. Argentina, 2800, 2832–2837, 2839. Blacks, 2810. Brazil, 2548, 2862–2864, 2869, 2878, 2886, 2888, 2891, 2953. Caribbean Area, 2778. Chile, 2844–2846, 2848, 2851. Colombia, 2804. Cuba, 2797. Dictatorships, 2844. Ecuador, 2808. Film, 2850. Jews, 2836. Labor and Laboring Classes, 2820. Mexican-American Border Region, 2692. Mexico, 2686, 2715–2717, 2720–2721, 2747, 2758, 2760. Peru, 2809–2810, 2820–2822. Uruguay, 2853. Women, 2704.

Musical Instruments. African Influences, 2819. Argentina, 2829. Brazil, 2897, 2915, 2927. Chile, 2852. Colonial History, 2730–2731, 2852. Mexico, 2716, 2728, 2760, 2762. Peru, 2819.
Musicals. Brazil, 2866, 2888, 2896. Colombia, 2331. Mexican Influences, 2733–2734. US, 2733–2734. *See Also* Zarzuelas.
Musicians, 2679–2680. Andean Region, 2826. Biography, 2826. Brazil, 2376, 2517, 2859, 2874, 2892, 2903, 2916, 2938, 2957. Caribbean Area, 2772, 2776. Chile, 2844. Colonial History, 2756. Dominican Republic, 943. Ethnic Identity, 2841. Interviews, 67. Jamaica, 2782. Jews, 2841. Mexico, 692, 2687, 2689, 2705, 2707, 2715, 2732, 2761, 2769. Rock Music, 2837.
Musicologists. Cuba, 2757. Mexico, 2757.
Musicology. Brazil, 2871, 2881, 2922, 2926, 2942, 2949, 2952, 2956. Cuba, 2796. Mexico, 2709, 2717, 2732, 2767.
Muslims, 419.
Mussolini, Benito, 1761.
Mystery Stories. *See* Detective and Mystery Stories.
Mysticism. Peru, 991.
Myths and Mythology. Andean Region, 225. Decorative Arts, 14. Incas, 283. Indigenous Art, 14. Mayas, 225. Mesoamerica, 225. Peru, 268.
Nahuas (indigenous group). Catholicism, 197. Codices, 201, 233, 243. Community Development, 220. Death, 219. Deities, 241. Epidemics, 233. Ethnic Groups and Ethnicity, 191. Ethnography, 222. Ethnohistory, 191, 195, 221. Governors, 195. Historiography, 243. Hunting, 228. Landowners, 224. Language and Languages, 197. Law and Legislation, 224. Medicine, 229, 233. Mexico, 208. Myths and Mythology, 225, 228. Political Conditions, 220. Regional Government, 220. Religion, 197, 476. Religious Life and Customs, 219, 228. Spanish Conquest, 192. US, 221. Wills, 224. Women, 224, 229. Writing, 197, 201, 219.
Nahuatl (language), 201. Books, 1751. Mexico, 219. Religion, 496. Social Structure, 496. Writing, 213.
Narborough, John, 1009.
Nariño, Colombia (dept.), 1135. Rural Conditions, 1144.
Narratives. Brazil, 1636. Wars of Independence, 1340.
Nascimento, Milton, 2885.

Natal, Brazil (city). Social History, 1541. Urbanization, 1541. World War II (1939–1945), 1541, 1544.
Nation-Building. *See* State-Building.
National Autonomy. *See* Autonomy.
National Characteristics, 24, 331, 406. Argentina, 2910. Bolivia, 3021. Brazil, 2910. Chile, 1002, 1241. Mexico, 533. Peru, 1187. Spain, 413. Venezuela, 1056. *See Also* National Identity.
National Defense. *See* National Security.
National Geographic Magazine, 892, 926–927.
National Identity, 2973, 3001. Argentina, 1406, 1412, 3035. Art, 81. Art History, 79, 81. Brazil, 133, 182, 1533, 1536, 1561, 1717. Chile, 103. Colombia, 1094, 1134, 3005. Cuba, 1912. Dominican Republic, 781. Mexico, 79, 2992. Paraguay, 1491, 1494, 1513. Periodicals, 1536. Peru, 3014. Philosophy, 2992, 3005. *See Also* National Characteristics.
National Patrimony. Cuba, 925. Mexico, 527.
National Security. Colombia, 1123.
Nationalism, 337, 3022. Argentina, 1292, 1344, 1372, 1382, 1430, 1432. Art, 81. Bolivia, 1228–1229. Brazil, 163, 1599, 2872. Chile, 3025. Colombia, 389, 1134. Economic Policy, 1468. Literary Criticism, 1938. Mexico, 81, 585, 615, 2990. Music, 2936. Panama, 780. Paraguay, 1201, 1492. Peru, 1187. Philosophy, 3041. Puerto Rico, 877, 893, 944, 953, 1938. Trinidad and Tobago, 914. Uruguay, 1510, 1519.
Nationbuilding. *See* State-Building.
Natural History. Argentina, 1451. Brazil, 188. Caribbean Area, 788. Paraguay, 1039. Pictorial Works, 16.
Natural Resources. Bolivia, 1228–1229. Mexico, 676.
Naufragios, 491.
Naval History. Brazil, 1620, 1633, 1694. Portugal, 1620. South America, 866. *See Also* Maritime History.
Navigation. Central America, 730. Pacific Ocean, 1743.
Nazi Influences. Argentina, 1370. Chile, 1253. Ecuador, 1150. *See Also* Nazism.
Nazis. *See* Nazism.
Nazism. Argentina, 1370, 1432. Brazil, 1698. Mexico, 650. *See Also* Nazi Influences.
Nederlandsche Oost-Indische Compagnie, 1624.

Neighborhood Associations. Argentina, 1394. Political Participation, 1394.
Neoliberalism, 424. Argentina, 1474. Art, 104. Chile, 104, 3025. Grenada, 942. Mexico, 666.
Neuquén, Argentina (prov.). Political History, 1458.
Neutrality. Argentina, 1478.
Neves, Tancredo, 1555.
New Jewel Movement (Grenada), 942.
New Mexico, US (state). Church History, 509. Colonial History, 499. Ethnic Groups and Ethnicity, 221. Ethnic Identity, 221. Folk Music, 2763. Franciscans, 499, 509. History, 560. Indigenous Peoples, 2736. Inquisition, 495. Marranos, 495. Musical History, 2763. Nahuas (indigenous group), 221. Slaves and Slavery, 2736. Songs, 2736.
New York, New York (city). Ethnography, 2840. Mexicans, 2769. Music, 2769. Tango, 2840.
Newspapers. Argentina, 1427. Art Criticism, 102. Bolivia, 102. Brazil, 1605, 1651, 1719. Colombia, 1108. Colonial History, 981. Communism and Communist Parties, 426. Cultural Development, 1719. Dominican Republic, 884, 941. Ecuador, 1151. Government, Resistance to, 1651. Independence Movements, 389. Mexico, 464, 592. Paraguay, 1491. Peronism, 1427. Peru, 1182. *See Also* Journalism.
Nezahualcóyotl, *King of Texcoco*, 1732.
Nicaragua. Ejército Popular Sandinista, 744.
Nicaragua. Guardia Nacional, 750, 761.
Nicoya Peninsula (Costa Rica). History, 712.
Niemeyer, Oscar, 174.
Nietzsche, Friedrich Wilhelm, 3030.
Nitrate Industry. Chile, 1249, 1280.
Nobility. Audiencia of Quito, 971. Colonial History, 203. Genealogy, 203.
Noé, Luis Felipe, 99.
Notaries. Venezuela, 1079.
Novás Calvo, Lino, 1944.
Nuevo Santander, New Spain (prov.). History, 487.
Núñez Cabeza de Vaca, Alvar, 491.
Nuns. Mexico, 33, 1720. Painting, 28.
Nutrition. Brazil, 1661. Chile, 1251.
Oaxaca, Mexico (state). Labor and Laboring Classes, 609. Railroads, 609.
Obregón, Álvaro, 702.
Oceanography, 332.
Odriozola Odriozola, Miguel Ángel, 48.
Ohtake, Tomie, 144.

Oiticica, Hélio, 124.
Oito Batutas (musical group), 2922.
Olderock, Ingrid, 1253.
Olympics. Mexico, 74.
Opera. Chile, 2842. European Influences, 2842. Mexico, 589, 2695, 2747, 2753–2754.
Operettas. *See* Musicals. *See* Zarzuelas.
Oral History. Argentina, 1333. Mexico, 661. Peronism, 1333. Peru, 1165.
Orbón, Julián, 2719.
Organización Montoneros (Argentina), 1310.
Organs (musical instrument). Mexico, 2730–2731, 2742.
Orinoco River Region (Venezuela and Colombia), 1083.
Orozco, Danilo, 2796.
Orozco, Gabriel, 83.
Orozco, Wistano Luis, 596.
Ortiz, Fernando, 2793.
Oruro, Bolivia (city). History, 1227. Modernity, 1227.
Oruro, Bolivia (dept.). Indigenous Peoples, 1203.
Otomí (indigenous group). Myths and Mythology, 225. Writing, 213.
Ouro Preto, Brazil (city). Abandoned Children, 1592. Church History, 1592. Social Conditions, 1592.
Outlaws. Mexico, 578.
Páez (indigenous group). Land Tenure, 290, 296.
Painters. Argentina, 99. Biography, 75. Brazil, 132, 134, 138, 148. British, 95. Costa Rica, 87. Cuba, 95. Ecuador, 61. Mexico, 75. Paraguay, 1495. Women, 87.
Painting, 22. Brazil, 134. Colombia, 19. Costa Rica, 87. Mexico, 40. Peru, 51, 56.
Palacios, Alfredo, 3039.
Palafox y Mendoza, Juan de, 2766.
Palenque Site (Mexico). Civilization, 543.
Palma, Ricardo, 3013–3014.
Palmira, Colombia (city). Marginalized Peoples, 1141.
Palomares López, Cecilio Pastor, 801.
Pampa, Argentina (prov.). *See* La Pampa, Argentina (prov.).
Pan-Africanism. Brazil, 2868. Caribbean Area, 889.
Pan-Americanism. History, 391.
Panama Canal. History, 780.
Panama Canal Treaties (1977), 780.
Pape, Lygia, 124.
Papel periódico ilustrado, 1126.
Paraguaná Peninsula, Venezuela. History, 1078.

Paraguayan War (1865–1870). Argentina/Brazil, 1489. Historiography, 1501. Newspapers, 1491. Oral History, 1498. Painters, 1495. Paraguay, 1490. Poetry, 2470. Political History, 1497.
Paraíba do Sul River Valley, Brazil. Atlantic Trade, 1567. Haitian Revolution (1787–1794), 1567. Slaves and Slavery, 1567.
Paraná, Brazil (state). Flowers, 178. Missions, 1637.
Parenthood. Costa Rica, 727.
Parinacochas, Peru (prov.). Indigenous Peoples, 304. Myths and Mythology, 304.
Paris, France (city). Brazilians, 1520.
Parliamentary Systems. *See* Political Systems.
Parnamirim Air Base (Brazil), 1541.
Partido Aprista Peruana. *See* APRA (Peru).
Partido Aprista Peruano. *See* APRA (Peru).
Partido Comunista de la Argentina, 754.
Partido Comunista do Brasil, 1521.
Partido Comunista Mexicano, 689.
Partido Liberal Mexicano, 618.
Partido Revolucionario de los Trabajadores, 1379, 1413.
Partido Socialista (Argentina), 1393.
Pasta, Paulo, 138.
Pasto, Colombia (dept.). Economic History, 1146. Local History, 1146. Social Conditions, 1146.
Pastures. Patagonia (region), 1255.
Patagonia, Argentina (prov.). Colonial History, 1442. Colonization, 1442. Cultural History, 1348. Germans, 1442. Immigrants, 1315, 1337, 1348. Indigenous/Non-Indigenous Relations, 1473. Language and Languages, 1337. Photography, 1315. Political Development, 1360. Race and Race Relations, 1473. Rural Development, 1315. State-Building, 1360. Welsh, 1337, 1348.
Paternalism. Chile, 1286. *See Also* Sexism.
Patronage, Political. *See* Clientelism.
Paz, Bolivia (city). *See* La Paz, Bolivia (city).
Paz, Octavio, 2299.
Peace. El Salvador, 745, 751.
Peace Corps (US), 1206.
Peacekeeping Forces. Brazil, 1545, 1639.
Peasant Movements. Mexico, 576.
Peasant Uprisings. Guatemala, 769.
Peasants. Music, 2796. Nicaragua, 772. Peru, 1176–1177, 1188.
Peddlers. *See* Informal Sector.
Pedro I, *Emperor of Brazil*, 1552, 1706.

Pedro II, *Emperor of Brazil*, 1553.
Pedrosa, Mário, 123. Interviews, 187.
Peforming Arts, 62.
Pellicer, Carlos, 85.
Pensions. Paraguay, 1501.
Penteado, João de Camargo, 1548.
Pereira, Edimilson de Almeida, 2528.
Pérez Prado, 2757.
Performing Arts. Andean Region, 2800. Argentina, 2800. Art History, 70. Caribbean Area, 1930. Chile, 2842. Feminism, 62. Interviews, 70. Mexico, 70. Political History, 70. Sexism, 62. Social Conditions, 70. Violence, 73.
Periodicals. Anarchism and Anarchists, 1353. Argentina, 1375. Brazil, 183, 1536. Catholicism, 1466. Children's Literature, 1466. Cooking, 1320. Discourse Analysis, 1353. Mexico, 528, 1736. Nationalism, 1292. Students, 183.
Pernambuco, Brazil (state). Intellectual History, 1582. Monuments, 1582.
Perón, Eva, 1389, 2084.
Perón, Evita. *See* Perón, Eva.
Perón, Juan Domingo, 1338, 1389–1390.
Peronism. Argentina, 1290, 1293, 1295, 1301, 1310, 1321, 1326, 1331, 1333, 1338, 1354, 1365, 1372, 1385, 1390, 1393, 1405, 1407, 1409, 1427, 1439, 1470, 3033, 3038, 3042. Biography, 1427. Catholic Church, 1432. Cultural History, 1415. European Influences, 1338. Exiles, 1472. Government, Resistance to, 1333. Historiography, 1365, 1416. Interviews, 1295. Labor and Laboring Classes, 1468. Musical History, 2839. Narratives, 1340. Nazism, 1432. Philosophy, 2978. Political Culture, 2829. Political Development, 1439. Political Ideology, 1439. Political Leadership, 1472, 1474. Political Violence, 1368. Regional Development, 1405, 1416. Socialism, 1393. Songs, 2830. Symbolism, 1415. Women, 1409.
Peru-Bolivian Confederation, 1216.
Pesticides. Central America, 743. Law and Legislation, 743.
Petroleum Industry and Trade. Bolivia, 1228–1229. Mexico, 565, 701. Venezuela, 1075, 1080–1081.
Pharmacy. Chile, 1276.
Philanthropists. Mexico, 513.
Philosophers, 2978. Argentina, 3036, 3038, 3042. Chile, 3026. Colombia, 1118. Cuba, 2980. Germany, 3009. Interviews, 3026. Peru, 3017.

Philosophy, 2959, 2965, 2970–2971, 2977–2978, 2980, 2987–2988. African Influences, 2998. Andean Region, 3008. Art, 98. Brazil, 1549. Caribbean Area, 2997, 2999. Colombia, 3003, 3007. Colonial Discourse, 3006. Colonial History, 3004. Colonization, 1549. Decolonization, 3008. French Influences, 3007. German Influences, 2963, 3036. Intellectual History, 2971. Liberation Theology, 2979. Linguistics, 2995. Literature, 2992. Mexico, 542, 2992–2993, 2995. National Identity, 2992. Peru, 3014, 3017. Poetry, 2148. Postmodernism, 3016. Spain, 2966. Uruguay, 2968, 3030. *See Also* Epistemology; Ethics.

Philosophy of Liberation. *See* Liberation Theology.

Photographers. Blacks, 96. Brazil, 161. Caribbean Area, 96.

Photography. Architecture, 161. Argentina, 1300, 1315, 1327. Blacks, 159. Bolivia, 1210. Brazil, 160, 1536. Caribbean Area, 926–927. Chile, 105. Collective Memory, 1327. Dictatorships, 105. Exhibitions, 160–161. Government, Resistance to, 105. Honduras, 746. Puerto Rico, 851, 892, 926. Race and Race Relations, 96. Slaves and Slavery, 168.

Physicians. Blacks, 979. Colonial History, 1752.

Piano. Mexico, 2693.

Piauí, Brazil (state). Leprosy, 1634.

Pichincha, Ecuador (prov.). Economic History, 970.

Pictorial Works. Brazil, 160.

Piglia, Ricardo, 2132.

Pinacoteca Marqués del Jaral de Berrio, 2715.

Pinglo Alva, Felipe, 2824.

Pino Suárez, José María, 672.

Pinochet, Augusto, 105.

Pioneer Life. *See* Frontier and Pioneer Life.

Pirates, 362. Great Britain, 790. Jamaica, 790. Mexico, 196. South America, 866. Viceroyalty of Río de la Plata (1776–1810), 1038. *See Also* Buccaneers; Smuggling.

Piro (indigenous group). Economic Conditions, 249. Land Tenure, 249.

Plantations. Barbados, 817. Brazil, 1535. British Caribbean, 794, 828. Cattle Raising and Trade, 1535. Children, 842. Honduras, 746. Industry and Industrialization, 829. Jamaica, 828–829, 831, 872. Pregnancy, 879. Saint-Domingue, 829. Slaves and Slavery, 1535. US, 794. *See Also* Haciendas.

Plata, Argentina (city). *See* La Plata, Argentina (city).

Playwrights. Argentina, 2318, 2326. Mexico, 2330, 2359. Puerto Rico, 1922.

Plebiscites. *See* Referendums.

Poetry. Argentina, 1332. Bolivia, 2144, 2164, 2191, 2280, 2288. Books, 180. Brazil, 2397, 2421, 2459, 2462, 2472, 2492, 2520–2521, 2533, 2541–2542. Caribbean Area, 2167. Colonial Literature, 1727. Ecuador, 2150, 2152, 2161, 2172, 2179, 2190, 2209, 2223, 2247–2248, 2268, 2270. Guatemala, 2227. Mexico, 2224. Nature, 2167. Panama, 1869. Paraguay, 2250. Physicians, 1752. Puerto Rico, 2148–2149, 2157. Religious Art, 2154.

Poets. Argentina, 2319. Brazil, 2461, 2521, 2540, 2913. Cuba, 1933. Dominican Republic, 936. Interviews, 67. Puerto Rico, 2149, 2157.

Police, 314, 320. Brazil, 1690, 1711. Chile, 1231. Corruption, 1219. Social History, 1711.

Political Boundaries. *See* Boundaries.

Political Campaigns. *See* Elections.

Political Candidates. *See* Politicians.

Political Conditions, 341, 406. Argentina, 1312, 1342, 1350, 1352, 1372, 1401. Art, 119. Bolivia, 1218. Brazil, 1556, 1657. Chile, 1232, 1243, 1267, 1282. Nicaragua, 762. Puerto Rico, 930. Venezuela, 118–119, 1072.

Political Corruption, 360. Airlines, 1560. Argentina, 1345. Bolivia, 1219. Brazil, 1524. Chile, 1255. Colombia, 1109. Colonial History, 371. Dominican Republic, 951. Mexico, 549. Venezuela, 1072.

Political Crimes. Argentina, 1457.

Political Culture, 346, 408. Argentina, 1363, 1422, 1445, 1474, 2830. Brazil, 1649, 2887. Chile, 1277. Gender Relations, 1363. Historiography, 1422. Mexico, 585. Rural Conditions, 1363.

Political Development. Argentina, 1314, 1316, 1325, 1360, 1376, 1388, 1402, 1411, 1414, 1439, 1441, 1459. Brazil, 1687. Caribbean Area, 809. Chile, 1232, 1245, 1275, 1277. Colombia, 1100–1101, 1104, 1109, 1121, 1125, 1144. Ecuador, 1157. Jamaica, 931.

Political Economy. Colombia, 1118. Venezuela, 1062. *See Also* Economic Policy.

Political Geography. Colombia, 1133.

Political History, 321, 330, 411–412, 415, 438, 1513. Argentina, 1018, 1031, 1290, 1293, 1307, 1311, 1314, 1329, 1349, 1351, 1362, 1376, 1389–1390, 1401–1402, 1410, 1414, 1419, 1430, 1458, 1480, 1486, 1488, 3043. Art History, 72. Assassinations, 924. Barbados, 821. Belize, 706. Bolivia, 1211, 1217, 1222, 3022. Brazil, 1529, 1540, 1546, 1569, 1580, 1605, 1632, 1642, 1660, 1692–1693, 1700, 1705. Caribbean Area, 844. Chile, 1010, 1243, 1245, 1247–1248, 1254, 1257. Church-State Relations, 1540. Colombia, 967, 1070, 1106, 1109, 1115, 1120, 1142. Colonial Administration, 1607. Costa Rica, 713, 738, 748–749, 753, 765–767, 770, 778. Cuba, 902, 909, 933. Dominican Republic, 786, 800, 806, 858, 885, 898, 907, 910, 924. Ecuador, 1152. El Salvador, 745, 751–752, 763. Historiography, 1452. Jamaica, 931, 948. Journalism, 1605. Law and Legislation, 1540. Mexico, 444, 537, 540, 549, 579, 599, 613, 616, 628, 644, 674, 680. Newspapers, 1605. Nicaragua, 761–762, 764. Paraguay, 1518. Peronism, 1372, 1470. Peru, 1172, 1185. Political Ideology, 1540. Popular Music, 2849. Printing Industry, 71. Puerto Rico, 782, 789, 795, 856, 893, 935, 944, 947, 953. Radicalism, 1407. Socialism and Socialist Parties, 1453. Sociology, 1311. Spanish Influences, 1366. Suriname, 911. Trinidad and Tobago, 913–914. Venezuela, 957, 1048–1050, 1052–1053, 1055, 1063, 1069, 1071, 1077, 1082, 3002.

Political Ideology, 3001. Argentina, 1310, 1332, 1364, 1439, 1452–1453, 1477. Brazil, 1540. Chile, 1254. Church-State Relations, 1540. Ecuador, 1152. El Salvador, 745. *See Also* Political Thought.

Political Institutions. Río de la Plata (region), 1041.

Political Leadership, 1076, 2985. Argentina, 1299, 1342, 1345, 1369, 1373, 1383, 1389, 1391, 1414, 1417, 1419, 1424, 1427, 1447, 1471–1472, 1480. Biography, 1471, 1555. Brazil, 1546, 1552, 1569, 1633, 1644. Chile, 1257, 1270. Colombia, 1121. Colonial History, 2985. Dominican Republic, 885. Mexico, 674. Peronism, 1427. Radicalism, 1417. Uruguay, 1504–1505, 1510, 1514.

Political Left, 343. Argentina, 1305, 1331, 1448. Bolivia, 1209. Brazil, 1551, 1655. Chile, 1232, 1237, 1248, 1270, 1276. Jamaica, 948. Literature, 1305. Peru, 1165.

Political Philosophy, 2969. Russian Influences, 1448. Student Movements, 693. Venezuela, 1071.

Political Movements. Argentina, 1382, 1444, 1461. Jamaica, 915. Mexico, 2989.

Political Participation, 341, 436, 2964. Andean Region, 2809. Argentina, 1047, 1386, 1399, 1461, 1471. Blacks, 2797. Bolivia, 2802. Brazil, 1628, 1638. Caribbean Area, 904. Chile, 1268, 1281, 1283. Colombia, 1089. Dominican Republic, 916. Elections, 699. Grenada, 942. Mexico, 598, 643, 666, 686. Peru, 1165. Universities, 638. Women, 390, 643, 916.

Political Parties. Argentina, 1311, 1364, 1370, 1445, 1488. Brazil, 1521. Chile, 1268, 1270, 1277, 1282. Colombia, 1089, 1106, 1119. Costa Rica, 748. Jamaica, 931. Mexico, 2990. Puerto Rico, 782. Radicalism, 1407, 1410, 1693. Venezuela, 1066, 1071.

Political Patronage. *See* Clientelism.

Political Philosophy, 2961, 2964–2965, 2972, 2975, 2981, 3001, 3044. Abolition (slavery), 2985. Anarchism and Anarchists, 2967. Argentina, 3033, 3035, 3037–3039, 3042–3043. Bolivia, 3018, 3020–3023. Caribbean Area, 2997–2998. Chile, 3024. Colombia, 3003, 3015. Colonial History, 2985. Cuba, 3000. German Influences, 3020. Guerrillas, 2962. Imperialism, 2975. Mexico, 552. Paraguay, 2967. Peru, 3010. Socialism and Socialist Parties, 3000, 3039. Uruguay, 2967, 3031–3032. Venezuela, 3002.

Political Prisoners. Argentina, 1309, 1428. Brazil, 1526, 1638, 1698. Chile, 2843. Interviews, 1428. Massacres, 1309. Paraguay, 1500. Puerto Rico, 877.

Political Reform, 321. Cuba, 2794.

Political Repression. Brazil, 1698.

Political Science. Colombia, 1101.

Political Systems. Mexico, 537. Venezuela, 1052.

Political Theory. Argentina, 1352.

Political Thought, 2959, 2975. Argentina, 1381. Bolivia, 3020, 3023. Brazil, 1692. Caribbean Area, 2998. Chile, 3024. Cuba, 933, 939. El Salvador, 759. Imperialism, 2975. Nicaragua, 742. Peronism, 1390. Puerto Rico, 890. Uruguay, 3032. *See Also* Political Ideology; Political Philosophy.

Political Violence, 316, 409–410, 416, 435, 438. Argentina, 1368, 1371, 1425. Brazil, 1705. Colombia, 1135. Colonial History,

986. Dominican Republic, 907. Guatemala, 775. Interviews, 1371. Mexico, 541. Peru, 1170. See Also Violence.
Politicians. Abolition (slavery), 1704. Brazil, 1704. Colombia, 1127. Education, 1716. Puerto Rico, 795, 899. Soccer, 1434. Venezuela, 1054, 1069.
Ponce, Puerto Rico (city). Commerce, 871. Slaves and Slavery, 876.
Poniatowska, Elena, 649.
Pontificia Universidad Javeriana. Facultad de Medicina, 1117.
Poor. Argentina, 1351. Chile, 1231, 1263, 1265.
Popayán, Colombia (city). Earthquakes, 1129. Local History, 1129. Public Health, 1129. Public Spaces, 1129.
Popul Vuh, 230.
Popular Art. Chile, 103. Colombia, 112. Mexico, 79.
Popular Culture, 2807. Alcohol and Alcoholism, 677. Argentina, 1431. Brazil, 1653, 2890. Colombia, 1130. Dominican Republic, 920. Mexico, 347. Narratives, 1636. Peru, 347, 2813–2814. Travel, 1560.
Popular Literature. Honduras, 1832–1833.
Popular Movements. See Social Movements.
Popular Music, 2678, 2680. Andean Region, 2809. Argentina, 2829, 2833, 2924. Bolivia, 2801–2802. Brazil, 2855, 2869, 2873–2874, 2876, 2878, 2887, 2890, 2894–2895, 2902, 2905, 2907, 2912, 2920–2926, 2928–2931, 2933, 2935, 2937–2938, 2941, 2943, 2948–2949, 2953–2955. Chile, 2844, 2847, 2849. Dominican Republic, 2775. Drug Traffic, 2703. Indigenous Influences, 2811. Labor and Laboring Classes, 2820. Mexican Americans, 2759. Mexico, 2686–2687, 2711, 2724, 2727, 2765. Peru, 2809, 2812–2814, 2820, 2823, 2825. Political Culture, 2887. Political History, 2849. Social Justice, 2682. US, 2711.
Popular Theater. Mexico, 2694. See Also Theater.
Population. Argentina, 1045. Brazil, 1648.
Population Growth. Brazil, 1622, 1715. Food Industry and Trade, 1688. Mexico, 441. See Also Birth Control.
Population Studies. See Demography.
Populism, 343, 436. Ecuador, 1160. Mexico, 2989–2990.
Portales, Diego José Víctor, 395.
Portillo, José López. See López Portillo, José.
Portinari, Cândido, 149.

Porto Alegre, Brazil (city). Music, 2870.
Portraits. Blacks, 159. Brazil, 132, 159. British Caribbean, 47, 826. Photography, 159.
Portuguese. Colonial History, 988. Peru, 988.
Portuguese Conquest. Brazil, 1615.
Portuguese Influences. Brazil, 1573, 1616, 1656, 1679. Mexico, 2749. Military History, 1679. Political History, 1623.
Positivism, 3013. Mexico, 552. Peru, 3013.
Postmodernism. Brazil, 2555. Political Philosophy, 3019.
Potosí, Bolivia (dept.). Colonization, 974.
Pottery. Peru, 58.
Pozo y Sucre, José del, 956.
Precolumbian Art, 2, 10. Art Collections, 57. Ceramics, 10. Colombia, 13. Ecuador, 13. Exhibitions, 1. Peru, 52, 57. Textiles and Textile Industry, 52. See Also Iconography.
Precolumbian Civilizations, 26. Archeology, 222. Architecture, 8. Art, 114. Chile, 294. Dyes and Dyeing, 22. Fish and Fishing, 250. Guatemala, 235. Inscriptions, 34. Mesoamerica, 222, 235. Mexico, 200, 223, 244. Murals, 9. Museums, 533. Painting, 5. Peru, 114. Philosophy, 2970, 3012. Urbanization, 9.
Precolumbian Sculpture. Mesoamerica, 202.
Pregnancy. Slaves and Slavery, 879.
Prehistory. See Archeology.
Presidential Systems. See Political Systems.
Presidents. Argentina, 1299, 1389–1390, 1410, 1418, 1424. Biography, 1390, 1410. Bolivia, 1217. Brazil, 1546, 1555, 1562. Colombia, 1120. Costa Rica, 738, 767, 770. Dominican Republic, 858, 885, 898. Mexico, 619, 628, 654, 690. Panama, 739. Uruguay, 1505, 1509. US, 690. Venezuela, 1055.
Press. See Mass Media.
Priests. See Clergy.
Prieto, Carlos, 2762.
Primary Education. See Elementary Education.
Prime Ministers. Trinidad and Tobago, 914.
Primer libro venezolano de literatura, ciencias y bellas artes, 1056.
Printers. See Printing Industry.
Printing Industry, 367. Brazil, 180. Colonial History, 981. Mexico, 71, 528. Political History, 71. Social History, 71.
Prints. Art History, 71. Mexico, 71.
Prisoners. Brazil, 1638. Chile, 1253. Mexico, 607.

Prisons. Education, 647. Mexico, 607, 650.
Private Enterprises. Argentina, 1426.
Private Schools. Cuba, 886.
Produce Trade. *See* Food Industry and Trade.
Propaganda, 417. Argentina, 981. Brazil, 1547. Film, 72. Mexico, 72, 635. Peru, 981, 1188.
Prostitution. Argentina, 1296, 1433. Jews, 1296. Mexico, 614, 663.
Protectionism. Jamaica, 868.
Protest Movements. *See* Protests.
Protesta (Buenos Aires), 1353.
Protesta Humana (Buenos Aires), 1353.
Protestant Churches. Chile, 1265.
Protestantism. Philosophy, 2960.
Protestants. Brazil, 1523, 1585, 1668. Dominican Republic, 894–895.
Protests. Brazil, 2506. Caribbean Area, 946. Colonial History, 731. Guatemala, 731.
Psychiatry. Argentina, 1483. Brazil, 1553.
Psychoanalysis. Argentina, 1483, 3037.
Psychology. Argentina, 1483. Biography, 1706.
Public Administration. Brazil, 1660, 1699. Mexico, 583.
Public Debt. Brazil, 1713. Colombia, 1100.
Public Education. Argentina, 1467, 1484. Brazil, 1661. Chile, 1258, 1260, 1264.
Public Finance, 366. Mexico, 485, 530, 601.
Public Health. Brazil, 1634, 1661, 1682, 1695, 1712. Chile, 1251, 1264, 1269. Colombia, 1107. Jamaica, 855. Mexico, 511, 553, 571, 574, 594, 663. Peru, 1166.
Public Opinion. Albania, 413. Brazil, 1692. Colombia, 389. Coups d'Etat, 1692. Mexico, 464, 566. Peru, 1195. Women's Rights, 634.
Public Opinion, US. Cuba, 945.
Public Policy. Mexico, 583.
Public Spaces. Brazil, 174.
Public Transportation. *See* Transportation.
Public Utilities. *See* Public Works.
Public Welfare. *See* Social Welfare.
Public Works. Argentina, 1426. Brazil, 169, 1661.
Publishers and Publishing. Argentina, 1357. Brazil, 180. Dominican Republic, 936. Mexico, 528. Poetry, 180.
Puebla, Mexico (city). Civilization, 593. Colonial History, 520. History, 620. Social History, 593. Social Life and Customs, 593.
Puebla, Mexico (state). Foreign Intervention, 545. Indigenous Peoples, 472. Sources, 545. Textiles and Textile Industry, 700. Women's Rights, 686.
Puerto Ricans. Dominican Republic, 952. US, 789, 918.
Puppets and Puppet Plays. Venezuela, 2322.
Purificación, Uruguay (city). History, 1506.
Quadros, Jânio, 1551.
Quechua (indigenous group). Catholiciism, 1725. Ecuador, 1159. Peru, 270.
Querétaro, Mexico (state). Catholic Church, 216–218. Church History, 513. Colonial History, 492, 513. Description and Travel, 447. Evangelistic Work, 217. Indigenous Peoples, 216–218. Land Tenure, 492. Local History, 447. Railroads, 639. Travelers, 447. Urban Development, 639.
Quetzalcoatl (Aztec deity), 241.
Quiché (indigenous group). History, 775.
Quijano, Carlos, 1516.
Quintanar, Héctor, 2698–2699.
Quiroga Santa Cruz, Marcelo, 1218.
Quito, Ecuador (city). Cabildos, 1153. History, 969. Regional Development, 1153.
Race and Race Relations, 2772, 2984. Antigua and Barbuda, 865. Argentina, 363, 1400, 1423, 1455, 1473, 1481. Art History, 92. Bahamas, 807. Barbados, 823. Belize, 706, 859. Bolivia, 1213–1214. Brazil, 423, 1559, 1659, 1683, 1697, 2854, 3029. Caribbean Area, 92, 824, 889. Colombia, 968, 1091, 1102, 1126, 3005. Cuba, 804, 849, 2794, 2797. Cultural Identity, 2794. Dominican Republic, 791, 908, 920. Jamaica, 816, 828, 836, 860, 931. Mexico, 363, 445, 563. Motherhood, 1695. Peru, 979, 1195. Philosophy, 2958, 3027, 3041. Photography, 96. Prisons, 1683. Puerto Rico, 854. US, 536. Viceroyalty of New Spain (1540–1821), 519. Viceroyalty of Peru (1542–1822), 976. Women, 830. *See Also* Eugenics; Racism.
Racism. Cuba, 804, 849. Dominican Republic, 781, 811. Haiti, 811. Mexico, 630. Scientific History, 853. *See Also* Race and Race Relations.
Radicalism. Argentina, 1322, 1373, 1407, 1410. Coups d'Etat, 1410. Political Parties, 1322. Youth, 1322.
Radio. Argentina, 1359. Bolivia, 1202. Brazil, 2912. Chile, 1285. Colombia, 1097, 1132. Mexico, 635. Propaganda, 635.
Radio Illimani (La Paz), 1202.
Railroads, 327. Argentina, 1426. Brazil, 1539, 1643, 1685. Construction Industry, 1539, 1685. Labor and Laboring Classes, 1539.

Mexico, 577, 609, 639. Puerto Rico, 847. Strikes and Lockouts, 609. Urbanization, 1643.
Rama, Angel, 2968.
Ramalho, Maria de Lourdes Nunes, 2564–2565.
Ramos, Nuno, 153.
Rangel, Lúcio, 2928.
Ranquel (indigenous group). Argentina, 1358. Indigenous/Non-Indigenous Relations, 277.
Rape. British Caribbean, 861.
Rastafarian Movement. Caribbean Area, 889. Jamaica, 915, 931.
Raymundo, Pedro, 2914.
Reading. Mexico, 1736.
Rebellions. See Insurrections.
Recife, Brazil (city). Photographers, 162. Photography, 162. Pictorial Works, 162. Police, 1711. Social Life and Customs, 2442.
Reclamation of Land. See Land Reform. See Land Tenure.
Reconquista, Argentina (city). Local History, 1464. Regional Development, 1464.
Redemocratization. See Democratization.
Redistribution of Wealth. See Income Distribution.
Reed, Dean, 2849.
Referendums. Venezuela, 1072.
Refugees. Communism and Communist Parties, 675. See Also Exiles.
Reggae Music, 2682.
Regional Development. Argentina, 1334, 1421, 1454, 1464. Bolivia, 1222. Brazil, 1537, 1703. Caribbean Area, 809. Chile, 1266. Colombia, 1104, 1135, 1140. Costa Rica, 215. Ecuador, 1154. Mesoamerica, 215. Mexico, 455, 459, 468, 579, 692, 696. Nicaragua, 215. Silver, 1614.
Regional Government. Argentina, 1293, 1298, 1356. Brazil, 1699, 1712. Mexico, 205.
Regional History. See Local History.
Regional Planning. Venezuela, 1078.
Regionalism, 337. Ecuador, 1154.
Reinaga, Fausto, 3019, 3027.
Religion. African Influences, 802. Audiencia of Chile, 1007. Caribbean Area, 2997. Colonial History, 977. Peru, 3014. Philosophy, 2959–2960.
Religion and Politics, 340, 347. Argentina, 1312, 1456. Brazil, 1585–1586, 1591. Caribbean Area, 802. Chile, 1233, 1271. Ecuador, 1152. Jamaica, 915. Mexico, 591.

Religious Art. Bolivia, 55, 1215. Chile, 252. Colombia, 19. Mexico, 28, 34. Nuns, 33. Puerto Rico, 2154. Women, 33.
Religious Life and Customs, 378, 512. Argentina, 1398. Brazil, 129, 1609, 1630. Caribbean Area, 802, 2786. Chile, 1271. Colombia, 1146. Colonial History, 481, 522, 733. Guatemala, 708, 733. Jamaica, 833, 2781. Mesoamerica, 207. Mexico, 32, 42, 444, 448. Río de la Plata (region), 1041. See Also Religion.
Religious Music, 1749, 2676. Brazil, 2877, 2897, 2915, 2919, 2939. Guatemala, 734. Guyana, 2783. Mexico, 2684, 2690, 2709, 2713, 2716, 2720, 2737–2738, 2740, 2742, 2752, 2758, 2766.
Repression, 316. Brazil, 1524.
Republicanism. Argentina, 1314, 1364. Colombia, 1101, 1141. Venezuela, 1077.
Research, 312. Colombia, 1142. Ecuador, 1155. Methodology, 345. See Also Bibliography.
Restoration. See Conservation and Restoration.
Return Migration. Mexico, 625–626. Spain, 317.
Reviews. See Art Criticism. See Film Criticism.
Revolution of the Comuneros. See Insurrection of the Comuneros (Paraguay, 1730–1735).
Revolutionaries. Argentina, 1033, 1295, 1330, 1379, 1383, 1391, 1440. Assassinations, 702. Autobiography, 664. Biography, 627. Cuba, 801, 875, 933, 954. Dominican Republic, 897, 900. Exiles, 664. Interviews, 645, 1295. Liberalism, 660. Mexico, 572, 578, 580, 600, 627–628, 647, 660, 664. Nicaragua, 742. Puerto Rico, 877. Uruguay, 1504, 1508, 1514. Women, 600, 1469.
Revolutionary Literature. Colombia, 1096.
Revolutions and Revolutionary Movements, 351, 399, 401, 407, 438, 2981. Argentina, 1295, 1319, 1323, 1325, 1330, 1340, 1354, 1366, 1379, 1413. Brazil, 1529, 1619, 1693. Chile, 1232. Collective Memory, 645. Colombia, 1096, 1115. Cuba, 784, 850, 870, 925, 932–933, 937–939, 1912. Dominican Republic, 897, 900. Ecuador, 1158. El Salvador, 763. Grenada, 942. Mexico, 451, 456, 469, 508, 540, 569, 621, 667, 702. Nicaragua, 750, 754, 764. Puerto Rico, 844. Radio, 635. Spanish Influences, 1366. Trade Unions, 1440. Venezuela, 1053, 1064, 1082. Women, 390, 629.

Reyes, Ernestina, 2773.
Reyes, Lucha, 2727.
Riaño, Juan Antonio de, 358.
Ribeiro, Maria, 2566.
Riedweg, Walter Stephan, 139.
Rimac River Valley (Peru). Folk Music, 2821. Indigenous Music, 2821. Land Use, 1162. Musical History, 2821.
Rio, João do, 1656.
Rio Branco, José Maria da Silva Paranhos Júnior, *Barão do*, 1633, 1674.
Río Cuarto, Argentina (city). Peronism, 1321. Political History, 1321.
Rio de Janeiro, Brazil (city). African Influences, 2882. Blacks, 2932–2933. Cemeteries, 1585. Church History, 1621. Cultural History, 1656. Freedmen, 1714. History, 1530. Jesuits, 1621. Labor and Laboring Classes, 1714. Music, 2928. Prisons, 1683. Race and Race Relations, 1683. Slaves and Slavery, 1714, 2882. Social Life and Customs, 2443. Street-Railroads, 1714. Transportation, 1714. Urbanization, 1680, 2882.
Rio de Janeiro, Brazil (state). Abolition (slavery), 1664. Beer Industry, 1689. Censuses, 1648. Coffee Industry and Trade, 1664. Immigrants, 1641. Italians, 1641. Political Conditions, 1699. Population, 1648. Public Administration, 1699. Railroads, 1643. Slaves and Slavery, 1664.
Río de la Plata (region). Bourbon Reforms, 1617. Colonization, 1027. Ethnic Groups and Ethnicity, 1594. Geographical History, 1043. History, 1019, 1034. Indigenous/Non-Indigenous Relations, 1594. Indigenous Peoples, 1017, 1590. Social Classes, 1594. Social Conditions, 1594.
Rio Grande do Sul, Brazil (state). Azoreans, 1595. Boundaries, 1596. Ethnic Groups and Ethnicity, 1595. Frontiers, 1596. Immigrants, 1595. International Relations, 1596.
Río Negro, Argentina (prov.). Political History, 1458.
Rioja, Argentina (prov.). *See* La Rioja, Argentina (prov.).
Ríos, Pedro, 1026.
Riots. Mexico, 508. Panama, 780. Saint Vincent and the Grenadines, 904.
Rites and Ceremonies. Colonial History, 20. Sacrifice, 235.
Roads. Mexico, 477.
Robbers. *See* Brigands and Robbers.
Rock Music. Argentina, 2832, 2837. Biography, 2837. Bolivia, 2801. Brazil, 2856.

Chile, 2851. Colombia, 1132. Dictatorships, 2825, 2851. Mexico, 2724, 2741, 2755. Musical History, 2832. Peru, 2812–2813, 2825. Political Participation, 2812. Social Classes, 2813.
Rockefeller, Nelson A., 417, 1566.
Rodó, José Carlos, 2971.
Rodó, José Enrique, 3030.
Rodríguez, Arsenio, 2787.
Rodríguez, Simón, 1085.
Rodríguez Cabrillo, Juan, 725.
Rodriguez Lozano, Mauel, 85.
Rojas, Gonzalo, 2300.
Romanies. Brazil, 1612. Slaves and Slavery, 1612.
Romanticism. Argentina, 1477, 3040.
Roncari, Amilcare, 589, 2753.
Roraima, Brazil (region). Colonial History, 1588. Indigenous/Non-Indigenous Relations, 1588. Slaves and Slavery, 1588.
Rosario, Argentina (city). Catholic Church, 1303. Collective Memory, 1429. Historiography, 1429. Modernization, 1303. National Identity, 1429. Social Conditions, 1303.
Rosas, Juan Manuel de, 395, 1316, 1346, 1364, 1369, 1419, 1485–1486.
Rosas, Juventino, 2718.
Royal African Company, 837.
Royalists. Uruguay, 1012.
Ruffato, Luiz, 2454.
Ruiz de Orellana, Garci, 994.
Rulers. *See* Kings and Rulers.
Rulfo, Juan, 649.
Rum Industry. Dominican Republic, 891.
Rural Conditions. Argentina, 1294, 1297, 1315. Brazil, 1705. Chile, 1237, 1263. Mexico, 676. Music, 2848. Peru, 1192.
Rural Development. Argentina, 1395, 1438. Brazil, 1554. El Salvador, 752. Mexico, 468.
Rural Sociology. Ecuador, 1159.
Russian Influences. Argentina, 1448.
Russian Revolution (1917–1921). Argentina, 1448.
Sabina, María, 1755.
Sacred Music. *See* Religious Music.
Sacred Space. Mexico, 8.
Sacrifice. Mesoamerica, 235.
Sahagún, Bernardino de, 222, 233, 243.
Salaries. *See* Wages.
Salas, Esteban, 2788.
Salsa. Peru, 2823. US, 2726.
Salta, Argentina (prov.). Military History, 1302.
Salvador, Brazil (city). Modernization, 1709. Regional Government, 1712.

Samba. African Influences, 2940. Brazil, 2862–2863, 2865, 2868, 2879, 2905, 2910, 2931–2932, 2940, 2943. Philosophy, 2944. Religious Life and Customs, 2908. Social History, 2901.

San Basilio del Palenque, Colombia (city). Blacks, 961.

San Javier, Uruguay (settlement). Migration, 1512.

San Juan, Argentina (prov.). Social History, 1022.

San Juan River (Nicaragua and Costa Rica). Discovery and Exploration, 723.

San Luis Potosí, Mexico (city). Epidemics, 594. History, 594. Labor and Laboring Classes, 558. Social History, 614. Water Supply, 594.

San Luis Potosí, Mexico (state). Commerce, 535. Economic History, 535. History, 610.

San Martín, José de, 1380, 1449.

San Miguel de Allende, Mexico (town). Expatriates, 637. Tourism, 637.

San Miguel de Tucumán, Argentina (city). Intellectual History, 1484. Public Education, 1484.

San Salvador de Jujuy, Argentina (town). Cabildos, 1356. History, 1020. Regional Government, 1356.

Sánchez, Luis Rafael, 1922.

Sánchez Navarro family, 498.

Sánchez Rodríguez, Limbano, 875.

Sánchez Santos, Trinidad, 622.

Sánchez Vázquez, Adolfo, 678.

Sandinistas (Nicaragua), 764. History, 750.

Sandino, Augusto César, 742.

Sanguinetti, Julio María, 1509.

Sanitation. See Public Health.

Santa Catarina, Brazil (state). Africans, 1710. Law and Legislation, 1623. Political History, 1623. Portuguese Influences, 1623.

Santa Catarina, Mexico (city). Colonial History, 214. Ethnic Identity, 214. Social History, 214.

Santa Cruz, Andrés, 1216.

Santa Cruz, Bolivia (dept.). Colonial History, 996. Historical Geography, 1000.

Santa Cruz de la Sierra, Bolivia (city). Autonomy, 1222. Commerce, 1205. History, 1205, 1207, 1222, 1224.

Santa Fe, Argentina (city). Freemasonry, 1308. Social Movements, 1308.

Santa Fe, Argentina (prov.). Collective Memory, 1429. Historiography, 1429. National Identity, 1429. Political History, 1458.

Santa Fe, New Mexico (city). Military History, 605.

Santa Juana, Chile (city). History, 1011.

Santa María González, Domingo, 1167.

Santa Rosalía, Mexico (town). History, 534.

Santana, María de los Ángeles, 901.

Santander, Colombia (dept.). Colonial History, 966. Economic Development, 1145. Political Development, 1145. Social Development, 1145. Social Life and Customs, 966.

Santería (cult), 2823.

Santiago, Chile (city). Art Criticism, 89. Intellectual History, 89.

Santiago, Cuba (city). Social History, 803.

Santos, Eduardo, 1120.

Santuario de Jesús Nazareno (Mexico), 30.

Santucho, Mario Roberto, 1413.

Sanuma (indigenous group). See Yanomamo (indigenous group).

Sanz, Francisco de Paula, 1960.

São Paulo, Brazil (city). Anarchism and Anarchists, 1548. Architecture, 167, 171, 1715. City Planning, 167. Education, 1548. French Influences, 171. Music, 2896. Urban History, 1715. Urbanization, 1715.

São Paulo, Brazil (state). Biography, 1630. Catholic Church, 1630. Coffee Industry and Trade, 1538. Cultural Development, 1538. Economic Development, 1538. Italians, 1669. Jews, 1646. Military Police, 1690. Religious Life and Customs, 1630.

Sargento, Nelson, 2865.

Sarmiento, Domingo Faustino, 1418, 1467, 1480, 2130.

Saving and Investment. Mexico, 691.

Schidlowsky, León, 2846.

Schindler Etchegaray, Jorge, 1276.

School Management and Organization. Chile, 1230.

Schools. Chile, 1230.

Science. Argentina, 1406. Brazil, 1557. Peru, 1182. Philosophy, 2966.

Science Fiction. Costa Rica, 1810. Peru, 1948, 2044. Puerto Rico, 1881.

Scientific History. Argentina, 1451, 1460. Brazil, 181. Medicine, 361. Mexico, 524, 565, 642. Peru, 979, 1164, 1182. South America, 997. Soviet Influences, 651.

Scientists. Mexico, 651.

Scots. Jamaica, 839.

Sculptors. Brazil, 128, 131, 135, 141.

Seasonal Farm Laborers Program, 661.

Secondary Education. Mexico, 671.

Security. See National Security.

Seeger, Pete, 2780.
Segall, Lasar, 149.
Segregation. Bahamas, 807. Belize, 859.
Self-Determination. *See* Autonomy. *See* Sovereignty.
Sendero Luminoso (guerrilla group), 298, 1165, 1170, 1177.
Separation. *See* Divorce.
Seventh-Day Adventists. Bolivia, 262.
Seville (Spain). Consulado, 386.
Sex and Sexual Relations. Argentina, 1296, 1306, 1404, 1433. Blacks, 1591. Bolivia, 999. British Caribbean, 861. Caribbean Area, 810. Colombia, 1138. Crime and Criminals, 852. Dominican Republic, 810. Ethics, 1433. Jamaica, 852. Mesoamerica, 237. Slaves and Slavery, 879. Social History, 810. Women, 1577, 1591. *See Also* Gender Relations.
Sex Roles. Argentina, 1433. Brazil, 1676. *See Also* Gender Roles.
Sexism. Art History, 62, 100. Dominican Republic, 811. Haiti, 811. Performing Arts, 62.
Shakespeare, William, 2310–2311.
Shamanism, 344.
Shantytowns. *See* Squatter Settlements.
Sheep. Patagonia (region), 1255.
Shining Path (guerrilla group). *See* Sendero Luminoso (guerrilla group).
Shipping. Espionage, 669. Mexico, 534, 669.
Short Stories. Argentina, 2077, 2087. Bolivia, 1953–1954, 1962–1964, 1967. Brazil, 2382, 2384, 2387–2388, 2390–2394, 2396–2397, 2399–2400, 2403–2408, 2412, 2415, 2417, 2420, 2423–2424. Colombia, 1981. Costa Rica, 1844, 1860. Ecuador, 1997, 1999. Guatemala, 1837–1838, 1840, 1851, 1859. Honduras, 1830, 1850. Nicaragua, 1842. Peru, 2006, 2019, 2030, 2051. Venezuela, 2060.
Sierra, Justo, 622.
Sierra Gorda, Mexico (region). Colonial History, 521.
Sigüenza y Góngora, Carlos de, 199, 1728.
Silva, Dora Ferreira da, 2530.
Silva, Luiz Inácio da. *See* Lula.
Silva, Myrta, 2773.
Silver, 387. Brazil, 1614. Colonial History, 523. Money, 339.
Silver Mines and Mining. Mexico, 523.
Silversmiths. Guatemala, 728.
Silverwork. Guatemala, 728.
Simonal, Wilson, 2895.

Sinaloa, Mexico (state). Economic Development, 676. Revolutions and Revolutionary Movements, 627. Women's Rights, 686.
Singers. Biography, 2814. Brazil, 2867, 2873, 2893, 2895, 2914, 2938. Caribbean Area, 2771. Cuba, 901. Dominican Republic, 943. Mexico, 2700, 2727, 2747. Peru, 2814. Puerto Rico, 2773.
Siqueiros, David Alfaro, 85.
Slaves and Slavery, 324, 376, 397. Antigua and Barbuda, 865. Barbados, 783, 813, 815, 817, 822–823. Biography, 831. Brazil, 168, 405, 1040, 1528, 1531, 1535, 1565, 1567, 1576, 1578, 1583, 1588, 1598, 1602, 1608, 1613, 1622, 1629, 1632, 1652, 1664, 1667, 1710. British Caribbean, 796, 808, 814, 825, 848, 861. Caribbean Area, 783, 794, 798, 813–814, 824, 837, 853. Cattle Raising and Trade, 1535. Child Abuse, 861. Childbirth, 879. Chile, 1004. Civil Rights, 814. Coffee Industry and Trade, 868. Collective Memory, 1571. Colombia, 968, 1103, 1140. Colonial History, 520. Communication, 823. Community Development, 1528. Cuba, 405, 812, 867. Cultural Identity, 1613. Exhibitions, 168. Freedom, 1583. Frontier and Pioneer Life, 1583. Genocide, 808. Geographical History, 1598. Guyana, 848. Insurrections, 823, 874, 881. Jamaica, 808, 822, 828–829, 831, 834, 839–840, 842, 879. Jesuits, 1621. Law and Legislation, 814, 822, 824, 837, 848, 876, 1004. Masculinity, 1677. Mexico, 196, 482, 520, 612, 812. Music, 2736. Oral History, 1571. Peru, 993. Plantations, 1535. Puerto Rico, 876. Rape, 861. Repression, 1629. Saint-Domingue, 829. Social Life and Customs, 831. Uruguay, 1040, 1515. US, 612, 794, 881. Violence, 796, 823. Women, 796, 832, 843, 879, 2986. Youth, 842.
Smuggling, 323. Mexican-American Border Region, 529.
Soberana Convención Revolucionaria (Mexico, 1914–1915), 623.
Soberón Sagredo, Agustín, 610.
Soccer. Argentina, 1394, 1434, 1462. Brazil, 1527, 1653, 1663, 2450. Cultural History, 1663. Cultural Identity, 1394. Historiography, 1462. Neighborhood Associations, 1394. Paraguay, 1513. Political Culture, 1434.
Social Anthropology. Brazil, 1533, 1559. Mexico, 466.

Social Change, 422. Barbados, 857. Chile, 1251. Education, 2828. Mexico, 538, 585, 643. Puerto Rico, 854. Women, 643.

Social Classes, 338, 423. Brazil, 1594, 1607, 1625. Colombia, 1124. Colonial History, 214. Dance, 2834. Dominican Republic, 920. Food, 679. Mexico, 470, 648. Musical History, 2848. Paraguay, 1493. Peru, 1191, 1195. Political Participation, 1628. Puerto Rico, 923. Rock Music, 2813. Spanish America, 381. Women, 2986.

Social Conditions, 406. Argentina, 308, 1047, 1303, 1350–1351, 1376, 1402, 1455. Bolivia, 1218, 3018. Brazil, 1558, 1570, 1592, 1594, 1625, 1680. Chile, 1237, 1243–1244, 1259, 1272–1273, 1278. Colombia, 1095, 1100, 1108, 1135. Colonial History, 214. Cuba, 793. Ecuador, 1156, 1159. Hispaniola, 811. Jamaica, 863. Mexico, 308, 448. Puerto Rico, 1942.

Social Conflict, 423. Argentina, 1313, 1325, 1425. Bolivia, 1228. Brazil, 1556. Chile, 1231, 1267. Colombia, 1113, 1141, 3007. Costa Rica, 748. Ecuador, 1156. Mexico, 446. Peru, 1178, 1193.

Social Control. Colonial History, 717. Mexico, 526, 614, 2994. Peru, 1195.

Social Customs. *See* Social Life and Customs.

Social Darwinism. Mexico, 542.

Social Development. Argentina, 1360, 1388. Brazil, 1533, 1561. Chile, 1236, 1260. Colombia, 1094, 1097, 1125–1126. Haiti, 878. Jamaica, 878.

Social History, 1102, 2987. Argentina, 1044–1045. Bahamas, 807. Barbados, 783. Bolivia, 1214, 1227. Brazil, 126, 1568, 1662. Caribbean Area, 788, 799, 810, 946. Central America, 755. Chile, 1001, 1008, 1279. Colombia, 966–967, 1102. Costa Rica, 707, 709, 748. Cuba, 845, 902. Dominican Republic, 800, 810. Film, 1568. Guyana, 848. Honduras, 710, 746. Jamaica, 828, 831, 834, 836, 841, 843. Mexico, 444, 504, 564, 1740. Nicaragua, 772. Paraguay, 1015. Peru, 1185. Printing Industry, 71. Puerto Rico, 854, 856. Suriname, 911. Uruguay, 1023. Venezuela, 3002.

Social Justice, 418. Central America, 760. Mexico, 578.

Social Life and Customs. Brazil, 2943. Chile, 247, 1008. Jamaica, 2781. Mexico, 446, 448, 573.

Social Media. Brazil, 2521, 2542. Puerto Rico, 1941, 1943. Songs, 2807.

Social Mobility. Ecuador, 1156.

Social Movements. Argentina, 1308, 1487. Brazil, 1565, 1632. Chile, 1239, 1264. Colombia, 1112, 1115, 1131, 1144. Cuba, 2797. Ecuador, 1157. Homosexuality, 1306. Mexico, 439, 446, 451, 472, 658, 680, 2989. Puerto Rico, 919.

Social Organization. *See* Social Structure.

Social Participation. Brazil, 1607. Puerto Rico, 1941.

Social Policy. Argentina, 1456. Brazil, 1635. Chile, 1264, 1284, 1286.

Social Realism. Cuba, 93.

Social Reform. Brazil, 1564. Mexico, 458. Uruguay, 1504.

Social Relations. *See* Social Life and Customs.

Social Security. Brazil, 1635. Chile, 1272.

Social Structure, 338. Colonial History, 359.

Social Thought, 2959, 2973. Mexico, 2989.

Social Welfare. Argentina, 308. Chile, 1260. Mexico, 308.

Socialism and Socialist Parties, 424, 912, 3044. Argentina, 1386, 1393, 1422, 1453, 1463, 1477, 3039. Art History, 93. Bolivia, 1209. Brazil, 1684. Cuba, 93, 3000. Education, 695. Grenada, 942. Historiography, 1422. Mexico, 671, 695. Political Ideology, 1453. Political Philosophy, 3000, 3039. Uruguay, 3031. Venezuela, 1055.

Socialist International, 1684.

Sociologists. Dominican Republic, 2999. Mexico, 2990.

Sociology. Bolivia, 3022. Mexico, 2990.

Soldiers. Bolivia, 1204. British Caribbean, 827. Colonial History, 1026. El Salvador, 776. Masculinity, 1677. Mexico, 585. Paraguay, 1493. Women, 776.

Soldiers, Spanish. Cuba, 869.

Somoza, Anastasio, 777.

Somoza Debayle, Lillian, 777.

Songs, 2675, 2807. Brazil, 2906, 2917. Chile, 2847. Cuba, 2787. Dictatorships, 2843, 2847. Mexico, 2689, 2706, 2758. Political Prisoners, 2843. Slaves and Slavery, 2736.

Sor Juana Inés de la Cruz. *See* Juana Inés de la Cruz, Sor.

Sorcery. *See* Witchcraft.

Sources. Venezuela, 1063.

Sovereignty. Argentina, 1025. Dominican Republic, 884, 896, 900, 952. Puerto Rico, 953. *See Also* Autonomy.

Soviet Influences. Mexico, 651.

Spain. Cortes (1810–1813), 335.

Spaniards. Argentina, 1387. Central America, 755. Cuba, 787, 869, 887, 903. Guatemala, 774. Immigrants, 1387. Mexico, 604. Peru, 980. Relations with Indigenous Peoples, 505, 726. Río de la Plata (region), 1027.

Spanish Civil War (1936–1939), 1547. Argentina, 1387. Mexico, 675.

Spanish Conquest, 26, 329, 374, 491, 1750. Argentina, 267. Bolivia, 995. Caribbean Area, 818, 820. Chile, 1003. Costa Rica, 215. Drama, 2313. Fiction, 1958. Historiography, 380. Land Settlement, 737. Language and Languages, 242. Mesoamerica, 215, 231. Mexico, 192, 231, 506, 515, 1744. Nicaragua, 215. Peru, 255, 1750. Soldiers, 1735. Violence, 986.

Spanish Influences. Argentina, 1366–1367. Brazil, 1616. Cuba, 787. Mexico, 514. *See Also* Castilian Influences.

Sports. Argentina, 1462. Brazil, 1527, 1653, 1663. Chile, 279. Colombia, 1130, 1136. Precolumbian Civilizations, 250. Puerto Rico, 944. Social History, 1527.

Squatter Settlements. Venezuela, 1087.

Standard of Living. *See* Cost and Standard of Living.

State, The, 330. Brazil, 1657. Peru, 1175.

State-Building, 401. Argentina, 1360. Chile, 1260. Costa Rica, 713. Mexico, 585, 597. Venezuela, 1048–1049.

State Violence. *See* Political Violence.

Statebuilding. *See* State-Building.

Statesmen. Dominican Republic, 862, 1051. Mexico, 616. Nicaragua, 762. Panama, 739. Puerto Rico, 899, 935.

Statistics. Argentina, 1384. History, 1384. Mexico, 597.

Storni, Alfonsina, 1476.

Street-Railroads. Brazil, 1714.

Strikes and Lockouts. Mexico, 609. Peru, 1193. Puerto Rico, 919.

Student Movements. Mexico, 439, 449, 638, 657, 665, 673, 693.

Students. Argentina, 1386. Art, 183. Brazil, 183. Colombia, 1092, 1112, 1138. Fiction, 1901. Newspapers, 183. Political Participation, 665, 693, 1386.

Substance Abuse. *See* Alcohol and Alcoholism.

Sugar Industry and Trade. Argentina, 1436. Barbados, 821. Bolivia, 1205. Brazil, 1691. Caribbean Area, 926. Jamaica, 840. Puerto Rico, 871, 883, 917, 919, 921–923, 926, 928, 949. Slaves and Slavery, 840.

Spanish Caribbean, 883. Strikes and Lockouts, 919. US, 921.

Suicide, 324.

Sumalavia, Ricardo, 2047.

Sundheim, Wilhelm, 329.

Suya (indigenous group). Ethnography, 2947. Music, 2947.

Symbolism. Argentina, 1415. *See Also* Symbolism (literature).

Symbolism (literature). Caribbean Area, 2174.

Syncretism. Amazon Basin, 246. Andean Region, 246. Mexico, 246.

Syrians. Argentina, 1396. Immigrants, 1396. Mexico, 700.

Tabasco, Mexico (state). Pirates, 196. Slaves and Slavery, 196. Women's Rights, 686.

Tacna, Peru (prov.). Warfare, 1166.

Taco, Gregorio, 975.

Tailyour, John, 839.

Tamaulipas, Mexico (state). Economic Conditions, 453. Regional Development, 453.

Tamayo, Rufino, 85.

Tango. Argentina, 1431, 1482, 2834–2835, 2910, 2924. Brazil, 2924. Cultural History, 1482, 2834, 2840. Musical History, 2835. Social Classes, 2834.

Tapia y Rivera, Alejandro, 1940.

Tarapacá, Chile (region). British, 1249.

Tarasco (indigenous group). Ethnic Groups and Ethnicity, 191. Ethnohistory, 191, 227. Indigenous/Non-Indigenous Relations, 227. Social History, 227.

Tarija, Bolivia (city). History, 1198. Independence Movements, 1198.

Tattooing. Mesoamerica, 202.

Tawantinsuyu (Inca Empire). Philosophy, 3011. Precolumbian Civilizations, 3011.

Taxation. Colombia, 965. Mexico, 587, 601, 608.

Taxes. *See* Taxation.

Taylor, Simon, 872.

Teatro de Amadores de Pernambuco, 2580.

Teatro Municipal (Buenos Aires), 2356.

Technological Development. Mexico, 443. Philosophy, 2968.

Technological Innovations. Mexico, 443.

Tegucigalpa, Honduras (city). Church History, 719. Colonial History, 719.

Tehuelche (indigenous group). Economic Conditions, 1473. History, 280.

Teixeira, Pedro, 1615.

Television. Dominican Republic, 920.

Téllez, Eduardo, 1786.

Ten Years' War (Cuba, 1868–1878), 875.
Tenochtitlán Site (Mexico). Urban History, 38.
Teotihuacán Site (Mexico). Artifacts, 9.
Teresa Cristina, *Empress, consort of Pedro II, Emperor of Brazil*, 1640.
Teresa, *of Avila, Saint*, 2293.
Terrorism, 409.
Texas, US (state). Evangelistic Work, 488. Folk Songs, 2759. Generals, 487. Indigenous/Non-Indigenous Relations, 488. Military History, 487.
Texcocans (indigenous group). Colonial History, 204. Cultural History, 204. Elites, 245. Historiography, 245. Nobility, 245. Political History, 204.
Texcoco de Mora, Mexico (city). Church History, 204. Colonial History, 194, 204, 223, 474. Indigenous Peoples, 204. Nobility, 194, 474. Spanish Conquest, 223.
Textbooks. Colombia, 1098.
Textile Industry. *See* Textiles and Textile Industry.
Textiles and Textile Industry. Colonial History, 694. Dyes and Dyeing, 22. Mexico, 639, 694, 700. Peru, 11, 52. Regional Development, 694.
Tezcucan (indigenous group). Community Development, 220. Political Conditions, 220. Regional Government, 220. Spanish Conquest, 223.
Theater. Argentina, 2355–2356. Brazil, 2896. Costa Rica, 2357. Italian Influences, 2585. Music, 2676, 2694, 2733–2734, 2787. Political Conditions, 1730. US, 2733–2734. *See Also* Popular Theater.
Theatro Municipal de São Paulo, 2574.
Theatro Sete de Abril (Pelotas, Brazil), 2582.
Tinguipaya, Bolivia (town). Indigenous Peoples, 287.
Tipografía del Comercio (Monterrey, Mexico), 528.
Tirado, Romualdo, 2733.
Tizón, María, 1338.
Tlatelolco, Mexico (zone). Colonial History, 214. Ethnic Identity, 214. Labor and Laboring Classes, 657. Massacres, 657. Social History, 214.
Toba (indigenous group). Dance, 2831.
Tojeira, José María, 1818.
Tojolaba (indigenous group). Guerrillas, 640.
Toltecs (indigenous group). Death, 219. Religious Life and Customs, 219.
Torquemada, Juan de, 241.
Torres, Camilo, 3015.

Torriente Brau, Pablo de la, 1907.
Torture. Brazil, 1524, 1666. Chile, 1253. Interviews, 1666. Paraguay, 1500.
Totalitarianism. *See* Authoritarianism.
Totatiche, Mexico (city). Historical Demography, 441.
Tourism. Israel, 429. Mexico, 637, 687. Peru, 1180.
Toussaint L'Ouverture, 805.
Towns. *See* Cities and Towns.
Traba, Marta, 1092.
Trabulse, Elías, 1720.
Trade. *See* Balance of Trade. *See* Commerce.
Trade Policy. Brazil, 1551.
Trade Unions. Argentina, 1440. Brazil, 1712. Chile, 1234, 1240, 1250. Interviews, 1440. Mexico, 699. Puerto Rico, 919. Revolutionaries, 1440.
Transnational Corporations. *See* Multinational Corporations.
Transportation, 327. Brazil, 1714.
Travel. *See* Description and Travel.
Travel Literature. Brazil, 2493.
Travelers. Brazil, 269, 300, 1520. Mexico, 1745. Music, 2777. Venezuela, 256. Women, 349, 573.
Travelers, European. Mexico, 543, 573.
Treaties. Argentina, 1355. Barbados, 821. Paraguay, 1499.
Treaty of Utrecht, 355.
Trials. Argentina, 1309. Massacres, 1309.
Triple Alliance War (1865–1870). *See* Paraguayan War (1865–1870).
Trolleys. *See* Street-Railroads.
Trujillo Molina, Rafael Leónidas, 888, 907–908, 910, 924, 941, 951, 1926.
Tsuru, Kiso, 648.
Tucumán, Argentina (prov.). Colonial History, 1042. Economic Development, 1436. Radicalism, 1407. Regional Development, 1436. Sugar Industry and Trade, 1436.
Tupac-Amaru, José Gabriel, 266, 992.
Túpac Amaru, Juan Bautista, 2080.
Tupamaros. *See* Movimiento de Liberación Nacional (Uruguay).
Tupi (indigenous group). Brazil, 269.
Tupinamba (indigenous group), 1572.
Turcios Lima, Luis Augusto., 775.
Tuxtlas Region (Mexico). Colonial History, 212. Geographical History, 212. Indigenous Peoples, 212.
TV. *See* Television.
Tzeltal (indigenous group). Social Movements, 658.

Umbanda (cult). Music, 2900. *See Also* African Influences.
UN. *See* United Nations.
Unidad Popular, 1250.
Unión Cívica Radical (Argentina), 1407, 1417.
Unión Federal Republicana (Venezuela), 1066.
United Brands Company. *See* United Fruit Company.
United Fruit Company, 333.
United Nations. Peacekeeping Forces, 1639.
United States. Agency for International Development, 1208.
United States. Federal Bureau of Investigation, 1150.
United States. Immigration Border Patrol, 653.
Universidad Autónoma de Yucatán, 568.
Universidad Central de Venezuela, 958.
Universidad de Chile, 103.
Universidad de Costa Rica, 2357.
Universidad de Guadalajara, 638.
Universidad Nacional Autónoma de México, 455.
Universidad Nacional de Córdoba, 1460.
Universidade de São Paulo, 183.
Universidade Federal do Rio Grande do Sul. Instituto de Artes, 137.
Universities. Art, 84. Mexico, 455, 638. *See Also* Higher Education.
University Reform. Colombia, 1112.
Urban Areas. Architecture, 8. Argentina, 1351. Bolivia, 1221, 2802. Chile, 2847. Soccer, 1462. Youth, 2802. *See Also* Urban Renewal.
Urban Development. Brazil, 1537. Mexico, 639.
Urban History. Brazil, 164, 166, 1525, 1680, 1703, 1715. Colombia, 964. Communism and Communist Parties, 1525.
Urban Planning. *See* City Planning.
Urban Renewal. Brazil, 167. Merchants, 666. *See Also* Urban Areas.
Urban Sociology. Brazil, 2882. Ecuador, 1159.
Urbanization. Argentina, 1334. Brazil, 164, 170, 1541, 1703, 1715. Colombia, 964. Mexico, 440, 442, 561. South America, 313.
Urquiza, Justo José de, 1299.
US Influences. Economic Conditions, 433.
U.S. Navy Steel Band, 2780.
Usumacinta River Valley (Guatemala and Mexico). Murals, 6.

Utopias. Argentina, 1297.
Valdés, José Manuel, 979.
Valente, Assis, 2909.
Valle del Cauca (dept.). Blacks, 1140.
Valle Iberlucea, Enrique del, 3039.
Valle y Caviedes, Juan del, 1752.
Vargas, Getúlio, 1546, 1569, 1687, 2573, 2575.
Vargas Llosa, Mario, 1947, 1949, 1951.
Varnhagen, Francisco Adolfo de, *Visconde de Porto Segur*, 1702.
Vaz Ferreira, Carlos, 3030.
Vázquez, José Antonio, 1743.
Vázquez y Sánchez Vizcaíno, Francisco Pablo, 465.
Vega, Garcilaso de la, 1722.
Vega, Jorge de la, 99.
Velasco Ibarra, José María, 1992.
Vélez Sárfield, Aurelia, 2130.
Veltfort, Anna, 1919.
Veracruz, Mexico (city). Economic History, 608. Fiscal Policy, 608. Military History, 688. Military Occupation, US, 688.
Veracruz, Mexico (state). Crime and Criminals, 650. Folk Music, 2707. Food Supply, 652. Land Reform, 489. Mexican Revolution (1910–1920), 652. Musical History, 2764. Nazism, 650. Prisons, 650. World War II (1939–1945), 650.
Veríssimo, Erico, 2372.
Vetancurt, Augustín de, 518.
Viceroyalty of New Granada (1718–1810). Diplomatic History, 963. Economic Conditions, 962. Economic Policy, 960. Military History, 973.
Viceroyalty of New Spain (1540–1821), 1750. Art, 18. Dance, 2714. Elites, 194, 474. Epidemics, 511. Ethnohistory, 198, 1721. Fiscal Policy, 485. Forced Migration, 501. Indigenous/Non-Indigenous Relations, 508. Indigenous Peoples, 194, 474, 1751. Insurrections, 516. Land Settlement, 473. Land Tenure, 489. Mestizos and Mestizaje, 519. Military, 475. Military History, 501. Music, 2709, 2713, 2715–2716, 2720, 2739, 2743, 2749, 2752, 2756, 2766. Musical Instruments, 2730–2731. Painting, 483. Poetry, 1746. Race and Race Relations, 483, 519, 526, 2994. Religious Life and Customs, 1741. Religious Music, 2723, 2737. Rites and Ceremonies, 522. Sex and Sexual Relations, 504. Slaves and Slavery, 482, 520. Smuggling, 529. Social Structure, 483, 526, 2994.

Viceroyalty of Peru (1542–1822), 1750. Art, 18. Educational Policy, 985. Religion, 976. Sex and Sexual Relations, 999. Social History, 999. Social Life and Customs, 1044. Sources, 975, 990.
Viceroyalty of Río de la Plata (1776–1810). Biography, 1016. Economic History, 1032. Foreign Intervention, British, 1037. Indigenous Peoples, 1024, 1036. Mass Media, 1019. Political History, 1023. Religious Life and Customs, 1042. Social Conditions, 1042. Social Life and Customs, 1044. Travelers, 1036. Women, 1019.
Viceroys. Argentina, 1032.
Villa, Pancho, 681.
Villa-Lobos, Heitor, 2861, 2888, 2936, 2950–2952, 2956.
Villagrá, Gaspar Pérez de, 1005.
Villancicos. Guatemala, 734.
Villanueva, Francisco Javier, 1342.
Violence, 316. Andean Region, 986. Argentina, 3034. Art, 73. Chile, 1231, 1263. Colombia, 1113. Music, 2805. Performing Arts, 73. Peru, 1170. Social Conditions, 1561. *See Also* Political Violence.
Virginity. *See* Sex and Sexual Relations.
Viscardo y Guzmán, Juan Pablo, 384.
Vitória, Brazil (city). Urbanization, 1703.
Voting. Bolivia, 1211. Chile, 1268. *See Also* Elections.
Vucetich, Juan, 320.
Wages. Peru, 1190.
Waldeck, Frédéric de, 543.
Walker, William, 753.
Wapisiana (indigenous group). Brazil, 281.
War of the Pacific (1879–1884), 394, 1167, 1194. Economic History, 1200. Peru, 1166, 1171.
War of the Triple Alliance. *See* Paraguayan War (1865–1870).
Warfare. Colombia, 1105.
Wars of Independence, 335, 351, 384, 393, 396. Argentina, 981, 1026, 1030–1031, 1033, 1046, 1302, 1319, 1323, 1340, 1350, 1355, 1361, 1380, 1391, 1447, 1449. Bolivia, 998, 1198, 1207, 1224. Brazil, 1696. Chile, 1002, 1238. Collective Memory, 1361. Colombia, 1094, 1105, 1128. Cuba, 850, 869–870, 875, 882, 909. Ecuador, 969, 973. Historiography, 1361. Medical Care, 869. Mexico, 210, 454, 456, 469, 538, 554, 572, 581, 588. Music, 2676. Paraguay, 1026. Peru, 981, 1172. Philosophy, 2974. Pirates, 866. Venezuela, 1048–1050, 1057, 1061, 1064–1065, 1077. Women, 390. *See Also* Independence Movements.
Water Distribution. Mexico, 703.
Water Rights. Peru, 1162.
Water Supply. Mexico, 468, 544, 703. Puerto Rico, 873.
Waterways. Mexico, 212.
Wealth. Colonial History, 484. Jamaica, 872. Mexico, 622.
Weaving. *See* Textiles and Textile Industry.
Welfare. *See* Social Welfare.
Welles, Sumner, 951.
Welsh. Argentina, 1300, 1348. Immigrants, 1348. Language and Languages, 1337. Photographs, 1339.
Williams, Eric Eustace, 913–914.
Wills. Mesoamerica, 226. Mexico, 226.
Wine and Wine Making. Argentina, 1459. Colonial History, 372.
Witchcraft. Audiencia of Chile, 1007.
Women. Antigua and Barbuda, 865. Argentina, 100, 1294, 1359, 1428, 1469, 1476. Artists, 63, 78, 100, 689. Barbados, 832. Biography, 1640. Brazil, 1558, 1676. Caribbean Area, 830. Chile, 1244, 1261, 1273, 1278. Chinese, 630. Colombia, 1136. Colonial History, 991, 2986. Description and Travel, 349. Dictatorships, 1428. Dominican Republic, 900, 906, 929, 936, 2775. Economic Conditions, 428. Ecuador, 1159. Education, 698. El Salvador, 776, 779. Entrepreneurs, 830, 832. Government, Resistance to, 1428. Guatemala, 708. Historiography, 390. Interviews, 1409, 1428. Jamaica, 843. Journalists, 686. Labor and Laboring Classes, 843, 1320. Law and Legislation, 830. Mass Media, 1359. Medicine, 229. Mesoamerica, 237. Mexico, 614, 617, 629, 643, 698, 2704. Middle Classes, 1320. Military, 1253. Music, 2704, 2902. Musicians, 2771, 2903. Painters, 87. Paraguay, 1493. Poetry, 2532. Political Participation, 1423, 1409. Political Prisoners, 1428. Radio, 1359. Regional Development, 1294. Religious Life and Customs, 708. Revolutionaries, 877. Revolutions and Revolutionary Movements, 1469. Rural Conditions, 1294. Singers, 2773. Slaves and Slavery, 2986. Social Change, 643. Social Classes, 2986. Social Conditions, 843. Travelers, 349. Violence, 865. Writers, 1476.
Women's Rights. Birth Control, 1404. Chile, 1239, 1273. Colombia, 1127. Dominican

Republic, 906. Mexico, 630, 634, 680, 686.
Wood Carving. Brazil, 143.
Working Class. *See* Labor and Laboring Classes.
World Cup (soccer), *Brazil, 1950*, 1663.
World War I (1914–1918), 412, 430. Argentina, 1387, 1478. Brazil, 1688, 1694. Chile, 1280. Mexico, 669. Peru, 1179.
World War II (1939–1945). Argentina, 1387. Brazil, 1541–1542, 1544, 1550, 1566, 1568, 1665, 1687. Ecuador, 1150. Foreign Policy, 1687. Mexico, 648.
Writers. Government, Resistance to, 1247. Interviews, 67. Mexico, 649. Panama, 1869. Puerto Rico, 1922. Uruguay, 2137.
Writers. *See* Authors.
Writing. Colonial History, 1597. Mexico, 201. Migration, 326.
Xalapa, Mexico (city). Musical History, 2764.
Ximénez, Francisco, 230.
Xingu River Valley (Brazil). Indigenous Art, 177.
Yañez, Octaviano, 2735.
Yanhuitlán, Mexico (convent). Colonial Architecture, 32. Religious Life and Customs, 31. Social Life and Customs, 31.
Yanoama (indigenous group). *See* Yanomamo (indigenous group).
Yanomami (indigenous group). *See* Yanomamo (indigenous group).
Yanomamo (indigenous group). Venezuela, 256.
Yaqui (indigenous group). Dictatorships, 672. Insurrections, 672. Mexico, 672.
Yawar Mallku (Blood of the Condor), 1206.
Youth. Argentina, 1399. Bolivia, 2802. Chile, 1283, 2849. Colombia, 1132, 1136. Dance, 2831. Drama, 2318. Peronism, 1386. Political Participation, 1399. Popular Music, 2785. Socialism and Socialist Parties, 1386.
YouTube (firm), 2807.
Yucatán, Mexico (state). Assassinations, 494. Borderlands, 209, 547. Caciques, 210. Colonial History, 236. Cultural Identity, 450. Education, 568. Epidemics, 590. Ethnic Groups and Ethnicity, 209, 547. Frontiers, 209, 547. Government, Resistance to, 494. History, 337. Immigrants, 546. Mayas, 209–210, 547. Merchants, 209, 547. Musical History, 2761. Musicians, 2765. Pirates, 196. Public Health, 590. Race and Race Relations, 209, 547. Slaves and Slavery, 196. Social Conditions, 210. Songs, 2765. Wars of Independence, 210. Women's Rights, 686.
Yucatán Peninsula. Colonial Administration, 517. Colonial History, 475. Description and Travel, 543. Indigenous Languages, 493. Political History, 517.
Zacatecas, Mexico (city). Mexican Revolution (1910–1920), 668, 681.
Zacatecas, Mexico (state). History, 477, 569. Mexican Revolution (1910–1920), 692. Newspapers, 551. Political History, 611.
Zapata, Emiliano, 645.
Zapatistas. *See* Ejército Zapatista de Liberación Nacional (Mexico).
Zapotec (indigenous group). Myths and Mythology, 225.
Zarzuelas. Mexico, 2694. *See Also* Musicals.
Zavaleta Mercado, René, 3022.
Zeballos, Estanislao, 1498.
Zulen, Pedro Salvino, 3017.
Zulia, Venezuela (state). Economic Development, 1080. Petroleum Industry and Trade, 1080. Sources, 1079.
Zurita, Raúl, 2304.

AUTHOR INDEX

¡A estudiar, a luchar! movimientos estudiantiles en Colombia y México, siglos XX y XXI, 439.
Abad Faciolince, Héctor Joaquín, 2635.
Abalo, Esteban, 1398.
Abdo Francis, Jorge, 623.
Abe, Marié, 2683.
Abella, Gonzalo, 1503.
Abello Vives, Alberto, 1102.
Abmeier, Angela, 1287.
Aboites, Luis, 440.
Abraldes, Daniel, 2973.
Abrego, Verónica, 1288.
Abréu, Dió-genes, 781.
Abreu, Jean Luiz Neves, 1611.
Abreu, Luciano Aronne de, 408.
Abreu, Martha, 1598.
Abreu, Sergior, 1489.
Abreu Cardet, José Miguel, 844, 909, 932.
Abril, Federico, 2352.
Abromeit, John, 436.
Absell, Christopher David, 1631.
Absi, Pascale, 1210.
Abstracciones: Nueva York, París, Cuenca, México, 69.
Abya-Yala (organization), 2152.
Academia Brasileira de Letras, 2434.
Academia Dominicana de la Historia, 884, 910.
Academia Nacional de la Historia (Venezuela), 1083.
Acevedo, Héctor Luis, 899.
Acevedo Puello, Rafael Enrique, 967.
Acevedo Tarazona, Álvaro, 439.
Achim, Miruna, 527.
Achugar, Hugo, 2182.
Acosta, José, 1871.
Acosta, José Virgilio, 1289.
Acosta, Miguel, 1800.
Acosta Cartagena, Alma, 1938.
Acri, Martín Alberto, 1031.
Actores del ritual en la Catedral de México, 2684.
Acuña D., Ángel, 247.
Acuña Ortega, Víctor Hugo, 738.
Acuña Prieto, Ruth Nohemí, 111.
Acuña Rodríguez, Olga Yanet, 1089.
Adamovsky, Ezequiel, 1415, 2829.
Adams, William Yewdale, 306.
Adaui Sicheri, Katya, 2006–2007.
Adet, Walter, 2138.
Adopte una Obra de Arte (program), 30.
Afolabi, Niyi, 2854.
Afro-Latin American studies: an introduction, 2958.
Agencia Española de Cooperación Internacional para el Desarrollo, 97.
Agrasánchez Jr., Rogelio, 2685.
Agua la boca: restaurantes de la Ciudad de México en el siglo XX, 624.
Agüero, Ana Clarisa, 313.
Aguerre, Enrique, 117.
Aguerre Core, Fernando, 1012.
Aguilar, José Roberto, 134.
Aguilar, Nelson, 134.
Aguilar Camín, Héctor, 1753.
Aguilar Mora, Jorge, 2959.
Aguilar Piedra, Raúl, 767.
Aguilar Rivera, José Antonio, 2989.
Aguilera, Carlos A., 1885, 1937.
Aguinaga, Luis Vicente de, 2183, 2297.
Aguirre, Ana Cecilia, 1398.
Aguirre, Carlos, 314, 319.
Aguirre, Coral, 1754.
Aguirre Arango, José Pedro, 1801.
Aguirre Lora, Georgina María Esther, 84.
Agustini, Delmira, 2184.
Aiello, Tânia, 185.
Aire de luz: cuentos cubanos del siglo XX, 1872.
Al Assal, Marianna Boghosian, 163.
Alanís Enciso, Fernando Saúl, 625–626.
Alarcón Amézquita, Saúl Armando, 627.
Alatorre, Antonio, 1720.
Alba, 2459.
Alba de la Vega, Víctor, 1802.
Alberdi, Juan Bautista, 1342.
Alberto Lleras Camargo y John F. Kennedy: amistad y política internacional: recuento de episodios de la Guerra Fría, la Alianza para el Progreso y el problema de Cuba, 1090.

Albiez, Sarah, 191, 227.
Albizu Campos, Pedro, 1938.
Albornoz, María Eugenia, 1001.
Albuquerque, Maria Betânia Barbosa, 1572.
Albuquerque, Wlamyra Ribeiro de, 1576.
Alcalá, Luisa Elena, 40.
O alcance da canção: estudos sobre música popular, 2855.
Alcântara, Paulo Henrique, 2556.
Alcántara Rojas, Berenice, 243.
Aldana de Hoyos, Leonardo, 2309.
Aldunate, Carlos, 294.
Alemán Iglesias, Javier, 883.
Alemán Salvador, María Gabriela, 1990.
Alemany Bay, Carmen, 2304.
Alexander, Rani T., 480.
Alexander, Ryan M., 628.
Alexandre, Ricardo, 2856.
Alfaro, Alfonso, 2991.
Alfaro, Eloy, 3009.
Alfaro Pareja, Francisco, 1048–1049.
Alfau Durán, Vetilio, 884.
Alge, Barbara, 2857–2858, 2911.
Aliaga, Juan Vicente, 62.
Aliaga-Buchenau, Ana-Isabel, 664.
Aljovín de Losada, Cristóbal, 1152.
Allard, Raúl, 1230.
Allier, Eugenia, 435.
Almada, Márcia, 126.
Almada, Selva, 2076–2077.
Almánzar Rodríguez, Armando, 1873.
Almario García, Óscar, 1091.
Almeida, Carina Santos de, 248.
Almeida, Jaime, 2686.
Alonso, Aldo Fabio, 1290.
Alonso, Angela, 1632, 1693.
Alonso, Nancy, 2630.
Alonso Coma, Ismael, 886.
Alonso González, José Luis, 1490.
Alonso Marchante, José Luis, 1291.
Alonso-Minutti, Ana R., 2687–2693, 2767.
Alou, Antoinette Tidjani, 889.
Alsina Júnior, João Paulo Soares, 1633.
Altable, Francisco, 473.
Altera Roma: art and empire from Mérida to México, 26.
Altesor, Sergio, 2119.
Altez, Rogelio, 399, 1050.
Alva Ixtlilxóchitl, Fernando de, 192.
Alva-Viale, Harold, 2139–2140.
Alvarado, Jaime, 2185.
Alvarado Chaparro, Dulce María de, 70.
Alvarado Meléndez, Marcelo, 3024.
Alvarado Tezozómoc, Fernando, 1751.
Alvarenga, Antonia Valtéria Melo, 1634.
Álvarez, Carlos Manuel, 1874.
Álvarez Álvarez, Luis, 845, 1920.
Álvarez Bravo, Paulo, 1231.
Álvarez-Curbelo, Silvia, 947.
Álvarez Delgado, Álvaro, 2330.
Álvarez Gila, Oscar, 311, 317.
Álvarez Hernández, Orlando, 2842.
Alvarez Lobo, Ricardo, 249.
Alvarez López, Luis, 844.
Álvarez-Uría, Fernando, 354.
Álvarez Vallejos, Rolando, 1283.
Álvarez Vergara, Marco, 1232.
Alvariño Atiénzar, Alberto, 954.
Alves, Jolinda de Moraes, 1635.
Alves, Salomão Pontes, 1660.
Alves-Bezerra, Wilson, 2460.
Amado, Janaína, 1573.
Amado Gonzáles, Donato, 316.
Amantino, Marcia, 1621, 1677.
Amaral, Aracy A., 152.
Amaro Peñaflores, René, 458.
Amaya, Vladimir, 2171.
Amayo, Enrique, 250.
América: cruce de miradas, 307.
América invertida: an anthology of emerging Uruguayan poets, 2587.
América y el Tratado de Utrecht de 1713, México, 2013, 355.
Ametrano, Lucía, 193.
Amores, Juan Bosco, 317.
Amorfino: canto mayor del montubio, 2806.
Amorim, Paulo Henrique, 1636.
Amoroso, Marta Rosa, 1637.
Ampuero, Fernando, 2008–2009.
Ampuero, María Fernanda, 1991.
Anaya Larios, José Rodolfo, 513.
Anderson, Barbara C., 22, 1747.
Andes, Stephen Joseph Carl, 421, 1233.
Andrade, Carlos Drummond de, 2461.
Andrade, Clara de, 2571.
Andrade, Gênese, 2462.
Andrade, Jairo, 1968.
Andrade, Mário de, 2461, 2859.
Andrade, Oswald de, 2462.
Andrade, Paulo, 2463, 2531.
Andrews, George Reid, 2958.
Andrioli, Luiz, 2382.
Andruetto, María Teresa, 2078.
Andújar, Rey Emmanuel, 1875.
Andújar Castillo, Francisco, 371.
Angarita Cáceres, Rafael Gonzalo, 272.
Ángel Molina A., Maria del, 601.
Angelo Mladinic, Gloria, 1261.
Angels, demons and the New World, 1739.

Angulo Morales, Alberto, 311.
Anjos, Augusto dos, 2464.
Anselm Eckart, S.J. e o Estado do Grão-Pará e Maranhão setecentista (1785), 1574.
Antes de Perón y antes de Frondizi: el nacionalismo económico y la revista *Servir*: 1936–1943, 1292.
Anthology of Spanish American thought and culture, 2959.
Anticona Cebrián, Juan Pablo, 2823.
Antigua (Guatemala). Ayuntamiento, 714.
Antigua (Guatemala). Cabildo, 714.
Antivilo Peña, Julia, 63.
Antologia da poesia erótica brasileira, 2465.
Antología de argumentos teatrales en Argentina 2003–2013, 2308.
Antología de teatro de La Guajira, 2309.
Antologia UBE, 2426.
Antonini, Blanca, 751.
Antropologia e performance: ensaios Napedra, 2569.
Antúnez, Damián Horacio, 1293.
Anzai, Leny Caselli, 1573.
Aparicio, Yvette, 2298.
Aponte Alsina, Marta, 1876.
Aponte-Ledée, Rafael, 2770.
Aportes a la construcción del país: selección de pensadores antioqueños, 3003.
Appelbaum, Nancy P., 1170.
Appratto, Roberto, 2120.
Aquino, Alfonso D', 2596.
Aquino, Alfredo, 2436.
Aragão, Isabel, 1638.
Aragão, Pedro de Moura, 2860.
Aramayo, Omar, 2141.
Arámbulo López, Carlos, 1946, 2010.
Arana Bustamante, Luis, 251.
Araújo, Carlos Eduardo Moreira de, 1680.
Araújo, Elian, 411.
Araújo, Emanoel, 181, 184.
Araújo, Gessé Almeida, 2570.
Araújo, Jeaneth Xavier de, 1619.
Araújo, Leusa, 2499.
Araujo Sánchez, Diego, 1992.
Araúz, Celestino Andrés, 739.
Araya, Sandra, 1993.
Araya Gómez, Rodrigo, 1234, 1267.
Araya Miranda, Jaime, 2186.
Arbitraria: muestrario de poesía y ensayo, 2142.
Arcanjo, Loque, 2861.
Arce, Alejandra de, 1294.
Arce, B. Christine, 629.
Archivo General de la Nación (Dominican Republic), 2999.

Archivo Histórico de Zacatecas (Mexico), 681.
Arcos Cabrera, Carlos, 1994.
Arellano, Julio, 276.
Arena, Carolyn, 813.
Arenas, Marco, 252.
Arenas-Carter, Rodrigo, 2176.
Arendt, Isabel Cristina, 326.
Argentina. Secretaría de Cultura, 1355, 1470.
Argüelles, Juan Domingo, 2145.
Argüello Mora, Manuel, 1803.
Arias, Hernán, 2079.
Arias, Patricia, 441.
Arias, Santa, 1741.
Arias Castro, Tomás Federico, 740.
Arias Vásquez, Andrés, 1092.
Aridjis, Homero, 1755, 2597, 2636.
Arismendi Miraballes, Andrea, 2187.
Aristizábal García, Diana Marcela, 1093.
Armas Asín, Fernando, 1162.
Armaza Pérez del Castillo, Hernando, 1197.
Arocena, Felipe, 406.
Arquivo Histórico Judaico Brasileiro. Núcleo de História Oral, 1646.
Arquivo Nacional (Brazil), 1660.
Arquivo Público do Estado do Rio de Janeiro, 1699.
Arraes, Ricardo, 1639.
Arreola, Guillermo, 1756.
Arriaga Jordán, Guillermo, 1757.
Arrioja Díaz Viruell, Luis Alberto, 597.
Arrosagaray, Enrique, 1295.
Arroyo Abad, Leticia, 356.
Arroyo de Jesús, Frances, 2354.
Arroyo Pizarro, Yolanda, 1877.
ArtCultura, 2862–2863.
Arte botânica no Paraná, 178.
Arteaga, Juan José, 1013.
Arteaga, Sonia, 2819.
Artesanos, artistas, artífices: la Escuela de Artes Aplicadas de la Universidad de Chile, 1928–1968, 103.
Artículos recopilados sobre la ocupación norteamericana de 1916, 884.
Artigas hoy: testimonios sobre historia Uruguaya, 1503.
Ascencio, Michaelle, 2058.
Ascencio Cedillo, Efraín, 2724.
Ashley, James Matthew, 2996.
Ashwell, Washington, 1014.
Asociación de Historiadores Latinoamericanistas Europeos, 399.
Asociación de Historiadores Latinoamericanistas Europeos. Congreso. 16th, San Fernando, Spain, 2011, 464.

Asociación de Historiadores Latinoamericanos y del Caribe. Congreso, 10th, Santo Domingo, 2011, 407.
Assad Cuellar, José, 2310.
Associação Indígena Kisêdjê, 2947.
Assumpção, Maurício Torres, 1520.
Assunção, Ademir, 2506.
Asymmetries: anthology of Peruvian poetry, 2588.
El Atlántico como frontera: mediaciones culturales entre Cuba y España, 1921.
Aubin, Myrian Ribeiro, 2864.
Augustine-Adams, Kif, 630.
Augusto Boal: arte, pedagogia e política, 2571.
Aurrecoechea, Juan Manuel, 631.
Autores baianos: um panorama = Bahianische autoren: ein panorama = Bahian authors: a panorama = Autores bahianos: un panorama, 2589.
Autoritarismo e cultura política, 408.
Autran, Lúcio, 2466.
El auxilio en las ciudades: instituciones, actores y modelos de protección social: Argentina y México: siglos XIX y XX, 308.
Avella, Aniello Angelo, 1640.
Avellaneda, Mercedes, 1015.
Ávila, Affonso, 127.
Avila, Jacqueline, 2694–2697.
Ávila Espinosa, Felipe Arturo, 632.
Ávila Juárez, José Óscar, 639.
Ávila Martínez, Alexander, 3004.
Avni, Haim, 1296.
Avski, Joseph, 1969.
Axt, Gunter, 1708.
Ayalá, Bernc, 741.
Ayala, Gabriel de, 1751.
Ayala Lafée-Wilbert, Cecilia, 1051.
Ayala Mora, Enrique, 1147–1148.
Ayerbe, Júlia Souza, 141, 152.
Azcona Pastor, José Manuel, 409, 413, 755, 787, 1297.
Azcuy Ameghino, Eduardo, 1504.
Azevedo, Carlito, 2467.
Bacal, Tatiana, 2930.
Bacelar, Jeferson, 1575.
Bacellar, Carlos de Almeida Prado, 334.
Backes, Marcelo, 2360.
Badano Gaona, Alondra, 1816.
Báez Martínez, Roberto, 242.
Balaguer, Joaquín, 885.
Balam Rodrigo, 2188–2189.
Balbín, Ricardo, 1471.
Balbino, Evaldo, 2427.
Balbuena, Bernardo de, 1740.

Balderrama Román, Rolando A., 994.
Balladares Rodríguez, Omar, 2190.
Ballesteros, Cacayo, 2598.
Ballón, Alejandra, 1181.
Banco Central de Costa Rica. Museos, 713.
Banco de la República (Colombia), 106.
Baptista, Anna Paola Pacheco, 149.
Baptista Gumucio, Mariano, 1217.
Baquero, Gastón, 1878.
Baradit, Jorger, 1235.
Barahona, Dorelia, 1860.
Barahona Riera, Macarena, 766.
Baranda, María, 2599.
Baratta, Maria Victoria, 1491.
Barbacci, Norma, 43.
Barbara, Vanessa, 2428.
Barbosa, Juliana dos Santos, 2865.
Barbosa, Mario, 470.
Barbosa Sánchez, Alma, 71.
Barceló Rodríguez, Alejandro, 2698–2699.
Barcelos, Fábio Campos, 1660.
Bárcenas García, Felipe, 528.
Barcos, María Fernanda, 1298.
Bardi, Lina Bo, 173.
Barela, Liliana, 414.
Barganhas e querelas da escravidão: tráfico, alforria e liberdade (séculos XVIII e XIX), 1576.
Barham Ode, Walid, 253.
Bari, Atílio, 2557.
Barja, Wagner, 140.
Barnes, William L., 3.
Barnett, Jeffrey C., 2614.
Barnett, Michael A., 915.
Barnitz, Jacqueline, 64.
Barón Biza, Jorge, 2637.
Baronetto, Luis Miguel, 1440.
Barradas, Efraín, 1879, 1922.
Barral, María Elena, 1041.
Barralaga de Olancho, Francisco, 1804.
Barrancos, Dora, 1433.
Barrão, 135.
Barrera-Agarwal, María Helena, 1149.
Barrera-Enderle, Alberto, 529.
Barrera Jurado, Gloria Stella, 107.
Barrero Cuellar, Edgar, 2962.
Barreto, Adriana, 136.
Barreto, Fernando, 2429.
Barreto, Maribel, 2114, 2133.
Barreto Constantín, Ana María, 1299.
Barriga López, Leonardo, 969.
Barrio Batista, Magrid, 886.
Barrios y periferia: espacios socioculturales, siglos XVI-XXI, 442.
Barroco: teoria e análise, 127.

Barrón Corvera, Jorge, 2700–2701.
Barrón Rollano, Vadik, 2191.
Barros, Antonio Evaldo Almeida, 1681.
Barros, Francisco Reinaldo Amorim de, 1546.
Barros, Manoel de, 2468.
Barros, Regina Teixeira de, 152.
Barros, Rubem Rabello Maciel de, 2866.
Barroso, Oswald, 2572.
Bartholazzi, Rosane Aparecida, 1641.
Bartra, Eli, 80.
Barzini, Jorge, 1300.
Basbaum, Ricardo, 179.
Baschetti, Roberto, 1301.
Basile, Marcello Otávio, 1670–1673.
Basile, María Verónica, 1399.
Baskes, Jeremy, 357.
Bastenier, Miguel Angel, 1102.
Bastos, Alcmeno, 2469.
Bastos, Rodrigo, 164.
La Batalla de la Tablada: 200 años; 1817–14 y 15 de abril - 2017; estudios, testimonios, documentos y bibliografía, 1198.
La Batalla de Salta: 20 de febrero de 1813, 1302.
Las batallas por la identidad: visiones de Rosario, 1303.
Batista Lemaire, Olivier, 1915.
Battcock, Clementina, 27.
Bauck, Sönke, 1304.
Baudry, Paul, 2011.
Bauer, Brian S., 254.
Bauer, Caroline Silveira, 410.
Bauer, Erin, 2702.
Bautista S., Rafael, 3018.
Bay, Carmen Alemany, 2304.
Bayer, Osvaldo, 1305.
Bayrón Toro, Fernando, 782.
Beatty, Edward N., 443.
Bebeacua, Francisco, 1503.
Beccar, Alejo, 2311.
Becerril Hernández, Carlos de Jesús, 530.
Beck, Hugo Humberto, 1024.
Becker, Marc, 1150.
Becker, Peter von, 77.
Beckles, Hilary, 783, 814.
Bedregal Villanueva, Juan Francisco, 995, 997.
Beerman, Eric, 358.
Beezley, William H., 444.
Bef, 1765, 1777.
Bejarano Pérez, Mariana Lucrecia, 2178.
Belevén, Harry, 2012.
Belgrano, Manuel, 1031.
Belisário, Waldemar, 148.

Bell, Elizabeth R., 2785.
Bell, Vikki, 98.
Bellatin, Mario, 1758–1761.
Belli, Carlos Germán, 2143, 2235.
Bellini, Lígia, 1577.
Bello, Javier, 2192.
Bellotto, Tony, 2361.
Belmonte Pijuán, Mauricio, 1199.
Beltramim, Fabiana, 159.
Beltrán, José, 1915.
Bem, Sueli de, 165.
Ben, Pablo, 1306.
Ben Othman, Adel, 846.
Benavides, Jorge Eduardo, 2013.
Benavides, Milagrito Alegría de, 276.
Bendaña, Alejandro, 742.
Bender, Wolfgang, 2781.
Benemérita Universidad Autónoma de Puebla. Dirección General de Fomento Editorial, 699.
Bengoa, José, 1236–1237.
Benítez Torres, Milton, 1995.
Bentancor, Orlando, 974.
Benton, Bradley, 192, 194–195, 474.
Beorlegui, Carlos, 2970.
Beovídez, José Luis, 1309.
Berbel, Márcia Regina, 1578.
Bergel, Martín, 1163.
Bergman, Ted L.L., 2703.
Berguño, Jorge, 1238.
Berguño Hurtado, Fernando, 1238.
Bermúdez Molina, Juan Alberto, 2768.
Bernal García, María Elena, 8.
Bernaschina, Paulo, 181.
Bernasconi, Eduardo Guillermo, 1307.
Berrian, Brenda F., 2771.
Berro Hontou, Ernesto, 1505.
Berro: la obra de un estadista, 1505.
Bertero, Eliana, 1308.
Bertero Gutiérrez, Mauro Alberto, 2144.
Bertonha, João Fábio, 1642.
Bertoni Lemus, Claudio, 2193.
Berute, Gabriel Santos, 1595.
Bescós, Roberto, 2194.
Bessa-Oliveira, Marcos Antônio, 2362.
Besse, Juan, 1354.
Betanzos, Lourdes, 2317.
Bethânia, Maria, 2473.
Betto, *Frei*, 2430.
Bezzubikoff Díaz, Evgueni, 2195.
Bialuschewski, Arne, 196.
Biblioteca Nacional Pedro Henríquez Ureña, 941.
El bicentenario de la independencia: legados y realizaciones a doscientos años, 1094.

Bienal Internacional de Asunción, *1st*, *Asunción, 2015*, 113.
Bilac, Jô, 2558–2559.
Bilbao Richter, José, 2080.
Binder, Axel, 1309.
Bindman, David, 47, 826.
Biondo, Gabriela Anahí, 1310.
Bioy Casares, Adolfo, 2081.
Bishop-Sanchez, Kathryn, 2867.
Bitrán, Arón, 2705.
Bitrán Goren, Yael, 2674, 2704.
Bittencourt, Rita Lenira de Freitas, 2470.
Blacha, Luis Ernesto, 1311.
Blackmore, Lisa, 118.
Blanco, Fernando A., 104.
Blanco, Jessica E., 1363.
Blanco Rodríguez, Juan Andrés, 887.
Blandón Guevara, Erick, 1805.
Bleichmar, Daniela, 16.
Bloch, Avital H., 531.
Blumenthal, Edward, 1312.
Bocanegra, Lidia, 675.
Bock, Ulrike, 475.
Bocskay, Stephen, 2868.
Bofill Pérez, María Antonia, 888.
Bohme, Susanna Rankin, 743.
Bohórquez, Abigael, 2196.
Bohórquez Barrera, Jesús, 960.
Böing, Raul, 178.
Boj, Oscar, 2162.
Bojórquez, Daniela, 1762.
Bojunga, Claudia Barroso Roquette-Pinto, 1536.
Bolaños-Salvatierra, Luis M., 2625.
Bolívar, Jorge, 3042.
Bolívar-Martí: pensamiento, vigencias y convergencias: antología, 3001.
Bollettino, Maria Alessandra, 827.
Bon, Henrique, 2383.
Bonacci, Giulia, 889.
Bonan, Amanda, 121.
Bonatti, Andrés, 1313.
Bonaudo, Marta, 1458.
Boneo, Martín Francisco, 1016.
Bonet, Juan Manuel, 69.
Bonet, María Teresa, 3033.
Bonevardi, Marcelo, 68.
Bonilla, Heraclio, 1100, 1200.
Bonilla López, Douglas, 744.
Bonnett, Piedad, 2333.
Boone, Elizabeth Hill, 4, 197, 476.
Booth, Eric, 2828.
Borges, Leonardo, 1506.
Borioli, Gabriela, 2318.
Borrero González, Edwin, 847.
Borrero Silva, María del Valle, 317.
Borsa Cattani, Icleia, 137.
Borsò, Vittoria, 538.
Borucki, Alex, 359.
Bosco, María Angélica, 2638.
Bosi, Viviana, 2520.
Bossa Nova canção: prospettive teoriche e analisi poetico-musicali, 2869.
Bossi, Osvaldo, 2082.
Botana, Natalio R., 1314.
Botelho, Joaquim Maria, 2426.
Botero Montoya, Luis Horacio, 389.
Boturini Benaducci, Lorenzo, 198, 1721.
Boucq, 2645.
Bowman, Henry Edward, 1315.
Bowman, Kirk S., 406.
Boyle, Peter, 2611.
Boza Villarreal, Alejandra, 713.
Bracco, Diego, 1017.
Bracho, Jorge, 1077.
Bradu, Fabienne, 2299–2300.
Braga, Isabel M.R. Mendes Drumond, 1579.
Braga, Reginaldo Gil, 2870.
Braga, Roberto Saturnino, 2384.
Bragança, Jomar, 128.
Brame, Fernando Ribeiro Conçalves, 1643.
Brandão, Ignácio de Loyola, 2423, 2436.
Brander, Leya Mira, 2388.
Bransboin, Hernán, 1316.
O Brasil colonial, 1580.
O Brasil na visualidade popular, 157.
Brasiliana: Journal for Brazilian Studies, 2871.
Braun, Herbert, 1095.
Bravo, María Celia, 1458.
Bravo, Mauribel, 1052.
Bravo Herrera, Fernanda Elisa, 1317.
Braz, Marcelo, 2943.
Brennan, Juan Arturo, 2705.
Brenner, Helmut, 2768.
Brescia, Marco, 2888.
Bresciani, Alberto, 2471.
Bretas, Rodrigo José Ferreira, 128.
Breve antología de poesía mexicana: impúdica, procaz, satírica y burlesca, 2145.
Breve noticia del recibimiento y permanencia de SS. MM. II. en la ciudad de Puebla: Puebla, tipografía de T.F. Neve, 1864, 532.
Brezzo, Liliana María, 1498.
Brian, Amber, 192, 199–200.
Brigagão, Clóvis, 1644.
Bringas, Alfredo, 2706.
Brites, Blanca, 137.
Brito, Alexandre, 2497.
Brito, Mário da Silva, 2462.

Brito, Ronaldo Correia de, 2385.
Brito Guadarrama, Baltazar, 201.
Brittenham, Claudia, 6.
Britto, Luiz, 2560.
Britto, Paulo Henriques, 2472, 2930.
Brizuela, Jean Carlos, 1069.
Brodsky, Adriana Mariel, 1318.
Broner, Martina, 2632.
Brown, Kendall W., 990.
Browne, Randy M., 848.
Bruni Celli, Marco Tulio, 1053.
Bruno, María Sol, 1399.
Bryce, Benjamin, 1412.
Buch, Esteban, 1415, 2830.
Bueno, Christina, 533.
Bueno, Guilherme, 149.
Buenos Aires noir, 2590.
Bulhões, Maria Amélia, 137, 151.
Bulmer-Thomas, V., 309.
Burciaga Campos, José Arturo, 477.
Burdick, Catherine, 202.
Burel, Hugo, 2121.
Burgi, Sergio, 161.
Burgos, Fernando, 1869.
Burgos, Julia de, 1935.
Burgos, Nidia, 2326.
Burke, Janet, 1744.
Burkhart, Louise M., 197, 476.
Burnard, Trevor G., 828–829.
Buscacio, Cesar Maia, 2872.
Bustamante, Maruja, 2308.
Bustamante Bermúdez, Gerardo, 2196.
Bustamante Paulino, Nicéforo, 255.
Bustamante Petit, Armando, 2014.
Bustamente Zamudio, Guillermo, 1989.
Busto Ibarra, Karina, 534.
Bustos, Ilda, 1440.
Bustos Argañaráz, Prudencio, 1319.
Buttó, Luis Alberto, 1059, 1068.
Buve, Raymundus Thomas Joseph, 579.
Caballero, Néstor, 2312.
Caballero Argáez, Carlos, 1090.
Caballero Arias, Hortensia, 256.
Cabanillas Cárdenas, Carlos Fernando, 1752.
Cabiya, Pedro, 1880.
Cabral, Astrid, 2386.
Cabral, Diogo de Carvalho, 1581.
Cabral, Salvador, 257.
Cabrera, Luis, 633.
Cabrera Hanna, Santiago, 1151.
Cabrera Peña, Miguel, 849.
Cacao: producción, consumo y comercio: del período prehispánico a la actualidad en América Latina, 310.

Cáceres, Alejandro, 2184.
Cáceres, Grecia, 2015.
Cáceres, Omar, 2600.
Cáceres Carenzo, Raúl, 2313.
Cacua Prada, Antonio, 1096.
Cádenas, Rafael, 2601–2602.
Caderno de poesias, 2473.
Cafiero, Flavio, 2387.
Caiafa, Janice, 2474.
Caistor, Nick, 2654.
Caixa Cultural Rio de Janeiro, 157.
Calcagno, Duilio Lorenzo, 425.
Calcanhotto, Adriana, 2496.
Caldera, Rafael, 1054.
Calderon Alcantar, Édgar Alejandro, 2709.
Caldo, Paula, 1320.
Caleb Acevedo, David, 1881.
Calles, Ariany, 1051.
Calles caminadas: anverso y reverso, 1239.
Calveyra, Arnaldo, 2603.
Calviño, Manuel, 2962.
Calvo, Julio, 276.
Camacho, Claudia Cristancho, 106.
Camacho, Ricardo, 2333.
Camacho Guizado, Eduardo, 2333.
Camaño Semprini, Rebeca, 1321–1322.
Camargo, Angélica Ricci, 2573.
Camargos, Marcia, 2574.
The Cambridge history of religions in Latin America, 2960.
Camerlengo, Camilla, 2203.
Camerón, Juan, 2197.
Camilletti, Stella, 2314.
Los caminos del Moncada, 784.
Camogli, Pablo, 1323.
Campos, Adalgisa Arantes, 129.
Campos, Adriana Pereira, 1622.
Campos, Haroldo de, 2462, 2547.
Campos, Paulo Mendes, 2431.
Campos Chavarría, Benjamín, 1806.
Campos García, Melchor, 478.
Campos Vera, Norma, 55.
Campuzano Arteta, Álvaro, 3010.
Canale, Dario, 1521.
Canção romântica: intimidade, mediação e identidade na América Latina, 2675.
Canciani, Leonardo, 1324.
Candia Gajá, Andrea, 2106.
Candina, Azun, 1240.
Candlin, Kit, 830.
Cañedo-Argüelles Fabrega, Teresa, 258, 307.
Cañedo Gamboa, Sergio Alejandro, 535.
Cánepa Koch, Gisela, 114.
Caneppele, Ismael, 2873.
Canfield, Martha L., 2214–2216.

Cano, Luis, 2315.
Cano Borrego, Pedro Damián, 715.
Cantarelli, Rodrigo, 1582.
Cantarino, Geraldo, 1645.
Cantarutti, Gabriel E., 254.
Cantera, Carmen Susana, 1019, 1325.
Cantet, Laurent, 1908.
Canton, Darío, 1326.
Cantos Cautivos, 2843.
Cantos de guerra y paz: la música en las independencias iberoamericanas (1800–1840), 2676.
Canuhé, Germán, 277.
Caparrós, Martín, 1874.
Capítulos provinciales de la Orden de la Merced en el Reino de Guatemala (1650–1754), 716.
Cappelletti, Angel J., 2961.
Caraballo, Jorge, 116.
Caramés, Diego, 1414.
Caratti, Jônatas Marques, 1583.
Carbajal López, David, 363.
Carballo, David M., 9.
Carbonero Gamundí, María Antònia, 2976.
Carcelén Reluz, Carlos Guillermo, 259.
Cardboard House Press, 2588.
Cardemil Lastra, Angélica, 1006.
Cardenal, Ernesto, 2198.
Cárdenas, Enrique, 562.
Cárdenas Franco, Adolfo, 1953.
Cárdenas Salazar, Sonia, 1127.
Cardia, Gringo, 2473.
Cardona Ishtar, 2707.
Cardoso, Vânia Zikán, 2584.
Cardoza Sáez, Ebert, 1068.
Cardozo Uzcátegui, Alejandro, 311, 1068, 1088.
Carella, Guiseppe Risisca, 2813.
Carey, Mark P., 1164.
Caribbean Irish connections: interdisciplinary perspectives, 785.
Carlo, Elias, 2604.
Carlson, Jerry W., 943.
Carmona Cruz, Aurelio, 260.
Carneiro, Maria Luiza Tucci, 1547.
Caro, María José, 2016.
Caro Cárdenas, Ricardo, 1165.
Carpinejar, 2475.
Carr Parúas, Fernando, 939.
Carranza Gálvez, Doris, 2199.
Carrascoza, João Anzanello, 2388.
Carredano, Consuelo, 2677.
Carreño Bolívar, Rubí, 2844.
Carreras Ares, Juan José, 2677.
Carrigan, William D., 536.

El carrusel atlántico: memorias y sensibilidades 1500–1950, 311.
Carsalade, Flávio de Lemos, 166.
Carta de chamada: relatos da imigração judaica em São Paulo de 1930 até 1942, 1646.
Cartaxo, Zalinda, 136.
Cartes Montory, Armando, 1002.
Carula, Karoline, 1682.
Caruso, Fernando, 2561.
Carvalho, Alessandra, 1692.
Carvalho, Danielle Crepaldi, 2403.
Carvalho, Hermínio Bello de, 2476, 2874.
Carvalho, Homero, 1954.
Carvalho, José Jorge de, 2875.
Carvalho, José Murilo de, 1657, 1670–1673.
Carvalho, Marco, 2363.
Carvalho, Pedro Henrique Varoni de, 2876.
Carvallo Torres, Guillermo Alejandro, 688.
Casa Amèrica a Catalunya, 94.
Casa de la Cultura Ecuatoriana "Benjamín Carrión", 2808.
Casadei, Eliza Bachega, 2575.
Casanova Rojas, Felipe, 1166.
Casas García, Juan Carlos, 591.
Caso Barrera, Laura, 310, 717.
Cassá, Roberto, 910.
Cassiani Herrera, Alfonso, 961.
Castagna, Paulo, 2877.
Castagnet, Martín Felipe, 2639.
Castañeda, Luis, 2017.
Castañeda de la Paz, María, 203.
Castañeda Murga, Juan, 50.
Castellanos, Julio, 2200.
Castellanos Moya, Horacio, 1807.
Castilho, Celso Thomas, 1565.
Castilla Urbano, Francisco, 350.
Castillo, Lisa Earl, 1576.
Castillo, Rodrigo, 2173.
Castillo Canché, Jorge I., 568.
Castillo Espinoza, Eduardo, 103.
Castillo Flores, Gabino, 2756.
Castillo-Garsow, Melissa, 2682.
Castillo Hernández, Mario Alberto, 243.
Castillo Olivares, Juan Jacobo, 639.
Castillo Ramírez, Daniel, 1166.
Castillo Ramírez, Guillermo, 634.
Castillo Troncoso, Alberto del, 414, 1327–1328.
Castrillón Gallego, Catalina, 1097.
Castro, Angela Maria Bezerra de, 2464.
Castro, Evandro Carlos Guilhon de, 1647.
Castro, Felipe, 2938.
Castro, Flávio, 2477.
Castro, Hebe Maria Mattos de, 1598.

Castro, J. Justin, 635.
Castro, Marcílio França, 2389.
Castro, Ruy, 2874, 2878–2879.
Castro Celada, Estuardo, 1808.
Castro García, Óscar, 1970.
Castro Mira, Santiago, 1970.
Castro R., Juan Pablo, 1996.
Casullo, Mariana, 1414.
Catálogo de obras de música del Archivo del Cabildo Catedral Metropolitano de México, 2708.
Cátedra Marta Traba, *Bogotá, 2010, semester 1*, 108.
De Catemahco a Tezcoco: origen y desarrollo de una ciudad indígena, 204.
Catena, Alberto, 3038.
Caudillos, política e instituciones en los orígenes de la nación argentina, 1329.
Caula, Nelson, 1503.
Cavalcanti, Geraldo Holanda, 2390.
Caviasca, Guillermo, 1330.
Cázares Puente, Eduardo, 479.
Celebración y sonoridad en las catedrales novohispanas, 2709.
Celis Galindo, Dante Guillermo, 1743.
100 anos de artes plásticas no Instituto de Artes da UFRGS: três ensaios, 137.
Ceniza enamorada: poetas salvadoreños de la resistencia, 2146.
O censo de 1906 do Rio de Janeiro, 1648.
Centeno, Juan, 1809.
Centeno Añeses, Carmen, 1923.
Cento Gómez, Elda, 850.
Centro de Arte Hélio Oiticica, 139.
Centro de Estudios Históricos (Mexico), 677.
Centro de Estudios La Mujer en la Historia de América Latina, 390.
Centro de Ilustração Botânica do Paraná, 178.
Centro de Investigación y Docencia Económicas, 343.
Centro de Preservação Cultural da USP, 175, 183.
Centro Journal, 890.
Centro para la Edición de Clásicos Españoles, 1742.
Centro Peninsular en Humanidades y Ciencias Sociales, 337.
Centro Rolando Morán, 775.
Cepeda Samudio, Alvaro, 1971.
Cerdá, Juan Manuel, 308.
Cerletti, Adriana, 2831.
Cerón Rengifo, Carmen Patricia, 1098.
Cerón Reyes, Roberto, 1246.
Cerón Soriano, Ahiremí Irene, 414.
Cerritos, Jorgelina, 2316.
Cerruti, Pedro, 3034.
Ceruso, Diego, 1331.
Cerutti Guldberg, Horacio, 2972.
Cervantes, Fernando, 1739.
Cervantes, Ignacio, 2791.
Cervera, Felipe Justo, 3035.
César, Chico, 2478.
Cestero, Tulio Manuel, 1882.
Chabrando, Victoria Anahí, 1399.
Chacal, 2479.
Chácara do Céu (Rio de Janeiro), 149.
The Chaco War: environment, ethnicity, and nationalism, 1201, 1492.
Chacón, Alfredo, 2201.
Chacón, Luis, 1810.
Chacón Hidalgo, Manuel Benito, 713.
Chagas, Jorge, 1507.
Chaires Zaragoza, Jorge, 537.
Chambouleyron, Rafael, 1522.
Chang, Jason Oliver, 445.
Chang-Rodríguez, Raquel, 1722.
Chasteen, John Charles, 2653.
Chauca Tapia, Roberto, 261.
Chaupis Torres, José, 394.
Chavajay, Pedro, 2162.
Chaves, Claudio Enrique, 1332.
Chaves, Gonzalo Leónidas, 1333.
Chaves, José Ricardo, 1811.
Chaves, Raquel, 2202.
Chávez, Alex E., 2710–2711.
Chávez, Joaquín Mauricio, 745.
Chávez, Rosa, 2203.
Chávez, Samuel Antonio, 262.
Chávez Camacho, Benjamín, 1955.
Chávez Chávez, Jorge, 621.
Chávez Frías, Hugo, 1055.
El Che en la psicología latinoamericana, 2962.
Cherñavsky, Analía, 2708.
Chesterton, Bridget María, 436, 1201, 1492–1494.
Chevalier, Nan, 1924.
Chez Checo, José, 891.
Chiappero, Rubén Osvaldo, 1334.
Chiara, Ana, 1507.
Chiaramonte, José Carlos, 1018, 1335.
Chicangana-Bayona, Yobenj Aucardo, 17.
Chile-Colombia: diálogos sobre sus trayectorias históricas, 1241.
Chile en el Perú: la ocupación a través de sus documentos, 1881–1884, 1167.
Chimalpahin Cuauhtlehuanitzin, Domingo Francisco de San Antón Muñón, 1751.
China y Perú: en el arte y la cultura, 1168.

Chiquichano, Nahuel, 1309.
Chiriboga, Fernando, 160.
Chirinos Arrieta, Eduardo, 2204.
Choque Canqui, Roberto, 263.
Chornik, Katia, 2843.
Choros de Garoto, 2880.
Christensen, Mark Z., 226.
Chust Calero, Manuel, 399.
Chután Alvarado, Edgar F., 714.
Cibotti, Ema, 312.
Cicerchia, Ricardo, 1336.
Cid Pérez, José, 2317.
Cienfuegos Salgado, David, 619.
150 años de Y Wladfa: ensayos sobre la historia de la colonización galesa en la Patagonia, 1337.
Cinemateca de Cuba, 97.
Cisneros, Gerardo, 455.
Cisneros, Renato, 2018.
Cisneros Stoianowski, Victoria, 455.
Citro, Silvia, 2831.
Ciudades sudamericanas como arenas culturales: artes y medios, barrios de élite y villas miseria, intelectuales y urbanistas: cómo ciudad y cultura se activan mutuamente: Bogotá, Brasilia, Buenos Aires, Caracas, Córdoba, La Plata, Lima, Montevideo, Quito, Recife, Río de Janeiro, Salvador, San Pablo, Santiago de Chile, 313.
Claps Arenas, María Eugenia, 557.
Clark, Blair, 22.
Clavé Almeida, Martín, 1745.
Clavigero, Francesco Saverio, 2991.
Cleary, Heather, 2609.
Cloppet, Ignacio Martín, 1338.
Coaguila, Jorge, 1947.
Cobo Borda, Juan Gustavo, 2205.
Cobo Paz, Natalia, 1129.
Codato, Adriano Nervo, 1658.
Coelho, Frederico Oliveira, 2930.
Coelho, Oliverio, 2083.
Coelho, Paulo, 2666–2667.
Coelho Neto, Eurelino Teixeira, 423.
Coelho Netto, J. Teixeira, 145.
Coester, Markus, 2781.
Cohen Suarez, Ananda, 51.
Cohen Ventura, Jacob, 1242.
Colantonio, Sonia, 1450.
Colanzi Serrate, Liliana, 2631.
Colección Barbosa-Stern, 54.
Colegio de México. Centro de Estudios Históricos, 446, 448.
Colegio de Michoacán, 242, 927.
Coleman, Kevin P., 746.

Collazo, Marcia, 1503.
Colmán Gutiérrez, Andrés, 2115.
Los colombianistas: una completa visión de los investigadores extranjeros que estudian a Colombia, 1099.
Colón González, José Luis, 899, 935.
La colonia galesa del Chubut en imágenes: de los comienzos al Centenario, 1339.
Colonia-independencia-revolución: genealogías, latencias y transformaciones en la escritura y las artes de México, 538.
Colonial and postcolonial change in Mesoamerica: archaeology as historical anthropology, 480.
Coloniality, religion, and the law in the early Iberian world, 1741.
Colonización, economía agrícola y empresarios en el noroeste de México: siglos XIX y XX, 539.
Colóquio Comunistas Brasileiros: Cultura Política e Produção Cultural *Universidade de São Paulo, Departamento de História, 2011*, 1649.
Coloquio Iberoamericano sobre Investigación Musical Ibermúsicas, *1st, México, 2015*, 2674.
Coloquio Internacional "1910: México entre Dos Épocas," *Paris, 2010*, 540.
Coloquio Internacional Delitos, Policías y Justicia en América Latina, *Santiago, Chile, 2013*, 314.
Coloquio Internacional El Antiimperialismo Latinoamericano: Discursos y Pácticas. Homenaje Augusto C. Sandino, *Managua, 2014*, 2975.
Coloquio La Presencia Africana en la Música de Guerrero, *4th, Chilpancingo de los Bravos, Mexico, 2011*, 2712.
Coloquio sobre Darwinismo en Europa y América *5th, Valdivia, Chile, 2013*, 315.
Combatir al otro: el Río de la Plata en épocas de antagonismos: 1776–1830, 1019.
Combès, Isabelle, 264–265.
Comisión Nacional del Uruguay para la UNESCO, 2853.
Como si no bastase ya ser: 15 narradoras peruanas, 2019.
El compañero que me atiende, 1883.
Una concepción atlántica del americanismo: en los pasos de François Chevalier, 636.
Conduru, Roberto, 138.
Conflicto, resistencia y negociación en la historia, 446.
Conflictos y tensiones en el Chile republicano, 1243.

Confluencias: dramaturgias serranas: recopilación en torno a los encuentros del Proyecto Pluja, 2318.
Conformación y retórica de los repertorios musicales catedralicios en la Nueva España, 2713.
Congreso Internacional Ciencias, Tecnologías y Culturas: Diálogo entre las Disciplinas del Conocimiento, Mirando al Futuro de América Latina y el Caribe, *3rd, Santiago, Chile, 2013*, 411.
Congreso Internacional de Escrituras Silenciadas, *4th, Cusco, Peru, 2014*, 316.
Congreso Internacional de Historia Regional, *12th, Ciudad Juárez, Mexico, 2009*, 621.
Congreso Internacional "La Tradición Clásica en la América de los Siglos XVI y XVII," *Madrid, 2014*, 1742.
Congreso Internacional Las Mujeres en los Procesos de Independencia de América Latina, *1st, Lima, 2013*, 390.
Congreso Internacional Nuevos Horizontes de Iberoamérica *1st, Mendoza, Argentina, 2013*, 411.
Congresso Internacional "Música, Cultura e Identidade no Bicentenário da Elevação do Brasil a Reino Unido," *São Paulo, 2015*, 2881.
Conjunto Cultural da República (Brasília). Museu Nacional, 140.
La conmemoración de la Revolución de Mayo: prensa gráfica, historia y política, siglos XIX–XXI, 1340.
Conover Blancas, Carlos, 718.
Consecuencias económicas de la independencia, 1100.
Consejo Nacional de Ciencia y Tecnología (Mexico), 927.
Constructing power and place in Mesoamerica: pre-Hispanic paintings from three regions, 5.
Contigo ni pan ni cebolla: debates y prácticas sobre el divorcio vincular en Argentina: 1932–1968, 1341.
Contreras, Carlos, 1185.
Cooper, Sara E., 2630.
Corcuera, Arturo, 2206.
Corcuera, Marco Antonio, 2207.
Corcuera, Ruth, 52.
Cordero, Karen, 78.
Cordero Michel, Emilio, 786.
Córdova, James M., 28.
Corella Ovares, Esteban, 713.
Cornejo Bouroncle, Jorge, 266.

Corominas, Alicia, 267.
Coronado Guel, Luis Edgardo, 461.
Coronel Quisbert, Cristóbal, 1202.
Corral Raigosa, Beatriz, 698.
Corrêa, Luiz Felipe de Seixas, 1700.
Corrêa, Maria Letícia, 1682.
Correa Rodríguez, Alejandro, 2714–2716.
Correspondencia de los diplomáticos franceses en Costa Rica (1889–1917), 747.
Correspondencia epistolar (1855–1881), 1342.
Corruption in the Iberian empires: greed, custom, and colonial networks, 360.
Corsaletti, Fabrício, 2432.
Cortázar, Julio, 2662.
Cortázar Velarde, Juan Carlos, 2020.
Cortés, Darío A., 2319.
Cortés, José Miguel G., 62.
Cortés González, Alejandro, 2208.
Cortés Guerrero, José David, 1094.
Cortés Koloffon, Adriana, 1723.
Cortés Máximo, Juan Carlos, 205, 208.
Cortés Navarro, Rocío, 373.
Cortesão, Jaime, 1584.
Cortez, Enrique E., 2030.
Cosentino, Olga, 2355.
Cosi, Claudio, 2869.
Cosse, Isabella, 1341.
Costa, Cecília, 2433.
Costa, Dilma Fátima Avellar Cabral da, 1660.
Costa, Dora Isabel Paiva da, 1650.
Costa, Edwaldo, 1651.
Costa, Heraldo Batista da, 1585.
Costa, Luana, 2938.
Costa, Margaret Jull, 2666.
Costa, Rafael Maul de Carvalho, 1652.
Costa, Ricardo Ramos, 2480.
Costa, Sabrina Studart Fontenele, 167.
Costa, Virgilio, 2433.
Costa, Walter Carlos, 2672.
Costa Filho, Odylo, 2433.
Costantini, Humberto, 2106.
Costin, Cathy Lynne, 10.
Cottyn, Hanne, 1203.
Coutinho, Araripe, 2481.
Coutinho, Maria do Carmo Strozzi, 1615.
Coutinho, Marina Henriques, 2576.
Coutinho, Renato Soares, 1653.
Couto, Caroline Peres, 2882.
Covert, Lisa Pinley, 637.
Cowan, Benjamin A., 1654.
Coy, Negma, 2162.
Cramaussel, Chantal, 363.
Crawford, Matthew James, 361.
Crenes Castro, Pedro, 1849.

Creni, Gisela, 180.
Crenzel, Emilio Ariel, 435.
Crespo Armáiz, Jorge Luis, 851, 892.
Crespo Granda, Andrea, 2209.
Cressoni, Fábio Eduardo, 1589.
Crewe, Ryan, 206.
Cribelli, Teresa, 182.
Cristi, Renato, 3025.
Cristóforis, Nadia Andrea de, 1343, 1387.
Croft, Jennifer, 2650.
Cruset, María Eugenia, 1344.
Cruz, Adelina Maria Alves Novaes e, 1569.
Cruz, Danielle Maia, 2883.
Cruz, Enrique Normando, 1020.
Cruz, Michel Garcia, 1898.
Cruz, Pablo, 53.
Cruz Gómez, Natalia, 1129.
Cruz Porchini, Dafne, 72, 81.
Cruz Santos, Martín, 893.
Cuadriello, Jaime, 40.
Cuando las armas hablan, los impresos luchan, la exclusion agrede...: violencia electoral en México, 1812–1912, 541.
Cuarenta años de investigación musical en México a través del CENIDIM, 2717.
Cuatro miradas: a propósito del *Primer Libro Venezolano de Literatura, Ciencias y Bellas Artes de 1895*, 1056.
Cuba on the verge: 12 writers on continuity and change in Havana and across the country, 1884.
Cuba y España: procesos migratorios e impronta perdurable (siglos XIX y XX), 787.
Cucchi, Laura, 1345.
Cuéllar Chávez, Bismark Alberto, 996.
Cuentos memorables venezolanos, 2059.
Cuerpo adentro: historias desde el clóset, 1997.
Cueto, Alonso, 2021.
Cuevas Murillo, Oscar, 569.
Culto a los ancestros, hechiceros y resistencia colonial: el case de Gragorio Taco, Arequipa, 1750, 975.
Cultura, arte e história: a contribuição dos jesuítas entre os séculos XVI e XIX, 1586.
Cummins, Tom, 1747.
Cunha, Jorge Luiz da, 326.
Cunha, Paulo Ribeiro da, 1655.
Cunha, Rubens da, 2482.
Cunill, Pedro, 1057.
Cunin, Elisabeth, 706.
Curatola, Marco, 347.
Curcó Cobos, Felipe, 2963.
Curso "Filósofos Justicialistas", *Buenos Aires, 2012*, 3042.
Curtis, Howard, 2642.
Cushman, Gregory T., 1169.
Cushner, Nicholas P., 970.
Cussen, Celia L., 976.
Cutrera, María Laura, 1346.
Cynovich, Carolina, 2122.
Czajka, Rodrigo, 1649.
Da cartografia do poder aos itinerários do saber, 181.
Da Orden, María Liliana, 1347.
Dagua Hurtado, Abelino, 288.
Dalby, Jonathan R., 852.
D'Alessandro Bello, María Elena, 1058.
d'Avila, Cristiane, 1656.
Dalla-Corte, Gabriela, 318.
Dalton, Roque, 2146.
Dámaso Martínez, Carlos, 1476.
Daniel, Claudio, 2483.
Dapieve, Arthur, 2391.
Darío, Rubén, 2301.
Daróz, Carlos Roberto Carvalho, 1587.
Darwin en (y desde) México, 542.
Dávalos López, Marcela, 442.
David, Sérgio Nazar, 2484.
Davidson, Christina Cecelia, 894–895.
Davidson, Russ, 625.
Davies, Drew Edward, 2708, 2713.
Davies, Jonathan Ceredig, 1348.
Dávila, Arturo, 2147.
Dávila, Numa, 2176.
Dávila Montoya, Alejandra, 27.
Dávila Munguía, Carmen Alicia, 642.
Davis, Helen R., 2084.
Dawsey, John C., 2569, 2584.
Day, Stuart Alexander, 457.
De Amberes al Cusco: el grabado europeo como fuente del arte virreinal, 54.
De Ferrari, Guillermina, 1925.
De Giuseppe, Massimo, 588.
De heroínas, fundadoras y ciudadanas: mujeres en la historia de Chile, 1244.
De la Fuente, Juan, 2210.
De la Garza, Armida, 2718.
De la hueste indiana al pretorianismo del siglo XX: relaciones civiles y militares en la historia de Venezuela, 1059.
de la Torre, Ricardo, 2719.
De León Olivares, Isabel Dolores, 896.
De música y cultura en la Nueva España y el México independiente: testimonios de innovación y pervivencia, 2720.
De qué va el cuento: antología del relato venezolano 2000–2012, 2060.

De Sarlo, Giulia, 1926.
Deconstrucción y genealogía del concepto de dignidad de los pueblos originarios en el pensamiento latinoamericano, 2964.
Deeny, Anna, 2595.
Degiovanangelo, Guillermo, 2320.
Degregori, Carlos Iván, 1170.
Dehne, Phillip, 412.
Dehouve, Danièle, 207.
Deij Prado, Macarena, 51.
Del Castillo, Lina, 49, 1101.
Del espacio cantábrico al mundo americano: perspectivas sobre migración, etnicidad y retorno, 317.
Del pensamiento continuo: apuntes de/sobre Norberto Griffa, 3036.
Del Priore, Mary, 1677.
Delgado, Jessica L., 481.
Delgado Benites, Francisco Javier, 1171.
Delgado Gonzales, Trifonio, 1204.
Delgado Rozo, Juan David, 1104.
Delgado Senior, Igor, 2061.
Deltoro, Antonio, 2211.
Democracia, otredad, melancolía: Roger Bartra ante la crítica, 2990.
Denis, Rafael Cardoso, 168.
Denis Molina, Carlos, 2321.
Dente, Miguel Angel, 2832.
Depestre Catony, Leonardo, 1907.
Depetris, Carolina, 337, 543.
Derbiz, Walter, 1347.
Derenji, Jussara da Silveira, 130.
La desamortización civil desde perspectivas plurales, 544.
As descobertas do Brasil: o olhar estrangeiro na construção da imagem do Brasil, 182.
Desde la historia: homenaje a Marta Bonaudo, 1349.
Desde la otra orilla: miradas extranjeras sobre Querétaro, 447.
DeSilva-Johnson, Lynne, 2613.
Despradel, Fidelio, 897.
Desquirón, Antonio, 89.
Desrosiers, Sophie, 11.
Los desterrados del paraíso: raza, pobreza y cultura en Cartagena de Indias, 1102.
Deustua, Raúl, 2212.
d'Horta, Vera, 156.
Di Benedetto, Antonio, 2632.
Di Donato, Dinapiera, 2605.
Di Giorgio, Marosa, 2606.
Di Lorenzo, José Luis, 3042.
Di Mauro, Daniel, 2322.
Di Meglio, Gabriel, 1350–1351.
Di Paolo, Rossella, 2213.
Di Pasquale, Mariano, 1352.
di Salvia, Daniela, 268.
Di Stefano, Mariana, 1353.
Di Stefano, Roberto, 340.
Di Tata Roitberg, Emilio, 2085.
"Diario de la navegación hecha por José Antonio Vázquez": contribución al conocimiento náutico de la ruta entre Filipinas y la Nueva España, 1743.
Dias, Antônio Gonçalves, 269, 2434.
Dias, Elaine, 132.
Dias, Maurício de Mello, 139.
Dias, Renato da Silva, 1619.
Dias & Riedweg, 139.
Díaz, Carla, 283.
Diaz, Josef, 18.
Diaz, Juan Diego, 2884.
Díaz, Martín, 1812.
Díaz, Mónica, 239, 989.
Díaz Araujo, Enrique, 1245.
Díaz Araya, Alberto, 1166.
Díaz Arias, David, 707, 713, 748–749.
Díaz Ayala, Cristóbal, 2787.
Díaz Bagú, Alberto, 2323.
Díaz Casas, María Camila, 1103.
Díaz del Castillo, Bernal, 1744.
Díaz-Duhalde, Sebastián, 1495.
Díaz Frene, Jaddiel, 2721.
Díaz Granados, José Luis, 1972.
Díaz Hernández, Magdalena, 482.
Díaz Munévar, Alexander, 1129.
Díaz Ordaz, Gustavo, 638.
Díaz Quiñonez, Arcadio, 2132.
Diéguez Caballero, Ileana, 73.
Diel, Lori Boornazian, 29.
16 de junio de 1955, bombardeo y masacre: imágenes, memorias, silencios, 1354.
Dillman, Jefferson, 788.
Dimensões e fronteiras do estado brasileiro no oitocentos, 1657.
Diniz, Clarissa, 168.
Diniz, Sheyla Castro, 2885.
Ditadura: o que resta da transição, 1658.
Las diversidades indígenas en Michoacán, 208.
Do Valongo à favela: imaginário e periferia, 168.
Dobel, Hilary Vaughn, 2657.
Döbrich, Wolfgang, 1523.
Documentos del gobierno de Carlos F. Morales Languasco 1903–1906, 898.
Documentos para la historia del general don Manuel Belgrano, 1355.
Documentos y testimonios históricos del sitio a Puebla de 1863, 545.

Dodson, Katrina, 2665.
Dolabela, Marcelo Gomes, 2485.
Dolhnikoff, Miriam, 1693.
Domingues, Petrônio, 1667, 1697.
Domínguez, Freddy, 1063.
Domínguez, Lourdes, 853.
Domínguez, Ramiro, 2134.
Domínguez Condezo, Víctor, 270.
Domínguez Hernández, Javier, 110.
Domínguez Paredes, Raúl Alejandro, 1356.
Domínguez Saldívar, Roger, 568.
Dominican Republic. Secretaría de Estado de Cultura, 941.
Donís Ríos, Manuel Alberto, 1060.
Donnell, Alison, 785.
Donoso, Sebastián I., 362.
Donoso Fritz, Karen, 395.
Donoso Rojas, Carlos, 1243.
Dormady, Jason H., 452.
Dorr, Kirstie A., 2809.
D'Orto, Alejandro, 2350.
Dos caminhos históricos aos processos culturais entre Brasil e Suriname, 1588.
Dotta Ostria, Mario, 1508.
Dougnac Rodríguez, Antonio, 1246.
Doval, Romina, 2086.
Dove, Stephen C., 2960.
Dr. Antonio Fernós Isern: de médico a constituyente, 899.
Drago, Margarita, 776.
Dramaturgia antioqueña, 1879–1963: antología, 2324.
Dramaturgia cubana contemporánea: antología, 2325.
Dramaturgias bahienses, 2326.
Dreher, Martin Norberto, 1659.
Drews, Pablo, 3030.
Drummond, Roberto, 2668.
Duany, Jorge, 789.
Duarte, Drika, 2486.
Duarte, Luis María, 1496.
Dubatti, Ricardo, 2341.
Duchesne, Frédéric, 975.
Duchesne Winter, Juan, 1927.
Dudeque, Norton, 2886, 2956.
Dughi, Pilar, 2022.
Dujovne, Alejandro, 1357.
Dulci, Tereza Maria Spyer, 391.
Dumaresq, Paulo Jorge, 2562.
Dumbarton Oaks, 10.
Dumett, Rafael, 2023.
Dumont, Henri, 853.
Dundes, Lauren, 791.
Dungy, Kathryn Renée, 854.
Dunkley, Daive A., 915.

Dunn, Christopher, 2887.
Dunn, Richard S., 831.
Duno Gottberg, Luis, 3002.
Dupey García, Elodie, 243.
Duprey Salgado, Néstor R., 899.
Duque Estrada Sacasa, Esteban, 750.
Duque Muñoz, Lucía, 1104.
Durán, Juan Guillermo, 1358.
Durán Ayanegui, Fernando, 1813.
Durán-Merk, Alma, 546.
Durán Moncada, Cristóbal Margarito, 2722.
Durand González, Guillermo, 1061.
Dutt, Rajeshwari, 209–210, 547.
Duverger, Christian, 211.
Earle, Rebecca, 483, 1105.
Earth, water and sky: a bilingual anthology of environmental poetry, 2591.
Eastman, Scott, 400.
Echavarren, Roberto, 2607.
Echevarría Cabán, Abdiel, 2148.
Echeverría, Maurice, 1814.
Eckart, Anselm, 1574.
La economía colonial de la Nueva Granada, 962.
Educação, sociedade e cultura na América portuguesa: estudos sobre a presença jesuítica, 1589.
Los efectos del liberalismo en México, siglo XIX, 548.
Ehlers S. Prestán, Sonia, 1815.
Ehrick, Christine, 1359.
Eielson, Jorge Eduardo, 2214–2216.
Eisner, Mark, 2619.
Eissa-Barroso, Francisco A., 963.
El Salvador, de la guerra civil a la paz negociada, 751.
El Youssef, Alain, 1567.
Eldridge, Michael, 2772.
Elecciones en el México del siglo XIX: las fuentes, 549.
Elementos identitarios de la imagen de España, América Latina y de su historia en Albania: análisis estructural y estudio de caso, 413.
Eli Rodríguez, Victoria, 2677.
Elías Caro, Jorge Enrique, 407.
Elliott, Richard George, 34.
Elmir, Cláudio P., 328.
Eloy, Horacio, 1247.
Emmer, Denise, 2487.
Empresa, empresarios e industrialización en las regiones de México, siglos XIX y XX, 639.
En el nudo del imperio: independencia y democracia en el Perú, 1172.

En la vastedad del "desierto" patagónico...: estado, prácticas y actores sociales (1884–1958), 1360.
Enchílame otras: comida mexicana en el siglo XIX, 550.
Enciso Contreras, José, 551, 569.
Encontro de Musicologia Histórica da UFRJ, 7th, Pirenópolis, Brazil, 2015, 2949.
Encontro: São Paulo, 2013, 2577.
Encuentro Iberoamericano de Jóvenes Musicólogos, 3rd, Sevilla, Spain, 2016, 2888.
Encuentro Internacional sobre Barroco, 5th, La Paz, 2009, 55.
Encuentro Latinoamericano de Historia Oral, 5th, San Salvador, 2013, 414.
Engel, Emily A., 1747.
Engel, Magali, 1682.
Engemann, Carlos, 1621.
Enríquez, Lucero, 2684, 2708, 2713.
Enriquez, Mariana, 2633.
Enríquez Perea, Alberto, 545.
Enríquez Rubio, Lucero, 2720.
Entrecopas: arte brasileira 1950–2014, 140.
Episodios de la cultura histórica argentina: celebraciones, imágenes y representaciones del pasado, siglos XIX y XX, 1361.
Erlich, Uriel, 1362.
Ernst Powell, Jessica, 2619.
Escallón, Eduardo, 1090.
Escalona Chádez, Israel, 787.
Escamilla, Iván, 355, 2991.
Escenarios y provocaciones: mujeres cuentistas de Panamá y México 1980–2014, 1816.
Escenas del yo flotante: Cuba: escrituras autobiográficas, 1885.
Escobar Galindo, David, 751.
Escobar Giraldo, Octavio, 1973.
Escobar Guzmán, Brenda, 1106.
Escobar Medrano, Jorge Enrique, 56.
Escobar Ohmstede, Antonio, 544, 548.
Escobar Velásquez, Mario, 1974.
Escola SESC de Ensino Médio (Rio de Janeiro), 2901.
Escolán Romero, Gabriel, 752.
Escribir las fuerzas: taller de dramaturgia Juárez 2014, 2327.
Escudero, Eduardo A., 1479.
Escudos, Jacinta, 1817.
Escuela de Gobierno Alberto Lleras Camargo, 1090.
Espacio público en Argentina, fines s. XIX-primera mitad s. XX: partidos, catolicismo, sociabilidad, 1363.

Espacios críticos habaneros del arte cubano: la década de 1950, 90.
Espacios en la historia: invención y transformación de los espacios sociales, 448.
Espartaco, Daniel, 1763.
Espejel Carbajal, Claudia, 242.
Espínola, Adriano, 2488.
Espínola, Ramón Emilio, 900.
Espinosa, Agustín, 30.
Espinosa, Carlos R., 971.
Espinosa, David, 449.
Espinosa, Gustavo, 2123.
Espinosa, Rafael, 2217.
Espinosa Fernández de Córdoba, Carlos, 1152.
Espinosa Mendoza, Norge, 1898.
Espinosa Ochoa, Francisco, 1998.
Espinoza, Eunice, 2169.
Espinoza, G. Antonio, 1173.
Espinoza Chávez, Agustín, 30.
Espinoza Córdova, María del Carmen, 50.
Espírito Santo, Cristina, 2577.
Esponda Jimeno, Víctor Manuel, 2751.
Esquinca, Bernardo, 1764.
Esquinca, Jorge, 2218, 2302.
Estação Pinacoteca, 153.
Estado e administração: a construção do Brasil independente (1822–1840), 1660.
Estephan, Sérgio, 2889.
Estermann, Josef, 3008.
La estética del suspenso: epistemología para una historia compartida, a partir de la obra de Walter Benjamín: lecturas latinoamericanas, 3009.
Estévez, Abilio, 1886.
Estrada, Chris, 2890.
Estrada Iguíniz, Margarita, 334.
Estrada Orrego, Victoria, 1107.
Estrada Saavedra, Marco, 640.
Estrada Valadez, Tania, 2723.
Estrella, Ana, 1999.
Estrella González, Alejandro, 552.
Estruch, Dolores, 1021.
Estudios y testimonios sobre el exilio español en México: una visión sobre su presencia en las humanidades, 641.
Estudos luso-brasileiros em iconografia musical, 2891.
Etchegoimberry, Delia, 1503.
Etchevarren, Javier, 2219.
Etnomusicologia no Brasil, 2892.
Etnorock: los rostros de una música global en el sur de México, 2724.
Eujanian, Alejandro C., 1361, 1364.
Evangelista, Ana Maria da Costa, 1661.

Evangelista, Olinda, 185.
Ewell, Barbara C., 2959.
Exiliados de la guerra civil española, en México: sociedad, política y ciencia, 642.
Extendiendo los límites: nuevas agendas en historia reciente, 415.
Eyal, Hillel, 484.
Fabião, Eleonora, 2577.
Fajardo Estrada, Ramón, 901.
Falabella, Fernanda, 294.
Falcón, Romana, 544, 579.
Falconí, Ana María, 2220.
Fallas Santana, Carmen Maria, 753.
Familias, movilidad y migración: América Latina y España, 318.
Familias pluriétnicas y mestizaje en la Nueva España y el Río de la Plata, 363.
Fanchin, Ana, 1022.
Fantini, Sérgio, 2392.
Faour, Rodrigo, 2893.
Farías, Matías, 1414.
Farías, Víctor, 1248.
Fariña, Soledad, 2221.
Faudree, Paja, 2725.
Favila Vázquez, Mariana, 212.
Fayad, Luis, 1975.
Feldman, Heidi Carolyn, 2810.
Felippe, Guilherme Galhegos, 271, 1590.
Felix, Nelson, 141.
Fernandes, João, 150.
Fernandes, Leandro Raniero, 2859.
Fernandes, María Lúcia Outeiro, 2531.
Fernandes, Rinaldo de, 2393.
Fernandes, Ronaldo Costa, 2489.
Fernández, Bernardo (Bef), 1765.
Fernández, Bertha, 2788.
Fernández, Laura, 1742.
Fernández, María Ángeles, 24.
Fernandez, Segundo J., 91.
Fernández, Severiano, 2178.
Fernández Aceves, María Teresa, 643.
Fernández Ampié, Guillermo, 2625.
Fernández Caminero, José, 1915.
Fernández Domingo, Jesús Ignacio, 846.
Fernández Hellmund, Paula D., 754.
Fernández Pavón, Marisol, 688.
Fernández Rosado, Ángela Altagracia, 407.
Fernández Sagastume, Mirian Leavel, 719–720.
Fernández Uribe, Carlos Arturo, 110.
Ferrando, Diego, 2350.
Ferrari, Jorge Luis, 1365.
Ferrari, Olgar, 2087.
Ferraris, María Carolina, 1366.
Ferraz, Eucanaã, 2490, 2516.

Ferraz, Francisco César Alves, 1679.
Ferreira, César, 1950.
Ferreira, Daniel, 1976.
Ferreira, Elisangela Oliveira, 1591.
Ferreira, Evandro Affonso, 2364.
Ferreira, Glória, 123.
Ferreira, Gustavo Alves Alonso, 2894–2895.
Ferreira, Jaci, 185.
Ferreira, Jorge Luiz, 1661.
Ferreira, Roquinaldo, 1662.
Ferreira Esparza, Carmen Adriana, 964.
Ferrer, Renée, 2114.
Ferrigni, Yoston, 1062.
Fetter, Bruna, 151.
Févola, Lucila Beatriz, 2222.
Fierros Hernández, Arturo, 553.
Figallo Lascano, Beatriz J., 1367.
Figueiredo, Lucas, 1524.
Figueiredo, Tatiana Longo, 2859.
Figueroa, Evelyn, 2819.
Filinich Orozco, Renzo, 2811.
Filosofía iberoamericana del siglo XX, 2965–2966.
Filosofía y sabiduría ancestral, 272.
Finchelstein, Federico, 1368, 3037.
Finegold, Andrew, 2.
Finzi, Alejandro, 2328.
Fiol-Matta, Licia, 2773.
Firbas, Paul, 2132.
La fiscalidad novohispana en el imperio español: conceptualizaciones, proyectos y contradicciones, 485.
Fischer, Brodwyn M., 1525.
Fischer, Luís Augusto, 2393, 2855.
Fitzpatrick-Behrens, Susan, 1174.
Flaherty, George F., 74.
La flama del tiempo: testimoniales y estudios poéticos, 2305.
Fleck, Eliane Cristina Deckmann, 1039.
Fleites, Alex, 1893.
Flint, Richard, 364, 486.
Florentino, Manolo, 1622.
Flores, Malva, 2306.
Flores, Tatiana, 92.
Flores Chávez, Pablo, 2223.
Flores Clair, Eduardo, 554.
Flores Lara, Mario, 2962.
Flores Zavala, Marco Antonio, 555.
Flórez Bolívar, Francisco Javier, 1102.
Folsom, Bradley, 487.
Fomento Cultural Banamex, 40.
Fonseca, Carolina, 1816.
Fonseca, Denise Sella, 2896.
Font Acevedo, Francisco, 1887.
Fontano Patán, Francisco, 556.

Forjando el tiempo: historia del metal en el Perú, 12.
Formación y gestión del estado en Chiapas: algunas aproximaciones históricas, 557.
Fornet, Jorge, 902.
Fornet-Betancourt, Raúl, 2970.
Forniés Casals, José Francisco, 316.
Forstall Comber, Biddy, 1249.
Forster, Ricardo, 3038.
Fortuna, Felipe, 2491.
Fos, Carlos, 2326, 2356.
Fowler, Will, 579.
Fradique, Teresa, 2584.
Fradkin, Raúl O., 1047, 1369, 1388.
Fraga, Gerson Wasen, 1663.
Fragoso, João Luís Ribeiro, 1580, 1622, 1664.
França, Jean Marcel Carvalho, 182.
France, Miranda, 2652.
Franceschi González, Napoleón, 1063.
Francisco, Marion, 2176.
Francisco Xavier Clavigero, un humanista entre dos mundos: entorno, pensamiento, y presencia, 2991.
Franco, Gladys, 2124.
Franco, Régulo, 12.
Franco, Renato, 1592.
Franco González, Luis, 2224.
Francos Lauredo, Aurelio, 903.
Françozo, Mariana de Campos, 1593.
Frank, Patrick, 64, 66, 99.
Fraser, Adrian, 904.
Frassani, Alessia, 31–32.
Freedom, power and sovereignty: the thought of Gordon K. Lewis, 2998.
Freidenson, Marilia, 1646.
Freilich de Segal, Alicia, 2062.
Freire, Marcelino, 2394, 2506.
Freitas, Artur, 142.
Freitas, Luana Ferreira de, 2672.
Freitas, Mariana Portas de, 2897.
Fresán, Rodrigo, 2640–2641.
Freston, Paul, 2960.
Frías, Susana R., 1045.
Frías Sarmiento, Eduardo, 539, 676.
Friedmann, Germán, 1370.
Fróes, Elson, 2492.
From the ashes of history: loss and recovery of archives and libraries in modern Latin America, 319.
Fronteiras: arte, imagem, história, 121.
La frontera en el mundo hispánico, 365.
Fryer, Christienna D., 855.
Fucé, Pablo, 1023.
Fuente, Alejandro de la, 2958.
Fuentes, Marisa J., 832.
Fuentes, Moisés Elías, 2625.
Fuentes, Pepe, 2845.
Fuentes Armadans, Claudio José, 1497.
Fuentes orales, emigración española y desarrollo socioeconómico en Centroamérica, 755.
Fugellie, Daniela, 2846.
Fumero Vargas, Patricia, 2357.
Fundação Bienal de São Paulo, 155.
Fundação Cultural do Estado da Bahia, 2589.
Fundação de Amparo à Pesquisa do Estado de São Paulo, 167.
Fundação Joaquim Nabuco, 162, 1582.
Fundación Global Democracia y Desarrollo, 1915.
Fundación Museos del Banco Central de Costa Rica, 87, 713.
Fundación Telefónica (Peru), 299.
Fundora, Ernesto, 2325.
Furia ideológica y violencia en la Argentina de los 70, 1371.
Furman, Rubén, 1372.
Fuster Lavín, Ana María, 1888.
Fux, Jacques, 2395.
Gabbay, Marcello Monteiro, 2898.
Gadea, Alina, 2024.
Gaguine, Daniel, 2832.
Galán, Jorge, 1818.
Galán-Guerrero, Luis Gabriel, 1108.
Galarza, Sergio, 2025.
Galasso, Norberto, 1373.
Galdames Rosas, Luis Alberto, 975.
Galeana de Valadés, Patricia, 325, 599, 680.
Galindo, David Rex, 488.
Gallo, Carlos Artur, 1526.
Gallo, Claudio Rodolfo, 1374.
Gallo, Edit Rosalía, 1375.
Gallo, Ezequiel, 1376.
Gallo, Oscar, 1107.
Gallo, Rubén, 1952.
Galván, Valeria, 1452.
Gálvez Suárez, Arnoldo, 1819.
Gambeta, Wilson, 1527.
Gambi Giménez, Esther, 1547.
Gamble Miller, Elizabeth, 2630.
Gamboa, Santiago, 2642.
Gámez, Moisés, 558.
Gámez Casado, Manuel, 721.
Gándara, Aída, 565.
Gander, Forrest, 2596.
Gangelhoff, Christine, 2774.
Gantús, Fausta, 541, 549.
Garavaglia, Juan Carlos, 330, 1377–1378.
Garavito Aguilar, Alejandra, 2227.
Garay, Gerardo, 2967.

Garcia, Cindy, 2726.
Garcia, Elisa Frühauf, 1594.
García, Gervasio Luis, 856.
García, Luis Eduardo, 2026.
Garcia, Marília, 2493.
García, Octavio, 482.
Garcia, Tânia da Costa, 2862.
García Alvarez, Alejandro, 887.
García Basalo, Javier F., 1467.
García Bergua, Ana, 1766–1767.
García-Crespo, Naida, 905.
García Cruzado, Eduardo, 329.
García de Germenos, Pilar, 76.
García de Sanjurjo, Raquel, 2125.
García Enríquez, Fernando Aníbal, 1205.
García Falcón, Marco, 2027–2028.
García Ferrari, Mercedes, 320.
García Jordán, Pilar, 338.
García Moreno, María Luisa, 870.
García Murillo, Julio, 76.
García Robayo, Margarita, 1977.
García-Robles, Jorge, 550.
García-Roza, Luiz Alfredo, 2365.
García Ruiz, Luis J., 489.
Garcia-Solek, Hélène, 2899.
García Vilar, Carmen, 2329.
García Yero, Olga, 845.
García Zambrano, Angel Julián, 8.
Gargarella, Roberto, 321.
Garí Barceló, Bernat, 1742.
Garone Gravier, Marina, 213, 243.
Garrandés, Alberto, 1872.
Garrard, Virginia, 2960.
Garrett, Victoria Lynn, 1027.
Garrigus, John D., 829.
Garro, Elena, 2330.
Garza, Mercedes de la, 238.
Garza Cabrera, Patricia de la, 2723.
Gasteazoro, Eva, 1820.
El gasto público en los imperios ibéricos, siglo XVIII, 366.
Gatto, Hebert, 3031.
Gaudichaud, Franck, 1250.
Gaune, Rafael, 1003.
Gautherot, Marcel, 161.
Gautier, Manuel Salvador, 1889.
Gavirati, Marcelo, 1337.
Gaytán, Marie Sarita, 2727.
Gazzolo, Ana María, 2212.
Geidel, Molly, 1206.
Gelman, Juan, 2106, 2225.
Gené, Juan Carlos, 2355.
Gentes das ilhas: trajetórias transatlânticas dos Açores ao Rio Grande de São Pedro entre as décadas de 1740 a 1790, 1595.
Geraldo, Sheila Cabo, 121.
Gerber Bicecci, Verónica, 1768, 2643.
Gerbner, Katharine, 833.
Gerchman, Clara, 154.
Gerchman, Rubens, 154.
Gerling, Vera Elisabeth, 538.
Germaná, Gabriela, 12.
Gerón, Cándido, 885, 906–907.
Gertopán, Susana, 2116–2117.
Gertz, René Ernaini, 1665.
Getselteris, Gonzalo, 1379.
Ghirardi, M. Mónica, 1044, 1450.
Giannini, Humberto, 3026.
Giannoni, Daniel, 12.
Giardinelli, Mempo, 2106.
Gibbings, Julie, 756.
Gidal, Marc, 2900.
Gigliotti, Carlos Alberto, 1380.
Gilard, Jacques, 1971.
Giménez, María José, 2659.
Giordano, Verónica, 1341.
Giorgi, Alvaro de, 1509.
Giorgi, Guido Ignacio, 1452.
Giraud, Paul-Henri, 540.
Giron, Luís Antônio, 2434.
Girondo, Oliverio, 2608–2609.
Gisbert, Teresa, 55.
Giusti, Miguel, 2987.
Glenadel, Paula, 2523.
La gloriosa batalla del 21 de octubre de 1863, 559.
Glover, Andrew, 2728.
Glück, Mario, 1381.
Gluzman, Georgina G., 100.
Godínez-Nivón, Daniel, 2626.
Godoy, Juan, 1382.
Godoy, Marcelo, 1666.
Goenaga, Francia Elena, 2664.
Goldemberg, Isaac, 2610.
Golden kingdoms: luxury arts in the ancient Americas, 1.
Goldman, Noemí, 1383.
Goldsmith Weil, Jael, 1251.
Golin, Tau, 1596.
Gomas, Otrova, 2063.
Gomes, Antonio Henrique de Castilho, 2901.
Gomes, Flávio dos Santos, 1528, 1667, 1697.
Gomes, Paulo César Ribeiro, 137.
Gomes, Rodrigo Cantos Savelli, 2902–2903.
Gómez, Cristóbal, 2158.
Gómez, Franco Lázaro, 82.
Gómez, José María, 2088.
Gómez, Juan Pablo, 757, 1866.
Gómez, Santiago Andrés, 1978.

Gómez Campuzano, Ricardo, 106.
Gómez Gómez, Mauricio Alejandro, 273.
Gómez Migliaro, Willy, 2226.
Gómez Muntané, María del Carmen, 2677.
Gómez Romero, Álex, 1742.
Gómez Sántiz, Isaías, 676.
Gómez Yoc, Byron, 2176.
Gómezgil R.S., Ignacio, 1743.
Gomezjurado Zevallos, Javier, 1153.
Gonçalves, André, 2494.
Gonçalves, Carlos Barros, 1668.
Gonçalves, Carlos Eduardo Soares, 2396.
Gonçalves, Leandro Pereira, 1698.
Gonçalves, Paulo Cesar, 1669.
Gonzalbo, Pilar, 214, 446, 448.
Gonzales, Felipe, 560.
González, Alejandra Soledad, 1399.
González, Arquímedes, 1821.
González, Carina, 2353.
González, Cristina Cruz, 33.
González, Hermann, 955.
González, José Eduardo, 2968.
González, Luis Felipe, 758.
González, Mariño, 1769.
González, Pablo Alonso, 93.
González, Soledad, 2318.
González, Wingston, 2227, 2307.
González Acosta, Alejandro, 2305.
González Alonso, Nuria, 755.
González Boixo, José C., 1724.
González Bollo, Hernán, 1384.
González Carré, Enrique, 274.
González Cruz, Edith, 459.
González de Noval, María Helena, 75.
González Errázuriz, Francisco Javier, 1252.
González García, Mónica, 2904.
González Gómez, Claudia, 592.
González Lapuente, Alberto, 2677.
González Leal, Miguel Ángel, 1154.
González Leyva, Alejandra, 46.
González Luna, Ana María, 588.
González Mafud, Ana María, 1920.
González Martínez, Elda Evangelina, 326.
González Milea, Alejandro, 561.
González Quesada, Alfons, 94.
González R., Juan Pablo, 2847.
González Ríos, Juanmanuel, 2149.
González Rissotto, Rodolfo, 1508.
González Sánchez, Carlos Alberto, 1597.
González Sarmiento, Luis, 1979.
González Serrano, Manuel, 75.
González Tenorio, Walter Jacinto, 2150.
González Undurraga, Carolina, 1004.
González Victoria, Rosa María, 464.
González y González, Luis, 644.

Good, Carl, 940.
Goodman, Walter, 95.
Goodridge, Sehon S., 857.
Gootenberg, Paul, 1175.
Gordienko, Abril, 1822.
Gorelik, Adrián, 313.
Gorza, Anabella, 1385.
Gould, Jeffrey L., 759.
Gouvêa, Maria de Fátima, 1580.
Goyas Mejía, Ramón, 676.
Goytia, Andrea, 284.
Grabois, Roberto, 1386.
Graça, Antônio Paulo, 2386.
Graciano, Osvaldo Fabián, 3039.
Graeff, Nina, 2905.
Graff Zivin, Erin, 2969.
Graham Soberón de Armida, María, 610.
A grammar of justice: the legacy of Ignacio Ellacuría, 2996.
Grandes financieros mexicanos, 562.
Las grandes guerras del siglo XX y la comunidad española de Buenos Aires, 1387.
Grassmann, Marcelo, 143.
Graubart, Karen B., 977.
Greaves, Lucy, 2638.
Green, W. John, 416.
Greene, Jack P., 834.
Greene, Oliver N., 2786.
Greene, Shane, 2812.
Gregory, Stephen, 2136.
Grewe, David, 563.
Griffa, Norberto L., 3036.
Griffin, Clive, 367.
Grigsby Vergara, William, 1823.
Grinberg, Keila, 1040.
GRISO (research group), 55.
Grossi, Florencia, 2975.
Grupo Proceso Pentágono: políticas de la intervención, 1969-1976-2015, 76.
Los grupos subalternos en el nordeste del Virreinato del Río de la Plata, 1024.
Guadarrama, Gloria, 308.
El Guairá literario, 2134.
Guardia, Sara Beatriz, 349, 390.
Guardino, Peter F., 564.
Guariglia, Osvaldo Norberto, 2965-2966.
Guarín Salazar, Milkiades, 2331.
Guebel, Daniel, 2332.
Guedea, Rogelio, 2296.
Guerini, Andréia, 2672.
Guerra, Wendy, 1890.
Guerra Ávila, Rogelio, 1824.
La guerra de la independencia en Santa Cruz de la Sierra, según sus historiadores, 1810-1825, 1207.

La Guerra del Paraguay en primera persona, 1498.
Guerra literária: panfletos da Independência (1820–1823), 1670–1673.
Guerra Vilaboy, Sérgio, 322.
Guerras de la historia argentina, 1388.
Guerrero, Ana Luisa, 2964.
Guerrero, Laureano, 1891.
Guerrero, Victoria, 2228.
Guerrero Rincón, Amado Antonio, 964.
Guerriera, Natalia, 1309.
Guerriero, Leila, 1884, 2663.
Guevara, Che, 912.
Guevara, Otoniel, 2146.
Guía, Germán, 1068.
Guía Comares de filosofía latinoamericana, 2970.
Guía MALI, 57.
Güich Rodríguez, José, 1948.
Guijarro Mora, Victor, 1297.
Guillén, Paul, 2151.
Guimarães Neto, Regina Beatriz, 414.
Guinea Diez, Gerardo, 1825.
Gullar, Ferreira, 2435, 2495.
Gullo, Marcelo, 1025.
Guran, Milton, 1598.
Guridi, Ricardo R., 2789.
Gusmán, Luis, 2089.
Gusmão, Alexandre de, 2669.
Gusmão, Milene Silveira, 122.
Gutérres Ludwig, Fabio André, 1340.
Gutfreind, Celso, 2497.
Gutiérrez-Álvarez, José A., 2740.
Gutiérrez Cruz, Sergio Nicolás, 557.
Gutiérrez Negrón, Sergio, 1892.
Gutiérrez Quintanilla, Lya, 645.
Gutiérrez Samanez, Julio Antonio, 58.
Gutiérrez Sanín, Francisco, 1109.
Gutiérrez Sanjuán, Luis, 411.
Gutiérrez Viñuales, Rodrigo, 335.
Güttner, Carlos Hermann, 1026.
Guy, Donna J., 1389, 1433.
Guzmán, Celene, 1770.
Guzmán, Ricardo, 565.
Guzmán Bravo, José Antonio, 2729–2731.
Guzmán Jasmen, Nancy, 1253.
Guzmán Suárez, M. Silvinar, 1390.
Hacer y deshacer el amor: 7 narradores cubanos contemporáneos, 1893.
Hacia una dramaturgia nacional: cinco autores del Teatro Libre, 2333.
Los hados de febrero: visiones artísticas de la Decena Trágica, 646.
Hahn, Daniel, 2670.
Haicai do Brasil, 2496.
Halac-Higashimori, Madeleine, 254.
Hales Dib, Jaime, 1254.
Halperín Donghi, Tulio, 1391.
Hamerly, Michael T., 1155.
Handler, Jerome S., 815.
Hangar Bicocca, 150.
Hanna, Mark G., 790.
Harambour, Alberto R., 1255.
Harari, Ianina, 1392.
Harmer, Tanya, 1256.
Harrison, Osvaldo di Paolo, 1928.
Harrison, Regina, 1725.
Harvey, Rosalind, 2646.
Harvey, Simon, 323.
Harvey Recharte, Katherine, 59.
Harvey Valencia, Armando, 59.
Hasbún, Rodrigo, 1956.
Hasgall, Alexander, 1457.
Hatfield, Charles Dean, 2971.
Hatun taki: poemas a la Madre Tierra y los abuelos, 2152.
Havilio, Iosi, 2090.
Hawkins, Timothy, 722.
Hay Festival, 1784.
Heatherton, Christina, 647.
Hébrard, Véronique, 636.
Hecker Filho, Paulo, 2497.
Heilman, Jaymie Patricia, 1176.
Heilman, Lawrence C., 1208.
Heinowitz, Cole, 2622.
Heinsfeld, Adelar, 1674.
Helg, Aline, 368.
Henderson, James D., 1110.
Henriques Neto, Afonso, 2397.
Henry E. Huntington Library and Art Gallery, 16.
Heredia, José Francisco, 1064.
Heredia, Verónica del Valle, 1399.
Heredia, Víctor, 2091.
Herik, Helder, 2498.
Heringer, Victor, 2366.
Herkenhoff, Paulo, 123, 144.
Hermosa Mantilla, Hernán, 2000.
Hernández, Claudia, 1826.
Hernández, David, 1827.
Hernández, Francisco, 2229.
Hernández, Patricia, 497.
Hernández, Ramona, 941.
Hernández, Ricardo, 1828.
Hernández Alvarado, Hilda G., 414.
Hernández Bencid, María Soledad, 1069.
Hernández Collazo, Edgar, 2790.
Hernández Figueroa, Alfredo Rafael, 898.
Hernández Fuentes, Miguel, 566.
Hernández Galindo, Sergio, 648.

Hernández González, Manuel, 956, 1065.
Hernández López, José de Jesús, 676.
Hernández Palomo, José Jesús, 990.
Hernández Pico, Juan, 760.
Hernández Rangel, Nelly Josefina, 1066.
Hernández Salván, Marta, 1929.
Hernández Silva, Héctor Cuauhtémoc, 572.
Herrera, Carlos-Miguel, 1393.
Herrera, Fernando, 1803.
Herrera, Olga U., 417.
Herrera Farfán, Nicolás Armando, 3015.
Herrera Gómez, Fernando, 2230.
Herrera León, Fabián, 684.
Hertz, Carmen, 1257.
Hertzman, Marc A., 324.
Herzog, Manoel, 2367.
Hess, Hans, 2906.
Heureaux, Ulises, 858.
Hidalgo Lehuedé, Jorge, 275, 294.
Hidalgo Pego, Mónica, 567.
Hikiji, Rose Satiko Gitirana, 2569.
Hill, Rowena, 2601.
Hillock Damm, Laura, 1006.
Hilst, Hilda, 2499.
Hinostroza, Rodolfo, 2029.
Hintzen, Amelia, 908.
Hiriart, Hugo, 1771.
Historia andina en Chile, 275.
Historia comparada de las migraciones en las Américas, 325.
Historia crítica de la poesía mexicana, 2296.
História da escola dos imigrantes italianos em terras brasileiras, 1675.
História da imigração: possibilidades e escrita, 326.
História das mulheres e do gênero em Minas Gerais, 1676.
Historia de Cuba, 909.
Historia de la educación en Chile, 1810–2010, 1258.
Historia de la educación superior en Yucatán: las instituciones (universidad, colegio e instituto), siglos XIX y XX, 568.
Historia de la música en España e Hispanoamérica, 2677.
Historia de las izquierdas bolivianas: archivos y documentos (1920-1940), 1209.
Historia de las relaciones diplomáticas Venezuela - Corea (1965–2015) = Han'guk kwa Penesuella kan ŭi 50-yŏn ujŏng, 1067.
História dos homens no Brasil, 1677.
História e cultura estudantil: revistas na USP, 183.
História e memória das ditaduras do século XX, 1678.

Historia general del pueblo dominicano, 910.
História militar: novos caminhos e novas abordagens, 1679.
Historia mínima de la expansión ferroviaria en América Latina, 327.
Historia política de Chile, 1810–2010, 1259–1260.
História urbana: memória, cultura e sociedade, 1680.
Historia y cultura en el mundo andino: homenaje a Henrique Urbano, 276.
Historias de mujeres inmigrantes de Magallanes: más importante que el oro, 1261.
Histórias do Maranhão em tempos de República, 1681.
Historicidad dialéctica: espacio y tiempo en nuestra América, 2972.
La historiografía costarricense en la primera década del siglo XXI: tendencias, avances e innovaciones, 707.
Hoblicua, 2500.
Hodge, Michael Jonathan Sessions, 542.
Hoefler, Walter, 2160.
Hoefte, Rosemarijn, 911.
Hofer, Jen, 2617.
Hoffmann, Odile, 706, 859.
Holtz, Raul, 186.
Hoobler, Ellen, 2.
Horn, Maja, 810.
Hörner, Erik, 1529.
Horowitz, Joel, 1394.
Hoz, Joaquín Viloria de la, 1111.
Huacuz Elías, María Guadalupe, 80.
Huamanchumo de la Cuba, Ofelia, 978.
Huberman, Silvio, 1395.
Huertas, Jorge, 2334.
Huidobro Salazar, María Gabriela, 1244.
Humphrey, Ted, 1744.
Hurtado de Mendoza Santander, William, 2231.
Hurtado Lores, Camilo, 2064.
Hutchinson, Sydney, 2775.
Hutton, Clinton A., 860, 915.
Huys, Johan Leuridan, 276.
Hyland, Steven, 1396.
Ianelli, Mariana, 2436.
Iannini, Nicolás, 1387.
Ibarra, Ana Carolina, 2991.
Ibarra Rojas, Eugenia, 215, 723.
Iber, Patrick, 418, 649.
Ideas, ideólogos e idearios en la construcción de la imagen peninsula, 450.
Ideas que cruzan el Atlántico: utopía y modernidad latinoamericana, 2973.

Idéias: Revista do Instituto de Filosofia e Ciências Humanas, 2907.
Identidad cultural colombiana: visiones de filósofos y pensadores en tiempos del bicentenario, 3005.
Identidad y pensamiento latinoamericano, 2974.
Ilarione, *da Bergamo, fra,* 1745.
Ildefonso, Miguel, 2232–2233.
Illades, Carlos, 451, 470.
Illades Aguiar, Lilián, 620.
Illanes O., María Angélica, 1273.
Illueca Sibauste, Jorge Enrique, 739.
Imágenes de la revolución industrial: Robert Gerstmann en las minas de Bolivia (1925–1936), 1210.
Imaginación visual y cultura en el Perú, 114.
El imaginario antiimperialista en América Latina, 2975.
Imagining histories of colonial Latin America: synoptic methods and practices, 369.
Imigração na América Latina: histórias de fracassos, 328.
The improbable conquest: sixteenth-century letters from the Río de la Plata, 1027.
Incendiar el presente: la narrativa peruana de la violencia política y el archivo (1984–1989), 2030.
El incesto republicano: relaciones civiles y militares en Venezuela, 1812–2012, 1068.
Inclán Fuentes, Carlos, 650.
Independencia, revolución y derecho: catorce miradas sobre las revoluciones de México, 569.
Indiana, Rita, 2644.
Iñigo Carrera, Nicolás, 1397.
Iñigo Madrigal, Luis, 1740.
Injusticias de género en un mundo globalizado: conversaciones con la teoría de Nancy Fraser, 2976.
Inniss, Tara A., 861.
Iño, Weimar Giovanni, 1227.
Inoa, Orlando, 862.
Inquisiciones: dimensiones comparadas (siglos XVI-XIX), 370.
Insausti, Santiago Joaquin, 1306.
Instituto Belgraniano Central (Buenos Aires), 1355.
Instituto Confucio (Universidad Ricardo Palma), 1168.
Instituto Cultural Itaú, 145.
Instituto de Estudios Peruanos, 299.
Instituto de Historia y Museo Militar (Paraguay), 1498.
Instituto de Investigaciones Dr. José María Luis Mora, 355, 927.
Instituto de la Cultura del Estado de Guanajuato, 30.
Instituto Nacional de Antropología e Historia (Mexico), 672, 2712, 2744.
Instituto Nacional de Estudios Históricos de la Revolución Mexicana, 469.
Instituto Nacional de Estudios Históricos de las Revoluciones de México, 599, 688.
Instituto Pereira Passos (Rio de Janeiro), 1648.
Instituto Venezolano de Investigaciones Científicas, 256.
Instituto Vladimir Herzog, 189.
Os intelectuais e a nação: educação, saúde e a construção de um Brasil moderno, 1682.
Inter American University of Puerto Rico. Metropolitan Campus. Centro Interamericano para el Estudio de las Dinámicas Políticas, 899.
Intereses extranjeros y nacionalismo en el noroeste de México, 1840–1920, 570.
International Association for the Study of Popular Music. Rama Latinoamericana, *10th, Córdoba, Argentina, 2012,* 2678.
International Congress of Americanists, *53rd, México, 2009,* 8.
International Congress of Americanists, *54th, Vienna, Austria, 2012,* 227.
International Congress on Traditional Asian Medicines (ICTAM) *9th, Kiel, Germany, August 6–12, 2017,* 375.
Inventário dos lugares de memória do tráfico Atlântico de escravos e da história dos africanos escravizados no Brasil, 1598.
Ipanema, Cybelle de, 1530.
Iparraguirre, Hilda, 588.
Iparraguirre, Sylvia, 2092.
Ipiña Melgar, Enrique, 1957.
Iracheta Cenecorta, Pilar, 442.
Irianni, Marcelino, 2093.
Iriarte, Flávia, 2398.
Iris, Manuel, 2234.
Irurozqui, Marta, 1211.
Irwin G., Domingo, 1068.
Isaenko, Anatoly V., 1494.
Islam and the Americas, 419.
Iturriaga de la Fuente, José N., 447.
Iyanaga, Michael, 2908.
Izaguirre, Matías, 1354.
Izhaki, Flávio, 2368.
Izquierdo, Isabel, 651.
J. Paul Getty Museum, 1.
Jablonski, Bernardo, 2561.

Jabor, Juliana, 2930.
Jacinto, Lizette, 620.
Jackson, Robert H., 490.
Jaffe, Noemi, 153.
Jaime, Juan Cruz, 1016.
Jaksic, Ivan, 1259–1260.
Jamilis, Amalia, 2094.
Jané, Óscar, 365.
Los japoneses en Bolivia: 110 años de historia de la inmigración japonesa en Bolivia, 1212.
Jara Jiménez, Cronwell, 2031.
Jaramillo Levi, Enrique, 1816, 1849.
Jardim, Ana Teresa, 2399.
Jarquín Ortega, María Teresa, 244.
Jáuregui, Carlos A., 491.
Jauregui, Gabriela, 1772.
Jayaram, Kiran, 811.
Jean, Martine, 1683.
Jemmott, Jenny M., 863.
Jerez Brenes, Verónica, 713.
Jesus, Nauk Maria de, 1614.
Jiménez, Orián, 968.
Jiménez Becerra, Absalón, 1112.
Jiménez Belmar, Bruno, 301.
Jiménez-Cavallé, Pedro, 2740.
Jiménez de la Espada, Marcos, 997.
Jiménez Emán, Gabriel, 2065.
Jiménez Gómez, Juan Ricardo, 216–218, 492.
Jiménez Marce, Rogelio, 571, 652.
Jiménez Reyes, Luis Carlos, 1104.
Jobim, Elizabeth, 146.
Jodorowsky, Alejandro, 2645.
Joffily, Mariana, 1684.
Johansson K., Patrick, 219.
Johnson, Benjamin D., 220.
Jones, Owen H., 724.
Jornadas de Historia sobre el Descubrimiento de América, 329.
Jornadas en Homenaje a Germán Canuhé, 1st, Universidad Nacional de La Pampa, 2014, 277.
Jornadas Internacionales de Historia de la Iglesia y las Religiosidades en el NOA, 4th, Cafayate, Argentina, 2013, 1398.
Jorrat, Jorge Raúl, 1326.
Jouve Martín, José Ramón, 979.
Jovine Bermúdez, Federico, 1894.
Jubithana-Fernand, Andrea Idelga, 1588.
Jufresa, Laia, 1773.
Júnior, Gonçalo, 2909.
Junttonen, Mary Black, 2799.
Jurado G., Ana María, 1829.
Just south of Zion: the Mormons in Mexico and its borderlands, 452.
Juventudes, políticas culturales y prácticas artísticas: fragmentos históricos sobre la década de 1980, 1399.
Kahlo, Frida, 77.
Kalil, Emilio, 139.
Kalmar, Fritz, 2125.
Kalyva, Eve, 65.
Kamiya, Alejandra, 2095.
Kang, S. Deborah, 653.
Karl, Robert A., 1113.
Karsburg, Alexandre de Oliveira, 1708.
Karush, Matthew Benjamin, 2833.
Kasl, Ronda, 40.
Katzew, Ilona, 40.
Kaz, Roberto, 2437.
Kazanjian, David, 392.
Keller, Renata, 420.
Kepecs, Susan, 480.
Kepp, Michael, 2438.
Kerber, Alessander, 2910.
Kercheval, Jesse Lee, 2587, 2591, 2615.
Kern, Margit, 34.
Kesey, Roy, 2648.
Khan, Aisha, 419.
Kiddle, Amelia M., 654.
Kietzmann Goldemberg, Deborah, 2423.
Kirby, Cristian, 105.
Kirst, Marcos Fernando, 2369.
Kisêdjê, Kamikia, 2947.
Klappenbach, Fernando, 1470.
Kobelinski, Michel, 1599.
Kociancich, Vlady, 2096.
Koegel, John, 2732–2734.
Kohan, Néstor, 912.
Kohl, Randall, 2735.
Kosack, Edward, 655.
Kosovski, Pedro, 2563.
Kovacic, Fabián, 2137.
Kozel, Andrés, 2975.
Kozer, José, 2611.
Kramer, Wendy, 714, 725–726.
Kremer, Harold, 1989.
Krimko, Stuart, 2612, 2628.
Kristal, Efraín, 1949.
Kruchin, Samuel, 169.
Krutitskaya, Anastasia, 2709.
Kucinski, Bernardo, 2370.
Kunimoto, Iyo, 1212.
Kunstforum Wien, 77.
Kunstmusik—Kolonialismus—Lateinamerika, 2911.
Kuntz Ficker, Sandra, 327.
Kury, Lorelai Brilhante, 188.
Kushner, Anna, 2649.
Kusunoki, Ricardo, 57.

La Fountain-Stokes, Lawrence, 1930.
La Rosa Corzo, Gabino, 853.
La Serna, Miguel, 1177–1178.
La Via, Stefano, 2869.
Labastida, Jaime, 2992.
Labinger, Andrea G., 2656.
Lacerda, Marcos, 2929.
Lago, Luiz Aranha Corrêa do, 1531.
Lagrotta, Miguel J., 1503.
Lagrou, Els, 302.
Laguna, Fernanda, 2612.
Laguna y Ortuña, Norma María, 43.
Lalo, Eduardo, 1931.
Lamadrid, Enrique R., 221, 2736.
Lamb, Valerie, 791.
Lamounier, Maria Lúcia, 1685.
Landaburu, Roberto E., 1400.
Landavazo Arias, Marco Antonio, 459.
Langa Pizarro, M. Mar, 2163.
Langue, Frédérique, 957.
Lanseros, Raquel, 2172.
Lanteri, Ana Laura, 1401–1402.
Lara, Boris, 1830.
Lara, Liliana, 2066.
Lara Cisneros, Gerardo, 370.
Lara Martínez, Rafael, 1867.
Lara Zavala, Hernán, 1774.
Largey, Michael D., 2779.
Largo, Eliana, 1239.
Larguía, Alejandro, 1403.
LaRosa, Michael, 1099.
Larrain, Ramiro, 2350.
Larson, Brooke, 1213.
Lasso, Marixa, 1102.
Lastra, Pedro, 2235.
Latin American bureaucracy and the state building process (1780–1860), 330.
A Latin American music reader: views from the south, 2679.
Laub, Michel, 2670.
Laudanna, Mayra, 143.
Laurencich, Alejandra, 2097.
Lavín, Mónica, 1816.
Lavín Cerda, Hernán, 2153.
Lavín Higuera, Valentín, 453.
Leal, Francisco, 2236.
Leal, Ildefonso, 958.
Leal, María del Rosario, 49.
Leão, Ricardo, 2501.
Lear, John, 656.
Leavitt-Alcántara, Brianna, 708.
Lebron, Maybell, 2237.
Lecca, Dante, 2238.
Ledesma Prietto, Nadia, 1404.
Leduc, Renato, 2239.
Lee, Thomas A., 2751.
Lee-Borges, José, 864.
The legacy of Eric Williams: Caribbean scholar and statesman, 913.
The legacy of Eric Williams: into the post-colonial moment, 914.
Legañoa Alonso, Jorge, 1055.
LeGrand, Cathleen, 2774, 2776.
Leitão, Miriam, 189.
Leite, Guto, 2855.
Lema, Yana Lucíla, 2152.
Lemaitre Ripoll, Julieta, 1131.
Lemes, Fernando Lobo, 1614.
Lemoine Villicaña, Ernesto, 572.
Lemos, Carlos Alberto Cerqueira, 170.
Lengwinat, Katrin, 2827.
Lenis Ballesteros, César Augusto, 1114.
Lenk, Wolfgang, 1600.
Lenti, Joseph U., 657.
Lentz, Mark W., 493–494.
León, Conchi, 2335.
León, Javier F., 2679.
León, Luis Miguel, 69.
León Portilla, Miguel, 222, 243.
León-Real Méndez, Nora Marisa, 573.
Leonard Percival Howell and the genesis of Rastafari, 915.
Leonardo Filho, 2442.
Leoni, María Silvia, 1405.
Lépiz Vega, Jonatan, 2240.
Lerner, Jaime, 2439.
Lerner, Sharon, 57.
Lesbre, Patrick, 223.
Lesman, Robert, 2630.
Levin, Orna, 2403.
Levin, Silvia, 2976.
Levine, Alex, 1406.
Levine, Frances, 495.
Levitas y sotanas en la edificación republicana: proceso político e ideas en tiempos de emancipación, 1069.
Levitin, Alexis, 2616, 2629.
Levy, Daniela Tonello, 1609.
Lewis, Stephen E., 658.
Leyva, Gustavo, 678.
Leza, José Máximo, 2677.
Libertella, Mauro, 2098.
Lichtmajer, Leandro, 1407.
Lida, Clara Eugenia, 2754.
Lida, Miranda, 1408.
Lightfoot, Natasha, 865.
Ligiéro, Zeca, 2571.
Lihn, Enrique, 2235.
Lima, Angélica Torres, 2502.
Lima, Chely, 2613.

Lima, Giuliana Souza de, 2912.
Lima, José Edson Schümann, 1699.
Lima, Oliveira, 1686.
Lima, Paolo de, 2303.
Lima, Ricardo Gomes, 158.
Lima, Samarone, 2503.
Lima, Sérgio Eduardo Moreira, 1615.
Limia Díaz, Ernesto, 835.
Limón Olvera, Silvia, 344.
Lineros Pérez, Cristian, 1006.
Lingold, Mary Caton, 2777.
Lira, José Tavares Correia de, 170, 175, 183.
Lírio, Vinícius da Silva, 2578.
Lisboa, Adriana, 2504.
Lisboa, Solange, 134.
Lisboa Junior, Luiz Americo, 2913.
Lisbona, Miguel, 659.
Liscia, María Herminia Beatriz di, 1409.
Lísias, Ricardo, 2400.
Liska, María Mercedes, 2834.
Lispector, Clarice, 1935, 2401, 2665.
Liu, Wenlong, 454.
Livesay, Daniel, 816, 836.
Lizárraga Sánchez, Salvador, 455.
Llano, Eduardo del, 1895.
Llorca-Jaña, Manuel, 1262.
Llorente, Renzo, 2977.
Llosa Vélez, Pedro José, 2032.
Lo Presti, Pablo Alberto, 1315, 1339.
Loaeza, Pablo García, 192, 1027.
Loaiza Becerra, Martha, 639.
Loayes, Wilson, 2162.
Loayza Portocarrero, José Antonio, 278.
Lobato, Sidney da Silva, 1532.
Lobo Wiehoff, Tatiana, 1831.
Local Church, global Church: Catholic activism in Latin America from *Rerum Novarum* to Vatican II, 421.
Lochery, Neill, 1687.
Lojo de Beuter, María Rosa, 2099–2100.
Lolo, Begoña, 2676.
Lomnitz-Adler, Claudio, 660.
Londoño Vélez, Santiago, 19.
Lopes, Israel, 2914.
Lopes, João Marcos, 175.
Lopes, Maria-Aparecida, 336, 1688.
Lopes, Rodrigo Garcia, 2505.
López, Amanda M., 574.
López, Atilio, 1440.
López, Guisela, 1851.
López, Patricio Antonio, 1746.
Lopez, Telê Porto Ancona, 2859.
López Alemany, Ignacio, 1750.
López Amaya, Zurelys, 2614.
López Austin, Alfredo, 225.

López Baquero, Patricio, 1156.
López Bauzá, Juan, 1896.
López Bohórquez, Alí Enrique, 1064.
López Calderón, Carme, 24.
López-Chávez, Celia, 1005.
López de Mariscal, Blanca, 573, 1726.
López Degregori, Carlos, 2241.
López-Durán, Fabiolar, 422.
López Franco, Roberto, 414.
López Guzmán, Lorena, 3015.
López Herrera, Luis Alberto, 2242.
López Maltez, Nicolás, 761.
López Méndez, Xel-Ha, 2243.
López Michelsen, Alfonso, 1115.
López Mills, Tedi, 1775.
López Moya, Martín de la Cruz, 2724.
López Ramírez Gastón, José Ignacio, 2813.
López Uribe, Cristina, 455.
López Velásquez, María Eugenia, 414.
López von Vriessen, Carlos, 279.
Lorenz, Federico G., 1388.
Lorenzo Río, María Dolores, 308.
Los Angeles County Museum of Art, 40.
Losada, Janaina Zito, 1533–1534.
Losada, Leandro, 1410.
Losada Cubillos, Jhon Jairo, 3005–3006.
Lourenço, Miguel Rodrigues, 370.
Lovell, W. George, 726.
Lovera, José Rafael, 331.
Lovera De-Sola, R.J., 1070.
Lovisolo, Jorge, 2978.
Löwy, Michael, 3010.
Loyola T., Manuel, 1283.
Loza, Mireya, 661.
Loza, Santiago, 2336.
Lozada Pérez, Hiram, 1897.
Lozano, Brenda, 1776.
Lozoya López, Ivette, 1263.
Lubeka, Tory, 2244.
Lucano, Juan Carlos, 2245.
Lucas, Glaura, 2915.
Lucas, Kintto, 1157.
Luchese, Terciane Ângela, 1675.
Lucido, Jennifer A., 36.
Lucien, Renée-Clémentine, 1932.
Ludlow, Leonor, 562.
Lühning, Angela, 2892, 2916, 2957.
Luján Muñoz, Jorge, 714.
Luker, Morgan James, 2835.
Lulalivre*Lulalivro, 2506.
Luna, Herbert, 2154.
Luna Sánchez, Patricia, 662.
Lund, Christopher C., 2669.
Luque, Matías, 2308.
Luque Ccota, Leoncio, 2155.

Lutas sociais, intelectuais e poder: problemas de história social, 423.
Lutz, Christopher H., 726.
Luz, Guilherme Amaral, 1611.
Luz, Rogerio, 2507.
Luza Melo, Armando, 1006.
Luzuriaga, Juan Carlos, 1028.
Lyons, Claire L., 26.
Lytton Regalado, Alexandra, 2175.
Mac Adam, Alfred J., 2645.
Mac-Clure Hortal, Óscar, 1264.
Macedo, Carlos Eduardo Martins, 2574.
Macedo, Dimas, 2508.
Maceira, Rodrigo, 2402.
Machado, Antônio de Alcântara, 2403.
Machado, José Lucio da Silva, 1535.
Machado, Maria Helena Pereira Toledo, 1565.
Machado, Nauro, 2509–2510.
Machado, Silvia de Ambrosis Pinheiro, 2917.
Machado de Assis: tradutor e traduzido, 2672.
Machado Neto, Diósnio, 2918–2919.
Macías Huerta, Adolfo, 2001.
Maciel, Diógenes André Vieira, 2564–2565.
Maciel, Maria Esther, 2440.
MacLachlan, Colin M., 444.
MacSweeney, Christina, 2643.
Madajczak, Julia, 496.
Maddalena, Pablo, 1411.
Made in Latin America: studies in popular music, 2680.
Madeira, Angélica, 147.
Madrigal Muñoz, Eduardo, 709, 727.
Maduro, Otto, 2979.
Maestro soberano: ensaios sobre Antonio Carlos Jobim, 2920.
Magaldi, Sábato, 2579.
Magalhães, Aline Montenegro, 1536.
Magalhães, Fábio, 189.
Magaloni Kerpel, Diana, 35, 243.
Maggi, Carlos, 1510.
Maggiori, Ernesto, 280.
Magri, Altair, 1511.
Maguiña, Alicia, 2814.
Maia, Circe, 2246.
Maia, Cláudia, 1676.
Maia, Delta Maria de Souza, 281.
Maison européenne de la photographie (Paris), 161.
Majluf, Natalia, 57.
Making citizens in Argentina, 1412.
Málaga Núñez Zeballos, Alejandro, 1182.
Maldonado, Antonio, 294.
Maldonado, Bernardita, 2247.
Maldonado Toral, Consuelo, 2358.
Malkún Castillejo, Willian, 1116.
Mallo, Ernesto, 2590.
Malpica Cuello, Antonio, 1777.
Malufe, Annita Costa, 2511.
Mañana hablarán de nosotros: antología del cuento cubano, 1898.
Mangan, Jane E., 980.
Mangiantini, Martín, 1413.
Manifestos and polemics in Latin American modern art, 66.
Manifiesto País, 119.
Manifiestos políticos argentinos: antología, 1414.
Manley, Elizabeth S., 916.
Mansilla, H.C.F., 3019–3021.
Mansilla, Miguel Ángel, 1265.
Manuel, Peter, 2778–2779.
Manuscript cultures of colonial Mexico and Peru: new questions and approaches, 1747.
El mar: percepciones, lecturas y contextos: una mirada cultural a los entornos marítimos, 332.
Maranhão, Salgado, 2512–2513.
Maranhão Sobrinho, 2514.
Marcallé Abréu, Roberto, 1899–1900.
La marchita, el escudo y el bombo: una historia cultural de los emblemas del peronismo, de Perón a Cristina Kirchner, 1415.
Marcilese, José, 1416.
Marco, Miguel Angel de, 1417–1418.
Marcondes, Ana Maria Barbosa de Faria, 148.
Marcos Padua, Reynaldo, 1938.
Marejada: antología de mujeres poetas del Magdalena, 2156.
Marentes Esquivel, Xochitl del Carmen, 692.
Margarita Quesada Schmidt: no a la realidad, 87.
María, Angélica, 2157.
Mariasch, Marina, 2101.
Mariazza F., Jaime, 12.
Marín, Carlos Alfredo, 1071.
Marín, Juan, 2158.
Marín Benítez, Ciro, 3011.
Marín López, Javier, 2737–2740.
Marín Sevilla, Desirée, 2248.
Marín Suárez, María Natalia, 1090.
Marinho Filho, Luiz, 2580.
Mário de Andrade e seus dois pintores: Lasar Segall e Cândido Portinari, 149.
Mariscal, Beatriz, 1746.
Marotta, Gary Michael, 436.

Marques, Ana Martins, 2515.
Marqués, René, 1938.
Marques, Teresa Cristina de Novaes, 1689.
Marquese, Rafael de Bivar, 1578.
Marquesini, Janaína, 2938.
Márquez, Marcelo, 2318.
Márquez Morfín, Lourdes, 497, 663.
Márquez Valderrama, Jorge, 1107.
Marreco Brescia, Rosana, 2888.
Marrero-Fente, Raúl, 1727, 1741.
Marroquín Lazo, Edwing, 2176.
Marsilli, María, 975.
Martí, Gerardo Marcelo, 1419.
Martin, Andrew R., 2780.
Martin, Guillemette, 1179.
Martin, James W., 333.
Martin, John Angus, 792.
Martín, María Pía, 1303.
Martin-Gropius-Bau (Berlin), 77.
Martínez, Cecilia, 282.
Martínez, Francisco José, 2965–2966.
Martinez, Françoise, 1214.
Martínez, Ignacio, 1420.
Martínez, Janicce, 1056.
Martínez, Jorge Oscar, 1440.
Martínez, José Pedro, 82.
Martínez, Patricia, 498.
Martínez, Virginia, 1512.
Martínez Arias, Jack, 2033.
Martínez Carmenate, Urbano, 1933.
Martínez Cereceda, José Luis, 283.
Martínez Curiel, Enrique, 676.
Martínez Elizalde, Jocelyn, 2305.
Martínez García, Gonzalo, 2848.
Martínez-Hernández, Laura, 2741.
Martínez Lillo, Pedro Antonio, 424.
Martínez López-Cano, María del Pilar, 485.
Martínez Meucci, Miguel Ángel, 1072.
Martínez Mottola, Fernando, 2067.
Martínez Rodríguez, Marcela, 575.
Martínez-San Miguel, Yolanda, 1934.
Martínez Teixeiro, Alva, 2530.
Martino, Daniel, 2081.
Martinovich, Francisco, 2158.
Martins, Alexandre, 1601.
Martins, Ana Cecilia, 182.
Martins, Ana Luiza Rios, 2921.
Martins, Bruno Viveiros, 2948.
Martins, Luiza Mara Braga, 2922.
Martins, Marcelo Thadeu Quintanilha, 1690.
Martins, Sérgio B., 150.
Martiren, Juan Luis, 1421.
Martocci, Federico, 1422.
Martos, Marco, 2169, 2249.

Marzal, Manuel María, 347.
Masera, Gustavo, 425.
Masés, Enrique, 1360, 1423.
Masi, Andrés Alberto, 1424.
Masís Olivas, Sergio, 2337.
Maslíah, Leo, 2126.
Massé, Gladys, 1045.
Massot, Vicente Gonzalo, 393.
Mata de López, Sara, 1425.
Matallana Rose, Gryzel, 2169.
Matamoros Hüeck, Bosco, 762.
Mate, Reyes, 2965–2966.
Mateo, Graciela, 1292.
Materyn, Diego, 1901.
Mateus, Susana Bastos, 370.
Matos, Paulo Teodoro de, 1595.
Matrimonio: intereses, afectos, conflictos: una aproximación desde la antropología, la historia y la demografía (siglos XVIII al XXI), 334.
Mattos, Cyro de, 2371.
Mattos, Martín Barea, 2615.
Mattos Cintrón, Wilfredo, 1902–1903.
Mauleón, Gustavo, 2742–2743.
Mauro, Diego Alejandro, 1349.
Máximo Castillo and the Mexican Revolution, 664.
Maxwell, Keely, 1180.
Mayer, Mirko Edgardo, 1426.
Mayer, Mónica, 78.
Mayer Celis, Leticia, 446.
Mayer Center Symposium, *12th, Denver Art Museum, 2012*, 20.
Mayes, April J., 811.
Máynez Vidal, Pilar, 243.
Mayor Mora, Alberto, 107.
Mayorga Quirós, Román, 751.
Mazzei de Grazia, Leonardo, 1266.
Mazzi Huaycucho, Víctor, 3012.
M'Bokolo, Elikia, 889.
Mc Evoy, Carmen, 1167, 1172.
McCalpin, Jermaine, 2998.
McCarthy, Matthew, 866.
McCloskey, Jason, 1750.
McCormick, Grace, 49.
McCracken, Ellen, 499.
McDowell, John H., 2807.
McDowell, Megan, 2633–2634, 2660.
McGarrity, Maria, 785.
McLean, Anne, 2635.
McManus, Stuart M., 500.
McNamara, Patrick J., 576.
McWhirter, George, 2597.
Medeiros, Lucas Viriato de, 2529.
Medina, Cuauhtémoc, 35.

Medina Bustos, José Marcos, 548.
Medina García, Jorge, 1832.
Medina García, Miguel Ángel, 577.
Medina Medina, Alejandra, 513.
Medina Vera, Heriberto, 917.
Medinaceli, Ximena, 1215.
Meeks, Brian, 2998.
Megías, Alicia, 1303.
Meglioli, Mauricio, 1480.
Mehl, Eva María, 501.
Meireles, Cildo, 150.
Meisel Roca, Adolfo, 962.
Mejía, Carlos A., 1833.
Mejía Burgos, Otto, 763.
Mejía de Mesa, Marietta, 1117.
Mejía Flores, José Francisco, 675.
Mejía Quintana, Oscar, 2974.
Meléndez, Edgardo, 890, 918.
Meléndez-Badillo, Jorell A., 919.
Meléndez M., Raúl, 1059.
Melgar, Mariano, 2159.
Melgar Bao, Ricardo, 426.
Mello, Cassandra, 2577.
Mello, Joana, 171.
Mello, Luiza, 135.
Mello, Magno Moraes, 1586.
Mello, Maria Ignez Cruz, 2903.
Mello, Marisa S., 135.
Melo, Érico, 1546.
Melo, José Evando Vieira de, 1691.
Melo, Rômulo César, 2404.
Melton-Villanueva, Miriam, 224.
Melvin, Karen, 369.
Memória e cultura: itinerários biográficos, trajetórias e relações geracionais, 122.
Memoria histórica del 68 en México: antología, 665.
Memorial da Resistência de São Paulo, 105.
Memorias de la independencia: España, Argentina y México en el primer centenario (1908–1910–1912), 335.
Memorias del caso peruano de esterilización forzada, 1181.
Memorias: Revista de la Maestría en Historia Social y Cultural de la UNAH, 710.
Mena, Miguel D., 1882.
Mendes, Anderson Fabrício Moreira, 1699.
Méndez, Danny, 920.
Méndez, Nora, 1834.
Méndez Chinchilla, Melvin, 2338.
Méndez Serrano, Manuel Reinaldo, 793.
Mendieta, Eduardo, 2979.
Mendieta, Pilar, 1227.
Mendiola García, Sandra C., 666.
Mendiondo, Miguel, 2326.

Mendívil, Julio, 2680, 2815–2816.
Mendonça, Manuela, 1618.
Mendonça, Martha, 2405.
Mendoza, Jesús Leticia, 502.
Mendoza, Rubén G., 36.
Mendoza Huerta, Yasbil Yanil Berenice, 2744.
Mendoza Muñoz, Jesús, 37, 503.
Mendoza Soriano, Reidezel, 578.
Menegat, Carla, 1040.
Meneses, Juan Diego Diaz, 2923.
Menezes, Andreia dos Santos, 2924.
Menz, Maximiliano Mac, 1602.
Mercado, Silvia D., 1427.
Mercado, Tununa, 2106.
Mercado Villalobos, Alejandro, 2745–2746.
Mercados en común: estudios sobre conexiones transnacionales, negocios y diplomacia en las Américas (siglos XIX y XX), 336.
Merced Hernández, Grisselle, 1935.
Merenson, Silvina, 1428.
Merhy, Sílvio, 2925.
Merino, Alicia de Los Ríos, 414.
Merino Acosta, Luz, 90.
Meriño Fuentes, María de los Ángeles, 803, 867.
Mérito, venalidad y corrupción en España y América, siglos XVII y XVIII, 371.
Merleaux, April, 921–922.
Mesa Chica, Darío, 1118.
Mesa Gisbert, Carlos D., 1958.
Messón, Omar, 1915.
Metropolitan Museum of Art (New York), 1, 40.
México en los setenta: ¿guerra sucia o terrorismo de estado?: hacia una política de la memoria, 667.
México... nunca más: expresiones artísticas y contextos socioculturales en una era postnacional, 79.
El México profundo en la gran década de desesperanza (1846–1856), 579.
Mexico. Secretaría de Marina, 688.
Meyer, Jean A., 456, 580.
Meyer, Pedro, 2510.
M.H. de Young Memorial Museum, 9.
Micett, Ingrid, 1068.
Michaud, Cécile, 54.
Michelena, José Antonio, 1904.
Micheletti, Maria Gabriela, 1429.
Michielin, Francisco, 2453.
Midence, Carlos, 764.
Mier Noriega y Guerra, José Servando Teresa de, 581.

Mijangos, Pablo, 591.
Mijares, Enrique, 2327.
Mikowsky, Solomon Gadles, 2791.
1964: 50 anos depois: a ditadura em debate, 1692.
1964: 50 Anos Depois (seminar), *São Paulo, 2014*, 1693.
1964: do golpe à democracia, 1693.
1914: definiendo el rumbo de una nación, 668.
Milano, Laura, 101.
Millán, Elizabeth, 2980.
Miller, Aragorn Storm, 1073.
Miller, Mary Ellen, 6.
Millones, Luis, 225, 344, 975.
Mills, Bill, 669.
Minaya, Julio, 2999.
Minchillo, Carlos Cortez, 2372.
Minga, Ana, 2616.
Minila, Jonathan, 1778.
Miño Grijalva, Manuel, 458, 972.
Mintz, Sidney Wilfred, 923.
Minutolo de Orsi, Cristina V., 1430.
Mira Caballos, Esteban, 372.
Mira Delli-Zotti, Guillermo Claudio, 415.
Miradas regionales: las regiones y la idea de nación en América Latina, siglos XIX y XX, 337.
Miranda, Ana, 269, 2423.
Miranda, Bruno Romero Ferreira, 1603.
Miranda, Marcos Paulo de Souza, 131.
Miranda, Ricardo, 2747.
Miranda, Wander Melo, 2473.
Miranda Neto, Manoel José de, 1604.
Miranda Nieto, Alejandro, 2748.
Mirisola, Marcelo, 2373.
Miró Ibars, Margarita, 2250.
Mistral, Gabriela, 2160.
Mitchell, Stephanie Evaline, 670.
Mitchell-Walthour, Gladys L., 3029.
Los mitos y sus tiempos: creencias y narraciones de Mesoamérica y los Andes, 225.
Miyashiro, Aldo, 2339.
Modelo 1972: 12 poetas ecuatorianos: (con los ojos también maravillados), 2161.
Modern, Rodolfo E., 2340.
Modern Mexican culture: critical foundations, 457.
Modernidade: coleção de arte brasileira Odorico Tavares, 184.
La modernización de la república: la prensa científica del Perú (1827–1829), 1182.
Moguel Pasquel, María Carolina, 582.
Molina, Matias M., 1605.
Molina, Paulina, 2704.
Molina, Raúl A., 1029.
Molina, Sergio, 2926.
Molina del Villar, América, 334.
Molina González, Ana, 939.
Molina Jiménez, Iván, 707, 765.
Molina Medina, Norbert, 1067.
Molina Palomino, Pablo, 2817.
Moncada González, Gisela, 583–584.
Mondolfi Gudat, Edgardo, 924.
Mondragón, Juan Carlos, 2127.
Monge Picado, María José, 87.
Monreal, Susana, 340.
Monroy, María Isabel, 610.
Monroy Bordon, Valentina, 455.
Monrroy, Gustavo, 1216.
Monsalve Pino, Margarita María, 108.
Monsalvo Mendoza, Edwin, 1119.
Montagnani, Tommaso, 2927.
Montaldo, Graciela R., 1431.
Montali, Lilia, 318.
Montás, Keiselim A., 1915.
Monteiro, Marcelo, 1694.
Monteiro, Marianna Francisca Martins, 2569.
Monteiro, Mário Ypiranga, 1537.
Monteith, Kathleen E.A., 868.
Montejo, Victor, 1835.
Montenegro, Antonio Torres, 414.
Montenegro, Carlos, 1217.
Montero, Carlos Guillermo, 88.
Montero, Mayra, 1905.
Montero Quispe, Raúl, 51.
Montes de Oca, Ignacio, 1432.
Montes de Oca Navas, Elvia, 671.
Montilla, Claudia, 2333.
Montini, Pablo, 1303.
Montoya Garay, Jhon Williams, 1104.
Montoya Gómez, María Victoria, 504.
Montt, Nahum, 1980.
Moore, Robin D., 2793.
Mora, Gerardo, 284.
Mora, Sergio de la, 2727.
Moraes, Eliane Robert, 2465.
Moraes, José Geraldo Vinci de, 2928.
Moraes, Julio Lucchesi, 1538.
Moraes, Reinaldo, 2441.
Moraes, Vinícius de, 2516.
Morales, Andrés, 1513, 2251.
Morales, Mario Roberto, 1868.
Morales Abril, Omar, 2749.
Morales Barrientos, Diego, 1286.
Morales Barrios, Luis Emilio, 1836.
Morales Benítez, Otto, 1120.
Morales C., María, 2252.
Morales Flores, Iván César, 2792.

Morales Santos, Francisco, 2253.
Morales Tejeda, Aida Liliana, 925.
Moralidades y comportamientos sexuales: Argentina, 1880–2011, 1433.
Morán, Elizabeth, 7.
Morán Ramos, Luis Daniel, 981.
Moraña, Mabel, 2990.
Moratelli, Thiago, 1539.
More, Anna Herron, 1728.
Moreira, María Verónica, 1434.
Moreira, Moraes, 2517.
Moreira, Regina da Luz, 1569.
Moreira Mazariegos, Axel Javier, 1837.
Moreiras, Alberto, 2981.
Morejón Arnaiz, Idalia, 1885.
Morelli, Rolando D.H., 1906.
Moreno, Alessandra Zorzetto, 1606.
Moreno, Alicia del Carmen, 1435.
Moreno, Iani del Rosario, 2359.
Moreno Lázaro, Javier, 427.
Moreno Luzón, Javier, 335.
Moreno Molina, Agustín, 1074.
Moreno Vázquez, José Israel, 2768.
Moreyra, Beatriz Inés, 308.
Morgado, Flávio, 2518.
Morong Reyes, Germán, 285.
Moroni, Delfina, 2975.
Morrone, Ariel J., 286.
Moscona, Myriam, 2254, 2617.
Moscovich, Cíntia, 2406.
Moser, Benjamin, 2665.
Mosquera, José E., 1121.
Mosquera Saravia, Javier, 1838.
Mota, Urariano, 2442.
Motta, Rodrigo Patto Sá, 408, 1649.
Moura, Aureliano Pinto de, 1708.
Moutinho, Marcelo, 2443.
Movimiento sindical en dictadura: fuentes para una historia del sindicalismo en Chile, 1973–1990, 1267.
Moya, Fernanda Nunes, 2681.
Moyano, Daniel, 1436.
Moyano, Marcelo, 1437.
Muaze, Mariana, 1567.
Muchnik, Daniel, 1371, 1438.
Mues Orts, Paula, 40.
Múgica, María Luisa, 1303.
Mujeres, feminismo y arte popular, 80.
Mujica, Mayte, 2034.
Mujica Pinilla, Ramón, 60.
Mularski, Jedrek, 2849.
Mulcahy, Matthew, 794.
Mulheres de outrora, bordados de agora, 185.
Mulino Giannattasio, Alexandra, 1056.
Müller, Regina Polo, 2569.
Mulligan, Joseph, 2627.
El mundo del trabajo urbano: trabajadores, cultura y prácticas laborales, 458.
El mundo latinoamericano como representación, siglos XIX–XX, 338.
Mundy, Barbara E., 38.
Munhoz, Raquel, 2938.
Muniz Neto, Mentor, 2444.
Muñoz, Víctor, 1839–1840.
Muñoz, Willy Oscar, 1945.
Muñoz Aguirre, Inés, 2068.
Muñoz Marín, Luis, 795.
Muñoz Mata, Laura, 926–927.
Muñoz Paz, María del Carmen, 728.
Muñoz Rivera, Luis, 795.
Muñoz Rojo, Fabián, 1503.
Muñoz Serrulla, María Teresa, 339.
Murillo Sandoval, Juan David, 1122.
Murueta, Marco Eduardo, 2962.
Museo de Arte Carrillo Gil, 86.
Museo de Arte de Lima, 57.
Museo de Arte Moderno (Mexico), 69.
Museo Mural Diego Rivera (México), 75.
Museo Nacional Centro de Arte Reina Sofía, 150.
Museo Nacional de Arte (Mexico), 81.
Museo Nacional de Artes Visuales de Montevideo (Uruguay), 116.
Museo Rufino Tamayo, 68.
Museu Afro Brasil, 181, 184.
Museu de Arte do Rio, 168.
Museu de Arte do Rio Grande do Sul Ado Malagoli, 186.
Museu de Arte Moderna do Rio de Janeiro, 152.
Museu Lasar Segall, 149.
Museu Oscar Niemeyer, 145.
Museu Paraense Emílio Goeldi, 1574.
Museu Serralves, 150.
Museum of International Folk Art (N.M.), 22.
Museus Castro Maya, 149.
Música, 2929.
Música indígena y contemporaneidad: nuevas facetas de la música en las sociedades tradicionales, 2750.
Música vernácula de Chiapas: antología, 2751.
Música y catedral: nuevos enfoques, viejas temáticas, 2752.
Mustakeem, Sowande' M., 796.
Myers, Jorge, 3040.
Myers, Robin, 2604.
Myrup, Erik, 1607.
Nahas, Ana Laura, 2445.

Najlis, Michele, 2255.
Nállim, Jorge, 1439.
Nandayapa, Mario, 82.
Napolitano, Marcos, 1649.
Narradores indígenas y mestizos de la época colonial (siglos XVI-XVII): zonas andina y mesoamerica, 373.
La narrativa de Jorge Eduardo Benavides: textos críticos, 1950.
Narrativa guatemalteca: antología, 1841.
Nascente, Gabriel José, 2519.
Nascimento, Elomar, 2407.
Nascimento, Evando, 2408.
Nascimento, Mara Regina do, 1611.
National Geographic Society (US), 304.
Native wills from the colonial Americas: dead giveaways in a New World, 226.
Naupari, Héctor, 2140.
Nava, Mariano, 1077.
Navajas Cortés, Esteban, 2333.
Navarrete, Otilia, 2256.
Navarrete, Sylvia, 69.
Navarrete Linares, Federico, 243.
Navarrete-Montalvo, Juan, 1262.
Navarro, Walter, 2446.
Navarro Carballo, José Ramón, 869.
Navarro Rodríguez, Sebastián Rafael, 1075.
Navas, Mykel, 1052.
Naves, Rodrigo, 141.
Naves, Santuza Cambraia, 2930.
Navia, Patricio, 1268.
Nazario Velasco, Rubén, 928.
Necochea López, Raúl, 1183.
Neder, Gizlene, 1540.
Negrín, Edith, 2239.
El negro Atilio: un trabajador, un líder sindical combativo, un militante político revolucionario: libro homenaje a 40 años de su asesinato, 1440.
Neira Samanez, Hugo, 374.
Neira Vilas, Xosé, 797.
Nejar, Carlos, 2374.
Nemer, José Alberto, 157.
Nemser, Daniel, 505.
Neruda, Pablo, 2618-2619.
Neste instante: novos olhares sobre a poesia brasileira dos anos 1970, 2520.
Nesvig, Martin Austin, 506.
Neto, Lira, 2931.
Nettel, Guadalupe, 1784, 2646.
Netto, Raymundo, 269.
Networks and trans-cultural exchange: slave trading in the South Atlantic, 1590-1867, 1608.
Neufeld, Stephen, 585.

Neves, Josélia, 2494.
Neves, Kátia Regina Felipini, 105.
Neves, Lúcia Maria Bastos Pereira das, 1657, 1670-1673.
Neves, Manuel, 116.
Newman, Simon P., 817.
Newton, Melanie J., 818.
Neyra Magagna, Ezio, 2035.
Ni vencedores ni vencidos: la Guerra del Pacífico en perspectiva histórica, 394.
Niaah, Jahlani, 915.
Nichols, James David, 586.
Nichols, Jason, 2682.
Nicolas, Vincent, 287.
Nikken, Pedro, 751.
Niño, Jairo Aníbal, 2333.
Nocera, Eduardo Luis, 1514.
Nogueira, Carlos, 2932.
Nogueira, Fátima, 1869.
Noguera, Renato, 2944.
Noguera Penso, Claudia, 2257.
Noguera Solano, Ricardo, 542.
Noreña, Aurora, 2258.
Noriega, Luis, 1981.
Noriega Bernuy, Julio, 2164.
Noriega Elío, Cecilia, 341.
Norman, York, 436.
Norões, Everardo, 2409.
Noronha, Isabela, 2375.
El norte de México y la historia regional: homenaje a Ignacio del Río, 459.
Norte: una antología, 1779.
Norton, Marcy, 507.
Nötzold, Ana Lúcia Vulfe, 248.
Novais, Fernando A., 1584.
Novas, José C., 929.
As novas regras do jogo: o sistema da arte no Brasil, 151.
Novinsky, Anita Waingort, 1609.
Nuestros reveses y victorias: causas y experiencias (1868-1958), 870.
Nuevas dramaturgias argentinas: obras de autores nacidos entre 1981-1990, 2341.
Nuevas iluminaciones: la larga trayectoria literaria de Enrique Jaramillo Levi, 1869.
Nuevas miradas sobre los antiguos michoacanos (México): un diálogo interdisciplinario (symposium), *Vienna, Austria, 2012*, 227.
Nuevos documentos de 1948: los proscriptos, 766.
Nuez, Iván de la, 1936.
Numhauser, Paulina, 316.
Núñez, Griselda, 2259.

Núñez, Jorge, 1076.
Núñez Sánchez, Jorge, 973.
Núñez Tapia, Francisco Alberto, 639.
Nuricumbo Aguilar, Rigoberto, 559.
Obando Villota, Lorena, 288.
Obejas, Achy, 2644.
Obermeier, Franz, 375, 1610.
Obregón, Clotilde María, 729.
Oca Building (São Paulo), 181.
O'Callaghan, Evelyn, 785.
Ocampo, Emilio, 1441.
Ochoa, Juan Sebastián, 2804.
Ochoa Serrano, Álvaro, 644.
Odone, María Carolina, 252.
O'Donnell, Pacho, 1030.
Odriozola Guillot, Miguel Ángel, 48.
Odriozola Odriozola, Miguel Ángel, 48.
Oesterheld, Héctor Germán, 2647.
Ohtake, Tomie, 144.
Oiticica Filho, César, 187.
Ojeda, Gabriel, 2260.
Ojeda, Mónica, 2002.
Olea, Catalina, 1273.
Olea Franco, Rafael, 646.
Oles, James, 39, 68.
Oliani, Luiz Otávio, 2521.
Oliva, Elena, 3027.
Olivar, José Alberto, 1069.
Olivé, León, 2965–2966.
Oliveira, Acauam, 2929.
Oliveira, Giovana Paiva de, 1541.
Oliveira, Reginaldo Gomes de, 1588.
Oliveira, Reinaldo, 2580.
Oliveira, Susane Rodrigues de, 289.
Olivera, Gastón Alejandro, 1442.
Oliveria, Dennison de, 1542.
Olivero, Romina, 2261.
Olivier, Guilhem, 228, 243.
Ollé, Carmen, 2036.
Olmedo, Ernesto, 1443.
Olmedo Zorrilla, Elvira, 1500.
Olmos Aguilera, Miguel, 2750.
Oloixarac, Pola, 2102, 2648.
Olveda, Jaime, 460.
Olvera Aguilar, Jorge, 639.
O'Malley, Gregory E., 798.
Omohundro Institute of Early American History & Culture, 837.
Onofre, Jonatas, 2522.
Op. Cit.: Revista del Centro de Investigaciones Históricas, 799, 930.
La opción republicana en el marco de las independencias: ideas, política e historiografía, 1797–1830, 1077.
Oramas León, Orlando, 1055.
Ordem crítica: a América portuguesa nas "fronteiras" do século XVIII, 1611.
El orden y el bajo pueblo: los regímenes de Portales y Rosas frente al mundo popular, 1829–1852, 395.
Ordóñez Iturralde, Wilman, 2806, 2808.
Orellana, Luis, 1265.
Ormachea Gutiérrez, Verónica, 1959.
Orosco, José Antonio, 2982.
Orozco, Gabriel, 83.
Orrego, Francisco, 315.
Ortega, María Teresa, 2594.
Ortega, Marxitania, 1780.
Ortega González, Carlos Alberto, 587.
Ortemberg, Pablo, 982.
Ortiz, Fernando, 2793.
Ortiz, Salvador, 1781.
Ortuño, Antonio, 1782–1783.
Ortuño Martínez, Bárbara, 1347.
Ortúzar, Diego, 1269.
Oseki-Dépré, Inês, 2523.
Ospina Ovalle, Carlos, 1123.
Ospital, María Silvia, 1292.
Ossa Santa Cruz, Juan Luis, 1259.
Ossio A., Juan M., 1747.
Osuna, Florencia, 1452.
Otero, Diego, 2037.
Otero-Cleves, Ana María, 348, 1124.
Otovo, Okezi T., 1695.
Otras miradas de las revoluciones mexicanas (1810–1910), 588.
El otro Belgrano: lejos del mito, cerca de una visión: escritos y documentos, 1031.
El otro rostro de la inversión extranjera: redes migratorias, empresa y crecimiento económico en México y América Latina, 427.
Los otros rebeldes novohispanos: imaginarios, discursos y cultura política de la subversión y la resistencia, 508.
Ovalle, Elizabeth, 2342.
Ovando, Gabriela, 1960.
Overmyer-Velázquez, Mark, 625.
Oviedo, José Miguel, 1748.
Oxford research encyclopedia of Latin American history, 800.
Oy, caramba!: an anthology of Jewish stories from Latin America, 2592.
Oyarzún, Kemy, 2262.
Pablo en Bohemia, 1907.
Pablo Hammeken, Luis de, 589, 2753–2754.
Pabón Villamizar, Silvano, 964.
Pacheco, Ana Paula Soares, 177.
Pacheco, Karina, 2038–2039.
Pacheco, Mariano, 1444.

Pacheco Rojas, José de la Cruz, 509.
Pacific Standard Time: LA/LA (project), 1, 16, 40.
Paço Imperial do Rio de Janeiro, 145.
Padilla, Carmella, 22.
Padilla, María Victoria, 1078.
Padilla Cárdenas, Gilberto, 97.
Padilla Jacobo, Abel, 676.
Padilla Ramos, Raquel, 672.
Padura Fuentes, Leonardo, 1908, 2649.
Páez, Silvio, 1842.
Pagán Vélez, Alexandra, 1909.
Pagés, Bernarda, 2103.
Pagliai, Lucila, 1342.
Painted in Mexico, 1700–1790: Pinxit Mexici, 40.
Paisaje y Diseño Urbano: Interdependencias Conceptuales en la Ciudad Mesoamericana, Precolonial y Colonial (conference), *México, 2009*, 8.
Paisajes culturales y patrimonio en el centro-norte de México, siglos XVII al XX, 461.
Paiva, Anabela, 1648.
Paiva, Asséde, 1612.
Paiva, Eduardo França, 1613.
Palabra viva del Libertador: legado ideológico y patriótico del Presidente Juan Rafael Mora para la Costa Rica en devenir, 767.
Palabras mayores: nueva narrativa mexicana, 1784.
Palabras para colgar en los árboles: breve selección de poesía guatemalteca, 2162.
Palácio das Artes (Belo Horizonte, Brazil), 145.
Palacios, Guillermo, 1543.
Palermo, Eduardo R., 1515.
Palermo Liñero, Edelsi, 925.
Palhares, Taisa Helena P., 141, 146.
Palma Alvarado, Daniel, 314, 395.
Palmer, Colin A., 913, 931.
Palmer Brown, Dionny Milena, 2178.
Palomares Ferrales, Eugenia, 801.
Palomino, Pablo, 2836.
Palominos Mandiola, Simón, 2818.
Palou, Pedro Ángel, 1785–1786.
Pan American Institute of Geography and History, 325.
Pancorvo Saliccetti, Anel, 12.
Panella, Claudio, 1470.
Pang, Bing'an, 882.
Pani, Erika, 462.
Papavero, Nelson, 1574.

Para além das Gerais: dinâmicas dos povos e instituições na América portuguesa Bahia, Goiás e Mato Grosso, 1614.
Parada, Maurício, 182.
Parada Ayala, Carlos, 2620.
Pardo, Cecilia, 57.
Paredes, Julio, 1982.
Paredes Cisneros, Santiago, 290.
Parisio, João Paulo, 2410.
Los parlamentos hispano-mapuches, 1593–1803: textos fundamentales, 1006.
Parodi, Claudia, 1749.
Parra, Eduardo Antonio, 1779.
Parra, Guillermo, 2593.
Parron, Tâmis, 1578.
Pasiones anticlericales: un recorrido iberoamericano, 340.
Pasolini, Ricardo, 1361.
Pasta, Paulo, 138.
Pastor, Marialba, 2684.
Pastor Bodmer, Beatriz, 396.
Pasztory, Esther, 2.
Paton, Diana, 802.
La patria albina: exilio, escritura y conversación en Lorenzo García Vega, 1937.
La patria organizada...: (antología de narrativa del nacionalismo puertorriqueño), 1938.
Patrimonio vivo de Uruguay: relevamiento de Candombe, 2853.
Paula, Romina, 2650.
Paulo, Heloísa, 1547.
Pauls, Alan, 2104.
Pavez Ojeda, Jorge, 1210.
Pavón, Armando, 641.
Pavoni, Norma L., 1445.
Paxton, Merideth, 5.
Payares, Gabriel, 2069.
Payàs, Gertrudis, 1006.
Payne Iglesias, Elizet, 713.
Paz, Juan Alberto, 2263.
Paz Esquerre, Eduardo, 291.
Paz Soldán, Edmundo, 1961–1963.
Pedreira, Flávia de Sá, 1544.
Pedro Teixeira, a Amazônia e o Tratado de Madri, 1615.
Pedrosa, Fernando, 415.
Pedrosa, Fernando Velôzo Gomes, 1545.
Pedrosa, Mário, 123, 187.
Peixoto, Alzira Vargas do Amaral, 1546, 1569.
Peixoto, Celina Vargas do Amaral, 1546.
Peixoto, Charles, 2524.
Peixoto, Fernanda Arêas, 313.
Peixoto, Luiz Felipe de Lima, 2933.

Pellanda, Luís Henrique, 2447–2448.
Peluffo, Luisa, 2264.
Peña, Alfonso, 67.
Pena, Felipe, 2449.
Peña, Hilario, 1787.
Peña Doria, Olga Martha, 1733.
Peña Hasbún, Paula, 1207, 1224.
Peña Núñez, Beatriz Carolina, 1729.
Pena Rodríguez, Alberto, 1547.
Penelu, Larissa, 423.
Peniche Moreno, Paola, 590.
Pensado, Jaime M., 673.
Pensado Leglise, María Patricia, 414.
Pensamiento Velasco, Juan, 1843.
Pensamiento visual contemporáneo, 108.
Pensar la modernidad política: propuestas desde la nueva historia política: antología, 341.
Pepe, Edward Charles, 2742–2743.
Pequeno, Fernanda, 124.
Peralta, Victoria, 1099, 1125.
Peralta Ruiz, Víctor, 1184.
Perearnau, Marcos, 2308.
Perednik, Jorge Santiago, 2621.
Pereira, Carlos Eduardo, 2934.
Pereira, Manuel, 1910.
Pereira, Simone Luci, 2675.
Pereira, Walter Luiz, 133.
Perera Díaz, Aisnara, 803, 867.
Peres, Ana Maria Clark, 2376.
Peres, Fernando Antonio, 1548.
Pérez, Cristián, 1270.
Pérez, Daniel Edgardo, 1371.
Pérez, Helvecia, 2853.
Pérez, Inés, 428.
Pérez, José, 1068.
Pérez, José Manuel Santos, 1616.
Pérez, Julián, 2040.
Pérez, Liliana Elizabeth, 292, 1315.
Pérez, Luis Marcelo, 2265.
Pérez, Manuel, 1749.
Pérez, Mirzam, 1730.
Pérez, Roberto Alexander, 2343.
Pérez Alacántara, Ivonne Andrea, 41.
Pérez Alencart, Alfredo, 2266.
Pérez Benavides, Amada Carolina, 1126.
Pérez Calderón, Ismael, 15.
Pérez Concepción, Hebert, 804.
Pérez Cortés, Sergio, 678.
Pérez Firmat, Gustavo, 1939.
Pérez Garay, Carlos Alberto, 3013.
Pérez Gaviria, Lina María, 1983.
Pérez González, Natalie Chelsea, 455.
Pérez Herrero, Pedro, 467.
Pérez Lizana, Sebastían, 301.

Pérez-Maricevich, Francisco, 2118, 2135.
Pérez Memén, Fernando, 805.
Pérez Morales, Edgardo, 968.
Pérez Ortiz, Luis Alejandro, 676.
Pérez Perdomo, Francisco, 2593.
Pérez Puente, Leticia, 2756.
Pérez Ramírez, Gustavo, 1158.
Pérez Rivero, Roberto, 932.
Pérez-Rosario, Vanessa, 809.
Pérez Sánchez, Yusleidy, 933.
Pérez Stocco, Sandra, 1446.
Pérez Toledo, Sonia, 458.
Pérez Vega, Ivette, 871.
Pérez-Yglesias, María, 1844.
Pereza, revolución y desarrollo empresarial en México: siglos XIX y XX, 463.
Perlingeiro, Camila, 144.
Perlingeiro, Max, 144.
Perón, Juan Domingo, 1390.
Perrone, Charles A., 2525–2528, 2531.
Perry, Marc D., 2794.
Perry, Zoë, 2667.
Perú, 1185.
Peru. Ministerio de Cultura, 299.
Pestana, Carla Gardina, 819.
Peters, Ana Paula, 2935.
Peters Solórzano, Gertrud, 768.
Peterson, Jeanette Favrot, 21.
Petit, Edgar, 120.
Petley, Christer, 872.
Petra, Adriana, 1414.
Petruccelli, Alejandro, 2837.
Pettigrew, William A., 837.
Peza, Carmen de la, 2755.
Pharao Hansen, Magnus, 496.
Phé-Funchal, Denise, 1845.
Phillips, Anthony de V., 857.
Philp, Marta, 1479.
Pico, Claudia Milena, 965.
Picó, Fernando, 873.
Pico de Coaña de Valicourt, Yago, 769.
Piczenik, José Luis, 429.
Piedade, Acácio Tadeu de Camargo, 2936.
Piedra Valdez, José, 342.
Pierce, Donna Lee, 20.
Pieroni, Agustín, 1032.
Pieroni, Geraldo, 1601.
Pierson, Pierre, 1846.
Pifarré, Francisco, 293.
Piglia, Ricardo, 2132, 2651.
Pigna, Felipe, 1033, 1447.
Pignatari, Décio, 2450.
Pillsbury, Joanne, 1.
Pimenta, Gabriel, 2411.
Pimenta, João Paulo G., 1696.

Pimentel, Jerónimo, 2041.
Pimentel Carranza, Eduardo, 50.
Pineda Mendoza, Raquel, 42.
Piñeiro, Claudia, 2652.
Pinheiro, Milton, 1658.
Pinho, Osmundo, 2937.
Pini, Valeria, 1308.
Pino, Amado del, 2325.
Pino, Fermín del, 274.
Pinto, Antonio J., 874.
Pinto, Paulo Roberto Margutti, 1549.
Pinto, Roxana, 1847.
Pinto, Surama Conde Sá, 1679.
Pinto Garia, Maria Elisa, 2805.
Pinto Vallejos, Julio, 395.
Pinzón de Lewin, Patricia, 1090, 1127.
Pinzón Ríos, Guadalupe, 332, 355, 730.
Pipitone, Ugo, 343.
Pires, Catarina, 181.
Pistorio, Raúl H., 1471.
Pita Pico, Roger, 966, 1128.
Pittaluga, Roberto, 1448.
Piza, Arthur Luiz, 2465.
Pizarnik, Alejandra, 2622.
Pizarro Larrea, Roberto, 395.
Plana, Manuel, 674.
Plástico bolha: antologia de poesia, 2529.
Plata S., Jorge, 2333.
Plaza Navamuel, Rodolfo Leandro, 1449.
Plaza Salgado, Camila Belén, 1007.
Pleitez, Tania, 2175.
Población y sociedad en tiempos de lucha por la emancipación: Córdoba, Argentina, en 1813, 1450.
Poder y privilegio: cabildos eclesiásticos en Nueva España, siglos XVI a XIX, 2756.
Podetti, José Ramiro, 3041.
Podgorny, Irina, 1451.
Podhajcer, Adil, 2800, 2838.
Poesia com deuses: estudos de Hídrias, de Dora Ferreira da Silva, 2530.
Poesia na era da internacionalização dos saberes: circulação, tradução, ensino e crítica no contexto contemporâneo, 2531.
Poesía paraguaya: antología esencial, 2163.
Poesía quechua en Bolivia: antología, 2164.
Poéticas de la traducción, 2664.
Pogolotti, Graziella, 1911.
Pohl, John M.D., 26.
Polanco, Edward Anthony, 229.
Polesso, Natália Borges, 2412.

Polifonía del Padre de la Patria: ciento treinta atisbos, narraciones y testimonios sobre el capitán general Don Juan Rafael Mora, presidente de la República de 1849 a 1859, 770.
Política y cultura durante el "Onganiato": nuevas perspectivas para la investigación de la presidencia de Juan Carlos Onganía (1966–1970), 1452.
Política y sociedad en el exilio republicano español, 675.
Políticas da raça: experiências e legados da abolição e da pós-emancipação no Brasil, 1697.
The politics of the second slavery, 397.
Pollack, Aaron, 731.
Polleri Sierra, Felipe, 2128.
Polo Acuña, José, 967.
Pompéia, Raul, 2671.
Ponce, David, 2845.
Ponce, Pilar, 371.
Ponce de León, Macarena, 1258.
Pons, Joe Ott, 2795.
Pontificia Universidad Católica del Perú. Centro Cultural, 54.
Pontificia Universidad Católica del Perú. Especialidad de Antropología, 114.
Pontificia Universidad Católica del Perú. Fondo Editorial, 2987.
Poole, Stafford, 198, 1721.
Popayán en el siglo XX: algunas perspectivas sobre su historia urbana, 1129.
Por la mano del hombre: prácticas y creencias sobre chamanismo y curandería en México y el Perú, 344.
Por una Iglesia libre en un mundo liberal: la obra y los tiempos de Clemente de Jesús Munguía, primer arzobispo de Michoacán (1810–1868), 591.
Porfírio, Pablo F. de A., 414.
Porley, Rodolfo, 1503.
Porras Sáenz, Cecilia, 2176, 2267.
Porro, Antonio, 1574.
Porro Gutiérrez, Jesús María, 307.
Portinari, Cândido, 149.
Porto Cabrales, Raúl, 1130.
Portocarrero Maisch, Gonzalo, 3014.
Portuondo Zúñiga, Olga, 95, 838.
Posgrado Centroamericano en Historia (Universidad de Costa Rica), 707.
Potts, Timothy F., 1.
Poy, Lucas, 1453.
Pozzi Albornoz, Ismael R., 1034.
Pradelli, Ángela, 2105.
Prado, Adélia, 2532.

Prado, Estuardo, 2176.
Prado, Fabrício Pereira, 1617.
Prata, Antonio, 2451.
Pre-Columbian Studies Symposium "Making Value, Making Meaning: Techné in the Pre-Columbian World," *Washington, D.C., 2010*, 10.
Preciado, Antonio, 2268.
Prehistoria en Chile: desde sus primeros habitantes hasta los Incas, 294.
Premio Mesoamericano de Poesía "Luis Cardoza y Aragón": diez años: antología, 2165.
Prêmio UFES de Literatura, *2nd, Vitória, Brazil, 2013–2014*, 2452.
Premo, Bianca, 983.
La prensa en el porfiriato: procesos políticos en Michoacán, diplomacia y actores sociales en México, 592.
La prensa: un actor sempiterno: de la Primera Guerra Mundial a la posmodernidad, 464.
Presas, Adela, 2676.
Presos políticos e perseguidos estrangeiros na era Vargas, 1698.
Preston, Douglas J., 711.
Prieto, Agustina, 1303.
Prieto, Guillermo, 593.
Prieto, Mercedes, 1159.
Prieto González, José Manuel, 1912.
Prignitz-Poda, Helga, 77.
Priori, Angelo, 1550.
Pro Ruiz, Juan, 330, 1349.
Problemas del desarrollo económico en el occidente de México: los recursos y sus usos en una perspectiva de largo plazo, siglos XIX y XX, 676.
Proctor, Frank T., 510.
Prodani, Anastasi, 413.
Projeto construtivo brasileiro na arte, 152.
Protocolos de escribanos en el Registro Principal del Estado Zulia (1790–1836): catálogo integral y extractos documentales, 1079.
A província fluminense: administração provincial no tempo do Império do Brasil, 1699.
Púa M., Giovanni, 3005.
Puchet, May, 117.
Pueblos indígenas en Latinoamérica: incorporación, conflicto, ciudadanía y representación siglo XIX, 398.
Puello Ch., Ricardo A., 1848.
Puente levadizo: vcinticuatro cuentistas de Panamá y España, 1849.
Puente Luna, José Carlos de la, 984–985.
Puerta Bautista, Lorena, 1080.
Puertas abiertas: antología de poesía centroamericana, 2166.
Puga, Vera, 1676.
Puig-Samper, Miguel Angel, 315.
Pujol, Jessica, 2459.
Pulecio Mariño, Enrique, 2333.
Pulido Esteva, Diego, 677.
Pulido Herráez, Begoña, 581.
Pulido Llano, Gabriela, 2757.
Puñales-Alpízar, Damaris, 1921.
Purcell Torretti, Fernando, 1241, 2850.
Pureco Ornelas, Alfredo, 676.
Putnam, Lara, 345, 934.
Quadrat, Samantha Viz, 1678.
Qué es el peronismo: una respuesta desde la filosofía, 3042.
Quelé, a voz da cor: biografia de Clementina de Jesus, 2938.
Queler, Jefferson J., 1551.
Quemé, Fabrizio, 2176.
Querejazu, Pedro, 102.
Querejazu Lewis, Roy, 295.
Quesada, Margarita, 87.
Quesada, Sarah, 376.
Quesada Monge, Rodrigo, 3028.
Quesada Vanegas, Gustavo, 2269.
Quezada Torres, María Teresa, 594.
Quichua Chaico, David, 1186.
Quila, Elizabeth, 2270.
Quiñones Aguilar, Ana Cielo, 107.
Quintanilla, Luis, 2626.
Quintanilla, Pablo, 3017.
Quintero, Ednodio, 2059.
Quintero Arredondo, Héctor, 3003.
Quinteros, Guillermo O., 1035, 1340.
La Quintiada (1912–1925): la rebelión indígena liderada por Manuel Quintín Lame en el Cauca: recopilación de fuentes primarias, 1131.
Quirarte, Vicente, 1788.
Quiroga, Néstor I., 230.
Quiroga Santa Cruz, Marcelo, 1218.
Quiroga Zuluaga, Marcela, 296.
Quirós Alcalá, Julio E., 795.
Quiroz Ávila, Rubén, 3017.
Quiroz Serrano, Rafael, 1081.
Quispe-Agnoli, Rocío, 297.
Rabelo Cartagena, José A., 1913–1914.
Radburn, Nicholas, 839.
Rafael Martínez Nadal: una vida, un ideal, 935.
Raíces cn otra tierra: el legado de Adolfo Sánchez Vázquez, 678.

Raizes medievais do Brasil moderno: ordens religiosas entre Portugal e o Brasil, 1618.
Ramacciotti, Karina Inés, 1341.
Ramalho, Maria de Lourdes Nunes, 2564–2565.
Ramírez, Camilo A., 2637.
Ramírez, Dixa, 936.
Ramírez, Paul Francis, 511.
Ramírez, Sergio, 2166, 2198.
Ramírez, Sócrates, 1082.
Ramírez, Susan E., 985.
Ramírez Braschi, Dardo, 1454.
Ramírez Cañedo, Elier, 939.
Ramírez G., María Teresa, 962.
Ramírez González, Clara Inés, 641.
Ramírez González, Imelda, 109.
Ramírez Samayoa, Gerardo, 716.
Ramos, Agustín, 1789.
Ramos, Antonio, 1850.
Ramos, Elizabeth Santos, 2377.
Ramos, Eloisa H. Capovilla da Luz, 326.
Ramos, Graciliano, 2377.
Ramos, José Miguel, 2848.
Ramos, Juan G., 2983.
Ramos, Juana M., 776.
Ramos, Nuno, 153.
Ramos, Rubén, 2167.
Ramos Aguirre, Francisco, 679.
Ramos-Izquierdo, Eduardo, 540.
Ramos Lara, María de la Paz, 595.
Ramos-Perea, Roberto, 1940.
Ramos Revillas, Antonio, 1790.
Ramos-Rodríguez, Froilán José, 1068.
Ramos Sucre, José Antonio, 2593.
Ran, Amalia, 2839.
Randall, Margaret, 2613.
Rangel, Joselo, 1791.
Rangel Lozano, Claudia E.G., 667.
Rangel Silva, José Alfredo, 596.
Raposo, Paulo, 2584.
Rappo Míguez, Susana Edith, 472.
Ratto, Silvia, 1455.
Rauch, Laura, 2356.
Raúl Zurita: alegoría de la desolación y la esperanza, 2304.
Rayes, Agustina, 312.
Re, Matteo, 409.
A reader in African-Jamaican music, dance and religion, 2781.
Rebollo-Gil, Guillermo, 1941–1943.
Rebuzzi, Solange, 2533.
Recalde, Héctor, 1456.
Reches, Ana Laura, 1399.
Recias, Matías, 2832.
Red Latinoamericana de Historia Oral, 414.
A red like no other: how cochineal colored the world: an epic story of art, culture, science, and trade, 22.
Redden, Andrew, 1739.
Regime der Anerkennung: Kämpfe um Wahrheit und Recht in der Aufarbeitung der argentinischen Militärdiktatur [Searching for recognition: the fight for law and rights in the historical reappraisal of the Argentine military dictatorship], 1457.
Registrar e imaginar la nación: la estadística durante la primera mitad del siglo XIX, 597.
Rêgo, Josoaldo Lima, 2534.
Reichert, Rafal B., 820.
Reid, Ahmed, 840.
Reily, Suzel Ana, 2939.
Reina, Leticia, 398, 598.
Reina Rodríguez, Carlos Arturo, 1132.
Reinato, Eduardo José, 1614.
Reis, Mateus Fávaro, 1516.
Relações internacionais do Brasil: antologia comentada de artigos da Revista do IHGB (1841–2004), 1700.
Relatos de mujeres nuevas, 1851.
Relatos del exilio: escritores argentinos en México: Humberto Costantini, Juan Gelman, Mempo Giardinelli y Tununa Mercado, 2106.
La religión en la esfera pública chilena: ¿laicidad o secularización?, 1271.
Remedi, Gustavo, 2988.
Rememorar los derroteros: la impronta de la formación artística en la UNAM, 84.
Rendall, Steven, 881.
Rendón Alarcón, Jorge, 678.
Rengifo, Francisca, 1258, 1260, 1272.
Rénique C., José Luis, 1187.
Repetto Málaga, Luis, 12.
Representaciones de la política: provincias, territorios y municipios (1860–1955), 1458.
Representações da fauna no Brasil: séculos XVI-XX, 188.
Representações do sertão: poder, cultura e identidades, 1619.
La República errante, 599.
Reséndez, Andrés, 377.
La resignificación del Nuevo Mundo: crónica, retórica y semántica en la América virreinal, 1749.
Resistir é preciso..., 189.
Restall, Matthew, 231.

Restauración de la obra maestra barroca de Taxco de Alarcón: legado y futuro de la iglesia de Santa Prisca = Restoring the Baroque masterpiece of Taxco de Alarcón: the legacy and future of Santa Prisca Church, 43.
Restiffe, Mauro, 153.
Restrepo David, Felipe, 2324.
Revilla Orías, Paola, 998.
Revista do Instituto de Estudos Brasileiros, 2940.
Revista USP, 2941.
Revista Vórtex, 2942.
La revolución de las mujeres en México, 680.
La Revolución en Zacatecas y la Batalla de 1914: a través de documentos inéditos del Archivo Histórico del Estado de Zacatecas (agosto de 1910-octubre de 1915), 681.
La revolución permanente: historia social de las mujeres en Chile, 1273.
Revolucionarias fueron todas, 600.
Las revoluciones en el largo siglo XIX latinoamericano, 399.
Rex Galindo, David, 365, 378, 512.
Rey Fajardo, José del, 959, 1083.
Reyes, Ana María, 1084.
Reyes Fragoso, Arturo, 624.
Reyes Hernández, Luis Angel, 2070.
Reynoso Bolaños, Arturo, 2991.
Reza, Germán A de la, 1133.
Rezzutti, Paulo, 1552.
Rhi Sausi Garavito, María José, 601.
Rhoades, Patricia Clare, 713.
Ribeiro, Ana Elisa, 2413.
Ribeiro, Daniele Corrêa, 1553.
Ribeiro, Eduardo Magalhães, 1554.
Ribeiro, Eneida Beraldi, 1609.
Ribeiro, José Augustor, 1555.
Ribeiro, José Iran, 1701.
Ribeiro, Júlio Naves, 2930.
Ribeiro, Maria, 2566.
Ribeiro, Renilson Rosa, 1702.
Ribeiro, Simone, 178.
Ribeiro, Trajano, 1644.
Ricca, Javier, 1517.
Rice, Prudence M., 232.
Richard Jorba, Rodolfo A., 1459.
Richards Mayo, Sandra, 2782.
Richardson, David, 1608.
Richter, Kim N., 1.
Riddle, Frances, 2639, 2663.
Riedweg, Walter Stephan, 139.
Riera, Daniel, 2107.
Rieznik, Marina, 1460.
Rinaud, Christian, 2707.
Rincón, Carlos, 1134.
Rincón Frías, Gabriel, 513.
Rincón Rubio, Luis M., 1079.
Rincón Serratos, Jazmín, 2758.
Rinke, Stefan H., 430, 1556.
Río, Ignacio del, 459, 570.
Riofrio, John D., 431.
Ríos, Edmundo de los, 2042.
Ríos, Patricia, 2350.
Ríos, Rubén Horacio, 3042.
Ríos Castaño, Victoria, 233.
Risco, Enrique del, 1883.
The rise of constitutional government in the Iberian Atlantic world: the impact of the Cádiz Constitution of 1812, 400.
Rivas Rojas, Raquel, 2071.
Rivaud Morayta, Amelia, 414.
Rivera, Gabriela, 2704.
Rivera, José Eustasio, 2653.
Rivera, Luis César, 2168.
Rivera Aguilar, Asucena, 639.
Rivera Cabrieles, Leticia, 688.
Rivera Cachique, Ronald, 115.
Rivera Garza, Cristina, 1784.
Rivera Martínez, Edgardo, 2043.
Rivera Mir, Sebastián, 682, 1274.
Rivera Rodríguez, Marialuz, 2168.
Roa Mascheroni, Mirta, 2134.
Robb, Matthew H., 9.
Roberts, Justin, 821.
Robertson, James Craufurd, 841.
Robin, Alena, 44.
Robledo, Víctor, 106.
Robles, Juan Manuel, 2044.
Robles Ortiz, Claudio, 1262.
Roca, Ignacio, 277.
Roca, Juan Manuel, 2271.
Roca, Pilar, 986.
Roca-Rey, Christabelle, 1188.
Rocca Torres, Luis, 2819.
Rocha, Simone, 1557.
Rocío García Olmedo, María del, 686.
Rodas Morales, Hugo, 3022.
Rodeiro, Luis Enrique, 1440.
Rodilla León, María José, 1731.
Rodrigues, Alexandre Marques, 2414–2415.
Rodrigues, Fernando da Silva, 1501, 1679.
Rodrigues, Jaime, 1620.
Rodrigues, Marcus Vinicius, 2416.
Rodrigues, Mário, 2453.
Rodriguez, Alberto, 2759.
Rodríguez, Carlos Armando, 13.
Rodríguez, Cynthia, 2674.
Rodríguez, Emilio Jorge, 2594.
Rodríguez, Gustavo, 2045.

Rodríguez, Jimena N., 1749.
Rodriguez, Manuel R., 947.
Rodríguez, María Graciela, 1354.
Rodríguez, María Guadalupe, 602.
Rodríguez, Miguel, 540.
Rodríguez, Rolando, 937–939.
Rodríguez Alcalá, Guido, 1498.
Rodríguez-Alegría, Enrique, 514.
Rodríguez Amaya, Fabio, 1971.
Rodríguez Carucci, Alberto, 3001.
Rodríguez Cascante, Francisco, 2997.
Rodríguez Caso, Juan Manuel, 542.
Rodríguez Cuadros, José Darío, 1135.
Rodríguez Díaz, María del Rosario, 592, 603.
Rodríguez García, Huascar, 1219.
Rodríguez García, Margarita, 531.
Rodriguez Iglesias, Legna, 2623.
Rodríguez Jáuregui, Luis, 515.
Rodríguez Joa, Mariela, 925.
Rodríguez La O, Raúl, 875.
Rodríguez Leytón, Nivardo, 3023.
Rodríguez Maglio, Leonardo Rafael, 3032.
Rodríguez Morel, Genaro, 910.
Rodríguez Moya, Inmaculada, 24.
Rodríguez O., Jaime E., 346.
Rodríguez Ostria, Gustavo, 1220.
Rodríguez Pérez, María Cristina, 668.
Rodríguez Quispe, Virgilio, 1221.
Rodríguez-Raga, Juan Carlos, 1108.
Rodríguez Romero, Agustina, 25.
Rodríguez Sáenz, Eugenia, 771.
Rodríguez-Sala, María Luisa, 1743.
Rodríguez Sirtori, Leonardo, 2269.
Roe, Michelle, 1852.
Roggero, Chiara, 2352.
Rohner, Fred, 2820–2821.
Roio, José Luiz del, 189.
Rojas, Agustín de, 2654.
Rojas, José Luis de, 234.
Rojas, Juan Ramón, 1853.
Rojas, Rafael, 940.
Rojas Guevara, Xiomara, 2272.
Rojas Huaynates, Joel, 3017.
Rojas Salas, Luis Eugenio, 2273.
Rojas Vásquez, Víctor Hernán, 1222.
Rojas Zolezzi, Enrique, 298.
Rojkind, Inés, 1461.
Roldán, Diego P., 1462.
Rollemberg, Denise, 1678.
Román, Alejandro, 2344.
Román Alarcón, Rigoberto Arturo, 539.
Romeiro, Adriana, 1586.
Romero, Fausto, 2003.
Romero, Jilma, 414.
Romero, Raúl R., 2822.
Romero, Ricardo, 2108.
Romero de Nohra, Flor, 1984.
Romero Delgado, Marta, 414.
Romero Galván, José Rubén, 243.
Romero Gil, Juan Manuel, 570.
Romero Ibarra, María Eugenia, 427.
Ronchi, Verónica, 1463.
Rondón Almeida, Carlos Enrique, 3007.
Ronsino, Hernán, 2655.
Roorda, Eric Paul, 806.
Root, William Pitt, 2618.
Roque, Randall, 2274.
Roque Baldovinos, Ricardo, 1870.
Roque Puente, Carlos Alberto, 461.
Rosa, Nei Vargas da, 151.
Rosabal Conejo, Ricardo, 1856.
Rosales Ayala, S. Héctor, 79.
Rosario Natal, Carmelo, 876.
Rosario Rivera, Raquel, 877.
Rosas Lauro, Claudia, 344.
Rosas Salas, Sergio Francisco, 465.
Rose, Juan Gonzalo, 2169.
Roselli, Manuel H., 1464.
Rosende, Mercedes, 2129.
Rosenmüller, Christoph, 360.
Rosenzvaig, Marcos, 2109.
Roskamp, Hans, 227.
Rossi, Claudia, 2275.
Rostoldo, Jadir Peçanha, 1703.
Los rostros de la tierra encantada: religión, evangelización y sincretismo en el Nuevo Mundo: homenaje a Manuel Marzal, S.J, 347.
Rostworowski de Diez Canseco, María, 299.
Roubina, Evguenia, 2760.
Roulet, Florencia, 1036.
Rovira, José Carlos, 1732.
Rovner, Eduardo, 2345.
Rowe, Erin Kathleen, 379.
Ruan, Felipe E., 380.
Ruano Ruano, Leticia, 466.
Rubé, Julio Horacio, 1465.
Rubens Gerchman: o rei do mau gosto, 154.
Rubinzal, Mariela, 1466.
Rubio, Joaquín, 12.
Rubio Apiolaza, Pablo, 424, 1243, 1275.
Rueda Estrada, Verónica, 772.
Ruffato, Luiz, 2454.
Rufinoni, Manoela Rossinetti, 172.
Rugemer, Edward B., 822.
Rugier, Marcelo, 1292.
Ruisánchez Serra, José Ramón, 2276.
Ruivo, Marina, 2378.
Ruiz, Rosaura, 315.

Ruiz Barrionuevo, Carmen, 1722.
Ruiz de Gordejuela Urquijo, Jesús, 604.
Ruiz Gutiérrez, Rosaura, 542.
Ruiz Medrano, Carlos Rubén, 461, 508.
Ruiz Patiño, Jorge Humberto, 1136.
Ruiz Pérez, Ignacio, 2277.
Ruiz Plaza, Guillermo, 1964.
Ruiz Rodríguez, Carlos, 2712.
Ruiz Rosas, Alonso, 2278.
Ruiz S., Carlos, 3025.
Ruiz Velazco, Víctor, 2279.
Ruiz Zamora, Agustín, 2796.
Rumos Itaú Cultural, 2577.
Rupp, Bettina, 151.
Rupprecht, Tobias, 432.
Russo, Alessandra, 23.
Rutter, Samuel, 2655.
Ruz, Mario Humberto, 450.
Ryden, David B., 840.
Sá, Lenita de, 2535.
Sábato, Hilda, 401.
Sabeh, Luiz, 1601.
Saccomanno, Guillermo, 2656.
Sáenz Andrade, Bruno, 2346.
Saer, Juan José, 2657.
Saffell, Cameron L., 605.
Sala i Vila, Núria, 1189.
Salas, Alberto Mario, 1037.
Salas, Lisbeth, 119.
Salazar, Braulio, 1854.
Salazar, Oswaldo, 1855.
Salazar Mora, Orlando, 747.
Salazar Salvo, Manuel, 1276.
Salazar Vergara, Gabriel, 1277.
Saldarriaga, Gregorio, 381.
Saldivar Arellano, Juan Manuel, 2823.
Sales, Tadeu José Gouveia de, 1704.
Salgado Hernández, Elizabeth Karina, 1137.
Salgado Ismodes, Italo, 1006.
Salinas, María Laura, 1024.
Salinas Sánchez, Alejandro, 1190.
Salinas Sandoval, María del Carmen, 606.
Salinas Toledo, Juan Luis, 1278.
Salinero, Gregorio, 516.
Sallas, Ana Luisa Fayet, 300.
Salles, Paulo de Tarso, 2956.
Salles, Ricardo, 1567.
Salluco Sirpa, Teodoro, 1223.
Salmerón Castro, Alicia, 341, 541.
Salmerón Sanginés, Pedro, 632, 683.
Salmón, Josefa, 2959.
Salomón Tarquini, Claudia, 277.
Salum-Flecha, Antonio, 1499.
Samacá Alonso, Gabriel David, 439.

Samaniego Román, Lorenzo A., 14.
Samba, cultura e sociedade: sambistas e trabalhadores entre a "questão social" e a questão cultural no Brasil, 2943.
O samba e a filosofia, 2944.
Sambrizzi, Alejandro, 1038.
Samis, Alexandre, 1698.
Sampaio, Antonio Carlos Jucá de, 1622.
Sampaio, Gabriela dos Reis, 1576.
San Francisco, Alejandro, 1279.
San Francisco A., Alexander, 301.
Sanabrais, Sofía, 45.
Sanabria, Luis Carlos, 2280.
Sanches, Helen Crystine Corrêa, 1708.
Sanches Neto, Miguel, 2455.
Sánchez, Aurelio, 525.
Sánchez, Carlos Alberto, 2993.
Sánchez, Diego Alonso, 2281.
Sanchez, Evelyne, 600.
Sánchez, João, 2509.
Sánchez, José Miguel, 2658.
Sánchez, Josué, 1792.
Sánchez, Manuel Gerardo, 2072.
Sánchez, Martín, 544.
Sánchez, Roberto, 1191.
Sánchez Andrés, Agustín, 467, 684.
Sánchez Baute, Alonso, 1985.
Sánchez Cerén, Salvador, 751.
Sánchez Cuervo, Juan Mario, 1986.
Sánchez de la O, María de Guadalupe, 607.
Sánchez Flores, Miguel Antonio, 2046.
Sánchez Hidalgo Hernández, Dora, 608.
Sánchez Labrador, José, 1039.
Sánchez León, Abelardo, 2282.
Sánchez Llorens, Mara, 173.
Sánchez-López, Virginia, 2740.
Sánchez Mondaca, Maximiliano, 2851.
Sánchez Mora, Alexánder, 732–733.
Sánchez Mota, Marcela, 1793.
Sánchez Novelo, Faulo M., 2761.
Sánchez Paredes, José, 347.
Sánchez Parra, Sergio Arturo, 439.
Sánchez Patzy, Mauricio, 2801.
Sánchez Prado, Ignacio M., 2990.
Sánchez Quesada, Leonel, 1856.
Sánchez Reséndiz, Victor Hugo, 468.
Sánchez Rodríguez, Limbano, 875.
Sánchez Román, José Antonio, 433.
Sánchez Santiró, Ernest, 366, 485.
Sánchez Serrano, Evangelina, 667.
Sánchez Tagle, Héctor, 685.
Sandoval, Carlos, 2060.
Sandoval Bacigalupo, Renato, 2283.
Saneaux, Sully, 941.
Sanglard, Gisele, 1680.

Sanhueza, Leonardo, 2284.
Sanhueza, Lorena, 294.
Sankhé Adebowale, Maimouna, 1944.
Santa Catarina, Brazil (state). Ministério Público Catarinense, 1708.
Santa Cruz: de legado dos jesuítas à pérola da Coroa, 1621.
Santa Cruz en la guerra de independencia: nuevas aproximaciones, 1224.
Sant'Anna, Alice, 2536.
Sant'Anna, Denise Bernuzzi de, 1558.
Sant'Anna, Sérgio, 2417.
Santiago, José de, 84.
Santiago, Luís, 1705.
Santiago, Silviano, 128.
Santiago, Sylvester, 2138.
Santibáñez, Julia, 2624.
Santibáñez Rebolledo, Camilo, 1280.
Santillán Flor, Elsy, 2172.
Santiváñez, Roger, 2170.
Santos, Eduardo, 1120.
Santos, Eugénio dos, 1706.
Santos, João Marinho dos, 1618.
Santos, Jocélio Teles dos, 1559.
Santos, Joel Rufino dos, 2581.
Santos, Klécio, 2582.
Santos, Marcel de Lima, 166.
Santos, Norma Breda dos, 434.
Santos, Raquel Costa, 122.
Santos, Roberto Corrêa dos, 2401.
Sanz Camañes, Porfirio, 365.
São Paulo, Brazil (state). Pinacoteca do Estado, 141, 152.
Saraiva, Alberto, 136.
Saraiva, Chico, 2945.
Saravia, Alejandro, 2659.
Sarazúa, Juan Carlos, 773.
Sarmiento, Antonio, 2285.
Sarmiento, Sixto, 2286.
Sarmiento da Silva, Érica, 1698.
Sarmiento Herencia, Rodrigo, 2824.
Sarmiento, los Estados Unidos y la educación pública, 1467.
Sarmiento Pacheco, Oliverio, 681.
Sarracino, Rodolfo, 402.
Sasaki, Daniel Leb, 1560.
Sasso, Rolando W., 1518.
Satomi, Alice Lumi, 2946.
Saucedo Estrada, Alán Saúl, 2762.
Saucedo González, José Isidro, 517.
Saunders, Gail, 807.
Saunders, Tanya L., 2797.
Savarino Roggero, Franco, 621.
Savino, Luis M., 1467.
Saxton-Ruiz, Gabriel T., 1950.

Scavone, Ricardo, 1225.
Schaefer, Sérgio, 2944.
Schaposchnik, Ana Edith, 987.
Schara, Julio César, 85.
Scheidt, Eduardo, 411.
Scherer, Andrew K., 235.
Schlesinger, María Elena, 1857.
Schlez, Mariano, 1019.
Schloesser de Paiz, Anabella, 1858.
Schmidhuber de la Mora, Guillermo, 1733.
Schmidt, Benito Bisso, 423.
Schmit, Roberto, 1329.
Schueler, Alessandra Frota Martinez, 1682.
Schultz, Anna, 2783.
Schulze, Frederik, 1707.
Schwaller, John Frederick, 518.
Schwaller, Robert C., 519.
Schwarcz, Lilia Moritz, 1561.
Schwartz, Jorge, 2462.
Schwarzböck, Silvia, 3043.
Schweblin, Samanta, 2660.
Scott, Ana Silvia Volpi, 1595.
Scott, David, 810, 942.
Scott, Paulo, 2537.
Sebadelhe, Zé Octávio, 2933.
Secchin, Antonio Carlos, 2538–2540.
Secreto, María Verónica, 403.
Sedano Ortega, Mauricio, 609.
Seeger, Anthony, 2947.
Segall, Lasar, 149.
Segato, Rita Laura, 2984.
Segundo índice antológico de la poesía salvadoreña, 2171.
Sekou, Lasana M., 2594.
Sellen, Adam T., 337, 450.
Sellers, Julie A., 943.
Sellers-García, Sylvia, 369.
Selva, Salomón de la, 2625.
Semán, Ernesto, 1468.
Seminário Contestado, Leituras e Significados, *Rio de Janeiro, 2012*, 1708.
Seminário Escravidão, Fronteiras e Relações Internacionais no Império do Brasil, *Universidade do Rio de Janeiro, 2011*, 1040.
Seminário "Imaginação da Terra: Memória e Utopia na Canção Popular e no Cinema Brasileiro," *Belo Horizonte, Brazil, 2008*, 2948.
Seminário Internacional Cultura, Arte e História, *Universidade Federal de Minas Gerais, 2010*, 1586.
Seminario Internacional Diálogos entre Brasil y Argentina: Historia e Historiografía, *Mariana, Brazil, 2013*, 1041.

Seminário Internacional "Nas Rotas do Império: Eixos Mercantis, Tráfico de Escravos e Relações Sociais no Mundo Português", *Universidade Federal do Rio de Janeiro, Programa de Pós-Graduação em História Social, 2006*, 1622.

Seminário Nacional 100 Anos da Guerra do Contestado, *Florianópolis, Brazil, 2012*, 1708.

Seminario Nacional de Teoría e Historia del Arte, *9th, Medellín, Colombia, 2012*, 110.

Senra, Nelson, 1648.

Sepúlveda, Juan, 1265.

Sepúlveda, Patricia Graciela, 1469.

Sepúlvela Díaz, Jairo, 301.

Sequeira, Jessica, 2631.

Serafini, Breno, 2456.

Serna Jiménez, Alfonso, 639.

Serra Puche, Mari Carmen, 675.

Serrano, Sol, 1258.

Serrano Catzim, José E., 568.

Serrano Sánchez, Raúl, 1997.

Serrera Contreras, Ramón María, 382.

Serviço Social do Comércio, 2901.

60 años: catálogo de publicaciones INEHRM (1953–2013), 469.

Sesenta años de lucha por el sufragio femenino en México, 1953–2013, 686.

Severi, Carlo, 302.

Shanahan, Maureen G., 1084.

Sharples, Jason T., 823.

Shaves-Ford Dunoyer, Robert, 1987.

Shaw, Jenny, 824.

Shchelchkov, A.A., 1209.

Sheinin, David, 1412.

Shellhorse, Adam Joseph, 2541.

Shepherd, Verene, 808.

Sheppard, Randal, 687.

Sheridan, Guillermo, 1799.

Shields, Tanya L., 914.

Shook, David, 2626.

Sibaja Amador, Patricia, 729.

Sibaja Chacón, Luis Fernando, 712.

Siciliano, Tatiana Oliveira, 2583.

Siegert, Yvette, 2622.

Sierra, María, 1349.

Sierra Silva, Pablo Miguel, 520.

Signs of power in Habsburg Spain and the New World, 1750.

Siguas, William, 2287.

Siles Quezada, Fernando Arturo, 985.

Silva, Aldo José Morais, 1709.

Silva, Augusto da, 1623.

Silva, Cidinha da, 2418.

Silva, Elcio Gomes da, 174.

Silva, Fabiana Bruce da, 162.

Silva, Filipa Ribeiro da, 1608, 1624.

Silva, José Bento Rosa da, 1710.

Silva, Juremir Machado da, 1562.

Silva, Lina Gorenstein Ferreira da, 1609.

Silva, Luiz Roberto Nascimento, 2542.

Silva, Wellington Barbosa da, 1711.

Silva Márquez, César, 1794.

Silva Yrigoyen, Mariana, 2347.

Silveira, Marco Antonio, 1041, 1625.

Silveira, Ronie Alexsandro Teles da, 2944.

Silvestre, Edney, 2419.

Silvestrin, Ricardo, 2543–2544.

Simon, Joshua David, 2985.

Simón Rodríguez: y las pedagogías emancipadoras en nuestra América, 1085.

Simonett, Helena, 2679.

Simposio Bienal de Historia Naval en México, *1st, Veracruz, Mexico; Distrito Federal, Mexico, 2014*, 688.

Simposio De colonia a república: economía, política e iglesia en Costa Rica (1709–1892), *Museos del Banco Central de Costa Rica, 2017*, 713.

Simposio Internacional de Jóvenes Investigadores del Barroco Iberamericano, *2nd, Castellón de la Plana, Spain, 2015*, 24.

Simpósio "Memória, Trabalho e Arquitetura," *São Paulo, 2010*, 175.

Simposio Nacional de Arte Rupestre, *4th, Ayacucho, Peru, 2010*, 15.

Simpósio Nacional de Musicologia da UFG, *5th, Pirenópolis, Brazil, 2015*, 2949.

Simpósio Nacional de Musicologia da UFG, *6th, Pirenópolis, Brazil, 2016*, 2949.

Simpósio Nacional de Musicologia da UFG, *7th, Pirenópolis, Brazil, 2017*, 2949.

Simpósio Nacional Villa-Lobos, *1st, Rio de Janeiro, 2015*, 2950.

Simpósio Nacional Villa-Lobos, *2nd, Rio de Janeiro, 2016*, 2951.

Simpósio Villa-Lobos, *3rd, São Paulo, 2017*, 2952.

Sinfonía de sal / Nunca cerrar los ojos, 2172.

Singer, Deborah, 734.

Sinning Téllez, Luz Guillermina, 111.

Siqueira, João Batista de Cancão, 2545.

Siqueira, José Jorge, 1680.

Siqueira, Sonia A., 1626.

Siracusano, Gabriela, 25.

Siscar, Marcos, 2546–2547.

Small, Daniele Avila, 2567.

Small Axe: A Caribbean Journal of Criticism, 809–810.

Smietniansky, Silvina, 1042.

Smith, James Clois, Jr., 2763.
Smith, Matthew J., 878.
Smith, Stephanie J., 689.
Smoke, flames, and the human body in Mesoamerican ritual practice, 235.
Snoey, Christian, 1742.
Soares, Órris, 2464.
Soares, Wellington, 2457.
Soberón Sagredo, Agustín, 610.
Sobral, Sonia, 2577.
Sobre los orígenes del peronismo: reseña histórica del Partido Justicialista de La Plata, 1945–1955, 1470.
Sobrevilla Perea, Natalia, 400.
Sochaczewski, Monique, 182.
Sociedad, política y cultura en Colombia siglos XVIII-XIX: (enfoques, problemas y tendencias), 967.
Socolow, Susan Migden, 2986.
Socorro, Milagros, 2073.
Sola, Lucia de, 2175.
Sola Ayape, Carlos, 675, 690.
Solano D., Sergio Paolo, 967.
Solano López, Francisco, 2647.
Solari, Ada, 313.
Solari, Amara, 236.
Soler, Ricardo, 1471.
Soler Durán, Alcira, 665.
Solís Carnicer, María del Mar, 1405.
Solís Hernández, Oliva, 639.
Soliz, Carmen, 1226.
Soliz Guzmán, Edgar, 2288.
Solorio Reyes, Víctor, 1795.
Solórzano Fonseca, Juan Carlos, 735.
Sombra roja: diecisiete poetas mexicanas (1964–1985), 2173.
Somohano Martínez, Lourdes, 521.
Somoza Debayle, Lillian, 777.
Sorín, Daniel, 1472.
Sosa, Norma, 1473.
Sosenski, Susana, 691.
Soto, Alvaro de, 751.
Soto, Ángel, 1281.
Soto Castro, Ignacio, 1268.
Soto Salazar, Limonar, 692.
Sotomayor, Antonio, 944.
Sotuyo Blanco, Pablo, 2891.
Soulas, Leo de, 1859.
Souroujon, Gastón, 1474.
Sousa, Avanete Pereira, 1614, 1712.
Sousa, Lisa, 237.
Sousa, Louise Gabler de, 1660.
Sousa, Márcia Regina Pereira de, 190.
Souto Anido, Carmen, 2798.
Souto-Maior, Valéria Andrade, 2564–2566.

Souto Mantecón, Matilde, 355, 485.
Souza, Enivalda Nunes Freitas e, 2530.
Souza, Iracy Conceição de, 2513.
Souza, Lécio Gomes de, 1043, 1627.
Souza e Mello, Marcia Eliane Alves de, 1628.
Souza Junior, José Alves de, 1629.
Spanish American music in New Mexico: the WPA era: folk songs, dance tunes, singing games, and guitar arrangements, 2763.
Spencer Espinosa, Christian, 2680.
Sperling, Rafael, 2420.
Spinelli, María Estela, 1361.
Stagnaro, Andrés, 1475.
Staines Cicero, Leticia, 5.
Starling, Heloisa Maria Murgel, 1524, 1561, 2473, 2948.
Stavans, Ilan, 2592, 2651.
Steen, Edla van, 2579.
Stefanoni, Pablo, 1209.
Stephens, Michelle, 92.
Stern, Steve J., 1170.
Storni, Alfonsina, 1476.
Stratton-Pruitt, Suzanne, 18.
The struggle for memory in Latin America: recent history and political violence, 435.
Stuven, Ana María, 1271.
Suárez, Patricia, 2348–2349.
Suárez Saavedra, Fernando, 999.
Suárez Salazar, Luis, 3000.
Sullón Barreto, Gleydi, 988.
Sumalavia, Ricardo, 2047.
Summerhill, William Roderick, 1713.
Superposiciones: arte latinoamericano en colecciones mexicanas, 68.
Suplemento literário de Minas Gerais, 2548.
Surdich, Francesco, 383.
Suya, Kambrinti, 2947.
Suya, Kokoyamãratxi, 2947.
Suya, Winti, 2947.
Swingen, Abigail L., 825.
Szkurka, Zsu, 1759–1761.
Tamayo, Guido Leonardo, 1988.
Tamayo-Acosta, Juan José, 779.
Tamez, Jared M., 452.
Taniya, Kyn, 2626.
Tapia, Carlos, 2274.
Taracena Arriola, Arturo, 337, 774.
Tarcus, Horacio, 1477.
Tarruella, Ramón D., 1478.
Tarso Salles, Paulo de, 2952.
Tasso, Alberto, 2289.
Tatis Pérez, Vladimir, 1915.
Tato, María Inés, 1387.

Tavares, Flavio, 1563.
Tavares, Zulmira Ribeiro, 2421.
Tavárez, David Eduardo, 197, 246, 476.
Tavarez, Fidel J., 384.
Tavárez Vales, Amarilis, 2174.
Taylor, William B., 522.
Teatro bajo mi piel = Theatre under my skin, 2175.
Teatro Libre de Bogotá, 2333.
Tedeschi, Losandro Antonio, 349.
Teel, Leonard Ray, 945.
Teelucksingh, Jerome, 946.
Teixeira, Melissa, 1564.
Teixeira, Virna, 2459.
Tejeiro, Clemencia, 1118.
Tejerina, Marcela Viviana, 1019.
Tejerina, Verónica, 2802.
Tellería Antelo, Paul, 1965.
Téllez, Yolanda, 1218.
Tena, Rafael, 1751.
Tenorio, Martha Lilia, 1720, 1734.
Teotihuacan: city of water, city of fire, 9.
Teperman, Ricardo Indig, 2953.
Ter Horst, Enrique, 751.
Terán, Oscar, 3044.
Terán Fuentes, Mariana, 611.
Tercera antología del cuento corto colombiano, 1989.
Terra, Paulo Cruz, 1714.
A terra do não-lugar: diálogos entre antropologia e performance, 2584.
Terrazas, Eduardo, 86.
Territorios de la historia, la política y la memoria, 1479.
Territorios de lo cotidiano, siglos XVI–XX: del antiguo Virreinato del Perú a la Argentina contemporánea, 1044.
Testimonios para no olvidar: entrevistas a víctimas de la dictadura, a 26 años del golpe, 1500.
Textos vivos: los pueblos indígenas de Guatemala en los escritos del Ejército Guerrillero de los Pobres - EGP, 775.
Tezza, Cristóvão, 2458.
Thales, Sérgio, 2568.
Thomas, José Luis, 2110.
Thompson, Krista A., 96.
Thorndike, Jennifer, 2048–2049.
Thornton, John K., 736.
Thouvenot, Marc, 243.
Tiburi, Marcia, 2379.
Ticlla Siles, Juan, 1198.
El tiempo de los dioses-tiempo: concepciones de Mesoamérica, 238.

Tiempos binarios: la Guerra Fría desde Puerto Rico y el Caribe, 947.
Tiempos de zozobra: miradas, rostros y latitudes de la revolución en Zacatecas, 692.
Tiesler, Vera, 235.
Timm, Birte, 948.
Tirado Rivera, Alexis Oscar, 949.
Tirado Villegas, Gloria, 693.
Titan Junior, Samuel, 161.
Tittler, Jonathan, 2610.
Titto, Ricardo de, 1480.
Tlaxcala: la invención de un convento, 46.
To be indio in colonial Spanish America, 239, 989.
Tobón Giraldo, Daniel Jerónimo, 110.
Tocornal, Constanza, 283.
Tokovinine, Alexandre, 240.
Tola, Raúl, 2050.
Toledo, Francisco, 2597.
Toledo, Roberto Pompeu de, 1715.
Tolerancia: sobre el fanatismo, la libertad y la comunicación entre culturas, 2987.
Tomamos la palabra: mujeres en la guerra civil de El Salvador: (1980–1992), 776.
Tomich, Dale W., 397.
Tooge, Marly D'Amaro Blasques, 2673.
Toral, Mario, 2235.
Torget, Andrew J., 612.
Tornando-se livre: agentes históricos e lutas sociais no processo de abolição, 1565.
Toro, Maria Stella, 1273.
Torre, Carlos de la Espinosa, 1160.
Torre, Mónica de la, 2600.
Torrente, Alvaro, 2677.
Torres, Camilo, 3015.
Torres, Magdalena de, 2129.
Torres, Oscar Flores, 463.
Torres, Rene, 2759.
Torres, Rosane dos Santos, 1716.
Torres Cendales, Leidy Jazmín, 1138.
Torres Dávila, Víctor Hugo, 1161.
Torres della Pina, José, 54.
Torres Dujisin, Isabel, 1282.
Torres Layan, Justo Avelino, 2178.
Torres Medina, Raúl Heliodoro, 2752.
Torres Rotondo, Carlos, 2825.
Torres Sánchez, Rafael, 366.
Torriente Brau, Pablo de la, 1907.
Toscana, David, 1796.
Tota, Antônio Pedro, 1566.
Tovar Bernal, Leonardo, 1139.
Tovar y de Teresa, Rafael, 613.
Townsend, Camilla, 241.

Los trabajadores de la ciudad de México, 1860–1950: textos en homenaje a Clara E. Lida, 470.
Uma tragédia americana: a Guerra do Paraguai sob novos olhares, 1501.
Trajano, José, 2453.
Transformations of populism in Europe and the Americas: history and recent tendencies, 436.
Transnational Hispaniola: new directions in Haitian and Dominican studies, 811.
Traversari, Gabriel, 777.
Un trébol de cuatro hojas: las juventudes comunistas de Chile en el siglo XX, 1283.
13 ficciones del país sin soldados, 1860.
Trejo Barajas, Dení, 459.
Trejo Contreras, Zulema, 548.
Trejo Luna, Adolfo, 611.
Trejo Rivera, Flor, 332.
Trejos Celis, Juliana, 107.
Trelles Paz, Diego, 2051–2052.
Trentmann, Frank, 348.
Tres crónicas mexicanas: textos recopilados por Domingo Chimalpáhin, 1751.
Trevisan, Armindo, 2549.
Trevisan, Dalton, 2422.
Trigo, Luciano, 2550.
30 x bienal: transformações na arte brasileira da 1a à 30a edição, 155.
Trotta, Felipe, 2954.
Truitt, Jonathan G., 226.
Trujillo Bolio, Mario A., 694.
Trujillo Holguín, Jesús Adolfo, 695.
Trujillo Muñoz, Gabriel, 696.
Trullen, Gustavo, 1507.
Tudo o que não foi: coletânea literária, 2423.
Tugny, Rosângela Pereira de, 2892, 2957.
Tulard, Jean, 1238.
Tunstall, Tricia, 2828.
Turin, Rodrigo, 1717.
Turle, Licko, 2571.
Turner, Guillermo, 1735.
Turner, Sasha, 879.
Tutino, John, 404, 523.
Tzoc, Manuel, 2162, 2176, 2267.
Tzoc Bucup, Manuel Gabriel, 2176.
Ugarte, Diego, 1861.
Ulhôa, Martha, 2675.
Ulloa, Antonio de, 990.
Ulloa, Daniel, 2290.
Ulloa Argüello, Warren, 1862.
Una y otra vez, Sarmiento, 1480.
Unamuno, Gonzalo, 2111.
UNAN-Managua, 414.
Undurraga Schüler, Verónica, 1008.
União Brasileira de Escritores, 2426.
Unidad de Investigaciones Jurídico Sociales "Gerardo Molina", 2974.
Unidad y variación cultural en Michoacán, 242.
Unión Campesina Emiliano Zapata Vive, 472.
Union latine, 55.
Universidad Autónoma de Ciudad Juárez, 2327.
Universidad Católica de Chile. Instituto de Historia, 1241.
Universidad Católica de Temuco, 1006.
Universidad Central de Venezuela. Facultad de Humanidades y Educación, 1056.
Universidad de Alcalá. Instituto de Estudios Latinoamericanos, 467.
Universidad de Costa Rica. Facultad de Ciencias Sociales, 707.
Universidad de los Andes (Bogotá). Departamento de Historia, 1241.
Universidad de los Andes (Bogotá). Departamento de Humanidades y Literatura, 2664.
Universidad de los Andes (Mérida, Venezuela). Centro de Estudios de África y Asia "José Manuel Briceño Monzillo", 1067.
Universidad de "San Martín de Porres", 390.
Universidad de "San Martín de Porres." Facultad de Ciencias de la Comunicación, Turismo y Sicología, 50, 276.
Universidad de Santiago de Chile, 411.
Universidad Estatal a Distancia (Costa Rica). Editorial, 2357.
Universidad Industrial de Santander, 272.
Universidad Internacional de Andalucía. Sede Santa María de La Rápida, 329.
Universidad Juárez del Estado de Durango. Instituto de Investigaciones Históricas, 602.
Universidad Michoacana. Instituto de Investigaciones Históricas, 208, 467, 592.
Universidad Nacional Autónoma de México, 79.
Universidad Nacional Autónoma de México. Centro de Investigaciones sobre América Latina y el Caribe, 675, 2972.
Universidad Nacional Autónoma de México. Coordinación General de Estudios de Posgrado, 212.
Universidad Nacional Autónoma de México. Facultad de Arquitectura, 455.

Universidad Nacional Autónoma de México. Instituto de Investigaciones Filológicas, 238, 243.
Universidad Nacional Autónoma de México. Instituto de Investigaciones Históricas, 242, 355.
Universidad Nacional Autónoma de México. Instituto de Investigaciones sobre la Universidad y la Educación, 84, 2756.
Universidad Nacional Autónoma de México. Museo Universitario Arte Contemporáneo, 76.
Universidad Nacional de Colombia. Cátedra Manuel Ancízar, 1094.
Universidad Nacional de Colombia. Comisión para la Celebración del Bicentenario de la Independencia, 1100.
Universidad Nacional de Colombia. Grupo de Investigación en Historia Económica y Social, 1100.
Universidad Nacional de Colombia. Grupo de Investigación Estudios sobre la Problemática Urbano-Regional, 1104.
Universidad Nacional de Cuyo, 411.
Universidad Ricardo Palma, 1168.
Universidad Simón Bolívar. Centro Latinoamericano de Estudios de Seguridad, 1088.
Universidade de Coimbra, 181.
Universidade de São Paulo. Departamento de História, 1649.
Universidade de São Paulo. Núcleo de Antropologia, Performance e Drama, 2569.
Universidade do Rio de Janeiro, 1040.
Universidade Federal de Minas Gerais, 2473.
Universidade Federal de Ouro Preto. Instituto de Ciências Humanas e Sociais, 1041.
Universidade Federal de Santa Catarina. Pós-Graduação em Estudos da Tradução, 2672.
Universidade Federal do Rio de Janeiro. Programa de Pós-Graduação em História Social, 1622.
Universidade Federal do Rio Grande do Sul. Instituto de Artes, 137.
El universo de Sahagún: pasado y presente, 2011, 243.
Urban, Loiva, 414.
Urbano, Henrique, 276.
Urbina, Maribel, 2305.
Urbina Carrasco, María Ximena, 1009.
Urías Horcasitas, Beatriz, 697.
Uribe, J. Alfredo, 315.
Uribe, Mauricio, 294.
Uribe Peguero, Eurípides Antonio, 950.
Uribe Soto, María de Lourdes, 614.
Uribe Trejo, Abraham, 639.
Urman, Andrea, 2350.
Urquiola, José Ignacio, 513.
Urquiola Flores, Rodrigo, 1966.
Urrutia, Jaime, 1192.
Urtecho, Mario, 1863.
Uruguay. Ministerio de Educación y Cultura, 2853.
Vadillo Vila, José, 2826.
Valarino de Cemboraín, Elizabeth, 2074.
Valdés, Carlos Manuel, 812.
Valdés, Zoé, 1916.
Valdés Castellanos, Guillermo, 471.
Valdés Sánchez, Servando, 784.
Valdez Garza, Dalia, 1736.
Valdivia, José Gabriel, 2159.
Valdivia Ortiz de Zárate, Veronica, 1284.
O Vale do Paraíba e o Império do Brasil nos quadros da segunda escravidão, 1567.
Valencia Llano, Alonso, 1140–1141.
Valenzuela, Jorge, 1946, 1951.
Valenzuela, Roberto Araya, 1262.
Valenzuela A., Eduardo, 385.
Valenzuela Márquez, Jaime, 1010.
Valenzuela Noguera, Ezequiel, 303.
Valerio Ulloa, Sergio, 639.
Valero Juan, Eva María, 1737, 2304.
Valiant, Seonaid, 615.
Valim, Alexandre Busko, 1568.
Valko, Marcelo, 1481.
Vall de la Ville, Keila, 2075.
Valladares Quijano, Manuel, 1193.
Valle-Castillo, Julio, 777.
Valle y Caviedes, Juan del, 1752.
Vallejo, Cesar, 2627.
Vallejo, Osiris, 1917.
Vallejo Corral, Raúl, 2004.
Valles Ruiz, Rosa María, 464.
Valles Salas, Beatriz Elena, 698.
Valobra, Adriana María, 1341, 1433.
Van Deusen, Nancy E., 991.
Van Young, Eric, 616.
Vanderhyden, Will, 2640–2641.
Vanegas Zubiría, Carlos Mario, 110.
Vannini de Gerulewicz, Marisa, 1086.
Vannucci, Alessandra, 2585.
Varanasi González, Julieta, 2764.
Varas, José Miguel, 1285.
Varela, Blanca, 2177.
Varela, Gustavo, 1482.
Vargas, Armando, 767, 770.
Vargas, Getúlio, 1569.
Vargas, Herom, 2678.

Vargas, Manuel, 1967.
Vargas, Maria Thereza, 2586.
Vargas, Virginia, 87.
Vargas Álvarez, Sebastián, 1142.
Vargas Arias, Claudio Antonio, 778.
Vargas Cetina, Gabriela, 2765.
Vargas Llosa, Mario, 1952.
Vargas Lozano, Gabriel, 678.
Vargas Valdez, Jesús, 664.
Vargascarreño, Hernán, 2156.
Vasconcellos, Colleen A., 842.
Vasconcelos, Cláudio Beserra de, 1570.
Vásconez, Javier, 2005.
Vásquez Bonilla, Vicente Antonio, 1864.
Vásquez Frías, Pastor, 880.
Vásquez Medina Luis, 1194.
Vásquez Monzón, Olga, 779.
Vásquez Pavéz, Pablo Favio, 414.
Vásquez Reyna, Noé, 2176.
Vassallo, Jaqueline, 370.
Vaudry-Brown, Peter, 2668.
Vaz, Sérgio, 2551.
Vázquez, Guillermo Javier, 1440.
Vázquez, José Antonio, 1743.
Vázquez, Lourdes Celina, 617.
Vázquez Franco, Guillermo, 1519.
Vázquez Toriz, Rosalía, 472.
Vázquez Valenzuela, David, 618.
Vecinos y pasantes: la movilidad en la colonia, 1045.
Veeser, Cyrus, 858.
Vega, Bernardo, 951.
Vega Farfán, Denisse, 2291.
Vega Jácome, Roy, 2292.
Vega Jácome, Selenco, 2053.
Vega Jiménez, Patricia, 464.
Vega Miche, Sara, 97.
Vega y Ortega, Rodrigo, 524.
Vegas, Federico, 2060.
22 mujeres 3: 21 cuentistas y una prologuista, 2129.
Vela del Campo, Juan Angel, 2677.
Velasco, Alejandro, 1087.
Velasco Castelán, Thalía Edith, 2723.
Velasco Gómez, Ambrosio, 641.
Velasco Mackenzie, Jorge, 2661.
Velázquez, Carmela, 713.
Velden, Felipe Ferreira Vander, 188.
Veloz Maggiolo, Marcio, 1918.
Velôzo Gomes Pedrosa, Fernando, 1501.
Veltfort, Anna, 1919.
Venancio Filho, Paulo, 146, 155.
Venator-Santiago, Charles R., 890.
Vendramini, José Eduardo, 2579.
Venegas Delgado, Hernán, 812.
Venegas Espinoza, Fernando, 1011.
Venegas Valdebenito, Hernán, 1286.
Venezuela y la Guerra Fría, 1088.
Ventura Rodríguez, María Teresa, 699.
Vera, Alejandro, 2852.
Vera, Héctor, 437.
La verdad: an international dialogue on hip hop Latinidades, 2682.
Verdade, fraternidade, arte: secessão de Dresden, Grupo 1919 e contemporâneos, 156.
Verduga, Demián, 2112.
Verolin, Irma, 2244.
Vezzetti, Hugo, 1483.
Vhiestrox Herbas, Herland, 1000.
Viajeras entre dos mundos, 349.
Viales Hurtado, Ronny José, 707.
Viana, Antonio Carlos, 2424.
Vianna, Marly de Almeida Gomes, 1698.
Vicente, Eduardo, 2955.
Vicente Guerrero (1782–1831): primero tuve patria...: recopilación documental, 619.
Vicentín, Matías, 1308.
Victoria Ojeda, Jorge, 525.
Vida en Puebla durante el segundo imperio mexicano: nuevas miradas, 620.
Vida indígena en la colonia: perspectivas etnohistóricas, 244.
Vidal, Gardenia, 1363.
Vidales Quintero, Mayra Lizzete, 676.
Vidargas del Moral, Juan Domingo, 570.
Video nas Aldeias (project), 2947.
Vieira, Fábio, 2552.
Vieira, Luiz, 152.
Viel Temperley, Héctor, 2628.
Viera, Eduardo, 2962.
Viera-Vargas, Hugo René, 2784.
Vieyra Sánchez, Lilia, 593.
Vigil, Mercedes, 2130.
Vignoli, Marcela, 1484.
Vila Vilar, Enriqueta, 386.
Viladrich, Anahí, 2840.
Vilar, Juan Antonio, 1485.
Vilar-Payá, Luisa, 2766–2767.
Vilcapoma Ignacio, José Carlos, 304.
Vilches, Elvira, 387.
Vilela, Ivan, 2941.
Villa-Flores, Javier, 319.
Villa-Forte, Leonardo, 2425.
Villa-Lobos, um compêndio: novos desafios interpretativos, 2956.
Villagrán San Millán, Martín R., 1046.
Villanueva, Francisco Javier, 1342.
Villarreal, Felipe, 2351.
Villarreal, Minerva Margarita, 2293.

Villavicencio Rojas, Josué Mario, 700.
Villavicencio Zarza, Frida Guadalupe, 242.
Villella, Peter B., 245.
Villena, Luis Antonio de, 2179.
Villena Vega, Nataly, 2019, 2054.
Villoro, Juan, 1784.
Vinson, Ben, 526, 2994.
Viotti Barbalato, Matías, 414.
Visiones de la conquista y la colonización de las Américas, 350.
Visiones históricas de la frontera: cruce de caminos: revoluciones y cambios culturales en México, 621.
Vistas cruzadas: los estudios latinoamericanos en Estados Unidos en los 90, vistos desde el Sur; un diálogo interdisciplinario, 2988.
Visual culture of the ancient Americas: contemporary perspectives, 2.
Vitz, Matthew, 701.
Vivas, Rodrigo, 125.
Vivir la modernidad en Oruro 1900–1930, 1227.
Vizcaíno, Santiago, 2629.
Vizcarra, Vanessa, 2352.
Voces de esclavitud y libertad: documentos y testimonios, Colombia, 1701–1833, 968.
Voces de la sierra: marimbas sencillas en Chiapas, 2768.
Volek, Emil, 1738.
Volpi Escalante, Jorge, 1797.
La voz que no marchita: breve selección de poesía costarricence, 2178.
Wahren, Cecilia, 2803.
Walker, Alexander, 1143.
Walker, Charles F., 992.
Walker, Christine, 843.
Walker, Tamara J., 993.
Wasserman, Renata R. Mautner, 2671.
Webb, Clive, 536.
Webre, Stephen, 737.
Webster, Susan Verdi, 61.
Wehling, Arno, 1708.
Weigel, Molly, 2608, 2621.
Weimer, Günter, 176.
Weimer, Rodrigo de Azevedo, 1571.
Weiner, Richard, 622.
Weintraub, Fabio, 2553.
Weis, Robert, 702.
Werlang, Guilherme, 2947.
West, Adrian, 2632.
Whipple, Pablo, 1195.
White, John Howard, 1502.
Wilbert, Werner, 1051.

Wilcock, Juan Rodolfo, 2353.
Wilde, Guillermo, 1024.
Williams, Fernando, 1337.
Williamson, Emily, 2769.
Wills Otero, Laura, 1108.
Wisnik, Guilherme, 150.
Witt, Marcos Antônio, 326, 328, 1718.
Wohl, Lillian M., 2841.
Woitowicz, Karina Janz, 1719.
Wolfe, Mikael, 703.
Wolff, Jennifer, 388.
Words & worlds turned around: indigenous Christianities in colonial Latin America, 246.
World Congress of Philosophy, *23rd, Athens, Greece, 2013*, 238.
World Monuments Fund (New York), 43.
World of Music (new series), 2957.
Wright, Micah, 952.
Wright, Thomas C., 351, 438.
Wrobel, Ronaldo, 2380.
Xerxenesky, Antônio, 2381.
Xilonen, Aura, 1798.
Xu shi cheng, 352.
Xu shi cheng ji = Volume of Xu Shicheng, 352.
¿Y el pueblo dónde está?: Contribuciones para una historia popular de la revolución de independencia en el Río de la Plata en el siglo XIX rioplatense, 1047.
Yaiku, 2947.
Yanez, Mirta, 2630.
Yaya, Isabel, 305.
Yepes Muñoz, Rubén Darío, 112.
Yie Garzón, Maite, 1144.
Yokota, Ryan Masaaki, 1196.
Yoss, 2658.
Young, Fernanda, 2554.
Young, Julia Grace Darling, 421, 704.
Young, Kevin A., 1228–1229.
Yrigoyen, José Carlos, 2055.
Yucatán, Mexico (state). Secretaría de la Cultura y las Artes, 2761.
Yuen Cárdenas, Hugo Antonio, 2056.
Yurman, Pablo, 1486.
Yushimito, Carlos, 2057.
Zachariadhes, Grimaldo Carneiro, 1692.
Zadro Wierna, Inés, 1302.
Zamboni, Olga, 2113.
Zambra, Alejandro, 2634.
Zamora, Margarita, 373.
Zamorano-Villarreal, Claudia Carolina, 705.
Zamudio Vega, Mario A., 223.
Zanca, José A., 340.
Zanon, Dalila, 1630.

Zanzio, Jorge, 2350.
Zapata, Claudia, 353.
Zapata, Cristóbal, 2179.
Zapata Giraldo, Juan Gonzalo, 1145.
Zapata Oliveras, Carlos R., 953.
Zaporta Pallarés, José, 716.
Zarama Rincón, Rosa Isabel, 1146.
Zárate Toscano, Verónica, 2995.
Zardetto, Carol, 1865.
Zavala, José Manuel, 1006.
Zebadúa Carbonell, Juan Pablo, 2724.
Zeferino, Augusto César, 1708.
Zegarra Medina, Raúl Eduardo, 3016.
Zelaya, Chester, 712.
Zeledón Cartín, Elías, 758.
Zeller, Ludwig, 2180.
Zequeira Motolongo, Alfonso, 954.
Zeter, Mary Jo, 2799.
Zeuske, Michael, 405, 881.
Zhongguo ren yu Guba du li zhan zheng = The Chinese and Cuba's independence wars, 882.
Zieleniec, Raquel, 2131.
Zimmermann, Klaus, 243.
Zink, Mirta, 1360.
Zoboli Pocebon, Ruthe, 2881.
Zondek, Verónica, 2160.
Zuba, Elizabeth, 2603.
Zubizarreta, Ignacio, 1487–1488.
Zular, Roberto, 2555.
Zulen, Pedro S., 3017.
Zuleta, María Cecilia, 336.
Zúñiga Arias, Ana Yolanda, 414.
Zúñiga C., Juan Cristóbal, 780.
Zurita, Raúl, 2181, 2294–2295, 2595.
Zuzulich, Jorge, 3036.